Looking for ways to integrate the Web into your curriculum?

ClassZone, McDougal Littell's textbook-companion Web site, is the solution! Online teaching support for you and engaging, interactive content for your students!

ClassZone is your online guide to
The Language of Literature

- Web links to help guide student's research
- Interactive activities for practice and comprehension
- Internet tutorial to help students conduct research on the Web
- Standardized test practice
- Teacher Center for classroom planning

Log on to ClassZone at classzone.com

With the purchase of *Language of Literature*, you have immediate access to ClassZone.

Teacher Access Code

MCDKLMLHLPIHU

Use this code to create your own user-name and password. Then, access both teacher only and student resources.

Student Access Code

MCDB7CIJVTGHL

Give this code to your class. Each student creates a unique username and password to access resources for students.

McDougal Littell

THE LANGUAGE OF
LITERATURE

TEACHER'S EDITION

Grade 6

McDougal Littell
A HOUGHTON MIFFLIN COMPANY
Evanston, Illinois • Boston • Dallas

ISBN 0-618-13664-9

1 2 3 4 5 6 7 8 9 – DWO – 06 05 04 03 02 01

THE LANGUAGE OF LITERATURE

Language and Literature: Skills

McDougal Littell offers you high-quality literature and the tools to build a solid foundation in the reading, writing, and grammar skills that your students will find essential throughout their lives.

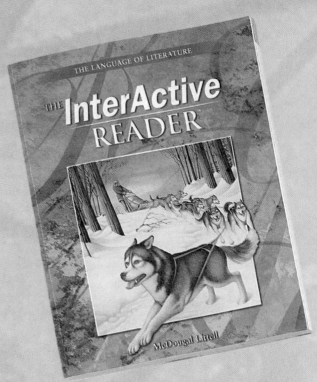

The Language of Literature

The Language of Literature provides high-quality classic and contemporary literature selections, supported by skills instruction and practice in grammar and writing skills. Literary concepts and active reading strategies are reinforced with numerous follow-up activities.

Literature Connections are complete novels and plays bound together with theme-related readings.

The InterActive Reader™

The InterActive Reader™ reinforces active reading strategies and encourages writing during reading. The consumable worktext takes core selections from **The Language of Literature** and breaks them down into manageable reading chunks to increase comprehension.

for a Lifetime

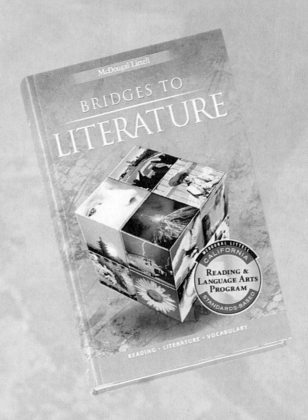

Language Network

Language Network teaches key grammar skills, provides a step-by-step approach to the writing process, and encourages oral communication skills. This up-to-date, comprehensive approach to grammar and composition reinforces skills using literary models and real-life examples.

Bridges to Literature

Bridges to Literature provides high-quality literature to less-proficient readers. This leveled series teaches grade-level skills through engaging and accessible selections, giving students the basics they need to transition successfully to a traditional on-level anthology.

Reading Options for Every Learning

Reading creates a foundation for success that supports your students through school, their careers, and the activities of everyday life. **The Language of Literature** helps you build better readers through diagnosis, instruction, application, and reteaching.

The ancient Romans built the world's first network of paved roads. These roads connected Rome with its conquered provinces across Europe. Roman roads were built primarily to permit the quick and safe movement of troops. However, the roads also had another **(29)** _____. They were designed to facilitate trade throughout the empire.

The greatest of the Roman roads was the Appian Way. Begun in 312 B.C., the Appian Way at first ran only as far as the military center of Capua. In time, however, the road was **(30)** _____. Eventually, it reached the port of Brindisi, on the Adriatic. This gave Rome a gateway to the Near East and its riches.

Roman roads are famous for being straight. In many cases, it would have been easier for the Romans to build roads around mountains and swamps instead of going through them. Yet, Romans chose the latter **(31)** _____. Preferring the most direct course, they scaled mountains and crossed swamps.

Romans built their roads essentially by hand. This was necessary, since they had no **(32)** _____. Working with picks, hammers, and shovels, they prepared roadbeds upon which they set down layers of mortar and stone. They topped their roads with paving stones of volcanic rock. The roads were usually crowned, or raised in the middle so that water would drain off. As a result, the roads were seldom **(33)** _____. They were the first "all-weather" roads ever built.

Roman emperors decreed that the roads should be well constructed, so they would remain serviceable for years. The roads were supposed to **(34)** _____. The roads did, in fact, prove durable. They needed no repair for many years, despite constant use. Many stretches remain today. Along them one can still see the ancient milestones erected to record the distance to Rome. These milestones also tell when the road was built and who reigned at that time. The stones are thus a source of **(35)** _____. Historians have learned much from studying them.

Go to the Next Page ▶

29. ○ a) purpose ○ d)
    ○ b) name ○ e)
    ○ c) entrance

30. ○ a) lighted ○ d) lev
    ○ b) taxed ○ e) ext
    ○ c) crossed

31. ○ a) material ○ d) amou
    ○ b) route ○ e) marke
    ○ c) date

32. ○ a) soldiers ○ d) ships
    ○ b) laws ○ e) station
    ○ c) machines

33. ○ a) traveled ○ d) divided
    ○ b) flooded ○ e) fenced
    ○ c) guarded

34. ○ a) turn ○ d) last
    ○ b) meet ○ e) narrow
    ○ c) rise

35. ○ a) disease ○ d) money
    ○ b) dust ○ e) information
    ○ c) shelter

Placement Test 5

Pretest from the *Reading Toolkit*

Bridges to Literature

*Provide accessible reading selections to less-proficient readers through the **Bridges to Literature** program. This transitional program gives students who have been diagnosed to be reading below grade level the skills they need to access a traditional on-level anthology successfully.*

Start with the *Reading Toolkit* to measure each student's reading ability and access materials for instruction of reading skills and strategies.

Need

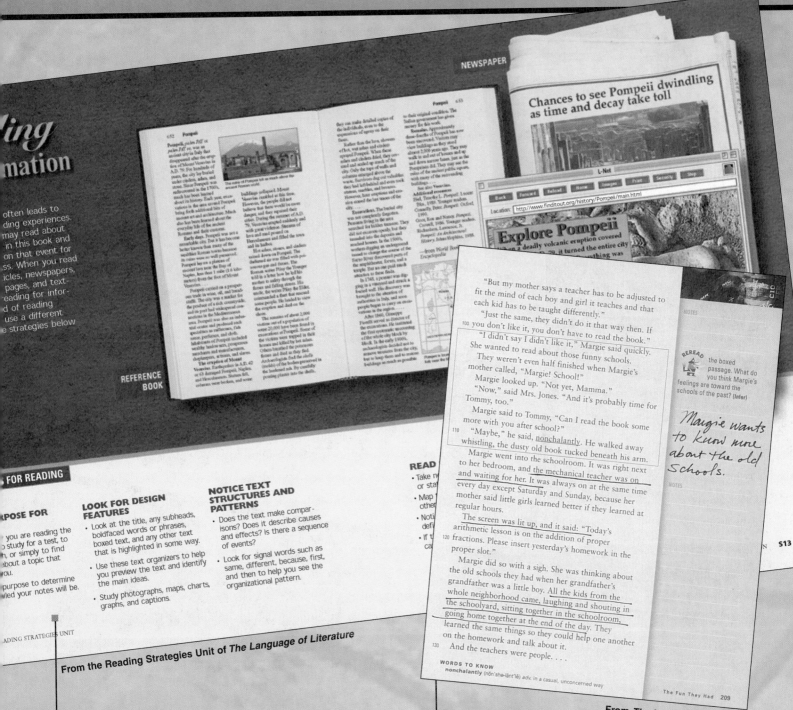

NEWSPAPER

Chances to see Pompeii dwindling as time and decay take toll

REFERENCE BOOK

Pompeii *pahm PAY* or *pahm PAY ee*, was an ancient city in Italy that disappeared after the eruption of Mount Vesuvius in A.D. 79. For hundreds of years, the city lay buried under cinders, ashes, and stone. Since Pompeii was rediscovered in the 1700's, much has been learned about its history. Each year, since it was first discovered...

...often leads to ...ding experiences. ...may read about ...in this book and ...on that event for ...s. When you read ...icles, newspapers, ...pages, and text-...reading for infor-...d of reading ...use a different ...e strategies below

Explore Pompeii

...S FOR READING

...RPOSE FOR

...you are reading the ...o study for a test, to ...h, or simply to find ...about a topic that ...you.

...purpose to determine ...iled your notes will be.

LOOK FOR DESIGN FEATURES
- Look at the title, any subheads, boldfaced words or phrases, boxed text, and any other text that is highlighted in some way.
- Use these text organizers to help you preview the text and identify the main ideas.
- Study photographs, maps, charts, graphs, and captions.

NOTICE TEXT STRUCTURES AND PATTERNS
- Does the text make compar-isons? Does it describe causes and effects? Is there a sequence of events?
- Look for signal words such as same, different, because, first, and then to help you see the organizational pattern.

...ADING STRATEGIES UNIT

From the Reading Strategies Unit of *The Language of Literature*

"But my mother says a teacher has to be adjusted to fit the mind of each boy and girl it teaches and that each kid has to be taught differently."

"Just the same, they didn't do it that way then. If
100 you don't like it, you don't have to read the book."

"I didn't say I didn't like it," Margie said quickly. She wanted to read about those funny schools.

They weren't even half finished when Margie's mother called, "Margie! School!"

Margie looked up. "Not yet, Mamma."

"Now," said Mrs. Jones. "And it's probably time for Tommy, too."

Margie said to Tommy, "Can I read the book some more with you after school?"

110 "Maybe," he said, nonchalantly. He walked away whistling, the dusty old book tucked beneath his arm.

Margie went into the schoolroom. It was right next to her bedroom, and the mechanical teacher was on and waiting for her. It was always on at the same time every day except Saturday and Sunday, because her mother said little girls learned better if they learned at regular hours.

The screen was lit up, and it said: "Today's arithmetic lesson is on the addition of proper
120 fractions. Please insert yesterday's homework in the proper slot."

Margie did so with a sigh. She was thinking about the old schools they had when her grandfather's grandfather was a little boy. All the kids from the whole neighborhood came, laughing and shouting in the schoolyard, sitting together in the schoolroom, going home together at the end of the day. They learned the same things so they could help one another on the homework and talk about it.

130 And the teachers were people. . . .

WORDS TO KNOW
nonchalantly (nŏn´shə-länt´lē) adv. in a casual, unconcerned way

READ...
- Take n... or sta...
- Map t... other...
- Noti... defi...
- If t... ca...

NOTES

REREAD the boxed passage. What do you think Margie's feelings are toward the schools of the past? (Infer)

Margie wants to know more about the old schools.

NOTES

S13

The Fun They Had 209

From *The InterActive Reader*™

Teach essential reading skills and strategies within the context of the selections in *The Language of Literature.* Innovative reading models offer additional strategies that support academic, functional, and recreational reading experiences that are essential to your students' success.

Give your students extra reading strategy practice with *The InterActive Reader*™. Students of all ability levels will benefit from the "mark-it-up" format as they read or re-read key literature selections found in the anthology.

The Reading and Writing Connection

The Language of Literature takes a step-by-step approach to the writing process that helps you teach your students how to think critically about what they read, incorporate important grammar and vocabulary skills, and organize their thoughts to become effective and successful writers.

Grammar in Context provides grammar practice through writing exercises that ask students to rewrite sentences related to the selection.

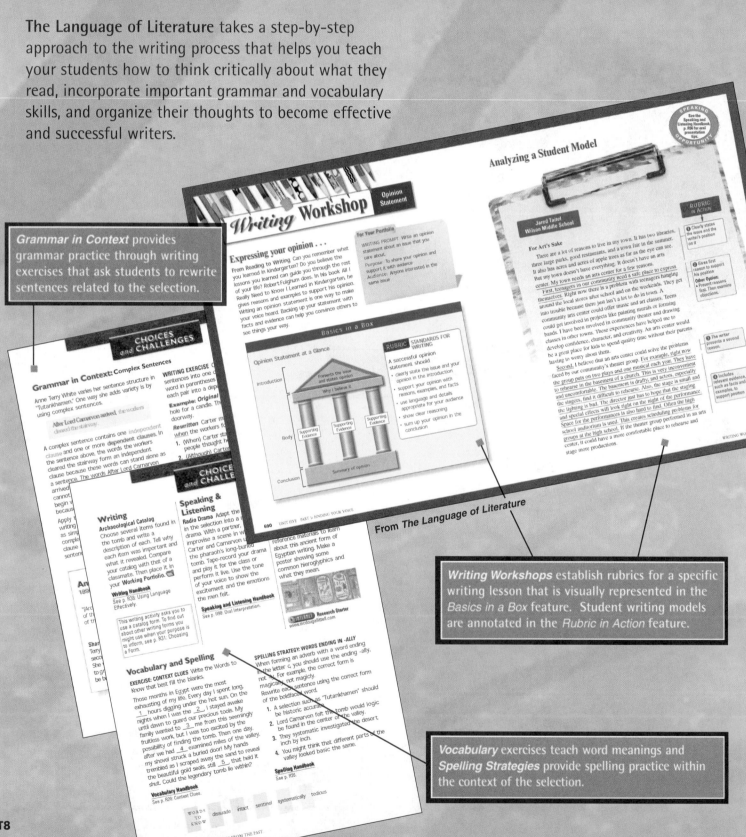

From The Language of Literature

Writing Workshops establish rubrics for a specific writing lesson that is visually represented in the *Basics in a Box* feature. Student writing models are annotated in the *Rubric in Action* feature.

Vocabulary exercises teach word meanings and *Spelling Strategies* provide spelling practice within the context of the selection.

Extensive Assessment Preparation

A full range of assessment options is available to meet your needs, including standardized test practice, reading skills assessment, and alternative assessment.

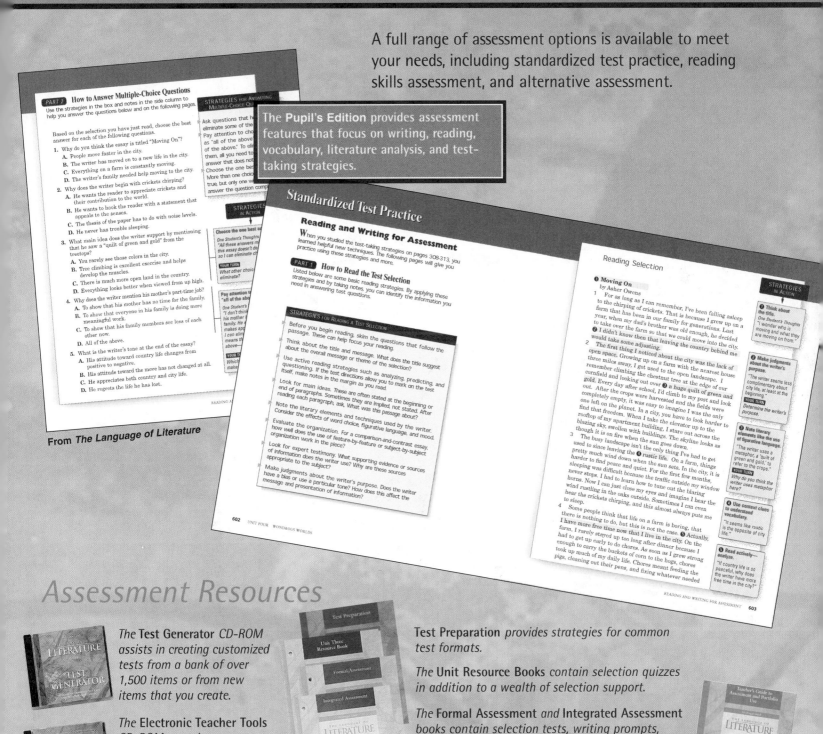

The Pupil's Edition provides assessment features that focus on writing, reading, vocabulary, literature analysis, and test-taking strategies.

From *The Language of Literature*

Assessment Resources

The **Test Generator** *CD-ROM assists in creating customized tests from a bank of over 1,500 items or from new items that you create.*

The **Electronic Teacher Tools** *CD-ROM contains assessment materials and other ancillary support that can be printed at your convenience.*

Test Preparation *provides strategies for common test formats.*

The **Unit Resource Books** *contain selection quizzes in addition to a wealth of selection support.*

The **Formal Assessment** *and* **Integrated Assessment** *books contain selection tests, writing prompts, practice questions, scoring rubrics, unit integrated assessment, and end-of-year integrated assessment.*

The **Teacher's Guide to Assessment and Portfolio Use** *contains portfolio assessment, writing rubrics, and other forms of open-ended assessment.*

Teaching Support for You —
The Language of Literature *Program Components*

Core Components

- The Language of Literature
  Pupil's Edition
- The Language of Literature
  Teacher's Edition

Teaching Resources

- Unit Resource Books
- Grammar, Usage, and Mechanics
  Book and Answer Key
- Vocabulary and Spelling Book
  and Answer Key
- Speaking and Listening Book
- Lesson Planning Guides
- English Learners/Students
  Acquiring English
  EL/SAE Spanish Study Guide
  EL/SAE Test Preparation
  *EL/SAE English Grammar Survival
  Kit Copymasters with Audio CD*
  *EL/SAE Teacher's Sourcebook for
  Language Development*

- Resource Management Guide
- Writing Research Reports
- Skills Transparencies
  Writing Transparencies
  Language Transparencies
  Fine Art Transparencies
  Literary Analysis Transparencies
  *Reading and Critical Thinking
  Transparencies*
- Assessment
  Formal Assessment
  Integrated Assessment
  Test Preparation
  *Teacher's Guide to Assessment
  and Portfolio Use*

Skill Support for Your Students

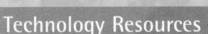

Reading Resources

- The InterActive Reader™ Pupil's Edition
- The InterActive Reader™ Teacher's Guide
- Reading Toolkit
- Literature Connections (novels with related readings)
- Literature Connections SourceBooks

Technology Resources

- Literature in Performance Video Series
- ClassZone with Online Lesson Planner
- Audio Library
- Test Generator
- Electronic Teacher Tools
- NetActivities
- Power Presentations
- Web site: www.mcdougallittell.com

Also Available:

- Bridges to Literature Pupil's Edition
- Bridges to Literature Teacher's Edition
- Language Network Pupil's Edition
- Language Network Teacher's Edition
- Nextext® Classic Retellings
- Nextext® Stories in History

McDougal Littell

THE LANGUAGE OF
LITERATURE

McDougal Littell

THE LANGUAGE OF
LITERATURE

Senior Consultants

Arthur N. Applebee

Andrea B. Bermúdez

Sheridan Blau

Rebekah Caplan

Peter Elbow

Susan Hynds

Judith A. Langer

James Marshall

McDougal Littell

A HOUGHTON MIFFLIN COMPANY

Evanston, Illinois • Boston • Dallas

Acknowledgments

Front Matter

Professional Publishing Services Company: Excerpt from "The Dog of Pompeii," from *The Donkey of God* by Louis Untermeyer. Published by arrangement with the Estate of Louis Untermeyer, Norma Anchin Untermeyer, c/o Professional Publishing Services Company. This permission is expressly granted by Laurence S. Untermeyer.

World Book Publishing: Excerpt from "Pompeii" by Erich S. Gruen, World Book Encyclopedia. Copyright © 2000 World Book, Inc. By permission of the publisher. www.worldbook.com

The Associated Press: Excerpt from "Chances to see Pompeii dwindling as time and decay take toll" by Candice Hughes, November 27, 1997. Reprinted with permission of The Associated Press.

Archaeology Magazine: Excerpt from "The Walls Speak" by Antonio Varone, *Archaeology*, March/April 1991. Copyright © 1991 by the Archaeological Institute of America. Reprinted with the permission of *Archaeology* Magazine.

Lensey Namioka: "The All-American Slurp" by Lensey Namioka, from *Visions,* edited by Donald R. Gallo. Copyright © 1987 by Lensey Namioka. Reprinted by permission of Lensey Namioka. All rights are reserved by the author.

Excerpt from "The All-American Slurp" by Lensey Namioka, from *Visions,* edited by Donald R. Gallo. Copyright © 1987 by Lensey Namioka. Reprinted by permission of Lensey Namioka. All rights are reserved by the author.

Unit One

Susan Bergholz Literary Services: "Eleven," from *Woman Hollering Creek and Other Stories* by Sandra Cisneros, published by Vintage Books, a division of Random House, Inc., and originally in hardcover by Random House, Inc. Copyright © 1991 by Sandra Cisneros. Reprinted by permission of Susan Bergholz Literary Services, New York. All rights reserved.

Continued on page R170

ISBN 0-618-13661-4

Senior Consultants

The senior consultants guided the conceptual development for *The Language of Literature* series. They participated actively in shaping prototype materials for major components, and they reviewed completed prototypes and/or completed units to ensure consistency with current research and the philosophy of the series.

Arthur N. Applebee Professor of Education, State University of New York at Albany; Director, Center for the Learning and Teaching of Literature; Senior Fellow, Center for Writing and Literacy

Andrea B. Bermúdez Professor of Studies in Language and Culture; Director, Research Center for Language and Culture; Chair, Foundations and Professional Studies, University of Houston–Clear Lake

Sheridan Blau Senior Lecturer in English and Education and former Director of Composition, University of California at Santa Barbara; Director, South Coast Writing Project; Director, Literature Institute for Teachers; Former President, National Council of Teachers of English

Rebekah Caplan Senior Associate for Language Arts for middle school and high school literacy, National Center on Education and the Economy, Washington, D.C.; served on the California State English Assessment Development Team for Language Arts; former co-director of the Bay Area Writing Project, University of California at Berkeley.

Peter Elbow Emeritus Professor of English, University of Massachusetts at Amherst; Fellow, Bard Center for Writing and Thinking

Susan Hynds Professor and Director of English Education, Syracuse University, Syracuse, New York

Judith A. Langer Professor of Education, State University of New York at Albany; Co-director, Center for the Learning and Teaching of Literature; Senior Fellow, Center for Writing and Literacy

James Marshall Professor of English and English Education; Chair, Division of Curriculum and Instruction, University of Iowa, Iowa City

Contributing Consultants

Linda Diamond Executive Vice-President, Consortium on Reading Excellence (CORE); co-author of *Building a Powerful Reading Program*. Ms. Diamond reviewed program components as part of the development of a teacher-training program designed to accompany those materials; she also reviewed and contributed to McDougal Littell's *Reading Toolkit*, the professional development component of the program.

William L. McBride Reading and Curriculum Specialist; former middle and high school English instructor. Dr. McBride reviewed prototype materials and served as a consultant on the development of the Reading Strategies Unit and the Reading Handbook.

Sharon Sicinski-Skeans, Assistant Professor of Reading, University of Houston–Clear Lake. Dr. Sicinski-Skeans served as primary consultant on *The InterActive Reader,* providing guidance on prototype development and reviewing final manuscript.

Multicultural Advisory Board

The multicultural advisers reviewed literature selections for appropriate content and made suggestions for teaching lessons in a multicultural classroom.

Dr. Joyce M. Bell Chairperson, English Department, Townview Magnet Center, Dallas, Texas

Dr. Eugenia W. Collier author; lecturer; Chairperson, Department of English and Language Arts and teacher of creative writing and American literature, Morgan State University, Maryland

Kathleen S. Fowler President, Palm Beach County Council of Teachers of English, Boca Raton Middle School, Boca Raton, Florida

Corey Lay ESL Department Chairperson, Chester Nimitz Middle School, Los Angeles Unified School District, Los Angles, California

Noreen M. Rodriguez Trainer for Hillsborough County School District's Staff Development Division; independent consultant, Gaither High School, Tampa, Florida

Michelle Dixon Thompson Seabreeze High School, Daytona Beach, Florida

Teacher Review Panels

The following educators provided ongoing review during the development of tables of contents, lesson design, and key components of the program.

CALIFORNIA

Steve Bass Eighth-Grade Team Leader, Meadowbrook Middle School, Poway Unified School District

Cynthia Brickey Eighth-Grade Academic Block Teacher, Kastner Intermediate School, Clovis Unified School District

Karen Buxton English Department Chairperson, Winston Churchill Middle School, San Juan School District

Sharon Cook Independent consultant, Fresno Unified School District

Bonnie Garrett Davis Middle School, Compton School District

Sally Jackson Madrona Middle School, Torrance Unified School District

Sharon Kerson Los Angeles Center for Enriched Studies, Los Angeles Unified School District

Gail Kidd Center Middle School, Azusa School District

continued on page R186

Manuscript Reviewers

The following educators reviewed prototype lessons and tables of contents during the development of the *Language of Literature* program.

William A. Battaglia Herman Intermediate School, San Jose, California

Hugh Delle Broadway McCullough High School, The Woodlands, Texas

Robert M. Bucan National Mine Middle School, Ishpeming, Michigan

Ann E. Clayton Department Chairperson for Language Arts, Rockway Middle School, Miami, Florida

Hillary Crain Diegueño Middle School, Encinitas, California

continued on page R187

vi

Student Panel

LITERATURE REVIEWERS

The following students read and evaluated selections to assess their appeal for the sixth-grade.

Ted Burke East Aurora Middle School, East Aurora, New York

Ian Graham Churchill Road Elementary School, McLean, Virginia

Melissa Hall Frenship Intermediate School, Wolfforth, Texas

Stephanie Liberati Hampton Middle School, Allison Park, Pennsylvania

Bridget McGuire St. John of the Cross, Western Springs, Illinois

Eileen Pablos-Velez Henry H. Filer Middle School, Hialeah, Florida

Nicole Putnam Rockway Middle School, Miami, Florida

Eli Shlaes Davidson Middle School, San Rafael, California

Theresa Sullivan St. Ann's School, Wilmington, Delaware

Christine Tran Foothill Middle School, Walnut Creek, California

Alexis Wong Foothill Middle School, Walnut Creek, California

ACTIVE READERS

The following students participated in the development of The Active Reader: Skills and Strategies pages in this book:

Ryane Griffis

Sean Mtunis

Carine Miranda

Michael Beaupre

Ricky Wong

Jillian DeBaie

Orlando Castillo

Brittany Regan

Talisa Murray

Chris McGarry

STUDENT MODEL WRITERS

The following students wrote the student models for Writing Workshop pages that appear in this book:

Daniel Kwan

Samantha Piwinski

Carolyn Nash

Tiffany George

Yoshio Adachi

M. McGoff

Weston Sager

Ben Wright

Jared Taitel

Katherine Helming

Table of Contents

Student Resource Bank

Reading Handbook
Vocabulary Handbook
Spelling Handbook
Writing Handbook
Grammar Handbook
Speaking and Listening Handbook
Research and Technology Handbook
Glossary of Literary and Reading Terms
Glossary of Words to Know in English and Spanish

Literature Connections

Each of the books in the *Literature Connections* series combines a novel or play with related readings—poems, stories, plays, personal essays, articles— that add new perspectives on the theme or subject matter of the longer work.

Listed below are some of the most popular choices to accompany the Grade 6 anthology:

The House of Dies Drear by Virginia Hamilton

Number the Stars by Lois Lowry

Taking Sides by Gary Soto

Dogsong by Gary Paulsen

The Glory Field by Walter Dean Myers

Tuck Everlasting* by Natalie Babbitt

Maniac Magee by Jerry Spinelli

The Call of the Wild* by Jack London

The Cay by Theodore Taylor

Dragonwings by Laurence Yep

Homecoming by Cynthia Voight

Roll of Thunder, Hear My Cry* by Mildred D. Taylor

*A Spanish version is also available.

THE LANGUAGE OF
LITERATURE

Reading Strategies Unit

Unit One

Tests of Courage

SOCIAL STUDIES CONNECTION

See Unit Six, "The Oral Tradition: Tales from the Ancient World to Today" for links to Unit One.

Unit Two

Growth and Change

SOCIAL STUDIES CONNECTION
See Unit Six, "The Oral Tradition: Tales from the Ancient World to Today" for links to Unit Two.

Unit Three

A Sense of Fairness

SOCIAL STUDIES CONNECTION

See Unit Six, "The Oral Tradition: Tales from the Ancient World to Today" for links to Unit Three.

Unit Four

Wondrous Worlds

SOCIAL STUDIES CONNECTION

See Unit Six, "The Oral Tradition: Tales from the Ancient World to Today" for links to Unit Four.

Unit Five

Making Your Mark

Part 2 Voices From the Past 696

GENRE FOCUS: HISTORICAL FICTION

UNIT WRAP-UP

SOCIAL STUDIES CONNECTION
See Unit Six, "The Oral Tradition: Tales from the Ancient World to Today" for links to Unit Five.

Unit Six

THE ORAL TRADITION:
Tales from the Ancient World to Today

The Language of Literature
Student Resource Bank

The Language of Literature
Teaching by Genre

The Language of Literature
Teaching by Genre

Poetry

Drama

Classical Myths

Oral Tradition

The Language of Literature
Special Features

Writing Workshops

Communication Workshops

Building Vocabulary

Standardized Test Practice

Successful readers must be able to understand a broad range of materials, from classic literature to web pages. This special unit may be used to introduce students to a variety of skills and strategies that will strengthen their comprehension and help them to become active readers. The four parts of the unit address specific skills and strategies.

- **Becoming an Active Reader** on pages S2-S3 presents and explains the key strategies for reading. Then pages S4-S5 model some of the important tools for reading such as a reader's notebook and a reading log.
- **Reading Literature** on pages S6-S7 introduces specific strategies for reading literature. Then on pages S8-S11 we see how two students applied the strategies to a literary model.
- **Reading for Information** on pages S12-S13 gives detailed strategies for reading for information. Pages S14-S19 show these strategies being applied to examples from reference books, magazines, newspapers, and web sites along with additional special strategies needed for each type.
- **Your Turn: Applying the Strategies** beginning on page S20 is an opportunity for students to apply the reading strategies. The literary selection presented here allows students to practice the skills on their own with a few questions to guide them.

Pacing
This unit can be used at many different times:
- To begin the study of literature
- To review specific reading strategies at any time during the year
- To practice active reading at any time using the Your Turn model
- To introduce strategies for reading for information
- To prepare students for the informative reading associated with writing research reports
- To review for many kinds of assessments

Becoming an Active Reader

Active readers comprehend what they read and connect it to their own lives. An active reader asks questions, forms opinions, and visualizes scenes. The strategies in this special unit and throughout the book will help you become an active reader of all kinds of materials.

McDougal Littell

THE LANGUAGE OF LITERATURE

PAT MORA
LOIS LOWRY
LAUREN YEP
AVI
GARY PAULSEN
HELEN KELLER
LANGSTON HUGHES
SANDRA CISNEROS
VIRGINIA HAMILTON

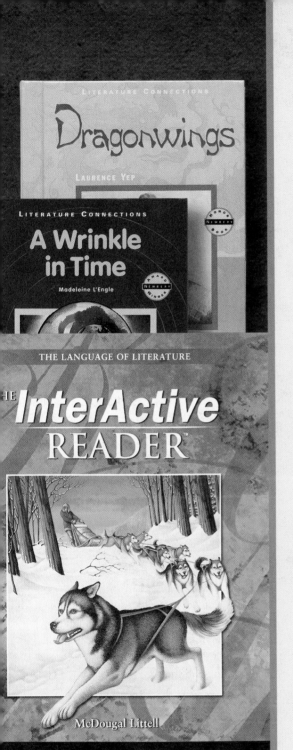

Active readers learn and apply reading strategies to get the most out of what they read. Whether you are reading for information or for enjoyment, pause from time to time and **monitor** your understanding of the material. Reread if necessary and **reflect** on what you have read. As you reflect, use one or more of these techniques.

PREDICT

Try to figure out what might happen next. Then read on to see how accurate your guesses were.

VISUALIZE

Picture the people, places, and events being described to help you understand what's happening.

CONNECT

Connect personally with what you're reading. Think of similarities between what is being described and what you have experienced, heard about, or read about.

QUESTION

Ask questions about events in the material you're reading. What happened? Why? How do the people involved feel about the events? Searching for reasons can help you feel closer to what you are reading.

CLARIFY

From time to time, review your understanding of what you read. You can do this by **summarizing** what you have read, identifying the **main idea,** and **making inferences—** drawing conclusions from the information you are given. Reread passages you don't understand. If you need to, consult a dictionary, glossary, or other source.

EVALUATE

Form opinions about what you read, both while you're reading and after you've finished. Develop your own ideas about people, places, and events.

READER'S NOTEBOOK

Putting your thoughts on paper can help you understand and connect with literature. Many readers record their ideas in a Reader's Notebook. You can use almost any kind of notebook for this purpose. This page describes two ways you can use your notebook.

① PREPARE TO READ

Complete the **📖 READER'S NOTEBOOK** activity on the Preparing to Read page of each literature lesson. This activity will help you apply an important skill as you read the literature selection.

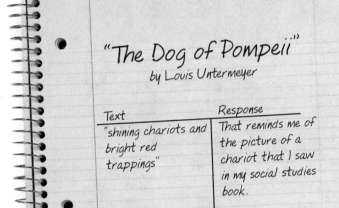

"The Dog of Pompeii"
by Louis Untermeyer

Text	Response
"shining chariots and bright red trappings"	That reminds me of the picture of a chariot that I saw in my social studies book.

② RECORD YOUR THOUGHTS

In your Reader's Notebook, record responses, connections, questions, sketches, and charts. Use your notebook before and after reading a selection as well as while you read. Jot down notes that might later be a springboard to your own writing.

Watch for other reminders about your Reader's Notebook throughout the textbook.

Shana Dawes
PORTFOLIO

Date	Project	Comments
10/21	Report on author Laurence Yep	Finished
11/7	Poem about Amelia Earhart	First and second drafts only
12/5	Research report on Pompeii	Notes and ideas

Personal Word List

<u>Word</u>: sham
<u>Selection</u>: The Dog of Pompeii
<u>Page</u>: S8 ("sham battles and athletic sports were free for the asking")
<u>Definition</u>: artificial, fake, not real

<u>Word</u>: stodgy
<u>Selection</u>: The Dog of Pompeii
<u>Page</u>: S9 ("A heavy supper made boys too restless and dogs too stodgy")
<u>Definition</u>: slow-moving from being filled up with food

Reading Log

Name: <u>Shana Dawes</u>

Date	Title/Author	Genre/Type	Time/Number of Pages
9/28	The Call of the Wild by Jack London	Novel	30 minutes/21 pages
10/4	American Snowboarder	Magazine	10 minutes/6 pages

WORKING PORTFOLIO

Artists and writers keep portfolios in which they store works in progress. Your portfolio can be a folder, a box, or a notebook. Add drafts of your writing experiments and notes on your goals as a reader and writer.

PERSONAL WORD LISTS

Vocabulary In your Reader's Notebook, you can add words you learn to a personal word list—a list of words you want to use.

Spelling Add words that are difficult to spell to a separate spelling list in your Reader's Notebook.

READING LOG

Keep track of how much you read and how often. You may be surprised at how many books and other materials you read in a year! Keep your reading log in your Reader's Notebook or on a worksheet your teacher provides for you.

Integrated Technology

Your involvement doesn't stop with the last line of the text. Use these technology products to further your study and understanding:

- **Literature in Performance videos**
- **NetActivities CD-ROM**
- **Audio Library**
- INTERNET ClassZone, McDougal Littell's companion Web site, at **www.mcdougallittell.com**

Reading Literature

When you read short stories, literary nonfiction, poems, plays, or myths, you are interacting with the literature in many ways. You may be enjoying the power of storytelling. You could be finding connections with your own life. You may even be encountering new ideas and experiences. The tips on this page will help you become an active reader of literature.

DRAMA

POETRY

STRATEGIES FOR READING

BEFORE READING

- Set a purpose for reading. What do you want to learn? Are you reading as part of an assignment or for fun? Establishing a purpose will help you focus.

- Preview the text by looking at the title and any images and captions. Try to **predict** what the literature will be about.

- Ask yourself if you can **connect** what you are reading with what you already know.

DURING READING

- Check your understanding of what you read. Can you restate the text in your own words?

- Try to **connect** what you're reading to your own life. Have you experienced similar events or emotions?

- **Question** what's happening in the literature. You may wonder about events and characters' feelings.

- **Visualize,** or create a mental picture of, what the author is describing.

- Pause from time to time to **predict** what will happen next.

HISTORICAL FICTION

THE
DOG OF
POMPEII
by Louis Untermeyer

Abd al-Rahman Ibrahima
from NOW IS YOUR TIME!

by Walter Dean Myers

BIOGRAPHY

In
the
LAND
of
SMALL
DRAGON

As told by
Dang Manh Kha
to Ann Nolan Clark

AFTER READING

- Review your predictions. Were they correct?
- Try to **summarize** the text. Give the main idea or the basic plot.
- Reflect on and **evaluate** what you have read. Did the reading fulfill your purpose?
- To **clarify** your understanding, write down opinions or thoughts about the piece, or discuss it with someone.

The story on these pages is part of a piece of historical fiction from Unit Five. Read the excerpt and record your responses to it in your **READER'S NOTEBOOK.** Then read the Strategies in Action columns to find out how two students applied the strategies for reading.

THE DOG OF POMPEII

by Louis Untermeyer

T ito and his dog Bimbo lived (if you could call it living) under the wall where it joined the inner gate. They really didn't live there; they just slept there. They lived anywhere. Pompeii was one of the gayest of the old Latin towns, but although Tito was never an unhappy boy, he was not exactly a merry one. The streets were always lively with shining chariots and bright red trappings; the open-air theaters rocked with laughing crowds; sham battles and athletic sports

Cave Canem [Beware of dog], Roman mosaic. Museo Archeologico Nazionale, Naples, Italy. Scala/Art Resource, New York.

were free for the asking in the great stadium. Once a year the Caesar[1] visited the pleasure city, and the fireworks lasted for days; the sacrifices[2] in the forum were better than a show. But Tito saw none of these things. He was blind—had been blind from birth. He was known to everyone in the poorer quarters. But no one could say how old he was; no one remembered his parents; no one could tell where he came from. Bimbo was another mystery. As long as people could remember seeing Tito—about twelve or thirteen years—they had seen Bimbo. Bimbo had never left his side. He was not only dog but nurse, pillow, playmate, mother, and father to Tito.

Ramón: *Tito and Bimbo are homeless, I guess. They must have a hard life.*
CONNECTING

Did I say Bimbo never left his master? (Perhaps I had better say comrade, for if anyone was the master, it was Bimbo.) I was wrong. Bimbo did trust Tito alone exactly three times a day. It was a fixed routine, a custom understood between boy and dog since the beginning of their friendship, and the way it worked was this: Early in the morning, shortly after dawn, while Tito was still dreaming, Bimbo would disappear. When Tito woke, Bimbo would be sitting quietly at his side, his ears cocked, his stump of a tail tapping the ground, and a fresh-baked bread—more like a large round roll—at his feet. Tito would stretch himself; Bimbo would yawn; then they would breakfast. At noon, no matter where they happened to be, Bimbo would put his paw on Tito's knee, and the two of them would return to the inner gate. Tito would curl up in the corner (almost like a dog) and go to sleep, while Bimbo, looking quite important (almost like a boy), would disappear again. In half an hour he'd be back with their lunch. Sometimes it would be a piece of fruit or a scrap of meat; often it was nothing but a dry crust. But sometimes there would be one of those flat, rich cakes, sprinkled with raisins and sugar, that Tito liked so much. At suppertime the same thing happened, although there was a little less of everything, for things were hard to snatch in the evening with the streets full of people. Besides, Bimbo didn't approve of too much food before going to sleep. A heavy supper made boys too restless and dogs too stodgy—and it was the business of a dog to sleep lightly with one ear open and muscles ready for action.

Shana: *I can imagine what the raisin cake looked and tasted like.*
VISUALIZING

---

1. **the Caesar** (sē′zər): the Roman emperor.
2. **sacrifices:** offerings of animals or objects to the gods.

Shana: Bimbo is just as important a character as Tito.
EVALUATING

But whether there was much or little, hot or cold, fresh or dry, food was always there. Tito never asked where it came from, and Bimbo never told him. There was plenty of rainwater in the hollows of soft stones; the old egg-woman at the corner sometimes gave him a cupful of strong goat's milk; in the grape season the fat winemaker let him have drippings of the mild juice. So there was no danger of going hungry or thirsty. There was plenty of everything in Pompeii if you knew where to find it—and if you had a dog like Bimbo.

Ramón: I like the art because it helps me imagine what the streets of Pompeii looked like.
VISUALIZING

The Sorceress and the Traveler. Mosaic from Pompeii, House of the Dioscuri. Museo Archeologico Nazionale, Naples, Italy. Scala/Art Resource, New York.

As I said before, Tito was not the merriest boy in Pompeii. He could not romp with the other youngsters and play hare and hounds and I spy and follow-your-master and ball-against-the-building and jackstones and kings and robbers with them. But that did not make him sorry for himself. If he could not see the sights that delighted the lads of Pompeii, he could hear and smell things they never noticed. He could really see more with his ears and nose than they could with their eyes. When he and Bimbo went out walking, he knew just where they were going and exactly what was happening.

"Ah," he'd sniff and say as they passed a handsome villa, "Glaucus Pansa is giving a grand dinner tonight. They're going to have three kinds of bread, and roast pigling, and stuffed goose, and a great stew—I think bear stew—and a fig pie." And Bimbo would note that this would be a good place to visit tomorrow.

Or, "H'm," Tito would murmur, half through his lips, half through his nostrils. "The wife of Marcus Lucretius is expecting her mother. She's shaking out every piece of goods in the house; she's going to use the best clothes—the ones she's been keeping in pine needles and camphor[3]—and there's an extra girl in the kitchen. Come, Bimbo, let's get out of the dust!"

Or, as they passed a small but elegant dwelling opposite the public baths, "Too bad! The tragic poet is ill again. It must be a bad fever this time, for they're trying smoke fumes instead of medicine. Whew! I'm glad I'm not a tragic poet!"

Or, as they neared the forum, "Mm-m! What good things they have in the macellum today!" (It really was a sort of butcher-grocer-marketplace, but Tito didn't know any better. He called it the macellum.) "Dates from Africa, and salt oysters from sea caves, and cuttlefish, and new honey, and sweet onions, and—ugh!—water-buffalo steaks. Come, let's see what's what in the forum." And Bimbo, just as curious as his comrade, hurried on. Being a dog, he trusted his ears and nose (like Tito) more than his eyes. And so the two of them entered the center of Pompeii.

---

3. **camphor** (kăm′fər): a strong-smelling substance used as a moth repellent.

Ramón: *I never thought about being able to "see" with your nose and ears. I wonder how many things I miss because I'm not paying attention.*
CONNECTING

Ramón: *What's a macellum? Oh, it's explained in the next sentence.*
CLARIFYING

The entire story can be found on pages 700–713. To practice reading strategies, go to "Your Turn" on pages S20–S31.

Reading for Information

Reading literature often leads to other kinds of reading experiences. For example, you may read about a historical event in this book and then do research on that event for social studies class. When you read encyclopedia articles, newspapers, magazines, Web pages, and text-books, you are reading for information. This kind of reading requires you to use a different set of skills. The strategies below will help you.

REFERENCE BOOK

652 Pompeii

Pompeii, *pahm PAY* or *pahm PAY ee,* was an ancient city in Italy that disappeared after the eruption of Mount Vesuvius in A.D. 79. For hundreds of years, the city lay buried under cinders, ashes, and stone. Since Pompeii was rediscovered in the 1700's, much has been learned about its history. Each year, excavations in the area around Pompeii bring forth additional bits of ancient art and architecture. Much also has been learned about the everyday life of the ancient Romans and their customs.

The ruins of Pompeii tell us much about the ancient Roman world.

Early days. Pompeii was not a remarkable city. But it has become better known than many of the wealthier Roman towns because its ruins were so well preserved. Pompeii lay on a plateau of ancient lava near the Bay of Naples, less than 1 mile (1.6 kilometers) from the foot of Mount Vesuvius. . . .

Pompeii carried on a prosperous trade in wine, oil, and breadstuffs. The city was a market for the produce of a rich countryside, and its port had widespread connections in the Mediterranean area. Pompeii was also an industrial center and produced such specialties as millstones, fish sauce, perfumes, and cloth. Inhabitants of Pompeii included wealthy landowners, prosperous merchants and manufacturers, shopkeepers, artisans, and slaves.

The eruption of Mount Vesuvius. Earthquakes in A.D. 62 or 63 damaged Pompeii, Naples, and Herculaneum. Statues fell, columns were broken, and some buildings collapsed. Mount Vesuvius rumbled at this time. However, the people did not believe that there would be more danger, and they repaired their cities. During the summer of A.D. 79, Vesuvius erupted suddenly and with great violence. Streams of lava and mud poured on Herculaneum and filled the town and its harbor.

Hot ashes, stones, and cinders rained down on Pompeii. The darkened air was filled with poisonous gas and fumes. The Roman writer Pliny the Younger told in a letter how he led his mother to safety through the fumes and falling stones. His uncle, the writer Pliny the Elder, commanded a fleet that rescued some people. He landed to view the eruption and died on the shore.

The remains of about 2,000 victims out of a population of some 20,000 have been found in excavations at Pompeii. Some of the victims were trapped in their homes and killed by hot ashes. Others breathed the poisonous fumes and died as they fled. Archaeologists find the *shells* (molds) of the bodies preserved in the hardened ash. By carefully pouring plaster into the shells,

STRATEGIES FOR READING

SET A PURPOSE FOR READING

- Decide why you are reading the material—to study for a test, to do research, or simply to find out more about a topic that interests you.

- Use your purpose to determine how detailed your notes will be.

LOOK FOR DESIGN FEATURES

- Look at the title, any subheads, boldfaced words or phrases, boxed text, and any other text that is highlighted in some way.

- Use these text organizers to help you preview the text and identify the main ideas.

- Study photographs, maps, charts, graphs, and captions.

NOTICE TEXT STRUCTURES AND PATTERNS

- Does the text make comparisons? Does it describe causes and effects? Is there a sequence of events?

- Look for signal words such as *same, different, because, first,* and *then* to help you see the organizational pattern.

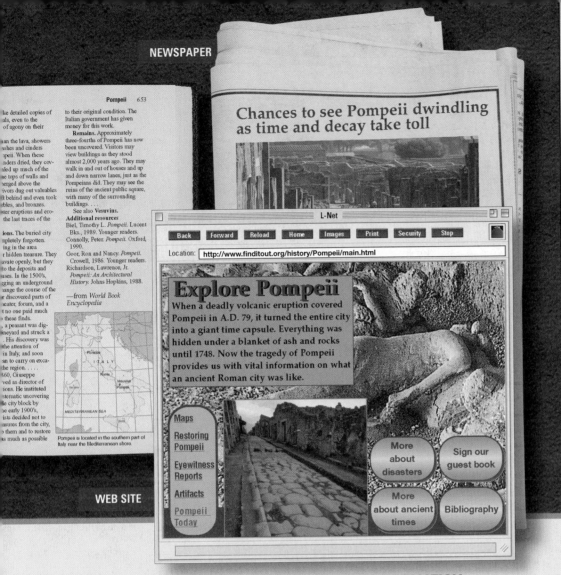

NEWSPAPER

Chances to see Pompeii dwindling as time and decay take toll

WEB SITE

Explore Pompeii

When a deadly volcanic eruption covered Pompeii in A.D. 79, it turned the entire city into a giant time capsule. Everything was hidden under a blanket of ash and rocks until 1748. Now the tragedy of Pompeii provides us with vital information on what an ancient Roman city was like.

Maps

Restoring Pompeii

Eyewitness Reports

Artifacts

Pompeii Today

More about disasters

Sign our guest book

More about ancient times

Bibliography

Location: http://www.finditout.org/history/Pompeii/main.html

Back · Forward · Reload · Home · Images · Print · Security · Stop

L-Net

READ SLOWLY AND CAREFULLY

- Take notes on the main ideas. Try to paraphrase, or state the information in your own words.
- Map the information by using a concept web or other graphic organizer.
- Notice unfamiliar words. These are sometimes defined in the text.
- If there are questions with the text, be sure you can answer them.

EVALUATE THE INFORMATION

- Think about what you have read. Does the text make sense? Is it complete?
- Summarize the information—give the main points in just a few words.

Encyclopedias, textbooks, and other reference books give reliable information. Use the tips on the previous pages and the strategies below to read the encyclopedia article. Then see how Shana and Ramón applied the strategies as they did research for a social studies project.

STRATEGIES FOR READING

(A) Read the heading and subheads.
Also, look at photographs, maps, and captions.

(B) Notice how the text is organized.
This article gives the main idea and then describes a sequence of events—the destruction and rediscovery of a city.

(C) Look for clues to difficult words.
This encyclopedia uses *italic type* for specialized terms and defines those terms in parentheses.

(D) Decide if you need to do more research.
The "See also" reference means the encyclopedia has an article on a related subject. The "Additional resources" section also recommends books on Pompeii for different age groups.

---

652   **Pompeii**

(A) Pompeii, *pahm PAY* or *pahm PAY ee,* was an ancient city in Italy that disappeared after the eruption of Mount Vesuvius in A.D. 79. For hundreds of years, the city lay buried under cinders, ashes, and stone. Since Pompeii was rediscovered in the 1700's, much has been learned about its history. Each year, excavations in the area around Pompeii bring forth additional bits of ancient art and architecture. Much also has been learned about the everyday life of the ancient Romans and their customs.

The ruins of Pompeii tell us much about the ancient Roman world.

(B) Early days. Pompeii was not a remarkable city. But it has become better known than many of the wealthier Roman towns because its ruins were so well preserved. Pompeii lay on a plateau of ancient lava near the Bay of Naples, less than 1 mile (1.6 kilometers) from the foot of Mount Vesuvius. . . .

Pompeii carried on a prosperous trade in wine, oil, and breadstuffs. The city was a market for the produce of a rich countryside, and its port had widespread connections in the Mediterranean area. Pompeii was also an industrial center and produced such specialties as millstones, fish sauce, perfumes, and cloth. Inhabitants of Pompeii included wealthy landowners, prosperous merchants and manufacturers, shopkeepers, artisans, and slaves.

The eruption of Mount Vesuvius. Earthquakes in A.D. 62 or 63 damaged Pompeii, Naples, and Herculaneum. Statues fell, columns were broken, and some buildings collapsed. Mount Vesuvius rumbled at this time. However, the people did not believe that there would be more danger, and they repaired their cities. During the summer of A.D. 79, Vesuvius erupted suddenly and with great violence. Streams of lava and mud poured on Herculaneum and filled the town and its harbor.

Hot ashes, stones, and cinders rained down on Pompeii. The darkened air was filled with poisonous gas and fumes. The Roman writer Pliny the Younger told in a letter how he led his mother to safety through the fumes and falling stones. His uncle, the writer Pliny the Elder, commanded a fleet that rescued some people. He landed to view the eruption and died on the shore.

The remains of about 2,000 victims out of a population of some 20,000 have been found in excavations at Pompeii. Some of the victims were trapped in their homes and killed by hot ashes. Others breathed the poisonous fumes and died as they fled. Archaeologists find the *shells* **(C)** (molds) of the bodies preserved in the hardened ash. By carefully pouring plaster into the shells, they can make detailed copies of the individuals, even to the expressions of agony on their faces.

Rather than the lava, showers of hot, wet ashes and cinders sprayed Pompeii. When these ashes and cinders dried, they covered and sealed up much of the city. Only the tops of walls and columns emerged above the waste. Survivors dug out valuables they had left behind and even took statues, marbles, and bronzes. However, later eruptions and erosion erased the last traces of the city. . . .

Excavations. The buried city was not completely forgotten. Peasants living in the area searched for hidden treasure. They did not excavate openly, but they tunneled into the deposits and reached houses. In the 1500's, workers digging an underground tunnel to change the course of the Sarno River discovered parts of the amphitheater, forum, and a temple. But no one paid much attention to these finds.

In 1748, a peasant was digging in a vineyard and struck a buried wall. His discovery was brought to the attention of authorities in Italy, and soon people began to carry on excavations in the region. . . . .

After 1860, Giuseppe Fiorelli served as director of the excavations. He instituted the first systematic uncovering of the whole city block by block. In the early 1900's, archaeologists decided not to remove treasures from the city, but to keep them and to restore buildings as much as possible to their original condition. The Italian government has given money for this work.

Remains. Approximately three-fourths of Pompeii has now been uncovered. Visitors may view buildings as they stood almost 2,000 years ago. They may walk in and out of houses and up and down narrow lanes, just as the Pompeians did. They may see the ruins of the ancient public square, with many of the surrounding buildings. . . .

D See also **Vesuvius.**

Additional resources

Biel, Timothy L. *Pompeii.* Lucent Bks., 1989. Younger readers.
Connolly, Peter. *Pompeii.* Oxford, 1990.
Goor, Ron and Nancy. *Pompeii.* Crowell, 1986. Younger readers.
Richardson, Lawrence, Jr. *Pompeii: An Architectural History.* Johns Hopkins, 1988.

—from *World Book Encyclopedia*

Pompeii is located in the southern part of Italy near the Mediterranean shore.

Newspaper and magazine articles are written to provide information, but they often entertain as well. As you read them, keep these strategies in mind.

STRATEGIES FOR READING

A **Study the headline.**
It will tell you the main idea.

B **Look at visuals and captions.**
Photographs, maps, and other graphics provide information.

C **Watch for organizational patterns.**
This article first describes an effect (Pompeii is "at risk of dying"). Read further to find the many causes of the problem. For more on text organization, see pages R106–R111 in the Reading Handbook.

D **Notice special features such as sidebars.**
Sidebars are mini-articles on related topics.

E **Pay attention to sources.**
Where did the writer get the information—from firsthand experience, from experts, or from people on the street?

A ## Chances to see Pompeii dwindling as time and decay take toll

B Tourists crowd the ancient streets of Pompeii.

By Candice Hughes
The Associated Press

C POMPEII, Italy—Pompeii is a city under siege, a city at risk of dying.

Again.

The ancient Roman town in the shadow of Mount Vesuvius has long been synonymous with tragedy. A powerful earthquake struck in A.D. 62. Sixteen years later, just as Pompeii was recovering, Vesuvius blew its top, burying the bustling city and killing thousands of people.

Time transformed disaster into another era's good fortune. A 20-foot-deep cocoon of volcanic ash preserved the city virtually intact, bestowing an unparalleled gift for future generations: intimate knowledge of day-to-day life in the ancient world. . . .

Pompeii is an unrivaled time machine that takes us back 2,000 years.

But the machine is breaking down. A ruthless array of forces . . . have taken a toll. And what is lost cannot be recovered.

E "Pompeii's death is not in one blow. It is slow, but sure," says Pietro Giovanni Guzzo, the archaeological superintendent of ancient Pompeii, which is a nationally administered district separate from the nearby modern town of Pompeii.

Wild dogs roam the ancient city, snapping and snarling at tourists. Weeds dislodge paving stones and mosaics. Sun and rain fade frescoes—some are now almost invisible, others gone for good. Rotting boards prop up crumbling

walls and barricades block off much of the city.

Most of the wall paintings, the colonnaded houses, the statues and mosaics are now off-limits. Only 34 acres are open—half of what visitors could see in the 1950s. . . .

Pompeii attracts tourists in ever-increasing numbers. Around 2 million people now visit every year. They jam into the few open houses, backpacks scraping against frescoes, fingers rubbing along painted walls, greedy hands scooping up morsels of marble as souvenirs.

Pompeii has just 150 guards, safely sinecured state workers prone to lounging in the shade.

A few glimmers of hope have appeared. Pompeii has sound management for the first time in decades and is about to get more money. World Monuments Watch, which calls Pompeii one of the planet's most imperiled cultural sites, is working on a master plan for conservation. . . .

"We can't wait another 10 years," says one of Italy's most prominent archaeologists, Andrea Carandini. "Because in another 10 years there won't be anything left."

The Walls Speak
by Elizabeth Gordon

The eruption of Mount Vesuvius preserved Pompeii—right down to the scribbles on its walls. The graffiti shown below were translated from the Latin by archaeologist Antonio Varone and first appeared in *Archaeology* magazine.

Sports
On the 25th and 26th of February, in Pompeii, there will be a show by Tiberius Claudius Verus, including combat against wild beasts, wrestling matches and sprinkling with scented water . . .

Loitering
This is not a place for idlers. Leave, you who have nothing to do

Politics
O Trebius Valens, vote for Ovidius Veiento as *aedile* [an elected official], and he in turn will support you

Verbal Abuse
Litus, you are a mediocre man

Graffiti
I am surprised, o wall, that you, who have to bear the weariness of so many writers, are still standing

Reading for Information
Web Sites

Web sites that are run by museums, libraries, universities, and government agencies are good sources of reliable information. Reading Web pages requires special strategies, as you will see here.

STRATEGIES FOR READING

A **Find the page's Web address.**
This is generally in a box at the top of your screen. Write down or bookmark the address in case you get lost while Web surfing.

B **Read the page's title.**
This will give you an idea of what the page is about.

C **Look for links to other parts of the site.**
Scan the menu options and decide which are most likely to have the information you need. Don't get lost following link after link. Use the Back button to retrace your steps when necessary.

D **Notice source citations.**
Some sites tell you where their information is from so you can decide whether it is reliable.

E **Write down important ideas and details.**
Try to paraphrase the text, or restate it in your own words. Then decide whether you need to consult other sources.

L-Net

| Back | Forward | Reload | Home | Images | Print | Security | Stop |

Location: http://www.finditout.org/history/Pompeii/main.html **A**

Explore Pompeii
When a deadly volcanic eruption covered Pompeii in A.D. 79, it turned the entire city into a giant time capsule. Everything was hidden under a blanket of ash and rocks until 1748. Now the tragedy of Pompeii provides us with vital information on what an ancient Roman city was like.

C
Maps
Restoring Pompeii
Eyewitness Reports
Artifacts
Pompeii Today

More about disasters
Sign guest b
More about ancient times
Bibliogr

D **Sources:** The Pompeii Forum Project at the University of Virginia, *World Book Encyclopedia, Journal of Archaeology.* **Last updated:** Jan. 9

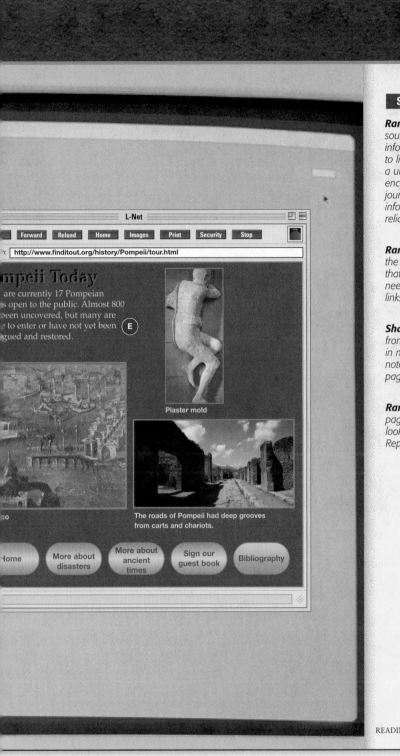

L-Net

Forward | Reload | Home | Images | Print | Security | Stop

http://www.finditout.org/history/Pompeii/tour.html

mpeii Today

are currently 17 Pompeian
s open to the public. Almost 800
been uncovered, but many are
e to enter or have not yet been Ⓔ
gued and restored.

Plaster mold

The roads of Pompeii had deep grooves
from carts and chariots.

Home | More about disasters | More about ancient times | Sign our guest book | Bibliography

STRATEGIES IN ACTION

Ramón: From the title, it sounds as if this site has information on what it was like to live in Pompeii. The site lists a university project, an encyclopedia, and a scientific journal as sources, so the information is likely to be reliable.

Ramón: I'm going to click on the Pompeii Today link because that sounds like it has what I need. I'll look at some other links later.

Shana: I might use information from the Pompeii Today page in my report, so I'll take some notes and write down the page's Web address.

Ramón: The Pompeii Today page doesn't have what I'm looking for, so I'll try Eyewitness Reports instead.

Your Turn
Applying the Strategies

As you read the following story, create a **Reader's Notebook** to help you understand and reflect on what you read. Prompts and questions in the margins will help you. For instructions on how to create a Reader's Notebook, see page S4.

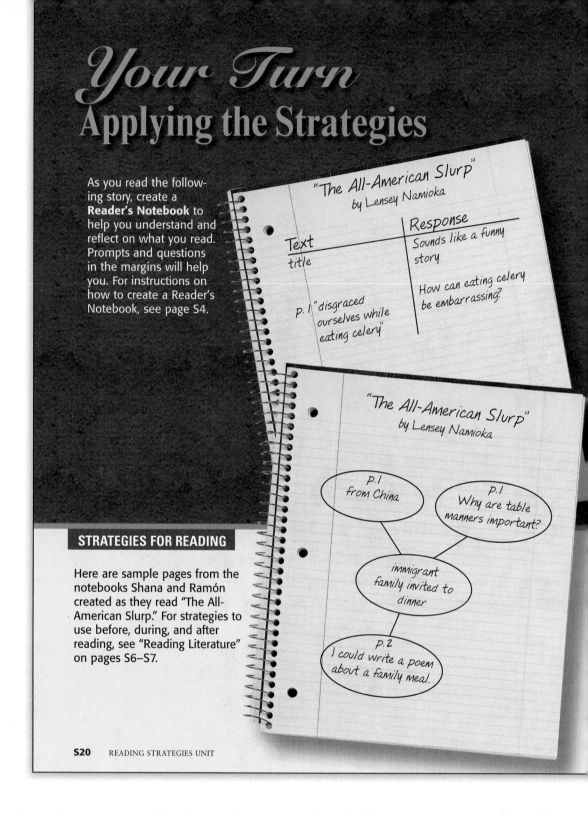

"The All-American Slurp"
by Lensey Namioka

Text	Response
title	Sounds like a funny story
p. 1 "disgraced ourselves while eating celery"	How can eating celery be embarrassing?

"The All-American Slurp"
by Lensey Namioka

- p. 1 from China
- p. 1 Why are table manners important?
- immigrant family invited to dinner
- p. 2 I could write a poem about a family meal.

STRATEGIES FOR READING

Here are sample pages from the notebooks Shana and Ramón created as they read "The All-American Slurp." For strategies to use before, during, and after reading, see "Reading Literature" on pages S6–S7.

The All-American SLURP

by Lensey Namioka

The first time our family was invited out to dinner in America, we disgraced ourselves while eating celery. We had emigrated to this country from China, and during our early days here we had a hard time with American table manners.

Applying the Strategies

Your Turn

In China we never ate celery raw, or any other kind of vegetable raw. We always had to disinfect the vegetables in boiling water first. When we were presented with our first relish tray, the raw celery caught us unprepared.

We had been invited to dinner by our neighbors, the Gleasons. After arriving at the house, we shook hands with our hosts and packed ourselves into a sofa. As our family of four sat stiffly in a row, my younger brother and I stole glances at our parents for a clue as to what to do next.

QUESTION ▶
Why do you think the family is so nervous?

Mrs. Gleason offered the relish tray to Mother. The tray looked pretty, with its tiny red radishes, curly sticks of carrots, and long, slender stalks of pale green celery. "Do try some of the celery, Mrs. Lin," she said. "It's from a local farmer, and it's sweet."

Mother picked up one of the green stalks, and Father followed suit. Then I picked up a stalk, and my brother did too. So there we sat, each with a stalk of celery in our right hand.

Mrs. Gleason kept smiling. "Would you like to try some of the dip, Mrs. Lin? It's my own recipe: sour cream and onion flakes, with a dash of Tabasco sauce."

Most Chinese don't care for dairy products, and in those days I wasn't even ready to drink fresh milk. Sour cream sounded perfectly revolting. Our family shook our heads in unison.

Mrs. Gleason went off with the relish tray to the other guests, and we carefully watched to see what they did. Everyone seemed to eat the raw vegetables quite happily.

Mother took a bite of her celery. *Crunch.* "It's not bad!" she whispered.

Father took a bite of his celery. *Crunch.* "Yes, it is good," he said, looking surprised.

EVALUATE ▶
Do the sound effects help you imagine the scene? Why or why not?

I took a bite, and then my brother. *Crunch, crunch.* It was more than good; it was delicious. Raw celery has a slight sparkle, a zingy taste that you don't get in cooked celery. When Mrs. Gleason came around with the relish tray, we each took another stalk of celery, except my brother. He took two.

There was only one problem: long strings ran through the length of the stalk, and they got caught in my teeth. When I help my mother in the kitchen, I always pull the strings out before slicing celery.

I pulled the strings out of my stalk. *Z-z-zip, z-z-zip.* My brother followed suit. *Z-z-zip, z-z-zip, z-z-zip.* To my left, my parents were

S22 READING STRATEGIES UNIT

taking care of their own stalks. *Z-z-zip, z-z-zip, z-z-zip.*

Suddenly I realized that there was dead silence except for our zipping. Looking up, I saw that the eyes of everyone in the room were on our family. Mr. and Mrs. Gleason, their daughter Meg, who was my friend, and their neighbors the Badels—they were all staring at us as we busily pulled the strings of our celery.

That wasn't the end of it. Mrs. Gleason announced that dinner was served and invited us to the dining table. It was lavishly covered with platters of food, but we couldn't see any chairs around the table. So we helpfully carried over some dining chairs and sat down. All the other guests just stood there.

Mrs. Gleason bent down and whispered to us, "This is a buffet dinner. You help yourselves to some food and eat it in the living room."

Our family beat a retreat back to the sofa as if chased by enemy soldiers. For the rest of the evening, too mortified to go back to the dining table, I nursed a bit of potato salad on my plate.

Next day Meg and I got on the school bus together. I wasn't sure how she would feel about me after the spectacle our family made at the party. But she was just the same as usual, and the only reference she made to the party was, "Hope you and your folks got enough to eat last night. You certainly didn't take very much. Mom never tries to figure out how much food to prepare. She just puts everything on the table and hopes for the best."

I began to relax. The Gleasons' dinner party wasn't so different from a Chinese meal after all. My mother also puts everything on the table and hopes for the best.

Meg was the first friend I had made after we came to America. I eventually got acquainted with a few other kids in school, but Meg was still the only real friend I had.

My brother didn't have any problems making friends. He spent all his time with some boys who were teaching him baseball, and in no time he could speak English much faster than I could—not better, but faster.

I worried more about making mistakes, and I spoke carefully, making sure I could say everything right before opening my mouth. At least I had a better accent than my parents, who never really got rid of their Chinese accent, even years later. My parents had both studied English in school before coming to America, but

◀ **CONNECT**
What connections can you make between this situation and a time you were embarrassed?

◀ **CLARIFY: SUMMARIZE**
How would you summarize the story so far?

what they had studied was mostly written English, not spoken.

Father's approach to English was a scientific one. Since Chinese verbs have no tense, he was fascinated by the way English verbs changed form according to whether they were in the present, past imperfect, perfect, pluperfect, future, or future perfect tense. He was always making diagrams of verbs and their inflections, and he looked for opportunities to show off his mastery of the pluperfect and future perfect tenses, his two favorites. "I shall have finished my project by Monday," he would say smugly.

Mother's approach was to memorize lists of polite phrases that would cover all possible social situations. She was constantly muttering things like "I'm fine, thank you. And you?" Once she accidentally stepped on someone's foot and hurriedly blurted, "Oh, that's quite all right!" Embarrassed by her slip, she resolved to do better next time. So when someone stepped on her foot, she cried, "You're welcome!"

In our own different ways, we made progress in learning English. But I had another worry, and that was my appearance. My brother didn't have to worry, since Mother bought him blue jeans for school, and he dressed like all the other boys. But she insisted that girls had to wear skirts. By the time she saw that Meg and the other girls were wearing jeans, it was too late. My school clothes were bought already, and we didn't have money left to buy new outfits for me. We had too many other things to buy first, like furniture, pots, and pans.

The first time I visited Meg's house, she took me upstairs to her room, and I wound up trying on her clothes. We were pretty much the same size, since Meg was shorter and thinner than average. Maybe that's how we became friends in the first place. Wearing Meg's jeans and T-shirt, I looked at myself in the mirror. I could almost pass for an American—from the back, anyway. At least the kids in school wouldn't stop and stare at me in the hallways, which was what they did when they saw me in my white blouse and navy blue skirt that went a couple of inches below the knees.

When Meg came to my house, I invited her to try on my Chinese dresses, the ones with a high collar and slits up the sides. Meg's eyes were bright as she looked at herself in the mirror. She struck several sultry poses, and we nearly fell over laughing.

EVALUATE ▶
Do you think it is fair that the mother buys skirts for the girl and jeans for the boy? Write down your opinion and the reasons for it.

The dinner party at the Gleasons' didn't stop my growing friendship with Meg. Things were getting better for me in other ways too. Mother finally bought me some jeans at the end of the month, when Father got his paycheck. She wasn't in any hurry about buying them at first, until I worked on her. This is what I did. Since we didn't have a car in those days, I often ran down to the neighborhood store to pick up things for her. The groceries cost less at a big supermarket, but the closest one was many blocks away. One day, when she ran out of flour, I offered to borrow a bike from our neighbor's son and buy a ten-pound bag of flour at the big supermarket. I mounted the boy's bike and waved to Mother. "I'll be back in five minutes!"

Before I started pedaling, I heard her voice behind me. "You can't go out in public like that! People can see all the way up to your thighs!"

"I'm sorry," I said innocently. "I thought you were in a hurry to get the flour." For dinner we were going to have pot-stickers (fried Chinese dumplings), and we needed a lot of flour.

"Couldn't you borrow a girl's bicycle?" complained Mother. "That way your skirt won't be pushed up."

"There aren't too many of those around," I said. "Almost all the girls wear jeans while riding a bike, so they don't see any point buying a girl's bike."

We didn't eat pot-stickers that evening, and Mother was thoughtful. Next day we took the bus downtown, and she bought me a pair of jeans. In the same week, my brother made the baseball team of his junior high school, Father started taking driving lessons, and Mother discovered rummage sales. We soon got all the furniture we needed, plus a dart board and a 1,000-piece jigsaw puzzle (fourteen hours later, we discovered that it was a 999-piece jigsaw puzzle). There was hope that the Lins might become a normal American family after all.

Then came our dinner at the Lakeview Restaurant.

The Lakeview was an expensive restaurant, one of those places where a headwaiter dressed in tails conducted you to your seat, and the only light came from candles and flaming desserts. In one corner of the room a lady harpist played tinkling melodies.

Father wanted to celebrate, because he had just been promoted. He worked for an electronics company, and after his English started improving, his superiors decided to appoint him

◀ **QUESTION**
Why does the mother buy jeans for the girl?

◀ **VISUALIZE**
Can you imagine what the restaurant looks and sounds like? You may want to make a sketch of the scene.

APPLYING THE STRATEGIES   **S25**

to a position more suited to his training. The promotion not only brought a higher salary but was also a tremendous boost to his pride.

Up to then we had eaten only in Chinese restaurants. Although my brother and I were becoming fond of hamburgers, my parents didn't care much for Western food, other than chow mein.

But this was a special occasion, and Father asked his coworkers to recommend a really elegant restaurant. So there we were at the Lakeview, stumbling after the headwaiter in the murky dining room.

At our table we were handed our menus, and they were so big that to read mine I almost had to stand up again. But why bother? It was mostly in French, anyway.

Father, being an engineer, was always systematic. He took out a pocket French dictionary. "They told me that most of the items would be in French, so I came prepared." He even had a pocket flashlight, the size of a marking pen. While Mother held the flashlight over the menu, he looked up the items that were in French.

"*Pâté en croûte*," he muttered. "Let's see . . . *pâté* is paste . . . *croûte* is crust . . . hmm . . . a paste in crust."

The waiter stood looking patient. I squirmed and died at least fifty times.

At long last Father gave up. "Why don't we just order four complete dinners at random?" he suggested.

"Isn't that risky?" asked Mother. "The French eat some rather peculiar things, I've heard."

"A Chinese can eat anything a Frenchman can eat," Father declared.

The soup arrived in a plate. How do you get soup up from a plate? I glanced at the other diners, but the ones at the nearby

PREDICT ▶
What do you think will happen? Jot down your predictions.

tables were not on their soup course, while the more distant ones were invisible in the darkness.

Fortunately my parents had studied books on Western etiquette before they came to America. "Tilt your plate," whispered my mother. "It's easier to spoon the soup up that way."

She was right. Tilting the plate did the trick. But the etiquette book didn't say anything about what you did after the soup reached your lips. As any respectable Chinese knows, the correct way to eat your soup is to slurp. This helps to cool the liquid and prevent you from burning your lips. It also shows your appreciation.

We showed our appreciation. *Shloop,* went my father. *Shloop,* went my mother. *Shloop, shloop,* went my brother, who was the hungriest.

The lady harpist stopped playing to take a rest. And in the silence, our family's consumption of soup suddenly seemed unnaturally loud. You know how it sounds on a rocky beach when the tide goes out and the water drains from all those little pools? They go *shloop, shloop, shloop.* That was the Lin family, eating soup.

At the next table a waiter was pouring wine. When a large *shloop* reached him, he froze. The bottle continued to pour, and red wine flooded the tabletop and into the lap of a customer. Even the customer didn't notice anything at first, being also hypnotized by the *shloop, shloop, shloop.*

It was too much. "I need to go to the toilet," I mumbled, jumping to my feet. A waiter, sensing my urgency, quickly directed me to the ladies' room.

I splashed cold water on my burning face, and as I dried myself with a paper towel, I stared into the mirror. In this perfumed ladies' room, with its pink-and-silver wallpaper and marbled sinks, I looked completely out of place. What was I

◀ **CONNECT**
How would you react if you heard someone in a fancy restaurant slurping soup?

◀ **CLARIFY: MAKE INFERENCES**
Why do you think the girl's face is "burning"? List two or three adjectives that describe how she is feeling.

APPLYING THE STRATEGIES   **S27**

A Kitchen on the Eve of a Festival, Zhou Jihe.
Courtesy of Foreign Languages Press, Beijing, China.

CONNECT ▲
*How is this picture similar to
or different from the kitchen in
your home?*

doing here? What was our family doing in the Lakeview Restaurant? In America?

The door to the ladies' room opened. A woman came in and glanced curiously at me. I retreated into one of the toilet cubicles and latched the door.

Time passed—maybe half an hour, maybe an hour. Then I heard the door open again, and my mother's voice. "Are you in there? You're not sick, are you?"

There was real concern in her voice. A girl can't leave her family just because they slurp their soup. Besides, the toilet cubicle had a few drawbacks as a permanent residence. "I'm all right," I said, undoing the latch.

Mother didn't tell me how the rest of the dinner went, and I didn't want to know. In the weeks following, I managed to push the whole thing into the back of my mind, where it jumped out at me only a few times a day. Even now, I turn hot all over when I think of the Lakeview Restaurant.

◀ **CLARIFY**
Why does the girl leave the cubicle?

But by the time we had been in this country for three months, our family was definitely making progress toward becoming Americanized. I remember my parents' first PTA meeting. Father wore a neat suit and tie, and Mother put on her first pair of high heels. She stumbled only once. They met my homeroom teacher and beamed as she told them that I would make honor roll soon at the rate I was going. Of course Chinese etiquette forced Father to say that I was a very stupid girl and Mother to protest that the teacher was showing favoritism toward me. But I could tell they were both very proud.

The day came when my parents announced that they wanted to give a dinner party. We had invited Chinese friends to eat with us before, but this dinner was going to be different. In addition to a Chinese-American family, we were going to invite the Gleasons.

"Gee, I can hardly wait to have dinner at your house," Meg said to me. "I just *love* Chinese food."

That was a relief. Mother was a good cook, but I wasn't sure if people who ate sour cream would also eat chicken gizzards stewed in soy sauce.

Mother decided not to take a chance with chicken gizzards. Since we had Western guests, she set the table with large dinner plates, which we never used in Chinese meals. In fact we didn't use individual plates at all but picked up food from the platters in the middle of the table and brought it directly to our rice bowls.

◀ **PREDICT**
What will happen when the Gleasons visit? Write down one or two predictions. Check them later to see if you were correct.

Following the practice of Chinese-American restaurants, Mother also placed large serving spoons on the platters.

The dinner started well. Mrs. Gleason exclaimed at the beautifully arranged dishes of food: the colorful candied fruit in the sweet-and-sour pork dish, the noodle-thin shreds of chicken meat stir-fried with tiny peas, and the glistening pink prawns in a ginger sauce.

At first I was too busy enjoying my food to notice how the guests were doing. But soon I remembered my duties. Sometimes guests were too polite to help themselves, and you had to serve them with more food.

I glanced at Meg, to see if she needed more food, and my eyes nearly popped out at the sight of her plate. It was piled with food: the sweet-and-sour meat pushed right against the chicken shreds, and the chicken sauce ran into the prawns. She had been taking food from a second dish before she finished eating her helping from the first!

Horrified, I turned to look at Mrs. Gleason. She was dumping rice out of her bowl and putting it on her dinner plate. Then she ladled prawns and gravy on top of the rice and mixed everything together, the way you mix sand, gravel, and cement to make concrete.

I couldn't bear to look any longer, and I turned to Mr. Gleason. He was chasing a pea around his plate. Several times he got it to the edge, but when he tried to pick it up with his chopsticks, it rolled back toward the center of the plate again. Finally he put down his chopsticks and picked up the pea with his fingers. He really did! A grown man!

All of us, our family and the Chinese guests, stopped eating to watch the activities of the Gleasons. I wanted to giggle. Then I caught my mother's eyes on me. She frowned and shook

CLARIFY ▶
How are the Lins' table manners different from the Gleasons'?

VISUALIZE ▶
Can you picture how the Gleasons look as they eat their dinner? List a few words that describe them, or make a sketch.

her head slightly, and I understood the message: the Gleasons were not used to Chinese ways, and they were just coping the best they could. For some reason I thought of celery strings.

When the main courses were finished, Mother brought out a platter of fruit. "I hope you weren't expecting a sweet dessert," she said. "Since the Chinese don't eat dessert, I didn't think to prepare any."

"Oh, I couldn't possibly eat dessert!" cried Mrs. Gleason. "I'm simply stuffed!"

Meg had different ideas. When the table was cleared, she announced that she and I were going for a walk. "I don't know about you, but I feel like dessert," she told me, when we were outside. "Come on; there's a Dairy Queen down the street. I could use a big chocolate milk shake!"

Although I didn't really want anything more to eat, I insisted on paying for the milk shakes. After all, I was still hostess.

Meg got her large chocolate milk shake, and I had a small one. Even so, she was finishing hers while I was only half done. Toward the end she pulled hard on her straws and went *shloop, shloop*.

"Do you always slurp when you eat a milk shake?" I asked, before I could stop myself.

Meg grinned. "Sure. All Americans slurp." ❖

◀ **QUESTION**
Why does the girl think of celery strings?

◀ **EVALUATE**
What is your opinion of the story? Would you recommend it to a friend?

Tests of Courage

There are many kinds of courage: for instance, physical courage, inner strength, and the courage it takes just to live every day. In Unit One, students will read about people who face various challenges—some internal, some external. This unit contains two parts, both of which contribute to the unit theme by examining the tests of courage people face, and particularly, their reactions to those tests.

——————— Part 1 ———————

The Courage to Be Me In this part, young people face one of life's greatest tests—knowing who you are and what is important to you. For example, in "Nadia the Willful," a young girl learns about the importance of custom, law, and family. In doing so, she teaches others what real strength is.

——————— Part 2 ———————

Courage in Action Another kind of courage is highlighted in the nonfiction, fiction, and poetry of this section. Feats of daring and danger challenge and bring out the best in the people and characters students will read about. For example, in "Matthew Henson at the Top of the World," a man risks everything in his quest for the North Pole.

UNIT ONE

Tests of Courage

All serious daring starts from within.

Eudora Welty
AMERICAN WRITER

© Reggie Holladay/SIS.

18

EXPLICIT INSTRUCTION **Viewing and Representing**

Untitled **by Reggie Holladay/SIS**

ART APPRECIATION
Instruction Explain that this illustration has some of the qualities of a photograph—its immediacy and realism—and some of the qualities of a painting. The artist has mixed realistic elements—the skateboarders and the wave itself—with imagination, so the boys on wheels appear to ride the waves.

Ask: Why do you think the artist shows skateboarders riding a wave instead of on a sidewalk?
Possible Response: Not only does it take physical courage to do the kinds of flips and tricks both skateboarders and surfers do, but also it takes courage to do things a little differently than most people do them. By putting the skateboarders in the setting of a large wave, the artist emphasizes the challenge facing them.

To help students explore the connections between the art, the quotation, and the unit theme, have them consider the following questions:

Ask: Who is the most courageous person you know or have read about? Why?
Students' responses will vary, but should provide reasons why they think the person they have chosen is courageous.

Ask: How would you paraphrase the quotation by Eudora Welty on page 18?
Possible Response: It's what's inside people that enables them to face challenges.

Ask: What kind of courage do you think the painting relates to?
Possible Response: The people in the painting must have physical courage and daring to perform the gravity-defying feats they do.

Ask: What kinds of stories and experiences might you expect to read about in this unit?
Possible Response: ones with strong people facing real or fictional challenges, some with action and physical danger

19

Features and Selections	Literary Analysis	Reading and Critical Thinking	Writing Opportunities
Tests of Courage **The Courage to Be Me**			
Learning the Language of Literature **Fiction**	Fiction, 21 Forms of Fiction, 21		
The Active Reader **Skills and Strategies**		Reading Fiction, 25	
SHORT STORY **Eleven** Difficulty Level: *Easy* Related Reading **Who's the New Kid?**	Character, 26, 28, 31 Main and Minor Characters, 28 Character Traits, 29	Connecting, 26, 28, 30, 31 Comparing Texts, 31 Read Aloud, 30	Tell a Friend, 32
SHORT STORY **President Cleveland, Where Are You?** Difficulty Level: *Average* Reading for Information **Trading Card Talk**	Plot, 34, 36, 38, 42, 44, 45 Review: Character, 45 Character Traits, 39	Sequence of Events, 34, 36, 38, 40, 42, 44, 45 True to Life, 47 Predicting, 43 Paraphrasing, 49 Paraphrasing, 48 Outlining, 50	Character Comparison, 46
SHORT STORY **Scout's Honor** Difficulty Level: *Easy*	Setting, 52, 54, 56, 57, 58, 60, 61, 64 Character Traits, 55 Influence of Setting, 63 Theme, 63	Visualizing, 52, 54, 56, 58, 62, 64 Comparing Texts, 64 Predicting, 59	Persuasive Letter, 65 Past Times, 66
SHORT STORY **Nadia the Willful** Difficulty Level: *Average* Related Reading **Life Doesn't Frighten Me** Building Vocabulary	Theme, 67, 68, 70, 71, 72, 73, 76	Recognizing Cause and Effect, 67, 68, 70, 72, 76 Comparing Texts, 76	Finding Theme, 77
Writing Workshop: Responding to Literature Standardized Test Practice		Analyzing a Student Model, 90 Patterns of Organization, 91	Writing Your Response to Literature, 92 Supporting Your Response, 93 Revision: Organization, 93

Features and Selections	Literary Analysis	Reading and Critical Thinking	Writing Opportunities
Courage in Action			
Learning the Language of Literature **Nonfiction**	Nonfiction, 96		
The Active Reader **Skills and Strategies**		Reading Nonfiction, 100	
BIOGRAPHY **Matthew Henson at the Top of the World** Difficulty Level: *Average* Related Reading: **Into Lucid Air**	Biography, 101, 102, 104, 106, 111 Point of View, 109	Identifying Main Idea and Details, 101, 102, 104, 105, 107, 110, 111 Comparing Texts, 111 Comparing Information, 106	Acceptance Speech, 112 Henson Autobiography, 112 Agreement with a Compound Subject, 113

Features and Selections	Literary Analysis	Reading and Critical Thinking	Writing Opportunities	
INFORMATIVE NONFICTION **Summer of Fire** **Difficulty Level:** *Average*	Informative Nonfiction, 114, 116, 118, 121 Imagery and Simile, 118	Chronological Order, 114, 116, 117, 118, 120, 121 Connect to Your Life, 114 Previewing, 116 Fact and Opinion, 119 Review: Main Idea and Details, 121	Causes and Effects, 122 Active and Passive Voice, 123	
SHORT STORY **Ghost of the Lagoon** **Difficulty Level:** *Average*	Conflict, 124, 126, 130, 132 Review: Plot, 132 Influence of Setting and Plot, 126, 128, 132	Predicting, 124, 126, 128, 130, 132	Battle Narrative, 133 Picturing Mako, 133	
AUTOBIOGRAPHY *from* **The Fun of It** **Difficulty Level:** *Challenging*	Autobiography, 135, 136, 138, 140, 142 Point of View, 139	Identifying the Author's Purpose, 135, 136, 138, 142 Standardized Test Practice, 143	Personality Profile, 143	
Reading for Information **Daring to Dream** **Building Vocabulary**		Reading a Magazine Article, 146, 146 Summarizing, 147		
AUTHOR STUDY **Gary Paulsen**				
ESSAY **Older Run** **Difficulty Level:** *Average* **A Life in the Day of Gary Paulsen**	Anecdote, 154, 156, 158, 161	Comparing Information, 151 Recognizing Causes and Effects, 154, 156, 157, 161 Author's Perspective, 159 Comparing Texts, 161 Fact and Opinion, 163, 163,		
MEMOIR *from* **Woodsong** **Difficulty Level:** *Average*	Memoir, 165, 166, 170 Imagery, 169	Questioning, 165, 166, 170 Read Aloud, 168 Paired Activity, 170		
The Author's Style **Author Study Project**	Key Style Points, 172	Active Reading, 172	Writing, 172 Henson and Paulsen, 173 Survival Kit, 173	
Writing Workshop: **Personal Experience Essay** **Standardized Test Practice**		Analyzing a Student Model, 177 Patterns of Organization, 177	Writing Your Personal Experience Essay, 179 Necessary Details, 180 Revision: Organization, 180	
Reflect and Assess	Discussing Setting, 183	Noting the Newsworthy, 182 Evaluating Reading Experiences, 182 Analyzing Nonfiction, 183	Comparing the Daring, 182 Noting the Newsworthy, 182 Portfolio Building, 183	

UNIT ONE
RESOURCE MANAGEMENT GUIDE
PART 1

To introduce the theme of this unit, use transparencies 1–3 in Fine Arts Transparencies.

	Unit Resource Book	Assessment	Integrated Technology and Media
Eleven pp. 26–33	• Summary p. 7 • Active Reading: Connecting p. 8 • Literary Analysis: Character p. 9 • Active Reading: Read Aloud p. 10 • Grammar p. 11 • Words to Know p. 12 • Selection Quiz p. 13	• Selection Test, Formal Assessment pp. 5–6 Test Generator	Audio Library
President Cleveland, Where Are You? pp. 34–47	• Summary p. 14 • Active Reading: Sequence of Events p. 15 • Literary Analysis: Plot p. 16 • Literary Analysis: Character Traits p. 17 • Grammar p. 18 • Words to Know p. 19 • Selection Quiz p. 20	• Selection Test, Formal Assessment pp. 7–8 Test Generator	Audio Library
Trading Card Talk pp. 48–51	• Paraphrasing p. 21 • Outlining p. 22		
Scout's Honor pp. 52–66	• Summary p. 23 • Active Reading: Visualizing p. 24 • Literary Analysis: Setting p. 25 • Literary Analysis: Character Traits p. 26 • Grammar p. 27 • Words to Know p. 28 • Selection Quiz p. 29	• Selection Test, Formal Assessment pp. 9–10 Test Generator	Audio Library Research Starter www.mcdougallittell.com
Nadia the Willful pp. 67–78	• Summary p. 30 • Active Reading: Cause and Effect p. 31 • Literary Analysis: Theme p. 32 • Literary Analysis: Theme and Conflict p. 33 • Grammar p. 34 • Words to Know p. 35 • Selection Quiz p. 36	• Selection Test, Formal Assessment pp. 11–12 Test Generator	Audio Library Research Starter www.mcdougallittell.com

Writing Workshop: Response to Literature

		Unit Assessment	**Unit Technology**
Unit One Resource Book • Prewriting p. 38 • Drafting and Elaboration p. 39 • Peer Response Guide p. 40 • Revising Organization and Ideas p. 41 • Revising, Editing, and Proofreading p. 42 • Student Models pp. 43–45 • Rubric for Evaluation p. 46	**Writing Coach** **Reading and Critical Thinking Transparencies** TR40 **Speaking and Listening Book** pp. 6–9, 12–13, 27–28	• Unit One, Part 1 Test, Formal Assessment pp. 13–14 Test Generator • Unit One: Integrated Assessment pp. 1–6	ClassZone www.mcdougallittell.com Electronic Teacher Tools

Additional Support

Literary Analysis Transparencies	Reading and Critical Thinking Transparencies	Language Transparencies	Writing Transparencies	Speaking and Listening Book
• Analyzing Character TR3	• Connecting TR2	• Daily Language SkillBuilder TR1 • Sentence Fragments TR32 • Prefixes TR57	• Levels of Language TR14	• Evaluating Reading Aloud p.14
• Plot TR5 • Setting TR6 • Conflict TR8	• Connecting TR2 • Venn Diagram TR35	• Daily Language SkillBuilder TR1 • Context Clues: Compare and Contrast, Cause and Effect TR54	• Transitional Words List TR10 • Locating Material in the Library TR41	
	• Paraphrasing TR19		• Using Internal Organizers of a Book TR43	
• Setting TR6	• Visualizing TR4	• Daily Language SkillBuilder TR2 • Verbs—Using Correct Verb Forms TR35 • Context Clues: Compare and Contrast, Cause and Effect TR54	• Writing Variables TR2 • Locating Information TR45–48	• Creating an Informative Presentation p. 25 • Guidelines: How to Analyze an Informative Presentation p. 26
• Theme TR7	• Cause and Effect TR5	• Daily Language SkillBuilder TR2 • Context Clues: Definition and Overview TR53	• Organizing Your Writing TR11 • Revising Problem Sentences TR20	• Evaluatiing Reading Aloud p. 14

ENGLISH LEARNERS / STUDENTS ACQUIRING ENGLISH

The **Spanish Study Guide,** pp. 1–15, includes language support for the following pages:
• Family and Community Involvement (per unit)

• Selection Summaries and Vocabulary
• Active Reading
• Literary Analysis

For **systematic instruction** in language skills, see:
• **Vocabulary and Spelling Book**
• **Grammar, Usage, and Mechanics Book**
• pacing chart on p. 19i

UNIT ONE
RESOURCE MANAGEMENT GUIDE
PART 2
To introduce the theme of this unit, use
transparencies 1–3 in Fine Arts Transparencies.

	Unit Resource Book	Assessment	Integrated Technology and Media
Matthew Henson at the Top of the World *pp. 101–113*	• Summary p. 47 • Active Reading: Main Idea-Details p. 48 • Literary Analysis: Biography p. 49 • Active Reading: Comparing Information p. 50 • Grammar p. 51 • Words to Know p. 52 • Selection Quiz p. 53	• Selection Test, Formal Assessment pp. 15–16 ◉ Test Generator	◯ Audio Library ◉ Research Starter www.mcdougallittell.com
Summer of Fire *pp. 114–123*	• Summary p. 54 • Active Reading: Chronological Order p. 55 • Literary Analysis: Informative Nonfiction p. 56 • Active Reading: Previewing p. 57 • Grammar p. 58 • Words to Know p. 59 • Selection Quiz p. 60	• Selection Test, Formal Assessment pp. 17–18 ◉ Test Generator	◯ Audio Library ◉ Research Starter www.mcdougallittell.com
Ghost of the Lagoon *pp. 124–134*	• Summary p. 61 • Active Reading: Predicting p. 62 • Literary Analysis: Conflict p. 63 • Literary Analysis: Setting p. 64 • Grammar p. 65 • Words to Know p. 66 • Selection Quiz p. 67	• Selection Test, Formal Assessment pp. 19–20 ◉ Test Generator	◯ Audio Library ◉ Research Starter www.mcdougallittell.com
from **The Fun of It** *pp. 135–144*	• Summary p. 68 • Active Reading: Author's Purpose p. 69 • Literary Analysis: Autobiography p. 70 • Literary Analysis: Point of View p. 71 • Grammar p. 72 • Words to Know p. 73 • Selection Quiz p. 74	• Selection Test, Formal Assessment pp. 21–22 ◉ Test Generator	◯ Audio Library ▭ Video: Literature in Performance, Video Resource Book pp. 3–9
Daring to Dream *pp. 145–148*	• Reading a Magazine Article p. 75 • Summarizing p. 76		
Older Run *pp. 154–162*	• Summary p. 78 • Active Reading: Cause-Effect p. 79 • Literary Analysis: Anecdote p. 80 • Active Reading: Author Perspective p. 81 • Grammar p. 82 • Words to Know p. 83 • Selection Quiz p. 84	• Selection Test, Formal Assessment pp. 23–24 ◉ Test Generator	◯ Audio Library ◉ NetActivities
from **Woodsong** *pp. 165–171*	• Summary p. 85 • Active Reading: Questioning p. 86 • Literary Analysis: Memoir p. 87 • Literary Analysis: Imagery p. 88 • Grammar p. 89 • Words to Know p. 90 • Selection Quiz p. 91	• Selection Test, Formal Assessment pp. 25–26 ◉ Test Generator	◯ Audio Library ◉ Research Starter www.mcdougallittell.com ◉ NetActivities

Writing Workshop: Personal Experience Essay

		Unit Assessment	Unit Technology
Unit One Resource Book • Prewriting p. 92 • Drafting and Elaboration p. 93 • Peer Response Guide p. 94 • Revising Organization and Ideas p. 95 • Revising, Editing, Proofreading p. 96 • Student Models pp. 97–99 • Rubric for Evaluation p. 100	◉ **Writing Coach** **Reading and Critical Thinking Transparencies** TR6 **Speaking and Listening Book** pp. 6–9, 12–13, 24–25	• Unit One, Part 2 Test, Formal Assessment pp. 27–28 ◉ Test Generator • Unit One: Integrated Assessment pp. 1–6	◉ ClassZone www.mcdougallittell.com ◉ Electronic Teacher Tools

Additional Support

Literary Analysis Transparencies	Reading and Critical Thinking Transparencies	Language Transparencies	Writing Transparencies	Speaking and Listening Book
• Biography TR10	• Main Idea and Supporting Details TR25	• Daily Language SkillBuilder TR3 • Subject-Verb Agreement TR37 • Context Clues: Definition and Overview TR53	• Note Taking TR49 • How to Paraphrase TR50 • How to Summarize TR51 • Paraphrasing and Summarizing TR52	• Writing Your Speech p. 8
	• Predicting TR7	• Daily Language SkillBuilder TR3	• Transitional Words List TR10 • Cause and Effect TR36 • How to Summarize TR51	• Creating a Persuasive Presentation p. 29 • Guidelines: How to Analyze a Persuasive Presentation p. 30
• Plot TR5 • Conflict TR8	• Predicting TR7	• Daily Language SkillBuilder TR4 • Subject-Verb Agreement TR37 • Learning and Remembering New Words TR65	• Short Story TR34	
• Autobiography TR11	• Author's Purpose and Audience TR8	• Daily Language SkillBuilder TR4 • Synonyms TR60	• Writing Variables TR2 • Effective Language TR15 • Character Sketch TR30	• Working in a Group p. 33
	• Skimming and Scanning TR47		• Locating Information TR45–48	
• Author's Style TR9 • Autobiography TR11		• Daily Language SkillBuilder TR5 • Subject-Verb Agreement TR37 • Context Clues: Definition and Overview TR53		
• Autobiography TR11 • Author's Purpose TR16	• Questioning TR9	• Daily Language SkillBuilder TR5 • Run-on Sentences TR33 • Context Clues: Definition and Overview TR53	• Structuring an Essay TR6	• Creating a Persuasive Presentation p. 29 • Guidelines: Evaluating a Persuasive Presentation p. 30

ENGLISH LEARNERS / STUDENTS ACQUIRING ENGLISH

The **Spanish Study Guide,** pp. 16–33, includes language support for the following pages:
• Family and Community Involvement (per unit)

• Selection Summaries and Vocabulary
• Active Reading
• Literary Analysis

For **systematic instruction** in language skills, see:
• **Vocabulary and Spelling Book**
• **Grammar, Usage, and Mechanics Book**
• pacing chart on p. 19i

INTEGRATING SKILLS INSTRUCTION PACING CHART

The *Language of Literature* offers several options for integrating language arts instruction and literature.

- Systematic instruction in grammar, vocabulary, and spelling is provided in the *Grammar, Usage, and Mechanics Book* and in the *Vocabulary and Spelling Book*. The pacing chart on the right shows when to use the lessons in these books.
- The Pupil's Edition provides grammar and vocabulary instruction in context. The examples for the grammar feature, *Grammar in Context,* arise from the selections and relate to the grammar focus for each unit. In addition each selection includes vocabulary words called *Words to Know.* Vocabulary practice occurs in *Choices and Challenges* at the end of each selection.
- The Teacher's Edition provides review and reinforcement of the grammar and vocabulary concepts through Explicit Instruction lessons. References to additional support in *Unit Resource Books* and other ancillaries are included at the end of appropriate lessons.

Grammar, Usage and Mechanics

From Grammar, Mechanics, and Usage Book

Chapter 1: Sentence and Its Parts
- Complete Subjects and Predicates
- Simple Subjects
- Simple Predicates, or Verbs
- Verb Phrases
- Compound Sentence Parts
- Kinds of Sentences
- Subjects in Unusual Order
- Complements: Subject Complements
- Complements: Objects of Verbs
- Fragments and Run-ons

Chapter 2: Nouns
Chapter 3: Pronouns
Chapter 4: Verbs
Chapter 5: Adjectives and Adverbs
Chapter 6: Prepositions, Conjunctions, Interjections
Chapter 7: Subject-Verb Agreement

For Ongoing Reference
Chapter 8: Capitalization
Chapter 9: Punctuation

Vocabulary
From Vocabulary and Spelling Book

Lesson 1: Context Clues
Lesson 2: Restatement Context Clues
Lesson 3: Contrast ContextClues
Lesson 4: Definition Context Clues
Lesson 5: Comparison Context Clues
Lesson 6: General Context Clues

Lesson 7: Prefixes and Base Words
Lesson 8: Prefixes and Base Words
Lesson 9: Base Words and Suffixes
Lesson 10: Base Words and Suffixes
Lesson 11: Anglo-Saxon Affixes and Base Words
Lesson 12: Roots and Word Families
Lesson 13: Roots and Word Familes
Lesson 14: Analyzing Roots and Affixes
Lesson 15: Analyzing Roots and Affixes
Lesson 16: Foreign Words in English
Lesson 17: Specialized Vocabulary
Lesson 18: Specialized Vocabulary
Lesson 19: Specialized Vocabulary
Lesson 20: Words with Multiple Meanings
Lesson 21: Synonyms
Lesson 22: Antonyms
Lesson 23: Denotation and Connotation
Lesson 24: Using a Thesaurus
Lesson 25: Idioms
Lesson 26: Similes and Metaphors
Lesson 27: Compound Words
Lesson 28: Homonyms
Lesson 29: Homophones and Easily Confused Words
Lesson 30: Homographs
Lesson 31: Analogies
Lesson 32: Using Your Strategies

Spelling
From Vocabulary and Spelling Book

Lesson 1: Silent *e* Words and Suffixes
Lesson 2: The Suffix *ance*
Lesson 3: Plural Words Ending in *o*
Lesson 4: Prefixes and Base Words
Lesson 5: Prefixes and Roots
Lesson 6: Words Ending with *ary*

Lesson 7: Soft and Hard *g*
Lesson 8: Review
Lesson 9: Final *y* words and Suffixes
Lesson 10: The Suffix *able*
Lesson 11: Words Ending with *al* + *ly*
Lesson 12: The Prefix *com*
Lesson 13: Forms of the Prefix *ad*
Lesson 14: Words Ending with *ory*
Lesson 15: Unstressed Syllables
Lesson 16: Review
Lesson 17: *VAC* Words
Lesson 18: Non-*VAC* Words
Lesson 19: Words Ending with *c* + *ally*
Lesson 20: The Prefix *ex*
Lesson 21: More Forms of the Prefix *ad*
Lesson 22: Base Word Changes
Lesson 23: Words Ending with *cious, cial,* or *cian*
Lesson 24: Review
Lesson 25: Greek Combining Forms
Lesson 26: Compound Words and Contractions
Lesson 27: The Suffix *ible*
Lesson 28: Forms of Prefix *ob* + *sub*
Lesson 29: Forms of Prefix *in*
Lesson 30: The Suffixes *ence* + *ent*
Lesson 31: Words Ending with *ize* + *ise*
Lesson 32: Review

Selection	SkillBuilder Sentences	Suggested Answers
Eleven	1. Don't you think it was unfair for Mrs. Price to make Rachel where the sweater? 2. The day might have been worse if Rachel had throne the sweater away at lunch time.	1. Don't you think it was unfair for Mrs. Price to make Rachel **wear** the sweater? 2. The day might have been worse if Rachel had **thrown** the sweater away at lunch time.
President Cleveland, Where Are You?	1. Boys went to the movies and trade cowboy cards for fun during the Depression. 2. All the boys wanted to be the first to completed their set.	1. Boys went to the movies and **traded** cowboy cards for fun during the Depression. 2. All the boys wanted to be the first to **complete** their set.
Scout's Honor	1. Before him and his friends went camping, they should have made a plan. 2. Their mothers helped they get ready.	1. Before **he** and his friends went camping, they should have made a plan. 2. Their mothers helped **them** get ready.
Nadia the Willful	1. Nadia was given the nickname "nadia the willful" because she was stubborn and had a quick temper. 2. when Nadia grew angry, only her brother hamed could calm her down.	1. Nadia was given the nickname "**Nadia** the **Willful**" because she was stubborn and had a quick temper. 2. **When** Nadia grew angry, only her brother **Hamed** could calm her down.
Matthew Henson at the Top of the World	1. Matthew Hensons first adventure was on a ship called the *Katie Hines*. 2. Their leaving for the North Pole tomorrow.	1. Matthew **Henson's** first adventure was on a ship called the *Katie Hines*. 2. **They're** leaving for the North Pole tomorrow.

Selection	SkillBuilder Sentences	Suggested Answers
Summer of Fire	1. The fire fighters did'nt think they could put out the fire at Yellowstone.	1. The fire fighters **didn't** think they could put out the fire at Yellowstone.
	2. The fire finally went out after burning for month's.	2. The fire finally went out after burning for **months.**
Ghost of the Lagoon	1. Mako's mother said "Hush! Would you bring trouble on us all?"	1. Mako's mother said, "Hush! Would you bring trouble on us all?"
	2. Did the ghost see Mako and Afa	2. Did the ghost see Mako and Afa**?**
from The Fun of It	1. amelia earhart was the first women to fly across the atlantic ocean.	1. **Amelia Earhart** was the first **woman** to fly across the **Atlantic Ocean.**
	2. she had some problems with her plane before landing in ireland.	2. **She** had some problems with her plane before landing in **Ireland.**
Older Run	1. While Paulsen was rubbing one dog's ears, another trotting up.	1. While Paulsen was rubbing one dog's ears, another **trotted** up.
	2. People still used the tracks though they were abandon.	2. People still used the tracks though they were **abandoned.**
from Woodsong	1. In the reegen ware Paulsen lives, there are lots of pine trees.	1. In the **region where** Paulsen lives, there are lots of pine trees.
	2. Bare hunting is aloud, but Paulsen does not hurt the bares.	2. **Bear** hunting is **allowed,** but Paulsen does not hurt the **bears.**

OVERVIEW

Students work in small groups to produce a news program featuring characters from the unit who took risks or made tough choices when faced with a challenge. Students collect characters' stories and compile them for a national evening newsmagazine broadcast.

Project at a glance The selections in Unit One feature characters who confront a challenge by taking a risk or making a tough choice. For this project, some students will assume the roles of characters in the stories and other students will interview them. Students will present the stories in a *60 Minutes*-type video newsmagazine format. Members of each group will share responsibilities for researching the topic, writing the script, narrating, conducting interviews, and taping their segment. Each topic should be well thought out with a focus on the challenge in the story, the events that led up to it, and the resulting choice made or risk taken. If your school has access to a video camera, the program might be videotaped for presentation. If not, staging will work just as well.

SCHEDULING

Individual segments should take no more than ten minutes. The entire "program" should run about 60 minutes. You may want to schedule the presentations over the course of 2–3 class periods. This project may take place over the course of the unit or at the end of the unit, depending on your scheduling purposes.

PROJECT OBJECTIVES

• To demonstrate the speaking and listening skills introduced in the activity
• To identify what a character learned by making a tough choice or taking a risk
• To conduct in-depth interviews with students playing character roles
• To write an original script synthesizing the events in a story
• To combine the story with those of other groups into a full-length newsmagazine

SUGGESTED GROUP SIZE

4–5 students per group

Video Newsmagazine

1 ▶ Getting Started

Explain that students will be working in small groups to plan and produce a video newsmagazine along the lines of *60 Minutes, Dateline,* or *20/20*. Each group will produce an interview segment with a character from a story in the unit. Characters will reveal what they learned by taking a risk or making a tough choice in the face of a difficult situation.

Have students watch one of the television shows mentioned above and note some key elements: background information, interviews, transitional statements made by the anchors, and introductory and concluding statements made by the reporters. Remind students that a real television show has the luxury of high-tech editing.

If video equipment is available, have someone videotape each of the segments when they are all ready. Students who cannot videotape can present their findings as if on live television.

Interviews should be well rehearsed. If you are using video equipment, arrange for interviewees to come to one taping at a specific time. Allow for extra time to complete the project.

Writing Workshop Connection

As a springboard, students may use the Writing Workshop assignment **Response to Literature,** p. 89, or **Personal Experience Essay,** p. 176, which they will complete in this unit.

2 ▶ Directing the Project

Preparing *(1 class period)* Divide students into groups of four or five. Have students choose their favorite stories from the unit. List main characters from the stories and the difficult choices or risks they took in the face of a challenge. Ask groups to write a brief description of the character, the choice or risk taken, and the resulting insight.

Assigning Roles

• Select two students to act as anchors.
• Assign one main character from a story, as well as minor characters for each group.
• Choose reporters to interview the main characters and writers to help the reporters prepare questions as well as an introduction and a concluding thought for the piece.
• Assign a "tech team" to work the video camera, build sets, and make cue cards.

▶ Have students brainstorm a list of interview questions for the main character. Meet with each group to help refine the script. Group members should "prep" the main character by asking him or her questions. Have students review their notes. They'll feel more comfortable knowing they have more than enough material to present. Review with students the Speaking and Listening Skills listed on the next page, as well as the interview tips found on page R105 of the Speaking and Listening Handbook at the back of the pupil

edition.
▶ Students should be aware of the guidelines for working in a group, found on pages R104–105 in the Speaking and Listening Handbook.

Practicing *(2 class periods)* Allow time for students to coordinate their interview and to rehearse. Tell students that giving and receiving feedback during the rehearsal stage is crucial. Refer to the tips in the Feedback Center.

▶ Anchors should briefly meet with groups to "prescreen" each interview so that they can write transitional statements, as well as an introduction and a conclusion.

Presenting *(2–3 class periods)* This project could culminate in a screening for the entire student body or just for your class.

▶ To begin, have students take a few deep breaths and focus on what they want to communicate. Anchors should look directly into the camera during the introduction, transitional statements, and conclusion of each piece. They should appear natural, using gestures and facial expressions that fit the content. Characters should use appropriate verbal and nonverbal cues that reflect the tone of their stories. Reporters should appear interested but neutral.

Teaching the Speaking and Listening Skills

The student is expected to:

Demonstrate effective communication skills that reflect such demands as interviewing, reporting, and requesting and providing information

Teaching Suggestions: Have students review the interview guidelines on page R105. Remind them that often an interviewer has to ask the same question in different ways to get the necessary information. Also tell students to take clear notes or tape the interview sessions to get a better idea of their subject's style and main points. Discuss the idea of the "objective reporter." In other words, reporters should present their findings in a balanced manner. They should also make sure that all main points are supported with evidence and examples from the stories.

Use appropriate rate, volume, pitch, and tone for the audience and the setting

Teaching Suggestions: Tell students to rehearse their parts several times in front of a mirror. They should speak at a comfortable pitch, placing emphasis on important words. Coach them on making their delivery fit their message, audience, and setting.

Understand the major ideas and supporting evidence in spoken messages

Teaching Suggestions: After the presentation, have the class reflect on the coherence of each piece. Did it make sense? Were major ideas supported by examples from the text? Were their insights and conclusions logical? Were the characters convincing? To check for understanding, have audience members identify the important event in the life of each featured character and summarize the character's discovery and insight.

Feedback Center

Students can use the following guidelines when giving and receiving feedback during this project:

Giving Feedback

▶ Ask questions concerning content, delivery, purpose, and point of view (for instance, is tone appropriate to purpose?)

▶ Provide feedback about the coherence and logic of the content, delivery, and overall impact on the listener.

▶ Comment on the verbal and nonverbal delivery (pitch, pace, volume, gestures, body language) and its impact on the listener.

▶ Respond to persuasive messages with questions, challenges, or affirmations.

▶ Question the evidence to support the speaker's claims and conclusions.

Receiving Feedback

▶ Listen to constructive criticism with an open mind.

▶ Use audience feedback and modify the presentation to clarify meaning or organization.

Assessing the Project

The following rubric can be used for group or individual assessment.

3 | Full Accomplishment

The group produced a news segment that showed what a character learned by taking a risk or making a difficult choice in the face of a challenging situation. Students worked effectively in a group and demonstrated all three of the Speaking and Listening Skills listed, including effective communication skills, appropriate delivery of information, and a logical presentation of the points.

2 | Substantial Accomplishment

The students produced a newsmagazine segment, but it lacked some key information or clarity of subject matter. Students worked in a group with adequate communication in organizing and fulfilling individual roles. Two out of three of the Speaking and Listening Skills were demonstrated.

1 | Little Accomplishment

The students' segment was incomplete or did not fulfill the requirements of the assignment. Organization of the presentation was unclear, and students did not fulfill group roles. Students demonstrated only one of the Speaking and Listening Skills.

The Literature You'll Read

The Concepts You'll Study

Vocabulary and Reading Comprehension
Vocabulary Focus: Using Context Clues
Connecting
Sequence of Events
Visualizing
Recognizing Cause and Effect

Literary Analysis
Genre Focus: Fiction
Character
Plot
Setting
Theme

Writing and Language Conventions
Writing Workshop: Response to Literature
Sentence Fragments
Four Kinds of Sentences
Subjects and Verbs
Direct Objects

Speaking and Listening
Original Letter Read Aloud
Scene Performance
Problem-Solution Presentation
Short Speech

LEARNING the Language of Literature

Fiction

A good story is a work of art. Like a beautiful painting, it springs from the imagination. It can be sparked by a memory, an experience, or even a dream.

Stories that come from a writer's imagination are called **fiction.** Two forms of fiction are the **short story** and the **novel.** These two forms are similar in some ways. For example, they both contain the main elements of **plot, character, setting,** and **theme.** Each form also has unique characteristics. These are shown in the chart below.

Forms of Fiction

short story
- usually focuses on a single idea
- is short enough to be read at one sitting

novel
- focuses on several ideas
- is a much longer work

21

Objectives
- understand the following literary terms:

fiction	conflict
short story	exposition
novel	rising action
plot	climax
character	falling action
setting	(resolution)
theme	

- understand and appreciate fiction
- recognize the distinguishing features of fiction

Teaching the Lesson

This lesson analyzes the forms and the elements of fiction and demonstrates how each of the elements contributes to the fictional work as a whole.

Introducing the Concepts
Have students think of an especially memorable film or television program they have seen recently that is fictional. Ask them to explain how this work would change if one of its most pivotal events had not happened, if the work had been set in a different time and place, or if one of the minor characters became the main character.

Use **Literary Analysis Transparencies,** pp. 1, 3, 5–7 for additional support.

EXPLICIT INSTRUCTION   Forms of Fiction

Instruction Tell students that the forms of fiction include short stories, novels, and novellas. (Explain that a novella is a very short novel.) Remind students that they have probably read both short stories and novels. A short story is usually focused on a single idea, with one or two main characters. A novel is a much longer work that is focused on several ideas, more than one or two main characters, and several minor characters. Have students estimate how

long it might take them to read an average short story and an average novel.
(Answers will vary, but the reading times for the short story should be shorter than those for the novel.)
Practice Construct a two-column chart on the board, with the following column heads: Short Story and Novel. Have students name titles of short stories and novels they have read. Write their suggestions in the chart. *(Suggestions will vary.)* When the chart is complete, ask

pairs of students to compare a novel and a short story they have read by discussing these topics:
- number of characters
- development of the characters (How much do they know about the characters?)
- plot development (How long a period does the story cover? How many events occur?)
Possible Responses: Responses will vary.

Presenting the Concepts
Plot

Point out to students that writers make plans for the framework of their story. This framework, called a plot, has a beginning, middle, and end.

YOUR TURN

Possible Response: The conflict is that, because of their unfamiliarity with American customs, the family behaves differently from the rest of the guests at the dinner party.

Plot

The series of events in a story is called the **plot.** Usually, a plot is built around a central **conflict**—a problem or struggle that drives the story. A conflict might be a life-or-death battle, or it might be just a disagreement between friends. Usually, the first part of a story tells about how the conflict becomes more complicated. The last part of a story tells about how the conflict is resolved.

> **PLOT**
>
> It [the dining table] was lavishly covered with platters of food, but we couldn't see any chairs around the table. So we helpfully carried over some dining chairs and sat down. All the other guests just stood there.
>
> —Lensey Namioka, "The All-American Slurp"

YOUR TURN The "we" in the passage at the right is a family that has recently emigrated from China. The family members are attending their first American dinner party. What conflict is introduced in the passage?

Most plots develop in four stages:

- **Exposition** This first stage introduces the characters and the setting. It also gives background information for the story. Often, the conflict is introduced during this stage.

- **Rising Action** During this stage, the story becomes more and more complicated as the conflict develops.

- **Climax** This is the turning point of the story—the most exciting part, when the outcome of the conflict is decided. A character may make a discovery or take an important action to solve the conflict. Often a change results.

- **Falling Action** The climax is usually followed by a falling action or resolution, in which loose ends are tied up before the story ends.

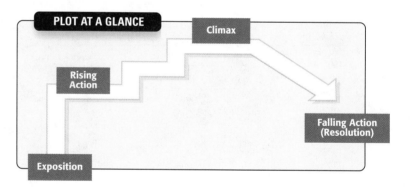

PLOT AT A GLANCE

Climax

Rising Action

Falling Action (Resolution)

Exposition

Character

Characters are the people, animals, and imaginary creatures who take part in the action of a story. Generally, the action centers on one important character. This is the **main character.** The other, less-important characters are called **minor characters.** They interact with the main character and help the story move along.

Characters are revealed by their **traits,** or qualities. Courageous, kind, and selfish are three examples of traits. You can learn about characters' traits by paying attention to their speech, thoughts, feelings, and actions; the speech, thoughts, and actions of other characters; the writer's direct statements about them; and their physical characteristics.

YOUR TURN In the story "Nadia the Willful," the main character is a young Bedouin girl with a reputation for being strong-willed. What details in the passage at the right show this character trait?

CHARACTER

And the less she was listened to, the less she was able to recall Hamed's face and voice. And the less she recalled, the more her temper raged within her, destroying the peace she had found.

By evening, she could stand it no longer. She went to where her father sat, staring into the desert, and stood before him.

"You will not rob me of my brother Hamed!" she cried, stamping her foot. "I will not let you!"

—Sue Alexander, "Nadia the Willful"

"Aaron wasn't quite certain what his mother would say. . . ."
—Myron Levoy, "Aaron's Gift"

". . . Mako's mother had food ready and waiting."
—Armstrong Sperry, "Ghost of the Lagoon"

". . . I had begun to really look at myself, . . ."
—Elizabeth Ellis, "Flowers and Freckle Cream"

"Margot stood alone. She was a very frail girl. . . ."
—Ray Bradbury, "All Summer in a Day"

LEARNING THE LANGUAGE OF LITERATURE **23**

Setting

The time and place in which a story occurs is called the **setting.** The time may be the past, the present, or the future; day or night; and any season. The place may be imaginary or real. A writer's vivid description helps readers picture the setting. Setting often plays a role in the conflicts that develop and how they are resolved. Setting can also influence characters' actions.

YOUR TURN Look at the passage at the right. When and where does this story take place? What words or phrases describe the setting?

Dong Kingman, *Station Platform*, from "Scout's Honor"

SETTING

Since I grew up in Brooklyn in the 1940s, the only grass I knew was in Ebbets Field where the Dodgers played. Otherwise, my world was made of slate pavements, streets of asphalt (or cobblestone), and skies full of tall buildings. The only thing "country" was a puny pin oak tree at our curb, which was noticed, mostly, by dogs.

—Avi, "Scout's Honor"

Theme

Theme is the meaning or moral of a story. Writers create themes to express their ideas about life and human nature. A theme in a short story might be "Good friends stand by each other," or "The harder something is to get, the greater the reward." Most themes are not stated openly. They become apparent as stories unfold. You can gather clues to a story's theme by thinking about

- the title
- the actions, thoughts, and words of the characters
- the conflicts in the story
- the setting and the images the writer creates

YOUR TURN Read the passage at the right. What do you think one theme of the story might be?

THEME

I splashed cold water on my burning face, and as I dried myself with a paper towel, I stared into the mirror. In this perfumed ladies' room, with its pink-and-silver wallpaper and marbled sinks, I looked completely out of place. What was I doing here? What was our family doing in the Lakeview Restaurant? In America?

—Lensey Namioka, "The All-American Slurp"

Reading Fiction

The world is full of stories that entertain and inform. Our favorite stories may be filled with interesting **characters,** far-away **places,** and exciting **events,** but all stories leave room for our imaginations. To get the most from every work of fiction you read, try using the strategies explained here.

How to Apply the Strategies

Preview the story and set a purpose for reading. Before you begin, look at the title and pictures. Skim through and read a few words on each page. Can you tell what the story is about? As you begin to learn the strategies and how to use them, stop from time to time to **monitor** how well they are working for you. If it helps your reading, modify the strategies as necessary to suit your needs.

CONNECT Do the characters share thoughts or experiences that you have had? Does the story remind you of an event or a person you've heard of or read about?

QUESTION Ask questions as the story unfolds. The events, characters, and ideas in the story should make sense to you.

PREDICT As you become more involved in the story, try to predict what will happen next. Look for clues that hint at events to come.

VISUALIZE As you read about a character, place, or event, pay attention to the descriptive details. Try to imagine how something might look, sound, feel, taste, or smell. Can you picture the setting in your mind? Is the action easy to imagine?

EVALUATE Think about the characters and their actions. Do they seem realistic? Also evaluate how well the writer is telling the story.

CLARIFY Remember to pause now and then to review what you've read. Reread when necessary. You also can take notes or discuss the story with a friend.

Here's how Ryane uses the strategies:

*"When I read fiction, I like to sit in a quiet place. I try to **visualize** how a person or place looks. When I see these characters and the problems they face, I **connect** the story to my own life. At different points in the story, I stop to **predict** what is happening. Sometimes, I become so lost in the story that I forget about time."*

OVERVIEW

Standards-Based Objectives
- understand and enjoy fiction by using strategies such as preview, connect, question, predict, visualize, evaluate, and clarify
- connect personal experiences to the experiences of characters in fiction

Teaching the Lesson

The strategies on this page will help students interpret fiction by focusing on useful strategies for understanding and connecting with what they read.

Presenting the Strategies
Point out that this page offers strategies for helping students get the most out of what they read.

📖 Use **Reading and Critical Thinking Transparencies,** p. 1, for additional support.

PREVIEW
Allow students time to preview several stories in their books. What conclusions did they draw about the content of each story? What clues did they use to help them figure this out?

CONNECT
Ask students to think about "The All-American Slurp." With which incidents did they particularly connect and why? How does this help them understand how the Lins felt?

Possible Response: Students may mention times when they did something embarrassing because they did not know a custom or way of doing something in an unfamiliar setting. Remembering their own embarrassments helps them understand why the Lins acted the way they did.

QUESTION and PREDICT
Remind students to ask themselves questions as they read, then predict what the answers might be, given the characters' personalities and the events of the story so far.

VISUALIZE
Remind students that picturing in their minds what is happening will make the story seem more real to them. Have students close their eyes and try to visualize the city scene described in the passage from "Scout's Honor."

EVALUATE
Remind students that their response to a story and its characters will often be based on their own experiences and interests.

CLARIFY
Discuss with students something they may have misread the first time they read a story. Ask how it affected their understanding of the story. If it didn't make sense, what did they do then?

This selection is included in the **Grade 6 InterActive Reader.**

Standards-Based Objectives

1. understand and appreciate a **short story**
2. identify qualities of **characters**
3. **connect** a story to prior knowledge and experiences
4. **read aloud** narrative text

Summary

Rachel wakes up on her eleventh birthday feeling as if she's still ten—and nine, and eight, and all the ages that came before. At school, what should be a happy day turns gloomy when the teacher insists that an ugly, unclaimed sweater belongs to Rachel. Mrs. Price puts the sweater in an embarrassing pile on Rachel's desk. Worse yet, she makes Rachel put the sweater on. It smells bad, it itches, it's full of germs—and Rachel, feeling all her years of childhood rattling around inside her, cries in front of the whole class. The classmate who is the real owner of the sweater finally claims it, while Rachel longs for the day to end.

Thematic Link

Rachel doesn't quite have the courage to stick up for herself regarding the sweater, but she is able to accept the younger self who cries in the face of injustice.

English Conventions Practice

Daily Language SkillBuilder

Have students **proofread** the display sentences on page 19k and write them correctly. The sentences also appear on Transparency 1 of **Language Transparencies.**

Preteaching Vocabulary

If you would like to preteach the WORDS TO KNOW for this selection, use the Explicit Instruction, page 27.

Eleven

by SANDRA CISNEROS

Connect to Your Life

Celebration Days As you may have guessed from the title, this story's main character has just turned 11 years old. What was turning 11 like for you? Or, what will turning 11 be like? On a sheet of paper, copy the diagram to the right. Then record words and phrases that you associate with being 11 years old. Share your diagram with a partner.

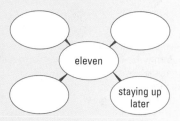

Build Background

The Child Inside When she was interviewed about this story in 1986, Sandra Cisneros commented that she sometimes feels 11 years old inside, even as an adult: "When I think how I see myself, I would have to be at age eleven. I know I'm thirty-two on the outside, but inside I'm eleven. I'm the girl in the picture with skinny arms and a crumpled shirt and crooked hair. I didn't like school because all they saw was the outside me."

WORDS TO KNOW
Vocabulary Preview
except   invisible
expect   sudden

Focus Your Reading

LITERARY ANALYSIS | **CHARACTER**

Characters are the people, animals, or imaginary creatures who take part in the action of a story. Usually one or two characters are the most important; they are called **main characters.** Less important characters are called **minor characters.** As you read this story, determine the **traits,** or qualities, of the main character by paying attention to

• her speech, thoughts, feelings, and actions
• the speech, thoughts, and actions of other characters
• the writer's direct statements about her
• descriptions of her physical characteristics

ACTIVE READING | **CONNECTING**

When reading a story makes you think about things you have experienced, you are **connecting.** Characters, settings, and events in a story may remind you of people you know, feelings you've had, or other stories you've read.

READER'S NOTEBOOK Make a chart like this one. As you read, jot down details about Rachel's 11th birthday in one column. In the other, jot down things in your own life that those details bring to mind.

LESSON RESOURCES

UNIT ONE RESOURCE BOOK, pp. 7–13

ASSESSMENT
Formal Assessment, pp. 5–6
Test Generator

SKILLS TRANSPARENCIES AND COPYMASTERS
Literary Analysis
• Analyzing Character, TR 3 (pp. 28, 31)
Reading and Critical Thinking
• Connecting, TR 2 (p. 28)

Language
• Daily Language SkillBuilder, TR 1 (p. 26)
• Sentence Fragments, TR 32 (p. 33)
• Prefixes, TR 57 (p. 27)
Writing
• Levels of Language, TR 14 (p. 32)
Speaking and Listening
• Evaluating Reading Aloud, p. 14 (p. 32)

INTEGRATED TECHNOLOGY
Audio Library

Visit our Web site:
www.mcdougallittell.com

For **systematic instruction** in language skills, see:
• **Vocabulary and Spelling Book**
• **Grammar, Usage, and Mechanics Book**
• pacing chart on p. 19i.

ELEVEN

by Sandra Cisneros

nine *one* *three* *two* *four* *seven* *five* *eight* *six* *O*

What they don't understand about birthdays and what they never tell you is that when you're eleven, you're also ten, and nine, and eight, and seven, and six, and five, and four, and three, and two, and one. And when you wake up on your eleventh birthday you expect to feel eleven, but you don't. You open your eyes and everything's just like yesterday, only it's today. And you don't feel eleven at all. You feel like you're still ten. And you are—underneath the year that makes you eleven.

Like some days you might say something stupid, and that's the part of you that's still ten. Or maybe some days you might need to sit on your mama's lap because you're scared, and that's the part of you that's five. And maybe one day when you're all grown up maybe you will need to cry like if you're three, and that's okay. That's what I tell Mama when she's sad and needs to cry. Maybe she's feeling three.

Because the way you grow old is kind of like an onion or like the rings inside a tree trunk or like my little wooden dolls that fit one inside the other, each year inside the next one. That's how being eleven years old is.

2

You don't feel eleven. Not right away. It takes a few days, weeks even, sometimes even months before you say Eleven when they ask you. And you don't feel smart eleven, not until you're almost twelve. That's the way it is.

Only today I wish I didn't have only eleven years rattling inside me like pennies in a tin Band-Aid box. Today I wish I was one hundred

---

WORDS TO KNOW **expect** (ĭk-spĕkt′) *v.* to look forward to something that is likely to occur

27

Differentiating Instruction

Less Proficient Readers
Guide students to use the title and art to infer that the story is about an eleventh birthday.

Set a Purpose Have students read to find out what Rachel (the "birthday girl") thinks people don't understand about birthdays. Ask why she thinks this way.

English Learners
1 Remind students that personal pronouns like *he, we,* and *they* are used in place of a noun or another pronoun and refer to a person or group of people. The narrator uses the pronouns *they* and *you* in the first paragraph, however, these pronouns are not referring to specific characters in the story. Make sure students understand that *they* refers to *people in general* (most likely adults or parents). The subject pronoun *you* refers to both the narrator and the reader.

Age is expressed in different ways in different languages. In Spanish, for example, "Yo tengo once años," literally means, "I have eleven years." Tell students that in English we say, "I am eleven," meaning, "I am eleven years old." Have students share how age is expressed in different languages.

Advanced Students
2 The narrator compares growing older to three things. Ask students what they are *(an onion, rings inside a tree trunk, and little wooden dolls that fit one inside the other).* Ask students if anyone knows what these types of comparisons are called. *(simile)* Ask students to come up with another comparison for age as they continue to read the story.

EXPLICIT INSTRUCTION ## Preteaching Vocabulary

WORDS TO KNOW
Teaching Strategy One way to figure out the meaning of an unfamiliar word is to break it into its parts and think about what the parts mean. **Prefixes** are word parts added to the beginning of a base word or a root that change its meaning.
in + visible = invisible
The prefix *in-* ("not") is combined with the base word *visible* ("able to be seen"), so the meaning of *invisible* must be "not able to be seen."

Practice Show students the two other story words below. Have them break each word into a prefix and a base or root word. Then have them tell what the prefix means and use a dictionary to find the meaning of the word. Finally, have them use each word in a sentence.

　　　　　except　　　expect

Use **Unit One Resource Book**, p. 12, for more practice.

For **systematic instruction** in vocabulary, see:
• Vocabulary and Spelling Book
• pacing chart on p. 19i.

Literary Analysis | CHARACTER

Sometimes a narrator will describe a character directly. At other times, readers can make inferences from what a character says, does, and thinks. Ask students to look for clues about Rachel. What do they know about her from her words, actions, and thoughts?

Possible Responses: She is thoughtful (she thinks about what birthdays mean); she is shy (she cannot speak up for herself); she is thin (she describes herself as "skinny").

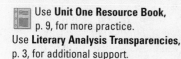 Use **Unit One Resource Book,** p. 9, for more practice.
Use **Literary Analysis Transparencies,** p. 3, for additional support.

Active Reading | CONNECTING

Tell students that although they may not have had the same experiences as Rachel, they can still connect with many parts of this story. Use the following questions to help them make connections to their own experiences:

• How would you describe Mrs. Price and Sylvia Saldívar? Have you ever known people like them?
• How does Rachel feel when she cannot fight back against Mrs. Price? Have you ever felt this way?

Use **Unit One Resource Book,** p. 8, for more practice.
Use **Reading and Critical Thinking Transparencies,** p. 2, for additional support.

ACTIVE READER

A CONNECT **Possible Response:** her voice.

B CONNECT **Possible Response:** Students may say that they've been embarrassed to cry in front of other people at one time or another.

---

and two instead of eleven because if I was one hundred and two I'd have known what to say when Mrs. Price put the red sweater on my desk. I would've known how to tell her it wasn't mine instead of just sitting there with that look on my face and nothing coming out of my mouth.

"Whose is this?" Mrs. Price says, and she holds the red sweater up in the air for all the class to see. "Whose? It's been sitting in the coatroom for a month."

"Not mine," says everybody. "Not me."

"It has to belong to somebody," Mrs. Price keeps saying, but nobody can remember. It's an ugly sweater with red plastic buttons and a collar and sleeves all stretched out like you could use it for a jump rope. It's maybe a thousand years old and even if it belonged to me I wouldn't say so.

Maybe because I'm skinny, maybe because she doesn't like me, that stupid Sylvia Saldívar says, "I think it belongs to Rachel." An ugly sweater like that, all raggedy and old, but Mrs. Price believes her. Mrs. Price takes the sweater and puts it right on my desk, but when I open my mouth nothing comes out.

"That's not, I don't, you're not . . . Not mine," I finally say in a little voice that was maybe me when I was four.

ACTIVE READER

(A) CONNECT What is it about Rachel's thoughts and actions that reminds you of a four-year-old?

"Of course it's yours," Mrs. Price says. "I remember you wearing it once." Because she's older and the teacher, she's right and I'm not.

Not mine, not mine, not mine, but Mrs. Price is already turning to page thirty-two, and math problem number four. I don't know why but all of a sudden I'm feeling sick inside, like the part

of me that's three wants to come out of my eyes, only I squeeze them shut tight and bite down on my teeth real hard and try to remember today I am eleven, eleven. Mama is making a cake for me for tonight, and when Papa comes home everybody will sing Happy birthday, happy birthday to you.

Only today I wish I didn't have only eleven years rattling inside me.

But when the sick feeling goes away and I open my eyes, the red sweater's still sitting there like a big red mountain. I move the red sweater to the corner of my desk with my ruler. I move my pencil and books and eraser as far from it as possible. I even move my chair a little to the right. Not mine, not mine, not mine.

In my head I'm thinking how long till lunchtime, how long till I can take the red sweater and throw it over the schoolyard fence, or leave it hanging on a parking meter, or bunch it up into a little ball and toss it in the alley. Except when math period ends, Mrs. Price says loud and in front of everybody, "Now, Rachel, that's enough," because she sees I've shoved the red sweater to the tippy-tip corner of my desk and it's hanging all over the edge like a waterfall, but I don't care.

"Rachel," Mrs. Price says. She says it like she's getting mad. "You put that sweater on right now and no more nonsense."

"But it's not—"

"Now!" Mrs. Price says.

This is when I wish I wasn't eleven, because all the years inside of me—ten, nine, eight, seven, six, five, four, three, two, and one—are pushing at the back of my eyes when I put one arm through one sleeve of the sweater that smells like cottage cheese, and then the other arm through the other and stand there with my arms apart like if the sweater hurts

WORDS
TO
KNOW

except (ĭk-sĕpt′) *prep.* other than; but

28

EXPLICIT INSTRUCTION Main and Minor Characters

Instruction Remind students that main characters are the most important people, animals, or imaginary creatures in stories or novels. Minor characters are the less important people, animals, and imaginary creatures who interact with the main characters and help move the plot along. Invite students to name the main and minor characters in their favorite books, stories, or movies. Then ask students if they can tell by reading through page 28 who

the main—or most important—character is in this story. Ask students to explain their answers. (*Rachel is the main character. She is the narrator and she is telling the story about herself.*)

Practice After reading the story, have students work in pairs to list all the characters in the story, tell whether each is a main or a minor character, and explain how each character is important in the story.

Possible Responses: Rachel is the main character: the story is all about her. Mrs. Price is a minor character: she has a conflict with Rachel. Sylvia Saldivan is a minor character: she tells Mrs. Price the sweater is Rachel's. Phyllis Lopez is a minor character: she remembers the sweater is hers.

Cake Window (Seven Cakes) (1970–1976), Wayne Thiebaud. Copyright © Wayne Thiebaud/Licensed by VAGA, New York.

me and it does, all itchy and full of germs that aren't even mine.

That's when everything I've been holding in since this morning, since when Mrs. Price put the sweater on my desk, finally lets go, and all of a <u>sudden</u> I'm crying in front of everybody. I wish I was <u>invisible</u> but I'm not. I'm eleven and it's my birthday today and I'm crying like I'm three in front of everybody. I put my head down on the desk and bury my face in my stupid clown-sweater arms. My face all hot and spit coming out of my mouth because I can't stop the little animal noises from coming out of me, until there aren't any more tears left in my eyes, and it's just my body shaking like when you have the hiccups, and my whole head hurts like when you drink milk too fast.

ACTIVE READER

CONNECT How does this description of crying relate to how you have experienced it?

But the worst part is right before the bell rings for lunch. That stupid Phyllis Lopez, who is even dumber than Sylvia Saldívar, says she remembers the red sweater is hers! I take it off right away and give it to her, only Mrs. Price pretends like everything's okay.

Today I'm eleven. There's a cake Mama's making for tonight, and when Papa comes home from work we'll eat it. There'll be candles and presents, and everybody will sing Happy birthday, happy birthday to you, Rachel, only it's too late.

I'm eleven today. I'm eleven, ten, nine, eight, seven, six, five, four, three, two, and one, but I wish I was one hundred and two. I wish I was anything but eleven, because I want today to be far away already, far away like a runaway balloon, like a tiny *o* in the sky, so tiny-tiny you have to close your eyes to see it. ❖

WORDS TO KNOW	**sudden** (sŭd′n) *adj.* happening without warning **invisible** (ĭn-vĭz′ə-bəl) *adj.* impossible to see; not visible

Differentiating Instruction

Less Proficient Readers
Ask students to paraphrase what Rachel thinks people don't understand about birthdays.

1 Ask students what they think Rachel means when she says, "all of a sudden I'm feeling sick inside, like the part of me that's three wants to come out of my eyes." Help them understand this refers back to what the narrator talked about on page 27, when she says that sometimes even grown-ups need to cry like three-year-olds.
Possible Response: People can be many ages at the same time. Sometimes they feel vulnerable and younger than they are, as Rachel does.

English Learners
2 Students should be able to infer the meaning of *tippy-tip* from the context. Have a volunteer point to the "tippy-tip corner" of his or her desk.

Advanced Students
Remind students that the climax of a story is the most exciting or interesting moment. Ask them to identify the climax of this story and tell how the events leading up to it build suspense.
Possible Response: The climax is when Rachel breaks down and cries. When she wakes up on her birthday and does not feel any older, readers wonder whether she will have a reason to act younger. The interaction between Mrs. Price and Rachel builds tension as Rachel becomes more upset. When Rachel feels all her younger selves pushing against the back of her eyes, readers can predict that she is about to cry.

EXPLICIT INSTRUCTION Character Traits

Instruction Write the following words on the board: *shy*, *outgoing*. Ask students which word they would use to describe Rachel and why. Explain that this word describes one of Rachel's traits, or qualities. Continue by telling students that when they describe what a character—or a real person—is like, they are describing traits. Remind students that they can learn about a character's traits by paying attention to the character's speech, thoughts, feelings, and actions; the writer's direct statements about the character; the speech, thoughts, and actions of other characters; and descriptions of physical characteristics.

Say, "Not all traits are stated directly. For example, Rachel never says, 'I really think a lot about things.' But readers can tell that she is thoughtful because of all the time she spends thinking about birthdays and how she sometimes feels like crying." Now ask students to name one of Rachel's physical traits from the story and explain how this trait was revealed. (*She is thin. She describes herself as skinny.*)
Practice Have students use page 9 of the **Unit One Resource Book** to record Rachel's and Mrs. Price's character traits and the story information that reveals each trait.

Possible Responses: Rachel—*Trait:* sensitive; *Evidence:* acts embarrassed at being singled out, cries after she is forced to wear the sweater. *Trait:* shy or inarticulate; *Evidence:* can't find the words to tell Mrs. Price that the sweater isn't hers. Mrs. Price—*Trait:* insensitive; *Evidence:* doesn't think about why Rachel would tell her the sweater isn't hers. *Trait:* bossy; *Evidence:* demands that Rachel put on the sweater.

 Use **Unit One Resource Book**, p. 9.

Active Reading [CONNECTING]

A Ask, "Have you ever worn clothing or a hair style that made you feel as if you were 'not yourself'? Why are such things important to a person's identity?"

Possible Response: Clothing and hair styles can make a statement about the kind of person we are or want to be. Although people should be judged on more than their appearance, it is hard to escape judgments based on looks.

Reading Skills and Strategies: COMPARE/CONTRAST

What are some similarities and differences between "Who's the New Kid?" and "Eleven"?

Possible Response: Both main characters are shy eleven-year-old girls. In both stories, the main character has a humiliating experience in school. Rachel's embarrassing experience revolves around a sweater, whereas the narrator in "Who's the New Kid?" is embarrassed because of a haircut. "Eleven" ends with Rachel wanting to escape, but "Who's the New Kid?" ends with a funny comment from the narrator's adult perspective.

Lois Lowry

Lois Lowry's father was an army dentist whose transfers kept her family on the move throughout her childhood. She was born in Hawaii and had lived in Pennsylvania and Tokyo by the time she started high school in New York. She went to college in Rhode Island before marrying a naval officer whose career again led her to move a lot. Later she graduated from the University of Southern Maine before beginning to write.

"WHO'S THE NEW KID?"
by Lois Lowry

Because of my father's job, my family moved a great deal. I was always (at least it felt like always!) the "new kid" in school.

I remember that when I was eleven years old, I was once again entering a brand-new school. And school had already begun. The kids had already gotten to know each other, had made friends, and had learned the teachers' names, the layout of the classrooms and the hallways, and the schedules.

A I arrived in the middle of the day, feeling very awkward and shy. I had had my hair cut the day before; it had been very long, and now it was very short, so I didn't even feel like myself. My mother took me to the school office, and they did the necessary paperwork to enroll me, and then she left me there. Someone took me to the classroom where I was supposed to be.

Everyone stared at me, of course, when I entered the room. One of the students—reacting to my very short hair, I suppose—called out, "Is it a boy or a girl?"

Do you know, that was *forty-four* years ago, that moment—yet I still remember how humiliating it felt.

But guess what. I still wear my hair very short. I think it's my way, now, of saying, "Nyah nyah. I don't care *what* you think."

EXPLICIT INSTRUCTION   Read Aloud

Instruction Use the first two paragraphs of "Who's the New Kid?" to model reading aloud using appropriate pacing, intonation, and expression. Explain to students that when they read aloud, they need to

- make sure they read at the right speed— not too quickly or too slowly
- use tone of voice to emphasize important ideas, make transitions clear, and help listeners understand what they are hearing

- use their voices to show the feelings the writer is expressing

Also explain that students need to make sure they can read words accurately and fluently and that they may have to practice reading difficult words. Knowing what a passage is about will also help them read aloud accurately. Ask, "When you're reading aloud, what clues in the text tell you when to stop and breathe?" (*the punctuation, such as commas and periods*)

Practice Have students work in pairs to

practice reading aloud another short passage from "Who's the New Kid?" Partners may team up with another pair to present their readings. As one student in the group reads, the others should listen and then ask questions about how the reader prepared the passage. Ask volunteers to read their passages to the rest of the class.

 Use **Unit One Resource Book,** p. 10.

Connect to the Literature

1. What Do You Think?
Do you sympathize with Rachel's feelings? Why or why not?

Comprehension Check
- What does Rachel think about the sweater?
- What does Rachel do after she puts on the sweater?

Think Critically

2. [ACTIVE READING] [CONNECTING]
Look at the notes you took in your [📖 READER'S NOTEBOOK]. What **connections** did you make between Rachel's birthday and your own recollections?

3. Why do you think the incident with the sweater affects Rachel so powerfully?

> **Think About:**
> - Rachel's feelings about turning 11
> - her description of the sweater
> - Mrs. Price's responses to Rachel

4. Does Mrs. Price treat Rachel unfairly, or does she just make an honest mistake? Explain.

5. When Rachel cries, it seems that her 11th birthday is ruined. If you were a friend of Rachel's, what would you say or do to help her feel better?

Extend Interpretations

6. [COMPARING TEXTS] Read "Who's the New Kid?" on page 30. What comparisons can you make between Lois Lowry's experience and Rachel's?

7. Critic's Corner One critic has said that Sandra Cisneros "makes the invisible, visible." How does Cisneros make Rachel's feelings "visible" to readers?

8. Connect to Life Do you think people of all ages share Rachel's feelings about becoming a year older? Discuss with your classmates your own thoughts about growing up.

Literary Analysis

 [CHARACTER] **Characters** are the people, animals, or imaginary creatures who take part in the action of a story. A story usually focuses on events in the life of the **main character.** The **minor characters** serve mainly to help move along the action. In "Eleven," Rachel is the main character and the teacher and students are minor characters. Just like real people, characters have **traits,** or qualities. For example, a character may be courageous, shy, friendly, stubborn, or sensitive. You can determine characters' traits by paying attention to these elements:

- their speech, thoughts, feelings, and actions
- the speech, thoughts, and actions of other characters
- the writers' direct statements about them
- descriptions of their physical characteristics

Group Activity Get together with three classmates. Have two members of your group pretend to be Rachel and Mrs. Price, discussing why they acted as they did about the sweater. As they hold their discussion, the other two group members should take notes about what traits, or qualities, they see in the characters' behavior and language. Afterward, compare your group's observations with another group's.

ELEVEN   **31**

Connect to the Literature

What Do You Think?
1. Possible Response: It is understandable that Rachel is so upset because she has been singled out and her teacher will not believe what she says.

Comprehension Check
- Rachel thinks the sweater is ugly and embarrassing and smells bad.
- After Rachel puts on the sweater, she begins to cry.

📖 Use Selection Quiz
Unit One Resource Book, p. 13.

Think Critically

2. Possible Response: It is easy to relate to feeling unfairly treated and embarrassed. These feelings are worse when your classmates do not stick up for you.

3. Possible Response: Rachel felt younger than 11 years old when she awakened. Maybe she went to school feeling sensitive. Not only is the sweater not hers, but she feels singled out, publicly wronged, and humiliated.

4. Possible Responses: Mrs. Price treats Rachel unfairly. She should see that Rachel is telling the truth and that Rachel is upset. She should know that it's Rachel's birthday. Or, Mrs. Price makes a mistake because she is too busy to notice Rachel's reactions. She thinks Rachel is acting silly about the sweater.

5. Possible Response: I would tell Rachel that other people understand how she feels. Also, she can still have a good birthday celebration with her family.

Literary Analysis

Character After the role-playing activity, groups may discuss whether the students who played the roles followed the story and acted in character for Mrs. Price and Rachel.

 Use **Literary Analysis Transparencies,** p. 3, for additional support.

Extend Interpretations

6. Comparing Texts Possible Response: Like Rachel, Lois Lowry felt misunderstood—in her case, when a student thought she might be a boy. Also like Rachel, she felt embarrassed and alone in front of the class when all the children stared at her.

7. Critic's Corner Possible Response: Rachel says that the sweater "hurts" her and describes it as "all itchy and full of germs that aren't even mine." When Rachel cries, Cisneros describes how it feels to have one's body overcome by sobs.

8. Connect to Life Students may say that they expect to feel older and wiser each year, and that they hope that people will remember their birthdays and do things to make it a special day.

Writing

Tell a Friend Students might begin by making a list of Rachel's traits. Remind them to use details from the story to make their descriptions convincing.

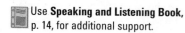
Use **Speaking and Listening Book,** p. 14, for additional support.

Speaking & Listening

Letter From Mrs. Price Remind students to put themselves in Mrs. Price's place and to tell the story from her point of view this time.

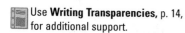
Use **Writing Transparencies,** p. 14, for additional support.

Research & Technology

Celebrate! After all students have created their posters, lead a class discussion on the similarities and differences in how birthdays are observed from family to family and country to country. Be sensitive to the fact that Jehovah's Witnesses do not celebrate birthdays, and allow any of these students to explain their beliefs.

Vocabulary and Spelling

EXERCISE: RESTATEMENT CLUES
1. sudden
2. invisible
3. except
4. expect

SPELLING STRATEGY
Answers will vary.

Writing

Tell a Friend If you had to describe Rachel to a friend, what would you say? What words would you use to tell about Rachel's qualities? Write a paragraph that describes Rachel. Use details from the story to support your description. Place your paragraph in your **Working Portfolio.** ▱

Writing Handbook
See p. R35: Paragraphs.

Speaking & Listening

Letter from Mrs. Price Mrs. Price has a difficult time dealing with Rachel and the fuss over the sweater. Pretend that you are Mrs. Price. Write a letter in which you tell a friend about your day. Read the letter to the class. As you read, use your voice and facial expressions to help listeners understand Mrs. Price's feelings. Also remember to read slowly and clearly so listeners will understand you.

Speaking and Listening Handbook
See p. R96: Practice.

Research & Technology

Celebrate! Birthday celebrations vary from country to country. Conduct research to find out about birthday celebrations in three other countries. Look for information in books and articles, and on the Internet. Then create a poster, using words and pictures to show the traditions you discovered. On the bottom of your poster, list the sources you used to find information.

A piñata is a traditional birthday decoration and game.

Vocabulary and Spelling

EXERCISE: RESTATEMENT CLUES On a sheet of paper, write the Word to Know that best completes each sentence.
1. With a _____ movement, Rachel pushed the sweater to the floor.
2. She could not read the letter because it was written with _____ ink.
3. No one _____ me knew that it was my birthday.
4. We _____ to have some chocolate cake at the party.

WORDS TO KNOW	except	expect	invisible	sudden

SPELLING STRATEGY: COMPOUND WORDS A compound word is made up of smaller words, called base words. These base words are joined together with no changes in spelling. Examples of compound words include *watermelon, football, ice cream,* and *brother-in-law.*

You can often figure out the meaning of a compound word from the meaning of its base words.

Make a list of all the compound words in "Eleven." Write down the base words that make up each one. Then use one of the base words to spell another compound word.

Example: waterfall = <u>water</u> + <u>fall</u>
<u>downfall</u>

Spelling Handbook
See p. R26.

CHOICES and CHALLENGES

Grammar in Context: Sentence Fragments

In "Eleven," Rachel becomes so frustrated that she speaks and thinks in broken pieces, or **fragments,** of a sentence.

> An ugly sweater like that, all raggedy and old. Mrs. Price puts it on my desk. "That's not, I don't, you're not . . . Not mine," I finally say in a little voice that was maybe me when I was four.

A sentence expresses a complete thought. A fragment is only a piece of a thought. Although fragments are rare in good writing, sometimes writers use them to communicate extreme emotion.

Usage Tip: The word *and, or, but,* or *like* at the beginning of a sentence may introduce a fragment. Try to avoid beginning a sentence with one of these words.

WRITING EXERCISE Rewrite each fragment as a complete sentence. You may add or delete words.

Example: *Original* Because nobody listened to me.

Rewritten Nobody listened to me.

1. Feels scared and small.
2. A little child.
3. Because nobody understands.
4. Tried to explain.

Connect to the Literature Reread the paragraph on page 28 that begins, "But when the sick feeling goes away . . ." Rewrite the paragraph so that it contains only complete sentences but remains packed with emotion.

Grammar Handbook
See p. R67: Writing Complete Sentences.

Sandra Cisneros
born 1954

"I'm trying to write the stories that haven't been written."

Traveling Years Sandra Cisneros moved frequently as a child, particularly between Chicago, the city where she was born, and Mexico, the country her father came from. "I didn't like school because we moved so much, and I was always new and funny looking," she says. As a writer, Cisneros has drawn on her childhood memories of her Spanish-speaking neighborhood in Chicago, especially in her award-winning book *The House on Mango Street.*

A Quiet Observer Cisneros was shy in school. "I never opened my mouth," she remembers, "except when the teacher called on me, the first time I'd speak all day." Her out-of-class reading sparked her interest in writing. After studying literature in college, Cisneros earned a master's degree and began to publish poems, essays, and short stories. She has won praise both in this country and overseas for her writing about Mexican Americans.

AUTHOR ACTIVITY
The Lone Daughter As the only daughter in a family with seven children, Sandra Cisneros often felt overlooked and misunderstood. In your opinion, which details in "Eleven" express these feelings? Share your ideas with your classmates.

Grammar in Context

Grammar in Context

WRITING EXERCISE
Possible Responses:

1. She feels scared and small.
2. A little child cried.
3. She feels lonely because nobody understands.
4. Rachel tried to explain.

Connect to the Literature
Paragraphs will vary, but should contain only complete sentences.

Sandra Cisneros

Sandra Cisneros says that she is "trying to write the stories that haven't been written"–stories of people in extended Latino families such as hers. Dedicated to promoting other Latina and Latino writers, Cisneros believes that the Spanish language has a great contribution to make to American literature.

Author Activity

The Lone Daughter Students may say that Rachel's feelings that people don't understand about birthdays come from Cisneros' experience.

EXPLICIT INSTRUCTION Grammar in Context

SENTENCE FRAGMENTS
Instruction Tell students that there are two basic ways to fix sentence fragments.

- **Add a subject or a verb.** A complete sentence must have a subject and a verb. Add the missing part to fix a fragment.
  FRAGMENT: The horrible red sweater
  REVISED: The horrible red sweater lay on Rachel's desk.
- **Join the fragment with a sentence.** Words such as *before, when, because, as, who, whose, which,* and *that* sometimes appear at the beginning of a fragment. A fragment like this can be joined to a related sentence.
  SENTENCE: Rachel didn't feel eleven.
  FRAGMENT: When she woke up
  REVISED: Rachel didn't feel eleven when she woke up.

Practice Ask students to rewrite these items, correcting any fragments.

1. Sometimes adults act silly. Because they feel as if they're three years old. *(silly, because)*
2. Which was why I cried. *(Everyone forgot my birthday, which)*

3. Was wishing her birthday would end. *(She was)*

 Use **Unit One Resource Book,** p. 11.

 For more instruction in correcting sentence fragments, see McDougal Littell's **Language Network,** Chapter 1.

For **systematic instruction** in grammar, see:
- **Grammar, Usage, and Mechanics Book**
- pacing chart on p. 19i.

Standards-Based Objectives

1. understand and appreciate a **short story**
2. understand the **plot** of a story
3. understand the **sequence of events** in fiction
4. understand **character traits**

Summary

Jerry and his friends are obsessed with cowboy cards. When Jerry's brother Armand asks him to chip in for a birthday gift for their father, Jerry holds back some money to spend on cards. But when Jerry gets to Lemire's store to buy them, he learns that the company is not making them anymore and is making president cards instead. Jerry races to catch his brother before he buys the birthday gift, so he can contribute more, but he is too late. He feels guilty. Later, when Jerry must again choose how to spend his money, he gives it to his brother, who needs money to attend a dance. Jerry deprives himself of being the first boy to collect a complete set of cards, thereby losing out on the grand prize of a baseball glove. But that's not the worst part. Now he must tell his best friend that he was responsible for the biggest braggart in town's winning the glove.

Thematic Link

After making a decision that benefits himself and regretting it, Jerry makes a courageous decision, and as a result, must face his friend's anger.

English Conventions Practice

Daily Language SkillBuilder

Have students **proofread** the display sentences on page 19k and write them correctly. The sentences also appear on Transparency 1 of **Language Transparencies.**

Preteaching Vocabulary

If you would like to preteach the WORDS TO KNOW for this selection, use the Explicit Instruction, page 35.

President Cleveland, Where Are You?

by ROBERT CORMIER

Connect to Your Life

Costly Choices Making your own choices takes courage. Think of a time when you chose to do something different from what someone else wanted or expected. Or think about someone in a book or movie who made a difficult choice. What was so difficult?

Build Background

HISTORY

"President Cleveland, Where Are You?" is set in the 1930s. In that decade, the United States suffered through the economic crisis now known as the Great Depression. Thousands of people lost their jobs, and banks and businesses closed all over the country.

Despite hard times, the 1930s was also a great decade for entertainment. Children enjoyed the Sunday "funny papers," four-hour movie matinees, and radio programs like *Little Orphan Annie* and *Dick Tracy*. Many children, like the boys in this story, collected trading cards that featured the heroes of movies and sports.

WORDS TO KNOW
Vocabulary Preview

allot	incredulous
betrayed	indignant
contempt	lethargy
divulge	obsess
dwindle	stalemate

Focus Your Reading

LITERARY ANALYSIS **PLOT**

The series of events in a story is called the **plot.** A plot usually revolves around a **conflict,** or problem, faced by the main character. Plots usually develop in four stages. During the **exposition** stage, the characters and setting are introduced. The conflict develops and the story becomes more complicated during the **rising action.** The **climax** is the turning point of the story. The **falling action** follows, as the characters deal with the conflict's resolution, and the story ends. As you read, try to identify the main conflict and its resolution.

ACTIVE READING **SEQUENCE OF EVENTS**

To understand a story, you must be able to follow the **sequence of events** in the plot. Look for events that help to move the plot along. Some may seem unimportant at first but turn out to be significant.

READER'S NOTEBOOK As you read, use a story wheel like the one at the right to keep track of six important events. The wheel will help you see how events move the plot forward.

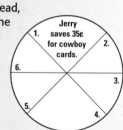

Jerry
1. saves 35¢ for cowboy cards.
2.
3.
4.
5.
6.

LESSON RESOURCES

UNIT ONE RESOURCE BOOK, pp. 14–20

ASSESSMENT
Formal Assessment, pp. 7–8
Test Generator

SKILLS TRANSPARENCIES AND COPYMASTERS
Literary Analysis
• Setting, TR 6 (p. 36)
• Plot, TR 5 (pp. 38, 45)
• Conflict, TR 8 (p. 38)

Reading and Critical Thinking
• Connecting, TR 2 (p. 45)
• Venn Diagram, TR 35 (p. 46)
Language
• Daily Language SkillBuilder, TR 1 (p. 34)
• Context Clues: Compare and Contrast, Cause and Effect, Example, TR 54 (p. 35)
Writing
• Transitional Words List, TR 10 (p. 46)
• Locating Material in the Library, TR 41 (p. 46)

INTEGRATED TECHNOLOGY
Audio Library

Visit our Web site:
www.mcdougallittell.com

For **systematic instruction** in language skills, see:
• **Vocabulary and Spelling Book**
• **Grammar, Usage, and Mechanics Book**
• pacing chart on p. 19i.

President Cleveland, WHERE ARE YOU?

BY ROBERT CORMIER

T HAT WAS THE AUTUMN OF THE COWBOY CARDS— Buck Jones and Tom Tyler and Hoot Gibson and especially Ken Maynard. The cards were available in those five-cent packages of gum: pink sticks, three together, covered with a sweet white powder. You couldn't blow bubbles with that particular gum, but it couldn't have mattered less. The cowboy cards were important—the pictures of those rock-faced men with eyes of blue steel.

On those wind-swept, leaf-tumbling afternoons, we gathered after school on the sidewalk in front of Lemire's Drugstore, across from St. Jude's Parochial School, and we swapped and bargained and matched for the cards. Because a Ken Maynard serial[1] was playing at the Globe every Saturday afternoon, he was the most popular cowboy of all, and one of his cards was worth at least ten of any other kind. Rollie Tremaine had a treasure of thirty or so, and he guarded them jealously. He'd match you for the other cards, but he risked his Ken Maynards only when the other kids threatened to leave him out of the competition altogether.

1. **serial** (sîr′ē-əl): a movie appearing in weekly parts.

Differentiating Instruction

Less Proficient Readers
Ask students about their hobbies or collections and then explain that this story is about card collecting, which has been a popular hobby for decades. Have students look at the picture and read the first two paragraphs. Ask them what kind of card collecting they think this selection will be about. *(The picture is of a president, but the paragraphs are about cowboys.)* Suggest to students that the selection might be about collecting more than one kind of card.
Set a Purpose Have students read to learn how Jerry, the main character, decides how to spend his money.

English Learners
Tell students that Buck Jones, Tom Tyler, Hoot Gibson, and Ken Maynard were movie stars who played cowboys in Westerns. Encourage students to use the context to figure out the meaning of proper nouns that may be unfamiliar, like "the Globe" (a theater), "Monument Comb Shop" (factory), and "Monument Men's Shop" (clothing store for men). What can students infer from the fact that both stores start with the word *Monument*? *(maybe that is the name of the town)*
 Point out that "swapped and bargained and matched" refers to how the boys traded and collected cards to get a complete set or the cards with the most value.

Use **Spanish Study Guide,** pp. 7–9, for additional support.

Advanced Students
Ask students to use Jerry's actions to infer what he is feeling and thinking when he makes his decisions.

EXPLICIT INSTRUCTION Preteaching Vocabulary

WORDS TO KNOW
Teaching Strategy Remind students that they can draw on **context clues** and their experiences to bring meaning to words. Write the following sentence on the chalkboard: This week my father earned extra money, so he was able to *allot* each of us an extra dime. Read the sentence aloud and point out that the word *so* sets up a cause-effect relationship. The father earned extra money, so he must have been able to *give* each one an extra dime. *Allot* means "to distribute to as a share."

Practice Have students use the context to find the meaning of each underlined word.
1. The <u>indignant</u> drivers honked at me as I darted in front of cars on my bicycle. *(angry)*
2. I was <u>incredulous</u> when my brother told me his unbelievable news. *(skeptical)*
3. My <u>lethargy</u> was so great I couldn't get out of bed. *(fatigue)*
4. My brother begged me to tell him the secret, but I refused to <u>divulge</u> it. *(reveal)*
5. Most students were excited by the team's victory, but I was <u>indifferent</u>. *(uninterested)*

Use **Unit One Resource Book,** p. 19, for more practice.

For **systematic instruction** in vocabulary, see:
• **Vocabulary and Spelling Book**
• pacing chart on p. 19i.

You could almost hate Rollie Tremaine. In the first place, he was the only son of Auguste Tremaine, who operated the Uptown Dry Goods Store, and he did not live in a tenement[2] but in a big white birthday cake of a house on Laurel Street. He was too fat to be effective in the football games between the Frenchtown Tigers and the North Side Knights, and he made us constantly aware of the jingle of coins in his pockets. He was able to stroll into Lemire's and casually select a quarter's worth of cowboy cards while the rest of us watched, aching with envy.

Once in a while I earned a nickel or dime by running errands or washing windows for blind old Mrs. Belander, or by finding pieces of copper, brass, and other valuable metals at the dump and selling them to the junkman. The coins clutched in my hand, I would race to Lemire's to buy a cowboy card or two, hoping that Ken Maynard would stare boldly out at me as I opened the pack. At one time, before a disastrous matching session with Roger Lussier (my best friend, except where the cards were involved), I owned five Ken Maynards and considered myself a millionaire, of sorts.

 One week I was particularly lucky; I had spent two afternoons washing floors for Mrs. Belander and received a quarter. Because my father had worked a full week at the shop, where a rush order for fancy combs had been received, he allotted my brothers and sisters and me an extra dime along with the usual ten cents for the Saturday-afternoon movie. Setting aside the movie fare, I found myself with a bonus of thirty-five cents, and I then planned to put Rollie Tremaine to shame the following Monday afternoon.

---

2. **tenement** (tĕn′ə-mənt): a low-rent or rundown apartment building.

WORDS
TO
KNOW

allot (ə-lŏt′) v. to parcel out to; distribute to

Monday was the best day to buy the cards because the candy man stopped at Lemire's every Monday morning to deliver the new assortments. There was nothing more exciting in the world than a fresh batch of card boxes. I rushed home from school that day and hurriedly changed my clothes, eager to set off for the store. As I burst through the doorway, letting the screen door slam behind me, my brother Armand blocked my way.

He was fourteen, three years older than I, and a freshman at Monument High School. He had recently become a stranger to me in many ways—indifferent to such matters as cowboy cards and the Frenchtown Tigers—and he carried himself with a mysterious dignity that was fractured now and then when his voice began shooting off in all directions like some kind of vocal fireworks.[3]

"Wait a minute, Jerry," he said. "I want to talk to you." He motioned me out of earshot of my mother, who was busy supervising the usual after-school skirmish[4] in the kitchen.

I sighed with impatience. In recent months Armand had become a figure of authority, siding with my father and mother occasionally. As the oldest son, he sometimes took advantage of his age and experience to issue rules and regulations.

"How much money have you got?" he whispered.

"You in some kind of trouble?" I asked, excitement rising in me as I remembered the blackmail plot of a movie at the Globe a month before.

He shook his head in annoyance. "Look," he said, "it's Pa's birthday tomorrow. I think we ought to chip in and buy him something. . . ."

I reached into my pocket and caressed the coins. "Here," I said carefully, pulling out a nickel. "If we all give a nickel, we should have enough to buy him something pretty nice."

He regarded me with contempt. "Rita already gave me fifteen cents, and I'm throwing in a quarter. Albert handed over a dime—all that's left of his birthday money. Is that all you can do—a nickel?"

"Aw, come on," I protested. "I haven't got a single Ken Maynard left, and I was going to buy some cards this afternoon."

"Ken Maynard!" he snorted. "Who's more important—him or your father?"

His question was unfair because he knew that there was no possible choice—"my father" had to be the only answer. My father was a huge man who believed in the things of the spirit. . . . He had worked at the Monument Comb Shop since the age of fourteen; his booming laugh—or grumble—greeted us each night when he returned from the factory. A steady worker when the shop had enough work, he quickened with gaiety on Friday nights and weekends, . . . and he was fond of making long speeches about the good things in life. In the middle of the Depression, for instance, he paid cash for a piano, of all things, and insisted that my twin sisters, Yolande and Yvette, take lessons once a week.

I took a dime from my pocket and handed it to Armand.

---

3. **vocal fireworks:** because Armand's voice is changing, its pitch varies unexpectedly from high to low.

4. **skirmish** (skûr′mĭsh): a minor battle or conflict.

WORDS TO KNOW · **contempt** (kən-tĕmpt′) n. the feeling produced by something disgraceful or worthless; scorn

37

Differentiating Instruction

English Learners

1 Explain that *dry goods store* is an old-fashioned name for a store that sells fabrics, clothing, and small household items like needles, buttons, and thread.

Less Proficient Readers

2 Ask students why Jerry might consider it "lucky" that his father worked a full week. *(Jobs and money are scarce because of the Depression.)* Ask students what types of jobs Jerry does to earn money to buy cowboy cards *(washes floors, washes windows, runs errands, and collects cans and metal).*

Set a Purpose Have students look for what changes when Jerry's dad is laid off. How does Jerry change? How does Jerry's father change?

Advanced Students

Have students read more about the Depression to understand what life was like during that period. Have a class discussion about what Jerry's family life might have been like and how they were affected by the Depression. Ask how growing up during this time would be different from growing up today.

Reading and Analyzing

Reading Skills and Strategies:
PREDICT

 Ask students to predict what Jerry will do now that he can't buy any cowboy cards.

Possible Response: He will give the money to Armand for the present for his father.

Active Reading

SEQUENCE OF EVENTS

Remind students that they can represent text information in different ways. Have them continue filling out their story maps with the events on this page.

Possible Responses: There are no more cowboy cards. Jerry hurries to give his brother more money. He is too late.

Literary Analysis **PLOT**

Remind students that the rising action of the story is the stage during which the conflict develops and the story becomes more complicated. Ask students what happens on page 39 that complicates the plot.

Possible Response: Jerry learns about the President cards. He is too late to give his brother more money.

Use **Literary Analysis Transparencies,** p. 5, for additional support.

Literary Analysis: CONFLICT

Analyze and discuss Jerry's conflict with students. Is it an internal conflict or an external one?

Possible Response: It has elements of both. It begins with an external conflict when Armand asks him for money and argues about how much he gives, but the conflict continues for Jerry as he thinks over the decision he made.

Use **Literary Analysis Transparencies,** p. 8, for additional support.

Whelan's Drug Store, Berenice Abbott. Photography Collection, Miriam and Ira D. Wallach Division of Art, Prints and Photographs, The New York Public Library, Astor, Lenox and Tilden Foundations.

WHEN I ARRIVED AT LEMIRE'S, I SENSED DISASTER IN THE AIR.

38

Elements of Plot: Rising Action

Instruction Review the plot graph on page 22 and remind remind students that during the rising action, a story becomes more complicated as the conflict develops. Ask students what happens on page 39 to cause Jerry to regret his decision not to give Armand all of his extra money. *(The cowboy cards have been discontinued, so Jerry doesn't need extra money.)* Discuss how this makes the plot more complicated.

Practice Have students work in small groups to discuss story events and details that show how the story conflict is becoming more complicated. Then have students record these details on page 16 of the **Unit One Resource Book,** in the box labeled Rising Action. Tell students to continue to fill in this box as the rising action continues.

Possible Responses: Jerry's conflict with Armand over the money has become more

complicated. Jerry learns that he does not need his extra twenty-five cents after all. Filled with guilt, he rushes to find Armand and his sisters. When he finds them, they have already bought their father's present. This only makes Jerry feel more guilty.

Use **Unit One Resource Book,** p. 16.

"Thanks, Jerry," he said. "I hate to take your last cent."

"That's all right," I replied, turning away and consoling myself with the thought that twenty cents was better than nothing at all.

When I arrived at Lemire's, I sensed disaster in the air. Roger Lussier was kicking disconsolately at a tin can in the gutter, and Rollie Tremaine sat sullenly on the steps in front of the store.

"Save your money," Roger said. He had known about my plans to splurge on the cards.

"What's the matter?" I asked.

"There's no more cowboy cards," Rollie Tremaine said. "The company's not making them any more."

"They're going to have President cards," Roger said, his face twisting with disgust. He pointed to the store window. "Look!"

A placard in the window announced: "Attention, Boys. Watch for the New Series. Presidents of the United States. Free in Each 5-Cent Package of Caramel Chew."

"President cards?" I asked, dismayed.

I read on: "Collect a Complete Set and Receive an Official Imitation Major League Baseball Glove, Embossed with Lefty Grove's Autograph."

Glove or no glove, who could become excited about Presidents, of all things?

Rollie Tremaine stared at the sign. "Benjamin Harrison,[5] for crying out loud," he said. "Why would I want Benjamin Harrison when I've got twenty-two Ken Maynards?"

I felt the warmth of guilt creep over me. I jingled the coins in my pocket, but the sound was hollow. No more Ken Maynards to buy.

"I'm going to buy a Mr. Goodbar," Rollie Tremaine decided.

I was without appetite, indifferent even to a Baby Ruth, which was my favorite. I thought of how I had betrayed Armand and, worst of all, my father.

"I'll see you after supper," I called over my shoulder to Roger as I hurried away toward home. I took the shortcut behind the church, although it involved leaping over a tall wooden fence, and I zigzagged recklessly through Mr. Thibodeau's garden, trying to outrace my guilt. I pounded up the steps and into the house, only to learn that Armand had already taken Yolande and Yvette uptown to shop for the birthday present.

I pedaled my bike furiously through the streets, ignoring the indignant horns of automobiles as I sliced through the traffic. Finally I saw Armand and my sisters emerge from the Monument Men's Shop. My heart sank when I spied the long, slim package that Armand was holding.

"Did you buy the present yet?" I asked, although I knew it was too late.

"Just now. A blue tie," Armand said. "What's the matter?"

"Nothing," I replied, my chest hurting.

He looked at me for a long moment. At first his eyes were hard, but then they softened. He smiled at me, almost sadly, and touched my arm. I turned away from him because I felt naked and exposed.

"It's all right," he said gently. "Maybe you've learned something." The words were gentle, but they held a curious dignity, the dignity remaining even when his voice suddenly cracked on the last syllable.

I wondered what was happening to me, because I did not know whether to laugh or cry.

---

5. **Benjamin Harrison:** president of the United States from 1889 to 1893.

| WORDS TO KNOW | **indignant** (ĭn-dĭg′nənt) *adj.* angry at something unjust, mean, or unworthy |

English Learners
Tell students that Major League baseball players are pictured on cards that people collect and trade.

Have students scan the page, looking for words they don't understand. Review "disconsolately," "splurge," "placard," "embossed," indifferent," "indignant," and "dignity."

Less Proficient Readers
[1] Ask students why Jerry feels guilty and why he feels he has betrayed his brother and father.
Possible Response: He kept some of his money to buy cards instead of giving it all to his brother to buy a present for their father's birthday.
[2] Ensure students understand Armand's reaction. Why were Armand's eyes hard at first and then softer? (At first Armand is angry, but then he understands why his brother acted as he did.) What else does Armand do that lets the reader know he is not mad at Jerry? (He smiles at Jerry and touches Jerry's arm; his voice is gentle.)

Advanced Students
What clues does the author give us about Jerry's character? (Sometimes he is thinking of himself but then realizes he is being selfish.) Why does Jerry feel "naked and exposed"? (He thinks his brother knows that he held money back for himself and now feels guilty.) What does the last line on page 39 tell us about Jerry, "I wondered what was happening to me, because I did not know whether to laugh or cry"? (Jerry's feelings conflict.) Have students talk about why Jerry might be both happy and sad. How is this evidence that Jerry may be growing up?

EXPLICIT INSTRUCTION ## Character Traits

Instruction Ask students to describe the difference between a main character and a minor character. (A main character is the most important character, usually the one who experiences the conflict. A minor character is less important but still moves the plot along and interacts with the main character.) Then ask students who the main character is in the story. (Jerry) Ask students to describe Jerry's traits. (competitive, imaginative, sensitive) Write the words on the board and discuss the story information that reveals these traits.

Practice Have pairs of students list the story characters and classify them as either main or minor. Then have partners list Jerry's traits and note the story information that reveals these traits.

Possible Responses: Main character: Jerry; minor characters: Rollie Tremaine; Roger Lussier; Jerry's father; Armand and Albert (Jerry's brothers); Rita, Yolande, and Yvette (Jerry's sisters). Jerry's traits—competitive: ongoing cowboy card battle; clever or energetic: works to earn money for cowboy

cards and is always racing or running somewhere; smart: saves his money; imaginative: sees himself in movie plots; sensitive: feels guilty about keeping his money.

Use **Unit One Resource Book,** p. 17, for more practice.

Literary Analysis: HUMOR

A Discuss the humorous tone the author has taken throughout this story. For example, he says, "We journeyed on our bicycles to the North Side, engaged three boys in a matching bout, and returned with five new presidents, including Chester Alan Arthur, who up to that time had been missing." Ask students if he really means the President himself had been missing. If not, what does he mean and why do they think he says it this way?

Possible Response: No, he means that President Arthur's *card* has not been seen around yet. The story event is funnier because it is described as though the president himself were missing.

Active Reader | SEQUENCE OF EVENTS

B Have students add the important information that Jerry learns about Armand on page 41 to their story maps.

Possible Response: Jerry learns that Armand is in love.

Sister Angela was amazed when, a week before Christmas vacation, everybody in the class submitted a history essay worthy of a high mark—in some cases as high as A minus. (Sister Angela did not believe that anyone in the world ever deserved an A.) She never learned— or at least she never let on that she knew—we all had become experts on the Presidents because of the cards we purchased at Lemire's. Each card contained a picture of a President and, on the reverse side, a summary of his career. We looked at those cards so often that the biographies imprinted themselves on our minds without effort. Even our street-corner conversations were filled with such information as the fact that James Madison was called "The Father of the Constitution," or that John Adams had intended to become a minister.

The President cards were a roaring success, and the cowboy cards were quickly forgotten. In the first place, we did not receive gum with the cards, but a kind of chewy caramel. The caramel could be tucked into a corner of your mouth, bulging your cheek in much the same manner as wads of tobacco bulged the mouths of baseball stars. In the second place, the competition for collecting the cards was fierce and frustrating—fierce because everyone was intent on being the first to send away for a baseball glove and frustrating because although there were only thirty-two Presidents, including Franklin Delano Roosevelt,[6] the variety at Lemire's was at a minimum. When the deliveryman left the boxes of cards at the store each Monday, we often discovered that one entire box was devoted to a single President—two weeks in a row the boxes contained nothing but Abraham Lincolns. One week Roger Lussier and I were the heroes of Frenchtown. We journeyed on our bicycles to

the North Side, engaged three boys in a matching bout, and returned with five new Presidents, including Chester Alan Arthur, who up to that time had been missing.

Perhaps to sharpen our desire, the card company sent a sample glove to Mr. Lemire, and it dangled, orange and sleek, in the window. I was half sick with longing, thinking of my old glove at home, which I had inherited from Armand. But Rollie Tremaine's desire for the glove outdistanced my own. He even got Mr. Lemire to agree to give the glove in the window to the first person to get a complete set of cards, so that precious time wouldn't be wasted waiting for the postman.

We were delighted at Rollie Tremaine's frustration, especially since he was only a substitute player for the Tigers. Once, after spending fifty cents on cards—all of which turned out to be Calvin Coolidge—he threw them to the ground, pulled some dollar bills out of his pocket, and said, "The heck with it. I'm going to buy a glove!"

"Not that glove," Roger Lussier said. "Not a glove with Lefty Grove's autograph. Look what it says at the bottom of the sign."

We all looked, although we knew the words by heart: "This Glove Is Not For Sale Anywhere."

Rollie Tremaine scrambled to pick up the cards from the sidewalk, pouting more than ever. After that he was quietly <u>obsessed</u> with the Presidents, hugging the cards close to his chest and refusing to tell us how many more he needed to complete his set.

I too was obsessed with the cards, because they had become things of comfort in a world

---

6. **Franklin Delano Roosevelt:** president of the United States from 1933 to 1945; president at the time of the story.

WORDS
TO   **obsess** (əb-sĕs′) *v.* to occupy the mind of; concern excessively
KNOW

that had suddenly grown dismal. After Christmas, a layoff at the shop had thrown my father out of work. He received no paycheck for four weeks, and the only income we had was from Armand's after-school job at the Blue and White Grocery Store—a job he lost finally when business dwindled as the layoff continued.

Although we had enough food and clothing—my father's credit had always been good, a matter of pride with him—the inactivity made my father restless and irritable. . . . The twins fell sick and went to the hospital to have their tonsils removed. My father was confident that he would return to work eventually and pay off his debts, but he seemed to age before our eyes.

When orders again were received at the comb shop and he returned to work, another disaster occurred, although I was the only one aware of it. Armand fell in love.

I discovered his situation by accident, when I happened to pick up a piece of paper that had fallen to the floor in the bedroom he and I shared. I frowned at the paper, puzzled.

"Dear Sally, When I look into your eyes the world stands still . . ."

The letter was snatched from my hands before I finished reading it.

"What's the big idea, snooping around?" Armand asked, his face crimson. "Can't a guy have any privacy?"

He had never mentioned privacy before. "It was on the floor," I said. "I didn't know it was a letter. Who's Sally?"

He flung himself across the bed. "You tell anybody and I'll muckalize you," he threatened. "Sally Knowlton."

Nobody in Frenchtown had a name like Knowlton.

"A girl from the North Side?" I asked, incredulous.

He rolled over and faced me, anger in his eyes, and a kind of despair, too.

"What's the matter with that? Think she's too good for me?" he asked. "I'm warning you, Jerry, if you tell anybody . . ."

"Don't worry," I said. Love had no particular place in my life; it seemed an unnecessary waste of time. And a girl from the North Side was so remote that for all practical purposes she did not exist. But I was curious. "What are you writing her a letter for? Did she leave town or something?"

"She hasn't left town," he answered. "I wasn't going to send it. I just felt like writing to her."

I was glad that I had never become involved with love—love that brought desperation to your eyes, that caused you to write letters you did not plan to send. Shrugging with indifference, I began to search in the closet for the old baseball glove. I found it on the shelf, under some old sneakers. The webbing was torn and the padding gone. I thought of the sting I would feel when a sharp grounder slapped into the glove, and I winced.

"You tell anybody about me and Sally and I'll—"

"I know. You'll muckalize me."

I did not divulge his secret and often shared his agony, particularly when he sat at the supper table and left my mother's special butterscotch pie untouched. I had never realized before how terrible love could be. But my compassion was short-lived, because I had other things to worry about: report cards due at Eastertime; the loss of income from old Mrs. Belander, who had gone to live with a daughter in Boston; and, of course, the Presidents.

WORDS	dwindle (dwĭn'dl) v. to become less and less
TO	incredulous (ĭn-krĕj'ə-ləs) adj. unbelieving
KNOW	divulge (dĭ-vŭlj') v. to reveal, especially something private or secret

41

Cross Curricular Link Social Studies

FRENCH AMERICANS Explorers from France were not the first Europeans to reach the Americas, but they played a major role in the early exploration of what is now the United States and Canada. Some came to trade with Native Americans. Others came to fight on the American side in the Revolution. From the late 17th to mid-18th centuries, about 15,000 Huguenots (French Protestants) came to escape religious persecution. Political refugees came following the French Revolution. Many French Canadians began to move to the United States in the mid-1800s to find work in the mills and factories. Most of them settled in New England.

The impact of French Americans has been great. Paul Revere, Alexander Hamilton, Henry David Thoreau, Henry Wadsworth Longfellow, and Jacqueline Bouvier Kennedy Onassis are just a few of the people of French heritage who have had a profound effect on the cultural, political, scientific, and humanitarian life of the United States.

Because a <u>stalemate</u> had been reached, the President cards were the dominant force in our lives—mine, Roger Lussier's, and Rollie Tremaine's. For three weeks, as the baseball season approached, each of us had a complete set—complete except for one President, Grover Cleveland. Each time a box of cards arrived at the store, we hurriedly bought them (as hurriedly as our funds allowed) and tore off the wrappers, only to be confronted by James Monroe or Martin Van Buren or someone else. But never Grover Cleveland, never the man who had been the twenty-second and the twenty-fourth President of the United States. We argued about Grover Cleveland. Should he be placed between Chester Alan Arthur and Benjamin Harrison as the twenty-second President, or did he belong between Benjamin Harrison and William McKinley as the twenty-fourth President? Was the card company playing fair? Roger Lussier brought up a horrifying possibility—did we need two Grover Clevelands to complete the set?

Indignant, we stormed Lemire's and protested to the harassed store owner, who had long since vowed never to stock a new **1** series. Muttering angrily, he searched his bills and receipts for a list of rules.

"All right," he announced. "Says here you only need one Grover Cleveland to finish the set. Now get out, all of you, unless you've got money to spend."

2 Outside the store, Rollie Tremaine picked up an empty tobacco tin and scaled it across the street. "Boy," he said. "I'd give five dollars for a Grover Cleveland."

When I returned home, I found Armand sitting on the piazza[7] steps, his chin in his hands. His mood of dejection mirrored my own, and I sat down beside him. We did not say anything for a while.

"Want to throw the ball around?" I asked.

He sighed, not bothering to answer.

"You sick?" I asked.

He stood up and hitched up his trousers, pulled at his ear, and finally told me what the matter was—there was a big dance next week at the high school, the Spring Promenade, and Sally had asked him to be her escort.

I shook my head at the folly of love. "Well, what's so bad about that?"

"How can I take Sally to a fancy dance?" he asked desperately. "I'd have to buy her a corsage. . . . And my shoes are practically falling apart. Pa's got too many worries now to buy me new shoes or give me money for flowers for a girl."

I nodded in sympathy. "Yeah," I said. "Look at me. Baseball time is almost here, and all I've got is that old glove. And no Grover Cleveland card yet . . ."

"Grover Cleveland?" he asked. "They've got some of those up on the North Side. Some kid was telling me there's a store that's got them. He says they're looking for Warren G. Harding."

"Holy smoke!" I said. "I've got an extra Warren G. Harding!" Pure joy sang in my veins. I ran to my bicycle, swung into the seat—and found that the front tire was flat.

"I'll help you fix it," Armand said.

Within half an hour I was at the North Side Drugstore, where several boys were matching cards on the sidewalk. Silently but blissfully I shouted: President Grover Cleveland, here I come!

---

7. **piazza** (pē-ăz′ə): porch.

| WORDS |
| TO |
| KNOW |

stalemate (stāl′māt′) *n.* a situation in which none of the people playing a game are able to win

42

Tenement Flats (Family Flats) (1934), Millard Sheets. National Museum of American Art, Washington, D.C./Art Resource, New York.

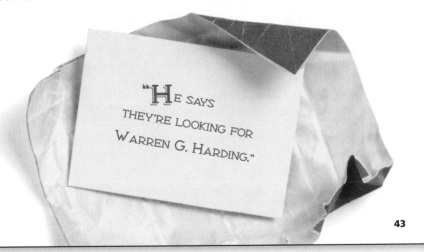

"HE SAYS THEY'RE LOOKING FOR WARREN G. HARDING."

43

Differentiating Instruction

Less Proficient Readers

1 Ask students why the store owner is angry.

Possible Response: He is tired of all the bother caused by the cards. The boys have probably been pestering him about missing cards and other things connected to the contest.

English Learners

Help students use context to find the meanings of the following:

2 *scaled*—context clue: *picked up, across the street;* meaning: "threw"

3 *corsage*—context clue: *flowers for a girl;* meaning: "small bouquet of flowers worn at the shoulder, waist, or wrist"

Less Proficient Readers

Be sure students understand that time passes after Jerry tries to get a Grover Cleveland card and before Armand leaves for the dance.

Check to see that students are aware that Jerry gets a Grover Cleveland card, sells it to Rollie, and gives the money to Armand, who buys a corsage.

Advanced Students

Have students discuss what details of the story are specific to the time period. What would had to have changed if the story had taken place earlier or later? How would changing these details affect the plot of the story?

Possible Responses: The movie showing at the Globe; the cowboys that were famous in the movies; details of the Depression; how many president cards they were looking for. Changing the time would change how much Jerry could spend on cards and on the amount of money his family has. If the story were after the Depression, his father would probably have a steady job and would therefore have money to buy Armand a corsage and something nice to wear for the dance. Instead, Jerry has to trade a card for the money.

EXPLICIT INSTRUCTION **Predicting**

Instruction Remind students that they can often predict, or guess, what will happen next in a story by using the facts in the story and their own experience. For example, point out that students might have been able to predict that Jerry would feel guilty when he only gave Armand a dime for his father's birthday present because most people feel guilty when they aren't as generous as they might have been, or were expected to be. Predicting that Jerry would feel guilty is based on readers' prior knowledge, or previous experience. Remind students to check their predictions by reading farther in a work to see what actually occurs.

Practice Draw a two-column chart on the board with these heads: Facts from the Story, My Own Experiences. Ask students to copy the chart on their own paper and work in pairs to make predictions about what Jerry will tell Roger about the baseball card. They can fill in the two columns of the chart to support their prediction. Have volunteer pairs share their predictions with the class.

Possible Responses: Responses will vary but should be based on story information.

Reading Skills and Strategies:
MAKE INFERENCES

A Ask what inference students can draw based on the fact that Armand went to the dance with a corsage in hand. Have them support their inferences with text evidence.

Answer: Jerry got the card, sold it to Rollie, and gave the money to Armand.

Reading Skills and Strategies:
CONNECT

Invite students to refer to relevant aspects of the story and to their own experiences to tell why they think Jerry isn't with the others practicing baseball.

Possible Responses: He didn't get the new glove, and his old glove isn't good enough to play with. His mind was on other things, and he didn't feel like playing.

Literary Analysis: CHARACTER

B Ask, "Why does Jerry have to confess to Roger?"

Possible Response: Roger is his friend and he doesn't like keeping secrets from him, especially about something as important as the Grover Cleveland card.

Active Reading
> **SEQUENCE OF EVENTS**

Ask students to complete their story maps.
Possible Response: Jerry tells Roger the truth.

Reading Skills and Strategies:
CONNECT

C Ask students to discuss why they think Jerry is still waiting for the good feeling.

Possible Response: Even though he did the right thing, it came at some cost—Roger wasn't happy with his decision, and the decision may have cost him his chance to play baseball.

A After Armand had left for the dance, all dressed up as if it were Sunday, the small green box containing the corsage under his arm, I sat on the railing of the piazza, letting my feet dangle. The neighborhood was quiet because the Frenchtown Tigers were at Daggett's Field, practicing for the first baseball game of the season.

I thought of Armand and the ridiculous expression on his face when he'd stood before the mirror in the bedroom. I'd avoided looking at his new black shoes. "Love," I muttered.

Spring had arrived in a sudden stampede of apple blossoms and fragrant breezes. Windows had been thrown open and dust mops had banged on the sills all day long as the women busied themselves with housecleaning. I was puzzled by my lethargy. Wasn't spring supposed to make everything bright and gay?

I turned at the sound of footsteps on the stairs. Roger Lussier greeted me with a sour face.

"I thought you were practicing with the Tigers," I said.

"Rollie Tremaine," he said. "I just couldn't stand him." He slammed his fist against the railing. "Jeez, why did he have to be the one to get a Grover Cleveland? You should see him showing off. He won't let anybody even touch that glove. . . ."

B I felt like Benedict Arnold[8] and knew that I had to confess what I had done.

"Roger," I said, "I got a Grover Cleveland card up on the North Side. I sold it to Rollie Tremaine for five dollars."

"Are you crazy?" he asked.

"I needed that five dollars. It was an—an emergency."

"Boy!" he said, looking down at the ground and shaking his head. "What did you have to do a thing like that for?"

I watched him as he turned away and began walking down the stairs.

"Hey, Roger!" I called.

He squinted up at me as if I were a stranger, someone he'd never seen before.

"What?" he asked, his voice flat.

"I had to do it," I said. "Honest."

He didn't answer. He headed toward the fence, searching for the board we had loosened to give us a secret passage.

I thought of my father and Armand and Rollie Tremaine and Grover Cleveland and wished that I could go away someplace far away. But there was no place to go.

Roger found the loose slat in the fence and slipped through. I felt betrayed: Weren't you supposed to feel good when you did something fine and noble?

A moment later, two hands gripped the top of the fence and Roger's face appeared. "Was it a real emergency?" he yelled.

"A real one!" I called. "Something important!"

His face dropped from sight and his voice reached me across the yard: "All right."

"See you tomorrow!" I yelled.

I swung my legs over the railing again. The gathering dusk began to soften the sharp edges of the fence, the rooftops, the distant church steeple. I sat there a long time, waiting for the good feeling to come. ❖

---

8. **Benedict Arnold:** an American general who became a traitor to his country's cause during the Revolutionary War.

WORDS TO KNOW	**lethargy** (lĕth′ər-jē) *n.* a lack of activity; sluggishness
	betrayed (bĭ-trād′) *adj.* made a fool of; tricked **betray** *v.*

44

EXPLICIT INSTRUCTION **Elements of Plot: Falling Action and Resolution**

Instruction Use the Reading Skills and Strategies: Make Inferences note in the green side column to help students figure out what happened after the climax. Tell students that the climax does not mean the end of the story. Often some very interesting events and information are found after the climax. This stage of the plot is called the falling action and resolution. During this stage, the loose ends of the story are tied up before the story ends. Ask students to think of loose ends and details

that have not yet been tied up. Help students understand that Roger's reaction to what Jerry did with the Grover Cleveland card and Jerry's own feelings about what he did are the focus of the falling action in this story.

Practice Have students check the predictions they made on page 43. Then have students find and record details that are part of the falling action. They can record this information on page 16 of the **Unit One Resource Book.**

Possible Response: Armand goes to the dance; Roger is angry at Jerry's decision; Jerry explains that his action was in response to an emergency; Roger finally accepts this reasoning. Jerry has mixed feelings about selling the card.

 Use **Unit One Resource Book,** p. 16.

Connect to the Literature

1. **What Do You Think?**
   What was your reaction to Jerry's decision to sell the Grover Cleveland card?

Comprehension Check
- Why do the other kids resent Rollie Tremaine?
- Why does Jerry want a full set of President cards?
- How does Jerry get the Grover Cleveland card?

Think Critically

2. How would you describe Jerry's feelings toward Armand? Support your answer with examples.

3. Why does Jerry say he felt "like Benedict Arnold" after Rollie got the new glove?

4. **ACTIVE READING** **SEQUENCE OF EVENTS**
   Look back over the story wheel you created in your **READER'S NOTEBOOK**. What events in Jerry's family life contribute to his decision to sell the card?

5. Why do you think the author chose to have the main character tell this story?

   Think About:
   - Jerry's desire for trading cards and a new baseball glove
   - his observations of his father and brother
   - his relationships with his friends

Extend Interpretations

6. **Different Perspectives** Imagine that the last scene of the story were told by Roger instead of Jerry. How would it be different? What might Roger say about his thoughts and feelings?

7. **Connect to Life** Near the end of the story, Jerry tells us, "I felt betrayed. Weren't you supposed to feel good when you did something fine and noble?" How would you answer this question? Explain your thinking.

Literary Analysis

PLOT The **plot** is the series of events in a story. Usually, the plot centers on a **conflict**—a problem faced by the main character. Most plots can be divided into four stages: the **exposition,** when characters and setting are introduced; **rising action,** when the story becomes more complicated and the conflict develops; the **climax,** when the story reaches a turning point, the main character makes an important discovery or choice, and the outcome of the conflict is decided; and **falling action,** when the character resolves the conflict. You can see Jerry begin to experience a conflict when he feels guilty about giving so little money for his father's birthday gift.

Paired Activity Copy the chart shown below. With a partner, go back through the story to fill in the chart. In the first box, identify the conflict. In the second box, identify the climax of the story. In the third box, state how the conflict is resolved. Use examples to support your ideas.

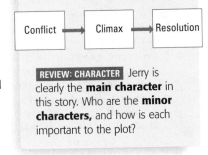

Conflict → Climax → Resolution

REVIEW: CHARACTER Jerry is clearly the **main character** in this story. Who are the **minor characters,** and how is each important to the plot?

Connect to the Literature

1. **What Do You Think?**
   Students may be surprised that Jerry sold the card when he needed it to get the baseball glove. They may also admire his selflessness and generosity toward his brother Armand.

Comprehension Check
- His family has money. He can buy almost anything he wants, and he flaunts his good fortune.
- If Jerry is the first to collect a full set of President cards, he will win a new baseball glove to replace his old one.
- Armand tells Jerry that boys on the North Side have a Grover Cleveland card to trade.

Use Selection Quiz **Unit One Resource Book,** p. 20.

Think Critically

2. **Possible Response:** Jerry feels that Armand has changed, assuming an authority Jerry sometimes resents. Yet he also admires Armand's dignity and gentleness following the tie incident, and he feels sympathy when he learns Armand has fallen in love with a girl from the upscale North Side.

3. **Possible Response:** Rollie was the last person the other kids would want to have the glove, yet Jerry in effect gave it to him.

4. **Possible Responses:** Jerry's father and brother lose their jobs, so money is tight. Jerry is sorry he did not contribute more toward the gift. Also, Jerry learns that Armand has a girlfriend from a wealthy area.

Use **Reading and Critical Thinking Transparencies,** p. 2, for additional support.

5. **Possible Response:** This lets Cormier tell the story through the eyes of a boy, to whom cards and a new baseball glove are very important. We better understand Jerry's feelings and decisions.

Literary Analysis

Plot Students' charts should include: Conflict: how to spend his money; Climax: Jerry sells the President card; Resolution: Jerry gives Armand the money he needs.

Use **Literary Analysis Transparencies,** p. 5, for additional support.

Extend Interpretations

6. **Different Perspectives** Students may say that Roger might talk about his frustration and anger with Jerry for selling the card to Rollie. Then Roger might realize that Jerry had done a good thing, and he would express his admiration.

7. **Connect to Life** Students may say that doing something "fine and noble" often involves sacrifice, risk, or discomfort. They might point to examples of firefighters, pioneers, and other heroes who risk their lives, health, or personal comfort to help others. They may also know from experience that doing something right is not always easy or socially rewarding. Sometimes, the "good feeling" is a sense of integrity or satisfaction, rather than happiness; it has to come from within, and it comes at a cost.

Writing

Character Comparison Students may say that Jerry and Armand both love their father. Jerry is interested in things like card collecting and baseball. Armand takes more responsibility and is interested in dating.

 Use **Writing Transparencies**, p. 10, for additional support

 Use **Reading and Critical Thinking Transparencies**, p. 35, for additional support.

Speaking & Listening

Dramatic Scene Scenes will vary, but should get across the information that Jerry received five dollars from the sale of the Grover Cleveland card, and that he wants Armand to have the money.

Research & Technology

Talking Cards Students may need support figuring out where to find the information they need. Allow time for small groups to share their research.

 Use **Writing Transparencies**, p. 41, for additional support.

Vocabulary

1. A
2. H
3. D
4. G
5. C
6. J
7. C
8. F
9. B
10. J

Writing

Character Comparison
In what ways are Jerry and Armand similar and different? Use a Venn diagram to record your thoughts. Then write a paragraph from the diagram. Be sure to support your ideas with details from the story.

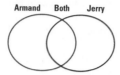

Place the comparison in your **Working Portfolio.**

Writing Handbook
See p. R36: Compare and Contrast.

Speaking & Listening

Dramatic Scene Imagine the conversation Jerry and Armand might have had when Jerry gave Armand the money from selling the card. What did Jerry say? How did Armand react? With a partner, write this scene. Then practice performing the scene, using gestures and facial expressions. Also make sure you are using the right tone of voice and speaking at the right speed and volume. When you and your partner feel you have practiced enough, perform the scene for your class.

Research & Technology

Talking Cards In this story you read about a time when children collected cards depicting cowboys and presidents. People still collect and trade cards. Research the types of trading cards that are available today, using the Internet, the library, or both. Write a paragraph or two describing your findings. If possible, include information about the cost of the cards. Under your paragraph, list the books, articles, or Web sites you used to find information.

Reading for INFORMATION
Read the article on p. 48 before writing your response.

Vocabulary

Choose the word or group of words that means the same, or nearly the same, as the underlined Word to Know.

1. To <u>allot</u> something is to—
   A distribute it   **B** demonstrate it
   C locate it   **D** auction it
2. If someone is <u>betrayed</u>, he or she is—
   F relieved   **G** frightened
   H cheated   **J** beloved
3. <u>Contempt</u> means—
   A concern   **B** silence
   C affection   **D** scorn
4. <u>Indignant</u> is another word for—
   F amused   **G** angry
   H accepted   **J** afraid
5. <u>Obsessed</u> means—
   A disgusted   **B** united
   C absorbed   **D** obligated
6. To <u>dwindle</u> is to—
   F balance   **G** overtake
   H discover   **J** decrease
7. <u>Incredulous</u> is another word for—
   A unreal   **B** intense
   C unbelieving   **D** overwhelmed
8. To <u>divulge</u> something is to—
   F reveal it   **G** disinfect it
   H understand it   **J** misplace it
9. A <u>stalemate</u> refers to a—
   A decision   **B** standoff
   C conclusion   **D** discussion
10. <u>Lethargy</u> means—
    F envy   **G** energy
    H ability   **J** inactivity

Vocabulary Handbook
See p. R22: Synonyms and Antonyms.

Grammar in Context: Four Kinds of Sentences

There are four basic types of sentences. Each serves a purpose.

A *declarative* sentence makes a statement.

An *imperative* sentence issues a request or a command.

An *exclamatory* sentence expresses strong emotion.

An *interrogative* sentence asks a question.

> "The company's not making any more." (declarative)
> "Look what it says at the bottom of the sign." (imperative)
> "There's no more cowboy cards!" (exclamatory)
> "What's the matter?" (interrogative)

Usage Tip: The subject of an imperative sentence is often the pronoun *you*. Usually it is not written but is implied or understood. For example, it is understood that "Wait a minute" really means "You wait a minute."

Apply to Your Writing: Exclamatory sentences "shout" at the reader. Use exclamatory sentences sparingly so that they will have more force.

WRITING EXERCISE Think about the short story "President Cleveland, Where Are You?" Write a paragraph about the Spring Promenade, to which Armand is going to escort Sally. In your paragraph, use one sentence of each of the four types.

Connect to the Literature Reread page 42. Find one complete sentence of each type—declarative, imperative, exclamatory, and interrogative.

Grammar Handbook
See p. R64: Quick Reference Punctuation.

Robert Cormier
1925–2000

"Even if I'd never been published, I would still be writing."

Starting Out As a boy in Leominster, Massachusetts, Robert Cormier's favorite place was the library. He published his first short story while he was a college student, and began his career working for a radio station and newspapers. Still, he recalls, "I regarded myself as a novelist who was a reporter in order to support his family." After writing adult novels, Cormier published *The Chocolate War*, the first of his acclaimed novels for young adults.

Criticism and Praise Some reviewers criticize Cormier's books because they deal with controversial issues such as crime and death. At times, people have even demanded that Cormier's novels be taken off library bookshelves. Other critics praise Cormier's stories for their realistic style and gripping plots.

AUTHOR ACTIVITY
True to Life In his writing, Cormier often uses realistic details seen from a young person's point of view. For example, Jerry describes Rollie Tremaine's home as "a big white birthday cake of a house." Read some of Cormier's other stories and look for details that seem to capture exactly how a character sees something. Make a list of these descriptions, writing them down in Cormier's own words.

Grammar in Context
WRITING EXERCISE
Answers will vary but should reflect students' understanding of the story, for example, that Armand is the narrator's brother, that the Spring Promenade is a big dance at the high school, or that Sally is a girl from the other side of town. Students' writing should include one of each of the four sentence types.

Connect to the Literature
Answers will vary, but each should be the correct type of sentence, chosen from the story.

Possible Responses:
Declarative: His mood of dejection mirrored my own, and I sat down beside him.
Imperative: Now get out, all of you, unless you've got money to spend.
Exclamatory: I've got an extra Warren G. Harding!
Interrogatory: How can I take Sally to a fancy dance?

Robert Cormier

Cormier has great respect for the young people he writes for. He says, "A lot of people underestimate that intelligent teenager out there. These kids today . . . are really far ahead of a lot of adults. They have been exposed to so much. Anybody who writes down to these people is making a mistake."

Author Activity

True to Life Give students ample time to find the Cormier stories. Lists should focus on descriptive language.

EXPLICIT INSTRUCTION Grammar in Context

PUNCTUATING FOUR KINDS OF SENTENCES
Instruction Tell students that they need to use correct punctuation to make their writing clear. Remind them that every sentence must start with a capital letter and end with either a period, a question mark, or an exclamation point.

Exercises Read each sentence aloud. Have students decide which end punctuation would best complete the sentence. (Tell students that some sentences could end with either a period or an exclamation point.)

1. Armand said, "Give me more money" *(! or .)*
2. I ran to Lemire's to buy more cards *(.)*
3. Did you give Armand five dollars *(?)*
4. You want to know what Rollie said when I gave him the money, don't you *(?)*
5. Get out of my way *(!)*

 Use **Unit One Resource Book**, p. 18.

 For more instruction in end punctuation, see McDougal Littell's *Language Network*, Chapter 9.

For **systematic instruction** in grammar, see:
- **Grammar, Usage, and Mechanics Book**
- pacing chart on p. 19i.

Standards-Based Objectives
- read to be informed
- read and analyze a magazine article
- learn to paraphrase
- make an outline

Connecting to the Literature

"Trading Card Talk" takes students into the world of card trading, which is central to "President Cleveland, Where Are You?" Since the time when that story took place, card trading has grown from a young person's hobby to a much more lucrative industry. Terminology and standards—and deception—have grown with it.

LESSON RESOURCES

UNIT ONE RESOURCE BOOK,
pp. 21–22

SKILLS TRANSPARENCIES AND COPYMASTERS
Reading and Critical Thinking
- Paraphrasing, TR 19 (p. 49)
Writing
- Using Internal Organizers of a Book, TR 43 (p. 51)

Magazine Article Source: *Boys' Life*

Trading Card Talk

by

Jay Johnson

★ ★ ★ ★ ★ ★ ★ ★ ★ ★ ★ ★ ★ ★ ★

To be a savvy card collector, you must know how to talk the talk.

1 Walking into a hobby card shop for the first time is like visiting another country. Everyone seems to be speaking a foreign language. But don't worry. You can learn card lingo right now. Once you do, chatting with another collector is easy.

Condition Is Critical

Before buying a card, you should find out what condition it's in. That goes for non-sports cards as well as for baseball and other types of sports cards.

2 A card in *mint* condition is perfect. It should look brand-new, no matter how old it is. Cards that are *near mint* have only one defect, or flaw. For instance, a worn corner or an off-center picture will knock a mint card down to near mint.

Most collectors don't want to buy cards newer than 10 years old unless they are mint or near mint. Older cards, printed before 1980 or so, can still be desirable even if they are in worse condition.

An *excellent* card may have several defects. It is worth about half as much as a mint version of the same card. For example, a card sometimes loses its gloss, or shine, as it gets older. Combine that problem with a couple of fuzzy, or frayed, corners, and you have a card that would rate an excellent grade. Many collectors who are on a budget prefer to collect excellent-grade cards. They are attractive, but cheaper.

EXPLICIT INSTRUCTION **Paraphrasing**

Instruction Tell students that to paraphrase is to put reading material into your own words. It is different from quoting a writer's exact words and identifying the writer and the source. Paraphrasing can help readers make sense of difficult material, and remember and understand written copy. Like summarizing, paraphrasing should capture the main ideas of the material.

Practice Have students work in pairs to complete the numbered activities on the pupil pages.

Possible Responses: See the side columns in the teacher's edition for possible responses to the activities.

Use **Unit One Resource Book,** p. 21, for support.

WHAT'S IT WORTH?

A mint card has no defects. The cards below have serious flaws that reduce their value. The defects include handwriting, a crease, and a bent corner.

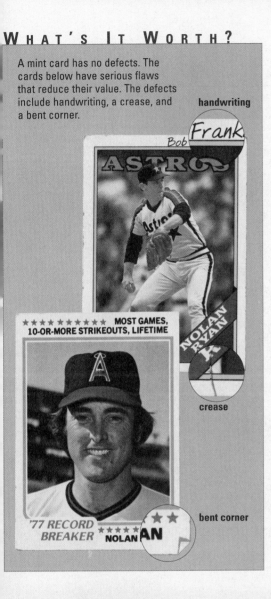

handwriting

crease

bent corner

When you write a paper or a research report, you need to support your ideas with information from different sources. You also need to give credit to those sources to avoid **plagiarism**—presenting someone else's work as your own. One way to avoid copying material is to rewrite it using your own words.

Paraphrasing

When you paraphrase, you restate an author's ideas in your own words. You will probably use simpler language than the author used. A well-written paraphrase is about the same length as the original text. It includes the **main ideas** and **supporting details.**

You may need to paraphrase a whole paragraph or just a few sentences for a report. Be sure to change the wording completely to avoid plagiarism.

YOUR TURN *Use the questions and activities below to help you learn how to paraphrase.*

❶ Read this paragraph carefully and identify its **main idea** and supporting details. Use **paraphrasing** to rewrite the paragraph in your own words. Your paraphrase should be 1–2 sentences long.

❷ Suppose you want to explain in a research report what a mint card is. You wouldn't use the exact words that the writer of this article used. Write a sentence in which you define *mint card* in your own words.

Reading for Information

Tell students that this article appeared in the magazine *Boys' Life.* Have students use the material in the right-hand column to help them learn to paraphrase. The following are possible responses to the questions and activities.

1 There is a special vocabulary for talking about trading cards that is easy to learn.

2 A mint card is one that looks just like it did when it came out of the factory.

Use **Reading and Critical Thinking Transparencies,** p. 19, for additional support.

Possible response to the practice activity in the minilesson on page 50.

I. A buyer should find out the condition of a card before buying it.

   A. A mint card is in perfect condition.

      1. A mint card should look new even if it isn't.

   B. Near mint cards have only one defect.

      1. Defects might be a worn corner or an off-center picture.

      2. One defect turns a mint card into a near mint card.

   C. An excellent card may have several defects.

      1. An excellent card may have lost its gloss or have fuzzy corners.

      2. An excellent card is worth about half as much as a mint card.

      3. Collectors on a budget prefer excellent cards because they are cheaper.

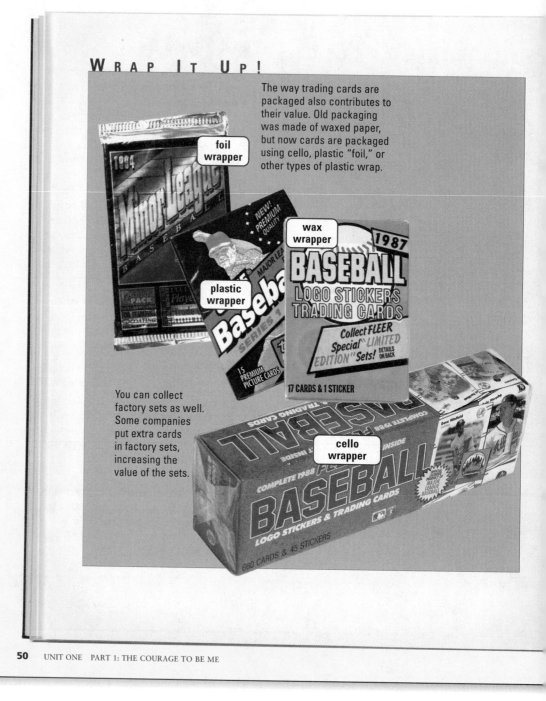

WRAP IT UP!

The way trading cards are packaged also contributes to their value. Old packaging was made of waxed paper, but now cards are packaged using cello, plastic "foil," or other types of plastic wrap.

foil wrapper

wax wrapper

plastic wrapper

cello wrapper

You can collect factory sets as well. Some companies put extra cards in factory sets, increasing the value of the sets.

EXPLICIT INSTRUCTION **Outlining**

Instruction Tell students that the organization and main points of an article will become clear when they outline an article. Introduce outlining to the class as a more formal organization for notes. Draw the following diagram on the board:

I. (main topic)

   A. (supporting detail)

   B. (supporting detail)

      1. (less important details)

Then say, "Roman numerals are used for main ideas, indented capital letters for supporting details, and indented numbers for less important details." Then say, "To outline, find the main ideas or topics and label each topic with a roman numeral. Under the main topic, indent and label subtopics or supporting details with capital letters. Under supporting details, indent and label less important but useful details with numbers."

Practice Have students work in pairs to outline the section of this article called "Condition Is Critical," on page 48.

Possible Responses: See the side column on this page of the teacher's edition for an outline of this section.

Use **Unit One Resource Book**, p. 22, for more practice.

❸ Leader of the Packs

New cards should always be mint. Words used to describe new cards deal not with condition, but with how the cards are packaged.

Not long ago, almost everything was sold in *wax packs.* Thick waxed paper was wrapped around 10 or 15 cards. The pack sold for 50 cents to $1. Wax packs aren't as popular anymore. People often opened the pack and removed the good cards. Then they resealed it by running a warm iron over the waxed paper. To stop that, card companies began wrapping packs with *cello,* short for cellophane, a thin plastic.

A *foil pack* is the same as a cello pack, except the wrapping is made of a shiny plastic that looks like aluminum foil. Cello and foil packs cannot be resealed so easily.

Another common package is a *jumbo pack.* It contains 25 to 35 cards, depending on the brand. The price is usually $1 to $2.

Make a Box Set

Larger packages of cards have their own terms. Experienced collectors often buy an entire box of 20 or 30 cello packs. They take care that the box is still wrapped with the factory seal, which means no one has removed any packages. The collector opens all the packages in the box and tries to assemble all the cards, making a *set.* Once he has put every card in numerical order, he has created a *hand-collated set.* That means the set was put together by hand, one card at a time.

A *factory set* is similar, except it is assembled by machine at a card company. Like boxes, factory sets usually are sold with a seal. Some companies put extra cards in factory sets, which can make the sets more valuable.

Before you buy, sell or trade cards, learn trading card lingo. That knowledge will help you enjoy this wonderful hobby.

Reading for Information *continued*

❸ Reread the section with the subheading "Leader of the Packs." Paraphrase this section by completing the following steps:

- Write the **main idea** of the section in your own words.
- List the **supporting details** and rewrite them in your own words.
- **Combine** the main idea and details you rewrote into a paragraph.
- Finally, **revise** your paragraph to make sure it reads smoothly and makes sense. You may need to **simplify** the language by replacing difficult words with more familiar ones.

Research & Technology
Activity Link: "President Cleveland, Where Are You?" p. 46. What new terms have you learned from reading "Trading Card Talk"? Locate nine special words or terms explained in the article. Then create a **glossary,** or dictionary, in which you define each term by paraphrasing information found in the article.

Reading for Information

3 Possible Response: Packaging, rather than condition, is most important with new cards. For a while, all cards were sold in wax packs. Manufacturers have replaced wax packaging with plastic to stop tampering. Foil is also used and is similar to plastic. Jumbo packs contain more cards than foil or plastic packs. The more cards in a pack, the higher the price.

Research & Technology

The Research & Technology activity on this page links with the Research & Technology section of Choices & Challenges on page 46 that follows "President Cleveland, Where Are You?"

Instruction Show students the glossary of this book or of other books as a model. Encourage them to notice how a glossary entry differs from a dictionary entry.

Practice Students should include 9 of the following words in a glossary for card collectors.

cello: thin plastic; short for cellophane
excellent: with several flaws
factory set: manufacturer-assembled complete set
foil pack: pack of cards wrapped in plastic made to look like foil
hand-collated set: collector-assembled complete set
jumbo pack: pack with 25 to 35 cards
mint: in perfect condition

near mint: with one flaw
set: all cards in a series
wax pack: pack of cards wrapped in wax paper

Use **Writing Transparencies,** p. 43, for additional support.

Standards-Based Objectives

1. understand and appreciate a **short story**
2. understand **setting** and its effect on characters and plot in a short story
3. use the reading strategy of **visualizing** to help understand setting, characters, and action
4. analyze the **effect of the qualities of the characters**
5. understand **plot development**
6. identify and analyze **theme**

Summary

The story's narrator joins the Boy Scouts because he believes the organization will "make a man" of him. He learns that moving up the Boy Scout ranks requires an overnight hike in the country. Consequently, he and two fellow Scouts leave their Brooklyn neighborhood to "rough it" in the woods for a night. On the advice of their scoutmaster, the boys decide to cross the George Washington Bridge by foot and camp in New Jersey. Poor planning and bad weather turn the trip into a fiasco. The boys wish to return home, but nobody wants to be the one to give up first. Finally the narrator gathers the courage to suggest that they go home, and the others eagerly agree. All vow to keep the details of their experience secret.

Thematic Link

Three city boys know that leaving their neighborhood for their first camping trip takes courage. They learn that being honest and able to admit defeat can take even more courage.

English Conventions Practice

Daily Language SkillBuilder

Have students **proofread** the display sentences on page 19k and write them correctly. The sentences also appear on Transparency 2 of **Language Transparencies.**

Preteaching Vocabulary

If you would like to preteach the WORDS TO KNOW for this selection, use the Explicit Instruction, page 53.

Scout's Honor

by AVI

Connect to Your Life

Tough Enough? Have you ever been faced with a difficult situation and felt you "chickened out"? Did other people seem braver than you? With a partner, discuss a situation like that from your own life. What lessons might be learned from your experience?

Build Background

HISTORY

"Scout's Honor" tells about three friends who go camping in an effort to meet a Boy Scout requirement. The first camping group of Boy Scouts was organized in Great Britain in 1908 by a soldier.

To become Scouts, boys must swear to live by the Scout Oath. In doing so they promise to give their best effort in everything they do; to respect their country, including its laws and natural resources; to help others; and to be honest and fair. They also promise to honor the Scout Motto—Be Prepared.

> **WORDS TO KNOW**
> **Vocabulary Preview**
>
> | | | |
> |---|---|---|
> | bellow | retort | suspicion |
> | envious | rival | vent |
> | immense | smugly | |
> | pummel | straddle | |

Focus Your Reading

LITERARY ANALYSIS **SETTING**

The **setting** of a story is the time and place of the action. The **time** may be past, present, or future; daytime or nighttime; and any season. The **place** may be real or imaginary. Sometimes setting is very important in a story. It may shape the characters or influence the conflict. For example, in "Scout's Honor," the main character must prove his camping abilities even though he lives in the heart of the city.

ACTIVE READING **VISUALIZING**

When you form a picture in your mind based on what you are reading, you are **visualizing.** To visualize, pay attention to descriptions of the setting as well as details about what the characters see, hear, and do.

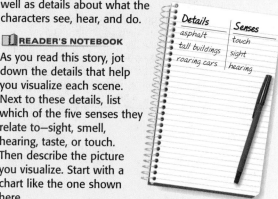

READER'S NOTEBOOK

As you read this story, jot down the details that help you visualize each scene. Next to these details, list which of the five senses they relate to—sight, smell, hearing, taste, or touch. Then describe the picture you visualize. Start with a chart like the one shown here.

LESSON RESOURCES

UNIT ONE RESOURCE BOOK, pp. 23–29

Formal Assessment, pp. 9–10

Test Generator

SKILLS TRANSPARENCIES AND COPYMASTERS

Literary Analysis
- Setting, TR 6 (pp. 56, 64)
- Reading and Critical Thinking
- Visualizing, TR 4 (p. 64)

Language
- Daily Language SkillBuilder, TR 2 (p. 52)
- Verbs—Using Correct Verb Forms, TR 35 (p. 66)

- Context Clues: Compare and Contrast, Cause and Effect, Example, TR 54 (p. 53)

Writing
- Writing Variables, TR 2 (p. 65)
- Locating Information Using Print References, TR 45 (p. 66)
- Locating Information Using Technical Resources, TR 46 (p. 66)
- Locating Information Using the Internet I and II, TR 47, 48 (p. 66)

Speaking and Listening
- Creating an Informative Presentation, p. 25 (p. 65)

- Guidelines: How to Analyze an Informative Presentation, p. 26 (p. 65)

INTEGRATED TECHNOLOGY
Audio Library
Internet: Research Starter

Visit our Web site:
www.mcdougallittell.com

For **systematic instruction** in language skills, see:
- **Vocabulary and Spelling Book**
- **Grammar, Usage, and Mechanics Book**
- pacing chart on p. 19i.

SCOUT'S HONOR

by Avi

The Scouting Trail, Norman Rockwell.
Art from the Archives of Brown & Bigelow,
Inc. and with permission from The Boy
Scouts of America.

Back in 1946,
when I was nine,
I worried that I wasn't
tough enough. That's why I
became a Boy Scout. Scouting,
I thought, would make a man of me.

Less Proficient Readers
Have students keep these questions in mind as they begin to read:
• Why do the boys go camping?
• What do the boys try to prove to one another?
• What does their first camping trip teach them?

Set a Purpose Have students read to find out how well-prepared the boys are for their first camping trip.

English Learners
Explain that Brooklyn is a borough, or section, of New York City, the country's largest city. The George Washington Bridge crosses the Hudson River, which separates New York and New Jersey.

Use **Spanish Study Guide,** pp. 10–12, for additional support.

Advanced Students
Explain that *irony* is the difference between what is expected and what actually exists or happens. As they read, have students look for details and situations that are ironic. Suggest they look to the story's title and setting.

Possible Responses: A "hike in the country" includes a subway ride and a busy bridge; the boys use the phrase "Scout's Honor" when promising to hide their experience from the scoutmaster.

English Learners
1 Tell students that "make a man of me" is an expression meaning "make me stronger or tougher." It reflects the stereotypical idea that one must be physically and emotionally tough in order to be a "real" man.

EXPLICIT INSTRUCTION **Preteaching Vocabulary**

WORDS TO KNOW
Teaching Strategy Remind students that they may be able to figure out the meaning of an unfamiliar word by using context clues. Use the model sentence to show students how they can clarify a word's meaning by finding a **comparison** or **contrast clue** to a familiar word. Tell them that comparisons are often signaled by words such as *like, as,* and *than* and contrasts by words like *although, but, yet, however,* and *on the other hand.*

Model Sentence:
His *bellow* was louder <u>than thunder</u>.

Practice Ask students to use comparison and contrast clues to define the underlined WORDS TO KNOW in the following sentences:

1. At first they were <u>rivals</u>, but then they worked together.
2. The bridge seemed as <u>immense</u> as a mountain range.
3. In the lean-to, they made a <u>vent</u> that worked like a chimney.

4. He felt <u>suspicion</u>, yet acted quite trusting.

Use **Unit One Resource Book,** p. 28, for more practice.

For **systematic instruction** in vocabulary, see:
• **Vocabulary and Spelling Book**
• pacing chart on p. 19i.

Reading and Analyzing

Reading Skills and Strategies:
PREVIEW

Ask students to read the title of the story. What does this phrase mean to them? What do they think the story will be about? As they read, they can modify their ideas about the story and the meaning of the title.

Active Reading | VISUALIZING |

Avi describes each location and incident in vivid detail. These details help readers to appreciate the boys' experience. Tell students to pause from time to time as they read. Encourage them to close their eyes and try to see, hear, touch, taste and smell each scene. Invite volunteers to describe mental images the text descriptions evoke.

Use **Unit One Resource Book**, p. 24, for more practice.

Literary Analysis | SETTING |

Encourage students to recognize and analyze details of the story's setting as they read. Tell students that setting is an important element of the story. It has a strong effect on characters and events and provides part of the story's humor. Students can keep a record of details of setting.

1 It didn't take long to reach Tenderfoot rank. You got that for joining. To move up to Second Class, however, you had to meet three requirements. Scout Spirit and Scout Participation had been cinchy. The third requirement, Scout Craft, meant I had to go on an overnight hike in the *country*. In other words, I had to leave Brooklyn, on my own, for the first time in my life.

Since I grew up in Brooklyn in the 1940s, the only grass I knew was in Ebbets Field where the Dodgers played. Otherwise, my world was made of slate pavements, streets of asphalt

Station Platform, Dong Kingman. Hirshhorn Museum and Sculpture Garden, Smithsonian Institution, gift of Joseph H. Hirshhorn, 1966. Photo: John Tennant.

2 (or cobblestone), and skies full of tall buildings. The only thing "country" was a puny pin oak tree at our curb, which was noticed, mostly, by dogs.

I asked Scoutmaster Brenkman where I could find some country. Now, whenever I saw Mr. Brenkman, who was a church pastor, he was dressed either in church black or Scout khaki. When he wore **3** black, he'd warn us against hellfire. When he wore khaki, he'd teach us how to build fires.

"Country," Scoutmaster Brenkman said in answer to my question, "is anywhere that has lots of trees and is not in the city. Many boys camp in the Palisades."

54   UNIT ONE   PART 1: THE COURAGE TO BE ME

EXPLICIT
INSTRUCTION   **Setting**

Instruction Tell students that the setting of a literary work is the time and place in which the plot unfolds. The time may be the past, present, or future; day or night; and any season or month. The place may be imaginary or real. Have students reread page 53 and identify the time of the setting. *(1946)*

Practice Have students read page 54 and identify and record details that describe the setting of Brooklyn. Remind students to continue to think about and record setting information as they read.
Possible Responses: Ebbets Field; slate pavements; streets of asphalt; skies full of tall buildings; one puny pin oak tree at the curb.

Use **Unit One Resource Book**, p. 25, for more practice.

"Where's that?"

"Just north of the city. It's a park in Jersey."

"Isn't that a zillion miles from here?"

"Take the subway to the George Washington Bridge, then hike across."

I thought for a moment, then asked, "How do I prove I went?"

Mr. Brenkman looked deeply shocked. "You wouldn't *lie*, would you? What about Scout's honor?"

"Yes, sir," I replied meekly.[1]

My two best friends were Philip Hossfender, whom we nick-named Horse, and Richard Macht, called Max because we were not great spellers. They were also Scouts, Tenderfoots like me.

Horse was a skinny little kid about half my size whose way of arguing was to ball up his fist and say, "Are you saying . . . ?" in a threatening tone.

Max was on the pudgy side, but he could talk his way out of a locked room. More importantly, he always seemed to have pocket money, which gave his talk real power.

I wasn't sure why, but being best friends meant we were <u>rivals</u> too. One of the reasons for my wanting to be tougher was a feeling that Horse was a lot tougher than I was, and that Max was a little tougher.

"I'm going camping in the Palisades next weekend," I casually informed them.

"How come?" Max challenged.

"Scout Craft," I replied.

"Oh, *that*," Horse said with a shrug.

"Look," I said, "I don't know about you, but I don't intend to be a Tenderfoot all my life. Anyway, doing stuff in the city is for sissies. Scouting is real camping. Besides, I like roughing it."

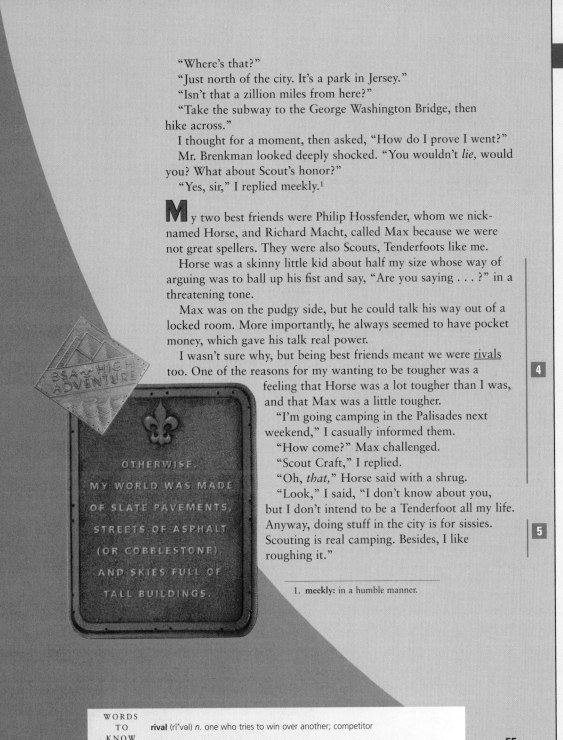

OTHERWISE,
MY WORLD WAS MADE
OF SLATE PAVEMENTS,
STREETS OF ASPHALT
(OR COBBLESTONE),
AND SKIES FULL OF
TALL BUILDINGS.

---

1. **meekly:** in a humble manner.

4

5

Differentiating Instruction

English Learners

Be sure that students understand what being a Boy Scout is and means. Refer to the "Build Background" section on page 52. Ask students if they know of or participate in similar groups.

1 Tell students that *cinchy* is an informal word meaning "easy." It comes from the noun *cinch*—"something effortless."

2 Explain that the word *puny* means small and sickly.

3 Tell students that *khaki* is a light brown color. The word also describes a sturdy cloth of this color or a uniform made of the cloth. Point out to students the irony here: The preacher/scoutmaster is warning against a kind of fire when he is a preacher and teaching kids how to build fires when he is a scoutmaster.

Less Proficient Readers

4 Ask the following questions to help students understand the characters' traits and motivations:

- According to the narrator, what is interesting about each friend's personality?
  Possible Response: Horse is small but tough and always using the phrase "Are you saying…?" Max is pudgy, a big talker, and always has money, which backs up his talk.
- What does the narrator say about his relationship with Horse and Max?
  Possible Response: They are best friends, yet they are always competing to determine who is the toughest.

English Learners

5 Tell students that *sissies* is a label used to insult people who seem timid or cowardly. *Roughing it* is an expression meaning "to endure uncomfortable conditions."

EXPLICIT INSTRUCTION ## Character Traits

Instruction Remind students that character traits are the qualities of a character. These include physical characteristics such as freckles, as well as other characteristics, such as courage or forgetfulness. Character traits are revealed through the character's own speech, thoughts, feelings, and actions; the writer's direct statements about the character; and the thoughts, speech, and actions of other characters. Ask students to describe the narrator, Horse, and Max. (*The narrator is a city boy who has never seen the country. He wants to*

be a Scout because it will make a man out of him. He sees himself as the least tough of the three boys. Horse is skinny and about half the size of the narrator; because of his size, he argues in a threatening voice; Max is pudgy, can talk his way out of a locked room, and always has money. None of the three boys is a good speller.) Ask students whether they learned about these traits from the characters themselves, from the writer, or from another character. (*from another character— the narrator*)

Practice Based on what they have read so far, have students write a brief description of the traits of each of the three boys.

Possible Responses: Horse is physically small; he acts tough. Max is pudgy; he's very clever with words. The narrator may be physically small; he's insecure about being tough.

Use **Unit One Resource Book,** p. 26, for more practice.

Literary Analysis: DIALOGUE

A This selection can help students to understand the important role dialogue can play in a story. Tell students that dialogue consists of the words characters speak aloud to one another. Explain that dialogue often reveals important information about characters and their relationships. Ask students what the characters are discussing in this paragraph and what their conversation reveals about their relationship.

Possible Response: They argue about who is tough enough to go camping. This passage shows that the characters are competitive and care about how they appear to one another.

Reading Skills and Strategies: QUESTION

Have students raise questions about the items the boys decide to bring. Do students believe the boys are well-prepared for a hike? Why, or why not?

Active Reading VISUALIZING

B Ask students to visualize the scene in which the boys become separated, first from the point of view of Max, then from the point of view of Horse and the narrator. What do they see? How do they feel?

Literary Analysis SETTING

Ask students to analyze and discuss the subway as a setting. How does this setting affect the characters and the events of the story? Ask students to think about how this scene sets the mood of the story.

Use **Literary Analysis Transparencies,** p. 6, for additional support.

"You saying I don't?" Horse snapped.

"I'm not saying nothing," I said.

They considered my idea. Finally, Horse said, "Yeah, well, I was going to do that, but I didn't think you guys were ready for it."

"I've been ready for *years*," Max protested.

"Then we're going, right?" I said.

They looked around at me. "If you can do it, I can do it," Max said.

"Yeah," Horse said thoughtfully.

The way they agreed made me nervous. Now I really was going to have to be tough.

We informed our folks that we were going camping overnight (which was true) and that the Scoutmaster was going with us—which was a lie. We did remember what Mr. Brenkman said about honesty, but we were baseball fans too, and since we were prepared to follow Scout law—being loyal, helpful, friendly, courteous, kind, obedient, cheerful, thrifty, brave, clean, *and* reverent—we figured a 900 batting average was not bad.

So Saturday morning we met at the High Street subway station. I got there first. Stuffed in my dad's army surplus knapsack was a blanket, a pillow, and a paper bag with three white-bread peanut-butter-and-jelly sandwiches—that is, lunch, supper, and Sunday breakfast. My pockets were full of stick matches. I had an old flashlight, and since I lived by the Scout motto—Be Prepared—I had brought along an umbrella. Finally, being a serious reader, I had the latest Marvel Family comics.

Horse arrived next, his arms barely managing to hold on to a mattress that seemed twice his size. As for food, he had four cans of beans jammed into his pockets.

Max came last. He was lugging a new knapsack that contained a cast-iron frying pan, a packet of hot dogs, and a box of saltine crackers—plus two bottles. One bottle was mustard, the other, celery soda. He also had a bag of Tootsie Rolls and a shiny hatchet. "To build a lean-to,"[2] he explained.

Max's prize possession, however, was an official Scout compass. "It's really swell," he told us. "You can't ever get lost with it. Got it at the Scout store."

"I hate that place," Horse informed us. "It's all new. Nothing real."

"This compass is real," Max retorted. "Points north all the time. You can get cheaper ones, but they point all different directions."

"What's so great about the north?" Horse said.

"That's always the way to go," Max insisted.

"Says who?" I demanded.

"Mr. Brenkman, dummy," Horse cried. "Anyway, there's always an arrow on maps pointing the way north."

"Cowboys live out west," I reminded them. They didn't care.

On the subway platform, we realized we did not know which station we were heading for. To find out, we studied the system map, which looked like a noodle factory hit by a

---

2. **lean-to:** a shelter with a flat, sloping roof.

WORDS TO KNOW **retort** (rĭ-tôrt′) *v.* to reply, especially in a quick or unkind way

---

Cross Curricular Link **Geography: Map Reading**

MAPS AND COMPASSES Just as Horse says, maps do usually feature an arrow pointing north. For thousands of years, people trying to understand where they are have looked to the north. People lost in the woods at night could find Polaris, the North Star, and find their way north. Hikers lost during the daylight hours could poke a stick in the ground at noon. In the northern hemisphere, the stick's shadow will always point north as sun shines on it from the south. The arrow on a map usually points to the geographic North Pole, a spot in the Arctic Ocean that marks the northern end of the earth's axis of rotation. The North Star is close to the north celestial pole, the highest point in the sky above the earthly North Pole.

The magnetic needle of a compass is attracted to the earth's magnetic poles—located near the geographic North and South Poles—where the earth's magnetic field is most intense. Most compasses are constructed of a circular dial that shows directions and a magnetized steel needle that always points north.

bomb. The place we wanted to go (north) was at the top of the map, so I had to hoist Horse onto my shoulders for a closer look. Since he refused to let go of his mattress—or the tin cans in his pockets—it wasn't easy. I asked him—in a kindly fashion—to put the mattress down.

No sooner did he find the station—168th Street—than our train arrived. We rushed on, only to have Horse scream, "My mattress!" He had left it on the platform. Just before the doors shut, he and I leaped off. Max, however, remained on the train. Helplessly, we watched as his horror-stricken face slid away from us. "Wait at the next station!" I <u>bellowed</u>. "Don't move!"

The next train took forever to come. Then it took even longer to get to the next stop. There was Max. All around him—like fake snow in a glass ball—were crumbs. He'd been so nervous he had eaten all his crackers.

"Didn't that make you thirsty?"

"I drank my soda."

I noticed streaks down his cheeks. Horse noticed them too. "You been crying?" he asked.

"Naw," Max said. "There was this water dripping from the tunnel roof. But, you said don't move, right? Well, I was just being obedient."

By the time we got on the next train—with all our possessions—we had been traveling for

an hour. But we had managed to go only one stop.

During the ride, I got hungry. I pulled out one of my sandwiches. With the jelly soaked through the bread, it looked like a limp scab.

Horse, <u>envious</u>, complained *he* was getting hungry.

"Eat some of your canned beans," I suggested.

He got out one can without ripping his pocket too badly. Then his face took on a mournful look.

"What's the matter?" I asked.

"Forgot to bring a can opener."

Max said, "In the old days, people opened cans with their teeth."

"You saying my teeth aren't strong?"

"I'm just talking about history!"

"You saying I don't know history?"

Always kind, I plopped half my sandwich into Horse's hand. He squashed it into his mouth and was quiet for the next fifteen minutes. It proved something I'd always believed: The best way to stop arguments is to get people to eat peanut butter sandwiches. They can't talk.

Then we became so absorbed in our Marvel Family comics we missed our station. We got to it only by coming back the other way. When we reached street level, the sky was dark.

"I knew it," Max announced. "It's going to rain."

"Don't worry," Horse said. "New Jersey is a

THE BEST WAY TO STOP ARGUMENTS IS TO GET PEOPLE TO EAT PEANUT BUTTER SANDWICHES. THEY CAN'T TALK.

| WORDS TO KNOW | **bellow** (bĕl′ō) *v.* to shout in a deep voice |
| | **envious** (ĕn′vē-əs) *adj.* jealous |

57

Reading and Analyzing

Reading Skills and Strategies:
PREDICT

Review with students what has happened on the trip so far. Ask them to predict what might happen as the boys continue on their journey. Students should be able to explain what details from the story help them to make their predictions.

Possible Response: Students might say that the trip will continue to be a disaster. The boys don't seem to know where they are going and they have already used up their food supplies.

Literary Analysis   SETTING

A Ask students why Horse feels it might not be raining in New Jersey. What does his suggestion reveal about his understanding of his surroundings?

Possible Response: He feels that because New Jersey is "a whole other state," it might not be raining. In saying this, he reveals that he does not understand they are close to home, despite the fact they are about to enter a different state.

Active Reading   VISUALIZING

B Ask students why the writer compares the boys to war refugees. What does this comparison help readers to visualize?

Possible Response: Like people fleeing their homes on short notice, the boys are burdened with too many belongings, and they don't seem to have a strong sense of where they are going.

Whitestone Bridge (1939), Ralston Crawford. Oil on canvas, 40¼ × 32˝. Memorial Art Gallery of the University of Rochester (New York) Marion Stratton Gould Fund (51.2).

whole other state. It probably won't be raining there."

"I brought an umbrella," I said <u>smugly</u>, though I wanted it to sound helpful. **A**

As we marched down 168th Street, heading for the George Washington Bridge, we looked like European war refugees.[3] Every few paces, Horse cried, "Hold it!" and adjusted his arms around his mattress. Each time we paused, Max pulled out his compass, peered at it, then announced, "Heading north!" **B**

I said, "The bridge goes from east to west."

"Maybe the bridge does," Max insisted with a show of his compass, "but guaranteed, *we* are going north." **1**

About then, the heel of my left foot, encased in a heavy rubber boot over an earth-crushing Buster Brown shoe, started to get sore. Things weren't going as I had hoped. Cheerfully, I tried to ignore the pain.

The closer we drew to the bridge, the more <u>immense</u> it seemed. And the clouds had become so thick, you couldn't see the top or the far side.

Max eyed the bridge with deep <u>suspicion</u>. "I'm not so sure we should go," he said.

"Why?"

"Maybe it doesn't have another side." **2**

We looked at him.

"No, seriously," Max explained, "they could have taken the Jersey side away, you know, for repairs."

"Cars are going across," I pointed out.

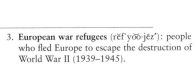

"MAYBE IT DOESN'T HAVE ANOTHER SIDE."

---

3. **European war refugees** (rĕf'yŏŏ-jēz'): people who fled Europe to escape the destruction of World War II (1939–1945).

WORDS	**smugly** (smŭg'lē) *adv.* in a very self-satisfied way
TO	**immense** (ĭ-mĕns') *adj.* huge; enormous
KNOW	**suspicion** (sə-spĭsh'ən) *n.* a feeling of doubt or mistrust

59

Differentiating Instruction

English Learners

1 Call students' attention to language that describes the boys' awkwardness and discomfort as they walk. Tell students to look for words that describe how the boys are feeling.

Less Proficient Readers

2 Ask students what Max fears as the boys approach the bridge. Why does he have this fear?

Set a Purpose Have students read to learn how each boy handles the most difficult part of the trip.

Advanced Students

Often, the characters in this story have taken on predictable roles that are funny in part because the reader anticipates how each character will react. Ask, "What predictable roles have the characters taken on?"

Possible Responses: Max persists in trying to use the compass even though he doesn't understand how to use it. Horse interprets comments as criticisms: "You saying I don't know?" "You saying my teeth aren't strong?" "You saying I'm not clean?" And then finally, "You saying I'm the one who's tough?"

EXPLICIT INSTRUCTION **Predicting**

Instruction Point out that students can make predictions, or logical guesses, about story events as they read. Their predictions should be based on what has happened so far in the story, as well as on what they know from their own experiences. Ask students whether they think the boys will cross the bridge.

Practice Have students write a prediction about whether the boys will cross the bridge or turn back. Have them support their predictions with story information and personal experiences.

Possible Responses: Students may predict that the boys will cross the bridge because they've worked hard to get this far; they've told their parents they would be gone overnight; they don't want to be failures. They may predict that the boys will turn back because they are miserable and they don't know what they are doing.

Reading Skills and Strategies:
QUESTION

A Ask students to question the narrator's hope that his friends have "chickened out," and why he feels better when he hears fear in Horse's voice.

Possible Response: Students might wonder if the narrator wants to quit, but does not want to be the first to suggest such a thing.

B Point out to students that Horse challenges one of his friends again with his favorite phrase: "You saying . . . ?" Ask what this response reveals about his character.

Possible Response: Students might wonder if it is a defensive response because he is really not as tough as he wants to appear.

Literary Analysis: HUMOR

C Sometimes a simple repeated detail can create humor in a story. Ask students: What is funny about Horse's mattress?

Possible Response: The mattress is big and awkward and a serious hiker would never have brought it.

Literary Analysis **SETTING**

D Why, according to Max, is the area of their campsite "just like Brooklyn"?

Possible Response: The area is near lots of buildings and is littered with garbage.

• What were they expecting?
Possible Response: "country"

• How does the campsite add to the humor of the story?
Possible Response: It is humorous because it is so different from what the boys imagined.

"They could be dropping off," he suggested.

"You would hear them splash," Horse argued.

"I'm going," I said. Trying to look brave, I started off on my own. My bravery didn't last long. The walkway was narrow. When I looked down, I saw only fog. I could feel the bridge tremble and sway. It wasn't long before I was convinced the bridge was about to collapse. Then a ray of hope struck me: Maybe the other guys had chickened out. If they had, I could quit because of *them*. I glanced back. My heart sank. They were coming.

After they caught up, Horse looked me in the eye and said, "If this bridge falls, I'm going to kill you."

A quarter of a mile farther across, I gazed around. We were completely fogged in.

"I think we're lost," I announced.

"What do we do?" Horse whispered. His voice was jagged with panic. That made me feel better.

"Don't worry," Max said. "I've got my compass." He pulled it out. "North is that way," he said, pointing in the direction we had been going.

Horse said, "You sure?"

"A Scout compass never lies," Max insisted.

"*We* lied," I reminded him.

"Yeah, but this is an official Scout compass," Max returned loyally.

"Come on," Max said and marched forward. Horse and I followed. In moments, we crossed a metal bar on the walkway. On one side, a sign proclaimed: NEW YORK; on the other, it said: NEW JERSEY.

"Holy smoke," Horse said with reverence as he straddled the bar. "Talk about being tough. We're in two states at the same time."

It began to rain. Max said, "Maybe it'll keep us clean."

"You saying I'm not clean?" Horse shot back.

Ever friendly, I put up my umbrella.

We went on—Max on one side, Horse on the other, me in the middle—trying to avoid the growing puddles. After a while, Max said, "Would you move the umbrella? Rain is coming down my neck."

"We're supposed to be roughing it," I said.

"Being in the middle isn't roughing it," Horse reminded me.

I folded the umbrella up so we all could get soaked equally.

"Hey!" I cried. "Look!" Staring up ahead, I could make out tollbooths and the dim outlines of buildings.

"Last one off the bridge is a rotten egg!" Horse shouted and began to run. The next second, he tripped and took off like an F-36 fighter plane. Unfortunately, he landed like a Hell-cat dive-bomber as his mattress unspooled before him and then slammed into a big puddle.

Max and I ran to help. Horse was damp. His mattress was soaked. When he tried to roll it up, water cascaded like Niagara Falls.

"Better leave it," Max said.

"It's what I sleep on at home," Horse said as he slung the soaking, dripping mass over his shoulder.

When we got off the bridge, we were in a small plaza. To the left was the roadway, full of roaring cars. In front of us, aside from the highway, there was nothing but buildings. Only to the right were there trees.

"North is that way," Max said, pointing toward the trees. We set off.

"How come you're limping?" Horse asked

WORDS
TO
KNOW

straddle (străd'l) *v.* to stand with a leg on either side of

60

EXPLICIT
INSTRUCTION **Setting**

Instruction Remind students that writers can change the setting throughout a single story. Ask students to identify the two main settings so far in this story. *(Brooklyn and the subway).* Now ask them where the characters are on page 60. *(on the bridge)*

Practice Have students record setting details that describe the bridge setting. Have them record details that answer questions such as, "What is it like on the bridge?" and "What do the boys see as they get off the bridge?"

Possible Responses: It is foggy; the bridge trembles and sways; a sign identifies the New York/New Jersey state boundary; it begins to rain; tollbooths and buildings appear at the end of the bridge. When the boys leave the bridge they are in a small plaza. On one side is a roadway full of cars, on the other side are buildings. There are also some trees.

 Use **Unit One Resource Book,** p. 25, for more practice.

me. My foot *was* killing me. All I said, though, was, "How come you keep rubbing your arm?"

"I'm keeping the blood moving."

We approached the grove of trees. "Wow," Horse exclaimed. "Country." But as we drew closer, what we found were discarded cans, bottles, and newspapers—plus an old mattress spring.

"Hey," Max cried, sounding relieved, "this is just like Brooklyn."

I said, "Let's find a decent place, make camp, and eat."

It was hard to find a campsite that didn't have junk. The growing dark didn't help. We had to settle for the place that had the least amount of garbage.

Max said, "If we build a lean-to, it'll keep us out of the rain." He and Horse went a short distance with the hatchet.

Seeing a tree they wanted, Max whacked at it. The hatchet bounced right out of his hand. There was not even a dent in the tree. Horse retrieved the hatchet and checked the blade. "Dull," he said.

"Think I'm going to carry something sharp and cut myself?" Max protested. They contented themselves with picking up branches.

I went in search of firewood, but everything was wet. When I finally gathered some twigs and tried to light them, the only thing that burned was my fingers.

Meanwhile, Horse and Max used their branches to build a lean-to directly over me. After many collapses—which didn't

I ALMOST SAID SOMETHING ABOUT GIVING UP, BUT AS FAR AS I COULD SEE, THE OTHER GUYS WERE STILL TOUGH.

help my work—they finally got the branches to stand in a shaky sort of way.

"Uh-oh," Horse said. "We forgot to bring something for a cover."

Max eyed me. "Didn't you say you brought a blanket?"

"No way!" I cried.

"All in favor of using the blanket!"

Horse and Max both cried, "Aye."

Only after I built up a mound of partially burned match sticks and lit *them,* did I get the fire going. It proved that where there's smoke there doesn't have to be much fire. The guys meanwhile draped my blanket over their branch construction. It collapsed twice.

About an hour after our arrival, the three of us were gathered inside the tiny space. There was a small fire, but more light came from my flickering flashlight.

"No more rain," Horse said with pride.

"Just smoke," I said, rubbing my stinging eyes.

"We need a <u>vent</u> hole," Horse pointed out.

"I could cut it with the hatchet," Max said.

"It's my mother's favorite blanket."

"And you took it?" Max said.

I nodded.

"You *are* tough," Horse said.

Besides having too much smoke in our eyes and being wet, tired, and in pain, we were starving. I almost said something about giving up, but as far as I could see, the other guys were still tough. **3**

61

Active Reading | VISUALIZING |

A Have students visualize the campsite after the food fight. What details help them to imagine how the boys look and feel?

Possible Responses: details of the wet, dripping beans; the mud; the wet blanket; the image of the boys picking wet beans off of each other

B Ask students to visualize how the boys must look to others when they are standing on the subway. Why might people back away from them?

Possible Response: They must look dirty and wet. They might also look suspicious carrying all their dirty, wet belongings.

Reading Skills and Strategies: CONNECT

C Ask students to think about how the boys' definition of *tough* has changed. How is this conversation both different from and similar to other conversations they have had on the subject of being tough? What has finally made the narrator the leader he wants to be?

Literary Analysis: CHARACTERS

D Discuss why the characters seem to feel a sense of relief at the end of the story, despite the fact that their trip was not what they wanted it to be. Was being good Boy Scouts what was most important to the boys?

Literary Analysis: HUMOR

Have students explain what elements create the most humor in the story. Do they believe it is the characters, the setting, the plot, or the writer's voice and style?

Number 8, 1949, Jackson Pollock. Neuberger Museum of Art, Purchase College, State University of New York, gift of Roy R. Neuberger. Photo: Jim Frank. Copyright © 2001 Pollock-Krasner Foundation/Artists Rights Society (ARS), New York.

Max put his frying pan atop my smoldering smoke. After dumping in the entire contents of his mustard bottle, he threw in the franks. Meanwhile, I bolted down my last sandwich.

"What am I going to eat?" Horse suddenly said.

"Your beans," I reminded him.

Max offered up his hatchet. "Here. Just chop off the top end of the can."

"Oh, right," Horse said. He selected a can, set it in front of him, levered himself onto his knees, then swung down—hard. There was an explosion. For a stunned moment, we just sat there, hands, face, and clothing dripping with beans.

A Suddenly Max shouted, "Food fight! Food fight!" and began to paw the stuff off and fling it around.

Having a food fight in a cafeteria is one thing. Having one in the middle of a soaking wet lean-to with cold beans during a dark, wet New Jersey night is another. In seconds, the lean-to was down, the fire kicked over, and Max's frankfurters dumped on the ground.

"The food!" Max screamed, and began to snatch up the franks. Coated with mustard, dirt, grass, and leaves, they looked positively prehistoric. Still, we wiped the franks clean on our pants then ate them—the franks, that is. Afterward, we picked beans off each other's clothes—the way monkeys help friends get rid of lice.

For dessert, Max shared some Tootsie Rolls. After Horse swallowed his sixteenth piece, he announced, "I don't feel so good."

The thought of his getting sick was too much. "Let's go home," I said, ashamed to look at the others. To my surprise—and relief—nobody objected.

Wet and cold, our way lit by my fast-fading flashlight, we gathered our belongings—most of them, anyway. As we made our way back

1

Influence of Setting

Instruction Have students think about the idea of "country." Ask, "Do you think characters who had grown up in the country would have considered this site at the end of the bridge to be the country? Why or why not?" *(People who live in the country would probably have considered this place to be part of the city because it is close to a big road and a parking lot. There is lots of traffic.)* Then ask, "Why did these characters think that the place out beyond the George Washington Bridge was country?" Finally, reread pages 54–55, where

the narrator is talking to Scoutmaster Brenkman. *(When the narrator asks where he can find some country, Mr. Brenkman says, "Country is anywhere that has lots of trees and is not in the city. Many boys camp in the Palisades. . . . Just north of the city. It's a park in Jersey.")*

Practice Have students write a paragraph describing how growing up in the city affected the way the characters thought about the country and how it affected their preparations for the camping trip.

Possible Responses: Because the characters grew up in the city, they didn't know much about the country. They didn't know how to prepare themselves to be in the country. They brought along some useful things, such as a compass, matches, a flashlight, and sandwiches. They also brought things that aren't usually used on a camping trip, such as a mattress and an umbrella. No one brought a can opener for the cans of food.

over the bridge, gusts of wind-blown rain pummeled us until I felt like a used-up punching bag. By the time we got to the subway station, my legs were melting fast. The other guys looked bad too. Other riders moved away from us. One of them murmured, "Juvenile delinquents." To cheer us up, I got out my comic books, but they had congealed into a lump of red, white, and blue pulp.

With the subways running slow, it took hours to get home. When we emerged from the High Street station, it was close to midnight.

Before we split up to go to our own homes, we just stood there on a street corner, embarrassed, trying to figure out how to end the day gracefully. I was the one who said, "Okay, I admit it. I'm not as tough as you guys. I gave up first."

Max shook his head. "Naw. I wanted to quit, but I wasn't tough enough to do it." He looked to Horse.

Horse made a fist. "You saying I'm the one who's tough?" he demanded. "I hate roughing it!"

"Me too," I said quickly.

"Same for me," Max said.

Horse said, "Only thing is, we just have to promise not to tell Mr. Brenkman."

Grinning with relief, we simultaneously[4] clasped hands. "No matter what," Max reminded us.

To which I added, "Scout's Honor." ❖

---

4. **simultaneously** (sī′məl-ta′nē-əs-lē): at the same time.

WORDS
TO **pummel** (pŭm′əl) v. to beat, as with the fists
KNOW

"I am a twin and that meant—and still means—sharing with my twin sister Emily. For example, usually it's me who tells the jokes while she laughs. Or, if we're at a party together, Emily does most of the talking, while I tend to be the listener.

When we were kids, one of her jobs was remembering. Thus, though we were in the same class from nursery school through seventh grade, Emily remembers our classmates' and teachers' names. I recall just my friends' names. In short, my memories of childhood are only of those things I did without her.

So, when asked to write a story about when I was young, I recalled the time I was trying to be a Boy Scout, my first attempt at an overnight camping trip. Emily wasn't there.

Keep in mind that 'Scout's Honor' is a piece of fiction. Though I can't recall the actual words we spoke, much less the moment to moment events, the broad outlines of that fiasco are true. What's more, I recall that, even then, we thought it was all pretty funny.

At the age when this story takes place—though I was a voracious reader—it had never occurred to me that I might become a writer. But I was an inventor of stories, which I—and my friends—acted out, much as described in my book Who Was That Masked Man, Anyway? *Only during high school, when I was told I was a bad writer, did I decide to prove that I could write. As for my twin sister, she too is a writer. She writes poetry and nonfiction. So you see, we still divide things up."*

Differentiating Instruction

Less Proficient Readers

1 The narrator is surprised that nobody objects to his suggestions. Ask students why he is surprised and if they were surprised as well.

Possible Response: The narrator is surprised because he never thought for a moment his friends weren't "tough." Students might say they picked up on clues that the other boys wanted to go.

Ask students to briefly summarize the events from when the characters step off the bridge to when they end up on street corners near their own homes.

English Learners

2 Be sure students understand why the writer repeats the phrase "Scout's Honor" at the end of the story. Ask them to flip back to page 55, when the scoutmaster uses it. What meaning does it have there? What meaning does it have here, when the boys use it?

Advanced Students

Avi writes this story from the point of view of an adult looking back on a childhood experience. Suggest that growing older and more distanced from events gives the writer a clearer understanding of himself and his friends. Ask students to explain how the story would be different if it were written from a child's perspective on events as they were unfolding. Invite them to back up their statements with details from the text.

Possible Response: The humor comes from the author's understanding of how foolish some of the boys' actions are. The writer seems to have understanding into why the boys behave in certain ways. A child talking about events as they unfold might not have this understanding.

EXPLICIT INSTRUCTION ## Theme

Instruction Remind the class that theme is the meaning or moral of a story. It is a message that the writer wishes to communicate to the reader. Write these three theme statements on the board: "Courage involves undergoing new experiences." "Admitting defeat takes more courage than pretending success." "Hiding your fear is harder than admitting your fear."

Practice Have students work in small groups to choose the theme they think best matches the story. Call on one member from each group to tell which theme the group has chosen and to explain the group's reasoning.

Possible Responses: Answers will vary. All three themes can be justified for this selection.

Connect to the Literature

1. What Do You Think?
Possible Response: Going home was a wise decision. The boys had already faced many challenges.

Comprehension Check
• They gather an assortment of ill-chosen items, such as cans without can openers, a mattress, a blanket, a hatchet, and a compass.
• **Possible Responses:** They get separated and lost on the subway; they run out of food; they get caught in the rain; they lack tools for creating warmth and shelter.
• They agree that they all really wanted to go home, but not all were tough enough to admit it; they agree that they won't tell Mr. Brenkman that they went home early.

Use Selection Quiz,
Unit One Resource Book, p. 29.

Think Critically

2. Possible Response: The main character doesn't want to be the first to suggest going home because he wants to appear tough in front of his friends. They probably feel the same way: though no one else suggests going home, no one protests when the narrator suggests leaving.

3. Possible Response: The main character may say later that admitting one's fears is tougher than just acting brave. Still, his wanting to keep his experience a secret shows that he hasn't completely changed his definition of toughness.

4. Responses should include specific details from the story. For example, the details about the familiar objects the boys carry with them should make it easy for students to visualize their belongings and the burdened, slow-moving way they begin their journey.

Use **Reading and Critical Thinking Transparencies,** p. 4, for additional support.

Literary Analysis

Setting Students' charts should show an understanding of the most important elements of the story's setting.

Use **Literary Analysis Transparencies,** p. 6, for additional support.

Connect to the Literature

1. What Do You Think?
What was your reaction to this story?

Comprehension Check
• How do the main character and his friends prepare for their camping trip?
• Name three difficulties they encounter.
• What do the boys agree about at the end of their trip?

Think Critically

2. Why do you think the main character doesn't want to be the first person to suggest going home? Do you think his friends feel the same way? Give examples from the story to support your answer.

3. Do you think the main character will think differently about being "tough enough" after his adventure in Palisades Park?

Think About:
• the main character's conversation with Max and Horse about the planned trip
• his thoughts just before crossing the bridge
• his friends' reaction when he suggests going home

4. **ACTIVE READING** **VISUALIZING**
How clear were the mental pictures you described in your **READER'S NOTEBOOK?** Discuss with a partner the **details** from your notebook and how they helped you to **visualize.**

Extend Interpretations

5. **COMPARING TEXTS** Scout Law requires the boys in this story to be "loyal, helpful, friendly, courteous, kind, obedient, cheerful, thrifty, brave, clean, and reverent." Evaluate the characters in this story and in "President Cleveland, Where Are You?" Which traits apply to each character? Explain.

6. **Connect to Life** At the end of the story, Max says he wants to quit but isn't tough enough to do it. Do you agree that sometimes it is harder to quit than to keep going? Explain.

Literary Analysis

SETTING The **setting** of a story is the time and place in which the action occurs. The **time** may be the past, present, or future; daytime or nighttime; and any season. The **place** may be real or imaginary. Along with facts about time and place, a setting includes **imagery** and **sensory details** that describe sights, sounds, and smells. Setting often affects the way conflicts develop and are resolved. It also can influence characters' actions.

Paired Activity Make a chart like the one shown below. Working with a partner, look back through the story and find details that suggest the story's setting. When your chart is complete, discuss your findings with another pair in the class. Consider:
• Which details tell you the most about the story's time and place?
• What parts of the setting are most important to the action of the story?
• How do details about the setting make the story

Details of Place
Brooklyn
Ebbets Field

Details of Time
1946

Extend Interpretations

5. Comparing Texts Students may respond that the three main characters in "Scout's Honor" possess all of these qualities, with the possible exceptions of obedient, clean, and reverent. They are not quite honest in their actions, but they are loyal and helpful friends to each other. The boys in "President Cleveland, Where Are You?" with the exception of Rollie Tremaine, also possess most of these qualities. In fact, the narrator's loyalty and kindness to his brother causes him no end of problems.

6. Connect to Life Students may respond that quitting is sometimes harder than continuing, because you might be embarrassed in front of your friends or face negative consequences such as losing a race or failing a test.

Writing

Persuasive Letter Think about the challenges the boys faced in going camping. Do you think the boys deserve to be promoted to Second Class Scouts? Write a letter to Mr. Brenkman explaining your opinion. Be sure to give clear reasons and story details to support your opinion. Place the letter in your **Working Portfolio.**

Writing Handbook
See p. R47: Persuasive Writing.

> This writing activity asks you to use the letter form. To find out about other writing forms you might use when your purpose is to persuade, see p. R31: Choosing a Form.

Speaking & Listening

Camping Do's and Don'ts The motto of the Boy Scouts of America is "Be Prepared." Unfortunately, the boys in the story were not prepared for their camping trip. Make a list of three ways in which the boys were unprepared. Then come up with ideas about what they might have done to be better prepared. Present your list of problems and recommendations to the class.

Speaking and Listening Handbook
See p. R96: Prepare-Practice-Present.

Research & Technology

Following a Map "Scout's Honor" takes place mainly in New York City. With a partner, look in an encyclopedia or an atlas to find a map of New York City, and use it to answer these questions: What river separates Manhattan and Brooklyn? What river separates Manhattan and New Jersey? The boys first got on a subway near the Brooklyn Bridge. They finally got off the subway near the George Washington Bridge. What is the approximate distance between these two bridges?

Vocabulary

EXERCISE: CONTEXT CLUES On a sheet of paper, write the Word to Know that best completes each sentence.

1. I began to _____ loudly at my friends to meet me at the next train station.
2. When we camped, we cut a _____ in our lean-to so that smoke could escape.
3. Horse is my _____, and we compete in everything; but he is my best friend.
4. Horse had to _____ a metal bar on the sidewalk to have one foot in New York and one in New Jersey.
5. "I brought an umbrella," he said _____, seeing that we were getting soaked.
6. Horse was _____ of the food we brought, since all he had was canned beans.
7. The harsh wind and rain continued to _____ our little group.
8. We Scouts stared at the bridge, not believing its _____ size.
9. Max just had to _____ in his own defense when we doubted his skill.
10. As we walked through the fog, we viewed our surroundings with _____.

Vocabulary Handbook
See p. R20: Context Clues.

WORDS TO KNOW	bellow	immense	retort	smugly	suspicion
	envious	pummel	rival	straddle	vent

Writing

Persuasive Letter Students' letters should focus on specific qualities the boys exhibit as they deal with the hardships of their journey. Tell students that a good persuasive letter should support ideas and opinions with solid facts and details and should address any objections Mr. Brenkman might raise.

 Use **Writing Transparencies**, p. 2, for additional support.

Speaking & Listening

Camping Do's and Don'ts The list of ways the boys weren't prepared should be clearly based on the story. Solutions should be realistic.

 Use **Speaking and Listening Book**, pp. 25 and 26, for additional support.

Research & Technology

Following a Map You may want to have students work in groups to complete this activity. If possible, bring a map of New York City into class and show students the areas discussed in the activity.

Vocabulary

1. bellow
2. vent
3. rival
4. straddle
5. smugly
6. envious
7. pummel
8. immense
9. retort
10. suspicion

Grammar in Context
WRITING EXERCISE
Answers will vary. Possible answers are shown.

1. My two best _friends_ (went) camping with me in the park.
2. With the subways running slow, the _trip_ home (took) hours.
3. _Horses_ (are) very intelligent animals.
4. The _bridge_ (spanned) the mighty river.

Author Activity

Past Times Students should review biographies, library catalogs, and online resources to locate information on Avi's other works. Students can look for quotes from Avi and information about Avi's life that give clues about his interests and the themes of his work. Have students analyze why certain historical periods might appeal to Avi.

 Use **Writing Transparencies,** p. 45–48, for additional support.

Grammar in Context: Subjects and Verbs

A sentence has two important parts: the **subject** and the **verb.** The subject "performs" the action of the verb. Verbs can express physical action, as in this example:

> I **pounded** up the steps into the house.

Verbs can also express a state of being:

> Scouting **is** real camping.

Usage Tip: Sometimes a sentence has a **verb phrase**—a **main verb** and one or more **helping verbs:**

> He <u>could talk</u> his way out of a locked room.

Apply to Your Writing Check your writing to be sure that your sentences contain both a subject and a verb.

WRITING EXERCISE Write a sentence using the subject provided. In each case, underline the subject and circle the verb.

Example: *Original* The overnight hike

Rewritten <u>The overnight hike</u> (turned) into a test of bravery.

1. My two best friends
2. The trip home
3. Horses
4. The bridge

Grammar Handbook
See p. R63: The Sentence and Its Parts.

Avi
born 1937

"Everybody has ideas. The vital question is, what do you do with them?"

Writing Relations Many of Avi's relatives, including both of his parents, were writers. Avi has said he learned more from reading books than from going to school. School was a struggle for Avi. Because of a learning problem, he had a hard time in class and once even flunked out. He found his first success as a writer during college, when one of his plays won a prize and was published.

Books and More Books Avi worked as a librarian for 25 years. Meanwhile, he made up stories for his own children. These stories eventually became his first book, *Things That Sometimes Happen.* Since then, Avi has published dozens of books, including two Newbery Honor Books, *The True Confessions of Charlotte Doyle* and *Nothing but the Truth.* Although Avi has earned a reputation as a historical novelist, he also writes spooky stories, science fiction, and humorous novels.

AUTHOR ACTIVITY
Past Times Do research to find out about the settings of some of Avi's historical novels. Choose the one you find most interesting and write a short report about why you would like to read a story that takes place in that era. Share your report with the class.

EXPLICIT INSTRUCTION ## Grammar in Context

VERB PHRASES: MAIN AND HELPING VERBS
Instruction Tell students that many verbs are single words but that sometimes a verb is made up of two or more words. The last word is the main verb; other words are helping verbs. Write the following examples on the board.

Helping Verb(s)	Main Verb	Verb
is	hiking	is hiking
has been	raining	has been raining
might have	made	might have made

Tell students that forms of the verbs *be, have,* and *do* are the most commonly used helping verbs. Explain that forms of *be, have,* and *do* can also be used as main verbs.
Example He <u>is</u> hiking. (helping verb)
He <u>is</u> a hiker. (main verb)
Practice Have students underline the subject and circle the verb, including the helping verbs. Note: One sentence contains no helping verbs.

1. <u>He</u> (was hoping) for success.
2. The camping <u>trip</u> (might have been) a mistake.

3. <u>They</u> (should have prepared) for rain.
4. <u>Avi</u> (was) a Boy Scout.
5. <u>He</u> (has been) remembering his childhood.

 Use **Unit One Resource Book,** p. 27.

For more instruction on the use of subjects, verbs, and predicates, see McDougal Littell's *Language Network,* Chapter 4.

For **systematic instruction** in grammar, see:
• **Grammar, Usage, and Mechanics Book**
• pacing chart on p. 19i.

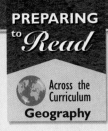

Nadia the Willful

by SUE ALEXANDER

Connect to Your Life

This story is set in the Sahara Desert. How does climate affect life in your region?

Build Background

Despite its harsh climate, the Sahara—the largest desert in the world—supports some 2.5 million people, as well as many kinds of plant and animal life.

Bone-dry and scorched by the sun, the Sahara Desert covers about 3.5 million square miles—an area about as large as the United States. It is sometimes called "the sea without water."

The climate is severe and dangerous. Food is scarce, sandstorms are common, and temperatures can reach 130°F.

Because the Sahara is so dry, heat disappears quickly at night. Temperatures can drop as much as 100°F when the sun goes down.

Rare oases (places with water and pasture) provide relief for people and animals.

Focus Your Reading

LITERARY ANALYSIS **THEME**

A **theme** is the meaning or moral of a story. The theme expresses the writer's ideas about life and human nature. Most themes are not directly stated. You can figure out the theme of a story by thinking about the title, characters, plot, and setting.

WORDS TO KNOW **Vocabulary Preview**
banish   bazaar   clan   decree   ponder

ACTIVE READING **RECOGNIZING CAUSE AND EFFECT**

When one event brings about, or causes, another, the two events are related as **cause and effect.** The event that happens first is the cause; the one that follows is the effect. Looking for examples of cause and effect can help you understand why a story unfolds in a particular way.

As you read this story, jot down notes in your **READER'S NOTEBOOK** about events that cause changes.

Standards-Based Objectives

1. understand and appreciate a **short story**
2. understand the **theme** of a story
3. understand how to **recognize cause and effect** in fiction

Summary

A young Bedouin girl (the Bedouin are a nomadic people of North Africa and the Middle East) has earned the nickname Nadia the Willful because of her quick temper. Her brother, Hamed, is the only one who can tame her temper, and when he disappears and is presumed dead, she is sad and angry. Her father, Tarik, decrees that no one shall speak Hamed's name. Nadia finds herself struggling with the loss of Hamed, and the only way she can keep his memory alive is to talk about him. She makes the brave decision to willfully disobey her father. In the end, Nadia shows her father how he can keep Hamed's memory alive.

Thematic Link

Making difficult decisions takes courage. In honoring the memory of her brother, the inner peace Nadia's memories brought her outweighed the threat of punishment from her father. Nadia's decision was true to herself and consistent with her character.

English Conventions Practice

Daily Language SkillBuilder

Have students **proofread** the display sentences on page 19k and write them correctly. The sentences also appear on Transparency 2 of **Language Transparencies.**

Preteaching Vocabulary

If you would like to preteach the WORDS TO KNOW for this selection, use the Explicit Instruction, page 68.

LESSON RESOURCES

UNIT ONE RESOURCE BOOK, pp. 30–36

ASSESSMENT
Formal Assessment, pp. 11–12
Test Generator

SKILLS TRANSPARENCIES AND COPYMASTERS
Literary Analysis
• Theme, TR 7 (p. 76)
Reading and Critical Thinking
• Cause and Effect, TR 5 (p. 76)

Language
• Daily Language SkillBuilder, TR 2 (p. 67)
• Context Clues: Definition and Overview, TR 53 (p. 68)
Writing
• Organizing Your Writing, TR 11 (p. 77)
• Revising Problem Sentences, TR 20 (p. 77)
Speaking and Listening
• Evaluating Reading Aloud, p. 14 (p. 77)

INTEGRATED TECHNOLOGY
Audio Library
Internet: Research Starter

Visit our Web site:
www.mcdougallittell.com

For **systematic instruction** in language skills, see:
• **Vocabulary and Spelling Book**
• **Grammar, Usage, and Mechanics Book**
• pacing chart on p. 19i.

Literary Analysis THEME

The theme of this unit is "The Courage to Be Me." Ask students what they think it means and how it might be connected to a story called "Nadia the Willful." (Discuss what it means to be willful.)

Possible Response: The theme might mean that sometimes it takes courage to be yourself, to do what you think is right. A willful person is one who is determined to achieve his or her goals or unwilling to give in. It can also mean "stubborn," and there is a fine line between determination and stubbornness. "Nadia the Willful" sounds like a story about someone who is determined to do things her way.

Active Reading RECOGNIZING CAUSE AND EFFECT

A Why is Nadia called "willful"? Why is her father "praised in every tent"?

Possible Responses: Nadia is stubborn and has a temper; her father is kind and gracious.

 Use **Unit One Resource Book,** p. 31, for more practice.

Reading Skills and Strategies: PREDICT

Ask students to predict how Hamed is able to calm Nadia.

Possible Response: He is able to calm her with his sense of humor.

Bedouins (about 1905–1906), John Singer Sargent. Watercolor, 18″ × 12″, The Brooklyn Museum, New York. Purchased by special subscription (09.814).

68

EXPLICIT INSTRUCTION **Preteaching Vocabulary**

WORDS TO KNOW

Teaching Strategy Point out the list of WORDS TO KNOW. Remind students that using **context clues** is one way to figure out unfamiliar words. Another strategy is to look them up in a **dictionary**.

- Help students to locate the first word, *bazaar*, in a dictionary.
- Ask a volunteer to read the definition(s) found.
- Locate the word *bazaar* on page 70.

- Help students to determine which definition fits the context of the sentence, using clues from the story.
- Ask students to write a definition for the word *bazaar* in their own words.

Practice Students should follow the above sequence for the other WORDS TO KNOW.

 Use **Unit One Resource Book,** p. 35, for more practice.

For **systematic instruction** in vocabulary, see:
- **Vocabulary and Spelling Book**
- pacing chart on p. 19i.

Nadia the Willful

by Sue Alexander

In the land of the drifting sands where the Bedouin move their tents to follow the fertile grasses, there lived a girl whose stubbornness and flashing temper caused her to be known throughout the desert as Nadia the Willful.

Nadia's father, the sheik Tarik, whose kindness and graciousness caused his name to be praised in every tent, did not know what to do with his willful daughter.

Only Hamed, the eldest of Nadia's six brothers and Tarik's favorite son, could calm Nadia's temper when it flashed.

Differentiating Instruction

Less Proficient Readers
Have students look up *Bedouin* and *sheik* in the dictionary. Based on these definitions, the first three paragraphs, and the painting by Sargent, have students describe the setting and Nadia's people in their own words. Tell students to keep this setting in mind as well as the culture of the Bedouin people as they read the story.

Set a Purpose Ask students to read on to find out what happens to Nadia's brother Hamed. Ask students to think about how the setting is important to what happens to Hamed.

English Learners
Tell students that this story is written in a formal, old-fashioned style so that it reads like a fable or myth—it teaches a lesson about life to the reader. The language also reflects the culture of the people in the story. Explain phrases like "Let no one utter Hamed's name," "Such is the way of Allah," and "Cease, I implore you."

Use **Spanish Study Guide**, pp. 13–15, for additional support.

Advanced Students
Ask students if they've ever heard the expression "to pick your battles." Ask them what they think it means. As they read this story, have them think about how Nadia decides to pick this battle with her father. Do they agree with her choice? Have they ever had to "pick a battle" in their families? Have students discuss and then write in their Reader's Notebook.

Cross Curricular Link Social Studies

BEDOUINS The Bedouins are an Arab people of the Sahara and the desert lands of the Middle East. The leader of a Bedouin tribe or clan is called a sheik. Bedouins live as nomads, or wanderers, searching the desert for oases (places with water and pasture) where they can settle with their goats, sheep, camels, and horses. When water becomes scarce, the group moves on. Life in the desert is hard and dangerous. Food is scarce, sandstorms are common, and temperatures can reach up to 130 degrees Fahrenheit.

Traditionally, Bedouins live in tents. Their diet includes meat and dairy products produced from their livestock, as well as rice and dates. When Bedouins want to acquire manufactured goods, they often trade their meat and dairy products with people in villages. During the past fifty years or so, some Middle Eastern nations have encouraged many Bedouins to settle in designated places. This has led many of them to give up their nomadic lifestyle and live in one place, seeking jobs and sending their children to school.

Literary Analysis: SETTING

Ⓐ Ask students to describe the desert setting of this story.

Possible Responses: There are some grassy areas surrounding the oases where the sheep graze. Pillars of wind and blowing sand separate the oases. Merchants travel by camel across the empty land.

Active Reading ┃ RECOGNIZING CAUSE AND EFFECT

Ⓑ Nadia and her father are struggling with intense feelings. What are those feelings, and what has caused them?

Possible Response: Nadia and her father are experiencing grief and sadness caused by the disappearance and presumed death of Hamed.

Ⓒ What are some of the situations that cause Nadia to remember Hamed, and what effect does this have on Nadia?

Possible Response: Some of the things that cause Nadia to remember Hamed are the games that her brothers play, the women weaving by the tents, and the shepherds with their flocks. They cause Nadia to feel unhappy, angry, and lonely.

Reading Skills and Strategies: EVALUATE

Ⓓ Have students evaluate Nadia's response to her brothers' game. Is speaking Hamed's name a wise thing for Nadia to do? Why or why not?

Possible Responses: Speaking Hamed's name might be good because Nadia needs to release her grief and frustration. It also helps her to remember him. It could also be bad because she is going against the wishes of her father.

"Oh, angry one," he would say, "shall we see how long you can stay that way?" And he would laugh and tease and pull at her dark hair until she laughed back. Then she would follow Hamed wherever he led.

One day before dawn, Hamed mounted his father's great white stallion and rode to the west to seek new grazing ground for the sheep. Nadia stood with her father at the edge of the oasis and watched him go.

Hamed did not return.

Ⓐ Nadia rode behind her father as he traveled across the desert from oasis to oasis, seeking Hamed.

Shepherds told them of seeing a great white stallion fleeing before the pillars of wind that stirred the sand. And they said that the horse carried no rider.

Passing merchants, their camels laden with spices and sweets for the <u>bazaar</u>, told of the emptiness of the desert they had crossed.

1 Tribesmen, strangers, everyone whom Tarik asked, sighed and gazed into the desert, saying, "Such is the will of Allah."[1]

𝒜t last Tarik knew in his heart that his favorite son, Hamed, had been claimed, as other Bedouin before him, by the drifting sands. And he told Nadia what he knew—that Hamed was dead.

Nadia screamed and wept and stamped the sand, crying, "Not even Allah will take Hamed from me!" until her father could bear no more and sternly bade her to silence.

Ⓑ Nadia's grief knew no bounds. She walked blindly through the oasis, neither seeing nor hearing those who would console her. And Tarik was silent. For days he sat inside his tent, speaking not at all and barely tasting the meals set before him.

Then, on the seventh day, Tarik came out of his tent. He called all his people to him, and when they were assembled, he spoke. "From this day forward," he said, "let no one utter Hamed's name. Punishment shall be swift for those who would remind me of what I have lost."

Each memory brought Hamed's name to Nadia's lips.

Hamed's mother wept at the <u>decree</u>. The people of the <u>clan</u> looked at one another uneasily. All could see the hardness that had settled on the sheik's face and the coldness in his eyes, and so they said nothing. But they obeyed.

Nadia, too, did as her father decreed, though each day held something to remind her of Hamed. As she passed her brothers at play, she remembered games Hamed had taught her. As she walked by the women weaving patches for the tents and heard them talking and laughing, she remembered tales Hamed had told her and how they had made her laugh. And as she watched the shepherds with their flock, she remembered the little black lamb Hamed had loved.

Ⓒ

---

1. **Allah** (ăl′ə): the name for God in the Islamic religion.

WORDS TO KNOW
bazaar (bə-zär′) *n.* in Middle Eastern countries, an outdoor market of small shops
decree (dĭ-krē′) *n.* an official order
clan (clăn) *n.* a family group

70

EXPLICIT INSTRUCTION Understanding Theme

Instruction Review the concept of theme with the class. Remind them that the theme of a selection is a message about life or human nature that the writer wishes to communicate to the reader. The theme can be inferred through clues such as the characters, the conflicts, important events, the lessons that characters learn, and key statements that the characters make. Ask, "Who is the main character in this story?" (*Nadia*) "Who are the other important characters?" (*Nadia's father,*

Tarik, and brother Hamed) What important events have occurred by the end of page 70?

Practice Write this question on the board and have students work in pairs to answer it: What important actions and events occur by the end of page 70? Invite students to share their answers. Then ask if they can think of any themes for this selection, or whether they think they need to read on.

Possible Responses: Important actions/events— Hamed calms Nadia's anger; Hamed rides off

to seek grazing lands and does not return; Tarik hunts for Hamed and comes to believe his son is dead; Hamed threatens punishment for anyone who speaks Hamed's name; Nadia remembers Hamed everywhere she goes. The theme might have something to do with the necessity to do what one needs to do even if it goes against a parent's wishes.

 Use **Unit One Resource Book,** p. 32, for more practice.

La caravane [The caravan] (1880), Alexandre-Gabriel Decamps. Louvre, Paris. Giraudon/Art Resource, New York.

Each memory brought Hamed's name to Nadia's lips, but she stilled the sound. And each time that she did so, her unhappiness grew until, finally, she could no longer contain it. She wept and raged at anyone and anything that crossed her path. Soon everyone at the oasis fled at her approach. And she was more lonely than she had ever been before.

One day, as Nadia passed the place where her brothers were playing, she stopped to watch them. They were playing one of the games that Hamed had taught her. But they were playing it wrong.

Without thinking, Nadia called out to them. "That is not the way! Hamed said that first you jump this way and then you jump back!"

Her brothers stopped their game and looked around in fear. Had Tarik heard Nadia say Hamed's name? But the sheik was nowhere to be seen.

"Teach us, Nadia, as our brother taught you," said her smallest brother.

And so she did. Then she told them of other games and how Hamed had taught her to play them. And as she spoke of Hamed, she felt an easing of the hurt within her.

D

Differentiating Instruction

Less Proficient Readers

1 Ask the following questions to be sure that students understand what has happened in the story so far:

- Why is Nadia called "willful"?
  Possible Response: She is stubborn and quick-tempered.
- What has happened to Hamed?
  Possible Response: He has disappeared into the desert.

English Learners

Students may not be familiar with the kind of life Bedouin people live. Have them look up the word *Bedouin* in the dictionary, and then list clues from the story to the lifestyle of the Bedouin.

Possible Responses: They live in tents, ride horses and camels, and are animal herders who migrate into the desert during the rainy winter and move back toward cultivated land in the dry summer months.

Have them look up the word *sheik (a religious official, or leader of an Arab family or village)* and note the words *clan* and *bazaar* defined at the bottom of page 70.

Advanced Students

Ask students why the setting and culture of the Bedouin people are essential to this story.

Possible Responses: If they were not nomads living in the desert, Hamed would not have been killed. If Tarik were not the leader, he would not have the power to order a decree.

Ask students to think about how this story might change if the setting were different. Would the theme, or lesson learned, change? Have students try to rewrite the story in a different setting while keeping the same theme. Would the story still work? Discuss the importance of setting and its impact on plot and theme.

EXPLICIT INSTRUCTION ## Understanding Theme

Instruction Review with students that characters' thoughts, words, feelings, and actions can help reveal the theme. Have students read the characters' words on pages 70 and 71. Then ask if any character's words on these pages seem especially important. Help students see that Tarik's proclamation is important because it is a formal statement and because it causes many strong feelings and reactions. Then ask how Nadia reacts to Tarik's statement, and whether any of her actions, thoughts, and feelings might be important.

Practice Have students work in pairs to discuss and note the characters' important

actions, thoughts, feelings, and words on pages 70–71.

Possible Responses: Actions: Nadia teaches her brothers to play a game using Hamed's rules. Thoughts and Feelings: Tarik is so sad about Hamed's death that he doesn't leave his tent for days. "Nadia's grief knew no bounds." She remembers her brother every day. She feels better when she speaks of Hamed. Words: Tarik proclaims that no one may utter Hamed's name. Nadia disobeys her father by speaking of Hamed to her brothers.

Use **Unit One Resource Book,** p. 32, for more practice.

Active Reading | **RECOGNIZING CAUSE AND EFFECT**

A What causes the conflict between Nadia and her mother and the other women in her clan?

Possible Response: Her mother and the other women are afraid to listen to Nadia talk about Hamed because of the sheik's decree. They fear Tarik's punishment.

B What effect does speaking about Hamed have on Nadia?

Possible Response: The more she talks about him, the clearer his memory becomes. Nadia becomes less angry and hurt, and finally comes to feel peace.

Literary Analysis: CONFLICT

C Ask students to describe the conflict Nadia is experiencing and how she resolves it.

Possible Response: Nadia is conflicted by her father's decree and her intense desire to talk about Hamed. She resolves the conflict by talking to her father about Hamed.

So she went on speaking of him.

She went to where the women sat at their loom and spoke of Hamed. She told them tales that Hamed had told her. And she told how he had made her laugh as he was telling them.

At first the women were afraid to listen to the willful girl and covered their ears, but after a time, they listened and laughed with her.

"Remember your father's promise of punishment!" Nadia's mother warned when she heard Nadia speaking of Hamed. "Cease, I implore you!"

A Nadia knew that her mother had reason to be afraid, for Tarik, in his grief and bitterness, had grown quick-tempered and sharp of tongue. But she did not know how to tell her mother that speaking of Hamed eased the pain she felt, and so she said only, "I will speak of my brother! I will!" And she ran away from the sound of her mother's voice.

She went to where the shepherds tended the flock and spoke of Hamed. The shepherds ran from her in fear and hid behind the sheep. But Nadia went on speaking. She told of Hamed's love for the little black lamb and how he had taught it to leap at his whistle. Soon the shepherds left off their hiding and came to listen. Then they told their own stories of Hamed and the little black lamb.

B The more Nadia spoke of Hamed, the clearer his face became in her mind. She could see his smile and the light in his eyes. She could hear his voice. And the clearer Hamed's voice and face became, the less Nadia hurt inside and the less her temper flashed. At last, she was filled with peace.

But her mother was still afraid for her willful daughter. Again and again she sought to quiet Nadia so that Tarik's bitterness would not be turned against her. And again and again Nadia tossed her head and went on speaking of Hamed.

Soon, all who listened could see Hamed's face clearly before them.

"I have spoken!" roared the sheik. "It shall be done!"

One day, the youngest shepherd came to Nadia's tent, calling, "Come, Nadia! See Hamed's black lamb; it has grown so big and strong!"

But it was not Nadia who came out of the tent.

It was Tarik.

On the sheik's face was a look more fierce than that of a desert hawk, and when he spoke, his words were as sharp as a scimitar.[2]

"I have forbidden my son's name to be said. And I promised punishment to whoever disobeyed my command. So shall it be. Before the sun sets and the moon casts its first shadow on the sand, you will be gone from this oasis—never to return."

"No!" cried Nadia, hearing her father's words.

"I have spoken!" roared the sheik. "It shall be done!"

Trembling, the shepherd went to gather his possessions.

_____

2. **scimitar** (sĭm′ĭ-tər): a curved sword.

EXPLICIT INSTRUCTION ## Understanding Theme

Instruction Remind students that the conflicts that the story characters face help reveal themes. Ask students to identify the conflicts Nadia and her father are experiencing. *(Nadia's conflict is between her wish to obey her father and her wish to talk about Hamed. Tarik's conflict is between his wish to be free of grief and his demand that his decree be obeyed.)*

Practice Have students work in pairs to list the conflicts in the story. Then have them underline the main conflict.

Possible Responses: Nadia is conflicted by her father's decree and her desire to talk about Hamed; her desire to obey her father is in conflict with her desire to lessen her pain. Tarik is conflicted by his love of Hamed and his wish to not hear his name. The main conflict is between Tarik and Nadia over how to lessen the pain of losing Hamed.

 Use **Unit One Resource Book**, p. 32, for more practice.

And the rest of the clan looked at one another uneasily and muttered among themselves.

In the hours that followed, fear of being <u>banished</u> to the desert made everyone turn away from Nadia as she tried to tell them of Hamed and the things he had done and said.

And the less she was listened to, the less she was able to recall Hamed's face and voice. And the less she recalled, the more her temper raged within her, destroying the peace she had found.

By evening, she could stand it no longer. She went to where her father sat, staring into the desert, and stood before him.

"You will not rob me of my brother Hamed!" she cried, stamping her foot. "I will not let you!"

Tarik looked at her, his eyes colder than the desert night.

But before he could utter a word, Nadia spoke again. "Can you recall Hamed's face? Can you still hear his voice?"

Tarik started in surprise, and his answer seemed to come unbidden to his lips. "No, I cannot! Day after day I have sat in this spot where I last saw Hamed, trying to remember the look, the sound, the happiness that was my beloved son—but I cannot."

And he wept.

Nadia's tone became gentle. "There is a way, honored father," she said. "Listen."

And she began to speak of Hamed. She told of walks she and Hamed had taken and of talks they had had. She told how he had taught her games, told her tales, and calmed her when she was angry. She told many things that she remembered, some happy and some sad.

And when she was done with the telling, she said gently, "Can you not recall him now, Father? Can you not see his face? Can you not hear his voice?"

Tarik nodded through his tears, and for the first time since Hamed had been gone, he smiled.

"Now you see," Nadia said, her tone more gentle than the softest of the desert breezes, "there is a way that Hamed can be with us still."

The sheik <u>pondered</u> what Nadia had said. After a long time, he spoke, and the sharpness was gone from his voice.

"You will not rob me of my brother Hamed!"

"Tell my people to come before me, Nadia," he said. "I have something to say to them."

When all were assembled, Tarik said, "From this day forward, let my daughter Nadia be known not as willful but as wise. And let her name be praised in every tent, for she has given me back my beloved son."

And so it was. The shepherd returned to his flock, kindness and graciousness returned to the oasis, and Nadia's name was praised in every tent. And Hamed lived again—in the hearts of all who remembered him. ❖

WORDS
TO
KNOW

banish (băn′ĭsh) v. to send away; exile
ponder (pŏn′dər) v. to think about carefully

73

Differentiating Instruction

English Learners
1 Explain to students what Nadia means by "rob me of my brother." Her father can not literally take her brother away because he is already dead, but by not allowing anyone to speak of Hamed, Tarik has taken away Nadia's memories of her brother. As her memories fade, so does the picture of her brother.

2 Help students understand the sentence construction when Nadia asks Tarik, "Can you not see his face? Can you not hear his voice?" Both sentences could be written, "Can't you see his face? Can't you hear his voice?" This re-write does not change the meaning, but it is less in keeping with the old-fashioned way Nadia talks. Make sure students understand that she is not speaking literally, but is asking her father to remember what Hamed looked and sounded like.

Less Proficient Readers
Have students summarize the events following Tarik's decree in their own words.
Possible Response: Nadia disobeys her father in order to remember Hamed. One of the shepherds uses Hamed's name when he thinks he's speaking to Nadia, but Tarik hears him and banishes him. This leads Nadia to confront her father. Tarik revokes the sentence when he understands that Nadia is right.

Advanced Students
Ask students if they believe that Nadia has become any less willful and to explain their answers.
Possible Responses: No, Nadia is still willful; her willfulness is what forced Tarik to reconsider his actions and to recognize her wisdom. Yes, she is now able to communicate her viewpoint to Tarik with gentle words.

EXPLICIT
INSTRUCTION **Understanding Theme**

Instruction Remind students that noting how characters change can help them identify the theme. Discuss with students how Nadia and Tarik have changed by the end of the story. (*In the beginning, Nadia is angry. She becomes even angrier when Hamed dies. She disobeys her father and is angry at him for telling her not to speak of Hamed. By the end of the story, she is calmly helping her father understand how speaking of Hamed lessens the pain of losing him. Tarik is angry at the beginning and punishes a man for speaking of Hamed. By the end, he is sad but has learned that speaking of Hamed is a good thing. Tarik is angry when Hamed dies and decrees that his name never be spoken again. At the end he realizes that Nadia's way of remembering Hamed can help lessen the pain.*)

Practice List the following theme statements on the board:

• Losing someone you love is painful, but remembering the good things about him or her helps ease the pain.
• To avoid pain, it's better to forget the people you love when they die.

Ask which statement is the better expression of the theme of the story. Have students discuss and justify their responses using information from the story.
Possible Response: Students should realize that the first theme statement above is a better expression of theme in "Nadia the Willful." Students should support their responses with story information.

 Use **Unit One Resource Book,** p. 33, for more practice in understanding theme.

Use the following questions to help students analyze and understand the poem.

• Think about the title of this poem and about a time when you had to overcome a fear. What qualities helped you succeed? What qualities do you need to succeed in life? Work with a group to generate a list.

Possible Responses: a kind heart, a good work ethic, self-confidence, faith, family, a good education

• Explain to students that a word, phrase, line, or group of lines repeated regularly in a poem is called a refrain. Ask them to identify this feature in this poem and to describe its effect.

Possible Response: "Life doesn't frighten me at all," with some variations, is the refrain. Each time the author mentions something that might be frightening, she repeats the refrain as if to convince herself that she is not scared.

• What mental image did you create as you read or heard this poem?

Possible Response: This poem creates a picture of a scared little girl in her room at night in the dark trying to be brave.

Maya Angelou

Born in 1928, Maya Angelou grew up in Stamps, Arkansas. She has worked as a dancer, singer, composer, writer, and teacher. She earned a National Book Award nomination for the first volume of her autobiography, *I Know Why the Caged Bird Sings,* and read an original poem at the inauguration of President Clinton in 1993.

Life Doesn't Frighten Me

by Maya Angelou

Shadows on the wall
Noises down the hall
Life doesn't frighten me at all
Bad dogs barking loud
5 Big ghosts in a cloud
Life doesn't frighten me at all.

Mean old Mother Goose
Lions on the loose
They don't frighten me at all
10 Dragons breathing flame
On my counterpane[1]
That doesn't frighten me at all,

I go boo
Make them shoo
15 I make fun
Way they run
I won't cry
So they fly
I just smile
20 They go wild
Life doesn't frighten me at all.

Tough guys in a fight
All alone at night
Life doesn't frighten me at all.

25 Panthers in the park
Strangers in the dark
No, they don't frighten me at all.

---

1. **counterpane** (koun′tər-pān′): bedspread.

Boy and Dog in a Johnnypump (1982), Jean-Michel Basquiat. Courtesy The Brant Foundation, Greenwich, Connecticut. Copyright © 2001 Artists Rights Society (ARS), New York/ADAGP, Paris.

That new classroom where
Boys all pull my hair
30 (Kissy little girls
With their hair in curls)
They don't frighten me at all.

Don't show me frogs and snakes
And listen for my scream,
35 If I'm afraid at all
It's only in my dreams.

I've got a magic charm
That I keep up my sleeve,
I can walk the ocean floor
40 And never have to breathe.

Life doesn't frighten me at all
Not at all
Not at all.
Life doesn't frighten me at all.

Advanced Students
Ask students to think about the tone of the poem and their own feelings about overcoming fear. Then have each student write a stanza about something that he or she thinks is frightening. Be sure students' stanzas reproduce the poem's defiant tone and its "doesn't frighten me at all" refrain.

Less Proficient Readers
1 To be sure students understand the poem, ask them how the poet deals with her fears.
Possible Response: She scares them away, laughs at them, and refuses to let them make her cry.
Set a Purpose As they read, ask students to identify the fears mentioned in "Life Doesn't Frighten Me" and the way the poet describes them.

English Learners
Help students to appreciate the qualities of free verse. Free verse is written like conversation, without a regular pattern of rhyme, rhythm, or line length. The vocabulary in the poem is not particularly difficult, so students should enjoy the beauty and sound of the language.

  Be sure students understand the meaning of this poem and how the poet deals with her fears. Explain that this poem is about all of the poet's fears, and that it is not meant to be taken literally.

EXPLICIT INSTRUCTION   Viewing and Representing

Boy and Dog in a Johnnypump
by Jean-Michel Basquiat

ART APPRECIATION
Instruction The Caribbean-American artist Jean-Michel Basquiat (1960–1988) was one of the best-known artists of the 1980s. This painting is from his early period, during which he often depicted skeleton-like figures, reflecting his obsession with death.

Practice Ask students to think about how this painting matches the mood or tone set in the poem. How does the style of the painting affect the mood?
Possible Response: The mood of the painting is scary because of the skeleton figures and the distorted features. The poem has a similar mood because it talks about magic charms, strangers in the dark, screams in the night, shadows and noises, dogs, and ghosts. Both make me think of something that could be frightening.

Connect to the Literature

1. What Do You Think?
Possible Response: Nadia's disobedience of Tarik's decree is brave and admirable because she ends up helping so many people.

Comprehension Check
- When Nadia first hears of her brother's death, she screams and weeps and will not let anyone console her.
- Tarik orders his people to never again speak of Hamed.
- Nadia likes to talk about Hamed because keeping his memory alive makes her grief easier to bear.

 Use Selection Quiz
Unit One Resource Book, p. 36.

Think Critically

2. **Possible Responses:** Nadia deserves to be called willful because she insists on saying and doing what she pleases. She is not willful; she is just honest about her feelings.

3. **Possible Response:** At first Nadia is very stubborn about her attitude. Over time, she learns to accept her brother's death and to confront Tarik in a calm and receptive way. In doing so, she becomes peaceful and wise.

4. **Possible Responses:** Nadia changes Tarik's mind because she is stubborn and refuses to back down. Nadia shows Tarik that silence does not erase grief and that remembering Hamed is both good and comforting.

 Use **Reading and Critical Thinking Transparencies,** p. 5, for additional support.

5. **Possible Responses:** Because Nadia is forbidden to speak of Hamed, she is frustrated and unhappy; because people are not allowed to speak of Hamed, they begin to forget him; because Nadia disobeys her father and begins to speak of Hamed, she begins to let go of her anger and grief.

Literary Analysis

Theme Students' lists should include some of the themes discussed throughout the story. Details and events listed should directly support each theme.

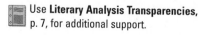 Use **Literary Analysis Transparencies,** p. 7, for additional support.

Connect to the Literature

1. What Do You Think?
What is your opinion of Nadia's behavior in the story?

Comprehension Check
- How does Nadia react at first to the news of Hamed's death?
- What order does Tarik give to his people?
- Why does Nadia like to talk about Hamed?

Think Critically

2. In your opinion, does Nadia deserve to be called willful? Why or why not?

3. How does Nadia change during the story? What causes the change?

4. Nadia's father promises to punish anyone who speaks Hamed's name. Why do you think Nadia is able to change her father's mind?

   Think About:
   - Nadia's character
   - her father's behavior after Hamed is lost
   - the effect Nadia's words have on other characters

5. **ACTIVE READING** **RECOGNIZING CAUSE AND EFFECT**
Think about the **cause-and-effect** relationships you recorded in your **READER'S NOTEBOOK.** Compare your observations with those of a classmate.

Extend Interpretations

6. **COMPARING TEXTS** Read "Life Doesn't Frighten Me" by Maya Angelou on page 74. Compare it to "Nadia the Willful." What do these two selections say about the qualities a person needs to deal with challenges? Which one offers better ideas about overcoming fears? Explain.

7. **Connect to Life** Nadia and Tarik have different ways of reacting to death. Do their differences bring to mind any differences between people that you know or have read about?

Literary Analysis

THEME A **theme** is the meaning or moral in a work of literature. Themes are usually lessons about life or human nature. Most themes are not directly stated. You can determine the theme of a story by paying attention to the **title;** the **characters** and their actions, thoughts, and words; the **plot;** and the **setting.**

In "Nadia the Willful," Nadia discovers that memories can help to ease the pain of losing someone close. This lesson is one of the story's themes.

Group Activity What themes can you find in "Nadia the Willful"? With a small group of classmates, review the story's plot and discuss the changes that take place. On a piece of paper, write down the messages that the plot suggests. Under each theme list the details and events in the story that support it.

Theme: Memories can help ease the pain of losing someone close.

Nadia talks about the game Hamed taught her and feels "an easing of the hurt."

Extend Interpretations

6. **Comparing Texts** Both selections suggest that people need strength and the ability to let go of their fears if they are to deal with challenges effectively. Students may say that "Life Doesn't Frighten Me" gives more examples of fears that the writer needs to overcome.

7. **Connect to Life** Students may suggest that Tarik is like other people who think that not talking about sad feelings will make those feelings go away, while Nadia is like people who feel that talking about something is better than keeping it bottled up inside them.

Writing

Finding Theme Determine the theme of another story you have read in your textbook. Then write a paragraph describing the theme. Begin the paragraph by clearly stating the theme. Include story information that supports the theme. Place your finished paragraph in your **Working Portfolio.**

Writing Handbook
See p. R35: Paragraphs.

Speaking & Listening

Tarik's Proclamation Now that Tarik has changed his mind, write a new proclamation, or order, that he might issue. Then read the proclamation aloud to the class. Before you present the proclamation, practice your reading to make sure your audience will be able to follow you. Also practice using facial expressions and the sound of your voice to help listeners understand and enjoy your performance.

Research & Technology

GEOGRAPHY

Conduct research to find out what kinds of animals live in the Sahara and how they adapt to the environment. How do they protect themselves? How do they keep cool? Create a chart to record your findings. Make sure you list the sources you used to find information.

Research and Technology Handbook
See p. R106: Getting Information Electronically.

INTERNET **Research Starter**
www.mcdougallittell.com

Writing

Finding Theme Remind students that they should support their themes using information about the conflicts that the characters experience and how the characters change.

 Use **Writing Transparencies,** pp. 11 and 20, for additional support.

Speaking & Listening

Tarik's Proclamation Students should look back at Tarik's original decree on page 70 to help them with the language and style. Encourage students to use the style of language from the selection.

 Use **Speaking and Listening Book,** p. 14, for additional support.

Research & Technology

Geography Allow students time in the library to research the topic more fully.

Vocabulary

EXERCISE: MEANING CLUES

1. decree
2. bazaar
3. ponder
4. clan
5. banish

VOCABULARY STRATEGY

1. bazaar
2. decree
3. clan
4. banish
5. ponder
Sentences will vary.

Vocabulary

EXERCISE: MEANING CLUES On a sheet of paper, write the Word to Know that is most clearly related to the idea in each sentence.

1. Angered by the theft of the horses, the sheik commanded that anyone found stealing a horse be punished.
2. The marketplace was packed with every imaginable item—blankets, saddles, robes of woven cloth, and even wooden toys for children.
3. Looking out at the horizon, Hamed sat and thought of the extraordinary size of the hot and silent desert.
4. When the families of the tribe camped at the oasis, they slept in tents and cooked their food over open fires.

5. Nadia could not survive in the desert alone, but she had to try because the members of the tribe would no longer let her live among them.

VOCABULARY STRATEGY: SYNONYMS On your paper, write the vocabulary word that is a synonym for each word. Then write a sentence using the word.

1. market
2. order
3. tribe
4. expel
5. think

Vocabulary Handbook
See p. R22: Synonyms and Antonyms.

WORDS TO KNOW	banish	bazaar	clan	decree	ponder

Multicultural Link **Remembering the Dead**

Tell students that different cultures respond to death in different ways. In some cultures, before a person is buried, people hold a wake, a gathering of relatives and friends to honor the person who died. Jewish people observe *shiva,* a seven-day mourning period that follows a funeral. During shiva, the immediate family stays at the home of the deceased, sitting on low stools or on the floor. They generally wear black clothes and refrain from normal activities, such as going to work or school. Friends and relatives visit, bringing food and keeping the mourners company. Ask students to think of other traditions and customs that various people have to remember the dead. They may want to think of books or movies that have depicted these customs.

Grammar in Context

WRITING EXERCISE
Possible Responses:

1. In the desert, Nadia <u>saw</u> the black lamb.
2. The sheik Tarik <u>learned</u> a valuable lesson.
3. Hamed <u>had taught</u> them games.
4. Nadia often <u>lost</u> her temper.
5. Nadia <u>disobeyed</u> her father.

Connect to the Literature
Possible Responses:

Responses will vary, but should show an understanding of direct objects and how to identify them.

Sue Alexander

In explaining why she writes for young people, Sue Alexander said, "because they have imaginations that soar, touched off by a word, a phrase, an image . . . a condition I share. To be able to provide a spark for this process gives me the greatest personal joy."

Grammar in Context: Direct Objects

In "Nadia the Willful," the author uses many **action verbs,** shown in red type below.

> She screamed. She wept. She stamped the sand.
> Nadia's grief knew no bounds.
> Nadia helped her father recall the face and voice of Hamed.

Sometimes an action verb also needs a **direct object** to "receive" its action. If a verb raises the question *what* or *whom,* a direct object may answer the question. Notice direct objects, shown in orange, below.

> *Incomplete* Hamed took. (Took what?)
> *Complete*   Hamed took a horse.
> *Incomplete* Nadia loved. (Loved whom?)
> *Complete*   Nadia loved her brother.

Usage Tip: Only an **action verb** can have a direct object.

WRITING EXERCISE Underline the verb. Ask *what* or *whom.* Then complete each sentence by writing a direct object.

Example: *Original* The clan said.

Rewritten The clan <u>said</u> nothing.

1. In the desert, Nadia saw.
2. The sheik Tarik learned.
3. Hamed had taught.
4. Nadia often lost.
5. Nadia disobeyed.

Connect to the Literature Look through the story to find three action verbs that raise the question *what* or *whom.* Then find the direct object of each of these verbs.

Grammar Handbook
See p. R63: The Sentence and Its Parts.

Sue Alexander
born 1933

"I write for young people because they have imaginations that soar . . ."

A Young Storyteller At the age of eight, Sue Alexander began writing stories for her friends. She says, "At that time I was small for my age (I still am) and very clumsy. So clumsy, in fact, that none of my classmates wanted me on their teams at recess time." One day Alexander spent recess time telling a made-up story to someone else who was not playing. Before her story was

finished, the rest of the class had come to listen. This incident sparked her great love of storytelling.

Worlds of Imagination Alexander says she would not trade writing for any other profession because writing satisfies her sense of fun and her need to share. Her fantasy stories all begin the same way—with how she feels about something. Her best-loved works include *World Famous Muriel* and *Lila on the Landing.*

Award-Winning Work Alexander's short stories have been published in *Weekly Reader* and other magazines for young readers. The book publication of *Nadia the Willful* won many honors, including one from the American Library Association in 1983.

Grammar in Context

DIRECT AND INDIRECT OBJECTS

Instruction Remind students that the indirect object of the verb usually tells to whom or for whom an action is done. Note that an indirect object never appears in any phrase beginning with the words *to* or *for.* Write the following sentence on the board: Hamed taught <u>Nadia</u> something important. Ask students to identify the indirect object in this sentence.

Practice Have students identify the indirect object in each of the following sentences.

1. Merchants traveling to the bazaar told <u>Tarik</u> stories of an empty desert.
2. Hamed's death brought <u>his family</u> much grief.
3. Nadia showed <u>her father</u> her courage.
4. Tarik gave <u>Nadia</u> a new name to honor her.
5. Nadia taught <u>her brothers</u> how to play Hamed's game correctly.
6. When Tarik raged at Nadia, she told <u>him</u> a story about Hamed.

7. Tarik said, "Nadia has given <u>me</u> back my beloved son."

 Use **Unit One Resource Book,** p. 34.

 For more instruction in direct and indirect objects, see McDougal Littell's *Language Network,* Chapter 1.

For **systematic instruction** in grammar, see:
• **Grammar, Usage, and Mechanics Book**
• pacing chart on p. 19i.

Building Vocabulary
Using Context Clues

How can you figure out the meaning of a word that is new to you? First think about the word's **context**—the other words around it. They can often be used as clues to help you understand what the word means.

> Max and I ran to help. Horse was damp. His mattress was soaked. When he tried to roll it up, water cascaded like Niagara Falls.
>
> —Avi, "Scout's Honor"

The meaning of **cascaded** is made clearer by the comparison to **Niagara Falls**, a huge and dramatic waterfall.

Strategies for Building Vocabulary

The clue in the example above is known as a **comparison clue.** The word's meaning is suggested by a comparison to something similar. Also helpful are **contrast clues,** places where writers point out differences between things or ideas. Contrast clues are often signaled by the words *although, but, however, unlike,* or *in contrast to.*

The following paragraphs explain some other types of context clues.

❶ Definition and Restatement Clues Often a tough word is followed by a definition or by a restatement of its meaning. Notice, for example, how the meaning of *banished* is restated in simpler language:

> Nadia knew that people feared being banished to the desert, sent away as outcasts.

The phrase "sent away as outcasts" suggests that to be banished is to be sent away.

❷ Example Clues Sometimes writers suggest the meanings of words with one or two examples. Notice how the meaning of *decree* is illustrated in the following sentence:

> People remembered some of Sheik Tarik's decrees, such as "From this day on, let my daughter be known as Nadia the Wise."

The example suggests that a decree is an official command.

❸ Description Clues When the meaning of a word is made clearer by descriptive details, you have a **description clue.** Look at the following passage.

> After that he was quietly obsessed with the Presidents, hugging the cards close to his chest . . .
> —Robert Cormier, "President Cleveland, Where Are You?"

The description suggests that *obsessed* means overly attached.

EXERCISE Use context clues to figure out the meanings of the underlined words. Identify each kind of context clue you used.

1. He had an attack of <u>lethargy</u>. In other words, he wasn't interested in anything.
2. The bridge was <u>immense</u>. Its top towered above the boys' heads.
3. At first, the boys looked at the bridge with <u>suspicion</u>, but later they decided to trust it.
4. They needed some kind of <u>vent</u>, such as a hole at the top of the tent, for the smoke.
5. Business began to <u>dwindle</u> like patches of snow melting in spring.

Building Vocabulary

Standards-Based Objectives
- use context to determine the meanings of words
- use a variety of types of context clues to determine the meanings of unfamiliar words

VOCABULARY EXERCISE
1. feeling of dullness or tiredness; definition and restatement clue
2. enormous, vast; description clue
3. distrust, doubt; contrast clue
4. opening; example clue
5. shrink steadily; comparison clue

 Use **Unit One Resource Book,** p. 37, for more practice.

Possible Objectives

You can use this selection to achieve one or more of the following objectives:

- enjoy independent reading (Option One)
- read and analyze literature with a group (Option Two)
- use the Reader's Notebook to formulate questions about literature (Option Three)
- write in response to literature (Option Three)

Summary

June feels safe in her life with her loving mother until the Tuesday she starts a swimming class and meets a bully who is also named June. The Other June ridicules her and bruises her with punches and pinches, turning her weeks into miserable countdowns toward Tuesday, which she calls "Awfulday." After the last swimming class, June believes that she is finally free of the Other June's bullying and insults. But when June and her mother move to another part of town, she discovers that there is no escape, for the Other June is a neighbor and a classmate in her new school. Faced with being bullied every day, June desperately faces her attacker in class. "No. No. No. No more," she declares, taking the Other June by surprise. The Other June backs away, and June knows that her days as a victim are over.

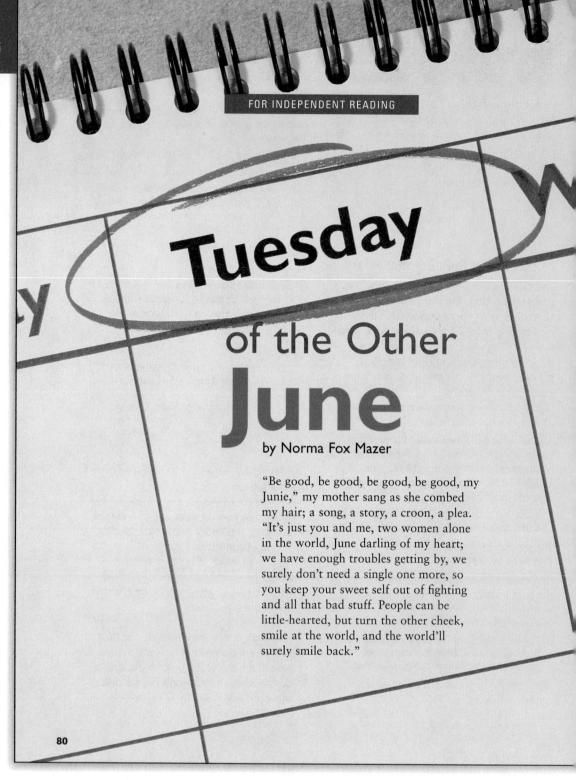

Tuesday
of the Other
June

by Norma Fox Mazer

"Be good, be good, be good, be good, my Junie," my mother sang as she combed my hair; a song, a story, a croon, a plea. "It's just you and me, two women alone in the world, June darling of my heart; we have enough troubles getting by, we surely don't need a single one more, so you keep your sweet self out of fighting and all that bad stuff. People can be little-hearted, but turn the other cheek, smile at the world, and the world'll surely smile back."

80

We stood in front of the mirror as she combed my hair, combed and brushed and smoothed. Her head came just above mine; she said when I grew another inch, she'd stand on a stool to brush my hair. "I'm not giving up this pleasure!" And she laughed her long honey laugh.

My mother was April, my grandmother had been May, I was June. "And someday," said my mother, "you'll have a daughter of your own. What will you name her?"

"January!" I'd yell when I was little. "February! No, November!" My mother laughed her honey laugh. She had little emerald eyes that warmed me like the sun.

Every day when I went to school, she went to work. "Sometimes I stop what I'm doing," she said, "lay down my tools, and stop everything, because all I can think about is you. Wondering what you're doing and if you need me. Now, Junie, if anyone ever bothers you—"

"—I walk away, run away, come on home as fast as my feet will take me," I recited.

"Yes. You come to me. You just bring me

The Case for More School Days, C. F. Payne. First appeared in *The Atlantic Monthly*.

your trouble, because I'm here on this earth to love you and take care of you."

I was safe with her. Still, sometimes I woke up at night and heard footsteps slowly creeping up the stairs. It wasn't my mother, she was asleep in the bed across the room, so it was robbers, thieves, and murderers, creeping slowly . . . slowly . . . slowly toward my bed.

I stuffed my hand into my mouth. If I screamed and woke her, she'd be tired at work tomorrow. The robbers and thieves filled the warm darkness and slipped across the floor more quietly than cats. Rigid under the covers, I stared at the shifting dark and bit my knuckles and never knew when I fell asleep again.

In the morning we sang in the kitchen. "Bill Grogan's goat! Was feelin' fine! Ate three red shirts, right off the line!" I made sandwiches for our lunches, she made pancakes for breakfast, but all she ate was one pancake and a cup of coffee. "Gotta fly, can't be late."

I wanted to be rich and take care of her. She worked too hard; her pretty hair had gray in it

Option One
Independent Reading
You might set aside time each week for independent reading to help your students approach the goal of reading 1 million words a year. During this time, you and all of your students would read for enjoyment. "Tuesday of the Other June" will appeal to many students and can be read independently in about fifteen minutes. If you want to encourage students to read for pleasure, you might forego any assignments related to this selection. Should you want to make assignments, Options Two and Three offer suggestions.

Option Two
Group Reading
You may assign students to groups or allow them to choose their own. Students can read the selection together, alternately reading sections aloud, or they can read independently and meet to cooperate in a project that portrays some element of the story.

Possible Projects
- Students can use information from the text to write personality portraits of the two Junes.
- Working in small groups, students can create a skit depicting June's first two days at her new school. This might include possible dialogue between the two Junes and should focus on June T.'s emotions and thoughts as implied by the author.
- Students can create a setting, such as a playground or a classroom, for a performance of the skit.

Art
Award-winning American illustrator C. F. Payne uses realism combined with distortion to make a point about the girl in this painting. The focus is on the expression on her face, seemingly a mixture of disgust and sarcasm.

- Ask students to describe the dilemma that June faces and to analyze in some detail the character of June.
- Tell students to read the selection, pausing at the end of column two, page 81. At that point, ask students to summarize in their Reader's Notebook the lesson that June's mother wants her to remember always. Have them write down any questions they have about the story so far or questions they would like to ask June.
  At the end of the story, students will return to their questions. Ask them to note if any of their questions have been answered and to write down any additional questions or comments they have about June or the story.
- Instead of acting out a possible conversation between the two Junes, students can write such a conversation in their Reader's Notebook.

that she joked about. "Someday," I said, "I'll buy you a real house, and you'll never work in a pot factory again."

"Such delicious plans," she said. She checked the windows to see if they were locked. "Do you have your key?"

I lifted it from the chain around my neck.

"And you'll come right home from school and—"

"—I won't light fires or let strangers into the house, and I won't tell anyone on the phone that I'm here alone," I finished for her.

"I know, I'm just your old worrywart mother." She kissed me twice, once on each cheek. "But you are my June, my only June, the only June."

She was wrong; there was another June. I met her when we stood next to each other at the edge of the pool the first day of swimming class in the Community Center.

"What's your name?" She had a deep growly voice.

"June. What's yours?"

She stared at me. "June."

"We have the same name."

"No we don't. June is my name, and I don't give you permission to use it. Your name is Fish Eyes." She pinched me hard. "Got it, Fish Eyes?"

The next Tuesday, the Other June again stood next to me at the edge of the pool. "What's your name?"

"June."

"Wrong. Your—name—is—Fish—Eyes."

"June."

"Fish Eyes, you are really stupid." She shoved me into the pool.

The swimming teacher looked up, frowning, from her chart. "No one in the water yet."

Later, in the locker room, I dressed quickly and wrapped my wet suit in the towel. The Other June pulled on her jeans. "You guys see

that bathing suit Fish Eyes was wearing? Her mother found it in a trash can."

"She did not!"

The Other June grabbed my fingers and twisted. "Where'd she find your bathing suit?"

"She bought it, let me go."

"Poor little stupid Fish Eyes is crying. Oh, boo hoo hoo, poor little Fish Eyes."

"Your name is Fish Eyes." She pinched me hard.

After that, everyone called me Fish Eyes. And every Tuesday, wherever I was, there was also the Other June—at the edge of the pool, in the pool, in the locker room. In the water, she swam alongside me, blowing and huffing, knocking into me. In the locker room, she stepped on my feet, pinched my arms, hid my blouse, and knotted my braids together. She had large square teeth; she was shorter than I was, but heavier, with bigger bones and square hands. If I met her outside on the street, carrying her bathing suit and towel, she'd walk toward me, smiling a square, friendly smile. "Oh well, if it isn't Fish Eyes." Then she'd punch me, blam! her whole solid weight hitting me.

I didn't know what to do about her. She was training me like a dog. After a few weeks of this, she only had to look at me, only had to growl, "I'm going to get you, Fish Eyes," for my heart to slink like a whipped dog down into my stomach. My arms were covered with bruises. When my mother noticed, I made up a story about tripping on the sidewalk.

My weeks were no longer Tuesday, Wednesday, Thursday, and so on. Tuesday was

82   UNIT ONE   PART 1: THE COURAGE TO BE ME

Awfulday. Wednesday was Badday. (The Tuesday bad feelings were still there.) Thursday was Betterday, and Friday was Safeday. Saturday was Goodday, but Sunday was Toosoonday, and Monday—Monday was nothing but the day before Awfulday.

I tried to slow down time. Especially on the weekends, I stayed close by my mother, doing everything with her, shopping, cooking, cleaning, going to the laundromat. "Aw, sweetie, go play with your friends."

"No, I'd rather be with you." I wouldn't look at the clock or listen to the radio (they were always telling you the date and the time). I did special magic things to keep the day from going away, rapping my knuckles six times on the bathroom door six times a day and never, ever touching the chipped place on my bureau. But always I woke up to the day before Tuesday, and always, no matter how many times I circled the worn spot in the living-room rug or counted twenty-five cracks in the ceiling, Monday disappeared and once again it was Tuesday.

The Other June got bored with calling me Fish Eyes. Buffalo Brain came next, but as soon as everyone knew that, she renamed me Turkey Nose.

Now at night it wasn't robbers creeping up the stairs, but the Other June, coming to torment me. When I finally fell asleep, I dreamed of kicking her, punching, biting, pinching. In the morning I remembered my dreams and felt brave and strong. And then I remembered all the things my mother had taught me and told me.

Be good, be good, be good; it's just us two women alone in the world. . . . Oh, but if it weren't, if my father wasn't long gone, if we'd had someone else to fall back on, if my mother's mother and daddy weren't dead all these years, if my father's daddy wanted to know us instead of being glad to forget us— oh, then I would have punched the Other June with a frisky heart, I would have grabbed her arm at poolside and bitten her like the dog she had made of me.

One night, when my mother came home from work, she said, "Junie, listen to this. We're moving!"

"Junie, listen to this. We're moving!"

Alaska, I thought. Florida. Arizona. Someplace far away and wonderful, someplace without the Other June.

"Wait till you hear this deal. We are going to be caretakers, trouble-shooters for an eight-family apartment building. Fifty-six Blue Hill Street. Not janitors; we don't do any of the heavy work. April and June, Trouble-shooters, Incorporated. If a tenant has a complaint or a problem, she comes to us and we either take care of it or call the janitor for service. And for that little bit of work, we get to live rent free!" She swept me around in a dance. "Okay? You like it? I do!"

So. Not anywhere else, really. All the same, maybe too far to go to swimming class? "Can we move right away? Today?"

"Gimme a break, sweetie. We've got to pack, do a thousand things. I've got to line up someone with a truck to help us. Six weeks, Saturday the fifteenth." She circled it on the calendar. It was the Saturday after the last day of swimming class.

Soon, we had boxes lying everywhere, filled with clothes and towels and glasses wrapped in newspaper. Bit by bit, we cleared the rooms,

Possible Activities
Independent Activities
• Have advanced students skim over the story, jotting down details about the relationship between June and her mother. Ask them to write in their Reader's Notebooks why they think the author emphasized the closeness of this relationship and what role this relationship played in the story as a whole.
• Have students review the Learning the Language of Literature and Active Reader pages 21–25. Ask them to note which skills and strategies they used while reading this selection.

Discussion Activities
• Use the questions formulated by the students as the start of a discussion about this story.
• Ask students how they felt about June T. finally standing up to the Other June. Do they feel that by doing so she let her mother down?

Assessment Opportunities
• You can assess student comprehension of the story by evaluating the questions they formulate in their Reader's Notebooks.
• You can use any of the discussion questions as essay questions.
• You can ask students to write an essay describing their interpretation of the story's central point.
• You can ask students to write a summary of the story.

84

leaving only what we needed right now. The dining-room table staggered on a bunched-up rug, our bureaus inched toward the front door like patient cows. On the calendar in the kitchen, my mother marked off the days until we moved, but the only days I thought about were Tuesdays—Awfuldays. Nothing else was real except the too fast passing of time, moving toward each Tuesday . . . away from Tuesday . . . toward Tuesday . . .

And it seemed to me that this would go on forever, that Tuesdays would come forever and I would be forever trapped by the side of the pool, the Other June whispering Buffalo Brain Fish Eyes Turkey Nose into my ear, while she ground her elbow into my side and smiled her square smile at the swimming teacher.

No more swimming class.
No more Awfuldays. . . .
No more Tuesdays.

And then it ended. It was the last day of swimming class. The last Tuesday. We had all passed our tests, and, as if in celebration, the Other June only pinched me twice. "And now," our swimming teacher said, "all of you are ready for the Advanced Class, which starts in just one month. I have a sign-up slip here. Please put your name down before you leave." Everyone but me crowded around. I went to the locker room and pulled on my clothes as fast as possible. The Other June burst through the door just as I was leaving. "Goodbye," I yelled, "good riddance to bad trash!" Before she could pinch me again, I ran past her and then ran all the way home, singing, "Goodbye . . . goodbye . . . goodbye, good riddance to bad trash!"

Later, my mother carefully untied the blue ribbon around my swimming class diploma. "Look at this! Well, isn't this wonderful! You are on your way, you might turn into an Olympic swimmer, you never know what life will bring."

"I don't want to take more lessons."

"Oh, sweetie, it's great to be a good swimmer." But then, looking into my face, she said, "No, no, no, don't worry, you don't have to."

The next morning, I woke up hungry for the first time in weeks. No more swimming class. No more Baddays and Awfuldays. No more Tuesdays of the Other June. In the kitchen, I made hot cocoa to go with my mother's corn muffins. "It's Wednesday, Mom," I said, stirring the cocoa. "My favorite day."

"Since when?"

"Since this morning." I turned on the radio so I could hear the announcer tell the time, the temperature, and the day.

Thursday for breakfast I made cinnamon toast, Friday my mother made pancakes, and on Saturday, before we moved, we ate the last slices of bread and cleaned out the peanut butter jar.

"Some breakfast," Tilly said. "Hello, you must be June." She shook my hand. She was a friend of my mother's from work; she wore big hoop earrings, sandals, and a skirt as dazzling as a rainbow. She came in a truck with John to help us move our things.

John shouted cheerfully at me, "So you're moving." An enormous man with a face covered with little brown bumps. Was he afraid his voice wouldn't travel the distance from his mouth to my ear? "You looking at my moles?" he shouted, and he heaved our big green flowered chair down the stairs. "Don't worry, they don't bite. Ha, ha, ha!" Behind him came my mother and Tilly balancing a bureau between them, and behind them I carried a lamp and the round, flowered Mexican tray that was my mother's favorite. She had found it at a garage sale and said it was as close to foreign travel as we would ever get.

The night before, we had loaded our car, stuffing in bags and boxes until there was barely room for the two of us. But it was only when we were in the car, when we drove past Abdo's Grocery, where they always gave us credit, when I turned for a last look at our street—it was only then that I understood we were truly going to live somewhere else, in another apartment, in another place mysteriously called Blue Hill Street.

Tilly's truck followed our car.

"Oh, I'm so excited," my mother said. She laughed. "You'd think we were going across the country."

Our old car wheezed up a long, steep hill. Blue Hill Street. I looked from one side to the other, trying to see everything.

My mother drove over the crest of the hill. "And now—ta da!—our new home."

"Which house? Which one?" I looked out the window and what I saw was the Other June. She was sprawled on the stoop of a pink house, lounging back on her elbows, legs outspread, her jaws working on a wad of gum. I slid down into the seat, but it was too late. I was sure she had seen me.

My mother turned into a driveway next to a big white building with a tiny porch. She leaned on the steering wheel. "See that window there, that's our living-room window . . . and that one over there, that's your bedroom . . . "

We went into the house, down a dim, cool hall. In our new apartment, the wooden floors clicked under our shoes, and my mother showed me everything. Her voice echoed in the empty rooms. I followed her around in a daze. Had I imagined seeing the Other June?

Maybe I'd seen another girl who looked like her. A double. That could happen.

"Ho yo, where do you want this chair?" John appeared in the doorway. We brought in boxes and bags and beds and stopped only to eat pizza and drink orange juice from the carton.

"June's so quiet, do you think she'll adjust all right?" I heard Tilly say to my mother.

"Oh, definitely. She'll make a wonderful adjustment. She's just getting used to things."

But I thought that if the Other June lived on the same street as I did, I would never get used to things.

That night I slept in my own bed, with my own pillow and blanket, but with floors that creaked in strange voices and walls with cracks I didn't recognize. I didn't feel either happy or unhappy. It was as if I were waiting for something.

Monday, when the principal of Blue Hill Street School left me in Mr. Morrisey's classroom, I knew what I'd been waiting for. In that room full of strange kids, there was one person I knew. She smiled her square smile, raised her hand, and said, "She can sit next to me, Mr. Morrisey."

"Very nice of you, June M. OK, June T., take your seat. I'll try not to get you two Junes mixed up."

I sat down next to her. She pinched my arm. "Good riddance to bad trash," she mocked.

I was back in the Tuesday swimming class, only now it was worse, because every day would be Awfulday. The pinching had already started. Soon, I knew, on the playground and in the halls, kids would pass me, grinning. "Hiya, Fish Eyes."

The Other June followed me around during recess that day, droning in my ear, "You are my slave, you must do everything I say, I am your master, say it, say, 'Yes, master, you are my master.'"

I pressed my lips together, clapped my hands over my ears, but without hope. Wasn't it only a matter of time before I said the hateful words?

"How was school?" my mother said that night.

"OK."

She put a pile of towels in a bureau drawer. "Try not to be sad about missing your old friends, sweetie; there'll be new ones."

The next morning, the Other June was waiting for me when I left the house. "Did your mother get you that blouse in the garbage dump?" She butted me, shoving me against a tree. "Don't you speak anymore, Fish Eyes?" Grabbing my chin in her hands, she pried open my mouth. "Oh, ha ha, I thought you lost your tongue."

"Oh, no! No. No. No. No more."

We went on to school. I sank down into my seat, my head on my arms. "June T., are you all right?" Mr. Morrisey asked. I nodded. My head was almost too heavy to lift.

The Other June went to the pencil sharpener. Round and round she whirled the handle. Walking back, looking at me, she held the three sharp pencils like three little knives.

Someone knocked on the door. Mr. Morrisey went out into the hall. Paper planes burst into the air, flying from desk to desk. Someone turned on a transistor radio. And the Other June, coming closer, smiled and licked her lips like a cat sleepily preparing to gulp down a mouse.

I remembered my dream of kicking her, punching, biting her like a dog.

Then my mother spoke quickly in my ear: Turn the other cheek, my Junie; smile at the world, and the world'll surely smile back.

But I had turned the other cheek and it was slapped. I had smiled and the world hadn't smiled back. I couldn't run home as fast as my feet would take me. I had to stay in school—and in school there was the Other June. Every morning, there would be the Other June, and every afternoon, and every day, all day, there would be the Other June.

She frisked down the aisle, stabbing the pencils in the air toward me. A boy stood up on his desk and bowed. "My fans," he said, "I greet you." My arm twitched and throbbed, as if the Other June's pencils had already poked through the skin. She came closer, smiling her Tuesday smile.

"No," I whispered, "no." The word took wings and flew me to my feet, in front of the Other June. "Noooooo." It flew out of my mouth into her surprised face.

The boy on the desk turned toward us. "You said something, my devoted fans?"

"No," I said to the Other June. "Oh, no! No. No. No. No more." I pushed away the hand that held the pencils.

The Other June's eyes opened, popped wide like the eyes of somebody in a cartoon. It made me laugh. The boy on the desk laughed, and then the other kids were laughing, too.

"No," I said again, because it felt so good to say it. "No, no, no, no." I leaned toward the Other June, put my finger against her chest. Her cheeks turned red, she squawked something—it sounded like "Eeeraaghyou!"—and she stepped back. She stepped away from me.

The door banged, the airplanes disappeared, and Mr. Morrisey walked to his desk. "OK. OK. Let's get back to work. Kevin Clark, how about it?" Kevin jumped off the desk, and

Mr. Morrisey picked up a piece of chalk. "All right, class—" He stopped and looked at me and the Other June. "You two Junes, what's going on there?"

I tried it again. My finger against her chest. Then the words. "No—more." And she stepped back another step. I sat down at my desk.

"June M.," Mr. Morrisey said.

She turned around, staring at him with that big-eyed cartoon look. After a moment she sat down at her desk with a loud slapping sound.

Even Mr. Morrisey laughed.

And sitting at my desk, twirling my braids, I knew this was the last Tuesday of the Other June. ❖

Primer Lesson
by Carl Sandburg

Look out how you use proud words.
When you let proud words go, it is
    not easy to call them back.
They wear long boots, hard boots; they
    walk off proud; they can't hear you
    calling—
Look out how you use proud words.

Norma Fox Mazer
born 1931

"I believe deeply and firmly that people should read what they want to read."

The Glories of Stories Norma Fox Mazer believes stories are a way to understand the world and the people in it. She says that readers of fiction "will find a world where people face troubles but act to help themselves."

Devoted to Her Craft Mazer's interest in writing started in high school when she was editor of her school paper and a correspondent for her town's newspaper. After a year at college, she married the novelist Harry Mazer. For ten years, she and her husband struggled to write while raising their four children. Today she is a widely recognized and prize-winning writer of fiction for young adults.

Keeping It Simple Mazer lives in New York but spends her summers in Canada, where she does without electricity, telephones, newspapers, radios, or indoor plumbing. About her writing, Mazer says, "I seem to deal in the ordinary, the everyday, the real. I should like in my writing to give meaning and emotion to ordinary moments. In my books and stories I want people to eat chocolate pudding, break a dish, yawn, look in a store window, wear socks with holes in them." Readers can encounter many of Mazer's true-to-life characters in works like *After the Rain*, a Newbery Honor Book.

Writing Workshop — Response to Literature

Sharing Responses to a Story . . .

From Reading to Writing People respond to stories in different ways. Your own experiences may be responsible for how you react to a character or how you interpret his or her actions. You might be drawn to the boys in "Scout's Honor" because you recognize the courage it took both to go on the trip and to return from it. You may identify with the young girl in "Eleven" and her desire to be some other age. Writing a **response to literature** can help you look closely at story elements such as character, setting, and plot. It also allows you to explore the deeper meaning of a story.

For Your Portfolio

WRITING PROMPT Write a response to a short work of literature in which you analyze a literary element and explain how it contributes to the meaning of a story.

Purpose: To share and explain your interpretation of a work of literature

Audience: Others who have read the story

Basics in a Box

Response to Literature at a Glance

Introduction
Introduces the title, author, and a clear statement of your focus

Body
Supports the response with evidence from the work

- Evidence
- examples from the story
- quotations
- specific reactions

Conclusion
Summarizes the response

RUBRIC STANDARDS FOR WRITING

A successful response to literature should

- include an introduction that names the literary work and the author
- tell enough about the work so that readers unfamiliar with it can understand your response
- focus on one element to analyze
- support your statements with quotations and details from the story
- summarize the response in the conclusion

Standards-Based Objectives

- write a 500- to 700-word response to literature
- use a written text as a model for writing
- revise a draft to add supporting details and quotations
- use correct subject-verb agreement
- deliver oral responses to literature

Introducing the Workshop

Response to Literature Discuss with students what a response to literature is: a composition in which the writer develops an interpretation of something he or she has read. Sometimes readers' own experiences influence how they react to a story's plot or setting or characters.

Ask students to think about a story or poem to which they had a strong response. Tell them to think about why they had particular feelings in response to the work and to think about how literary elements influenced their reactions.

Basics in a Box

Using the Graphic A personal response to literature begins with an introduction, which clearly expresses the writer's response. The body of the essay focuses on one main element and contains several examples, or evidence, from the poem or story to support the interpretation. The conclusion summarizes or restates the response.

Presenting the Rubric To help students better understand the assignment, review the Standards for Writing a Successful Response to Literature. You may also want to share with them the complete rubric, which describes several levels of proficiency. Use the rubric to evaluate students' writing.

 See **Unit One Resource Book**, p. 46.

 For more instruction on essential writing skills, see McDougal Littell's *Language Network*, Chapters 10–17.

 Power Presentation

To engage students visually, use **Power Presentation** 1, Response to Literature.

LESSON RESOURCES

USING PRINT RESOURCES

Unit One Resource Book
- Prewriting, p. 38
- Drafting and Elaboration, p. 39
- Peer Response, p. 40
- Revising Organization and Ideas, p. 41
- Revising, Editing, and Proofreading, p. 42
- Student Models, pp. 43–45
- Rubric, p. 46

Reading and Critical Thinking
- Horizontal Category Chart, TR 40 (p. 91)

Speaking and Listening
- Understanding Audience and Purpose, pp. 6–7 (p. 94)
- Developing and Delivering a Presentation, pp. 8–9, pp. 12–13 (p. 94)
- Creating and Analyzing an Oral Response, pp. 27–28 (p. 94)

INTEGRATED TECHNOLOGY

Writing Coach CD-ROM
Visit our Web site:
www.mcdougallittell.com

Analyzing a Student Model

Responding to "Scout's Honor"
In the student model, the writer remarks on the nature of friendship and how shared experiences and even hardships make friendship stronger.

Have students read the model and discuss what makes it a successful personal response. Then discuss the Rubric in Action. Point out key words and phrases in the model that correspond to the elements mentioned in the Rubric in Action.

1. Ask why it is important to name the title and the author in the introduction.
   Possible Response: By naming the title and author, the writer makes clear the subject that he is writing about.

2. Ask students why it is important for the writer to provide details about the story.
   Possible Response: The writer provides details as evidence to support and justify his interpretation.

3. Ask students what they expect the rest of the paper will be like based on this thesis sentence.
   Possible Response: The writer will probably give examples of courageous and honorable behavior on the part of the boys. He will show them to be good scouts, but he will also show them to be good friends to each other.

4. Ask students how the quotation from Max reveals something important about him.
   Possible Response: The quotation shows that Max is willing to admit his fear, meaning he is able to show his real feelings to his friends. It also means that when he does go across the bridge, he is doing something brave.

5. Point out to students that the writer says that the narrator "acts" brave, even though he hopes that one of the other boys will call off the trip so they will all have an excuse not to go.

Analyzing a Student Model

SPEAKING
OPPORTUNITY
See the Speaking and Listening Handbook, p. R96 for oral presentation tips.

Daniel Kwan
Sullivan Junior High

RUBRIC
IN ACTION

Responding to "Scout's Honor"

"Scout's Honor," a short story by Avi, is about three nine-year-old boys from the city, overcoming their fears of going out to camp in the country. On their trip they learn about friendship and courage, and they come to understand the meaning of "scout's honor."

❶ Names the title and author, and clearly states the focus of the analysis in the introduction

The narrator of the story worries that he isn't tough enough, so he decides to try to become a Second Class Boy Scout. To reach Second Class, he has to meet three requirements. The hardest of the requirements is Scout Craft, which means he has to go on an overnight hike in the country. The narrator asks two of his friends if they want to go along, and they agree. When the three boys reach the bridge that will take them from the city to the country, they get nervous, but none of them will admit it. The three boys eventually cross the bridge, but they are disappointed when they realize the "country" is littered with bottles and cans just like the city is. When the rain begins to fall and their food supply runs out in a matter of hours, the three boys all want to go home, but none of them wants to be the first to say they should leave. Avi shows how courage and honor are not only part of a scout's duty but also important to friendship.

❷ The writer gives a brief summary of the work so that readers unfamiliar with it can understand the interpretation.

❸ Mentions thesis statement and sets up structure of the analysis

All three of the friends want to be courageous, but I could sense that the three boys were all a little nervous before they set out on their journey when Horse said, "Yeah, well, I was going to do that, but I didn't think you guys were ready for it." It seems like he is blaming the other two for not being tough enough to spend a night in the country when he is really the one who is scared. Max is the first one to admit he's afraid when the boys reach the bridge. "I'm not so sure we should go," he said. "Maybe it doesn't have another side." The narrator tries to act brave and begins crossing the bridge. He hopes his friends won't follow so he will have an excuse to turn back, but they are right behind him.

❹ Uses quotations as textual evidence of the boys' emotions

❺ Exhibits understanding and insight into the boys' actions

90   UNIT ONE   PART 1: THE COURAGE TO BE ME

5. Ask students how the writer
supports the claim that the
friendship shared by the boys is
really strong.
Possible Responses: Horse and Max
don't blame the narrator. They all
share in the decision to return home.
6. Ask students to explain the theme of
the story.
Possible Responses: Hardships
can make the bonds of friendship
grow stronger. It takes courage to
admit fear.

Finally, the narrator admits his fear and says, "Let's go home." To his surprise, no one objects, and the three begin their trip home. It is this part of the story that shows me how close the three boys have become. Their friendship is really strong. Horse and Max don't make fun of the narrator for suggesting that they go home. Instead, they all agree that their trip has been a failure. "I wanted to quit, but I wasn't tough enough to do it," said Max. "You saying I'm the one who's tough?" said Horse, which makes all of them feel comfortable with their decision to quit the journey and head home.

❻ Uses examples to support the interpretation

This story showed me what friends can mean to each other and that being able to admit when you are scared takes more courage than pretending to be tough. I think all three of the boys are scared from the start, and they want to turn back. They don't want to let the others down, so they just keep on going. If the narrator had not made the suggestion to go home, it is possible that the trip would have turned into a disaster. The story also showed me that creating a bond by admitting failure was a more important experience than creating a bond by faking toughness. The story is not about a trip to the country; it is a story about friendship and the bonds it can form. Even the last words of the story, "Scout's Honor," show that keeping a pledge to one's friends is every bit as important as performing the tasks to move up to Second Class.

❼ Summarizes the interpretation in the conclusion and presents a clear premise

EXPLICIT INSTRUCTION **Patterns of Organization**

PICTURING TEXT STRUCTURE

Instruction One way to structure a response to literature is to describe several of the literary elements in the story in order to decide which one to focus on.

Practice Have students analyze the text of the student model by making a chart that allows them to comment on the main literary elements of the story and how the writer handled them. In one column they can list the elements: plot, character, setting, and theme. In a second column, they should note what comments the writer made about those elements. Here is a sample.

Literary Element	Comments of the Writer
Plot	3 boys go camping
Character	boys show fear and courage
Setting	boys leave city to go to country
Theme	"scout's honor" means doing one's duty but also honoring one's friends

The writer of this response chose to focus his paper on theme. Tell students that they can make a similar chart to plan their compositions. You might suggest that they complete their chart as they read the literature to which they are responding, or that they use a chart to organize their notes.

Use **Reading and Critical Thinking Transparencies,** p. 40, for additional support.

Prewriting

Choosing a Subject

If, after they have read the suggestions in the Idea Bank, students are still having difficulty choosing a story to respond to, offer the following suggestions:

- If you can't think of a character with whom you identify, think about a character whom you admire. It might be someone who possesses traits on which you would like to model yourself.
- Consider responding to a character whose actions you found somehow disturbing or unworthy of respect. Explain your response with examples of similar situations in which you behaved differently.

Planning Your Response to Literature

1. As students reread, have them ask themselves, "If I were a character in this story, who would I be and why?"
2. Tell students to jot down examples of situations that they have experienced that are somehow similar to those that the character in the story experienced.
3. Remind students that while they freewrite, they shouldn't be concerned with spelling. The purpose of this exercise is to get their feelings down on paper.
4. Help students by clarifying for them whether their intended audience should be peers, a teacher, or someone else.

Drafting

The student model represents just one effective way for students to organize their responses to literature. Suggest that they start with the introduction to get the basics down on paper and to state their response and basic interpretation. Then they can begin the work of supporting their ideas with examples.

IDEA Bank

1. Your Working Portfolio
Look for ideas in the **Writing** activities you completed earlier.

2. Mirror Image
Choose the story in the unit that is the opposite of your life or that portrays a character that is unlike you. Analyze the story or the character.

3. Literary Journal
Keep a journal of your responses to literature that you read both in and out of school. Write about a story or poem to which you responded strongly.

Have a question?

See the **Writing Handbook.**
Using Peer Response, p. R33
Elaboration, p. R37

See **Language Network.**
Prewriting, p. 264
Drafting, p. 267

Writing Your Response to Literature

❶ Prewriting

The golden rule of writing is to write what you care about.
—Jerry Spinelli, author of *Maniac Magee*

In selecting a story for your analysis, recall the short stories you have read recently. Think about memorable characters, events, moods, and settings. Choose the story you would like to write about. See the **Idea Bank** in the margin for more suggestions. After you choose a story, follow the steps below.

Planning Your Response to Literature

1. **Carefully reread the short story.** Notice the passages in the story that seem important and that you can relate to. Jot down notes about insights that you have as you read and quotations that interest or puzzle you. Ask: What did I think about the whole story? What affected me most? How did the author get me to respond in this way?

2. **Freewrite about the story.** Give yourself time to write down all of your thoughts and ideas about the story.

3. **Choose a focus.** Look back at your notes and your freewriting. Which element stands out? You can focus on plot, theme, character, or something else.

4. **Gather evidence.** Which quotations and details from the work support your interpretation? Which contradict it? Find passages and examples in the text that will help you make your points.

❷ Drafting

Begin writing your analysis with the idea that you will revise it later. Use the following points to help you organize your interpretation.

- Write an **introduction** that includes the title, the author's name, the focus of your essay, and a short summary of the story.

Ask Your Peer Reader

- What ideas came through most clearly in my writing?
- Did I provide enough information about the story?
- Where do I need more evidence? What information is unclear?

- In the **body,** explain your thoughts about the element you are analyzing. Support your ideas with details from the story, such as specific examples and quotations.
- Restate the most important ideas of your analysis in the **conclusion.**

❸ Revising

TARGET SKILL ▶ SUPPORTING YOUR RESPONSE *"I think the main character is brave."* If you had written this statement, your readers probably couldn't tell how or why you came to this conclusion. Adding quotations and details from the story can support your response statement.

> I could sense that the three boys were all a little nervous before they set out on their journey. *when Horse said, "Yeah, well, I was going to do that, but I didn't think you guys were ready for it."*

❹ Editing and Proofreading

TARGET SKILL ▶ SUBJECT-VERB AGREEMENT In a sentence, verbs must agree with their subjects. A singular subject agrees with the singular form of a verb, and a plural subject agrees with the plural verb form. Compound subjects—two or more nouns or pronouns joined by *and*—require a plural verb form. When you proofread your response, check to make sure that all your subjects and verbs agree.

> The narrator ask two of his friends if they wants to go along, and they agrees.

❺ Reflecting

FOR YOUR WORKING PORTFOLIO How did writing about the short story help you to understand it? Did your ideas about the story change as you wrote your essay? Attach your answers to your finished work. Save your response to literature in your **Working Portfolio.**

SPELLING
From Writing

 As you revise your work, look back at the words you misspelled and determine why you made the errors you did. For additional help, refer to the strategies and generalizations in the **Spelling Handbook** on page R26.

Need Revising Help?

Review the **Rubric,** p. 89
Consider **peer reader** comments
Check **Revision Guidelines,** p. R31

Puzzled about Agreement?

See the **Grammar Handbook,** Making Subjects and Verbs Agree, p. R68

See **Language Network.** Elaboration, p. 323

SPEAKING Opportunity

Turn your written response into an oral presentation.

Publishing IDEAS

- Set up a panel of students who wrote responses to the same short story. Videotape the panel discussion of students for classmates who did not write about that story.
- Sketch a scene from the story to accompany your response. Display your essay.

INTERNET Research Starter www.mcdougallittell.com

Revising
SUPPORTING YOUR RESPONSE

Ask volunteers to share a key sentence from their responses to literature. The sentence should express the writer's personal response. Then ask the class to make suggestions for more precise words that will make the response clearer and stronger. Remind students to back up their responses with examples from the story.

Editing and Proofreading
SUBJECT-VERB AGREEMENT

Go over the example with students, pointing out that the *s* at the end of the first verb, *begins,* means that it is a singular form and agrees with the singular subject, *she.*

The verb *feels* at the end of the sentence is also a singular verb. It agrees with the subject *everyone.* If this confuses students because *everyone* refers to more than one person, remind them that *everyone* is a collective pronoun. Collective nouns and pronouns, such as *class* or *everyone,* take a singular verb.

Reflecting

As students write their responses to literature, encourage them to consider what they learned about themselves by considering how their ideas had changed.

Option
TEACHING TIP

Suggest that students think of three examples that illustrate their response to the story they have chosen. Then have them show you the three examples and help them choose the one that is the strongest.

ORGANIZATION

Instruction Remind students that a well-chosen quotation or a specific detail can reveal a character's personality more quickly and accurately than an entire paragraph of description. Adding quotations and details to their responses can convince the reader of their point.

Practice Ask students to look at their responses for opportunities to add quotations from the literary work. Ask them to circle the quotations that they already use, and have them add at least three new quotations to their papers.

RUBRIC

3 Full Accomplishment Student has several quotations that support his or her response and has added three additional quotations.

2 Substantial Accomplishment Student has a few quotations to support his or her response and has added another one or two.

1 Little or Partial Accomplishment Student has a quotation or two and may have added one more. Response appears to be unsupported by real evidence from the text.

See the **Research and Technology Handbook,** pp. R108–109, for information about formatting documents using word processing skills.

Use **Unit One Resource Book,** p. 41, to give students practice in improving the organization and consistency of ideas in their writing..

Have students read through the passage once before correcting the errors. Then show students how they can figure out the correct answer to Question 1 by reviewing the spellings of *except* and *accept*.

Answers:
1. D; 2. C; 3. B; 4. B; 5. A; 6. A

Standardized Test Practice

Mixed Review

In the beginning of the story, no one can control Nadia <u>except</u> her
⁽¹⁾ brother Hamed. After his death, she really <u>missed</u> him. <u>Then she afraid</u>
⁽²⁾ ⁽³⁾
<u>of losing her memories of him.</u> Nadia begins to disobey her father by speaking her brother's name and telling stories about him. When the shepherd is overheard saying Hamed's name, <u>Nadia showed courage</u> by
⁽⁴⁾ standing up to her father. Finally, both <u>Nadia and her father agrees</u> that
⁽⁵⁾ talking about Hamed keeps his memory alive. <u>Nadia's stubbornness</u>
⁽⁶⁾ <u>brings about good. By the end of the story.</u>

Review Your Skills

Use the passage and the questions that follow it to check how well you remember the language conventions you've learned in previous grades.

1. What is the correct spelling in sentence 1?
   A. accept
   B. exept
   C. expect
   D. Correct as is

2. What is the correct verb tense in sentence 2?
   A. missing
   B. will miss
   C. misses
   D. Correct as is

3. How is sentence 3 best written?
   A. She afraid, loses her memories of him.
   B. Then she becomes afraid of losing her memories of him.
   C. Then she becomes afraid. Loses her memories of him.
   D. Correct as is

4. What is the correct verb tense in sentence 4?
   A. show
   B. shows
   C. shown
   D. Correct as is

5. How is sentence 5 best written?
   A. Nadia and her father agree
   B. Nadia's father agrees
   C. Nadia's father agree
   D. Correct as is

6. How is sentence 6 best written?
   A. Nadia's stubbornness brings about good by the end of the story.
   B. Nadia's stubbornness brings. About good by the end of the story.
   C. Nadia's stubbornness brings about. Good by the end of the story.
   D. Correct as is

Self-Assessment

Check your own answers in the **Grammar Handbook.**

Writing Complete Sentences, p. R67

Using Verbs Correctly, p. R76

EXPLICIT INSTRUCTION **Speaking Opportunity**

Prepare Once students have written their response to a piece of literature, they can share that response with an audience. Refer students to page R104 of the Speaking and Listening Handbook at the back of this book for tips on presenting their responses.

Present Have students present their responses to the class. They should strive to demonstrate their understanding of the work, evidence for their interpretation, and enthusiasm for the piece of literature.

RUBRIC

3 **Full Accomplishment** Student provides insight into the literary work, cites specific textual references in support of his or her interpretation, and supports judgments with plenty of evidence.

2 **Substantial Accomplishment** Student introduces the literary work, includes some textual references, and offers some evidence in support of his or her position.

1 **Little or Partial Accomplishment** Student selects a work that he or she partially

understands and tries to offer some evidence for the stated response.

Use **Speaking and Listening Book,** pp. 6–9, 12–13, 27–28, for additional support in preparing an oral response.

PART 2
Courage
in Action

Meeting Standards

UNIT ONE
PART 2

The Literature You'll Read

The Concepts You'll Study

Vocabulary and Reading Comprehension
Vocabulary Focus: Analyzing Word Parts
Identifying Main Idea and Details
Chronological Order
Predicting
Identifying the Author's Purpose
Recognizing Causes and Effects
Facts and Opinions
Questioning

Writing and Language Conventions
Writing Workshop: Personal Experience Essay
Compound Subjects and Compound Predicates
Active Voice and Passive Voice
Predicate Nouns and Predicate Adjectives
Subjects in Unusual Order
Subject-Verb Agreement
Varying Sentence Length

Literary Analysis
Genre Focus: Nonfiction
Biography
Informative Nonfiction
Conflict
Autobiography
Anecdote
Memoir

Speaking and Listening
Acceptance Speech
Oral Opinion Statement
Scene Performance
Group Discussion
Persuasive Speech

Standards-Based Objectives
- understand the following literary terms:
  - nonfiction
  - biography
  - autobiography
  - expository (formal) essay
  - personal (informal) essay
  - persuasive essay
  - informative article
  - interview
- understand and appreciate nonfiction
- understand literary forms by recognizing and distinguishing between biographies and autobiographies

Teaching the Lesson

This lesson defines nonfiction and analyzes five different types of nonfiction writing.

Introducing the Concepts
Have students think about a work of nonfiction they have recently read, such as a newspaper article, a true story about a famous person, or an article in a science magazine. Ask them to explain why they read it and what they learned from it.

 Use **Literary Analysis Transparencies,** pp. 10–11, 16, for additional support.

*N*onfiction

> *I write about anything that interests me—dogs, horses, forests, birds, mysteries, life in other countries. . . . The most important aspect is that [the subjects] interest me very much, because then I want to share them with other people.*
>
> —*Patricia Lauber, writer*

Chances are, you've read some nonfiction today. **Nonfiction** is writing that is about real people, places, and events. The nature magazine you may have on your desk or the school bulletin you may have in your backpack are both examples of nonfiction. A newspaper article, a set of instructions, and an encyclopedia article are also nonfiction. Nonfiction contains factual information—information that can be proved to be true. A writer can select and organize this information in any number of ways to suit his or her purpose.

Key Forms of Nonfiction
- biography
- autobiography
- essay
- informative article
- interview

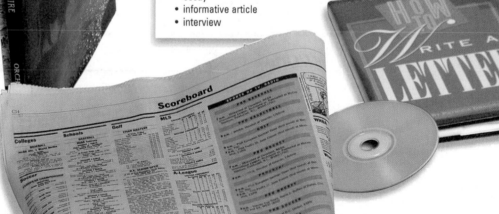

Biography

A **biography** is the story of a person's life, told by someone else. The person whose life is being described is called the subject. A biography is usually written in the **third-person point of view,** using pronouns such as *she, he, her,* and *him.* Whenever possible, the writer, or **biographer,** gets information by conducting interviews with people who have known the subject. Biographers also learn a great deal by reading letters, books, and diaries.

A short biography of the African-American explorer Matthew Henson is included in this book. As you will see, biographies contain some of the same elements as fiction, such as **character** and **setting.** Unlike fiction, the purpose of a biography is to present an accurate account of the subject's life.

YOUR TURN What do the details in the passage above to the right tell you about Henson's life?

Autobiography

An **autobiography** is the story of a person's life, told by that person. Autobiographies are almost always written in the **first-person point of view,** using pronouns like *I* and *me.* An autobiography is usually book length because it covers a long period in the writer's life. Shorter types of autobiographical writing include **journals, diaries, letters,** and **memoirs.**

YOUR TURN What words in the passage at the right let you know that it is from an autobiography rather than a biography?

BIOGRAPHY

Matthew Henson was born on August 8, 1866, in Charles County, Maryland, some forty-four miles south of Washington, D.C. His parents were poor, free tenant farmers who barely eked a living from the sandy soil. The Civil War had ended the year before Matthew was born, bringing with it a great deal of bitterness on the part of former slave-owners.

—Jim Haskins,
"Matthew Henson at the
Top of the World"

AUTOBIOGRAPHY

I could not move, would not have time to react. I knew I had nothing to say about it. One blow would break my neck. Whether I lived or died depended on him, on his thinking, on his ideas about me—whether I was worth the bother or not.

—Gary Paulsen,
Woodsong

**Presenting the Concepts
Biography**
Have students think about a famous person they would like to write about. Ask them to tell why this person interests them and what kinds of information they would want to include in a biography.

YOUR TURN
Possible Response: The author gives Henson's date of birth and describes in some detail the place of his birth. He also describes the situation of Henson's family and the cultural and social climate of the era.

Autobiography
Ask students if they have ever kept a journal or diary about the events in their own lives. Explain that this is a common form of autobiographical writing. Ask if students know of any personal diaries or journals that have become famous.

YOUR TURN
Possible Response: The author's use of the first-person pronoun "I," his use of the possessive pronoun "my," and the word "me"

Essay

An **essay** is a short work of nonfiction that deals with one subject. Essays are often found in newspapers and magazines. The purpose of an essay might be to express an opinion, to entertain or persuade the reader, or to describe an incident that has special significance for the writer. Three common types of essays are **expository** (formal), **personal** (informal), and **persuasive.** Formal essays use scholarly, formal language and discuss serious subjects. Informal essays have a conversational tone and present the feelings and observations of the writer.

ESSAY

expository

- tightly structured
- formal style
- presents or explains information and ideas

The ancient Greeks were horrified by hydras, sea dragons with nine or more heads. As centuries passed, only seven-headed hydras were seen. The seventeenth-century naturalist Edward Topsell included a picture of a hydra in *The Historie of Serpents*.

—Rhoda Blumberg,
The Truth About Dragons

personal

- looser structure
- personal style
- expresses writer's thoughts and feelings

My business is to make readers from non-readers, and if you think it's easy, then join me anytime and see how, where and why it's done. On the "where" front, I have slept on a lot of floors and couches, and on the "why" front I recall the kinder, gentler America that was proposed several years ago.

—Gary Soto,
"Who Is Your Reader?"

persuasive

- develops arguments
- tries to persuade readers to adopt a viewpoint or perspective

If the white man wants to live in peace with the Indian, he can live in peace. There need be no trouble. Treat all men alike. Give them the same law. Give them all an even chance to live and grow.

All men are made by the same Great Spirit Chief. They are all brothers. The earth is the mother of all people, and all people should have equal rights upon it.

—Chief Joseph,
"Chief Joseph Speaks"

Informative Article

Informative articles provide facts about a subject. **Newspaper** and **magazine articles** and **feature stories** are examples of informative nonfiction. Other types of informational materials are textbooks, encyclopedias, and books on single subjects such as car repair, sports history, or juggling.

YOUR TURN What factual information does the passage at the right provide about forest fires in Yellowstone National Park?

INFORMATIVE ARTICLE

On June 23 lightning started a fire near Shoshone Lake in the southern part of the park. On June 25 another bolt of lightning started a fire in the northwest. These fires did not go out, and no one tried to put them out.

—Patricia Lauber, "Summer of Fire"

Interview

Have you ever interviewed anyone? If you have, you probably know how interesting and exciting an interview can be. An **interview** is a conversation in which one person asks questions of another person to get information. The interviewer takes notes or records the conversation on audiotape or videotape in order to write an accurate account of what was said. An interview with the writer Gary Paulsen appears on page 153.

INTERVIEW

Q: *You wrote your best-known works while you were running dogs. Where did you find the time?*

A: With the dogs, you run them just four hours on, then four hours off. When they were sleeping those four hours, I'd sit by my campfire and write longhand.

Q: *What is your favorite thing to write about?*

A: Almost always, it's about making personal discoveries while struggling to survive in the great outdoors.

—"Talking with Gary Paulsen"

Informative Article
Ask students to think about why they would want to read informative nonfiction. Have them describe situations in which such works could be helpful.

YOUR TURN
Possible Responses: The passage tells the reader that a forest fire started in the southern part of the park on June 23 and in the northwest on June 25. Both fires were started by lightning strikes.

Interview
Ask students to think about one living person they would like to interview. Have them discuss what specific information they would want to get from the interview.

OVERVIEW

Standards-Based Objectives
• use a variety of strategies to read and appreciate nonfiction
• use graphic representations and cues to understand nonfiction

Teaching the Lesson

The strategies on this page will help students understand the upcoming nonfiction selections in this and other units.

Presenting the Strategies
Make sure students understand that there are different strategies for reading different kinds of nonfiction. For example, biography and autobiography are narrative forms of nonfiction and require strategies similar to those for reading fiction. Essays, informative articles, and interviews demand strategies geared more toward analyzing and evaluating a writer's reasoning and purpose.

Use **Reading and Critical Thinking Transparencies,** p. 1, for additional support.

PREVIEW
Remind students that the organization of a piece of nonfiction into sections with headings can provide an outline of the content. Words in boldface type often highlight the most important ideas presented in the article. Photographs, diagrams, and charts all give information at a glance.

FIGURE OUT THE ORGANIZATION
Tell students that before they read a piece of nonfiction, it is a good idea to figure out how it is presented: for instance, chronologically or by topic. Knowing how a piece is organized will help them understand and evaluate the author's points.

---

*R*eading Nonfiction

Nonfiction writing informs us about real people, places, and events. **Autobiographies, biographies, essays, informative articles,** and **interviews** provide answers to our questions and facts at our fingertips. The reading strategies explained here can help you to understand and enjoy many types of nonfiction.

How to Apply the Strategies

Preview the selection. Look at the title, the pictures or diagrams, and any subtitles. Also look at words and phrases in boldface or italic type. All of these features will help you get an idea of what the selection is about. As you read, stop now and then to **predict** what will come next.

Figure out the organization. In a biography or an autobiography, the organization is probably chronological—events are presented in the order in which they happened. Other selections may be organized around ideas the author wants to discuss. Dates and signal words, such as *before, after, next,* and *last,* may clarify the sequence of events.

Summarize the main idea. A **main idea** is the most important point about the topic. **Details** include words, phrases, or sentences that explain the main idea. You should summarize main ideas, or rewrite them in your own words, to help you understand and remember them.

Distinguish facts from opinions. Facts are statements that can be proved, such as, "There are 24 hours in a day." Opinions are statements that cannot be proved. They simply express a person's beliefs. Writers of nonfiction sometimes present opinions as if they were facts. Be sure you recognize the difference.

Evaluate what you read. When you evaluate what you read, you make a judgment about it. With nonfiction, you may need to evaluate a writer's opinions and how he or she supports them. Ask yourself: Do the writer's ideas seem reasonable? Does the writer use facts and examples to support ideas and opinions?

Here's how Sean uses the strategies:

*"Last year I wrote a report on horses. I had to read all sorts of magazines, books, and encyclopedias. As I skimmed the material, I looked for **main ideas** and **details. I evaluated** what I was reading by thinking about whether the author explained things well. After, I asked myself what I remembered most."*

SUMMARIZE THE MAIN IDEA
Tell students that they should look for the main ideas of a selection and facts that support them. They should be able to identify the most important facts and details in a selection.

DISTINGUISH FACTS FROM OPINIONS
Pick out statements from the selection and present them to the class. Ask students to determine whether each statement is a fact supported by evidence or an opinion held by the author.

EVALUATE WHAT YOU READ
Tell students that the above strategies will help them make judgments about what they read. Ask them to keep these questions in mind: What did you like or dislike about the article? Was the explanation clear and factual? Do you need to seek other sources of information?

Matthew Henson at the Top of the World

by JIM HASKINS

Connect to Your Life

What images come to mind when you think of the word *explorer?*

Build Background

In 1908, Matthew Henson joined Commander Robert E. Peary's expedition. Their goal was to be the first people in history to reach the North Pole. In their search, they were assisted by Eskimos known as Inuit.

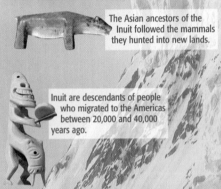

The Asian ancestors of the Inuit followed the mammals they hunted into new lands.

Inuit are descendants of people who migrated to the Americas between 20,000 and 40,000 years ago.

Migration Routes, 40,000–10,000 B.C.

Arctic Ocean

ASIA

NORTH AMERICA

Bering Strait

Atlantic Ocean

Pacific Ocean

SOUTH AMERICA

☐ Glacier ice, 12,000 B.C.
☐ Connecting land mass
← Possible land migration routes
◄-- Possible water migration routes

Focus Your Reading

LITERARY ANALYSIS **BIOGRAPHY**

A **biography** is the story of a person's life, written by another person. Biographers take information from many sources, including interviews, diaries, and letters. As you read, think about the sources the author might have used.

WORDS TO KNOW **Vocabulary Preview**

apt	menial	stamina	tyranny
ardent	proposition	surveyor	validate
deprivation	resentful		

ACTIVE READING **IDENTIFYING MAIN IDEA AND DETAILS**

In most nonfiction writing, you can figure out the writer's most important points by identifying the **main idea,** or central message, of each paragraph. The main idea may be stated in a sentence or two at any point in the paragraph. Other times, you must figure out the main idea using the **details** in the paragraph. In your 📖 READER'S NOTEBOOK jot down the main ideas of three paragraphs. Below each main idea, note supporting details— such as facts or examples—that tell more about the main idea.

This selection is included in the **Grade 6 InterActive Reader.**

Standards-Based Objectives

1. understand and appreciate a **biography**
2. identify, clarify, and connect **main ideas and details**
3. **compare information**
4. identify **point of view**

Summary

Born in 1866, Matthew Henson grew up with a hunger for adventure. He had a hard childhood and went to school for only a few years. At the age of 14, he became a cabin boy on a ship and began exploring the world. In 1887, he signed on as the servant of Robert E. Peary, a naval officer and explorer. Four years later, Henson and Peary sailed off to the first of their five expeditions to the Arctic. The fifth expedition, in 1908, had as its goal the North Pole, which had never been reached before. Seven explorers and forty-one Eskimos began the grueling Arctic journey. Frostbite, exhaustion, and death reduced the party until only Peary, Henson, and four Eskimos remained. On April 6, 1908, Peary concluded that the group had reached the North Pole, and he asked Henson to place the U.S. flag on the spot. Upon his return to the United States, Peary became a hero for his achievement, but because Henson was African American, his own contribution was not honored until much later.

Thematic Link

Henson demonstrated great courage during his Arctic explorations and in his everyday life as an African American.

English Conventions Practice

Daily Language SkillBuilder

Have students **proofread** the display sentences on page 19k and write them correctly. The sentences also appear on Transparency 3 of **Language Transparencies.**

Preteaching Vocabulary

If you would like to preteach the WORDS TO KNOW for this selection, use the Explicit Instruction, page 102.

Literary Analysis `BIOGRAPHY`

Remind students that the writer of a biography gathers information from many sources. Some of this information is presented in the writer's own words. Other information is quoted directly from the source. Have students examine the text on page 102. What sources has Jim Haskins used for the information presented here?

Possible Responses: The writer has drawn on his own knowledge and research about explorers in the American West to make general statements and comparisons with Arctic exploration. He has quoted from the writing of Donald MacMillan, an Arctic explorer who knew Matthew Henson. He may have consulted birth records to find the date and place of Henson's birth, and a map to find the distance between Charles County and Washington, D.C.

📖 Use **Unit One Resource Book,** p. 49, for more practice.

Active Reading   `IDENTIFYING MAIN IDEA AND DETAILS`

Ask students to identify the main idea of the opening paragraph. Then ask them to list several details that support the main idea.

Possible Response: Main idea—Matthew Henson had great stamina and courage. Details—Henson explored the North Pole with Robert Peary. In the Arctic, explorers could not count on finding water or game, and spring did not bring warmth; Donald MacMillan said that Henson was the most valuable member of Peary's expedition.

MATTHEW HENSON AT THE
TOP OF THE WORLD

by Jim Haskins

 While the explorers of the American West faced many dangers in their travels, at least game and water were usually plentiful; and if winter with its cold and snow overtook them, they could, in time, expect warmth and spring. For Matthew Henson, in his explorations with Robert Peary at the North Pole, this was hardly the case. In many ways, to forge ahead into the icy Arctic took far greater <u>stamina</u> and courage than did the earlier explorers' travels, and Henson possessed such hardiness. As Donald MacMillan, a member of the expedition [journey toward a goal], was later to write: "Peary knew Matt Henson's real worth. . . . Highly respected by the Eskimos,[1] he was easily the most popular man on board ship. . . . Henson . . . was of more real value to our Commander than [expedition members] Bartlett, Marvin, Borup, Goodsell and myself all put together. Matthew Henson went to the Pole with Peary because he was a better man than any one of us."

Matthew Henson was born on August 8, 1866, in Charles County, Maryland, some forty-four miles south of Washington, D.C. His parents were poor, free tenant

---

1. **Eskimos:** a term used throughout this account to refer to the native peoples of the Arctic; the Eskimos of Greenland, such as those who traveled on Peary's expeditions, call themselves Inuit, as do the Eskimos of Canada.

WORDS
TO
KNOW   **stamina** (stăm′ə-nə) *n.* the strength to withstand hardship

102

WORDS TO KNOW
Teaching Strategy If students can't find the meaning of an unfamiliar word from context, they can use a **dictionary** to look up the word. Many words will have more than one meaning listed. Students can use **context clues** to determine which is the correct meaning for that context.

Exercises Each of the sentences contains one of the WORDS TO KNOW for this selection. Have students look up each underlined word

and use the context of the sentence to decide which dictionary meaning is appropriate.
1. Even at the age of five, Eileen was very <u>apt</u> at playing the violin.
2. Jon gets bored watching sports on television, but he is <u>ardent</u> about playing sports himself.
3. Most of our plants died of water <u>deprivation</u> while my family was on vacation.
4. What do you think of Aisha's <u>proposition</u> that we have pizza for lunch?

5. Joan claims she made 47 jump shots in a row, but she has no witness to <u>validate</u> her feat.

 Use **Unit One Resource Book,** p. 52, for more practice.

For **systematic instruction** in vocabulary, see:
• **Vocabulary and Spelling Book**
• pacing chart on p. 19i.

Matthew Henson
in animal furs that
protected him from
the Arctic cold.

Differentiating Instruction

Less Proficient Readers

Ask students to describe what they think the North Pole is like. Tell them that they are going to read about Matthew Henson, a member of the first group ever to reach the North Pole. Have them preview the photographs in the selection, which show Henson and Peary and some of the tools they used in their expedition.

Set a Purpose Have students read to find out about Henson's childhood.

English Learners

Students may benefit from background information about the history of the United States during the late 1800s. They may need help understanding references to slavery, the Ku Klux Klan, and Reconstruction.

 Explain that *hardly* is a negative word meaning "not at all."

Use **Spanish Study Guide,** pp. 16–18, for additional support.

Advanced Students

Have students look for passages that describe hardships in Henson's life. Ask them to think about how Henson reacted to each hardship. Does his way of dealing with challenges and setbacks provide some insight into how he became one of the first people to reach the North Pole?

**Reading Skills and Strategies:
SUMMARIZE**

A Ask students to monitor their own comprehension by summarizing why the Hensons moved to Washington, D.C.

Possible Response: The Hensons were tenant farmers in the South after the Civil War. Former slave owners resented the new independence of African Americans, and the Ku Klux Klan terrorized the former slaves. The Hensons moved north to avoid the Klan and to search for better opportunities.

Literary Analysis **BIOGRAPHY**

B Ask students what kind of source the author might have used to gather the information in this paragraph. Have them explain their answers.

Possible Response: The information probably came from Henson's own writings or memoirs. The paragraph discusses Henson's feelings about his situation as a teenager. It also describes experiences he had at the restaurant. This kind of information could only have come from Henson himself.

ACTIVE READER

C QUESTION **Possible Response:** Henson wanted adventure and decided to seek it at sea.

Literary Analysis: CHARACTER

D Ask students what details the author uses to characterize Matthew Henson in this paragraph.

Possible Response: Henson impressed his boss at the store, who recognized that he was "bright and hard working." Henson eagerly accepted Peary's offer despite the hazards involved; this shows that Henson was eager for adventure and was not afraid of challenges.

farmers[2] who barely eked a living from the sandy soil. The Civil War had ended the year before Matthew was born, bringing with it a great deal of bitterness on the part of former slave-owners. One manifestation of this hostility was the terrorist activity on the part of the Ku Klux Klan[3] in Maryland. Many free and newly freed blacks had suffered at the hands of this band of night riders.[4] Matthew's father, Lemuel Henson, felt it was only a matter of time before the Klan turned its **A** vengeful eyes on his family. That, and the fact that by farming he was barely able to support them, caused him to decide to move north to Washington, D.C.

B At first things went well for the Henson family, but then Matthew's mother died and his father found himself unable to care for Matthew. The seven-year-old boy was sent to live with his uncle, a kindly man who welcomed him and enrolled him in the N Street School. Six years later, however, another blow fell; his uncle himself fell upon hard times and could no longer support Matthew. The boy couldn't return to his father, because Lemuel had recently died. Alone, homeless, and penniless, Matthew was forced to fend for himself.

Matthew Henson was a bright boy and a hard worker, although he had only a sixth-grade education. Calling upon his own resourcefulness, he found a job as a dish-washer in a small restaurant owned by a woman named Janey Moore. When Janey discovered that Matthew had no place to stay, she fixed a cot for him in the kitchen; Matthew had found a home again.

Matthew Henson didn't want to spend his life waiting on people and washing dishes, however, no matter how kind Janey was. He had seen enough of the world through his schoolbooks to want more, to want adventure. This desire was reinforced by the men who frequented the restaurant—sailors from many ports, who spun tales of life on the ocean and of strange and wonderful places. As Henson listened, wide-eyed, to their stories, he decided, as had so many boys before him, that the life of a sailor with its adventures and dangers was for him. Having made up his mind, the fourteen-year-old packed up what little he owned, bade good-bye to Janey, and was off to Baltimore to find a ship.

ACTIVE READER

QUESTION What is the main idea of the paragraph you have just read?

Although Matthew Henson's early life seems harsh, in many ways he was very lucky. When he arrived in Baltimore, he signed on as a cabin boy on the *Katie Hines,* the master of which was a Captain Childs. For many sailors at that time, life at sea was brutal and filled with hard work, deprivation, and a "taste of the cat": whipping. The captains of many vessels were petty despots, ruling with an iron hand and having little regard for a seaman's health or safety. Matthew was fortunate to find just the opposite in Childs.

---

2. **tenant farmers:** people who farm land rented from others.

3. **Ku Klux Klan** (kōō′ klŭks klăn′): a secret society, organized in the South after the Civil War, that used terrorism to reassert the power of whites.

4. **night riders:** mounted and usually masked white men who committed acts of terror against African Americans during the period following the Civil War.

WORDS
TO
KNOW   **deprivation** (dĕp′rə-vā′shən) *n.* a lack of what is needed for survival or comfort

---

Main Idea and Supporting Details

Instruction Remind students that a paragraph is a group of sentences about one idea, called the main idea. Say, "The main idea may be stated in a topic sentence of a paragraph. The topic sentence is often the first sentence, but it may be the last sentence or any other. Other sentences in the paragraph add supporting details to explain or tell more about the main idea."

Write the following steps on the board and tell students to use them to find main ideas:
1. Look for a topic sentence.
2. Notice how other sentences add information about the main idea.

Next, have students read along silently as you read aloud the last paragraph on page 104 ("Although Matthew . . ."). Ask students what idea most of the sentences are about. *(Henson was in many ways very lucky despite his harsh early life.)*

Practice Have students work in pairs to find a sentence in this paragraph that states the main idea. Also have partners list the details that tell more about the main idea.

Possible Responses: Main Idea Sentence: "Although Matthew Henson's early life seems harsh, in many ways he was very lucky." Supporting Details: got a job when he arrived in Baltimore, found a job at sea, the captain of the *Katie Hines* was kind and cared about his crew.

 Use **Unit One Resource Book,** p. 48, for more practice.

Captain Childs took the boy under his wing. Although Matthew of course had to do the work he was assigned, Captain Childs took a fatherly interest in him. Having an excellent private library on the ship, the captain saw to Matthew's education, insisting that he read widely in geography, history, mathematics, and literature while they were at sea.

The years on the *Katie Hines* were good ones for Matthew Henson. During that time he saw China, Japan, the Philippines, France, Africa, and southern Russia; he sailed through the Arctic to Murmansk. But in 1885 it all ended; Captain Childs fell ill and died at sea. Unable to face staying on the *Katie Hines* under a new skipper, Matthew left the ship at Baltimore and found a place on a fishing schooner bound for Newfoundland.

Now, for the first time, Henson encountered the kind of unthinking cruelty and <u>tyranny</u> so often found on ships at that time. The ship was filthy, the crew surly and <u>resentful</u> of their black shipmate, and the captain a dictator. As soon as he was able, Matthew left the ship in Canada and made his way back to the United States, finally arriving in Washington, D.C., only to find that things there had changed during the years he had been at sea.

Opportunities for blacks had been limited when Henson had left Washington in 1871, but by the time he returned they were almost nonexistent. Post–Civil War reconstruction had failed, bringing with its failure a great deal of bitter resentment toward blacks. Jobs were scarce, and the few available were <u>menial</u> ones. Matthew finally found a job as a stock clerk in

A sextant (center) and other navigational instruments of Robert Peary.

a clothing and hat store, B. H. Steinmetz and Sons, bitterly wondering if this was how he was to spend the rest of his life. But his luck was still holding.

Steinmetz recognized that Matthew Henson was bright and hard working. One day Lieutenant Robert E. Peary, a young navy officer, walked into the store, looking for tropical hats. After being shown a number of hats, Peary unexpectedly offered Henson a job as his personal servant. Steinmetz had recommended him, Peary said, but the job wouldn't be easy. He was bound for Nicaragua to head an engineering survey team. Would Matthew be willing to put up with the discomforts and hazards of such a trip? Thinking of the adventure and opportunities offered, Henson eagerly said yes, little realizing that a partnership had just been formed that would span years and be filled with exploration, danger, and fame.

WORDS TO KNOW	**tyranny** (tĭr′ə-nē) *n.* an extremely harsh or unjust government or authority
	resentful (rĭ-zĕnt′fəl) *adj.* angry due to a feeling of being treated unfairly
	menial (mē′nē-əl) *adj.* fit for a servant

105

Literary Analysis `BIOGRAPHY`

A Have students notice the sources that the author has drawn upon for these quotations—a letter from Peary to his mother and the words of Matthew Henson, perhaps from Henson's own writing or quoted in the writing of someone who knew Henson. Point out the skillful way in which Haskins has made a link between the two unrelated sources. Henson was not thinking of Peary's letter when he said these words, but the biographer sees a common theme in the sources and shows readers the relationship.

Reading Skills and Strategies: ANALYZE

B Ask students to explain why they think Henson was willing to accompany Peary even without pay.

Possible Response: Henson was so excited about the prospect of exploring the Arctic that money did not matter.

`ACTIVE READER`

C **CLARIFY** The main idea appears at the beginning of the paragraph.

Literary Analysis: SETTING

Ask students to list details about the Arctic setting in which Peary and Henson did their exploring.

Possible Responses: expeditions between 1891 and 1908, Greenland, populated by Eskimos, 50 degrees below zero, leads in the ice

---

Robert E. Peary was born in Cresson, Pennsylvania, in 1856 but was raised in Maine, where his mother had returned after his father's death in 1859. After graduating from Bowdoin College, Peary worked as a <u>surveyor</u> for four years and in 1881 joined the navy's corps of civil engineers. One result of his travels for the navy and of his reading was an <u>ardent</u> desire for adventure. "I shall not be satisfied," Peary wrote to his mother, "until my name is known from one end of the earth to the other." This was a goal Matthew Henson could understand. As he later said, "I recognized in [Peary] the qualities that made me willing to engage myself in his service." In November 1887, Henson and Peary set sail for Nicaragua, along with forty-five other engineers and a hundred black Jamaicans.

Peary's job was to study the feasibility[5] of digging a canal across Nicaragua (that canal that would later be dug across the Isthmus of Panama).[6] The survey took until June of 1888, when the surveying party headed back to the United States. Henson knew he had done a good job for Peary, but even as they started north, Peary said nothing to him about

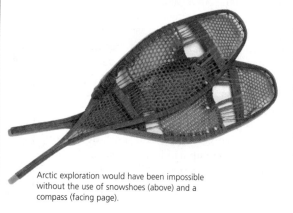

Arctic exploration would have been impossible without the use of snowshoes (above) and a compass (facing page).

continuing on as his servant. It was a great surprise, then, when one day Peary approached Henson with a <u>proposition</u>. He wanted to try to raise money for an expedition to the Arctic, and he wanted Henson to accompany him. Henson quickly accepted, saying he would go whether Peary could pay him or not.

"It was in June, 1891, that I started on my first trip to the Arctic regions, as a member of what was known as the 'North Greenland Expedition,'" Matthew Henson later wrote. So began the first of five expeditions on which Henson would accompany Peary.

`ACTIVE READER`

CLARIFY Does the main idea appear at the beginning, the middle, or the end of this paragraph?

During this first trip to Greenland, on a ship named *Kite*, Peary discovered how valuable Henson was to any expedition. He reported that Henson was able to establish "a friendly relationship with the Eskimos, who believed him to be somehow related to them because of his brown skin. . . ." Peary's expedition was also greatly aided by Henson's expert handling of the Eskimos, dogs, and equipment. Henson also hunted with the Eskimos for meat for the expedition and cooked under the supervision of Josephine Peary, Robert's wife. On the expedition's return to New York, September 24, 1892, Peary wrote, "Henson, my faithful colored boy, a hard worker and <u>apt</u> at anything, . . . showed himself . . . the equal of others in the party."

This first expedition to the Arctic led to several others, but it was with the 1905

---

5. **feasibility** (fē′zə-bĭl′ĭ-tē): possibility of being completed successfully.
6. **Isthmus** (ĭs′məs) **of Panama:** a narrow strip of land connecting the North and South American continents.

WORDS TO KNOW	
surveyor (sər-vā′ər) *n.* a person who determines land boundaries by measuring angles and distances
ardent (är′dnt) *adj.* full of enthusiasm or devotion
proposition (prŏp′ə-zĭsh′ən) *n.* a plan offered for acceptance
apt (ăpt) *adj.* quick to learn or understand

106

Instruction Tell students that comparing ideas in the texts they read will help them better understand the ideas. After students read about Robert Peary in the first paragraph on page 106, have them compare the information with what they learned about Matthew Henson on pages 102 and 104. Discuss with students some of the similarities and differences between Henson and Peary in terms of family life, education, and dreams. (*Both men lost father early on; Henson's family was poor; Peary's family was not poor. Henson had only a sixth-grade*

education; Peary graduated college. Both men dreamed about lives of adventure.) Next, draw a Venn diagram on the board to compare Henson and Peary. Ask a volunteer to enter one item for each of the three sections.

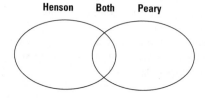

Henson   Both   Peary

Practice Have students work in pairs to copy the diagram from the board and fill it in with details about Henson and Peary.

Possible Responses: Henson: grew up poor, worked as a cabin boy on a ship, had very little education, worked mainly menial jobs. Peary: was not poor, attended college, joined the navy, worked as a surveyor and naval civil engineer. Both: lost their fathers, loved to read, had experience at sea, wanted a life of adventure.

 Use **Unit One Resource Book**, p. 50, for additional support.

expedition that Peary first tried to find that mystical point, the North Pole, the sole goal of the 1908 expedition.

On July 6, 1908, the *Roosevelt* sailed from New York City. Aboard it were the supplies and men for an expedition to reach the North Pole. Accompanying Peary were Captain Robert Bartlett and Ross Marvin, who had been with Peary on earlier expeditions; George Borup, a young graduate from Yale and the youngest member of the group; Donald MacMillan, a teacher; and a doctor, J. W. Goodsell. And, of course, Matthew Henson. In Greenland the group was joined by forty-one Eskimos and 246 dogs, plus the supplies. "The ship," Henson wrote, "is now in a most perfect state of dirtiness." On September 5, the *Roosevelt* arrived at Cape Sheridan, and the group began preparing for their journey, moving supplies north to Cape Columbia by dog sled to establish a base camp. Peary named the camp Crane City in honor of Zenas Crane, who had contributed $10,000 to the expedition.

The plan was to have two men, Bartlett and Borup, go ahead of the rest of the group to cut a trail stretching from the base camp to the North Pole. On February 28, the two men set out, and on March 1, the remainder of the expedition started north, following the trail Bartlett and Borup had cut the day before. At first, trouble seemed to plague them. On the first day, three of the sledges[7] broke, Henson's among them. Fortunately, Henson was able to repair them, despite the fact that it was nearly 50 degrees below zero.

As the days passed, further trouble came the way of the expedition. Several times they encountered leads—open channels of water— and were forced to wait until the ice closed over before proceeding. On March 14, Peary decided to send Donald MacMillan and Dr. Goodsell back to the base camp.

"IT WAS IN JUNE, 1891, THAT I STARTED ON MY FIRST TRIP TO THE ARCTIC REGIONS, AS A MEMBER OF WHAT WAS KNOWN AS THE 'NORTH GREENLAND EXPEDITION.'"

MacMillan could hardly walk, because he had frozen a heel when his foot had slipped into one of the leads. Dr. Goodsell was exhausted. As the expedition went on, more men were sent back due to exhaustion and frostbite. George Borup was sent back on March 20, and, on the 26th, so was Ross Marvin.

Although the expedition had encountered problems with subzero temperatures, with open water, and in handling the dogs, they had had no real injuries. On Ross Marvin's return trip to the base camp, however, he met with tragedy. On his journey, Marvin was accompanied by two Eskimos. He told them that he would go ahead to scout the trail. About an hour later, the Eskimos came upon a hole in the ice; floating in it was Marvin's coat. Marvin had gone through thin ice and, unable to save himself, had drowned or frozen. The Peary expedition had suffered its first—and fortunately its last—fatality.

---

7. **sledges:** sleds pulled by dogs.

Take this opportunity to discuss questions or comments students have at this point. Have them add these to their notebooks with answers.

Reading Skills and Strategies:
ANALYZE

A Ask students to explain why Peary put part of an American flag and two letters in the jar that he left at the pole.

Possible Responses: Peary wanted to record the expedition's discovery; he wanted the world to know that his expedition had made it to the pole first; he wanted to claim any land at the pole for the United States.

Literary Analysis:
PRIMARY AND SECONDARY SOURCES

Primary sources, such as diaries and letters, convey first-hand knowledge of an event or a period. Secondary sources, such as biographies and textbooks, are removed from the events they describe. Point out the italicized passages in the text. Ask students to identify them as either primary or secondary sources.

Answer: primary sources

Ask students why they think Haskins and other writers might include quotations from primary sources in their work.

Possible Responses: Primary sources give readers a taste of the historical period; they bring characters to life because readers can "hear" their voices; they support the writer's own statements and conclusions.

Reading Skills and Strategies:
PREDICT

Ask students to predict what will happen once Peary's proofs about reaching the North Pole are validated.

By April 1, Peary had sent back all of the original expedition except for four Eskimos and Matthew Henson. When Bartlett, the last man to be sent back, asked Peary why he didn't also send Henson, Peary replied, "I can't get along without him." The remnant of the original group pushed on.

We had been travelling eighteen to twenty hours out of every twenty-four. Man, that was killing work! Forced marches all the time. From all our other expeditions we had found out that we couldn't carry food for more than fifty days, fifty-five at a pinch. . . .

We used to travel by night and sleep in the warmest part of the day. I was ahead most of the time with two of the Eskimos.

So Matthew Henson described the grueling journey. Finally, on the morning of April 6, Peary called a halt. Henson wrote: "I was driving ahead and was swinging around to the right. . . . The Commander, who was about 50 feet behind me, called to me and said we would go into camp. . . ." In fact, both Henson and Peary felt they might have reached the Pole already. That day, Peary took readings with a sextant[8] and determined that they were within three miles of the Pole. Later he sledged ten miles north and found he was traveling south; to return to camp, Peary would have to return north and then head south in another direction—something that could only happen at the North Pole. To be absolutely sure, the next day Peary again took readings from solar observations. It was the North Pole, he was sure.

On that day Robert Peary had Matthew Henson plant the American flag at the North Pole. Peary then cut a piece from the flag and placed it and two letters in a glass jar that he left at the Pole. The letters read:

90 N. Lat., North Pole
April 6, 1909

Arrived here today, 27 marches from C. Columbia.

I have with me 5 men, Matthew Henson, colored, Ootah, Egingwah, Seegloo, and Ooqueah, Eskimos; 5 sledges and 38 dogs. My ship, the S.S. Roosevelt, is in winter quarters at Cape Sheridan, 90 miles east of Columbia.

The expedition under my command which has succeeded in reaching the Pole is under the auspices of the Peary Arctic Club of New York City, and has been fitted out and sent north by members and friends of the Club for the purpose of securing this geographical prize, if possible, for the honor and prestige of the United States of America.

The officers of the Club are Thomas H. Hubbard of New York, President; Zenas Crane, of Mass., Vice-president; Herbert L. Bridgman, of New York, Secretary and Treasurer.

I start back for Cape Columbia tomorrow.
Robert E. Peary
United States Navy

90 N. Lat., North Pole
April 6, 1909

I have today hoisted the national ensign of the United States of America at this place, which my observations indicate to be the North Polar axis of the earth, and have formally taken possession of the entire region, and adjacent, for and in the name of the President of the United States of America.

---

8. **sextant:** an instrument used to measure the positions of heavenly bodies.

Robert Peary (second from right) and Henson (far right) on board ship with other members of an expedition, 1909.

I leave this record and United States flag in possession.

Robert E. Peary
United States Navy

Having accomplished their goal, the small group set out on the return journey. It was, Matthew Henson wrote, "17 days of haste, toil, and misery. . . . We crossed lead after lead, sometimes like a bareback rider in the circus, balancing on cake after cake of ice." Finally they reached the *Roosevelt*, where they could rest and eat well at last. The Pole had been conquered!

During the return trip to New York City, Henson became increasingly puzzled by Peary's behavior. "Not once in [three weeks]," Henson wrote, "did he speak a word to me. Then he . . .

ordered me to get to work. Not a word about the North Pole or anything connected with it." Even when the *Roosevelt* docked in New York in September of 1909, Peary remained withdrawn and silent, saying little to the press and quickly withdrawing to his home in Maine.

The ostensible[9] reason for his silence was that when the group returned to New York, they learned that Dr. Frederick A. Cook was claiming that *he* had gone to the North Pole—and done so before Peary reached it. Peary told his friends that he wished to wait for his own proofs to be validated by the scientific societies before he spoke. He felt sure that Cook would not be able to present the kinds of evidence that he could present, and so it proved.

---

9. **ostensible** (ŏ-stĕn′sə-bəl): claimed, but not necessarily true.

WORDS TO KNOW   **validate** (văl′ĭ-dāt′) *v.* to show to be correct

109

Active Reading | IDENTIFYING MAIN IDEA AND DETAILS

A Ask students to state the main idea of this paragraph in their own words. Then have them list supporting details.

Possible Response: Main Idea: Henson was not recognized for his contribution for many years. Details: He worked in a variety of unrelated jobs. His friends tried to get his work recognized. In 1937 he was invited to join the Explorers Club. In 1944 he received a medal from Congress.

Active Reading: AUTHOR'S PURPOSE

Ask students what the author's purpose for writing this biography was.

Possible Responses: to describe Henson's contributions; to right the wrong done to Henson when his contributions were ignored; to make sure that Henson is not forgotten

RELATED READING

Poet Walt Whitman (1819–1892) once said, "The United States themselves are essentially the greatest poem." He loved the vastness and variety of his country and its people. Whitman published his first and most famous collection of poems, *Leaves of Grass,* in 1855. During the Civil War he volunteered in an army hospital. His poems "When Lilacs Last in the Dooryard Bloom'd" and "O Captain! My Captain!" deal with the death of Lincoln.

Ask students to describe in their own words the feelings expressed in "Into Lucid Air." Would Matthew Henson have understood these feelings?

Possible Response: The poem expresses a love of wide-open spaces. Henson would have understood this love because he himself had a strong desire to explore the world around him.

On December 15, Peary was declared the first to reach the North Pole; Cook could not present adequate evidence that he had made the discovery. Peary and Bartlett were awarded gold medals by the National Geographic Society; Henson was not. Because Henson was black, his contributions to the expedition were not recognized for many years.

A After 1909, Henson worked in a variety of jobs. For a while, he was a parking-garage attendant in Brooklyn, and at the age of forty-six, he became a clerk in the U.S. customshouse in Lower Manhattan. In the meantime, friends tried again and again to have his contributions to the expedition recognized. At last, in 1937, nearly thirty years after the expedition, he was invited to join the Explorers Club in New York, and in 1944, Congress authorized a medal for all of the men on the expedition, including Matthew Henson.

After his death in New York City on March 9, 1955, another lasting tribute was made to Henson's endeavors. In 1961, his home state of Maryland placed a bronze tablet in memory of him in the state house. It reads, in part:

MATTHEW ALEXANDER HENSON

Co-discoverer of the North Pole
with Admiral Robert Edwin Peary
April 6, 1909

Son of Maryland, exemplification of courage, fortitude, and patriotism, whose valiant deeds of noble devotion under the command of Admiral Robert Edwin Peary, in pioneer Arctic exploration and discovery, established everlasting prestige and glory for his state and country ❖

RELATED READING

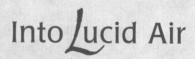

Into Lucid Air

by Walt Whitman

I inhale great draughts of space,
The east and the west are mine, and the north
and the south are mine.

---

lucid (loó-sĭd): clear and easy to see through.
draughts (drăfts): big gulps or breaths; also gusty air currents.

EXPLICIT INSTRUCTION | Main Idea and Supporting Details

Instruction Remind students that the main idea of a paragraph may be either stated or implied. Have them explain how to determine the main idea of a paragraph if the main idea is not stated. (*Figure out what main idea the writer is suggesting. Decide what main idea connects the sentences of the paragraph.*) Next, have students reread the second paragraph on page 110 ("After 1909. . . "). Ask students if there seems to be a stated main idea. (*no*) Discuss with students what most of the sentences in this paragraph are about. (*Henson's life after his journey to the North Pole*)

Practice Use the Active Reading: Identifying Main Idea and Details note in the green side column to give students practice. Have students work in pairs to complete the activity.

Possible Response: See side column.

 Use **Unit One Resource Book,** p. 48, for more practice.

Connect to the Literature

1. **What Do You Think?**
In reading about Matthew Henson's life, what impressed you the most?

Comprehension Check
• Why did Henson leave his job at the restaurant?
• What was Henson's first job with Peary?
• Why wasn't Henson honored for his contributions to the North Pole expedition?

Think Critically

2. What words best describe Matthew Henson?

3. **ACTIVE READING IDENTIFYING MAIN IDEA AND DETAILS**
Look at the **main ideas** and supporting **details** you noted in your **READER'S NOTEBOOK.** How do the details support each main idea?

4. How would you describe the relationship between Peary and Henson?

Think About:
• what traits, or qualities, they had in common
• their years of taking risks together
• any descriptions of each other in their writings

5. If Robert Peary had asked Matthew Henson to accompany him on another expedition after 1909, do you think Henson would have? Why or why not?

Extend Interpretations

6. **COMPARING TEXTS** Compare the courage of Matthew Henson with the courage of the main character in "Nadia the Willful" on page 67. How are they similar and different?

7. **Connect to Life** How might Matthew Henson be a role model for people today? Explain your answer.

Literary Analysis

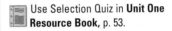 A **biography** is the story of a person's life, written by another person, called the biographer. A biographer's purpose is to accurately portray the life of his or her subject in a way that is also entertaining to read. The biographer takes information about the subject from many sources, including interviews, diaries, and letters. Then he or she combines this information with descriptive words and phrases, as Haskins did in this example:

His parents were poor, free tenant farmers who barely eked a living from the sandy soil.

A biography is usually written in the **third-person point of view,** using pronouns such as *she, he, her,* and *him.*

Activity Choose three paragraphs from the selection that describe part of Henson's life you found interesting. Then make a list of descriptive words and phrases that Haskins used to turn basic facts into a lively and interesting story.

"spun tales"
"wide-eyed"

Connect to the Literature

1. **What Do You Think?**
Possible Response: Henson risked his life to go where no one had gone before.

Comprehension Check
• He wanted to become a sailor and left to find work on a ship.
• He was Peary's personal servant during a trip to Nicaragua.
• He was not honored because of his race.

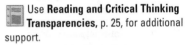 Use Selection Quiz in **Unit One Resource Book,** p. 53.

Think Critically

2. **Possible Responses:** brave, fearless, capable, curious, adventurous

3. Responses will vary, but details given should support the main ideas.

Use **Reading and Critical Thinking Transparencies,** p. 25, for additional support.

4. **Possible Responses:** Henson and Peary had similar values and goals; because of this they respected each other. Peary's behavior after they reached the North Pole was insulting to Henson. The two could never be close because Henson was Peary's employee.

5. **Possible Responses:** Yes, because Henson wanted to go on expeditions for the adventure. No, since Henson was insulted by Peary, he would not risk his life again.

Literary Analysis

Biography Responses will vary, but should include adjectives, adverbs, and vivid verbs.

Use **Literary Analysis Transparencies,** p. 10, for additional support.

Extend Interpretations

6. **Comparing Texts** Both characters took risks to accomplish goals that were important to them. Henson risked his life to explore the harsh Arctic environment, and Nadia risked her relationship with her father in order to keep her brother's memory alive. Henson's courage was mainly physical in nature, while Nadia's was the courage of her moral convictions.

7. **Connect to Life** Henson could be a good role model because, despite many obstacles, he accomplished something no one else had done before. He was brave and had a sense of adventure.

Writing

Henson Autobiography To get students started, suggest they skim the story to find the sections that were most interesting to them. Students should choose passages from these sections.

Speaking & Listening

Acceptance Speech Students' speeches should reflect the events in the biography as well as Henson's character and personality. To get students started, suggest that they locate an acceptance speech in the library to use as a model.

 Use the **Speaking and Listening Book,** p. 8, for additional support.

Research & Technology

Social Studies To extend this activity, have students use the results of their research to create a web site about the Inuit. Their site can include links to other, related sites that they discovered during their research.

 Use **Writing Transparencies,** pp. 49–52, for additional support.

Vocabulary
EXERCISE

1. deprivation
2. resentful
3. surveyor
4. validate
5. menial
6. tyranny
7. ardent
8. proposition
9. apt
10. stamina

Writing

Henson Autobiography Imagine that you are Matthew Henson and that you are writing the story of your own life. Choose two paragraphs from "Matthew Henson at the Top of the World" that tell about Henson's life. Rewrite these paragraphs in the first-person point of view, replacing third-person pronouns such as *he* and *his* with first-person pronouns such as *I* and *my.* Place your writing in your **Working Portfolio.**

Speaking & Listening

Acceptance Speech In 1937, Matthew Henson was invited to join the Explorers Club in New York. Write a short acceptance speech that Henson might have given to that group. Include the thoughts and feelings he might have had. Practice reading the speech aloud several times. Make sure your voice is loud enough and your pacing is slow enough. When you are ready, present your speech to the class.

Speaking and Listening Handbook
See p. R96: Organization and Delivery.

Research & Technology

SOCIAL STUDIES Prepare a classroom display on the history and the current lifestyle of the Inuit. You can find information in magazines, nonfiction books, or on the Internet. Write brief descriptions of Inuit life today and of the history of the Inuit. Include visual aids such as photos and images of Inuit art.

Research and Technology Handbook
See p. R106: Getting Information Electronically.

INTERNET Research Starter
www.mcdougallittell.com

Vocabulary

EXERCISE: SYNONYMS On a sheet of paper, write the Word to Know that can best replace the boldfaced word in each sentence.

1. For sailors in the 1800s, life at sea meant hard work and **shortages.**
2. The attention shown to Matthew Henson made some crew members **angry.**
3. Robert Peary worked as a **measurer** of boundaries.
4. After returning from the North Pole, Peary had to wait for scientific societies to **confirm** his discoveries.
5. After Henson's adventures, he found only **undesirable** jobs available.
6. Some of the crew feared the **cruelty** of their demanding captain.
7. Both Peary and Henson felt an **enthusiastic** desire for adventure.
8. Peary had a **plan** for an expedition to the Arctic.
9. Peary described Henson as a hard worker who was **quick-witted.**
10. The Inuit admired Henson's **endurance** in dealing with the Arctic weather.

Vocabulary Handbook
See p. R20: Context Clues.

WORDS TO KNOW	apt ardent	deprivation menial	proposition resentful	stamina surveyor	tyranny validate

Grammar in Context: Compound Subjects and Compound Verbs

Using a **compound subject** or a **compound verb** can help a writer say more in fewer words. Instead of writing two separate sentences—one about Henson and one about Peary—Jim Haskins often combines the two subjects into one.

> In November 1887, Henson and Peary set sail for Nicaragua.

A **compound subject** has two or more **subjects**. A **compound verb** has two or more **main verbs**, as shown below in green.

> Henson drove ahead and swung around to the right.

Usage Tip: The word *and, or,* or *but* is often used in a sentence to join compound elements, such as two subjects or two verbs.

WRITING EXERCISE Combine each pair of sentences by writing one complete sentence that has either a compound subject or a compound verb.

Example: *Original* Bartlett went ahead of the rest of the group. Borup went ahead of the rest of the group too.

Rewritten <u>Bartlett and Borup</u> went ahead of the rest of the group.

1. On February 28, the two men set out. They cut the trail for the others.
2. Donald MacMillan injured his foot. He returned to base camp.
3. Subzero temperatures caused problems. The dogs caused problems too.

Grammar Handbook
See p. R68: Making Subjects and Verbs Agree.

Jim Haskins
born 1941

"It has always seemed to me that the truth is not just 'stranger than fiction,' but also more interesting."

True Tales Important African-American figures in history, politics, entertainment, and sports have been the subjects of Jim Haskins's books. All of his works are nonfiction because Haskins prefers true stories to made-up ones. He has said, "It seems to me that the more you know about the real world, the better off you are."

Writing with a Mission Although Haskins learned to read early in his childhood, the public library in his Alabama hometown did not welcome black children. He stayed home and learned to rely on his family's encyclopedia. Explaining why African Americans have usually been his subjects, he says, "I want children today, black and white, to be able to find books about black people and black history in case they want to read them." Haskins has written more than 100 books, which have received a number of citations and awards, including the Coretta Scott King Award.

AUTHOR ACTIVITY
Explorers Galore Read another short biography of an explorer in Jim Haskins's book *Against All Opposition: Black Explorers in America.* Compare traits of the main character with those of Matthew Henson. Create a poster telling about his or her most courageous actions.

MATTHEW HENSON AT THE TOP OF THE WORLD **113**

Grammar in Context
WRITING EXERCISE
Possible Responses:
1. On February 28, the two men set out and cut the trail for the others.
2. Donald MacMillan injured his foot and returned to base camp.
3. Subzero temperatures and the dogs caused problems.

Jim Haskins

In addition to being a respected writer of children's literature, Jim Haskins has written books for adults, including a number of biographies of famous African-American performers, such as Nat King Cole, Richard Pryor, and Scott Joplin. Haskins's book, *The Cotton Club,* was the inspiration for Francis Ford Coppola's 1984 film of the same name.

Author Activity

Explorers Galore Allow time for students to research and prepare their posters and to share them with the class.

EXPLICIT INSTRUCTION **Grammar in Context**

AGREEMENT WITH A COMPOUND SUBJECT
Instruction Often two related sentences can be combined into one sentence with a compound subject. Compound subjects joined with the conjunction *and* are plural and take a plural verb. Write the following example on the board and point out to students how the verb changes in the revised sentence.
AWKWARD: Peary <u>was</u> honored by the National Geographic Society. Bartlett <u>was</u> also honored by the National Geographic Society.
REVISED: Peary <u>and</u> Bartlett <u>were</u> honored by the National Geographic Society.

Practice Have students combine each set of sentences into one sentence with a compound subject.
1. Donald MacMillan was sent back to the base camp. Dr. Goodsell was sent back to the camp. George Borup was sent back, too.
2. I am interested in learning more about Matthew Henson. Geena is also interested in learning more about him.
3. Was Ootah a member of the first expedition to reach the North Pole? Was Egingwah a member of the expedition? Were Seegloo and Ooqueah members of the expedition?

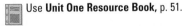 Use **Unit One Resource Book,** p. 51.

 For more instruction in compound subjects, see McDougal Littell's *Language Network,* Chapter 1.

For **systematic instruction** in grammar, see:
- **Grammar, Usage, and Mechanics Book**
- pacing chart on p. 19i.

This selection is included in the **Grade 6 InterActive Reader.**

Standards-Based Objectives

1. understand and appreciate **informative nonfiction**
2. understand and identify **chronological order**
3. identify **structural features** and use features to locate information
4. recognize **fact and opinion**
5. identify **literary devices** (imagery and simile)

Active Reading Summary

In the summer of 1988, fires raged out of control in Yellowstone National Park. Initially, the fires were allowed to burn, but at a certain point, park officials began worrying about the scale of the destruction, and efforts were made to control the fires. Fire fighters could not stop or slow the fires, but were able to save the buildings around Old Faithful. Though it seemed like total devastation to outsiders, the fires only burned in one third of the park, and the new growth that resulted promoted the flourishing of certain birds, animals, and plants.

Thematic Link

The hundreds of fire fighters who worked to save Yellowstone exemplified courage in action by risking their lives as they tried to halt the destruction of the forest.

Summer of Fire

by PATRICIA LAUBER

Connect to Your Life

Fighting Fires What do you know about wilderness fires? In a chart like the one below, record what you already know about wilderness fires, and what you want to learn.

What I Know	What I Want to Learn	What I Learned
1. Wilderness fires can spread quickly		

Build Background

BIOLOGY

In wilderness areas, fires can be started by lightning as well as by humans. Park managers must decide whether to let fires burn or put them out, because some fires are not necessarily harmful. Burned plant material renews nutrients in the soil, and fire can clear away old branches so that sunlight may reach the ground.

Large fires, however, can destroy huge areas of forest and threaten people who live or work nearby. That is what happened in Yellowstone National Park during the very dry summer of 1988. Despite the damage done in the fires, today Yellowstone is recovering well. Some species that had been rare before the fire are now thriving.

WORDS TO KNOW **Vocabulary Preview**

bear	geyser	threaten	veer
canopy	merge	tinder	withering
ember	oxygen		

Focus Your Reading

LITERARY ANALYSIS **INFORMATIVE NONFICTION**

The purpose of **informative nonfiction** is to provide factual information about real people, places, and events. Forms of informative nonfiction include newspaper and magazine articles, history and science books, and encyclopedias.

ACTIVE READING **CHRONOLOGICAL ORDER**

The order in which events happen in time is called **chronological order.** Stories or articles that are written in chronological order move forward in time from one event to another. Signal words, such as *before, after, first,* and *next,* and dates indicate the order of events.

READER'S NOTEBOOK As you read "Summer of Fire," notice that many paragraphs mention dates. Use a chart like the one below to keep track of events. Be sure to include signal words and dates that help show chronological order.

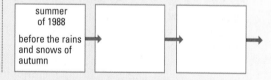

summer of 1988

before the rains and snows of autumn

SUMMER OF FIRE

by
Patricia
Lauber

The summer of 1988 was hot and dry in much of the United States.

115

Reading and Analyzing

Reading Skills and Strategies:
PREVIEW

Ask students to read the title page and headlines and to look at the photographs, captions, and map. Ask what they think the selection is about.

Possible Response: It is about a large forest fire.

Active Reading

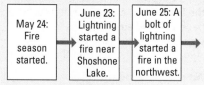

Ask students to begin their charts in their Reader's Notebooks. Their charts should include information such as the following:

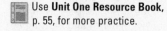

May 24: Fire season started. → June 23: Lightning started a fire near Shoshone Lake. → June 25: A bolt of lightning started a fire in the northwest.

Use **Unit One Resource Book,** p. 55, for more practice.

Literary Analysis

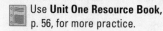

Explain that the author starts by giving an overview, then, on page 117, starts giving details. Ask, "What caused the first fires of the summer?"

Answer: lightning strikes

Use **Unit One Resource Book,** p. 56, for more practice.

Literary Analysis: MAIN IDEA

A Ask students to determine the main idea of this paragraph and how that idea is supported with details.

Possible Response: Main Idea: It was a hot, dry time. Details: The sun blazed, fields baked and crops withered, water dried up, the earth cracked.

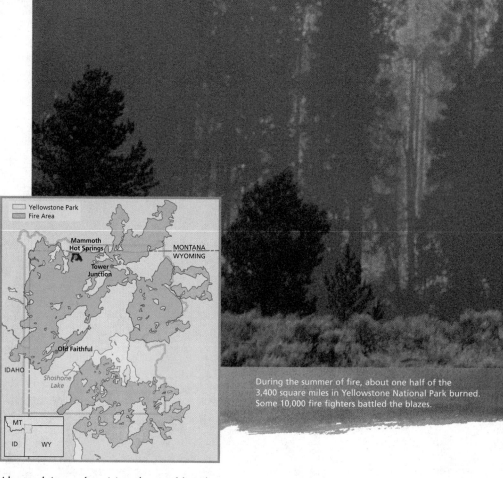

Yellowstone Park
Fire Area

Mammoth Hot Springs

Tower Junction

MONTANA
WYOMING

Old Faithful

IDAHO

Shoshone Lake

MT
ID   WY

During the summer of fire, about one half of the 3,400 square miles in Yellowstone National Park burned. Some 10,000 fire fighters battled the blazes.

A Above plains and prairies, the sun blazed out of an ever blue sky, baking fields and <u>withering</u> crops. Ponds and streams dried up. Rivers shrank. In places the very earth cracked open as underground water supplies dwindled away.

Farther west, forests were <u>tinder</u> dry. Sometimes skies grew dark with storm clouds. Thunder growled and lightning crackled, but little rain fell. Lightning strikes started forest fires that raged across the Rockies and other ranges with the roar of jumbo jets on take-off. Night skies turned red and yellow where flames soared 300 feet into the air. Smoke, carried on the winds, darkened skies as far away as Spokane and Minneapolis–St. Paul. Airline passengers, flying high above the fires, could smell the smoke. Before the rains and snows of autumn came, 2,600,000 acres had burned in the West and Alaska, an area twice the size of Delaware.

WORDS
TO
KNOW

withering (wĭth'ər-ĭng) *adj.* causing to dry out and shrivel up; wilting **wither** *v.*
tinder (tĭn'dər) *n.* a material, such as dry twigs, that is used to start a fire because it burns easily

116

EXPLICIT INSTRUCTION **Previewing Structural Features**

Instruction Explain that before students read an informational article, they can get a general idea of what it's about by previewing it—looking at the features of the article. List the following steps for previewing on the board:
- Read the title and any subtitles.
- Look at pictures, graphs, maps, or tables.
- Read captions and labels.
- Read the first few paragraphs.

Have students find examples of these features in the article. Then ask a volunteer to read aloud the title and the large-type sentence below it. Point out the photographs used in the article and ask volunteers to read aloud the captions.

Practice Have students work in small groups to complete the previewing activities you listed on the board. Encourage groups to take notes on the information provided in the various features. Then have groups write a paragraph that describes what they expect to learn about in this article. Ask groups to share their paragraphs with the class.

Possible Response: We will learn about a big forest fire that burned in the summer of 1988 in Montana, Idaho, and Wyoming. We will learn how the fire affected the forest and how it was put out.

 Use **Unit One Resource Book,** p. 57, for more practice.

Many people
thought you couldn't
set fire to the
forest if you tried.

Violent winds and extreme heat made
fire fighters' work exhausting.

In Yellowstone the fire season started on May 24, when lightning struck a tree in the northeastern part of the park. The fire stayed small. Rain fell later in the day and put it out. That was what usually happened. In Yellowstone, winters are long and cold, summers short and often rainy. Many people thought you couldn't set fire to the forest if you tried.

On June 23 lightning started a fire near Shoshone Lake in the southern part of the park. On June 25 another bolt of lightning started a fire in the northwest. These fires did not go out, and no one tried to put them out. Park policy was to let wildfires burn unless they <u>threatened</u> lives or property. Also, there seemed no reason to worry about the fires. Although winters in the 1980s had been dry, with little snow, summers had been unusually wet. The summer of 1988 was expected to be wet too.

1

WORDS
TO
KNOW   **threaten** (thrĕt'n) v. to be a danger to

117

Differentiating Instruction

Less Proficient Readers
1 Suggest that the first part of the selection concludes here. Student summaries of the passage might mention the earth drying and cracking, the lightning, the smoke being carried far and wide, and the number of acres burned.
Set a Purpose Ask students to read on to learn how and why the fires spread.

English Learners
Check to see that students are familiar with names in the selection and their locations on a map. Some of these places are noted on the map of Yellowstone on page 116. On a map, locate with your students the following areas: Rockies, Spokane, Minneapolis-St. Paul, the West, Alaska, Delaware, Yellowstone, Shoshone Lake, Old Faithful, Targee National Forest, Madison, Mammoth Hot Springs, and Tower Junction. Have students use the maps to estimate the distances referred to in the selection; Spokane is about 500 miles from Yellowstone, and Minneapolis-St. Paul is nearly 1,000 miles away.

Advanced Students
Nonfictional accounts can be written in a very engaging way. Ask students to find in the selection the action verbs the author uses to help make the account exciting (*"thunder growled and lightning crackled," "fires . . . raged," "flames soared," "helicopters and airplanes attacked," "winds whipped," "flames galloped," "boulders exploded," "fires jumped," "embers . . . shot a mile or more ahead," "the fire raced"*). Ask students what other techniques the author uses to create excitement (*comparisons, such as, "forest fires that raged . . . with the roar of jumbo jets taking off," and the feeling of "war" created on page 118 as the firefighters, helicopters, and airplanes "attack"*).

EXPLICIT INSTRUCTION **Chronological Order**

Instruction Ask a volunteer to explain chronological order. (*the order in which events occur*) Remind students that chronological order is a common pattern of organization for an informational article. Tell students to listen for words that tell when something happened as you read aloud this sentence: "Before the rains and snows of autumn came, 2,600,000 [two million, six hundred thousand] acres had burned." Ask students to identify the words. (*before, autumn*) Then explain that dates and keywords, such as *before, after, first, next,* are clues that an article

is written in chronological order. Ask volunteers to identify keywords and dates on page 117. (*May 24, when, later, June 23, June 25*)
Practice Use the Active Reading: Chronological Order note in the green side column to give students practice in understanding chronological order.
Possible Responses: See the side column note for information students might record in their charts.
Use **Unit One Resource Book**, p. 55, for more practice.

SUMMER OF FIRE   **117**

Active Reading
CHRONOLOGICAL ORDER

Ask students to update their charts with facts from these pages. They should include information like the following.

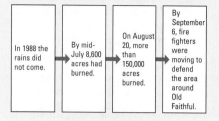

In 1988 the rains did not come.	By mid-July 8,600 acres had burned.	On August 20, more than 150,000 acres burned.	By September 6, fire fighters were moving to defend the area around Old Faithful.

Literary Analysis: SPATIAL ORDER

A Remind students that a place may be described according to its layout, for example, from right to left, from north to south, or from top to bottom. Show a map of the region that includes the places mentioned in this selection. Have students describe the events of the fire in spatial order.

Reading Skills and Strategies: VISUALIZE

B Read aloud from the top of the column to this point and ask students to describe their own mental image of the fire.

Literary Analysis
INFORMATIVE NONFICTION

Ask students to describe what fire fighters did to protect the area around Old Faithful.

Possible Response: Planes dropped chemicals, and fire fighters on the ground wet down buildings.

But in 1988 the rains of summer did not come. The Shoshone and other fires blazed and spread. By mid-July, 8,600 acres had burned. Park officials decided that all fires should be put out, no matter whether they were wildfires or caused by human carelessness.

Fire fighters arrived by the hundreds to attack fires from the ground. Helicopters and airplanes attacked from above. But new fires started in the park. In 1988 Yellowstone had more than 50 lightning strikes, twice the normal number. Fires in neighboring national forests swept into the park. Old fires burned on. And still the rains did not come.

Cold fronts passed through, bringing winds of hurricane force with gusts of 60 to 80 miles an hour. Winds whipped and spread the fires and fed them oxygen, which fires must have to keep burning. Big fires met, merged, and became even bigger fires. In forests flames galloped through the tops, or crowns, of trees, through the canopy. Snags—dead trees that are still standing—burned like Roman candles.[1] Boulders exploded in the heat. Sheets of flame leaped forward. Gigantic clouds of smoke ringed the horizon, looking like thunderheads,[2] only bigger. There were days when the sun was no brighter than a full moon.

Fires jumped rivers, roads, canyons, parking lots. Glowing embers, some the size of a man's fist, shot a mile or more ahead, starting new fires. Flames were roaring through the park at

a rate of four or five miles a day. One fire ran 14 miles in only four hours. On August 20, a day known as Black Saturday, more than 150,000 acres burned inside the park and in neighboring forests. The 2,000 fire fighters could no more put out these fires than they could have stopped a hurricane. But what they

---

1. **Roman candles:** fireworks that shoot out showers of sparks and balls of fire.
2. **thunderheads:** the spreading upper parts of thunderclouds.

There were days when the sun was no brighter than a full moon.

By August, more than 50 individual fires had merged into eight huge ones.
(Right) Fire fighters drenched the historic Old Faithful Inn to protect it from advancing fires.

WORDS TO KNOW

oxygen (ŏk'sĭ-jən) *n.* one of the gases that make up air, needed for nearly all burning
merge (mûrj) *v.* to combine or unite
canopy (kăn'ə-pē) *n.* a rooflike cover; the covering formed by the branches and leaves of trees in a forest
ember (ĕm'bər) *n.* a small glowing bit of burning wood

118

EXPLICIT INSTRUCTION

Imagery and Simile

Instruction Tell students that imagery and figurative language help readers visualize people, places, and events. Review the definitions of imagery and simile. (*Imagery—language that appeals to a reader's five senses. Simile—a comparison of two things that have something in common using the word* like *or* as.) Then list these two sentences on the board: *The fire raced through the forests like a running herd of buffalo. The fire spread quickly.* Ask, "Which sentence uses a simile to describe the fire?"

Discuss what a running herd of buffalo might be like. (*loud, creating clouds of dust, fast, spreading outward*) Also discuss which sentence is more vivid.

Practice Have students work in small groups to find examples of imagery and figurative language in the paragraph on page 118 that begins "Cold fronts passed." Have students create a two-column chart with the headings *Similes* and *Imagery* and use it to record examples. In the imagery column, students

should identify the sense each example appeals to. In the simile column, students should identify the two things being compared in each example.

Possible Responses: Similes: "Snags . . . burned like Roman candles," "Gigantic clouds of smoke ringed the horizon, looking like thunderheads." Imagery: winds whipped, flames galloped, boulders exploded, sheets of flame leaped forward, sun was no brighter than a full moon. These appeal to readers' sense of sight.

could do was defend the park communities— the information centers and the buildings where people slept, ate, and shopped.

By September 6 fire fighters were moving in to defend the area around the park's most famous <u>geyser</u>, Old Faithful. The geyser itself could not be harmed by fire, but the buildings around it could. One of them, the Old Faithful Inn, was the world's largest log building. Now one of the eight major fires in the park was <u>bearing</u> down on it.

Called the North Fork fire, it had started in the Targhee National Forest on July 22, when a careless woodcutter threw away a lighted cigarette. Driven by shifting winds, the fire raced into Yellowstone, turned back into Targhee, neared the town of West Yellowstone, then <u>veered</u> back into the park. There it jumped roads and rivers, snarling its way through the crossroads at Madison on August 15. By the afternoon of September 7 it was approaching Old Faithful. Long before they could see the flames, fire fighters heard the fire's deep rumble and saw a churning wall of dark smoke towering skyward.

Planes dropped chemicals to damp down fires. On the ground weary fire fighters were wetting down buildings.

The fire came on, a mass of red flames whipped by winds gusting up to 50 miles an hour. Sparks and embers were everywhere, flying over the inn, parking lots, and geyser, and setting fire to the woods beyond. At the last moment the wind shifted and the fire turned to the northeast, away from Old Faithful.

Saturday, September 10, began as another bad day. One arm of the North Fork fire was threatening park headquarters at Mammoth

A

B

WORDS
TO
KNOW

geyser (gī′zər) *n.* a natural hot spring that at times spouts water and steam into the air
bear (bâr) *v.* to move forcefully; push
veer (vîr) *v.* to turn aside; swerve

119

Active Reading

CHRONOLOGICAL ORDER

Have students complete the charts in their Reader's Notebooks.

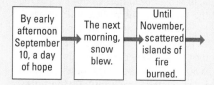

By early afternoon September 10, a day of hope → The next morning, snow blew. → Until November, scattered islands of fire burned. →

Literary Analysis:
SUPPORTING DETAILS

A Ask students to determine the main idea of this paragraph and how that idea is supported with details.

Possible Response: Main Idea: It seemed like the park must lie in ruins, but that was not so. Details: Geysers, steam vents, and hot springs were unharmed, communities were saved, nearly two-thirds of the park was untouched by fire.

Reading Skills and Strategies:
MONITOR

Ask students to monitor their comprehension. If there was any part of the text they did not understand, encourage them to reread it aloud, use reference aids, search for clues, or ask questions.

Even as old forests lay fallen, new plant life was taking root. In some areas, green grass began to sprout just two weeks after the fires.

Hot Springs, and another arm was a quarter of a mile from Tower Junction. The forecast was for winds of up to 60 miles an hour. But the sky was thick with clouds, and the temperature was falling.

By early afternoon, September 10 had turned into a day of hope. Rain was drenching the area around Old Faithful. The next morning snow blew along the streets of West Yellowstone. It sifted through blackened forests and dusted herds of bison and elk. Scattered islands of fire would burn until November blanketed them in snow. But the worst was over.

A At long last the summer of fire had ended. During it, eight major fires and many smaller ones had burned in Yellowstone. To people who had watched the fires on television news, it seemed the park must lie in ruins. But this was not so. The geysers, steam vents, and hot springs were unharmed. Park communities had been saved. Nearly two-thirds of the park had not even been touched by fire.

It was true that many once-green areas were now black and gray. Yet it was also true that they were not ruined. Instead, they were beginning again, starting over, as they had many times in the past. Fire has always been part of the Yellowstone region. Wildfire has shaped the landscape and renewed it. ❖

120 UNIT ONE PART 2: COURAGE IN ACTION

Connect to the Literature

1. What Do You Think?
What did you find most dramatic in this article?

Comprehension Check
- How did the 1988 fires in Yellowstone start?
- Why were fire fighters unable to stop the fires?
- How were the fires finally put out?

Think Critically

2. Why does Lauber say that Yellowstone was not ruined by the fires of 1988?

> **Think About:**
> - what was damaged
> - what was saved
> - what happened after the fires

3. Do you agree or disagree with the position that fire helps wilderness areas? Support your point of view.

4. ACTIVE READING | CHRONOLOGICAL ORDER
With a partner, take turns retelling the events of the selection in your own words. Use the chart you made in your ■READER'S NOTEBOOK to help you.

5. What skills and traits, or qualities, do you think a fire fighter needed in order to control the Yellowstone fires of 1988?

Extend Interpretations

6. The Writer's Style Lauber has said, "I believe that the best science books have a story line: that one thing leads to another . . ." Do you think that "Summer of Fire" has a story line? Explain.

7. Connect to Life In the last column of the chart you made for the Connect to Your Life activity on page 114, record any new information you learned about wilderness fires. What was most surprising to you? Explain.

Literary Analysis

INFORMATIVE NONFICTION

Newspapers and magazine articles, and the writing found in textbooks and encyclopedias, are all types of **informative nonfiction.** The main purpose of informative nonfiction is to give readers factual information about real people, places, and events. In this selection, Patricia Lauber's main purpose is to give readers factual information about the forest fires that burned in Yellowstone National Park in the summer of 1988.

Activity Make a time line like the one below. Go back through the selection and use the time line to record dates, facts, and events.

REVIEW: MAIN IDEA AND DETAILS

The **main idea** of a paragraph is the most important idea. The main idea is often stated in one sentence. The other sentences give **details** that explain or tell more about the main idea.

Connect to the Literature

1. What Do You Think?
Possible Responses: Students might respond to the drama of the fire fighters battling the blazes, the fierce winds that whip flames through the park, or merging fires that set forests ablaze and cause rocks to explode.

Comprehension Check
- Most were started by lightning bolts. One big one was started when a woodcutter threw down a lit cigarette.
- Extremely dry conditions, twice the normal number of lightning strikes, and high winds made the fires impossible to stop.
- Rain and snow in September finally put out the fires in November.

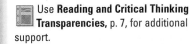 Use Selection Quiz
Unit One Resource Book, p. 60.

Think Critically

2. Although thousands of acres burned, almost two thirds of the park was untouched by fire. The fires did not damage the park's geysers, hot springs, or steam vents. All major park buildings were saved. After the fires, the forests and other areas began to regenerate.

3. Answers will vary. Students should support their opinions. They may agree that fire helps wilderness areas, saying that lightning is a natural force, and that after a forest burns, it regenerates. Or, they may argue that what burns cannot be quickly replaced.

4. Answers will vary.

■ Use **Reading and Critical Thinking Transparencies,** p. 7, for additional support.

5. Possible Response: The fire fighters needed courage, physical strength and stamina, good communication skills, and training in how to fight forest fires.

Literary Analysis

Informative Nonfiction Time lines should include the dates of major events over the course of the fire.

Extend Interpretations

6. The Writer's Style Possible Responses: Students may say that the article has a story line because one event leads to another, like events in a story's plot. As the fires spread, tension mounts as readers wonder how far the fires will burn, how much damage they will do, and how they will be stopped. On the other hand, students may argue that the article does not have characters other than the generic fire fighters.

7. Connect to Life Students should explain why their choices surprised them.

Writing

Causes and Effects Answers will vary, but should include facts from the selection, such as lightning strikes, human carelessness, drought, high winds, and park policy as causes, and widespread burning causing extreme alteration of habitat as effect.

 Use **Writing Transparencies,** pp. 10, 36 and 51, for additional support.

Speaking & Listening

Opinion Statement To help students get started, have them list the effects of letting natural fires burn and then decide how they feel about this policy. Remind them that they need to support their positions with evidence. Students may want to do library research to gather supporting evidence.

 Use **Speaking and Listening Book,** pp. 29 and 30, for additional support.

Research & Technology

Forest Features If there is a forested area near the school or students' homes, students might enjoy studying it, rather than doing research in books or on the Internet. They should bring binoculars and field guides with them if available, and be prepared to make drawings or take photos of the plants and animals they find. They will need to spend time in quiet observation, and should be careful not to disturb the area.

Vocabulary
EXERCISE

1. oxygen
2. ember
3. tinder
4. merge
5. bear
6. withering
7. veer
8. threaten
9. canopy
10. geyser

Writing

Causes and Effects What have you learned about forest fires? Write a paragraph that describes some causes and possible effects of fires.
To prepare for writing, make a chart or web of your thoughts. Place your paragraph in your **Working Portfolio.**

Writing Handbook
See p. R44: Cause and Effect.

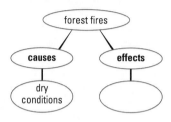

Speaking & Listening

Opinion Statement Based on "Summer of Fire," what is your opinion of the policy "let natural fires burn"? Do you agree or disagree with this policy? With a partner who feels the same way, write up a list of arguments that support your opinion. Be sure to use facts and information from the story as support. Then present your opinion to the class. Start your presentation with a clear statement of your position and then offer your supporting information.

Speaking and Listening Handbook
See p. R100: Persuasive Presentations.

Research & Technology

Forest Features Forests are complicated ecosystems made up of plants and animals of many kinds. Research the ecology of a typical North American forest to find out about the plants and animals that live there. Then create a poster showing the different parts of a forest community. Include a key that identifies each plant and animal. Also include a list of the sources you used to find information.

Research and Technology Handbook
See p. R106: Getting Information Electronically.

INTERNET Research Starter
www.mcdougallittell.com

Vocabulary

EXERCISE: CONTEXT CLUES On a sheet of paper, write the Word to Know that best completes each sentence.

1. To burn, a fire needs both fuel and _____ from the air.
2. A glowing _____ can fly out of one fire and start another one nearby.
3. Small, dry branches burn quickly and are often used as _____ to get a fire started.
4. A group of small fires can _____ to become a large fire.
5. Forced onward by the wind, the fire seemed to _____ down on the building.
6. During one hot, dry summer, the sun shone with a _____ heat.
7. A change in the wind can cause a fire to _____ in a different direction.
8. Wildfires can _____ homes or other valuable property.
9. The branches of the treetops create a _____ over the forest floor.
10. A _____ like Old Faithful shoots out hot water and steam from deep inside the earth.

Vocabulary Handbook
See p. R20: Context Clues.

WORDS TO KNOW	bear canopy	ember geyser	merge oxygen	threaten tinder	veer withering

Grammar in Context: Active Voice and Passive Voice

In **active-voice** sentences, the subject performs the action. In **passive-voice** sentences, the subject does not perform the action. Instead, the subject is acted upon by outside forces.

> **The smoke** blackened **their faces.** (active voice)
> **Their faces** were blackened by **the smoke.** (passive voice)

Notice the directness of the first sentence. In the second sentence the subject is merely acted upon by outside forces.

Apply to Your Writing: To strengthen your writing, rewrite passive-voice sentences in the active voice. Note the difference between these two sentences:

First draft The wildfires were put out.

Revision Exhausted fire fighters put out the wildfires.

WRITING EXERCISE Rewrite each sentence in the active voice.

Example: *Original* Millions of acres were burned by the fire.

Rewritten The fire raged over millions of acres.

1. Night skies were made red and yellow by the flames.
2. Forest fires are often caused by human carelessness.
3. The geyser could not be harmed by fire.

Connect to the Literature Reread page 118. Locate three powerful active-voice sentences. Notice how effectively the active voice communicates action. Then write five sentences about something dramatic or intense that happened to you. Use the active voice in your sentences.

Grammar Handbook
See p. R62: Parts of Speech.

Patricia Lauber
born 1924

"Some of my books are fiction, some are nonfiction, but all are based on what I've seen around me."

A Natural Writer Patricia Lauber has said, "I don't think that I 'became' a writer; I think I was born wanting to write." After graduating from Wellesley College, she became a writer and editor. Later she became a consultant to the science resource center of the Smithsonian Institution. Lauber has written more than 70 nonfiction books on topics ranging from the Ice Age to the Congo.

Endless Honors Lauber has won many awards for her writing. In 1983, she received the *Washington Post*/Children's Book Guild Award for her overall contribution to children's nonfiction literature. In 1987 she won a Newbery Honor Award for *Volcano: The Eruption and Healing of Mount St. Helens.*

AUTHOR ACTIVITY
Never a Dull Moment Lauber is often praised for her ability to make factual information dramatic and exciting. Read or look over some other nonfiction works by Patricia Lauber. How does she make science and history interesting? Share your thoughts with your classmates.

Grammar in Context
WRITING EXERCISE
Possible Responses

1. The flames turned the night skies red and yellow.
2. Human carelessness often causes fires.
3. Fire could not harm the geyser.

Connect to the Literature
Answers will vary, but each of the five sentences should be written in the active voice.

Patricia Lauber

An author best known for her award-winning nonfiction, Patricia Lauber has also written fiction, including a series of books about a dog named Clarence, who likes to watch television, catch burglars, and drink cod-liver oil. The character of Clarence is based on her own dog. The first book of the series is *Clarence, the TV Dog.*

Author Activity

Never a Dull Moment Students might point out that Lauber chooses interesting topics, includes real-life details, and writes as if she were telling a story.

EXPLICIT INSTRUCTION Grammar in Context

ACTIVE VOICE AND PASSIVE VOICE
Instruction Remind students that sentences can be in either the active or passive voice. Tell students that though the active voice is often preferable because it conveys action more directly and immediately, the passive voice is useful in the following cases:
• to avoid placing blame
  Passive: A mistake was made.
  Active: You made a mistake.
• to focus attention on the action rather than on the performer of the action

Passive: The fires were extinguished by the end of November.
Active: Snow extinguished the fires by the end of November.
• when the performer of the action is unknown
  Passive: The fire was started on July 22.
  Active: Someone started the fire on July 22.
Practice Have students rewrite each of the following sentences in the active voice.

1. The flames were extinguished by fire fighters.

2. Great damage was inflicted by the fires.
3. Meadows were seen by rangers where there were once forests.
4. The story was written in an exciting way.

 Use **Unit One Resource Book,** p. 58.

> For **systematic instruction** in grammar, see:
> • **Grammar, Usage, and Mechanics Book**
> • pacing chart on p. 19i.

This selection is included in the **Grade 6 InterActive Reader.**

Standards-Based Objectives

1. understand and appreciate a **short story**
2. understand and identify **conflict** in a short story
3. **predicting** the action as the author describes it
4. analyze **influence of setting** on plot

Summary

Mako grew up on the island of Bora Bora listening to his grandfather's stories about the shark Tupa—the "ghost of the lagoon." One of the most haunting stories tells how Tupa killed Mako's father. Mako's grandfather tells him that the king is offering a reward for Tupa's capture. Both for revenge and for the reward, Mako decides to kill Tupa. One day while out gathering bananas, Mako and his dog Afa encounter the ghost. When Afa is threatened, Mako fights for him, and in the process, kills Tupa.

Thematic Link

Courage comes from deep inside us, and often is found when one least expects it. Mako shows a great deal of courage in this story as he fights for the life of his beloved dog, Afa. Through this event, he discovers the tremendous bravery and courage he never knew he had.

English Conventions Practice

Daily Language SkillBuilder

Have students **proofread** the display sentences on page 19k and write them correctly. The sentences also appear on Transparency 4 of **Language Transparencies.**

Preteaching Vocabulary

If you would like to preteach the WORDS TO KNOW for this selection, use the Explicit Instruction, page 125.

Ghost of the Lagoon

by ARMSTRONG SPERRY

Connect to Your Life

Brave Deeds Think of someone you know or have read about who has been courageous. What risks did he or she take? What dreams or ideas made this person take these risks?

Build Background

GEOGRAPHY

This story of danger and courage is set on Bora Bora, a small volcanic island in the southern Pacific Ocean. Bora Bora is surrounded by coral reefs—underwater ridges made of a stony material. Coral reefs provide a home and food for many kinds of ocean life, including sharks. Sharks play an important role, eating small animals and plants, and leaving behind food scraps that nourish other reef life.

WORDS TO KNOW Vocabulary Preview

expedition	lagoon	reef
harpoon	phosphorus	

Focus Your Reading

LITERARY ANALYSIS **CONFLICT**

Almost every story centers on an important **conflict,** or struggle, that the main character faces. A struggle may be between a character and an outside force, such as a dangerous animal, a storm, or another character. Sometimes a struggle may go on inside a character's mind. For example, a character may have to make a difficult decision. As you read this story, look for examples of conflicts.

ACTIVE READING **PREDICTING**

When you try to figure out what will happen next in a story, you are **predicting.** For example, if you are reading a story about a contest between two friends, you might try to guess who will win. To make a prediction in a story, combine facts from the story with what you know from experience. After you make a prediction, you can then read on to find out if it is correct.

READER'S NOTEBOOK As you read "Ghost of the Lagoon," pause to jot down predictions about what will happen next and about how the story will end.

LESSON RESOURCES

UNIT ONE RESOURCE BOOK, pp. 61–67

ASSESSMENT
Formal Assessment, pp. 19–20
Test Generator

SKILLS TRANSPARENCIES AND COPYMASTERS
Literary Analysis
• Plot, TR 5 (p. 128)
• Conflict, TR 8 (p. 132)

Reading and Critical Thinking
• Predicting, TR 7 (pp. 128, 132)
Language
• Daily Language SkillBuilder, TR 4 (p. 124)
• Subject-Verb Agreement, TR 37 (p. 134)
• Learning and Remembering New Words, TR 65 (p. 125)
Writing
• Short Story, TR 34 (p. 133)

INTEGRATED TECHNOLOGY
Audio Library
Internet: Research Starter

Visit our Web site:
www.mcdougallittell.com

For **systematic instruction** in language skills, see:
• **Vocabulary and Spelling Book**
• **Grammar, Usage, and Mechanics Book**
• pacing chart on p. 19i.

Ghost
of the
Lagoon

by Armstrong Sperry

The island of Bora Bora,
where Mako lived, is far away
in the South Pacific. It is not a
large island—you can paddle
around it in a single day—but
the main body of it rises
straight out of the sea, very
high into the air, like a castle.
Waterfalls trail down the faces
of the cliffs. As you look
upward, you see wild goats
leaping from crag to crag.

© Cheryl Cooper, 1995.

125

Literary Analysis `CONFLICT`

Remind students that a conflict is a problem or struggle. What conflict are the people of Bora Bora facing?

Possible Response: The people face the terror of Tupa. He destroys their fishing nets and takes their gifts of food.

Often in short stories, the main character faces a personal conflict. It may be an external or an internal conflict. Ask what conflict(s) they think Mako will face in this story.

Possible Responses: Mako may have to fight Tupa. He may have to overcome his fear of Tupa.

 Use **Unit One Resource Book,** p. 63, for more practice.

Active Reading `PREDICTING`

A Tupa is referred to as both a "ghost" and a "monster." Have students predict what they think Tupa really is.

Possible Responses: a ghost, a sea creature, a shark or whale

Ask students to predict what Mako will do. Remind them to use clues from the story.

Possible Response: Mako will find the ghost and capture it so he can collect the reward offered by the king.

 Use **Unit One Resource Book,** p. 62, for more practice.

Reading Skills and Strategies: QUESTION

Ask students to think about the legends Mako has heard about Tupa. Have students raise a list of questions that Mako might have about Tupa.

Possible Responses: What is Tupa? Why is he killing people? Where does he live? Does he really exist? Can he really be captured if he is a ghost?

Mako had been born on the very edge of the sea, and most of his waking hours were spent in the waters of the lagoon, which was nearly enclosed by the two outstretched arms of the island. He was very clever with his hands; he had made a harpoon that was as straight as an arrow and tipped with five pointed iron spears. He had made a canoe, hollowing it out of a tree. It wasn't a very big canoe—only a little longer than his own height. It had an outrigger, a sort of balancing pole, fastened to one side to keep the boat from tipping over. The canoe was just large enough to hold Mako and his little dog, Afa. They were great companions, these two.

One evening Mako lay stretched at full length on the pandanus mats, listening to Grandfather's voice. Overhead, stars shone in the dark sky. From far off came the thunder of the surf on the reef.

The old man was speaking of Tupa, the ghost of the lagoon. Ever since the boy could remember, he had heard tales of this terrible **A** monster. Frightened fishermen, returning from the reef at midnight, spoke of the ghost. Over the evening fires, old men told endless tales about the monster.

Tupa seemed to think the lagoon of Bora Bora belonged to him. The natives left presents of food for him out on the reef: a dead goat, a chicken, or a pig. The presents always disappeared mysteriously, but everyone felt sure that it was Tupa who carried them away. Still, in spite of all this food, the nets of the fishermen were torn during the night, the fish stolen. What an appetite Tupa seemed to have!

Not many people had ever seen the ghost of the lagoon. Grandfather was one of the few who had.

"What does he really look like, Grandfather?" the boy asked, for the hundredth time.

The old man shook his head solemnly. The light from the cook fire glistened on his white hair. "Tupa lives in the great caves of the reef. He is longer than this house. There is a sail on his back, not large but terrible to see, for it burns with a white fire. Once, when I was fishing beyond the reef at night, I saw him come up right under another canoe—"

"What happened then?" Mako asked. He half rose on one elbow. This was a story he had not heard before.

The old man's voice dropped to a whisper. "Tupa dragged the canoe right under the water—and the water boiled with white flame. The three fishermen in it were never seen again. Fine swimmers they were, too."

Grandfather shook his head. "It is bad fortune even to speak of Tupa. There is evil in his very name."

"But King Opu Nui has offered a reward for his capture," the boy pointed out.

"Thirty acres of fine coconut land, and a sailing canoe as well," said the old man. "But who ever heard of laying hands on a ghost?"

Mako's eyes glistened. "Thirty acres of land and a sailing canoe. How I should love to win that reward!"

Grandfather nodded, but Mako's mother scolded her son for such foolish talk. "Be quiet now, son, and go to sleep. Grandfather has

> "It is bad fortune even to speak of Tupa."

WORDS
TO
KNOW

lagoon (lə-gōōn′) *n.* a shallow body of water separated from a sea by sandbars or coral reefs

harpoon (här-pōōn′) *n.* a spearlike weapon used to hunt large fish

reef (rēf) *n.* a ridge of rocks, sand, or coral near the surface of water

126

EXPLICIT INSTRUCTION Influence of Setting

Instruction Ask volunteers to explain what readers learn about a story during the exposition stage of the plot. (*information about the setting, the characters, and the conflict; background information*) Ask, "What did you learn about the setting on pages 125–126?" (*Setting is a faraway island called Bora Bora. Island is small and steep. There are waterfalls and wild goats. There's a lagoon with a ghost in it.*) Then ask students to name the characters they learn about and to tell which is the main character. (*characters: Mako, Mako's mother*

and grandfather; Mako is the main character)

Practice Have students create a two-column chart with these headings: Details about the Setting, Details about the Main Character. Then have students work in pairs to fill in details and information from pages 125 and 126. Remind students to include in the Main Character column any information about Mako's skills and talents.

Possible Responses: Setting: small island called Bora Bora; rises out of sea; waterfalls trail down the cliffs; wild goats live on

mountain tops; there's a lagoon with a ghost in it; people travel by canoes; reef full of caves. Main Character: Mako is a young boy; grew up on the island; spent lots of time in the water; made a canoe and a harpoon; has a dog named Afa; listens to his grandfather's stories; wants to win the reward for capturing Tupa.

 Use **Unit One Resource Book,** p. 64, for more practice.

Tahitian Woman and Boy (1889), Paul Gauguin. Oil on canvas, 37¼″ × 24¼″, Norton Simon Art Foundation, Pasadena, California. Gift of Mr. Norton Simon, 1976.

EXPLICIT INSTRUCTION · Influence of Setting

Instruction Use the Literary Analysis: Conflict note in the green side column to discuss the conflict so far. Next, explain that the setting of a story—where and when it takes place—can contribute to the conflict. Continue by saying, "Sometimes a conflict occurs because the story takes place in a dangerous place, such as a treacherous mountain, or in a dangerous time, such as during a terrible storm. A conflict might also happen because of how people live in a particular place, for example, how they get food or the transportation they use." Next, ask, "What do you learn about how people live on the island? How do the islanders travel and get food?" (*travel by boat, catch fish for food*) Explain that these are setting details. Tell students, "The islanders need to go out on the sea to catch fish, so the sea is important to them, but it is also where Tupa lives." Ask students if the setting of this story helps bring about the conflict. Discuss students' ideas.

Practice Write this question on the board: How does the setting of this story contribute to the conflict? Have students work in small groups to write an answer to the question.

Possible Responses: The islanders need to go out on the sea in boats to catch fish. Tupa destroys their nets and has attacked fishermen. Being on the water is necessary for the islanders, but it puts them in danger of being attacked by Tupa and creates a conflict for the islanders.

Reading Skills and Strategies: CONNECT

Have students think about the relationship Mako has with Afa. Ask them to think of a pet, friend, or sibling with whom they share a similar relationship. Ask them to use their knowledge of this relationship to discuss how Mako feels about Afa.

Literary Analysis: PLOT

 Explain to students that the large initial letter marks a division in the organization of the story. Information given up to this point will lead to further action. Ask students to recall what has happened in the story so far.

Possible Response: The setting has been established, grandfather has told the legend of Mako's father, Mako has claimed he will seek revenge on Tupa.

Use **Literary Analysis Transparencies,** p. 5, for additional support.

Active Reading PREDICTING

Explain to students that good readers continue making and adjusting their predictions as they read. Ask students to adjust their previous predictions.

Possible Responses: Mako will meet up with Tupa. He will fight Tupa.

Use **Reading and Critical Thinking Transparencies,** p. 7, for additional support.

Reading Skills and Strategies: VISUALIZE

B Remind students that authors often use imagery to help the reader develop a mental picture. Ask students to identify which detail words help them to visualize this scene.

Possible Responses: broad green blades, golden ripe, nest of soft leaves, swift slash

---

told you that it is bad fortune to speak of Tupa. Alas, how well we have learned that lesson! Your father—" She stopped herself.

"What of my father?" the boy asked quickly. And now he sat up straight on the mats.

"Tell him, Grandfather," his mother whispered.

The old man cleared his throat and poked at the fire. A little shower of sparks whirled up into the darkness.

"Your father," he explained gently, "was one of the three fishermen in the canoe that Tupa destroyed." His words fell upon the air like stones dropped into a deep well.

Mako shivered. He brushed back the hair from his damp forehead. Then he squared his shoulders and cried fiercely, "I shall slay Tupa and win the king's reward!" He rose to his knees, his slim body tense, his eyes flashing in the firelight.

"Hush!" his mother said. "Go to sleep now. Enough of such foolish talk. Would you bring trouble upon us all?"

Mako lay down again upon the mats. He rolled over on his side and closed his eyes, but sleep was long in coming.

The palm trees whispered above the dark lagoon, and far out on the reef the sea thundered.

The boy was slow to wake up the next morning. The ghost of Tupa had played through his dreams, making him restless. And so it was almost noon before Mako sat up on the mats and stretched himself. He called Afa, and the boy and his dog ran down to the lagoon for their morning swim.

Perhaps ghosts were only old men's stories, anyway!

When they returned to the house, wide-awake and hungry, Mako's mother had food ready and waiting.

"These are the last of our bananas," she told him. "I wish you would paddle out to the reef this afternoon and bring back a new bunch."

The boy agreed eagerly. Nothing pleased him more than such an errand, which would take him to a little island on the outer reef, half a mile from shore. It was one of Mako's favorite playgrounds, and there bananas and oranges grew in great plenty.

"Come, Afa," he called, gulping the last mouthful. "We're going on an expedition." He picked up his long-bladed knife and seized his spear. A minute later, he dashed across the white sand, where his canoe was drawn up beyond the water's reach.

Afa barked at his heels. He was all white except for a black spot over each eye. Wherever Mako went, there went Afa also. Now the little dog leaped into the bow of the canoe, his tail wagging with delight. The boy shoved the canoe into the water and climbed aboard. Then, picking up his paddle, he thrust it into the water. The canoe shot ahead. Its sharp bow cut through the green water of the lagoon like a knife through cheese. And so clear was the water that Mako could see the coral gardens, forty feet below him, growing in the sand. The shadow of the canoe moved over them.

A school of fish swept by like silver arrows. He saw scarlet rock cod with ruby eyes and the head of a conger eel peering out from a cavern in the coral. The boy thought suddenly of Tupa, ghost of the lagoon. On such a bright day it was hard to believe in ghosts of any

---

EXPLICIT INSTRUCTION Influence of Setting

Instruction Review the islanders' conflict with Tupa. (*He destroys their fishing nets and eats their offerings.*) Then ask, "What does Mako learn about Tupa that directly affects him?" (*Tupa killed Mako's father.*) Next, discuss how Mako's conflict is different from the islanders' conflict with Tupa. (*Mako's father was killed by Tupa, and Mako wants to seek revenge for this.*) Remind students that the setting can contribute to the conflict. Then ask what Mako's mother

asks Mako to do. (*go to another island to gather bananas*) Next, say, "In this part of the story, you learn another detail of the setting—that the bananas Mako gathers grow on another island. You also learn that Mako must use a canoe to get them." Ask students why Mako's trip to the other island might be dangerous.

Practice Have students work in pairs to write an answer to this last question. Then have partners share their answers with the class.

Possible Response: The trip might be dangerous because Mako may run into Tupa as he canoes to and from the other island.

 Use **Unit One Resource Book,** p. 64, for more practice.

sort. The fierce sunlight drove away all thought of them. Perhaps ghosts were only old men's stories, anyway!

Mako's eyes came to rest upon his spear—the spear that he had made with his own hands—the spear that was as straight and true as an arrow. He remembered his vow of the night before. Could a ghost be killed with a spear? Some night, when all the village was sleeping, Mako swore to himself that he would find out! He would paddle out to the reef and challenge Tupa! Perhaps tonight. Why not? He caught his breath at the thought. A shiver ran down his back. His hands were tense on the paddle.

As the canoe drew away from shore, the boy saw the coral reef that, above all others, had always interested him. It was of white coral—a long slim shape that rose slightly above the surface of the water. It looked very much like a shark. There was a ridge on the back that the boy could pretend was a dorsal fin, while up near one end were two dark holes that looked like eyes!

Times without number the boy had practiced spearing this make-believe shark, aiming always for the eyes, the most vulnerable spot. So true and straight had his aim become that the spear would pass right into the eyeholes without even touching the sides of the coral. Mako had named the coral reef Tupa.

This morning, as he paddled past it, he shook his fist and called, "Ho, Mister Tupa! Just wait till I get my bananas. When I come back, I'll make short work of you!"

Afa followed his master's words with a sharp bark. He knew Mako was excited about something.

The bow of the canoe touched the sand of the little island where the bananas grew. Afa leaped ashore and ran barking into the jungle, now on this trail, now on that. Clouds of sea birds whirled from their nests into the air with angry cries.

Mako climbed into the shallow water, waded ashore, and pulled his canoe up on the beach. Then, picking up his banana knife, he followed Afa. In the jungle the light was so dense and green that the boy felt as if he were moving underwater. Ferns grew higher than his head. The branches of the trees formed a green roof over him. A flock of parakeets fled on swift wings. Somewhere a wild pig crashed through the undergrowth while Afa dashed away in pursuit. Mako paused anxiously. Armed only with his banana knife, he had no desire to meet the wild pig. The pig, it seemed, had no desire to meet him, either.

Then, ahead of him, the boy saw the broad green blades of a banana tree. A bunch of bananas, golden ripe, was growing out of the top.

At the foot of the tree he made a nest of soft leaves for the bunch to fall upon. In this way the fruit wouldn't be crushed. Then with a swift slash of his blade he cut the stem. The bananas fell to the earth with a dull thud. He found two more bunches.

Then he thought, "I might as well get some oranges while I'm here. Those little rusty ones are sweeter than any that grow on Bora Bora."

So he set about making a net out of palm leaves to carry the oranges. As he worked, his swift fingers moving in and out among the strong green leaves, he could hear Afa's excited barks off in the jungle. That was just like Afa, always barking at something: a bird, a fish, a wild pig. He never caught anything, either. Still, no boy ever had a finer companion.

The palm net took longer to make than Mako had realized. By the time it was finished

A

B

English Learners

1 Help students distinguish between the word *bow* meaning "the front of a boat," its homophone (to bend at the waist as a salute or show of respect), and its homograms (e.g., a weapon used to shoot arrows).

2 Ask students to try to figure out the meaning of "times without number" *(too many times to count).*

Less Proficient Readers

Ask students to describe what Mako learned from his grandfather's story and what he vowed on hearing it.

Possible Response: Mako's father was one of the three fishermen killed by Tupa. Mako vowed to kill Tupa.

Set a Purpose Tell students to look for a conflict as they read.

Advanced Students

Have students look up the word *mako* in a dictionary. *(It is a kind of shark, and the word comes from the Maori language.)* Have them discuss why they think the author might have given the boy in this story the name *Mako*.

Ask students to jot down the events the author uses to build suspense on these two pages.

Possible Responses: The story makes Mako shiver and become tense; the palm trees are whispering and the sea thunders; the ghost of Tupa is in his dreams; the thought of challenging Tupa makes Mako shiver; Afa barks because he knows Mako is excited about something; Mako pretends the coral reef is Tupa and practices throwing his spear at it; the wild pig makes Mako anxious; the palm net takes longer to make than Mako expected.

Ask students to predict how the story will end.

Possible Responses: The great white shark will kill Afa; Mako will fight the shark and rescue Afa; Mako will kill Tupa.

Literary Analysis: CONFLICT

A Remind students that an internal conflict is a struggle within a character's mind. What is the internal conflict Mako is facing?

Possible Response: Mako fears losing Afa and fears that Tupa will kill him. He has to decide if he is willing to risk his life to fight for Afa.

B Remind students that an external conflict is a struggle between a character and an outside force. What is the external conflict Mako is facing?

Answer: Mako is fighting with the white shark, Tupa. He is fighting for his life and the life of his dog, Afa.

How does Mako resolve his conflicts, both internal and external, in this story?

Answers: Mako resolves the internal conflict by deciding to try to save Afa and fight Tupa. He resolves the external conflict by killing Tupa in the fight.

Reading Skills and Strategies: EVALUATE

Ask students to analyze Mako's decision. Do they agree with him? Why or why not? Have students write responses in their Reader's Notebooks. Students may meet in small groups to discuss their responses.

---

and filled with oranges, the jungle was dark and gloomy. Night comes quickly and without warning in the islands of the tropics.

Mako carried the fruit down to the shore and loaded it into the canoe. Then he whistled to Afa. The dog came bounding out of the bush, wagging his tail.

"Hurry!" Mako scolded. "We won't be home before the dark comes."

The little dog leaped into the bow of the canoe, and Mako came aboard. Night seemed to rise up from the surface of the water and swallow them. On the distant shore of Bora Bora, cook fires were being lighted. The first star twinkled just over the dark mountains. Mako dug his paddle into the water, and the canoe leaped ahead.

1 The dark water was alive with <u>phosphorus</u>. The bow of the canoe seemed to cut through a pale liquid fire. Each dip of the paddle trailed streamers of light. As the canoe approached the coral reef, the boy called, "Ho, Tupa! It's too late tonight to teach you your lesson. But I'll come back tomorrow." The coral shark glistened in the darkness.

And then, suddenly, Mako's breath caught in his throat. His hands felt weak. Just beyond the fin of the coral Tupa, there was another fin—a huge one. It had never been there before. And—could he believe his eyes? It was moving.

The boy stopped paddling. He dashed his hand across his eyes. Afa began to bark furiously. The great white fin, shaped like a small sail, glowed with phosphorescent light. Then Mako knew. Here was Tupa—the real Tupa—ghost of the lagoon!

2 His knees felt weak. He tried to cry out, but his voice died in his throat. The great shark was circling slowly around the canoe. With each circle, it moved closer and closer. Now the boy could see the phosphorescent glow of the great shark's sides. As it moved in closer, he saw the yellow eyes, the gill slits in its throat.

Afa leaped from one side of the canoe to the other. In sudden anger Mako leaned forward to grab the dog and shake him soundly. Afa wriggled out of his grasp as Mako tried to catch him, and the shift in weight tipped the canoe on one side. The outrigger rose from the water. In another second they would be overboard. The boy threw his weight over quickly to balance the canoe, but with a loud splash Afa fell over into the dark water.

Mako stared after him in dismay. The little dog, instead of swimming back to the canoe, had headed for the distant shore. And there was the great white shark—very near.

"Afa! Afa! Come back! Come quickly!" Mako shouted.

The little dog turned back toward the canoe. He was swimming with all his strength. Mako leaned forward. Could Afa make it? Swiftly the boy seized his spear. Bracing himself, he stood upright. There was no weakness in him now. His dog, his companion, was in danger of instant death.

Afa was swimming desperately to reach the canoe. The white shark had paused in his circling to gather speed for the attack. Mako raised his arm, took aim. In that instant the shark charged. Mako's arm flashed forward. All his strength was behind that thrust. The spear drove straight and true, right into the great shark's eye. Mad with pain and rage, Tupa whipped about, lashing the water in fury.

> One flip of that tail could overturn the canoe.

| WORDS TO KNOW | **phosphorus** (fŏs'fər-əs) *n.* a substance that glows with a yellowish or white light |

130

Cross Curricular Link **Science**

CORAL REEFS A coral reef is an underwater ridge of stone built up by the skeletons of many tiny sea animals. These reefs provide homes and food to many ocean creatures. These ridges form only in tropical or subtropical waters, where the surface waters are always warm.

There are three types of coral reefs: fringing reefs, which extend from the shore with little or no water between reef and shore; barrier reefs, which occur offshore, with a channel between reef and land; and atolls, which are typically a ring of coral islands around a shallow lagoon.

Bora Bora is a small island, covering less than 15 square miles (39 sq. km). It is in the South Pacific, and is surrounded by coral reefs.

The world's largest coral reef is the Great Barrier Reef, stretching for more than 1,250 miles (2,000 km) along Australia's northeastern coast. This reef is actually a chain of coral reefs in the Coral Sea. The reef is home to hundreds of species of coral in a beautiful range of colors and shapes. The reef also supports larger water animals, including about two thousand species of fish.

The canoe rocked back and forth. Mako struggled to keep his balance as he drew back the spear by the cord fastened to his wrist.

He bent over to seize Afa and drag him aboard. Then he stood up, not a moment too soon. Once again the shark charged. Once again Mako threw his spear, this time at the other eye. The spear found its mark. Blinded and weak from loss of blood, Tupa rolled to the surface, turned slightly on his side. Was he dead?

Mako knew how clever sharks could be, and he was taking no chances. Scarcely daring to breathe, he paddled toward the still body. He saw the faintest motion of the great tail. The shark was still alive. The boy knew that one flip of that tail could overturn the canoe and send him and Afa into the water, where Tupa could destroy them.

Swiftly, yet calmly, Mako stood upright and braced himself firmly. Then, murmuring a silent prayer to the shark god, he threw his spear for the last time. Downward, swift as sound, the spear plunged into a white shoulder.

Peering over the side of the canoe, Mako could see the great fish turn over far below the surface. Then slowly, slowly, the great shark rose to the surface of the lagoon. There he floated, half on one side.

Tupa was dead.

Mako flung back his head and shouted for joy. Hitching a strong line about the shark's tail, the boy began to paddle toward the shore of Bora Bora. The dorsal fin, burning with the white fire of phosphorus, trailed after the canoe.

Men were running down the beaches of Bora Bora, shouting as they leaped into their canoes and put out across the lagoon. Their cries reached the boy's ears across the water.

"It is Tupa—ghost of the lagoon," he heard them shout. "Mako has killed him!"

That night, as the tired boy lay on the pandanus mats listening to the distant thunder of the sea, he heard Grandfather singing a new song. It was the song which would be sung the next day at the feast which King Opu Nui would give in Mako's honor. The boy saw his mother bending over the cook fire. The stars leaned close, winking like friendly eyes. Grandfather's voice reached him now from a great distance, "Thirty acres of land and a sailing canoe. . . ." ❖

Tahitian Landscape (1891), Paul Gauguin. The Minneapolis Institute of Arts.

Connect to the Literature

1. What Do You Think?
Possible Responses: It was exciting that Mako had a chance to kill Tupa. It was scary when Mako's dog, Afa, fell into the water.

Comprehension Check
- Mako lives on Bora Bora, an island in the South Pacific.
- When Mako returns from collecting bananas, he meets, fights, and kills Tupa.
- Mako is rewarded with thirty acres and a canoe.

Use Selection Quiz
Unit One Resource Book, p. 67.

Think Critically

2. Possible Response: When Mako realized Tupa was swimming toward him, he probably felt scared. He was probably also excited at the chance to kill the shark.

3. Answers will vary.

Use **Reading and Critical Thinking Transparencies,** p. 7, for additional support.

4. Possible Responses: Mako would still have tried to kill Tupa to avenge his father's death. Or, without the immediate threat to Afa, Mako would have been too frightened of Tupa to try to kill him.

5. Possible Responses: The desire to save Afa made Mako brave and strong. Mako had practiced spearing on the reef. Mako wanted to avenge his father's death.

Literary Analysis

Conflict Students' responses should reflect the conflicts evident in the story. Students should also be able to tell how each conflict fits in the plot of the story.

Use **Literary Analysis Transparencies,** p. 8, for additional support.

Connect to the Literature

1. What Do You Think?
What was your reaction to Mako's fight with Tupa?

Comprehension Check
- Where does Mako live?
- What happens when Mako returns from collecting bananas?
- What is Mako's reward?

Think Critically

2. How do you think Mako felt when he realized that Tupa was swimming toward him?

3. **ACTIVE READING** **PREDICTING**
Look at the predictions you wrote in your **READER'S NOTEBOOK**. How well do they match the actual events in the story?

4. What if Mako's dog were not in danger? Do you think Mako still would have tried to kill Tupa? Why or why not?

5. Why do you think Mako is able to defeat Tupa?
Think About:
- his reasons for fighting Tupa
- his abilities and experience
- the histories of both Tupa and Mako

Extend Interpretations

6. Critic's Corner Theresa Sullivan, a member of the student board that reviewed the stories in this book, says, "I liked how this story was scary and not scary at the same time." Do you agree with her comment? Explain.

7. Connect to Life Do you think that you could act as courageously as Mako does? In what kind of situation would you take such a great risk?

Literary Analysis

CONFLICT Almost every story is built around an important **conflict,** or struggle, that the main character must face. A conflict may be between a character and an outside force. A conflict may also happen inside the mind of a character, when he or she must make a difficult decision. In "Ghost of the Lagoon," the main character, Mako, faces a conflict with an outside force—the shark called Tupa.

Group Activity In a small group, look through "Ghost of the Lagoon" and jot down as many conflicts as you can find. Afterward, discuss how these conflicts helped the plot of the story move forward. Share your ideas with the class.

SETTING In the story you just read, the island **setting** plays an important role in the conflict. Because Mako lives on an island, he often travels by boat. He paddles his canoe around the island the way other kids ride bicycles around their neighborhoods. When Mako's mother asks him to bring home some bananas, he travels by canoe to a small island to get them. As a result, he comes face to face with Tupa.

Extend Interpretations

6. Critic's Corner Possible Responses: Yes, it was scary when Mako and Tupa were attacking each other; but on the other hand it was not scary because you could guess Mako would be okay in the end. No, it was scary all the way through because you could never be sure that both Mako and Afa would be all right.

7. Connect to Life Anyone would hope that they could be as courageous as Mako is in this story. Someone might take such a great risk if a person or animal they loved was in danger.

CHOICES and CHALLENGES

Writing

Battle Narrative Imagine that Mako is now an old man. Write the story of Mako's battle with Tupa from Mako's point of view. You might begin your story with a sentence like this: "When I was just a boy, I fought the greatest battle of my life." Include details that tell how Mako felt and what he saw, heard, and did. Try to create a sense of excitement in your story. Keep this story in your **Working Portfolio.**

Writing Handbook
See p. R41: Narrative Writing.

Speaking & Listening

Presenting Characters In a group of three, assign the roles of Mako, his father, and his grandfather. Make up a scene in which these characters discuss how Tupa affected each of their lives. You might want to first brainstorm ideas about how each character was affected by Tupa. Then work together to write the conversation between the characters. After you've finished writing, practice performing your dialogue. Then present it to the class.

Research & Technology

Jaws Sharks have swum the ocean waters for hundreds of millions of years. If you were going to write a report on sharks, what would you want to know about them? Write a list of five questions you have about sharks. Also list three information sources you might use to answer these questions.

 INTERNET Research Starter
www.mcdougallittell.com

Art Connection

Picturing Mako French artist Paul Gauguin fell in love with Tahiti and spent his last years there. Look again at the painting *Tahitian Woman and Boy* on page 127. How well do you think the portrait fits the characters of Mako and his mother? Support your opinion with story information and your own reasons.

Vocabulary and Spelling

EXERCISE: WORD MEANING Write the Word to Know that best fits each definition.

1. a ridge of rocks or coral
2. a glowing substance
3. a shallow body of water
4. a journey
5. a spearlike weapon

Vocabulary Handbook
See p. R20: Context Clues.

WORDS TO KNOW	expedition	harpoon
	lagoon	phosphorus
	reef	

SPELLING STRATEGY: THE $\overline{oo}$ SOUND The long vowel sound $\overline{oo}$ is most often spelled *oo*. Sometimes, however, it is spelled *ue, ew, ou,* or *oe*. Rewrite the following sentences using the correct spelling of each boldfaced word.

1. Would **yoo** like to swim in the **lagoun?**
2. When he **thrue** the **harpewn,** his aim was **troo.**
3. She **knou** how to guide the **canoo thrue** the reef.

Spelling Handbook
See p. R26.

GHOST OF THE LAGOON **133**

Writing

Battle Narrative Remind students that in a narrative account they would pretend to be Mako and would tell the story in the first-person point of view. Students may want to reread pages 130–131 to recall the details of Mako's battle with Tupa.

Use **Writing Transparencies**, p. 34, for additional support.

Speaking & Listening

Presenting Characters Students should reread the story to familiarize themselves with the character they have been assigned. Have them observe that character's point of view during the rereading. Allow students time to practice their scene prior to the performance.

Research & Technology

Jaws Before they can come up with questions, students may need to read an article that gives general background information on sharks.

Art Connection

Picturing Mako Students may think the characters in Gauguin's painting look a lot like Mako and his mother due to their physical attributes. Students may find their mental pictures of Mako and his mother do not look like the painting.

Vocabulary and Spelling
EXERCISE: WORD MEANING
1. reef
2. phosphorus
3. lagoon
4. expedition
5. harpoon

SPELLING STRATEGY
1. you, lagoon
2. threw, harpoon, true
3. knew, canoe, through

Grammar in Context

WRITING EXERCISE
Possible Responses:

1. The oranges tasted sweet.
2. Mako's grandfather was proud.
3. The jungle was a scary place.
4. Opu Nui was the king.

Note: If students write "The oranges fell from the tree," review the distinction between linking and action verbs.

If students write "The jungle was scary", review the difference between predicate nouns and adjectives.

Armstrong Sperry

Armstrong Sperry was educated at the Yale School of Fine Arts and the New York Art Students League before studying art in Paris. He started his career in publishing as an illustrator before combining his artistic talent with writing children's books. He has illustrated almost all of his numerous books and stories.

Author Activity

South Seas Sights Students will need to visit the school or public library to gather books written and illustrated by Armstrong Sperry.

Grammar in Context: Predicate Nouns and Predicate Adjectives

Predicate nouns and predicate adjectives tell more about the subject. Sentences with predicate nouns and adjectives do not express action. Instead, a **predicate noun** follows a linking verb and renames the subject. A predicate adjective follows a **linking verb** and describes the subject. Notice the predicate noun, shown in red, and predicate adjective, in orange.

> In his imagination, the coral became a killer shark.
> His hands were tense on the paddle.

Here are some common linking verbs:
am, are, is, was, were, been, grow, become, remains, feels, tastes, smells, looks, sounds, seems, appears

WRITING EXERCISE Write each subject below. Add a linking verb and a predicate adjective that describes the subject.

Example: *Original* Little Afa

Rewritten Little Afa seems brave.

1. The oranges
2. Mako's grandfather

Write each subject below. Add a linking verb and a predicate noun that renames the subject.

Example: *Original* Fear

Rewritten Fear is an enemy.

3. The jungle
4. Opu Nui

Armstrong Sperry
1897–1976

"The world which belongs to the artist is a world to which few scientists possess the key."

A World Traveler Armstrong Sperry once said that a writer "should tell his story clearly, in a supple prose that leaves his reader—young or old—wondering 'What happens next?'" Sperry had an advantage in writing stories with exciting plots—he traveled widely in Europe, North America, and the West Indies. Inspired by his grandfather's stories of visits to the South Pacific, Sperry spent two years in French Polynesia. There he learned French and Tahitian and gathered information for many of his books.

Literary Adventures Sperry's talent for writing adventure stories set in exotic places led to the success of his book *Call It Courage.* This novel, based on a legend of the South Pacific, was awarded the Newbery Medal in 1941. Sperry's book *The Rain Forest* received the Boys' Clubs of America Junior Book Award in 1949.

AUTHOR ACTIVITY
South Seas Sights Armstrong Sperry was not only a writer but an artist. In fact, he illustrated nearly all of his many books and stories. Find one of Sperry's books that includes his own drawings of the South Pacific. How do these images compare with the setting he describes in "Ghost of the Lagoon"? Present your findings to the class.

Grammar in Context

PREDICATE NOUNS AND PREDICATE ADJECTIVES
Instruction Remind students that predicate nouns and predicate adjectives follow a verb and are part of the predicate. In sentences with predicate nouns or adjectives, the verb is a linking verb. The predicate noun or predicate adjective renames or describes the subject. List the following sentences on the chalkboard:
Mako felt courageous.
Afa was a little, white dog.
Ask students to identify the predicate noun and/or predicate adjective in each sentence.

(courageous, dog)
Practice Have students make three columns on their papers: Subject, Linking Verb, and Predicate Noun/Adjective. Have them find these parts in each numbered sentence that follows and write them in the proper columns. After the predicate word, students should write *n* or *adj* to indicate whether it is a noun or an adjective. Have students include helping verbs in the linking verb column.
1. Life on Bora Bora seems peaceful.
2. Mako's grandfather was a gentle old man.

3. Mako's expedition sounds like fun.
4. Tupa was a great white shark.
5. Mako became a hero.

 Use **Unit One Resource Book,** p. 65.

 For more instruction in predicate nouns and predicate adjectives, see McDougal Littell's *Language Network,* Chapter 5.

For **systematic instruction** in grammar, see:
• **Grammar, Usage, and Mechanics Book**
• pacing chart on p. 19i.

from **The Fun of It**

by AMELIA EARHART

Connect to Your Life

Flying! What exciting goal would you like to accomplish in your lifetime? What would be good preparation for accomplishing this dream?

Build Background

HISTORY

Amelia Earhart was a pioneer in aviation, or flight. Wilbur and Orville Wright had made the first successful flight in 1903. In 1908, Earhart saw an airplane for the first time. She began watching military pilots practice flying. Later, she took flying lessons from Neta Snook. Earhart passed her pilot's test in 1922. Although Earhart had other jobs, she flew whenever possible. Soon she had set an unofficial record for women by flying to 14,000 feet—nearly three miles high.

In June 1928, Earhart became the first woman to fly across the Atlantic Ocean, as a passenger. Four years later she made her famous solo flight across the Atlantic Ocean. Earhart went on to make other flights that were firsts for both men and women.

In 1937, Earhart set a new goal: to become the first woman to fly around the world. During the flight, she, her plane, and her navigator disappeared. To this day, Earhart remains famous for her courage, her achievements, and the mystery surrounding her last flight.

> WORDS TO KNOW **Vocabulary Preview**
>
> accumulate   faculty   hospitality   sufficient
> altitude   fleeting   margin   vessel
> extent   fluctuation

Focus Your Reading

LITERARY ANALYSIS   **AUTOBIOGRAPHY**

An **autobiography** is the story of a person's life, told by that person. Listen for Earhart's voice in this detail from her autobiography:

> *And then something happened that has never occurred in my twelve years of flying. The altimeter . . . failed.*

Only Earhart would know that her altimeter, a device that shows how high the plane is flying, had never failed before. As you read, notice other details that could only be told by someone with firsthand experience.

ACTIVE READING   **IDENTIFYING THE AUTHOR'S PURPOSE**

An **author's purpose** is his or her reason for creating a particular work. The purpose may be to **entertain,** to **inform,** to **explain,** to **express an opinion,** or to **persuade** readers to do or believe something. An author may have more than one purpose, but usually one is the most important.

READER'S NOTEBOOK   As you read, look for clues to Earhart's purpose for writing. Identify at least three sentences that show the author's purpose, and record them.

Standards-Based Objectives

1. understand and appreciate an **autobiography**
2. understand **author's purpose** in an autobiography
3. recognize difference between first- and third-person **point of view**

Summary

Amelia Earhart describes her solo flight across the Atlantic, beginning with her successful takeoff from the coast of Newfoundland and ending with her unplanned but safe landing in a pasture in Northern Ireland. During the long night, she must deal with broken instruments, ice on the plane's wings, storms, fog, and a fire in the exhaust system.

Thematic Link

Amelia Earhart embodies courage in action as she makes her solo flight across the Atlantic, putting thoughts of herself behind concern for her plane and her mission.

English Conventions Practice

Daily Language SkillBuilder

Have students **proofread** the display sentences on page 19k and write them correctly. The sentences also appear on Transparency 4 of **Language Transparencies.**

Preteaching Vocabulary

If you would like to preteach the WORDS TO KNOW for this selection, use the Explicit Instruction, page 136.

LESSON RESOURCES

UNIT ONE RESOURCE BOOK, pp. 68–74

ASSESSMENT
Formal Assessment, pp. 21–22
Test Generator

SKILLS TRANSPARENCIES AND COPYMASTERS
Literary Analysis
• Autobiography, TR 11 (pp. 138, 142)
Reading and Critical Thinking
• Author's Purpose and Audience, TR 8 (p. 142)

Language
• Daily Language SkillBuilder, TR 4 (p. 135)
• Synonyms, TR 60 (p. 136)
Writing
• Writing Variables, TR 2 (p. 143)
• Effective Language, TR 15 (p. 143)
• Character Sketch, TR 30 (p. 143)
Speaking and Listening
• Working in a Group, p. 33 (p. 143)

INTEGRATED TECHNOLOGY
Audio Library
Video: Literature in Performance
• *Amelia Earhart.* See **Video Resource Book,** pp. 3–9

Visit our Web site:
www.mcdougallittell.com

For **systematic instruction** in language skills, see:
• **Vocabulary and Spelling Book**
• **Grammar, Usage, and Mechanics Book**
• pacing chart on p. 19i.

Reading and Analyzing

Active Reading

IDENTIFYING AUTHOR'S PURPOSE

Let students know that being aware of the author's purpose helps them read more critically. Ask students to choose a sentence on this page that illustrates the author's purpose, and to write it and the purpose in their Reader's Notebooks.

Possible Response: "At twelve minutes after seven, I gave her the gun." The author's main purpose is to inform. Students may also say that her purpose is to entertain, because she has used action to get the reader's attention and interest.

 Use **Unit One Resource Book,** p.69, for more practice.

Literary Analysis   **AUTOBIOGRAPHY**

Remind students that this is a factual account written by the narrator. Ask students why they think Earhart called her book *The Fun of It*.

Possible Response: She enjoyed flying.

 Use **Unit One Resource Book,** p.70, for more practice.

Literary Analysis: NARRATIVE NONFICTION

Let students know that narrative nonfiction deals with real people and events, but it is written to be read and experienced like fiction. Ask students to notice details on this page that make it seem like fiction.

Possible Responses: She jumps right into the events without preliminaries; she creates suspense when she says that something happened that had never happened before.

f r o m

(Right) Amelia Earhart in the cockpit of her plane. (Above) Earhart made her historic solo flight across the Atlantic in this red Lockheed Vega.

136

EXPLICIT INSTRUCTION ## Preteaching Vocabulary

WORDS TO KNOW

Teaching Strategy Remind students to draw on their knowledge of words to bring meaning to other words in context. Tell students they will sometimes find a word's meaning by reading a **synonym** in the same sentence or one near it.

I was looking for a boat. I spotted one <u>vessel</u> in the distance.

Tell students they can figure out the meaning of the word *vessel* from knowing the word *boat*.

Practice Have students write the sentences and circle the synonym of the underlined word.

1. My <u>course</u> put me on a route eastward across the Atlantic. *(route)*
2. I had a <u>fleeting</u> worry about the plane, but it was passing. *(passing)*
3. I needed to <u>accumulate</u>, or gather, plenty of money to finance the trip. *(gather)*
4. It was difficult to find a good <u>altitude</u>—each height had its own problems. *(height)*

 Use **Unit One Resource Book,** p. 73, for more practice.

For **systematic instruction** in vocabulary, see:
• **Vocabulary and Spelling Book**
• pacing chart on p. 19i.

The FUN of It

by Amelia Earhart

The southwest wind was nearly right for the runway. At twelve minutes after seven, I gave her the gun. The plane gathered speed, and despite the heavy load rose easily.

A minute later I was headed out to sea.

For several hours there was fair weather with a lingering sunset. And then the moon came up over a low bank of clouds. For those first hours I was flying at about 12,000 feet. And then something happened that has never occurred in my twelve years of flying. The altimeter,[1] the instrument which records height above ground, failed. Suddenly the hands swung around the dial uselessly and I knew the instrument was out of commission for the rest of the flight.

---

1. **altimeter** (ăl-tĭm′ĭ-tər).

137

Differentiating Instruction

English Learners
This selection includes some specialized vocabulary. You might post a picture of an airplane with explanatory notes for words such as *tachometer, course, altitude, gyro compass, manifold,* and *gauge.* Have students study the picture before they read the selection.

1 Students may not know that *gave her the gun* means that Earhart increased the amount of fuel going to the engine so it would speed up.

2 The phrase *out of commission* means that the instrument was broken.

Use **Spanish Study Guide,** pp. 25–27, for additional support.

Less Proficient Readers
Have students keep these questions in mind as they read:
• Who is the narrator of the selection?
• Where did she leave from and where is she headed?
• What problems does she encounter?

Advanced Students
Amelia Earhart is a celebrated figure in American history. Have students do one of the following: read a biography of Amelia Earhart, research and compare the instruments pilots have today with those Earhart had available to her, read about other early notable pilots such as Wilbur and Orville Wright and Charles Lindbergh, or construct a time line to show the key aeronautical events of the last 100 years.

Active Reading | IDENTIFYING AUTHOR'S PURPOSE

Ask students to find a sentence on this page that shows the author's purpose. Have them write the sentence and its purpose in their Reader's Notebooks.

Possible Response: "Instrument-flying cannot be done safely very near the surface with the equipment we have today." It is written to inform.

📋 Use **Reading and Critical Thinking Transparencies**, p. 8, for additional support.

Literary Analysis: CONFLICT

Review the text in the second column of this page. Was Earhart's conflict with another person or with her situation?

Possible Response: It was with her situation and herself. If she flew too high, she got ice on her wings. If she flew too low, she was in fog, and in danger of going into the water.

Reading Skills and Strategies: CLARIFY

Make sure students understand that Earhart started her trip in Newfoundland, and that she is flying east across the Atlantic. Ask them to locate Newfoundland on a map and tell why she chose that place.

Possible Response: It is farthest east and would give her the shortest trip.

Literary Analysis | AUTOBIOGRAPHY

A Ask students to identify what detail in this paragraph would only have been known by the person experiencing it.

Possible Response: The last sentence concerns her feelings about having looked at the flames. No one else would be aware of that.

📋 Use **Literary Analysis Transparencies**, p. 11, for additional support.

About 11:30, the moon disappeared behind some clouds, and I ran into rather a severe storm with lightning, and I was considerably buffeted about, and with difficulty held my course. In fact, I probably got off my course at this point to some <u>extent</u> because it was very rough. This lasted for at least an hour. Then I flew on in calmer weather though in the midst of clouds. Once I saw the moon for a <u>fleeting</u> instant and thought I could pull out on top of the clouds, so I climbed for half an hour when suddenly I realized I was picking up ice.

I knew by the climb of the ship which was not as fast as usual that it was <u>accumulating</u> a weight of ice. Then I saw slush on the windowpane. In addition, my tachometer,[2] the instrument which registers revolutions per minute of the motor, picked up ice and spun around the dial.

In such a situation one has to get into warmer air, so I went down hoping the ice would melt. I descended until I could see the waves breaking although I could not tell exactly how far I was above them. I kept flying here until fog came down so low that I dared not keep on at such an <u>altitude</u>. Instrument-flying[3] cannot be done safely very near the surface with the equipment we have today.

---

2. **tachometer** (tă-kŏm'ĭ-tər).
3. **instrument-flying** (ĭn'strə-mənt-flī'ĭng): piloting an airplane by relying on instrument readings rather than on one's view of the ground.

WORDS TO KNOW
extent (ĭk-stĕnt') *n.* an amount or degree
fleeting (flē'tĭng) *adj.* passing quickly
accumulate (ə-kyōōm'yə-lāt') *v.* to gather or pile up
altitude (ăl'tĭ-tōōd') *n.* an object's height above a particular level, such as ground level or sea level

Her pilot's license showed Earhart wearing her leather flight helmet.

There was nothing left but to seek a middle ground, that is, to fly under the altitude at which I picked up ice and over the water by a <u>sufficient</u> <u>margin</u>. This would have been much easier to do had I been able to know my height

Later, I tried going up again with the same result. So I gave up, just plowing through the "soup" and not looking out of the cockpit again until morning came. I depended on the instruments there to tell me the position of the plane in space, as under these conditions human <u>faculties</u> fail. Had I not been equipped with the best I could never have succeeded. The gyro compass,[4] which is freest of all from <u>fluctuations</u>, was a real life-saver.

About four hours out of Newfoundland, I noticed that the flames were coming through a broken weld in the manifold ring.[5] I knew that it would grow worse as the night wore on. However, the metal was very heavy and I hoped it would last until I reached land. I was indeed sorry that I had looked at the break at all because the flames appeared so much worse at night than they did in the daytime.

As daylight dawned, I found myself between two layers of clouds, the first very high, probably 20,000 feet, the lower ones little fluffy white clouds near the water. This was the first sight of the sea in daylight.

I noticed from the blowing foam that there was a northwest wind. The little white clouds soon grew packed and resembled a vast snow field. I could see on the leading edge of my wings particles of ice which had not yet melted. Soon I went a little higher and ran into another bank of clouds. I was in these for at

---

4. **gyro** (jī′rō) **compass:** a compass that keeps its north-south alignment by means of a spinning disk instead of a magnetic needle.

5. **manifold** (măn′ə-fōld′) **ring:** a seal in the engine's exhaust system.

WORDS
TO
KNOW

sufficient (sə-fĭsh′ənt) *adj.* being enough; adequate
margin (mär′jĭn) *n.* an amount or distance that allows for safety
faculty (făk′əl-tē) *n.* any of the powers of the mind
fluctuation (flŭk′chōō-ā′shən) *n.* an irregular movement or change

139

Differentiating Instruction

English Learners

1 If students do not understand the word *buffeted*, point out the context "rather a severe storm" and "with difficulty held my course." See if they can figure out that *buffeted* means "struck against forcefully" or "battered."

Less Proficient Readers

2 Ask students whether they know why the plane would pick up ice when it went higher. Can they think of something on earth that demonstrates the same principle?

Possible Response: Temperature decreases with increasing altitude. There is snow and ice at the top of mountains when there isn't any down below.

3 Be sure students understand that Earhart was writing in 1932 when airplanes were much more basic than they are now.

4 Review events thus far with students: Earhart took off from Newfoundland, lost the use of her altimeter, ran into a storm, picked up ice on her wings, ran into fog, and had a fire to worry about.

Set a Purpose As they continue to read, have students think about Earhart's attitude to danger.

Advanced Students

Ask students to speculate on why Earhart chose to fly at night.

Possible Response: Responses will vary but may relate to weather conditions for the departure or flight.

EXPLICIT INSTRUCTION Point of View

Instruction Ask students who is telling this story about Amelia Earhart. *(She is telling the story about herself.)* Then review with students the definition of point of view: the perspective or position from which an experience or story is told. Remind students of the two basic types of point of view: First-person— told from the author's or main character's personal perspective, using the pronouns *I, me,* and *we.* Third-person—told from the perspective of a person outside the story, using the pronouns *he, she,* and *they.* Explain that autobiographies use first-person point of view, and biographies use third-person point of view. Ask volunteers to read aloud sentences on page 138 and 139 with first-person pronouns in them.

Practice Use the Literary Analysis: Autobiography note in the green side column to discuss how the first-person point of view affects the story. Have students write their responses to the activity in this note.

Possible Responses: See the side column note for possible responses.

Use **Unit One Resource Book,** p. 71, for more practice.

Earhart ended her transatlantic flight in the green fields of Ireland.

least an hour and then came out in a clear space again over the white snow fields.

By this time, the upper layer was thin enough for the sun to come through, and it was as dazzling as on real snow. I had dark glasses but it was too much for me even so, and I came down through the lower layer to fly in the shade, as it were.

Anyway, ten hours had passed, and I wished to see the water lest[6] I was passing a boat. I had seen one <u>vessel</u> shortly after I left Harbour Grace. I blinked my navigation lights[7] but apparently no one saw me as I was flying high. Then I picked up either a fishing vessel or an oil tanker off the coast of Ireland, but those were the only two I saw until I met a fleet near the coast.

From then on I met sunshine and low hanging clouds, most of which I kept under even though they were very near the water.

A By the way, I didn't bother much about food for myself. The really important thing was fuel for the engine. It drank some 350 gallons of gasoline. My own trans-Atlantic rations consisted of one can of tomato juice which I punctured and sipped through a straw.

Of course, the last two hours were the hardest. My exhaust manifold was vibrating very badly, and then I turned on the reserve tanks and found the gauge[8] leaking. I decided I should come down at the very nearest place, wherever it was. I had flown a set compass course all night. Now I changed to due east and decided to head for Ireland. I did not wish to miss the tip of Ireland and the weather was such I couldn't see very far. I thought I must be south of the course, for I had been told by the weather man in New York that I might find rain south of my course. There was a wind which might blow it on, so when I ran into the storm I thought that I was in this weather spoken of. Then when I saw the northwest wind, I was

---

6. **lest:** in case.

7. **navigation lights:** lights on the wings and tail of an airplane, which allow the plane to be seen in the dark.

8. **gauge** (gāj): an instrument for measuring or indicating an amount—in this case, the instrument that shows how much fuel is in the fuel tanks.

WORDS TO KNOW   **vessel** (vĕs′əl) *n.* a boat or ship

sure I must be south. As it happened, I probably was exactly on my course, and I think I hit Ireland about the middle.

I started down the coast and found thunderstorms lower in the hills. Not having the altimeter and not knowing the country, I was afraid to plow through those lest I hit one of the mountains, so I turned north where the weather seemed to be better and soon came across a railroad which I followed hoping it would lead me to a city, where there might be an airport.

The first place I encountered was Londonderry, and I circled it hoping to locate a landing field but found lovely pastures instead. I succeeded in frightening all the cattle in the county, I think, as I came down low several times before finally landing in a long, sloping meadow. I couldn't have asked for better landing facilities, as far as that.

There ended the flight and my happy adventure. Beyond it lay further adventures of hospitality and kindness at the hands of my friends in England, France and America. ❖

An Irish farm family looked on as Earhart read messages of congratulations.

| WORDS TO KNOW | **hospitality** (hŏs′pĭ-tăl′ĭ-tē) *n.* a friendly and generous attitude toward guests |

141

Less Proficient Readers
Be sure students understand that Harbor Grace is the place Earhart left from in Newfoundland, and that Londonderry is her landing point in Ireland (now in Northern Ireland).

1 Ask students to discuss why Earhart's last two hours might have been the hardest.
Possible Response: She was probably very tired, and her plane was having problems.

Ask students to draw a map showing Newfoundland and Ireland, and to plot Earhart's course, including her final change of direction.

English Learners
Be sure students understand that the phrase "It drank some 350 gallons" is referring to the engine. The engine doesn't literally drink but uses that much fuel. Also, be sure students understand that sufficient fuel is important because Earhart cannot stop for more. The purpose of the flight is to cross the Atlantic Ocean, so there is nowhere to refuel while over the water.

Advanced Students
Jane Mendelsohn wrote a novel in 1996 inspired by the life of Amelia Earhart titled, *I Was Amelia Earhart*. In it she describes solo flying as isolated, antisocial, and uncomfortable because one can't eat well, read a book, dance, or do many other things. Yet Earhart called her solo flight a "happy adventure." Have students write a paragraph about why Earhart might have called this flight a "happy adventure."
Possible Responses: The human fascination with doing things that have never been done before; the excitement of taking risks; and the joy of making friends in different countries.

EXPLICIT INSTRUCTION **Viewing and Representing**

ART APPRECIATION Students will have noticed that this selection is enhanced by numerous photographs—of Amelia Earhart, her plane, her destination, and her pilot's license.
Instruction Point out that photographs can make a time period come alive in a more immediate way than text. Photographs present details that might be very tedious to read if written out. Ask, "Where can you find the year Earhart received her pilot's license?" *(in the photograph on page 139)*

Practice Ask students to work in small groups. Have them describe how the photographs in the selection help to represent or extend the text's meanings. Have them list all the information they can discover in the photographs. Then have them cross out information that is also in the text. What is presented in the photos only? Groups can then compare their lists.

Connect to the Literature

1. What Do You Think?

Possible Responses: Students may say they would have felt challenged by the problems and thrilled by the achievement. They might also say they would have been scared to be flying alone, without important instruments, through storms and ice.

Comprehension Check

- Earhart was flying across the Atlantic Ocean from Canada to Europe. She took off from Harbour Grace, in Newfoundland, and landed in Londonderry, Ireland (now in Northern Ireland).
- She took off at 7:12 P.M. and landed the next day.
- Without the altimeter, Earhart could not tell how high she was flying. She had to rely on her judgment to stay above the waves and beneath the level at which the plane picked up ice.

 Use Selection Quiz
Unit One Resource Book, p. 74.

Think Critically

2. Possible Response: Earhart knows about planes and engines, geography, and weather. She can also fly, navigate, and write. She is courageous, resourceful, flexible, outgoing, and appreciative of other people's hospitality. She seems to view life as a "happy adventure."

3. Possible Response: Earhart's main purpose was to inform readers about her flight.

Use **Reading and Critical Thinking Transparencies,** p. 8, for additional support.

4. Possible Response: The first-person point of view allows Earhart to speak directly to readers and tell her thoughts and impressions. For example, when she is landing she gives the reader a sense of the dangers she faced, and what it felt like to land in the countryside.

5. Possible Response: Because Amelia Earhart was a pioneer, it was important for her to share her stories. She was able to describe experiences that were unfamiliar to most people. It also gave her an opportunity to be a role model, especially for women.

Connect to the Literature

1. What Do You Think? If you were in Earhart's place, how would you have felt?

Comprehension Check
- Where was Earhart flying?
- When did her flight begin and end?
- Why was the loss of the altimeter so significant?

Think Critically

2. Based on this story, what kind of person do you think Amelia Earhart was?

Think About:
- her personal traits and skills
- the way in which she tells a story
- how she responded to each problem on the flight

3. ACTIVE READING IDENTIFYING THE AUTHOR'S PURPOSE What do you think was Earhart's main purpose for writing this story? To support your answer, refer to the notes you made in your READER'S NOTEBOOK.

4. How does hearing this story from Earhart herself make the story come alive? Look back through the selection to find details that support your answer.

5. Amelia Earhart wrote several books and articles, and toured giving lectures. Why do you think it was so important for her to tell others about her flying?

Extend Interpretations

6. What If? Imagine that Amelia Earhart had grown up later in the 20th century. What kinds of goals might she be dreaming about and accomplishing today?

7. Connect to Life Think about how you might write your own autobiography. What would be the most dramatic event to include? What would be your purpose?

Literary Analysis

AUTOBIOGRAPHY

An **autobiography** is the story of a person's life, told by that person. Autobiography is usually written from the **first-person point of view,** meaning that the writer uses first-person pronouns to tell the story.

At twelve minutes after seven, I gave [the plane] the gun. . . . A minute later I was headed out to sea.

Since autobiographies are about real people and real events, they are a form of **nonfiction.** Types of autobiography include **journals, travelogues, diaries,** and **memoirs.**

Paired Activity Working with a partner, go back through the story and create a flight log for Earhart's trip. A log is a set of entries that describe time, weather, position, routine events, unusual events, and problems during the course of a trip. The time might be general, for example, "dawn."

FLIGHT LOG:
TRANSATLANTIC
CROSSING

A. Earhart.

7:12 P.M. Fair weather.
Took off solo from
Harbour Grace,
Newfoundland.
No problems.
Headed out to sea.

Literary Analysis

Autobiography Logs should include details of take-off, landing, and problems encountered on the way. Where possible, times and positions should be included.

Use **Literary Analysis Transparencies,** p. 11, for additional support.

Extend Interpretations

6. What If? Answers will vary widely but should reflect an understanding of Earhart's vision, competence, determination, and courage. Today Earhart might be an astronaut, for example, or someone who searches the rain forest for plants that will help make a cure for cancer.

7. Connect to Life Answers will vary. Students may say that they would like to share favorite stories, allow others to learn from their experiences, and introduce readers to people they would never otherwise meet.

Writing

Personality Profile Write a profile of Earhart's personality, using details from the selection. First use a web to organize your ideas. Place your profile in your **Working Portfolio.**

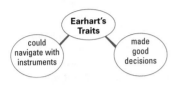

Writing Handbook
See page R37: Elaboration.

This writing activity asks you to inform readers about Amelia Earhart. To find out about writing forms you might use when your purpose is to inform, see p. R31: Choosing a Form.

Speaking & Listening

Video Viewing View the video biography of Amelia Earhart. In a small group, discuss what seeing and hearing Earhart adds to your impressions of her character. Why do you think people continue to find her inspiring? Support your answer.

VIDEO: Literature in Performance

Amelia Earhart

Research & Technology

Following Earhart's Lead In 1994 Vicki Van Meter became the youngest pilot to make a flight across the Atlantic Ocean. Find out about other record-breaking pilots. Make a chart showing the names of the pilots, the records they broke, and the dates of their accomplishments.

Reading for INFORMATION
As part of your research, read the magazine article "Daring to Dream" on p. 145.

Vocabulary

EXERCISE: RESTATEMENT CLUES On a sheet of paper, write the Word to Know that best completes each sentence. Then write a sentence of your own using this word.

1. The _____ of a flight is its length.
2. When you catch a _____ glimpse of the moon, you see it for a brief moment.
3. The plane began to _____ speed, going faster and faster.
4. The _____ of a plane is its flying height.
5. If the fuel in a plane's tank is _____, then the plane can land safely.
6. A plane that is above the ground by too small a _____ is flying too low.
7. A person who has lost the _____ of sight cannot see well.
8. Flying into the storm, the pilot noticed a _____, or change, in altitude.
9. A fishing _____ is a kind of boat.
10. Earhart's friends in England showed _____ by welcoming her.

Vocabulary Handbook
See p. R20: Context Clues.

WORDS TO KNOW				
accumulate	extent	fleeting	hospitality	sufficient
altitude	faculty	fluctuation	margin	vessel

Writing

Personality Profile Responses will vary but should include some of the following information: she was a skilled pilot, understood weather and its effect on the plane, had confidence in her abilities, put concern for her plane ahead of herself, enjoyed adventure, was both daring and careful.

 Use **Writing Transparencies,** pp. 2, 15, and 30, for additional support.

Speaking & Listening

Video Viewing Responses will vary, but should include that seeing her on video makes the viewer feel more connected to her.

 Use the **Speaking and Listening Book,** pp. 33, for additional support.

Research & Technology

Following Earhart's Lead Students might find this information in an almanac or book of records.

 Use **Writing Transparencies,** pp. 44, 45 for additional support.

Vocabulary
EXERCISE
1. extent
2. fleeting
3. accumulate
4. altitude
5. sufficient
6. margin
7. faculty
8. fluctuation
9. vessel
10. hospitality

Grammar in Context

WRITING EXERCISE
Students' sentences will vary. Accept sentences that use subjects in unusual order.

Connect to the Literature
The author uses the first and third methods.

Amelia Earhart

Because of her great achievements and the mystery surrounding her disappearance during her round-the-world trip, interest in Amelia Earhart has never waned. In 1997, a Texas woman named Linda Finch, using the same type of airplane as Earhart, completed the trip. It is believed that Earhart's plane went down near Howland Island in the Pacific, meaning Earhart had completed about three-fourths of her journey.

Grammar in Context: Subjects in Unusual Order

One way to make your writing more conversational—more like real speech—is to put the **subjects** of your sentences in different positions. There are many ways to do this. Here are four examples:

1. The word *there* or *here* at the beginning of a sentence usually means that the subject will follow the **verb**.

   > **There** ended my flight and happy adventure.

2. Sometimes the first words of a sentence are words of introduction, and the subject comes later.

   > **By the way, I didn't** bother much about food for myself.

3. Switching the usual subject-verb order, even without using *there* or *here,* is another way to add variety.

   > **Directly into the storm** flew the plane.

4. A question may not only switch the order of the subject and verb but may split up a verb phrase.

   > **Statement:** Amelia Earhart flew **her plane over the Atlantic.**
   > **Question: Where** did Amelia Earhart fly **her plane?**

WRITING EXERCISE Recall a time in your life when you acted bravely, or remember a story you have read about someone else's brave actions. Write five sentences about the experience, using the methods discussed above to add variety to the sentences.

Connect to the Literature Reread the first two paragraphs on page 139. Look for sentence subjects in different positions. Does the author use any of the methods discussed in the lesson?

Amelia Earhart
1897–1937?

"Women must try to do things as men have tried."

Breaking the Mold Amelia Earhart was born in Kansas. As children she and her sisters shocked their community by wearing pants and doing things usually done only by boys—things like hiking and sledding. Amelia even built a roller coaster in her backyard so that she could feel as if she were flying. As a young woman, she worked on airplane engines to pay for flying time. She also worked at several other jobs, but flying was always her passion.

Setting New Standards In accepting an award for her famous transatlantic solo flight, Earhart said, "I hope that the flight has meant something to women in aviation. If it has, I shall feel it was justified." Earhart published two memoirs in her lifetime, and some of her writings about her life and flying were published after her death. During her last flight—an attempt to fly around the world—she disappeared at sea.

EXPLICIT INSTRUCTION Grammar in Context

SUBJECTS IN UNUSUAL ORDER
Instruction Tell students that to find the subject of a question or an exclamation, they can change the question or exclamation into a statement: *Was Amelia Earhart the first woman to fly across the Atlantic?* becomes *Amelia Earhart was the first woman to fly across the Atlantic. Amelia Earhart* is the subject of the verb *was. Wasn't she something!* becomes *She wasn't something. She* is the subject of the verb *wasn't.*

For imperative sentences, explain that the word *you* is usually understood to be the subject, because the command is aimed at that person: *Get on the plane!* means *You get on the plane! You* is the subject of the verb *get.*
Practice Ask students to circle the subject in each of the following sentences. If *you* is understood, they should write *you.*
1. Did Earhart fly with Lindbergh? (Earhart)
2. Be sure to notice where she landed. (you)
3. Was she a great pilot! (she)

4. Did you read about the ice on the wings? (you)

 Use **Unit One Resource Book,** p. 72.

 For more instruction in finding the subject, see McDougal Littell's *Language Network,* Chapter 1.

For **systematic instruction** in grammar, see:
- **Grammar, Usage, and Mechanics Book**
- pacing chart on p. 19i.

Source: *American Girl*

Daring to Dream

Adapted from *Taking Flight, My Story*

by **Vicki Van Meter** with **Dan Gutman**

Dreams can come true. Just ask Vicki Van Meter, 13, of Meadville, Pennsylvania. Vicki's amazing adventures began with a simple wish: to become an astronaut.

To encourage Vicki's soaring spirit, her father suggested that Vicki take flying lessons when she was ten years old. Less than two years later, Vicki became the youngest girl to pilot a plane across America!

The following summer, a new challenge called to Vicki: flying across the Atlantic Ocean. Vicki's sixth-grade graduation was on June 3, 1994, and the next day she took off to pilot a plane to Scotland. "I knew one thing for sure," Vicki says. "Writing an essay on my summer vacation would be a breeze!"

Since Vicki was too young to fly alone, an adult pilot accompanied her on the flight across America, and on the flight across the Atlantic. But Vicki did all the flying herself. What follows is Vicki's account of her incredible journey across the ocean.

Vicki Van Meter,
record-breaking pilot

Reading for Information

Writers often use text organizers and other structural features to clarify and explain ideas. **Maps, time lines,** and **photographs** are used to organize information visually. Other features include **subheadings,** the large-type words that introduce sections of a work, and **captions.**

READING FOR INFORMATION **145**

1 The information following the title indicates that what is to follow is an adaptation from a longer piece of writing—the writer's autobiography, *Taking Flight, My Story.*

2 The subheadings ("Day 1: We're Off!" etc.) provide information about the events of Vicki's trip. Readers learn that the trip lasted three days and that as the trip went on, Vicki encountered more and more trouble.

3 The map provides detailed information about Vicki's route. Readers learn exactly where the trip began and ended, the stops Vicki made, when she flew over land and when she flew over water, and how far she flew each day of the trip.

Reading for Information *continued*

Reading a Magazine Article

Looking at text organizers and features, such as subheadings, sidebars, photographs, and captions, can help you figure out what an article is about. These features can also provide information that isn't in the body of the article, such as related facts or personal details.

YOUR TURN Use the following questions and activities to identify and use the features in this article and use them to get information.

❶ The **title** of a magazine article may be followed by a note explaining the **source** of the article or by a short summary of the article. What information follows this title?

❷ The words in highlighted type that begin a new section within an article are called a **subheading.** A subheading helps the reader understand the important ideas in the text that follows. What important ideas are identified by the subheadings in this article?

❸ A **map** can give clues to the topic of an article. A **map key** is a list of symbols that help you understand the information on the map. What do you learn about the article from this map?

❷ Day 1: We're off!

Along the way, I heard commercial pilots flying above us who were talking about me on the radio. They didn't know I was listening in on the same frequency.

"Hey, where's that little girl who's flying across the ocean?" they were saying.

I answered, "This is 127 Sierra, the girl who's flying across the ocean. Hi!"

Day 2: Trouble

We were a little over an hour into the flight when I noticed we were picking up some ice on the wings.

If we kept going like that, the ice would become so heavy that the plane wouldn't be able to fly.

"This is really starting to build up," I said to Curt. "Let's get on top of this stuff," he replied.

I pulled back on the yoke, but the nose of the plane didn't go up. Not a foot. We had waited too long.

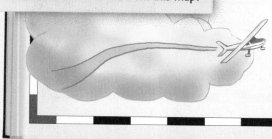

EXPLICIT
INSTRUCTION **Reading a Magazine Article**

Instruction Tell students that they can get information from magazine articles not only by reading the text but also by looking closely at special features, such as titles, pictures, captions, and maps. Ask, "What kinds of features are found on page 145 that are not part of the text of the article?" *(article title, where article came from, authors' names, photograph, caption)* On pages 146–147, point out the large-type headings (Day 1: We're off!, etc.) and explain that these headings tell about the sections of the article that follow them. Finally, ask volunteers to

identify other features in the article. *(map, map key, another photo and caption, sidebar)*

Practice Have students work in pairs to read and complete the numbered activities on the pupil pages.

Possible Responses: See the side columns in the teacher's edition for answers to the activities on the pupil pages.

Use **Unit One Resource Book,**
p. 75, for more practice.

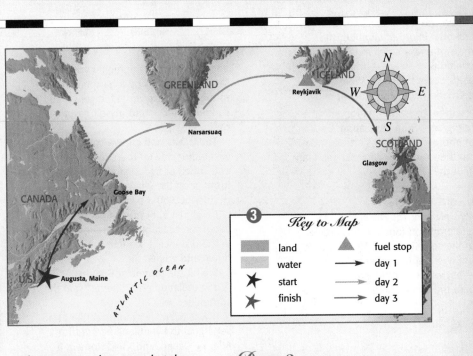

Key to Map

③

▢	land	▲	fuel stop
▢	water	→	day 1
★	start	→	day 2
★	finish	→	day 3

There was no place to go but down. If we dropped below the clouds, the air would be warmer, and hopefully it would melt the ice.

I brought Harmony down to 7,000 feet, and then 5,000 feet, but the air was thick with clouds. I came down to 3,000 feet, then 2,000 feet, then 1,000 feet. Still there were clouds— and a real danger of crashing.

Finally, at 800 feet over the water, we broke out from the clouds. We kept going at 500 feet. Soon the ice was gone. The crisis was past.

Day 3: More trouble

The first hours were smooth, but then we found ourselves flying through clouds and I noticed ice forming on the wings. Not again!

I had to take Harmony all the way up to 13,500 feet before we popped out of the top of the clouds and the sun began to melt the ice.

Just as it's risky flying too low, it's also risky flying very high. The atmosphere surrounding the earth

Main Idea(s): Vicki Van Meter has always been interested in flying. Vicki Van Meter created a challenge for herself when she was 13: to fly across the Atlantic Ocean.

Details: She wanted to become an astronaut. Her father suggested she learn how to fly a plane. She became the youngest pilot to cross America.

Day 1

Main Idea(s): Other pilots knew about Vicki's flight and were talking about her on the radio.

Details: One pilot said, "Hey, where's that little girl who's flying across the ocean?"

Day 2

Main Idea(s): On the second day, ice on the plane's wings caused trouble.

Details: The ice started to build up and make the plane heavy. Vicki tried to fly higher but the plane wouldn't go up. Vicki had to bring the plane very low to melt the ice. There was a danger of crashing.

Day 3

Main Idea(s): On the third day, ice on the wings caused more trouble.

Details: Vicki flew very high to let the sun melt the ice. There is a lack of oxygen at high altitudes and Vicki felt tired and couldn't breathe well. She had to suffer through it to be safe.

Summaries will vary.

EXPLICIT INSTRUCTION **Summarizing**

Instruction Tell students that a good way to make sure they understand the articles they read is to summarize them. Explain that a summary contains the most important information in an article. Say, "To summarize an article, you need to create a shortened version in your own words. You can do this by first figuring out the main idea of the whole article and then finding the important supporting details." Write these steps for determining the main idea of an article on the board and explain each step to students:

1 Note the main idea of each paragraph.
2 Find the 3 or 4 most important ideas in your list of main ideas.
3 Use these ideas to figure out the main idea of the whole article.

Say, "A good summary is accurate and does not include less important details."

Practice Have students work in pairs to identify the main ideas and details in the four different sections of this article: the introduction on page 145, and the information about each day of the trip on pages 146, 146–147, and 147–148. Then have partners use this information to write a summary of "Daring to Dream."

Possible Responses: See the side column on this page for possible responses.

Use **Unit One Resource Book**, p. 76, for more practice.

4 The sidebar gives specific details about Vicki's journey, such as the distance from beginning to end, the type of plane Vicki flew, who her copilot was, and a description of some special gear she used.

5 You learn that the article is about a young girl who is a pilot. That she's broken a record with her flying. You can guess that the article will be about her record-breaking flight. You also learn that she is younger than 17 and that even though she's broken a record, she still can't get her pilot's license until she is older.

Reading for Information *continued*

4 A **sidebar** is a box that shows additional information about the article's topic. A sidebar might include definitions of special terms or more details about the topic. What information does this sidebar show?

5 A **caption** gives information about a photograph or an illustration. Look at the photographs in this article and read their captions. What do you learn about the article?

Research & Technology
Activity Link: from *The Fun of It*, **p. 143.** Using information found in this article and in the selection from *The Fun of It*, prepare two graphics—maps or time lines—that will help other students compare the two flights.

becomes thinner the higher you go. My body was having a hard time due to the lack of oxygen. I felt very tired suddenly, and found myself gasping for breath.

There was nothing we could do. It was either stay up there in the thin air and suffer, or fly lower and risk ice forming on the wings again. We decided it would be safer to suffer.

I had just about reached my limit when the coast of Scotland appeared in the distance. I brought the plane down and gulped air.

We hit the tarmac at 6:30 P.M. "Congratulations, 127 Sierra," said the controller.

It was over. Six months earlier I had set a goal to fly a plane across the Atlantic Ocean, and I had done it. It felt great. Better than great. It felt awesome.

4

The Journey: Maine to Scotland

Distance: 3,105 miles over the freezing waters of the North Atlantic

Plane: A single-engine Cessna named Harmony. My call name was 127 Sierra.

Copilot: Curt Arnspiger, age 38

Important piece of emergency gear: Curt and I wore suits that were red and rubbery the entire trip. They were uncomfortable, but would keep us warm and afloat for 24 hours in case we had to land in water.

5 Despite her experience, Vicki can't get her pilot's license until she's 17.

EXPLICIT INSTRUCTION **Research & Technology**

The Research & Technology activity on this page links to the Research & Technology activity from the Choices & Challenges section following the excerpt from *The Fun of It* on page 143.

Instruction As they do the Research & Technology activity, students may use print sources or CD-ROM encyclopedias to find more information. If your school computer is connected to the Internet, help students refine searches by noting specific keywords. For example, "pilot records" or "speed records" are better search

phrases than "pilots" or "aeronautics," both of which are too broad.

Application Have students take informal notes before they decide how to organize their charts. In that way, they will be better able to decide which kinds of information to include.

Use **Writing Transparencies,** pp. 45–48, for additional support.

Building Vocabulary
Analyzing Word Parts

Did you know that when you speak English, you are also, in a way, speaking Greek, Latin, and other languages? Many English words have origins in these languages.

For example, the word hospitality is related to the Latin word *hospes*, meaning "guest."

Latin:	**hospes** *(guest)*
English:	**hospitality**
	hospital
	hospice
	host

> There ended the flight and my happy adventure. Beyond it lay further adventures of hospitality and kindness at the hands of my friends in England, France and America.
>
> —Amelia Earhart,
> *The Fun of It*

Strategies for Building Vocabulary

A **root** is a word part from which various words can be formed. *Hospit,* the root of *hospitality,* is an example of a Latin root. If you know certain roots, or base words, you can figure out the meanings of new words.

❶ **Understanding Word Families** Words that have the same root make up a **word family.** Such words usually have related meanings. For example, the Greek root *graph,* meaning "writing," is found in the related

words *autograph* (a person's signature or handwriting), *biography* (the written story of a person's life), and *graphite* (a mineral used in pencils).

❷ **Remembering Roots** Think of roots as clues that will lead you to the meanings of new words. The charts on this page show some common Greek and Latin roots. Notice how the meanings of the example words are related to the meanings of their roots.

Greek Root	Meaning	Word Family
aster, astr	star	asteroid (a small object in outer space) astronomy (the study of outer space)
geo	earth	geography (the study of earth's features) geode (a hollow, crystal-filled rock)
tele	far, distant	telephone (a device for transmitting sounds) television (a device for transmitting pictures)

Latin Root	Meaning	Word Family
mal	bad	malfunction (a failure to function) malady (an illness)
srib, script	write	scribble (to write hurriedly) description (a picture in words)
ten, tent	hold, keep	detention (a holding in custody) tenure (permanent holding of a job)

EXERCISE Identify a root in each word, and tell what the root means. Then use the word in a sentence. Use a dictionary if you need help.

1. prescription
2. malicious
3. tenacious
4. telecommunication
5. astronaut

Standards-Based Objectives
• understand how words are built from roots
• apply meanings of root words in order to comprehend

VOCABULARY EXERCISE
Sentences given are examples.
1. script; write; A doctor writes many prescriptions in one day.
2. mal; bad; His actions were mean and malicious.
3. ten; hold; Melanie is the most tenacious player I have ever seen; she never gives up.
4. tele; far, distant; Telecommunication allows people all over the world to speak to each other.
5. aster, astr; star; The astronaut just returned after nine weeks at the space station.

 Use **Unit One Resource Book,** p. 77.

Standards-Based Objectives
- appreciate the works of a contemporary American writer for young adults
- analyze the effect of personal experiences on Paulsen's writing
- explore some of the works Paulsen has written during his career

The Author Study puts the focus on one particular writer, examining his life and works in detail. By using the Author Study, students can develop the ability to compare and contrast a writer's experience with his or her literary output.

Author Study **GARY PAULSEN**

born 1939

CONTENTS

A Writer of Adventure

"If I can write a story, it's because of actually going, being there, and doing those things. It's more than 'Write what you know.' It's kind of like: Write what you are!"

LOST AND FOUND

Born into a military family in Minneapolis in 1939, Paulsen was raised by his aunts and grandmother and was shuffled around from school to school. Never a dedicated student, and without a permanent home or friends, young Paulsen found few opportunities in school and couldn't manage to fit in. Luckily, he reached a turning point in his early teens that

His LIFE and TIMES

1939
Born May 17 in Minneapolis, Minnesota

1953
Receives first library card

1955
Joins a carnival

1957
Graduates from high school

1940 — 1950 — 1960

1941–1945
United States in World War II

1951
Rock-and-roll is first used as a term to describe music.

1955
Bus boycott begins in Montgomery, Alabama.

150

changed his life. On a cold winter night he went into a library just to warm up. There a librarian offered him a library card, a book, and a chance to get as many books as he wanted, as long as he brought them back. As Paulsen tells it, "It was as though I had been dying of thirst and the librarian handed me a five-gallon bucket of water."

ALWAYS AN EXPLORER

Through his reading Paulsen developed a taste for action and adventure. In his teens, he worked on a farm, hunted and tracked animals, and even joined a carnival. Not surprisingly, his eagerness to experience new things stayed with him in the years ahead. As an adult, Paulsen held jobs as a teacher, engineer, soldier, actor, rancher, truck driver, professional archer, singer, and sailor. All the while he continued reading and exploring the world through stories. And with each new book and new adventure, Paulsen's desire to tell his own stories grew.

Did You Know?

- Gary Paulsen has written more than 130 books.
- He has raced in the Iditarod twice.
- His wife, Ruth, has illustrated some of his books.
- He once rode his motorcycle from New Mexico to Alaska.
- He travels around the world on his sailboat.
- He has covered 22,000 miles by sled.

Childhood
A Paulsen's father was a Danish immigrant who served on General Patton's staff in Europe during World War II. His mother worked in a munitions plant in Chicago. In 1946, Paulsen and his mother traveled to the Philippines, where he met his father for the first time. In one interview, Paulsen noted, "I became a street kid in Manila when I was around seven." Elsewhere he comments: "After we returned to the States [in 1949], we moved around constantly. I lived in every state. The longest time I spent in one school was for about five months." He also says, "I grew up in a small Minnesota town. I was an 'at risk' kid, as they are called now, and a poor student. I actually flunked the ninth grade." In another interview he comments: "School was a nightmare because I was unbelievably shy, and terrible at sports. I had no friends, and teachers ridiculed me."

Reading
B Paulsen adds another comment to his story about starting to read: "Over the course of two years, [the librarian] got me reading. I can't even imagine what would have happened to me without her. First it was a book a month, then a book every three weeks. Eventually it was two books a week. I would get Zane Grey westerns or books by Edgar Rice Burroughs, and she would slip in a Melville or a Dickens, or something. When I brought them back, she would ask me what I thought. It was incredible."

| 1966 Moves to Hollywood | 1968 Publishes first novel, *Some Birds Don't Fly* | 1971 Marries artist Ruth Wright | 1983 Races in his first Iditarod | 1986 *Dogsong* is named a Newbery Honor Book. | 1999 Lives and works mostly on board his sailboat |

1970 — 1980 — 1990 — 2000

| 1965–1973 U.S. ground troops in Vietnam War | 1979 Hostage crisis begins in Iran. | 1987 AIDS quilt is displayed to raise awareness. | 1995 Internet becomes widely available. | 1998 President Clinton is impeached. |

GARY PAULSEN **151**

Comparing Information

Instruction After students have read pages 150 and 151, ask them to compare the information about Paulsen with what they learned about Matthew Henson and Robert Peary in "Matthew Henson at the Top of the World." Ask, "How are these three men similar?" (*They were all raised without one or both parents. Both Henson and Paulsen had erratic educational experiences. They all developed a love for books and reading, as well as adventure. All three worked as sailors.*) Then discuss with students how reading was important in the lives of all three men.

Practice Have students work in pairs to write a short report that describes how books and reading were important to Paulsen, Peary, and Henson.

Possible Responses: Students' reports should include one or more of the following points: reading about faraway places inspired each to want to lead an adventurous life; both Henson and Paulsen were introduced to books by an older mentor; all three experienced adventure in their lives.

Author Study GARY PAULSEN

Career

C Paulsen describes his first job in writing this way: "I wrote a totally fictitious resume, which landed me an associate editorship on a men's magazine in Hollywood, California. It took them about two days to find out that I knew nothing about publishing. I didn't know what a lay-out sheet was, let alone how to do one. My secretary—who was all of nineteen years old—edited my first three issues. They could see I was serious about wanting to learn, and they were willing to teach me. We published some excellent writers—Steinbeck, Bradbury, Ellison—which was great training and exposure for me."

Dogsled Racing

D Paulsen stopped writing shortly after the publication of his novel *Winterkill* in 1977, when he was sued for libel. He went back to living off a 60-mile trap line in the Minnesota wilderness. One day he was given four sled dogs so that he could work his line more easily. From then on, he was hooked on dogsled racing. At one point he took off for seven days on a completely free romp across northern Minnesota, with only a few beaver carcasses for food. Later, after he went on to run the Iditarod, he rediscovered the joy of writing and began producing books again.

Reverence for Life

E The Iditarod taught Paulsen a new reverence for life. In one interview he commented: "The Iditarod may sound like a macho thrill, but it's the opposite. You go where death goes, and death doesn't give a damn about macho. Besides, the last two races were won by women. Here's something that was brought home to me: macho is a lie. It's . . . garbage. Core toughness and compassion are the opposite of macho. The absence of fear comes with knowledge, not strength or bravura. More people should be telling this to young people, instead of 'climb the highest mountain and kill something.'"

A NEW CALLING

C To learn the art of writing, Paulsen decided he needed to be in Hollywood, if only to be near other writers. Once he arrived, he talked his way into a job with an ad agency and worked on his writing at night. At last he had found his true calling. His skills as a writer developed slowly, but with hard work and the advice of fellow writers, Paulsen developed his own voice and style.

INTO THE NORTH

D In order to write full-time, Paulsen returned to Minnesota, settled into an isolated cabin, and began living off the land. After one winter there, Paulsen had completed his first novel, *Some Birds Don't Fly*. He enjoyed living in the woods and hunting for food, but he decided to move farther north to train for **E** the Iditarod, the famous trans-Alaska dogsled race. Even while training day and night in the cold, Paulsen continued writing. He also grew to love and admire his sled dogs so much that he found he could never kill another animal. Today Paulsen is one of America's most prolific and popular writers. He and his wife, the illustrator Ruth Wright Paulsen, share a Southwestern ranch and a houseboat anchored off the coast of California.

Paulsen with Cookie, one of his favorite companions and lead sled dog.

TALKING WITH GARY PAULSEN

Gary Paulsen loves to respond to letters. Here's his response to some frequently asked questions.

Q: **What is your favorite thing to write about?**

A: Almost always, it's about making personal discoveries while struggling to survive in the great outdoors. When I go into the wilderness, I like to go it alone. That way, I can pay close attention to things around me, which helps make my writing more realistic. I become very wolflike. Wolves see and listen to every single thing.

Q: **Getting your first library card was your passport to becoming a reader. Do you still read as much as you did then?**

A: I read like a wolf eats. I read myself to sleep every night. And I don't think any of the good things that have happened to me would have been possible without that librarian and libraries in general.

Q: **Your childhood sounds hard, and you were a poor student, so how did you learn to write so well?**

A: Initially, I wasn't very good at it. But I was determined to get to the place where I could express my thoughts on paper—I had so many stories to tell! I had already tried a lot of jobs. Once I decided to be a writer,

I realized I had a lot to learn. I started to focus on writing with the same energies and efforts that I used training dogs. So we're talking 18- to 20-hour days, completely committed to work. I still work that way, and the end result is there's a lot of books out there.

Q: **Your adventurous life sounds like the plot of a Gary Paulsen novel. Is a lot of you in your stories?**

A: That's true of a lot of authors, you use what you are. Your life becomes your material.

Q: **You wrote your best-known works while you were still running dogs. Where did you find the time?**

A: With the dogs, you run them just four hours on, then four hours off. When they were sleeping those four hours, I'd sit by my campfire and write longhand.

Q: **Do you like writing better than the other jobs you tried?**

A: Absolutely. To be able to portray things I see and hear in writing is a privilege.

 **Author Link**
www.mcdougallittell.com

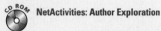 **NetActivities: Author Exploration**

Audience

F Paulsen claims that he writes for young adults because they are the only ones who can still change the world for the better. He notes that it is "artistically fruitless to write for adults. Adults created the mess which we are struggling to outlive. Adults have their minds set. Art reaches out for newness, and adults aren't new. And adults aren't truthful. . . . I'm betting that young people have the answers."

Autobiography

G Paulsen has written an autobiographical book, *Eastern Sun, Winter Moon.* It recounts some of his horrifying experiences as a child, including seeing a plane crash in the Pacific Ocean and its screaming passengers torn to shreds by sharks. One reviewer called it "a raw portrayal of a child thrown into the horrors of war and the adult world."

Attitude

H Paulsen notes: "I write because it's all I can do. Every time I've tried to do something else I cannot, and have to come back to writing, though often I hate it—hate it and love it. It's much like being a slave, I suppose, and in slavery there is a kind of freedom that I find in writing: a perverse thing. I'm not 'motivated.' . . . Nor am I particularly driven. I write because it's all there is."

GARY PAULSEN **153**

Standards-Based Objectives

1. understand and appreciate a **short story**
2. understand **anecdote** in a short story
3. identify effect of the **author's perspective**
4. recognize **cause-effect relationships**

Summary

While training his sled dogs, author Gary Paulsen gets into trouble. Caught in a precarious situation on a dangerous railroad trestle, he is forced to free the dogs from their harness. He is surprised and disheartened to see them disappear promptly into the woods. Miles from home, he begins the long trudge back, feeling abandoned. The lead dog, however, brings back the others, as she had on a previous occasion, and Paulsen gains new respect for her.

Thematic Link

Paulsen shows courage in action as he deals with a difficult turn of events. Though he finds himself alone on a frigid night in the Minnesota woods, he refuses to panic, and his patience is soon rewarded.

English Conventions Practice

Daily Language SkillBuilder

Have students **proofread** the display sentences on page 19k and write them correctly. The sentences also appear on Transparency 5 of **Language Transparencies.**

Preteaching Vocabulary

If you would like to preteach the WORDS TO KNOW for this selection, use the Explicit Instruction, page 155.

PREPARING to **Read** ESSAY

Older Run

by GARY PAULSEN

Connect to Your Life

Not Alone! Think about a time when you felt alone. Did someone come to help you? Describe the experience to a partner.

Build Background

HISTORY Mushing, or sled racing, is one of the oldest official sports in Canada. It was registered in 1908, even before hockey!

In recent years, long-distance racing and touring in the wilderness have become popular. "Sled" dogs are often hooked to skiers, bicycles, or four-wheelers.

WORDS TO KNOW
Vocabulary Preview

anticipate	ricochet
embankment	seasoned
exceeding	spectator
maneuver	transpire
marvel	trestle

Focus Your Reading

LITERARY ANALYSIS **ANECDOTE**

An **anecdote** is a short, entertaining story or report about one event. The event and characters can be either real or fictional. Paulsen's essay "Older Run" is an anecdote about a day in his life of training sled dogs. As you read, notice smaller anecdotes, or amusing events, within the larger one.

ACTIVE READING **RECOGNIZING CAUSES AND EFFECTS**

Two events have a **cause and effect** relationship when one event brings about the other. The event that happens first in time is the cause. The second event is the effect. Paying attention to causes and effects will help you understand why an event happened or what happened as a result of an event. As you read "Older Run," take notes in your **READER'S NOTEBOOK** about the causes and effects the author describes.

LESSON RESOURCES

INTEGRATED TECHNOLOGY
Audio Library

Visit our Web site:
www.mcdougallittell.com

For **systematic instruction** in language skills, see:
• **Vocabulary and Spelling Book**
• **Grammar, Usage, and Mechanics Book**
• pacing chart on p. 19i.

Older Run

by Gary Paulsen

Illustrations by Ruth Wright Paulsen

"HELP."

It was, in an impossible situation on an impossible night in an impossible life, the only possible thing to say.

I had never been in such an untenable,[1] completely bizarre situation.

The night had started easy, ridiculously easy, and I should have taken warning from the ease. Generally, when running dogs and sleds, a good moment or two will be followed by eight or nine hours of panic and disaster.

---

1. **untenable** (ŭn-tĕn′ə-bəl): impossible to maintain or defend.

155

Differentiating Instruction

Less Proficient Readers
Help students understand the action by mapping out the various times represented by parts of the text. For example, the story starts after Paulsen is abandoned; it then switches back to the beginning of his midnight adventure and follows it through to its conclusion, then jumps to the conversation he has with his wife about what happened.

English Learners
Ask students to think of the roles dogs play in different cultures. Answers may include: companions, guide dogs for blind people, research, or police and drug enforcement helpers. In some cultures dogs are used for transportation. In this story, dogsledding is a sport, although the author also uses dogs for transportation when he is trapping other animals.

Advanced Students
Have students consider the relationship between Paulsen and his dogs in the selection. Are the dogs characters? Ask students to write a paragraph comparing this animal/human relationship with friendships they have between themselves and their friends.

EXPLICIT INSTRUCTION Preteaching Vocabulary

WORDS TO KNOW
Teaching Strategy Explain to students that sometimes they can determine the meaning of an unfamiliar word by examining **examples** that might be given in the text. If they see the sentence "The dog did many tricky maneuvers, such as leaping backwards, twisting her body, and ducking quickly," students should be able to guess that a maneuver is a movement or change in direction.

Practice The following sentences use examples to explain some of the WORDS TO KNOW. Have students write a definition of each underlined word based on the examples given.
1. Spectators, whether they are football fans or innocent people at crime scenes, are often affected by what they see.
2. Embankments, such as those that protect castles, raise roadbeds, or cover underground houses, often change drainage patterns.

3. Trestles, whether they support railroad or highway bridges, require careful engineering.

Use **Unit One Resource Book**, p. 83, for more practice.

For **systematic instruction** in vocabulary, see:
• **Vocabulary and Spelling Book**
• pacing chart on p. 19i.

Help students understand the story by drawing a rough diagram of the trestle. Use the diagram to show how the dogs run out on the trestle, how Paulsen falls off the sled, and how he releases the dogs one by one. Ask students to speculate on what might happen after the dogs are released.

Active Reading

| RECOGNIZING CAUSES |
| AND EFFECTS |

Remind students that when one event brings about another, the events are said to have a cause and effect relationship. Ask students to identify events that are related by cause and effect as they read this selection.

 Use **Unit One Resource Book,** p. 79, for more practice.

Literary Analysis **ANECDOTE**

Ⓐ Have students retell the passage about getting the dogs harnessed and starting off as a distinct anecdote. Point out that personal essays such as the selection they are reading are often composed of many shorter anecdotes.

 Use **Unit One Resource Book,** p. 80, for more practice.

Reading Skills and Strategies:
VISUALIZE

Ⓑ Ask students to sit with their eyes closed and visualize the scene where the author takes the dogs into the forest while you read it to them. Then ask them to describe mental images that the text descriptions evoked.

It was early on in training Cookie's pups. They were already trained, knew how to run, where to run, when to run and were having a ball. I was still in that phase of my life when I thought I had some semblance of control over the team, did not yet understand that the dogs ran the show—all of it—and, if I was extremely lucky and didn't hit a tree, I was allowed to hang on the back of the sled and be a spectator. The problem was that my education was coming so slowly that I had fallen behind the dogs—say a couple of years— and it was becoming difficult to keep up.

This night had begun cleanly, wonderfully. It was midwinter, clear, fifteen or twenty below, a full moon—absolutely beautiful. I put Cookie on the front end and took three of the seasoned dogs and six of the pups, a total of ten dogs, counting Cookie.

Exceeding seven dogs was risky—more than seven dogs meant it would be difficult to stop them or control them, in fact it could not be done unless they wanted to stop—but I knew that and loaded the sled heavily with gear and four fifty-pound sacks of dog meat to help me control them.

WORDS	**spectator** (spĕk′tā′tər) *n.* someone who watches an event
TO	**seasoned** (sē′zənd) *adj.* made skillful by practice; experienced **season** *v.*
KNOW	**exceeding** (ĭk-sē′dĭng) *n.* having more than **exceed** *v.*

156

EXPLICIT INSTRUCTION ## Viewing and Representing

Illustration for "Older Run"
by Ruth Paulsen

ART APPRECIATION Ruth Paulsen, Gary Paulsen's wife, frequently contributes original artwork to his exciting adventure stories.

Instruction Tell students that sometimes what artists choose not to show is as important as what they do show. In this picture, shadow plays an essential role. Ask how the artist has used shadow to highlight the action on a moonlit night. *(The form on the sled is dark and obscured, so the viewer's eye is caught by the* dogs in front, which are the most active part of the illustration.)

Practice Ask students to explain how the picture would be different if it showed action taking place at noon.

Possible Response: It might include more detail—for example, the features of the man on the sled—and more color. It would not be so stark—that is, the extremes of light and shadow would not be so pronounced.

Cookie held the gang line[2] out while I harnessed the rest of them, the pups last because they were so excited they kept jumping over the gang line and getting tangled, and when I popped the quick-release holding the sled to a post near the kennel we snapped out in good order.

That's how I thought of it—almost in a stuffy English manner. *Ahh yes, we left the kennel in good order, everything quite, that is to say, quite properly lined up.*

The weight of the sled did not seem to bother them at all. This, of course, should have been a warning to me, a caution that I had exceeded my limits of ability and understanding, but it was a smashing night (still in the English mode), clear and quite, that is to say, quite beautiful, and I gave them their head (as if I had any choice).

We climbed the shallow hills out back of the kennel and moved into the forest. I had a plan to run a hundred miles—take twelve, fourteen hours with a rest stop—and see how the young dogs did with a slightly longer run. They had been to fifty twice and I didn't <u>anticipate</u> any difficulty. If they did get tired, I would just stop for a day and play—God knows I was carrying enough extra food.

I also decided to make it an "open" run and stay away from thick forests and winding trails. Young dogs tend to forget themselves in the excitement and sometimes run into trees on tight corners because they don't remember to swing out. It doesn't hurt them much, but it isn't pleasant and running should, of all things, be fun for them.

So I took the railroad grades. In northern Minnesota there used to be trains through the forests for hauling wood and supplies to the logging camps and to service the hundreds of small towns. Most of the towns are gone now, and much of the wood is hauled on trucks, but the railroad grades are still there.

In a decision so correct it seems impossible that government could have made it, they decided to pull the tracks and ties off the <u>embankments</u> and maintain them for wilderness trails. In the summer they use them for bicycles and hikers, in the winter for skiers and snowmobilers and now dogsledders.

The trails make for classic runs. It's possible to leave the kennel and run a week, hundreds and hundreds of miles, without seeing the same country twice.

The one problem is the <u>trestles</u>. Minnesota is a land of lakes and rivers and every eight or ten miles the trains would cross a river. They made wooden trestles for the tracks and the trestles are still there. They are open, some of them sixty or seventy feet high, and bare wood—although they took the tracks themselves off so it was possible to see down through the ties.

Because they were open they would not hold snow so the snowmobile clubs covered them with one-inch treated plywood to close them in and provide a base for the snow.

The first few times we crossed one, the dogs hesitated, especially on the higher ones, but I took it easy and the older dogs figured it out and passed confidence to the team and it worked all right.

We had by this time run the trestles many times, knew where each one was, and the dogs whizzed across when we came to them.

Until now.

---

2. **gang line:** the rope by which a team of sled dogs are attached to a sled.

WORDS
TO
KNOW

anticipate (ăn-tĭs′ə-pāt′) *v.* to look forward to; foresee
embankment (ĕm-băngk′mənt) *n.* a long mound of earth or stone, sometimes built
to raise a roadway or railroad above the surrounding land
trestle (trĕs′əl) *n.* a framework built to support a bridge

157

Literary Analysis: DESCRIPTION

A Have students identify elements of description in the passage about coming to the trestle.

Possible Response: Paulsen mentions "a quiet brook kept open by small warm springs winding through a stand of elegant spruce and tall Norway pines." He adds that it was a place "to make you whisper and think of churches."

Literary Analysis: HUMOR

B Ask students whether they find the description of the accident humorous or frightening, and ask them to explain their reasoning.

Possible Responses: The description is humorous, because the event is compared to something that might happen in a slapstick comedy, and Paulsen uses exaggerated language (for example, "ricocheted neatly into space, and dropped . . . headfirst, driving in like a falling arrow") and understatement ("I, however, did not stop.") Another humorous element is his belief that he is still on the sled when he is actually "upside down in the snowbank."

Literary Analysis   ANECDOTE

C Have students review the selection to this point and identify individual anecdotes within the larger personal essay that is "Older Run."

Possible Responses: Harnessing the dogs and setting out, the accident at the trestle, unharnessing the dogs, watching them disappear.

Literary Analysis: SUSPENSE

D Ask students to identify details that Paulsen uses to create suspense—that is, the things that slow the story down at this point.

Possible Response: He discusses the sled, having tea, how far away home is, his wish to meet the person who stole the plywood, and how he pulls the sled for a while along the railroad way.

Twenty-five miles into the run, smoking through the moonlight, we came to a trestle over an open rushing river. I had turned my head lamp off to let them run in the moonlight, which they preferred, and was thinking ahead, way ahead of a place we were going to camp to rest the pups. It was one of the most beautiful places I had ever seen, a quiet brook kept open by small warm springs, winding through a stand of elegant spruce and tall Norway pines. It was a place to make you whisper and think of churches, and I liked to stop and sit by a fire, and I was thinking of how it would be to camp there and be peaceful when the dogs suddenly stopped.

Dead in the middle of the trestle.

I hit the brakes with my right foot and almost killed myself. Some maniac had come and stolen all the plywood from the trestle and when I jammed the two hardened steel teeth of the brake down instead of sliding on the plywood surface to a gradual stop, they caught on an open cross tie and stopped the sled instantly.

I, however, did not stop.

In a maneuver that would have looked right in an old Mack Sennett[3] comedy, I slammed into the cross handlebar with my stomach, drove all the wind out of my lungs, flew up and over the sled in a cartwheel, hit to the right of the wheel dogs, bounced once on the iron-hard cross ties of the trestle, ricocheted neatly into space, and dropped twenty feet into a snow bank next to the river, headfirst, driving in like a falling arrow.

All of this occurred so fast I couldn't mentally keep up with it and still somehow thought that I must be on the sled when I was upside down in the snow bank. As it was I had hit perfectly. Had I gone a few feet farther I would have landed in the river and probably have drowned or frozen, ten feet sooner and I would have missed the snow bank and hit the bare packed ice, which would have broken my neck. It was the only place for me to land and not kill myself, but at the moment I was having trouble feeling gratitude.

I pushed my way out of the snow, cleared my eyes—it had happened so fast I hadn't had time to close them and they were full of snow—and peered up at the underside of the trestle where I could look through the ties and see the team still standing there, the dogs balanced precariously, teetering over open space.

"Easy," I called up. "Just easy now. Easy, easy, easy . . ."

Cookie had hit the trestle without stopping and run out, thinking that's what I wanted, until the whole team was out on the open ties. What stopped her was the pups. Somehow the adult dogs had kept up, stepping on the ties as fast as possible to keep going, but the young dogs had less experience and had tripped and gone down. Thank heaven they weren't injured and Cookie stopped when she felt them fall.

But the problem was still there. The team was spread along the trestle, each dog on a tie, and it seemed an impossible situation. To swing a dog team around requires a great deal of space. If they are dragged back on top of each other they get dreadfully tangled and tend to fight, and I couldn't imagine a dogfight at night with ten dogs on a narrow railroad trestle twenty feet off the ground.

An answer did not come to me immediately. I climbed the bank back up onto the trestle.

---

3. **Mack Sennett:** an early director of silent movies, especially slapstick comedies.

| WORDS TO KNOW | **maneuver** (mə-nōō'vər) *n.* a movement or change in direction |
| | **ricochet** (rĭk'ə-shā') *v.* to bounce off a surface |

Cookie was frozen out in front of the team holding them, her back legs jammed against one cross tie and her front feet clawed on the one in front, and the snow hook had fallen in the impact of the stop and had set itself in the ties under the sled so the team was held in place while I decided what to do.

I couldn't turn them around.

I couldn't drive them over the trestle without injuring dogs.

"I can't do anything," I said aloud to Cookie, who was looking back at me waiting for me to solve the thing. "It's impossible . . ."

You, her eyes said, *got us into this, and you'd better get us out.*

Her message hung that way for half a minute, my thoughts whirling, and I finally decided the only way to do it was to release each dog, one at a time, and let them go forward or backward on their own. I thought briefly of carrying them out, one by one, but I had no extra rope to tie them (it was the last run I made without carrying the extra rope) when I got across the trestle.

I would have to let them go.

I started with the older dogs. I let them loose and set the ties and was amazed to see that each of them went on across the trestle— the longer way—rather than turn and go back. They didn't hesitate but set out, moving carefully from tie to tie until they were across. Whereupon they didn't stop and instead, as I had feared, took off down the railroad grade. They had been here before and knew the way home. I let the young dogs go then and they were slower and more frightened, especially when they looked down, but as soon as they crossed they took off as well and vanished in

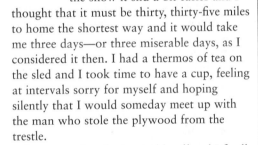

"Easy," I called up. "Just easy now. Easy, easy, easy . . ."

the night as they tried to catch up with the rest of the dogs.

"Well," I said to Cookie. "It's you and me . . ."

I let her loose and was amazed to see her take off after the team. We were good friends, had been for years, and I was sure she would stay with me, but she was gone in an instant.

"*Traitor.*" I said it with great feeling. The truth is she could not have pulled the sled anyway. It was too heavy for one dog. But it would have been nice to have company. I worried that they would have trouble, get injured somehow, run out on a highway and get hit by a car. It was like watching my body leave me, my family, and I gathered up the gang line and unhooked the snow hook and dragged the sled across the trestle. Once I got it on the snow it slid a bit easier and I thought that it must be thirty, thirty-five miles to home the shortest way and it would take me three days—or three miserable days, as I considered it then. I had a thermos of tea on the sled and I took time to have a cup, feeling at intervals sorry for myself and hoping silently that I would someday meet up with the man who stole the plywood from the trestle.

It was putting the inevitable off and I finally accepted it and put away the thermos and moved to the front of the sled and put the gang line around my waist and started pulling. Once it broke free it slid well enough and I set a slow pace. I had thought of hiding the sled in some way and coming back for it later but it was coming on a weekend and the snowmobilers would be on the trails and there

C

D

Differentiating Instruction

Less Proficient Readers
Give students guidance and practice in paraphrasing and summarizing text to recall and organize ideas. Have them summarize the action that takes place after Paulsen has fallen from the bridge.

Possible Response: Paulsen determines that the only way to get out of the situation is to let the dogs loose from their harnesses so that each can get off the bridge individually. As he lets each go, it disappears into the night. Even his favorite dog, Cookie, runs after the others. He is disappointed and feels alone but drags the sled off the bridge and has a cup of tea while he thinks over his situation.

English Learners
Discuss with students the meaning of any phrases they do not understand, which might include: "twenty five miles into the run" (*after we had gone 25 miles*); "smoking through the moonlight" (*going fast through the moonlight*); *maniac* (*crazy person*); *whereupon* (*after which*); "with great feeling" (*with a lot of emotion*); "putting the inevitable off" (*delaying even though what will happen next is certain*).

Advanced Students
Ask students what they would do in Paulsen's situation. Do they agree with him in letting each dog loose? Have students predict what will happen and how Paulsen gets the sled home. Have students support their predictions. After reading, check to see who made the correct predictions and ask students why they think the dogs returned.

EXPLICIT INSTRUCTION ## Author's Perspective

Instruction Explain to students that every author has a different perspective or way of seeing the world. Say, "Think of a child going to visit the doctor. The child and the child's parent might describe the same visit using different details and a different tone because each has a different perspective on, or way of understanding, the visit." Next, ask "How does Gary Paulsen seem to feel about the dogs? Does he think they are just work animals, or does he view them as sensitive and intelligent creatures, almost like humans?"

(*Paulsen respects his dogs as his equals.*) Then ask students to point out sections in the text that show Paulsen's perspective on his dogs. (*Students might point out the way Paulsen talks to and understands Cookie on page 159.*)

Practice Have students find and record other passages that show Paulsen's perspective on animals. After reading the story, ask students to share their lists and describe Paulsen's perspective.

Possible Responses: On page 159, Paulsen feels betrayed when Cookie runs away. "'*Traitor!* . . . [i]t would have been nice to have company.'" On page 160, Paulsen is proud of his dogs, "'I know it sounds insane. . . . I've never heard of anything like it.'"

Use **Unit One Resource Book,** p. 81, for more practice.

Reading and Analyzing

Literary Analysis: SARCASM

A Explain that sarcasm is a type of humor that depends on biting wit directed against a particular individual. Ask students to examine the passage in which the dogs return to Paulsen to find examples of sarcasm.

Possible Response: Paulsen's questions "Get lonely?" and "What is this? Loyalty?" are sarcastic.

Reading Skills and Strategies: EVALUATE

B Have students evaluate the text to determine Paulsen's feelings when Cookie brings the team back to him.

Possible Response: He is very moved emotionally by Cookie's intelligence and loyalty to him; he says that he has a lump "the size of a football" in his throat.

Reading Skills and Strategies: PREDICT

Ask students to predict the changes Paulsen will make as he continues his training of dogs after the incident described in "Older Run."

Possible Response: He will have more faith in Cookie and he will carry an extra length of rope for emergencies.

---

were hundreds of them. Surely, the sled—boiled white ash and oak with plastic runner shoes—would be too tempting.

I pulled half an hour on the embankment, trudging along—it seemed like a week—and I developed an updated gratitude for the dogs; their effortless strides covered miles so fast that I felt like with my own puny efforts I was on a treadmill. It seemed to take ten minutes to pass a tree.

Fifteen more minutes, I thought, *then I'll take a break.* I had also decided to throw out some of the dog food and let the wolves have it. It was commercial meat and had cost money but at the rate I was moving I wouldn't get it home until I was an old man anyway.

Ten minutes passed and I said to heck with it and sat down on the sled and was sitting there, sipping half a cup of tea, when I heard a sound and Minto, a large red dog who had a pointed face, came trotting up and sat down facing me.

"Hello," I said. "Get lonely?"

He cocked his head and I petted him, and while rubbing his ears another dog, named Winston, trotted up.

"What is this?" I asked. "Loyalty?"

The truth is they shouldn't have been there. I had lost dogs several times and had them leave me and run home. Trapline teams,[4] or teams that are lived with and enjoyed recreationally, sometimes are trained to stay with the musher;[5] and indeed Cookie had brought a team to me when I was injured once while trapping. But that is rare. Mostly they go home. And race teams, trained for only one thing, to go and go and never stop, simply do not come back. These were not trapline dogs but race dogs, and while I sat <u>marveling</u>

at them four more came back, then one more, then the last two pups and, finally, Cookie.

I stood and spread out the gang line and hooked up their harnesses, which were still on the dogs, putting Cookie in first and then the rest, and I wanted to say something and I finally did manage to get "thank you" out. But in truth I couldn't speak. I had a lump the size of a football in my throat. I stood on the back of the sled and they lined out and took off and I still wondered how it could be.

I do not know what happened out there—although some of the dogs had slight wounds in the end of their ears clearly made by bites. I did not see nor could I even guess what had <u>transpired</u>.

I know how it looked. I had been alone, Cookie had run after them, and they had come back. All of them, some bleeding slightly from bitten ears. They all got in harness and we finished the run in good order and when I was sitting in the kitchen later, sipping a cup of hot soup and trying to explain it to Ruth, I shook my head.

"I know it sounds insane but it looked like Cookie went after them, caught them and sent them back to me. I've never heard of anything like it."

"Well, if it looks like a duck, quacks like a duck, and walks like a duck . . ."

I nodded. "I agree, but it's so incredible."

"I don't know about that, but I do know one thing."

"What's that?"

"You aren't paying her nearly enough . . ." ❖

---

4. **trapline teams:** teams of working sled dogs that provide transportation for animal trappers.

5. **musher:** a person who drives a dogsled.

| WORDS TO KNOW | **marvel** (mär′vəl) *v.* to feel amazement or wonder at the sight of |
| | **transpire** (trăn-spīr′) *v.* to happen; occur |

160

Connect to the Literature

1. **What Do You Think?**
How did you feel
when the dogs
returned?

Comprehension Check
• What causes Paulsen's
accident?
• Why does Paulsen let the
dogs go?
• What does Paulsen say race
teams are trained to do?

Think Critically

2. What does Paulsen mean when he says, "I was still
in that phase of my life when I thought I had some
semblance of control over the team, did not yet
understand that the dogs ran the show . . ."?

3. **ACTIVE READING** **RECOGNIZING CAUSES
AND EFFECTS**

Look back at the causes and effects you listed in your
READER'S NOTEBOOK. Compare your list with a
classmate's.

4. How did reading Paulsen's story make you see the
connection between dogs and people in a new way?

Extend Interpretations

5. **COMPARING TEXTS** In the story "Ghost of the
Lagoon," on page 124, the main character faces
danger together with a very loyal dog. How are the
situations in that story and in "Older Run" similar
or different?

6. **Different Perspectives** What do you think happened to
the dogs when they ran away? What made them come
back? Retell the scene after the accident from Cookie's
point of view. Use details from the story and your own
imagination.

7. **Connect to Life** Do you have qualities of an adventurer?
Use examples from the story and from your own
experience to explain your opinion.

Literary Analysis

ANECDOTE An **anecdote** is a
short, entertaining story, either
fiction or **nonfiction,** about a
single event. Usually an
anecdote is rich with small
details.

Writers often use an anecdote
to throw a spotlight on a
character. For example, in "Older
Run," Paulsen uses an anecdote
to show readers some traits of
Cookie, his favorite dog. Notice
what traits are shown in the
following detail:

*Cookie had hit the trestle
without stopping and run out,
thinking that's what I wanted,
until the whole team was out
on the open ties. What stopped
her was the pups.*

Group Activity With a small
group, brainstorm some traits of
both Cookie and Gary Paulsen.
Choose a group member to
record your ideas in two webs.
Then have the group's recorder
add a detail from the anecdote
that would help readers to see
each trait.

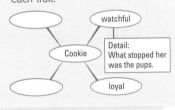

Connect to the Literature

What Do You Think?

1. **Possible Responses:** I felt relieved,
surprised, justified in my confidence
in dogs, and glad for Paulsen.

Comprehension Check
• Someone has stolen the plywood
decking from the trestle.
• There is not enough room on the
trestle to swing the team around.
• They are trained to keep going and
not come back to the sled.

 Use Selection Quiz, **Unit One
Resource Book,** p. 84.

Think Critically

2. **Possible Response:** He means that
he once believed that he could
control the dogs, but he now knows
that a sled driver has little if any real
control over the dogs.

3. **Possible Responses:** If two students
list different causes for the same
effect, or different effects of the
same cause, have them go back
through the story to double check
their work.

4. **Possible Responses:** It made me
realize that dogs care about people
in very intelligent and sophisticated
ways, even though people
sometimes underestimate them.

Literary Analysis

Anecdote Students' webs should accurately and appropriately depict character traits of both Cookie and Paulsen.
They should include details from the
story that illustrate the given traits.
Traits that might be mentioned include:
Cookie: intelligence, loyalty, a can-do
attitude; Paulsen: love of risk and
adventure, coolness under stress,
gratitude towards loyalty.

 Use **Literary Analysis Transparencies,**
pp. 9 and 11, for additional support.

Extend Interpretations

5. **Comparing Texts** Responses should note
similarities and differences between the two
animal stories. **To make this activity more
challenging,** ask students to write a new story
in which the characters in the two stories meet,
tell their tales, and compare and contrast their
experiences.

6. **Different Perspectives** Responses should
plausibly explain what the dogs were doing in
the interval in which they were absent, focusing
on Cookie's role in bringing them back.

To get students started on this activity, reread
the end of the story aloud.

7. **Connect to Life** Responses should indicate what
the qualities of an adventurer are and provide
appropriate details from the story and from
personal experience to support statements
made. **To make this activity easier,** hold a
discussion in which students explore what it
takes to be an adventurer. Then suggest that
students base their writing on some of the
themes and ideas worked out in class.

Grammar in Context

WRITING EXERCISE

Responses will vary. Possible responses are shown.

1. The trails lead to an open field.
2. The bear bothers the dogs.
3. The raven pecks the puppies away from the food pan.

Connect to the Literature

Pairs include: It was, They were/knew/were having, I was, I thought, I had, I did (not yet) understand, dogs ran, I was, I didn't hit, I was allowed, problem was, education was coming, I had fallen, it was becoming.

Vocabulary

EXERCISE A

1. d
2. c
3. b
4. c
5. d
6. c
7. d
8. a
9. c
10. b

EXERCISE B

Accept tips that make sense and use at least five of the WORDS TO KNOW.

Grammar in Context: Subject-Verb Agreement

If a subject is singular, its verb must also be singular. If a subject is plural, its verb must also be plural. This is what is meant by **subject-verb agreement.**

> **Singular: One** dog **jumps** ahead.
> **Plural: Two** dogs **jump** ahead.

Notice that adding an *s* makes a subject plural: "one dog," but "two dogs." Notice that adding an *s* makes a verb singular: "one dog jumps," but "two dogs jump." Some common verbs, like *to be, to go,* and *to have,* follow their own rules for changing number.

Usage Tip: The verb should always agree in number with the subject. Don't be confused by the position of the subject or the verb, or by the words that fall between them:

> **There were** still **problems.**
> (**Think "Problems were** still **there.")**

Vocabulary

EXERCISE A: WORD RECOGNITION On your paper, write the letter of the word that does not belong with the other words in each set. Use a dictionary if you need help.

1. (a) embankment (b) dam (c) levee (d) bridge
2. (a) spectator (b) onlooker (c) player (d) witness
3. (a) motion (b) crash (c) maneuver (d) action
4. (a) trestle (b) support (c) guide (d) structure
5. (a) accustomed (b) seasoned (c) skillful (d) new

WRITING EXERCISE Rewrite each sentence. Change each singular subject to plural, and each plural subject to singular. Then make the verb agree with the changed subject.

Example: *Original* The dog seems nervous.

Rewritten The dogs seem nervous.

1. The trail leads to an open field.
2. The bears bother the dogs.
3. The ravens peck the puppies away from the food pan.

Connect to the Literature Read the first paragraph on page 156 of the story. Notice the agreement between subjects and verbs in the paragraph. Then list all of the agreeing pairs.

Grammar Handbook
See p. R68: Making Subjects and Verbs Agree.

6. (a) surpassing (b) excelling (c) satisfying (d) exceeding
7. (a) anticipate (b) expect (c) foresee (d) ignore
8. (a) land (b) rebound (c) ricochet (d) bounce
9. (a) happen (b) occur (c) miss (d) transpire
10. (a) marvel (b) thin (c) ponder (d) muse

EXERCISE B Write some tips for sports safety. Use at least five of the Words to Know.

Vocabulary Handbook
See p. R22: Synonyms and Antonyms.

WORDS TO KNOW				
anticipate embankment	exceeding maneuver	marvel ricochet	seasoned spectator	transpire trestle

---

EXPLICIT INSTRUCTION Grammar in Context

SUBJECT-VERB AGREEMENT

Instruction Remind students that a pronoun is a word used *in place of* a noun. The singular pronouns used as subjects are *I, you, he, she, it.* The plural pronouns used as subjects are *we, you, they.* Pronouns, like all subjects, must agree with the verb. That is, if the pronoun is singular, the verb must also be singular. Write the following examples on the chalkboard:
SINGULAR: I am a dog. PLURAL: We are dogs.
SINGULAR: You are a dog. PLURAL: You are dogs.
SINGULAR: He/She is a dog.

PLURAL: They are dogs.
Point out to students that in some cases, the verb stays the same whether the pronoun is singular or plural.

Practice Have students change singular pronouns to plural and plural to singular, and then make the verb agree with the subject.

1. They love to run more than anything. (*She/He loves*)
2. I was ready to go anywhere on that sled. (*We were*)
3. We bounce off the trestle and fall in a snowbank. (*I bounce*)

4. You are the best dog in the world. (*You are*)
5. She was more loyal than Paulsen thought. (*They were*)

 Use **Unit One Resource Book,** p. 82.

 For more instruction in subject-verb agreement, see McDougal Littell's *Language Network,* Chapter 7.

For **systematic instruction** in grammar, see:
• **Grammar, Usage, and Mechanics Book**
• pacing chart on p. 19i.

A LIFE IN THE DAY OF GARY PAULSEN

Active Reading

FACTS AND OPINIONS

Point out to students that nonfiction often contains both facts and opinions. For example, a writer of nonfiction may present an opinion and support it with facts. Distinguishing fact from opinion is an important skill for readers to learn. Once readers identify a writer's opinions, they can better understand his or her personality, as well as his or her perspective on the world.

Students should think about what they learn about Gary Paulsen from reading his opinions and distinguishing them from facts.

PREPARING to *Read*

Focus Your Reading

ACTIVE READING | **FACTS AND OPINIONS**

Writers of nonfiction often combine facts and opinions to achieve their purpose. A **fact** is a statement that can be proven. Here's an example of a fact:

Gary Paulsen was born in 1939.

An **opinion** is a statement of thought, feeling, or belief. An opinion shows what someone thinks about a subject. Example:

People watch too much television.

Although an opinion may be based on facts, it is not a fact itself.

📖 **READER'S NOTEBOOK** As you read, jot down examples of facts and opinions.

At 5:30 A.M. I have a bowl of oatmeal, then I go to work. First up, I stow all the gear away. Then I take the covers off the sails and fire the engine up to get out of the harbor. I hate the motor—once it's off, there's silence. I have a steering vane so I can go below and cook or sit and write. Sailing is an inherently beautiful thing. To me it's like dancing with the wind and the water; it's like running with wolves—a perfect meeting of man and nature.

We all have the capability to work out of our minds, and I think we obstruct that constantly. So much of my life, and perhaps everybody's life, is television and traffic jams and trivia. A hundred yards into the woods on the back of a dog team, or the moment you clear the breakwaters in the harbors, all that is gone: my head clears and I feel calm. I have a radio but I frequently turn the darn thing off for a couple of days.

On the boat there is nothing, and I know I work better that way. I think that the writer in the city, with the traffic and the parties and the theater, is at a disadvantage, because the distractions are so enormous. I work in the city when I have to, but I find it really hard. I don't need much. The way I live is nobody's idea of luxury, but that's the way I like it. I use a battery to charge my laptop and I just head out to sea. Sometimes I go 150 miles out and 150 miles back; sometimes I head out and keep right on going.

I live on a diet of gruel because of my heart condition: no meat, no cheese, no fish; just beans and rice and marshmallows for treats, because they're fat free. I eat two meals a day and drink decaffeinated coffee—my cholesterol level has dropped to near normal.

I write all morning, then I have a two-hour break to answer mail. I get around 400 letters a day from children and I have a secretary in New York who helps me answer them all. I owe a great deal to dogs and a

A LIFE IN THE DAY OF GARY PAULSEN **163**

Fact and Opinion

Instruction Remind students that even though an autobiography is nonfiction, it usually contains more than just facts. The author usually includes his or her opinions about people, events, and places. Review with students the difference between a fact (*a statement that can be proven*) and an opinion (*a statement of someone's beliefs or feelings that cannot be proven*). Next, have students reread the first paragraph of "A Life in the Day of Gary

Paulsen" and ask volunteers to identify facts and opinions in it. (*Facts—Paulsen has a bowl of oatmeal at 5:30 A.M. then goes to work. He stows all the gear, takes the covers off the sails, and fires up the engine. Opinions— Paulsen hates the motor. Sailing is an inherently beautiful thing.*)

Practice Tell students to create a two-column chart, with columns labeled Fact and Opinion. Have students work in pairs to find five facts

and five opinions in the selection and record them in their charts.

Possible Responses: Opinions: Page 163: "Sailing is an inherently beautiful thing." "I think that the writer in the city"; Page 164: "It helps them to know you care." Facts: Page 163: "I have a steering vane"; Page 164: "Recently I was sailing"; Once a year."

1. **Possible Response:** It is a life of danger, loneliness, freedom, and closeness to nature.
2. Responses will vary but should indicate an understanding of the difference between fact and opinion.
3. **Possible Responses:** He eats gruel, just beans and rice, whereas it seems he once was a hunter and ate meat. He takes time to answer mail sent to him by his fans. He once needed company to keep him from getting lonely, but now he does not. He no longer pursues awards and money.

great deal to children, and I try to help both of those species. A lot of what I write is fiction based on my life. I spent my whole childhood running away. A lot of kids know this through my books, so I look for mail from kids in the same situation. It helps them to know you care. I'll try and get in touch with their school to let them know this child is in trouble. I'm aware I might be the only person they've told. I got a letter once from a girl who said, "My only friends in the world are your books."

Recently I was sailing down the Baja strip of Mexico from California. It's about 900 miles, with no anchorage, and it's very rough. I got caught in a storm and two other boats were lost. I talked to them over the radio before they went down. There was no way I could physically help them. Sometimes writing is that way. You want to reach out and make things right.

I'm not interested in money. I don't even know what I make. I give it all to my wife and she's very happy. I have all I want. Once a year I buy three new pairs of jeans and three denim shirts. I do have a jacket and tie for occasions, but I still got kicked out of the Savoy in London once.

I don't get lonely. There was a time when I lusted over having somebody who I could turn to and say, "Look at that!" I'd be leaning over the bow strip to touch the dolphins swimming alongside the boat. One time, three of them somersaulted in the air and crashed into the water, which was golden with the sinking sun. It was the most beautiful thing, and I felt so happy I just wanted to tell someone. But I realized that I'm telling it through my writing the whole time.

Occasionally I've tried to get people to go with me, but rarely do they understand. A lot of what I do is extreme. Sometimes Ruth meets me. She likes to fly to the pretty places and miss the slog [long, hard work]; for me, the slog is the beauty. I have no goal, no destination. I used to think I should be fulfilled by awards or by earning a million dollars, but with age has come some kind of self-knowledge. My rewards are less tangible: they're the killer whales who reared up out of the water to look at me. Or a 15-knot wind across my beam. Those are my moments of pure joy. ❖

THINKING through the LITERATURE

1. What is your impression of life on a sailboat?
2. **ACTIVE READING** **FACTS AND OPINIONS**
   With a partner, share the list of facts and opinions you wrote in your **READER'S NOTEBOOK**. Discuss the evidence the author uses to support his opinions.
3. Aside from living on a sailboat, what lifestyle changes do you see in Paulsen from the time he began writing to the time described in this article?

from **Woodsong**

by GARY PAULSEN

Connect to Your Life

In the Wild In the wilderness of Minnesota, wild animals, such as bears, were a part of Gary Paulsen's everyday life. With a small group, discuss what wild animals live in your region.

Build Background

GEOGRAPHY

Thick forests once covered 70 percent of Minnesota. Today, forests cover only about 35 percent of the state. Minnesota's most spectacular woods can be found in the 3 million-acre Superior National Forest, north of Lake Superior. The northern and northeastern sections of the state are the most rugged. In this region, people are scarce, but wild animals are plentiful. One of the few states where timber wolves still roam free, Minnesota is also home to white-tailed deer, beavers, and black bears.

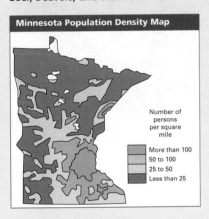

Minnesota Population Density Map

Number of persons per square mile

- More than 100
- 50 to 100
- 25 to 50
- Less than 25

WORDS TO KNOW **Vocabulary Preview**

| menace | novelty | predator | rummaging | scavenging |

Focus Your Reading

LITERARY ANALYSIS   MEMOIR

A **memoir** is a writer's description of his or her own memories. It is a type of **autobiography,** or self-told life story. Because a memoir is written about real people and real events, it is **nonfiction.** To make their stories interesting, writers of memoirs and autobiographies combine facts about their lives with language that appeals to a reader's senses of sight, sound, smell, taste, and touch. As you read, look for descriptions that appeal to your five senses.

ACTIVE READING   QUESTIONING

Good readers ask questions when they read in order to understand what is happening in a piece of nonfiction. As you read the excerpt from *Woodsong,* pause to ask questions about what is happening in the selection and about the author's ideas. Here are some questions you might ask yourself as you read:

- Why did things happen the way they did?

- What are the writer's feelings or opinions about the subject?

Jot down your questions in your
READER'S NOTEBOOK. Also note any confusing words, statements, or ideas.

This selection is included in the **Grade 6 InterActive Reader.**

Standards-Based Objectives

1. understand and appreciate a **memoir**
2. use the reading strategy of **questioning** to understand and analyze characters
3. recognize **imagery** and its effects

Summary

So many bears search for food outside Gary Paulsen's Minnesota cabin that he gives them nicknames and treats them like pets. One day, as Paulsen is burning trash that includes food scraps, the smell attracts a male bear nicknamed Scarhead. In his eagerness to get at the food, Scarhead rips up the enclosure where the trash is burned. When Paulsen angrily and unthinkingly tosses a stick at Scarhead, the bear turns on him. Paulsen, knowing that the creature can kill him with one blow, waits helplessly while Scarhead decides his fate. The bear chooses not to attack, and Paulsen hurries to get his rifle. He is about to shoot Scarhead—and then he realizes that the bear not only has spared his life but has reminded him to respect his fellow animals. Humbled and wiser, Paulsen puts the gun away.

Thematic Link

Paulsen once again demonstrates the ability to keep cool under stress—or at least to get a grip on himself before he commits an angry act he would regret. This is a form of courage in action.

English Conventions Practice

Daily Language SkillBuilder

Have students **proofread** the display sentences on page 19k and write them correctly. The sentences also appear on Transparency 5 of **Language Transparencies.**

Preteaching Vocabulary

If you would like to preteach the WORDS TO KNOW for this selection, use the Explicit Instruction, page 167.

LESSON RESOURCES

UNIT ONE RESOURCE BOOK, pp. 85–91

ASSESSMENT
Formal Assessment, pp. 25–26
Test Generator

SKILLS TRANSPARENCIES AND COPYMASTERS
Literary Analysis
- Author's Purpose, TR 16 (p. 168)
- Autobiography, TR 11 (p. 170)
Reading and Critical Thinking
- Questioning, TR 9 (p. 170)

Language
- Daily Language SkillBuilder, TR 5 (p. 165)
- Run-on Sentences, TR 33 (p. 171)
- Context Clues: Definition and Overview, TR 53 (p. 167)
Writing
- Structuring an Essay, TR 6 (p. 173)
Speaking and Listening
- Creating a Persuasive Presentation, p. 29 (p. 173)
- Guidelines: Evaluating a Persuasive Presentation, p. 30 (p. 173)

INTEGRATED TECHNOLOGY
Audio Library
Internet: Research Starter

Visit our Web site:
www.mcdougallittell.com

For **systematic instruction** in language skills, see:
- **Vocabulary and Spelling Book**
- **Grammar, Usage, and Mechanics Book**
- pacing chart on p. 19i.

Literary Analysis **MEMOIR**

Tell students that the language in "Woodsong" may remind them of fiction or ordinary storytelling rather than non-fiction, such as essays or news reports. Ask them to look for examples of a story-telling style on the first page. How are these examples different from what one might expect in a newspaper report?

Possible Response: Examples of story-telling style include: "We have bear trouble"; "Spring, when the bears come, is the worst"; "they are hungry beyond caution." The examples use more colorful, dramatic language than newspaper reports might.

 Use **Unit One Resource Book**, p. 87, for more practice.

Active Reading **QUESTIONING**

Ask students to form and revise questions arising from reading the material on the first page of the selection and to discuss them.

Possible Response: Why doesn't Paulsen build a strong enclosure to keep out the bears? How did his wife feel about being chased by a bear? What do the bears do when they annoy the dogs?

 Use **Unit One Resource Book**, p. 86, for more practice.

Literary Analysis: SENSORY DETAILS

Point out that a key part of Paulsen's story is the attraction that the smell of meat has for animals. Ask students to watch for details about smells as they read the story.

Wabana-Wagamuman

FROM WOOD SONG
BY GARY PAULSEN

Wabana-Wagamuman [Bear in the forest] (1989), Tom Uttech. Oil on canvas, courtesy of Struve Gallery, Chicago.

166 UNIT ONE **AUTHOR STUDY**

EXPLICIT INSTRUCTION ## Viewing and Representing

by Tom Uttech

ART APPRECIATION Tom Uttech's haunting woodland paintings are inspired by the wilderness regions of North America. The title of this painting is in the Chippewa (or Ojibwa) language.

Instruction Have students describe how the illustrator's choice of elements helps to represent and extend the meaning of the text. As an example, point out that the painter has chosen to show the bear as a small part of the picture.

Ask what effect this has on the viewer. *(It makes the viewer appreciate that the bear is just part of a larger natural world.)*

Practice Ask students to make a prediction about the message of the story based on the message of the picture.

Possible Response: Both the picture and the story are about animals as part of a larger world. In the story, humans are included with the animals in that world.

In Woodsong *Gary Paulsen describes his life as a trapper in the woods of northern Minnesota. He lived with his wife, Ruth, and his son, James, in a small cabin that did not have plumbing or electricity. At the time, Paulsen was not writing stories but simply learning the ways of the woods. This episode describes one of the lessons he learned.*

We have bear trouble. Because we feed processed meat to the dogs, there is always the smell of meat over the kennel. In the summer it can be a bit high[1] because the dogs like to "save" their food sometimes for a day or two or four—burying it to dig up later. We live on the edge of wilderness, and consequently the meat smell brings any number of visitors from the woods.

Skunks abound, and foxes and coyotes and wolves and weasels—all predators. We once had an eagle live over the kennel for more than a week, scavenging from the dogs, and a crazy group of ravens has pretty much taken over the puppy pen. Ravens are protected by the state, and they seem to know it. When I walk toward the puppy pen with the buckets of meat, it's a tossup to see who gets it—the pups or the birds. They have actually pecked the puppies away from the food pans until they have gone through and taken what they want.

Spring, when the bears come, is the worst. They have been in hibernation through the winter, and they are hungry beyond caution. The meat smell draws them like flies, and we frequently have two or three around the kennel at the same time. Typically they do not bother us much—although my wife had a bear chase her from the garden to the house one morning—but they do bother the dogs.

---

1. **it can be a bit high:** the smell can be rather strong.

WORDS
TO
KNOW

predator (prĕd′ə-tər) *n.* an animal that hunts other animals for food
scavenging (skăv′ən-jĭng) *adj.* searching for discarded scraps **scavenge** *v.*

167

Reading and Analyzing

Reading Skills and Strategies:
PREDICT

A Remind students that as they read, good readers gather information and combine it with what they know from their own experience to predict. Ask them to predict what might happen next.
Possible Response: The bear may injure Paulsen (he has described how a bear already killed two dogs).

Literary Analysis: CHARACTER TRAITS

Instruct students in analyzing characters, including their traits. Ask what they can conclude about Paulsen from these actions: (1) He throws a stick at the bear; (2) he wants to kill the bear; (3) he decides not to kill the bear.
Possible Responses: (1) He is impulsive; (2) he responds with anger when challenged; (3) he has a merciful, thoughtful side to his personality.

Reading Skills and Strategies:
AUTHOR'S PURPOSE

Guide students to identify effects of the author's purpose. On the board, draw a circle with four circles clustered around it. In the center circle write "Author's Purpose." In the circles around it, write: "To Entertain," "To Inform," "To Express an Opinion," and "To Persuade." Explain that the outer circles represent purposes that an author may have in writing a work, though often writers have more than one purpose. Ask what purposes they believe Paulsen had in writing the selection.
Possible Response: Paulsen wrote to entertain readers, to inform them about a way of life different from their own, and to express his opinion about the place of humans in nature.

Use **Literary Analysis Transparencies,** p. 16, for additional support.

They are so big and strong that the dogs fear them, and the bears trade on this fear to get their food. It's common to see them scare a dog into his house and take his food. Twice we have had dogs killed by rough bear swats that broke their necks—and the bears took their food.

We have evolved[2] an uneasy peace with them, but there is the problem of familiarity. The first time you see a bear in the kennel it is a <u>novelty</u>, but when the same ones are there day after day, you wind up naming some of them (old Notch-Ear, Billy-Jo, etc.). There gets to be a too-relaxed attitude. We started to treat them like pets.

1 A major mistake.

There was a large male around the kennel for a week or so. He had a white streak across his head, which I guessed was a wound scar from some hunter—bear hunting is allowed here. He wasn't all that bad, so we didn't mind him. He would frighten the dogs and take their hidden stashes now and then, but he didn't harm them, and we became accustomed to him hanging around. We called him Scarhead, and now and again we would joke about him as if he were one of the yard animals.

At this time we had three cats, forty-two dogs, fifteen or twenty chickens, eight ducks, nineteen large white geese, a few banty hens, **2** ten fryers which we'd raised from chicks and couldn't (as my wife put it) "snuff and eat," and six woods-wise goats.

The bears, strangely, didn't bother any of the yard animals. There must have been a rule, or some order to the way they lived, because they would hit the kennel and steal from the dogs but leave the chickens and goats and other yard stock completely alone—although you would have had a hard time convincing the goats of this fact. The goats spent a great deal of time with their back hair up, whuffing

and blowing snot at the bears—and at the dogs, who would *gladly* have eaten them. The goats never really believed in the truce.

There is not a dump or landfill to take our trash to, and so we separate it—organic, inorganic[3]—and deal with it ourselves. We burn the paper in a screened enclosure, and it is fairly efficient; but it's impossible to get all the food particles off wrapping paper, so when it's burned, the food particles burn with it.

And give off a burnt food smell.

And nothing draws bears like burning food. It must be that they have learned to understand human dumps—where they spend a great deal of time foraging. And they learn amazingly fast. In Alaska, for instance, the bears already know that the sound of a moose hunter's hunt means there will be a fresh gut pile when the hunter cleans the moose. They come at a run when they hear the shot. It's often a close race to see if the hunter will get to the moose before the bears take it away. . . .

Because we're on the south edge of the wilderness area, we try to wait until there is a northerly breeze before we burn, so the food smell will carry south, but it doesn't always help. Sometimes bears, wolves, and other predators are already south, working the sheep farms down where it is more settled—they take a terrible toll[4] of sheep—and we catch them on the way back through.

That's what happened one July morning.

---

2. **evolved** (ĭ-vŏlvd´): developed by a series of small changes.

3. **organic** (ôr-găn´ĭk), **inorganic** (ĭn´ôr-găn´ĭk): on the one hand, things made of plant or animal material; and on the other, things made of material that has never been alive.

4. **take a terrible toll:** destroy a large number.

WORDS
TO
KNOW **novelty** (nŏv´əl-tē) *n.* something new and unusual

168

EXPLICIT INSTRUCTION **Read Aloud**

Instruction Use the second paragraph on page 167 that begins "Skunks abound." to model reading aloud using appropriate pacing, intonation, and expression. Explain to students that when they read aloud, they need to
- make sure they read at the right speed—not too quickly or too slowly—so that listeners will be able to understand them
- use tone of voice to emphasize important ideas, make transitions clear, and help listeners understand what they are hearing

- use their voices to show the feelings and the mood the writer is expressing
Say, "You need to make sure you can read words accurately. You may have to look up difficult words in a dictionary to figure out pronunciation and then practice reading them." Also explain that knowing what a passage is about and paying attention to punctuation marks will help them read aloud accurately. Ask, "When you're reading aloud, which punctuation marks tell you when to stop and breathe?" *(commas, periods, dashes)*

Practice Have students work in pairs to practice reading aloud another short passage from the story. Partners may team up with another pair to present their readings. As one student in the group reads, the others should listen and then ask questions about how the reader prepared the passage. Ask volunteers to read their passages to the rest of the class.

Scarhead had been gone for two or three days, and the breeze was right, so I went to burn the trash. I fired it off and went back into the house for a moment—not more than two minutes. When I came back out, Scarhead was in the burn area. His tracks (directly through the tomatoes in the garden) showed he'd come from the south.

He was having a grand time. The fire didn't bother him. He was trying to reach a paw in around the edges of flame to get at whatever smelled so good. He had torn things apart quite a bit—ripped one side off the burn enclosure—and I was having a bad day, and it made me mad.

I was standing across the burning fire from him, and without thinking—because I was so used to him—I picked up a stick, threw it at him, and yelled, "Get out of here."

I have made many mistakes in my life, and will probably make many more, but I hope never to throw a stick at a bear again.

In one rolling motion—the muscles seemed to move within the skin so fast that I couldn't take half a breath—he turned and came for me. Close. I could smell his breath and see the red around the sides of his eyes. Close on me he stopped and raised on his back legs and hung over me, his forelegs and paws hanging down, weaving back and forth gently as he took his time and decided whether or not to tear my head off.

I could not move, would not have time to react. I knew I had nothing to say about it. One blow would break my neck. Whether I lived or died depended on him, on his thinking, on his ideas about me—whether I was worth the bother or not.

I did not think then.

Looking back on it, I don't remember having one coherent[5] thought when it was happening. All I knew was terrible <u>menace</u>. His eyes looked very small as he studied me. He looked down on me for what seemed hours. I did not move, did not breathe, did not think or do anything.

And he lowered.

Perhaps I was not worth the trouble. He lowered slowly and turned back to the trash, and I walked backward halfway to the house and then ran—anger growing now—and took the rifle from the gun rack by the door and came back out.

He was still there, <u>rummaging</u> through the trash. I worked the bolt and fed a cartridge in and aimed at the place where you kill bears and began to squeeze. In raw anger, I began to take up the four pounds of pull necessary to send death into him.

And stopped.

Kill him for what?

That thought crept in.

Kill him for what?

For not killing me? For letting me know it is wrong to throw sticks at four-hundred-pound bears? For not hurting me, for not killing me, I should kill him? I lowered the rifle and ejected the shell and put the gun away. I hope Scarhead is still alive. For what he taught me, I hope he lives long and is very happy, because I learned then—looking up at him while he made up his mind whether or not to end me—that when it is all boiled down, I am nothing more and nothing less than any other animal in the woods. ❖

---

5. **coherent** (kō-hîr′ənt): clear; logical.

WORDS
TO
KNOW
menace (mĕn′ĭs) *n.* a possible danger; threat
rummaging (rŭm′ĭ-jĭng) *adj.* searching thoroughly **rummage** *v.*

169

Connect to the Literature

1. What Do You Think?
Possible responses include: suspenseful, surprising, interesting, merciful, entertaining.

Comprehension Check
- He began naming them.
- He threw a stick at him.
- Scarhead ran over to him and almost killed him.

 Use Selection Quiz, **Unit One Resource Book,** p. 91.

Think Critically

2. Possible Responses: Students may have been able to answer all their questions. If any students still have unanswered questions, have them work together to go back through the story and find answers.

 Use **Reading and Critical Thinking Transparencies,** p. 9, for additional support.

3. Possible Responses: He could have built a strong enclosure around the property, lured the bears away somewhere else by putting food out, or discouraged them with an electric fence.

4. Most students will say that they learned that the risks of interactions with wild animals make living in the wilderness dangerous, and that wild animals need to be left alone as much as possible.

Literary Analysis

Memoir Responses should list appropriate details and demonstrate an understanding of their importance to the story. To get students started on this activity, list a few details, such as the smell of the meat the dogs bury, the reaction of the goats to the bears, and the smell of the bear's breath.

Use **Literary Analysis Transparencies,** p. 11, for additional support.

Connect to the Literature

1. What Do You Think?
Close your eyes for a moment, and think of five words that describe the selection. Compare your list with those of other classmates.

Comprehension Check
- What does Paulsen say he did that showed "a too-relaxed attitude" toward the bears?
- What mistake did Paulsen make when he saw Scarhead sniffing the burning trash?
- What happened when Paulsen confronted Scarhead?

Think Critically

2. ACTIVE READING   QUESTIONING
Look back at questions you wrote in your ▮ READER'S NOTEBOOK. Were you able to answer your questions by reading further? If not, what questions do you still have?

3. Faced with the problem of bears hanging around his home, what might Paulsen have done differently?

4. How did reading Paulsen's account affect your impression of living in the wilderness?

Extend Interpretations

5. Different Perspectives The story from *Woodsong* takes place at an earlier time than "Older Run." How do Paulsen's views of animal behavior differ between the two stories? How do you think his opinion may have been affected by dogsled racing?

6. Connect to Life Animals such as skunks, insects, raccoons, and crows are sometimes called "pests" because they interfere with humans. Discuss some problems you know about that come from human and wildlife interaction. What might be done to help solve these problems?

Literary Analysis

MEMOIR   A **memoir** is a writer's account of memories of true events in his or her own life. It is a type of **autobiography.** A memoir does not tell about a person's entire life, but includes one or more life-changing events. These events are usually told in the **first-person point of view,** using the pronouns *I, we, me,* and *us. Woodsong* is a memoir about one period in Gary Paulsen's life.

Because a memoir is written about real people and real events, it falls in the larger genre of **nonfiction.**

Paired Activity With a partner, look through the piece from *Woodsong.* Work together to list details that could only be told by someone who experienced them. Try retelling the story to each other without these details. What happened to the memoir in your retelling? Together, write a paragraph telling why the details you chose are so important to the story.

Details Only Paulsen Could Know

"ripped one side off the burn enclosure"

Extend Interpretations

5. Different Perspectives Students may say that Paulsen seems to have gained much more respect for animals and for their intelligence at the end of "Older Run." In the earlier story he is more focused on his own needs as a human being, and is not thinking as much about what animals need and want as he is by the end of the later story.

6. Connect to Life Wild animals sometimes attack people, pets, and farm animals; eat crops; destroy property; and spread disease. People can build fences, set humane traps, and learn ways of adjusting to the presence of animals.

CHOICES and CHALLENGES

Grammar in Context: Varying Sentence Length

Read the following passage from *Woodsong.* Pay attention to the length of the sentences—very long, short, short, and, at the end, a short **fragment.**

> **The first time you see a bear in the kennel it is a novelty, but when the same ones are there day after day, you wind up naming some of them (Old Notch-Ear, Billy-Jo, etc.). There gets to be a too-relaxed attitude. We started to treat them like pets.** A major mistake.

Paulsen creates drama not only with word choice but also with sentence length. He allows tension to build as sentences run long. Then he stops short, creating a dramatic pause, and ends with a broken thought.

When you write, be sure to use a variety of short and long sentences. Listen to their rhythm. As you revise, look for places to let your reader's imagination run with a long sentence. Also find places to pause.

Usage Tip: As you create variety, remember to watch out for sentence fragments and for run-on sentences. Fragments are not complete thoughts. They can be used sparingly to create emphasis. Run-on sentences will confuse your readers. Complete sentences, with proper punctuation, will give your writing the most clarity.

WRITING EXERCISE Rewrite the following paragraph so that it contains just five correctly punctuated sentences of varying length. Change words and punctuation as necessary.

> **We once had an eagle. The eagle lived near our house. The eagle flew over our yard. The cats were afraid of the eagle. The eagle was afraid of nothing. That's what we thought. Crows lived nearby. Crows flew around the eagle. They cawed at it. They yelled at it. They teased it. The crows were smaller than the eagle. They chased the eagle away.**

Grammar Handbook

See p. R67: Writing Complete Sentences.

Vocabulary

EXERCISE A: MEANING CLUES On your paper, write the word or phrase that best completes each sentence.

1. A **predator** is an animal that eats _______.
   (a) grass and fruits (b) vegetables
   (c) other animals
2. You can see bears **scavenging** in _______.
   (a) garbage piles (b) streams (c) caves
3. An animal that is a **menace** is _______.
   (a) harmless (b) dangerous (c) helpful
4. A polar bear is a **novelty** in _______.
   (a) Alaska (b) a zoo (c) Africa
5. A **rummaging** bear will _______.
   (a) make a mess (b) leave quickly
   (c) disappear without a trace

Vocabulary Handbook

See p. R20: Context Clues.

EXERCISE B Copy and fill in the chart below to analyze the word *predator.* Create similar charts for *menace* and *novelty.*

Definition of *predator*	Examples of predators	Use of *predator* in selection	Synonym of *predator*

Vocabulary Handbook

See p. R23: Denotative and Connotative Meaning; p. R22: Synonyms and Antonyms.

Grammar in Context

WRITING EXERCISE

Possible Responses:

Paragraphs will vary, but should include all the information in five sentences with correct punctuation.

Vocabulary

EXERCISE A

1. c
2. a
3. b
4. c
5. a

EXERCISE B

Definition of *Predator:*
An animal that hunts other animals for food
Examples of Predators:
skunks, foxes, coyotes, wolves, weasels
Use of *Predator* in Selection:
"Skunks abound, and foxes and coyotes and wolves and weasels—all predators."
Synonym of *Predator:*
hunter

EXPLICIT INSTRUCTION Grammar in Context

CORRECTING RUN-ON SENTENCES

Instruction Explain that there are three common ways to correct run-on sentences: add a comma and the word *and;* make two or more sentences out of one run-on sentence; or divide the run-on sentence with a semicolon. To demonstrate these methods, write the following on the board:

RUN-ON SENTENCE They have been in hibernation the meat smell draws them like flies.

USE A COMMA AND *AND* They have been in hibernation, and the meat smell draws them like flies.

MAKE TWO SENTENCES They have been in hibernation. The meat smell draws them like flies.

USE A SEMICOLON They have been in hibernation; the meat smell draws them like flies.

Practice Have students correct the following run-on sentences using each of the three methods suggested.

1. They are strong the dogs fear them.
2. We called him Scarhead we would joke about him he was like one of the yard animals.
3. I picked up a stick I threw it I was too used to him.

Use **Unit One Resource Book,** p. 89.

For more instruction in in correcting run-on sentences, see McDougal Littell's ***Language Network,*** Chapter 1.

For **systematic instruction** in grammar, see:
- **Grammar, Usage, and Mechanics Book**
- pacing chart on p. 19i.

Students will be made aware of Paulsen's style through the Key Style Points and will find examples in the author study.

Key Style Points

Possible Responses:

Sensory Details. Paulsen sees the way the muscles ripple under the bear's skin and the red around its eyes; he can smell its breath.

Vivid Verbs. slammed, drove, flew, hit, bounced

Precise Nouns. brook, springs, spruce, Norway pines

Applications

1. Active Reading Examples should represent sensory details, vivid verbs, and precise nouns. If necessary, begin the activity by helping students to choose one example of each type as a class activity.

2. Writing Students should prewrite a short summary of the experience they want to describe. They should build on their prewriting exercise by adding sensory details, vivid verbs, and precise nouns.

3. Speaking and Listening Students should demonstrate appropriate speaking and listening skills in this activity.

The Author's Style

Paulsen's Precise Language

Paulsen has said he searches for "that particular word, that phrase that would describe that particular light in the North Country." Like the focus device on a camera, precise language helps a writer create a sharp image. Notice how Paulsen's precise language brings each scene to life.

Key Style Points

Sensory Details Paulsen makes readers feel, see, hear, smell, and even taste a scene. What sensations do these words from *Woodsong* create?

Vivid Verbs To make the action in a story more exciting, writers like Paulsen use vivid verbs. Vivid verbs are precise instead of vague, active rather than passive, and fresh instead of dull or overly used. What powerful verbs do you notice in this description from "Older Run"?

Precise Nouns Because of Paulsen's expert knowledge of the outdoors, he chooses the precise nouns that make a setting real. In this scene from "Older Run," what precise names of things does Paulsen use?

> ### Sensory Details
> In one rolling motion—the muscles seemed to move within the skin so fast that I couldn't take half a breath—he turned and came for me. Close. I could smell his breath and see the red around the sides of his eyes.
> —*Woodsong*

> ### Vivid Verbs
> . . . I slammed into the cross handlebar with my stomach, drove all the wind out of my lungs, flew up and over the sled in a cartwheel, hit to the right of the wheel dogs, bounced once on the iron-hard cross ties of the trestle . . .
> —"Older Run"

> ### Precise Nouns
> . . . a quiet brook kept open by small warm springs, winding through a stand of elegant spruce and tall Norway pines.
> —"Older Run"

Applications

1. Active Reading Look back at the selections in this author study. Find two examples for each of the three types of precise language.

2. Writing Think of an exciting or scary experience you have had. Write about the experience using three types of precise language. Underline details that appeal to the five senses.

3. Speaking and Listening Choose a paragraph from a Paulsen work that has plenty of strong, active verbs. Read it aloud, using the sound of your voice to show the author's feelings and attitudes.

Writing

Henson and Paulsen Explorer Matthew Henson and author Gary Paulsen have many traits in common. Review the information about Matthew Henson on page 102 of this book and about Gary Paulsen on pages 150–153. Make a list of the ways in which these men had similar lives and dreams. Write a short report about them using this information. Place your report in your **Working Portfolio.**

Writing Handbook
See p. R43: Explanatory Writing.

Speaking & Listening

An Author's Idea In "A Life in the Day of Gary Paulsen" you read about some of Paulsen's ideas and feelings. Choose one of the ideas that you strongly agree or disagree with. Create an oral presentation describing your opinion. Begin by clearly stating your viewpoint. Then use information from the selection and from your own experience to support your opinion. Present your ideas to the class.

Speaking and Listening Handbook
See p. R100: Persuasive Presentations.

Research & Technology

Become an Expert Use non-fiction books, the Internet, and other media to help you find information on one of the following:

- search-and-rescue work
- sailing
- the Iditarod

Use this information to write a report giving basic information about your topic.

 INTERNET **Research Starter**
www.mcdougallittell.com

Author Study Project

Survival Kit

What basic things do humans need to survive? Create a kit that could help a human being survive harsh conditions.

❶ Brainstorm a List In a group of three or four students, brainstorm a list of items to include in a survival kit. Start with 20 items, then cut the list to 12. How will you decide which are most important?

> Survival Kit
> compass
> food
> water

❷ Assemble the Kit Create the kit by collecting actual items, finding magazine pictures, or making drawings. Include cards that tell the use or importance of each item.

> Kit Item:
> compass: tells directions, helps orient toward familiar path

❸ Write a Report Create a written report that includes a summary of your favorite Gary Paulsen survival story and a description of the survival challenges in Paulsen's own life.

❹ Present the Kit Display your kit where class members can view it. Give a group presentation, or post your writing and images onto a Web page or electronic slide-show.

GARY PAULSEN **173**

Writing

Henson and Paulsen Student's reports should show in-depth knowledge of Henson and Paulsen, based on the information in the selections. The comparisons should be clear and well-supported.

 Use **Writing Transparencies,** p. 6, for additional support.

Speaking & Listening

An Author's Idea Have students review the list of facts and opinions they made as they read the selection to help them choose a topic.

Use **Speaking and Listening Book,** pp. 29–30, for additional support.

Research & Technology

Become an Expert Students may wish to work in pairs or small groups on one of the topics. Other sources of information include sailing, sporting, and popular news magazines. Allow plenty of time for research and provide support for online research.

 Use **Writing Transparencies,** pp. 47–48, for additional support.

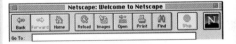

Author Study Project

SURVIVAL KIT
Before students begin, discuss the kind of challenges people face under harsh conditions. Begin with the basic need for food, water, clothing, and shelter. Then add the need for medical supplies, communication equipment, and various tools. Written reports should correlate various items in the kit with survival challenges in the Paulsen story.

Other Works by GARY PAULSEN

Putting characters in difficult situations is what author Gary Paulsen does best. Drawing from his own experiences living in the wilderness, Paulsen writes novels of human survival. His is a world in which determination triumphs over hostile forces, both in nature and in society. Readers love his characters' narrow escapes and grueling tests of endurance.

Hatchet 1987
Newbery Honor Book

In *Hatchet*, Paulsen tells the story of 13-year-old Brian Robeson, the sole survivor of a plane crash. Brian must use his wits to survive in the Canadian wilderness. Paulsen says the idea for *Hatchet* came from a time when he almost crashed in a small plane. He also wanted to write about a young person taking care of himself. "I decided to take a city boy, put him in a wild environment, and then see what happened."

Dogsong 1985
Newbery Honor Book

Motivated by vivid dreams, 14-year-old Russel Susskit attempts to escape the modern ways of his Eskimo village in order to discover his own path. A dogsled trek across the frozen Alaska wilderness becomes a journey of the spirit as he struggles to confront himself and the forces of nature around him.

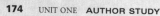

The Winter Room 1989

Newbery Honor Book

Set in the 1930s, this novel tells the story of Eldon, a young boy growing up on a remote Minnesota farm. On cold nights, Eldon, his brother Wayne, and the rest of the family gather in the winter room to listen to their Uncle David's stories of superheroes. One night Uncle David tells the story "The Woodcutter." The boys soon discover the truth about their elderly uncle and his tales.

The Voyage of the Frog 1989

Fourteen-year-old David Alspeth wants only to scatter the ashes of his recently deceased uncle over the sea when he sets out in his sailboat. But when a storm hits, David is stranded. With little water and just seven cans of food, David must survive many days on his own as he learns to understand himself and his uncle.

Soldier's Heart 1998

Paulsen based this historical novel on the real life of Charley Goddard, a 15-year-old farm boy who faked his age in order to join the First Minnesota Volunteers and fight in the Civil War. Only after Charley's first battle does he realize the horror of combat. By then, it is too late to turn back, and he can only hope to get out alive. Paulsen fills the book with true accounts of Civil War battles. He shows readers the gore and panic that produce "soldier's heart," an 1800s term used to describe the lasting mental and emotional damages of war.

Standards-Based Objectives
- write a 500- to 700-word personal experience essay
- use a written text as a model for writing
- revise a draft to add details
- use correct subject and object pronouns
- deliver a personal experience presentation

Introducing the Workshop

Personal Experience Essay Discuss with students what a personal experience essay is—a composition in which the writer describes something that he or she has done. Tell students that the personal experience they write about should have some significance in their life. It could be something that taught them an important lesson about themselves or about someone who plays a key role in their life.

Basics in a Box
Using the Graphic A personal experience essay should begin with an introduction that clearly states the experience and grabs the reader's attention. In the middle part, the writer should use vivid details and dialogue to bring the experience to life. This part is also where the writer should explain the importance of the experience. In the end, the writer should describe the outcome of the experience and express his or her feelings about it.

Presenting the Rubric To help students better understand the assignment, review the Standards for Writing a Successful Personal Experience Essay. You may also want to share with them the complete rubric, which describes several levels of proficiency.

 See **Unit One Resource Book**, p. 100.

 For more instruction on essential writing skills, see McDougal Littell's *Language Network*, Chapters 10–17.

 Power Presentation

To engage students visually, use **Power Presentation** 2, Personal Experience Essay

---

Writing Workshop — Personal Experience Essay

Telling your story . . .

From Reading to Writing In *Woodsong,* Gary Paulsen tells us that he never felt quite the same after he came face to face with a grizzly bear. He learned a lot about himself from this experience. Maybe you haven't met a bear in your backyard, but other incidents have probably affected you. Writing a **personal experience essay** can help you see how your experiences have shaped the way you think and what you believe is important.

For Your Portfolio

WRITING PROMPT Write an essay about a personal experience that was important to you.

Purpose: To share and explain an experience from your life
Audience: Your family members, classmates, and friends

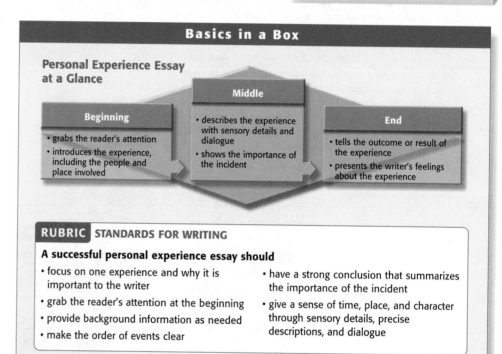

Basics in a Box

Personal Experience Essay at a Glance

Beginning
- grabs the reader's attention
- introduces the experience, including the people and place involved

Middle
- describes the experience with sensory details and dialogue
- shows the importance of the incident

End
- tells the outcome or result of the experience
- presents the writer's feelings about the experience

RUBRIC STANDARDS FOR WRITING

A successful personal experience essay should
- focus on one experience and why it is important to the writer
- grab the reader's attention at the beginning
- provide background information as needed
- make the order of events clear
- have a strong conclusion that summarizes the importance of the incident
- give a sense of time, place, and character through sensory details, precise descriptions, and dialogue

---

LESSON RESOURCES

USING PRINT RESOURCES
Unit One Resource Book
- Prewriting, p. 92
- Drafting and Elaboration, p. 93
- Peer Response, p. 94
- Revising Organization and Ideas, p. 95
- Revising, Editing, and Proofreading, p. 96
- Student Models, p. 97–99
- Rubric, p. 100

Reading and Critical Thinking
- Chronological Order, TR 6 (p. 177)

Speaking and Listening
- Understanding Audience and Purpose, pp. 6–7 (p. 181)
- Developing and Delivering a Presentation, pp. 8–9, pp. 12–13 (p. 181)
- Creating and Analyzing a Narrative Presentation, pp. 23–24 (p. 181)

INTEGRATED TECHNOLOGY
Writing Coach CD-ROM
Visit our Web site:
www.mcdougallittell.com

Analyzing a Student Model

SPEAKING OPPORTUNITY — See the Speaking and Listening Handbook, p. R96 for oral presentation tips.

Samantha Piwinski
Somerville Charter School

Courage in the Water

"Remember to respect the ocean. It's a little cranky this year!" Uncle Ray said. "So you've got to be careful and watch to see what color flag the lifeguards raise!"

It was August of 1991 and my family was getting ready to take its yearly summer vacation at my uncle's beach house in York Beach, Maine. My brother, Curtis, held the phone as we listened to Uncle Ray's warning about the flag system. If there is an undertow, a red flag is raised from the beach. If the water is rough, there is a yellow flag, and if the water is calm, then the flag is blue. That's how you know it is safe. We knew this by heart.

We promised Uncle Ray we'd watch for the flag.

On our first morning, we awoke early. Gulls cried overhead as we drank orange juice on the porch and stared out at the glimmering horizon. Uncle Ray had already packed our sandwiches. "Now remember the flag," he ordered. I nodded. Curtis was busy packing his CDs into his favorite purple knapsack.

When we arrived at the beach, the sun blazed down on our cheeks as our feet melted into the hot sand. I helped my mother unpack my supplies. I looked around for Curtis, but he was already racing toward the water. "Be careful!" my father called after him.

Curtis dove into the water first. I followed. The cold water pierced my skin. Seaweed tangled in between my toes. I tried to call Curtis, but he was far away, laughing, riding the waves. I could see the beautiful, warm, sandy shore in the distance. I struggled to find the ocean floor. My feet reached for ground but it seemed to fall away as soon as I touched it. Then all of the sudden I remembered the flag. My eyes scanned the beach. The flag hadn't been raised yet. We had no way of knowing what the undertow was like.

"Curtis, the flag!" I yelled.

He didn't hear me. "The waves are awesome!" Curtis yelled. "C'mon!"

I told myself to calm down and went into the water. Soon, we were up to our knees riding the waves, when a really big wave rushed over us, knocking us headfirst into the salty water. For a

RUBRIC IN ACTION

1 Begins with dialogue to engage the interest of the reader
Other option:
• Use questions.

2 Writer states place and time of year to establish setting.

3 Supporting details provide necessary information for readers to understand story.

4 Transitional phrases help readers follow order of events.

5 Precise verbs describe setting and show the danger in the situation.

Teaching the Lesson

Analyzing a Student Model

Courage in the Water
In the student model, the writer tells about the time when she and her brother were rescued after getting caught in a strong undertow while swimming in the ocean. After students read the model, discuss what makes this essay compelling. Then discuss the Rubric in Action.

1 Ask why dialogue is an effective way to begin a personal experience essay.
   Possible Response: Dialogue draws the reader in because it allows one to be in the middle of the action.

2 Ask students why it's important to establish the setting early on.
   Possible Response: These important facts help readers visualize what they are reading.

3 Background information is critical here because readers need to know the system of different colored flags in order to understand what happens later.

4 Ask students how transitional phrases help readers follow the order of events.
   Possible Response: Transitional phrases clarify the placement in time of key events.

5 Have students look for other precise verbs in the student model. Encourage students to talk about the impact of precise verbs and to think about how they paint a detailed picture that engages readers.
   Possible Responses: Other vivid verbs include *rushed, knocked, smothered, pounded,* and *struggled.*

EXPLICIT INSTRUCTION Patterns of Organization

PICTURING TEXT STRUCTURE
Instruction Like the writer of the student model, some writers start a personal experience essay with a key piece of dialogue. Other writers begin by describing the first event and telling what hap-pened in chronological order. The writer of the student model uses both techniques.

Practice Have students analyze the text structure of the student model by making a diagram showing how the writer organized her essay.

Use **Reading and Critical Thinking Transparencies,** p. 6, for additional support.

Curtis gets warning from uncle over phone. → At beach, uncle repeats warning. → Writer and brother head for beach. → They get knocked down by waves. → They yell for help.

They are rescued by man and lifeguard. → Family greets writer and brother. → Curtis says ocean could take someone's life away. → Writer and brother take rescue classes. → They befriend man who rescued them.

6 Ask students to tell which details create suspense and fear.

Possible Response: The phrase ". . . being smothered by a thick black blanket" creates suspense. The phrase ". . . only silence surrounded me" gives me a clear idea of how alone and scared the writer must have felt.

7 Have students discuss how staying focused on the rescue keeps the reader's attention.

Possible Response: By describing the rescue step-by-step, the writer almost recreates the feeling of being there watching them being rescued.

8 A conclusion that echoes what was said in the beginning can be especially effective. Ask students to think about why this technique works so well in the student model.

Possible Response: The opening paragraph includes the quotation from Uncle Joey about respecting the ocean. The conclusion refers to Uncle Joey's comment by paraphrasing his thoughts on the ocean's moods. This repetition emphasizes the message of this essay—that people must respect the power of the ocean.

---

moment, I couldn't see anything. I felt as though I were being smothered by a thick black blanket. A whoosh of water pounded in my ears. I could feel myself being pulled backward by the powerful undertow. When I surfaced, only silence surrounded me. Finally, I spotted Curtis floating far away.

"Swim in!" I yelled.

"Help! I can't!" he called back. "The undertow's too strong!" He began yelling for help. Eventually, I started to yell, too. Curtis was right. The ocean was too powerful. I struggled, and began to swallow water.

From out of nowhere, a man was swimming toward us. I could see he had white hair and he was wearing his glasses! He reached out to save me first. We fought our way through the steep waves toward Curtis. Then I saw a lifeguard running toward us from the beach. The old man held me and I grabbed hold of Curtis's arm. Before I knew it, the lifeguard threw in a yellow buoy. Curtis, the old man, and I shared it until another lifeguard arrived on a boat. He told Curtis to hold on to a blue buoy.

As the lifeguards pulled us in, I remember them telling me to hold on tight. When a big wave came, they pulled me out of the water so my head wouldn't go under.

Eventually, we arrived on the shore. My whole family surrounded us. Curtis's lips were blue. He said that the ocean was strong enough to take a life away. I agreed.

We stayed at the beach until we caught our breath. Afterward, we went back to Uncle Ray's cottage. Even Ed, the old man, came with us. He told us that he had been a champion swimmer when he was a boy. He also admitted that he had just lost his glasses. Later, my parents sent him a check for the glasses. They felt they needed to do something for him because of what he did for us.

When I think back to that day, it makes me feel good to know that a stranger would risk his life to try and save my brother and me. Curtis and I still love to swim, and we still go to York Beach. But now, things are a little different. We both have taken swimming rescue classes and we always pay attention to the flag. Just as Uncle Ray said, the ocean has moods—sometimes it's calm, other times it's angry. As for Ed, he has become a special person to our family. When we visit him each summer, we reminisce about the day when he became a champion swimmer again and saved a couple of kids.

6 Vivid details and sensory language create a feeling of suspense and fear.

7 The narrative stays focused on the rescue. No unnecessary details are included.

8 Conclusion explains the importance of the experience and presents a summary linked to the purpose of the essay.

Writing Your Personal Experience Essay

❶ Prewriting

You can only learn to be a better writer by actually writing.
—Doris Lessing, novelist and short story writer

Begin by thinking about major experiences in your life. **Brainstorm** a list of events from your past that were happy, sad, frightening, or humorous. Look through your photo album or talk to older family members to help you remember. See the **Idea Bank** in the margin for more suggestions. After you have chosen an incident, follow the steps below.

Planning Your Personal Experience Essay

▶ **1. Freewrite about the experience.** Write down your memories about the experience. Why is it important? Will you be comfortable sharing it?

▶ **2. Gather details.** Try to remember the details of your experience and your feelings at the time. Who was there? Was the weather important? What was on your mind?

▶ **3. Explore its importance.** What is the main point of the experience? Why was it important in your life? Did you learn a lesson? Did you realize something about yourself or someone else?

▶ **4. Tell your story aloud.** Describe the experience to friends before you write it down. They may have questions about details that are important to the story. Take notes about their reactions.

❷ Drafting

Once you start writing, don't worry about making your essay look or sound perfect. You can fix it later. Just get your ideas written down. Include details as they come to you.

- Use story elements—**plot, character,** and **setting.**
- Use **dialogue, figurative language,** words that appeal to the senses, and **precise verbs.** For example, instead of using the verb *drink,* think of a verb that describes the action more exactly, such as *sip, guzzle, gulp,* or *slurp.*
- Organize your essay. Usually, **chronological order** is the clearest method of organization. Build suspense if you can.

IDEA Bank

1. Your Working Portfolio 📁
Look for ideas in the **Writing** activities you completed earlier.

2. Time Travel
Find your class photograph from an earlier grade. With a friend or alone, try to name each person in the group. This will lead you to think of what happened that year in school and out of school. Choose one event to write about.

3. Memory Lane
Watch home movies or look through old family photographs for reminders of significant events in your past. Then decide which one would make a good story to share with others.

Have a question?

See the **Writing Handbook.**
Elaboration, p. R37
Chronological Order, p. R42

Ask Your Peer Reader

- How could I make the beginning of my essay more interesting?
- Why do you think this experience was important to me?
- Which parts of my essay are confusing?
- How could I improve the ending?
- What was your favorite part? Why?

Guiding Student Writing

Prewriting
Choosing an Event
If students are having difficulty choosing an event after they have read the suggestions in the Idea Bank, make the following suggestions:

- Think of something that you wanted to learn how to do but were afraid to try. What happened when you actually learned? What did you learn about yourself? How was this event important to you in a deeper way?
- Look through your souvenirs at home. Think about family trips or outings that were especially meaningful. How does the souvenir remind you of this experience? Why did you save it?

Planning Your Personal Experience Essay

1. As students write down their memories, have them think about why this memory stands out and why the event has had a lasting effect.

2. As students gather details, tell them to use precise verbs and nouns that capture the experience.

3. While thinking about the importance of the experience, students might consider the element of surprise associated with learning something new about themselves.

4. Tell listeners to hold their questions until the storyteller is finished telling the story.

Drafting
Suggest that students use either a graphic organizer or an outline to plan their essay. Tell them to place the events in chronological order within the diagram or on the outline.

Revising
NECESSARY DETAILS

Invite volunteers to choose a paragraph from their personal experience essay that contains details. Tell them to read it aloud. Ask listeners to give positive feedback, naming details that helped them understand the experience. Then ask listeners to identify any unnecessary details.

Editing and Proofreading
SUBJECT AND OBJECT PRONOUNS

Remind students that when a sentence contains a compound subject, one way to figure out the correct pronoun is to omit one part of the subject.
For example, *[Susan and] I went ice skating last Tuesday.*
Jesse passed the dessert tray to [Darrell and] me.

Reflecting

Encourage students to remember why they chose to write about this particular experience, and not some others. Tell them to think about what this experience revealed about themselves.

Option
TEACHING TIP

Suggest that partners read each other's essays. Tell students that when they finish reading the essay, they will write down the significance of the event or experience that they have just read about. Then have partners discuss whether the intended message of the essay was made clear.

Need revising help?

Review the Rubric, p. 176

Consider **peer reader** comments

Check **Revision Guidelines,** p. R31

See **Language Network,** Revising, p. 269–270.

SPELLING From Writing

As you revise your work, look back at the words you misspelled and determine why you made the errors you did. For additional help, refer to the strategies and generalizations in the **Spelling Handbook** on page R26.

Pronoun problems?

See the **Grammar Handbook,** Pronoun Case, p. R73.

SPEAKING Opportunity

Turn your essay into an oral presentation.

Publishing IDEAS

- Transform your personal experience essay into a comic strip that combines words and pictures to tell the story.
- With a few of your classmates, create a multimedia presentation to share your personal experience essays.

INTERNET

Publishing Options
www.mcdougallittell.com

---

❸ Revising
TARGET SKILL ▶ NECESSARY DETAILS Your essay must include details that make your reader understand what happened and why it is important. Details that are not important can confuse or bore your reader. If a detail does not add necessary information, leave it out. For example, if you are telling about something that happened at the fair one Saturday afternoon, it is probably not necessary to include information about someone who called later that day just to chat.

> As the lifeguards pulled us in, I remember them telling me to hold on tight. When a big wave came, they pulled me out of the water so my head wouldn't go under. ~~Still, my hair got soaked, and it made me mad because salt water is hard to wash out.~~

❹ Editing and Proofreading
TARGET SKILL ▶ SUBJECT AND OBJECT PRONOUNS It is easy to misuse pronouns. In conversation, you might say, *Me and my friend went downtown,* instead of *My friend and I went downtown.* However, in your writing it is important to use the following pronouns as subjects of sentences: *I, we, you, he, she, it, they.* Use the following as object pronouns: *me, us, you, him, her, it, them.*

> Curtis, the old man, and me shared it until another lifeguard arrived on a boat.

❺ Reflecting
FOR YOUR WORKING PORTFOLIO How did writing about the experience help you to see the event more clearly? Why is telling about a personal experience a good way to make a point? Attach your answers to your finished essay. Save your personal experience essay in your **Working Portfolio.**

EXPLICIT INSTRUCTION Revision

ORGANIZATION

Instruction Remind students that in a well-organized composition, using details to support main ideas strengthens their essays and makes it easier for readers to follow what they want to say. Unnecessary details, however, can confuse or annoy the reader. They can detract from the desired focus of the essay.

Practice Ask students to read their essays looking for extraneous or unnecessary details. They should delete any details that do not contribute to the focus of their essay.

See the **Research and Technology Handbook,** pp. R108–109, for information about formatting documents using word processing skills.

Use **Unit One Resource Book,** p. 95, to give students practice in improving the organization and consistency of ideas in their writing.

Standardized Test Practice

Mixed Review

Last January 4th, I sat in the doctor's waiting room waiting for the news. When my parents and the doctor came back into the room, I could tell by <u>there</u> expressions that the news <u>weren't</u> too bad. Finally, <u>they gave I</u> all the information that I had been asking for. When I understood my condition, I felt as if a <u>wait</u> had been lifted off my shoulders. My parents suggested <u>us</u> stop by my grandparents' house on the way home and tell them the news. I had caught impetigo, which is serious, but can be treated with medicine. Thank goodness <u>dr. perez</u> has so much experience!

(1) there (2) weren't (3) they gave I (4) wait (5) us (6) dr. perez

1. What is the correct spelling in item 1?
   A. they're
   B. their
   C. they are
   D. Correct as is

2. What is the correct verb form in item 2?
   A. were not
   B. wasnt
   C. wasn't
   D. Correct as is

3. What is the correct pronoun usage in item 3?
   A. they gave me
   B. them gave me
   C. them gave I
   D. Correct as is

4. What is the correct spelling in item 4?
   A. waight
   B. weight
   C. wieght
   D. Correct as is

5. What is the correct pronoun usage in item 5?
   A. them and me
   B. we
   C. they and I
   D. Correct as is

6. How is item 6 best written?
   A. dr. Perez
   B. doctor Perez
   C. Dr. Perez
   D. Correct as is

Demonstrate how students can eliminate incorrect choices for the first question.

A. This choice is incorrect because *they're* is a contraction for *they are* which doesn't make sense in the sentence.

B. This is the correct choice because *their* is a possessive pronoun referring to the writer's parents and the doctor.

C. This choice is incorrect because what is needed here is a possessive pronoun, not a pronoun and a verb.

D. The sentence is not correct as is. The writer needs to be more careful in using *there* and *their*. *There* refers to a place; *their* is a possessive pronoun.

Answers:
1. B; 2. C; 3. A; 4. B; 5. B; 6. C

EXPLICIT INSTRUCTION Speaking Opportunity

Prepare Once students have written their personal experience essay, they can plan to present it to an audience. Refer students to pages R102–103 of the Speaking and Listening Handbook at the back of this book for tips on presenting their personal experience essay.

Present Have students present their essays to the class. They should strive to make an interesting narrative that includes a setting and a plot and that uses narrative devices such as dialogue, suspense, or description.

RUBRIC

3 Full Accomplishment Student relates a strong, coherent incident, using sensory details and concrete language to develop the plot and the characters. Student uses narrative devices such as dialogue or suspense.

2 Substantial Accomplishment Student relays one event and includes some narrative devices to enliven the presentation. Student includes some sensory details and concrete language.

1 Little or Partial Accomplishment Student tells a somewhat confusing story and does not use narrative devices such as dialogue or suspense.

Use **Speaking and Listening Book,** pp. 6–9, 12–13, 23–24, for additional support in presenting a personal experience essay.

Standards-Based Objectives

- reflect on unit themes and use personal knowledge and experience to comprehend
- review literary analysis skills used in the unit
- represent text information in different ways, such as in a graphic organizer
- assess and build portfolios

Reflecting on Theme

OPTION 1

A successful response will

- rank a set of five characters in the selection according to the given criteria
- make an effective nomination of one of the characters on the list as number one
- present good reasons for the choice of the nominated individual
- clarify and support spoken ideas with evidence, elaborations, and examples

OPTION 2

A successful response will

- summarize in headlines the examples of courage demonstrated by characters in the unit
- use descriptive language in retelling the selected incidents
- demonstrate overall understanding of the effect of courage in various situations

OPTION 3

Have students prepare for the discussion by writing quick answers to the questions asked. They should jot down a few examples with which they can illustrate their answers when they discuss them with other class members. In the discussions, students should connect their own experiences, information, insights, and ideas with the experiences of others.

Self Assessment

Students' writing should take a stand one way or the other and support the position with appropriate examples. To get students started on this activity, have them discuss the meaning of the phrase "from within."

Tests of Courage

In the stories in this unit, characters show courage by speaking out, by facing unexpected challenges, and by struggling with forces of nature. What did you learn from their experiences? What kinds of adventures do you like to read about? Explore these questions by completing one or more of the options in each of the following sections.

© Reggie Holladay/SIS.

Reflecting on Theme

OPTION 1

Comparing the Daring Many of the characters in Unit One face difficult—and sometimes dangerous—conflicts. Which five characters or real-life people do you think were the most daring? Rank them in order, from 1 (most daring) to 5. Write a brief speech to nominate your number one choice for the title Most Daring. Give supporting reasons why.

OPTION 2

Noting the Newsworthy A young girl disobeys her father's orders. In so doing, she helps both herself and an entire clan. Firefighters battle blazes that threaten the country's oldest national park. The characters and people in this unit take risks and make difficult choices. Write a one-page newsletter about four or five challenges portrayed in Unit One. Use headlines that tell how the characters or real people showed courage. Tell what happened as a result of their courageous acts. Display or distribute your newsletter for the class.

OPTION 3

Evaluating Reading Experiences Discuss the following questions with your classmates: Which selections in this unit did you like best? Why did you like those the best? Which pieces of literature convey a message or lesson that you think is important? Support your opinions with examples.

Self ASSESSMENT

📖 READER'S NOTEBOOK

Consider the quotation at the beginning of the unit: "All serious daring starts from within." Write a few paragraphs in response. Support your ideas with examples from the selections in the unit.

REVIEWING YOUR PERSONAL
WORD List

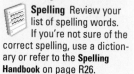

Vocabulary Review the new words you learned in this unit. If necessary, use a dictionary to check the meaning of each word.

Spelling Review your list of spelling words. If you're not sure of the correct spelling, use a dictionary or refer to the **Spelling Handbook** on page R26.

Reviewing Literary Concepts

OPTION 1

Discussing Setting The Unit One selections are set in different time periods and in places all over the world. Choose five selections and make a set of ten cards. Write each title on a different card. Next, write each setting on a different card. With a partner, match the titles with their settings, and discuss how setting affects action in each selection. Which settings present characters with the most exciting risks? Then move the cards to mix titles and settings. Discuss how the selections' events might be different in the new settings.

OPTION 2

Analyzing Nonfiction Most of the selections in Part 2 of this unit are nonfiction. There are many different kinds of nonfiction, with different purposes and characteristics. Make a list of the different kinds of nonfiction that appear in Part 2 of the unit, and write a brief explanation of the characteristics of each kind.

Portfolio Building

- **Choices and Challenges—Writing** Several of the writing assignments in this unit asked you to present descriptions of characters or to compare characters. Choose the one that you think best captures the spirit of the character you described. Attach a cover note explaining the reasons for your choice, and place it in your **Presentation Portfolio.**

- **Writing Workshops** In this unit you wrote a Response to Literature. You also wrote a Personal Experience Essay. Reread these two pieces and decide which one better shows your strengths as a writer. Explain your choice in a cover note, attach it to the piece, and place it in your **Presentation Portfolio.**

- **Additional Activities** Think back to any of the assignments you completed for **Speaking & Listening** and **Research & Technology.** Keep a record in your portfolio of any assignments that you especially enjoyed, found helpful, or would like to do further work on.

Self ASSESSMENT

READER'S NOTEBOOK

On a sheet of paper, copy the following literary terms introduced in this unit. Next to each term, jot down a brief definition. If you don't understand a particular term very well, look it up in the **Glossary of Literary and Reading Terms** on page R116.

character	informative nonfiction
plot	
setting	biography
theme	autobiography
exposition	essay
conflict	anecdote
climax	memoir
resolution	primary source
rising action	interview
falling action	

Self ASSESSMENT

At this point, you may be just beginning your **Presentation Portfolio.** Are the pieces you have chosen ones you think you'll keep, or do you think you'll be replacing them as the year goes on?

Setting GOALS

As you worked through the reading and writing activities in this unit, you probably identified certain skills you would like to develop. Make a list of skills and concepts you'd like to work on in the next unit.

Reviewing Literary Concepts

OPTION 1

Photocopy Unit One Resource Book, page 101, to provide students a graphic organizer for analyzing and comparing selection settings.

OPTION 2

A successful response will
- identify correctly all of the nonfiction in the unit.
- include an explanation of the characteristics of each.

Portfolio Building

Students should evaluate the items in their Working Portfolios and choose pieces that represent their highest quality work for their Presentation Portfolios.

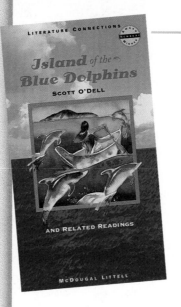

LITERATURE CONNECTIONS
Island of the Blue Dolphins

BY SCOTT O'DELL

In this novel, Karana, a Native American teenage girl, survives 18 years alone on an island off the Southern California coast. Loosely based on a true incident of the 1800s, the story comes alive with details about coastal wildlife, survival skills, and Chumash culture. Karana's courage carries her through danger to a better understanding of herself. Rich description and high drama won this novel a Newbery Medal among its many awards.

These thematically related readings are provided along with *Island of the Blue Dolphins:*

The Dolphin Walking Stick
BY GEORGIANA VALOYCE-SANCHEZ

from **The World of the Sea Otter**
BY STEFANI PAINE

The Ice-Hearts
BY JOSEPH BRUCHAC

Courage
BY DUDLEY RANDALL

from **The Girl with the White Flag**
BY TOMIKO HIGA

Staying Alive
BY DAVID WAGONER

Change
BY CHARLOTTE ZOLOTOW

More Choices

Call It Courage
BY ARMSTRONG SPERRY
A shy young man proves his courage by setting out to sea alone.

Where the Buffaloes Begin
BY OLAF BAKER
A young boy's journey to find the lake where the buffaloes begin becomes a wild ride through the night to save his people.

My Side of the Mountain
BY JEAN CRAIGHEAD GEORGE
A teenage hero survives the wilderness.

Seth of the Lion People
BY BONNIE PRYOR
Seth, an orphaned boy with a lame leg, courageously leaves his cave clan and makes his way home.

Heads or Tails: Stories from the Sixth Grade
BY JACK GANTOS
Young Jack faces backyard alligators, a mean sister, a pesky brother, and a secret crush.

Taking Flight: My Story
BY VICKI VAN METER
The youngest pilot to cross the Atlantic

LITERATURE CONNECTIONS
Trouble River

By Betsy Byars

Dewey Martin, a 12-year-old boy living in the 1800s, is left behind to tend the family farm while his parents go to Hunter City. Fearing a Comanche raid, Dewey, his grandmother, and their dog Charlie set off on a small raft. Akin to Huckleberry Finn and company, the trio face a river of difficulties in their struggle to reunite with Dewey's parents. Byars's ability to create believable young characters makes this an exciting read.

These thematically related readings are provided along with *Trouble River*:

from **Buffalo Gals: Women of the Old West**
By Brandon Marie Miller

from **On the Way Home**
By Laura Ingalls Wilder

Favorite Frontier Songs
Traditional

Old Sly Eye
By Russell Gordon Carter

Points of View
By Ishmael Reed

Song for Smooth Waters
Native American song

Granny Squannit and the Bad Young Man
By Joseph Bruchac

Social Studies Connection

The Boy of the Painted Cave
By Justin Denzel
A deformed boy who was cast out of his clan at birth faces many trials and survives to become a shaman of the tribe.

The Magic Amulet
By William Steele
During prehistoric times, Tragg must fend for himself after he is abandoned by his clan.

Maroo of the Winter Caves
By Ann Turnbull
Maroo, a girl of the Ice Age, must save her family from an icy winter.

Warrior Scarlet
By Rosemary Sutcliff
Set in the Bronze Age, a young boy with one arm sets out to prove to his grandfather that he can become a warrior.

Lobo of the Tasaday: A Stone Age Boy Meets the Modern World
By John Nance
Lobo and his people, who had been living in a stone age culture, must learn to adapt to the modern world.

Growth and Change

One thing is certain: nothing remains the same. By the time you read this, things will have changed in the world from the way they were a minute ago. That is a fact of existence. It's how we respond to growth and change that counts. Is it a threat to be feared or a challenge to be welcomed? This unit contains two parts, both of which highlight not only where we come from, but also where we are going as we grow and change.

—————— **Part 1** ——————

The Need to Belong Being part of something—a family, a group, a culture—buffers the pain of growth and change that all must face. Misery may love company, as the old saying goes, but so does joy. In "Chinatown," a young man tries to find just where he fits in as he approaches his young adulthood. This answer will give him the roots he needs in order to grow strong.

—————— **Part 2** ——————

Home and Heritage We all come from somewhere as we begin life's journey, and this heritage is one of the things that makes us who we are. The characters in these selections come from many different "homes," be they physical or spiritual. In "The Circuit," a young boy's frequent moves make it difficult for him to have a sense of home.

GROWTH

You start out with one thing, end

up with another, and nothing's

like it used to be, not even the future.

Rita Dove
American poet

David Peikon, *Spring Fair, Old Westbury Gardens*
30" x 40", Acrylic on canvas ©1998.
Courtesy of the Mark Humphrey Gallery,
Southampton, New York.

186

AND CHANGE

Making Connections

To help students explore the connections between the art, the quotation, and the unit theme, have them consider the following questions:

Ask: Think about a change in your life. How did it help you to grow?
Possible Response: Students' responses will vary, but should connect to the positive aspects of change.

Ask: Do you agree with Rita Dove's quotation about change?
Possible Response: Students may say they would agree with her statement, because change is constantly going on and always will, even in the future.

Ask: What aspect of growth and change do you think the painting portrays?
Possible Response: The young people in the painting may be friends attending an event in their community. Our friends and communities often shape the way we grow and change.

Ask: What kinds of stories and experiences might you expect to read about in this unit?
Possible Response: stories about people who learn important lessons about living as they grow and change

Features and Selections	Literary Analysis	Reading and Critical Thinking	Writing Opportunities	
Growth and Change **The Need to Belong**			Art Appreciation, 186	
Learning the Language of Literature Poetry	Poetry, 189			
The Active Reader Skills and Strategies		Reading Poetry, 193		
POETRY I'm Nobody! Who Are You? It Seems I Test People Growing Pains **Difficulty Level:** *Average*	Figurative Language, 194, 196, 198 Simile, 195 Metaphor, 196 Sentence Structure, 197	Making Inferences, 194, 196, 198	Letter to the Poet, 199	
Reading for Information Calling All "Nobodies"		Elaborating, 201, 201 Taking Notes, 203		
POETRY Three Haiku **Difficulty Level:** *Easy*	Haiku, 205, 206, 207	Noting Sensory Details, 205, 206, 207	Your Own Haiku, 208	
SHORT STORY All Summer in a Day **Difficulty Level:** *Easy* **Related Reading** Change	Science Fiction, 209, 210, 214, 216 Literary Devices, 211 Influence of Setting, 213 Understanding Theme, 215, 216 Changes, 218	Evaluating Story Elements, 209, 210, 214, 216 Comparing Texts, 216	Character Contrasts, 217	
MEMOIR Chinatown, *from* The Lost Garden **Difficulty Level:** *Average* **Building Vocabulary** **Related Reading** Same Song/La misma canción	Primary Source, 219, 220, 226, 227 Imagery and Figurative Language, 223	Distinguishing Fact from Opinion, 219, 220, 222, 226, 227 Comparing Texts, 227 Text Organization: Spatial Order, 221 Text Organization: Comparison and Contrast Order, 224, 225	Paired Activity, 227 The Outsider, 228 Text Organization: Spatial Order 221	
Writing Workshop: Original Poem **Standardized Test Practice**		Analyzing Published Student Models, 237 Patterns of Organization, 237	Writing Your Poem, 239 Using Sound Devices, 240 Revision: Word Choice, 240	

LEGEND   DLS – Daily Language SkillBuilder   Green type – Teacher's Edition

Speaking and Listening Viewing and Representing	Research and Technology	Grammar, Usage, and Mechanics	Vocabulary
Portrait of a Speaker, 199 Outsiders, 200	Poetry Poster, 199 Outsiders, 200	DLS, 194	
	Research and Technology: Activity Link, 204, 204		
Pioneering Poets, 208 Recycled Haiku, 208	Pioneering Poets, 208	DLS, 205	

Plot Comparison, 217
Art Appreciation, 212
	Science, 217
	Changes, 218
		Replacing Nouns with
		  Pronouns, 218
		DLS, 209
		Using the Right Pronoun Case,
		  218
			Using Context Clues, 210, 217

Story Recommendation, 228
Common Theme, 229
	Immigrant Communities, 228
	Common Theme, 229
		Proper Nouns, 229
		DLS, 219
		Concrete and Abstract Nouns,
		  229
			Antonyms, 228
			Spelling the sh Sound, 228
			Using Synonyms and
			  Antonyms, 230
			Using a Word Web, 220

Speaking Opportunity, 241		Consistent Verb Tense, 240 Standardized Test Practice, 241	

Features and Selections	Literary Analysis	Reading and Critical Thinking	Writing Opportunities	
Growth and Change **Home and Heritage**				
Learning the Language of Literature Character and Setting	Character and Setting, 243			
The Active Reader Skills and Strategies		Predicting, 247		
SHORT STORY Aaron's Gift **Difficulty Level:** *Challenging*	Character Traits, 248, 250, 252, 256, 257 Traits and Plot, 251, 252 Traits and Conflict, 255 Traits and Resolution, 256	Predicting, 248, 250, 252, 257 Comparing Texts, 257 Visualizing, 253	Story Summary, 258	
Reading for Information Your Family's History Will Come Alive		Reading a Web Site, 261, 261	Keyword Searches, 262	
SHORT STORY The Circuit **Difficulty Level:** *Average* **Related Reading** the 1st	Literary Devices, 264, 266, 272 Personification, 266, 269 Simile, 267 Imagery, 268, 269	Making Inferences, 264, 266, 268, 270, 272 Visualizing, 270 Read Aloud, 271 Comparing Texts, 272	Letter to Mr. Lema, 273 Between Two Languages, 274	
MEMOIR Oh Broom, Get to Work **Difficulty Level:** *Easy*	Point of View, 275, 276, 278, 280, 281 Imagery and Figurative Language, 277, 279	Connecting, 275, 276, 280, 281 Read Aloud, 280	Personality Profile, 282 Internment Camps, 283	
POETRY Western Wagons Night Journey **Difficulty Level:** *Average* **Building Vocabulary** **Related Reading** Saguaro	Sound Devices, 284, 286, 287 Rhyme and Repetition, 285 Rhythm, 286	Reading Aloud, 284, 286, 287 Comparing Texts, 287	Travel Poem, 288	
Writing Workshop: Character Sketch **Standardized Test Practice**		Analyzing a Student Model, 299 Patterns of Organization, 299	Planning Your Character Sketch, 301 Adding Dialogue, 302 Revision: Organization, 302	
Reflect and Assess	Thinking About Figurative Language, 305 Analyzing a Character, 305	Evaluating Growth, 304 Producing a Proposal, 304	Producing a Proposal, 304 Relating to the Theme, 304 Portfolio Building, 305	

UNIT TWO
RESOURCE MANAGEMENT GUIDE
PART 1

To introduce the theme of this unit, use
transparencies 4–6 in Fine Arts Transparencies.

	Unit Resource Book	Assessment	Integrated Technology and Media
I'm Nobody! Who Are You? It Seems I Test People Growing Pains *pp. 194–200*	• Active Reading: Making Inferences p. 4 • Literary Analysis: Figurative Language p. 5	• Selection Test, Formal Assessment pp. 29–30 ⊙ Test Generator	⌒ Audio Library
Calling All Nobodies *pp. 201–204*	• Elaborating p. 6 • Taking Notes p. 7		
Three Haiku *pp. 205–208*	• Active Reading: Noting Sensory Details p. 8 • Literary Analysis: Haiku p. 9	• Selection Test, Formal Assessment pp. 31–32 ⊙ Test Generator	⌒ Audio Library
All Summer in a Day *pp. 209–218*	• Summary p. 10 • Active Reading: Evaluating Story Elements p. 11 • Literary Analysis: Science Fiction p. 12 • Literary Analysis: Understanding Theme p. 13 • Grammar p. 14 • Words to Know p. 15 • Selection Quiz p. 16	• Selection Test, Formal Assessment pp. 33–34 ⊙ Test Generator	⌒ Audio Library ▭ Video: Literature in Performance, Video Resource Book pp. 11–18 ⌕ Research Starter www.mcdougallittell.com
Chinatown, *from* **The Lost Garden** *pp. 219–229*	• Summary p. 17 • Active Reading: Distinguishing Fact from Opinion p. 18 • Literary Analysis: Primary Source p. 19 • Active Reading: Comparison and Contrast Order p. 20 • Grammar p. 21 • Words to Know p. 22 • Selection Quiz p. 23	• Selection Test, Formal Assessment pp. 35–36 ⊙ Test Generator	⌒ Audio Library ⌕ Research Starter www.mcdougallittell.com

Writing Workshop: Original Poem

		Unit Assessment	*Unit Technology*
Unit Two Resource Book • Prewriting p. 25 • Drafting and Elaboration p. 26 • Peer Response Guide pp. 27–28 • Revising, Editing, and Proofreading p. 29 • Student Models pp. 30–32 • Rubric for Evaluation p. 33	⊙ **Writing Coach** **Writing Transparencies** TR17 **Reading and Critical Thinking Transparencies** TR39 **Speaking and Listening Book** pp. 9, 14	• Unit Two, Part 1 Test, Formal Assessment pp. 37–40 ⊙ Test Generator • Unit Two: Integrated Assessment pp. 7–12	⌕ ClassZone www.mcdougallittell.com ⊙ Electronic Teacher Tools

Additional Support

Literary Analysis Transparencies	Reading and Critical Thinking Transparencies	Language Transparencies	Writing Transparencies	Speaking and Listening Book
• Poetry: Figurative Language TR19	• Making Inferences TR10	• Daily Language SkillBuilder TR6		• Creating an Informative Presentation p. 25 • Guidelines: How to Analyze an Informative Presentation p. 26
			• Elaborating TR13 • Note Taking TR49	
	• Noting Sensory Details TR11	• Daily Language SkillBuilder TR6	• Cluster Diagram for Poem TR35	
	• Evaluating TR12	• Daily Language SkillBuilder TR7	• Transitional Words List TR10 • Showing, Not Telling TR22	• Working in a Group p. 33
• Primary/Secondary Source TR14	• Distinguishing Fact from Opinion TR26	• Daily Language SkillBuilder TR7	• Writing Variables TR2	• Creating a Persuasive Presentation p. 29 • Guidelines: How to Analyze a Persuasive Presentation p. 30

ENGLISH LEARNERS / STUDENTS ACQUIRING ENGLISH

The **Spanish Study Guide,** pp. 34–48, includes language support for the following pages:
• Family and Community Involvement (per unit)

• Selection Summaries and Vocabulary
• Active Reading
• Literary Analysis

For **systematic instruction** in language skills, see:
• **Vocabulary and Spelling Book**
• **Grammar, Usage, and Mechanics Book**
• pacing chart on p. 187i

UNIT TWO
RESOURCE MANAGEMENT GUIDE
PART 2

To introduce the theme of this unit, use transparencies 4–6 in Fine Arts Transparencies.

	Unit Resource Book	Assessment	Integrated Technology and Media
Aaron's Gift *pp. 248–259*	• Summary p. 34 • Active Reading: Predicting p. 35 • Literary Analysis: Character Traits p. 36 • Literary Analysis: Character Traits and Plot p. 37 • Grammar p. 38 • Words to Know p. 39 • Selection Quiz p. 40	• Selection Test, Formal Assessment pp. 39–40 ⊙ Test Generator	⌒ Audio Library
Your Family's History Will Come Alive *pp. 260–263*	• Reading a Web Site p. 41 • Keyword Searching p. 42		
The Circuit *pp. 264–274*	• Summary p. 43 • Active Reading: Making Inferences p. 44 • Literary Analysis: Literary Devices p. 45 • Active Reading: Visualizing p. 46 • Grammar p. 47 • Words to Know p. 48 • Selection Quiz p. 49	• Selection Test, Formal Assessment pp. 41–42 ⊙ Test Generator	⌒ Audio Library
Oh Broom, Get to Work *pp. 275–283*	• Summary p. 50 • Active Reading: Connecting p. 51 • Literary Analysis: Point of View p. 52 • Literary Analysis: Imagery and Figurative Language p. 53 • Grammar p. 54 • Words to Know p. 55 • Selection Quiz p. 56	• Selection Test, Formal Assessment pp. 43–44 ⊙ Test Generator	⌒ Audio Library
Western Wagons Night Journey *pp. 284–288*	• Active Reading: Reading Aloud p. 57 • Literary Analysis: Sound Devices p. 58	• Selection Test, Formal Assessment pp. 45–46 ⊙ Test Generator	⌒ Audio Library

Writing Workshop: Character Sketch

		Unit Assessment	Unit Technology
Unit Two Resource Book • Prewriting p. 60 • Drafting and Elaboration p. 61 • Peer Response Guide p. 62 • Revising Organization and Ideas p. 63 • Revising, Editing, and Proofreading p. 64 • Student Models pp. 65–67 • Rubric for Evaluation p. 68	⊙ **Writing Coach** **Writing Transparencies** TR24 **Reading and Critical Thinking Transparencies** TR37 **Speaking and Listening Book** pp. 6–9, 12–13, 23–24	• Unit Two, Part 2 Test, Formal Assessment pp. 47–48 ⊙ Test Generator • Unit Two: Integrated Assessment pp. 7–12	⊙ ClassZone www.mcdougallittell.com ⊙ Electronic Teacher Tools

Additional Support

Literary Analysis Transparencies	Reading and Critical Thinking Transparencies	Language Transparencies	Writing Transparencies	Speaking and Listening Book
	• Predicting TR7	• Daily Language SkillBuilder TR8 • Verbs: Using Correct Forms TR35 • Context Clues: Definition and Overview TR53	• How to Summarize TR51	• Creating an Informative Presentation p. 25 • Guidelines: How to Analyze an Informative Presentation p. 26
• Primary/Secondary Source TR14			• Locating Information: Using the Internet I and II TR47–48	
	• Making Inferences TR10	• Daily Language SkillBuilder TR8 • Avoiding Illogical Shifts in Tense TR36 • Context Clues: Definition and Overview TR53	• Effective Language TR15	• Creating a Persuasive Presentation p. 29 • Guidelines: How to Analyze a Persuasive Presentation p. 30
• Narrator and Point of View TR22	• Connecting TR2	• Daily Language SkillBuilder TR9 • Context Clues: Compare and Contrast, Cause and Effect, Example TR54	• Effective Language TR15 • Character Sketch TR30	
• Poetry: Sound Devices TR20		• Daily Language SkillBuilder TR9	• Writing Variables TR2 • Poem TR35	

ENGLISH LEARNERS / STUDENTS ACQUIRING ENGLISH

The **Spanish Study Guide,** pp. 49–60, includes language support for the following pages:
• Family and Community Involvement (per unit)

• Selection Summaries and Vocabulary
• Active Reading
• Literary Analysis

For **systematic instruction** in language skills, see:
• **Vocabulary and Spelling Book**
• **Grammar, Usage, and Mechanics Book**
• pacing chart on p. 187 i

The *Language of Literature* offers several options for integrating language arts instruction and literature.

- Systematic instruction in grammar, vocabulary, and spelling is provided in the *Grammar, Usage, and Mechanics Book* and in the *Vocabulary and Spelling Book*. The pacing chart on the right shows when to use the lessons in these books.

- The Pupil's Edition provides grammar and vocabulary instruction in context. The examples for the grammar feature, *Grammar in Context*, arise from the selections and relate to the grammar focus for each unit. In addition each selection includes vocabulary words called *Words to Know*. Vocabulary practice occurs in *Choices and Challenges* at the end of each selection.

- The Teacher's Edition provides review and reinforcement of the grammar and vocabulary concepts through Explicit Instruction lessons. References to additional support in *Unit Resource Books* and other ancillaries are included at the end of appropriate lessons.

Grammar, Usage and Mechanics
From Grammar, Mechanics, and Usage Book

Chapter 1: Sentence and Its Parts

Chapter 2: Nouns
- What Is a Noun?
- Singular and Plural Nouns
- Possessive Nouns
- Nouns and Their Jobs

Chapter 3: Pronouns
- What Is a Pronoun?
- Subject Pronouns
- Object Pronouns
- Possessive Pronouns
- Reflexive and Intensive Pronouns
- Interrogatives and Demonstratives
- Pronoun-Antecedent Agreement
- Indefinite Pronoun Agreement
- Pronoun Problems
- More Pronoun Problems

Chapter 4: Verbs
- What Is a Verb?
- Action Verbs and Objects
- Linking Verbs and Predicate Words
- Principal Parts of Verbs
- Irregular Verbs
- Simple Tenses
- Perfect Tenses
- Using Verb Tenses
- Troublesome Verb Pairs

Chapter 5: Adjectives and Adverbs
Chapter 6: Prepositions, Conjunctions, Interjections
Chapter 7: Subject-Verb Agreement

For Ongoing Reference
Chapter 8: Capitalization
Chapter 9: Punctuation

Vocabulary
From Vocabulary and Spelling Book

Lesson 1: Context Clues
Lesson 2: Restatement Clues
Lesson 3: Contrast Clues
Lesson 4: Definition Clues
Lesson 5: Comparison Clues
Lesson 6: General Context Clues

Lesson 7: Prefixes and Base Words
Lesson 8: Prefixes and Base Words
Lesson 9: Base Words and Suffixes
Lesson 10: Base Words and Suffixes
Lesson 11: Anglo-Saxon Affixes and Base Words
Lesson 12: Roots and Word Families
Lesson 13: Roots and Word Familes

Lesson 14: Roots and Affixes
Lesson 15: Roots and Affixes
Lesson 16: Foreign Words in English
Lesson 17: Specialized Vocabulary
Lesson 18: Specialized Vocabulary
Lesson 19: Specialized Vocabulary
Lesson 20: Words with Multiple Meanings
Lesson 21: Synonyms
Lesson 22: Antonyms
Lesson 23: Denotation and Connotation
Lesson 24: Using a Thesaurus
Lesson 25: Idioms
Lesson 26: Similes and Metaphors
Lesson 27: Compound Words
Lesson 28: Homonyms
Lesson 29: Homophones and Easily Confused Words
Lesson 30: Homographs
Lesson 31: Analogies
Lesson 32: Using a Dictionary
Lesson 33: Using a Pronounciation Key
Lesson 34: Using a Specialized Dictionary

Spelling
From Vocabulary and Spelling Book

Lesson 1: Silent *e* Words and Suffixes
Lesson 2: The Suffix *ance*
Lesson 3: Plural Words Ending in *o*
Lesson 4: Prefixes and Base Words
Lesson 5: Prefixes and Roots
Lesson 6: Words Ending with *ary*

Lesson 7: Soft and Hard *g*
Lesson 8: Review
Lesson 9: Final *y* words and Suffixes
Lesson 10: The Suffix *able*
Lesson 11: Words Ending with *al + ly*
Lesson 12: The Prefix *com*
Lesson 13: Forms of the Prefix *ad*

Lesson 14: Words Ending with *ory*
Lesson 15: Unstressed Syllables
Lesson 16: Review
Lesson 17: *VAC* Words
Lesson 18: Non-*VAC* Words
Lesson 19: Words Ending with *c + ally*
Lesson 20: The Prefix *ex*
Lesson 21: More Forms of the Prefix *ad*
Lesson 22: Base Word Changes
Lesson 23: Words Ending with *cious, cial,* or *cian*
Lesson 24: Review
Lesson 25: Greek Combining Forms
Lesson 26: Compound Words and Contractions
Lesson 27: The Suffix *ible*
Lesson 28: Forms of Prefix *ob + sub*
Lesson 29: Forms of Prefix *in*
Lesson 30: The Suffixes *ence + ent*
Lesson 31: Words Ending with *ize + ise*
Lesson 32: Review

Selection	SkillBuilder Sentences	Suggested Answers
I'm Nobody! Who Are You? It Seems I Test People Growing Pains	1. Her laughter fill the room. 2. Things has gone wrong in the past.	1. Her laughter **fills** the room. 2. Things **have** gone wrong in the past.
Three Haiku	1. The Milky Way are a galaxy, or a group of stars. 2. Henry doesn't thinks that he can write haiku.	1. The Milky Way **is** a galaxy, or a group of stars. 2. Henry doesn't **think** that he can write haiku.
All Summer in a Day	1. Tho Bradbury says, "A thousand forests had bin crushed under the rain," there are no forests on Venus. 2. They still rememberd the sun as a gold coin in the ski.	1. **Though** Bradbury says, "A thousand forests had **been** crushed under the rain," there are no forests on Venus. 2. They still **remembered** the sun as a gold coin in the **sky**.
Chinatown	1. The fair housing laws maked it illegal to deny someone housing because of race. 2. When he is a kid, Laurence Yep was asked to sing a song in Chinese even though he didn't read the language.	1. The fair housing laws **made** it illegal to deny someone housing because of race. 2. When he **was** a kid, Laurence Yep was asked to sing a song in Chinese even though he didn't read the language.

Selection	SkillBuilder Sentences	Suggested Answers
Aaron's Gift	**1.** Aarons grandmother lived in the Ukraine as a young girl.	**1. Aaron's** grandmother lived in the Ukraine as a young girl.
	2. Gift's that come from the heart are the most treasured kind.	**2. Gifts** that come from the heart are the most treasured kind.
The Circuit	**1.** Panchito and Roberto run and hid in the vineyard yesterday.	**1.** Panchito and Roberto **ran** and hid in the vineyard yesterday.
	2. Mr. Lema is a kind teacher who caring about Panchito.	**2.** Mr. Lema is a kind teacher who **cares** about Panchito.
Oh Broom, Get to Work	**1.** Can you teach me a magic trick with the broom	**1.** Can you teach me a magic trick with the broom?
	2. Watch out	**2.** Watch out!
Western Wagons / Night Journey	**1.** The Benéts say them will starve and freeze.	**1.** The Benéts say **they** will starve and freeze.
	2. As I ride on the train, me view the beautiful scenery.	**2.** As I ride on the train, **I** view the beautiful scenery.

OVERVIEW

Students conduct research and surveys to analyze the current image of children as portrayed by the media. They present their findings in a Media Panel Discussion.

Project at a glance The selections in Unit Two focus on the issues of identity and change. For this project, students will work in small groups to investigate how different forms of the media portray children and whether that portrayal is accurate. Each group will look at ads in a selected medium (magazines, television, newspaper, or radio). Then each group will conduct a survey to see if others think this image is accurate. They will also interview their peers (children) to find how they feel about their own image in the media. Group members will form panels to discuss their findings.

SCHEDULING

Panel discussions should take anywhere from 15 to 20 minutes. You may want to schedule the discussions over the course of this unit, or at the end of this unit depending on your purposes.

PROJECT OBJECTIVES

• To demonstrate the speaking and listening skills introduced in the activity
• To analyze the various images of children presented in the media
• To develop media awareness and critical-thinking skills
• To research various media and to interview people about the image presented by the media
• To draw conclusions about the image presented by the media
• To contribute to a panel discussion and present their findings

SUGGESTED GROUP SIZE

5–6 students per group

Media Panel Discussion

1 Getting Started

Think about the resources available to you and about how you want to structure the project. If you have access to video and audio equipment, students can include television and radio in their investigations and presentations. Since students will be handing out surveys, you may want to make arrangements to use your school's photocopier.

Also decide whether you want to create evaluation forms. If so, have those ready at the end of the project.

Gather a wide selection of magazines and newspapers to get students started. Make sure the collection includes some aimed at children, some aimed at adults, some hard news, and some gossip papers. Find a few extreme examples that you can discuss later.

You can assign each group a bulletin board, or a section of one, on which to display their final projects. Projects might also be displayed in the main hall or lobby of the school.

If you are including videotaping as part of the project, you will need a television to view parts of the presentation. Make arrangements for one well ahead of time.

Writing Workshop Connection

As a springboard, students may use the Writing Workshop assignment **Problem-Solution Essay**, p. 430.

2 Directing the Project

Preparing *(2 class periods)* Explain that students will be working in groups to research how the media portray children and to draw conclusions about the accuracy of this image. Each group will analyze images of children in a different form of media (television, radio, print ads, or magazines). Groups will also interview teens and adults to find out whether they think that the children in the media are representative of all children. Groups will draw a conclusion based on the information and present their findings and supporting arguments in panel discussions. The panels will be composed of one representative from each media group. Panel members will share, explore, and compare their findings.

Assigning Roles Divide students into groups. Assign these roles for each group (students can have more than one role):

• presenter
• researcher
• surveyor

• interviewer
• materials collector
• writer
• moderator

▶ Have students browse through magazines to find children in ads. Discuss whether all children look like the one(s) in the ads, whether the ad gives a negative or positive impression of children, and whether this represents an accurate picture. Talk about what conclusions might be drawn by people who don't have much contact with children.

▶ Have students research advertising in their group's medium and write a description of the most common type of child they find. They will then create and conduct a survey by asking questions such as, "Children are often portrayed in the _____ media as _____. Do you think this is a fair and/or accurate image of children in general?"

▶ Encourage groups to survey as many types and ages of people as they can and to keep track of the results. You might hold a brief class discussion about the results and conclusions of the project. Before doing so, review with students the Speaking and Listening Skills listed on the next page.

Practicing *(1 class period)* Help students form panels. Since each student will be participating in a panel, everyone is expected to speak knowledgeably about his or her group's findings.

▶ During the rehearsal stage, check to make sure all the panels are running smoothly. Tell students that giving and receiving feedback during this stage is crucial. Refer them to the tips in the Feedback Center.

Presenting *(1 class period)* This project could culminate in a schoolwide presentation.

▶ **EVALUATION** Let students know that they will be rating their own performances as well as those of other members after the discussions. You can hand out evaluation sheets at the end of the discussions.

Teaching the Speaking and Listening Skills

The student is expected to:

Monitor and seek clarification as needed

Teaching Suggestions: Tell students that they can take an active role in their own learning. This means monitoring their own understanding and asking for clarification if necessary. Remind them that it is likely that if they don't understand something, others may not understand it either. Tell the panelists that, during the discussion, they will be expected to ask questions of one another, challenge claims made by the speaker(s), and ask for clarification if they don't understand.

Evaluate a spoken message in terms of its content, credibility, and delivery

Teaching Suggestions: Tell students that, whether they are listening to a radio program, watching television, reading a magazine, or listening to a live presentation, they must evaluate the speaker and the message. To do this, they should keep the following questions in mind: Is the delivery effective (clear and direct)? Is the presentation well organized? Is the research up-to-date and from credible sources? Are the main ideas supported by good evidence? Does the speaker present a fair description of the material, or is there a detectable bias that affects the message?

Identify facts, identify opinions, and distinguish the two

Teaching Suggestions: Tell students that to become educated consumers they need to be on the lookout for opinions presented as facts. Remind students that facts are statements that can be proved, while opinions express the judgments or feelings of the speaker and cannot be proved. During the panel discussion, have students try to distinguish facts from opinions. Can they identify judgmental statements or opinions presented as facts? If so, they should seek clarification from the speaker as to the validity of the statement or evidence to support the claim.

Feedback Center

Students can use the following guidelines when giving and receiving feedback during this project:

Giving Feedback

▶ Ask questions concerning content, delivery, purpose, and point of view (for instance, does the speaker have a detectable bias?).

▶ Provide feedback about the coherence and logic of the content, delivery, and overall impact on the listener.

▶ Comment on the verbal and nonverbal delivery (pitch, pace, volume, gestures, body language) and its impact on the listener.

▶ Respond to persuasive messages with questions, challenges, or affirmations.

▶ Question the evidence to support the speaker's claims and conclusions.

Receiving Feedback

▶ Listen to constructive criticism with an open mind.

▶ Use audience feedback and modify the presentation to clarify meaning or organization.

 Assessing the Project

The following rubric can be used for group or individual assessment.

3 *Full Accomplishment*

The group followed directions to create a coherent description of children as portrayed by the media and used this successfully as the basis for a survey. Group members drew coherent conclusions and presented their information in an organized fashion in their panel discussion. Statements and claims were well supported by facts. All of the Speaking and Listening Skills were demonstrated.

2 *Substantial Accomplishment*

The group created a description, completed a survey, and drew adequate conclusions based on this information. Most of the information students presented in panel discussions was supported, and speakers were reasonably prepared. Two out of three of the Speaking and Listening Skills were demonstrated.

1 *Little Accomplishment*

The group's description and/or survey was incomplete or did not fulfill the requirements of the assignment. Panelists were unprepared, and their presentation seemed to lack several key elements. Only one of the Speaking and Listening Skills was demonstrated.

PART 1
The Need to Belong

Meeting Standards

The Literature You'll Read

The Concepts You'll Study

Vocabulary and Reading Comprehension
Vocabulary Focus: Using Synonyms and Antonyms
Making Inferences
Noting Sensory Details
Evaluating
Distinguishing Fact from Opinion

Writing and Language Conventions
Writing Workshop: Original Poem
Replacing Nouns with Personal Pronouns
Proper Nouns

Literary Analysis
Genre Focus: Poetry
Figurative Language
Haiku
Science Fiction
Primary Source

Speaking and Listening
Description of a Poem's Speaker
Haiku Read-Aloud
Group Discussion
Story Review

188

Poetry

There are pictures in poems and poems in pictures.

—William Scarborough, translator

You probably recognize **poetry** when you see it, even if you can't really explain what poetry is. Poetry looks different from prose because it is organized into lines instead of paragraphs. To understand a poem, you need to think about the way the words look on the page, the way the words sound together, and the images, or mental pictures, they create. The shapes, sounds, and images in a poem work together to express the poem's meaning.

There are many different styles of poetry. Most poems contain at least some, if not all, of the elements listed below.

Key Elements of Poetry
- form
- sound
- imagery
- figurative language

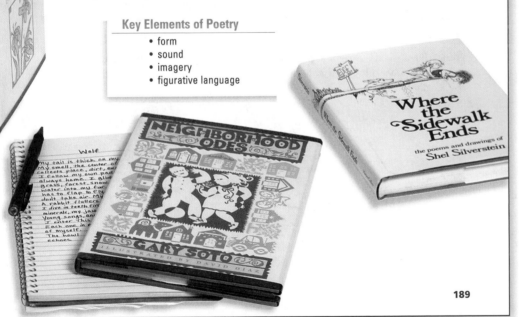

Standards-Based Objectives
- understand the following literary terms:

form	alliteration
line	speaker
stanza	imagery
free verse	figurative language
sound	simile
rhyme	metaphor
rhythm	personification
repetition	

- understand and appreciate poetry
- recognize the distinguishing features of poetry

Teaching the Lesson

This lesson analyzes the basic elements of poetry and shows how they work together in a poem to produce emotion, tone, and meaning.

Introducing the Concepts
Ask students to think about a poem or a song—a poem set to music—they have recently read or heard. Have them describe what makes that poem or song memorable.

Use **Literary Analysis Transparencies,** p. 17–21, for additional support.

189

Presenting the Concepts
Form

Have students look through the book to discover some of the different forms that poems can take. Ask them to point out the most unusual examples.

YOUR TURN

Possible Response: The first of the two stanzas contains five lines, which make up a sentence. The second stanza contains four lines, which also make up a sentence. Most of the lines are very short—only two or three words long.

Form

The way a poem looks on the page is called its **form.** Poems are made up of **lines.** In some cases, these lines are arranged in groups, called **stanzas.** Some poetry is written in strict patterns. Other poetry, called **free verse,** is not. Three elements related to form are line length, punctuation, and sentence structure.

- **Line length** A line may be just a few words long or it may be an entire sentence. Many poems include a combination of long and short lines. Poets use line length to suggest meaning in their poems. For example, long lines may suggest a sense of drama, energy, or force. Short lines may suggest quietness or stillness.
- **Punctuation** Some poets follow traditional rules of punctuation while others break these rules on purpose. Punctuation is often used, or not used, to emphasize the feelings in a poem.
- **Sentence Structure** The way words are arranged in sentences also conveys meaning in poems. The two sentences below use the same words but different arrangements. How does the emphasis change in the second sentence?

> I heard a lonely sound in the night.
> In the night, I heard a lonely sound.

As you read a poem, ask yourself how the form, line length, and punctuation reflect the subject and its meaning. Also think about the arrangement of words in sentences.

YOUR TURN Read the excerpt at the top right from "Change" by Charlotte Zolotow. Can you describe its form? Refer to the numbers of lines and stanzas and to the line lengths.

FORM

The summer
still hangs
heavy and sweet
with sunlight
as it did last year.

The autumn
still comes
showering gold and crimson
as it did last year.

— Charlotte Zolotow,
"Change"

Examples of a poetic form called limerick appear on p. 564.

The poetic form called haiku appears on p. 206.

The sonnet is a poetic form consisting of 14 lines.

Sound

Poems, like songs, depend on **sound** to help express meaning and emotions. When you analyze a poem, be sure to read it aloud at least once so you can hear the musical qualities it contains. The sound of poetry comes from rhyme, rhythm, and repetition.

- **Rhyme** is the repetition of similar sounds at the ends of words, for example, *moon* and *June.* Many poems contain rhyming words at the ends of lines. Rhyme helps express meaning in a poem by linking words, ideas, and feelings.
- **Rhythm** is the pattern of stressed and unstressed syllables in a poem. Stressed syllables are read with more emphasis, and unstressed syllables are read with less emphasis. Rhythm helps express the feelings and ideas in a poem. For example, a fast rhythm can create a sense of excitement, fear, or comedy. A slow rhythm can suggest sadness, loneliness, or peacefulness.

YOUR TURN Read aloud the lines at the right from "The Walrus and the Carpenter." Listen for the stressed (´) and unstressed (˘) syllables.

- **Repetition** is the use of sounds, words, phrases, or whole lines more than once. A poet may use repetition to emphasize an idea or a feeling. **Alliteration** is the repetition of consonant sounds at the beginning of two or more words. This is another technique poets use to emphasize meaning. Look at the lines at the right from "Life Doesn't Frighten Me." In the first line, two words begin with an *m* sound. Find an example of alliteration in the second line.

As you read a poem, listen for the patterns of sounds and think about how they convey ideas and feelings.

RHYME AND REPETITION

Shadows on the wall
Noises down the hall
Life doesn't frighten me at all
Bad dogs barking loud
Big ghosts in a cloud
Life doesn't frighten me at all.

— Maya Angelou,
"Life Doesn't Frighten Me"

RHYTHM

The sea was wet as wet could be,
The sands were dry as dry.

— Lewis Carroll,
"The Walrus and the Carpenter"

ALLITERATION

Mean old Mother Goose
Lions on the loose

— Maya Angelou,
"Life Doesn't Frighten Me"

Making Connections

Sound
Explain to students that sound devices in poetry can help make the poem's meaning more vivid and the emotion of the work more apparent.

Rhyme/Rhythm
Ask two volunteers to select a rhyming poem from this unit to read aloud. The first reader should use his or her voice to stress the rhyme; the second reader should emphasize the rhythm.

YOUR TURN
Students may benefit from reading the lines aloud in a small group setting.

Repetition
Have students think about a familiar nursery rhyme or the lyrics to a song. Ask them to note which word or words are repeated.

Alliteration
Point out to students that the use of alliteration in poetry makes the language more musical and easier to remember.

Imagery and Figurative Language

Poets use words and phrases to create mental pictures, or images, in readers' minds. These pictures help the reader understand the thoughts, feelings, and ideas the poet is writing about. Words and phrases that appeal to a reader's five senses—sight, hearing, smell, taste, and touch—are called **imagery.** Examples of imagery: blistering sun, piercing rain, cotton-candy clouds.

Another way that poets create clear and powerful images is through figurative language. **Figurative language** is made up of words and phrases that present ordinary things in new and unusual ways. Similes, metaphors, and personification are common types of figurative language.

> ### FIGURATIVE LANGUAGE
> Look out how you use proud words.
> When you let proud words go, it is not easy to call them back.
> They wear long boots, hard boots; they walk off proud; they can't hear you calling—
> Look out how you use proud words.
>
> —Carl Sandburg,
> "Primer Lesson"

- A **simile** is a comparison of two things that have something in common. A simile usually contains the word *like* or *as.* Example: Her eyes are green as emeralds.
- A **metaphor** is another kind of comparison. A metaphor does not contain the word *like* or *as.* Instead, it states that one thing actually is something else. Example: Her eyes are emeralds.
- **Personification** is a kind of figurative language in which an animal, object, or idea is given human qualities. It is described as if it were human. Example: The sun wrapped its warm arms round my shoulders.

YOUR TURN What does the "they" in the poem above represent? What human qualities do "they" have?

Tone and Speaker

The **tone** of a poem is the poet's attitude toward his or her subject. For example, the tone might be serious, sad, humorous, or angry. You can identify the tone by paying attention to the images in a poem and to the poet's **word choice.** Remember that even words that are close in meaning can express slightly different feelings. The **speaker** in a poem is the voice of the poem, the person who seems to be saying the words. The speaker is not necessarily the poet; he or she could be a character in the poem.

From "It Seems I Test People"

Reading Poetry

People often write poetry to express feelings. A poem's **form, sound, imagery, figurative language,** and **speaker** all work together to help the reader imagine the experience the poet is sharing. The following reading strategies can help you get the most from every poem.

How to Apply the Strategies

Preview the poem and read it aloud a few times. Notice the poem's form: its shape on the page, the number of lines, and whether the lines are divided into stanzas. As you read, listen for rhymes and rhythm and for the overall sound of the words.

Visualize the images. Create mental pictures of the images you find in the poem. Do the images remind you of your own feelings and experiences? How do the images contribute to the overall effect of the poem?

Think about words and phrases. Think about how the poet's choice of words adds to the meaning or feeling of the poem. What words or phrases create emotions in you? Are there any words or phrases that you find surprising or unexpected?

Make inferences. Use your own knowledge and details in the poem to make logical guesses about a poem's meaning. You can make inferences about the images in a poem and about the speaker's attitudes and personality.

Consider the poem's theme. Ask: What message is the poet trying to send or help me understand?

Here's how Carine uses the strategies:

*"Usually, I read a poem aloud so I can get a feel for the sound and rhythm. This helps me **visualize** the images. I sometimes memorize a poem and it becomes mine forever."*

THE ACTIVE READER **193**

LET YOUR UNDERSTANDING GROW
Explain that perhaps the most important thing about a poem is the effect it has on its readers. Students should allow themselves to connect to poems.

I'm Nobody! Who Are You?

by EMILY DICKINSON

It Seems I Test People

by JAMES BERRY

Growing Pains

by JEAN LITTLE

Connect to Your Life

Fitting In How important do you think it is to belong? Do you think it is better to "go with the flow" or to make your presence known?

Build Background

Breaking Tradition Emily Dickinson was born in 1830. At that time, almost all poets wrote in strict forms, using traditional rhythms and rhyme schemes.

Dickinson's poetry paved the way for new, unstructured forms, like free verse—poetry without regular patterns of rhythm, rhyme, or line length. Free verse sounds more like the way people speak, and it became popular in the 20th century. "It Seems I Test People" and "Growing Pains" are examples of free verse.

Focus Your Reading

LITERARY ANALYSIS · FIGURATIVE LANGUAGE

Poets use **figurative language** to convey feelings, ideas, and thoughts. Two common types of figurative language are similes and metaphors.

A **simile** is a comparison that uses the word *like* or *as.*
Example: **The sun is like a shiny penny.** A **metaphor** is a similar kind of comparison but without the word *like* or *as.* Instead, one thing is spoken of as if it actually were something else.
Example: **The sun is a shiny penny.**

As you read the following poems, look carefully at the use of similes and metaphors.

ACTIVE READING · MAKING INFERENCES

An **inference** is a logical guess you make based on a writer's words and on your own knowledge and experience. By making inferences, you can fill in details about what you are reading. Consider, for example, the second line of "It Seems I Test People":

my voice having tones of thunder

As you probably know from your own experience, thunder is loud. You can infer that the speaker's voice is loud and booming.

As you read these poems, make inferences about the figurative language you find. Record your inferences in your
📖 READER'S NOTEBOOK.

I'm Nobody! Who Are You?

by Emily Dickinson

I'm Nobody! Who are you?
Are you—Nobody—Too?
Then there's a pair of us!
Don't tell! they'd advertise—
    you know!

5 How dreary—to be—Somebody!
How public—like a Frog—
To tell one's name—
    the livelong June—
To an admiring Bog!

Clara in Front of Hydrangeas and Mirror (1978),
Norman Locks.

THINKING *through the* LITERATURE

1. How does the speaker in this poem feel about being "Nobody" instead of "Somebody"?

2. According to the speaker, how is a "Somebody" like a frog?

3. What do you think are the pros and cons of being well-known and of being unknown?

POEMS BY DICKINSON, BERRY, AND LITTLE   **195**

Ask students to make inferences in answer to the following questions and explain their reasoning:

Is the speaker of Berry's poem a gloomy or a cheerful person?

Possible Response: He is a cheerful person: he speaks of laughing and suggests that he is ready to greet people with a hello.

(A) In Little's poem, is the relationship between the speaker and her mother generally calm or stormy?

Possible Response: It seems to be stormy: the speaker says that her mother is "forever nagging." Later she says she often yells at her mother.

Use **Unit Two Resource Book,** p. 4, for more practice. Use **Reading and Critical Thinking Transparencies,** p. 10, for additional support.

Literary Analysis

FIGURATIVE LANGUAGE

To help students appreciate the importance of literary devices such as figurative language, ask them to rewrite the second stanza of "It Seems I Test People"—without using figurative language.

Possible Response: I always expect people to move away when I approach. I always wait to see changes taking place as a result of my entering. Though I am friendly, people leave when I arrive. It seems I make people think about serious issues when I approach.

Use **Unit Two Resource Book,** p. 5, for more practice. Use **Literary Analysis Transparencies,** p. 19, for additional support.

It Seems I Test People

by James Berry

Freedom Now, Charles White. Collection of the California African American Museum of Art and Culture, Los Angeles; courtesy Heritage Gallery, Los Angeles.

My skin sun-mixed like basic earth
my voice having tones of thunder
my laughter working all of me as I laugh
my walk motioning strong swings
5   it seems I test people

Always awaiting a move
waiting always to recreate my view
my eyes packed with hellos behind them
my arrival bringing departures
10   it seems I test people

Instruction Read the poem aloud and discuss what it's about. Invite students to point out any confusing parts of the poem, and help them with their understanding. You might suggest that students think of the first four lines in the first stanza as a list of the speaker's qualities that seem to test people, or make them feel uncomfortable.

Next, review the definition of metaphor and how it is different from a simile. (*A metaphor compares two things but doesn't use* like *or* as. *Instead, it states that one thing actually is something else.*) Write this sentence on the board and ask students to change the simile into a metaphor: *His voice sounds like thunder.* (*His voice is thunder.*) Point out that metaphors are not always as clear as they are in the example students wrote. Ask students to identify the metaphor in each stanza of the poem. (*my voice having tones of thunder; my eyes packed with hellos behind them*)

Practice Have pairs of students quote a metaphor in the poem, identify the two things being compared, and describe how the two things are similar.

Possible Responses: Metaphor: "my voice having tones of thunder." The poet is comparing the sound of his voice to thunder. Like thunder, the voice is low, powerful, and rumbling.

Use **Unit Two Resource Book,** p. 5, for additional support.

GROWING PAINS

Mother got mad at me tonight and bawled me out.
She said I was lazy and self-centered.
She said my room was a pigsty.
She said she was sick and tired of forever nagging
    but I gave her no choice.
5   She went on and on until I began to cry.
I hate crying in front of people. It was horrible.

I got away, though, and went to bed and it was over.
I knew things would be okay in the morning;
Stiff with being sorry, too polite, but okay.
10 I was glad to be by myself.

Then she came to my room and apologized.
She explained, too.
Things had gone wrong all day at the store.
She hadn't had a letter from my sister and she was
    worried.
15 Dad had also done something to hurt her.
She even told me about that.
Then *she* cried.
I kept saying, "It's all right. Don't worry."
And wishing she'd stop.

20 I'm just a kid.
I can forgive her getting mad at me. That's easy.
But her sadness . . .
I don't know what to do with her sadness.
I yell at her often, "You don't understand me!"
25 But I don't want to have to understand her.
That's expecting too much.

by
Jean Little

A

Differentiating Instruction

Less Proficient Readers
In order to help students analyze characters, including their traits, motivations, and relationships, have students point out examples of the contrast between the speaker's intentions (motivations) and his actual effect on people.
Possible Response: "My laughter working all of me as I laugh" contrasts with "It seems I test people" and "my eyes packed with hellos" contrasts with "my arrival bringing departures."

English Learners
Make sure students understand the structure of the poem. In each stanza the first four lines tell something about the speaker, and the last line tells the effect of the qualities that have been listed.

Advanced Students
Inform students that good writers have a way of helping the reader get to know their characters in just a few lines. Ask students to find details in "Growing Pains" that help them to know the speaker and/or the mother and to explain what these details reveal.
Possible Responses: The speaker hates "crying in front of people" (line 6); "I knew things would be okay in the morning; / Stiff with being sorry, too polite, but okay" (lines 8–9). She's been through this sort of interaction with her mother before; "Things had gone wrong all day at the store. / She hadn't . . . Dad had . . . hurt her" (lines 13–15). The mother has several stressful things going on in her life and relies heavily on the daughter for support.

EXPLICIT INSTRUCTION   Sentence Structure

Instruction Read the poem aloud and discuss what it's about. Invite students to point out any confusing parts of the poem, and help them with their understanding. Discuss how this poem sounds different from "It Seems I Test People," and point out that "Growing Pains" has a conversational style—the poem sounds the way people speak. Remind students that poets use sentence structure to convey meaning in their poems. In this poem, the poet has made sure that her sentences

sound like the natural speech of a young person. Ask students to point out words and lines that sound typical of someone their age.
Practice Have small groups discuss how they picture the speaker—What is she like? How does she feel? What is her relationship with her mother? What is her life like? Then have students work alone to write a description of the speaker, using lines from the poem to support their ideas.

Possible Responses: Students should support their ideas with quotations from the poem. Descriptions might include these ideas: The speaker is a young girl who has had an argument with her mother. She feels bad about the fight and about what her mother said to her. She feels worried about her mother, and she feels like she knows too much about her mother's life—more than she wants to know. Her mother's sadness scares her.

Connect to the Literature

What Do You Think?
1. Responses will vary. Some students may be reminded of relationships in their own lives. Others may respond by saying that the speaker should be more understanding of her mother.

Comprehension Check
- When he arrives, people depart.
- The mother said that the speaker was lazy and selfish, that the speaker's room was messy, and that the speaker gave the mother no choice but to nag.
- The mother expects too much by expecting the speaker, a child, to understand her.

Think Critically
2. **Possible Response:** Some students may say that the speaker feels overwhelmed by the mother's sadness and also feels responsible for making the mother happy.
3. **Possible Response:** Some students may say that the growing pains are those of becoming an adult and having to see one's parents as people with problems. Others may interpret "growing pains" more literally, as the pain of being yelled at by your mother.
4. Responses should list specific inferences made and mention reasons why personal experiences helped to make those inferences.

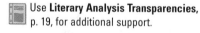 Use **Reading and Critical Thinking Transparencies,** p. 10, for additional support.

Literary Analysis

Figurative Language Responses should reflect an understanding of similes and metaphors and of the specific comparisons being made.

Use **Literary Analysis Transparencies,** p. 19, for additional support.

Connect to the Literature

1. What Do You Think? What do you think about the relationship between the speaker and the mother in "Growing Pains"?

Comprehension Check
- What happens when the speaker in "It Seems I Test People" arrives somewhere?
- What did the mother say when she "bawled out" the child in "Growing Pains"?
- What does the speaker in "Growing Pains" think is "expecting too much"?

Think Critically

2. Why do you think the speaker in "Growing Pains" finds the mother's sadness harder to accept than her anger?

   Think About:
   - what the speaker means by "I don't know what to do with her sadness"
   - the speaker's reaction to the mother's anger
   - the speaker's comment "I'm just a kid"

3. What do you think are the "growing pains" referred to in the poem's title? Support your answer with examples from the poem.

4. **ACTIVE READING** | **MAKING INFERENCES**
   Compare the **inferences** you recorded in your **READER'S NOTEBOOK** with those of a classmate. Discuss how your own experience helped you make the inferences.

Extend Interpretations

5. **What If?** What do you think would happen if the speakers of these three poems met? What would they talk about?

6. **Connect to Life** Which of the poems best expresses your own feelings about growing up and fitting in? Explain your answer.

Literary Analysis

FIGURATIVE LANGUAGE Poets use figurative language to convey feelings and ideas through vivid images. Two kinds of **figurative language** are similes and metaphors. Both are comparisons of things that have something in common, even though they may not be much alike on the surface.

In a **simile** a comparison is made using the word *like* or *as*. Example: The room was dark as a cave.

A **metaphor** is a direct comparison, without *like* or *as*. Example: The room was a dark cave.

You can figure out how similes and metaphors show meaning in a poem by asking yourself these questions:
- What image does the comparison create?
- What does the image say about the subject of the poem?

Emily Dickinson uses a simile to compare a person who seeks fame to a frog that croaks all day long. By doing so, she creates a negative image of fame-seekers as boring show-offs.

Paired Activity Choose a simile or a metaphor from one of the poems you read. With a partner, use the two questions listed above to discuss the comparison.

Extend Interpretations

5. **What If?** One possible response is that Dickinson's speaker and Little's speaker would have much in common to talk about, but Berry's speaker might be so brash that he would make the others keep silent. To get students started on this activity, have them divide into groups of three and role-play the various speakers.

6. **Connect to Life** Responses may indicate any one of the three poems. Many students will probably pick "Growing Pains" because it deals with a young person's thoughts and feelings. Explanations should be thoughtful and well reasoned.

Writing

Letter to the Poet Write a letter to Emily Dickinson telling her what you liked or disliked about her poem. Be specific in your letter by discussing particular words, images, punctuation, or ideas. Support your opinions with reasons and quotations from the poem. Place your letter in your **Working Portfolio.**

Dear Emily Dickinson,
I really like your simile in "I'm Nobody! Who Are You." People who brag are a little bit like croaking frogs. These people never seem to stop talking, and they always say the same things.

Speaking & Listening

Portrait of a Speaker What do you learn about the speaker in "Growing Pains"? Is she sensitive or selfish? Is she happy? How does she feel about her mother? Create a presentation that tells about the speaker. First, decide how you would describe the speaker. Then identify the information in the poem that supports your description. Present your ideas and support to the class. Be sure to include quotations from the poem in your presentation.

Speaking and Listening Handbook
See p. R96: Informative Presentations.

Research & Technology

Poetry Poster There are many books of poetry in your school and local libraries. Browse through a few books to find a poem you really like. Then find biographical information about the poet, such as the date of birth and how he or she became a poet. Next, create a poster showing the poem. Include a section for the poet's biographical information. You might also want to add illustrations.

Communities across the nation have celebrated Poetry Month with magnetic bulletin boards where passersby can compose their own poems.

Reading for INFORMATION
 As part of your preparation, read "Calling All 'Nobodies'" on page 201.

Writing

Letter to the Poet Responses should cite specific points in the poem and support the opinions given with sound reasoning. To make this activity more challenging, ask students to add a response from Dickinson defending her poem against any objections raised to it.

Speaking & Listening

Portrait of a Speaker To help students get started, have them review the description of the speaker they wrote earlier. Tell them to be sure to find examples in the poem to support their ideas about the speaker. Remind students that their presentation should last between 5 and 10 minutes.

Use the **Speaking and Listening Book,** pp. 25 and 26, for additional support.

Research & Technology

Poetry Poster Tell students that they may be able to find biographical information in reference books that a librarian can help them find and in newspaper and magazine articles.

Emily Dickinson

In 1862, Dickinson sent some poems to a professional writer, Thomas Wentworth Higginson, asking him if he thought them worthwhile. He did not think them worth publishing, but he was intrigued enough to write to her and even visit her. He later reported: "I was never with any one who drained my nerve power so much. Without touching her, she drew from me. I am glad not to live near her."

Author Activity

Outsiders Students may work in small groups to choose and discuss poems. Allow ample time for research in the school or public library.

James Berry

A teacher as well as an author, James Berry conducts writing workshops for children. Besides *When I Dance,* another of his books has won an award: *A Thief in the Village and Other Stories,* a 1988 Coretta Scott King Award honor book. It is told from the point of view of a Jamaican child, and it grew out of his own childhood experiences.

Jean Little

Jean Little's eye problems prevent her from reading now, but she continues to write with the help of a talking computer. Little gives the following advice to young writers: "Read and write a lot. You have a storehouse in your head. If you don't put anything in it, there's nothing to draw on."

Emily Dickinson
1830–1886

"a Book, is only the Heart's Portrait—every Page a Pulse."

Shut-in Emily Dickinson was born in Amherst, Massachusetts, where she lived her whole life. She gradually withdrew from society until she became a total recluse, never leaving her home. Though she rarely spoke to strangers, she got along well with the neighborhood children. She would lower them treats of gingerbread in a basket from her second-floor window.

From Nobody to Somebody Dickinson's poetry was practically unknown in her lifetime. She published only seven poems. After her death, however, her sister found a collection of nearly 1,800 poems in her room. Now many people consider Dickinson one of the greatest American poets.

AUTHOR ACTIVITY

Outsiders Read some other works that express feelings of not belonging. You might read *Nilda* by Nicholasa Mohr or *The Whispering Wind: Poetry by Young American Indians,* edited by Terry Allen. Choose a favorite work and discuss with a group why you like it.

James Berry
born 1925

"It's the function of writers and poets to bring in the left-out side of the human family."

A Remembered Childhood James Berry moved to England in 1948 but never forgot his youth in Jamaica. The poems in *When I Dance,* which won a *Signal* Poetry Award, are written in Caribbean dialect. These rhythmic, humorous poems focus on the good and the bad parts of daily life and on the uniqueness of the individual. According to one poem, "Nobody can get into my clothes for me / or feel my fall for me, or do my running. / Nobody hears my music for me, either."

Jean Little
born 1932

"The single most important thing that I have done to help myself become an able writer is to read."

Writing from Experience Jean Little's poems and stories are based on her own experiences and portray young people's lives realistically. Little was legally blind at birth. By fourth grade, her vision had improved enough for her to attend regular classes. Many of her characters have physical disabilities, such as cerebral palsy or blindness. Although there are no magical cures in Little's books, her characters learn to cope and survive.

Source: *The New York Times*

Living • Arts

Calling All "Nobodies"

SPECIAL REPORT

by Francis X. Clines

Washington, March 16, 1998—If there is a more lyrical way to celebrate the approaching millennium than by letting an average American recite T. S. Eliot's "The Love Song of J. Alfred Prufrock," then Robert Pinsky, poet laureate of the United States, is dedicated to finding it.

In the meantime, Mr. Pinsky rates it an offbeat contender for a poetry archive he plans to begin building next month as a kind of soul-print of the nation for future cultural historians. All sorts of ordinary citizens from all the states will be invited to record audio- and videotape recitations of their favorite poems as a measure of the nation's "collective cultural consciousness" at the millennial turning.

"A gift to the nation's future," Mr. Pinsky said as he outlined his big plans to invite Americans to try out for the poesy pool. About 1,200 of them will make the final cut, but tens of thousands of others will be put into a database.

Beau Sia, 19, reads poetry in a New York cafe.

Reading for Information

A newspaper article that includes only facts can be boring. Sensory details, personal anecdotes, and direct quotes can add variety, fill out a story, and expand on ideas. A writer who elaborates on basic information creates a stronger, more informative piece.

Elaborating

To **elaborate** is to work something out with great care and detail, to develop it completely. In writing, you elaborate when you support or develop a main idea with details—facts, descriptions, explanations, examples and stories, or quotations. By including such details you can create a vivid mental image for the reader.

YOUR TURN *Use this article with the questions and activities below to identify elaboration and to practice elaborating.*

① The writer describes Mr. Pinsky's archive as "a kind of soul-print of the nation for future cultural historians." A quotation from Mr. Pinsky and other details elaborate on that thought. Find another example in the article where a quotation provides more detail.

READING FOR INFORMATION **201**

EXPLICIT INSTRUCTION Elaborating

Instruction Tell the class that when a writer elaborates, he or she supports or develops a main idea with facts, descriptions, details, stories, examples, or quotations. Explain that these techniques help make writing lively and interesting. Have students reread the section of the article on page 201 with the blue bracket around it. Point out that in the first sentence, the writer explains that Robert Pinsky plans to create a poetry archive. Ask students to find in this section an example of how an explanation is used to elaborate on this information. ("All sorts of ordinary citizens from all the states will be invited to record . . . at the millennial turning.")

Practice Have students work in pairs to read and complete the numbered activities on the pupil pages.

Possible Responses: See the side columns in the teacher's edition for answers to the activities on the pupil pages.

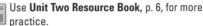 Use **Unit Two Resource Book,** p. 6, for more practice.

Poet laureates Robert Pinsky (left) and Rita Dove (far right) with Hillary Rodham Clinton at a Washington poetry contest.

2 "Poetry slows me down, makes me think, and it touches my heart," explained one of the most avid archive participants, Louise Hartzog, 97, a Sunday school teacher in Greenwood, S.C., with a prodigious[1] memory for a lifetime of favorite poets. She can speak riffs that dart from Wordsworth to Dorothy Parker. She laughingly applies some Emily Dickinson to explain her archive credentials:

"I'm Nobody! Who are you?
Are you—Nobody—too?
Then there's the pair of us!"

Mr. Pinsky thought of the archive as a way to play off the mass cultural events that will be center stage during the millennial celebrations. "The pleasure and admiration for the mass arts, I believe, creates an appetite, in reaction, for a kind of art that is personal and individual," he said. "Poetry is individual; it's a voice."

The archive will invite people to say why they chose their particular poems. "And the explanations are wonderful," Mr. Pinsky said of some early samplings here at the Library of Congress where the archive is to be stored.

Professional poets need not apply. The only requirement is that volunteers not read their own poetry, a simple rule that Mr. Pinsky is confident will guarantee the broadest mix of great poets read by ordinary enthusiasts.

The Favorite Poem Archive will be one of the humbler, least graphic markings of the nation's millennium celebration. But Mr. Pinsky is

---

1. **prodigious** (prə-dĭj′əs): enormous, of impressive size.

convinced it will be one of the better heeded across time as an educational tool. From his travels, he already expects tens of thousands of volunteers to wind up in the database that will describe precisely what sorts of people like what sorts of poems these days, and why.

③ Even without a formal announcement, word of mouth has already prompted more than 800 poetry lovers to offer their voice and favorite poem. There is an Alaska woman who uses poetry to stave off depression in the long winters; she wants to read Stevie Smith's "Not Waving But Drowning." There is a retired Maryland parole officer who regularly recited Langston Hughes's "Hold Fast to Dreams" for his troubled clients.

"It isn't so much the people and it isn't so much the poems," said Mr. Pinsky. "It's the relationship between the person and the poem, the attachment, that makes it interesting."

Mr. Pinsky will make all final decisions with the help of the Library of Congress and the New England Foundation for the Arts. The archive formally begins its work on April 1, 1998, at Town Hall in New York, where the Academy of American Poets **④** will line up a motley chorus—from an immigrant using poetry in his literacy training to some more public voices like Ed Bradley of "60 Minutes."

"I'm not particularly interested in celebrities," the laureate said. "The point of all this has to do not with celebrity but with our life together as Americans."

Reading for Information *continued*

② A writer can elaborate through the careful choice of descriptive words. For example, using vivid adjectives and sensory details of sound, smell, and taste to describe a meal can help build a complete mental picture of the event. What words and phrases does the writer use to describe Louise Hartzog as she quoted Emily Dickinson? How do the writer's descriptive words, combined with the facts of her age and occupation, create a more detailed image of Louise Hartzog?

③ A **fact** is any piece of information that can be proved true. Which facts in this paragraph help support Mr. Pinsky's expectation that tens of thousands of readings will eventually be placed in the database?

④ A writer may include a story or example to elaborate on a thought, making what you read easier to understand. Here, the writer uses the phrase "motley chorus," meaning a mixed group, to describe the people who will contribute to the poetry archive. What specific examples did the writer include in the article to show that the contributors are indeed a mixed group?

2 He says that she "laughingly" quotes Dickinson. The suggestion that she is laughing at herself and at her own credentials combines with the facts of her advanced age to suggest a spry, sharp-witted person.

3 Hundreds of poetry lovers found out about the project and responded even before a formal announcement was made. The writer cites two examples, a woman in Alaska and a man in Maryland.

4 The writer includes the specific examples of an immigrant using poetry in literacy training and a figure from the national news media.

 Use **Writing Transparencies,** p. 49, for additional support.

---

^{EXPLICIT}
^{INSTRUCTION} **Taking Notes**

Instruction Tell students that they can record and understand information in the articles and books they read by taking notes. Say, "When taking notes, you should look for the most important information and record it in a form that is easier to understand and remember." Also tell students that the notes they take may be in the form of whole sentences or words and phrases—the form doesn't matter as long as students are able to understand the notes when they read them later. Next, explain that to take notes, students first

need to read the entire article and then go back to find and record main ideas and supporting details in each paragraph or section. Ask a volunteer to identify the main idea in the paragraph on page 201 that begins, "In the meantime." Then ask volunteers to identify supporting details. Write the information on the board.

(Main idea: Robert Pinsky, the poet laureate of the U.S., plans to create a poetry archive. Details: Ordinary citizens from all over the U.S. will be invited to participate; They'll record

themselves reading favorite poems on audio-tape or videotape.)

Practice Have students take notes on the rest of the article, using page 7 of the **Unit Two Resource Book,** to record their notes.

Possible Responses: See the answer key in the back of the **Unit Two Resource Book** for possible responses.

 Use **Unit Two Resource Book,** p. 7.

Some Americans eminent in civic life, on the other hand, must be included, Mr. Pinsky said. "Whitman had this vision of poetry as holding together a country that might be fragmented," he explained. "So certain figures that have to do with our life together, our communal life, should be well-represented: a civil rights leader, someone who works with the home-less." But he guarantees that 85 percent of the archive participants will be the Dickinsonian nobodies who crave and read poetry in their lives.

"One of the beautiful things about the art of poetry is that the medium is the human body as its voice, but not necessarily the artist's body," Mr. Pinsky said of his search for the nobodies. "When you say a poem by Whitman or Dickinson, your voice is that artist's medium."

> **Research & Technology**
> **Activity Link: "I'm Nobody! Who Are You?," "It Seems I Test People," "Growing Pains," p. 199.** What poems do you know? Which one would you submit to an archive such as Mr. Pinsky's? Read several of your favorites aloud before making your final choice. Write a brief description of what the poem means to you. Elaborate, giving details or examples that help explain why the poem is important to you. With your classmates, create a poetry archive for your class. Record each student's favorite poem on audiotape, videotape, or in writing.

Peter McClenahan reads his favorite poem, "Kubla Khan," by Samuel Taylor Coleridge, at a poetry reading in Brookline, Massachusetts.

204   UNIT TWO   PART 1: THE NEED TO BELONG

EXPLICIT INSTRUCTION **Research & Technology**

Instruction Students can start the activity by reviewing poems in this textbook that appeal to them. They can also think about poems they have read in previous years of study. You may wish to provide some sources for students to look through—anthologies of popular poems or of poems for young people. Stress the requirement that they read their poems aloud before making their final choice, as their opinions of which is their favorite may shift as they experience the poem in oral presentation. Point out the connection between the assignment and the Reading for Information questions in their text. Both deal with elaboration of a description.

Practice Students can take turns recording their favorite poems for the archive. Each student should add a brief description of what is appealing about the poem he or she has chosen. If you wish to have students record their choices in writing, you may want to have them compile the poems in a book, either handwritten or produced on a computer.

Three Haiku

by BASHŌ, ISSA, *and* RAYMOND R. PATTERSON

Connect to Your Life

Capture the Moment The unusual poems you are about to read capture moments that have been meaningful to three poets. With a partner, choose an object in the room. Then, on your own, try to observe that object as though you were seeing it for the first time. List five words that describe the object. Compare lists with your partner. Did the two of you describe the object in different ways?

Build Background

HISTORY

Japanese poets have been writing haiku for several hundred years. Western poets learned of the haiku form in 1868, when Japan was reopened to the West. There had been no trade or communication between the two cultures for 250 years. After World War II, growing interest in Japanese culture made the haiku form popular in the United States.

Focus Your Reading

LITERARY ANALYSIS   HAIKU

A **haiku** is a three-line, unrhymed poem. In Japanese haiku, the first and third lines contain five syllables, and the second line contains seven syllables. (Haiku written in English or translated into English may have different numbers of syllables.)

> 1 2 3 4 5
> When the wind passes
>
> 1 2 3 4 5 6 7
> The sparrows in the branches
>
> 1 2 3 4 5
> They cling so tightly.

As you read these three poems, think about how a haiku describes a single moment with a few chosen words.

ACTIVE READING   NOTING SENSORY DETAILS

One way that haiku convey meaning is through sensory details, or imagery. A **sensory detail** is a word or phrase that helps the reader imagine the look, feel, sound, taste, or smell of something.

📖 **READER'S NOTEBOOK** As you read the three haiku, pay attention to the images and sensory details in each one. Identify the main image in each poem and record it in your notebook. Then list the sensory details that you find.

THREE HAIKU **205**

Standards-Based Objectives

1. understand and appreciate a **poem**
2. understand the **poetic form, haiku**
3. use the reading strategy of **noting sensory details** to help understand the poem

Summary

The poet Bashō describes feeling so different in his new clothing that he feels he must look like a completely different person. Issa tells of the beauty of the Milky Way as seen through holes punched in a paper screen or wall. Raymond Patterson suggests that the sunlight on his grandmother's knees is like a yellow quilt.

Thematic Link

Each haiku explores one way in which people feel a sense of belonging to life: in their appearance, in their appreciation of nature, or in the relationship they have with beloved relatives.

English Conventions Practice

Daily Language SkillBuilder

Have students **proofread** the display sentences on page 187k and write them correctly. The sentences also appear on Transparency 6 of **Language Transparencies**.

LESSON RESOURCES

UNIT TWO RESOURCE BOOK, pp. 8–9

ASSESSMENT
Formal Assessment, pp. 31–32
Test Generator

SKILLS TRANSPARENCIES AND COPYMASTERS
Reading and Critical Thinking
• Noting Sensory Details, TR 11 (p. 207)

Language
• Daily Language SkillBuilder, TR 6 (p. 205)
Writing
• Cluster Diagram for Poem, TR 35 (p. 208)

INTEGRATED TECHNOLOGY
Audio Library

Visit our Web site:
www.mcdougallittell.com

For **systematic instruction** in language skills, see:
• **Vocabulary and Spelling Book**
• **Grammar, Usage, and Mechanics Book**
• pacing chart on p. 187i.

Three Haiku

In my new clothing
I feel so different
I must
Look like someone else.

BY BASHŌ

Beautiful, seen through holes
Made in a paper screen:
The Milky Way.

BY ISSA

Glory, Glory . . .

Across Grandmother's knees
A kindly sun
Laid a yellow quilt.

BY RAYMOND R. PATTERSON

Incense wrapper (Edo period, Japan; 17th–18th centuries) attributed to Ogata Korin, 1658–1716. Wrapper mounted on hanging scroll, ink and color on gold-ground paper, 33 × 24.1 cm, The Art Institute of Chicago, Russell Tyson Purchase Fund (1966.470). Photograph © 1994, The Art Institute of Chicago, all rights reserved.

206   UNIT TWO   PART 1: THE NEED TO BELONG

Multicultural Link   **Traditional Poetry**

Many nations have forms of poetry, like haiku, that are traditionally linked to their culture. For example, India has its Sanskrit poetry, which began some 4,000 years ago. Its most ancient form is the *Veda,* the hymns to the gods. Vedic poets used meter, rhyme, and onomatopoeia. Their poetic form was the basis of classical Sanskrit poetry, which followed after the Vedas. The great epics of classical Sanskrit include the *Mahabharata,* which has one hundred thousand couplets! Greece's oldest traditional poetry is the Homeric epics, composed orally by poets who probably lived around 700 B.C. It lives on: One recent poet, Nikos Kazantzakis, wrote a 33,333-line continuation of the Homeric poems.

Norway and Iceland have the poems of Old Norse, written in two styles, the Eddic and Skaldic. These arose as early as A.D. 800–1000. One Skaldic poem, *Draumkvædet* (The Dream Vision), was composed around 1200 and then passed down from singer to singer until the 1800s, when it was finally written down.

Connect to the Literature

1. **What Do You Think?** Read the poems slowly a second or third time. Do you notice or feel anything that you didn't notice or feel in your first reading? Discuss your reactions with a partner.

Think Critically

2. **ACTIVE READING** **NOTING SENSORY DETAILS**
   Look back at the images and details you listed in your **READER'S NOTEBOOK**. Exchange notes with a partner and discuss other words or images that you could add.

3. Think about Bashō's haiku and the saying "Clothes make the man." Do you think the haiku and the saying have the same message? Explain your answer.

4. Which haiku best conveys the experience of being in a special place? Support your choice with details from the poem.

   Think About:
   - which sensory details in the poems present the clearest images
   - how many of the five senses each poem appeals to

Extend Interpretations

5. **What If?** Traditionally, haiku have no titles. Suppose you were asked to make up titles for the first two poems. What would your titles be?

6. **Connect to Life** Revisit the list you made in the Connect to Your Life activity on page 205. Write a haiku about the object you observed, using as many words from your list as possible.

7. **Art Connection** The artwork pictured on page 206 is a Japanese incense wrapper from the late 1600s. It was made by painting on thick gold paper. By decorating a wrapper—something intended to be thrown away—with a lovely work of art, the artist suggests that beauty passes away quickly. How might this idea apply to the images in haiku?

Literary Analysis

HAIKU The **haiku** is a traditional form of Japanese poetry. It presents a single moment, feeling, or object in three unrhymed lines. In traditional haiku, the first and third lines contain five syllables, and the second line contains seven syllables.

Originally, haiku were written to convey images of nature, but poets have used the form to write about everything from furniture to construction work.

Paired Activity With a partner, copy the three haiku in this lesson on a sheet of paper. Count the syllables in each line. (Keep in mind that haiku translated into English or written in English may not have the traditional pattern of five, seven, and five syllables.) Discuss with your partner the message that each haiku conveys to you.

Connect to the Literature

1. **What Do You Think?**
   Responses will vary. Some students will say that they noticed a feeling of peacefulness the second time they read the haiku. Others may comment on the way the poets paint scenes using just a few descriptive details.

Think Critically

2. Have students note whether they used all their senses in choosing words to fill in their web.

3. Most students will respond that the saying and the haiku have the same message, because both say that putting on certain clothes can make you look and feel different. The wearer changes to fit the image of the clothes he or she puts on.

4. Responses will vary. Students should cite the senses that they used when reading their chosen haiku.

   Use **Reading and Critical Thinking Transparencies**, p. 11, for additional support.

Literary Analysis

Haiku Students should be able to distinguish individual syllables and count them accurately. They should also discuss their personal experiences of the various haiku.

Extend Interpretations

5. **What If? Possible Responses:** "The Imposter," "Night Sky." To get students started on this activity, read them these sample responses and have them come up with others.

6. **Connect to Life** Responses will vary. Students should include as many words from their Reader's Notebook list as possible. To get students started on this activity, have them write a single sentence about the object they observed, using the words from their list, and then try to write the sentence in haiku form.

7. **Art Connection Possible Response:** Both the life of the wrapper and the actual haiku are brief, as is the moment considered in a haiku.

Writing

Your Own Haiku Responses should include the topics of growth and change and be presented in the haiku form. To get students started on this activity, discuss with them ways in which they have changed over the past few years.

 Use **Writing Transparencies,** p. 35, for additional support.

Speaking & Listening

Recycled Haiku Haiku generated in the activity should make sense. To make this activity easier, allow students to use some blank cards that can be filled in as needed to complete a haiku.

Author Activity

Pioneering Poets Have students work in special "poet research teams." Each team could be assigned a poet and each student on the team could have the task of finding out something about the poet from a different source.

Issa

During especially difficult periods of his youth, Issa would flee to the outdoors. Thus as a child he learned to associate the natural world with freedom, imagination, and possibility.

Bashō

Born Matsuo Menefusa, Bashō had no source of income except for his art. He frequently taught poetry writing and judged poetry contests.

Raymond R. Patterson

Patterson's most popular work, *Riot Rimes U.S.A.,* is an 85-poem sequence that depicts the Harlem riot of 1965.

Writing

Your Own Haiku Try writing three haiku of your own. Write about things that suggest growth and change. Place the haiku in your **Working Portfolio.**

Speaking & Listening

Recycled Haiku Write each word in the three haiku on a separate card. Then, compose several new haiku using the words on the cards, plus a few of your own. Read your poems to the rest of the class.

Author Activity

Pioneering Poets Who were some other important haiku poets? What did they write? Use your library to find out. Read examples of their work to the class.

Issa
1763–1827

A Life of Tragedy Issa, born Kobayashi Nobuyuki, led a life full of poverty, illness, and tragedy. His mother died when he was three, and his stepmother mistreated him. At age 13, he left home for Edo (now Tokyo). There he studied haiku and took the pen name Issa (meaning "cup of tea"). The poet's first wife died young, and only one of his many children survived infancy. Issa's troubles helped him understand the struggles of ordinary people. His haiku use simple language to describe everyday subjects with great sensitivity.

Raymond R. Patterson
born 1929

". . . a poem written is a poem discovered."

Teacher, Writer Raymond Patterson was born in New York City. After college, he worked in social services and taught English in public schools. In 1968 Patterson became a lecturer in English at City College in New York, where he is now professor emeritus. He received a Borestone Mountain Award in 1950 and a National Endowment for the Arts grant.

Bashō
1644–1694

A Wandering Poet Matsuo Bashō is considered one of Japan's greatest poets. The son of a samurai, he worked as the companion of a noble family's son. When the son died, Bashō was greatly upset. He left the family's service and became a wandering poet. His innovations in haiku influenced many later poets. He created strict rules for the form and preferred to write about nature, especially the seasons. In addition to the haiku for which he is famous, Bashō wrote many beautiful travel diaries.

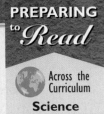
SHORT STORY

All Summer in a Day

by RAY BRADBURY

Connect to Your Life

How do weather and temperature affect you?

Build Background

"All Summer in a Day" is set on Venus, the second planet from the sun.

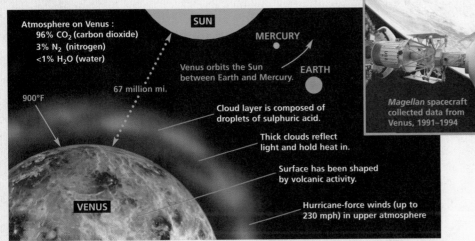

SUN

MERCURY

EARTH

Venus orbits the Sun between Earth and Mercury.

Atmosphere on Venus :
96% CO_2 (carbon dioxide)
3% N_2 (nitrogen)
<1% H_2O (water)

67 million mi.

900°F

Cloud layer is composed of droplets of sulphuric acid.

Thick clouds reflect light and hold heat in.

Surface has been shaped by volcanic activity.

Hurricane-force winds (up to 230 mph) in upper atmosphere

VENUS

Magellan spacecraft collected data from Venus, 1991–1994

Focus Your Reading

LITERARY ANALYSIS SCIENCE FICTION

Stories that are based on advances in science and technology are called **science fiction.** Many of these stories are set in the future and in imaginary places. As you read this story, look for:

- unusual settings
- effects of science or technology
- messages about the future

Also think about what the theme of this story might be.

ACTIVE READING EVALUATING

To **evaluate** a story is to make a judgment about it. Saying that a story is good or bad is too general. Instead, you should focus your evaluation on specific elements in the story, such as the characters, plot, and setting. As you read "All Summer in a Day," evaluate whether the plot is realistic and the characters are believable. Record your judgments in your **READER'S NOTEBOOK**, and be sure to support them with reasons.

WORDS TO KNOW **Vocabulary Preview**

apparatus   resilient   tumultuously
concussion   savor

This selection is included in the **Grade 6 InterActive Reader.**

Standards-Based Objectives

1. understand and appreciate a **short story**
2. appreciate **science fiction**
3. use the reading strategy of **evaluating** to help understand a short story
4. explain the effect of common literary devices
5. analyze the influence of settings on plot
6. understand and analyze theme

Summary

Margot's classmates resent her because she seems to be different. They were born on rainy Venus, but Margot comes from Earth and can remember what the sun was like. As the story opens, the sun is about to shine—as it does for one hour every seven years. Margot yearns to see it, but moments before it appears, her classmates lock her in a closet. After their hour of sunlit play, her classmates suddenly think of her and let her out. They have gained a new understanding of her need for the sun.

Thematic Link

To whom does Margot belong? To the underground dwellers on rain-swept Venus, or to the Earth dwellers who enjoy the blue sky and sun? Her play-mates give her a definitive answer, but in so doing, discover that they, too, still belong to the Earth they have never known.

English Conventions Practice

Daily Language SkillBuilder

Have students **proofread** the display sentences on page 187k and write them correctly. The sentences also appear on Transparency 7 of **Language Transparencies.**

Preteaching Vocabulary

If you would like to preteach the WORDS TO KNOW for this selection, use the Explicit Instruction, page 210.

LESSON RESOURCES

UNIT TWO RESOURCE BOOK, pp. 10–16

ASSESSMENT
Formal Assessment, pp. 33–34
Test Generator

SKILLS TRANSPARENCIES AND COPYMASTERS
Reading and Critical Thinking
- Evaluating, TR 12 (pp. 210, 216)

Language
- Daily Language SkillBuilder, TR 7 (p. 209)

Writing
- Transitional Words List, TR 10 (p. 217)
- Showing, Not Telling, TR 22 (p. 217)

Speaking and Listening
- Working in a Group, p. 33 (p. 217)

INTEGRATED TECHNOLOGY
Audio Library

Video: Literature in Performance
- "All Summer in a Day," see **Video Resource Book,** pp. 11–18

Internet: Research Starter

Visit our Web site:
www.mcdougallittell.com

For **systematic instruction** in language skills, see:
- **Vocabulary and Spelling Book**
- **Grammar, Usage, and Mechanics Book**
- pacing chart on p. 187i.

Reading and Analyzing

Reading Skills and Strategies:
MAKING INFERENCES

Briefly describe the situation of the people who live on Venus in this story, without mentioning how Margot is shut in the closet. Explain that according to the story, the people on Venus see the sun for only one hour every seven years. Ask students how the young people on Venus who could not remember ever seeing the sun would feel as they waited for it to reappear.
Possible Responses: eager, full of wonder and curiosity, perhaps fearful

Active Reading | EVALUATING |

Write the following questions on the board to help students evaluate the story during and after reading: Are believable reasons given for the actions of the characters? Is the end of the story satisfying? Why or why not?

Use **Reading and Critical Thinking Transparencies,** p. 12, for additional support.

Literary Analysis | SCIENCE FICTION |

Students should be able to identify the purposes of different types of texts. Point out that though we now know enough about Venus to see that Bradbury's story could not take place on that planet, his story is still of value. It says something about who we are as humans and what we need—including basic things like the sun and under-standing of one another's differences. Ask students to look for other insights about people as they read this story.

Use **Unit Two Resource Book,** p. 12, for more practice.

ALL SUMMER IN A DAY
BY RAY BRADBURY

Detail of *The Sower* (1888), Vincent van Gogh. Oil on canvas, Rijksmuseum Kroeller-Mueller, Otterlo, The Netherlands, Erich Lessing/Art Resource, New York. Photo copyright © Erich Lessing.

Background photo copyright © 1994 Thomas Wiewandt.

210

EXPLICIT INSTRUCTION **Preteaching Vocabulary**

WORDS TO KNOW
Teaching Strategy Remind students that when they come across an unfamiliar word, they should examine the **context** carefully to see if they can infer the word's meaning. Write the following sentence on the chalkboard:
Though he knew little about machines, he managed to get the underline{apparatus} to work.
Point out that the context suggests that an apparatus is a kind of machine.

Practice Have students use context clues to infer the meanings of the underlined WORDS

TO KNOW in the following sentences:
1. The flowers were springy and <u>resilient</u>, and they bounced back when bent over by the rain.
2. With wild shrieking and shouting, the children spilled <u>tumultuously</u> out of the school.
3. Margot planned to sit quietly in the sunlight and happily <u>savor</u> its warmth.
4. The storms shook and rattled the buildings with repeated <u>concussions</u>.

 Use **Unit Two Resource Book,** p. 15, for more practice.

For **systematic instruction** in vocabulary, see:
• **Vocabulary and Spelling Book**
• pacing chart on p. 187i.

"Ready?"

"Ready."

"Now?"

"Soon."

"Do the scientists really know? Will it happen today, will it?"

"Look, look; see for yourself!"

The children pressed to each other like so many roses, so many weeds, intermixed, peering out for a look at the hidden sun.

It rained.

It had been raining for seven years; thousands upon thousands of days compounded and filled from one end to the other with rain, with the drum and gush of water, with the sweet crystal fall of showers and the <u>concussion</u> of storms so heavy they were tidal waves come over the islands. A thousand forests had been crushed under the rain and grown up a thousand times to be crushed again. And this was the way life was forever on the planet Venus, and this was the schoolroom of the children of the rocket men and women who had come to a raining world to set up civilization and live out their lives.

"It's stopping, it's stopping!"

"Yes, yes!"

Margot stood apart from them, from these children who could never remember a time when there wasn't rain and rain and rain. They were all nine years old, and if there had been a day, seven years ago, when the sun came out for an hour and showed its face to the stunned world, they could not recall. Sometimes, at night, she heard them stir, in remembrance, and she knew they were dreaming and remembering gold or a yellow crayon or a coin large enough to buy the world with. She knew that they thought they remembered a warmness, like a blushing in the face, in the body, in the arms and legs and trembling hands. But then they always awoke to the tatting drum, the endless shaking down of clear bead necklaces upon the roof, the walk, the gardens, the forest; and their dreams were gone.

It had been raining for seven years; thousands upon thousands of days . . .

All day yesterday they had read in class about the sun, about how like a lemon it was and how hot. And they had written small stories or essays or poems about it:

I think the sun is a flower,
That blooms for just one hour.

That was Margot's poem, read in a quiet voice in the still classroom while the rain was falling outside.

"Aw, you didn't write that!" protested one of the boys.

"I did," said Margot. "I *did.*"

"William!" said the teacher.

But that was yesterday. Now, the rain was slackening, and the children were crushed to the great thick windows.

"Where's teacher?"

"She'll be back."

"She'd better hurry; we'll miss it!"

They turned on themselves, like a feverish wheel, all tumbling spokes.

Margot stood alone. She was a very frail girl who looked as if she had been lost in the rain for years, and the rain had washed out the blue from her eyes and the red from her mouth and the yellow from her hair. She was an old photograph dusted from an album, whitened away;

WORDS TO KNOW	**concussion** (kən-kŭsh′ən) *n.* a strong shaking

211

Differentiating Instruction

Less Proficient Readers

Set a Purpose Ask students to discuss how they feel when someone shows them dislike and what they do when they dislike someone. Then have them read to find out why Margot's classmates dislike her and how they treat her.

English Learners

The author's language may confuse students if they interpret it literally. Review the relevant concepts of similes and metaphors as explained on page 192. Make sure students understand the meaning of the following phrases:

• "The sweet crystal fall of showers and the concussion of storms"

• "clear bead necklaces upon the roof"

• "She was an old photograph"

Then have the students find examples of similes and metaphors for the sun. Have students try to write similes and metaphors that are different from those in the story.

Use **Spanish Study Guide,** pp. 43–45, for additional support.

Advanced Students

Have students research Venus to see if it is actually similar to the way that Bradbury describes it in his story. This story was written in 1954, and we now know more about Venus. Our current knowledge makes the story very unbelievable. Ask, "How does our current knowledge of Venus change the story?"

Possible Responses: The climate of Venus is not hospitable to life at all. The skies are consistently covered with clouds, and the planet is bombarded by horrible storms. One year (the time it takes to orbit the sun) on Venus is 225 Earth days long; one day on Venus (the time it takes for the planet to rotate once on its axis) is 243 Earth days long, which makes one day on Venus longer than one year.

EXPLICIT INSTRUCTION **Literary Devices**

Instruction List the following two sentences on the board: *The sun is like a lemon. The sun is a flower that blooms quickly and then dies.* Ask students which sentence contains a simile (*the first*) and which contains a metaphor (*the second*). Remind students that a writer uses literary devices, such as similes and metaphors, to help readers create mental images and to help them understand the writer's meaning. Discuss what two things are being compared in each sentence and what qualities each comparison gives the sun. (*sun is bright yellow; sun is beautiful but short-lived*) Then review the definitions of simile and metaphor. (*simile—a comparison of two things using the word* like *or* as; *metaphor—a comparison of two things that doesn't use* like *or* as. *Instead, it states that one thing actually is something else*)

Practice Have students work in pairs to find five other examples of figurative language in the selection. Partners should record each literary device and the page they found it on, identify the type of device, and note the items being compared and the qualities being shown by the comparison.

Possible Responses: Similes: "[She] looked as if she had been lost in the rain for years." (p. 211) Margot looked pale, washed out, colorless; "It's like a penny, . . . It's like a fire." (p. 212) The sun is shiny and hot. Metaphors: "She was an old photograph. . . ." (p. 211) Margot looked pale and faded; "[The jungle] was a nest of octopuses." (p. 214) The jungle was full of tangled vines.

Reading and Analyzing

Reading Skills and Strategies:
RECOGNIZE CAUSE AND EFFECT

Tell students that certain words indicate cause and effect relationships: *because, therefore, so,* and others. Remind them that sometimes cause and effect is shown indirectly, without the use of these marker words. Ask them to use marker words and inferences to find the causes behind the children's dislike of Margot.

Possible Responses: They dislike her because she will not play games with them or sing with them unless they sing about the sun and the summer. She has seen the sun and remembers what it was like.

Literary Analysis: SIMILES

Ⓐ Remind students that a comparison of two things is called a simile if *like* or *as* is used. Have students identify similes in this dialogue.

Possible Response: "Like a penny" and "like a fire in the stove" are both similes.

Reading Skills and Strategies:
PREDICT

Ⓑ Point out that one of the things that good readers do is ask questions about the outcome of the story. These questions are a first step toward predicting what will happen—a way of exploring several possible outcomes. Ask students to formulate questions about what will happen once Margot is locked in the closet.

Possible Responses: Will she get out? Will she miss the sun? How will the other students feel afterward if she fails to see the sun?

Wee Maureen (1926), Robert Henri. Oil on canvas, 24″ × 20″. Courtesy of the Pennsylvania Academy of the Fine Arts, Philadelphia. Gift of Mrs. Herbert Cameron Morris. Acct. no. 1962.17.1.

and if she spoke at all, her voice would be a ghost. Now she stood, separate, staring at the rain and the loud, wet world beyond the huge glass.

"What're *you* looking at?" said William.

Margot said nothing.

"Speak when you're spoken to." He gave her a shove. But she did not move; rather, she let herself be moved only by him and nothing else.

They edged away from her; they would not look at her. She felt them go away. And this was because she would play no games with them in the echoing tunnels of the underground city. If they tagged her and ran, she stood blinking after them and did not follow. When the class sang songs about happiness and life and games, her lips barely moved. Only when they sang about the sun and the summer did her lips move as she watched the drenched windows.

And then, of course, the biggest crime of all was that she had come here only five years ago from Earth, and she remembered the sun and the way the sun was and the sky was when she was four, in Ohio. And they, they had been on Venus all their lives, and they had been only two years old when last the sun came out and had long since forgotten the color and heat of it and the way that it really was. But Margot remembered.

"It's like a penny," she said once, eyes closed.

"No, it's not!" the children cried.

"It's like a fire," she said, "in the stove."

"You're lying; you don't remember!" cried the children.

But she remembered and stood quietly apart from all of them and watched the patterning windows. And once, a month ago, she had refused to shower in the school shower rooms, had clutched her hands to her ears and over her head, screaming the water mustn't touch her head. So after that, dimly, dimly, she sensed

---

EXPLICIT INSTRUCTION **Viewing and Representing**

Wee Maureen
by Robert Henri

ART APPRECIATION American artist Robert Henri (1865–1929) loved to paint pictures of children. However, his pictures never idealized children or childhood, but tried to express the emotions children actually experience.

Instruction Point out that portrait paintings use color, light, and the sitter's pose to describe the sitter. Ask students what kind of person Wee Maureen might be. (*She seems like an open person who is not shy, because of the way the artist painted her facing him and looking straight at him.*)

Practice Compare the painting to Bradbury's description of Margot on pp. 211–212.

Possible Response: The girl in the picture has a washed out, "whitened" look, like Margot. Both the girl in the painting and Margot have blonde hair and blue eyes.

it; she was different, and they knew her difference and kept away.

There was talk that her father and mother were taking her back to Earth next year; it seemed vital to her that they do so, though it would mean the loss of thousands of dollars to her family. And so, the children hated her for all these reasons, of big and little consequence. They hated her pale, snow face, her waiting silence, her thinness, and her possible future.

"Get away!" The boy gave her another push. "What're you waiting for?"

Then, for the first time, she turned and looked at him. And what she was waiting for was in her eyes.

"Well, don't wait around here!" cried the boy, savagely. "You won't see nothing!"

Her lips moved.

"Nothing!" he cried. "It was all a joke, wasn't it?" He turned to the other children. "Nothing's happening today. *Is* it?"

They all blinked at him and then, understanding, laughed and shook their heads. "Nothing, nothing!"

"Oh, but," Margot whispered, her eyes helpless. "But, this is the day, the scientists predict, they say, they *know*, the sun . . ."

"All a joke!" said the boy and seized her roughly. "Hey, everyone, let's put her in a closet before teacher comes!"

"No," said Margot, falling back.

They surged about her, caught her up, and bore her, protesting and then pleading and then crying, back into a tunnel, a room, a closet, where they slammed and locked the door. They stood looking at the door and saw it tremble from her beating and throwing herself against it. They heard her muffled cries. Then, smiling, they turned and went out and back down the tunnel, just as the teacher arrived.

"Ready, children?" She glanced at her watch.
"Yes!" said everyone.
"Are we all here?"
"Yes!"
The rain slackened still more.
They crowded to the huge door.
The rain stopped.

It was as if, in the midst of a film concerning an avalanche, a tornado, a hurricane, a volcanic eruption, something had, first, gone wrong with the sound <u>apparatus</u>, thus muffling and finally cutting off all noise, all of the blasts and repercussions and thunders, and then, secondly, ripped the film from the projector and inserted in its place a peaceful tropical slide which did not move or tremor. The world ground to a standstill. The silence was so immense and unbelievable that you felt that your ears had been stuffed or you had lost your hearing altogether. The children put their hands to their ears. They stood apart. The door slid back, and the smell of the silent, waiting world came in to them.

The sun came out.

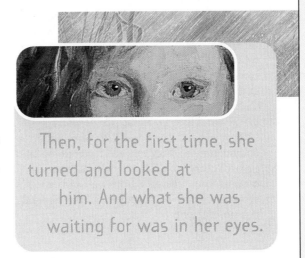

Then, for the first time, she turned and looked at him. And what she was waiting for was in her eyes.

WORDS TO KNOW **apparatus** (ăp′ə-rā′təs) *n.* a device or set of equipment used for a specific purpose

213

Literary Analysis SCIENCE FICTION

Remind students that one of the features of science fiction is the description of unusual settings, especially on other planets or in future times. Ask students to identify descriptions on this page that show that the writing is science fiction.

Possible Responses: The Venusian jungle is like "a nest of octopuses, clustering up great arms of fleshlike weed, wavering . . . It was the color of rubber and ash." The floor of the jungle is described as a mattress that "sighs and squeaks under them, resilient and alive." When the rain comes back it is described as falling "in tons and avalanches everywhere and forever."

Active Reading EVALUATING

Ask students to evaluate the children's actions by answering these questions:

- Is the description of the children's response to the Venusian "spring" accurate? Explain.

  Possible Response: Yes; it would be very natural for children to run and shout in the sunlight when they had a chance.

- What is the author suggesting when he says that one of the children "gave a little cry" when he or she remembered Margot?

  Possible Response: He is suggesting that the child felt remorse for having shut Margot away and forgotten her.

- Is it believable that the children cannot look at each other as they think about having left Margot in the closet?

  Possible Response: Yes, because they are feeling extreme shame for what they have done. It was only when they experienced how wonderful the sun was that they could understand why Margot acted so strangely.

It was the color of flaming bronze, and it was very large. And the sky around it was a blazing blue tile color. And the jungle burned with sunlight as the children, released from their spell, rushed out, yelling, into the summertime.

"Now, don't go too far," called the teacher after them. "You've only one hour, you know. You wouldn't want to get caught out!"

But they were running and turning their faces up to the sky and feeling the sun on their cheeks like a warm iron; they were taking off their jackets and letting the sun burn their arms.

"Oh, it's better than the sun lamps, isn't it?"

"Much, much better!"

They stopped running and stood in the great jungle that covered Venus, that grew and never stopped growing, <u>tumultuously</u>, even as you watched it. It was a nest of octopuses, clustering up great arms of fleshlike weed, wavering, flowering in this brief spring. It was the color of rubber and ash, this jungle, from the many years without sun. It was the color of stones and white cheeses and ink.

The children lay out, laughing, on the jungle mattress and heard it sigh and squeak under them, <u>resilient</u> and alive. They ran among the trees, they slipped and fell, they pushed each other, they played hide-and-seek and tag; but most of all they squinted at the sun until tears ran down their faces, they put their hands up at that yellowness and that amazing blueness, and they breathed of the fresh, fresh air and listened and listened to the silence which suspended them in a blessed sea of no sound and no motion. They looked at everything and <u>savored</u> everything. Then, wildly, like animals escaped from their caves, they ran and ran in shouting circles. They ran for an hour and did not stop running.

And then—

In the midst of their running, one of the girls wailed.

Everyone stopped.

The girl, standing in the open, held out her hand.

"Oh, look, look," she said, trembling.

They came slowly to look at her opened palm.

In the center of it, cupped and huge, was a single raindrop.

She began to cry, looking at it.

They glanced quickly at the sky.

"Oh. Oh."

A few cold drops fell on their noses and their cheeks and their mouths. The sun faded behind a stir of mist. A wind blew cool around them. They turned and started to walk back toward the underground house, their hands at their sides, their smiles vanishing away.

A boom of thunder startled them, and like leaves before a new hurricane, they tumbled upon each other and ran. Lightning struck ten miles away, five miles away, a mile, a half mile. The sky darkened into midnight in a flash.

They stood in the doorway of the underground for a moment until it was raining hard. Then they closed the door and heard the gigantic sound of the rain falling in tons and avalanches everywhere and forever.

"Will it be seven more years?"

"Yes. Seven."

Then one of them gave a little cry.

"Margot!"

"What?"

"She's still in the closet where we locked her."

"Margot."

They stood as if someone had driven them, like so many stakes, into the floor. They looked

---

WORDS	**tumultuously** (tōō-mŭl′chōō-əs-lē) *adv.* in a wild and disorderly way
TO	**resilient** (rĭ-zĭl′yənt) *adj.* flexible and springy
KNOW	**savor** (sā′vər) *v.* to take great pleasure in

214

EXPLICIT INSTRUCTION **Evaluating Story Elements**

Instruction Tell students that to evaluate or critique a story means to make judgments about the story. Explain that when readers evaluate a story, they judge how well the writing measures up to their expectations or standards. Then they make specific statements that summarize their judgments. Say, "The first step in evaluating a short story is to examine and judge its parts—its characters, setting, and plot. You can use questions to help you evaluate." List the questions that follow on the board.

1. How realistic are the characters?
2. Would real people act and speak that way?
3. Are the details of setting accurate and believable?
4. How believable is the plot?

Tell students that when they state or write evaluations, they should make specific statements that can be supported with facts and examples.

Practice Have students work in pairs to answer the questions on the board.

Possible Responses: Responses will vary. Students should realize that although the story is science fiction, the characters and their actions are realistic. The setting is accurate and fitting for the story. The plot events are believable. All answers should be supported.

 Use **Unit Two Resource Book,** p. 11, for more practice.

at each other and then looked away. They glanced out at the world that was raining now and raining and raining steadily. They could not meet each other's glances. Their faces were solemn and pale. They looked at their hands and feet, their faces down.

"Margot."

One of the girls said, "Well . . . ?"

No one moved.

"Go on," whispered the girl.

They walked slowly down the hall in the sound of cold rain. They turned through the doorway to the room, in the sound of the storm and thunder, lightning on their faces, blue and terrible. They walked over to the closet door slowly and stood by it.

Behind the closet door was only silence.

They unlocked the door, even more slowly, and let Margot out. ❖

RELATED READING

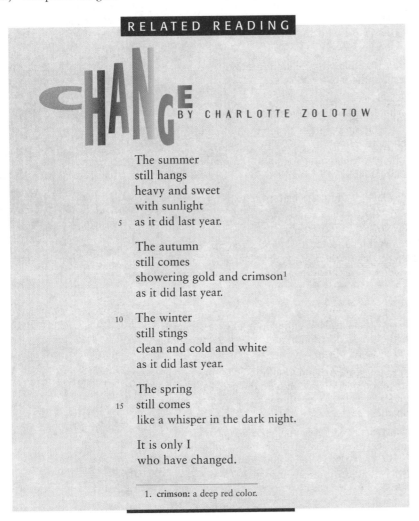

CHANGE
BY CHARLOTTE ZOLOTOW

The summer
still hangs
heavy and sweet
with sunlight
5   as it did last year.

The autumn
still comes
showering gold and crimson[1]
as it did last year.

10 The winter
still stings
clean and cold and white
as it did last year.

The spring
15 still comes
like a whisper in the dark night.

It is only I
who have changed.

---

1. **crimson:** a deep red color.

Connect to the Literature

1. What Do You Think?
Students may respond that they felt sorry for Margot at the end of the story, that Margot must feel sad that she missed the sun, and that the other children seem to feel badly about what they did to Margot.

Comprehension Check
• The story takes place on Venus in the future.
• Margot was living on Earth until five years ago, whereas the other children were born on Venus.
• Margot is locked in a closet.

📑 Use Selection Quiz,
Unit Two Resource Book, p. 16.

Think Critically

2. Possible Response: They envy her experiences in the sunlight.

3. Possible Response: After experiencing the sun, the children seem to understand Margot better and why she misses Earth so much. Now that they understand why Margot is different from them, they act guilty and serious about locking her in the closet.

4. Possible Responses: The relationship may improve because now everyone has seen the sun and the children feel guilty about locking Margot in the closet. The relationship may get worse because Margot may not be able to forgive or forget their cruel treatment of her.

5. Possible Responses: Responses will vary, but students might say that the plot, characters, and actions are believable despite the fantastic elements in the story. Students' evaluations should be supported with facts, reasons, and examples.

📑 Use **Reading and Critical Thinking Transparencies,** p. 12, for additional support.

Literary Analysis

Theme Responses will vary but should show an understanding of how themes are shown through different story elements.

Connect to the Literature

1. What Do You Think?
Discuss the end of the story. How do you think Margot feels? How do you think the other children feel?

Comprehension Check
• Where and when does the story take place?
• Why is Margot the only child who remembers the sun?
• Where is Margot when the sun comes out?

Think Critically

2. In your opinion, why do Margot's classmates play a prank on her?

3. How do you think the children feel about Margot at the end of the story?

> **Think About:**
> • what Margot misses most about Earth
> • the children's reaction when the hour ends and it starts to rain
> • how the children feel when they remember where Margot is

4. Predict Margot's future relationship with her classmates.

5. ACTIVE READING EVALUATING
With a partner, look over the notes you made in your 📖 **READER'S NOTEBOOK.** Is the plot of the story realistic? Are the characters and their actions believable?

Extend Interpretations

6. Different Perspectives If one of Margot's classmates were the story's narrator, how do you think he or she would describe Margot?

7. COMPARING TEXTS Read Charlotte Zolotow's poem "Change" on page 215. Compare the speaker's feeling about changes in the weather with Margot's reactions to weather.

8. Connect to Life Margot is unable to adapt to life on Venus. Discuss some kinds of changes that can be hard to accept. What can people do to help themselves adjust to those changes?

Literary Analysis

SCIENCE FICTION Fiction based on real or possible effects of progress in science and technology is called **science fiction.** Much science fiction is set in the future and in places where humans have never lived. The problems the characters face, however, are usually similar to the problems people face today.

THEME **Theme** is the meaning or moral of a story. Most themes are lessons about life or human nature. You can determine the theme of a story by analyzing
• the title
• the actions, thoughts, and words of the characters
• the conflicts in the story
• the setting and the images the author creates

In Bradbury's story, a group of children play a prank on a classmate. Only later do they realize how cruel they have been. The idea that a prank can be terribly cruel is one of the story's themes.

Group Activity With a group of classmates, find other themes in "All Summer in a Day." Could any of the details about the future be part of a theme? List your themes and the information from the story that helped you determine each one.

Extend Interpretations

6. Different Perspectives Student responses will vary, but should include some of the description from pages 211–212. To help students get started on this, ask them whether the classmate is describing Margot at the beginning or at the end of the story.

7. Comparing Texts Possible Response: The speaker in the poem finds the predictability of the seasons reassuring. Margot is frustrated by the predictability of the weather on Venus, and is anxious to see the sun.

8. Connect to Life Possible Response: Moving, changing schools, and a new member of the family are examples of changes that might be hard to accept. To get students started on this activity, discuss the need for communication, support from family and friends, and willingness to find new friends or just good features in new situations.

Writing

Character Contrasts In what ways are Margot and her classmates different? Use a chart like the one shown here to list the differences. Then write a paragraph about how these differences create conflict in the story. Place your paragraph in your **Working Portfolio.**

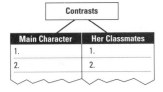

Main Character	Her Classmates
1.	1.
2.	2.

Writing Handbook
See p. R35: Paragraphs.

Speaking & Listening

Plot Comparison As you view the film of "All Summer in a Day," take notes in a sequence-of-events chart. Afterward, compare and contrast the plot of the film with that of the short story. With a small group, discuss why you think the filmmakers changed Bradbury's story.

VIDEO: Literature in Performance

"All Summer in a Day"

Research & Technology

SCIENCE

Conduct research on Venus or another planet to create a factsheet. Look through books, encyclopedias, articles, or Web sites to find facts about the planet. Your factsheet could include the following information, or other information you find interesting:

- the planet's size
- weather and atmosphere
- surface features

Be sure to list on your factsheet the information sources you used.

Research and Technology Handbook
See p. R106: Getting Information Electronically.

 INTERNET Research Starter
www.mcdougallittell.com

Vocabulary

EXERCISE: CONTEXT CLUES On your paper, write the Words to Know that best fill the blanks.

Instead of sleeping, Jamie shined a flashlight on the pages of his new science fiction book and began to __1__ the first chapter. The main character, Samma, was in trouble. Her spaceship's engine and other mechanical __2__ were malfunctioning. An explosion rocked the ship with a powerful __3__. Samma steered toward the nearest planet, and jumped ship. Her jet packs carried her into the planet's atmosphere, where she was tossed __4__ by strong winds. Jamie was glad to read that Samma landed safely, with the rainy planet's __5__ surface cushioning her fall.

Vocabulary Handbook
See p. R22: Synonyms and Antonyms.

WORDS TO KNOW	apparatus	concussion	resilient	savor	tumultuously

---

Writing

Character Contrasts Charts should list relevant contrasting characteristics. To get students started on this activity, have them skim the passage of the selection in which Margot is described.

 Use **Writing Transparencies,** pp. 10 and 22, for additional support.

Speaking & Listening

Plot Comparison You may suggest that students circle any events in their charts that take place in the film but not in the short story to help them get started. You might also suggest that students list events or details that were not included in the film.

Use the **Speaking and Listening Book,** p. 33, for additional support.

Research & Technology

Science Factsheets should demonstrate research and present facts effectively.

Vocabulary

EXERCISE
1. savor
2. apparatus
3. concussion
4. tumultuously
5. resilient

Grammar in Context
WRITING EXERCISE
Responses will vary. Possible responses
are shown.
1. Margot remembered the sun. She
   said it was like fire in a stove.
2. The children watched the rain. They
   shouted when it stopped.
3. The class locked Margot in. They
   watched the door as she shook it.

Connect to the Literature
Accept all paragraphs where nouns
are replaced with pronouns. Students
should notice how substituting all pronouns makes the paragraph vague.

Ray Bradbury
Ray Bradbury has won many awards
for science fiction and fantasy writing.
Unlike some other science fiction writers who are dazzled by high-tech gadgets, Bradbury is concerned with how
technology and science affect ordinary
people.

Author Activity
Changes Responses should demonstrate a solid acquaintance with the
two short stories and focus on a comparison of the effects of scientific
change as reflected in each story.

Grammar in Context: Replacing Nouns with Personal Pronouns

By repeating **personal pronouns** rather than
using specific names or other nouns, Ray
Bradbury creates the scary sense of a mob
overpowering an individual.

> They edged away from her; they would not
> look at her. She felt them go away.

Personal pronouns take different forms
depending on how they function in sentences.
A **subject pronoun** functions as the subject of
a sentence. Subject pronouns include the
following words: *I, we, he, she, it, they, you.*

An **object pronoun** can function as a direct
object, as an indirect object, or as the object of
a preposition. The following words are object
pronouns: *me, us, him, her, it, them, you.*

WRITING EXERCISE Rewrite each pair of sentences.
Choose effective places to replace nouns with
personal pronouns.

Example: *Original* Margot was different from
other children. The children didn't like Margot.

Rewritten Margot was different from them. They
didn't like her.

1. Margot remembered the sun. Margot said the
   sun was like fire in a stove.
2. The children watched the rain. The children
   shouted when the rain stopped.
3. The class locked Margot in. The class watched
   the door as Margot shook the door.

Connect to the Literature In a paragraph from the
story, replace nouns with pronouns. What effect
is lost?

Grammar Handbook
See p. R71: Using Nouns and Pronouns.

Ray Bradbury
born 1920

*"I don't need an alarm clock.
My ideas wake me."*

Imaginary Worlds As a boy in Illinois, Ray
Bradbury had a passion for adventure stories,
secret-code rings, and comic strips. He started
writing to create imaginary worlds of his own. In
these worlds, Bradbury says, "I could be
excellent all to myself."

First Love By the time he was in high school,
Bradbury was writing about a thousand words a
day. He wrote and illustrated his own
magazines. About his early writing, Bradbury
says, "I was in love with everything I did. I did

not warm to a subject, I boiled over." In the
early 1940s, he began selling his stories.

A Grown-Up Child Though he writes about
future technology and space travel, Bradbury is
a bit old-fashioned. He has never learned to
drive a car, preferring to get around by riding a
bicycle. According to one critic, Bradbury is "the
grown-up child who still remembers, still
believes."

AUTHOR ACTIVITY

Changes Many of Bradbury's writings explore
the impact of scientific developments on
people. Find copies of his short stories "The
Flying Machine" and "The Million-Year Picnic"
and read the two stories. Compare the effects
that scientific changes have on the lives of the
stories' characters.

218   UNIT TWO   PART 1: THE NEED TO BELONG

EXPLICIT
INSTRUCTION **Grammar in Context**

USING THE RIGHT PRONOUN CASE
Instruction Explain to students that pronouns
come in different forms, called *cases.* Write the
following examples on the chalkboard:
Subject: <u>They</u> shut Margot in the closet.
Possessive: Margot did not join <u>their</u> games.
Object: No wonder she disliked <u>them</u>!
    Point out to students how the form of the
pronoun changes depending on its use in the
sentence. Write the following list on the board
to help students understand pronoun case use:

Subject forms: *I, you, he, she, it, we, you, they*
Possessive forms: *My, mine, your(s), his,
her(s), its, our(s), their(s)*
Object forms: *me, you, him, her, it, us, you, them*
Practice Have students change the pronoun
in parentheses to the correct form.
1. (Them) thought she was strange.
2. (Her) did not join in their games.
3. We now know more about (it) climate.
4. It does not have a jungle on (its).
5. (Your) would not want to live as they did.

 Use **Unit Two Resource Book,** p. 14.

For more instruction in pronoun case, see
McDougal Littell's ***Language Network,***
Chapter 3.

For **systematic instruction** in grammar, see:
 • **Grammar, Usage and Mechanics Book**
 • pacing chart on p. 187i.

Chinatown *from* The Lost Garden

by LAURENCE YEP

This selection is included in the
Grade 6 InterActive Reader.

Connect to Your Life

Map Your Community What are the characteristics of your own neighborhood or community? Draw a simple map of your community, labeling the parts that are important to you. Share your map with a partner.

Build Background

HISTORY

In the 1800s the Chinese population in California rose dramatically. As the Chinese-American population grew, many people began to view the newcomers as an economic burden. Laws were passed to restrict Chinese immigration. Other laws isolated Chinese Americans in communities called Chinatowns.

Not until the 1960s were immigration laws changed to end bias based on race. Fair housing laws were passed that allowed Chinese Americans to live where they wished.

WORDS TO KNOW	Vocabulary Preview	
entice	remotely	tenement
gaudy	shunned	vulgar
immensely	stereotype	
palatial	taboo	

Focus Your Reading

LITERARY ANALYSIS **PRIMARY SOURCE**

Information comes from various kinds of sources. A **primary source** provides direct, firsthand knowledge. Autobiographies, journals, diaries, letters, and memoirs are all primary sources. "Chinatown" is a primary source because it is Laurence Yep's account of his own personal experience. As you read "Chinatown," notice how the details that Yep remembers help you understand what life was like for one Chinese American in San Francisco during the 1950s.

ACTIVE READING **DISTINGUISHING FACT FROM OPINION**

A **fact** is a statement that can be proved, such as "U.S. teens watch an average of 20 hours of television a week." An **opinion** is a statement that expresses a person's beliefs or feelings. "U.S. teens watch too much television" is one person's opinion. You can tell a fact from an opinion by asking yourself, Can this statement be proved, or does it express what one person believes?

Facts
Opinions
There is little plant life in Chinatown.

READER'S NOTEBOOK
As you read "Chinatown," list in your notebook at least three facts and three opinions that you find.

Standards-Based Objectives

1. understand and appreciate a **memoir**
2. recognize **primary sources**
3. **distinguish fact from opinion**
4. analyze text that uses the **comparison and contrast organizational pattern;** the spatial organizational pattern
5. use a variety of organizational patterns: **spatial**
6. explain the **effects of common literary devices**

Summary

In this memoir of his childhood in San Francisco, writer Laurence Yep describes how he felt like an outsider. Although he is Chinese American, Yep lived outside of Chinatown and did not learn how to speak Chinese. As a result, he missed the jokes that his friends told each other in Chinese. He didn't understand the different rules that governed the games Chinese boys played. Unlike the rest of his family, he wasn't a natural athlete. As he remembers feeling like an outsider, Yep also recalls wrestling with questions about his identity.

Thematic Link

Laurence Yep struggles to achieve a sense of belonging. As a Chinese American living in an African-American neighborhood, Yep explores Chinatown as an outsider. He tries to understand where he fits in.

English Conventions Practice

Daily Language SkillBuilder

Have students **proofread** the display sentences on page 187k and write them correctly. The sentences also appear on Transparency 7 of **Language Transparencies.**

Preteaching Vocabulary

If you would like to preteach the WORDS TO KNOW for this selection, use the Explicit Instruction, page 220.

LESSON RESOURCES

UNIT TWO RESOURCE BOOK, pp. 18–23

ASSESSMENT
Formal Assessment, pp. 35–36

SKILLS TRANSPARENCIES AND COPYMASTERS
Literary Analysis
• Primary/Secondary Source, TR 14 (pp. 220, 227)
Reading and Critical Thinking
• Distinguishing Fact from Opinion, TR 26 (pp. 220, 227)

Language
• Daily Language SkillBuilder, TR 7 (p. 219)
Writing
• Writing Variables, TR 2 (p. 228)
Speaking and Listening
• Creating a Persuasive Presentation, p. 29 (p. 228)
• Guidelines: How to Analyze a Persuasive Presentation, p. 30 (p. 228)

INTEGRATED TECHNOLOGY
Audio Library
Internet: Research Starter

Visit our Web site:
www.mcdougallittell.com

For **systematic instruction** in language skills, see:
• **Vocabulary and Spelling Book**
• **Grammar, Usage, and Mechanics Book**
• pacing chart on p. 187i.

Reading Skills and Strategies:
PREVIEW

Briefly summarize "Chinatown," without identifying the main theme—Yep's struggle to find his place in the world. Have students look through the story. Ask them to make predictions about what they think the selection will be about. Have them establish a purpose for reading.

Literary Analysis   `PRIMARY SOURCE`

Have students begin a list of the details that indicate "Chinatown" is a primary source. Engage them in a discussion about other works they have read that are primary sources.

Use **Unit Two Resource Book,** p. 19, for more practice. Use **Literary Analysis Transparencies,** p. 14, for additional support.

Active Reading   `DISTINGUISHING FACT FROM OPINION`

Distinguishing fact from opinion is an important reading skill. Once you identify a writer's opinions, you can better understand his or her personality, as well as his or her perspective on the world. As they read, tell students to think about what they know about Laurence Yep from tracking his opinions and distinguishing them from the facts.

Possible Response: It is a *fact* that Yep's parents and brother were athletic. It is a *fact* that Yep was not as athletic as his family, but it is Yep's *opinion* that his lack of athletic ability made him a major disappointment to his family.

Use **Unit Two Resource Book,** p. 18, for more practice. Use **Reading and Critical Thinking Transparencies,** p. 26, for additional support.

Chinatown

from
*The
Lost
Garden*

by Laurence Yep

Celebration, Chinatown (1940), Dong Kingman.
Private collection.

220   UNIT TWO   PART 1: THE NEED TO BELONG

EXPLICIT INSTRUCTION **Preteaching Vocabulary**

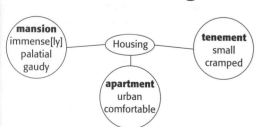

WORDS TO KNOW
Teaching Strategy Call students' attention to the list of WORDS TO KNOW. Tell them that making a **word web** can help them understand and remember the meanings of unfamiliar words.
- Write the word web on the board.
- Ask a volunteer to explain how the words in each circle are related.
- Discuss the relationships of the words.

(The main headings are types of housing; the words under them are words that describe each type.)
Practice Have students use the same kind of web with another WORD TO KNOW.

 Use **Unit Two Resource Book,** p. 22, for more practice.

For **systematic instruction** in vocabulary, see:
- **Vocabulary and Spelling Book**
- pacing chart on p. 187i.

This selection is a chapter from Laurence Yep's memoir The Lost Garden. *Yep grew up as a Chinese American in an African-American neighborhood of San Francisco. He attended school in Chinatown, although he did not speak or understand Chinese. His lack of knowledge of Chinese, among other things, made him an outsider in Chinatown—sometimes even among his friends.*

If Uncle Francis and other members of our family left Chinatown to explore America, my experience was the reverse because I was always going into Chinatown to explore the streets and perhaps find the key to the pieces of the puzzle. But the search only seemed to increase the number of pieces.

When I was a boy, Chinatown was much more like a small town than it is now. It was small not only in terms of population but in physical area as well. Its boundaries were pretty well set by Pacific Avenue on the north next to the Italian neighborhood of North Beach, Kearny Street on the east, Sacramento Street on the south, and Stockton Street on the west—an area only of a few city blocks.

There is a <u>stereotype</u> that the Chinese lived in Chinatown because they wanted to. The fact was that before the fair housing laws[1] they often had no choice.

For years there was a little cottage on an ivy-covered hill in the southwest corner of Chinatown just above the Stockton tunnel. There was—and still is—very little plant life in Chinatown, so the only color green I saw was the paint on my school. The kind of green that is alive—lawns, bushes, and trees—was something I had to leave Chinatown to see, except for that ivy-covered slope. On windy days, the ivy itself would stir and move like a living sea; and overlooking the ivy was a

cottage that was charm itself. However, as much as I admired the house—on occasion I was disloyal enough to the Pearl Apartments to want to live in it—I knew it wasn't for us. My Auntie Mary had once tried to rent it and had been refused because she was Chinese.

Out of some forty-five or so students in my class, I was one of the few who lived outside of Chinatown. Now, thanks to the fair housing laws that were passed in the 1960s, almost none of my former classmates live there; and

There is a stereotype that the Chinese lived in Chinatown because they wanted to.

Chinatown itself has spilled out of its traditional boundaries.

When I was a boy, though, we could see the results of white money and power on three sides of us. To the east we could stare up at the high-rise office buildings of the business district; and to the west, up the steep streets, were the fancy hotels of Nob Hill.[2] Southward lay downtown and the fancy department stores.

Grant Avenue led directly to downtown; but for years I always thought of the Stockton tunnel as the symbolic end to Chinatown. When it had been cut right through a hill, my father and his young friends had held foot races through it after midnight, hooting and hollering so that the echoes seemed to be the

---

1. **fair housing laws:** the civil rights acts of 1964 and 1968, which outlawed racial discrimination in the sale and rental of property, private as well as public.
2. **Nob Hill:** a wealthy neighborhood in northeastern San Francisco. It adjoins Chinatown and is noted for its large luxury hotels, such as the Fairmont and the Mark Hopkins.

WORDS TO KNOW · **stereotype** (stĕr′ē-ə-tīp′) *n.* a fixed idea, especially about the way a group of people looks or acts

221

Reading and Analyzing

Literary Analysis: MEMOIR

Ask students to give two examples that show that "Chinatown" is a memoir—a story about a person's life told by that person.

Possible Responses: Yep's story about following his friend Harold on his paper route shows that this is based on his childhood and therefore is a memoir. His story about his friend Paul is another example.

Literary Analysis: POINT OF VIEW

Ask students to identify the point of view of the selection, first-person or third-person, and explain how they know this.

Possible Response: The selection is written from the first-person point of view. The author uses the first-person pronouns *I* and *me*. He is writing a memoir about his own childhood experiences.

Active Reading | DISTINGUISHING FACT FROM OPINION

Ⓐ Ask students to identify one thing that Yep says about the Chinatown projects that is a fact and one thing that is an opinion.

Possible Response: Yep presents a fact when he says that many of his schoolmates lived in the Chinatown projects. He gives an opinion when he says that he wasn't sure if living there was any better than living in the projects near his family's store.

Detail. Young Chinese Americans enjoy a view of San Francisco Bay and the Bay Bridge. Courtesy California Historical Society, San Francisco.

222 UNIT TWO PART 1: THE NEED TO BELONG

cheers of a huge crowd. The rich white world began just on the other side of the tunnel.

There were also invisible barriers that separated the wealthy whites from the Chinese who cleaned their apartments or waited on

The world looked just the same whether it was a Chinese eye or an American one.

their tables. The Chinese could see and even touch the good life; but they could not join in.

One of my classmates, Harold, had a paper route on Nob Hill. I still find it hard to believe that, up hills that angled some forty degrees or so, he carried a kind of poncho loaded with papers in front and back. But he did that every afternoon. Once I went along with him; and I followed him into one of the fanciest hotels on Nob Hill, past the elaborately uniformed doorman, over the plush carpets, under the ornate chandeliers, and around in back, down concrete hallways as bleak as the ones in the Chinatown housing projects that were painted a cheap, <u>gaudy</u> yellow—a shade which my friend referred to as "landlord yellow." Harold would deliver the afternoon newspapers to the laundrymen and other workers. And with my friend that day, I wandered all around the roots of that <u>palatial</u> dream of wealth.

When the poncho was flat, my friend and I returned to his <u>tenement</u> apartment where there was only one toilet to a floor; and the toilet lacked both a door and toilet paper. When you went, you brought in your own toilet paper. Nothing could be done about the door except changing your attitude about privacy.

Many of my schoolmates lived in the Chinatown projects, and I wasn't sure if life was any better in them than life in the projects near our store. Another newspaper carrier named Paul lived there. As the oldest boy, Paul was expected to look after his younger brothers and sisters while his parents worked—a common practice among many Chinese families. However, as a result, Paul had failed to develop many social skills let alone improve his English. I remember the nun sending him out on an errand and then asking the rest of the class to act as his special friend—which was easy for her to say because she was an adult.

As far as I knew, he hung around with his own group in the projects rather than with anyone from school. His group, though, must have been pretty rough because one of them threw a knife that "accidentally" hit Paul in the eye. Fortunately, there was a charity that arranged an operation; and he was given a new eye from someone who had recently died.

We never knew the identity of the donor, but Paul amused himself by claiming it was a rich white. First, he would clap a hand over his new eye and roll his remaining Chinese eye around. Then he would put his hand over his old one and gaze around elaborately with his new American eye. And then he would announce to us that the world looked just the same whether it was a Chinese eye or an American one.

Paul had shot up early and was a giant compared to the rest of us. When he ran, he looked like an ostrich with arms. He would kick out his legs explosively while his arms flailed the air, so it was hard not to laugh; but we didn't because he was also <u>immensely</u> strong.

WORDS
TO
KNOW

gaudy (gô′dē) *adj.* bright and showy in a way that displays bad taste
palatial (pə-lā′shəl) *adj.* large and richly decorated, like a palace
tenement (tĕn′ə-mənt) *n.* a crowded, rundown apartment building
immensely (ĭ-mĕns′lē) *adv.* to a great extent; enormously

223

The playground at St. Mary's was only a concrete basketball court below. Up above, there was a kind of patio between the convent and the school where the younger children could play. However, the nuns were so worried about our knocking one another down that they forbade us to run during recess. About the only thing we could play under those conditions was a kind of slow-motion tag.

At noon, we could go across the street to the Chinese Playground—the playground where my father had once been the director. In those days, it consisted of levels. The first level near the alley that became known as Hang Ah Alley was a volleyball and a tennis court. Down the steps was the next level with a sandbox (which was usually full of fleas), a small director's building, a Ping-Pong table, an area covered by tan bark that housed a slide, a set of bars, and a set of swings and other simple equipment. The level next to the Chinese Baptist church was the basketball court.

We had Physical Education once a week there. The playground director taught the boys, and I suppose the nun handled the girls. Sometimes it was calisthenics; other times it was baseball played with a tennis ball on the tennis court. There was no pitcher. Rather, the "batter" threw up the ball and hit it with his fist. Because of his size and added arm strength from his own paper route, Paul could hit a home run almost every time, sending the tennis ball flying over the high wire mesh fence.

However, my experience was frequently the reverse. Because the present director knew that my father had once been the director of the playground, he was always urging me on to one disaster after another.

The worst happened when he wasn't present, though. In third grade, we had a very sweet nun, Sister Bridget, who used to play kickball with us. Kickball was like baseball except that the pitcher bowled a ball the size of a basketball over the ground and the "batter" kicked it. One time someone kicked a ball so that it rolled foul. Retrieving it, I threw it to Sister; but as fate would have it, she had turned her head right at that moment to look at something else. I wound up hitting her in the head; and though there was no physical harm, I broke her glasses. Even though my parents paid for replacements, the rest of my class treated me as if I were taboo for striking a nun. I learned what it meant to be shunned and to be invisible.

The only sport that I was remotely good at was football.

The experience also reinforced my belief that I was terrible at sports. Despite all the practice and coaching from my father, I was hopeless when it came to catching any ball in any shape or size. Nor could I dribble a basketball, even though my father sometimes kept me practicing in the little courtyard until it was almost too dark to see.

The only sport that I was remotely good at was football. Having worked and lifted crates in the store made me fairly strong. As a result, I was a good lineman at blocking and rushing—like my hero, Leo Nomellini. However, I was still hopeless at catching a pass. I still remember one game where I dropped three touchdown passes in a row. I was so bad that our opponents stopped covering me. Our quarterback, unable to resist a wide-open target, persisted in

WORDS	**taboo** (tə-bōō′) *adj.* not to be noticed or mentioned
TO	**shunned** (shŭnd) *adj.* avoided; shut out **shun** *v.*
KNOW	**remotely** (rĭ-mōt′lē) *adv.* to a small degree; slightly

224

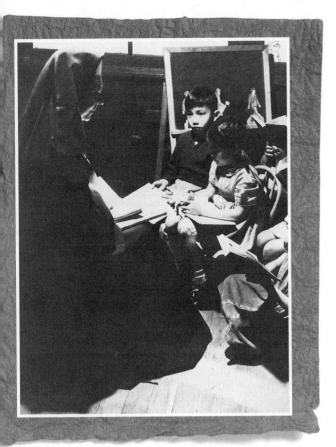

Detail. Chinese-American children reading with their teacher.
Courtesy California Historical Society, San Francisco.

very site of most of my failures. I often felt as if I were a major disappointment to my family.

Moreover, my lack of Chinese made me an outsider in Chinatown—sometimes even among my friends. Since it was a Catholic school taught by nuns, my friends would always tell dirty jokes in Chinese so the nuns wouldn't understand. However, neither did I, so I missed out on a good deal of humor when I was a boy. What Chinese I did pick up was the Chinese that got spoken in the playground—mostly insults and vulgar names.

There were times even with a good friend like Harold when I felt different. Though Harold and I would go see American war movies, he could also open up a closet and show me the exotic Chinese weapons his father, a gardener, would fashion in his spare time, and I could sense a gulf between my experience and that of Harold. It was as if we belonged to two different worlds.

throwing to me—and I dropped yet a fourth pass that could have been a touchdown.

The fact that my whole family was athletic only added to my disgrace. My father had played both basketball and football. My mother had also played basketball as well as being a track star, winning gold medals at the Chinese Olympics—a track event held for Chinese Americans. My brother was also excellent at basketball as well as bowling. Even worse, my father had coached championship teams when he had been a director at Chinese Playground—the

Even my friends' games and entertainments in Chinatown could sometimes take their own different spin. They weren't quite like the games I saw American boys playing on television or read about in Homer Price. Handball was played with the all-purpose tennis ball against a brick wall in the courtyard.

Nor do I remember anyone ever drawing a circle with chalk and shooting marbles in the American way. Instead, someone would set up

WORDS TO KNOW **vulgar** (vŭl′gər) *adj.* crudely disrespectful and displaying bad taste

225

Literary Analysis | PRIMARY SOURCE |

Ask students to explain why "Chinatown" is a primary source.

Possible Response: Yep writes about his own experiences growing up in Chinatown. He conveys facts about life in San Francisco during the 1950's based on firsthand knowledge.

Active Reading | DISTINGUISHING FACT FROM OPINION |

Ⓐ Ask students to identify one fact and one opinion in this paragraph.

Possible Response: It is a fact that the other kids sang in Chinese. It is Yep's opinion that the audience was charmed with the costumed Chinese children.

Reading Skills and Strategies: MAKING INFERENCES

Engage students in a discussion of the last two paragraphs. Ask them to think about why there is a change in Yep's feelings about dressing up.

Possible Response: Yep is more concerned at this point with figuring out who he is than he is with trying on a different identity. He feels that his own identity is a puzzle, and he wants to find the missing pieces and put them all together.

marbles on one side of the basketball court at St. Mary's and invite the others to try to hit them. If they did, they got the marbles. If they didn't, the boy would quickly snatch up their shooters. The ideal spot, of course, was where irregularities in the paving created bumps or dips to protect the owner's marbles. At times, one edge of the courtyard would resemble a bazaar with different boys trying to <u>entice</u> shooters to try their particular setup with various shouted jingles.

Other times, they would set up baseball or football cards. Trading cards weren't meant to be collector's items but were used like marbles. In the case of cards, the shooter would send a card flying with a flick of the wrist. Mint cards[3] did not always fly the truest; and certain cards with the right bends and folds became deadly treasures.

But that sense of being different became sharpest the time I was asked to sing. Our school had a quartet that they sent around to build goodwill. The two girls and two boys dressed up in outfits that were meant to be Chinese: the girls in colored silk pajamas and headdresses with pom-poms, the boys in robes with black vests and caps topped by red knobs.

How could I pretend to be somebody else when I didn't even know who I was?

However, one day in December, one of the boys took sick, so the nuns chose me to take his place. Musical ability was not a consideration; the fit of the costume was the important thing. We were brought to sing before a group of elderly people. I can remember following a cowboy with an accordion and a cowgirl with a short, spangled skirt who sang Christmas carols with a country twang.

Then we were ushered out on the small stage and I could look out at the sea of elderly faces. I think they were quite charmed with the costumed Chinese children. Opening their mouths, the others began to sing in Chinese. Now during all this, no one had bothered to find out if I could sing, let alone sing in Chinese. I recognized the tune as "Silent Night" but the words were all in Chinese. I tried to fake it, but I was always one note and one pretend-syllable behind the others. Then they swung into "It Came Upon a Midnight Clear." This time they sang in English, so I tried to sing along and ranged all over the musical scale except the notes I was supposed to be singing. Finally, one of the girls elbowed me in the ribs and from the side of her mouth, she whispered fiercely, "Just mouth the words."

Up until then I had enjoyed putting on costumes and even had a variety of hats, including cowboy and Robin Hood outfits as well as a French Foreign Legion hat and a Roman helmet; but the experience cured me of wanting to dress up and be something else. How could I pretend to be somebody else when I didn't even know who I was?

In trying to find solutions, I had created more pieces to the puzzle: the athlete's son who was not an athlete, the boy who got "A's" in Chinese school without learning Chinese, the boy who could sing neither in key nor in Chinese with everyone else. ❖

---

3. **mint cards:** freshly unwrapped trading cards, not yet damaged by handling.

| WORDS TO KNOW | **entice** (ĕn-tīs´) v. to lure; to attract with promise of some reward |

Connect to the Literature

1. What Do You Think?
As you read this selection, what thoughts did you have about Yep's childhood?

Comprehension Check
- According to Yep, what stereotype exists about Chinese Americans living in Chinatown?
- How did Yep feel about his athletic abilities as a child?
- Why was it difficult for Yep to perform in the school quartet?

Think Critically

2. Yep writes, "In trying to find solutions, I had created more pieces to the puzzle." How would you describe the puzzle he was trying to solve?

Think About:
- the community in which he lived
- his parents' expectations
- the language barrier

3. What are some ways in which Yep might have handled his problem of feeling like an outsider?

4. **ACTIVE READING** **DISTINGUISHING FACT FROM OPINION** Look over the **facts** and **opinions** you listed in your **READER'S NOTEBOOK**. Trade lists with a classmate and discuss how each of you knew what was fact and what was opinion.

Extend Interpretations

5. **COMPARING TEXTS** Ray Bradbury's story "All Summer in a Day" on page 209 is science fiction, while Laurence Yep's "Chinatown" is a retelling of his own memories. What account do you feel gives a more powerful sense of being torn between two worlds? What phrases in each selection create this feeling?

6. **Different Perspectives** How would "Chinatown" be different if Yep's story were told by someone other than Yep himself? Support your answer with details from the selection.

7. **Connect to Life** Laurence Yep longed to fit into the culture in which he lived. Later, however, he learned to appreciate his Chinese heritage. How important do you think it is for people to know and understand their heritage? Explain your opinion.

Literary Analysis

 A **primary source** provides direct, firsthand knowledge to the reader. "Chinatown" is a primary source because in it, Laurence Yep tells about things he has experienced personally. Primary sources are valuable for research because they provide eyewitness accounts by people who lived through particular times or events.

A **secondary source** is an account of events by someone who did not experience them directly. Authors of secondary sources get their information through research, not personal experience. Biographies and most newspaper articles are examples of secondary sources.

Paired Activity Become a "primary source" by writing on a sheet of paper some memories of your life. Then trade papers with a partner. After reading your partner's work, become a "secondary source" by rewriting it in your own words. (You may ask questions to gather more information.) Read the two versions to the class. Discuss the differences you notice in the two types of sources.

CHINATOWN **227**

Connect to the Literature

1. What Do You Think?
Responses will vary but should address the fact that Yep felt out of place in his own world.

Comprehension Check
- They lived in Chinatown because they wanted to, not because they were forced to.
- He was ashamed because he didn't excel at sports.
- He couldn't carry a tune and didn't know the Chinese language.

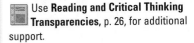 Use Selection Quiz **Unit Two Resource Book**, p. 23.

Think Critically

2. Most students will say that the puzzle Yep is trying to solve has to do with finding out who he is and where he fits in.

3. Some students may suggest that he could have learned more about his Chinese heritage. He could have learned the language.

4. Answers will vary, but should demonstrate the criteria students used to decide whether a piece of information was a fact or an opinion.

 Use **Reading and Critical Thinking Transparencies**, p. 26, for additional support.

Literary Analysis

Primary Source Students' primary sources should be written in the first-person, while their secondary sources should be written in the third-person. Both versions should include details that reveal something about the time and place in which students live.

Use **Literary Analysis Transparencies**, p. 14, for additional support.

Extend Interpretations

5. **Comparing Texts** Answers will vary. Phrases chosen should support students' choices.

6. **Different Perspectives** Students should understand that if the story had been told by someone else, the reader would not know as much about Yep's feelings.

7. **Connect to Life** Responses will vary. Students may stress that it is important to know about where you came from and to belong to a community of people who have a similar cultural background. Other students may say that it is important to fit into the culture in which you live, even if it is different from your original culture.

Writing

The Outsider Students' paragraphs should include the fact that Yep was less athletic than the rest of his family and that he didn't live in Chinatown or speak Chinese. Students might also mention that Yep didn't understand the different rules of the games Chinese boys played.

 Use **Writing Transparencies,** p. 2, for additional support.

Speaking & Listening

Story Recommendation Students might get started by listing the reasons why they liked or didn't like the story and identifying examples in the story that support these reasons.

 Use the **Speaking and Listening Book,** pp. 29 and 30, for additional support.

Research & Technology

Immigrant Communities Students could work in small groups on this assignment. Each student picks one form of research, such as travel guides, encyclopedias, or the Internet. Students do their research individually, taking notes as they read. When they finish their research, all group members convene to share their information. Students decide as a group how to organize their poster. The finished product should capture the highlights and the flavor of the neighborhood.

 Use **Writing Transparencies,** pp. 47-48, for additional support.

Vocabulary and Spelling
EXERCISE: ANTONYMS

1. vulgar
2. tenement
3. palatial
4. gaudy
5. entice
6. shunned
7. immensely
8. remotely
9. stereotype
10. taboo

SPELLING STRATEGY
Possible Responses:

se*lecti*on, popu*lati*on, bu*she*s, tradition-al, plu*sh*, *sh*ade, so*ci*al, spe*ci*al, *sh*ot, condi*ti*on, me*sh*, *sh*unned, *sh*ooter, *sh*arpest, u*sh*ered, solu*ti*ons

---

Writing

The Outsider In this story, Yep tells about some of the reasons he felt like an outsider as a boy. Write a paragraph that summarizes the main reasons that Yep felt this way. Browse through the story to find places where he compares himself to his classmates, friends, and family. Use this information as support in your paragraph. Place your paragraph in your **Working Portfolio.**

Writing Handbook
See p. R44: Cause and Effect.

> This writing activity asks you to write a summary. To find out about longer writing forms you might use when your purpose is to inform, see p. R31: Choosing a Form.

Speaking & Listening

Story Recommendation
Memoirs are often especially interesting because they are true stories. Did you find this memoir interesting? Create a presentation based on your opinion of this story. First, develop a clear statement of your opinion. Then give reasons and information from the memoir to support it. Be clear about why you did or did not like the story. Next, practice delivering your presentation in a strong voice. When you are ready, deliver your presentation to the class.

Speaking and Listening Handbook
See p. R96.

Research & Technology

Immigrant Communities Like San Francisco's Chinatown, Japantown in San Francisco and Little Italy in New York City have become tourist attractions because of their unique shops, restaurants, and appearance. Use the Internet, travel guides, or an encyclopedia to research another well-known city neighborhood settled by immigrants. Make a poster that describes the history of the neighborhood.

INTERNET Research Starter
www.mcdougallittell.com

Vocabulary and Spelling

EXERCISE: ANTONYMS On a sheet of paper, write the Words to Know with meanings most nearly opposite to the meanings of the words below.

1. polite
2. mansion
3. tiny
4. plain
5. repel
6. welcomed
7. barely
8. certainly
9. fact
10. acceptable

Vocabulary Handbook
See p. R22: Synonyms and Antonyms.

SPELLING STRATEGY: THE |SH| SOUND The |sh| sound, as in *shun*, is usually spelled with the two letters *sh*. The |sh| sound can also be spelled *ti*, as in *palatial, ci,* as in *special,* and *ss,* as in *pressure.*

Find at least seven words from "Chinatown" that have the |sh| sound. Write the words on your paper, and underline the spelling of |sh| in each word.

Spelling Handbook
See p. R26.

WORDS TO KNOW					
entice	immensely	remotely	stereotype	tenement
gaudy	palatial	shunned	taboo	vulgar

Grammar in Context: Proper Nouns

Laurence Yep uses specific names of people, places, and even songs to create a vivid picture of his childhood:

> One of my classmates, Harold, had a paper route on Nob Hill.

A **common noun** is a general name for a person, place, thing, or idea. A **proper noun** is the name of a specific person, place, thing, or idea. Notice the proper nouns in red.

uncle	Uncle Francis
hill	Nob Hill
song	Blue Moon
time	December

Usage Tip: Remember that proper nouns are capitalized; common nouns are not.

Apply to Your Writing: For vivid description, replace common nouns with proper nouns where possible.

WRITING EXERCISE Replace common nouns with proper nouns in the following sentences.

Example: *Original* The choir from our school will travel to another city.

Rewritten The Riverside School Chorus will travel to Atlanta.

1. We like to help our teacher.
2. Our school is on a street.
3. Our principal does a lot for our community.

Connect to the Literature Make a list of proper nouns in "Chinatown." Beside each one, write a common noun that could replace it.

Grammar Handbook
See p. R81: Correcting Capitalization.

Laurence Yep
born 1948

"Chinatown is not so much a place as a state of mind—or to be more accurate, a state of heart. . . ."

Making the Grade Laurence Yep began writing in school, when a teacher promised an A to any student who published an article in a national magazine. He earned the A with a science-fiction story that he sold for a penny per word.

An Outsider Yep's first book, *Sweetwater,* is about a young man who belongs to a minority group of transplanted aliens on another planet. According to Yep, "Probably the reason that

much of my writing has found its way to a teenage audience is that I'm always pursuing the theme of being an outsider—an alien—and many teenagers feel they're aliens." Yep also writes realistic and historical fiction. His novel *Dragonwings* has received 15 awards, including selection as a Newbery Honor Book.

AUTHOR ACTIVITY
Common Theme In much of his writing, Laurence Yep explores what it's like to be an outsider. Read one of his other stories or books and then describe it to a small group of classmates. With the group, discuss how Yep conveys the experience of being an outsider. Compare the feelings of his characters with Yep's own feelings about being an outsider in "Chinatown."

Grammar in Context
WRITING EXERCISE
Possible Responses:

1. Oscar and I like to help Mr. Gomez.
2. Lincoln School is on Park Drive.
3. Mrs. Lee does a lot for San Francisco.

Connect to the Literature
Some proper nouns that students might find are *Pacific Avenue* (street), *Auntie Mary* (aunt or relative), *Nob Hill* (neighborhood), *St. Mary's* (a school), and *Hang Ah Alley* (a playground).

Laurence Yep

A third-generation Chinese American, Laurence Yep sharpened his understanding of Chinese traditions and ideas through reading. Many of his books, including *Child of the Owl* and *Sea Glass,* focus on characters caught between two cultures. Yep has taught at various schools, including the University of California at Berkeley and the University of California at Santa Barbara, where he was a writer in residence.

Author Activity

Common Theme Give students adequate time to find, read, and discuss other Yep stories.

EXPLICIT INSTRUCTION Grammar in Context

CONCRETE AND ABSTRACT NOUNS
Instruction Explain that every noun is either concrete or abstract. A concrete noun names something that can be perceived with the senses: *banana, perfume, heat.* An abstract noun names an idea, quality, or characteristic: *justice, beauty, happiness.* Whether concrete or abstract, precise nouns make writing clearer.
Concrete and General: *furniture;* **Concrete and Precise:** *sofa;* **Abstract and General:** *feeling;* **Abstract and Precise:** *anger*

Practice Have students complete each sentence with a more precise form of the general noun in parentheses.
1. I'd like to learn more about (a religion). *(Buddhism)*
2. Our goal for the year is (a quality). *(peace)*
3. (A characteristic) is very important for people who work with the sick. *(compassion)*

 Use **Unit Two Resource Book,** p. 21.

 For more instruction in using precise nouns, see McDougal Littell's *Language Network,* Chapter 2.

For **systematic instruction** in grammar, see:
- **Grammar, Usage and Mechanics Book**
- pacing chart on p. 187i.

Standards-Based Objectives
- understand the relation of word meanings in synonyms and antonyms
- learn to choose exact synonyms and antonyms for words

VOCABULARY EXERCISE
Possible answers:
1. icy; boiling
2. giving; stingy
3. shabby; neat
4. frightening; calming
5. elderly; young
6. nasty; loving
7. uncomplicated; complicated
8. gorgeous; ugly
9. calm; disorderly
10. corrupt; honorable

 Use **Unit Two Resource Book,** p. 24.

Building Vocabulary
Using Synonyms and Antonyms

Being able to use vivid and precise language is an important skill for a writer. Words that have similar meanings are **synonyms.** Words with opposite meanings are **antonyms.**

Which synonym do you think has the power of and the meaning closest to *vulgar?*

> What Chinese I did pick up was the Chinese that got spoken in the playground—mostly insults and vulgar names.
>
> —Laurence Yep, "Chinatown"

synonyms:	rude	crude
	disrespectful	disgusting
	impolite	distasteful

Strategies for Building Vocabulary

Words not only express meaning, they help readers to feel a certain way. For example, suppose *vulgar* was replaced by the word *unpleasant* in the sentence above by Laurence Yep.

Notice how *unpleasant* does not have the suggestive power of *vulgar. Vulgar* expresses a strong feeling of disgust. *Unpleasant* suggests only mild discomfort. Writers learn to use these differences to express shades of meaning, or **connotations.**

❶ **Understand Synonyms** Notice the word *immensely* in the following passage.

> He would kick out his legs explosively while his arms flailed the air, so it was hard not to laugh; but we didn't because he was so immensely strong.
>
> —Laurence Yep, "Chinatown"

Now replace the word *immensely* with the word *very*. Although the words have similar meanings, notice that *very* does not create as strong a picture of the character. A better synonym for *immensely* might be *tremendously.* It has the same power.

❷ **Choose Exact Antonyms** Reread the passage and think of a word that would be an exact antonym of the word *immensely.* The root word *immense* gives a picture of something extremely large.

An opposite word also needs to express an extreme idea. For example, *faintly* might work. The word *faint* refers to something extremely weak or barely visible, just as the word *immense* refers to something that is not just big, but gigantic.

EXERCISE For each word below, write one synonym and one antonym. Try to make your choices vivid and precise.

1. freezing
2. generous
3. sloppy
4. terrifying
5. old
6. hateful
7. simple
8. beautiful
9. peaceful
10. evil

Flowers and Freckle Cream

BY ELIZABETH ELLIS

Siri (1970), Andrew Wyeth.
Tempera on panel, 30″ × 30½″.
Collection of the Brandywine
River Museum, Chadds Ford,
Pennsylvania. Copyright © 1970
Andrew Wyeth.

When I was a kid about twelve years old, I was already as tall as I am now, and I had a lot of freckles. I had reached the age when I had begun to really look at myself in the mirror, and I was underwhelmed.[1] Apparently my mother was too, because sometimes she'd look at me and shake her head and say, "You can't make a silk purse out of a sow's ear."[2]

I had a cousin whose name was Janette Elizabeth, and Janette Elizabeth looked exactly like her name sounds. She had a waist so small that men could put their hands around it . . . and they did. She had waist-length naturally curly blond hair too, but to me her unforgivable sin was that she had a flawless peaches-and-cream complexion. I couldn't help comparing myself with her and thinking that my life would be a lot different if I had beautiful skin too—skin that was all one color.

And then, in the back pages of Janette Elizabeth's *True Confessions* magazine, I found the answer: an advertisement for freckle-remover cream. I knew that I could afford it if I saved my

---

1. **underwhelmed:** not impressed.
2. **a silk purse out of a sow's ear:** something beautiful and of high quality from something inferior or ugly.

Possible Objectives
You can use this selection to achieve one or more of the following objectives:
- enjoy independent reading (Option One)
- read and analyze literature with a group (Option Two)
- use the Reader's Notebook to write in response to literature (Option Three)

Summary
The narrator of this story looks back at herself as a freckled, awkward twelve-year-old. Envious of her cousin Janette Elizabeth's beautiful skin, the narrator sends away for freckle-removing cream. When the package finally arrives, she puts the cream on before going outside to hoe tobacco. The cream turns out to have disastrous effects when exposed to the sun: at the end of the day, the narrator has even more freckles than before! Horrified at her reflection in the mirror, she runs weeping from the house. Her grandfather, learning what has happened, tells her, "But child, there are all kinds of flowers, and they are all beautiful." She responds, "I've never seen a flower with freckles!" and retreats in misery to her room. The next morning she finds a freckled tiger lily on her pillow, placed there by her grandfather.

Art
The painter of *Siri,* Andrew Wyeth, born in 1917 in Pennsylvania, is known for his paintings of ordinary people in a realistic style. Many of his paintings focus on the loneliness of people and their environments. Siri Ericson, the subject of this painting, was from Cushing, Maine, near the Wyeth family's summer home. Andrew's father was the well-known book illustrator N.C. Wyeth, and Andrew's son Jamie is also an artist.

Option One
Independent Reading

You might set aside time each week for independent reading to help your students approach the goal of reading 1 million words a year. During this time, you and your students would read for enjoyment. "Flowers and Freckle Cream" can be read independently in 30 minutes or so. To encourage students to read for pleasure, consider making no assignments related to this selection. However, Options Two and Three offer suggestions in case you do want to make assignments.

Option Two
Group Reading

You may assign students to groups or allow them to choose their own. Students can read the selection together, alternately reading sections aloud, or they can read independently and meet to cooperate in a project that portrays some element of the story.

Possible Projects

- Pairs of students can write the dialogue for a possible conversation between the narrator and her grandfather after she sees the lily on her pillow. They can focus on the lesson she may have learned from her grandfather and how it will affect her future actions. They can perform the conversation for the rest of the class.

- Students can collaboratively create a setting for the performance of the dialogue, choosing one of the locations mentioned in the story.

Option Three
Reader's Notebook

- Ask students to describe the character of the narrator and to analyze in some detail why the freckle cream is so important to her.

- Ask students to read the selection, pausing at the end of the first column on page 231. At that point, ask students to predict what they think is going to happen in the rest of the story. Have them write their predictions in their Reader's Notebook. Have them also write any questions they have so far about the events, the characters, or the language of the story. At the end of the story, students will return to their predictions. Ask them to note if their predictions were accurate.

Superb Lilies #2 (1966), Alex Katz. Oil on canvas, 72″ × 144″. Courtesy of Robert Miller Gallery, New York. Copyright © 1996 Alex Katz/Licensed by VAGA, New York.

money, and I did. The ad assured me that the product would arrive in a "plain brown wrapper." Plain brown freckle color. For three weeks I went to the mailbox every day precisely at the time the mail was delivered. I knew that if someone else in my family got the mail, I would never hear the end of it. There was no way that they would let me open the box in private. Finally, after three weeks of scheduling my entire day around the mail truck's arrival, my package came.

I went to my room with it, sat on the edge of my bed, and opened it. I was sure that I was looking at a miracle. But I had gotten so worked up about the magical package that I couldn't bring myself to put the cream on. What if it didn't work? What would I do then?

I fell asleep that night without even trying the stuff. And when I got up the next morning and looked at my freckles in the mirror, I said, "Elizabeth, this is silly. You have to do it now!" I smeared the cream all over my body. There wasn't as much of it as I had thought there would be, and I could see that I was going to need a part-time job to keep me in freckle remover.

Later that day I took my hoe and went with my brother and cousins to the head of the holler[3] to hoe tobacco, as we did nearly every day in the summer. Of course, when you stay out hoeing tobacco all day, you're not working in the shade. And there was something important I hadn't realized about freckle remover: if you wear it in the sun, it seems to have a reverse effect. Instead of developing a peaches-and-cream complexion, you just get more and darker freckles.

By the end of the day I looked as though I had leopard blood in my veins, although I didn't realize it yet. When I came back to the house, my family, knowing nothing about the freckle-remover cream, began to say things like, "I've never seen you with that many freckles before." When I saw myself in the mirror, I dissolved into tears and hid in the bathroom.

My mother called me to the dinner table, but I ignored her. When she came to the

---

3. **head of the holler:** dialect for "head of the hollow," the end of a small valley.

bathroom door and demanded that I come out and eat, I burst out the door and ran by her, crying. I ran out to the well house[4] and threw myself down, and I was still sobbing when my grandfather came out to see what was wrong with me. I told him about how I'd sent for the freckle remover, and he didn't laugh—though he did suggest that one might get equally good results from burying a dead black cat when the moon was full.

It was clear that Grandpa didn't understand, so I tried to explain why I didn't want to have freckles and why I felt so inadequate when I compared my appearance with Janette Elizabeth's. He looked at me in stunned surprise, shook his head, and said, "But child, there are all kinds of flowers, and they are all beautiful." I said, "I've never seen a flower with freckles!" and ran back to my room, slamming the door.

When my mother came and knocked, I told her to go away. She started to say the kinds of things that parents say at times like that, but my grandfather said, "Nancy, leave the child alone." She was a grown-up, but he was her father. So she left me alone.

I don't know where Grandpa found it. It isn't at all common in the mountains where we lived then. But I know he put it in my room because my mother told me later. I had cried myself to sleep that night, and when I opened my swollen, sticky eyes the next morning, the first thing I saw, lying on the pillow next to my head, was a tiger lily. ❖

---

4. **well house:** a shed covering a deep hole from which water is drawn.

Elizabeth Ellis
born 1943

"Sometimes I feel guilty because I have so much fun."

Dallas Librarian Elizabeth Ellis was born in Kentucky and grew up in Tennessee, amid the Appalachian Mountains. After graduating from college she worked for 10 years as a children's librarian in Dallas, Texas. There, she says, "I realized it was the storytelling part of my job that I enjoyed the most—and the card-filing part that I liked the least."

Telling Tales In 1979, after attending the National Storytelling Festival in Tennessee, and realizing that people made their living telling stories, Ellis left the library and became a storyteller. For the past 16 years, she has charmed audiences of all ages with more than 500 stories about Texas, Appalachia, personal experiences, and—her favorite—unknown heroic women. Ellis performs throughout North America at festivals, schools, and libraries.

Too Much Fun? Many of Ellis's stories she heard from her grandfather, a circuit-riding minister who collected stories as he traveled. The story "Flowers and Freckle Cream" is based on her experiences while spending summers with her grandfather in Kentucky. She resides in Dallas, where she continues to share her stories. "It's a charming way to make a living. Sometimes I feel guilty because I have so much fun."

Possible Activities
Independent Activities
- Have advanced students skim over the story, noting details, facts and descriptions about the narrator's relationship with her family. Ask them to write in their Reader's Notebook their analysis of the relationship between the narrator and her grandfather and what this relationship reveals about both characters.
- Have students review the Active Reader page, p. 193, in Unit Two. Ask them to note which skills and strategies they used while reading this selection.

Discussion Activities
- Use the questions formulated by the students in their Reader's Notebooks as the start of a discussion about this story.
- Ask students if they think that the narrator's perception of herself will change as a result of this experience. If so, how do they think her actions will change?

Assessment Opportunities
- You can assess students' comprehension of the story by evaluating the questions they formulate in their Reader's Notebook.
- You can use any of the discussion questions as essay questions.
- You can have students turn one of their Reader's Notebook entries into an essay.

Art
Superb Lilies #2 was painted by Alex Katz, born in 1927 in Brooklyn, New York. He has often painted colossal pictures of flowers, working directly from nature. The 6-by-12-foot canvas shown on page 232 was one of his experiments in size and scale.

Elizabeth Ellis

Elizabeth Ellis conducts workshops to teach other people how to develop their skills in storytelling. Two of the little-known heroic women featured in Ellis's stories are Deborah Sampson, who disguised herself as a man to serve in the Revolutionary War, and Delia Akeley, a pioneer explorer in Africa around the turn of the last century.

Same Song
by Pat Mora

While my sixteen-year-old son sleeps,
my twelve-year-old daughter
stumbles into the bathroom at six a.m.
plugs in the curling iron
5 squeezes into faded jeans
curls her hair carefully
strokes Aztec Blue shadow on her eyelids
smooths Frosted Mauve blusher on her cheeks
outlines her mouth in Neon Pink
10 peers into the mirror, mirror on the wall
frowns at her face, her eyes, her skin,
not fair.

At night this daughter
stumbles off to bed at nine
15 eyes half-shut while my son
jogs a mile in the cold dark
then lifts weights in the garage
curls and bench presses
expanding biceps, triceps, pectorals,
20 one-handed push-ups, one hundred sit-ups
peers into that mirror, mirror and frowns too.

La misma canción

translated by Ina Cumpiano

A los dieciséis, mi hijo duerme
mientras que mi hija, que tiene doce,
a tropiezos llega al baño a las seis de la mañana
enchufa el rizador de pelo
5 se apretuja en sus mahones descoloridos
se riza el cabello con todo cuidado,
se pinta los párpados de Azul Azteca,
se acaricia en la mejilla un color de Malva Escarcha
se traza la boca de Rosa Neón
10 se escudriña en el espejo . . . espejo, espejo, dime espejo . . .
frunce la frente al verse la cara, los ojos, la piel;
no hay justicia.

Por la noche esta hija
a tropiezos cae a la cama a las nueve
15 los ojos los tiene a medio cerrar mientras mi hijo
corre una milla en la fría oscuridad
luego levanta pesas en el garaje . . .
cosa de arranque y de envión
y de expandir los biceps, los triceps, los pectorales,
20 de hacer tracciones de una mano, cien sentadas
se examina en el espejo, espejo, espejo, dime espejo,
y también frunce la frente.

Standards-Based Objectives
- write an original poem
- use a written text as a model for writing
- revise a draft to add sound devices
- use verb tenses consistently
- deliver an original poem orally

Introducing the Workshop

Original Poem Discuss with students some of their favorite poems. You might suggest poetry by Shel Silverstein, Jack Prelutsky, or Maya Angelou. Engage students in a discussion about why certain poems are especially appealing. Encourage students to talk about the rhythm of the language, the sound of particular words together, and the images that those words convey.

Basics in a Box
Using the Graphic Explain to students that a poem contains certain elements. It begins with an idea. That idea is expressed with precise words that clearly represent the idea. Figurative language, including metaphor, simile, and personification, are also used to express the idea. Poems also contain "sound effects" made by words with the same beginning or ending sound, words with the same vowel sound, and words that sound like what they mean.

Presenting the Rubric To better understand the assignment, students may refer to the Standards for Writing a Successful Poem. You may also want to share with them the complete rubric, which describes several levels of proficiency.

 See **Unit Two Resource Book**, p. 33.

 For more instruction on essential writing skills, see McDougal Littell's *Language Network*, Chapters 10–17.

 Power Presentation

To engage students visually, use **Power Presentation 1**, Original Poem.

Writing Workshop — Original Poem

Convey meaning in a poem . . .

From Reading to Writing Good poems capture a mood and convey a feeling. They can take any form and can be written about anything imaginable—a feeling such as joy or sorrow, an image such as a beautiful sunset, or an everyday object such as an old tire lying by the side of the road. James Berry's poem "It Seems I Test People" shares the speaker's ideas about what others think of him. Jean Little's poem "Growing Pains" explores how upsetting it can be when people act differently from the way you expect. Writing an **original poem** gives you a chance to share your feelings and create pictures in the minds of your readers with carefully chosen words.

Basics in a Box

Poetry at a Glance

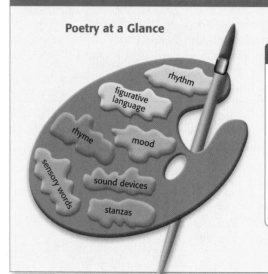

RUBRIC STANDARDS FOR WRITING

A successful poem should
- focus on a single experience, idea, or feeling
- use precise, sensory words in a fresh, interesting way
- include figurative language such as similes and metaphors
- include sound devices such as alliteration and rhyme to support the meaning of the poem

236 UNIT TWO   PART 1: THE NEED TO BELONG

LESSON RESOURCES

USING PRINT RESOURCES
Unit Two Resource Book
- Prewriting, p. 25
- Drafting, p. 26
- Peer Response, pp. 27–28
- Revising, Editing, and Proofreading, p. 29
- Student Models, pp. 30–32
- Rubric, p. 33

Writing
- Figurative Language and Sound Devices, TR 17 (p. 240)

Reading and Critical Thinking
- Sequence Chain, TR 39 (p. 237)

Speaking and Listening
- Emphasizing Points for the Listener, pp. 9 (p. 241)
- Evaluating Reading Aloud, pp. 14 (p. 241)

INTEGRATED TECHNOLOGY

Writing Coach CD-ROM
Visit our Web site:
www.mcdougallittell.com

Analyzing Published Student Models

SPEAKING OPPORTUNITY — See the Speaking and Listening Handbook, p. R96 for oral presentation tips.

Carolyn Nash
published in *Stone Soup* magazine

Whistle

A sleepy <u>darkness</u> coats my bedroom,
    <u>seeping</u> into the corners and <u>wrapping</u> me in a
        <u>blanket</u> of night.
Like snowflakes aimlessly swirling through the air,
    memories flood through my mind
    of times vanished and years past.
I remember, like remembering a dream,
    <u>sitting on my father's lap, in the first days of spring.</u>
His whistle, calm and soft,
    would sail with the wind and sing with the birds,
    <u>wrapping around trees like a satin ribbon.</u>
My head tucked gently under his chin,
    I listened to the music,
    as it mingled among the clouds.
In time, the birds would flock around us,
    their angel <u>wings</u> painted <u>with</u> brilliant colors,
    and they <u>would</u> <u>watch</u> over us.

In the first days of this spring,
    I will walk past the trees
    and whistle my own songs to the birds
And every note that soars through the branches,
    will carry higher than the last,
    until the birds flock to me,
    and we sing together.

RUBRIC IN ACTION

1 Uses precise sensory words

2 Focuses on a single experience

3 Uses an unexpected simile comparing her father's whistle to a satin ribbon

4 Alliteration with the *w* sound draws attention to the line.

5 The writer creates a separate stanza to indicate a shift in time (past to future).

Other Options
- Do not use separate stanzas.
- Use a rhyme scheme.

Teaching the Lesson

Analyzing the Model
Whistle

The first student model is a poem about a memory associated with early spring. As spring approaches, the writer recalls her father's whistle. She remembers that his whistle was in harmony with the wind, the birds, and the trees. At the end of the poem, the writer links her memory to the present as she says that *she* will whistle to the birds this spring.

Have a volunteer read the poem aloud. Then discuss the Rubric in Action with students. Point out key words and phrases in the student model that correspond to the elements mentioned in the Rubric in Action.

1 Ask students to identify some precise, sensory words that the poet uses.
   Possible Responses: snowflakes aimlessly swirling; memories flood. . .

2 Ask students why it is effective to begin a poem with a single experience.
   Possible Response: Readers are immediately drawn into the poem by the clear focus.

3 Ask what elements of a satin ribbon the poet emphasizes in this comparison.
   Possible Responses: its smoothness, its length, its softness

4 Ask students to find other examples of alliteration.
   Possible Responses: *memories* and *mind, will, walk,* and *whistle*

5 Ask students to identify what the poet describes in the new stanza.
   Possible Response: How she will whistle like her father did when spring comes

---

Patterns of Organization

EXPLICIT INSTRUCTION

PICTURING TEXT STRUCTURE

Instruction One way to structure a poem is to list the images that come to mind as one considers the topic. The poet arranges the images in a particular order to suit the feeling and meaning of the poem. In "Whistle" the images flow smoothly from one to the next.

Practice Have students analyze the organization of the student model by making a sequence chain like the one shown.

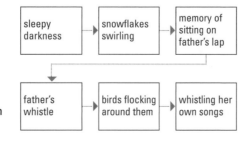

 Use **Reading and Critical Thinking Transparencies,** p. 39, for additional support.

Analyzing the Model

Animal

In the second model, the poet writes about his experience learning how to hit a baseball. He uses the image of a caged animal to represent his own feelings of being trapped and wanting to get out and show that he can play.

1 Ask students to explain the comparison between the poem's speaker and a caged animal.

   Possible Response: The speaker might feel restricted by the rules of the game. He just wants to play the game he loves.

2 Ask students what the internal rhyme "link clinks" makes them think of.

   Possible Response: I can almost hear the rattling of the chain link fence behind the batter.

3 Ask students how the dialogue draws readers into the poem.

   Possible Response: The dialogue helps create the sense of a real ballgame.

4 Ask students what these repeated words describe.

   Possible Response: The actions of a batter waiting for a pitch.

5 Ask students to describe the effect of alternating between dialogue and regular wording.

   Possible Response: The back-and-forth of dialogue and regular wording mimics the rhythm of the pitcher and the batter.

6 Ask students why the poet might have repeated the cage metaphor.

   Possible Response: to show that the speaker only feels free (out of the cage) when he is actually playing the game

Cody Banks
published in *Stone Soup* magazine

Animal

Coaches train me
to play a game I like.
They put me in a cage.
I'm the animal.
I want out.
I want to play.
Give me a bat;
I'll show you.

Chain link clinks
in the wind.
"Batter, batter, batter!"
someone yells.
I don't hear it.
Sounds like silence.
I know it's not.

Step, step, step.
Dig, dig, dig.
Twirl, twirl, twirl the bat.
Wiggle, wiggle, wiggle.
"Swing, batter!"
I don't.
"Ball one."
"Swing, batter!"
I don't.
"Ball two."
"Swing, batter!"
I do.
"Strike one!"

Eye to eye
across the field
with the pitcher.
He claws the ball.
He throws and it's mine.
Boom!
It's outta there.
Crowd screams.
Sounds like silence.
But I know it's not.

I performed.
Now, I'm in the cage.
Trained to play a game I like.

RUBRIC
IN ACTION

❶ Uses a metaphor to introduce his theme, comparing himself to an animal in a cage

❷ Rhymed words within the line create sound effects.

❸ Dialogue helps readers experience the speaker's feeling.

❹ The writer uses repetition to speed up the rhythm.

❺ The writer alternates between dialogue and regular wording to build rhythm and tension.

❻ The cage metaphor appears again, bringing the poem full circle.

Writing Your Poem

❶ Prewriting

Poetry = the best words in the best order.
—Samuel Taylor Coleridge, poet

Chances are that there is a poet inside you. Start noticing words and phrases that capture your imagination because of their sound, rhythm, or meaning. **List** things you see, hear, taste, touch, and smell during the day. **Jot down** your feelings. See the **Idea Bank** in the margin for more suggestions. After you choose a subject, follow the steps below.

Planning Your Poem

▶ 1. **Freewrite about your subject.** Write as much as you can about your subject. Let your ideas flow. Experiment with images, ideas, words, and meanings. Keep the ones you like and add new ones.

▶ 2. **Choose a focus.** Which word, line, or image captures your attention? Which makes you think of interesting images and ideas? Look for one powerful line that can be the focus of your poem.

▶ 3. **Decide on the mood.** Do you want your poem to be happy or sad? humorous or thoughtful? How will you accomplish this? Will you use rhyme or free verse? Will your poem be written in phrases or complete sentences?

❷ Drafting

Now you can begin putting your images and words into a poem. Most poets rewrite their poems several times, so don't worry if your poem doesn't sound perfect at first.

- **Find the poem within the poem.** Experiment by rearranging words. Try using different line lengths. Cut out extra words until you are left with the strongest ones.
- **Play with images.** Create images with precise verbs, nouns, and adjectives and with sensory details. Try using similes and metaphors to make a comparison between two things.
- **Read your poem aloud.** Listen for vowel and consonant sounds that create a certain mood or effect. Decide what sound devices fit your subject.

Ask Your Peer Reader

- How did you feel when you read my poem? What was the overall mood?
- What ideas or meanings did you get from my poem?
- Which words helped you to picture what I was describing?

IDEA Bank

1. Your Working Portfolio 📁
Look for ideas in the **Writing** activities that you completed earlier.

2. Borrowed Quotes
Listen carefully to people's conversations. Choose a line of dialogue that you find interesting. Use it as the first line of your poem.

3. Who Am I?
Write a poem that captures how you think people see you and feel about you. Ask friends, family, and classmates for ideas.

Have a question?

See the **Writing Handbook**
Using Language Effectively, p. R38
Descriptive Writing, p. R39

See **Language Network**
Imagery and Figurative Language, p. 352

Guiding Student Writing

Prewriting

Choosing a Subject
If after reading the Idea Bank students have difficulty choosing a subject for their poem, suggest that they try the following:

- Make a list of personal experiences that you find yourself thinking about often. Choose one that you think would lend itself well to comparisons and vivid language.
- Think of an idea that you would like to express. It can be serious, sad, funny, or silly.

Planning Your Poem

1. As students freewrite, check in with individuals to see who needs direction. Encourage hesitant writers to go forward with their ideas. Remind students not to be judgmental of their own ideas as they freewrite. Tell them they will make decisions once they are finished freewriting.

2. Tell students that focusing a poem simply means emphasizing what part of the subject readers will notice most. For example, In "Whistle," the poet focused on her memory of her father's whistling.

3. Remind students that poets create mood in many ways: by choosing words carefully, by the use of certain images and comparisons, and by the sound of words—rhythm, repetition, and possibly rhyme. Also remind students that poems don't have to rhyme.

Drafting

Remind students that the words that make up a poem should evoke its topic. Suggest that students brainstorm words and phrases that bring to mind the subject of their poem. For example, a poem about a warm spring day might include words such as *swaying leaves*, *soft breeze*, *sunshine soaked sky*, and so on.

Revising
USING SOUND DEVICES

Ask students to work with a partner to take turns reading aloud their poems to each other. Tell the partner who is listening to offer praise for words that evoke the topic of the poem and give suggestions for additional or alternative words that would enhance the poem.

 Use **Writing Transparencies,** p. 17, for additional support.

Editing and Proofreading
CONSISTENT VERB TENSE

Tell students that they don't have to limit themselves to the same tense within a poem but the tenses they use should be correct. Suggest that they reread "Whistle" and notice the different verb tenses. Point out that the writer uses the device of memory to make it clear that she is writing about the past. Tell students that they may change tenses within a poem, but they must make the transitions clear.

Reflecting

Encourage students to write an entry in their Reader's Notebook about the experience of writing their poem. Tell them that they will not have to share this entry with anyone else, so they should feel free to write candidly about their experience.

Option
TEACHING TIP

When students are finished writing their poems, invite volunteers to put together a poetry magazine featuring poems by class members or their favorite works by published poets. Distribute the booklet to other classes or organize a poetry reading.

Need revising help?

Review the **Rubric,** p. 236.

Consider **peer reader** comments.

Check **Revision Guidelines,** p. R31.

SPELLING
From Writing

As you revise your work, look back at the words you misspelled and determine why you made the errors you did. For additional help, refer to the strategies and generalizations in the **Spelling Handbook** on page R26.

Stumped by verb tense?

See the **Grammar Handbook,** Using Verbs Correctly, p. R76.

Publishing
IDEAS

• Find pictures that illustrate the subject of your poem. Lay out a page with your poem and these visual images.

• Perform your poem. Use dramatic movement to draw attention to important ideas in the poem. Choose music to play in the background.

◉ **INTERNET**

Publishing Options
www.mcdougallittell.com

240   UNIT TWO   PART 1: THE NEED TO BELONG

---

❸ Revising

TARGET SKILL ► **USING SOUND DEVICES** As you read your work aloud, listen to the sounds. **Alliteration,** the repetition of beginning consonant sounds, may speed up the rhythm and help add meaning. For instance, in a poem about a snake, you might use words beginning with *s. The snake slithers slowly . . .* The *s* sound makes your listener think of the hissing of a snake.

> with   wind
> would sail ~~on~~ the ~~breeze~~ and sing with the birds,
>
> wrapping around trees like a satin ribbon.

❹ Editing and Proofreading

TARGET SKILL ► **CONSISTENT VERB TENSE** It's easy to get confused about verb tense when you are writing a poem or telling a story. This is especially true if your subject thinks about the future or remembers the past. Go through your poem and look at all your verbs. Use the same tense when two or more actions occur at the same time or in sequence.

> He claws the ball.
> *throws*
> He ~~threw~~ and it's mine.
>
> Boom!
>
> It's outta there.
> *screams*
> Crowd ~~screamed~~.

❺ Reflecting

FOR YOUR WORKING PORTFOLIO How did writing a poem help you understand how you felt? What did you learn about poetry that you didn't know before? Attach your answers to your finished poem. Save your original poem in your **Working Portfolio.**

EXPLICIT INSTRUCTION **Revision**

WORD CHOICE

Instruction Remind students that it is important to revise even the specific words one uses in a composition. Especially in poetry, each word matters, and the sound devices one uses, such as alliteration, are important in establishing the effect the writer wants to have on the reader. Ask students why the words *with* and *wind* were substituted for *on* and *breeze.*

Practice Ask students to reexamine their poems, reading them aloud to determine whether some words should be substituted for others. They can consider adding more alliteration, assonance (repeated vowel sounds), or rhyme.

See the **Research and Technology Handbook,** pp. R108-109, for information about formatting documents using word processing skills.

Mixed Review

> Before I started to write my poem I sat down in the kitchen and
> (1)
> looked around. I pick an apple up off of the table. When I looked at it
> (2)
> closely, I could see my reflection. Then I bit into it. The first bite made
> (3)
> my taste buds water. The taste was incredible. The flesh of the fruit
> (4)
> snapped and crunched under my teeth. I breathed deeply. The apple's
> (5)   (6)
> smell were delicate and sweet.

1. How is sentence 1 best written?
   A. Before I started, to write my poem I sat down in the kitchen and looked around.
   B. Before I started to write my poem, I sat down in the kitchen and looked around.
   C. Before I started to write my poem I sat down, in the kitchen and looked around.
   D. Correct as is

2. What is the correct verb tense in sentence 2?
   A. I picked
   B. I was picking
   C. I was going to pick
   D. Correct as is

3. What is the correct verb tense in sentence 3?
   A. bite
   B. biting
   C. bitten
   D. Correct as is

4. What is the correct spelling in sentence 4?
   A. increduble
   B. incredouble
   C. incredible
   D. Correct as is

5. What is the correct spelling in sentence 5?
   A. breethed
   B. brethed
   C. breathd
   D. Correct as is

6. How is sentence 6 best written?
   A. apple's smell was delicate
   B. apple's smell is delicate
   C. apple's smell are delicate
   D. Correct as is

Review Your Skills

Use the passage and the questions that follow it to check how well you remember the language conventions you've learned in previous grades.

Self-Assessment

Check your own answers in the **Grammar Handbook.**

Quick Reference: Punctuation, p. R64

Making Subjects and Verbs Agree, p. R68

Using Verbs Correctly, R76

Tell students to read the passage completely before they begin to correct the errors. Then explain that B is the correct answer to the first question because the introductory prepositional phrase is "Before I started to write my poem."

Answers: 1. B; 2. A; 3. D; 4. C; 5. D; 6. A

EXPLICIT INSTRUCTION Speaking Opportunity

Prepare Once students have written their poem, they can read it aloud to an audience. Refer students to page R102 of the Speaking and Listening Handbook at the back of this book for tips on presenting their poem.

Present Have students present their poems to the class. They should strive to create a mood and to evoke emotion from the audience.

RUBRIC

3 Full Accomplishment Student uses precise language and sensory details to create a mood. Student speaks clearly, enunciating each word, using pacing and expression to convey emotion.

2 Substantial Accomplishment Student uses precise language and sensory details to create a mood. Student occasionally varies expression or pacing to convey meaning.

1 Little or Partial Accomplishment Student occasionally uses a precise word or a sensory detail within the poem. Student reads with little expression and shows little variety in tone of voice or pacing.

Use **Speaking and Listening Book,** pp. 9, 14, for additional support in presenting a poem.

PART 2
Home and Heritage

Meeting Standards

The Literature You'll Read

The Concepts You'll Study

Vocabulary and Reading Comprehension
Vocabulary Focus: Homonyms and Homophones
Predicting
Making Inferences
Connecting
Reading Aloud

Literary Analysis
Literary Focus: Character and Setting
Character Traits
Literary Devices
Point of View
Sound Devices

Writing and Language Conventions
Writing Workshop: Character Sketch
Vivid Verbs
Past and Present Verb Tenses
Action Verbs

Speaking and Listening
Character Traits Presentation
Persuasive Speech
Monologue
Poem Recital

242

LEARNING the Language of Literature

Character and Setting

> *I've been asked if I always like my characters.*
> *It goes deeper than that. I have to understand them.*
>
> —Jean Fritz, writer

Who are your favorite story characters? Are they just like you or completely different? Some story characters seem so real that you can actually imagine having conversations with them or introducing them to your friends. Like people, characters have personalities, which you learn about by noticing the things the characters do, think, feel, and say.

Characters are the people, animals, and imaginary creatures who take part in the action of a story. They live in a world created by the writer. This world is the story's **setting**—the place and time in which the story takes place.

Writers choose words carefully and use words in special ways to make stories come alive for readers. Using **imagery** and **figurative language**, writers help readers visualize settings and understand characters' feelings and actions.

Seattle, Washington

243

Character Traits

Point out to students that they can learn about a character in the same ways they might learn about a real person: through the character's words and actions, through the words and actions of other characters, and through direct statements about the character.

YOUR TURN

Possible Response: She seems to be frail, colorless, isolated, and not very lively. The author's descriptions of her appearance and her attitude convey these traits.

Character Traits

When you first get to know people, you learn about them in different ways. Perhaps you watch their actions and listen to what they say. You probably notice their physical appearance. You may also listen to what others say about them. These are the same methods readers use to learn about character **traits,** or qualities. When you read a story, look for clues to each character's traits by paying attention to:

- the character's speech, thoughts, feelings, and actions
- the speech, thoughts, and actions of other characters
- the writer's direct statements about the character
- descriptions of the character's physical appearance

Some words you might use to talk about a character's traits include *brave, generous, cruel,* and *selfish.*

YOUR TURN The above passage at the right contains details about Margot, the main character of "All Summer in a Day." What are some of her character traits? How do you know?

CHARACTER TRAITS

Margot stood alone. She was a very frail girl who looked as if she had been lost in the rain for years, and the rain had washed out the blue from her eyes and the red from her mouth and the yellow from her hair. She was an old photograph dusted from an album, whitened away; and if she spoke at all, her voice would be a ghost. Now she stood, separate, staring at the rain and the loud, wet world beyond the huge glass.

—Ray Bradbury, "All Summer in a Day"

From "All Summer in a Day"

Character Traits and Plot

You've learned that character **traits,** or qualities, help you understand a character's personality. Traits also affect the **plot** of a story. As you know, story characters carry out the action of a story and move the plot along. The characters' traits influence the actions they take and the way the plot develops. The characters' traits also influence the way the main conflict is resolved.

The chart below shows a conflict that a character might face and two examples of how different traits affect the resolution of the conflict.

Conflict	Two examples of how traits affect the resolution of the conflict
A character must decide whether to stand up for a friend who is being teased by a group of popular students or ignore her friend so she will be accepted by these students.	If the character is **loyal** and **strong-willed,** she may resolve the conflict by defending her friend.
	If she is **insecure** and **unhappy,** she may choose to ignore her friend and hope the other students will like her for this.

YOUR TURN In the excerpt above to the right, what conflict exists? What are some of Mrs. Pearce's character traits? How do her traits seem to affect the way she deals with this conflict?

TRAITS AND PLOT

"I'm sorry, madam, you can't bring that dog in here," the guard said.

Mrs. Pearce was a very determined old lady. She looked the porter in the eye.

"Now, see here, young man. That dog has walked twenty miles from St. Killan to get to my granddaughter. Heaven knows how he knew she was here, but it's plain he knows. And he ought to have his rights!"

—Joan Aiken, "Lob's Girl"

From "Aaron's Gift"

From "Tuesday of the Other June"

Character Traits and Plot
Have students mention some memorable characters they have read about and the qualities or traits that made them memorable. Discuss whether these traits affected the conflict or the resolution of the story.

YOUR TURN
Possible Response: Mrs. Pearce wants to bring a dog somewhere, but a guard tells her she can't. Her traits include determination, outspokenness, and willfulness. She stands up to the guard instead of backing down because she is determined and strong-willed.

LEARNING THE LANGUAGE OF LITERATURE   **245**

Describing Setting and Characters
List the following sentences on the board: The trees and plants were very pale. The map was confusing. The sun set behind the mountains.

Have students compare these sentences with the examples of imagery, simile, and personification. Discuss which versions are more vivid and interesting.

YOUR TURN
Possible Response: In the simile, a map is being compared to a noodle factory hit by a bomb. The mountains are given arms that can reach out and a mouth that can swallow.

Describing Setting and Characters

Poets are not the only writers who use imagery and figurative language in their work. Writers of fiction and nonfiction also use these **literary devices** to communicate ordinary things in fresh ways. These devices help readers picture the settings and events in stories and understand how characters feel. Some different types of literary devices are described below.

Imagery is language that appeals to the reader's five senses—sight, hearing, smell, taste, and touch. Writers use imagery to draw readers into a scene.

Figurative language is language that expresses ideas beyond the exact meanings of the words. A writer may use figurative language to describe settings, characters, events, or feelings in new and memorable ways. Two types of figurative language are listed below.

- A **simile** is a comparison of two things that have some of the same qualities. A simile usually contains a word such as *like* or *as*.
- **Personification** is a kind of figurative language in which an animal, object, or idea is given human qualities and is described as if it were human.

In poetry, a simile or image may be the most important part of a poem. In fact, it may be the subject of a poem. In prose, figurative language and imagery are only a small part of a longer work.

YOUR TURN Read the excerpts above. What two things are being compared in the example of simile? What human features are given to the mountains in the example of personification?

DESCRIBING SETTING AND CHARACTERS

IMAGERY

It was the color of rubber and ash, this jungle, from many years without sun. It was the color of stones and white cheeses and ink.

—Ray Bradbury, "All Summer in a Day"

SIMILE

. . . we studied the system map, which looked like a noodle factory hit by a bomb.

—Avi, "Scout's Honor"

PERSONIFICATION

Finally the mountains around the valley reached out and swallowed the sun.

—Francisco Jiménez, "The Circuit"

Detail of 1. Frederic Edwin Church, American, 1826–1900. *Twilight in the Wilderness,* 1860s. Oil on canvas, 101.6 x 162.6 cm. © The Cleveland Museum of Art, 1999, Mr. and Mrs. William H. Marlatt Fund, 1965.233

The Active Reader: Skills and Strategies

Predicting

You're about to leave the house, and you hear thunder rumbling in the distance. You look up, and the sky is dark and overcast. You predict that it will rain, and you decide to wear a raincoat. Predicting means thinking about what might happen in the future on the basis of clues. An active reader can also predict, or make a logical guess about, a story's outcome.

How to Apply the Strategy

To **PREDICT,** an active reader will:
• Note clues and details
• Think about what will happen next
• **Connect** new information to prior knowledge
• **Evaluate** and revise the prediction
• Use a chart like this one to help you make predictions:

clues + prior experience	prediction	new details	revised prediction

Try It Now!

Read the example below. Predict what will happen next.

> Then [the pigeon] strutted over to the crumbs, its head bobbing forth-back, forth-back, as if it were marching a little in front of the rest of the body—perfectly normal, except for that half-open wing which seemed to make the bird stagger sideways every so often.
> The pigeon began eating the crumbs as Aaron quickly unbuttoned his shirt and pulled it off. Very slowly, he edged toward the bird, . . .
>
> —Myron Levoy, "Aaron's Gift"

Here's how Mike uses the strategies:

*"To **predict** what will happen in 'Aaron's Gift,' I look for clues in the title, illustrations, and the story. I think about the details—the injured pigeon and Aaron removing his shirt. These lead me to predict that Aaron will capture the bird."*

OVERVIEW

Standards-Based Objectives
• make predictions and support them with textual evidence and prior knowledge
• use clues and details to make and revise predictions

Teaching the Lesson

The strategies on this page will help students apply the skill of predicting to the fiction selections they read.

Presenting the Strategies
PREDICT
Make sure students understand predicting and supporting their predictions with evidence and their own prior knowledge by discussing the incident described in the box on this page.

CONNECT
The combination of what they read and what they already know from their own experience of life is the key that allows good readers to make predictions.

EVALUATE
Remind students that predictions can change as new information is presented in the story. Adding details will help them to revise and refine their predictions as they continue to read. Ask, "What new details might be added to the thunder incident described in the box that could change your prediction?"
Possible Response: As you go to get a raincoat, you notice that the rain has stopped and the sun has come out suddenly.

Aaron's Gift

by MYRON LEVOY

Standards-Based Objectives

1. understand and appreciate a **short story**
2. identify **characters traits** and motives
3. understand the **effect of character traits** in a story
4. use **predicting** to help understand the traits, motivations, and changes in the main character

Summary

While roller-skating in the park, Aaron Kandel finds a pigeon with a broken wing. Aaron brings "Pidge" home, certain that his bird-loving grandmother will be pleased. As Pidge's wing heals, Aaron begins training him to be a carrier pigeon. When a neighborhood gang hears about the pigeon, they offer to let Aaron join if he will let them use Pidge as their mascot. When Aaron appears at the gang meeting, the boys build a fire and try to throw his bird into it. Aaron rescues Pidge, but the bird flies away during the struggle. Aaron is heartbroken because he had planned to give Pidge to his grandmother for her birthday, believing that the pigeon would replace the beloved pet goat she had as a girl in the Ukraine—a goat that was cruelly killed. Aaron runs home and tearfully tells his family about his own encounter with cruelty and about the loss of his grandmother's gift. Instead of being disappointed, Aaron's grandmother tells him that he has given her a greater gift than the pigeon. Aaron later understands that he has given the gift of freedom.

Thematic Link

Understanding one's home and heritage helps a person develop fully. In this story, Aaron learns more about himself through Pidge and his grandmother, helping him to grow and to develop his character.

English Conventions Practice

Daily Language SkillBuilder

Have students **proofread** the display sentences on page 187k and write them correctly. The sentences also appear on Transparency 8 of **Language Transparencies**.

Connect to Your Life

The Best Gifts in Life What is the best gift you ever gave or received, or heard about someone else giving? What made that gift so special?

Build Background

HISTORY

In this story, the main character's grandmother grew up in a Jewish village in the Ukraine, once a part of Russia. During the late 19th century, Jews in the Ukraine lived in constant fear of Cossacks—soldiers loyal to the ruler. These soldiers frequently attacked Jewish communities in raids known as pogroms.

A 19th-century Ukrainian family gathering.

WORDS TO KNOW
Vocabulary Preview

assassinate   stoop
frenzied   thrashing
mascot

Focus Your Reading

LITERARY ANALYSIS **CHARACTER TRAITS**

You can determine a character's **traits,** or qualities, by paying attention to the way the character thinks, acts, and feels and by thinking about what the character says. The **actions** a character takes in a story are based on his or her traits. As you read "Aaron's Gift," figure out his traits and notice how they affect his actions.

ACTIVE READING **PREDICTING**

When you try to guess what might happen next, you are **predicting.** To make predictions, look for the following information:

- details that tell you what the characters are like
- details about the setting, from the story and the illustrations
- conflicts that hint at what might happen next

READER'S NOTEBOOK As you read, pause to jot down at least three predictions about what will happen later in the story. Note the reasons for your predictions.

LESSON RESOURCES

Aaron's Gift

by Myron Levoy

Detail of *Autumn* (1980–1981), Craig McPherson. Oil on canvas, 54″ × 48″, Museum of the City of New York (83.4), gift of the American Institute of Arts and Letters.

249

Ask students to think about the kind of boy Aaron is and to provide examples from the text to support their answers.

Possible Response: Aaron is kind and gentle: he talks softly to the pigeon.

 Use **Unit Two Resource Book,** p. 36 for more practice.

Active Reading PREDICTING

Ask students to use the name of the story and what has happened so far to predict what Aaron's gift might be.

Possible Responses: Maybe Aaron's "gift" is the pigeon he got; Maybe he will give the pigeon away.

Use **Unit Two Resource Book,** p. 35 for more practice. Use **Reading and Critical Thinking Transparencies,** p. 7, for additional support.

Reading Skills and Strategies: IMAGERY

A Noting sensory words is a strategy that can help students visualize as they read. In this description, ask students to find examples of how things look, sound, feel, smell, or taste.

Possible Responses: See the pigeon fluttering in a frenzied dance. Hear the beating and jerking of wings and the clacking of skates. Feel or taste the cookie crumbs.

ACTIVE READER

B **PREDICT** **Possible Response:** Aaron will take the pigeon home and fix its wing.

A aron Kandel had come to Tompkins Square Park to roller-skate, for the streets near Second Avenue were always too crowded with children and peddlers and old ladies and baby buggies. Though few children had bicycles in those days, almost every child owned a pair of roller skates. And Aaron was, it must be said, a Class A, triple-fantastic roller skater.

Aaron skated back and forth on the wide walkway of the park, pretending he was an aviator in an air race zooming around pylons,[1] which were actually two lampposts. During his third lap around the racecourse, he noticed a pigeon on the grass, behaving very strangely. Aaron skated to the line of benches, then climbed over onto the lawn.

The pigeon was trying to fly, but all it could manage was to flutter and turn round and round in a large circle, as if it were performing a <u>frenzied</u> dance. The left wing was only half open and was beating in a clumsy, jerking fashion; it was clearly broken.

Luckily, Aaron hadn't eaten the cookies he'd stuffed into his pocket before he'd gone clacking down the three flights of stairs from his apartment, his skates already on. He broke a cookie into small crumbs and tossed some toward the pigeon. "Here pidge, here pidge," he called. The pigeon spotted the cookie crumbs and, after a moment, stopped <u>thrashing</u> about. It folded its wings as best it could, but the broken wing still stuck half out. Then it strutted over to the crumbs, its head bobbing forth-back, forth-back, as if it were marching a little in front of the rest of the

body—perfectly normal, except for that half-open wing which seemed to make the bird stagger sideways every so often.

The pigeon began eating the crumbs as Aaron quickly unbuttoned his shirt and pulled it off. Very slowly, he edged toward the bird, making little kissing sounds like the ones he heard his grandmother make when she fed the sparrows on the back fire escape.

Then suddenly Aaron plunged. The shirt, in both hands, came down like a torn parachute.

The pigeon beat its wings, but Aaron held the shirt to the ground, and the bird couldn't escape. Aaron felt under the shirt, gently, and gently took hold of the wounded pigeon.

"Yes, yes, pidge," he said, very softly. "There's a good boy. Good pigeon, good."

The pigeon struggled in his hands, but little by little Aaron managed to soothe it. "Good boy, pidge. That's your new name. Pidge. I'm gonna take you home, Pidge. Yes, yes, *ssh*. Good boy. I'm gonna fix you up. Easy, Pidge, easy does it. Easy, boy."

Aaron squeezed through an opening between the row of benches and skated slowly out of the park, while holding the pigeon carefully with both hands as if it were one of his mother's rare, precious cups from the old country. How fast the pigeon's heart was beating! Was he afraid? Or did all pigeons' hearts beat fast?

"*That's your new name. Pidge.*"

ACTIVE READER

PREDICT What will Aaron do with the pigeon?

---

1. **pylons** (pī′lŏnz′): towers marking turning points for airplanes in a race.

W O R D S
T O
K N O W

frenzied (frĕn′zēd) *adj.* wildly excited; frantic
thrashing (thrăsh′ĭng) *n.* moving wildly   **thrash** *v.*

250

Instruction Write these words on the board: *brave, generous, helpful, kind, cruel, selfish.* Explain that these are some words students might use to describe a character's traits—or what a character is like. Ask students if they know any movie or story characters they could describe using these words. Have volunteers describe the words or actions that revealed the movie or story character's traits. Then remind students that they can determine a story character's traits by paying attention to what a character says, thinks, feels, and does;

how other characters react to the character; and the writer's direct statements about the character. After students have read pages 250 and 251, have them brainstorm words that describe Aaron. Write the words on the board. (*active, athletic, alert, thoughtful, patient, kind, gentle, caring, concerned*) Then have students summarize the words, actions, and descriptions that helped them figure out Aaron's traits.

Practice Have students use page 36 of the **Unit Two Resource Book** to record Aaron's traits so far and to note the information that revealed these traits.

Possible Responses: Observant: Aaron notices the pigeon. Kind: Aaron takes care of the injured bird. Active, Athletic: Aaron is an excellent skater.

Use **Unit Two Resource Book,** p. 36

Bobby (ca. 1943), Jack Humphrey. Oil on masonite. Copyright© The Humphrey Estate. From the collection of John Corey.

It was fortunate that Aaron was an excellent skater, for he had to skate six blocks to his apartment, over broken pavement and sudden gratings and curbs and cobblestones. But when he reached home, he asked Noreen Callahan, who was playing on the <u>stoop</u>, to take off his skates for him. He would not chance going up three flights on roller skates this time.

"Is he sick?" asked Noreen.

"Broken wing," said Aaron. "I'm gonna fix him up and make him into a carrier pigeon[2] or something."

"Can I watch?" asked Noreen.

"Watch what?"

"The operation. I'm gonna be a nurse when I grow up."

"OK," said Aaron. "You can even help. You can help hold him while I fix him up."

Aaron wasn't quite certain what his mother would say about his newfound pet, but he was pretty sure he knew what his grandmother would think. His grandmother had lived with them ever since his grandfather had died three years ago. And she fed the sparrows and jays and crows and robins on the back fire escape with every spare crumb she could find. In fact, Aaron noticed that she sometimes created crumbs where they didn't exist, by squeezing and tearing pieces of her breakfast roll when his mother wasn't looking.

Aaron didn't really understand his grandmother, for he often saw her by the window having long conversations with the birds, telling them about her days as a little girl in the Ukraine. And once he saw her take her mirror from her handbag and hold it out toward the birds. She told Aaron that she wanted them to see how beautiful they were. Very strange. But Aaron did know that she would love Pidge, because she loved everything.

2. **carrier pigeon:** a pigeon trained to carry messages from place to place.

WORDS
TO
KNOW
stoop (sto͞op) *n.* a small porch outside the main door of a building

251

Reading Skills and Strategies: CLARIFY

Good readers are able to monitor their own comprehension as they read. One way to do that is by clarifying a confusing passage as you read it.

A Ask students to summarize this paragraph to help them clarify and comprehend.

Possible Response: Aaron's mother allowed him to keep the pigeon temporarily because it was sick and she could relate to it being all alone in the world.

Literary Analysis
CHARACTER TRAITS

B Ask students to think about Aaron's strong desire to be a part of the club. What does this tell them about Aaron?

Possible Response: It may mean that Aaron does not have many friends, that he is lonely, and that he wants desperately to be accepted by the older boys.

Active Reading | PREDICTING

C Ask students to predict what Aaron will give his grandmother for her birthday. As they read, have them check their predictions.

Possible Responses: Aaron might make a gift, like a box or a drawing. He might give his grandmother Pidge.

Literary Analysis: POINT OF VIEW

D So far, this story has been told as though the narrator knows Aaron's thoughts. Now the point of view expands. Whose thoughts and feelings are revealed by the narrator in the next three paragraphs?

Possible Response: the grandmother's

A To his surprise, his mother said he could keep the pigeon, temporarily, because it was sick, and we were all strangers in the land of Egypt,[3] and it might not be bad for Aaron to have a pet. *Temporarily.*

The wing was surprisingly easy to fix, for the break showed clearly and Pidge was remarkably patient and still, as if he knew he was being helped. Or perhaps he was just exhausted from all the thrashing about he had done. Two Popsicle sticks served as splints, and strips from an old undershirt were used to tie them in place. Another strip held the wing to the bird's body.

Aaron's father arrived home and stared at the pigeon. Aaron waited for the expected storm. But instead, Mr. Kandel asked, "Who *did* this?"

"Me," said Aaron. "And Noreen Callahan."

"Sophie!" he called to his wife. "Did you see this! Ten years old and it's better than Dr. Belasco could do. He's a genius!"

1 As the days passed, Aaron began training Pidge to be a carrier pigeon. He tied a little cardboard tube to Pidge's left leg and stuck tiny rolled-up sheets of paper with secret messages into it: THE ENEMY IS ATTACKING AT DAWN. Or: THE GUNS ARE HIDDEN IN THE TRUNK OF THE CAR. Or: VINCENT DEMARCO IS A BRITISH SPY. Then Aaron would set Pidge down at one end of the living room and put some popcorn at the other end. And Pidge would waddle slowly across the room, cooing softly, while the ends of his bandages trailed along the floor.

At the other end of the room, one of Aaron's friends would take out the message, stick a new one in, turn Pidge around, and aim him at the popcorn that Aaron put down on his side of the room.

And Pidge grew fat and contented on all the popcorn and crumbs and corn and crackers and Aaron's grandmother's breakfast rolls.

Aaron had told all the children about Pidge, but he only let his very best friends come up and play carrier pigeon with him. But telling everyone had been a mistake. A group of older boys from down the block had a club— Aaron's mother called it a gang—and Aaron had longed to join as he had never longed for anything else. To be with them and share their secrets, the secrets of older boys. To be able to enter their clubhouse shack on the empty lot on the next street. To know the password and swear the secret oath. To belong.

About a month after Aaron had brought the pigeon home, Carl, the gang leader, walked over to Aaron in the street and told him he could be a member if he'd bring the pigeon down to be the club <u>mascot</u>. Aaron couldn't believe it; he immediately raced home to get Pidge. But his mother told Aaron to stay away from those boys, or else. And Aaron, miserable, argued with his mother and pleaded and cried and coaxed. It was no use. Not with those boys. No.

---

3. **we were all . . . Egypt:** a reference to the biblical command to the Hebrews "Love ye therefore the stranger: for ye were strangers in the land of Egypt" (Deuteronomy 10:19).

WORDS TO KNOW — **mascot** (măs'kŏt') *n.* a person, an animal, or an object that is believed to bring good luck, especially one serving as the symbol of an organization (such as a sports team)

252

Character Traits

Instruction Read aloud the passage on page 252 that begins, "The wing was surprisingly easy to fix" and ends, "'He's a genius!'" Then ask students what they learn about Aaron and his father in this passage. (*Aaron is resourceful and skillful; he could be a doctor; his father is proud of him.*) Next, ask students to describe other things Aaron does on this page and what traits these actions reveal. (*Aaron trains Pidge—he is patient and caring; Aaron makes up a game—he is creative and imaginative;*

Aaron tells all his friends about Pidge—he is proud and excited about Pidge.) Now read aloud the passage on page 252 that begins, "A group of older boys" and ends at the bottom of the page. Discuss with students the conflict this introduces. (*Aaron wants to join the club but his mother won't let him.*) Use the Literary Analysis: Character Traits note in the green column to discuss the traits revealed in this passage.

Practice Have students use page 36 of the **Unit Two Resource Book** to record any new traits they have learned about Aaron up to this point, as well as the story information that revealed these traits.

Possible Responses: Resourceful and skillful: Aaron made a splint out of Popsicle sticks. Lonely: Aaron desperately wants to join the gang.

 Use **Unit Two Resource Book**, p. 36

Aaron's mother tried to change the subject. She told him that it would soon be his grandmother's sixtieth birthday, a very special birthday indeed, and all the family from Brooklyn and the East Side would be coming to their apartment for a dinner and celebration. Would Aaron try to build something or make something for Grandma? A present made with his own hands would be nice. A decorated box for her hairpins or a crayon picture for her room or anything he liked.

In a flash Aaron knew what to give her: Pidge! Pidge would be her present! Pidge with his wing healed, who might be able to carry messages for her to the doctor or his Aunt Rachel or other people his grandmother seemed to go to a lot. It would be a surprise for everyone. And Pidge would make up for what had happened to Grandma when she'd been a little girl in the Ukraine, wherever that was.

Often, in the evening, Aaron's grandmother would talk about the old days long ago in the Ukraine, in the same way that she talked to the birds on the back fire escape. She had lived in a village near a place called Kishinev[4] with hundreds of other poor peasant families like her own. Things hadn't been too bad under someone called Czar Alexander the Second,[5] whom Aaron always pictured as a tall, handsome man in a gold uniform. But Alexander the Second was <u>assassinated</u>, and Alexander the Third,[6] whom Aaron pictured as an ugly man in a black cape, became the czar. And the Jewish people of the Ukraine had no peace anymore.

In a flash Aaron knew what to give her.

One day, a thundering of horses was heard coming toward the village from the direction of Kishinev. "The Cossacks! The Cossacks!" someone had shouted. The czar's horsemen! Quickly, quickly, everyone in Aaron's grandmother's family had climbed down to the cellar through a little trap door hidden under a mat in the big central room of their shack. But his grandmother's pet goat, whom she'd loved as much as Aaron loved Pidge and more, had to be left above, because if it had made a sound in the cellar, they would never have lived to see the next morning. They all hid under the wood in the woodbin and waited, hardly breathing.

Suddenly, from above, they heard shouts and calls and screams at a distance. And then the noise was in their house. Boots pounding on the floor, and everything breaking and crashing overhead. The smell of smoke and the shouts of a dozen men.

The terror went on for an hour, and then the sound of horses' hooves faded into the distance. They waited another hour to make sure, and then the father went up out of the cellar and the rest of the family followed. The door to the house had been torn from its hinges, and every piece of furniture was broken. Every window, every dish, every stitch of clothing was totally destroyed, and one wall had been completely bashed in. And on the

---

4. **Kishinev** (kĭsh'ə-nĕf'): a city (known today as Chisinau) that is now the capital of the country of Moldova.

5. **Czar Alexander the Second:** emperor of Russia from 1855 to 1881.

6. **Alexander the Third:** emperor of Russia from 1881 to 1894.

WORDS TO KNOW **assassinate** (ə-săs'ə-nāt') *v.* to murder by surprise attack for political reasons

253

D

EXPLICIT INSTRUCTION **Reading Strategy: Visualizing**

Instruction Tell students that visualizing is a technique they can use to remember and enjoy the stories they read. Explain that when they visualize, they form a picture in their minds of what they are reading. They imagine, for example, what a character or place looks like by using details of description from the story. Tell students that they can visualize as they read by paying attention to descriptions of settings, characters, and events.

Practice Review the Build Background section on page 248 to help students understand the part of the world from which Aaron's grandmother came. Then read aloud the passage about Aaron's grandmother's experience in the Ukraine (beginning on page 253, "Often, in the evening", and continuing on page 254). Have students close their eyes as you read and try to imagine the characters, settings, and events. After reading, discuss with students which parts of the passage were especially vivid for them.

Possible Responses: Responses will vary.

ACTIVE READER

A CLARIFY Possible Response: She was the victim of an attack, or *pogrom*, by Cossack soldiers. As she and her family hid in the cellar, the soldiers destroyed everything in their house and killed her pet goat.

Reading Skills and Strategies:
IMAGERY

Ask students to identify the sensory details used in the description of the *pogrom* and to describe the effect of these details.

Possible Responses: Details include: shouts and calls and screams at a distance, boots pounding, everything breaking and crashing, the smell of smoke, shouts of a dozen men, the sound of horses' hooves fading into the distance, the goat lying quietly, a young girl weeping. These details support the terror and horror of the scene being described.

ACTIVE READER

B PREDICT Possible Responses: Carl will try to hurt Pidge. Carl will use Pidge to force Aaron to do something he does not want to do.

Literary Analysis:
PLOT

C The plot has been building toward a climactic event. Have students identify the turning point in this section and discuss how this event may influence the story's conclusion.

Possible Response: The gang is trying to kill Pidge. This leads to a turning point because Aaron really wants to be in the gang, and yet he loves Pidge and is looking forward to giving him to his grandmother. When Aaron "leap[s] right across the fire at Carl," he is choosing to defend Pidge rather than to belong to the gang.

Backyards, Brooklyn (1932), Ogden Minton Pleissner. Oil on canvas, 24″ × 30¼″, The Metropolitan Museum of Art, New York. Arthur Hoppock Hearn Fund, 1932 (32.80.2).

floor was the goat, lying quietly. Aaron's grandmother, who was just a little girl of eight at the time, had wept over the goat all day and all night and could not be consoled.

ACTIVE READER

CLARIFY What happened to Aaron's grandmother?

But they had been lucky. For other houses had been burned to the ground. And everywhere, not goats alone, nor sheep, but men and women and children lay quietly on the ground. The word for this sort of massacre, Aaron had learned, was *pogrom*. It had been a pogrom. And the men on the

horses were Cossacks. Hated word. Cossacks.

And so Pidge would replace that goat of long ago. A pigeon on Second Avenue where no one needed trap doors or secret escape passages or woodpiles to hide under. A pigeon for his grandmother's sixtieth birthday. *Oh wing, heal quickly so my grandmother can send you flying to everywhere she wants!*

But a few days later, Aaron met Carl in the street again. And Carl told Aaron that there was going to be a meeting that afternoon in which a map was going to be drawn up to show where a secret treasure lay buried on the

---

EXPLICIT INSTRUCTION Viewing and Representing

Backyards, Brooklyn
by Ogden Minton Pleissner

ART APPRECIATION As a boy growing up in Brooklyn, Ogden Minton Pleissner (1905–1983) drew constantly. After finishing art school in 1929, he lived and worked in a studio where he painted this backyard scene.

Instruction The art chosen to illustrate a story can help the reader understand the setting. Ask students to describe the neighborhood in this painting. How does it help them visualize the setting for this story?

Possible Responses: The tenement houses are three-story buildings, similar to the one Aaron lives in. The houses are covered with vines and face the street. The backyards show clotheslines, trees, fenced yards with gates, and plenty of places for birds to land. I can imagine Aaron's grandmother on a fire escape feeding those birds. The neighborhood looks like it comes from the time period of the story.

empty lot. "Bring the pigeon and you can come into the shack. We got a badge for you. A new kinda membership badge with a secret code on the back."

Aaron ran home, his heart pounding almost as fast as the pigeon's. He took Pidge in his hands and carried him out the door while his mother was busy in the kitchen making stuffed cabbage, his father's favorite dish. And by the time he reached the street, Aaron had decided to take the bandages off. Pidge would look like a real pigeon again, and none of the older boys would laugh or call him a bundle of rags.

Gently, gently he removed the bandages and the splints and put them in his pocket in case he should need them again. But Pidge seemed to hold his wing properly in place.

When he reached the empty lot, Aaron walked up to the shack, then hesitated. Four bigger boys were there. After a moment, Carl came out and commanded Aaron to hand Pidge over.

ACTIVE READER

PREDICT What will happen to Pidge?

"Be careful," said Aaron. "I just took the bandages off."

"Oh sure, don't worry," said Carl. By now Pidge was used to people holding him, and he remained calm in Carl's hands.

"OK," said Carl. "Give him the badge." And one of the older boys handed Aaron his badge with the code on the back. "Now light the fire," said Carl.

"What . . . what fire?" asked Aaron.

"The fire. You'll see," Carl answered.

"You didn't say nothing about a fire," said Aaron. "You didn't say nothing to—"

"Hey!" said Carl. "I'm the leader here. And you don't talk unless I tell you that you have p'mission. Light the fire, Al."

The boy named Al went out to the side of the shack, where some wood and cardboard and old newspapers had been piled into a huge mound. He struck a match and held it to the newspapers.

"OK," said Carl. "Let's get 'er good and hot. Blow on it. Everybody blow."

Aaron's eyes stung from the smoke, but he blew alongside the others, going from side to side as the smoke shifted toward them and away.

"Let's fan it," said Al. In a few minutes, the fire was crackling and glowing with a bright yellow-orange flame.

"Get me the rope," said Carl. One of the boys brought Carl some cord and Carl, without a word, wound it twice around the pigeon, so that its wings were tight against its body.

"What . . . what are you *doing!*" shouted Aaron. "You're hurting his wing!"

"Don't worry about his wing," said Carl. "We're gonna throw him into the fire. And when we do, we're gonna swear an oath of loyalty to—"

"No! *No!*" shouted Aaron, moving toward Carl.

"Grab him!" called Carl. "Don't let him get the pigeon!"

But Aaron had leaped right across the fire at Carl, taking him completely by surprise. He threw Carl back against the shack and hit out at his face with both fists. Carl slid down to the ground, and the pigeon rolled out of his hands. Aaron scooped up the pigeon and ran,

Gently, gently he removed the bandages.

(C)

English Learners

1 Point out that Carl uses ungrammatical (*We got* instead of *We have*) and informal (*kinda* instead of *kind of*) language when talking to Aaron. Ask students how this affects readers' perception of Carl.

Less Proficient Readers

Ask students the following questions to help guide them through the reading:

- Where did Aaron's grandmother live when she was a little girl? (*She lived in a village near Kishinev in the Ukraine.*)
- Why do you think the passage about Aaron's grandmother and her goat is included in the story?

Possible Responses: It helps explain why Aaron wants to give her the pigeon for her birthday. It helps us to understand Aaron's grandmother and her relationship with Aaron.

Advanced Students

As students read the remainder of the story, have them discuss the significance of the parallel between the story about Aaron and the story about his grandmother. How are the two stories similar? What purpose do these parallel stories serve?

Possible Responses: Both stories are concerned with the experiences of young children who must deal with violence and with the loss of a pet. The parallel stories strengthen the bond between Aaron and his grandmother and explain why Aaron decides to give Pidge to his grandmother as a birthday present.

EXPLICIT INSTRUCTION **Traits and Conflict**

Instruction Remind students of the central conflict of this story so far: Aaron desperately wants to join the older boys' club, but his mother won't let him. Refer to page 255, and ask students what Aaron does that makes this conflict more complicated. (*Aaron disobeys his mother and takes Pidge to a meeting with the boys in the club.*) Ask students if they are surprised that Aaron brought Pidge to the meeting with the boys. Discuss students' reactions.

Practice Have students review the traits they recorded on page 36 of the **Unit Two Resource Book** and use these traits to explain why they were, or were not, surprised by Aaron's actions.

Possible Responses: Students might be surprised because Aaron has been so responsible in the story. They may not be surprised because they know that Aaron very much wants to belong to this club.

 Use **Unit Two Resource Book**, p. 36

A Ask students if they agree or disagree with Aaron's calling the boys Cossacks. Have them explain their point of view.

Possible Responses: Students may agree with Aaron because the boys are behaving in a violent and destructive way like Cossacks; they are trying to kill the pigeon, just as the Cossacks killed the grandmother's goat. They may disagree because the boys are not killing thousands of people with government support, as the Cossacks did; they are just being mean to one boy and his pet.

Reading Skills and Strategies:
QUESTION

Ask students to imagine they are in Carl's gang and to respond to the dramatic scene between the gang and Aaron by generating questions the gang may have asked after they reassembled in their clubhouse.

Possible Responses: What are Cossacks? Why was Aaron yelling that at us? Why did the bird mean so much to him? Do you think Aaron is crazy?

Literary Analysis
CHARACTER TRAITS

Encountering difficult situations often helps people to grow and mature. Ask students if they feel Aaron's character was strengthened by his run-in with the gang. Have them meet with a partner and discuss how the author shows this new strength.

Possible Responses: Yes; Aaron's character was strengthened because he realizes that belonging to a gang is not really important. Aaron also sees that setting the pigeon free was a better gift than the pigeon itself.

---

pretending he was on roller skates so that he would go faster and faster. And as he ran across the lot he pulled the cord off Pidge and tried to find a place, *any* place, to hide him. But the boys were on top of him, and the pigeon slipped from Aaron's hands.

"Get him!" shouted Carl.

A Aaron thought of the worst, the most horrible thing he could shout at the boys. "Cossacks!" he screamed. "You're all Cossacks!"

Two boys held Aaron back while the others tried to catch the pigeon. Pidge fluttered along the ground just out of reach, skittering one way and then the other. Then the boys came at him from two directions. But suddenly Pidge beat his wings in rhythm, and rose up, up, over the roof of the nearest tenement, up over Second Avenue toward the park.

With the pigeon gone, the boys turned toward Aaron and tackled him to the ground and punched him and tore his clothes and punched him some more. Aaron twisted and turned and kicked and punched back, shouting "Cossacks! Cossacks!" And somehow the word gave him the strength to tear away from them.

When Aaron reached home, he tried to go past the kitchen quickly so his mother wouldn't see his bloody face and torn clothing. But it was no use; his father was home from work early that night and was seated in the living room. In a moment Aaron was surrounded by his mother, father, and grandmother, and in another moment he had told them everything that had happened, the words tumbling out between his broken sobs. Told them of the present he had planned, of the pigeon for a goat, of the gang, of the badge with the secret code on the back, of the shack, and the fire, and the pigeon's flight over the tenement roof.

And Aaron's grandmother kissed him and thanked him for his present which was even better than the pigeon.

"What present?" asked Aaron, trying to stop the series of sobs.

> Pidge beat his wings in rhythm, and rose.

And his grandmother opened her pocketbook and handed Aaron her mirror and asked him to look. But all Aaron saw was his dirty, bruised face and his torn shirt.

Aaron thought he understood, and then, again, he thought he didn't. How could she be so happy when there really was no present? And why pretend that there was?

Later that night, just before he fell asleep, Aaron tried to imagine what his grandmother might have done with the pigeon. She would have fed it, and she certainly would have talked to it, as she did to all the birds, and . . . and then she would have let it go free. Yes, of course. Pidge's flight to freedom must have been the gift that had made his grandmother so happy. Her goat has escaped from the Cossacks at last, Aaron thought, half dreaming. And he fell asleep with a smile. ❖

EXPLICIT INSTRUCTION ## Traits and Resolution

Instruction Ask students, "What is the climax of the conflict Aaron experiences between wanting to join the boys' club and not wanting to disobey his mother?" *(Aaron disobeys his mother and brings Pidge to the club meeting. Then he finds out what the boys want to do to Pidge. He realizes he cares more about Pidge than he does about being in the club, and he fights to save Pidge. He calls the boys "Cossacks.")* Ask students if Aaron's actions in this part of the story display any of the traits they listed on page 36 of the **Unit Two**

Resource Book. *(active, athletic—he gets away from the gang boys on skates; caring, concerned—he risks his own safety for Pidge.)* Then ask if students learned about any new traits of Aaron's in this section. *(courage—he acts so Pidge can escape; quick learner—he sees through the boys).*

Practice Tell students to imagine that Aaron decided not to save Pidge so he could be in the club. Have groups of students discuss what traits these feelings and actions reveal.

Possible Responses: Cowardice, cruelty, lack of compassion, selfishness, insecurity.

 Use **Unit Two Resource Book,** p. 37, for more practice.

Connect to the Literature

1. **What Do You Think?**
   What scene, object, or character stands out most in your memory of this story?

   Comprehension Check
   • What does Aaron notice about the pigeon he finds in the park?
   • Why does Aaron want to give his grandmother the pigeon?
   • How does the pigeon escape danger?

Think Critically

2. **ACTIVE READING PREDICTING**
   How accurate were the **predictions** in your **READER'S NOTEBOOK?** Discuss with a classmate the **details** in the story that either helped or misled you.

3. What kind of person is Aaron? Describe his character and values.

   Think About:
   • his feelings about the gang
   • his behavior toward Pidge
   • his relationships with his family and with his friend Noreen

4. How does Aaron's heritage affect his encounter with the gang members at the end of the story?

5. In your opinion, what is Aaron's gift to his grandmother? Explain your answer.

Extend Interpretations

6. **COMPARING TEXTS** Look back at the other selections in this book in which animals play important roles: "Ghost of the Lagoon" on page 124 and the excerpt from *Woodsong* on page 165. Compare and contrast the role of Tupa or Scarhead with the role of Pidge in "Aaron's Gift."

7. **Connect to Life** Compare Aaron's gift with the gift you discussed in Connect to Your Life on page 248. How is Aaron's gift similar to or different from the gift you chose?

Literary Analysis

CHARACTER TRAITS Readers can learn about a character's **traits,** or qualities, by paying attention to:

• the character's speech, thoughts, feelings, and actions

• the speech, thoughts, and actions of other characters

• the writer's direct statements about the character

• descriptions of the character's physical appearance

The **actions** a character takes are the result of his or her traits. For example, in "Aaron's Gift" you learn that Aaron is an unselfish and caring person from the way he treats Pidge. Because he is unselfish and caring, he chooses to rescue Pidge from the gang.

In this passage from the story, you can learn about the grandmother's traits from Aaron's thoughts about her.

But Aaron did know that she would love Pidge, because she loved everything.

Paired Activity Working with a partner, make a chart like the one below. Use the chart to record information from the story about Aaron. Then use information from the chart to write a description of Aaron's traits.

Information About Aaron	
Character's Thoughts, Speech, or Actions	He broke a cookie into small crumbs....
Thoughts, Speech, Actions of Others	
Author's Direct Comments	
Physical Descriptions	

AARON'S GIFT   **257**

Connect to the Literature

1. **What Do You Think?**
   Responses will vary. Some students may cite Pidge flying away from danger as the most memorable scene.

Comprehension Check
• The pigeon has a broken wing.
• Aaron wants the pigeon to replace the pet goat that was killed in a *pogrom* when his grandmother was a girl. He also thinks that the pigeon can be helpful to her by carrying messages.
• The pigeon flies over the tenement buildings toward the park.

 Use Selection Quiz **Unit Two Resource Book,** p. 40.

Think Critically

2. Have students note whether they used all the information available to them when they made their predictions.

3. **Possible Responses:** Aaron is a caring, thoughtful boy. He fixes Pidge's broken wing, plans to give his grandmother the best gift he can think of, and shares an important task with Noreen.

4. **Possible Responses:** Aaron's knowledge of his grandmother's life in the Ukraine makes him react strongly to being bullied by the members of Carl's gang. He thinks that the bullies are like the Cossacks who hurt his grandmother. He wants to protect Pidge at all costs because his grandmother's favorite childhood pet was killed and he has decided to replace it.

5. Most students will say that giving Pidge his freedom was Aaron's gift to his grandmother. Some will also say that Aaron's bravery and determination to save Pidge's life is his gift.

Extend Interpretations

6. **Comparing Texts Possible Responses:** Pidge helps Aaron to realize his potential as a caring person and teaches him a valuable lesson about bravery, determination, and the gift of freedom. Tupa threatens the safety of Mako and Afa and teaches Mako a valuable lesson about bravery, determination, and heroism. Scarhead threatens the safety of Paulsen at first but teaches him a valuable lesson about the need for respect and distance in dealing with wild animals.

7. **Connect to Life** Students' responses will vary based on the gift they discussed. Students should support their answers with reasons why Aaron's gift is similar to or different from the gifts they chose.

Literary Analysis

Character Traits Students should complete the chart with examples from the story. Descriptions of Aaron should be based on information recorded in students' charts.

Writing

Story Summary Students should complete the sequence chart prior to writing their summary. They may want to work with a partner to complete the chart, and then work individually to write the summary.

 Use **Writing Transparencies**, p. 51, for additional support.

Speaking & Listening

Presenting Aaron Students may want to begin by listing as many of Aaron's traits as they can (or by reviewing lists they have already created) and then choosing from this list the traits they will present.

 Use the **Speaking and Listening Book**, pp. 25 and 26, for additional support.

Research & Technology

Let's Talk Students may wish to work in small groups to interview an older person. They can take turns asking questions, or they can designate a spokesperson to ask questions prepared by the group.

Vocabulary and Spelling

STANDARDIZED TEST PRACTICE

1. C
2. G
3. C
4. J
5. A

SPELLING STRATEGY

1. says, birthdays
2. flies, families
3. stayed, qualified; staying, qualifying

Writing

Story Summary Filling in a sequence-of-events chart can help you understand "Aaron's Gift." Make a chart like the one shown here. Record one important event in each box. Add boxes and events until you have described the entire story. Then use your chart as a reference to write a summary of "Aaron's Gift." Place your summary in your **Working Portfolio.**

Event 1	Event 2	Event 3
Aaron finds a wounded pigeon.		

Speaking & Listening

Presenting Aaron Develop a presentation on Aaron's traits and how you learned about them. Begin your presentation with a clear description of three to five of Aaron's most important traits. Support your ideas about Aaron's traits with detailed evidence from the story. Rehearse your presentation a few times to make sure your voice is clear and loud enough. When you feel you are ready, deliver your presentation to the class.

Speaking and Listening Handbook
See p. R99: Informative Presentations.

Research & Technology

Let's Talk With your teacher's guidance, arrange to interview an older person to find out what life was like when he or she was your age. Then write up the best parts of the interview. Use library resources, such as encyclopedias and almanacs, or Web sites to add factual background. Include at least two of these sources. Be sure to list the information sources you used.

Research and Technology Handbook
See p. R105: Conducting Interviews.

Reading *for* INFORMATION
Read "Your Family's History Will Come Alive" on p. 260 before you begin your research.

Vocabulary and Spelling

STANDARDIZED TEST PRACTICE

Choose the word or group of words that means the same, or nearly the same, as the underlined Word to Know.

1. A <u>stoop</u> is a—
   - **A** stool
   - **B** boat
   - **C** porch
   - **D** coop
2. <u>Frenzied</u> means—
   - **F** thoughtful
   - **G** frantic
   - **H** relieved
   - **J** fragile
3. A <u>mascot</u> is a kind of—
   - **A** forest
   - **B** skirt
   - **C** symbol
   - **D** memory
4. To <u>assassinate</u> is to—
   - **F** witness
   - **G** assist
   - **H** protect
   - **J** murder
5. <u>Thrashing</u> is another word for—
   - **A** moving wildly
   - **B** jumping up
   - **C** falling down
   - **D** moving quickly

Vocabulary Handbook
See p. R22: Synonyms and Antonyms.

SPELLING STRATEGY: FINAL *Y* WORDS AND SUFFIXES
The spelling of some nouns and verbs ending in y changes when a suffix is added. When the letter before a final *y* is a vowel, the *y* does not change when a suffix is added, as in *plays*. When the letter before a final *y* is a consonant, change the *y* to *i* when adding *-es* or *-ed*, as in *frenzied*. When adding the suffix *-ing,* do not change the *y* to *i*, as in *carrying*.

1. Add the suffix *-s* to the following words.
   say   birthday
2. Add the suffix *-es* to the following words.
   fly   family
3. Add the suffixes *-ed* and *-ing* to the following words.
   stay   qualify

Spelling Handbook
See p. R26.

CHOICES and CHALLENGES

Grammar in Context: Vivid Verbs

Myron Levoy paints a colorful picture of the action in "Aaron's Gift." Notice his use of **vivid verbs,** shown in red type below:

> And Pidge would **waddle slowly** across the room, **cooing softly,** while the ends of his bandages **trailed** along the floor.

Suppose Levoy had used the verb "to move" in place of *waddle* above. The word *move* doesn't add any detail to the description. The sentences above would become dull and the vivid picture of the injured pigeon would be lost.

Apply to Your Writing: Replace dull, overused verbs with vivid verbs to add color and vitality to your writing.

WRITING EXERCISE Rewrite each sentence. Replace the underlined <u>verbs</u> with vivid verbs.

Example: *Original* Aaron's eyes <u>hurt</u> from the smoke.

Rewritten Aaron's eyes stung from the smoke.

1. Smoke <u>moved</u> toward them and away.
2. Aaron <u>ran</u> right across the fire to rescue Pidge.
3. Carl <u>fell</u> to the ground, and the pigeon <u>dropped</u> out of his hands.
4. Pidge <u>moved</u> along the ground and <u>walked</u> one way and then the other.

Connect to the Literature Reread the last page of "Aaron's Gift." Make a list of vivid verbs.

Grammar Handbook
See p. R76: Using Verbs Correctly.

Myron Levoy
born 1930

"My continuing concern has been for the 'outsider,' the loner."

Engineer Turned Writer Myron Levoy was born in New York City in 1930 and worked as a chemical engineer before becoming a professional writer. In describing his poetry, plays, and short stories, he says, "My continuing concern has been for the 'outsider,' the loner."

Between Two Worlds In *Alan and Naomi,* Levoy writes about a Jewish boy facing anti-Semitism who befriends a troubled refugee girl. In another novel, *A Shadow Like a Leopard,* Levoy depicts a boy from the ghetto who is torn between two worlds. Each of these people, says Levoy, must grow and struggle to discover who he or she is.

Critical Success In 1982, A *Shadow Like a Leopard* was named one of the best books for young adults by the American Library Association. *The Witch of Fourth Street and Other Stories,* from which "Aaron's Gift" is taken, was named a *Book World* honor book.

AUTHOR ACTIVITY
New York Childhood "Aaron's Gift" takes place on New York City's Lower East Side. Find out what neighborhood of New York City Levoy grew up in. Research what the area was like when he was a child in the 1930s and 1940s. Discuss with a group the autobiographical details found in the setting of "Aaron's Gift" and other Levoy works you've read.

Grammar in Context

WRITING EXERCISE
Possible Responses:

1. Smoke **shifted** toward them and away.
2. Aaron **leaped** right across the fire to rescue Pidge.
3. Carl **slid** to the ground, and the pigeon **rolled** out of his hands.
4. Pidge **fluttered** along the ground and **skittered** one way and then the other.

Connect to the Literature
Answers will vary. Vivid verbs include: pulled, slipped, screamed, held, catch, fluttered, skittering, beat, rose, tackled, punched, tore, twisted, turned, kicked, shouting, tear, surrounded, tumbling, kissed, thanked, understood, pretend, imagine, escaped, dreaming.

Myron Levoy

The title of Myron Levoy's book *The Witch of Fourth Street and Other Stories* refers to East Fourth Street on New York City's Lower East Side. The book's eight stories portray events in the lives of immigrants who lived in that area during the 1920s.

Author Activity

New York Childhood Students will need time and support to research Myron Levoy, his childhood, and the neighborhoods of New York City's Lower East Side.

EXPLICIT INSTRUCTION **Grammar in Context**

VERB PHRASES: MAIN AND HELPING VERBS
Instruction Remind students that a verb may be a single word or a group of words. When a verb is made up of two or more words, the last word is the main verb. Other words are helping verbs. Write this sentence on the board: *Aaron was planning.*

Have students identify the main verb *(planning)* and helping verb *(was).* Remind students that the main and helping verbs are not always next to each other in a sentence. (Example—Mother *has* never *liked* Carl's gang)

Practice Have students locate sentences from "Aaron's Gift" that contain more than one verb. Have them write the sentences down, identifying the main and helping verbs in each.

 Use **Unit Two Resource Book,** p. 38

 For more instruction in main and helping verbs, see McDougal Littell's *Language Network,* Chapter 4.

For **systematic instruction** in grammar, see:
• **Grammar, Usage, and Mechanics Book**
• pacing chart on p. 187i.

Standards-Based Objectives
- read and analyze news sources
- recognize distinctive characteristics of primary and secondary sources
- become aware of material available on the Internet
- find out about the American Family Immigration History Center

Connecting to the Literature
Reading the Internet article "Your Family's History Will Come Alive" can help your students connect with characters like Aaron's grandmother in "Aaron's Gift." It is likely that Aaron's grandmother immigrated to the United States between 1892 and 1924, the years of the American Family Immigration History Center's research project, since many Jews left the Ukraine during those years. As students learn personal facts about immigrants, they may be able to make connections to Aaron's grandmother and other immigrant characters they read about.

LESSON RESOURCES

UNIT TWO RESOURCE BOOK,
pp. 41–42

SKILLS TRANSPARENCIES AND COPYMASTERS
Literary Analysis
- Primary/Secondary Source, TR 14 (p. 261)

Writing
- Locating Information Using the Internet I and II, TR 47–48 (p. 262)

Source: *Statue of Liberty–Ellis Island Foundation, Inc.*

YOUR Family's History WILL COME Alive

Welcome to the American Family Immigration History Center

MANIFEST OF ALIEN IMMIGRANTS FOR THE COMMISSIONER OF IMMIGRATION

SEARCH FOR A PASSENGER

ELLIS ISLAND PASSENGER RECORDS

© Edwin Schlossberg Incorporated

click for enlargement

[Who We Are] [History Center] [Wall of Honor]
[Ellis Museum] [Hot Links]
[Contact Us][Home]

The Statue of Liberty–Ellis Island Foundation, Inc. has announced the development of an exciting new family genealogy[1] facility. To be housed in the Ellis Island Immigration Museum, **The American Family Immigration History Center**™ will use state-of-the-art interactive computer technology to bring the immigration records on ancestors who came to this country as long as a century ago to one's fingertips.

Over 113 million Americans are presently engaged in family history research. This innovative center will provide guidance to both adults and children in the fascinating task of tracing one's roots.

---

1. **genealogy** (jē′nē-ŏl′ə-jē): the study or research of ancestry and family history.

Tell students that this site tells about a project underway to help millions of families research their own ancestors' immigration to the United States. As they read through the article, have them use the information in the right hand column as a guide to gathering and interpreting information. If students have access to the Internet, they may want to visit the Statue of Liberty–Ellis Island Foundation.

Use **Literary Analysis Transparencies,** p. 14, for additional support.

Reading a Web Site
The following are possible responses to the five questions and activities.

1 The links allow you to go other pages of The American Family Immigration History Center site.

2 The primary data source is the manifest from the ship. It is a handwritten list of all the passengers on the ship, along with some information about each passenger. The original documents are on microfilm at the National Archives and Records Administration.

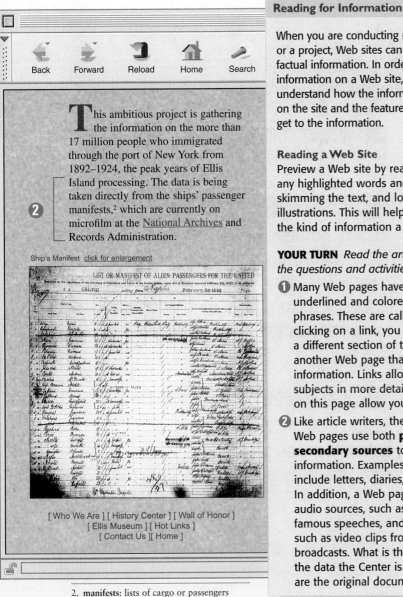

Back Forward Reload Home Search

❷ This ambitious project is gathering the information on the more than 17 million people who immigrated through the port of New York from 1892–1924, the peak years of Ellis Island processing. The data is being taken directly from the ships' passenger manifests,[2] which are currently on microfilm at the National Archives and Records Administration.

Ship's Manifest click for enlargement

LIST OR MANIFEST OF ALIEN PASSENGERS FOR THE UNITED

[Who We Are] [History Center] [Wall of Honor]
[Ellis Museum] [Hot Links]
[Contact Us][Home]

2. **manifests:** lists of cargo or passengers carried by a ship or airplane.

Reading for Information

When you are conducting research for a report or a project, Web sites can be good sources of factual information. In order to find information on a Web site, you need to understand how the information is organized on the site and the features you can use to get to the information.

Reading a Web Site
Preview a Web site by reading the title and any highlighted words and phrases, skimming the text, and looking at any illustrations. This will help you understand the kind of information a Web site contains.

YOUR TURN *Read the article and complete the questions and activities below.*

❶ Many Web pages have icons, pictures, or underlined and colored words and phrases. These are called **links.** By clicking on a link, you immediately go to a different section of the Web page or to another Web page that contains related information. Links allow you to explore subjects in more detail. What do the links on this page allow you to do?

❷ Like article writers, the people who create Web pages use both **primary** and **secondary sources** to provide information. Examples of primary sources include letters, diaries, and record books. In addition, a Web page may include audio sources, such as recordings of famous speeches, and video sources, such as video clips from television news broadcasts. What is the primary source of the data the Center is gathering? Where are the original documents?

EXPLICIT INSTRUCTION Reading a Web Site

Instruction Discuss with students how reading a Web article is both similar to and different from reading a print article. Explain that like a print article, a Web article has other features in addition to the text that provide information, such as pictures, titles, captions, and charts. Then explain that unlike a print article, a Web article may have sound effects, short movies, and links to other sites and pages. Write the word *links* on the board and ask students to share what they know about links.

Explain that links are connections to other parts of a Web site or to other Web sites. Links may be a list of terms, highlighted words in running text, or icons. Ask students to identify places where links are found on the Web site above. Finally, remind students that when reading Web sites, they may be distracted by the electronic features—the sounds, movies, advertisements, and links. Suggest that they keep a piece of paper with them when reading Web sites. If a link seems interesting but

has nothing to do with their topic, they can write down the address and go back to it later in their free time.

Practice Have students read and complete the numbered activities on the pupil pages.

Possible Responses: See the side columns in the teacher's edition for answers to the activities on the pupil pages.

Use **Unit Two Resource Book,** p. 41, for more practice.

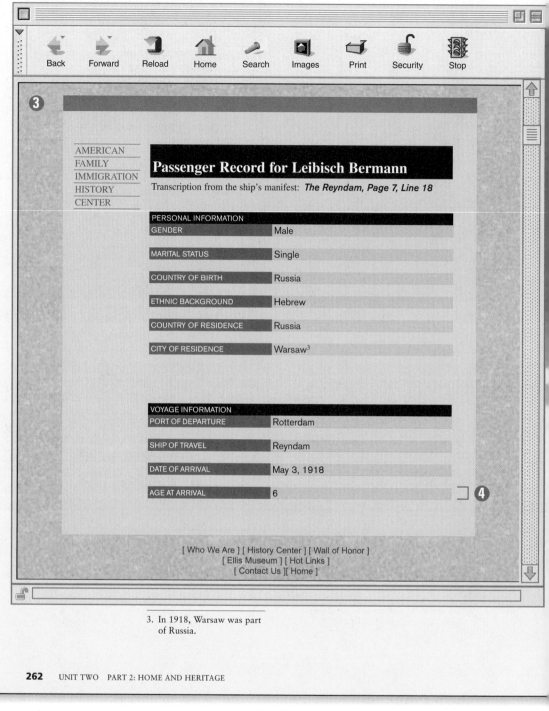

Back **Forward** **Reload** **Home** **Search** **Images** **Print** **Security** **Stop**

③

AMERICAN
FAMILY
IMMIGRATION
HISTORY
CENTER

Passenger Record for Leibisch Bermann

Transcription from the ship's manifest: *The Reyndam, Page 7, Line 18*

PERSONAL INFORMATION

GENDER	Male
MARITAL STATUS	Single
COUNTRY OF BIRTH	Russia
ETHNIC BACKGROUND	Hebrew
COUNTRY OF RESIDENCE	Russia
CITY OF RESIDENCE	Warsaw[3]

VOYAGE INFORMATION

PORT OF DEPARTURE	Rotterdam
SHIP OF TRAVEL	Reyndam
DATE OF ARRIVAL	May 3, 1918
AGE AT ARRIVAL	6

④

[Who We Are] [History Center] [Wall of Honor]
[Ellis Museum] [Hot Links]
[Contact Us][Home]

3. In 1918, Warsaw was part
of Russia.

262   UNIT TWO   PART 2: HOME AND HERITAGE

Keyword Searches

Instruction Ask students if they have conducted keyword searches on the Web and how they go about these searches. Then explain that one way to find information about a topic is to search the Web using keywords and a search engine. Say, "The first step in conducting a keyword search is to create a list of keywords that will help you find the information you need." Then explain that keywords must be chosen carefully in order to get the most useful results from an online search. For example, if a student is looking for information on the history of the New York Yankees baseball team, he or she should not start with a term like "sports" or "baseball" because these are too general. A more useful search term might be "New York Yankees" or "baseball history." Tell students that before they create a list of keywords, they need to have some general background knowledge on their topic. They can get this by reading magazine, newspaper, or encyclopedia articles.

Practice Have partners choose a research topic and come up with a list of 6–10 keywords related to this topic. If possible, allow partners to test their top three keywords on a search engine and judge the results.

Possible Responses: Responses will vary depending on the topics chosen. Invite students to share their lists and tell which terms they think would be most useful.

Use **Unit Two Resource Book,** p. 42, for more practice. Use **Writing Transparencies,** pp. 47 and 48, for additional support.

These valuable documents are, for the first time, being digitized, scanned, and entered into an electronic database for easy access. The information will cover 11 fields of information, including:

- Immigrant's given name
- Immigrant's surname[4]
- Ship name
- Port of origin
- Arrival date
- Line number on manifest
- Gender
- Age
- Marital status
- Nationality
- Last residence (town and country)

For a nominal fee, visitors will be given the opportunity to receive a printout of their family's data as well as a scanned reproduction of the original ship's manifest on which their ancestor's entry appears, and a picture of the ship on which he or she arrived.

[Who We Are] [History Center] [Wall of Honor]
[Ellis Museum] [Hot Links]
[Contact Us][Home]

---

4. **surname:** a family name; a shared name that identifies the members of a family.

Reading for Information *continued*

3 Compare this image with the image of the original manifest on page 261. What are some differences between the primary source and the typed record? Why might you want to read both an original document and its typed copy on a database?

4 This record states that Leibisch Bermann arrived in the United States on May 3, 1918. How old was he? What would you need to do to find out the date of his birth? List some primary and secondary sources you might use to find out more about Ellis Island immigrants.

5 Suppose you visit this site and tell a relative what you learned. You describe the center's purpose and the type of information it provides. Are you a primary source or a secondary source of information about the center? Explain. If you wanted more information about the center, what other sources might you check?

Research & Technology
Activity Link: "Aaron's Gift," p. 258. Ellis Island was a center for immigration for over 60 years. Use the Internet to find more information about this historic site. First, brainstorm with a partner a list of search terms. Choose two or three terms you think will be most helpful and begin your search. Find information to answer these questions: How many immigrants came through Ellis Island? What kinds of exhibits are at the museum?

---

3 The original manifest is handwritten in cursive, while the Internet image is typed. The original has all the information about a passenger following his/her name, and the image has a chart format. You might want to read both the original and the typed copy so that you could verify the information. The original might have some additional information that didn't fit the chart. It is also interesting to see your ancestor's name on the original document.

4 Leibisch Bermann was 6 years old when he arrived in the United States. You cannot figure out Leibisch Bermann's birthday with the information from this chart. To find the date of his birth, you would need to talk to someone who knew him, get a copy of his birth certificate, or search the original of the manifest to see if it was listed there.

5 You would be a secondary source if you were telling someone about the site. The site itself is the primary source. If more information is wanted about the Immigration Center, you could write them a letter, visit Ellis Island, or call them. Usually this information can be found on the Internet site.

Connecting to Life Ask students if any of them have visited Ellis Island. Invite them to share stories, memories, and photographs from their trips to Ellis Island. Have them discuss how their trips added to their understanding of family history, immigration, and the diverse culture of the United States.

EXPLICIT INSTRUCTION ## Research & Technology

This activity links to the Research & Technology activity of the Choices & Challenges section on page 258, following "Aaron's Gift," in which students interview an older person.

Instruction Students will need time and support to come up with a list of search terms. Remind students that if their search terms are too general, they will get long lists of Web sites unrelated to their subject. Tell students to write down the address of the sites they use in their research.

Application Students may want to present their findings to their classmates through an oral presentation. They may also want to create fact cards showing the questions they researched, the answers they found, and the names and addresses of the Web sites they used.

This selection is included in the **Grade 6 InterActive Reader.**

This selection appears in Spanish in the **Spanish Study Guide.**

Standards-Based Objectives

1. understand and appreciate a **short story**
2. understand author's use of **description**
3. explain the effects of common **literary devices** (personification, simile, imagery)
4. **Read aloud** narrative text
5. use the reading strategy of **making inferences** to help understand the traits, motivations, relationships, and changes of the main character

Summary

Panchito, a young Mexican-American boy, tells this story about life on "the circuit" in California—the regular route from harvest to harvest that migrant farm workers travel. As the story begins, Panchito's family have finished picking strawberries and are packing their jalopy with their few possessions. They find their next job picking grapes near Fresno, where an old garage serves as their temporary home. Each day Panchito and his older brother, Roberto, work alongside their father. When grape season ends in November, Panchito is free to enter sixth grade. On his first day at school, he feels shy and awkward at having to speak English for the first time in months. His teacher, Mr. Lema, is eager to help. Soon they form a friendship, and Panchito is thrilled when Mr. Lema offers to teach him the trumpet. He hurries home to tell his parents, only to find it is time to move again.

Thematic Link

When a family moves, many aspects of home and heritage change. In this story, Panchito struggles with frequent moves, but the love of his family is constant. The opportunities of education become more highly valued.

English Conventions Practice

Daily Language SkillBuilder

Have students **proofread** the display sentences on page 187k and write them correctly. The sentences also appear on Transparency 8 of **Language Transparencies.**

The Circuit

by FRANCISCO JIMÉNEZ

Connect to Your Life

Moving Day How would frequent moves affect your emotions, your experiences in school, and your friendships?

Build Background

SOCIAL STUDIES

This story is about the problems faced by Panchito, a young Mexican American boy in a family of migrant farm workers in California. Migrant farm workers are laborers who migrate, or move, from one agricultural area to another in search of work. The workers often move in a circuit—a regular route of travel—that follows the harvest seasons in different places.

California

• Santa Rosa
San Francisco
• Fresno
Pacific Ocean
CALIFORNIA
N W E S
• Los Angeles
Miles 0 80 160

This map shows the great distances that migrant workers may travel looking for work in California. Much of "The Circuit" takes place in Fresno.

WORDS TO KNOW Vocabulary Preview

| hesitantly | jalopy | vineyard |
| instinct | surplus | |

Focus Your Reading

LITERARY ANALYSIS **LITERARY DEVICES**

One way that writers make their stories come alive for readers is by using **literary devices,** such as **imagery, similes,** and **personification.** Literary devices help readers understand a character's life and surroundings. They also help readers form mental pictures of a story's setting and events. Look for examples of imagery and figurative language as you read.

ACTIVE READING **MAKING INFERENCES**

When you **make inferences,** you figure out what the writer means but is not stating directly. From the description below, you can infer that Panchito is hot, tired, and thirsty.

I was completely soaked in sweat, and my mouth felt as if I had been chewing on a handkerchief.

To make inferences, use the following strategies:

- Look for **details** that the writer provides about the characters, setting, and events.
- Think about what you already know about the topic.
- Connect to experiences from your own life.

READER'S NOTEBOOK As you read, jot down at least two inferences about each character.

264   UNIT TWO   PART 2: HOME AND HERITAGE

LESSON RESOURCES

UNIT TWO RESOURCE BOOK, pp. 43-49

ASSESSMENT
Formal Assessment, pp. 41–42
Test Generator

SKILLS TRANSPARENCIES AND COPYMASTERS
Reading and Critical Thinking
- Making Inferences, TR 10 (p. 272)
Language
- Daily Language SkillBuilder, TR 8 (p. 264)

- Avoiding Illogical Shifts in Tense, TR 36 (p. 274)
- Context Clues: Definition and Overview, TR 53 (p. 265)
Writing
- Effective Language, TR 15 (p. 273)
Speaking and Listening
- Creating a Persuasive Presentation, p. 29 (p. 273)
- Guidelines: How to Analyze a Persuasive Presentation, p. 30 (p. 273)

INTEGRATED TECHNOLOGY
Audio Library

Visit our Web site:
www.mcdougallittell.com

For **systematic instruction** in language skills, see:
- **Vocabulary and Spelling Book**
- **Grammar, Usage, and Mechanics Book**
- pacing chart on p. 187i.

The Circuit

by

Francisco Jiménez

Hot Day in the Field © 1999 Richard Haynes.

It was that time of year again. Ito, the strawberry sharecropper, did not smile. It was natural. The peak of the strawberry season was over and the last few days the workers, most of them *braceros*,[1] were not picking as many boxes as they had during the months of June and July.

As the last days of August disappeared, so did the number of *braceros*. Sunday, only one—the best picker—came to work. I liked him. Sometimes we talked during our half-hour lunch break. That is how I found out he was from Jalisco,[2] the same state in Mexico my family was from. That Sunday was the last time I saw him.

---

1. *braceros* (brä-sĕʹrôs) *Spanish:* Hispanic farm workers.
2. **Jalisco** (hä-lēsʹkô).

EXPLICIT INSTRUCTION — Preteaching Vocabulary

WORDS TO KNOW

Teaching Strategy Remind students that there are several strategies to use when they encounter unfamiliar words in reading. Using a **dictionary** can help students determine meanings for words they don't know. Combining **context clues** with meanings listed in the dictionary will help students determine the correct meaning for each word.

Practice Each of the following sentences contains one of the WORDS TO KNOW. Have students look up each underlined word and use the context of the sentence to decide which dictionary meaning is appropriate.

1. Panchito responded <u>hesitantly</u> when Mr. Lema called on him.
2. Papa was so proud of his old <u>jalopy</u>.
3. Papa worked long, hard hours in the <u>vineyard</u>.
4. Mama bought the cookpot at the army <u>surplus</u> store.
5. Upon seeing the school bus, our first <u>instinct</u> was to hide.

 Use **Unit Two Resource Book,** p. 48, for more practice.

For **systematic instruction** in vocabulary, see:
- **Vocabulary and Spelling Book**
- pacing chart on p. 187i.

Literary Analysis **LITERARY DEVICES**

A Ask students to explain what they know about Papa from reading the description of how he chose his car.

Possible Response: Papa is a proud man, knowledgeable, cautious, and patient.

 Use **Unit Two Resource Book,** p. 45, for more practice.

Active Reading **MAKING INFERENCES**

B Why does finding a blue necktie behind the rear seat of the car make Papa think that an important man must have owned the car?

Possible Response: In Papa's experience, the only men who wore neckties were important people.

Use **Unit Two Resource Book,** p. 44, for more practice. Use **Reading and Critical Thinking Transparencies,** p. 10, for additional support.

Literary Analysis: SYMBOLISM

C The family has two cherished possessions: the car and the cookpot. Ask what these two objects may symbolize.

Possible Response: The car may be a symbol of the family's constant travel. The cookpot may symbolize stability. Wherever they live, they will always have the cookpot.

Literary Analysis **LITERARY DEVICES**

D Have students explain how the author's description of the garage helps them to draw a mental image.

Possible Response: The garage is old, dilapidated, and dark. There is no electricity or furniture. This makes it seem sad and lonely.

When the sun had tired and sunk behind the mountains, Ito signaled us that it was time to go home. *"Ya esora,"*[3] he yelled in his broken Spanish. Those were the words I waited for twelve hours a day, every day, seven days a week, week after week. And the thought of not hearing them again saddened me.

As we drove home, Papa did not say a word. With both hands on the wheel, he stared at the dirt road. My older brother, Roberto, was also silent. He leaned his head back and closed his eyes. Once in a while he cleared from his throat the dust that blew in from outside.

Yes, it was that time of year. When I opened the front door to the shack, I stopped. Everything we owned was neatly packed in cardboard boxes. Suddenly I felt even more the weight of hours, days, weeks, and months of work. I sat down on a box. The thought of having to move to Fresno and knowing what was in store for me there brought tears to my eyes.

That night I could not sleep. I lay in bed thinking about how much I hated this move.

A little before five o'clock in the morning, Papa woke everyone up. A few minutes later, the yelling and screaming of my little brothers and sisters, for whom the move was a great adventure, broke the silence of dawn. Shortly, the barking of the dogs accompanied them.

While we packed the breakfast dishes, Papa went outside to start the "Carcanchita." That was the name Papa gave his old '38 black Plymouth. He bought it in a used-car lot in Santa Rosa in the winter of 1949. Papa was very proud of his car. *"Mi Carcanchita,"*[4] my little jalopy, he called it. He had a right to be proud of it. He spent a lot of time looking at other cars before buying this one. When he finally chose the "Carcanchita," he checked it thoroughly before driving it out of the car lot.

A

He examined every inch of the car. He listened to the motor, tilting his head from side to side like a parrot, trying to detect any noises that spelled car trouble. After being satisfied with the looks and sounds of the car, Papa then insisted on knowing who the original owner was. He never did find out from the car salesman. But he bought the car anyway. Papa figured the original owner must have been an important man, because behind the rear seat of the car he found a blue necktie.

Papa parked the car out in front and left the motor running. *"Listo,"*[5] he yelled. Without saying a word, Roberto and I began to carry the boxes out to the car. Roberto carried the two big boxes and I carried the smaller ones. Papa then threw the mattress on top of the car roof and tied it with ropes to the front and rear bumpers.

Everything was packed except Mama's pot. It was an old large galvanized pot she had picked up at an army surplus store in Santa Maria the year I was born. The pot was full of dents and nicks, and the more dents and nicks it had, the more Mama liked it. *"Mi olla,"*[6] she used to say proudly.

I held the front door open as Mama carefully carried out her pot by both handles, making sure not to spill the cooked beans. When she

---

3. **Ya esora:** a made-up spelling for the sharecropper's pronunciation of the Spanish expression *Ya es hora* (yä′ĕs-ô′rä), which means "It is time."
4. *Mi Carcanchita* (mē kär-kän-chē′tä) *Spanish:* jalopy.
5. *listo* (lē′stô) *Spanish:* ready.
6. *mi olla* (mē ô′yä) *Spanish:* my pot.

| WORDS TO KNOW | **jalopy** (jə-lŏp′ē) *n.* a shabby old car |
| | **surplus** (sûr′pləs) *n.* extra material or supplies; leftovers |

Instruction Explain to students that writers use imagery and figurative language to create vivid pictures in readers' minds of settings, characters, and events. Invite students to name different types of figurative language. Then remind students that personification is one type of figurative language, and ask volunteers to define personification. *(a type of figurative language in which an animal, object, or idea is given human qualities and is described as if it were human)* Have students listen for

an example of personification as you read aloud the first sentence on page 266. Ask a volunteer to identify the example *(The sun had tired)*.

Practice Write these questions on the board and have students work in pairs to answer them.

1. What is personified in this sentence?
2. What human qualities is the object given?
3. What is the writer trying to show about the object?

Possible Responses: The sun is personified. It has feelings—the feeling of being tired. The writer may be saying that the sun setting is like a person going to sleep.

 Use **Unit Two Resource Book,** p. 45, for more practice.

got to the car, Papa reached out to help her with it. Roberto opened the rear car door, and Papa gently placed it on the floor behind the front seat. All of us then climbed in. Papa sighed, wiped the sweat off his forehead with his sleeve, and said wearily: *"Es todo."*[7]

> Around
>
> nine o'clock
>
> the temperature
>
> had risen to almost
>
> one hundred
>
> degrees.

As we drove away, I felt a lump in my throat. I turned around and looked at our little shack for the last time.

At sunset we drove into a labor camp near Fresno. Since Papa did not speak English, Mama asked the camp foreman if he needed any more workers. "We don't need no more," said the foreman, scratching his head. "Check with Sullivan down the road. Can't miss him. He lives in a big white house with a fence around it."

When we got there, Mama walked up to the house. She went through a white gate, past a row of rose bushes, up the stairs to the front door. She rang the doorbell. The porch light went on and a tall husky man came out. They exchanged a few words. After the man went in, Mama clasped her hands and hurried back to the car. "We have work! Mr. Sullivan said we can stay there the whole season," she said, gasping and pointing to an old garage near the stables.

The garage was worn out by the years. It had no windows. The walls, eaten by termites, strained to support the roof full of holes. The loose dirt floor, populated by earthworms, looked like a gray road map.

That night, by the light of a kerosene lamp, we unpacked and cleaned our new home. Roberto swept away the loose dirt, leaving the hard ground. Papa plugged the holes in the walls with old newspapers and tin can tops. Mama fed my little brothers and sisters. Papa and Roberto then brought in the mattress and placed it in the far corner of the garage. "Mama, you and the little ones sleep on the mattress. Roberto, Panchito, and I will sleep outside under the trees," Papa said.

Early next morning Mr. Sullivan showed us where his crop was, and after breakfast, Papa, Roberto, and I headed for the vineyard to pick.

Around nine o'clock the temperature had risen to almost one hundred degrees. I was completely soaked in sweat, and my mouth felt as if I had been chewing on a handkerchief.

---

7. *Es todo* (ĕs tô′dô) *Spanish:* That's everything.

WORDS
TO
KNOW

vineyard (vĭn′yərd) *n.* an area where grapevines have been planted

267

Differentiating Instruction

English Learners
1 Remind students that *since* can mean both "from the time" and "because." Ask them which meaning is intended here (*because*).

Less Proficient Readers
2 Ask students what the family's new living quarters are like.
Possible Response: The garage is old and falling down, with a dirt floor, no electricity, and a roof full of holes.
Ask students these questions to make sure they understand the story so far:
• What event occurs in Panchito's family as the story begins? (*They are preparing to move.*)
• How do the members of the family respond to the prospect of moving? (*Papa and Roberto are silent and thoughtful, Panchito hates the move, and the younger children are excited.*)
Set a Purpose As students continue to read, they should look for descriptions of the family's next home.

Advanced Students
César Chávez and other advocates have fought for better living conditions for migrant workers in California. Their work has resulted in improved conditions. Nevertheless, there are still many places in California where workers live in substandard conditions. Have students locate information about migrant workers. How many migrants come to California each year? From what states or countries do these workers come?

Have students imagine a conversation with César Chávez and have them brainstorm ways that they might help migrant workers around their own state and community.

EXPLICIT INSTRUCTION Simile

Instruction Tell students that writers often use a type of figurative language called a simile to create vivid and fresh images in readers' minds. Remind students that a simile compares two unlike things using the word *like* or *as*. Ask students to find a simile in the second paragraph of the second column on page 267. (*"The loose dirt floor, populated by earthworms, looked like a gray road map."*) Ask students what two things are being compared in the simile. (*the dirt floor and a road map*) Discuss with students what they imagine the

floor looks like. Then write this sentence on the board: The loose dirt floor, populated with earthworms, was messy-looking. Ask students if this sentence creates as strong an image as the writer's simile. Discuss responses.
Practice Write these questions on the board and have students work in pairs to answer them:
1. What two things are being compared in the simile?
2. How are these two things alike?

Possible Responses: A dirt floor and a road map are being compared. The floor has lines all over it made by earthworms. The lines look like lines on a road map: curvy and messy.

Use **Unit Two Resource Book,** p. 45, for additional support.

Reading and Analyzing

Literary Analysis | **LITERARY DEVICES**

(A) Have students find the details the author uses to describe the difficult working conditions of Panchito and his family.

Possible Responses: Panchito was soaked in sweat, his mouth felt as if he had been chewing on a handkerchief, and he fell on the hot, sandy ground.

Active Reading | **MAKING INFERENCES**

(B) Ask students to explain why Papa is so alarmed when the school bus comes by.

Possible Response: Since by law all children must go to school, Papa may be frightened that the bus driver will report him for not sending his sons to school.

**Reading Skills and Strategies:
CONNECT**

(C) Ask students whether they have ever "ached all over" from hard work or exercise. If so, have them describe how it felt and tell what they did to feel better.

**Reading Skills and Strategies:
EVALUATE**

Tell students that as they've read this story, they've probably formed some opinions about migrant farm workers. Ask students to think about Francisco Jiménez's purpose for writing this story, and to choose several events from the story to evaluate.

Possible Responses: Students may select any event in the story, but may choose to talk about loading the car or Panchito's fall caused by the heat. They should express emotions and opinions about these events. Students should conclude that Jiménez wants his reader to know the harsh realities of the migrant farm worker's life.

(A) I walked over to the end of the row, picked up the jug of water we had brought, and began drinking. "Don't drink too much; you'll get sick," Roberto shouted. No sooner had he said that than I felt sick to my stomach. I dropped to my knees and let the jug roll off my hands. I remained motionless with my eyes glued on the hot, sandy ground. All I could hear was the drone of insects. Slowly I began to recover. I poured water over my face and neck and watched the black mud run down my arms and hit the ground.

I still felt a little dizzy when we took a break to eat lunch. It was past two o'clock and we sat underneath a large walnut tree that was on the side of the road. While we ate, Papa jotted down the number of boxes we had picked. Roberto drew designs on the ground with a stick. Suddenly I noticed Papa's face turn pale as he looked down the road. "Here **(B)** comes the school bus," he whispered loudly in alarm. Instinctively, Roberto and I ran and hid in the vineyards. We did not want to get in trouble for not going to school. The yellow **1** bus stopped in front of Mr. Sullivan's house. Two neatly dressed boys about my age got off. They carried books under their arms. After they crossed the street, the bus drove away. Roberto and I came out from hiding and joined Papa. "*Tienen que tener cuidado,*"[8] he warned us.

After lunch we went back to work. The sun kept beating down. The buzzing insects, the wet sweat, and the hot dry dust made the afternoon seem to last forever. Finally the mountains around the valley reached out and swallowed the sun. Within an hour it was too dark to continue picking. The vines blanketed the grapes, making it difficult to see the bunches. "*Vámonos,*"[9] said Papa, signaling to us that it was time to quit work. Papa then took out a pencil and began to figure out how much we had earned our first day. He wrote

down numbers, crossed some out, wrote down some more. "*Quince,*"[10] he murmured.

When we arrived home, we took a cold shower underneath a waterhose. We then sat down to eat dinner around some wooden crates that served as a table. Mama had cooked a special meal for us. We had rice and tortillas with *carne con chile,*[11] my favorite dish.

The next morning I could hardly move. My body ached all over. I felt little control over my arms and legs. This feeling went on every morning for days, until my muscles finally got used to the work.

It was Monday, the first week of November. The grape season was over and I could now go to school. I woke up early that morning and lay in bed, looking at the stars and savoring the thought of not going to work and of starting sixth grade for the first time that year. Since I could not sleep, I decided to get up and join Papa and Roberto at breakfast. I sat at the table across from Roberto, but I kept my head down. I did not want to look up and face him. I knew he was sad. He was not going to school today. He was not going tomorrow, or next week, or next month. He would not go until the cotton season was over, and that was sometime in February. I rubbed my hands together and watched the dry, acid-stained skin fall to the floor in little rolls.

When Papa and Roberto left for work, I felt relief. I walked to the top of a small grade next

---

8. *Tienen que tener cuidado* (tyĕ-nĕn' kĕ tĕ-nĕr' kwē-dä'dô) *Spanish:* you have to be careful.

9. *Vámonos* (vä'mô-nôs) *Spanish:* Let's go.

10. *Quince* (kēn'sĕ) *Spanish:* fifteen.

11. *carne con chile* (kär'nĕ kôn chē'lĕ) *Spanish:* a mixture of meat and spicy red peppers.

EXPLICIT INSTRUCTION **Imagery**

Instruction Read aloud to students the paragraph that begins at the bottom of page 267. ("Around nine o'clock.") Ask students to identify the examples of imagery. *("I was completely soaked in sweat, and my mouth felt as if I had been chewing on a handkerchief.")* Ask students what images and ideas came to their minds as they listened. Next discuss why the writer might have decided to use this imagery instead of just saying, "I was hot and my mouth was dry." *(This sentence would tell the truth but it would not be very colorful. It would not help readers visualize the scene.)*

Practice Have students find and copy one example of imagery and explain what is being described and what senses the example appeals to.

Possible Response: Example: "My mouth felt as if I had been chewing on a handkerchief." What it Describes: How thirsty Panchito felt. Senses Used: touch, taste

 Use **Unit Two Resource Book,** p. 45, for more practice.

Harvest Hope
© 1999 Richard Haynes.

269

Less Proficient Readers

Ask students the following questions to make sure they understand the story:

• What happened to Panchito as he worked in the vineyard?

• What happened when the school bus came by?

• How much time passes between the beginning of the story and the first day that Roberto attends school?

• Why is it suddenly possible for Roberto to attend school in November?

Advanced Students

Ask students to think about Panchito and his first day at school. How do they think he feels? What will it be like for Panchito at school?

Possible Response: Panchito is happy about going to school because he doesn't have to work. It will probably be difficult for Panchito at school because he doesn't know anyone, and he hasn't been in school for a while. Maybe he'll feel embarrassed and wish he were home with his big brother.

English Learners

1 When the school bus comes for the first time, Panchito and Roberto hide at the sight of it. However, later on in the story, Panchito seems excited to go to school. This seeming conflict may be confusing to some students. Ask the students why Panchito displays such different emotions.

Possible Response: Panchito wants to go to school, but he needs to work to help the family out financially. They are working when they first see the bus, and he and his family could get in trouble if he is caught not going to school. The next time he talks about school and takes the bus, his working season is over, so there is no more fear of getting in trouble.

Imagery and Personification

Instruction Read aloud the first four sentences in the third paragraph on page 268. ("After lunch") Ask students to identify the examples of imagery and personification in this description. *(Imagery: the buzzing insects, the wet sweat, and the hot dry dust; Personification: "Finally the mountains around the valley reached out and swallowed the sun.")* Discuss with students what elements of the story the figurative language helps them visualize—setting, characters, or events? *(setting)* Have students look at other examples of imagery and

figurative language that they have recorded so far and discuss which story elements these examples help them visualize.

Practice Copy on the board the examples of imagery and the example of personification in the paragraph on page 268. For each example of imagery, have students explain what is being described and what senses the examples appeal to. For the example of personification, have them explain what human qualities are given to the sun.

Possible Responses: Example: the buzzing insects. What it Describes: *the sounds of insects.* Senses Used: *hearing.* Example: the wet sweat, the hot dry dust. What They Describe: *the physical feelings of working in the hot sun.* Senses Used: *touch.* Personification: *Finally the mountains around the valley reached out and swallowed the sun.* Human qualities: *arms, ability, to swallow.*

Use **Unit Two Resource Book,** p. 45, for more practice.

A In this section, Panchito says he feels nervous and empty. Ask students to infer why he feels this way.

Possible Response: Everyone is ignoring him, and he's not sure he will like school or be able to do well.

Reading Skills and Strategies:
EVALUATE

Have students discuss how people treat Panchito on his first day at school.

Possible Responses: The other students and the woman in the principal's office seem unfriendly and indifferent; the teacher seems more sympathetic.

Reading Skills and Strategies:
CONNECT

Ask students to recall their first day at a new school and the feelings and expectations they had. Ask them to discuss how their experiences were similar to or different from Panchito's.

Possible Responses: Students may say that they felt alone and afraid just like Panchito and didn't like to read aloud either. They may say that they didn't feel like Panchito because all the kids were experiencing the same things.

Literary Analysis:
CHARACTER TRAITS

B Have students describe the kind of person Mr. Lema is.

Possible Response: He is enthusiastic, polite, sensitive, and caring.

---

to the shack and watched the "Carcanchita" disappear in the distance in a cloud of dust.

Two hours later, around eight o'clock, I stood by the side of the road waiting for school bus number twenty. When it arrived I climbed in. No one noticed me. Everyone was busy either talking or yelling. I sat in an empty seat in the back.

> I was
> startled.
> I had not
> heard English
> for months.

A When the bus stopped in front of the school, I felt very nervous. I looked out the bus window and saw boys and girls carrying books under their arms. I felt empty. I put my hands in my pants pockets and walked to the principal's office. When I entered I heard a woman's voice say: "May I help you?" I was startled. I had not heard English for months. For a few seconds I remained speechless. I looked at the lady who waited for an answer. My first <u>instinct</u> was to answer her in Spanish, but I held back. Finally, after struggling for English words I managed to tell her that I

wanted to enroll in the sixth grade. After answering many questions, I was led to the classroom.

Mr. Lema, the sixth-grade teacher, greeted me and assigned me a desk. He then introduced me to the class. I was so nervous and scared at that moment when everyone's eyes were on me that I wished I were with Papa and Roberto picking cotton. After taking roll, Mr. Lema gave the class the assignment for the first hour. "The first thing we have to do this morning is finish reading the story we began yesterday," he said enthusiastically. He walked up to me, handed me an English book, and asked me to read. "We are on page 125," he said politely. When I heard this, I felt my blood rush to my head; I felt dizzy. "Would you like to read?" he asked <u>hesitantly</u>. I opened the book to page 125. My mouth was dry. My eyes began to water. I could not begin. "You can read later," Mr. Lema said understandingly.

For the rest of the reading period, I kept getting angrier and angrier with myself. I should have read, I thought to myself.

During recess I went into the restroom and opened my English book to page 125. I began to read in a low voice, pretending I was in class. There were many words I did not know. I closed the book and headed back to the classroom.

Mr. Lema was sitting at his desk correcting papers. When I entered he looked up at me and smiled. I felt better. I walked up to him and asked if he could help me with the new words. "Gladly," he said.

The rest of the month I spent my lunch hours working on English with Mr. Lema, my best friend at school.

WORDS TO KNOW	**instinct** (ĭn'stĭngkt') *n.* a natural or automatic way of behaving
	hesitantly (hĕz'ĭ-tənt-lē) *adv.* with pauses or uncertainty

270

Instruction Remind students that writers use figurative language and imagery to help readers visualize—or create mental pictures of—characters, scenes, and events in a story. Visualizing helps readers remember a selection because details remain clear in their minds. Encourage students to visualize by paying attention to descriptions of a selection's setting, as well as to details about what the characters see, hear, and do. Ask volunteers to describe some of the elements they visualized as they read "The Circuit."

Practice Have students choose one example of imagery or figurative language from the story and write a paragraph describing what they visualized as they read it. Invite students to share their paragraphs.

Possible Responses: Responses will vary.

Use **Unit Two Resource Book**, p. 46, for more practice.

One Friday during lunch hour, Mr. Lema asked me to take a walk with him to the music room. "Do you like music?" he asked me as we entered the building.

"Yes, I like Mexican *corridos*,"[12] I answered. He then picked up a trumpet, blew on it and handed it to me. The sound gave me goose bumps. I knew that sound. I had heard it in many Mexican *corridos*. "How would you like to learn how to play it?" he asked. He must have read my face, because before I could answer, he added:

2

"I'll teach you how to play it during our lunch hours."

That day I could hardly wait to get home to tell Papa and Mama the great news. As I got off the bus, my little brothers and sisters ran up to meet me. They were yelling and screaming. I thought they were happy to see me, but when I opened the door to our shack, I saw that everything we owned was neatly packed in cardboard boxes. ❖

12. *corridos* (kô-rē′dôs) *Spanish:* slow, romantic songs.

RELATED READING

the 1st

by Lucille Clifton

what I remember about that day
is boxes stacked across the walk
and couch springs curling through the air
and drawers and tables balanced on the curb
and us, hollering,
leaping up and around
happy to have a playground;

nothing about the emptied rooms
nothing about the emptied family

Connect to the Literature

1. What Do You Think?
Many students will respond that the ending surprised them. Others will respond that they found it sad that Panchito's family's move will prevent him from learning to play the trumpet, which he was very excited about.

Comprehension Check
• The peak of the strawberry season is over, and the family has to move to an area where there are crops to be picked.
• He must pick cotton to help support the family.
• Panchito's family has to move again.

Use Selection Quiz **Unit Two Resource Book,** p. 49.

Think Critically

2. Have students note whether they used all the evidence available to them when they made inferences.
3. **Possible Response:** He is hardworking at school and in the fields. Also, he is sensitive, emotional, and shy.
4. **Possible Responses:** Yes; the memory of Mr. Lema's kindness and generosity can make Panchito trust other teachers. Also, Mr Lema taught Panchito an important lesson about how fun learning could be.
5. **Possible Response:** His experiences make the story more realistic, because he knows what it's like to move a lot and to work in the fields and to continue attending school.

Literary Analysis

Literary Devices Students should work cooperatively to complete the chart. When all groups have completed the work, they may want to share their charts with the whole class.

Connect to the Literature

1. What Do You Think? How did you react to the end of the story? Explain.

Comprehension Check
• Why does Panchito's family have to move to Fresno?
• Why can't Roberto join Panchito at school?
• Why won't Mr. Lema be able to teach Panchito the trumpet?

Think Critically

2. **ACTIVE READING   MAKING INFERENCES**
How did the **inferences** you made in your **READER'S NOTEBOOK** help you know or understand the characters? Compare your inferences with a classmate's and discuss the details from the story that helped you.

3. How would you describe Panchito, the narrator of the story?
   Think About:
   • his attitude toward work and school
   • his feelings about his brother
   • his feelings about frequent moves

4. Do you think the narrator's friendship with Mr. Lema will have a lasting effect? Explain why or why not.

5. Francisco Jiménez's parents were migrant farm workers when he was young. Do you think he could have written this story without these firsthand experiences? Explain.

Extend Interpretations

6. **COMPARING TEXTS** Compare and contrast the feelings about moving that are expressed in "The Circuit" and the Literary Link poem "the 1st" on page 271.

7. **The Writer's Style** Jiménez uses many words in the story from the first language of Panchito and his family. Panchito frequently uses a Spanish word and then explains its meaning. What do you think the use of the original language adds to the story?

8. **Connect to Life** Revisit your response to the Connect to Your Life activity on page 264. After reading the story, what are your feelings about moving? Have they changed? Explain your response.

272 UNIT TWO   PART 2: HOME AND HERITAGE

Literary Analysis

LITERARY DEVICES Writers use **literary devices** to create vivid pictures of settings, events, and characters in readers' minds. Two types of literary devices are imagery and similes.

Words that appeal to readers' senses are called **imagery.** Writers use imagery to help readers imagine how things look, feel, smell, taste, and sound. A **simile** is a comparison of two things that have some of the same qualities. A simile usually contains a word such as *like, as,* or *resembles.* Notice the use of imagery and the simile in this excerpt from "The Circuit."

The walls, eaten by termites, strained to support the roof full of holes. The loose dirt floor, populated by earthworms, looked like a gray road map.

Group Activity With a group, find descriptive passages from the story and read them aloud. Identify which senses the details appeal to. Also identify whether the description is of a person, a place, or an action. Record the group's answers in a chart like the one shown.

Details	Senses Used	Description of a . . .
drone of insects	hearing	place

Extend Interpretations

6. **Comparing Texts** Possible Response: In both selections, moving is seen as damaging. In the poem, the narrator as a younger person didn't realize the unhappiness connected with moving; in the story, Panchito, though young, is sad about the frequent moves.

7. **The Writer's Style** Possible Response: The Spanish words help remind you that even though most of the story is written in English, the family's first language is Spanish. It says in the story that Papa doesn't speak any English, and when Panchito starts school he realizes he hasn't heard English spoken for months, so the family probably uses only Spanish when they talk among themselves.

8. **Connect to Life** Responses will vary, but students should discuss their feelings about moving and relate them to their earlier thoughts. They should explain if and why their feelings have changed after reading the story.

Writing

Letter to Mr. Lema Write the letter that Panchito might send to Mr. Lema from the next town along the circuit. Use what you learned about Panchito from the story to make the letter seem like something Panchito would write. Place the letter in your **Working Portfolio.**

> Dear Mr. Lema,
> How are you? I just started at a new school. The practices we used to do at lunchtime have made my English much better. I read aloud in class today.

Writing Handbook
See p. R38: Using Language Effectively

Speaking & Listening

Persuasive Speech Prepare a speech to convince members of a committee to begin a program that gives school supplies and books to families that do migrant farm work. Clearly explain your opinions and ideas. Use what you learned from the story about the lives of migrant farming families to support your ideas. Practice your speech to make sure you are speaking clearly and with the right tone of voice. Then give your speech to the class.

Speaking and Listening Handbook
See p. R100: Persuasive Presentations.

Research & Technology

Farm Workers' Rights Who was Cesar Chavez? How did he affect the lives of migrant farm workers? Conduct research to learn about this influential man. Find books about Chavez or refer to an encyclopedia or Web site to get information. Then write a paragraph describing how he helped migrant farm workers. Under your paragraph, include a list of the information sources you used.

Research and Technology Handbook
See p. R106: Getting Information Electronically.

Vocabulary

STANDARDIZED TEST PRACTICE

Choose the word or group of words that means the same, or nearly the same, as the underlined Word to Know.

1. Panchito crept into the classroom underlined hesitantly. **Hesitantly** means—
   A with grace **B** with uncertainty
   C with eagerness **D** with humor

2. Mama's pots and pans were underlined surplus items. **Surplus** means—
   F leftover **G** expensive
   H sturdy **J** plain

3. Papa worked long hours working in the underlined vineyard. **Vineyard** means—
   A rain forest **B** rock quarry
   C apple orchard **D** grape farm

4. When he saw the school bus, Roberto's underlined instinct was to hide. **Instinct** means—
   F friendly feeling **G** hurtful feeling
   H natural feeling **J** sad feeling

5. Panchito's family had to have a underlined jalopy in order to follow the harvests. **Jalopy** is a—
   A clock **B** calendar
   C computer **D** car

Vocabulary Handbook
See p. R20: Context Clues.

Writing

Letter to Mr. Lema Students should review the style of a friendly letter before beginning. They should also keep their writing consistent with the style of Panchito's language.

 Use **Writing Transparencies**, p. 15, for additional support.

Speaking & Listening

Persuasive Speech Students may want to include statistics and visual aids in their presentations. Time and support may be needed to research this topic in the library.

Use the **Speaking and Listening Book,** pp. 29 and 30, for additional support.

Research & Technology

Farm Workers' Rights Students may want to work with a partner to research Cesar Chavez and to write their essays.

Vocabulary

STANDARDIZED TEST PRACTICE

1. B
2. F
3. D
4. H
5. D

Grammar in Context

WRITING EXERCISE

Answers

1. During recess I went to the library and opened my English book to page 125.
2. There were many words I did not know.
3. I closed the book and headed back.
4. I walked up to him and asked if he could help.

Francisco Jiménez

In 1973, Francisco Jiménez won an annual award from Arizona Quarterly for "The Circuit." He has also received a Ford Foundation grant and the Distinguished Leadership in Education Award from the California Teachers Association. His work appears widely in periodicals and in anthologies. In 1998, Jiménez's collected stories, *The Circuit: Stories from the Life of a Migrant Child,* won the coveted Boston Globe-Horn Book Award for fiction.

Author Activity

Between Two Languages Students may want to talk to classmates and others in the community who are bilingual. They may also need library time to locate and read other books by Francisco Jiménez.

Grammar in Context: Past and Present Verb Tenses

A story told in the **present tense** relates events that seem to be occurring now.

> Here comes the school bus.

A story told in the **past tense** relates events that have already occurred.

> The school bus stopped at my house.

Francisco Jiménez draws the reader into a past-tense world of memory in "The Circuit":

> When I opened the front door to the shack, I stopped. Everything we owned was neatly packed in cardboard boxes. Suddenly I felt even more the weight of hours, days, weeks, and months of work. I sat down on a box.

Usage Tip: In general, when telling a story, choose one tense and stay with it.

> Present Tense: The grape season is over and I can go to school.
> Past Tense: The grape season was over and I could go to school.

WRITING EXERCISE Rewrite the following sentences using a consistent tense.

Example: *Original* Papa wipes the sweat off his forehead and said wearily: *"Es todo."*

Rewritten Papa wiped the sweat off his forehead and said wearily: *"Es todo."*

1. During recess I go to the library and opened my English book to page 125.
2. There were many words I do not know.
3. I close the book and headed back.
4. I walk up to him and asked if he could help.

Grammar Handbook
See p. R76: Using Verbs Correctly.

Francisco Jiménez
born 1943

"Learning and knowledge were the only stable things in my life."

Migrant Childhood Francisco Jiménez was born in Mexico. He immigrated to the United States with his parents in 1947. Jiménez's parents were farm workers, and he helped them in the fields. Like Panchito, Jiménez enjoyed school because it meant he didn't have to pick crops. He also realized that school would help him escape "the circuit."

Professor and Writer A guidance counselor helped Jiménez get a scholarship to attend college. Jiménez now teaches Spanish and literature at the University of Santa Clara in California. "The Circuit" comes from his book *The Circuit: Stories from the Life of a Migrant Child,* which contains other stories about Panchito and his family.

AUTHOR ACTIVITY
Between Two Languages How does Jiménez's knowledge of languages and his experience of learning affect his writing? Reread "The Circuit" and look at other stories by Jiménez. Write a paragraph explaining how the author's bilingual ability helps his storytelling.

EXPLICIT INSTRUCTION **Grammar in Context**

FUTURE VERB TENSE
Instruction Verbs that tell about something that will happen in the future are in the future tense. One way to check to see if you are writing in future tense is to see if the word *tomorrow* makes sense in your sentence. Write the following sentence on the board: *Panchito will go to school when he gets to the next town.*

Ask students if this sentence is in the future tense, and help them to see that they could write, "*Tomorrow* Panchito *will go* to school . . ."
Practice Ask students to write a short paragraph in the future tense, describing the next place on the circuit that Panchito's family will work. Students may want to include information about the farm work, Panchito's new home, or Panchito's experiences at a new school.

 Use **Unit Two Resource Book,** p. 47.

 For more instruction on future tense verbs, see McDougal Littell's ***Language Network,*** Chapter 4.

For **systematic instruction** in grammar, see:
• **Grammar, Usage, and Mechanics Book**
• pacing chart on p. 187i.

Oh Broom, Get to Work

by YOSHIKO UCHIDA (yō′shē-kō ōō-chē′dä)

Connect to Your Life

Houseguests This selection tells how a girl reacts to having too many visitors in her home. How would you deal with an unwanted guest?

Build Background

Immigrant Life Author Yoshiko Uchida and her sister, Keiko (kā′kō), grew up near San Francisco, California. Uchida's parents were issei (ēs′sā′)—Japanese immigrants to the United States—who welcomed many household guests. They were eager to help Japanese students who had come to study in this country. Most of their visitors were students at the University of California or other area schools.

Like this student at the Pacific School of Religion, many guests of the Uchidas were studying to become Christian ministers.

Focus Your Reading

LITERARY ANALYSIS **POINT OF VIEW**
A writer chooses a **point of view** as a way of presenting events. The **narrator** is the voice or character that tells about the events. Most stories and nonfiction works are told from either a first-person or a third-person point of view. In a work told from a **first-person point of view**, the narrator participates in the events that he or she describes. The narrator uses the pronouns *I*, *me*, and *we*, as in this passage from the selection you are about to read:

> *I knew if I looked at Keiko we would both explode. But I did. And we did.*

As you read "Oh Broom, Get to Work," consider how the use of a first-person point of view affects the presentation of the events.

ACTIVE READING **CONNECTING**
When you relate your reading to things you already know or to events in your own life, you are making **connections.** Connecting can help you understand the people that you read about.

READER'S NOTEBOOK As you read this selection, ask yourself, What does this remind me of? Jot down at least three ways in which you connect the selection with your own knowledge or experience.

WORDS TO KNOW
Vocabulary Preview

audacious	indifferent
deprive	intrusion
devise	laden
dispense	pious
dread	pompous

OH BROOM, GET TO WORK   **275**

Standards-Based Objectives

1. understand and appreciate a **memoir**
2. understand **point of view** and its effect on a story
3. use **connecting** to help understand a story
4. explain the effects of common **literary devices**
5. **read aloud** narrative and expository text

Summary

Yoshiko Uchida reaches back to her childhood to recall the steady parade of Japanese visitors who came to her parents' home in California. In the author's view, all these visitors—with a few rare exceptions—were boring. Uchida's mother was unfailingly kind to the guests, a trait not shared by her resentful daughter. In fact, Uchida gleefully relates that she once followed an old Japanese tradition for getting rid of unwanted visitors: she put an upside-down broom with a cloth draped over it in view of a tiresome guest. When he saw it, he knew he was not wanted and soon departed.

Thematic Link

Uchida's home life helped her to appreciate her heritage, which included a tradition of courtesy and hospitality toward guests. The humor in her story arises from her refusal as a child to practice those family traditions even while she is slowly absorbing them.

English Conventions Practice

Daily Language SkillBuilder

Have students **proofread** the display sentences on page 187k and write them correctly. The sentences also appear on Transparency 9 of **Language Transparencies.**

Preteaching Vocabulary

If you would like to preteach the WORDS TO KNOW for this selection, use the Explicit Instruction, page 276.

LESSON RESOURCES

UNIT TWO RESOURCE BOOK, pp. 50–56

ASSESSMENT
Formal Assessment, pp. 43–44
Test Generator

SKILLS TRANSPARENCIES AND COPYMASTERS
Literary Analysis
• Narrator and Point of View, TR 22 (p. 276)
Reading and Critical Thinking
• Connecting, TR 2 (p. 276)

Language
• Daily Language SkillBuilder, TR 9 (p. 275)
• Context Clues: Compare and Contrast, Cause and Effect, Example, TR 54 (p. 276)
Writing
• Effective Language, TR 15 (p. 282)
• Character Sketch, TR 30 (p. 282)

INTEGRATED TECHNOLOGY
Audio Library

Visit our website:
www.mcdougallittell.com

For **systematic instruction** in language skills, see:
• **Vocabulary and Spelling Book**
• **Grammar, Usage, and Mechanics Book**
• pacing chart on p. 187i.

Reading and Analyzing

Literary Analysis | POINT OF VIEW

Explain to students that the selection is written in the first-person, which means that the narrator uses the pronouns *I*, *me*, *mine*, and sometimes *we*, *us*, and *our*. Have students think, as they read, about how the story would be different if it were written in the third-person.

Use **Unit Two Resource Book**, p. 48 for more practice. Use **Literary Analysis Transparencies**, p. 22, for additional support.

Active Reading | CONNECTING

Students should be able to compare the text to their own experiences. Suggest ways in which they can do this: They can recall times they have had visitors in their own homes; they can recall when they had difficulty restraining their laughter; they can think of annoying things their parents do.

Use **Unit Two Resource Book**, p. 51 for more practice.
Use **Reading and Critical Thinking Transparencies**, p. 2, for additional support.

Reading Skills and Strategies: EVALUATE

Remind students to evaluate the story as they read—to ask if its characters behave in believable ways, to consider whether or not they enjoy it, and to reflect on whether or not they agree with the central theme. Point out that standing back to think about a selection is an important part of any reading experience.

Oh Broom,

EXPLICIT INSTRUCTION **Preteaching Vocabulary**

WORDS TO KNOW
Teaching Strategy Explain to students that **examples** sometimes give valuable clues to the meaning of an unfamiliar word. In the sentence "Soldiers, astronauts, and mountain climbers all must be dauntless at times," students should be able to figure out from the examples that *dauntless* means "bold."
Practice The following sentences use examples to explain some of the WORDS TO KNOW.

Have students write a definition of each underlined word based on the examples given.
1. Nightmares and thoughts of monsters cause <u>dread</u> in some children.
2. Robbers, thieves, and cheats all <u>deprive</u> people of their money.
3. Doctors, nurses, and pharmacists can legally <u>dispense</u> medicines to people.

4. After bursting in on a church service and crashing a party, he became known for his <u>intrusions</u>.
5. Edison and Einstein were famous because they <u>devised</u> new things or ideas.

Use **Unit Two Resource Book**, p. 55, for more practice.

For **systematic instruction** in vocabulary, see:
• **Vocabulary and Spelling Book**
• pacing chart on p. 187i.

Get to Work

by Yoshiko Uchida

I was on my way home from school when I found it. A little dead sparrow. It lay still and stiff, its legs thrust in the air like two sticks. It was the first dead creature I had seen close up, and it filled me with both dread and fascination.

I knew what I would do. I would give the bird a nice funeral. Mama would find a piece of soft red silk for me from her bag of sewing scraps. I would wrap the bird in a silken shroud,[1] put it in a candy box, and bury it beneath the peach tree. Maybe I would have Mama say a prayer for it, like the minister did at real funerals.

I picked up the bird carefully, cupping it in both hands, and ran home. I rushed through the kitchen and flung open the swinging door to the dining room.

"Look, Mama! I found a dead sparrow!"

But Mama was busy. She was sitting in the easy chair, knitting quietly. Sitting across from her on the sofa was a squat blob of a man—balding and gray—as silent as a mushroom.

The only sound was the soft ticking of the Chelsea clock on the mantel above the fireplace. I could see dust motes floating in the shaft of late afternoon sun that filtered in from the small west window.

Poor Mama was stuck with company again. She and the guest had both run out of things to say, but the visitor didn't want to leave.

Poor Mama was stuck with company again.

"Hello, Yo Chan," my mother called. She seemed happy for the intrusion. "How was school today?"

But all I thought was, company again! It wasn't the first time a visitor had deprived me of my mother's time and attention, and I was tired of having them intrude into our lives uninvited. I stomped out of the living room without even a word of greeting to our guest, and knew I would have to bury the sparrow by myself.

Mama might have sung a Japanese hymn for me in her high, slightly off-key voice, and she certainly would have offered a better prayer than I could devise. But I did the best I could.

"Dear Heavenly Father," I began. "Please bless this little bird. It never hurt anybody. Thank you. Amen."

1. **shroud** (shroud): a cloth used to wrap a body for burial.

WORDS TO KNOW

dread (drĕd) *n.* deep fear; terror
intrusion (ĭn-trōō'zhən) *n.* an act of coming in rudely or inappropriately
deprive (dĭ-prīv') *v.* to take something away from
devise (dĭ-vīz') *v.* to form or plan in the mind; think up

Differentiating Instruction

Less Proficient Readers

Set a Purpose Explain to students that the story is based on the problems a girl has with visitors to her family's home. Ask them to identify two kinds of visitors to Uchida's home as they read.

1 Students are learning that each sentence must contain a subject and a predicate so the sentence fragments may confuse them. Ask students to find the sentence fragment in the first paragraph and then decide what part of the sentence is missing. *("A little dead sparrow." It has no verb.)*

English Learners

- Point out the illustration of the broom and the cloth on page 276. Tell students that the story mentions a Japanese superstition: If you drape a cloth over a broom and stand it upside down, an unwelcome visitor will leave.
- If the class includes students with Japanese backgrounds, encourage them to share information on Japanese customs, foods, and language.

Use **Spanish Study Guide,** pp. 55–57, for additional support.

Advanced Students

Students should be able to connect, compare, and contrast themes as they read. One of the themes of the story is caring about others. Ask students to find evidence of this theme as they read.

Possible Response: Yoshiko cares greatly about the little bird she finds on the way home from school. She does not care as much about visitors to her home, but her mother and father do.

EXPLICIT INSTRUCTION Imagery and Figurative Language

Instruction Remind students that nonfiction writers also use figurative language and imagery to make their writing interesting and memorable. Review the definitions of imagery (*language that appeals to a reader's senses*), simile (*a comparison that uses the word* like *or* as), and metaphor (*a comparison, without* like *or* as, *that states that one thing actually is another).* Next, list these sentences on the board and have students identify them as examples of imagery, simile, or metaphor: The old house was like a museum. *(simile)* The kitchen was warm and filled with the smell of baking bread. *(imagery)* The shadows were monsters ready to reach out and grab me. *(metaphor)* Now read the first paragraph of the selection to students and ask them to identify the simile and what two things are being compared. *(Simile: "its legs thrust in the air like two sticks" The legs of a dead sparrow are compared with two sticks sticking up out of the ground.)*

Practice Have students work in pairs to find and identify other examples of imagery and figurative language on this page. Have them record these examples.

Possible Responses: Imagery: "a piece of soft red silk"; "wrap the bird in a silken shroud, put it in a candy box, and bury it beneath the peach tree." Simile: "as silent as a mushroom." Metaphor: "a squat blob of a man."

Use **Unit Two Resource Book,** p. 53, for more practice.

I buried the box beneath a mound of soft, loose dirt, picked a few nasturtiums to lay on top, and made a cross out of two small twigs.

The gray-blob mushroom was just another of the countless visitors, usually from Japan, who came to see my parents. They were both graduates of Doshisha, one of Japan's leading Christian universities, and had close ties with many of its professors. This meant that many of our visitors were ministers or young men studying to become ministers at the Pacific School of Religion in Berkeley.

Once in a while, one of the visitors would be a pleasant surprise. Like the Reverend Kimura, who sang the books of the Bible to the tune of an old folk song.

1 *"Mah-tai, Mah-ko, Luka, Yoha-neh-deh-un . . ."* he sang out in a loud, clear voice. *"Shito, Roma, Corinto, Zen-ko-sho . . ."* He clapped in time as he sang.

I saw Mama's eyes light up as she listened, and soon she joined in, clapping and singing and laughing at the pure joy of it.

Mama surprised me sometimes. She could be a lot of fun depending on whom she was with. It was too bad, I thought, that so much of the time she had to be serious and proper, while visiting ministers smothered her with their <u>pious</u> attitudes.

To me they were all achingly and endlessly boring. It was only once in a great while that a Reverend Kimura turned up, like a red jelly bean in a jar full of black licorice.

A One <u>pompous</u> minister from Japan not only stayed overnight, which was bad enough, but left his dirty bathwater in the tub for Mama to wash out.

Yoshiko Uchida (right) and her older sister, Keiko, in the 1920s. Courtesy of the Bancroft Library, Berkeley, California.

"What nerve!" Keiko fumed.

"I'll say!" I echoed.

But Mama explained that in Japan everyone washed and rinsed outside the tub and got in just to soak. "That way the water in the tub stays clean, and you leave it for the next person."

Mama got down on her knees to wash out the tub, saying, "We're lucky he didn't try to wash himself outside the tub and flood the bathroom."

Some kind of luck, I thought. | **2**

WORDS TO KNOW	**pious** (pī′əs) *adj.* showing religious feeling, especially in a way designed to draw attention
	pompous (pŏm′pəs) *adj.* having excessive self-esteem or showing exaggerated dignity

I didn't feel at all lucky about the seminary[2] students who often dropped in, plunked themselves down on our sofa, and stayed until they were invited to have supper with us.

"Poor boys, they're lonely and homesick," Mama would say.

"They just need some of Mama's kind heart and good cooking," Papa would add. And if they needed some fatherly advice, he was more than willing to <u>dispense</u> plenty of that as well.

Both my parents had grown up poor, and they also knew what it was to be lonely. They cared deeply about other people and were always ready to lend a helping hand to anyone. Mama couldn't bear to think of her children ever being less than kind and caring.

"Don't ever be <u>indifferent</u>," she would say to Keiko and me. "That's the worst fault of all."

It was a fault she certainly never had. She would even send vitamins or herbs to some ailing person she had just met at the dentist's waiting room.

On holidays all the Japanese students from the Pacific School of Religion—sometimes as many as five or six—were invited to dinner. Keiko and I always complained shamelessly when they came.

"Aw, Mama . . . do you *have* to invite them?"

But we knew what we were expected to do. We flicked the dust cloth over the furniture, added extra boards to the dining room table so it filled up the entire room, and set it with Mama's good linen tablecloth and the company china.

If it was to be a turkey dinner, we put out the large plates and good silverware. If it was a sukiyaki[3] dinner, we put out the rice bowls, smaller dishes, and black lacquer[4] chopsticks.

The men came in their best clothes, their squeaky shoes shined, their hair smelling of camellia hair oil. Papa didn't cook much else, but he was an expert when it came to making sukiyaki, and cooked it right at the table with gas piped in from the kitchen stove. As the men arrived, he would start the fat sizzling in the small iron pan.

Soon Mama would bring out huge platters <u>laden</u> with thin slivers of beef, slices of bean curd[5] cake, scallions, bamboo shoots, spinach, celery, and yam noodle threads. Then Papa would combine a little of everything in broth flavored with soy sauce, sugar, and wine, and the mouth-watering smells would drift through the entire house.

One evening in the middle of a sukiyaki dinner, one of the guests, Mr. Okada, suddenly rose from the table and hurried into the kitchen. We all stopped eating as the scholarly Mr. Okada vanished without explanation.

"Mama," I began, "he's going the wrong way if he has to . . ."

Mama stopped me with a firm hand on my knee. My sister and I looked at each other. What did he want in the kitchen anyway? More rice? Water? What?

It seemed a half hour before Mr. Okada finally reappeared. But he was smiling and seemed much happier.

---

2. **seminary** (sĕm′ə-nĕr′ē): a school for the training of priests, ministers, or rabbis.

3. **sukiyaki** (soō′kē-yä′kē): a Japanese dish of sliced meat, bean curd, and vegetables seasoned and fried together.

4. **lacquer** (lăk′ər): a shiny substance used as a decorative coating on wooden objects.

5. **bean curd:** a food made from soybeans—also known as tofu.

WORDS TO KNOW	
dispense (dĭ-spĕns′) v. to give out; distribute	
indifferent (ĭn-dĭf′ər-ənt) adj. not interested; unconcerned	
laden (lād′n) adj. weighed down; heavy	

279

Active Reading CONNECTING

Ⓐ Ask students to describe real-life situations in which someone told a joke that brought a great deal of laughter from a group. Ask, "What effect does it have on a gathering when someone tells a successful, entertaining joke?"

Possible Response: It makes everyone feel more relaxed and at home.

Ask what it says about Yoshiko's father that he loved to talk and tell jokes and stories.

Possible Response: He enjoyed putting guests at ease in his house.

Literary Analysis POINT OF VIEW

Ⓑ Point of view does not just involve using particular pronouns. It also involves presenting a story with a particular view, or perspective. Ask students to pretend they are the visitor and retell the broom incident from his point of view. Get them started by discussing how the visitor might feel after he left the house.

Possible Response: "At a house I was visiting the other day, a little girl did something very rude. She put a cloth over a broom and stood it upside down. She made sure it was in a spot where I could see it. I was insulted and of course left immediately."

Reading Skills and Strategies: MAKE INFERENCES

Ⓒ Ask students whether they think Yoshiko learned anything from the incident with the broom. Have them explain the inference they drew.

Possible Response: No; Yoshiko seems to have thought that she was fully justified in driving away the stranger, even at the risk of seeming rude.

"I'm sorry," he murmured, "but it was so warm I had to remove my winter undershirt." He wiped his face with a big handkerchief and added, "I feel much better now."

I knew if I looked at Keiko we would both explode. But I did. And we did. We laughed so hard we had to leave the table and rush into the kitchen holding our sides. Keiko and I often got the giggles at company dinners, and the harder we tried to stop, the harder we laughed. The only solution was for us not ever to glance at each other if we felt the giggles coming on.

In spite of all our grumbling, Keiko and I often enjoyed ourselves at these dinners. Sometimes it was Papa who provided the laughs. He loved to talk, and everyone always liked listening to his stories. Sometimes he would tell a joke he had heard at the office:

Ⓐ A visitor from Japan looked up at the sky. "Beautiful pigeons!" he says to a native San Franciscan.

"No, no," answers the native. "Those aren't pigeons, they're gulls."

The visitor replies, smiling, "Well, gulls or boys, they're beautiful pigeons!"

Much laughter all around.

After dinner Papa liked to gather everyone around the piano. He had a good baritone voice, often sang solos at church, and even organized the church choir. Keiko played the piano, and we sang everything from "Old Black Joe"[6] to "In the Good Old Summertime."

Sometimes Keiko and I added to the entertainment by playing duets for our guests —a fairly <u>audacious</u> act since most of the time I hadn't practiced all week. It never occurred to me then, but I suppose we were just as boring to them as they so often seemed to us.

I once thought I'd found the perfect solution for getting rid of unwanted guests. Mrs. Wasa, who was like an adopted grandmother, told me one day of an old Japanese superstition.

"If you want someone to leave," she said, "just drape a cloth over the bristles of a broom and stand it upside down. It always works!"

I filed that wonderful bit of information inside my head, and the very next time Mama was trapped in the living room with another silent mushroom, I gave it a try. I did just as Mrs. Wasa instructed and stood the broom at the crack of the swinging door leading to the dining and living rooms.

"Oh, broom," I murmured. "Get to work!"

I kept a watchful eye on our visitor, and before too long, he actually got up and left.

"Mama, it worked! It worked!" I shouted, dancing into the living room with the broom. "He left! I got him to leave!"

But Mama was horrified.

"*Mah*, Yo Chan," she said. "You put the broom at the doorway where he could see?"

I nodded. "I didn't think he'd notice."

Only then did I realize that our visitor had not only seen the broom, but had probably left because he knew a few Japanese superstitions himself.

I'd always thought the seminary on the hill was bent on endlessly churning out dull ministers to try my soul. But that afternoon I felt as though I'd evened the score just a little. ❖

Before too long, he actually got up and left.

---

6. **"Old Black Joe":** a song by Stephen Foster (1826–1864), a composer of songs celebrating life in the Old South.

WORDS
TO
KNOW

audacious (ô-dā´shəs) *adj.* fearlessly and recklessly daring; bold

---

Instruction Read aloud the first five paragraphs of the selection as students listen. Model reading with appropriate pacing, intonation, and expression. For example, the passage about finding the dead sparrow might be read in a quiet, reflective voice, while the passage in which the narrator talks about the bird's funeral might be read as if she were talking conversationally to herself. When you have finished, remind students why you read in certain ways. Say, "I read the dialogue 'Look Mama! I found a dead sparrow!' in a loud and enthusiastic voice because the content is enthusiastic. I dropped my voice tone at 'But Mama was busy' because the narrator has come in on a scene that is very quiet. Why else do you think I read in a louder voice when the narrator tells her mother about the dead sparrow?" *(The sentences end with exclamation points.)*

Practice Have students work in pairs to practice reading aloud a passage from the selection. Remind them to think about punctuation, such as question marks and exclamation points, as well as pause marks like periods and commas; voice level for the content of dialogue; and intonation to express judgment, sadness, joy, disgust, etc. Have pairs raise their hands when they are ready to have you listen to them read.

Connect to the Literature

1. **What Do You Think?**
   What is your opinion of young Yoshiko Uchida's behavior?

   Comprehension Check
   - Who were the family's visitors?
   - In what ways did the visitors annoy Yoshiko?
   - At the end of the selection, why did the visitor leave?

Think Critically

2. **ACTIVE READING CONNECTING**
   With a group of classmates, discuss the connections that you recorded in your READER'S NOTEBOOK. Did you and your classmates relate to Yoshiko's situation?

3. In your opinion, how well did Yoshiko cope with her family's many visitors?

   Think About:
   - her descriptions of the visitors and the activities the family shared with them
   - her feelings toward her family
   - the expectations her parents had of her

4. Yoshiko's mother used to say, "Don't ever be indifferent. That's the worst fault of all." Why might being indifferent be such a terrible fault?

Extend Interpretations

5. **The Writer's Style** Uchida uses **sensory details,** or imagery, to make her writing interesting. Phrases such as "hair smelling of camellia hair oil" appeal to the reader's senses. Find other examples of sensory details in the selection and record them in a chart like the one shown. Note which sense or senses each detail uses.

Sensory Details	Sense(s) Used
hair smelling of camellia hair oil	smell

6. **Connect to Life** What is your idea of the perfect host and the perfect guest? Using ideas from the story and from your own experience, describe them.

Literary Analysis

POINT OF VIEW When events are told from a **first-person point of view,** the **narrator** (the person or character who tells about them) is involved in the events. The narrator refers to himself or herself as *I* or *me.* Memoirs and autobiographies are usually told from a first-person point of view.

When events are told from a **third-person point of view,** the narrator describes the events but does not take part in them. A third-person narrator refers to all the people or characters in the story as *he, she,* or *they.* The story "All Summer in a Day" is told from a third-person point of view. In this sentence from that story, the narrator describes the actions of Margot and her classmates:

If they tagged her and ran, she stood blinking after them.

Biographies are usually told from a third-person point of view.

Group Activity With a group of classmates, choose a short (one- or two-paragraph) scene from "Oh Broom, Get to Work." Write three retellings of the scene from different points of view. Try telling it from the mother's point of view (first person), a visitor's point of view (first person), or the point of view of a narrator not involved in the events (third person).

Connect to the Literature

1. **What Do You Think?**
   Responses will vary, but may include that she was selfish or impatient.

Comprehension Check
- They were seminary students or ministers from Japan.
- They take her mother's attention; they come uninvited and they stay too long; they make extra work for the Uchidas.
- Yoshiko, following an old Japanese superstition that is supposed to cause unwelcome guests to leave, turned a broom upside down and covered it with a cloth. The guest saw the broom and left because he knew the same superstition.

Use Selection Quiz,
Unit Two Resource Book, p. 56.

Think Critically

2. **Possible Responses:** Yes; I've had many dinners with my parents' friends when I was so bored I wanted to shout. Also I hate when my mother starts cleaning the house for "company." My friend and I once started laughing in the library. We tried to stop and we couldn't.

3. **Possible Response:** Yoshiko deals effectively with her family's many visitors. She lets her parents know that the visitors bore her, but she doesn't mean to be rude.

4. **Possible Response:** Being indifferent is an even worse fault than being mean—if you are indifferent towards someone, you don't even think the person is worth talking to.

Literary Analysis

Point of View Students should be able to shift from one point of view to another, and should also understand the difference between first-person and third-person tellings of an event.

Extend Interpretations

5. **The Writer's Style Possible Responses:** "The soft ticking of the Chelsea clock" appeals to the sense of hearing. "Dust motes floating in the shaft of late afternoon sun" and "like a red jellybean in a jar full of black licorice" appeal to the sense of sight.
   You may wish to have students work in small groups to find examples of sensory details.

6. **Connect to Life** Students may say that the perfect guest is one who is entertaining but doesn't stay too long, and that the perfect host is one who is kind and generous and doesn't rush the guests to leave. To get students started on this assignment, review with them the things that Yoshiko does not like about guests.

Writing

Personality Profile Profiles should accurately sum up Yoshiko's personality, citing instances from the story in support of statements made, and including both good and bad qualities. To get students started on this activity, have them skim the selection and jot down good qualities and bad as they refresh their memories by reading.

 Use **Writing Transparencies,** pp. 15 and 30, for additional support.

Speaking & Listening

Monologue Monologues should tell about a scene from the point of view of the speaker.

Research & Technology

What's for Dinner? Menus should accurately describe dishes at a Japanese dinner. A good source of information for this activity, aside from cookbooks featuring Japanese cooking exclusively, would be Asian or international cookbooks that include Japanese recipes.

Vocabulary

STANDARDIZED TEST PRACTICE

1. C
2. M
3. B
4. J
5. C
6. L
7. A
8. K
9. D
10. K

Writing

Personality Profile A profile is a description of a person's most important traits and actions. Write a profile of young Yoshiko. What was she like? What were her good and not-so-good points? Use precise verbs, nouns, and adjectives to create a strong image of Yoshiko. Place the profile in your **Working Portfolio.**

Writing Handbook
See p. R34: Building Blocks of Good Writing.

Speaking & Listening

Monologue A monologue is a speech made by a character in a story. In a monologue, a character describes his or her thoughts and feelings. Choose a scene from this selection and rewrite it as a monologue delivered by one of the characters in the scene. Then practice performing the monologue, using gestures and facial expressions to help convey feelings. When you are ready, perform your monologue for the class.

Speaking and Listening Handbook
See p. R34: Oral Interpretation.

Research & Technology

What's for Dinner? The Uchidas sometimes served their guests sukiyaki. What are some other Japanese dishes the Uchidas might have served? Using cookbooks and books about Japanese culture, create a menu for a Japanese dinner. Include a description of each dish on your menu.

Vocabulary

STANDARDIZED TEST PRACTICE

Choose the word or group of words that means the same, or nearly the same, as the underlined Word to Know.

1. A feeling of <u>dread</u>
   A daring   B hunger
   C fear   D pride

2. A sudden <u>intrusion</u>
   J invitation K reward
   L accident   M attack

3. A <u>pious</u> minister
   A polite   B devout
   C humble   D stern

4. To <u>devise</u> a plan
   J form   K execute
   L dislike   M support

5. An <u>indifferent</u> audience
   A eager   B intelligent
   C uninterested D unusual

6. To <u>dispense</u> medicine
   J practice   K measure
   L distribute M swallow

7. A <u>pompous</u> public speaker
   A conceited   B popular
   C humorous   D shy

8. To <u>deprive</u> someone of happiness
   J cure   K rob
   L teach   M write

9. A pail <u>laden</u> with sand
   A sprinkled   B white
   C ready   D heavy

10. An <u>audacious</u> act
    J admirable   K adventurous
    L unpleasant   M unforgivable

Vocabulary Handbook
See p. R22: Synonyms and Antonyms.

CHOICES *and* CHALLENGES

Grammar in Context: Action Verbs

Author Yoshiko Uchida uses **action verbs** to show a child's energy and excitement in "Oh Broom, Get to Work."

> I rushed through the kitchen and flung open the swinging door. . . .

Compare these sentences:

> I felt in a big hurry.
> I rushed through the kitchen.

The second sentence, which uses an action verb, is more forceful and vivid than the first.

Usage Tip: An **action verb** can show **physical action**, or an **action of the mind:**

> They cared deeply about other people.

WRITING EXERCISE Rewrite each sentence using action verbs.

Example: *Original* Yo Chan seemed rude.
Rewritten Yo Chan fidgeted.
1. The sukiyaki was delicious.
2. The man seemed so dull.
3. Our conversation felt uncomfortable.
4. Mother's song sounded sweet.

Connect to the Literature Look back at the selection to find more examples of action verbs. Find two examples of verbs showing physical action, and two examples of verbs that show action of the mind.

Grammar Handbook
See p. R62: Parts of Speech.

Yoshiko Uchida
1921–1992

"I write to celebrate our common humanity, for the basic elements of humanity are present in all our strivings."

Leading Family An author and educator, Yoshiko Uchida grew up in Berkeley, California. Her parents—leaders of Berkeley's Japanese-American community—filled their home with homesick seminary students, ministers, and graduates of Doshisha University.

War Experiences After the United States declared war on Japan in 1941, many Japanese Americans were arrested and placed in internment camps. The Uchidas were split up and sent to camps in Montana and Utah.

"Don't Think in Terms of Labels" Though Uchida's parents taught their daughters Japanese customs, the family's loyalty to the United States was strong. In 1984 Uchida said that she hoped that children could be "caring human beings who don't think in terms of labels—foreigners or Asians or whatever—but think of people as human beings."

AUTHOR ACTIVITY
Internment Camps Yoshiko Uchida's first successful writings were about her family's experiences during World War II. Find a copy of her autobiography *The Invisible Thread,* from which "Oh Broom, Get to Work" is taken. Read about her experiences in an internment camp during the war, and write a paragraph describing what happened.

Grammar in Context
WRITING EXERCISE
Possible Responses:

1. We gobbled up the delicious sukiyaki.
2. The dull man said nothing.
3. Our conversation included uncomfortable topics.
4. Mother sang a sweet song.

Connect to the Literature
Possible Responses: Verbs chosen will vary. wash, rinsed (physical action); thought, meant (action of the mind)

Yoshiko Uchida

Uchida's big break came when she followed the advice of an editor at *The New Yorker* magazine, who suggested that Uchida write about her experiences in the internment camps. In time, she also began to explore her other experiences as an American-born daughter of Japanese parents.

Author Activity

Internment Camps Responses should indicate acquaintance with Uchida's autobiography and focus on her experiences in the internment camp, summarizing them in an intelligible fashion. Students may find more information about Uchida's internment years in her book *Desert Exile: The Uprooting of a Japanese American Family.*

EXPLICIT INSTRUCTION **Grammar in Context**

TWO KINDS OF LINKING VERBS
Instruction Explain to students that a linking verb links a word in the predicate to the subject. (*I am happy to see you.*) There are two kinds of linking verbs: forms of the verb *be* (*am, is, are, was, were, been, being*) and verbs that express condition (*look, smell, feel, sound, taste, grow, appear, become, seem*). The second kind of linking verb may also be used as an action verb. Discuss these examples with students:
LINKING The sky <u>appears</u> blue.
ACTION The sun <u>appears</u> at dawn.

LINKING The meat <u>tasted</u> delicious.
ACTION I <u>tasted</u> the delicious meat.
Point out that a linking verb expresses a state of being, not an action. Say, "If you can substitute a form of the verb *be* for a verb, that verb is a linking verb."
Practice Have students copy the following sentences and indicate whether the verbs in them are action verbs or linking verbs. Answers are given in parentheses.
1. Yo Chan remained happy. *(linking)*
2. She grew sick of the visits. *(linking)*

3. She looked for the broom. *(action)*
4. She smelled the sukiyaki her dad made. *(action)*

 Use **Unit Two Resource Book,** p. 54, for more practice.

 For more instruction in linking verbs, see McDougal Littell's *Language Network,* Chapter 4.

For **systematic instruction** in grammar, see:
• **Grammar, Usage, and Mechanics Book**
• pacing chart on p. 187i.

Standards-Based Objectives

1. understand and appreciate a **poem**
2. understand poet's use of **sound devices** (rhyme, repetition, rhythm)
3. use **reading aloud** to better understand poetry

Summary

The two poems in this selection deal with travel across the western United States. In the first, Stephen Vincent Benét describes westward expansion in an easy-going rhyme reminiscent of a traditional song. In the second, Theodore Roethke recounts in lilting verse an experience of traveling westward by train.

Thematic Link

Benét and Roethke are concerned with the nature of our homeland, the United States. While Benét revels in the legends of expansion that form the mythic history of our heritage, Roethke focuses on its physical beauty.

English Conventions Practice

Daily Language SkillBuilder

Have students **proofread** the display sentences on page 187k and write them correctly. The sentences also appear on Transparency 9 of **Language Transparencies.**

Western Wagons
by STEPHEN VINCENT BENÉT

Night Journey
by THEODORE ROETHKE

Connect to Your Life

In what ways do you think travel changes you or helps you grow?

Build Background

The two poems you are about to read describe experiences of travelers in the West. The ease and popularity of westward travel has increased with its speed.

Before 1850 A pioneer family might live out of the interior of a Conestoga wagon. **Travel time, New York to San Francisco: over two months**

After 1850 Rail passengers could travel in comfortable trains, complete with dining cars. **New York to San Francisco: less than one week**

After 1920 The popularity of cars led to the construction of a national highway network. **New York to San Francisco: two and a half days, not including stops**

After 1970 Jet travel became the preferred method of cross-country travel. **New York to San Francisco: about five hours**

Transportation Milestones

1807	1831	1869	1908	1958
Robert Fulton invents the steamboat.	First U.S. steam railroad for passengers opens.	First U.S. transcontinental railroad completed.	Henry Ford begins mass producing automobiles.	First domestic jet passenger service.

Focus Your Reading

LITERARY ANALYSIS | **SOUND DEVICES**

Rhyme, rhythm, and repetition are sound devices that can add feeling and music to poetry. Words that end with the same sound are said to **rhyme.** Many poems also have **rhythm**—a pattern of stressed and unstressed syllables. (Stressed syllables are spoken with more emphasis.) The use of a word, phrase, or even a stanza more than once is called **repetition.**

ACTIVE READING | **READING ALOUD**

Poets choose and arrange words to create the sounds they want listeners to hear. Try reading these two poems aloud. Pay attention to the patterns of sounds that you hear. In your **READER'S NOTEBOOK** list at least three pairs of lines that end with rhyming words.

LESSON RESOURCES

UNIT TWO RESOURCE BOOK, pp. 57–58

ASSESSMENT
Formal Assessment, pp. 45–46
Test Generator

SKILLS TRANSPARENCIES AND COPYMASTERS
Literary Analysis
- Poetry: Sound Devices, TR 20 (p. 286)

Language
- Daily Language SkillBuilder, TR 9 (p. 284)

Writing
- Writing Variables, TR 2 (p. 288)
- Poem, TR 35 (p. 288)

INTEGRATED TECHNOLOGY
Audio Library

Visit our Web site:
www.mcdougallittell.com

For **systematic instruction** in language skills, see:
- **Grammar, Usage, and Mechanics Book**
- **Vocabulary and Spelling Book**
- pacing chart on p. 187i.

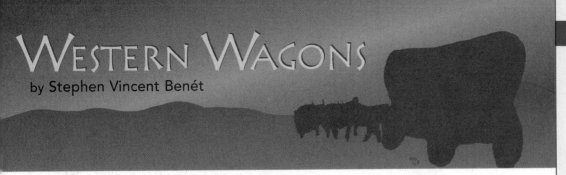

WESTERN WAGONS

by Stephen Vincent Benét

They went with axe and rifle, when the trail was still to blaze,
They went with wife and children, in the prairie-schooner days,
With banjo and with frying pan—Susanna, don't you cry!
For I'm off to California to get rich out there or die!

5 We've broken land and cleared it, but we're tired of where we are.
They say that wild Nebraska is a better place by far.
There's gold in far Wyoming, there's black earth in Ioway,
So pack up the kids and blankets, for we're moving out today!

The cowards never started and the weak died on the road,
10 And all across the continent the endless campfires glowed.
We'd taken land and settled—but a traveler passed by—
And we're going West tomorrow—Lordy, never ask us why!

We're going West tomorrow, where the promises can't fail.
O'er the hills in legions, boys, and crowd the dusty trail!
15 We shall starve and freeze and suffer. We shall die, and tame the lands.
But we're going West tomorrow, with our fortune in our hands.

THINKING *through the* LITERATURE

1. **Comprehension Check** What things are the pioneers taking with them?

2. On the basis of the poem, what kind of people do you think pioneers are?

3. Recall your responses to the question in Connect to Your Life on page 284. How do you think the people in this poem will be changed by their experiences on the trail?

Less Proficient Readers
Set a Purpose Ask students to read to find out how the writers of the poems use sound to express their thoughts about traveling west.

English Learners
Help students read the rhyming words at the end of the lines in the poems. They may not perceive at first, for instance, that *road* and *glowed* are rhymes.

The students may not realize that *Iowa* was changed to *Ioway* in the 7th line of the poem. Ask, "Why do you think that the poet spelled the name of the state Iowa incorrectly?"

Possible Responses: The poet changed the spelling of the word so that it would sound like the "slang" language that the settlers used. Or, the poet changed the spelling of the word so that it would rhyme with *today* in line 8.

 Use **Spanish Study Guide,** pp. 58–60, for additional support.

Advanced Students
Students may be interested in reading other poetry by Roethke. The poem "The Sloth," about that slow-moving animal, is amusing and appropriate for advanced readers. Other students might enjoy "A Nonsense Song," a love poem written by Stephen Vincent Benét for his wife.

Thinking through the Literature

1. **Comprehension Check** They are taking tools, rifles, musical instruments, and household goods.
2. **Possible Responses:** strong, hardy, adaptable, independent, restless
3. Responses will vary, but should include reasonable predictions.

EXPLICIT INSTRUCTION Rhyme and Repetition

Instruction Ask volunteers to define *rhyme* and *repetition*. (Rhyme: the repetition of similar sounds at the ends of words; Repetition: the use of sounds, words, phrases, or whole lines more than once in a poem.) Then ask volunteers to read aloud pairs of lines that rhyme in "Western Wagons." Point out that the use of rhyme links ideas in the line pairs within a stanza. Discuss how rhyme makes the poem sound different from prose. Next, ask a volunteer to identify examples of repetition in

the poem. *(Repetition: "We're going West tomorrow")* Discuss with students why the poet might have repeated these lines and what the repetition shows about the speaker's attitude toward the subject. *(repeated for emphasis, possibly to show the pioneers' determination)*

Practice Have students find and record other examples of rhyme and repetition in "Western Wagons."

Possible Responses: Rhyme: "They went with axe and rifle, when the trail was still to blaze, They went with wife and children, in the prairie-schooner days." Repetition: "We're going West tomorrow"; "They went with"; "We shall."

 Use **Unit Two Resource Book,** p. 58.

286 UNIT TWO PART 2

Reading and Analyzing

Active Reading [READING ALOUD]

The key to appreciating both poems in this selection will be reading them aloud. Benét's poem has long, musical sounding lines full of vivid imagery and dialect of the Old West. Students should find reading it out loud highly entertaining. The Roethke poem has a clickety-clack rhythm that mimics a rushing train. This will become clear to students as they interpret the poem aloud. Have students take turns reading stanzas of Benét's poem. Break up the Roethke poem according to sense in the following portions: lines 1–5; 6–11; 12–15; 16–19; 20–23; and line 24 to the end.

Use **Unit Two Resource Book**, p. 57 for more practice.

Literary Analysis [SOUND DEVICES]

After reading the poems aloud with students, point out that the rhythm in "Night Journey" is much like that of the rocking train described in the first two lines. The shortness of the lines and the strong rhymes that cap them reinforce this rhythm. Ask students to compare and contrast the sound devices used in "Night Journey" and "Western Wagons."

Possible Response: The lines in "Western Wagons" are long and musical, while the lines in "Night Journey" are short and clipped. Both poems use strong rhyme. There is also repetition, such as in "Western Wagons" the repeat phrase "We're going West tomorrow."

Use **Literary Analysis Transparencies**, p. 20, for additional support

NIGHT JOURNEY
by Theodore Roethke

Twilight in the Wilderness, by Frederick Edwin Church, American (1826–1900), Oil on canvas, 101.6 x 162.6 cm, © 1999 The Cleveland Museum of Art, Mr. and Mrs. William H. Marlatt Fund, 1965.233.

Now as the train bears west,
Its rhythm rocks the earth,
And from my Pullman berth
I stare into the night
5   While others take their rest.
Bridges of iron lace,
A suddenness of trees,
A lap of mountain mist
All cross my line of sight,
10 Then a bleak wasted place,
And a lake below my knees.
Full on my neck I feel
The straining at a curve;
My muscles move with steel,

15 I wake in every nerve.
I watch a beacon swing
From dark to blazing bright,
We thunder through ravines
And gullies washed with light.
20 Beyond the mountain pass
Mist deepens on the pane,
We rush into a rain
That rattles double glass.
Wheels shake the roadbed stone,
25 The pistons jerk and shove,
I stay up half the night
To see the land I love.

EXPLICIT INSTRUCTION **Rhythm**

Instruction Remind students that rhythm is the pattern of stressed and unstressed syllables in a poem. Now read aloud the first five lines of "Night Journey," emphasizing the rhythm with your voice. Copy one or two lines on the board and show students how to mark stressed and unstressed syllables.

Its rhythm rocks the earth,
And from my Pullman berth

Then read the entire poem aloud with students, emphasizing the rhythm by using voice and clapping. Use the Literary Analysis: Sound

Devices note in the green side column to continue discussing rhythm.

Practice Have students work in pairs to copy two lines from "Night Journey" and mark the stressed and unstressed syllables.

Possible Responses
We thunder through ravines,
And gullies washed with light.

Use **Unit Two Resource Book**, p. 58, for more practice.

Connect to the Literature

1. **What Do You Think?**
   What are your impressions of the speaker of "Night Journey"?

   Comprehension Check
   • Where is the speaker?
   • What is the speaker doing?
   • Name at least three things that the speaker sees, hears, or feels.

Think Critically

2. How do you think the speaker of "Night Journey" will feel about the end of his or her trip?

3. **ACTIVE READING** **READING ALOUD**
   Share with a partner the pairs of rhyming lines you listed in your **READER'S NOTEBOOK**. Discuss the effects created by the rhymes in the two poems.

4. How is seeing the world from a moving train different from experiencing it on foot or from a horse-drawn wagon?

   Think About:
   • the achievements and hardships of the pioneers
   • the observations that the speaker of "Night Journey" makes from the train
   • your own experiences traveling on foot versus traveling by car, bus, or subway

5. Which of the journeys presented in these poems would you most like to go on? Explain your response.

Extend Interpretations

6. **COMPARING TEXTS** Compare and contrast the journeys in "Western Wagons" and "Night Journey" with the journey of Amelia Earhart in the selection from *The Fun of It* (page 135). How are the travelers' experiences and reasons for traveling similar? How are they different?

7. **Connect to Life** Do you think you have to leave home to go on a journey or to explore? Why or why not?

Literary Analysis

SOUND DEVICES The sound of a poem reinforces its meaning and the mood, or feeling, in the poem. Rhyme, rhythm, and repetition are sound devices used in poetry.

Rhyme Words that end with the same sounds are said to rhyme. Poets sometimes emphasize words or ideas by using rhyme.

Rhythm Rhythm is a pattern of stressed and unstressed syllables. The rhythm of a poem may be closely connected to the subject of the poem. In "Night Journey," the fast and regular rhythm helps the reader imagine the sounds of a train.

Repetition The use of a word or phrase more than once is called repetition. Repetition helps the poet to emphasize an idea or convey a certain feeling. In "Western Wagons," the repetition of "we're going West tomorrow" emphasizes the pioneers' determination.

Paired Activity Copy the four lines from "Night Journey" that begin with the word *I*. With a partner, answer these questions: Are these lines an example of rhyme, rhythm, or repetition? Explain your answer. What is described in each of the four lines? How is this different from what is described in the rest of the poem?

Connect to the Literature

1. **What Do You Think?**
   Possible Responses: The speaker is very observant and thoughtful. He enjoys traveling.

Comprehension Check
• He's on a train.
• He's staying up at night to look out the window of the train.
• The speaker sees bridges, trees, mountains, a lake, a beacon. The speaker hears the thunder of the wheels and the rattling of the window glass. He feels the rocking of the train and a straining of his neck muscles as it goes around a curve.

Think Critically

2. **Possible Response:** The speaker will be sad that the journey is over.

3. Responses will vary. Students might note that the rhymes in the first poem add a song-like quality. In the second, they might comment on the rocking, regularity that imitates the train.

4. **Possible Response:** Train travel only allows you to catch glimpses of the outside world instead of being able to take in the scenery at your leisure. Also, the train shelters you from the rain and other external conditions that you would experience in a wagon or on foot.

5. Responses will vary but should be supported with explanations.

Literary Analysis

Sound Devices The lines are an example of repetition; in each line, the pronoun *I* is used at the beginning. Most of the other lines describe the movement of the train or what the speaker sees outside the window. These four lines describe the speaker's actions.

Extend Interpretations

6. **Comparing Texts** Responses will vary, and should include the idea of adventure in all three works of literature. To get students started on this activity, have them turn back to the story of Amelia Earhart in "The Fun of It" and skim it to refresh their memories. Suggest they take notes as they skim.

7. **Connect to Life** Responses will vary. Some students may feel that they can learn much about a place from books and the media without actually going there, or that books and films allow you to go on a journey into the imagination. Other students may feel that it is necessary to have new experiences in person in order to learn about something.

Writing

Travel Poem Responses should focus on growth and change brought about by traveling. They should exhibit one or more of the sound devices listed.

 Use **Writing Transparencies,** pp. 2 and 35, for additional support.

Speaking & Listening

Poetry Reading Suggest to students that they memorize the poem two lines at a time.

Research & Technology

Social Studies Responses should include maps showing road and rail routes. A good source of information for this activity is *The First Transcontinental Railroad,* by John Debo Galloway (New York: Dorset Press, 1989).

Writing

Travel Poem Write a poem about a journey you have taken. Your poem could describe a trip to a faraway place or just to the grocery store. Try using sound devices in your poem. Place your poem in your **Working Portfolio.**

Writing Handbook

This writing activity asks you to use the poem form. To find out about other forms you might use when your purpose is to describe, see p. R31: Choosing a Form.

Speaking & Listening

Poetry Reading Work with a partner to memorize all or part of one of the poems you just read. Once you both know the words, practice reciting it, paying attention to the rhythms and rhymes in the poem. You and your partner can take turns reading lines aloud. When you are ready, recite the poem to the class together, using the tone of your voice to make the poem interesting for your audience.

Research & Technology

SOCIAL STUDIES

By the end of the 1800s, roads and railways crisscrossed the United States. With a partner, research the development of these transportation networks. Study historical atlases, and create a historical transportation map showing road and rail routes. Label key routes and intersections.

Research and Technology Handbook See p. R107: Library Computer Services.

Stephen Vincent Benét
1898–1943

A Literary Family Stephen Vincent Benét grew up in a family of writers. His father and grandfather had kept written records of their wartime experiences, and the family encouraged the literary interests of its younger members. Benét's brother and sister also became writers. Benét published his first book when he was just 17. In 1920 Benét received a fellowship that allowed him to study in France. During a later stay in France, Benét wrote his Pulitzer Prize-winning poem *John Brown's Body.* Stephen and his wife, Rosemary Benét, often combined their writing talents, especially when bringing stories from American history to life for children.

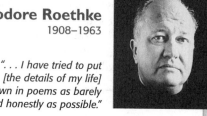

Theodore Roethke
1908–1963

". . . I have tried to put [the details of my life] down in poems as barely and honestly as possible."

Childhood Theodore Roethke's father owned a floral business. Roethke grew up helping to tend the flowers in the family greenhouse. His father's death when Roethke was 14 affected the poet deeply. Much of his poetry explores his memories of his father.

Self Direction After graduating from the University of Michigan, Roethke supported himself by teaching in colleges. In 1947 he went west to take a job at the University of Washington in Seattle. He enjoyed teaching and was a favorite of his students, a number of whom became important poets themselves. In 1954, Roethke was awarded the Pulitzer Prize for his collection *The Waking.*

Building Vocabulary
Homonyms and Homophones

Words can have many meanings. Words like *pound* (a measure of weight) and *pound* (to beat) are called **homonyms.** They have the same spelling and sound but different meanings. Some words that sound the same have different spellings and different meanings. These are **homophones.**

Homonyms	
examples: *row, row*	
same	• spelling
	• pronunciation
different	• meaning

Homophones	
examples: *or, oar*	
same	• pronunciation
different	• spelling
	• meaning

> . . . when he reached home, he asked Noreen Callahan, who was playing on the stoop, to take off his skates for him.
>
> —Myron Levoy, *"Aaron's Gift"*

In this passage, **stoop** means: *a small porch or platform at the entrance of a home.*

But **stoop** can also mean: *to bend down.*

Strategies for Building Vocabulary

Homonyms and homophones can be confusing to readers, and can plague writers. In most cases the **context** makes clear the correct meaning of a homonym.

For example, in the Levoy passage above, it is clear that *stoop* is the noun that means "a small porch," not the verb meaning "to bend down."

❶ **Understand Homonyms** There may be times when you see a familiar word in a new context that just doesn't make sense.

How many meanings can you think of for the word *bark?* You know "the dog's bark," and "the tree's bark." What about "We set sail in a bark"? You can either consider **context** or use a **dictionary** to determine that *bark* also means "a sailing ship."

❷ **Use Homophones in Your Writing** The most difficult thing about using homophones in writing is that many common words are homophones (*our, hour; write, right*). Use these words freely in your first drafts without worrying about spelling. Then, in revising, check carefully for homophones. See whether the words you chose match their contexts.

If you find different spellings hard to remember, you can keep a chart of hints such as the one on this page.

Homophones	Hints
here	in this place
hear	hear with the ear
herd	the shepherd's flock
heard	past tense of hear
their	belonging to them
they're	they are
there	there, not here

❸ **Word Play** You can also use homonyms and homophones creatively in your writing, for humor and for fun. Many poets, ad copywriters, and even comedians use pairs of words as puns: *Which witch? The nose knows!*

EXERCISE Look up each word's meaning in a dictionary. Then find the meaning of either a homonym or a homophone. Jot down both definitions, along with a sentence using each one. Tell whether you have used homonyms or homophones.

1.	pair	**6.**	piece
2.	weather	**7.**	lie
3.	desert	**8.**	mean
4.	shore	**9.**	past
5.	mind	**10.**	brake

BUILDING VOCABULARY **289**

Standards-Based Objectives
- understand the relationship of word meanings in homonyms and homophones
- understand the differences between homonyms and homophones

VOCABULARY EXERCISE

Answers will vary. Sample answers are given for items 1–3.

1. *pair* Two corresponding persons or items, similar in form or function, and matched or associated
   pear An edible fruit; homophones
   This pair of shoes doesn't fit me any more.
   Would you like an apple or a pear in your lunch?
2. *weather* The state of the atmosphere at a given time or place
   whether A word used to show alternatives; homophones
   I hope the weather is good for our picnic.
   Do you know whether Olivia is bringing her sister?
3. *desert* 1. abandon; Latin *deserere*; *desert* 2. something deserved; Old French *deservir*; homonyms
   We can't desert our friends who are lost.
   Jail was their just desert after their terrible crimes.

 Use **Unit Two Resource Book,** p. 59.

Possible Objectives

You can use this selection to achieve one or more of the following objectives:

- enjoy independent reading (Option One)
- read and analyze literature with a group (Option Two)
- use the Reader's Notebook to formulate questions about literature (Option Three)
- write in response to literature (Option Three)

Summary

In 1947, Mary is almost eleven and dreading her birthday. It means that she and her cousin Roger Deer Leg, like other eleven-year-old Kaws, have to undergo an endurance test called Ta-Na-E-Ka, or "the flowering of adult-hood." For five days and nights, they will have to survive alone in the woods. Mary and Roger are prepared by their grandfather, who teaches them which berries and insects to eat and tells them tales of Ta-Na-E-Ka in the past. They complain and cannot see how this tradition fits into modern American life. As the first day of Ta-Na-E-Ka draws near, Mary decides that she cannot eat grasshoppers and berries. Formulating a plan, she borrows five dollars from her teacher.

Mary and Roger set off into the woods and separate according to the rules. Mary heads for the river where she knows she will find a marina. She uses some of the five dollars to buy herself breakfast at a restaurant. Later, when the owner has gone for the night, she sneaks into the restaurant to sleep. Discovered by the owner the next morning, she explains about Ta-Na-E-Ka and he offers to let her stay for the five days. When Mary returns home, she finds Roger exhausted; of course, she looks suspiciously healthy. Mary confesses what she did and, to her surprise, her grandfather praises her for her insight into survival in the modern world.

Ta-Na-E-Ka

Children at Play, Oscar Howe. © 1983 Adelheid Howe.

BY MARY WHITEBIRD

290

As my birthday drew closer, I had awful nightmares about it. I was reaching the age at which all Kaw Indians had to participate in Ta-Na-E-Ka.

Well, not all Kaws. Many of the younger families on the reservation were beginning to give up the old customs. But my grandfather, Amos Deer Leg, was devoted to tradition. He still wore handmade beaded moccasins instead of shoes and kept his iron-gray hair in tight braids. He could speak English, but he spoke it only with white men. With his family he used a Sioux dialect.[1]

Grandfather was one of the last living Indians (he died in 1953, when he was eighty-one) who actually fought against the U.S. Cavalry. Not only did he fight, he was wounded in a skirmish at Rose Creek—a famous encounter in which the celebrated Kaw chief Flat Nose lost his life. At the time, my grandfather was only eleven years old.

Eleven was a magic word among the Kaws. It was the time of Ta-Na-E-Ka, the "flowering of adulthood." It was the age, my grandfather informed us hundreds of times, "when a boy could prove himself to be a warrior and a girl took the first steps to womanhood."

"I don't want to be a warrior," my cousin, Roger Deer Leg, confided to me. "I'm going to become an accountant."

"None of the other tribes make girls go through the endurance ritual," I complained to my mother.

"It won't be as bad as you think, Mary," my mother said, ignoring my protests. "Once you've gone through it, you'll certainly never forget it. You'll be proud."

I even complained to my teacher, Mrs. Richardson, feeling that, as a white woman, she would side with me.

She didn't. "All of us have rituals of one kind or another," Mrs. Richardson said. "And look at it this way: How many girls have the opportunity to compete on equal terms with boys? Don't look down on your heritage."

Heritage, indeed! I had no intention of living on a reservation for the rest of my life. I was a good student. I loved school. My fantasies were about knights in armor and fair ladies in flowing gowns, being saved from dragons. It never once occurred to me that being an Indian was exciting.

But I've always thought that the Kaw were the originators of the women's liberation movement. No other Indian tribe—and I've spent half a lifetime researching the subject—treated women more "equally" than the Kaw. Unlike most of the sub-tribes of the Sioux Nation, the Kaw allowed men and women to eat together. And hundreds of years before we were "acculturated,"[2] a Kaw woman had the right to refuse a prospective husband even if her father arranged the match.

The wisest women (generally wisdom was equated with age) often sat in tribal councils. Furthermore, most Kaw legends revolve around "Good Woman," a kind of supersquaw, a Joan of Arc[3] of the high plains. Good Woman led Kaw warriors into battle after battle, from which they always seemed to emerge victorious.

And girls as well as boys were required to undergo Ta-Na-E-Ka.

---

1. **Sioux** (sōō) dialect: a language spoken by Native Americans of the Great Plains.
2. **acculturated** (ə-kŭl′chə-rā′tĭd): made to adopt another people's culture—in this case, the culture of European Americans.
3. **Joan of Arc**: French heroine of the early 1400s. At age 17, she led her country's army against the English and drove them out of the city of Orléans.

TA-NA-E-KA **291**

Reading the Selection

Option One
Independent Reading
You might set aside time each week for independent reading to help your students approach the goal of reading 1 million words a year. During this time, you and all of your students would read for enjoyment. "Ta-Na-E-Ka" will appeal to many students and can be read independently in about thirty minutes. If you want to encourage students to read for pleasure, you might forego any assignments related to this selection. Should you want to make assignments, Options Two and Three offer suggestions.

Option Two
Group Reading
You may assign students to groups or allow them to choose their own. Students can read the selection together, alternately reading sections aloud, or they can read independently and meet to cooperate in a project that portrays some element of the story.

Possible Projects
- Using elements from the story, students can write the script for a speech Mary gives at school after completing Ta-Na-E-Ka. In it, she can explain what she did and what she learned about herself and her heritage through the experience. Students can present the speech to the class.
- Students can illustrate the various story characters, add captions giving their important traits, and add speech-bubbles with especially characteristic quotations from the story.

Option Three
Reader's Notebook

- Ask students to describe the setting of "Ta-Na-E-Ka" and to describe the character of Mary in detail.
- Tell students to read the selection, pausing at the end of the first column on page 292. At that point, ask them to summarize in their Reader's Notebook their initial impressions of the story and of the two children. Have them write down any questions they have about the story or any questions they would like to ask Mary. At the end of the story, students will return to their questions. Ask them to note if any of their questions have been answered and to write down additional questions they have.
- Instead of presenting a speech to the class, students can write such a speech in their Reader's Notebooks.

The actual ceremony varied from tribe to tribe, but since the Indians' life on the plains was dedicated to survival, Ta-Na-E-Ka was a test of survival.

"Endurance is the loftiest[4] virtue of the Indian," my grandfather explained. "To survive, we must endure. When I was a boy, Ta-Na-E-Ka was more than the mere symbol it is now. We were painted white with the juice of a sacred herb and sent naked into the wilderness without so much as a knife. We couldn't return until the white had worn off. It wouldn't wash off. It took almost 18 days, and during that time we had to stay alive, trapping food, eating insects and roots and berries, and watching out for enemies. And we did have enemies—both the white soldiers and the Omaha warriors, who were always trying to capture Kaw boys and girls undergoing their endurance test. It was an exciting time."

"What happened if you couldn't make it?" Roger asked. He was born only three days after I was, and we were being trained for Ta-Na-E-Ka together. I was happy to know he was frightened, too.

"Many didn't return," Grandfather said. "Only the strongest and shrewdest.[5] Mothers were not allowed to weep over those who didn't return. If a Kaw couldn't survive, he or she wasn't worth weeping over. It was our way."

"What a lot of hooey," Roger whispered. "I'd give anything to get out of it."

"I don't see how we have any choice," I replied.

Roger gave my arm a little squeeze. "Well, it's only five days."

Five days! Maybe it was better than being painted white and sent out naked for eighteen days. But not much better.

We were to be sent, barefoot and in bathing suits, into the woods. Even our very traditional parents put their foot down when Grandfather suggested we go naked. For five days we'd have to live off the land, keeping warm as best we could, getting food where we could. It was May, but on the northernmost reaches of the Missouri River the days were still chilly and the nights were fiercely cold.

Grandfather was in charge of the month's training for Ta-Na-E-Ka. One day he caught a grasshopper and demonstrated how to pull its legs and wings off in one flick of the fingers and how to swallow it.

I felt sick, and Roger turned green. "It's a darn good thing it's 1947," I told Roger teasingly. "You'd make a terrible warrior." Roger just grimaced.[6]

I knew one thing. This particular Kaw Indian girl wasn't going to swallow a grasshopper no matter how hungry she got. And then I had an idea. Why hadn't I thought of it before? It would have saved nights of bad dreams about squooshy grasshoppers.

I headed straight for my teacher's house. "Mrs. Richardson," I said, "would you lend me five dollars?"

"Five dollars!" she exclaimed. "What for?"

"You remember the ceremony I talked about?"

"Ta-Na-E-Ka. Of course. Your parents have written me and asked me to excuse you from school so you can participate in it."

---

4. **loftiest:** highest; most noble.

5. **shrewdest:** most clever.

6. **grimaced** (grĭm'ĭst): made a disgusted face.

292

"Well, I need some things for the ceremony," I replied, in a half-truth. "I don't want to ask my parents for the money."

"It's not a crime to borrow money, Mary. But how can you pay it back?"

"I'll baby-sit for you ten times."

"That's more than fair," she said, going to her purse and handing me a crisp, new five-dollar bill. I'd never had that much money at once.

"I'm happy to know the money's going to be put to a good use," Mrs. Richardson said.

A few days later the ritual began with a long speech from my grandfather about how we had reached the age of decision, how we now had to fend for ourselves and prove that we could survive the most horrendous of ordeals. All the friends and relatives who had gathered at our house for dinner made jokes about their own Ta-Na-E-Ka experiences. They all advised us to fill up now, since for the next five days we'd be gorging[7] ourselves on crickets. Neither Roger nor I was very hungry. "I'll probably laugh about this when I'm an accountant," Roger said, trembling.

"Are you trembling?" I asked.

"What do you think?"

"I'm happy to know boys tremble, too," I said.

At six the next morning, we kissed our parents and went off to the woods. "Which side do you want?" Roger asked. According to the rules, Roger and I would stake out "territories" in separate areas of the woods, and we weren't to communicate during the entire ordeal.

"I'll go toward the river, if it's okay with you," I said.

This particular Kaw Indian girl wasn't going to swallow a grasshopper no matter how hungry she got.

"Sure," Roger answered. "What difference does it make?"

To me, it made a lot of difference. There was a marina a few miles up the river, and there were boats moored there. At least, I hoped so. I figured that a boat was a better place to sleep than under a pile of leaves.

"Why do you keep holding your head?" Roger asked.

"Oh, nothing. Just nervous," I told him. Actually, I was afraid I'd lose the five-dollar bill, which I had tucked into my hair with a bobby pin. As we came to a fork in the trail, Roger shook my hand. "Good luck, Mary."

"*N'ko-n'ta,*" I said. It was the Kaw word for "courage."

The sun was shining and it was warm, but my bare feet began to hurt immediately. I spied one of the berry bushes Grandfather had told us about. "You're lucky," he had said. "The berries are ripe in the spring, and they are delicious and nourishing." They were orange and fat, and I popped one into my mouth.

Argh! I spat it out. It was awful and bitter, and even grasshoppers were probably better tasting, although I never intended to find out.

I sat down to rest my feet. A rabbit hopped out from under the berry bush. He nuzzled the berry I'd spat out and ate it. He picked another one and ate that, too. He liked them. He looked at me, twitching his nose. I watched a red-headed woodpecker bore into an elm tree, and I caught a glimpse of a civet cat[8]

---

7. **gorging** (gôr'jĭng): filling with food; stuffing.
8. **civet** (sĭv'ĭt) **cat:** a spotted skunk.

Possible Activities

Independent Activities

- Have advanced students scan the story, jotting down details, facts, and descriptions about the narrator's attitude towards her heritage. Ask them to write in their Reader's Notebooks their analysis of her true feelings before and after the ritual and to note any significant changes that occur during the story. Remind them to consider carefully the passages in which the narrator informs the reader about the Kaw people. Ask students to consider what these passages reveal about the narrator's feelings.

- Have students review the Learning the Language of Literature and Active Reader pages, pp. 243–247. Ask them to note which skills and strategies they used while reading this selection.

Discussion Activities

- Use the questions formulated by the students in their Reader's Notebooks as the start of a discussion about this story.

- Ask students to consider what rituals in their lives might signal coming of age as the Ta-Na-E-Ka did for Mary and Roger.

Assessment Opportunities

- You can assess student comprehension of the story by evaluating the questions they formulate in their Reader's Notebook.

- You can use any of the discussion questions as essay questions.

- You can have students turn any one of their Reader's Notebook entries into an essay. Ask them to expand and clarify their ideas in the essay.

- You can have students write a summary of the selection.

waddling through some twigs. All of a sudden I realized I was no longer frightened. Ta-Na-E-Ka might be more fun than I'd anticipated. I got up and headed toward the marina.

"Not one boat," I said to myself dejectedly. But the restaurant on the shore, "Ernie's Riverside," was open. I walked in, feeling silly in my bathing suit. The man at the counter was big and tough-looking. He wore a sweatshirt with the words "Fort Sheridan, 1944," and he had only three fingers on one of his hands. He asked me what I wanted.

"A hamburger and a milkshake," I said, holding the five-dollar bill in my hand so he'd know I had money.

"That's a pretty heavy breakfast, honey," he murmured.

"That's what I always have for breakfast," I lied.

"Forty-five cents," he said, bringing me the food. (Back in 1947, hamburgers were twenty-five cents and milkshakes were twenty cents.) "Delicious," I thought. "Better'n grasshoppers—and Grandfather never once mentioned that I couldn't eat hamburgers."

While I was eating, I had a grand idea. Why not sleep in the restaurant? I went to the ladies room and made sure the window was unlocked. Then I went back outside and played along the riverbank, watching the water birds and trying to identify each one. I planned to look for a beaver dam the next day.

The restaurant closed at sunset, and I watched the three-fingered man drive away. Then I climbed in the unlocked window. There was a night light on, so I didn't turn on any lights. But there was a radio on the counter. I turned it on to a music program. It was warm in the restaurant, and I was hungry. I helped myself to a glass of milk and a piece of pie,

> I walked in, feeling silly in my bathing suit.

intending to keep a list of what I'd eaten so I could leave money. I also planned to get up early, sneak out through the window, and head for the woods before the three-fingered man returned. I turned off the radio, wrapped myself in the man's apron, and in spite of the hardness of the floor, fell asleep.

"What the heck are you doing here, kid?" It was the man's voice.

It was morning. I'd overslept. I was scared.

"Hold it, kid. I just wanna know what you're doing here. You lost? You must be from the reservation. Your folks must be worried sick about you. Do they have a phone?"

"Yes, yes," I answered. "But don't call them."

I was shivering. The man, who told me his name was Ernie, made me a cup of hot chocolate while I explained about Ta-Na-E-Ka.

"Darnedest thing I ever heard," he said, when I was through. "Lived next to the reservation all my life and this is the first I've heard of Ta-Na whatever-you-call-it." He looked at me, all goose bumps in my bathing suit. "Pretty silly thing to do to a kid," he muttered.

That was just what I'd been thinking for months, but when Ernie said it, I became angry. "No, it isn't silly. It's a custom of the Kaw. We've been doing this for hundreds of years. My mother and my grandfather and everybody in my family went through this ceremony. It's why the Kaw are great warriors."

"Okay, great warrior," Ernie chuckled, "suit yourself. And, if you want to stick around, it's okay with me." Ernie went to the broom closet and tossed me a bundle. "That's the lost-and-found closet," he said. "Stuff people left on boats. Maybe there's something to keep you warm."

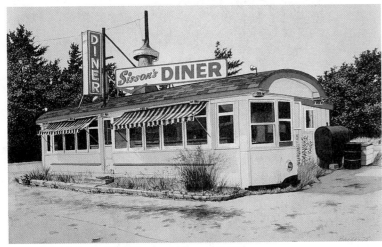

Sisson's Diner, John Baeder, 7⅝" x 11", watercolor on paper, © 1977.

The sweater fitted loosely, but it felt good. I felt good. And I'd found a new friend. Most important, I was surviving Ta-Na-E-Ka.

My grandfather had said the experience would be filled with adventure, and I was having my fill. And Grandfather had never said we couldn't accept hospitality.

I stayed at Ernie's Riverside for the entire period. In the mornings I went into the woods and watched the animals and picked flowers for each of the tables in Ernie's. I had never felt better. I was up early enough to watch the sun rise on the Missouri, and I went to bed after it set. I ate everything I wanted—insisting that Ernie take all my money for the food. "I'll keep this in trust for you, Mary," Ernie promised, "in case you are ever desperate for five dollars." (He did, too, but that's another story.)

I was sorry when the five days were over. I'd enjoyed every minute with Ernie. He taught me how to make Western omelets and to make Chili Ernie Style (still one of my favorite dishes). And I told Ernie all about the legends of the Kaw. I hadn't realized I knew so much about my people.

But Ta-Na-E-Ka was over, and as I approached my house, at about nine-thirty in the evening, I became nervous all over again. What if Grandfather asked me about the berries and the grasshoppers? And my feet were hardly cut. I hadn't lost a pound and my hair was combed.

"They'll be so happy to see me," I told myself hopefully, "that they won't ask too many questions."

I opened the door. My grandfather was in the front room. He was wearing the ceremonial beaded deerskin shirt which had belonged to *his* grandfather. "*N'g'da'ma,*" he said. "Welcome back."

I embraced my parents warmly, letting go only when I saw my cousin Roger sprawled on the couch. His eyes were red and swollen. He'd lost weight. His feet were an unsightly mass of blood and blisters, and he was moaning: "I made it, see. I made it. I'm a warrior. A warrior."

My grandfather looked at me strangely. I was clean, obviously well-fed, and radiantly healthy. My parents got the message. My uncle and aunt gazed at me with hostility.

Finally my grandfather asked, "What did you eat to keep you so well?"

I sucked in my breath and blurted out the truth: "Hamburgers and milkshakes."

"Hamburgers!" my grandfather growled.

"Milkshakes!" Roger moaned.

"You didn't say we *had* to eat grasshoppers," I said sheepishly.

"Tell us all about your Ta-Na-E-Ka," my grandfather commanded.

I told them everything, from borrowing the five dollars, to Ernie's kindness, to observing the beaver.

"That's not what I trained you for," my grandfather said sadly.

I stood up. "Grandfather, I learned that Ta-Na-E-Ka *is* important. I didn't think so during training. I was scared stiff of it. I handled it my way. And I learned I had nothing to be afraid of. There's no reason in 1947 to eat grasshoppers when you can eat a hamburger."

I was inwardly shocked at my own audacity. But I liked it. "Grandfather, I'll bet you never ate one of those rotten berries yourself."

Grandfather laughed! He laughed aloud! My mother and father and aunt and uncle were all dumbfounded. Grandfather never laughed. Never.

"Those berries—they are terrible," Grandfather admitted. "I could never swallow them. I found a dead deer on the first day of my Ta-Na-E-Ka—shot by a soldier, probably—and he kept my belly full for the entire period of the test!"

Grandfather stopped laughing. "We should send you out again," he said.

I looked at Roger. "You're pretty smart, Mary," Roger groaned. "I'd never have thought of what you did."

"Accountants just have to be good at arithmetic," I said comfortingly. "I'm terrible at arithmetic."

Roger tried to smile but couldn't. My grandfather called me to him. "You should have done what your cousin did. But I think you are more alert to what is happening to our people today than we are. I think you would have passed the test under any circumstances, in any time. Somehow, you know how to exist in a world that wasn't made for Indians. I don't think you're going to have any trouble surviving."

Grandfather wasn't entirely right. But I'll tell about that another time. ❖

Background: The Kaw Nation

Homeland Mary Whitebird is a member of the Kaw, or Kansa, Nation—a Native American group related to the Sioux. The names *Kaw* and *Kansa* both mean "people of the south wind." The original homeland of the Kansa was the plains of what is now Kansas. There they hunted buffalo and farmed. They lived in domed lodges made of wood, reeds, and earth.

Contact and Clash Because the Kansas and Missouri rivers were important means of transportation, the Kansa were among the first Native Americans of the plains to meet European explorers. In the early 1700s many Kansa began to die from smallpox carried by the Europeans. In the early 1800s the Kansa lost much of their land in treaties with the United States government. Later the government forced them onto a reservation in Oklahoma, where many of the nation's members live today.

SAGUARO

BY FRANK ASCH

Stand
still.
Grow
slow.
Lift
high
your arms to the sun.
Stand
still.
Grow
slow.
Lift
high
your
flowers to the sky.
Stand
still.
Grow
slow.
Hold
tight
your
water
inside.
Stand
still.
Grow
slow
and let your roots spread wide and let your roots spread wide.

Standards-Based Objectives

- write a 500- to 700-word character sketch
- use a written text as a model for writing
- revise a draft to add dialogue
- use possessive nouns and pronouns correctly
- deliver an oral presentation about a character sketch

Introducing the Workshop

Character Sketch Discuss with students some character sketches that they have read. Elicit from students the kinds of details that make a character sketch memorable. Have students talk about funny, unusual, or fascinating traits and anecdotes that add to a good character sketch. Point out that while it is fun to read about famous people, sometimes it is even more inspiring to read about everyday people who have done extraordinary things.

Basics in a Box

Using the Graphic Tell students that the elements that make up a character sketch blend together to create a vivid and complete portrait. All of the components are equally important. Just as the viewer of a sculpture walks around the piece to see it in its entirety, the reader of a character sketch needs to see as many facets of a person as possible.

Presenting the Rubric To better understand the assignment, students can refer to the Standards for Writing a Successful Character Sketch. You may also want to share with them the complete rubric, which describes several levels of proficiency.

 See **Unit Two Resource Book,** p. 68.

 For more instruction on essential writing skills, see McDougal Littell's *Language Network,* Chapters 10–17.

 Power Presentation

To engage students visually, use **Power Presentation 2,** Character Sketch.

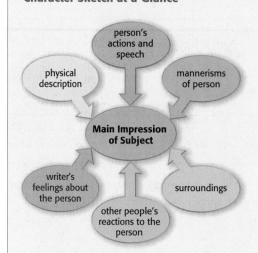

Writing Workshop — Character Sketch

Describing a character ...

From Reading to Writing A character sketch is a portrait of a person drawn in words. It describes what he or she is like, inside and out. In "The Circuit," Francisco Jiménez shows Panchito's life as a young migrant worker. In "Aaron's Gift," Myron Levoy draws the portrait of a caring and brave boy who risks his own safety to rescue a pigeon. A good **character sketch** describes the personality and the physical appearance of a person. The person may be a real person or a story character.

For Your Portfolio

WRITING PROMPT Write a character sketch of someone you know or admire.

Purpose: To help readers understand an individual's personality

Audience: Classmates, family, or general readers

Basics in a Box

Character Sketch at a Glance

- physical description
- person's actions and speech
- mannerisms of person
- writer's feelings about the person
- surroundings
- other people's reactions to the person
- **Main Impression of Subject**

RUBRIC STANDARDS FOR WRITING

A successful character sketch should

- present a vivid picture of the personality and physical appearance of the person
- give a main impression of the person
- include dialogue, mannerisms, descriptions and other devices that show, rather than tell, what the person is like
- reveal the writer's response to the person
- place the person in surroundings that help readers understand him or her
- have a clear structure, a strong beginning, and a strong conclusion

---

LESSON RESOURCES

USING PRINT RESOURCES
Unit Two Resource Book
- Prewriting, p. 60
- Drafting and Elaboration, p. 61
- Peer Response Guide, p. 62
- Revising Organization and Ideas, p. 63
- Revising, Editing, and Proofreading, p. 64
- Student Models, pp. 65–67
- Rubric for Evaluation, p. 68

Writing
- Dialogue, TR 24 (p. 302)

Reading and Critical Thinking
- Spider Map/Mind Map, TR 37 (p. 299)

Speaking and Listening
- Understanding Audience and Purpose, pp. 6–7 (p. 303)
- Developing and Delivering a Presentation, pp. 8–9, 12–13 (p. 303)

- Creating and Analyzing a Narrative Presentation, pp. 23–24 (p. 303)

INTEGRATED TECHNOLOGY

Writing Coach CD-ROM

Visit our Web site:
www.mcdougallittell.com

Analyzing a Student Model

SPEAKING OPPORTUNITY See the Speaking and Listening Handbook, p. R96 for oral presentation tips.

Tiffany George
Princess Anne Middle School

The Nurse: A Character Sketch

Grandma's friends call her "The Nurse" because she is always taking care of people. People come to her when they are not feeling well or when they need some support. She holds their hands and speaks softly to them, as though they were members of her own family. I know people are comforted by the warmth and strength in her green eyes, the way she leans in and listens, and the patience in her voice. There is a picture of her mother hanging in her house. She has the same high cheekbones and serious expression. Although she is in her seventies, Grandma has no wrinkles. She still looks young, even with all the responsibility on her shoulders. I know my grandfather appreciates everything she does, even if he cannot show it.

For seven years my grandmother has taken care of my grandfather—almost twenty-four hours a day, seven days a week. He is unable to take care of himself because he has Alzheimer's disease and recently suffered a stroke. Grandma felt that he needed more care than the nursing home could provide, so she decided to care for him herself. Because of this, she rarely gets to go to church anymore. If she needs to run an errand, she has to arrange for a relative to come and care for my grandfather or do the errand for her. She never leaves my grandfather alone.

Every morning, after she has had her cup of tea, Grandma makes my grandfather's bed and coaxes him to roll over so she can wash him up. "Rise and shine!" she announces as she opens the shutters to let the sun in. After that she helps him get ready for the day. She keeps him company when he eats his meals. Sometimes she just watches him. Often she will gently rub his back or smooth his hair.

RUBRIC IN ACTION

1 Attention-getting beginning describes an important characteristic and presents the thesis statement.

2 States important mannerisms using precise verbs, nouns, and adjectives

Other Option:
- Use a quotation to introduce main impression.

3 Presents person's physical appearance

4 Explains the person's situation

5 Writer includes specific details. She places the person in surroundings that show personality.

Teaching the Lesson

Analyzing the Model
The Nurse: A Character Sketch

The student model is a character sketch of the writer's grandmother. The writer lovingly calls her grandmother "the nurse" not because she is a real nurse, but because she provides care to so many people. The writer tells how her grandmother has devoted herself to caring for her husband, who has Alzheimer's disease. The writer describes a typical day in Grandma's life. The writer shows her affection and admiration by saying that even though they are the same height now, she still looks up to her grandmother.

Have a volunteer read the model aloud and discuss the Rubric in Action with students. Point out the key words and phrases in the student model that correspond to the elements mentioned in the Rubric in Action.

1/2 Ask why it is effective to begin with one of the character's important traits. What are three significant aspects of the character's personality mentioned in the first few sentences?

Possible Response: Readers can get a clear picture of the strength the person conveys. She speaks softly, is a good listener, and is patient.

3/4 Ask students to discuss the effect of the physical description and the explanation of the situation.

Possible Response: The physical description helps me to visualize the writer's grandmother and her actions; the explanation of the situation, the grandmother's life.

5 What details show her strength and warmth?

Possible Response: She speaks cheerfully despite her husband's illness; she thinks he needs more care than a nursing home can give.

EXPLICIT INSTRUCTION **Patterns of Organization**

PICTURING TEXT STRUCTURE

Instruction While vivid description and strong examples are critical to a successful character sketch, the structure—the way in which the ideas are organized—also plays a key role.

Practice Have students analyze the structure of the student model by making a diagram to show how the writer organized her character sketch. The following chart is an example.

Use **Reading and Critical Thinking Transparencies,** TR 37, for additional support.

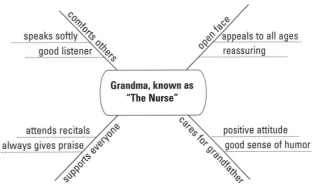

comforts others — speaks softly, good listener

open face — appeals to all ages, reassuring

Grandma, known as "The Nurse"

attends recitals, always gives praise — supports everyone

cares for grandfather — positive attitude, good sense of humor

6 Have students imagine this part of the character sketch without the dialogue. How would it be different?

Possible Response: If the writer just described what her grandmother said, instead of using dialogue, this part wouldn't have been as lively. The dialogue adds a bright, spontaneous element to the description. It helps me to imagine her grandmother talking.

7 Ask students to tell why the final details are important.

Possible Response: The final details tell more about the writer's relationship with her grandmother. Most of the character sketch tells about how her grandmother cares for others, especially for her grandfather, but the end shows how her grandmother expresses her love for the writer. It also shows how the writer feels toward her grandmother.

Sometimes, when he doesn't do what she tells him to do, she will good-naturedly say, "Stop, or I'll fetch the fly-swatter!" Then they share a laugh. She shakes all over and throws her head back when she laughs. Her laughter can fill a whole room.

Grandma makes people feel good just by being there for them. In the four years that I have been playing piano, she hasn't missed even one of my recitals. Whenever I've messed up, she says, "I didn't notice. It sounded good to me!" Grandma shows her whole family the same love and patience she shows my grandfather. She supports me so I show her respect. Even though I am as tall as she is now, about 5'3", I still look up to her!

> **6** Uses dialogue to show what the person is like

> **7** Ends with a detailed summary linked to the purpose of the sketch

Writing Your Character Sketch

❶ Prewriting

A writer should create living people.
—Ernest Hemingway, American writer

Write down the names of people you respect or admire. Consider family members, friends, teachers, neighbors, or others in your community. What makes them interesting? Is it how they look or act? Do they have an interesting past or unusual hobbies? Do they have a quirky habit or have they made a great accomplishment in their lives? What about someone who always makes you laugh or whom you know you can trust? See the **Idea Bank** in the margin for more suggestions.

Planning Your Character Sketch

1. **Choose your subject.** Look over your list of interesting people. Choose the one who stands out the most. This is your subject.

2. **Get to know your subject.** Collect details about how the person looks, dresses, talks, and moves. Then list characteristics such as talents, hobbies, likes, and dislikes. Also note how others react to your subject. If you don't know your subject, you may want to talk to others who do, or interview the person yourself. Use a chart like the one below to organize your information.

How subject looks	What subject says	What subject does	How others react

3. **Decide on a focus.** What qualities do you want to focus on? What is your main feeling about the person? What do you want your readers to know about him or her? Before you begin writing, focus on the two or three traits, or qualities, that best describe your subject.

4. **Choose a setting or situation for your subject.** Showing how your subject reacts in a situation can help show his or her personality. Which setting will best show how your subject acts around others? Which setting will reveal what your subject is really like?

❷ Drafting

Close your eyes for a minute and just think about your subject. What do you have to say about him or her? Start writing down your thoughts in any order. You don't have to make it sound perfect. Just get it all down on the page. Later on, you will develop an attention-getting introduction, a detailed body section, and a solid conclusion.

- **Show rather than tell.** Good writing doesn't just tell readers what's going on. It lets them see for themselves by including vivid details, incidents, and dialogue. For example, the narrator in "The Nurse" shows her grandmother's patience and devotion when she describes how her grandmother spends each day taking care of her grandfather.

IDEA Bank

1. Your Working Portfolio
Look for ideas in the **Writing** activities you completed earlier.

2. Changing Places
Think about people with whom you would like to switch places for a day or two. Choose as your subject the person you would most like to be.

3. Real-Life Characters
Make a list of your favorite characters from the works that you've read. Then think of people in real life who interest you for the same reasons. Choose the person most similar to a favorite character.

Have a question?

See the **Writing Handbook**
Using Language Effectively, p. R38
Descriptive Writing, p. R39
See **Language Network**
Building Compositions, p. 311

Ask Your Peer Reader

- How do you think I feel about this person?
- How would you describe the person's personality?
- What details help you picture the person?
- Was there anything that confused you about my essay?

Prewriting
Choosing a Subject
If after reading the Idea Bank students have difficulty choosing a subject for their character sketch, suggest that they try the following:

- List three people who you think are especially strong and confident. Write down examples of things they have done that illustrate their strength.
- Think about someone you know who has a job that you would like to do. Think about why that job seems appealing and why he or she is good at doing it.

Planning Your Character Sketch

1. Remind students that the person who stands out most may not necessarily be the one with the most exciting job but the one who, overall, has the most interesting or admirable personality.
2. After students have collected details about the person, suggest that they write a journal entry from that person's point of view.
3. Once students have chosen the two or three qualities that they will focus on, have them list two examples showing each of those traits.
4. Remind students to use dialogue to show how their subject acts in different situations.

Drafting
Suggest that students trade rough drafts with a partner. Have partners read each other's drafts and make suggestions for more dialogue, more vivid physical descriptions, clearer examples of character traits, and so on.

Revising
ADDING DIALOGUE

To help students locate places to insert dialogue, suggest that they look for a passage with a description that seems a little dull. Tell them that adding dialogue will make the subject of their character sketch appear more real to readers.

Use **Writing Transparencies,** p. 24, for additional support. Use **Unit Two Resource Book,** p. 63, to give students practice in improving the organization and consistency of ideas in their writing.

Editing and Proofreading
POSSESSIVE NOUNS AND PRONOUNS

Remind students to be careful not to confuse possessive pronouns with contractions. For example:

The soccer team played *its* last game.

It's a beautiful day for a picnic.

Explain that in the first sentence, *its* is a possessive pronoun, and it does not have an apostrophe. In the second sentence, *It's* is a contraction, which stands for *It is.*

Reflecting

Encourage students to think about what they learned about their subjects and whether they feel differently about a person as a result of writing a character sketch.

Option
TEACHING TIP

Suggest that each student prepare a copy of their character sketch for the person who is the subject of the writing. Encourage students to make the copies especially neat, place each in a folder, and make a date to present it to the person about whom it was written.

Need revising help?

Review the **Rubric,** p. 298

Consider **peer reader** comments

Check **Revision Guidelines,** p. R31

See **Language Network** Punctuating Quotations, p. 214

SPELLING From Writing

As you revise your work, look back at the words you misspelled and determine why you made the errors you did. For additional help, refer to the strategies and generalizations in the **Spelling Handbook** on page R26.

Puzzled by the possessive form?

See the **Grammar Handbook** Using Nouns and Pronouns, p. R71

SPEAKING Opportunity

Turn your sketch into an oral presentation.

Publishing IDEAS

- Create a photo essay by gathering pictures that show a person's character traits. Write captions for each photo.
- Collect slides and rewrite your sketch as narration for a slide show.

(●) INTERNET

Publishing Options www.mcdougallittell.com

- **Remember your focus** A good character sketch gives a picture of a person that is so complete that readers can predict how she or he would behave in other situations. As you write, ask yourself, "Will this help the reader better understand my subject?"

❸ Revising

TARGET SKILL ▶ **ADDING DIALOGUE** Reading the exact words that a person says can tell you a lot about his or her personality. As you revise your character sketch, look for places where you can add dialogue. For example, if you are trying to show that the person has a great sense of humor, quote something funny that the person said.

Sometimes when he doesn't do what she tells him to do, she will good-naturedly ~~tell him to stop.~~

say, "Stop, or I'll fetch the fly swatter!"

❹ Editing and Proofreading

TARGET SKILL ▶ **POSSESSIVE NOUNS AND PRONOUNS** Possessive nouns show who or what owns something. For most singular possessive nouns, place the apostrophe before the *s,* as in *one boy's book.* For plural nouns that end in the letter *s,* place the apostrophe after the *s,* as in *all of the girls' pictures.* Possessive pronouns, such as *my, mine, his, her,* and *our,* do not have apostrophes.

Every morning, after she has had her cup of tea, Grandma makes my grandfather's bed and coaxes him to roll over so she can wash him up.

❺ Reflecting

FOR YOUR WORKING PORTFOLIO If your character sketch is about someone you didn't know, what surprising thing did you learn about the person while doing this assignment? What other people would you like to sketch? Why? Attach your answers to your finished character sketch. Save your character sketch in your **Working Portfolio.**

EXPLICIT INSTRUCTION Revision

ORGANIZATION

Instruction Remind students that a well-chosen piece of dialogue can sometimes reveal a character's personality more quickly and more accurately than an entire paragraph of description. Discuss the difference between writing that a person is selfish and quoting that person as saying, "What's mine is mine. What's yours is mine. My needs are more important than anyone else's."

Practice Ask students to look at their character sketches for places where they can add dialogue to bring their writing to life. Have them circle the quotations they already use, and have them add at least three new quotations to their papers.

RUBRIC

3 Full Accomplishment Student uses several quotations that reflect the personality of a character and has added three additional quotations.

2 Substantial Accomplishment Student uses a few quotations to demonstrate the personality of a character and has added another one or two.

1 Little or Partial Accomplishment Student neglects to use quotations to demonstrate the personality of a character.

See the **Research and Technology Handbook,** pp. R108-109, for information about formatting documents using word processing skills.

Standardized Test Practice

Mixed Review

Often a character I'm reading about reminds me of someone I know. My aunt Bessie reminds me of mama (1) in "Oh Broom, Get to Work." Because she is hospitable. (2) Her house is a true home. She always welcome (3) visitors to her house. Even if my Grandpa Joe and Cousin Sal arrives (4) at an inconvenient time she always ask (5) them to sit down and have some refreshments. When she invites guests over, she cooks. their favorite foods. (6) Aunt Bessies (7) favorite saying is, "Happiness is doubled when you share what you have."

1. How is sentence 1 best written?
   - A. My Aunt Bessie reminds me of Mama
   - B. My Aunt Bessie reminds me of mama
   - C. My aunt Bessie reminds me of Mama
   - D. Correct as is
2. How is sentence 2 best written?
   - A. She is hospitable.
   - B. Bessie is hospitable.
   - C. Because Bessie is hospitable.
   - D. Correct as is
3. How is sentence 3 best written?
   - A. She always will welcome
   - B. She always welcoming
   - C. She always welcomes
   - D. Correct as is
4. How is item 4 best written?
   - A. Grandpa Joe and Cousin Sal is arriving
   - B. Grandpa Joe and Cousin Sal arrive
   - C. Grandpa Joe and Cousin Sal are arriving
   - D. Correct as is
5. How is item 5 best written?
   - A. she always asked
   - B. she always did ask
   - C. she always asks
   - D. Correct as is
6. How is item 6 best written?
   - A. When she invites guests over, She cooks their favorite foods.
   - B. When she invites guests. Over she cooks their favorite foods.
   - C. When she invites guests over, she cooks their favorite foods.
   - D. Correct as is
7. What is the correct possessive form in sentence 7?
   - A. Aunt Bessie's
   - B. Aunt Bessies'
   - C. Aunt Bessie's'
   - D. Correct as is

Review Your Skills

Use the passage and the questions that follow it to check how well you remember the language conventions you've learned in previous grades.

Self-Assessment

Check your own answers in the **Grammar Handbook.**

Quick Reference: Capitalization, p. R66

Writing Complete Sentences, p. R67

Making Subjects and Verbs Agree, p. R68

Standardized Test Practice

Demonstrate how students can eliminate incorrect choices for the first question.

A. This choice is correct because *Aunt* and *Mama* are capitalized.

B. This choice is incorrect because Mama is not capitalized.

C. This choice is incorrect because *aunt* is not capitalized.

D. The original version is incorrect because neither *aunt* nor *mama* is capitalized.

Answers:
1. A, **2.** A, **3.** C, **4.** B, **5.** C, **6.** C, **7.** A

EXPLICIT INSTRUCTION Speaking Opportunity

Prepare Once students have written their character sketch, they can plan to present it to an audience. Refer students to pages R102-103 of the Speaking and Listening Handbook at the back of this book for tips on presenting their character sketch.

Present Have students present their character sketches to the class. They should strive to portray an interesting character through the use of narrative devices such as dialogue, suspense, or description.

RUBRIC

3 Full Accomplishment Student presents a vivid picture, including dialogue and descriptions of actions that show rather than tell about the person. Student indicates his or her reaction to the person being written about.

2 Substantial Accomplishment Student presents enough details for the reader to get an impression of the person. Student indicates his or her reaction to the person being written about.

1 Little or Partial Accomplishment Student gives a somewhat sketchy account of the person and does not include many details. Student does not explain why this person is important to him or her.

Use **Speaking and Listening Book,** pp. 6–9, 12–13, 23–24, for additional support in presenting a character sketch.

Standards-Based Objectives
- reflect on unit themes
- determine a text's main or major ideas
- connect, compare, and contrast ideas, themes, and issues across texts
- review literary analysis skills used in the unit
- assess and build portfolios

Reflecting on Theme

Option 1
A successful response will
- identify qualities that show growth or maturity in the characters in this unit
- evaluate the growth of four characters
- include productive spoken interaction with a partner

Option 2
A successful response will
- analyze the selections in the unit according to their adaptability to a television format
- develop a proposal presenting the selections in terms of the growth and change of the characters
- paraphrase and summarize text to recall, inform, or organize ideas
- support choices with logical reasoning

Option 3
A successful response will
- relate the chosen selections with the theme of each part of the unit and with the overall unit theme
- give appropriate reasons for opinions given
- present ideas in clear and grammatically correct prose

Self Assessment
Students should demonstrate active assessment of their work on a chosen option. They should be able to connect their own experiences with the possible experiences of others. Extend the activity by having students present their responses orally.

Growth and Change

The selections in this unit are about growth and change in people, in society, and in the natural world. On the basis of your reading, what do you think causes growth and change? How do growth and change make people feel? Explore these questions by completing one or more of the options in each of the following sections.

Reflecting on Theme

OPTION 1

Evaluating Growth What qualities do you think are signs of growth in a person? Make a list of the qualities shown by characters in this unit, as well as other qualities that you think are signs of growth or maturity. Use the list to evaluate four of the characters. In your opinion, which character grows the most as events unfold? Discuss your choice with a partner.

OPTION 2

Producing a Proposal Pretend that your class is a TV production company. Your job is to produce a series of hour-long shows called "Growth and Change," aimed at viewers your age. With two classmates, decide which selections in the unit would make the best television programs. Write a proposal in which you summarize the selections and give reasons for your choices.

OPTION 3

Relating to the Theme Choose one selection from each part of the unit. Write a paragraph about each selection, telling how it illustrates the theme of the part in which it appears—"The Need to Belong" or "Home and Heritage." Be sure to support your ideas with examples from the selection. Then write another paragraph about each selection, telling how it relates to the unit theme "Growth and Change."

Self ASSESSMENT

📖 **READER'S NOTEBOOK**

Imagine that another class is about to try the activities at the left. Write a brief note recommending the activity you chose. Explain what completing the activity revealed to you about the theme "Growth and Change." What might the other class want to do differently from the way you did it?

REVIEWING YOUR PERSONAL WORD List

Vocabulary Review the new words you learned in this unit. If necessary, use a dictionary to check the meaning of each word.

Spelling Review your list of spelling words. If you're not sure of the correct spelling, use a dictionary or refer to the **Spelling Handbook** on page R26.

Reviewing Literary Concepts

OPTION 1

Thinking About Figurative Language Many writers of stories and poems use figurative language to convey meaning and vivid images to readers. Make a list of the titles of this unit's selections. Next to each title, record examples of figurative language or sensory details that you thought were particularly effective. Then circle titles of selections you liked best.

OPTION 2

Analyzing a Character Choose one character from each selection in this unit (except for poems). Then use a chart like the one below to show the character's traits. Which character do you think you came to know best? Explain your choice.

Portfolio Building

- **Choices and Challenges—Writing** A few of the writing assignments in this unit were invitations to write poems. From your responses, choose the one in which you feel you expressed yourself the best. Write a note explaining the reasons for your choice. Then attach the note to the poem and place it in your **Presentation Portfolio.**

- **Writing Workshops** In this unit you wrote a poem. You also wrote a character sketch. Reread these two pieces and decide which you think shows a better use of vivid language and sensory details. Write a cover note explaining the reasons for your choice, attach it to the piece, and place it in your **Presentation Portfolio.**

- **Additional Activities** Think back to the assignments you completed for **Speaking & Listening** and **Research & Technology.** Keep a record in your portfolio of any assignments that you especially enjoyed, found helpful, or would like to do further work on.

Self ASSESSMENT

 **READER'S NOTEBOOK**

On a sheet of paper, copy the following literary terms introduced in this unit. Next to each term, jot down a brief definition. If you don't understand a term very well, refer to the **Glossary of Literary and Reading Terms** on page R116.

figurative
 language
simile
metaphor
science
 fiction
haiku
free verse

character traits
dialogue
description
point of view
rhyme
rhythm
repetition

Self ASSESSMENT

At this point, you should have several pieces in your portfolio. Consider the different types of writing that are represented. What other types of writing do you want to add to your portfolio?

Setting GOALS

What one problem are you having with reading or writing that you would like to work on? What will you do to improve in this area? Write your answers on a sheet of colored paper. Use it as a reminder while you are working on the next unit.

Reviewing Literary Concepts

Option 1

A successful response will
- list the titles of the unit completely and correctly
- determine and record examples of figurative or sensory details
- indicate which selections the student liked best

Option 2

Use the Unit Two Resource Book, page 69, to provide students a ready-made, full-depth chart for recording and analyzing character traits.

Portfolio Building

Students should evaluate the items in their Working Portfolios and choose pieces that represent their highest quality work for their Presentation Portfolios.

Before students write their notes, remind them that they will be reviewing their notes months from now. They should indicate their reasons clearly so that they will be able to understand them when reviewing them in the future.

Self Assessment and Setting Goals

Point out to students that part of the process of building any kind of portfolio is checking to ensure its breadth and depth of coverage. An assessment activity of this type helps to monitor the variety of materials in the portfolio.

Give the following examples of problems students may be having: visualizing as they read; pausing or rereading to clarify; making active predictions as they read; keeping structures in their writing parallel; using appropriate verb tenses.

LITERATURE CONNECTIONS
Dragonwings

BY LAURENCE YEP

In this historical novel about the risks of growth and change, a young Chinese immigrant comes to San Francisco to join his father. Father and son encounter prejudice and danger and meet new friends. Along with relatives already settled in Chinatown, they learn how to preserve heritage while pursuing long-held dreams. Laurence Yep draws on historical documents from the early 1900s in this Newbery Honor Book.

These thematically related readings are provided along with *Dragonwings:*

The Flying Machine
BY RAY BRADBURY

"The Chinese Must Go"
BY BERNARD A. WEISBERGER

Crazy Boys
BY BEVERLY McLOUGHLAND

Ginger for the Heart
BY PAUL YEE

The Skydivers
BY JOSEPH COLIN MURPHY

The Story of an Eyewitness
BY JACK LONDON

More Choices

Charlie Pippin
BY CANDY DAWSON BOYD
Eleven-year-old Chartrueuse (Charlie for short), an African American child, learns the importance of making peace within his family.

The Great Gilly Hopkins
BY KATHERINE PATERSON
Gilly Hopkins, a troubled foster child used to fighting her own battles, never thought she would find a real family. When she does, she discovers what true strength is.

Homesick: My Own Story
BY JEAN FRITZ
Jean, an American child, shares her memories about growing up in China.

Sarah, Plain and Tall
BY PATRICIA MacLACHLAN
Sarah has always lived by the sea, but she gives up her home for a new life as a mother on the prairie.

On the Banks of Plum Creek
BY LAURA INGALLS WILDER
The Ingalls family faces adversity in their dugout home on the banks of Plum Creek in Minnesota. Laura, her parents, and her sisters weather blizzards, grasshopper plagues, and leeches in this ongoing tale of strength and courage.

Roll of Thunder, Hear My Cry

BY MILDRED D. TAYLOR

Set in Mississippi during the Great Depression, Mildred Taylor's novel describes the members of the Logan family and their relationships with the land, their neighbors, and each other. When disturbing actions threaten their close-knit family, the Logans draw together in a fight to keep their 400-acre cotton farm.

These thematically related readings are provided along with *Roll of Thunder, Hear My Cry*:

from **Growing Up in the Great Depression**
BY RICHARD WORMSER

Depression
BY ISABEL JOSHLIN GLASER

The Stolen Party
BY LILIANA HEKER
TRANSLATED BY ALBERTO MANGUEL

from **Black Women in White America**
BY GERDA LERNER

Incident
BY COUNTEE CULLEN

Equal Opportunity
BY JIM WONG-CHU

The Clearing
BY JESSE STUART

The Five-Dollar Dive
BY YVONNE NELSON-PERRY

Social Studies Connection

The Crest and the Hide and Other African Stories
BY HAROLD COURLANDER
Each short story describes a brave and important act by a noble African man.

The Egyptian Cinderella
BY SHIRLEY CLIMO
In this Egyptian version of the classic tale, young Rhodopis's world changes when she meets a handsome pharaoh.

Mara, Daughter of the Nile
BY ELOISE JARVIS MCGRAW
Life around 1550 B.C. can be difficult. Follow the trials and tribulations of 17-year-old Mara, an Egyptian slave girl.

Nefertiti: The Mystery Queen
BY BURNHAM HOLMES
Accompanied by illustrations, this tale recounts Nefertiti's changing life from the queen's own point of view.

Mother Crocodile: An Uncle Amadou Tale from Senegal
BY ROSA GUY
In this fable, Mother Crocodile's children learn to use her folk tales and wise stories to get out of trouble.

The Standardized Test Practice feature provides practice in taking standardized tests. As students work through this lesson, they will learn strategies for reading comprehension questions, multiple-choice questions, and essay and short-answer questions. Boxed strategies located alongside the text will help guide students through the activities. These strategies model processes students can use as they take standardized tests.

STANDARDS-BASED OBJECTIVES

- understand and apply strategies for reading a test selection
- recognize literary techniques in a test selection
- understand and apply strategies for answering multiple-choice questions about a test selection
- respond to a writing prompt and present ideas in a logical order
- understand and apply strategies for revising and proofreading a test response

Standardized Test Practice

Reading and Writing for Assessment

Throughout middle school, you will be tested on your ability to read and understand many different kinds of reading selections. The following pages will give you test-taking strategies. Practice applying these strategies by working through the following models.

PART 1 **How to Read the Test Selection**

In many tests, you will read a passage and then answer multiple-choice questions. Applying the following basic test-taking strategies can help you focus on the right information.

STRATEGIES FOR READING A TEST SELECTION

▸ **Before you begin reading, skim the questions that follow the passage.** These can help focus your reading.

▸ **Use active reading strategies such as analyzing, predicting, and questioning.** Make notes in the margin only if the test directions allow you to mark on the test itself.

▸ **Think about the title, the message, and the theme.** What does the title suggest about the overall selection? What larger lesson can you draw from the passage?

▸ **Look for main ideas.** These are often stated at the beginning or end of paragraphs. Sometimes they are implied, not stated. After reading each paragraph, ask, What was this passage about?

▸ **Examine the sequence of ideas.** Are the ideas developed in chronological order, order of importance, or in some other way?

▸ **Evaluate literary elements and techniques used by the writer.** How well does the writer use tone (writer's attitude toward the subject), point of view, figurative language, or other elements to create a certain effect or to get the message across?

▸ **Unlock word meanings.** Use context clues and word parts to help you unlock the meaning of unfamiliar words.

Reading Selection

❶ Why Don't They Roam?
by Patricia Akhimie

1   Have you ever seen a buffalo? Maybe you've seen one in a zoo or on the back of an old nickel. Only a few hundred years ago it was not uncommon for the American plains to turn to ❷ black seas with the millions of moving heads of the buffalo herds. Now, it is unusual to see many buffalo. What led to the decrease in population?

2   With a thick woolly hide, humped back, and curved horns, the buffalo is hard to mistake for any other animal. However, the North American buffalo is not really a buffalo at all! The true name of the American buffalo is "bison." Some believe bison are called buffalo because the name French explorers gave the animals—"boeufs" (buhf) for their resemblance to cattle—was mispronounced by English settlers as "buffalo."

3   The prehistoric ancestors of the modern buffalo came to North America from Asia about 200,000 years ago during the last ice age. At that time there was a land bridge between Asia and what is now Alaska. ❸ These buffalo evolved in the new climate and multiplied to number in the millions, roaming in herds over the plains.

4   The herds were hunted by nomadic Native Americans, who revered and honored the animal. Every part of the buffalo was valuable to them. They used buffalo skin, horns, and bones in everyday life. Almost all of the buffalo could be eaten as food, or made into clothes or tools.

5   Native American hunting did not hurt the buffalo population, which numbered in the tens of millions. However, with the arrival of the first Europeans in the 1500s things began to change. Spanish explorers introduced horses. By the 1800s horses were being used by the Native Americans to chase or quickly corner the buffalo. Soon guns replaced the bow and arrow, creating a much deadlier hunter.

6   ❹ The number of buffalo began to fall as the number of hunters began to rise. White settlers continued to arrive throughout the 1800s. Fur traders and trappers found a

---

❶ Think about the title.

ONE STUDENT'S THOUGHTS

"I wonder who 'they' are. Maybe they're animals, because people don't usually roam."

---

❷ Evaluate the effectiveness of figurative language.

"The writer compares herds of buffalo to black seas. It creates an impression in the reader's mind."

YOUR TURN
Determine the writer's purpose.

---

❸ Look for main ideas.

"It's amazing that there were so many buffalo once. What happened to them?"

YOUR TURN
Find one or two other key ideas in this selection.

---

❹ Read actively by asking questions.

"How were the Native Americans affected when so many buffalo were killed?"

Begin by previewing the text. Then read through the multiple-choice questions on page 311. As you read each question, ask students what they will need to look for as they read.

1 Students might recognize the title as coming from the old song "Home on the Range," in particular the lyrics, "O, give me a home, where the buffalo roam . . .'"

2 Discuss ways in which the buffalo were like a black sea: they seemed to roll like waves and go on forever.

YOUR TURN By using this image, the writer is able to show how immense the buffalo herds were. This helps the reader understand the magnitude of the destruction of this natural resource.

3 To help students understand what the main idea is, read these examples and ask students if they are main ideas or not: A picture of the buffalo used to appear on the nickel (no); the arrival of the Europeans signaled a change in the fate of the buffalo herds (yes); in 1872, President Grant created Yellowstone Park (no).

YOUR TURN At one time, there were millions of buffalo; now there are only a few thousand. Native Americans hunted the buffalo and used every bit of the animal. Legislators and researchers have taken action to increase the number of buffalo.

4 Ask students to formulate other questions such as: Why were the carcasses left to rot? What did the Native Americans use to replace the buffalo as food? What else is being done today to protect buffalo?

5 Remind students that sometimes they will encounter words they do not understand in the text. First they should determine whether the word is important to understanding the selection. If not, they may not need to spend time determining its meaning. However, if it relates to a key event or idea in the selection, they should take a few minutes to apply their reading strategies to decipher it:

- Look at the surrounding words and sentences for context clues, such as examples, restatement, and definitions.
- Use word parts such as prefixes, suffixes, and roots to determine the meaning of the word.
- Try out different meanings for the word in the sentence. If the meaning is still not clear, make a prediction, then read on to see if there are more clues later in the selection.

6 Other words that convey the writer's tone are *revered, shocking, did a lot of damage,* and *"civilized"* (the quotation marks suggest irony).

YOUR TURN The writer talks about the enormous effort that was needed to preserve the buffalo at all.

7 Point out that skimming the questions before they read will help students find the information they need to answer the questions later on.

YOUR TURN The writer mentions Native Americans' hunting as a contrast to the wasteful ways in which white settlers used the buffalo, almost causing its extinction.

Check Your Understanding

Have students use the following questions to test their understanding of the selection before they answer the questions in their texts.

- What is the topic of the selection?
- What is the writer's attitude toward the subject?
- For what purpose did the author probably write the selection?
- Did the selection answer all your questions about the subject? If not, what questions remain unanswered?

good business in selling buffalo meat and hides.

7   Train companies also did a lot of damage. The demand for buffalo products, like fur coats and decorative horns, increased. The railroads promoted shooting buffalo for sport from the windows of the moving train. What is perhaps more shocking is that most of the ❺ carcasses were not eaten, but instead left behind to rot.

8   By the 1860s buffalo hunting had become popular. The famous "Buffalo Bill" Cody killed over four thousand in two years. The destruction of the buffalo was considered a way to hurt Native Americans who still fought with the settlers. Killing the buffalo would take away their source of food and way of life. The settlers thought this would force the Native Americans to become "civilized."

9   Only a few thousand buffalo remained by 1880, but they were still hunted. In 1872, the United States Congress had created Yellowstone, the world's first national park, to preserve America's scenery and wildlife. However, the herds continued to decline, because poachers snuck into the park and shot them. In 1894, there were only twenty buffalo in all of Yellowstone!

10   Shocked by the ❻ tragic drop in numbers, Congress passed a law against poaching in 1902, but the buffalo herd remained small. Through the efforts of some important animal researchers, buffaloes from ranches and zoos were sent to Yellowstone to increase the herds, and to establish other wild herds on protected land.

11   Today there are over two thousand American bison in Yellowstone, with other smaller herds across the country. The buffalo very nearly became extinct in a short period of time. From the loss of so many great animals, we should learn a lesson not to abuse nature's resources.

❺ **Use context clues to understand vocabulary.**

"It seems like *carcasses* means the dead bodies of the buffalo."

❻ **Look for examples of tone.**

"Words like *tragic* show the attitude of the writer toward the subject."

YOUR TURN
How else does the writer get her point across?

❼ **Skim the questions that follow the passage.**

"There was a question about what led to the killing off of the buffalo. The selection mentions hunting by Native Americans and white settlers, as well as damage from railroad expansion."

YOUR TURN
Why does the writer mention Native Americans' hunting if it didn't harm the population?

How to Answer Multiple-Choice Questions

Use the strategies and notes in the side column to help you answer the questions below and on the following pages.

Based on the selection you have just read, choose the best answer for each of the following questions.

1. Why does the writer include statistics?

   A. Research reports are supposed to include statistics.

   B. to support her statement that the buffalo almost became extinct

   C. to show that the land could not support the herds

   D. to convince the reader that she is telling the truth

2. In paragraph 7, why does the writer say that the fact that the carcasses were not eaten is more shocking than the way the buffalo were killed?

   A. She thinks the killing was pointless.

   B. She thinks it was a hazard to the environment.

   C. She does not believe in killing animals of any kind.

   D. She thinks people should have eaten the buffalo.

3. According to the writer, what did a lot of damage to the buffalo population?

   A. the land bridge

   B. famine

   C. disease

   D. train companies

4. What seems to be the writer's attitude toward the buffalo?

   A. She doesn't feel strongly about the buffalo.

   B. She respects the buffalo and wants to protect it.

   C. She thinks it is fair to kill animals for any reason.

   D. She feels the buffalo were a nuisance to begin with.

5. How does the title of the article relate to the article's theme?

   A. It does not relate to the theme.

   B. It refers to the population decrease of the Native Americans on the open plains.

   C. It refers to the settlers who built their houses on the open plains.

   D. It raises the question of what happened to the buffalo.

STRATEGIES FOR ANSWERING MULTIPLE-CHOICE QUESTIONS

▸ **Ask questions** that help you eliminate some of the choices.

▸ **Pay attention** to choices such as "all of the above" or "none of the above." To eliminate them, all you need to find is one answer that doesn't fit.

▸ **Skim your notes.** Details you noticed as you read may provide answers.

STRATEGIES IN ACTION

↓

Skim your notes.

ONE STUDENT'S THOUGHTS

"She doesn't mention disease. I can eliminate choice *C*."

YOUR TURN

What other choices can you eliminate?

Ask questions. *What makes sense in the real world?*

"She might have been talking about the Native American population but one usually uses the word *roam* to refer to animals, especially buffalo. I can eliminate choice *B*."

YOUR TURN

Which other choice doesn't make sense?

Multiple-Choice Questions

1. B
2. A
3. D

YOUR TURN Choice A can be eliminated because the selection says the land bridge was the way the buffalo got to America; Choice B can be eliminated because the author does not mention famine. That leaves Choice D, the correct option.

4. B
5. D

YOUR TURN She might mean the settlers, but the title asks why they *don't* roam. The settlers were people who came from other areas—roamed—to find new land. So option C can be eliminated.

Short-Answer Question

The writer wants to persuade people to respect nature's resources, not abuse them. She does so by using the near-extinction of the buffalo as an example.

YOUR TURN The writer's tone is one clue that she wants to persuade people to respect nature. She is appalled at the way the buffalo was nearly brought to extinction by the carelessness of white settlers.

Essay Question

When tens of millions of buffalo roamed the plains, the Native Americans who lived there were never at a loss for food. They hunted the massive animals, using hide, horns, bones, and meat for food, clothes, tools, and other necessities. Because they killed only as many as they needed, the buffalo herds did not decline. It was this way for thousands of years.

When Europeans reached America, things changed. They also hunted the buffalo for meat, hides, and other products, but in such huge numbers that the herds began to dwindle. This meant that the Native Americans could no longer pursue their own way of life. Buffalo became scarce, and Native Americans had to compete with white hunters. Without their traditional source of food and skins, the Native Americans' way of life changed forever.

YOUR TURN The main points are the decline of the buffalo herd and the reasons for this decline, as well as the fact that without the buffalo, the Native Americans could no longer live the way they had lived for centuries.

PART 3 **How to Respond in Writing**

You may be asked to write answers to questions about a reading passage. **Short-answer questions** often ask you to answer in a sentence or two. **Essay questions** require a fully developed piece of writing.

Short-Answer Question

STRATEGIES FOR RESPONDING TO SHORT-ANSWER QUESTIONS

▸ **Identify key words** in the writing prompt that tell you the ideas to discuss. Make sure you know what each word means.
▸ **State your response directly** and to the point.
▸ **Support your ideas** using evidence from the selection.
▸ **Use correct grammar.**

Sample Question

Answer the following question in one or two sentences.

Explain what you think the writer's purpose was in researching and reporting on the history of the buffalo.

Essay Question

STRATEGIES FOR ANSWERING ESSAY QUESTIONS

▸ **Look for direction words** in the writing prompt such as *essay, analyze, describe,* or *compare and contrast.*
▸ **List the points** you want to make before beginning to write.
▸ **Write an introduction** that presents your main point.
▸ **Develop your ideas** by using evidence from the selection.
▸ **Write a conclusion** that summarizes your points.
▸ **Check your work for correct grammar.**

Sample Prompt

Write an essay in which you explain how the killing of so many buffalo affected the Native Americans' way of life.

STRATEGIES IN ACTION

Identify Key Words

ONE STUDENT'S THOUGHTS

"The key words are *explain* and *purpose.* This means that I'll have to decide why the writer wrote the article and tell why I think that way."

YOUR TURN
What clues to the writer's purpose can you find in the selection?

Look for Direction Words

ONE STUDENT'S THOUGHTS

"The important words are *essay* and *explain.* This means I'll have to create a fully developed piece of writing that explains the connections between things."

YOUR TURN
What are the main points you will need to cover?

PART 4

How to Revise, Edit, and Proofread a Test Response

Here is a student's first draft in response to the essay prompt at the bottom of page 312. Read and answer the multiple-choice questions that follow.

1	The Native Americans centered their lives around the
2	buffalo. The decline in the buffalo population hurt the
3	Native Americans.
4	Tribes might have had to travel and look elsewhere for
5	food. Because of this, they would not be able easily to
6	defend themselves and their land against them.

STRATEGIES FOR REVISING, EDITING, AND PROOFREADING

▶ **Read the passage carefully.**
▶ **Note the parts that are confusing** or don't make sense. What kinds of errors do they signal?
▶ **Look for errors** in grammar, usage, spelling, and capitalization. Common errors include:
  • run-on sentences
  • sentence fragments
  • lack of subject-verb agreement
  • lack of transition words

1. What is the BEST way to combine the sentences in lines 1-3 ("The Native Americans . . . the Native Americans.")?

   A. Because Americans centered their lives around the buffalo, the declining buffalo population hurt them.

   B. Since the Native Americans centered their lives around the buffalo, but the declining population hurt them.

   C. Even though the Native Americans centered their lives around the buffalo, the declining population hurt them.

   D. Make no change.

2. The BEST way to make the connection between paragraphs clear would be to add which of the following words to the beginning of line 4 ("Tribes might have . . .")?

   A. However,

   B. For example,

   C. In conclusion,

   D. Make no change.

3. What is the BEST change, if any, to the sentence in lines 5 and 6 ("Because of this . . . against them.")?

   A. Because of this, the white settlers would not be able easily to defend themselves and their land against the Native Americans.

   B. Because of this, they would not be able easily to defend themselves and their land against the white settlers.

   C. Because of this, they would not be able easily to defend themselves and their land against the Native Americans.

   D. Make no change.

Answers
1. A
2. B
3. B

Check Your Understanding
Have students reread their own response to the short-answer and essay questions. Then have them use the following questions to guide them as they revise and edit their own work.

• Have I responded directly to the direction words in the writing prompt?
• Have I presented the points I wanted to make?
• Have I begun with an interesting introduction?
• Have I supported my ideas with evidence from the selection?
• Have I presented my ideas in a logical order?
• Have I written a conclusion that summarizes my points?
• Have I used correct grammar?

A Sense of Fairness

The selections in Unit Three present characters, both real and fictional, who have had to come to terms with unfair situations. The unit is divided into two parts: Part 1, "Between Friends," and Part 2, "Breaking Barriers." Selections in both parts contribute to the unit theme by presenting the many ways in which people fight to bring a sense of fairness to the world.

—————— Part 1 ——————

Between Friends The selections in Part 1 focus on how friendship often helps people move past an argument or quarrel. A good strong friendship can also serve as a buffer to the hardships and unfair situations presented by life. In *Damon and Pythias,* a remarkable friendship sends out ripples felt throughout an entire kingdom.

—————— Part 2 ——————

Breaking Barriers Part 2 further develops the theme of fairness in the larger world. How do we overcome the barriers each of us must face? An African prince struggles against the unfairness of slavery in America in "Abd al-Rahman Ibrahima." In "from *The Story of My Life,*" readers meet Helen Keller—blind, deaf, and unable to speak—who went on to become one of the most memorable achievers of her century.

UNIT THREE

A Sense of Fairness

We

must

move

past

indecision

to

action.

Dr. Martin Luther King, Jr.

American civil-rights leader

314

EXPLICIT INSTRUCTION Viewing and Representing

Pushball
by Pavel Varfolomeevic Kusnezov

ART APPRECIATION

Instruction Pushball is a game in which two opposing teams attempt to push a heavy ball—which is 6 feet in diameter—across a goal. Explain that the painter has used brush strokes that give the painting a sense of movement. The colors form a halo around the ball, as if to indicate movement. There is also a sense of looseness and movement in the figures of the players themselves.

Practice Ask, "Why would a painting showing a competitive game be a good illustration for a unit named 'A Sense of Fairness'"?

Possible Responses: When you play games, it is important that everyone plays fairly and follows the rules. It might also mean that people need to work together and rely on teamwork to make the world a fairer place.

Pushball, Pavel Kusnetzov, Tretiakov Gallery, Moscow, Russia/Superstock. Copyright © Estate of Pavel Kusnetzov/Licensed by VAGA, New York, NY.

315

To help students explore the connections between the art, the quotation, and the unit theme, have them consider the following questions:

Ask: What do you think Dr. Martin Luther King, Jr. means in this quotation?

Possible Response: He may mean that it's not enough to just say that something is unfair. It's important to do something about it.

Ask: How would you define "A Sense of Fairness"?

Possible Response: Students may say that a sense of fairness is the idea that everybody should have a fair chance and an equal opportunity.

Ask: What do you think the people in the picture are doing, and how does it relate to a sense of fairness?

Possible Response: The people seem to be trying to lift a large, round, heavy object—possibly a symbol for the world. If each person does her or his fair share, the task can be done. Otherwise, it is hopeless. They also seem to be playing a game. In order to have fun, they must agree on the rules for fair play.

Features and Selections	Literary Analysis	Reading and Critical Thinking	Writing Opportunities	
A Sense of Fairness Between Friends				
Learning the Language of Literature **Drama**	Drama, 317			
The Active Reader **Skills and Strategies**		Reading Drama, 321		
DRAMA **Damon and Pythias** Difficulty Level: *Average*	Stage Directions, 322, 324, 328, 330 Review: Theme, 330 Understanding Theme, 324, 326, 328, 329	Story Mapping, 322, 324, 328, 330 Comparing Texts, 330	Comparing Characters, 331 Precise Description, 331	
SHORT STORY **Cricket in the Road** Difficulty Level: *Average* Related Reading **Mean Song**	Dialogue, 333, 334, 337 Review: Setting, 337 Character Traits, 336	Predicting, 333, 334, 337 Author Activity, 339	Dramatic Dialogue, 338	
Reading for Information **Peers Talk It Out**		Summarizing, 341, 341 Reading a Newspaper Article, 340		
POETRY **The Quarrel Fable** Difficulty Level: *Average* **Building Vocabulary** Related Reading: **Analysis of Baseball**	Narrative Poetry, 343, 344, 345, 346	Connecting, 343, 344, 346 Comparing Texts, 346	Conversation Poem, 347	
Writing Workshop: Comparison-and-Contrast Essay **Standardized Test Practice**		Analyzing a Student Model, 356 Picturing Text Structure, 357	Writing Your Comparison-and-Contrast Essay, 358 Elaborating with Examples and Details, 359 Revision: Organization, 359	

Breaking Barriers				
Learning the Language of Literature **Autobiography and Biography**	Autobiography and Biography, 362			
The Active Reader **Skills and Strategies**		Chronological Order, 364		
BIOGRAPHY **Abd al-Rahman Ibrahima,** *from* **Now Is Your Time!** Difficulty Level: *Challenging* Related Reading **The Wolf and the House Dog**	Sources of Information, 365, 366, 370, 374, 378 Biography, 378 Point of View, 370 Identifying Tone, 368, 371	Chronological Order, 365, 366, 372, 378 Comparing Texts, 378 Author Activity, 380 Main Idea of the Selection, 375 Connecting Main Ideas, 377	Persuasive Pamphlet, 379	

LEGEND   DLS – Daily Language SkillBuilder   Green type – Teacher's Edition

Features and Selections	Literary Analysis	Reading and Critical Thinking	Writing Opportunities	
AUTOBIOGRAPHY *from* The Story of My Life **Difficulty Level: *Challenging***	Imagery, 381 Autobiography, 385, 382, 383, 384, 385	Clarifying, 381, 382, 384, 385 Implied Main Idea, 384 Author Activity, 387	Her Own Words, 386	
Reading for Information High-tech Helping Hands		Forming and Revising Research Questions, 388, 389 Connecting Main Ideas, 389		
POETRY Street Corner Flight/Alas en la esquina Words Like Freedom **Difficulty Level: *Average*** **Building Vocabulary**	Tone, 391, 392, 394, 395 Review: Repetition, 395 Tone and Word Choice, 392, 394 Meaning and Line Length, 393	Making Inferences About the Speaker, 391, 392, 394, 395 Comparing Texts, 395	Concept Poem, 396	
AUTHOR STUDY Gary Soto				
SHORT STORY The School Play **Difficulty Level: *Easy***	Tone, 402, 404, 409, Character Traits, 405	Monitoring Reading Strategies, 402, 404, 408, 409 Comparing Texts, 409		
POETRY Ode to My Library **Difficulty Level: *Easy***	Imagery, 411, 412, 414, 415	Visualizing, 411, 412, 415		
ESSAY Who Are Your Readers?	Audience, 416			
MEMOIR The Jacket **Difficulty Level: *Average***	Humor, 418, 420, 424 Activity, 424 Review: Simile, 424 Imagery and Figurative Language, 420	Identifying the Author's Purpose, 418, 420, 424		
The Author's Style Author Study Project	Key Style Points, 426	Active Reading, 426	Writing, 426 Embarrassing Moments Gallery, 427 Author Study Project, 427	
Writing Workshop: **Problem-Solution** Essay **Standardized Test Practice**		Analyzing a Student Model, 431 Patterns of Organization, 432	Writing Your Problem-Solution Essay, 433 Supporting Ideas with Examples, 434 Revision: Organization, 434	
Reflect and Assess	Reviewing Literary Concepts, 437	Finding Inspiration, 436 Making a Top-Ten List, 436	Portfolio Building, 437	

LEGEND   DLS – Daily Language SkillBuilder   Green type – Teacher's Edition

UNIT THREE
RESOURCE MANAGEMENT GUIDE
PART 1
To introduce the theme of this unit, use
transparencies 7–9 in Fine Arts Transparencies

	Unit Resource Book	Assessment	Integrated Technology and Media
Damon and Pythias *pp. 322–332*	• Summary p. 4 • Active Reading: Story Mapping p. 5 • Literary Analysis: Stage Directions p. 6 • Literary Analysis: Understanding Theme p. 7 • Grammar p. 8 • Words to Know p. 9 • Selection Quiz p. 10	• Selection Test, Formal Assessment pp. 49–50 ◉ Test Generator	◯ Audio Library
Cricket in the Road *pp. 333–339*	• Summary p. 11 • Active Reading: Predicting p.12 • Literary Analysis: Dialogue p. 13 • Literary Analysis: Character Traits p. 14 • Grammar p. 15 • Words to Know p. 16 • Selection Quiz p. 17	• Selection Test, Formal Assessment pp. 51–52 ◉ Test Generator	◯ Audio Library
Peers Talk It Out *pp. 340–342*	• Summarizing p. 18 • Reading a Newspaper Article p. 19		
The Quarrel **Fable** *pp. 343–347*	• Active Reading: Connecting p. 20 • Literary Analysis: Narrative Poetry p. 21	• Selection Test, Formal Assessment pp. 53–54 ◉ Test Generator	◯ Audio Library

Writing Workshop: Comparison-and-Contrast Essay

		Unit Assessment	**Unit Technology**
Unit Three Resource Book • Prewriting p. 23 • Drafting and Elaboration p. 24 • Peer Response Guide p. 25 • Organizational Patterns: Comparison and Contrast Writing p. 26 • Revising, Editing, and Proofreading p. 27 • Student Models p. 28–30 • Rubric for Evaluation p. 31	◉ **Writing Coach** **Reading and Critical Thinking Transparencies** TR35 **Speaking and Listening Book** pp. 6–9, 12–13, 25–26	• Unit Three, Part 1 Test, Formal Assessment pp. 55–56 ◉ Test Generator • Unit Three: Integrated Assessment pp. 13–18	◈ ClassZone www.mcdougallittell.com ◉ Electronic Teacher Tools

Additional Support

Literary Analysis Transparencies	Reading and Critical Thinking Transparencies	Language Transparencies	Writing Transparencies	Speaking and Listening Book
• Drama: Stage Directions TR23	• Summarizing (Story Map) TR13	• Daily Language SkillBuilder TR10 • Verbs—Using Correct Verb Forms TR35	• Writing Variables TR2 • Transitional Words List TR10	• Creating an Oral Response p. 27 • Guidelines: How to Analyze an Oral Response p. 28
• Dialogue TR24	• Predicting TR7 • Compare and Contrast TR17	• Daily Language SkillBuilder TR10 • Verbs—Using Correct Verb Forms TR35 • Context Clues: Compare and Contrast, Cause and Effect, Example TR54	• Dialogue TR24	• Creating an Informative Presentation p. 25 • Guidelines: How to Analyze an Informative Presentation p. 26
			• How to Summarize TR51	
• Theme TR7	• Connecting TR2	• Daily Language SkillBuilder TR11	• Dialogue TR24 • Poem TR35	

ENGLISH LEARNERS / STUDENTS ACQUIRING ENGLISH

The **Spanish Study Guide,** pp. 61–72, includes language support for the following pages:
• Family and Community Involvement (per unit)

• Selection Summaries and Vocabulary
• Active Reading
• Literary Analysis

For **systematic instruction** in language skills, see:
• **Vocabulary and Spelling Book**
• **Grammar, Usage, and Mechanics Book**
• pacing chart on p. 315i

UNIT THREE
RESOURCE MANAGEMENT GUIDE
PART 2
CONTINUED

To introduce the theme of this unit, use transparencies 7–9 in Fine Arts Transparencies.

	Unit Resource Book	Assessment	Integrated Technology and Media
Abd al-Rahman Ibrahima, *from* **Now Is Your Time!** pp. 365–380	• Summary p. 32 • Active Reading: Chronological Order p. 33 • Literary Analysis: Sources of Information p. 34 • Active Reading: Connecting Main Ideas p. 35 • Grammar p. 36 • Words to Know p. 37 • Selection Quiz p. 38	• Selection Test, Formal Assessment pp. 57–58 ◉ Test Generator	◉ Audio Library ◉ Research Starter www.mcdougallittell.com
from **The Story of My Life** pp. 381–387	• Summary p. 39 • Active Reading: Clarifying p. 40 • Literary Analysis: Imagery p. 41 • Active Reading: Main Idea-Details p. 42 • Grammar p. 43 • Words to Know p. 44 • Selection Quiz p. 45	• Selection Test, Formal Assessment pp. 59–60 ◉ Test Generator	◉ Audio Library
High-Tech Helping Hands pp. 388–390	• Forming and Revising Research Questions p. 46 • Connecting Main Ideas p. 47		
Street Corner Flight/ Alas en la esquina Words Like Freedom pp. 391–396	• Active Reading: Making Inferences About the Speaker p. 48 • Literary Analysis: Tone p. 49	• Selection Test, Formal Assessment pp. 61–62 ◉ Test Generator	◉ Audio Library
The School Play pp. 402–410	• Summary p. 51 • Active Reading: Monitoring p. 52 • Literary Analysis: Tone p. 53 • Literary Analysis: Character Traits p. 54 • Grammar p. 55 • Words to Know p. 56 • Selection Quiz p. 57	• Selection Test, Formal Assessment pp. 63–64 ◉ Test Generator	◉ Audio Library ◉ NetActivities
Ode to My Library pp. 411–415	• Active Reading: Visualizing p. 58 • Literary Analysis: Imagery p. 59	• Selection Test, Formal Assessment pp. 65–66 ◉ Test Generator	◉ Audio Library ◉ NetActivities
The Jacket pp. 418–425	• Summary p. 60 • Active Reading: Author's Purpose p. 61 • Literary Analysis: Humor p. 62 • Literary Analysis: Imagery and Figurative Language p. 63 • Grammar p. 64 • Words to Know p. 65 • Selection Quiz p. 66	• Selection Test, Formal Assessment pp. 66–67 ◉ Test Generator	◉ Audio Library ▬ Video: Literature in Performance, Video Resource Book pp. 19–24 ◉ NetActivities

Writing Workshop: Problem-Solution Essay		Unit Assessment	Unit Technology
Unit Three Resource Book • Prewriting p. 67 • Drafting and Elaboration p. 68 • Peer Response Guide p. 69 • Organizational Patterns: Order of Importance p. 70 • Revising, Editing, Proofreading p. 71 • Student Models pp. 72–74 • Rubric for Evaluation p. 75	◉ **Writing Coach** **Writing Transparencies** TR6 **Speaking and Listening Book** pp. 6–9, 12–13, 31–32	• Unit Three, Part 2 Test, Formal Assessment pp. 69–70 ◉ Test Generator • Unit Three: Integrated Assessment pp. 13–18	◉ ClassZone www.mcdougallittell.com ◉ Electronic Teacher Tools

Additional Support

Literary Analysis Transparencies	Reading and Critical Thinking Transparencies	Language Transparencies	Writing Transparencies	Speaking and Listening Book
• Primary/Secondary Source TR14	• Chronological Order TR6	• Daily Language SkillBuilder TR11 • Avoiding Errors in the Use of Modifiers TR41 • Word Parts: Roots and Base Words, Prefixes, Suffixes TR56-58	• How to Summarize TR51	• Creating a Persuasive Presentation p. 29 • Guidelines: How to Analyze a Persuasive Presentation p. 30
	• Noting Sensory Details TR11	• Daily Language SkillBuilder TR12 • Double Negatives TR43 • Learning and Remembering New Words TR65		• Evaluating Reading Aloud p. 14
			• Generating Research Questions TR40 • Locating Material in the Library TR41	
• Poetry: Speaker TR21		• Daily Language SkillBuilder TR12	• Writing Variables TR2 • Figurative Language and Sound Devices TR17 • Poem TR35 • Crediting Sources TR55	
• Tone TR25	• Strategies for Reading TR1	• Daily Language SkillBuilder TR13 • Comparison of Regular and Irregular Adjectives and Adverbs TR42 • Context Clues: Definition and Overview TR53		
	• Visualizing TR4 • Cluster Diagram TR38	• Daily Language SkillBuilder TR13	• Combining Sentences Using Conjunctions TR19	
	• Author's Purpose and Audience TR8	• Daily Language SkillBuilder TR14 • Context Clues: Definition and Overview TR53	• Structuring the Essay TR6 • Figurative Language and Sound Devices TR17 • Personal Experience Essay TR25	• Creating a Persuasive Presentation p. 29 • Guidelines: How to Analyze a Persuasive Presentation p. 30

ENGLISH LEARNERS / STUDENTS ACQUIRING ENGLISH

The **Spanish Study Guide**, pp. 73–90, includes language support for the following pages:
• Family and Community Involvement (per unit)

• Selection Summaries and Vocabulary
• Active Reading
• Literary Analysis

For **systematic instruction** in language skills, see:
• **Vocabulary and Spelling Book**
• **Grammar, Usage, and Mechanics Book**
• pacing chart on p. 315i

INTEGRATING SKILLS INSTRUCTION PACING CHART

The *Language of Literature* offers several options for integrating language arts instruction and literature.

- Systematic instruction in grammar, vocabulary, and spelling is provided in the *Grammar, Usage, and Mechanics Book* and in the *Vocabulary and Spelling Book.* The pacing chart on the right shows when to use the lessons in these books.
- The Pupil's Edition provides grammar and vocabulary instruction in context. The examples for the grammar feature, *Grammar in Context,* arise from the selections and relate to the grammar focus for each unit. In addition each selection includes vocabulary words called *Words to Know.* Vocabulary practice occurs in *Choices and Challenges* at the end of each selection.
- The Teacher's Edition provides review and reinforcement of the grammar and vocabulary concepts through Explicit Instruction lessons. References to additional support in *Unit Resource Books* and other ancillaries are included at the end of appropriate lessons.

Grammar, Usage and Mechanics

From Grammar, Mechanics, and Usage Book

Chapter 1: Sentence and Its Parts
Chapter 2: Nouns
Chapter 3: Pronouns
Chapter 4: Verbs

Chapter 5: Adjectives and Adverbs
- What Is an Adjective?
- Predicate Adjectives
- Other Words Used as Adjectives
- What Is an Adverb?
- Making Comparisons
- Adjective or Adverb?
- Avoiding Double Negatives

Chapter 6: Prepositions, Conjunctions, Interjections
Chapter 7: Subject-Verb Agreement

For Ongoing Reference
Chapter 8: Capitalization
Chapter 9: Punctuation

Vocabulary
From Vocabulary and Spelling Book

Lesson 1: Context Clues
Lesson 2: Restatement Clues
Lesson 3: Contrast Clues
Lesson 4: Definition Clues
Lesson 5: Comparison Clues
Lesson 6: General Context Clues
Lesson 7: Prefixes and Base Words
Lesson 8: Prefixes and Base Words
Lesson 9: Base Words and Suffixes
Lesson 10: Base Words and Suffixes
Lesson 11: Anglo-Saxon Affixes and Base Words
Lesson 12: Roots and Word Families
Lesson 13: Roots and Word Familes

Lesson 14: Roots and Affixes
Lesson 15: Roots and Affixes
Lesson 16: Foreign Words in English
Lesson 17: Specialized Vocabulary
Lesson 18: Specialized Vocabulary
Lesson 19: Specialized Vocabulary

Lesson 20: Words with Multiple Meanings
Lesson 21: Synonyms
Lesson 22: Antonyms
Lesson 23: Denotation and Connotation
Lesson 24: Using a Thesaurus
Lesson 25: Idioms
Lesson 26: Similes and Metaphors
Lesson 27: Compound Words
Lesson 28: Homonyms
Lesson 29: Homophones and Easily Confused Words
Lesson 30: Homographs
Lesson 31: Analogies
Lesson 32: Using a Dictionary
Lesson 33: Using a Pronounciation Key
Lesson 34: Using a Specialized Dictionary

Spelling
From Vocabulary and Spelling Book

Lesson 1: Silent *e* Words and Suffixes
Lesson 2: The Suffix *ance*
Lesson 3: Plural Words Ending in *o*
Lesson 4: Prefixes and Base Words
Lesson 5: Prefixes and Roots
Lesson 6: Words Ending with *ary*
Lesson 7: Soft and Hard *g*
Lesson 8: Review
Lesson 9: Final *y* words and Suffixes
Lesson 10: The Suffix *able*
Lesson 11: Words Ending with *al + ly*
Lesson 12: The Prefix *com*
Lesson 13: Forms of the Prefix *ad*

Lesson 14: Words Ending with *ory*
Lesson 15: Unstressed Syllables
Lesson 16: Review
Lesson 17: *VAC* Words
Lesson 18: Non-*VAC* Words
Lesson 19: Words Ending with *c + ally*

Lesson 20: The Prefix *ex*
Lesson 21: More Forms of the Prefix *ad*
Lesson 22: Base Word Changes
Lesson 23: Words Ending with *cious, cial,* or *cian*
Lesson 24: Review
Lesson 25: Greek Combining Forms
Lesson 26: Compound Words and Contractions
Lesson 27: The Suffix *ible*
Lesson 28: Forms of Prefix *ob + sub*
Lesson 29: Forms of Prefix *in*
Lesson 30: The Suffixes *ence + ent*
Lesson 31: Words Ending with *ize + ise*
Lesson 32: Review

Selection	SkillBuilder Sentences	Suggested Answers
Damon and Pythias	**1.** Fan Kissen wrote playes for childrens.	**1.** Fan Kissen wrote **plays** for **children**.
	2. Mans jumped out of the bushs and tied his foots to a tree.	**2.** **Men** jumped out of the **bushes** and tied his **feet** to a tree.
Cricket in the Road	**1.** Selo, Vern, and Amy likes to play cricket.	**1.** Selo, Vern, and Amy **like** to play cricket.
	2. Selo throw the bat and ball in the bushes.	**2.** Selo **throws** the bat and ball in the bushes.
The Quarrel	**1.** I will have quarreled with my brother, but we soon were friends again.	**1.** I **had** quarreled with my brother, but we soon were friends again.
Fable	**2.** You be not as small as I be.	**2.** You **are** not as small as I **am**.
Abd al-Rahman Ibrahima	**1.** Them were brought as slaves to America.	**1.** **They** were brought as slaves to America.
	2. Him and her went back to Africa.	**2.** **He** and **she** went back to Africa.
from The Story of My Life	**1.** Helen Keller couldn't read nothing when Miss Sullivan became her teacher.	**1.** Helen Keller couldn't read **anything** when Miss Sullivan became her teacher.
	2. Miss Sullivan never gave up on nobody.	**2.** Miss Sullivan never gave up on **anybody**.

Selection	SkillBuilder Sentences	Suggested Answers
Street Corner Flight/Alas en la esquina Words Like Freedom	**1.** The young frightened child clung tightly to his sister's dirty scarred hand. **2.** His mother sobbing and scared fought silently against the cold rushing water.	**1.** The young, frightened child clung tightly to his sister's dirty, scarred hand. **2.** His mother, sobbing and scared, fought silently against the cold, rushing water.
The School Play	**1.** I like most of Gary Soto's stories, because I don't always understand them. **2.** I love to read poetry, or I really enjoy writing my own poems.	**1.** I like most of Gary Soto's stories, **but** I don't always understand them. **2.** I love to read poetry, **and** I really enjoy writing my own poems.
Ode to My Library	**1.** you think that the author paints a vivid picture of the library? **2.** the author mentions the Incas, he says that they lived two steps from heaven.	**1.** **Don't** you think that the author paints a vivid picture of the library? **2.** **When** the author mentions the Incas, he says that they lived two steps from heaven.
The Jacket	**1.** Gary Soto had always felt that his ugly jacket has been the cause of his unhappiness. **2.** Even though he hated the jacket, Soto continues to wear it and even calls it his "brother."	**1.** Gary Soto had always felt that his ugly jacket **was** the cause of his unhappiness. **2.** Even though he hated the jacket, Soto **continued** to wear it and even **called** it his "brother."

OVERVIEW

Students work in small groups to present a persuasive speech on community involvement.

Points at a glance The selections in Unit Three focus on fairness. For this project, each group of students will identify an issue they feel is unfair in their school or community and deliver a speech proposing a way for the community to get involved. The issue could be anything from helping the handicapped (see "High-tech Helping Hands") to solving quarrels among students (see selections in Part 1). Students will research their idea, gather evidence, and write a persuasive speech. Members of each group will share responsibilities for researching the topic, writing the speech, and conducting interviews. Each topic should be well thought out, with a focus on a workable solution. Each student will present part of the speech so that everyone has a chance to speak.

SCHEDULING

Each group should take no more than ten minutes to present its persuasive speech. You may want to schedule the speeches over the course of 2–3 class periods. This project may take place over the course of the unit or at the end of the unit, depending on your scheduling purposes.

PROJECT OBJECTIVES

• To demonstrate the speaking and listening skills introduced in the activity
• To write a persuasive speech communicating the importance of solving a particular issue
• To present a convincing and workable plan
• To conduct in-depth research on their idea
• To effectively combine all parts of the speech into a coherent presentation

SUGGESTED GROUP SIZE

4–5 students per group

Persuasive Speech

1 Getting Started

Explain that students will be working in small groups to write and present a persuasive speech on community involvement. For some ideas on issues, see the Selections Overview for summaries of the stories in this unit.

Gather back copies of the op-ed section of local newspapers that deal with community issues. You might want to videotape a legislative session from a cable television channel so that students can get a flavor of the nature of persuasion. Also make sure students are familiar with the characteristics of a persuasive speech, found in the Speaking and Listening Handbook, pages R100–101.

You can have students give their speeches in your classroom. There should be chairs available for audience members and, if possible, a lectern from which students can address the audience. A row of chairs for group members should be positioned next to the lectern. You might invite other classes, parents, or teachers to act as judges or audience members. For their convenience, schedule any adults well ahead of time.

Writing Workshop Connection

As a springboard, students may use the Writing Workshop assignment **Problem-Solution Essay,** p. 430, which they will complete in Part 2 of this unit.

2 Directing the Project

Preparing *(1 class period)* As a class, have students discuss the issues covered in this unit, as well as any other issues in their school or community that they feel are unfair. Discuss the need for community involvement and the different forms it can take.

▶ Divide students into groups of four or five. Tell students that each person will write and present a segment of the speech so that everyone has a chance to speak. You can have students divide the speech into a five-paragraph essay format. For example, one student will write and present the introduction, another student will cover a body paragraph, and so on.

Assigning Roles Roles might include writer, interviewer, researcher, and so on. You might want to choose one student to write and present an introduction and conclusion for the entire class presentation (or you could fill this position yourself).

▶ Meet with groups after they have their ideas. Make sure there are no duplications. Later, help students write and refine the speech, identify visual aids, or just make suggestions about the project as a whole.

▶ Well before the presentation, have students check to make sure that all of their main points are supported with facts and examples. Also review with students the Speaking and Listening Skills listed on the next page.

Practicing *(1 class period)* You should leave enough time for groups to rehearse. The individual parts should have a similar feel and tone. Tell students that giving and receiving feedback during the rehearsal stage is crucial. Refer to the tips in the Feedback Center.

▶ Remind students that the point of a persuasive speech is to convince. Therefore, they should appear enthusiastic yet natural. Speakers should use gestures and facial expressions to fit the content. Their tone of voice should be loud enough to be heard but not so loud that they are shouting. If students are using visual aids such as posters, these should be neat and visible to the audience.

Presenting *(1–2 class periods)* This project could culminate in a presentation for the entire student body or just for your class.

▶ To begin, have students take a few deep breaths and focus on what they want to communicate. If they are using visual aids such as posters, these should be ready and on hand. Students should be seated in order of appearance next to the lectern so that they can quickly take the stage.

Teaching the Speaking and Listening Skills

The student is expected to:

Clarify and support spoken ideas with evidence, elaborations, and examples

Teaching Suggestions: Remind students that they are trying to persuade people who either have no opinion or who disagree with their own opinion. Evidence, including facts and statistics, expert testimony, and details such as sensory details make their ideas clearer and more convincing.

Set a purpose for listening

Teaching Suggestions: Discuss with students the purpose for listening to this speech. They might be listening to understand a different point of view, to learn something new, to solve a problem in their school or community, or to choose the best idea presented.

Eliminate barriers to effective listening

Teaching Suggestions: Tell students that barriers can prevent the listener from receiving the speaker's message. Review these strategies:

- Remove distracting noises
- Rein in your mind if it starts to wander
- List questions that occur to you as you listen
- Keep your eyes on the speaker
- Be aware of personal bias about the speaker or the message

Analyze a speaker's persuasive techniques and credibility

Teaching Suggestions: Remind the student audience that an important part of critical listening is recognizing persuasive devices. These often involve faulty reasoning and might include inaccurate generalizations, either/or reasoning, bandwagon, or snob appeal. (These can be found in the Speaking and Listening Handbook, pages R103–104.) Have students assess the credibility of the speaker. Does the speaker appear knowledgeable about the subject matter? Has he or she done the necessary research? Are the claims and ideas backed up with facts and evidence?

Feedback Center

Students can use the following guidelines when giving and receiving feedback during this project:

Giving Feedback

▶ Ask questions concerning content, delivery, purpose, and point of view (for instance, is tone appropriate to purpose?).

▶ Provide feedback about the coherence and logic of the content, delivery, and overall impact on the listener.

▶ Comment on the verbal and nonverbal delivery (pitch, pace, volume, gestures, body language) and its impact on the listener.

▶ Respond to persuasive messages with questions, challenges, or affirmations.

▶ Question evidence to support the speaker's claims and conclusions.

Receiving Feedback

▶ Listen to constructive criticism with an open mind.

▶ Use audience feedback and modify the presentation to clarify meaning or organization.

▶ 3 Assessing the Project

The following rubric can be used for group or individual assessment.

3 *Full Accomplishment*

The group presented a persuasive speech that included a convincing plan for solving a particular issue. The ideas were well supported with evidence and clearly organized. Students worked effectively in a group and demonstrated all of the Speaking and Listening Skills listed, including effective communication skills, appropriate delivery of information, and logical presentation of the points.

2 *Substantial Accomplishment*

The group presented a persuasive speech, but it lacked focus or clarity of subject matter. There was some supporting evidence, but the speech lacked coherence. Two to three of the Speaking and Listening Skills were demonstrated.

1 *Little Accomplishment*

The group's segment was incomplete or did not fulfill the requirements of the assignment. The speech lacked a persuasive tone, the arguments were not supported, and only one of the Speaking and Listening Skills was demonstrated.

PART 1
Between
Friends

Meeting Standards

The Literature You'll Read

The Concepts You'll Study

Vocabulary and Reading Comprehension
Vocabulary Focus: Understanding Analogies
Story-Mapping
Predicting
Connecting

Writing and Language Conventions
Writing Workshop: Comparison-and-Contrast
   Essay
Using Adjectives for Precise Description
Using Adverbs for Excitement

Literary Analysis
Genre Focus: Drama
Stage Directions
Dialogue
Narrative Poetry

Speaking and Listening
Interpretation of a Play
Oral Report
Dramatic Reading

316

LEARNING the Language of Literature

Drama

> *You need three things in the theatre—the play, the actors, and the audience, and each must give something.*
> —Kenneth Haigh, writer

The stage is set. The lights begin to dim. As the heavy velvet curtain rises, a hush falls over the audience. One by one the actors take the stage. The drama is about to unfold.

When you go to a movie, watch a program on television, or see a play in a theater, you are experiencing a drama. A **drama** is a story that is meant to be acted out for an audience. It is written in a special form called a **script,** in which **lines** are written out for the characters to speak. All dramas share the elements of **stage directions, plot, character,** and **dialogue.**

Key Elements of Drama
- stage directions
- plot
- character
- dialogue

317

Standards-Based Objectives
- understand and identify the following literary terms:
  - drama
  - stage directions
  - upstage
  - downstage
  - stage right
  - stage left
  - scenery
  - plot
  - conflict
  - climax
  - rising action
  - falling action
  - resolution
  - scenes
  - acts
  - main characters
  - minor characters
  - narrator
  - dialogue
- understand and appreciate drama
- appreciate a writer's craft
- compare communication in different forms such as contrasting a dramatic performance with a print version of the same story.

Teaching the Lesson

This lesson helps students understand and appreciate drama by defining and explaining its key elements.

Introducing the Concepts
Have students think about a play or musical they have seen performed on stage. Ask them to describe how they felt as the curtain rose and the play began. How does this experience compare with the feeling of being in a movie theater? If some of the students have participated in plays, ask them to describe their experiences from a behind-the-scenes perspective.

Presenting the Concepts
Stage Directions

With students, discuss what kinds of scenery and props they would need in order to create the proper setting and mood for a dramatization of "Oh Broom, Get to Work," or one of the other selections in Unit 2.

YOUR TURN

Possible Response: The stage directions in this excerpt reveal the numbers mine as an eerie, dark but wondrous place. They also give the actors clues about how their voices should sound in such a place and the kind of movements they should make to reinforce a mood of awe.

Stage Directions

Stage directions are instructions for the actors, the director, and the stage crew. They are usually printed in italics in the script and might be enclosed in parentheses. Stage directions can tell the actors to move **upstage** or **downstage** or whether to enter and exit **stage right** or **stage left.** In addition, stage directions might describe an actor's tone of voice, the scenery, and the props. **Scenery** can include painted screens, backdrops, or other materials that help turn an ordinary stage into a different world. **Props** are objects that actors use during the play, such as books, telephones, or canes.

YOUR TURN How do stage directions in the excerpt to the right help create a mood for the scene?

STAGE DIRECTIONS

Dodecahedron. We're here. This is the numbers mine. *(Lights up a little, revealing Little Men digging and chopping, shoveling and scraping.)* Right this way and watch your step. *(His voice echoes and reverberates. Iridescent and glittery numbers seem to sparkle from everywhere.)*

—Norton Juster and Susan Nanus, *The Phantom Tollbooth*

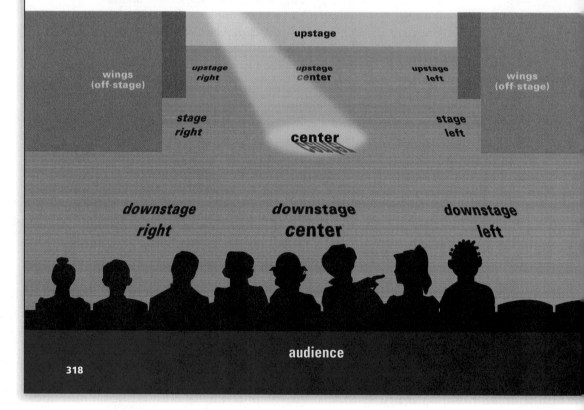

Plot

Just as in fiction, **plot** in drama is made up of a series of main events in which a **conflict** develops, reaches a peak (**climax**), and then is resolved (**resolution**). (For more information about plot, see pages 443–445.) Just as a book is divided into chapters, the action in a drama is divided into **scenes.** When the setting or time changes, a new scene begins. Sometimes two or more scenes are grouped into an **act.**

YOUR TURN What conflict is suggested by the lines to the right from *Damon and Pythias?*

> ### PLOT
>
> **King** *(hard, cruel).* So, Pythias! They tell me you do not approve of the laws I make.
>
> **Pythias.** I am not alone, Your Majesty, in thinking your laws are cruel. But you rule the people with such an iron hand that they dare not complain.
>
> —Fan Kissen, *Damon and Pythias*

Characters

In a drama, the main characters and minor characters are listed in the cast of characters at the beginning of the script. Brief descriptions of the characters might also be included. **Main characters** are the most important characters in the play. The **minor characters** interact with the main character and help to further the plot. Sometimes there is a **narrator.** The narrator does not usually take part in the action. He or she sets the scene for the drama and might comment on what happens.

YOUR TURN Damon and Pythias are main characters in a play. What qualities do they show in the excerpt at the right?

> ### CHARACTERS
>
> **Narrator.** When Damon heard that his friend Pythias had been thrown into prison and the severe punishment that was to follow, he was heartbroken. He rushed to the prison and persuaded the guard to let him speak to his friend.
>
> **Damon.** Oh, Pythias! How terrible to find you here! I wish I could do something to save you!
>
> **Pythias.** Nothing can save me, Damon, my dear friend. I am prepared to die. But there is one thought that troubles me greatly.
>
> **Damon.** What is it? I will do anything to help you.
>
> **Pythias.** I'm worried about what will happen to my mother and my sister when I'm gone.
>
> —Fan Kissen,
> *Damon and Pythias*

From *Damon and Pythias*

Plot

Remind students that the plot of a play contains the same elements as the plot of a short story or novel. The action in a play, however, is usually divided into acts, which are made up of several scenes each.

YOUR TURN

Possible Response: The conflict in this excerpt is between the king, who has made unjust and cruel laws, and Pythias, who has spoken out against these laws.

Characters

Explain to students that many plays provide a list of the cast of characters. Ask students to discuss why this would be helpful to the audience or the reader. Have them consider how it helps them identify characters and the relationships between them.

YOUR TURN

Possible Response: Damon exhibits compassion and determination. Pythias demonstrates bravery and loyalty.

Dialogue

Divide students into pairs. Have each pair create and write a dialogue between two players who are about to start off on an adventurous journey. Ask for volunteers to perform their dialogue for the class.

YOUR TURN

Possible Response: This dialogue reveals that since Rhyme and Reason left, things have not been going smoothly. There is a difference of opinion about letting them return. It reveals that Humbug sides with whomever states an opinion and that Milo would like Rhyme and Reason to return while Azaz cannot see their return as a possibility.

Dialogue

Conversation, or **dialogue,** between the characters is what makes up most of a dramatic script. As a reader, you can get to know the characters' thoughts and feelings through the dialogue as the action of the drama takes place.

YOUR TURN What can you tell about the plot or the characters from reading the dialogue to the right?

DIALOGUE

Milo. Maybe you should let Rhyme and Reason return.

Azaz. How nice that would be. Even if they were a bother at times, things always went so well when they were here. But I'm afraid it can't be done.

Humbug. Certainly not. Can't be done.

Milo. Why not?

Humbug. (*Now siding with Milo.*) Why not, indeed?

Azaz. Much too difficult.

Humbug. Of course, much too difficult.

Milo. You could, if you really wanted to.

Humbug. By all means, if you really wanted to, you could.

—Norton Juster and Susan Nanus,
The Phantom Tollbooth

From
The Phantom Tollbooth

The Active Reader: Skills and Strategies

Reading Drama

A drama can be as exciting on the page as it is on the stage. To read drama, you must be able to visualize the play as it unfolds. Exciting **characters** and **dialogue,** powerful **themes,** interesting **plots,** and detailed **stage directions** can all come alive as you read. The reading strategies explained here can help you get the most from every play.

How to Apply the Strategies

Read the play silently. Before you read the play aloud with others, read it to yourself. You need to know the entire plot and understand the characters before you perform the play.

Read the stage directions carefully. Stage directions tell you where and when each scene is happening and help you understand the characters and the plot.

Get to know the characters. In a play, a character's words and actions tell you what he or she is like. Read the dialogue carefully.

Keep track of the plot. The plot of a play usually centers on a main conflict that the characters try to resolve. A story map is a chart that can help you keep track of the characters and events in the play.

Story Map for *Damon and Pythias*	
Characters:	Setting:
Conflict:	
Event 1: Damon challenges the king. Event 2: Event 3:	
Climax:	Resolution:

Read the play aloud with others. When you read a part, let yourself become the character. Be ready with your lines and read only the words your character says. Do not read the stage directions aloud.

Here's how Ricky uses the strategies:

*"When I read a play, I preview the stage directions and **visualize** how a character looks and acts. Sometimes I make a **story map** to keep track of the plot."*

THE ACTIVE READER **321**

OVERVIEW

Standards-Based Objectives
- understand and appreciate drama by analyzing elements of plot, character, setting, and theme
- identify stage directions to visualize the play as it unfolds
- use story mapping to keep track of the plot

Teaching the Lesson

Presenting the Strategies
The strategies on this page will help students interpret drama by focusing on the basic elements of its structure.

1 Read the Play, Including Stage Directions
Explain that in following any kind of directions, it is important to read them in their entirety before proceeding. This helps the reader to form the "big picture."

2 Get to Know the Characters
It is the interpretation of a character's words and actions that makes a play come alive. In order to do a thorough job, actors should get to know the characters they portray. Have small groups brainstorm a list of questions about each character: Who is the character? What does the he/she look like? What does she/he like? Is he/she a "good guy" or "bad guy" in the play—or neither? What makes you say that? Students may then work in small groups to come up with answers that describe each of the characters.

3 Keep Track of the Plot
What has happened? What is going to happen? In figuring out how a character reacts to a particular incident, for example, it's important that the reader keeps straight which events have already taken place and which haven't. A story map can help them to keep these events in order.

As students read *Damon and Pythias,* have them keep track of which events lead to the climax, what the climax is, and what events make up the resolution.

Use **Reading and Critical Thinking Transparencies,** p. 13, for additional support.

Summary

Damon and Pythias are best friends who openly criticize Sicily's evil king. When Pythias criticizes the king to his face, he is thrown in prison and sentenced to death. Pythias's only wish is to see his mother and sister before he dies. Damon offers to take his friend's place in prison so that he may travel to see them. Curious to test the limits of their friendship, the king agrees to this arrangement. Pythias makes the trip home safely but is attacked by robbers on his return journey. He arrives just before the execution and finds Damon—who has believed in Pythias throughout his absence—ready to die in his place. The king is so impressed by their loyalty and friendship that he sets both men free.

Thematic Link

Damon and Pythias demonstrate both a willingness to speak up for justice and a depth of trust. So powerful is this example of true friendship that it has survived in legend and literature to this day.

Editor's Note: With the permission of the author or copyright holder, the following alterations have been made to the text: The announcer has been deleted from the Cast of Characters and the announcer's only speech has been deleted from the beginning of the play.

Damon and Pythias

by FAN KISSEN

Long, dry summers made it pleasant to spend time outside. Greeks built vast outdoor theaters and held drama festivals, where playwrights and actors competed for prizes.

Connect to Your Life

What evidence of ancient Greek culture do you see in your world today?

Build Background

Wherever the ancient Greeks traveled, they brought their culture. More than two thousand years ago, in settlements as far apart as Spain, North Africa, and Asia Minor, communities spoke Greek, performed Greek plays, and built temples in the Greek style. The city of Syracuse, where the famous friends Damon and Pythias lived, was one of the most powerful of these colonies.

Because steep, rocky mountains made land travel difficult, the ancient Greeks became expert sea travelers. They explored in boats such as this *trireme,* powered by about 170 rowers.

Focus Your Reading

LITERARY ANALYSIS **STAGE DIRECTIONS**

The script of a play includes **stage directions.** These are instructions to the performers, the director, and the stage crew. Stage directions provide suggestions about music, sound effects, scenery, lighting, mood, and action.

ACTIVE READING **STORY-MAPPING**

A **story map** shows the most important elements in a story.

READER'S NOTEBOOK
As you read, make a story map for the play. Start by writing down the title and author, then complete a chart like the one shown.

Characters: Damon Pythias King
Setting:
Conflict:
Key Events:
1.
2.

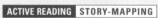

LESSON RESOURCES

DAMON

AND

PYTHIAS

RETOLD BY FAN KISSEN

Top: Detail of statue of Diadoumenos (440 B.C.), unknown artist. Roman copy of Greek original, pentelic marble, The Metropolitan Museum of Art, Fletcher Fund, 1925 (25.78.56). Copyright © The Metropolitan Museum of Art.
Bottom: Detail of Chiron the centaur teaching Achilles to play the lyre (first to third century A.D.), Roman fresco from Pompeii, Museo Archeologico Nazionale, Naples, Italy. Photo copyright © Erich Lessing/Art Resource, New York.

Reading Skills and Strategies:
PREVIEW

Briefly summarize the events of the story, omitting the conclusion. Have students speculate on what the ending of the story might be, based on what you have told them.

Literary Analysis `STAGE DIRECTIONS`

Point out that the first stage direction refers to sounds that occur before the narrative actually begins. Ask students why the sounds are called for.

Possible Response: The sounds are intended to get the audience's attention at the beginning of the play. Point out that other stage directions describe background music—used to show changes in point of view or scene changes—and the tone of voice in which lines are spoken. Have students analyze each stage direction as they read to determine what purpose each one serves.

Use **Unit Three Resource Book,** p. 6, for more practice. Use **Literary Analysis Transparencies,** p. 23, for additional support.

Active Reading `STORY MAPPING`

Point out that the stage directions that refer to music will help with story mapping: they signal the end of a scene. Explain that each scene will have at least one key event to be summarized on the story map.

Use **Unit Three Resource Book,** p. 5, for more practice. Use **Reading and Critical Thinking Transparencies,** p. 13, for additional support.

`ACTIVE READER`

A **CLARIFY** Response: Pythias tells the king that his laws are cruel but that the people are afraid to speak out. The king sends Pythias to prison.

CAST OF CHARACTERS

Damon	**Mother**
Pythias	**Narrator**
King	**First Voice**
Soldier	**Second Voice**
First Robber	**Third Voice**
Second Robber	

(Sound: Iron door opens and shuts. Key in lock.)
(Music: Up full and out.)

Narrator. Long, long ago there lived on the island of Sicily[1] two young men named Damon and Pythias.[2] They were known far and wide for the strong friendship each had for the other. Their names have come down to our own times to mean true friendship. You may hear it said of two persons:

First Voice. Those two? Why, they're like Damon and Pythias!

Narrator. The king of that country was a cruel tyrant. He made cruel laws, and he showed no mercy toward anyone who broke his laws. Now, you might very well wonder:

Second Voice. Why didn't the people rebel?

Narrator. Well, the people didn't dare rebel because they feared the king's great and powerful army. No one dared say a word against the king or his laws—except Damon and Pythias. One day a soldier overheard Pythias speaking against a new law the king had proclaimed.

Soldier. Ho, there! Who are you that dares to speak so about our king?

Pythias *(unafraid)*. I am called Pythias.

Soldier. Don't you know it is a crime to speak against the king or his laws? You are under arrest! Come and tell this opinion of yours to the king's face!

(Music: A few short bars in and out.)

Narrator. When Pythias was brought before the king, he showed no fear. He stood straight and quiet before the throne.

King *(hard, cruel)*. So, Pythias! They tell me you do not approve of the laws I make.

Pythias. I am not alone, Your Majesty, in thinking your laws are cruel. But you rule the

---

1. **Sicily** (sĭs′ə-lē): large island off the southern tip of Italy.
2. **Damon** (dā′mən) . . . **Pythias** (pĭth′ē-əs).

EXPLICIT INSTRUCTION ## Understanding Theme

Instruction Review theme with students: theme is the meaning or moral of a story. It is a message about life or human nature that the writer shares with the reader. Most themes are unstated; students must infer a theme by thinking about the conflict in a story, the characters and their actions, the way characters change, important things characters say, and the lessons they learn. Next, tell students that as they read "Damon and Pythias," they should note important details about characters and plot. After they have finished reading and noting details, they should ask themselves what message the writer is trying to give in this story.

Practice After students have read through the bottom of page 325, have them write notes about who the important characters are and about any important events that have taken place in the story so far.

Possible Responses: Important characters—Damon, Pythias, the king. Important events—Pythias speaks up to the king, telling him that people don't like the way he rules; the king sentences Pythias to death; Damon offers to take Pythias' place in prison so Pythias can travel to see his mother and sister.

For more practice, use **Unit Three Resource Book,** p. 7.

people with such an iron hand that they dare not complain.

King (*angry*). But you have the daring to complain for them! Have they appointed you their champion?

Pythias. No, Your Majesty. I speak for myself alone. I have no wish to make trouble for anyone. But I am not afraid to tell you that the people are suffering under your rule. They want to have a voice in making the laws for themselves. You do not allow them to speak up for themselves.

King. In other words, you are calling me a tyrant! Well, you shall learn for yourself how a tyrant treats a rebel! Soldier! Throw this man into prison!

ACTIVE READER

CLARIFY Summarize the conversation between Pythias and the king.

Soldier. At once, Your Majesty! Don't try to resist, Pythias!

Pythias. I know better than to try to resist a soldier of the king! And for how long am I to remain in prison, Your Majesty, merely for speaking out for the people?

King (*cruel*). Not for very long, Pythias. Two weeks from today, at noon, you shall be put to death in the public square as an example to anyone else who may dare to question my laws or acts. Off to prison with him, soldier!

(*Music: In briefly and out.*)

Narrator. When Damon heard that his friend Pythias had been thrown into prison and the severe punishment that was to follow, he was heartbroken. He rushed to the prison and persuaded the guard to let him speak to his friend.

Damon. Oh, Pythias! How terrible to find you here! I wish I could do something to save you!

Pythias. Nothing can save me, Damon, my dear friend. I am prepared to die. But there is one thought that troubles me greatly.

Damon. What is it? I will do anything to help you.

Pythias. I'm worried about what will happen to my mother and my sister when I'm gone. **4**

Damon. I'll take care of them, Pythias, as if they were my own mother and sister.

Pythias. Thank you, Damon. I have money to leave them. But there are other things I must arrange. If only I could go to see them before I die! But they live two days' journey from here, you know.

Damon. I'll go to the king and beg him to give you your freedom for a few days. You'll give your word to return at the end of that time. Everyone in Sicily knows you for a man who has never broken his word. **5**

Pythias. Do you believe for one moment that the king would let me leave this prison, no matter how good my word may have been all my life?

Damon. I'll tell him that I shall take your place in this prison cell. I'll tell him that if you do not return by the appointed day, he may kill me in your place!

Differentiating Instruction

Less Proficient Readers
Ask students to describe Pythias.
Possible Responses: Pythias is brave or foolish; idealistic or naive; stubborn or ready to die for a principle.

1 Point out to the students that italic words enclosed in parentheses after a character's name are not meant to be read aloud. They are called stage directions, and they help the actors know what actions to perform, at what volume to speak, and what tone of voice to use. Have students find examples of stage directions regarding tone on page 326. (*Damon has a "begging" tone of voice, and the King has an "astonished" tone of voice.*)

English Learners
You may want to discuss the meanings of sentences with unusual phrases or construction such as, "Their names have come down to our own times to mean true friendship." *Come down* refers to the way that stories and anecdotes pass from generation to generation.
Explain the following idioms to students:
2 *iron hand:* harsh authority or rule
3 *to have a voice in:* to participate in, to be able to express an opinion about
4 *when I'm gone:* after I'm dead
5 *to break one's word:* to go back on or break a promise

Advanced Students
Point out to students that the penalty of death that Pythias faces is undeniably harsh. Ask students if they believe it is right for a ruler to punish those who speak out against his laws. Have students debate whether any kind of punishment is justifiable in this situation.

Multicultural Link Other Legendary Friendships

One of the oldest friendships described in world literature is that of Gilgamesh and Enkidu. The epic that tells this story is Mesopotamian and dates from some time in the third millennium B.C. The Hebrew Bible, at a somewhat later date, describes David and Jonathan as the best of friends. In one notable incident, Jonathan protects David against Jonathan's father, Saul, when Saul wants to kill David.

Another legend from Greek times is the friendship of Orestes and Pylades. When they have been captured by an evil king, one is to be killed and the other spared if he will take letters back to his homeland. Each insists that the other be the one to carry the letters. Eventually they both win their freedom.

The medieval legend of Amis and Amiloun is told in a French epic poem. At one point in the epic, Amiloun learns from an angel that Amis can be cured of leprosy if Amiloun will sacrifice his own children. Relying on his faith in God, Amiloun slays his children and cures Amis. His children then miraculously come back to life.

Reading and Analyzing

ACTIVE READER

A **EVALUATE** Response: It sets up the situation where Pythias must return on time or his friend will be killed in his place.

Reading Skills and Strategies: PREDICT

B Point out to students that the king has set a date for Pythias' return. Ask them how they think that might become important in the story.
Possible Response: Pythias' failure to return before the set time will test Damon's trust in his friend.

Literary Analysis: NARRATOR

C Ask students why the writer used a narrator to tell these events rather than have actors act them out.
Possible Response: It would take a lot of time to convey the long discussion between Damon and Pythias and the information about Pythias' long journey. The lines by the narrator allow the writer to keep the story moving at a rapid pace.

Literary Analysis: DIALOGUE

D Ask students to explain why the writer uses lines of dialogue among voices to evaluate Pythias' decision.
Possible Response: The dialogue of the different voices of the townspeople makes the ideas more lively and interesting.

Detail of procession of the court of Emperor Augustus (about 13–9 B.C.), unknown Roman artist. Museum of the Ara Pacis, Rome, Nimatallah/Art Resource, New York.

Pythias. No, no, Damon! You must not do such a foolish thing! I cannot—I will not—let you do this! Damon! Damon! Don't go! (*to himself*) Damon, my friend! You may find yourself in a cell beside me!

(*Music: In briefly and out.*)

Damon (*begging*). Your Majesty! I beg of you! Let Pythias go home for a few days to bid farewell to his mother and sister. He gives his word that he will return at your appointed time. Everyone knows that his word can be trusted.

King. In ordinary business affairs—perhaps. But he is now a man under sentence of death. To free him even for a few days would strain his honesty—any man's honesty—too far. Pythias would never return here! I consider him a traitor, but I'm certain he's no fool.

Damon. Your Majesty! I will take his place in the prison until he comes back. If he does not return, then you may take my life in his place.

King (*astonished*). What did you say, Damon?

Damon. I'm so certain of Pythias that I am offering to die in his place if he fails to return on time.

King. I can't believe you mean it!

ACTIVE READER
EVALUATE How does this scene help move the plot along?
A

Damon. I do mean it, Your Majesty.

King. You make me very curious, Damon, so curious that I'm willing to put you and Pythias to the test. This exchange of prisoners will be made. But Pythias must be back two weeks from today, at noon.

EXPLICIT INSTRUCTION **Understanding Theme**

Instruction Remind students that in order to figure out a theme, they must pay attention to, and pick up clues from, the conflict, the characters, and the characters' actions. Ask students to describe important events on pages 326–327. (*Damon asks the king to let Pythias go free for a few days to see his family. The king refuses but allows Pythias to leave prison and Damon to take his place. The king gives a time limit for when Pythias must return.*) Explain that sometimes clues to a theme come from statements made by the characters or by the writer. Tell stu-

dents that they should look for statements about big ideas, such as freedom, honesty, or friendship. Ask students what big ideas have been discussed by characters in the play so far. Help students see that on page 324, the narrator talks about friendship, and Pythias and the king talk about ruling justly on page 325. Ask students if any statements about big ideas are made on pages 326–327. If necessary, prompt students by asking what the king says about honesty. (*To free a man who is sentenced to death, even for a few days, would strain his honesty.*) Ask

Damon. Thank you, Your Majesty!

King. The order with my official seal[3] shall go by your own hand, Damon. But I warn you, if your friend does not return on time, you shall surely die in his place! I shall show no mercy!

(Music: In briefly and out.)

Narrator. Pythias did not like the king's bargain with Damon. He did not like to leave his friend in prison with the chance that he might lose his life if something went wrong. But at last Damon persuaded him to leave, and Pythias set out for his home. More than a week went by. The day set for the death sentence drew near. Pythias did not return. Everyone in the city knew of the condition on which the king had permitted Pythias to go home. Everywhere people met, the talk was sure to turn to the two friends.

First Voice. Do you suppose Pythias will come back?

Second Voice. Why should he stick his head under the king's axe once he's escaped?

Third Voice. Still, would an honorable man like Pythias let such a good friend die for him?

First Voice. There's no telling what a man will do when it's a question of his own life against another's.

Second Voice. But if Pythias doesn't come back before the time is up, he will be killing his friend.

Third Voice. Well, there's still a few days' time. I, for one, am certain that Pythias will return in time.

---

3. **official seal:** mark or stamp that shows that the order came from the king.

Active Reading | STORY MAPPING

Remind students to be alert to the introduction of minor characters such as the mother and the robbers. These characters should all be included on the list of characters in the story map.

Literary Analysis: SUSPENSE

Tell students that a common way to create suspense is to use an event that slows down the action. This kind of dramatic device provides an obstacle and often brings on a crisis. The robbers serve such a function in the legend of Damon and Pythias. Ask students what the action of the legend would be like without the robbers.

Possible Response: Without the robbers, Pythias would have returned to the city a day early. There would have been no dramatic delay in which Damon's faith in his friend was tested to the utmost; and probably the king would not have been as impressed by Damon's loyalty as he was.

ACTIVE READER

A **QUESTION** Because Pythias is tied up, he can't get back to save Damon.

Literary Analysis | STAGE DIRECTIONS

B Point out that it is a common technique in radio plays to make a character's voice fade out to indicate passing time or a break in the action. Ask what the stage direction "fade" is intended to show in this scene.

Possible Response: It shows that Pythias's protests continued for longer than the time we have heard them.

Second Voice. And I am just as certain that he will not. Friendship is friendship, but a man's own life is something stronger, I say!

Narrator. Two days before the time was up, the king himself visited Damon in his prison cell.

(Sound: Iron door unlocked and opened.)

King *(mocking)*. You see now, Damon, that you were a fool to make this bargain. Your friend has tricked you! He will not come back here to be killed! He has deserted you!

Damon *(calm and firm)*. I have faith in my friend. I know he will return.

King *(mocking)*. We shall see!

(Sound: Iron door shut and locked.)

Narrator. Meanwhile, when Pythias reached the home of his family, he arranged his business affairs so that his mother and sister would be able to live comfortably for the rest of their years. Then he said a last farewell to them before starting back to the city.

Mother *(in tears)*. Pythias, it will take you only two days to get back. Stay another day, I beg you!

Pythias. I dare not stay longer, Mother. Remember, Damon is locked up in my prison cell while I'm gone. Please don't make it harder for me! Farewell! Don't weep for me. My death may help to bring better days for all our people.

Narrator. So Pythias began his return journey in plenty of time. But bad luck struck him on the very first day. At twilight, as he walked along a lonely stretch of woodland, a rough voice called:

First Robber. Not so fast there, young man! Stop!

Pythias *(startled)*. Oh! What is it? What do you want?

Second Robber. Your money bags.

Pythias. My money bags? I have only this small bag of coins. I shall need them for some last favors, perhaps, before I die.

First Robber. What do you mean, before you die? We don't mean to kill you, only to take your money.

Pythias. I'll give you my money, only don't delay me any longer. I am to die by the king's order three days from now. If I don't return to prison on time, my friend must die in my place.

First Robber. A likely story! What man would be fool enough to go back to prison ready to die?

Second Robber. And what man would be fool enough to die for you?

First Robber. We'll take your money, all right. And we'll tie you up while we get away.

ACTIVE READER

QUESTION Why is the robbery such a serious problem?

Pythias *(begging)*. No! No! I must get back to free my friend! *(fade)* I must go back!

Narrator. But the two robbers took Pythias' money, tied him to a tree, and went off as fast as they could. Pythias struggled to free himself. He cried out for help as loud as he could for a long time. But no one traveled through that lonesome woodland after dark. The sun had been up for many hours before he finally managed to

---

EXPLICIT INSTRUCTION **Understanding Theme**

Instruction Remind students that statements about big ideas are often clues to the theme. Point out this line at the top of the page 328: "Friendship is friendship, but a man's own life is something stronger, I say!" Ask students to compare this to what the king says about honesty on page 326. How are these ideas similar? (*Both men believe that honor and friendship could never be as important to a man as his own life.*) Next, point out that Damon's line on page 328 ("I have faith in my friend. I know

he will return.") shows that Damon does not agree with the king's view of friendship and honor. Ask students, "If Pythias doesn't return to the king, could the Second Voice's statement be the theme of the story?" (*yes*)

Practice Have students note important actions and statements on pages 328–329.

Possible Responses: Actions—Pythias sees his mother; he refuses to stay longer because he doesn't want Damon in any more danger; robbers delay Pythias' trip back; Pythias returns in

time to save Damon; the king decides not to kill Pythias. Statements—"Friendship is friendship, but a man's life is something stronger, I say!"; "What man would be fool enough to go back to prison ready to die?"; "I would have died for you gladly, my friend."; "But I would give all my money and power for one friend like Damon or Pythias!"

For more practice, use **Unit Three Resource Book,** p. 7.

free himself from the ropes that had tied him to the tree. He lay on the ground, hardly able to breathe.

(Music: In briefly and out.)

Narrator. After a while Pythias got to his feet. Weak and dizzy from hunger and thirst and his struggle to free himself, he set off again. Day and night he traveled without stopping, desperately trying to reach the city in time to save Damon's life.

(Music: Up and out.)

Narrator. On the last day, half an hour before noon, Damon's hands were tied behind his back, and he was taken into the public square. The people muttered angrily as Damon was led in by the jailer. Then the king entered and seated himself on a high platform.

(Sound: Crowd voices in and hold under single voices.)

Soldier *(loud)*. Long live the king!

First Voice *(low)*. The longer he lives, the more miserable our lives will be!

King *(loud, mocking)*. Well, Damon, your lifetime is nearly up. Where is your good friend Pythias now?

Damon *(firm)*. I have faith in my friend. If he has not returned, I'm certain it is through no fault of his own.

King *(mocking)*. The sun is almost overhead. The shadow is almost at the noon mark. And still your friend has not returned to give you back your life!

Damon *(quiet)*. I am ready, and happy, to die in his place.

King *(harsh)*. And you shall, Damon! Jailer, lead the prisoner to the—

(Sound: Crowd voices up to a roar, then under.)

First Voice *(over noise)*. Look! It's Pythias!

Second Voice *(over noise)*. Pythias has come back!

Pythias *(breathless)*. Let me through! Damon!

Damon. Pythias!

Pythias. Thank the gods I'm not too late!

Damon *(quiet, sincere)*. I would have died for you gladly, my friend.

Crowd Voices *(loud, demanding)*. Set them free! Set them both free!

King *(loud)*. People of the city! *(crowd voices out)* Never in all my life have I seen such faith and friendship, such loyalty between men. There are many among you who call me harsh and cruel. But I cannot kill any man who proves such strong and true friendship for another. Damon and Pythias, I set you both free. *(roar of approval from crowd)* I am king. I command a great army. I have stores of gold and precious jewels. But I would give all my money and my power for one friend like Damon or Pythias! |1|

(Sound: Roar of approval from crowd up briefly and out.)

(Music: Up and out.) ❖

Differentiating Instruction

English Learners

1 Observe that *stores* has a different meaning here than the usual one. Ask students to use the context to infer the meaning. *(Here* stores *refers to "supplies that are put away for the future on reserve" and not to "a place where merchandise is sold.")*

Less Proficient Readers

Ask students the following questions:

• Who was put to death at the end of the story? *(No one was put to death.)*

• How does Pythias' return save Pythias as well as Damon? **Possible Response:** The king is so impressed by the friendship of the two that he decides to set them both free.

Advanced Students

Have students discuss whether they think it fits the king's cruel character to be so impressed by the friendship between Damon and Pythias that he spares them both.

Possible Responses: Some may argue that the decision of the king to spare both Damon and Pythias is highly unlikely. If a politician or tyrant is cruel enough to put someone to death for speaking against the government, he or she probably does not have enough goodness to appreciate friendship and loyalty. Others may say that the king would be very aware that he had no true friends and might indeed highly value a display of true friendship.

Understanding Theme

EXPLICIT INSTRUCTION

Instruction Tell students that once they have determined the message a writer is trying to convey, they need to put that message in their own words. Review the important events in the story, and ask students what big ideas were discussed *(friendship, honesty, human nature)*. Then list these four questions on the board: (1) Which character changed the most during the play? (2) How did this character change? (3) What lesson did this character learn? (4) What message is the writer trying to give?

Practice Have students work in pairs to answer these questions, and then use their answers to determine themes of this drama. Tell students to note the story information that suggested the themes they discussed. Remind students that an author may present more than one theme.

Possible Responses: (1) The king changed the most. (2) He went from being cruel and untrusting to being kinder. (3) He learned that some friends will die for each other and that friendship is more valuable and rarer than

wealth or power. (4) Friendship is very important. Possible themes: Friendship is rarer and more valuable than power or wealth. A good friend will never let you down. True friends never doubt each other. A true friend is a rare thing.

For more practice, use **Unit Three Resource Book,** p. 7.

Connect to the Literature

1. What Do You Think?
Possible Response: I felt relieved during the king's speech, though I had guessed that both Damon and Pythias would be safe in the end.

Comprehension Check

- He is arrested because he speaks out against one of the king's laws.
- Damon agrees to stay in prison while Pythias visits his family. If Pythias does not return, Damon will be killed in his place.
- Even the ordinarily merciless king cannot kill two people who have such a strong friendship that they are willing to die for one another.

 Use Selection Quiz,
Unit Three Resource Book, p. 10.

Think Critically

2. Possible Response: They trust each other completely and keep their promises. Damon gives up his freedom, and possibly his life, for his friend. Pythias leaves his family early to make sure he gets to the city on time.

3. Possible Response: It is a generous thing to do but it is also foolish, because something could happen to Pythias (as it almost does). They both could have died. If I loved a friend that much I might be willing to take that risk.

4. Possible Responses: Damon is a greater hero, because he volunteers to trade places with Pythias; Pythias is a greater hero, because he speaks up against the king and keeps his promise; both are equally heroic.

5. Possible Responses: This story shows the values of friendship, honor, and trust; the king discovers that friendship is more important than wealth or power.

6. Responses should include that the turning point, or climax, comes when Pythias returns.

Use **Reading and Critical Thinking Transparencies**, p. 13, for additional support.

Connect to the Literature

1. What Do You Think?
What effect did the final scene have on you?

Comprehension Check
- Why is Pythias arrested?
- What bargain does the king strike with Damon?
- Why does the king free Damon and Pythias?

Think Critically

2. How would you describe the friendship between Damon and Pythias? Use examples from the play to support your answer.

3. Think about Damon's offer. Do you think taking Pythias's place is a wise and generous thing to do? What would you do if you were in Damon's position?

4. Who do you think is more of a hero—Damon or Pythias? Why?

5. What values do you think this story shows and supports?

> **Think About:**
> - Damon's bargain with the king
> - Pythias's words as he leaves his mother
> - the king's speech at the end of the play

6. **ACTIVE READING** **STORY-MAPPING**
Look at the story map you made in your **READER'S NOTEBOOK**. What would you say is the turning point of the story? Compare your story map with that of a classmate.

Extend Interpretations

7. **COMPARING TEXTS** Think back to how Nadia sought to keep her brother's memory alive in "Nadia the Willful" (page 67). How is her effort similar to Damon's effort to help Pythias? How would you compare the way these two characters face authority figures?

8. Connect to Life Imagine Damon and Pythias in our society today. What issues might they stand up for?

Literary Analysis

Stage Directions Responses will vary but should indicate awareness of how the stage directions contribute to the reader's knowledge of the characters and the changes in setting and time.

Use **Literary Analysis Transparencies**, p. 23, for additional support.

Extend Interpretations

7. Comparing Texts Nadia had a strong bond with her brother, and Damon and Pythias were as close as brothers. Both Nadia and Damon were willing to stand up to authority when they felt authority figures were acting unfairly.

8. Connect to Life Possible Response: Damon and Pythias would stand up for free speech and political participation. They might lead voter registration drives, uncover conspiracies, or seek to free political prisoners.

Literary Analysis

STAGE DIRECTIONS In the script of a play, instructions to the performers, the director, and the stage crew are called **stage directions.** Stage directions provide information about when and where the play takes place and give clues about characters and plot. Stage directions can help you **visualize** the play.

Group Activity In a small group, go back through the play and read the stage directions. Discuss what you learned from these directions. What did they tell you about the characters? What did they tell you about the plot events? Did they help you visualize the setting? Then, make a three-column chart like the one shown.

Directions about characters	Directions about plot events	Directions about setting
Damon: "calm and firm"		

REVIEW: THEME The **theme** of a literary work is the meaning or moral of the story. Writers create themes to express their ideas about life or human nature. Think about what theme this line might suggest: "I would give all my money and my power for one friend like Damon or Pythias!"

Writing

Comparing Characters
Compare and contrast the traits of Damon and Pythias. First, make a two-column chart. In one column, list Damon's traits. In the other, list those of Pythias. What do the two characters have in common? How are they different? Using information from the chart, write a paragraph or two that answers these questions. Begin with a statement of your main idea. Include specific details from the story to explain your main idea. Place your writing in your **Working Portfolio.**

Writing Handbook
See p. R43: Compare and Contrast.

> To find out about forms you might use use when your purpose is to inform, See p. R31: Choosing a Form.

Speaking & Listening

Speaking of Friendship What message about friendship does "Damon and Pythias" contain? How would you state this message in one or two sentences? Present your ideas to the class orally. First, come up with a sentence or two that summarizes the play's message about friendship. Then use examples from the play and your own experience to support your ideas. Practice your presentation to make sure you are speaking slowly and clearly. Then deliver your presentation to the class.

Speaking and Listening Handbook
See p. R100: Oral Response to Literature.

Research & Technology

Exploring Ancient Greece
"Damon and Pythias" is set in ancient Greece. The ancient Greeks are responsible for many great achievements in science, philosophy, and the arts. Conduct research to find out about one area of life in ancient Greece, such as family life, religion, education, or recreation. Use Web sites, articles, and books to gather information on your topic. Then create a poster that includes pictures and written information about your topic. On a separate piece of paper, list the sources you used to find your information.

Research and Technology Handbook
See p. R106: Getting Information Electronically.

Art Connection

Precise Description During the fifth century B.C., Greek sculptors began creating figures with lifelike poses and expressions. Look at the statue below. What details seem realistic? How would you describe his features and the expression on the face? Try to use precise verbs, nouns, and adjectives in your description.

Writing Handbook
See p. R38: Using Language Effectively.

Writing

Comparing Characters Responses may mention Damon's somewhat stubborn determination to help his friend and Pythias's intense concern for others, even at the risk of his own welfare. To get students started on this activity, set up a model chart on the blackboard and fill in some of the characteristics of Damon and Pythias, as volunteered by students.

 Use **Writing Transparencies,** pp. 2, 10, for additional support.

Speaking & Listening

Speaking of Friendship To get students started, have them review the notes they took about the story using their story maps. Also have them reread the story to look for statements about friendship.

 Use **Speaking and Listening Book,** pp. 27, 28, for additional support.

Research & Technology

Exploring Ancient Greece Allow students time to conduct research in the library and on the Internet.

Art Connection

Precise Description Student responses will vary but may include the idea that the smooth soft curves of the face and the glance of the eyes look realistic and that the expression looks sad or thoughtful.

Grammar in Context

WRITING EXERCISE Answers will vary. Possible answers are shown.

1. The King of Sicily was a cruel man who made unfair laws.
2. As Pythias walked the endless trail, he heard a booming voice.
3. Pythias set off on his most grueling day of travel.
4. Damon was ecstatic that his friend returned at the exact hour.
5. There were never such devoted friends as these.

Connect to the Literature

Answers will vary.

Fan Kissen

Fan Kissen was an elementary school teacher in New York before she began writing radio scripts. However, after she started working on station WNYE, run by the board of education, her writing began to fill more of her time. During her long scriptwriting career she won seven first place prizes for her educational radio plays. Some of her many volumes of collected scripts appeared as supplementary readers published by Houghton Mifflin between 1949 and 1961.

Grammar in Context: Using Adjectives for Precise Description

In the opening line of *Damon and Pythias,* the narrator tells us that

> ...there lived on the island of Sicily two young men named Damon and Pythias.

The words shown in red above are **adjectives.** Adjectives are words used to describe a noun or pronoun. They tell **how many, what kind,** or **which one** about the word they modify. The adjective *two,* for example, tells how many young men there are. The adjective *young* tells what kind of men they are. In the following examples, the adjectives tell you which one the writer is talking about:

> So Pythias began his return journey. . . .
> On the last day, half an hour before noon, . . .

Apply to Your Writing Choose precise adjectives that give necessary information. They should help your description paint a clear picture.

WRITING EXERCISE Find the adjectives in each sentence. Replace each one with a more specific adjective that tells what kind, how many, or which one.

Example: *Original* Pythias was a good man who fought the king's large army.

Rewritten Pythias was a brave man who fought the king's well-trained army.

1. The King of Sicily was a bad man who made bad laws.
2. As Pythias walked the long trail, he heard a loud voice.
3. Pythias set off on his worst day of travel.
4. Damon was happy that his friend returned at the perfect hour.
5. There were never such good friends as these.

Grammar Handbook
See p. R38: Using Language Effectively.

Connect to the Literature Reread one page of the play, paying attention to the stage directions. List the adjectives you find in stage directions only.

Fan Kissen
born 1904

Legendary Literature Fanny "Fan" Kissen was born in New York City and spent most of her career there. A former elementary school teacher, she became a successful radio scriptwriter. For 17 years she had her own award-winning radio series, *Tales from the Four Winds.* In this popular show she dramatized world folk tales and legends. Her plays, which are written as radio scripts, always include instructions for music and sound effects.

Travels and Tales Kissen visited the lands in which many of her stories take place. Her travels took her throughout Europe, South America, and the Near East. Most of her books are collections of plays written as radio scripts, including *The Straw Ox and Other Plays* and *The Bag of Fire and Other Plays.* In addition to writing radio plays, Kissen wrote several biographies of little-known historical figures for young people.

Grammar in Context

FORMING ADJECTIVES FROM VERBS

Instruction Students should understand how they can form adjectives from verbs by creating participles. The simplest way to do this is to add *-ing* to the verb to form the present participle. For example, by adding *-ing* to *mutter,* the adjective *muttering,* as in the phrase "the muttering crowd," is created. The past participle is formed by adding *-ed* to the verb, as in "The *muttered* complaints reached the king."

Practice Have students form adjectives from the underlined verbs in these sentences:

1. The <u>terrify</u> man ran down the road. *(terrified)*
2. The <u>roar</u> crowd surprised the king. *(roaring)*
3. The <u>demand</u> voices were loud. *(demanding)*
4. The <u>amaze</u> king spared Pythias. *(amazed)*
5. The <u>rejoice</u> friends went home. *(rejoicing)*

 Use **Unit Three Resource Book,** p. 8, for more practice.

 For more instruction in in forming adjectives from verbs, see McDougal Littell's **Language Network,** Chapter 5.

For **systematic instruction** in grammar, see:
- **Grammar, Usage, and Mechanics Book**
- pacing chart on p. 315i.

Cricket in the Road

by MICHAEL ANTHONY

Connect to Your Life

Fighting Words In the story you are about to read, a boy becomes upset with his friends over a game. Recall a disagreement you have had with a friend or a disagreement that you have read about. What caused it? How was it settled?

Build Background

GEOGRAPHY

The setting of this story is the village of Mayaro on the island of Trinidad. Trinidad is one of two islands that make up a country called Trinidad and Tobago, in the Caribbean Sea. Its climate is hot and humid, with a rainy season that lasts from about late May until December. Trinidad and Tobago was a colony of Great Britain until 1962 and still has many British customs. Cricket, a game somewhat like baseball, is popular in both countries.

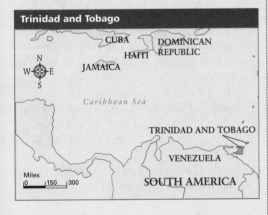

Trinidad and Tobago

CUBA
HAITI — DOMINICAN REPUBLIC
JAMAICA
Caribbean Sea
TRINIDAD AND TOBAGO
VENEZUELA
Miles
0   150   300
SOUTH AMERICA

WORDS TO KNOW	Vocabulary Preview	
dumbfounded	peal	tumult
fume	torrent	

Focus Your Reading

LITERARY ANALYSIS **DIALOGUE**

The words that characters in a story speak aloud are called **dialogue**. Dialogue helps to move the plot along. It also helps to reveal the personalities of the characters. In "Cricket in the Road," you will notice that some of the dialogue is not standard English. This is because many people in Trinidad speak Trinidad English, a form of English that has been influenced by French and Spanish.

ACTIVE READING **PREDICTING**

When you make guesses about the outcome of a story, you are **predicting**. To make predictions, combine information from the story with your own knowledge. Look for the following story information to help you make predictions:

- details that help you understand what the characters are like
- conflicts that give clues about what might happen next

As you read, pause to write your predictions in your ▢▮READER'S NOTEBOOK. Also note the reasons for your predictions.

Standards-Based Objectives
- understand and appreciate a **short story**
- understand author's use of **dialogue**
- use **predicting** to help understand a story better
- understand **character traits**

Summary
During the long rainy season, Selo, Amy, and Vern play cricket whenever there is a break in the rain. One day, the children argue, and Selo throws the bat and ball away. For many months, Amy and Vern don't play with Selo. But when the sun comes out, all is forgiven, and they let Selo bat first.

Thematic Link
An argument between friends is the subject of this story, in which a young boy learns the cost of rash anger and learns that one should never be too quick to judge what is or isn't fair.

English Conventions Practice

Daily Language SkillBuilder

Have students **proofread** the display sentences on page 315k and write them correctly. The sentences also appear on Transparency 10 of **Language Transparencies**.

Preteaching Vocabulary
If you would like to preteach the WORDS TO KNOW for this selection, use the Explicit Instruction, page 334.

LESSON RESOURCES

Reading Skills and Strategies:
PREVIEW

Have students look over the illustrations
and skim a few paragraphs. Ask them to
tell what they think the story is about.

Set a Purpose Have students read to
see if their predictions were correct.

Literary Analysis **DIALOGUE**

(A) Remind students that dialogue can
give the reader a sense of the characters.
Ask what the dialogue in this section tells
the reader about the characters.

Possible Response: The characters'
words show they are excited and how
easily they can get angry at one another.

Use **Unit Three Resource Book,**
p. 13, for more practice.
Use **Literary Analysis Transparencies,** p. 24,
for additional support.

Active Reading **PREDICTING**

Ask if students predicted that the children would argue. What information did
they use to predict this?

Possible Response: The children all
want to be first.

Use **Unit Three Resource Book,**
p. 12, for more practice.
Use **Reading and Critical Thinking
Transparencies,** p. 17, for additional
support.

Literary Analysis: CONFLICT

Explain that internal conflict is a struggle within a character; external conflict
is a struggle between a character and
something outside himself or herself.
Ask which type of conflict Selo's argument with Amy and Vern represents.

Answer: external

CRICKET in the ROAD

by Michael Anthony

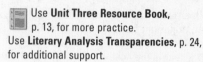

In the rainy season we got few chances to play cricket in the road, for whenever we were at the game, the rains came down, chasing us into the yard again. That was the way it was in Mayaro in the rainy season. The skies were always overcast, and over the sea the rain clouds hung low and gray and scowling, and the winds blew in and whipped angrily through the palms. And when the winds were strongest and raging, the low-hanging clouds would become dense and black, and the sea would roar, and the torrents of rain would come sweeping with all their tumult upon us.

We had just run in from the rain. Amy and Vern from next door were in good spirits and laughing, for oddly enough they seemed to enjoy the downpour as much as playing cricket in the road. Amy was in our yard, giggling and pretending to drink the falling rain, with her face all wet and her clothes drenched, and Vern, who was sheltering under the eaves,[1] excitedly jumped out to join her. "Rain, rain, go to Spain," they shouted. And presently their mother, who must have heard the noise and knew, appeared from next door, and Vern and Amy vanished through the hedge.

I stood there, depressed about the rain, and then I put Vern's bat and ball underneath the house and went indoors. "Stupes!" I said to myself. I had been batting when the rains came down. It was only when *I* was batting that the rains came down! I wiped my feet so I wouldn't soil the sheets and went up on the bed. I was sitting, sad, and wishing that the rain would really go away—go to Spain, as Vern said—when my heart seemed to jump out of me. A deafening peal of thunder struck across the sky.

Quickly I closed the window. The rain hammered awfully on the rooftop, and I kept tense for the thunder which I knew would break again and for the unearthly flashes of lightning.

Secretly I was afraid of the violent weather. I was afraid of the rain, and of the thunder and

---

1. **eaves** (ēvz): overhanging edges of a roof.

WORDS	**torrent** (tôr′ənt) *n.* a heavy downpour
TO	**tumult** (tōō′mŭlt′) *n.* a noisy uproar
KNOW	**peal** (pēl) *n.* a loud burst of noise

334

**EXPLICIT
INSTRUCTION** **Preteaching Vocabulary**

WORDS TO KNOW
Teaching Strategy Students should be able to
apply knowledge of context to recognize words.
Tell students that often the context gives clues
to a word's meaning. **Comparison and contrast
clues** compare or contrast an unfamiliar word
with known words and phrases. These clues
may be introduced by the words *like, as, similar
to, but, not, although, however,* or *on the other
hand.* Write the following example on the
board: The storm caused a tumult, but was not
as loud as I had feared.

Show students how the contrast clue contained in the sentence should lead them to
infer that *tumult* means a loud noise.

Practice Have students infer the meanings of
the underlined words from the context clues:

1. The torrent soon slowed to a trickle of
water.
2. Although at first he was dumbfounded, Vern
soon understood what Selo was doing.
3. I fumed for months, but then my anger
cooled.

4. The peals of thunder in Trinidad were like
the clanging of fierce bells.

Use **Unit Three Resource Book,** p. 16, for more
practice.

For **systematic instruction** in vocabulary, see:
• **Vocabulary and Spelling Book**
• pacing chart on p. 315i.

the lightning that came with them, and of the sea beating against the headlands,[2] and of the storm winds, and of everything being so deathlike when the rains were gone. I started[3] again at another flash of lightning, and before I had recovered from this, yet another terrifying peal of thunder hit the air. I screamed. I heard my mother running into the room. Thunder struck again, and I dashed under the bed.

"Selo! Selo! First bat!" Vern shouted from the road. The rains had ceased and the sun had come out, but I was not quite recovered yet. I brought myself reluctantly to look out from the front door, and there was Vern, grinning and impatient and beckoning to me.

"First bat," he said. And as if noting my indifference, he looked toward Amy, who was just coming out to play. "Who second bat?" he said.

"Me!" I said.

"Me!" shouted Amy almost at the same time.

"Amy second bat," Vern said.

"No, I said 'Me' first," I protested.

Vern grew impatient while Amy and I argued. Then an idea seemed to strike him. He took out a penny from his pocket. "Toss for it," he said. "What you want?"

"Heads," I called.

"Tail," cried Amy. "Tail bound to come!"[4]

The coin went up in the air, fell down and overturned, showing tail.

"I'm *not* playing!" I cried, stung. And as that did not seem to disturb enough, I ran toward

Schoolboys, Frané Lessac. From *Caribbean Canvas*, Macmillan Press, Ltd. By permission of the artist.

where I had put Vern's bat and ball and disappeared with them behind our house. Then I flung them with all my strength into the bushes.

When I came back to the front of the house, Vern was standing there <u>dumbfounded</u>. "Selo, where's the bat and ball?" he said.

I was <u>fuming</u>. "I don't know about *any* bat and ball!"

---

2. **headlands:** points of land that jut out into the water.

3. **started:** jumped suddenly in surprise.

4. **Toss for it. . . . Tail bound to come!:** Vern is flipping a coin to determine who will bat second. Selo calls that it will come up heads, so Amy roots for it to come up tails.

WORDS TO KNOW

dumbfounded (dŭm′foun′dĭd) *adj.* speechless with shock; astonished **dumbfound** *v.*
fume (fyōōm) *v.* to burn with anger

335

Reading and Analyzing

Literary Analysis: DIALECT

A Explain to students that a dialect is a variety of a language that can be found in a specific region. It differs from the standard form of the language in important ways. Point out these pieces of dialect: "He throw them away" and "Who second bat?" They are Trinidad dialect for the Standard English "He threw them away" and "Who's batting second" or "Who's second at bat?" Much of the dialogue of the story is written in dialect; however, the narration is written in Standard English. Ask students how you would say, "You first bat" in Standard English.

Possible Response: "You be first [at] bat." OR "You bat first."

Reading Skills and Strategies: MAKE JUDGMENTS

Ask students to make a judgment about whether Selo does the right thing in walking away from the game when he is angry. On what do they base this judgment?

Possible Responses: Some may say Selo is foolish to make his friends angry over such a silly thing. Some may say he avoids a worse confrontation by walking away. Students may say that their judgments are based on their own experience.

RELATED READING

Use the following questions to help students analyze the poem.
- What kind of mood do the nonsense words suggest? *(anger)*
- Suggest a meaning for one of the lines of nonsense words in the poem. *(Responses will vary.)*

"Tell on him," Amy cried. "He throw them away."

Vern's mouth twisted into a forced smile. "What's an old bat and ball," he said.

But as he walked out of the yard, I saw tears glinting from the corners of his eyes.

For the rest of that rainy season, we never played cricket in the road again. Sometimes the rains ceased and the sun came out brightly, and I heard the voices of Amy and Vern on the other side of the fence. At such times I would go out into the road and whistle to myself, hoping they would hear me and come out, but they never did, and I knew they were still very angry and would never forgive me.

And so the rainy season went on. And it was as fearful as ever with the thunder and lightning and waves roaring in the bay, and the strong winds. But the people who talked of all this said that was the way Mayaro was, and they laughed about it. And sometimes when through the rain and even thunder I heard Vern's voice on the other side of the fence, shouting "Rain, rain, go to Spain," it puzzled

me how it could be so. For often I had made up my mind I would be brave, but when the thunder cracked I always dashed under the bed.

It was the beginning of the new year when I saw Vern and Amy again. The rainy season was, happily, long past, and the day was hot and bright, and as I walked toward home I saw that I was walking toward Vern and Amy just about to start cricket in the road. My heart thumped violently. They looked strange and new, as if they had gone away, far, and did not want to come back anymore. They did not notice me until I came up quite near, and then I saw Amy start, her face all lit up.

"Vern—" she cried, "Vern look—look Selo!"

Embarrassed, I looked at the ground and at the trees, and at the orange sky, and I was so happy I did not know what to say. Vern stared at me, a strange grin on his face. He was ripping the cellophane paper off a brand new bat.

"Selo, here—*you* first bat," he said gleefully. **A**

And I cried as though it were raining and I was afraid. ❖

RELATED READING

Mean Song
by Eve Merriam

Snickles and podes,
Ribble and grodes:
That's what I wish you.

A nox in the groot,
A root in the stoot
And a gock in the forebeshaw, too.

Keep out of sight
For fear that I might
Glom you a gravely snave.

Don't show your face
Around any place
Or you'll get one flack snack in the bave.

EXPLICIT INSTRUCTION **Character Traits**

Instruction Remind students that a character trait is a quality that a character shows, such as honesty, greed, or bravery. Explain that readers can make logical guesses about character traits by examining the character's actions, thoughts, words, and feelings; by examining what other characters say about a character; and by examining the author's direct statements about the character. Next, read aloud from "'Selo! Selo!'" to "overturned, showing tail." on page 335. Tell students that Vern's words, thoughts, and actions in this pas-

sage reveal information about his personality. Ask, "What traits are revealed in this section? What specific information reveals them?" *(leadership—Vern organizes game and tries to solve argument; impatience—he is impatient about starting the game and about the argument; fair—figures out a fair way to solve the argument.)*

Practice Have students work in pairs to reread from "'I'm not playing,'" on page 335 to "from the corners of his eyes" on page 336. Tell pairs to identify and list Vern's and Selo's

traits and the information that reveals each trait.

Possible Responses: Vern—tolerant, forgiving: he doesn't tell on Selo; sensitive: he cries. Selo—childish, poor sport: won't abide by coin toss, takes ball and bat, lies about taking them.

📖 Use **Unit Three Resource Book**, p. 14, for more practice.

Connect to the Literature

1. What Do You Think?
What were your thoughts about the three friends as you finished reading?

Comprehension Check
- Why do Selo and Amy argue?
- How does Vern try to resolve their disagreement?
- How is the disagreement finally resolved?

Think Critically

2. It is obvious that Selo wants to play with Vern and Amy. Why, then, do you think he is reluctant to talk to them after the disagreement occurs?

3. In what ways are Selo and Vern alike? In what ways are they different?

> **Think About:**
> - their actions during the downpour
> - the way they determine the batting order
> - their reactions to seeing each other after the rainy season

4. **ACTIVE READING** **PREDICTING**
Look at the notes you made in your
READER'S NOTEBOOK. How do your predictions compare with the events of the story? Share your notes with a partner.

Extend Interpretations

5. What If? If Vern had not reached out to Selo, what do you think would have happened to their friendship?

6. Connect to Life In your opinion, what is the fairest and fastest way to settle a disagreement between friends? Support your opinion with ideas from "Cricket in the Road" as well as the experience you discussed before reading.

Literary Analysis

DIALOGUE In a story, spoken language is called **dialogue.** In "Cricket in the Road," the author writes the dialogue of the characters just as it would sound. This lets you "hear" how the characters speak. It also helps you to understand their feelings, actions, and traits.

Paired Activity With a partner, look over the story. Discuss how the dialogue helps the author tell the story. How would the story have been different if the author had used descriptions in place of dialogue?

REVIEW: SETTING The **setting** of a story is the time and place of the action. How does the setting of "Cricket in the Road" affect the characters?

Connect to the Literature

1. What Do You Think?
Responses will vary. Students may say that the three friends seem to have decided that friendship is more important than anything else. They may say that Amy's warmth, Vern's generosity, and Selo's tears prove how important the friendship was to all involved. Some students may say that Selo acted like a bad sport, and that Amy and Vern showed they were good friends when they forgave him for this.

Comprehension Check
- Both think they should be second bat.
- Vern tries to resolve the disagreement between Amy and Selo by tossing a coin.
- The quarrel is finally resolved when Vern makes the first move, letting Selo use his new bat first.

Use Selection Quiz,
Unit Three Resource Book, p. 17.

Think Critically

2. Possible Response: Selo is afraid that Amy and Vern will not want to play with him any more. He is embarrassed about and ashamed of his behavior.

3. Possible Response: Selo and Vern enjoy many of the same activities, such as cricket, but are very different in temperament. Vern enjoys the rainy season, for example, while Selo is terrified of the thunder and lightning.

4. Answers will vary.

Use **Reading and Critical Thinking Transparencies,** p. 7, for additional support.

Literary Analysis

Dialogue Students should be aware that the dialogue makes the story more vivid and lively, as well as giving it a flavor of the region in which the action takes place.

Use **Literary Analysis Transparencies,** p. 24, for additional support.

Extend Interpretations

5. What If? Possible Responses: If Vern had not reached out to Selo, the two boys would never have been reunited; or Selo would eventually have swallowed his pride and apologized to Amy and Vern.

6. Connect to Life Responses will vary. Make sure that the students include ideas from the selection and from their own experience.

Writing

Dramatic Dialogue Responses should indicate an accurate understanding of how the disagreement started and reflect the underlying causes of the problem in the suggested remedies. To get students started on this activity, have them hold improvised role-playing discussions in groups of three.

 Use **Writing Transparencies,** p. 24, for additional support.

Speaking & Listening

Game Plan Remind students to look at books, articles, and Web sites for information. Also, remind them to refine their questions if they are having trouble finding answers.

 Use **Speaking and Listening Book,** pp. 25, 26, for additional support.

Research & Technology

Friend or Foe? To get students started tell them to think about how they and their friends and family members resolve conflicts.

Vocabulary

STANDARDIZED TEST PRACTICE

1. B
2. F
3. C
4. H
5. D

SPELLING STRATEGY

Responses will vary. Accept all mnemonic devices that correctly use a word with a silent letter.

Writing

Dramatic Dialogue At the end of "Cricket in the Road," Amy and Vern forgive Selo. What kind of conversation might these three friends have about their disagreement? What would each person say in such a conversation? Continue the story by writing a dialogue in which Selo, Amy, and Vern talk about their disagreement. Use what you know about the characters to write what you think each one would say. Place your dialogue in your **Working Portfolio.**

Writing Handbook
See p. R41: Narrative Writing.

Vocabulary

STANDARDIZED TEST PRACTICE

Choose the word or group of words that means the same, or nearly the same, as the underlined Word to Know in each sentence.

1. A <u>torrent</u> of rain forced the children to end their game of cricket. <u>Torrent</u> means a—
   A tiny cloud   **B** heavy downpour
   C light mist   **D** large puddle

2. As they played loudly in the rain, Vern and Amy created a <u>tumult</u>. <u>Tumult</u> means a—
   F disturbance   **G** partnership
   H tunnel   **J** picture

3. When he heard a <u>peal</u> of thunder, Selo crawled under his bed. <u>Peal</u> means a—
   A gentle whisper   **B** peaceful song
   C loud burst of noise **D** distant echo

4. Vern was <u>dumbfounded</u> by Selo's actions. <u>Dumbfounded</u> means—
   F furious   **G** delighted
   H speechless   **J** wounded

Speaking & Listening

Game Plan Research the game of cricket and prepare a short oral report on it. Begin by listing questions you have about the game, such as "How is cricket played?" or "How does cricket compare to baseball?" Choose the question that most interests you and conduct research to answer it. Use your question and the information you find as the basis of your report. You might want to include diagrams and pictures in your presentation. Practice your presentation several times, and then deliver it to the class.

Speaking and Listening Handbook
See p. R99: Informative Presentations.

Research & Technology

Friend or Foe? What makes a friendship strong? Can friends disagree and still remain friends? How can friends who disagree still work or play together? With three or four classmates, brainstorm a list of ways to resolve conflicts, to calm down when angry, and to renew a friendship. Then look for information in newspapers, magazines, and nonfiction books to add more methods to your list. Write a report on conflict resolution using some of the techniques you listed.

Reading for INFORMATION
As part of your research, read "Peers Talk It Out" on p. 340.

---

5. After Selo lost his opportunity to bat first, he <u>fumed.</u> <u>Fumed</u> means—
   A smiled with joy   **B** cried in pain
   C fled in shame   **D** burned with anger

SPELLING STRATEGY: SILENT LETTERS Many words are difficult to spell because they contain silent consonants. Such words include *dumbfounded, whistle, crumb, answer,* and *sign.* You can invent your own catchy reminder to help you remember difficult spellings. These reminders are called *mnemonic devices.* Here is an example:

> *Dumb, thumb, and crumb*
> *All have a letter that's mum.*
> *To spell them correctly,*
> *End each with a "b."*

Create your own mnemonic device for a word that contains a silent letter.

Spelling Handbook
See p. R26.

Grammar in Context: Using Adverbs for Excitement

In "Cricket in the Road," Michael Anthony describes Selo's reaction to a thunderstorm. Notice how the words in red type add excitement and clarity to the writing:

> Quickly I closed the window. The rain hammered awfully on the rooftop, and I kept tense for the thunder which I knew would break again and for the unearthly flashes of lightning.
>
> Secretly I was afraid of the violent weather.

The words shown in red above are **adverbs.** An adverb modifies, or describes, a verb, an adjective, or another adverb. An adverb answers the question *how, when, where,* or *to what extent* about the word it modifies.

WRITING EXERCISE Rewrite each of the sentences, adding an adverb that answers the question in parentheses.

Example: *Original* The winds whipped (how?) through the palms.
Rewritten The winds whipped fiercely through the palms.

1. I screamed (how?) when the thunder pealed.
2. I wanted to bat (when?).
3. The thunder was (how?) loud.
4. My heart thumped (how?).
5. Selo felt (to what extent?) terrified.

Connect to the Literature Find four more exciting adverbs from "Cricket in the Road."

Grammar Handbook
See p. R78: Using Modifiers Effectively.

Michael Anthony
born 1932

"I feel very strongly about the brotherhood of mankind."

Island Life Michael Anthony writes tales about life on the island of Trinidad. His stories offer readers a taste of Caribbean culture and a chance to consider the most important things in life—like friendship. His other works include *The Games Were Coming* and *Green Days by the River.*

Jobs and Journeys Born in Mayaro, in Trinidad and Tobago, Anthony began working in an iron foundry at the age of 15. Eight years later he went to England, where he held a variety of factory jobs and eventually became a journalist. From England he went to Brazil. After a two-year stay, he and his wife and four children returned to Trinidad to live.

Hoping for Peace The selection you have just read is from a short story collection that is also titled *Cricket in the Road.* Anthony has published novels and poems as well as stories. An optimist who would like to see all the nations of the world join together to become one strong nation, he says, "One of my main hopes is that human beings will find a way to live together without friction."

AUTHOR ACTIVITY
Caribbean View Read another one of Anthony's stories that is set in Trinidad. Look for details about the setting of the island and the customs of its people. What are your impressions of everyday life in Trinidad? Draw a scene based on Anthony's descriptions.

Grammar in Context
WRITING EXERCISE
Answers will vary. Sample answers follow.
1. I screamed loudly when the thunder pealed.
2. I wanted to bat first.
3. The thunder was very loud.
4. My heart thumped fiercely.
5. Selo felt extremely terrified.

Connect to the Literature
Possible Response: brightly, reluctantly, angrily, excitedly

Michael Anthony

Anthony is also very interested in space exploration. "I sometimes find the mystery of the universe too much to bear," he says. "I do consider [humanity's] quest for knowledge vital and, in fact, inevitable."

Author Activity

Caribbean View Allow time for students to find and read Anthony's stories, to discuss their impressions, and to make their drawings.

EXPLICIT INSTRUCTION ## Grammar in Context

IDENTIFYING ADVERBS Instruction Remind students that an adverb is a word used to modify a verb, an adjective, or another adverb. Adverbs tell how, when, where, or to what extent. Write the sentence below on the board, and point out that *extremely* modifies the adjective *rainy* by telling to what extent: Trinidad can be extremely rainy.
Practice Ask students to identify the adverbs and the words they modify in the following sentences:

1. Selo's life was fearfully full of thunder. (*fearfully* modifies *full*)
2. It rained hard in Mayaro. (*hard* modifies *rained*)
3. Selo wept very gratefully. (*gratefully* modifies *wept,* and *very* modifies *gratefully*)
4. Selo, Amy, and Vern played happily and peacefully. (*happily* and *peacefully* both modify *played*)

 Use **Unit Three Resource Book,** p. 16.

 For more instruction in identifying adverbs and the words they modify, see McDougal Littell's *Language Network,* Chapter 5.

For **systematic instruction** in grammar, see:
• **Grammar, Usage, and Mechanics Book**
• pacing chart on p. 315i.

Reading *for* INFORMATION
NEWSPAPER ARTICLE
Real World Link to "Cricket in the Road"

Standards-Based Objectives
- read and analyze a newspaper article
- practice summarizing information from text
- examine the concept of peer mediation

Connecting to the Literature
"Peers Talk It Out" presents the notion that in many situations it is young people who can best solve disputes between their peers. By connecting this real-world idea to what students have just read in "Cricket in the Road," students can explore the way the fictitious argument in the short story reflects disputes and misunderstandings that go on around them every day.

LESSON RESOURCES

UNIT THREE RESOURCE BOOK
PP. 18–19

SKILLS TRANSPARENCIES AND COPYMASTERS

Writing
- How to Summarize, TR 51 (p. 342)

Source: *The Dallas Morning News*

Metro·Region

❶ Peers Talk It Out

SPECIAL REPORT

by Janis Leibs Dworkis

❷ Does a 10-year-old really know enough to help other students solve their problems? Can he understand more than one side of an issue? Can she be fair and impartial if she knows the students involved?

About 10 percent of the 85,000 schools in the United States offer some form of peer mediation. The Dallas Independent School District offers peer mediation in about half of its almost 200 schools. And almost every school district in the Dallas–Fort Worth area offers a similar program in at least some of its schools.

The peer mediation concept is simple: two or more students who have a disagreement talk over their problem in front of one or two of their peers, with no adults present. The peer mediators, who remain neutral, help the students come to a mutually agreeable solution.

At the Nathaniel Hawthorne Elementary School, sixth graders Earnestine Glosson (front left) and Rocio De Leon (front right) mediate a misunderstanding between fourth graders Laura Rios and Quaniqua Davis (back, left and right).

EXPLICIT INSTRUCTION **Reading a Newspaper Article**

Instruction Tell students they can get information from newspaper articles not only by reading the text but also by looking closely at special features, such as the article title, maps, photographs, captions, and quotations shown in large type (called pulled quotations). List these features on the board and ask, "What kinds of features do you find on pages 340–343 that are not part of the text of the article?" (*article title, name of the newspaper section, photograph, caption, pulled quotation*) Explain that these features often give extra information and details not offered in the text and may help students better understand the text. Also explain that they can preview an article to decide whether it will be useful for their research by looking at the features. Tell students that to examine features, they should read any captions, look at pictures and maps, read pulled quotations, and think about what each feature tells them about the subject of the article.

Practice Have students work in pairs to identify the features in this article and write a description of the information contained in each feature.

Possible Responses: Answers will vary. Students should be able to identify these features and use them to gather information: title, photograph, caption, pulled quotation.

 Use **Unit Three Resource Book,** p. 19, for more practice.

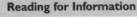

A good way to make sure you understand the articles you read is to **summarize** them. When you summarize, you pay attention to the most important information in an article. Being able to summarize information will help you when you conduct research and when you study for tests.

Summarizing
To summarize a piece of writing, you need to create a shortened version of the text in your own words. First, determine the **main idea** of the whole article. Then find important **supporting details**. A good summary is accurate, reads smoothly, and does not include less important details.

YOUR TURN *Use the activities below to help you summarize the article.*

1 Before you read the article, preview it by looking at the title and at any headings, photographs, and captions. What do you think this article is about?

2 Next, read the article. Write down the main idea or the most important information in each paragraph. After reading, edit your notes so there are only three or four main points. Use these points to determine the main idea of the whole article. What do you think is the most important information in these paragraphs?

Reading for Information

Students may be familiar with the notion of peer mediation already if their school has such a program in place. If so, ask them to approach the concept as if it were new to them. As you examine the article with students, have them use the material in the right-hand column as a guide to reading newspaper articles. The following are possible responses to the numbered activities.

1 The article is about peer mediators and the idea that peer mediators can solve many problems between young people more effectively than adults can.

2 Ideas about the most important information will vary. Possible ideas: First paragraph—Can young people truly help each other solve their problems? Second paragraph—10 percent of the 85,000 schools in the United States offer some form of peer mediation; the Dallas Independent School District has peer mediation in about half of its 200 schools; almost every school district in the Dallas-Fort Worth area offers a similar program in at least some of its schools. Third paragraph—The idea behind peer mediation is that students who have a disagreement discuss it in front of peer mediators. The mediators help students find solutions.

EXPLICIT INSTRUCTION **Summarizing**

Instruction Tell students that they can help themselves remember and understand the articles they read by summarizing them. Explain that a summary is a shortened version of a text, written in students' own words, that includes only the most important ideas and details of the article. Tell students that they can summarize an article by first figuring out the main idea of the whole article and then finding the important supporting details. Write these steps for summarizing on the board: " (1) Note the main idea of each paragraph.

(2) Find the three to four most important ideas in your list of main ideas. (3) Use these ideas to figure out the main idea of the entire article. (4) Go back through the story and find supporting details."

Tell students that after they gather this information, they can use it to write a shortened version of the article. Remind students that a good summary is accurate and does not include less important details.

Practice Have students work in pairs to read and complete the numbered activities on the student pages.

Possible Responses: See the side columns in the teacher's edition for answers to activities.

Use **Unit Three Resource Book**, p. 18, for more practice.

3 The paragraphs give an example of how peer mediation works in one elementary school. They suggest that mediation works because peers listen well and understand the issues involved.

Use **Writing Transparencies,** p. 51, for additional support.

Peer mediators don't dictate an outcome. If no solution can be found, which rarely happens, the mediation ends. Although peer mediators usually address problems related to rumors, gossip or other friendship issues, they have also handled problems related to racism and gangs.

Once the peer mediators are trained and put into action, they tend to be very successful. According to the National Institute for Dispute Resolution, peer mediation programs have reduced the need for adult

> **"If they had been sent to an adult, . . . they would probably just have been told not to do a fight."**

intervention in student conflicts by up to 80 percent in some schools. Some experts say that's because students can understand the problems other students face better than adults can.

Sixth-grader Rocio De Leon is serving her third year as a student mediator at Hawthorne. She remembers one particular mediation involving five or six fourth-grade girls who were fighting about some rumors circulating around school.

"We listened to what they had to say real well. That's so important in mediation. And we asked them what they wanted to have happen. They decided they just wanted to be friends. And they still are very good friends," Rocio says.

"If they had been sent to an adult, instead of coming to mediation, they would probably just have been told not to do a fight. But the adult wouldn't really understand them. It's a lot easier for a child to understand because you're talking to a person who is actually your age and having some of the same problems as you are."

Those who work with peer mediation hope that, in the long run, these problem-solving skills will lessen the occurrence of fighting—not only at school, but elsewhere, too.

Reading for Information *continued*

3 After you've determined the main idea of the article, reread the article. This time, look for supporting details that help make the main idea more understandable. How do these paragraphs help explain peer mediation?

Research & Technology
Activity Link: "Cricket in the Road," p. 338. After finalizing your list of important ideas and supporting details, write a three- or four-sentence summary of "Peers Talk It Out." Then add a brief description of how peer mediation might have worked for Vern, Amy, and Selo. How could they have used peer mediation to settle their argument?

342 UNIT THREE   PART 1: BETWEEN FRIENDS

Research & Technology

Instruction The Research & Technology activity on this page links the newspaper article to the story "Cricket in the Road." As students practice the summarizing skills called for here, they will gain an understanding of the process of peer mediation. They will then be able to apply that knowledge to the situation in the story. First, make sure that students understand what a peer is. They should realize that their peers are those who are approximately their own age and from their own basic background. For instance, a peer would be someone from their school.

After students have had a chance to summarize "Peers Talk It Out," review peer mediation with them. Observe that peer mediators do not dictate an outcome. Their success comes through listening and making all parties feel heard. Once those who are in dispute feel heard, they can move on to a solution that feels fair to everyone.

Practice Ask students to focus on what Vern, Amy, and Selo might have said if they told their peers about their argument. Airing feelings would have been part of a solution.

The Quarrel

by ELEANOR FARJEON

Fable

by RALPH WALDO EMERSON

Connect to Your Life

Despite Our Differences At one time or another, nearly everyone has had a fight or disagreement that seemed impossible to resolve. Can you think of a time when you felt like you and someone else would never see eye to eye, but still you managed to work things out? What happened? How did you come to a resolution?

Build Background

Poems with a Past Narrative poems are poems that tell stories. Long ago, people often told stories in the form of poems because the rhythm of the poetry helped them to learn and remember the stories. As a result, people who did not read were able to pass on the beliefs, tales, and lessons they most valued by learning, and then sharing, narrative poems. All narrative poetry comes from this important tradition, from epic poems that tell about grand adventures of heroes to brief poems like the ones you are about to read.

The *Ellesmere Manuscript* contains Geoffrey Chaucer's 14th-century poem *The Canterbury Tales.*

Detail from Chaucer's *Canterbury Tales*, Ellesmere Manuscript (Facsimile Edition) (1911). Private collection/Bridgeman Art Library.

Focus Your Reading

LITERARY ANALYSIS NARRATIVE POETRY

Poetry that tells a story is called **narrative poetry.** Like any story, a narrative poem contains **characters**, a **setting,** and a **plot.** For example, the plot of each poem you are about to read involves characters who have a quarrel and then come to a resolution.

ACTIVE READING CONNECTING

When your reading brings to mind things you know about or have experienced, you are **connecting.** As you read these poems, think about ways in which you can relate to the events described in the poems.

READER'S NOTEBOOK After you read each poem, think about the connections you can make between the experiences of the characters and your own knowledge or experiences. Record the details that triggered these connections, as well as your own related thoughts.

Standards-Based Objectives

1. understand and appreciate a **narrative poem**
2. understand author's use of **theme** in a narrative poem
3. Use **connecting** to help understand the theme better

Summary

In "The Quarrel," two siblings have a dispute that ends when one generously admits to being in the wrong and proposes that they end the quarrel. In "Fable," the mountain and the squirrel also quarrel, and the mountain calls the squirrel a "little prig." The squirrel points out that being small has its advantages and insists upon respect.

Thematic Link

These two selections continue the theme of fairness between friends. In "The Quarrel," the poet explores the value of rising above petty disagreement. In "Fable," the poet uses a fictitious argument to point out that power and ability do not always belong to the large or mighty.

English Conventions Practice

Daily Language SkillBuilder

Have students proofread the display sentences on page 315k and write them correctly. The sentences also appear on Transparency 11 of **Language Transparencies.**

LESSON RESOURCES

UNIT THREE RESOURCE BOOK
pp. 20–21

ASSESSMENT
Formal Assessment, pp. 53–54
Test Generator

SKILLS TRANSPARENCIES AND COPYMASTERS
Literary Analysis
• Theme, TR 7 (pp. 344, 346)

Reading and Critical Thinking
• Connecting, TR 2 (pp. 344, 346)
Language
• Daily Language SkillBuilder, TR 11 (p. 343)
Writing
• Dialogue, TR 24 (p. 347)
• Poem, TR 35 (p. 347)

INTEGRATED TECHNOLOGY
Audio Library

Visit our Web site:
www.mcdougallittell.com

For **systematic instruction** in language skills, see:
• **Vocabulary and Spelling Book**
• **Grammar, Usage, and Mechanics Book**
• pacing chart on p. 315i.

Literary Analysis

NARRATIVE POETRY

Have students paraphrase the events of both poems, tell who the characters are, and describe any details of settings. Then ask them to give a statement of the theme for each poem.

Use **Unit Three Resource Book**, p. 21, for more practice. Use **Literary Analysis Transparencies**, p. 7, for additional support.

Active Reading **CONNECTING**

Ask students to connect the selections to at least one thing in their own lives. Suggest that they use a chart to note their connections.

Use **Unit Three Resource Book**, p. 20, for more practice. Use **Reading and Critical Thinking Transparencies**, p. 2, for additional support.

Thinking through the Literature

1. **Comprehension Check: Possible Response:** Two siblings have a quarrel, then make up.
2. **Possible Response:** They weren't even quarreling about anything important (they can't remember what started it), the quarrel seems like it will ruin the day, and the brother just wants it to be over.
3. **Possible Response:** The last line says that the brother's position was the right one to take in this situation.

THE Quarrel
by Eleanor Farjeon

Two Birds, One Worm (1989), © William Wegman. Watercolor on paper, 11" × 14".

I quarreled with my brother,
I don't know what about,
One thing led to another
And somehow we fell out.
5   The start of it was slight,
The end of it was strong,
He said he was right,
I knew he was wrong!
We hated one another.
10   The afternoon turned black.
Then suddenly my brother
Thumped me on the back,
And said, "Oh, come along!
We can't go on all night—
15   I was in the wrong."
So he was in the right.

THINKING *through the* LITERATURE

1. **Comprehension Check** What happens in this poem?
2. Why do you think the brother tries to end the quarrel?
   Think About:
   • what the speaker says about the cause of the quarrel
   • the effects of the quarrel
   • the brother's words to the speaker
3. What does the last line of the poem mean?

344

EXPLICIT INSTRUCTION **Viewing and Representing**

Two Birds, One Worm
by William Wegman

ART APPRECIATION William Wegman's simple watercolor is full of the drama of natural life. Wegman is perhaps best known for his photographs of Weimaraners dressed as people, but in this work, two birds compete over their dinner.

Instruction Point out how simple the watercolor image is and yet how full of meaning it is. Ask students to explain how it echoes the theme of the poem "The Quarrel." *(The painting, like the poem, is about a dispute between two creatures.)*

Practice Ask students how the quarrel in the watercolor could have the same outcome as the quarrel in the poem.

Possible Response: If one bird decided to give in to the other, and if the second bird decided to share the worm, then the two birds would stop their quarrel.

Fable
by Ralph Waldo Emerson

Sunrise at Fujiyama, Japan (1928), Lillian Miller
(1885–1943). Woodblock print, 37.3 × 51.6 cm,
Lillian Miller Collection, Scripps College, Claremont.
Photo: G+B Photo, Pasadena, Calif.

The mountain and the squirrel
Had a quarrel,
And the former[1] called the latter[2] "Little Prig";
Bun replied,
5 "You are doubtless very big;
But all sorts of things and weather
Must be taken in together,
To make up a year
And a sphere.
10 And I think it no disgrace
To occupy my place.
If I'm not so large as you,
You are not so small as I,
And not half so spry.[3]
15 I'll not deny you make
A very pretty squirrel track;
Talents differ; all is well and wisely put;
If I cannot carry forests on my back,
Neither can you crack a nut."

---

1. **former:** the first of two things.
2. **latter:** the second of two things.
3. **spry:** lively and active.

Connect to the Literature

1. What Do You Think?
Possible Response: The squirrel has good sense to stand up for itself with such a calm and reasonable argument.

Comprehension Check
• The mountain is big and supports forests (home to the squirrel).
• The squirrel is small and spry and can crack nuts (impossible for the mountain).

Think Critically

2. Responses will vary, but the message is something to this effect: Everyone has necessary talents, so it is foolish to quarrel over who is most important. The squirrel responds to the mountain's insult ("Little Prig," line 3) by telling the mountain that they are each valuable. Each is uniquely valuable, so it is pointless to insult each other and quarrel over who is most important.

3. Possible Response: The squirrel is self-confident, outspoken, fair, reasonable, thoughtful, expressive, and so on. Though small, the squirrel stands up for itself to the mountain; it knows and values its own talents while acknowledging the mountain's talents.

4. Responses will vary. Students might identify with the sibling characters in "The Quarrel," who lost track of why they were fighting. Alternately, they may identify with the squirrel in "Fable," which stood up for itself in response to an insult.

🖥 Use **Reading and Critical Thinking Transparencies**, p. 2, for additional support.

Literary Analysis

Narrative Poetry Students should concentrate on presenting poems calmly and deliberately so that their messages, or themes, can be understood. To make this activity more challenging, have students work in larger groups and pantomime the action of the poems as they recite.

🖥 Use **Literary Analysis Transparencies**, p. 7, for additional support.

Connect to the Literature

1. What Do You Think?
How did you react to the words of the squirrel?

Comprehension Check
• What are named as the mountain's most important traits?
• What does the squirrel name as its most important traits?

Think Critically

2. What do you think is the main message of the squirrel's speech?

Think About:
• the differences between the squirrel and the mountain
• the unique qualities of each
• the last two lines of the poem

3. How would you describe the squirrel in "Fable"? Support your answer by referring to the poem.

4. **ACTIVE READING** **MAKING CONNECTIONS**
Which poem did you relate to more? Give reasons for your answer based on the details you recorded in your 📖 **READER'S NOTEBOOK**.

Extend Interpretations

5. **COMPARING TEXTS** Compare the quarrels in these poems with the quarrel in "Cricket in the Road" on page 333. How are they similar? What are the biggest differences? Support your opinions with details from the selections.

6. Connect to Life After reading these poems, what helpful tips for resolving a real argument can you offer? Use words and examples from the poem to elaborate on your tips.

Literary Analysis

NARRATIVE POETRY Poetry that tells a story is called **narrative poetry.** Like other stories, a narrative poem includes **characters,** a **setting,** and a **plot.** Narrative poetry may contain such elements of poetry as **rhyme, rhythm, imagery,** and **personification.** The description of the mountain "carrying a forest on its back" is an example of imagery. It is also an example of personification, or giving human qualities to something that is not human.

Paired Activity Working with a partner, prepare one of these poems each for a dramatic reading to your class. First, practice reciting the poem for each other. Read in a way that brings to life the characters in the poem and the action of the plot. Speak slowly and make sure your words are clear and distinct.

Extend Interpretations

5. Comparing Texts Possible Responses:
Differences: "The Quarrel" does not give details about the disagreement, where "Cricket in the Road" does. The brother capitulates in "The Quarrel," and the characters in "Cricket" make up, while the squirrel defends itself. Similarities: Both poems and the story say the quarrels are foolish or pointless, the issues insignificant or invalid, and the division between characters hurtful and unnecessary.

6. Connect to Life Responses will vary. The poems could encourage combatants to consider the importance of what they argue about; the damage that may result; the value of others, despite differences; the possibility of giving in to end a stalemate; and the possibility of standing up for themselves calmly and rationally when points of view differ.

Writing

Conversation Poem Think of a disagreement you've had with a friend or a family member. Then write a narrative poem about it. Include in your poem the thoughts and feelings you had at the time of the disagreement. Also use dialogue in your poem. Place your finished poem in your **Working Portfolio.**

Writing Handbook
See p. R39: Descriptive Writing.

Speaking & Listening

Dramatic Reading Present a dramatic reading of the poem you wrote for the writing activity on this page. Use facial expressions, gestures, and the tone of your voice to show the feelings in the poem. Rehearse your dramatic reading several times. Then present it to the class.

Speaking and Listening Handbook
See p. R98: Oral Interpretation.

Research & Technology

Friendship Quotations
Friendship is a subject that many famous people have written and talked about. In the library, locate a book of quotations and look up the subject of friendship or friends. Find two or three quotations that are especially interesting and write them down. Be sure to include information about where the quotations came from. Create a friendship wall with classmates and display your quotations on the wall.

Writing

Conversational Poem To give students another example of the use of conversational-style and dialogue in a poem, have them reread the poem "Growing Pains," on page 197. Point out that "Growing Pains" is serious, while "The Quarrel" and "Fable" are not so serious. Tell students they can choose the tone and mood of their poem.

Use **Writing Transparencies,** pp. 24, 35, for additional support.

Speaking & Listening

Dramatic Reading Suggest students perform their reading for a friend to get feedback on their performance and tips for improvement.

Research & Technology

Friendship Quotations Allow students time to find quotations that appeal to them. Invite students to explore books of quotations to find quotations on other topics of interest to them.

Eleanor Farjeon

When Farjeon began her writing at age seven, she did not bother with pen and paper. Instead she began tapping away at her father's typewriter as if she knew she had to hurry to finish seventy years' worth of writing!

Ralph Waldo Emerson

Though Emerson is now known mostly for his philosophy, his poetry was once highly regarded. American writer Nathaniel Hawthorne said of him that he admired Emerson "as a poet of deep beauty . . . but sought nothing from him as a philosopher."

Eleanor Farjeon
1881–1965

"It would have been . . . as unnatural not to read as not to eat."

Ralph Waldo Emerson
1803–1882

"Nothing great was ever achieved without enthusiasm."

A Passion for Words Eleanor Farjeon grew up in London, England. She gained much of her education at home, by reading books in her father's library and talking with the writers and stage performers who were family friends. She began writing poems and stories when she was seven. At 16, she co-wrote a libretto (the script for an opera) that was performed at London's famous Royal Academy of Music.

International Success Although Farjeon lived and wrote in England, her work was read and enjoyed in many countries. She wrote for more than 70 years, publishing poems, short stories, and novels. Her poems are often included in collections of favorite verse for children.

Claims to Fame Emerson was one of the most famous poets and thinkers of the 19th century. Trained as a minister, he later dedicated himself to writing and lecturing about his ideas on religion, nature, and society. Some of Emerson's beliefs are expressed in his well-known essay "Self-Reliance," which encourages people to make up their own minds about what they believe to be right.

A Lasting Influence Emerson's friends and followers included poet Walt Whitman and writer Henry David Thoreau. In his poetry, Emerson used clearer images, simpler words, and freer verse forms than most of the poets before him. His style helped shape modern poetry.

Building Vocabulary

Standards-Based Objectives

- identify the relation of word meanings in analogies
- recognize a variety of types of word relationships

VOCABULARY EXERCISE

1. line
2. moist
3. hero
4. love
5. book

 Use **Unit Three Resource Book,** p. 22.

Building Vocabulary
Understanding Analogies

An **analogy** contains two word pairs. The words in each pair have similar relationships. Words may be related as synonyms or as antonyms, for example, or one word might describe another. Analogies can help you understand these word relationships.

> Sitting across from her on the sofa was a squat blob of a man—balding and gray— as silent as a mushroom. . . .
> —Yoshiko Uchida, "Oh Broom, Get to Work"

The word *squat* means "short and thick; low and broad."

Squat is to mushroom as tall is to skyscraper.

Written in a formal way, an analogy looks like this:

SQUAT : MUSHROOM ∷ tall : skyscraper

Notice that in both pairs, the relationship is descriptive.

Strategies for Building Vocabulary

The following tips can help you understand and complete analogies.

❶ **Read Analogies** The words *happy* and *contented* are **synonyms,** as are the words *sad* and *depressed.* An analogy for these word pairs would be written this way:

HAPPY : CONTENTED :: sad : depressed

You would read the statement like this:

> Happy **relates to** contented as sad **relates to** depressed.

On a test, you might be asked to complete an analogy by filling in the appropriate word:

HAPPY : CONTENTED :: sad : __?__

❷ **State the Relationship** In completing an analogy, it helps to read it aloud, restating it more precisely. For example, if the words are synonyms, you can use the phrase "means almost the same as." If the words are antonyms, say "means the opposite of."

SILENT : NOISY :: sad : __?__

Say the analogy as though it were a sentence:

> Silent **means the opposite of** noisy as sad **means the opposite of** what?

❸ **Review Your Choice** First, determine the relationship expressed in the first word pair. Next, choose a word to complete the second word pair. Finally, test your choice by reading the complete statement. For example:

> Silent **means the opposite of** noisy as sad **means the opposite of** happy.

Here are some common word relationships.

Relationship	Example
Synonyms	BIG : LARGE :: shiny : bright
Antonyms	FRIEND : ENEMY :: bottom : top
Part to Whole	LEAF : TREE :: spoke : wheel
Item to Category	POODLE : DOG :: daisy : flower
Descriptive	ROUND : CIRCLE :: pointy : arrow

EXERCISE For each exercise write a word that completes the analogy.

1. ROUND : CIRCLE :: straight : __?__
2. BIG : LARGE :: damp : __?__
3. FRIEND : ENEMY :: coward : __?__
4. PUSH : SHOVE :: like : __?__
5. LEAF : TREE :: page : __?__

The Southpaw
by Judith Viorst

Dear Richard,

Don't invite me to your birthday party because I'm not coming. And give back the Disneyland sweat shirt I said you could wear. If I'm not good enough to play on your team, I'm not good enough to be friends with.

Your former friend, Janet

P.S. I hope when you go to the dentist he finds twenty cavities.

Dear Janet,

Here is your stupid Disneyland sweat shirt, if that's how you're going to be. I want my comic books now—finished or not. No girl has ever played on the Mapes Street baseball team, and as long as I'm captain, no girl ever will.

Your former friend, Richard

P.S. I hope when you go for your checkup you need a tetanus shot.

THE SOUTHPAW **349**

Possible Objectives

- enjoy independent reading (Option One)
- read and analyze literature with a group (Option Two)
- use the Reader's Notebook to formulate questions about literature (Option Three)
- write in response to literature (Option Four)

Summary

This story is told through the exchange of letters between two friends who are arguing about the right of one of them to play on the neighborhood baseball team. Richard is the captain of the Mapes Street baseball team. Janet is his friend who wants to play on the team. She has been left out because she is a girl. Janet tries to blackmail Richard into putting her on the team by taking back things she'd given him, such as her sweatshirt, and by not inviting him for ice cream. Richard continues to refuse. As the summer wears on, however, his team loses game after game and his players drop out one by one. Finally, he is forced to ask Janet to play on the team, which she agrees to do only if she can pitch and the other neighborhood girls can play as well.

Reading the Selection

Option One
Independent Reading

You might set aside time each week for independent reading to help your students approach the goal of reading 1 million words a year. During this time, you and your students would read for enjoyment. "The Southpaw" can be read independently in 20 minutes or so. To encourage students to read for pleasure, consider making no assignments related to this selection. However, Options Two and Three offer suggestions in case you do want to make assignments.

Option Two
Group Reading
You may assign students to groups or allow them to choose their own. Students can read the selection together, alternately reading sections aloud, or they can read independently and meet to cooperate in a project that portrays some element of the story.

Possible Projects
- Students can collaborate on writing, in letter form, a different ending to the story in which Richard and Janet do not reach an agreement.
- Students can role-play an interview of Janet and Richard by a reporter for the school newspaper following Janet's first game.

Art Appreciation
The painting on this page by Katherine Desjardins captures the feeling of conversations between friends. What are they saying? Who is saying what to whom?

While the people in the painting are realistic looking, the background isn't. Sometimes the shapes seem to link the friends, and sometimes they seem to separate them.

Ask: Why do you think this artwork has been chosen to illustrate "The Southpaw"?

Untitled (Radiation) (1998), Katherine Desjardins. Oil and resin on wood, 24" × 24". Photograph courtesy of Dan Soper.

Why don't you forget about baseball and learn something nice like knitting?

I understand you're the laughingstock of New Jersey.

Dear Richard,

I'm changing my goldfish's name from Richard to Stanley. Don't count on my vote for class president next year. Just because I'm a member of the ballet club doesn't mean I'm not a terrific ballplayer.

Your former friend, Janet

P.S. I see you lost your first game, 28–0.

Dear Janet,

I'm not saving any more seats for you on the bus. For all I care you can stand the whole way to school. Why don't you forget about baseball and learn something nice like knitting?

Your former friend, Richard

P.S. Wait until Wednesday.

Dear Richard,

My father said I could call someone to go with us for a ride and hot-fudge sundaes. In case you didn't notice, I didn't call you.

Your former friend, Janet

P.S. I see you lost your second game, 34–0.

Dear Janet,

Remember when I took the laces out of my blue-and-white sneakers and gave them to you? I want them back.

Your former friend, Richard

P.S. Wait until Friday.

Dear Richard,

Congratulations on your unbroken record. Eight straight losses, wow! I understand you're the laughingstock of New Jersey.

Your former friend, Janet

P.S. Why don't you and your team forget about baseball and learn something nice like knitting, maybe?

Dear Janet,

Here's the silver horseback-riding trophy that you gave me. I don't think I want to keep it anymore.

Your former friend, Richard

P.S. I didn't think you'd be the kind who'd kick a man when he's down.

Dear Richard,

I wasn't kicking exactly. I was kicking back.

Your former friend, Janet

P.S. In case you were wondering my batting average is .345.

Dear Janet,

Alfie is having his tonsils out tomorrow. We might be able to let you catch next week.

Richard

Dear Richard,

I pitch.

Janet

Dear Janet,

Joel is moving to Kansas and Danny sprained his wrist. How about a permanent place in the outfield?

Richard

Dear Richard,

I pitch.

Janet

THE SOUTHPAW   351

Art Note

The collage on this page, *Corrugated Catcher* by Saul Steinberg, takes a humorous look at baseball. The Romanian-born artist (1914–1999) was a keen observer of American culture, often using his sense of humor to comment on life in cartoons for the *New Yorker* magazine. This collage, which features the material often found in shipping boxes, has a light, whimsical attitude, which matches the tone of Viorst's storytelling style.

Corrugated Catcher (1954), Saul Steinberg, 29" × 20", courtesy of Jason Van Dalen. Copyright © 2001 Estate of Saul Steinberg/Artists Rights Society (ARS), New York.

I'll give you first base. That's my final offer.   I pitch.

Dear Janet,

   Ronnie caught the chicken pox and Leo broke his toe and Elwood has these stupid violin lessons. I'll give you first base. That's my final offer.

   Richard

Dear Richard,

   Susan Reilly plays first base, Marilyn Jackson catches, Ethel Kahn plays center field, I pitch. It's a package deal.

   Janet

P.S. Sorry about your 12-game losing streak.

Dear Janet,

   Please! Not Marilyn Jackson.

   Richard

Dear Richard,

   Nobody ever said that I was unreasonable. How about Lizzie Martindale instead?

   Janet

Dear Janet,

   At least could you call your goldfish Richard again?

   Your friend, Richard ❖

Judith Viorst
born 1931

"I always, always, always wanted to be a writer."

A Lifelong Writer Judith Viorst began writing poetry as a young child. "I took my writing very seriously," she says, "and thought everything I wrote was a masterpiece." After college she worked as an editor and journalist. While raising her children, she discovered that motherhood provided an endless source of material. The names and antics of her three sons made their way into her writing for children—most famously in her classic picture book *Alexander and the Terrible, Horrible, No Good, Very Bad Day.* This book was recently made into a musical, for which Viorst wrote many of the lyrics.

On the Go Viorst's writing is praised for its unique sense of humor and its sympathetic portrayals of life's everyday struggles. "It helps to understand that the losses of life . . . are part of the human condition," Viorst says. For nearly 40 years she has lived in Washington, D.C., with her husband, Milton Viorst, who is also a writer. Energetic and organized, she usually seems to be doing several things at the same time: once she cooked an entire chicken dinner while on the phone answering questions for a radio show. She has written dozens of books, ranging from collections of comic poetry to serious nonfiction books about psychology.

THE SOUTHPAW **353**

Possible Activities
Independent Activities
• Have advanced students skim over the story, noting details, facts, and descriptions about the friendship between Richard and Janet. Ask them to write in their Reader's Notebook their analysis of the relationship between these two characters and what it reveals about each.
• Have students review the Learning the Language of Literature and Active Reader pages, pp. 317–321. Ask them to note which skills and strategies they used while reading this selection.

Discussion Activities
• Use the questions formulated by the students in their Reader's Notebooks as the start of a discussion about this story.
• Ask students how they feel about Richard finally asking Janet to save the team from utter disgrace. Would they have done the same thing in his place?

Assessment Opportunities
• You can assess students' comprehension of the story by evaluating the questions they formulate in their Reader's Notebook.
• You can use one of the discussion questions given above as an essay question.
• You can choose one of the Reader's Notebook activities, given on page 351, and ask students to write their responses in essay form.
• You can ask students to summarize the story.

Judith Viorst

Judith Viorst's three children are perhaps the greatest source of inspiration for her writing. She wrote several of her books in response to problems that one or another of her own children was facing. Although she knew the books wouldn't solve their problems, she hoped that the books would help her boys "laugh at their problems, or look at them in less troubled, less hopeless ways."

Among the books that she wrote with her own children in mind are *I'll Fix Anthony,* which she wrote for her son Nick who bore the brunt of his older brother Anthony's teasing, and *Sunday Morning,* which features Anthony and Nick in a series of early morning adventures while their parents are still sleeping.

Analysis of Baseball

by
May Swenson

It's about
the ball,
the bat,
and the mitt.
5 Ball hits
bat, or it
hits mitt.
Bat doesn't
hit ball, bat
10 meets it.
Ball bounces
off bat, flies
air, or thuds
ground (dud)
15 or it
fits mitt.

Bat waits
for ball
to mate.
20 Ball hates
to take bat's
bait. Ball
flirts, bat's
late, don't
25 keep the date.
Ball goes in
(thwack) to mitt,
and goes out
(thwack) back
30 to mitt.

Ball fits
mitt, but
not all
the time.
35 Sometimes
ball gets hit
(pow) when bat
meets it,
and sails
40 to a place
where mitt
has to quit
in disgrace.
That's about
45 the bases
loaded,
about 40,000
fans exploded.

It's about
50 the ball,
the bat,
the mitt,
the bases
and the fans.
55 It's done
on a diamond,
and for fun.
It's about
home, and it's
60 about run.

Writing Workshop

Comparison-and-Contrast Essay

Pointing out similarities and differences . . .

From Reading to Writing When you read about Damon and Pythias and about Janet and Richard, you might think that their friendships are very different. The mythological friends are on the same side of a conflict. The modern-day friends are on opposite sides. However, both sets of friends share an important similarity: their friendship really matters to them. Writing a **comparison-and-contrast essay** helps you examine how two subjects are similar and different and deepens your understanding of both subjects.

For Your Portfolio

WRITING PROMPT Write a comparison-and-contrast essay about two subjects that interest you.

Purpose: To inform, explain, or clarify
Audience: Anyone interested in your subjects

Basics in a Box

Comparison-and-Contrast Essay at a Glance

Introduction	Body	Conclusion
• introduces the **subjects** being compared • tells the **purpose** for the comparison	explains similarities and differences Subject A only — Both subjects — Subject B only	• summarizes the comparison • explains new understanding

RUBRIC STANDARDS FOR WRITING

A successful comparison-and-contrast essay should

- introduce the subjects being compared
- state a clear purpose for the comparison
- include both similarities and differences and support each statement with examples and details
- follow a clear organizational pattern
- include transitional words and phrases to make similarities and differences clear
- summarize the comparison in a conclusion linked to the purpose of the essay

---

LESSON RESOURCES

USING PRINT RESOURCES
Unit Six Resource Book
- Prewriting, p. 23
- Drafting and Elaborating, p. 24
- Peer Response Guide, p. 25
- Organizational Patterns, p. 26
- Revising, Editing, and Proofreading, p. 27
- Student Models, pp. 28–30
- Rubric for Evaluation, p. 31

Reading and Critical Thinking
- Venn Diagram, TR 35 (p. 357)
Speaking and Listening
- Understanding Audience and Purpose, pp. 6–7 (p. 360)
- Developing and Delivering a Presentation, pp. 8–9, 12–13 (p. 360)
- Creating and Analyzing an Informative Presentation, pp. 25–26 (p. 360)

INTEGRATED TECHNOLOGY
Writing Coach CD-ROM
Visit our Web site:
www.mcdougallittell.com

Writing Workshop
Comparison-and-Contrast Essay

Standards-Based Objectives
- write a 500- to 700-word comparison-and-contrast essay
- use a comparison-contrast text as a model for writing
- revise a draft to add examples and details
- make comparisons using adjectives
- deliver an informative presentation

Introducing the Workshop

Comparison-and-Contrast Essay
Help students to see that any two subjects can be compared in a comparison-and-contrast essay—it might be two people, two things, or two events. Lead a class discussion to brainstorm possible subjects for comparisons. Choosing two subjects that are too similar or too different does not make a very effective comparison essay.

Basics in a Box
Using the Graphic The elements of a comparison-and-contrast essay are shown in the graphic. Students should note that the introduction and conclusion are particularly important because they make the reader aware of the point of the essay. The introduction sets up the reason for the comparison, and the conclusion explains what new understanding can come from the comparison. Point out the Venn diagram that forms the body of the essay, and remind students of other times they have used this format.

Presenting the Rubric To help students better understand the assignment, review the Standards for Writing a Successful Comparison-and-Contrast Essay. You may also want to share with them the complete rubric, which describes several levels of proficiency.

 See **Unit Three Resource Book**, p. 31.

 For more instruction on essential writing skills, see McDougal Littell's *Language Network*, Chapters 10–17.

 Power Presentation

To engage students visually, use **Power Presentation 2**, Comparison-and-Contrast Essay.

Analyzing the Model

My Two Countries

In this essay, the writer compares her native country of Japan to the United States, where she currently lives. The essay focuses on two main areas—transportation and shopping. She offers the reader a closer look at these two elements in terms of their similarities and differences.

Have students read the model and discuss what makes it a successful comparison-and-contrast essay. Then discuss the Rubric in Action. Point out key sections of the model that correspond to the elements mentioned in the Rubric in Action.

1 Ask why it is important to state the subjects being compared.

Possible Response: The reader will know exactly what the essay is about and can activate any prior knowledge about the subjects.

2 Discuss how a subject-by-subject organization would differ from a feature-by-feature organization.

Possible Response: Instead of analyzing all aspects of transportation, then going on to shopping, a subject-by-subject organization would first tell about Japan, discussing features, and then talk about the United States covering the same features.

3 Have students discuss how the author knew these specific facts and how they will gather facts for their own essays.

Possible Response: The author has lived in both countries, and she may have talked to experts or read a book to gather specific facts. Students should indicate that those would be good strategies for them to use as well.

4 Ask students to summarize one of the differences stated in this section.

Possible Response: Most people in Japan get to work by using public transportation. In the United States, most people drive cars.

5 Ask students to suggest other key words that could signal a transition.

Possible Responses: However; Not all; In the United States

Analyzing a Student Model

SPEAKING OPPORTUNITY
See the Speaking and Listening Handbook, p. R96 for oral presentation tips.

**Yoshio Adachi
St. Walter's School**

My Two Countries

I am lucky because I am only ten and I have lived in two countries—Japan and the United States. When I first moved to the United States, I was very shocked at how different it is from my homeland. Japan is one of the oldest empires in the world. It is a small country, located on a chain of islands in the Pacific Ocean. Much of the land is crowded with people. The United States, however, is a young country and is the fourth largest country in the world. As a result, it is quieter, even in cities. The two countries also share similarities and differences—in the areas of transportation and shopping. Comparing these features can help us to understand each country better.

First of all, both countries have public transportation. In Japan, most people don't have cars. Therefore, public transportation, such as subways and trains, must be convenient. There are 12 different subway lines with over 125 train stations in Tokyo alone. People also ride bicycles or walk to stores or to work. In contrast, most Americans have their own cars. They would rather drive than wait for a train or a bus. Even though many Americans do use public transportation, it is not as convenient as it is in Japan. The distance between the stations and American homes makes it more difficult.

There are also similarities and differences in what is called "rush hour." In both Japan and the United States, rush hour is hectic. In Japan, most people ride the train to work. The train gets crowded quickly, and many people must stand. Most subway and train companies hire people called "pushers" who work only during the rush hour. The pusher's job is to push people into the train so the doors will close. When the train stops at a station and the doors open, slowly the crowd of people surges forward. The pusher pushes the rest of the people onto the train before the doors close. In contrast, the American rush hour is mostly a problem for people driving cars. Usually there is only one person in a car and the cars clog the streets. Many Americans try to find shortcuts that will help them get to work faster. Both Japanese and Americans are often frustrated by the start of their work day.

RUBRIC IN ACTION

❶ Introduces the subjects being compared in a way that engages the reader's interest

❷ Clearly states the purpose of the composition and uses a feature-by-feature organization

Other option:
• Use a subject-by-subject organization.

❸ Specific facts support points of comparison and show the writer's knowledge of the subject.

❹ Detailed examples and precise language help make differences clear.

❺ Transitions signal differences and unify the paragraph.

6 Ask students to identify the sentence that summarizes the significant differences between the two countries.

Answer: The differences in transportation and shopping help to make each culture unique.

7 Ask students what the student writer has learned from living in two countries.

Possible Responses: The writer has learned that people are similar, no matter where you go.

Differences in transportation lead to differences in shopping styles. Both Japanese and American people buy most of their groceries in stores. However, the Japanese shop for food items at individual stores. There are many small shops, which usually sell just one thing. There are fish stores, butchers, or bakeries. Many of these small shops are open in the front and are just a few feet from the street. Every day, Japanese people shop for their supper. The shop owners call out to invite people to buy. Taking public transportation doesn't let people "stock up" as Americans do with their big cars. In the United States, many Americans shop just once a week. Storing food in large refrigerators and freezers allows them to plan ahead for a week or more.

Another way to shop in Japan is by vending machine. Vending machines are very popular because it's easy for people taking public transportation to use them. There is probably one on every street corner. Similar to the United States, the vending machines in Japan hold drinks. Soda and tea are common, but some machines have soup. Iced coffee and tea are Japanese favorites. In contrast, there are fewer vending machines in the United States. There are also fewer drink choices in the machines that do exist.

The differences in transportation and shopping help to make each culture unique. But these are not the only things. Japan is a very traditional society that has worked hard to take care of the large number of people living in such a small place. The United States is a very young country with plenty of space. However, having lived in both places, one thing I have learned is that people are people wherever you go. The language and styles may be different, but the people are the same. The friends I have made in the United States are very much like my friends in Japan—loyal, smart, and willing to help me learn more about the beauty of a country.

6 The conclusion summarizes significant differences and relates to the purpose of the essay.

7 The writer shows the importance of the comparison.

EXPLICIT INSTRUCTION **Patterns of Organization**

PICTURING TEXT STRUCTURE

Instruction One way to structure a good comparison-and-contrast essay is to have students complete a Venn diagram showing the unique features of each subject and the things the subjects have in common.

Practice Have students analyze the organization of the student model by constructing a Venn diagram to illustrate how the writer organized the essay, such as in the sample shown here.

Use **Unit Three Resource Book,** p. 35, to help students use and revise the comparision and contrast organizational pattern. Use **Reading and Critical Thinking Transparencies,** p. 35, for additional support.

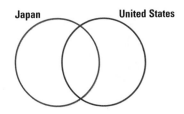

Japan   United States

Prewriting

Choosing Two Subjects to Compare

If after reading the Idea Bank students have difficulty choosing subjects for their comparison-and-contrast essay, suggest they try the following:

- go back to the brainstormed lists of subjects from the beginning of the lesson
- think about people, places, and things in their own lives that interest them
- share ideas with a partner

Planning Your Comparison-and-Contrast Essay

1. Tell students that their essay will be more meaningful if they have a reason for comparing and contrasting two subjects. Help them to think about what those reasons might be.

2. Ask students to brainstorm some of the similarities and differences. Then have them focus in on a couple that will help them achieve their chosen purpose. This will make each student's essay easier to write because it will be more focused.

3. Ask students to work individually to complete a Venn diagram or chart listing the similarities and differences for the features they have decided on. Remind them to keep it simple and focused on their purpose.

4. Remind them of the student sample and the discussion held earlier concerning feature-by-feature and subject-by-subject organizational methods. Use the graphic to help students think about which method may be best for their essay.

Drafting

Once students have completed their Venn diagram or chart and decided on the organizational pattern, they should be ready to write their first draft.

IDEA Bank

1. Your Working Portfolio

Look for ideas in the **Writing** activities that you completed earlier.

2. Inventions

Set out to compare products new and old, such as CDs with records, or videos with filmstrips. Ask family members for help in getting ideas for writing your comparison.

3. Favorite Activities

Compare and contrast features of two of your favorite hobbies or sports or other activities.

Have a question?

See the **Writing Handbook.**

Transitions, p. R36

Elaboration, p. R37

Compare and Contrast, p. R43

See **Language Network,** Compare-and-Contrast Order, pp. 306–307.

Ask Your Peer Reader

- Was my reason for comparison clear?
- Did I support my statements with facts and examples?
- Is my organization consistent?

Writing Your Comparison-and-Contrast Essay

❶ Prewriting

Begin by **listing** stories, characters, objects, or people you want to compare. See the **Idea Bank** for more suggestions. Then follow the steps below.

Planning Your Comparison-and-Contrast Essay

▶ 1. **Decide on your purpose.** Why do you want to compare and contrast your two subjects? Do you want to understand something better? Do you want to make a decision?

▶ 2. **Look at key features of your subjects.** Which features do you want to focus on? Which comparisons will help you support your purpose?

▶ 3. **Generate similarities and differences.** Use a Venn diagram or a chart to record similarities and differences.

Feature	Similar	Different
population	both have large populations	in Japan, more crowded because less land
transportation	both have public transportation	fewer Japanese own cars

▶ 4. **Choose your organization.** You can compare and contrast two subjects by describing all the features of one subject and then all the features of the other subject. This is the **subject-by-subject** method. You can also discuss the features one by one, first in one subject, then in the other. This is the **feature-by-feature** approach.

Subject by Subject	Feature by Feature
Subject A	Feature 1
feature 1	subject A
feature 2	subject B
Subject B	Feature 2
feature 1	subject A
feature 2	subject B

❷ Drafting

Begin drafting your essay using the organizational pattern you chose. For either pattern, you will need an introduction, body, and conclusion.

- Your **introduction** should identify the subjects you are comparing and state your purpose.
- In the **body,** you should begin a new paragraph for each subject, if using the

subject-by-subject pattern, or for each feature, if using the feature-by-feature pattern. Use examples and details for support. Use transitions to link your ideas.

- Your **conclusion** should summarize your comparison and connect to the purpose you identified earlier.

❸ Revising

TARGET SKILL ▶ ELABORATING WITH EXAMPLES AND OTHER DETAILS When making comparisons, you must provide examples to support your statements. Giving one example may save several sentences of explanation and allow your reader to visualize what you are saying. For example, instead of saying one movie was better than another, you might describe the reaction of the audience: *Everyone yawned through the first movie.*

In Japan, most people don't have cars. Therefore, public transportation, such as subways and trains, must be convenient. *There are 12 different subway lines with over 125 train stations in Tokyo alone.*

❹ Editing and Proofreading

TARGET SKILL ▶ COMPARING WITH ADJECTIVES Adjectives such as *fast, faster,* and *fastest* signal a comparison. The comparative form of the adjective is often created by adding *–er.* To compare more than two items, use the superlative form by adding *–est* to the adjective. Some adjectives have irregular comparative or superlative forms, and some show degrees of comparison when the word *less, least, more,* or *most* is placed before them.

As a result, it is ~~more quiet~~ *quieter,* even in cities.

❺ Reflecting

FOR YOUR WORKING PORTFOLIO What did you learn about your subjects by comparing them? What other subjects would you like to compare and contrast? Attach your answers to your finished essay. Save your comparison-and-contrast essay in your **Working Portfolio.**

Need revising help?

Review the **Rubric,** p. 355

Consider **peer reader** comments

Check **Revision Guidelines,** p. R31

SPELLING
From Writing

As you revise your work, look back at the words you misspelled and determine why you made the errors you did. For additional help, refer to the strategies and generalizations in the **Spelling Handbook** on page R26.

Unclear about comparatives and superlatives?

See the **Grammar Handbook,** Using Modifiers Effectively, p. R78.

See **Language Network,** Making Comparisons, p. 133.

SPEAKING
Opportunity

Turn your essay into an oral presentation.

Publishing
IDEAS

- Make a chart to show the differences and similarities between your subjects, and present your essay as a speech.
- Print out your essay on the computer and insert diagrams and illustrations to help emphasize important points. Hang your essay on the bulletin board.

🔗 **INTERNET**

Publishing Options
www.mcdougallittell.com

Revising
ELABORATING WITH
EXAMPLES AND OTHER DETAILS

Look at the two examples given, and help students to see how much more powerful the sentences with examples and details are. Ask for a volunteer to share a sentence from his or her essay. Model how to elaborate using examples and details. Ask students to work with a partner to elaborate in their own essays.

Editing and Proofreading
COMPARING
WITH ADJECTIVES

Ask students to read through their own essays looking for comparative and superlative forms of adjectives. Have them check to see if they've used the forms correctly and to edit as necessary.

Reflecting

🗂 Encourage students to be specific in reflecting about their essay writing. Ask them to describe what they learned in detail and to suggest other subjects they would like to explore.

Option
TEACHING TIP

It is sometimes difficult for students to compare and contrast subjects in a meaningful way. It may be helpful for you to think about authentic purposes for writing comparison-and-contrast essays and to include these suggestions early in the essay writing process. For example, if students choose to compare two books, the purpose might be to provide classmates with information about the books so that they could choose one of them for a particular class assignment.

EXPLICIT INSTRUCTION Revision

ORGANIZATION

Instruction Remind students that in a well-organized composition, ideas within the body of the paper need to be supported with examples and other details. Have students think of at least one more example that they can add to their comparison-and-contrast essays and share that example with a partner.

Practice Ask students to read each of the paragraphs in the body of their essays to find places where an additional example would make their comparison-and-contrast essays stronger and more convincing.

RUBRIC

3 **Full Accomplishment** Student supports comparisons and contrasts with examples, which are drawn from the work and are complete and accurate.

2 **Substantial Accomplishment** Student uses a few examples throughout the paper to support comparisons and contrasts.

Examples are drawn from the work and are reasonably complete and accurate.

1 **Little or Partial Accomplishment** Student has limited support for the comparisons and contrasts that he or she draws. The examples that are used are incomplete or inaccurate.

See the **Research and Technology Handbook,** pp. R108-109, for information about formatting documents using word processing skills.

Ask students to read the entire passage prior to correcting the errors. Then demonstrate how students can eliminate incorrect choices for the first question.

An apostrophe is used to show possession or in a contraction. There is no possession in this sentence, and there are no contractions, so no apostrophe is needed. Therefore A and C are incorrect. When making a word plural that ends in *y*, the *y* is changed to *i* and *-es* is added. Therefore, B is incorrect. The correct response is D.

Answers:

1. D, **2.** A, **3.** A, **4.** C, **5.** D, **6.** B

Standardized Test Practice

Mixed Review

There are many differences between the book and the movie version of *Father, Dancing*. The book has stronger characters whose <u>personalities</u> ⁽¹⁾ are fully developed. The director of the movie must have thought that having big-name actors would make up for a lack of character development. The plot of the book is also <u>best</u> than the one in the movie, ⁽²⁾ because <u>some scenes they leave out are important</u>. On the other hand, ⁽³⁾ the movie has flashy special effects. However, <u>effects has less meaning</u> ⁽⁴⁾ than plot. In my opinion, the <u>book is</u> more interesting than the movie, ⁽⁵⁾ even though the movie was <u>the more expensive</u> production in the history ⁽⁶⁾ of Hollywood.

1. How is sentence 1 best written?
   A. personalities'
   B. personalitys
   C. personality's
   D. Correct as is

2. What is the correct form of the adjective in item 2?
   A. better
   B. more good
   C. most good
   D. Correct as is

3. How is item 3 best written?
   A. some scenes the movie leaves out are important.
   B. some scenes the book leaves out are important.
   C. some scenes we leave out are important.
   D. Correct as is

4. How is sentence 4 best written?
   A. effects had less meaning
   B. effects has had less meaning
   C. effects have less meaning
   D. Correct as is

5. How is item 5 best written?
   A. book are
   B. book were
   C. books were
   D. Correct as is

6. What is the correct form of the adjective in item 6?
   A. the expensivest
   B. the most expensive
   C. the expensiver
   D. Correct as is

Review Your Skills

Use the passage and the questions that follow it to check how well you remember the language conventions you've learned in previous grades.

Self-Assessment

Check your own answers in the **Grammar Handbook.**

Making Subjects and Verbs Agree, p. R68

Using Nouns and Pronouns, p. R71

Using Modifiers Effectively, p. R78

EXPLICIT INSTRUCTION Speaking Opportunity

Prepare Once students have written their comparison-and-contrast essay, they can plan to present it to an audience. Refer students to pages R100–102 of the Speaking and Listening Handbook at the back of this book for tips on planning and presenting their comparison-and-contrast essay.

Present Have students present their comparison-and-contrast essays to the class. They should strive to support their statements with details and examples and use transitions to make similarities and differences clear.

RUBRIC

3 Full Accomplishment Student presents a well-organized, logical comparison of two subjects. Similarities and differences are well supported with details or examples.

2 Substantial Accomplishment Student compares and contrasts two subjects and supports points with some details or examples.

1 Little or Partial Accomplishment Student has difficulty organizing the subjects' similarities and differences and does not treat each of the two subjects equally. Not all points are supported with details or examples.

Use **Speaking and Listening Book,** pp. 6–9, 12–13, 25–26, for additional support in presenting a character sketch.

The Literature You'll Read

The Concepts You'll Study

Vocabulary and Reading Comprehension
Vocabulary Focus: Prefixes and Suffixes
Chronological Order
Clarifying
Making Inferences About the Speaker
Monitoring Reading Strategies
Visualizing
Identifying the Author's Purpose

Writing and Language Conventions
Writing Workshop: Problem-Solution Essay
Comparing with Adjectives
Avoiding Confusion with Negatives
Choosing Adjective or Adverb
Describing with Prepositional Phrases

Literary Analysis
Genre Focus: Autobiography and Biography
Sources of Information
Imagery
Tone
Humor

Speaking and Listening
Persuasive Speech
Autobiography Read-Aloud
Original Poem Read-Aloud
Film Review

OVERVIEW

Standards-Based Objectives
- understand and identify the following literary terms:
  - autobiography
  - biography
  - first-person point of view
  - third-person point of view
  - primary source
  - secondary source
  - author's perspective
  - bias
  - tone
- understand and appreciate autobiographies and biographies
- recognize the distinguishing features of autobiography and biography
- describe how the author's perspective or point of view affects the text

Teaching the Lesson

This lesson analyzes the basic elements of autobiographies and biographies and explains how the two types of nonfiction differ from each other.

Introducing the Concepts
Ask students to think about an event or incident from their own lives that they might want to write about. Ask for volunteers to share their topic, a possible opening sentence, and the reason they would want to write about this experience.

Presenting the Concepts
Point of View

Explain to students that an autobiography, which is written in the first-person point of view, often includes the author's feelings and thoughts. In a biography, written in the third person point-of-view, the writer tells about the experiences of the subject's life in the writer's own style and language. Although readers learn about a subject's personality in a biography, they don't find out as much about the subject's feelings and thoughts.

YOUR TURN
Possible Response: The use of the pronouns *I* and *me* indicates that this excerpt is autobiographical.

Use **Literary Analysis Transparencies,** pp. 10, 11, 14, 22, 25, for additional support.

LEARNING the Language of *Literature*

Autobiography and Biography

> *[Before I write a biography, a] character in history will suddenly step right out of the past and demand a book. Once my character and I reach an understanding, then I begin the detective work.*
>
> —Jean Fritz, writer

Autobiographies and **biographies** are two types of nonfiction that tell a life story. The main difference between them is in who does the telling. In an autobiography, the writer tells the story of his or her own life. A biography, however, is the story of someone's life written by another person. The stories the author chooses to include in a biography may help readers to understand the **author's perspective** on his or her subject, and the **author's purpose** for writing.

Point of View

Autobiographies are usually written from the **first-person point of view.** The writer tells about his or her own personal experiences and uses first-person pronouns such as *I*, *me*, and *we*. Biographies, on the other hand, are usually written from the **third-person point of view.** You know a piece is a biography because the writer is outside the story and uses third-person pronouns such as *he, she,* and *they.*

YOUR TURN Is this excerpt from *The Story of My Life* by Helen Keller autobiographical or biographical? Which words in the excerpt helped you know this?

POINT OF VIEW

I did not know what the future held of marvel or surprise for me. Anger and bitterness had preyed upon me continually for weeks and a deep languor had succeeded this passionate struggle.

The Story of My Life by Helen Keller

Primary and Secondary Sources

In order to gather information about a person's life, biographers and other writers of nonfiction use primary and secondary sources. A **primary source** is a firsthand account of an event, written by someone who actually witnessed the event. Primary sources include **autobiographies, journals, diaries, memoirs,** and **letters.** A **secondary source** is an account based on other sources and not on the source writer's own experiences. Examples of secondary sources include **articles, reference books, reports,** and **biographies.**

Libraries are a good place to start looking for primary and secondary sources. The Internet also features good primary and secondary sources on a variety of subjects. For example, you can use the Internet to find interesting material on Helen Keller. If you decide to use an online source, always make sure it is reliable.

YOUR TURN What kinds of sources might the author have used to write this biography of Ibrahima, the son of an African chief?

SOURCES

For Ibrahima there was confusion and pain. What was he to do? A few months before, he had been a learned man and a leader among his people. Now he was a captive in a strange land where he neither spoke the language nor understood the customs. Was he never to see his family again? Were his sons forever lost to him?

As a Fula, Ibrahima wore his hair long; Foster insisted that it be cut. Ibrahima's clothing had been taken from him, and his sandals. Now the last remaining symbol of his people, his long hair, had been taken as well.

—Walter Dean Myers,
"Abd al-Rahman Ibrahima," from *Now Is Your Time!*

From "Abd al-Rahman Ibrahima"

Author's Perspective

The way an author sees the world is called the **author's perspective.** The author's ideas, attitudes, feelings, beliefs, and values can often be understood through the **tone** of his or her writing. Other clues to the author's perspective include the author's direct statements, the ways in which the author describes important individuals, and the author's background. In nonfiction, it is important to look for the author's **biases,** or preferences and prejudices. Recognizing bias will help you determine the **author's purpose** for writing, and help you decide if the author's ideas are fair and truthful.

Primary and Secondary Sources
Ask students to create a plan for researching the life of Albert Einstein, or another famous person they would like to know about. What kind of information would they need to write a biography of this person? Where might they find this information?

YOUR TURN
Possible Response: The author may have used secondary sources, such as biographies of slaves and former slaves and reference books on life in Africa and on slavery. The author may also have used primary sources, such as memoirs and autobiographies of slaves and former slaves, legal documents that describe the rights of slave owners, and journals and diaries written by both slave owners and abolitionists.

Author's Perspective
Discuss with students how an author's attitudes, feelings, beliefs, and values could affect the way he or she writes about a subject.

OVERVIEW

Standards-Based Objectives
- develop effective strategies, such as using a time line, for understanding chronological order
- learn to use a text's structure or progression of ideas such as chronology to locate and recall information

Teaching the Lesson

The strategies on this page will help students understand and recognize chronological order.

Presenting the Strategies
Help students understand the strategies by asking for volunteers to read them aloud. Emphasize to students that they will be using these skills as they read various selections in this book.

SKIM FOR WORDS THAT SIGNAL TIME
Remind students that when they see words like *first, second, next, then, finally, after, before,* and *soon,* they should stop and clearly place the event being signaled in its chronology.

Use **Reading and Critical Thinking Transparencies,** p. 6, for additional support.

QUESTION AND CLARIFY
Tell students that by asking themselves when an event takes place in relation to another event, they can clarify what is happening. Using a time line will help them keep these events in chronological order.

EVALUATE
Sometimes a story is not told in chronological order. For example, a writer might alternate current events with flashbacks. In that case, it is up to the reader to put the pieces of information together in a meaningful way.

Chronological Order

Have you ever asked an older relative about your family's history? If so, he or she may have said something like this: "My father was born in 1910 in Great Britain. Then when he was eight, he moved to the United States." When events are presented as they occurred in time, they are said to be in chronological order. Understanding the order of events can help you keep track of information.

How to Apply the Skill

To understand **chronological order,** an active reader will
- Skim the selection for dates and words that signal time
- Ask **questions** about what happens first, next, last
- **Clarify** the sequence of events with a time line
- **Evaluate** whether the order of events make sense

Try It Now!

The time line below shows some of the events described in "Abd al-Rahman Ibrahima." How can a time line like this one help you keep track of events?

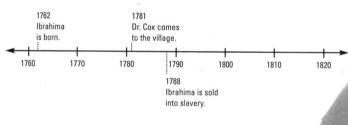

1762
Ibrahima
is born.

1781
Dr. Cox comes
to the village.

1760   1770   1780   1790   1800   1810   1820

1788
Ibrahima is sold
into slavery.

Here's how Jillian uses the strategies:

"When I read 'Abd al-Rahman Ibrahima,' I looked for dates. I took notes on major events and time periods.

*"Sometimes while reading I make a time line that starts when someone was born. I mark the time line with even spaces, every 5, 10, or 20 years. Then I add the events. I can then **clarify** the order of events by seeing what happened in what sequence."*

Abd al-Rahman Ibrahima
from Now Is Your Time!

by WALTER DEAN MYERS

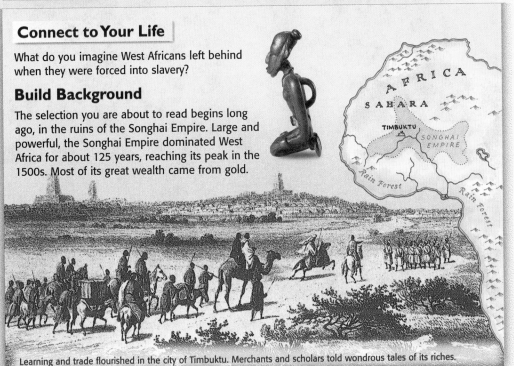

Connect to Your Life

What do you imagine West Africans left behind when they were forced into slavery?

Build Background

The selection you are about to read begins long ago, in the ruins of the Songhai Empire. Large and powerful, the Songhai Empire dominated West Africa for about 125 years, reaching its peak in the 1500s. Most of its great wealth came from gold.

Learning and trade flourished in the city of Timbuktu. Merchants and scholars told wondrous tales of its riches.

Focus Your Reading

LITERARY ANALYSIS   SOURCES OF INFORMATION

A **primary source,** such as a diary or a letter, presents firsthand knowledge based on the writer's own experience. "Abd al-Rahman Ibrahima" is a **secondary source** because the information it contains comes from sources other than the writer's own experience.

WORDS TO KNOW   Vocabulary Preview

bondage	inhabitant	prosper	status
chaos	premise	reservation	trek
dynasty	procedure		

ACTIVE READING   CHRONOLOGICAL ORDER

Chronological order is the order in which events happen in time. In some narratives, events are related in chronological order. Other narratives move backward and forward in time.

READER'S NOTEBOOK "Abd al-Rahman Ibrahima" covers one man's life from his birth in 1762 to his death in 1829. Make a time line to keep track of events. As you read, write in the years and events mentioned in the selection.

This selection is included in the **Grade 7 InterActive Reader.**

Standards-Based Objectives
- understand and appreciate a **biography**
- understand author's use of **sources of information**
- use **chronological order** to help understand the sequence of events in a biography
- identify **tone**
- recognize **point of view** in biography
- recognize **main idea**
- **connect and clarify** main ideas

Summary
Abd al-Rahman Ibrahima was born in Africa in 1762, the son of a Fula chieftain. Ibrahima was captured during an intertribal battle, sold to slave traders, and shipped to America. There, a Mississippi farmer named Thomas Foster bought him. To Foster, the African's claims to nobility meant nothing—he was simply a possession. After 20 years as a slave, he met John Cox, an Irish doctor who had lived with the Fula in Africa years before. Cox began a campaign to free Ibrahima. The African gained his freedom through the intervention of the Moroccan and American governments. In 1829, Ibrahima sailed with his wife to return to his homeland. He never reached his people, however. He died in the West African colony of Liberia that year.

Thematic Link
The story of Ibrahima and Dr. Cox shows how people can break through the barriers of culture to find a common human bond that transcends all.

English Conventions Practice

Daily Language SkillBuilder

Have students **proofread** the display sentences on page 315k and write them correctly. The sentences also appear on Transparency 11 of **Language Transparencies.**

Preteaching Vocabulary

If you would like to preteach the WORDS TO KNOW for this selection, use the Explicit Instruction, page 367.

LESSON RESOURCES

UNIT THREE RESOURCE BOOK, pp. 32–38

ASSESSMENT
Formal Assessment, pp. 57–58
Test Generator

SKILLS TRANSPARENCIES AND COPYMASTERS
Literary Analysis
- Primary/Secondary Source, TR 14 (pp. 370, 378)

Reading and Critical Thinking
- Chronological Order, TR 6 (pp. 372, 378, 380)

Language
- Daily Language SkillBuilder, TR 11 (p. 365)
- Avoiding Errors in the Use of Modifiers, TR 41 (p. 380)
- Word Parts: Roots and Base Words, Prefixes, Suffixes, TR 56–58 (p. 367)

Writing
- How to Summarize, TR 51 (p. 379)

Speaking and Listening
- Creating a Persuasive Presentation, p. 29 (p. 379)
- Guidelines: How to Analyze a Persuasive Presentation, p. 30 (p. 379)

INTEGRATED TECHNOLOGY
Audio Library
Internet: Research Starter

Visit our Web site:
www.mcdougallittell.com

For **systematic instruction** in language skills, see:
- **Vocabulary and Spelling Book**
- **Grammar, Usage, and Mechanics Book**
- pacing chart on p. 315i.

Reading and Analyzing

Active Reading

CHRONOLOGICAL ORDER

Have students give examples of narratives (either in print or in films) that are told in chronological order. Then have them give contrasting examples of narratives told in non-chronological order. They may be able to think of narratives that use flashbacks, for example. Then explain that "Abd al-Rahman Ibrahima" is written in chronological order. Ask them to consider, as they read, how flashbacks might have been used to tell the story.

 Use **Unit Three Resource Book**, p. 33, for more practice.

Literary Analysis

SOURCES OF INFORMATION

Ask students to think, as they read, about the kinds of primary sources Walter Dean Myers might have used to get the facts for this biography. When they have finished reading, discuss these possible sources with them and discuss which would be reliable and which would not.

Possible Response: Myers might have consulted newspaper accounts of the time, government documents, records of abolitionist societies, and personal letters. Students should be aware that some sources might not be as trustworthy as others because they are based on incomplete information or personal opinion.

 Use **Unit Three Resource Book**, p. 34, for more practice.

Into Bondage (1936), Aaron Douglas. Oil on canvas, 60 3/8" x 60 1/2". In the collection of The Corcoran Gallery of Art, Washington, D.C. Museum purchase and partial gift from Thurlow Evans Tibbs. The Evans Tibbs Collection.

366   UNIT THREE   PART 2: BREAKING BARRIERS

EXPLICIT INSTRUCTION Viewing and Representing

Into Bondage
by Aaron Douglas

ART APPRECIATION This mural by Harlem Renaissance artist Aaron Douglas (1899–1979) depicts the enslavement of Africans and their removal from their homeland. The 60-by-60-inch mural was commissioned for the Texas Centennial Exposition in 1936.

Instruction Explain that the artist has included several symbolic elements in his painting. Symbolic elements can often be recognized because they depart from strict realism. Point out that ships in the painting are probably intended to be symbols, as they are not shown in correct scale, and would not be sailing at full speed directly for the coast. Ask students what the ships represent. (*The ships represent the voyage away from the African homeland into bondage in the Americas.*)

Practice Ask students what the star represents.

Possible Response: It may represent the distant hope of achieving freedom again.

Abd al-Rahman Ibrahima

from NOW IS YOUR TIME!

by Walter Dean Myers

. . . The Africans came from many countries, and from many cultures. Like the Native Americans, they established their territories based on centuries of tradition. Most, but not all, of the Africans who were brought to the colonies came from central and West Africa. Among them was a man named Abd al-Rahman Ibrahima.

Literary Analysis: PLOT

(A) Explain to students that a story's plot usually begins with an exposition, in which an author provides background for understanding the story and sets up the story's major conflict. Ask students what important information is provided in the exposition of this selection.

Possible Response: The exposition gives important background information about how life in Africa changed drastically after the arrival of European invaders. This background will be important in understanding what happens to Ibrahima.

ACTIVE READER

(B) CLARIFY Make sure that students' responses indicate an awareness of how privileged Ibrahima's life has been so far.

Literary Analysis: IMAGERY

(C) Have a volunteer read aloud the description of John Coates Cox. Ask students what mental image forms in their minds as they listen to the description.

Possible Response: He is a small man with a patch over one eye who hobbles on one leg into the village, favoring a leg with a wound that is badly infected.

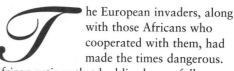

(A) The European invaders, along with those Africans who cooperated with them, had made the times dangerous. African nations that had lived peacefully together for centuries now eyed each other warily. Slight insults led to major battles. Bands of outlaws roamed the countryside attacking the small villages, kidnapping those unfortunate enough to have wandered from the protection of their people. The stories that came from the coast were frightening. Those kidnapped were taken to the sea and sold to whites, put on boats, and taken across the sea. No one knew what happened then.

Abd al-Rahman Ibrahima was born in 1762 in Fouta Djallon, a district of the present country of Guinea.[1] It is a beautiful land of green mountains rising majestically from grassy plains, a land rich with minerals, especially bauxite.

Ibrahima was a member of the powerful and influential Fula people and a son of one of their chieftains. The religion of Islam had swept across Africa centuries before, and the young Ibrahima was raised in the tradition of the Moslems.[2]

The Fula were taller and lighter in complexion than the other <u>inhabitants</u> of Africa's west coast; they had silky hair, which they often wore long. A pastoral[3] people, the Fula had a complex system of government, with the state divided into nine provinces and each province divided again into smaller districts. Each province had its chief and its subchiefs.

1

As the son of a chief, Ibrahima was expected to assume a role of political leadership when he came of age. He would also be expected to set a moral example and to be well versed in his religion. When he reached twelve he was sent to Timbuktu[4] to study.

Under the Songhai[5] <u>dynasty</u> leader Askia the Great, Timbuktu had become a center of learning and one of the largest cities in the Songhai Empire. The young Ibrahima knew he was privileged to attend the best-known school in West Africa. Large and sophisticated, with wide, tree-lined streets, the city attracted scholars from Africa, Europe, and Asia. Islamic law, medicine, and mathematics were taught to the young men destined to become the leaders of their nations. It was a good place for a young man to be. The city was well guarded, too. It had to be, to prevent the <u>chaos</u> that, more and more, dominated African life nearer the coast.

Ibrahima learned first to recite from the Koran, the Moslem holy book, and then to read it in Arabic. From the Koran, it was felt, came all other knowledge. After Ibrahima had finished his studies in Timbuktu, he returned to Fouta Djallon to continue to prepare himself to be a chief.

ACTIVE READER

CLARIFY What was Ibrahima's life like up to this point?

The Fula had little contact with whites, and what little contact they did have was filled with

(B)

---

1. **Fouta Djallon** (fūt′ə-jə-lōn′). . . **Guinea** (gĭn′ē): Fouta Djallon is a small, mountainous region in Guinea, a small nation on the west coast of Africa.

2. **Islam** (ĭs-läm′). . . **Moslems** (mŏz′ləmz): refers to the Moslem merchants who traveled the gold-salt routes of wealthy West African empires and introduced Islam to the region. (A Moslem is a believer in the religion of Islam.)

3. **pastoral** (păs′tər-əl): having a way of life based on raising livestock.

4. **Timbuktu** (tĭm′bŭk-tōō′): now known as Tombouctou, a city in the part of Africa now known as Mali.

5. **Songhai** (sông′hī′): a West African empire that thrived in the 1400s and 1500s.

WORDS
TO
KNOW

inhabitant (ĭn-hăb′ĭ-tənt) *n.* someone living in a particular place
dynasty (dī′nə-stē) *n.* a series of rulers who are members of the same family
chaos (kā′ŏs) *n.* a state of great disorder

368

Identifying Tone

Instruction Remind students that the tone of a selection is the author's attitude toward his or her subject. For example, a tone may be admiring or angry, sad or amused. Students can determine tone by figuring out the subject and examining the author's word choice. Have students reread the third and fourth paragraphs on page 368. Then ask these questions: Who or what is the subject of these paragraphs? (*Ibrahima and the Fula*) How would you describe the author's tone, or attitude, toward

the subject of these paragraphs? (*admiring and positive*) Which words or phrases helped you identify the tone? (*"powerful and influential," "complex system of government"*)

Practice Tell students to reread the paragraph on page 368 that begins, "Under the Songhai dynasty." Then have students work in pairs to identify the subject and describe the tone of the paragraph. Students should give examples from the paragraph to support their answers.

Possible Responses: Subject—the city of Timbuktu; tone—respectful and admiring; examples from text—"center of learning," "large and sophisticated," "city attracted scholars."

danger. So when, in 1781, a white man claiming to be a ship's surgeon stumbled into one of their villages, they were greatly surprised.

John Coates Cox hardly appeared to be a threat. A slight man, blind in one eye, he had been lost for days in the forested regions bordering the mountains. He had injured his leg, and it had become badly infected as he tried to find help. By the time he was found and brought to the Fula chiefs, he was more dead than alive.

Dr. Cox, an Irishman, told of being separated from a hunting party that had left from a ship on which he had sailed as ship's surgeon. The Fula chief decided that he would help Cox. He was taken into a hut, and a healer was assigned the task of curing his infected leg.

During the months Dr. Cox stayed with the Fula, he met Ibrahima, now a tall, brown-skinned youth who had reached manhood. His bearing reflected his <u>status</u> as the son of a major chief. Dr. Cox had learned some Fulani, the Fula language, and the two men spoke. Ibrahima was doubtless curious about the white man's world, and Dr. Cox was as impressed by Ibrahima's education as he had been by the kindness of his people.

When Dr. Cox was well enough to leave, he was provided with a guard; but before he left, he warned the Fula about the danger of venturing too near the ships that docked off the coast of Guinea. The white doctor knew that the ships were there to take captives.

Cox and Ibrahima embraced fondly and said their good-byes, thinking they would never meet again.

Ibrahima married and became the father of several children. He was in his mid-twenties when he found himself leading the Fula cavalry in their war with the Mandingo.[6]

The first battles went well, with the enemy retreating before the advancing Fula. The foot warriors attacked first, breaking the enemy's ranks and making them easy prey for the well-trained Fula cavalry. With the enemy in full rout[7] the infantry returned to their towns while the horsemen, led by Ibrahima, chased the remaining stragglers. The Fula fought their enemies with spears, bows, slings, swords, and courage.

His bearing reflected his status as the son of a major chief.

The path of pursuit led along a path that narrowed sharply as the forests thickened. The fleeing warriors disappeared into the forest that covered a sharply rising mountain. Thinking the enemy had gone for good, Ibrahima felt it would be useless to chase them further.

"We could not see them," he would write later.

But against his better judgment, he decided to look for them. The horsemen dismounted at the foot of a hill and began the steep climb on

---

6. **Mandingo** (măn-dĭng′gō): a member of any of various peoples of West Africa.

7. **in full rout:** in complete retreat.

WORDS TO KNOW   **status** (stā′təs) *n.* one's position in society; rank

369

Cross Curricular Link History

WEST AFRICAN TRIBES Inhabited West Africa is formed of two zones: the savanna, or grasslands, in the interior and the rain forest along the coast. In the savanna, there are three main groups of people: the Mande, including the Bambara, the Malinke, the Soninke, and others; the Voltaic group, including the Senufo, Lobi, Grunshi, Dogon, and Mossi; and the non-Muslim peoples of northern Nigeria, Niger, and Cameroon. Mingled with these non-Muslim tribes are the Muslim Fula or Fulani, the tribe to which Ibrahima belonged. (The enemies of the Fula, the Mandingo, belong to the Mande group.)

Along the Nigerian coast are found the Igbo, Ibibio, Edo, and Yoruba, and to the west can be found the Edo, Yorba, Fon, Ewe, Ga, Ashanti, Anyi, Fanti, Kru, Mende, Dyula, and the Wolof people.

Generally the people of the savanna were herders and used horses for transport, as did Ibrahima's people. The rain forest was unsuitable for both cattle and horses, so people there survived by farming in forest clearings and by trade.

Literary Analysis: RISING ACTION

Explain to students that the term *rising action* refers to the part of a plot in which the story becomes more complicated. Ask students to identify the point at which they can see a clear example of rising action.

Possible Response: The moment at which Ibrahima is captured is clearly an example of rising action.

Reading Skills and Strategies: SUMMARIZE

A Have students summarize how Ibrahima came to be captured.

Possible Response: He was leading the Fula against another people, the Mandingo. Although the Mandingo seemed to be retreating, they were actually leading the Fula into a trap. Ibrahima tried to escape with his soldiers, and then to defend himself, but he was knocked unconscious.

Literary Analysis

SOURCES OF INFORMATION

Have students speculate about what sources Myers might have used to reconstruct what happened to Ibrahima during the attack on the Mandingo.

Possible Response: He might have used an account by someone Ibrahima talked to in America.

Use **Literary Analysis Transparencies,** p. 14, for additional support.

Reading Skills and Strategies: PREDICT

Ask students to predict what will happen when Ibrahima is captured.

Possible Response: Students should be able to predict that Ibrahima will be sold into slavery.

---

foot. Halfway up the hill the Fula realized they had been lured into a trap! Ibrahima heard the rifles firing, saw the smoke from the powder and the men about him falling to the ground, screaming in agony. Some died instantly. Many horses, hit by the gunfire, thrashed about in pain and panic. The firing was coming from both sides, and Ibrahima ordered his men to the top of the hill, where they could, if time and Allah permitted it, try a charge using the speed and momentum of their remaining horses.

A Ibrahima was among the first to mount, and urged his animal onward. The enemy warriors came out of the forests, some with bows and arrows, others with muskets that he knew they had obtained from the Europeans. The courage of the Fula could not match the fury of the guns. Ibrahima called out to his men to save themselves, to flee as they could. Many tried to escape, rushing madly past the guns. Few survived.

Those who did clustered about their young leader, determined to make one last, desperate stand. Ibrahima was hit in the back by an arrow, but the aim was not true and the arrow merely cut his broad shoulder. Then something smashed against his head from the rear.

The next thing Ibrahima knew was that he was choking. Then he felt himself being lifted from water. He tried to move his arms, but they had been fastened securely behind his back. He had been captured.

1 When he came to his full senses, he looked around him. Those of his noble cavalry who had not been captured were already dead. Ibrahima was unsteady on his legs as his clothes and sandals were stripped from him. The victorious Mandingo warriors now pushed him roughly into file with his men. They began the long <u>trek</u> that would lead them to the sea.

In Fouta Djallon being captured by the enemy meant being forced to do someone else's bidding,[8] sometimes for years. If you could get a message to your people, you could, perhaps, buy your freedom. Otherwise, it was only if you were well liked, or if you married one of your captor's women, that you would be allowed to go free or to live like a free person.

Ibrahima sensed that things would not go well for him.

The journey to the sea took weeks. Ibrahima was tied to other men, with ropes around their necks. Each day they walked from dawn to dusk. Those who were slow were knocked brutally to the ground. Some of those who could no longer walk were speared and left to die in agony. It was the lucky ones who were killed outright if they fell.

The journey to the sea took weeks. Ibrahima was tied to other men, with ropes around their necks.

When they reached the sea, they remained bound hand and foot. There were men and women tied together. Small children clung to their mothers as they waited for the boats to come and the bargaining to begin.

---

8. **do someone else's bidding:** follow another's orders.

WORDS
TO
KNOW

trek (trĕk) *n.* a slow, difficult journey

370

Point of View

Instruction Ask a volunteer to explain the difference between a biography and an autobiography. (*In a biography, someone else writes about the person. In an autobiography, the person writes about his or her own life.*) Tell students that one way to tell an autobiography from a biography is to look at the point of view. Display the following chart on the board as you explain these points: Biographies are written from a third-person point of view, using third-person pronouns such as *he* or *she* to tell about someone else's life. Autobiographies are

written from a first-person point of view. The writer uses first-person pronouns such as *I* and *me* to tell about his or her own life.

Biography	Autobiography
• third-person point of view	• first-person point of view
• *he, she*	• *I, me*

Ask, "Who is the narrator or speaker in the selection? Is Ibrahima telling his own story, or is someone else telling it? (*someone else—Walter Dean Myers*) What is the point of view? Which pronouns on page 370 show this?" (*third person; he, his*)

Practice Have students write how this biography would be different if Ibrahima had written it himself. What new information would be included?

Possible Responses: It would include Ibrahima's own thoughts and feelings. Examples will vary.

Mecklenberg County: High Cotton Mother and Child (1978), Romare Bearden. Courtesy of the Estate of Romare Bearden.
Copyright © Romare Bearden Foundation/Licensed by VAGA, New York, NY.

Ibrahima, listening to the conversations of the men who held him captive, could understand those who spoke Arabic. These Africans were a low class of men, made powerful by the guns they had been given, made evil by the white man's goods. But it didn't matter who was evil and who was good. It only mattered who held the gun.

Ibrahima was inspected on the shore, then put into irons and herded into a small boat that took him out to a ship that was larger than any he had ever seen.

The ship onto which Ibrahima was taken was already crowded with black captives. Some shook in fear; others, still tied, fought by hurling their bodies at their captors. The beating and the killing continued until the ones who were left knew that their lot was hopeless.

On board the ship there were more whites with guns, who shoved them toward the open hatch. Some of the Africans hesitated at the hatch, and were clubbed down and pushed belowdecks.

It was dark beneath the deck, and difficult to breathe. Bodies were pressed close against other bodies. In the section of the ship he was in, men prayed to various gods in various languages. It seemed that the whites would never stop pushing men into the already crowded space. Two sailors pushed the Africans into position so that each would lie in the smallest space possible. The sailors panted and sweated as they untied the men and then chained them to a railing that ran the length of the ship.

The ship rolled against its mooring as the anchor was lifted, and the journey began. The

EXPLICIT INSTRUCTION **Identifying Tone**

Instruction Remind students that the tone of a selection is the author's attitude toward his or her subject. Students can determine tone by figuring out the subject and examining the author's word choice. Have students reread the paragraphs on pages 371 and 372 that describe the slave ship. When students have finished reading, ask "What is the subject of these paragraphs? (*conditions on the ship*) How would you describe the author's tone? (*angry, disgusted, horrified*) Next, tell stu-

dents that although selections generally have one overall tone, tone may vary from one paragraph or section to another. This happens because the subjects of paragraphs vary. Ask whether the tone of the section you have been discussing is the same as or different from the tone they identified earlier (*different*). Follow up by asking why the tone changes. (*The author first wrote about an impressive city, and now he is writing about the awful conditions on the ship.*)

Practice Have pairs of students write a paragraph that describes the tone of this section and gives examples that show the tone.
Possible Responses: Tone—disgusted, horrified. Examples—"vomiting upon themselves in the wretched darkness," "irons cutting into their legs," "gasping for air."

A **CHRONOLOGICAL ORDER**
Possible Response: The Africans were crammed into small spaces and chained. Once a day they were taken on deck to exercise and be fed beans or rice and yams and water. Many of them got sick and died.

Literary Analysis: PLOT

Ask students to explain why the sale of Ibrahima as a slave is an important moment in the plot.

Possible Response: It is at this point in the plot that the complete change in his life begins to become clear.

B **CLARIFY** Ibrahima had no way to get back to Africa, and he was being held in captivity. He didn't know where he was. He though he might die if he escaped.

Active Reading

CHRONOLOGICAL ORDER

Write the following list of events and have students determine the order in which they take place:

• Ibrahima is whipped. (4)
• Ibrahima is sold to Foster. (1)
• Ibrahima escapes. (5)
• Ibrahima tries to explain who he is to Foster. (2)
• Ibrahima decides to work for Foster. (6)
• Ibrahima's hair is cut. (3)

Use **Reading and Critical Thinking Transparencies**, p. 6, for additional support.

---

boards of the ship creaked and moaned as it lifted and fell in the sea. Some of the men got sick, vomiting upon themselves in the wretched darkness. They lay cramped, muscles aching, irons cutting into their legs and wrists, gasping for air.

Once a day they would be brought out on deck and made to jump about for exercise. They were each given a handful of either beans or rice cooked with yams, and water from a cask. The white sailors looked hardly better than the Africans, but it was they who held the guns.

Illness and the stifling conditions on the ships caused many deaths. How many depended largely on how fast the ships could be loaded with Africans and how long the voyage from Africa took. It was not unusual for 10 percent of the Africans to die if the trip took longer than the usual twenty-five to thirty-five days.

Ibrahima, now twenty-six years old, reached Mississippi in 1788. As the ship approached land, the Africans were brought onto the deck and fed. Some had oil put on their skins so they would look better; their sores were treated or covered with pitch. Then they were given garments to wear in an obvious effort to improve their appearance.

In your own words, describe the sequence of events of Ibrahima's journey by ship.

Although Ibrahima could not speak English, he understood he was being bargained for. The white man who stood on the platform with him made him turn around, and several other white men neared him, touched his limbs, examined his teeth, looked into his eyes, and made him move about.

Thomas Foster, a tobacco grower and a hard-working man, had come from South Carolina with his family and had settled on the rich lands that took their minerals from the Mississippi River. He already held one captive, a young boy. In August 1788 he bought two more. One of them was named Sambo, which means "second son." The other was Ibrahima.

For Ibrahima there was confusion and pain. What was he to do?

Foster agreed to pay $930 for the two Africans. He paid $150 down and signed an agreement to pay another $250 the following January and the remaining $530 in January of the following year.

When Ibrahima arrived at Foster's farm, he tried to find someone who could explain to the white man who he was—the son of a chief. He wanted to offer a ransom for his own release, but Foster wasn't interested. He understood, perhaps from the boy whom he had purchased previously, that this new African was claiming to be an important person. Foster had probably never heard of the Fula or their culture; he had paid good money for the African, and wasn't about to give him up. Foster gave Ibrahima a new name: He called him Prince.

For Ibrahima there was confusion and pain. What was he to do? A few months before, he had been a learned man and a leader among his people. Now he was a captive in a strange land where he neither spoke the language nor understood the customs. Was he never to see his family again? Were his sons forever lost to him?

As a Fula, Ibrahima wore his hair long; Foster insisted that it be cut. Ibrahima's clothing had been taken from him, and his sandals. Now the last remaining symbol of his people, his long hair, had been taken as well.

He was told to work in the fields. He refused, and he was tied and whipped. The sting of the whip across his naked flesh was terribly painful, but it was nothing like the pain he felt within. The whippings forced him to work.

For Ibrahima this was not life, but a mockery of life. There was the waking in the morning and the sleeping at night; he worked, he ate, but this was not life. What was more, he could not see an end to it. It was this feeling that made him attempt to escape.

Ibrahima escaped to the backwoods regions of Natchez.[9] He hid there, eating wild berries and fruit, not daring to show his face to any man, white or black. There was no telling who could be trusted. Sometimes he saw men with dogs and knew they were searching for runaways, perhaps him.

Where was he to run? What was he to do? He didn't know the country, he didn't know how far it was from Fouta Djallon or how to get back to his homeland. He could tell that this place was ruled by white men who held him in captivity. The other blacks he had seen were from all parts of Africa. Some he recognized by their tribal markings, some he did not. None were allowed to speak their native tongues around the white men. Some already knew nothing of the languages of their people.

As time passed, Ibrahima's despair deepened. His choices were simple. He could stay in the woods and probably die, or he could submit his body back into bondage. There is no place in Islamic law for a man to take his own life. Ibrahima returned to Thomas Foster.

Foster still owed money to the man from whom he had purchased Ibrahima. The debt would remain whether he still possessed the African or not. Foster was undoubtedly glad to see that the African had returned. Thin, nearly starving, Ibrahima was put to work.

ACTIVE READER

CLARIFY Summarize the reasons that Ibrahima remained with Thomas Foster.

Ibrahima submitted himself to the will of Thomas Foster. He was a captive, held in bondage not only by Foster but by the society in which he found himself. Ibrahima maintained his beliefs in the religion of Islam and kept its rituals as best he could. He was determined to be the same person he had always been: Abd al-Rahman Ibrahima of Fouta Djallon and of the proud Fula people.

By 1807 the area had become the Mississippi Territory. Ibrahima was forty-five and had been in bondage for twenty years. During those years he met and married a woman whom Foster had purchased, and they began to raise a family. Fouta Djallon was more and more distant, and he had become resigned to the idea that he would never see it or his family again.

Thomas Foster had grown wealthy and had become an important man in the territory. At forty-five Ibrahima was considered old. He was less useful to Foster, who now let the tall African grow a few vegetables on a side plot and sell them in town, since there was

---

9. **Natchez** (năch′ĭz): an early settlement in what is now the state of Mississippi.

WORDS TO KNOW **bondage** (bŏn′dĭj) *n.* slavery

373

Cross Curricular Link **History**

SLAVERY IN UNITED STATES HISTORY The first captive Africans arrived in Virginia in 1619. As the settlers there did not have any legal provision for slave ownership, these first captives were viewed as indentured servants. However, the legal device of perpetual servitude was soon established. By 1681 there were 2,000 African slaves in Virginia.

The colonies (later states) of the South developed economies dependent upon slave labor to produce their major cash crops: tobacco, rice, and cotton. Because tobacco rapidly exhausted the soil, it was failing as a cash crop by the time of the Revolution, and it seemed at that time that slavery would fade out. However, the boom in cotton production reversed this trend, and by 1860 there were some 4,441,000 slaves in the southern states. Thus, slavery can be linked to the plantation economy of the southern states. The division between the slave holding states of the South and the free states of the North was one of the tensions—though not the only one—that led to the Civil War.

Differentiating Instruction

English Learners

1 Make sure students understand the implied meaning of the word *life* in the phrase "this was not life." Point out that Ibrahima is still alive but feels that his life is meaningless and unbearable.

Less Proficient Readers

2 Check students' understanding by asking them to explain why Ibrahima does not simply go home to Africa after escaping from Foster.

Possible Response: Ibrahima has no way to get transportation back to Africa. He has no money and no friends to help him, and he is stranded in the white-controlled territory of Mississippi in the late 1700s.

Advanced Students

Slavery was a common practice in the United States in the late 1700s. In the modern world, it has been eliminated in the United States and in most other countries. Sadly, it still exists today in some parts of the world in the forms of sweatshops or actual bondage. Students may want to research the history of slavery and learn about places where this practice persists today.

Explain to students that falling action in a narrative occurs after the climax or turning point. Have them discuss when the falling action begins in the story of Ibrahima.

Possible Responses: Some may say that the falling action begins after Ibrahima's unsuccessful attempt to escape from Foster. Others may say that it occurs after Ibrahima meets Dr. Cox.

Literary Analysis

SOURCES OF INFORMATION

A Point out that Myers describes the basic premise of slavery as "a premise that Foster *must have believed* without reservation" (emphasis added). Ask why Myers made his statement about Foster's belief in these words.

Possible Response: Myers did not have any primary sources that could definitely support his statement about Foster's belief, so he is letting us know that this statement is an inference on his part, based on the evidence of Foster's behavior.

Literary Analysis: BIOGRAPHY

Students should be able to identify the purposes of different types of texts. Ask students what Walter Dean Myers's purpose was in writing this biography of Ibrahima's life.

Possible Responses: Myers wanted to tell an interesting story about a remarkable man whose life was totally changed by slavery, but who managed to hold on to his identity as a cultured person, free in spirit, if not in fact; Myers wanted to make us appreciate our own liberty and to increase our respect for the rights of others.

---

nowhere in the territory that the black man could go where he would not be captured by some other white man and returned.

It was during one of these visits to town that Ibrahima saw a white man who looked familiar. The smallish man walked slowly and with a limp. Ibrahima cautiously approached the man and spoke to him. The man looked closely at Ibrahima, then spoke his name. It was Dr. Cox.

The two men shook hands, and Dr. Cox, who now lived in the territory, took Ibrahima to his home. John Cox had not prospered over the years, but he was still hopeful. He listened carefully as Ibrahima told his story—the battle near Fouta Djallon, the defeat, the long journey across the Atlantic Ocean, and, finally, his sale to Thomas Foster and the years of labor.

Dr. Cox and Ibrahima went to the Foster plantation. Meeting with Foster, he explained how he had met the tall black man. Surely, he reasoned, knowing that Ibrahima was of royal blood, Foster would free him? The answer was a firm, but polite, no. No amount of pleading would make Foster change his mind. It didn't matter that Dr. Cox had supported what Ibrahima had told Foster so many years before, that he was a prince. To Foster the man was merely his property.

Dr. Cox had to leave the man whose people had saved his life, but he told Ibrahima that he would never stop working for his freedom.

Andrew Marschalk, the son of a Dutch baker, was a printer, a pioneer in his field, and a man of great curiosity. By the time Marschalk heard about it, Cox had told a great many people in the Natchez district the story of African royalty being held in slavery in America. Marschalk was fascinated. He

suggested that Ibrahima write a letter to his people, telling them of his whereabouts and asking them to ransom him. But Ibrahima had not been to his homeland in twenty years. The people there were still being captured by slave traders. He would have to send a messenger who knew the countryside, and who knew the Fula. Where would he find such a man?

For a long time Ibrahima did nothing. Finally, some time after the death of Dr. Cox in 1816, Ibrahima wrote the letter that Marschalk suggested. He had little faith in the procedure but felt he had nothing to lose. Marschalk was surprised when Ibrahima appeared with the letter written neatly in Arabic. Since one place in Africa was the same as the next to Marschalk, he sent the letter not to Fouta Djallon but to Morocco.

The government of Morocco did not know Ibrahima but understood from his letter that he was a Moslem. Moroccan officials, in a letter to President James Monroe, pleaded for the release of Ibrahima. The letter reached Henry Clay, the American secretary of state.

The United States had recently ended a bitter war with Tripoli in North Africa and welcomed the idea of establishing good relations with Morocco, another North African country. Clay wrote to Foster about Ibrahima.

Foster resented the idea of releasing Ibrahima. The very idea that the government of Morocco had written to Clay and discussed a religion that Ibrahima shared with other Africans gave Ibrahima a past that Foster had long denied, a past as honorable as Foster's.

WORDS TO KNOW	**prosper** (prŏs'pər) *v.* to be successful; thrive **procedure** (prə-sē'jər) *n.* a course of action

This idea challenged a basic <u>premise</u> of slavery—a premise that Foster must have believed without <u>reservation</u>: that the Africans had been nothing but savages, with no humanity or human feelings, and therefore it was all right to enslave them. But after more letters and pressure from the State Department, Foster agreed to release Ibrahima if he could be assured that Ibrahima would leave the country and return to Fouta Djallon.

Many people who believed that slavery was wrong also believed that Africans could not live among white Americans. The American Colonization Society had been formed expressly to send freed Africans back to Africa. The society bought land, and a colony called Liberia was established on the west coast of Africa. Foster was assured that Ibrahima would be sent there.

By then Ibrahima's cause had been taken up by a number of abolitionist[10] groups in the North as well as by many free Africans. They raised money to buy his wife's freedom as well.

On February 7, 1829, Ibrahima and his wife sailed on the ship *Harriet* for Africa. The ship reached Liberia, and Ibrahima now had to find a way to reach his people again. He never found that way. Abd al-Rahman Ibrahima died in Liberia in July 1829.

Who was Ibrahima? He was one of millions of Africans taken by force from their native lands. He was the son of a chief, a warrior, and a scholar. But to Ibrahima the only thing that mattered was that he had lost his freedom. If he had been a herder in Fouta Djallon, or an artist in Benin, or a farmer along the Gambia, it would have been the same. Ibrahima was an African who loved freedom no less than other beings on earth. And he was denied that freedom. ❖

---

10. **abolitionist** (ăb′ə-lĭsh′ə-nĭst): favoring the end of slavery.

WORDS TO KNOW	**premise** (prĕm′ĭs) *n.* an idea that forms the basis of an argument **reservation** (rĕz′ər-vā′shən) *n.* a doubt; an exception

375

The WOLF and the HOUSE DOG

by Aesop

Use the following questions to help students analyze and understand the fable.

1. Why does the idea of living as a House Dog appeal to the Wolf at first?

Possible Response: He thinks of all the wonderful things he would have to eat.

2. Why does the Wolf decide that being a House Dog is not so wonderful?

Possible Response: He asks about the place on the Dog's neck that is worn away by the collar and finds out that the House Dog is not always free.

Aesop

The name Aesop is given to a legendary figure associated with animal fables that arose in Greece at least as early as the fifth century B.C. Various writers invented "facts" about him, but there is no reason to accept any of these biographical details as true.

The first collection of fables said to be by Aesop was made by Demetrius Phalareus in the fourth century B.C. The fables were retold by many writers thereafter. One of the most well-known retellers was Jean de La Fontaine, a French poet of the seventeenth century.

*T*here once was a Wolf who got very little to eat because the Dogs of the village were so wide awake and watchful. He was really nothing but skin and bones, and it made him very downhearted to think of it.

One night this Wolf happened to fall in with a fine fat House Dog who had wandered a little too far from home. The Wolf would gladly have eaten him then and there, but the House Dog looked strong enough to leave his marks should he try it. So the Wolf spoke very humbly to the Dog, complimenting him on his fine appearance.

"You can be as well-fed as I am if you want to," replied the Dog. "Leave the woods; there you live miserably. Why, you have to fight hard for every bite you get. Follow my example and you will get along beautifully."

"What must I do?" asked the Wolf.

"Hardly anything," answered the House Dog. "Chase people who carry canes, bark at beggars, and fawn on the people of the house. In return you will get tidbits of every kind, chicken bones, choice bits of meat, sugar, cake and much more besides, not to speak of kind words and caresses."

EXPLICIT INSTRUCTION Viewing and Representation

Dog
by Alberto Giacometti

ART APPRECIATION The art of Alberto Giacometti (1901–1966) includes sculptures, paintings, and poetry. His later sculptures are characterized by the extreme thinness, seen in his statue of the dog reproduced here.

Instruction Point out that the sculptor used lines and shapes to express a mood or emotion in his sculpture of the dog. The page designer chose this sculpture specifically because those lines and shapes, and the mood or emotion they express, represent the mood and emotion of the text.

Practice Ask students what mood the sculpture expresses and how it represents or extends the meaning of the text.

Possible Response: The bowed head of the sculpture makes the dog look downtrodden and expresses the lack of freedom of the dog in the fable.

Dog, Alberto Giacometti. Hirshhorn Museum and Sculpture Garden, Smithsonian Institution, gift of Joseph H. Hirshhorn, 1966. Photo: Ricardo Blanc. Copyright © 2001 Artists Rights Society (ARS), New York/ADAGP, Paris.

The Wolf had such a beautiful vision of his coming happiness that he almost wept. But just then he noticed that the hair on the Dog's neck was worn and the skin chafed.

"What's that on your neck?"

"Nothing at all," replied the Dog.

"What! Nothing!"

5 "Oh, just a trifle!"

"But please tell me."

"Perhaps you see the mark of the collar to which my chain is fastened."

"What! A chain!" cried the Wolf. "Don't you go wherever you please?"

"Not always! But what's the difference?" replied the Dog.

"All the difference in the world! I don't care a rap for your feasts and I wouldn't take all the tender young lambs in the world at that price." And away ran the Wolf to the woods. **6**

There is nothing worth so much as liberty. ❖ **7**

Connect to the Literature

1. What Do You Think?
Responses will vary. Students might say that Ibrahima's life shows the terrible cost of slavery—that a human being could be treated as property. They might say that Ibrahima should be proud of who he was and where he came from, regardless of the position he held in American society

Comprehension Check
- The Mandingos capture Ibrahima and sell him to the whites, who put him on a slave ship bound for the United States.
- He becomes enslaved to Thomas Foster.
- There is no way he could have gotten back there, even if he had escaped.

 Use Selection Quiz
Unit Three Resource Book, p. 38.

Think Critically

2. Possible Response: Dr. Cox might have told Foster about how the Fula people had taken care of him when he was injured, and about how educated Ibrahima was. He might have added that Foster's basic premise—that these people were savages without human feelings—was untrue.

3. Answers will vary, but should include the inhumanity of enslaving another person.

4. Students' retellings will vary, but should be in chronological order.

 Use **Reading and Critical Thinking Transparencies,** p. 6, for additional support.

5. Responses will vary. Students should support their answers with details from the selection, comparing what they now know to what they knew before they began reading.

Literary Analysis

Sources of Information Students' lists should indicate an understanding of what sources are secondary and what sources are primary. They should list appropriate sources, such as school records and letters to friends.

Use **Literary Analysis Transparencies,** p. 14, for additional support.

Connect to the Literature

1. What Do You Think?
If you could say one thing about Ibrahima's life, what would it be?

Comprehension Check
- How does Ibrahima come to be sold into slavery?
- What happens to Ibrahima in the United States?
- Why doesn't Ibrahima return to his home in Fouta Djallon?

Think Critically

2. Walter Dean Myers notes that Thomas Foster must have believed deeply in the "basic premise of slavery" to treat Ibrahima as he did. What do you think Dr. Cox would say to Foster about those beliefs?

> **Think About:**
> - Dr. Cox's experiences in Fouta Djallon
> - his relationship with Ibrahima
> - his parting words to Ibrahima

3. If you were teaching this selection, what two or three main ideas would you want your students to remember?

4. **ACTIVE READING** **CHRONOLOGICAL ORDER**
With a partner, take turns retelling the story of Ibrahima's life in your own words. Refer to the time line you made in your 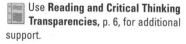 **READER'S NOTEBOOK** to keep track of chronological order.

5. What information about slavery did you find most surprising or disturbing?

Extend Interpretations

6. **COMPARING TEXTS** Read "The Wolf and the House Dog" on page 376. What ideas about freedom does this fable present? Do you think Ibrahima would agree with these ideas? Why?

7. **Connect to Life** Many people go to great lengths to find out about their backgrounds and ancestors. Why do you think finding out about their pasts matters so much to some people?

Extend Interpretations

6. Comparing Texts Possible Response: The fable's moral says that nothing is better than freedom. Ibrahima would agree, since he had to live most of his life without it.

7. Connect to Life Possible Response: People want to know about their heritage to understand who they are and where they came from. Ibrahima's knowledge of his heritage helped him preserve his dignity while he was a slave.

Literary Analysis

SOURCES OF INFORMATION The writer of a biography may use both primary and secondary sources to find out about a person's life. **Primary sources,** such as journals, diaries, and letters, convey firsthand knowledge. **Secondary sources,** such as other biographies and reference books, convey secondhand knowledge.

Group Activity What kinds of sources might a biographer use in order to find out about your life? In a small group, make a list of primary and secondary sources that you think would be helpful.

Primary Sources:
• photographs

Secondary Sources:
• school newspaper

BIOGRAPHY A **biography** is the story of a person's life written by another person. Biographies are usually written in the **third-person point of view,** using pronouns such as *he, she,* and *they.* The selection you have just read is a biography of Abd al-Rahman Ibrahima, written by Walter Dean Myers.

Writing

Persuasive Pamphlet Suppose that Andrew Marschalk, the Dutch printer who helped Ibrahima send a letter to Africa, is preparing a pamphlet that argues against slavery. Summarize Ibrahima's story for the pamphlet. In your summary, include the important points from the biography and the details that Walter Dean Myers used to support them. Remember that your summary should be in your own words. Place it in your **Working Portfolio.**

Speaking & Listening

Speaking of Justice What issue in your school or community do you feel strongly about? Pick one issue and create a presentation about it. Begin by developing a clear statement of your opinion on the issue. Then gather support and evidence for your opinion. You may need to do some research or interview a few people to get the evidence you need. You may also want to include photographs or other visual displays. Practice presenting the information in a loud, strong voice. Then deliver your presentation to the class.

Speaking and Listening Handbook
See p. R100: Persuasive Presentations.

Research & Technology

SOCIAL STUDIES

Research the Songhai Empire, along with the kingdoms of Benin, Kush, Kanem-Bornu, Ethiopia, and Mali. Then make a map of Africa, showing the region that each kingdom occupied and the period in which each existed. Add images that represent each kingdom.

 INTERNET **Research Starter**
www.mcdougallittell.com

Vocabulary

An analogy contains two pairs of words that are related in the same way. Consider this example:

LARGE : HUGE :: quiet : silent

This analogy is read as

"*Large* is to *huge* as *quiet* is to *silent.*"
The two pairs of words are related because they are pairs of synonyms.

For each analogy, figure out the relationship between the words in the first pair. Then, decide which Word to Know best completes the second pair of words.

1. NOISE : UPROAR :: _____ : resident
2. IDEA : OPINION :: _____ : doubt
3. FILTHY : CLEAN :: _____ : calmness
4. REGION : AREA :: _____ : rank
5. RESPONSE : ANSWER :: _____ : hike
6. TRUTH : FALSEHOOD :: _____ : freedom
7. SHUT : OPEN :: _____ : lose
8. FRIEND : COMPANION :: _____ : method
9. DECORATION : ORNAMENT :: _____ : belief
10. CAR : AUTOMOBILE :: _____ : empire

Vocabulary Handbook
See p. R24: Analogies.

WORDS TO KNOW					
	bondage	dynasty	premise	prosper	status
	chaos	inhabitant	procedure	reservation	trek

Writing

Persuasive Pamphlet Summaries should outline the story in a coherent fashion. To get students started on this activity, have them skim the story, taking notes as they read.

 Use **Writing Transparencies,** p. 51, for additional support.

Speaking & Listening

Speaking of Justice After students have chosen an issue to speak about, suggest they freewrite about their feelings and opinions. Also suggest they develop a list of questions they need to answer to help them gather more information about the issue.

Use the **Speaking and Listening Book,** pp. 29, 30, for additional support.

Research & Technology

Social Studies Student maps should be copied or traced from an actual printed map and should show the approximate boundaries of the kingdoms in question accurately. Labels should be clear and appropriate. A good source of information for this activity might be historical atlases or history texts that include information about the history of West Africa.

Vocabulary

1. inhabitant
2. reservation
3. chaos
4. status
5. trek
6. bondage
7. prosper
8. procedure
9. premise
10. dynasty

Grammar in Context

WRITING EXERCISE

1. older
2. more painful
3. saddest

Walter Dean Myers

Among the many challenges Myers overcame as a child was a speech impediment. As an adult he has struggled to find his way through the creative process, and has weathered personal difficulties such as divorce. His output includes stories and novels about his childhood home, the Harlem section of New York City. One of his poems recently won the Michael Printz Award. He has remarried and today lives in Jersey City, New Jersey.

Author Activity

Heroic Tales Students' time lines should show a clear understanding of chronological order and isolate the main events of the selected biography.

Use **Reading and Critical Thinking Transparencies,** p. 6, for additional support.

Grammar in Context: Comparing with Adjectives

"Abd al-Rahman Ibrahima" contains many **adjectives** that compare people, things, or ideas. Notice how the words in red type add drama:

> . . . a ship that was larger than any he had ever seen.
> Fouta Djallon was more and more distant.

Writers use the **comparative form** of an adjective to compare one thing to another. For many adjectives, you can form the comparative by adding *-er* to the end of the word. For others, you need to place the word *less, more, better,* or *worse* in front of the adjective.

The **superlative form** of an adjective compares something to two or more things, or to an entire group or category of things. Form the superlative by adding *-est* to the adjective or by using the words *most, least, best,* or *worst.*

> Timbuktu became the largest city in the Songhai Empire.
> Ibrahima attended the best-known school.

WRITING EXERCISE Rewrite each sentence. Add the adjective form defined in parentheses.

Example: *Original* The Fula were the (superlative of *tall*) people.

Rewritten The Fula were the tallest people.

1. Now that he was (comparative of *old*), Ibrahima tended his own garden.
2. It was (comparative of *painful*) to starve in the woods than to live in slavery.
3. The (superlative of *sad*) part of the story was when Ibrahima died.

Grammar Handbook
See p. R78: Using Modifiers Effectively.

Walter Dean Myers
born 1937

". . . I want to . . . touch the lives of my characters and, through them, those of my readers."

Early Obstacles The early years of Walter Dean Myers's life were marked by hardship. When this West Virginia native was two years old, his mother died. He was put into foster care at the age of three. As Myers grew into a bright and talented teenager in New York City's Harlem, he turned to writing as a way of expressing himself. In 1970, after a brief period in the army and a series of unsatisfying jobs, Myers became an editor for a publishing company. He wrote part-time for several years, and in 1977 he began to write full-time.

Many Talents Best known for his young people's novels about Harlem youth, Myers has also written ghost stories, adventure tales, modern fairy tales, and nonfiction. The selection "Abd al-Rahman Ibrahima" is a chapter from the nonfiction book *Now Is Your Time! The African-American Struggle for Freedom.* This book, like Myers's novels *Slam, Fallen Angels, The Young Landlords,* and *Motown and Didi: A Love Story,* won a Coretta Scott King Award. His novels *Somewhere in the Darkness* and *Scorpions* were Newbery Honor Books.

AUTHOR ACTIVITY

Heroic Tales Read another extraordinary life story in *Now Is Your Time!* Prepare a time line of the biography and a series of illustrations covering major events in the subject's life. Hang them on a bulletin board in your classroom.

380 UNIT THREE PART 2: BREAKING BARRIERS

EXPLICIT INSTRUCTION **Grammar in Context**

AVOIDING DOUBLE COMPARATIVES AND SUPERLATIVES

Instruction Remind students that they should use the comparative form of a modifier (an adjective or an adverb) to compare two things and the superlative form to compare more than two things. For most one-syllable modifiers and some two-syllable modifiers, add *-er* to form the comparative and *-est* to form the superlative (braver, bravest; shallower, shallowest). With other two-syllable modifiers, use *more* for the comparative and *most* for the superlative forms (more calmly, most calmly). Point out

that using *more* and *-er* or *most* and *-est* together results in a double comparative *(more faster)* or double superlative *(most fastest).* Both should be avoided.

Practice Have students replace the underlined double comparatives and superlatives in these sentences with the correct form.

1. The Fula had a <u>more complexer</u> form of government than many societies of that time. *(more complex)*
2. Timbuktu was one of the <u>most importantest</u> cities in Africa. *(most important)*

3. Dr. Cox was <u>more harmlesser</u> than the Fula expected. *(more harmless)*
4. Ibrahima rode <u>more faster</u> than his men. *(faster)*

 Use **Unit Three Resource Book,** p. 36.

 For more instruction on avoiding double comparatives and superlatives, see McDougal Littell's **Language Network,** Chapter 5.

For **systematic instruction** in grammar, see:
• **Grammar, Usage, and Mechanics Book**
• pacing chart on p. 315i.

from The Story of My Life
by HELEN KELLER

Connect to Your Life

Aha! In the selection you are about to read, Helen Keller describes a childhood experience when she had an exciting breakthrough. Think of a time when you were suddenly able to do or understand something important. What happened? What did it feel like?

Build Background

HISTORY

Thomas Gallaudet and Laurent Clerc established the first American school for the hearing impaired in Hartford, Connecticut, in 1817. Gallaudet and Clerc also developed a new sign language that combined elements of French Sign Language with other sign languages in use in the United States. This new sign language eventually became American Sign Language (ASL). ASL combines signs, gestures, facial expressions, and a hand alphabet. It is now the fourth most used language in the United States.

American Sign Language Manual Alphabet

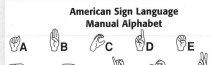

WORDS TO KNOW **Vocabulary Preview**

bitterness	persist	repentance	sentiment	tangible
impress	prey	reveal	succeed	vainly

Focus Your Reading

LITERARY ANALYSIS **IMAGERY**

Words and phrases that help readers see, hear, taste, smell, and feel what a writer is describing are called **imagery**. Note the details related to sight and touch in this line from the selection:

> *The afternoon sun penetrated the mass of honeysuckle that covered the porch.*

As you read, look for other details that help you understand Helen Keller's childhood experiences.

ACTIVE READING **CLARIFYING**

When you stop to quickly review events or unfamiliar words while you are reading, you are **clarifying.** Clarifying can help you find answers to any questions you might have. It can also help you make sense of what you read.

READER'S NOTEBOOK As you read, stop every two or three paragraphs to clarify what you have just read. Record the main events of the selection.

> Helen has a temper tantrum.
> Teacher (Anne) arrives.

THE STORY OF MY LIFE **381**

This selection is included in the **Grade 6 InterActive Reader.**

Standards-Based Objectives
- understand and appreciate an **autobiography** (Literary Analysis)
- understand author's use of **sensory details** (Literary Analysis)
- use **clarifying** as a reading strategy to help understand autobiography better (Active Reading)
- understand **implied main idea**

Summary
In this excerpt from Helen Keller's autobiography, *The Story of My Life,* Helen recounts the beginning of her relationship with her teacher, Miss Anne Sullivan. She tells of the day Miss Sullivan arrived, and how she taught Helen to sign the names of familiar objects. Helen remembers that normal feelings and emotions were not part of her life at the time, and how that changed as she realized the power that came with knowing objects had names.

Thematic Link
Helen Keller lived at a time when many deaf and blind people were institutionalized and never learned to function in the wider world. Because of Anne Sullivan's and Helen's determination, these women were able to break an important barrier for people with disabilities of all kinds. This short excerpt offers readers the hope that perhaps their own barriers can be overcome.

English Conventions Practice

Daily Language SkillBuilder

Have students **proofread** the display sentences on page 315k and write them correctly. The sentences also appear on Transparency 12 of **Language Transparencies.**

Preteaching Vocabulary
If you would like to preteach the WORDS TO KNOW for this selection, use the Explicit Instruction, page 382.

LESSON RESOURCES

UNIT THREE RESOURCE BOOK, pp. 39–45

ASSESSMENT
Formal Assessment, pp. 59–60
Test Generator

SKILLS TRANSPARENCIES AND COPYMASTERS
Reading and Critical Thinking
- Noting Sensory Details, TR 11 (pp. 382, 385)

Language
- Daily Language SkillBuilder, TR 12 (p. 381)
- Double Negatives, TR 43 (p. 387)
- Learning and Remembering New Words, TR 65 (p. 382)

Speaking and Listening
- Evaluating Reading Aloud, p. 14 (p. 386)

INTEGRATED TECHNOLOGY
Audio Library

Visit our Web site:
www.mcdougallittell.com

For **systematic instruction** in language skills, see:
- **Vocabulary and Spelling Book**
- **Grammar, Usage, and Mechanics Book**
- pacing chart on p. 315i.

from The Story of My Life

by Helen Keller

Reading and Analyzing

Literary Analysis IMAGERY

 A Since Helen can neither see nor hear, she relies on her other senses. Ask what examples show her use of the sense of touch in this paragraph. **Possible Responses:** The sun touched her face; her fingers touched the leaves and blossoms.

Use **Unit Three Resource Book**, p. 41, for more practice. Use **Reading and Critical Thinking Transparencies**, p. 11, for additional support.

Active Reading CLARIFYING

B Ask students to think about the analogy Helen makes between herself before schooling and a ship in a dense fog. Ask them to explain how they think Helen felt before her education. **Possible Response:** Helen was searching for something more, yet didn't know what it was or how to find it.

Use **Unit Three Resource Book**, p. 40, for more practice.

Reading Skills and Strategies: EVALUATE

C Ask students to speculate why Miss Sullivan began to teach Helen by signing such words as *doll, pin, hat,* and *cup.* **Possible Response:** She began with words for objects that Helen was familiar with and that Helen used regularly.

Literary Analysis: CHARACTER TRAITS

Have students describe Miss Sullivan. **Possible Responses:** She is patient, intelligent, persistent, and kind.

EXPLICIT INSTRUCTION **Preteaching Vocabulary**

WORDS TO KNOW

Teaching Strategy Remind students that among the strategies for learning the meanings of words are **using context clues** and **using a dictionary.** Have students find the word *tangible* on page 383. Have students first analyze the word for recognizable word parts. Then ask them to read the sentence the word appears in and try to find context clues that define it. If they find none, have students look up the word in a dictionary.

Practice Divide the class into pairs or small groups, giving each pair or group one of the words from the WORDS TO KNOW list. Ask students to define each word by first analyzing the word for familiar word parts, then looking for context clues, and finally using the dictionary if no context clues exist. Have them write the words and definitions on the board. Then have students work individually to write a descriptive paragraph using as many of the WORDS TO KNOW as possible.

Use **Unit Three Resource Book**, p. 44, for more practice.

For **systematic instruction** in vocabulary, see:
- **Vocabulary and Spelling Book**
- pacing chart on p. 315i.

The most important day I remember in all my life is the one on which my teacher, Anne Mansfield Sullivan, came to me. I am filled with wonder when I consider the immeasurable contrasts between the two lives which it connects. It was the third of March, 1887, three months before I was seven years old.

On the afternoon of that eventful day, I stood on the porch, dumb, expectant. I guessed vaguely from my mother's signs and from the hurrying to and fro in the house that something unusual was about to happen, so I went to the door and waited on the steps. The afternoon sun penetrated the mass of honeysuckle that covered the porch, and fell on my upturned face. My fingers lingered almost unconsciously on the familiar leaves and blossoms which had just come forth to greet the sweet southern spring. I did not know what the future held of marvel or surprise for me. Anger and <u>bitterness</u> had <u>preyed</u> upon me continually for weeks and a deep languor had <u>succeeded</u> this passionate struggle.

Have you ever been at sea in a dense fog, when it seemed as if a <u>tangible</u> white darkness shut you in, and the great ship, tense and anxious, groped her way toward the shore with plummet and sounding-line,[1] and you waited with beating heart for something to happen? I was like that ship before my education began, only I was without compass or sounding-line, and had no way of knowing how near the harbor was. "Light! Give me light!" was the wordless cry of my soul, and the light of love shone on me in that very hour.

I felt approaching footsteps. I stretched out my hand as I supposed to my mother. Someone took it, and I was caught up and held close in the arms of her who had come to <u>reveal</u> all things to me, and, more than all things else, to love me.

The morning after my teacher came she led me into her room and gave me a doll. The little blind children at the Perkins Institution had sent it and Laura Bridgman had dressed it; but I did not know this until afterward. When I had played with it a little while, Miss Sullivan slowly spelled into my hand the word "d-o-l-l." I was at once interested in this finger play and tried to imitate it. When I finally succeeded in making the letters correctly I was flushed with childish pleasure and pride. Running downstairs to my mother I held up my hand and made the letters for *doll*. I did not know that I was spelling a word or even that words existed; I was simply making my fingers go in monkey-like imitation. In the days that followed I learned to spell in this uncomprehending way a great many words, among them *pin, hat, cup* and a few verbs like *sit, stand,* and *walk*. But my teacher had been with me several weeks before I understood that everything has a name.

One day, while I was playing with my new doll, Miss Sullivan put my big rag doll into my lap also, spelled "d-o-l-l" and tried to make me understand that "d-o-l-l" applied to both. Earlier in the day we had had a tussle[2] over the words "m-u-g" and "w-a-t-e-r." Miss Sullivan

---

1. **plummet** (plŭm′ĭt) **and sounding-line:** a metal weight tied to the end of a rope, used to determine water depth.

2. **tussle** (tŭs′əl): a rough struggle.

WORDS TO KNOW	**bitterness** (bĭt′ər-nĭs) *n.* a feeling of disgust or resentment
	prey (prā) *v.* to have a harmful effect
	succeed (sək-sēd′) *v.* to come after; follow
	tangible (tăn′jə-bəl) *adj.* able to be touched or grasped
	reveal (rĭ-vēl′) *v.* to bring to view; to show

383

Literary Analysis IMAGERY

Ask students to think about how Helen Keller made sense of her world without her senses of sight and sound. What words does she use to help us understand her silent world?

Possible Responses: warm sunshine, hop and skip with pleasure, fragrance of honeysuckle, cool stream gushed

Active Reading CLARIFYING

Have students summarize the events that led Helen to realize she had emotions.

Possible Response: Miss Sullivan begins to teach Helen to sign, Helen and Miss Sullivan argue over *mug* and *water,* and Helen breaks the doll. They walk to the well-house where Helen finally understands *water.* Upon returning home, Helen touches many objects, eager to learn their names. She tries to put the doll back together and realizes she feels sorry for what she's done.

Reading Skills and Strategies: QUESTION

Ask students to brainstorm a list of questions that Helen might have asked Miss Sullivan once Helen understood language and was able to sign fluently.

Possible Responses: Answers will vary, but should reflect the kinds of things someone who had lived in silence for so long would ask once he or she had discovered language.

Reading Skills and Strategies: MAKE JUDGMENTS

Ask students to reflect on why Helen Keller chose to recall these particular events in her life. Ask them to write down several reasons and then to discuss them with a partner.

---

had tried to <u>impress</u> upon me that "m-u-g" is *mug* and that "w-a-t-e-r" is *water,* but I <u>persisted</u> in confounding[3] the two. In despair she had dropped the subject for the time, only to renew it at the first opportunity. I became impatient at her repeated attempts and, seizing the new doll, I dashed it upon the floor. I was keenly delighted when I felt the fragments of the broken doll at my feet. Neither sorrow nor regret followed my passionate outburst. I had not loved the doll. In the still, dark world in which I lived there was no strong <u>sentiment</u> or tenderness. I felt my teacher sweep the fragments to one side of the hearth and I had a sense of satisfaction that the cause of my discomfort was removed. She brought me my hat, and I knew I was going out into the warm sunshine. This thought, if a wordless sensation may be called a thought, made me hop and skip with pleasure.

We walked down the path to the well-house, attracted by the fragrance of the honeysuckle with which it was covered. Someone was drawing water and my teacher placed my hand under the spout. As the cool stream gushed over one hand she spelled into the other the word *water,* first slowly, then rapidly. I stood still, my whole attention fixed upon the motions of her fingers. Suddenly I felt a misty consciousness as of something forgotten—a thrill of returning thought; and somehow the mystery of language was revealed to me. I knew then that "w-a-t-e-r"

meant the wonderful cool something that was flowing over my hand. That living word awakened my soul, gave it light, hope, joy, set it free! There were barriers still, it is true, but barriers that could in time be swept away.

I left the well-house eager to learn. Everything had a name, and each name gave birth to a new thought. As we returned to the house every object which I touched seemed to quiver with life. That was because I saw everything with the strange, new sight that had come to me. On entering the door I remembered the doll I had broken. I felt my way to the hearth and picked up the pieces. I tried <u>vainly</u> to put them together. Then my eyes filled with tears; for I realized what I had done, and for the first time I felt <u>repentance</u> and sorrow.

I learned a great many new words that day. I do not remember what they all were; but I do know that *mother, father, sister, teacher* were among them—words that were to make the world blossom for me, "like Aaron's rod, with flowers."[4] It would have been difficult to find a happier child than I was as I lay in my crib at the close of that eventful day and lived over the joys it had brought me, and for the first time longed for a new day to come. ❖

---

3. **confounding:** confusing.
4. **"like Aaron's rod, with flowers":** a reference to a passage of the Bible in which a wooden rod miraculously bears flowers and fruit (Numbers 17:8).

WORDS TO KNOW	
	impress (ĭm-prĕs') *v.* to implant firmly in the mind; convey vividly
	persist (pər-sĭst') *v.* to continue stubbornly
	sentiment (sĕn'tə-mənt) *n.* emotion
	vainly (vān'lē) *adv.* without success
	repentance (rĭ-pĕn'təns) *n.* a regret for past behavior

384

EXPLICIT INSTRUCTION Implied Main Idea

Instruction Remind students that the main idea of a selection is what most of the paragraphs are about. The main idea may be stated as a thesis statement in the introduction or as a summarizing statement in the conclusion. Sometimes the main idea is unstated, and readers must infer the main idea by thinking about the information in the selection. Tell students that the main idea of the excerpt from *The Story of My Life* is unstated.

Practice Have students work in small groups to come up with main idea statements for this selection and give examples from the text to support their main ideas.

Possible Responses: Main idea of selection— Helen Keller's life changed drastically after Anne Sullivan became her teacher. Supporting details—Before Sullivan arrived, Keller felt as if she were in a "dense fog." She could not communicate clearly. She did not know the names of everyday objects. She did

not feel emotionally attached to the world. After Sullivan arrived, Keller learned to spell words with her fingers. She learned the names of things. She felt happy and excited, and she became aware of her own emotions and those of others.

Use **Unit Three Resource Book,** p. 42, for more practice.

Connect to the Literature

1. **What Do You Think?**
In reading about Helen Keller's experience, what impressed you the most?

Comprehension Check
• What made Helen's world "still" and "dark"?
• How old was Helen when her teacher arrived?
• What happened at the well-house?

Think Critically

2. **ACTIVE READING** **CLARIFYING**
How did her teacher's arrival affect Helen Keller's life? To support your answer, refer to the notes you made in your **READER'S NOTEBOOK**.

3. How would you describe Helen's life before she learned to use words? How would you describe it afterward?

4. Why did Helen's feelings about the doll change?

5. Based on this selection, what kind of person do you think Helen Keller was as a young girl?

   Think About:
   • the difficulties she faced
   • what she learned
   • her feelings about her teacher

6. How does reading Helen's own words make the events come alive? Support your answer with details from the selection.

Extend Interpretations

7. **Different Perspectives** Suppose that Helen's teacher, Anne Sullivan, had written about these events. What would be different about her account?

8. **Connect to Life** Imagine that Keller were a child today. How might her life be different?

Literary Analysis

IMAGERY The words and phrases that writers use to help readers imagine that they can see, hear, taste, smell, and feel what is being described are called **imagery.** Keller uses imagery to help her readers understand her experiences. For example, writing that the "sun . . . fell on my upturned face" appeals to the reader's sense of touch, or feeling. It helps the reader imagine the sun's warmth.

Paired Activity Working with a partner, look back through the selection to find sensory details. Record them on a chart as shown. Do you find details for every sense? What senses are triggered most often?

Sensory Details	
Smell	
Touch	sun . . . fell on my upturned face
Taste	
Sight	
Hearing	

AUTOBIOGRAPHY
An **autobiography** is the story of a person's life, told by that person. Autobiographies are usually written in the **first-person point of view,** using pronouns such as *I, me,* and *we.* The selection you have just read was taken from Helen Keller's autobiography.

Connect to the Literature

1. **What Do You Think?**
Possible Responses: Students might be impressed by the anger and bitterness Keller felt before her teacher's arrival, by Sullivan's patience and skill, or by the speed of Helen's learning.

Comprehension Check
• Helen Keller could not see, hear, or speak.
• Helen was six years old, almost seven, when her teacher arrived.
• Helen understood for the first time that things have names.

Use Selection Quiz **Unit Three Resource Book,** p. 45.

Think Critically

2. **Possible Response:** Before her teacher's arrival, Helen Keller could not express thoughts or feelings. Afterwards, Keller could communicate with sign language.

3. **Possible Response:** Helen's life before she learned to communicate was "dark" and "still." After she began to learn words, the world opened up to her.

4. **Possible Response:** Helen seemed to realize that the doll, being a gift, represented someone else's concern for her, something she could not understand before she had experienced her teacher's gift of love and language.

5. **Possible Response:** Helen was angry and bitter before she learned to communicate, but she was also intelligent, determined, successful, and grateful for love and for opportunities.

6. **Possible Response:** We feel what it was like for Helen to be deaf, blind, and mute. For example, she notices what honeysuckle leaves feel like; she also uses the "ship at sea in a dense fog" analogy to help the reader understand what her early life was like.

Extend Interpretations

7. **Different Perspectives** Sullivan probably would have described Helen, both upon meeting her and as she watched her progress. She would also have described her own feelings and thoughts about working with Helen, but would have known less about Helen's thoughts and feelings.

8. **Connect to Life** Today, Helen would have many more public resources available to her, for example, Braille signs in many buildings, a communicating keyboard, and specially trained teachers in school settings. She probably would not have a teacher living with her family and constantly available. She still would have to learn to live with her disabilities because there are still no cures for many types of blindness and deafness.

Literary Analysis

Imagery Students may find that smell, touch, and taste are triggered more often, since those senses are more acutely developed in Helen.

Use **Reading and Critical Thinking Transparencies,** p. 11, for additional support.

Writing

Her Own Words Suggest students go back through the story and take notes on Helen Keller's life before and after the arrival of Anne Sullivan.

Speaking & Listening

Reading a Life Allow students plenty of time to practice reading and incorporating expressions and gestures. Remind them to use a dictionary to help them pronounce any unfamiliar words.

 Use the **Speaking and Listening Book,** p. 14, for additional support.

Research & Technology

Helping Hands To make this activity easier, have students work in small groups to brainstorm helping occupations and to classify them according to kinds of help they provide, for example, medical, educational, and so on. Have them choose from their lists the careers they will write about.

Vocabulary

STANDARDIZED TEST PRACTICE

Students should complete the chart as modeled, using the WORDS TO KNOW.

EXERCISE Students should write their own definitions prior to using a dictionary.

Writing

Her Own Words In the first sentence of the selection you just read, Helen Keller states, "The most important day I remember in all my life is the one on which my teacher, Anne Sullivan, came to me." Why do you think this was the most important day in Helen Keller's life? What happened as a result of this day? Write a paragraph or two that answers these questions. Place your paragraph in your **Working Portfolio.**

Writing Handbook
See p. R43: Explanatory Writing.

Speaking & Listening

Reading a Life Choose a short section from "The Story of My Life" to read aloud. Practice reading it to make sure you can accurately read every word. As you practice, add facial expressions and gestures that will help an audience understand and enjoy the text. When you are ready, present the reading to the class. Be sure to read slowly and in a voice everyone can hear.

Speaking and Listening Handbook
See p. R98: Oral Interpretation.

Research & Technology

Helping Hands Helen Keller felt lonely and frustrated before help arrived in the form of her teacher, Anne Sullivan. Conduct research to find out about careers that focus on helping people overcome challenges. What careers focus on finding new and innovative ways of helping others? Whom do they help? What types of help do they provide? Use books, articles, and the Internet to find information on three "helping" careers. Write a short report about these careers.

Reading for INFORMATION
Read "High-tech Helping Hands" on p. 388 before searching for information about people who work to help others.

Vocabulary

STANDARDIZED TEST PRACTICE

VOCABULARY STRATEGY: WORD ORIGINS On your paper, complete a chart like the one below. Use a dictionary to research the definition and origin, or etymology, of each Word to Know below. Then use each word in a sentence related to the story. *Reveal* has been started for you as an example.

Word	Definition	Origin	Sentence
reveal	to make known	Middle English: *revelen;* Old French *reveler;* Latin *revēlāre;* (re- + *vēlāre,* to cover)	

WORDS TO KNOW				
bitterness	persist		repentance	sentiment	tangible
impress	prey		reveal	succeed	vainly

EXERCISE: PREFIXES AND SUFFIXES Think about how knowing the origins of words can help you understand new words. Use the chart that you created to help you write definitions for *sentimental* and *impression.* Check your definitions in a dictionary.

Vocabulary Handbook
See p. R22: Word Origins.

Grammar in Context: Avoiding Confusion with Negatives

In *The Story of My Life* Helen Keller remarks:

> I did not know what the future held of marvel or surprise for me.

The word in red is a **negative**. A negative is a word that says "no." It "negates," or reverses, the meaning of the words around it. Negatives include *no, not, none, nothing, nobody, never,* and *nowhere.*

Writers and speakers of standard English never use two negatives together in the same sentence. That kind of construction, called a **double negative,** actually reverses the meaning of the negative. If Helen Keller had written, "I did not know nothing of what the future held," her words would lose their meaning. "I did not know nothing" is an awkward way of saying, "I knew something."

WRITING EXERCISE Rewrite each sentence using the negative in parentheses.

Example: *Original* Helen knew what to expect from her new teacher. (not)

Rewritten Helen did not know what to expect from her new teacher.

1. Helen guessed right away what the letters meant. (not)
2. Helen was horrified when she realized the doll was broken. (not)
3. She felt tenderness for the doll. (no)
4. At first Helen cared about the irritation she caused others. (nothing)

Grammar Handbook

See p. R78: Using Modifiers Effectively.

Grammar in Context
WRITING EXERCISE
Possible Responses:

1. Helen could not guess what the letters meant right away.
2. Helen was not horrified when she realized the doll was broken.
3. She felt no tenderness for the doll.
4. At first Helen cared nothing about the irritation she caused others.

Author Activity

Vivid Words Students will need access to the book *The Story of My Life.* It might be advantageous to have multiple copies available for students to work cooperatively on this activity. If only one copy is available, you may want to read other sections aloud.

Helen Keller
1880–1968

"Life is either a daring adventure, or nothing."

Silent Darkness Helen Keller was born in Tuscumbia, Alabama. Before she turned two, an illness left her blind and deaf. As a child, she invented 60 signs to identify objects and people.

A Life-Changing Visitor The director of the famous Perkins Institute for the Blind sent Anne Mansfield Sullivan to be a teacher for Helen. Sullivan herself had been nearly blind, but she had undergone operations that partially restored her sight. With patience and hard work, Sullivan won Keller's trust and became not only her teacher but her friend for life.

Education and Activism With Sullivan's help, Keller attended schools for the blind and deaf, and graduated from Radcliffe College, part of Harvard University. She wrote, lectured, and traveled the world, working for the rights of women, the poor, and the blind and deaf. In 1964, Keller received the Presidential Medal of Freedom from President Johnson.

AUTHOR ACTIVITY
Vivid Words Read further in *The Story of My Life.* How do you think Keller's early experiences might have affected her writing style?

THE STORY OF MY LIFE **387**

EXPLICIT INSTRUCTION Grammar in Context

CORRECTING DOUBLE NEGATIVES

Instruction Explain that the word *not* is an adverb that often causes problems. *Not* is a negative, a word that says "no." It changes the meaning of the verb, making it negative. When two negatives appear in one sentence, they result in a double negative. Remind students that many contractions contain the word *not,* represented as *n't.* It's easy to forget that contractions with an *n't* are negatives and should not be combined with words meaning "not." Write the following sentence on the board:

Helen Keller didn't have no fun before she learned words. Ask students to identify the double negative *(didn't, no)* and to correct the sentence.

Practice Ask students to eliminate each double negative in the following sentences.

1. It wasn't never easy for Helen to learn to read. *(wasn't easy; was never easy)*
2. Miss Sullivan wouldn't not give up; she was persistent. *(wouldn't give up; would not give up)*

3. Helen didn't not think she could go to college. *(didn't think; did not think)*

 Use **Unit Three Resource Book,** p. 43.

 For more instruction in compound subject and predicates, see McDougal Littell's **Language Network,** Chapter 5.

For **systematic instruction** in grammar, see:
- **Grammar, Usage, and Mechanics Book**
- pacing chart on p. 315i.

Standards-Based Objectives
- read for information
- read and analyze a magazine article and its features
- form and revise research questions
- connect main ideas
- learn about inventions that help people with disabilities

Connecting to the Literature
An article such as "High-Tech Helping Hands" can help students make connections to nonfiction works such as "The Story of My Life." As students read this article, ask them to think about how some of these high-tech inventions could have helped Helen Keller. They may also want to think of other high-tech inventions that could have helped Keller as she learned to read, write, and communicate with others.

LESSON RESOURCES

UNIT THREE RESOURCE BOOK, pp. 46–47

Writing
- Generating Research Questions, TR 40 (p. 389)
- Locating Material in the Library, TR 41 (p. 390)

Magazine Article Source: *National Geographic World*

HIGH-TECH HELPING HANDS

By Jane R. McGoldrick

KIDS HELP RESEARCHERS INVENT HIGH-TECH TOOLS FOR PEOPLE WITH DISABILITIES.

C. J. Marconi's hand motions are "read" by his gloves and then displayed on a computer monitor.

EXPLICIT INSTRUCTION ## Forming and Revising Research Questions

Instruction Remind students that when they begin to research a topic, they often have a question in their minds that they want to answer. Tell students to pretend they are going to conduct research on the life of Helen Keller after reading the selection from *The Story of My Life.* Ask students to come up with questions they could answer through research, and list these on the board. (*Examples: How long was Helen Keller a student of Anne Sullivan? What happened to Helen Keller when she grew up?*) Write the

following question on the board: What happened to Helen Keller when she grew up? Tell students that if they were to research this question, they might find a lot of information—more than they could use for a report. They also might find out about a particular episode in Keller's life that they want to explore further. As a result, students might change their original question to focus on this episode. Tell students that in order to form research questions, they need to know something about the topic; they may need to

read an encyclopedia article to get background information that will help them ask questions.

Practice Have students work in pairs to read and complete the numbered activities on the student pages.

Possible Responses: See the side columns in the teacher's edition for answers to the activities on the student pages.

 Use **Unit Three Resource Book,** p. 46, for more practice.

POWER USERS

Power users, techno testers—kids like C. J. Marconi, 12, are both. Through a program in Wilmington, Delaware, C. J. and others ages 9 and up test high-tech devices designed to assist people with disabilities like their own. Here, C. J., who is deaf, tests a computer sign-language system. As C. J. makes the sign for "cat," his gloves "read" the sign. The figure on the monitor behind him is starting to mimic his movements.

SIGN ON! IT'S CHAT TIME

"It's cool—and a good learning tool, too," says C. J. of Fort Meyers, Florida. That's his description of the sign-language recognition and animation system he tested while staying in Delaware. The system displays an animated figure on a monitor. The figure mimics signs made by a tester. Researchers hope the system eventually will allow any person who doesn't sign to "speak" with someone who does sign. As the nonsigner types or speaks, a computer converts the words into signs. The signer "reads" the monitor. As the signer replies, the computer converts the signs into spoken or written words.

TESTING HANDS AND ARMS

When Krista Caudill tested a finger-spelling robot hand she immediately put her finger on the problem. The robot hand shifted into neutral between each letter it spelled, creating unnatural delays. Now, thanks to Krista's help, engineers are refining the motions.

Reading for Information

When you begin researching a topic, keep a specific question in mind. However, you may find that as you answer one question, your research raises new questions.

Forming and Revising Research Questions
Asking questions about a topic will help guide your research. Once you have chosen a topic, think of a specific question you have about it. Then begin your research by looking for information that will answer the question.

For example, your research question might be "What was life like in the 19th century for people who were disabled?" Then, as you do further research, you gradually revise the question to be more focused. Your final research question might be, "In the 19th century, what support and devices were available to people who were hearing-impaired?"

YOUR TURN *Use this article with the questions and activities below to help you learn how to form and revise research questions.*

1 Before you read this article, scan the title and the photos. What questions come to mind? List two or three questions you would like to have answered.

 Suppose that after scanning this photo you wondered: "Who is this person and why is he wearing those gloves?" After reading the caption and the article, you learn more—C. J. Marconi is testing gloves that "read" sign language. Yet this doesn't explain everything about C. J. and his work. Write one or two questions about C. J. that go beyond the simple who-and-why question.

Reading for Information

Tell students that this magazine article appeared in *National Geographic World,* as noted in the line that begins "Magazine Article Source." As they read through the article, have them use the material in the right-hand column as a guide to reading. The following are possible responses to the four numbered activities.

1 Students should preview the article prior to reading, taking note of the title and photograph. They may want to look at the photograph on the next page as well. The questions they generate should be prompted by their preview.
Possible Responses: What kinds of inventions exist for helping people with disabilities? How did these kids get involved with helping researchers? How do these inventions help people with disabilities?

2 Students should generate more questions based on the photograph on page 388 and on the information from the article.
Possible Responses: How do the gloves that C. J. is wearing help deaf people communicate? Are the gloves wired to the computer?

Use **Writing Transparencies,** p. 40, for additional support.

EXPLICIT INSTRUCTION Connecting Main Ideas

Instruction Remind students that often they can better understand the important ideas in one selection by connecting them to important ideas in another, related selection. Next, review the main idea of the selection from *The Story of My Life:* Helen Keller's world changed drastically due to the teachings of Anne Sullivan. Help students determine the main idea of "High-Tech Helping Hands." (*Kids with disabilities are helping companies test high-tech devices designed to assist people with disabilities.*) Discuss with students the similarities between the two selections.

What do these two selections have in common? Have students think about Helen Keller's experiences as a child and the experiences of the people mentioned in the article. How are the experiences similar and different? When you read about how disabled kids are being helped today, did it help you understand how lonely Helen Keller felt?

Practice Have students work in pairs to compare the effect Anne Sullivan had on Helen Keller's life with the effect technology has on the lives of the young people in the article.

Possible Responses: Responses will vary but students should point out that Anne Sullivan opened up the world for Helen Keller just as the technology has helped young people be more a part of the world. The main difference is how much more is available to people with disabilities today

Use **Unit Three Resource Book,** p. 47, for more practice.

3 Students' questions should reflect details presented in the paragraph. **Possible Responses:** What is finger spelling, and how do people learn to do it? How did kids like Krista get involved with research? How are these inventions marketed and sold?

4 Students should think of questions that this article has prompted yet are not explicitly discussed in the article. **Possible Responses:** What kinds of video games could people with disabilities play? What is cerebral palsy, and what inventions help people who have it?

Reading for Information *continued*

3 This paragraph includes information about a girl who helps engineers develop and test equipment. What detailed and specific research question might you ask about this topic?

4 Sometimes during research you find yourself attracted to a topic that differs from your original focus. For example, suppose your original question was "In what ways is technology used to help people with disabilities?" After reading about Julia Nelson, you might decide instead to ask, "How do people with physical disabilities stay fit?" That's fine, especially if you find the topic more interesting, and think others will, too. Think of one or two new focus questions that this article raises.

Research & Technology
Activity Link: from *The Story of My Life*, p. 386. Review the article and consider this focus question: "What devices, services, or training available today could have helped Helen Keller as a child?" Research how children with disabilities similar to Helen Keller's are given help, support, and training. Write a brief report of your findings.

"THE PEOPLE I WORK WITH REALLY VALUE MY OPINION. IT MAKES ME FEEL GOOD THAT PEOPLE CAN LEARN FROM ME."
KRISTA CAUDILL

 Krista is deaf and blind. To communicate, she often uses fingerspelling—forming shapes that stand for letters in the palm of the hand of her "listener." Krista helps engineers who work at the A.I. DuPont Institute in Wilmington, Delaware. They develop and test equipment to help people with disabilities. Krista is one of about a dozen young people with disabilities from the area who serve as consumer researchers before the devices are ready to be sold.

"We ask the researchers to attend team meetings and give us ongoing feedback," says director Richard Foulds. "They're a major part of our team."

Bern Gavlick, 16, has been testing a robot arm that attaches to his wheelchair. Because of his cerebral palsy, Bern cannot easily control the movements of his limbs. The arm can take a book off a shelf or open a door for him. Julia Nelson, 16, also has cerebral palsy. She tested a video game system designed for fun and fitness. "I love trying out the latest products," says Julia. "As a disabled teen, I'm looking to a future of trying to be independent," she adds. "It gives me hope that there are people working on products to help me achieve that goal."

EXPLICIT INSTRUCTION **Research & Technology**

The Research & Technology activity on this page links to the activity on page 386 from the Choices & Challenges following the excerpt from *The Story of My Life.*

Instruction This article will serve as a starting point for researching the focus question; however, students will need time and support with print and electronic sources to gather additional information. Remind students of the requirements for writing a brief report. Students may benefit from working with a partner on this activity.

Practice Students may want to do further research using one of the questions they generated during the reading of this magazine article, and share their research with the class.

Use **Writing Transparencies**, p. 41, for additional support.

Street Corner Flight

by NORMA LANDA FLORES

Words Like Freedom

by LANGSTON HUGHES

Connect to Your Life

To Be Free What comes to mind when you think about freedom? What words and images express your thoughts and feelings about what it means to be free? Use a web like the one shown to explore your ideas.

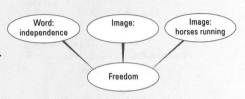

Build Background

Words to Live By People have always struggled toward great ideals and imagined better ways of living. From national anthems to poems to simple proverbs, these ideals are often expressed in words and images. The Declaration of Independence proclaimed the importance of "life, liberty, and the pursuit of happiness." A famous African-American spiritual sang out hope for a time when slaves would "cross the mighty river" and know freedom. In the poems you are about to read, Langston Hughes and Norma Landa Flores use images and words to convey their thoughts about freedom.

Focus Your Reading

LITERARY ANALYSIS   TONE

A poet's attitude toward his or her subject is called **tone.** Words that can be used to describe different tones include *angry, sad,* and *humorous.* You can figure out the tone of a poem by paying attention to the images in it and to the poet's **word choice.** As you read, look for words and phrases that help you understand tone.

ACTIVE READING   MAKING INFERENCES ABOUT THE SPEAKER

An **inference** is a logical guess based on evidence. The **speaker** of the poem is the voice that "talks" to the reader. A poem's speaker is not necessarily the poet. When you make inferences about the speaker, you are making logical guesses about the speaker's beliefs, attitudes, and feelings.

READER'S NOTEBOOK As you read each poem, jot down any inferences you can make about the speaker. Also note evidence to support your inferences.

Standards-Based Objectives
- understand and appreciate a **poem**
- understand author's use of **speaker**
- **make inferences** to help understand poetry
- define how **tone or meaning** is conveyed through **word choice** and **line length.**

Summary
In "Street Corner Flight," Norma Landa Flores describes a city scene: two small boys release pigeons to fly away free. From her descriptive language, we get the image of the birds' view from the air, and we feel the sense of flying free, away from the problems and woes that must be facing the young boys. In "Words Like Freedom," the poet Langston Hughes provides powerful images. He evokes the deep significance the words *Freedom* and *Liberty* hold for the speaker. By looking at both poems, the reader gets a sense of how freedom may mean different things to different people—and for different reasons.

Thematic Link
The ways to break barriers are as many and as varied as the barriers themselves. Overcoming the barriers to liberty and freedom is a major theme in literature, as it is in life.

English Conventions Practice

Daily Language SkillBuilder

Have students **proofread** the display sentences on page 315k and write them correctly. The sentences also appear on Transparency 12 of **Language Transparencies.**

STREET CORNER FLIGHT / WORDS LIKE FREEDOM   **391**

LESSON RESOURCES

UNIT THREE RESOURCE BOOK, pp. 48–49

ASSESSMENT
Formal Assessment, pp. 61–62
Test Generator

SKILLS TRANSPARENCIES AND COPYMASTERS
Literary Analysis
- Poetry: Speaker, TR 21 (pp. 394, 395)

Language
- Daily Language SkillBuilder, TR 12 (p. 391)

Writing
- Writing Variables, TR 2 (p. 396)
- Figurative Language and Sound Devices, TR 17 (p. 396)
- Poem, TR 35 (p. 396)
- Crediting Sources, TR 55 (p. 396)

INTEGRATED TECHNOLOGY
Audio Library

Visit our Web site:
www.mcdougallittell.com

For **systematic instruction** in language skills, see:
- **Vocabulary and Spelling Book**
- **Grammar, Usage, and Mechanics Book**
- pacing chart on p. 315i.

Explain to students that the poet's choice of words helps develop the tone of the poem. You might have students write a list of words and phrases that sound powerful or that they respond to. Students can use this list to determine the tone.

 Use **Unit Three Resource Book**, p. 49, for more practice.

Active Reading

MAKING INFERENCES ABOUT THE SPEAKER

Ask students to draw inferences about who the speaker is and to support the inferences with evidence from the poem.

Possible Responses: The speaker may be the poet herself remembering how it was when she grew up in a similar place. She may have seen boys releasing pigeons and written this poem to portray the feeling she had of wanting to fly to freedom like the pigeons.

 Use **Unit Three Resource Book**, p. 48, for more practice.

Thinking through the Literature

1. **Comprehension Check** The boys set the pigeons free and they fly away.
2. **Think Critically** They are probably excited, sad, envious, and wishful.

Street CORNER Flight

by Norma Landa Flores

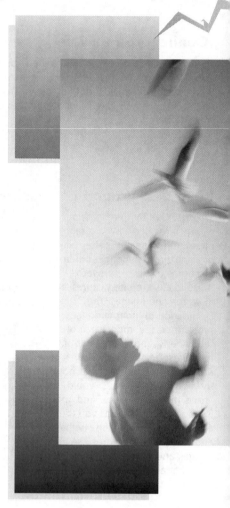

From this side . . .
   of their concrete barrio
    two small boys hold
     fat white pigeons
5   trapped in their trembling hands.

Then,
  gently,
   not disturbing
    their powers of flight,
10   release them
into the air.

They were free
  to glide above
   rushing traffic
15   soar beyond
     labyrinths of
food stamps . . . loneliness . . . and want.

They were free
  to fly
20   toward the other side . . .
a world away.

THINKING *through the* LITERATURE

1. **Comprehension Check** What happens to the pigeons in "Street Corner Flight"?
2. **Think Critically** What do you think the boys in the poem are feeling?

EXPLICIT INSTRUCTION **Tone and Word Choice**

Instruction Read aloud "Street Corner Flight" to students, and discuss what it is about. Invite students to point out anything they find confusing, and help them with their understanding. Then tell students that the tone of a poem is the poet's attitude toward his or her subject. For example, a tone can be admiring or angry, amused or sad. Explain that students can determine the tone by figuring out the subject of a poem and analyzing the words and phrases the poet uses to write about the subject. Ask students to identify the subject of the poem above (*two boys in their neighborhood*).

Practice Have students work in pairs. Ask students to describe the tone of the poem. Then ask students to name words and phrases that show this tone.

Possible Responses: sad, frustrated, defeated ("concrete barrio," "trapped," "food stamps . . . loneliness . . . and want"); gentle, caring, sympathetic, hopeful ("gently," "not disturbing," "They were free," "soar beyond," "a world away")

 Use **Unit Three Resource Book**, p. 49, for more practice.

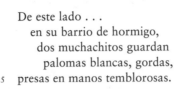

Alas en la esquina

translated by F. E. Albi

De este lado . . .
  en su barrio de hormigo,
    dos muchachitos guardan
     palomas blancas, gordas,
5 presas en manos temblorosas.

En ese entonces,
  suavemente,
    sin contener
     sus ganas de volar,
10   las sueltan
en el aire.

Y fueron libres
  de planear por encima
    del loco trafico,
15   y subir mas alla de
      laberintos
de estampillas de comida . . . soledad . . .
    y miseria.

Libres
  de volar
20   hacia el otro lado . . .
un mundo aparte.

Literary Analysis TONE

Remind students that the tone of a poem shows the poet's feelings about the subject. Ask students to think about how the poet feels about freedom.

Possible Responses: Students may say that the poet feels freedom is beautiful.

Active Reading

MAKING INFERENCES ABOUT THE SPEAKER

Ask students to draw inferences about what the speaker is trying to tell the reader. What evidence in the text supports those inferences?

Possible Responses: The speaker is telling the reader that simple words like *freedom* and *liberty* mean different things to different people. To the speaker, they are precious and powerful words that cause strong responses and emotions.

 Use **Literary Analysis Transparencies,** p. 21, for additional support.

Literary Analysis: REPETITION

The repetition of a word or phrase in a poem is often used to make a point. Ask students to identify the repetition in this poem and to interpret its meaning.

Possible Response: The repetition is of the phrase "There are words like." The poet may be using those words to remind the reader that there are many words we hear regularly and don't think about, but these words have very special meaning to some people.

Words Like FREEDOM

by Langston Hughes

There are words like *Freedom*
Sweet and wonderful to say.
On my heartstrings freedom sings
All day everyday.

There are words like *Liberty*
That almost make me cry.
If you had known what I know
You would know why.

Freedom Now, (1965), Reginald Gammon. Acrylic on board, 101.6 cm x 76.2 cm.

EXPLICIT INSTRUCTION Tone and Word Choice

Instruction Read aloud "Words Like Freedom" to students and discuss what it is about. Invite students to point out anything they find confusing, and help them with their understanding. Then remind students that the tone of a poem is the poet's attitude toward his or her subject. Continue by reminding students that they can determine the tone by figuring out the subject of a poem and analyzing the words and phrases the poet uses to describe the subject.

Practice Ask students to describe the tone of "Words Like Freedom." Then ask students to read aloud the language in the poem that conveys the tone they identified.

Possible Responses: happy ("Sweet and wonderful." "On my heartstrings freedom sings."); sad, wistful, nostalgic ("make me cry." "If you had known . . . You would know why")

 Use **Unit Three Resource Book,** p. 49, for more practice.

Connect to the Literature

1. **What Do You Think?**
After reading "Words Like Freedom," what image stays in your mind?

   Comprehension Check
   • What effects do words like *freedom* and *liberty* have on the poem's speaker?

Think Critically

2. How would you describe the mood, or feeling, of "Words Like Freedom"?

3. What experiences might have made the poem's speaker appreciate freedom and liberty?

   Think About:
   • times when you appreciate freedom and liberty
   • events in history linked to these words
   • emotions the speaker implies

4. **ACTIVE READING** **MAKING INFERENCES ABOUT THE SPEAKER**
   Who do you imagine is the speaker in each poem? To support your answers, refer to the notes in your
   📖 **READER'S NOTEBOOK.** What lines from the poems support your ideas?

Extend Interpretations

5. **COMPARING TEXTS** Choose either "Street Corner Flight" or "Words Like Freedom" and compare it with "I'm Nobody! Who Are You?," "It Seems I Test People," or "Growing Pains" (page 194). Compare the poetic form, use of figurative language, and theme, or message, of the two poems.

6. **What If?** Imagine that the speaker in "Words Like Freedom" could talk to the boys in "Street Corner Flight." What advice might he give them?

7. **Connect to Life** What new impressions or understandings of freedom did you gain from these poems? Share your thoughts with your classmates.

Literary Analysis

TONE A poet's attitude toward his or her subject is called **tone.** The words and images a poet chooses help to create the tone, which might be joyful, sad, or angry, among other possibilities. You can identify the tone of a poem by paying attention to the poet's **word choice** and images.

Paired Activity Working with a partner, go back through the poems. Look for words and phrases that help you understand the tone of each poem. Create a chart like the one below to identify the tone, and quote words and lines that show this tone.

"*Street Corner Flight*"

TONE	EVIDENCE
sympathetic sad	"foodstamps... loneliness... and want."

REVIEW: REPETITION The use of a sound, word, or phrase more than once is called **repetition.** Poets use repetition to draw special attention to certain ideas, sounds, or feelings.

Connect to the Literature

1. **What Do You Think?**
   Answers will vary.

Comprehension Check
• They make the speaker both happy and sad.

Think Critically

2. **Possible Response:** The mood is one of celebration mixed with the sadness of remembering.

3. **Possible Response:** If the speaker is African American, he may be remembering slavery and thinking about racism.

4. **Possible Response:** The speaker in "Words Like Freedom" is probably an adult African American, possibly Hughes himself. The speaker in "Street Corner Flight" is probably an adult, an observer who might or might not be the poet, possibly poor and/or Hispanic, since (s)he seems to understand the boys and their situation.

 Use **Literary Analysis Transparencies,** p. 21, for additional support.

Literary Analysis

Tone As students work with their partners, encourage them to write down only those words and phrases that seem especially strong or meaningful. Have them think about the experiences, thoughts, and feelings they had when reading the poems to help them understand the tone.

Extend Interpretations

5. **Comparing Texts** Answers will vary depending on the poems students choose to compare, but they should be able to support their comparisons with evidence from the poems.

6. **What If?** Students might say the speaker in "Words Like Freedom" would tell the boys to value freedom; to learn from others' examples how to become free; to go to school, work hard, organize to live in better conditions as they grow up, and so on. He might also offer to help them.

7. **Connect to Life** Students may realize that poverty traps people: to be free, people need opportunities and options, and some people don't have those. Some people cannot take freedom for granted, and when they gain it, they rejoice in it.

Writing

Concept Poem Encourage students to select a word that has an emotional meaning to them. Remind them that poetry can rhyme or it can be free verse.

 Use **Writing Transparencies,** pp. 2, 17, 35, for additional support.

Speaking & Listening

Sharing Your Poem As an alternative, you might suggest students exchange poems with a partner and read the partner's poem to the class.

Research & Technology

Famous Freedom Words If your school's computer has an encyclopedia program, you may want to provide students the opportunity to look for freedom quotations there.

 Use **Writing Transparencies,** p. 55, for additional support.

Author Activity

Read On Provide students with time to gather and read more works by Hughes. Students can work in small groups to discuss the major themes and topics in Hughes's work.

Writing

Concept Poem *Liberty* and *freedom* are meaningful words to the speaker in "Words Like Freedom." What word holds meaning for you? Here are some examples of meaningful words: *friendship, honor, truth, hope.* Write a poem about your word. Place your poem in your **Working Portfolio.**

Writing Handbook

> This activity asks you to use the poem form. To find out about other writing forms you might use when your purpose is to describe, see p. R31: Choosing a Form.

Speaking & Listening

Sharing Your Poem Read aloud the poem you wrote for the writing activity on this page. Practice reading it several times to make sure your voice will be heard by all your classmates. Also practice reading at the right rate—not too fast! When you are ready, read your poem to your class.

Speaking and Listening Handbook
See p. R98: Oral Interpretation.

Research & Technology

Famous Freedom Words In a book of quotations, look up *freedom.* Choose quotations that seem particularly meaningful and create a poster of famous sayings about freedom. Be sure to credit the person who said, wrote, or sang each line.

Langston Hughes
1902–1967

"My soul has grown deep like the rivers."

A Legend in His Time Born in Joplin, Missouri, Hughes had a lonely childhood during which his family moved often. After graduating from Lincoln University, he lived outside New York City and held odd jobs while writing poetry. Eventually, his works included poetry, songs, plays, short stories, novels, nonfiction, and a newspaper column. Hughes became a key figure in the Harlem Renaissance, the great literary movement that blossomed in New York City's Harlem during the 1920s.

AUTHOR ACTIVITY
Read On Read several more poems by Langston Hughes. With classmates, identify and discuss some of the themes, or important messages, that you see in his work.

Norma Landa Flores

"Out of midnight's cold winter air illusions become realities."

Winning Words At the time Norma Landa Flores wrote "Street Corner Flight," she was a student in California's lower San Joaquín Valley. She submitted entries to a writing contest sponsored by the Chicano Studies Department of Bakersfield College in Bakersfield, California. "Street Corner Flight" was one of several winning poems by Flores (another, "Through a Blue Room's Door," is quoted above). These poems were later published in *Sighs and Songs of Aztlán,* an anthology of new Chicano literature.

Building Vocabulary
Analyzing Word Parts: Prefixes and Suffixes

When you read a word you don't recognize, look for a **base word** you do know. Then look for a familiar **prefix**, a word part attached before the base word, or a familiar **suffix**, a word part attached to the end of the word.

> Bands of outlaws roamed the countryside . . . kidnapping those unfortunate enough to have wandered from the protection of their people.
> —Walter Dean Myers,
> "Abd al-Rahman Ibrahima"

You can divide the word into three parts to help determine its meaning.

```
                  unfortunate
prefix un- means "not"    |    suffix -ate means "having or filled with"
              base word fortune means "luck"
```

Put the three parts together to determine the meaning of *unfortunate*: "not having luck."

Strategies for Building Vocabulary

Knowing the meanings of common prefixes and suffixes can help you understand new words. Here are some strategies for using prefixes and suffixes.

❶ Take the Word Apart To find the meaning of an unfamiliar word, divide it into parts. Think about the meaning of the prefix, the base word, and/or the suffix. Guess at a definition. Then check to see if it makes sense in context. Look at the following example:

> The Fula were taller and lighter in complexion than the other inhabitants of Africa's west coast; . . .
> —Walter Dean Myers,
> "Abd al-Rahman Ibrahima"

You can divide the word *inhabitants* into three parts as shown:

Prefix	Base Word	Suffix
in-	*habit*	*-ants*
"in, into"	"dwell"	"those who"

❷ Learn Common Prefixes and Suffixes You may already be familiar with many prefixes and suffixes. The following charts contain some of the most common ones.

Prefix	Meanings	Example
ex-	out, from	export
in-	in, into, not	incite
pre-	before	preface
pro-	forward, favoring	propose
re-	again, back	rebound
trans-	across, beyond	transmit
un-	not, opposite of	unhappy

Suffix	Meanings	Example
-al	of, like	trivial
-ant, -ent	one who	dominant
-ist	one performing or believing in	bicyclist
-ion, -tion	act or state of	suspension
-ous, -ious	marked by	pompous
-less	without	hopeless
-ment	act or state of	contentment

EXERCISE Divide each word to show its base word, prefix, and suffix. Then write a possible definition of the word. Use a dictionary to review the actual definition.

1. renewal
2. expression
3. proactive
4. insubstantial
5. abandonment

Standards-Based Objectives
- understand the meanings of prefixes and suffixes
- apply meanings of prefixes and suffixes to understand unfamiliar words

VOCABULARY EXERCISE
Possible Answers:
1. re/new/al—the act of making new again
2. ex/press/ion—the act of setting forth in words
3. pro/active—acting in advance (to deal with an expected difficulty)
4. in/substant/ial—of, or related to, having no substance or material
5. ab/andon/ment—the state of withdrawing support from

 Use **Unit Three Resource Book**, p. 50, for additional practice.

Author Study GARY SOTO

Standards-Based Objectives
- **appreciate** the works of a contemporary author and poet
- interpret the possible **influences of personal events** in Soto's life on his writing
- look at the **descriptive writing** techniques used by Soto

The Author Study offers a special opportunity for students to focus on the work of a popular contemporary author. Students will be exposed to information about Soto's life, which will give them insight into the person behind the stories. They will explore some aspects of the author's craft and apply these to their own writing.

CONTENTS

From Field to Fame

"Because I believe in literature and the depth of living it adds to our years, my task is to start Chicanos reading."

born 1952

CARDBOARD IN HIS SHOES

Gary Soto was born in Fresno, California, in a neighborhood surrounded by the factories where many of his relatives worked. His grandparents had left Mexico in 1914, but almost 40 years later the family was still struggling. Soto remembers walking around with cardboard in his shoes and wearing "socks with holes big enough to be ski masks." When Soto was five, his family moved to a new neighborhood. Soon afterward, his father was

Gary, his brother Rick (left), and sister Debra in 1957

His LIFE and TIMES

| 1952 Born April 12 in Fresno, California | 1957 Father dies. | 1970–1974 Attends college; begins to write poetry |

Gary, age six

| **1950** | **1960** | **1970** |

| 1957 Soviets launch Sputnik satellite. | 1963 President Kennedy is assassinated. | 1965–1973 U.S. ground troops in Vietnam War |

killed in an accident while helping to re-roof a friend's house. After the funeral, Soto recalls going into an empty room in the still-new house and making as much noise as possible so that "I could not hear the things in my heart."

HARD LABOR

As a child, Soto first wanted to be a priest, then a hobo, and even a paleontologist, a scientist who studies dinosaurs. But one of his first real jobs was picking grapes. When he was younger he had played in the vineyards while his mother worked, but he had no idea how difficult the work truly was. He soon found out when, as an adolescent, he began to pick grapes himself. Soto picked grapes off and on until he was 15. Later on, he and his brother hoed and chopped cotton, earning $1.25 an hour for work that was backbreaking. Soto also worked in car washes and at a tire factory.

AN ARTIST AWAKENS

While growing up, Soto had no great love of school, and his teachers considered him difficult. "I was no good at school," he recalls. "I could not sing, do art, or figure out math problems. I was deathly scared of the stage, yet jealous when my

Did You Know?

- Soto has met more than 300,000 teachers and students.
- When he visits schools, he often joins students in playing baseball and basketball, singing, and performing plays.
- He produced an award-winning film, *The Pool Party*.
- He wrote the words for an opera called *Nerd-Landia*.

Gary at age 20, around the time he started writing poetry

Family Struggles

A Most of Soto's family worked in the Sun-Maid Raisin factory on Braly Street where the author lived when he was a boy. Soto's grandfather, grandmother, father, three uncles, an aunt, and a dog—who accompanied his grandfather, a security guard, on rounds—worked at this factory.

Making a Living

B Soto began looking for work when he was still a boy. His search began one year when he tried to get the neighbors to pay him for raking leaves—in the summer when there were no leaves on the ground! He found some odd jobs, such as going to the store and weeding, to earn a little spending money. When he was older, he picked grapes with his mother each summer. It was hard, backbreaking work, and the pay was low, but it allowed Soto to buy new clothes for the next school year. One summer, he and his brother Rick got jobs chopping cotton—dusty, hot, and difficult work.

Poetry

C Soto's family was largely uneducated, and there were few books in his house when he was growing up. No one encouraged him to read. He began writing poetry in college after discovering a book of poems that made him think, "This is terrific: I'd like to do something like this." Soto was influenced and guided by the poet Philip Levine, his writing instructor at California State University, Fresno. His first poems were for adults, but in 1990, he began writing books of poetry for young people.

1975
Marries Carolyn Sadako Oda

1977
Publishes first book, *The Elements of San Joaquín*

1990
Publishes *Baseball in April*, his first book for young readers

1995
Is a finalist for the National Book Award

1980

1990

2000

1979
Egypt and Israel sign peace agreement.

1989–1990
Cold War between U.S. and USSR ends.

1993
South Africa adopts majority rule constitution.

1997
U.S. spacecraft transmits pictures from Mars.

GARY SOTO **399**

School Visits

D Soto says that one of his goals is to get Chicano kids reading. He wants to encourage them to read, partly because there was no one there to encourage him when he was a child. He enjoys spending time with young people and frequently visits with them at schools. Many of his stories reflect real issues that a lot of kids face, and this encourages students to connect with him.

friends got up on the stage and sang with gusto." His thoughts about school changed, however, when he received his draft notice for the Vietnam War in 1970. As a college student, Soto would be able to put off entering the army, so he enrolled at Fresno City College. During his second year, he discovered poetry. On his own, he read a poem called "Unwanted" that expressed many of his own feelings of being alone and isolated. This inspired him to write poetry of his own. Three years later, he won a national prize for his poetry.

A WRITER ON THE ROAD

Today, Soto is an important American poet and writer. He is also dedicated to working with young people. He travels around California and **D** the Southwest to promote Chicano literacy and literature. Although Soto has won much praise for his writing for adult audiences, he has become even better known by young readers. "I think I'm very childlike," he says, "and I often write youthful poems. It's sort of a silly act, writing itself . . . I like the youth in my poetry, sort of a craziness. For me that's really important. I don't want to take a dreary look at the world." Soto lives in Berkeley, California, with his wife and daughter.

Gary Soto visits with students at the Washington School in Cloverdale, California.

400

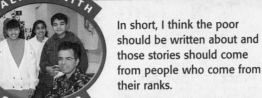

TALKING WITH GARY SOTO

Gary Soto loves traveling around to schools and meeting students.

Q: Do you ever write in Spanish or just English?

A: Like most writers who have two languages, I choose to write in only one. English is my writing language. I leave the Spanish translations to Spanish experts.

E **Q:** Which do you find easier to write—fiction or poetry?

A: I find it easier to write fiction, although poetry is what I truly love to write. My style of poetry is narrative (each poem has a story), so I guess I like to tell stories. With poetry, as opposed to fiction, I enjoy the challenge of telling that story with minimum words that still sound musical to my ear.

F **Q:** One of the kids in my class didn't realize that you are Mexican, too, and he got really angry about one of your stories. He thought the story made it seem like all Mexicans were poor, or not educated. Have other people reacted to any of your stories like that? What do you say when they do?

A: Some of my characters are in fact poor, but there is nothing wrong about seeing poor people march across the page, especially if these people happen to be Chicano/Mexican American. People go to extremes to stay away from the poor, while in my own personal life I go to extremes to be with them. I'm thinking of my church, where most of our members are day laborers, domestic helpers, baby sitters, roofers, gardeners.

In short, I think the poor should be written about and those stories should come from people who come from their ranks.

Q: Have you ever experienced stage fright like the character Robert in "The School Play"?

A: Yes, I did, age 10 and in fifth grade. Cast as a Gold Rush 49er, I was supposed to say, "I have the glasses." But I was so busy admiring my costume beard that I forgot what to say. The beard, I remember, was red.

G **Q:** The characters in your stories seem so true to life. Are they based on people in your family and people you know?

A: Yes, in books such as *Living Up the Street* and *A Summer Life* I have drawn on my childhood and, thus, the unavoidable presence of family, which, at times, was wild as pirates. While we may lament that our childhoods are boring, they in fact become the stuff of poems and storytelling. This is particularly true if you grew up poor, where there were not a lot of material gifts. Instead, the work of invention was at hand. What does my family think of this? Well, they don't really read my work, so they're not fully aware of how they've been brought to the page.

INTERNET Author Link
www.mcdougallittell.com

CD ROM NetActivities: Author Exploration

Variety
E Soto is currently writing novels, plays, essays, and poetry for adults and young readers. His passion at the moment is writing plays. He feels it is natural for contemporary writers to try their hand at many kinds of writing, and says he is still "mulling over my intentions."

Chicano Influence
F Soto's themes are universal and speak to all adolescents, but his stories are clearly set in Mexican-American communities. He calls himself a Chicano and says he feels a certain obligation to that ethnic group. He includes many Spanish words in his writings because these are a part of the memories he draws from when he writes.

Grandmother
G A major influence in Soto's life was his grandmother, and even though she may not read his work, she is proud of him. She worked for over twenty years at the Sun-Maid Raisin factory to make a meager living for her family. She would stand at a conveyor belt, plucking out leaves and pebbles from raisins on their way to being boxed. She is the subject of some of Soto's poems, and his admiration for her shows through in his work.

The School Play

by GARY SOTO

Standards-Based Objectives

- understand and appreciate a **short story**
- understand author's use of **tone**
- use **monitoring reading strategies** as an aid to understanding
- identify **character traits**

Summary

In this short story, author Gary Soto tells about a boy who is assigned a small speaking part in a school play. Although Robert knows his two lines well, he must deliver them to Belinda, the classroom bully, known for beating up boys and even taking on a pit bull terrier! Despite Belinda's menacing presence, Robert is determined to deliver his lines flawlessly and please his teacher, his family, and himself.

Thematic Link

Bullies like Belinda create barriers by making others feel inferior. Robert must overcome his fear of Belinda, as well as his own fear of failure, and prove to himself that he can perform without making mistakes.

English Conventions Practice

Daily Language SkillBuilder

Have students **proofread** the display sentences on page 315k and write them correctly. The sentences also appear on Transparency 13 of **Language Transparencies.**

Connect to Your Life

You're On! Think back to your own experiences of performing or speaking to a group. What do you remember most?

Build Background

HISTORY

In "The School Play," a class is preparing to perform *The Last Stand,* a play based on a tragic incident. In 1846 a group of about 90 pioneers from Illinois and nearby states set out for California. The group was led by George and Jacob Donner.

When trying to cross the Sierra Nevada mountain range in eastern California, the Donner party became snowbound, and the travelers ran out of food. Many began dying of starvation.

In their desperation, some of the remaining members of the party resorted to eating the bodies of the dead to survive. Only 47 made it through that grim winter. Donner Pass is now a national landmark.

WORDS TO KNOW
Vocabulary Preview

depleted	quiver	smirk
prop	relentless	

Focus Your Reading

LITERARY ANALYSIS TONE

The attitude that a writer has toward his or her subject is called **tone.** The tone can be humorous, sad, serious, frightening, or a combination of attitudes.

ACTIVE READING MONITORING READING STRATEGIES

You may be halfway through a story when you realize that you've forgotten who a certain character is, or that you don't understand what happened in a particular scene. To avoid these problems, it is helpful to **monitor** how you are reading. Pause every so often as you read. If you lose track of the characters, go back to an earlier scene to reread for details.

📖 READER'S NOTEBOOK   As you read, refer to the strategies in this chart. Make note of places where one or more of the strategies helped your understanding.

Reading Strategies	
Questioning	Question what happens as you read.
Connecting	Connect personally with the story.
Predicting	Predict what might happen next.
Clarifying	Stop occasionally for a quick review.
Visualizing	Form mental images of the story.
Evaluating	Form opinions about the story.

LESSON RESOURCES

UNIT THREE RESOURCE BOOK, pp. 51–57

ASSESSMENT
Formal Assessment, pp. 63–64
Test Generator

SKILLS TRANSPARENCIES AND COPYMASTERS
Literary Analysis
- Tone, TR 25 (pp. 404, 409)

Reading and Critical Thinking
- Strategies for Reading, TR 1 (pp. 404, 408, 409)
Language
- Daily Language SkillBuilder, TR 13 (p. 402)
- Comparison of Regular and Irregular Adjectives and Adverbs, TR 42 (p. 410)
- Context Clues: Definition and Overview, TR 53 (p. 403)

INTEGRATED TECHNOLOGY
Audio Library

Visit our Web site:
www.mcdougallittell.com

For **systematic instruction** in language skills, see:
- **Vocabulary and Spelling Book**
- **Grammar, Usage, and Mechanics Book**
- pacing chart on p. 315i.

THE SCHOOL PLAY

BY GARY SOTO

In the school play at the end of his sixth-grade year, all Robert Suarez had to remember to say was, "Nothing's wrong. I can see," to a pioneer woman, who was really Belinda Lopez. Instead of a pioneer woman, Belinda was one of the toughest girls since the beginning of the world. She was known to slap boys and grind their faces into the grass so that they bit into chunks of wormy earth. More than once Robert had witnessed Belinda staring down the janitor's pit bull, who licked his frothing chops but didn't dare mess with her.

The class rehearsed for three weeks, at first without costumes. Early one morning Mrs. Bunnin wobbled into the classroom lugging a large cardboard box. She wiped her brow and said, "Thanks for the help, Robert."

Robert was at his desk scribbling a ballpoint tattoo that spelled DUDE on the tops of his knuckles. He looked up and stared, blinking at his teacher. "Oh, did you need some help?" he asked.

"NOTHING'S

WRONG.

I CAN SEE."

She rolled her eyes at him and told him to stop writing on his skin. "You'll look like a criminal," she scolded.

Robert stuffed his hands into his pockets as he rose from his seat. "What's in the box?" he asked.

She muttered under her breath. She popped open the taped top and brought out skirts, hats, snowshoes, scarves, and vests. She tossed Robert a red beard, which he held up to his face, thinking it made him look handsome.

"I like it," Robert said. He sneezed and ran his hand across his moist nose.

His classmates were coming into the classroom and looked at Robert in awe. "That's bad," Ruben said. "What do I get?"

Mrs. Bunnin threw him a wrinkled shirt. Ruben raised it to his chest and said, "My dad could wear this. Can I give it to him after the play is done?"

Mrs. Bunnin turned away in silence.

Most of the actors didn't have speaking

THE SCHOOL PLAY **403**

Differentiating Instruction

Less Proficient Readers
Have students keep these questions in mind as they read:
- Who are the main characters in the story?
- What is the setting of the story?
- What is the major problem, or conflict?

English Learners
Point out the phrase, in the first paragraph, "licked his frothing chops." Explain that *to lick one's chops* means "to anticipate excitedly." *Chops* is slang for "mouth." Therefore, to lick one's chops originally meant to lick one's lips in anticipation of food. Explain that this is just one example of the idioms and slang words used throughout this story.

Use **Spanish Study Guide**, pp. 82–84, for additional support.

Advanced Students
As students read, have them keep track of the many exaggerations used by the author. Have them work in pairs to come up with additional exaggerations that could be used to create the same impression.

EXPLICIT INSTRUCTION Preteaching Vocabulary

WORDS TO KNOW
Call students' attention to the list of WORDS TO KNOW. Remind them that sometimes they can define an unfamiliar word by looking for words around it that **restate** or **define** the word. Use the model to demonstrate the strategy of using restatement clues.
Model: When you act in a play, someone is responsible for the *props*. That person collects and keeps track of all the objects that appear on stage.

Teaching Strategy
- Write the model sentence on the board.
- Ask a volunteer to read the sentence aloud.
- Ask students to define the word *props*.
- Ask students to identify the restatement clue that helped them figure out the meaning of the word *props*.

Practice Have students, working in pairs, look up the rest of the WORDS TO KNOW and write sentences with restatement clues.

Use **Unit Three Resource Book**, p. 56, for more practice.

For **systematic instruction** in vocabulary, see:
- **Vocabulary and Spelling Book**
- pacing chart on p. 315i.

Literary Analysis **TONE**

Ask students to consider the author's tone and think about how it contributes to the effect of the text. Have students identify words, phrases, and sentences that reflect the tone of the story.

Possible Response: The tone is humorous and a little scary. When Belinda says, "Sucka, is there something wrong with your eye-balls?" it's funny. But because she's so tough, Belinda might have beaten up Robert if he made a mistake, so that was a little scary.

📖 Use **Unit Three Resource Book**, p. 53, for more practice. Use **Literary Analysis Transparencies**, p. 25, for additional support.

Active Reading
MONITORING READING STRATEGIES

Remind students that when you monitor something, you keep track of it. As you read, sometimes you need to go back and reread certain parts in order to keep track of what's going on. Model monitoring by saying that now that Belinda's been fooling around with her line, you forget what she's really supposed to say to Robert. Have students go back and find her actual line.

📖 Use **Unit Three Resource Book**, p. 52, for more practice. Use **Reading and Critical Thinking Transparencies** p.1, for additional support.

Literary Analysis: **CHARACTER TRAITS**

Who are the main characters and what do you know about their traits?

Possible Response: The main characters are Robert, Belinda, and Mrs. Bunnin. Robert must be a good speller, because he got a speaking part in the play. He's nervous about his part and intimidated by Belinda, who is a bully. Mrs. Bunnin is a tough, wise teacher.

The Old and the New Year (1953), Pablo Picasso. Musée d'Art et d'Histoire, St. Denis, France. Giraudon/Art Resource, New York. Copyright © 2001 Estate of Pablo Picasso/Artists Rights Society (ARS), New York.

EXPLICIT INSTRUCTION Viewing and Representing

The Old and the New Year
by Pablo Picasso

ART APPRECIATION Spanish artist Pablo Picasso (1881–1973) is one of the 20th century's most important artists. Picasso created a wealth of paintings, sculptures, etchings, and ceramics.
Instruction Discuss the subject matter of this work of art. Ask students to interpret what they see. (*I think you could look at this work of art in two ways. First, you could say that a young boy is removing a mask of an old man. Maybe the boy is imagining what it might be like to be old. Or you could interpret it to mean that the old man is looking for the young boy inside of himself. Maybe the painting is a statement about the child inside all of us.*)
Practice Ask students to relate this work of art to "The School Play."
Possible Response: Like the boy in the painting, Robert wears a mask when he is in the play. Acting is like wearing a mask and pretending to be someone else.

parts. They just got cutout crepe-paper snowflakes to pin to their shirts or crepe-paper leaves to wear.

During the blizzard in which Robert delivered his line, Belinda asked, "Is there something wrong with your eyes?" Robert looked at the audience, which at the moment was a classroom of empty chairs, a dented world globe that had been dropped by almost everyone, one limp flag, one wastebasket, and a picture of George Washington, whose eyes followed you around the room when you got up to sharpen your pencil. Robert answered, "Nothing's wrong. I can see."

Mrs. Bunnin, biting on the end of her pencil, said, "Louder, both of you."

Belinda stepped up, nostrils flaring so that the shadows on her nose quivered, and said louder, "Sucka, is there something wrong with your eye-balls?"

"Nothing's wrong. I can see."

"Louder! Make sure the audience can hear you," Mrs. Bunnin directed. She tapped her pencil hard against the desk. She scolded, "Robert, I'm not going to tell you again to quit fooling with the beard."

"It's itchy."

"We can't do anything about that. Actors need props. You're an actor. Now try again."

Robert and Belinda stood center stage as they waited for Mrs. Bunnin to call "Action!" When she did, Belinda approached Robert slowly. "Sucka face, is there anything wrong with your mug?" Belinda asked. Her eyes were squinted in anger. For a moment Robert saw his head grinding into the playground grass.

"NOTHING'S

WRONG.

I CAN SEE."

"Nothing's wrong. I can see."

Robert giggled behind his red beard. Belinda popped her gum and smirked. She stood with her hands on her hips.

"What? What did you say?" Mrs. Bunnin asked, pulling off her glasses. "Are you chewing gum, Belinda?"

"No, Mrs. Bunnin," Belinda lied. "I just forgot my lines."

Belinda turned to face the snowflake boys clumped together in the back. She rolled out her tongue, on which rested a ball of gray gum, depleted of sweetness under her relentless chomp. She whispered "sucka" and giggled so that her nose quivered dark shadows.

The play, *The Last Stand*, was about the Donner party just before they got hungry and started eating each other. Everyone who scored at least twelve out of fifteen on their spelling tests got to say at least one line. Everyone else had to stand and be trees or snowflakes.

Mrs. Bunnin wanted the play to be a success. She couldn't risk having kids with bad memories on stage. The nonspeaking trees and snowflakes stood humming snow flurries, blistering wind, and hail, which they produced by clacking their teeth.

Robert's mother was proud of him because he was living up to the legend of Robert De Niro,[1] for whom he was named. Over dinner he said, "Nothing's wrong. I can see," when his brother asked him to pass the dishtowel,

---

1. **Robert De Niro** (də nîr'ō): a well-known American movie actor.

WORDS TO KNOW	**quiver** (kwĭv'ər) v. to shake with a rapid trembling movement
	prop (prŏp) n. an object an actor uses in a play
	smirk (smûrk) v. to smile in an insulting, self-satisfied manner
	depleted (dĭ-plē'tĭd) adj. emptied; drained **deplete** v.
	relentless (rĭ-lĕnt'lĭs) adj. refusing to stop or give up

405

Reading Skills and Strategies:
MAKE INFERENCES

(A) Ask students to make an inference about Robert's feelings based on what he tells David he wants to be when he grows up.

Possible Response: Robert is probably afraid that David would laugh if he told him the truth—that he wants to be someone with a great memory who answers questions for people. Instead, Robert says something that makes him sound tough.

Literary Analysis: SLANG

(B) Have students note Robert's use of the word *buck* to refer to the dollar bill he finds. Ask them to identify some other slang words used to refer to money.

Possible Responses: loot, dead presidents, dinero, greenbacks

Reading Skills and Strategies:
PREDICT

(C) Ask students to make a prediction about what Robert will do when it's his turn to speak.

Possible Response: Robert will probably make a mistake because he's so nervous.

Reading Skills and Strategies:
CONNECT

(C) Can you understand how Robert is feeling? Have you ever been in a play or performed on stage? How did you feel right before the performance?

Possible Responses: Many students will, like Robert, say that they felt nervous and excited and worried that they might make a mistake. Others will say that they felt confident and excited.

their communal napkin. His sister said, "It's your turn to do dishes," and he said, "Nothing's wrong. I can see." His dog, Queenie, begged him for more than water and a dog biscuit. He touched his dog's own hairy beard and said, "Nothing's wrong. I can see."

One warm spring night, Robert lay on his back in the backyard, counting shooting stars. He was up to three when David, a friend who was really his brother's friend, hopped the fence and asked, "What's the matter with you?"

"Nothing's wrong. I can see," Robert answered. He sat up, feeling good because the line came naturally, without much thought. He leaned back on his elbow and asked David what he wanted to be when he grew up.

"I don't know yet," David said, plucking at the grass. "Maybe a fighter pilot. What do you want to be?"

"I want to guard the president. I could wrestle the assassins and be on television. But I'd pin those dudes, and people would say, 'That's him, our hero.'" David plucked at a stalk of grass and thought deeply.

Robert thought of telling David that he really wanted to be someone with a supergreat memory, who could recall facts that most people thought were unimportant. He didn't know if there was such a job, but he thought it would be great to sit at home by the telephone waiting for scientists to call him and ask hard questions.

The three weeks passed quickly. The day before the play, Robert felt happy as he walked home from school with no homework. As he turned onto his street, he found a dollar floating over the currents of wind.

"A buck," he screamed to himself. He snapped it up and looked for others. But he didn't find any more. It was his lucky day,

though. At recess he had hit a home run on a fluke bunt—a fluke because the catcher had kicked the ball, another player had thrown it into center field, and the pitcher wasn't looking when Robert slowed down at third, then burst home with dust flying behind him.

That night, it was his sister's turn to do the dishes. They had eaten enchiladas with the works, so she slaved with suds up to her elbows. Robert bathed in bubble bath, the suds peaked high like the Donner Pass. He thought about how full he was and how those poor people had had nothing to eat but snow. I can live on nothing, he thought and whistled like wind through a mountain pass, raking flat the suds with his palm.

The next day, after lunch, he was ready for the play, red beard in hand and his one line trembling on his lips. Classes herded into the auditorium. As the actors dressed and argued about stepping on each other's feet, Robert stood near a cardboard barrel full of toys, whispering over and over to himself, "Nothing's wrong. I can see." He was hot, itchy, and confused when he tied on the beard. He sneezed when a strand of the beard entered his nostril. He said louder, "Nothing's wrong. I can see," but the words seemed to get caught in the beard. "Nothing, no, no. I can see great," he said louder, then under his breath because the words seemed wrong. "Nothing's wrong, can't you see? Nothing's wrong. I can see you." Worried, he approached Belinda and asked if she remembered his line. Balling her hand into a fist, Belinda warned, "Sucka, I'm gonna bury your ugly face in the ground if you mess up."

"I won't," Robert said as he walked away. He bit a nail and looked into the barrel of toys. A clown's mask stared back at him. He

"NOTHING'S

WRONG.

I CAN SEE."

prayed that his line would come back to him. He would hate to disappoint his teacher and didn't like the thought of his face being rubbed into spiky grass.

The curtain parted slightly, and the principal came out smiling onto the stage. She said some words about pioneer history and then, stern faced, warned the audience not to scrape the

chairs on the just-waxed floor. The principal then introduced Mrs. Bunnin, who told the audience about how they had rehearsed for weeks.

Meanwhile, the class stood quietly in place with lunchtime spaghetti on their breath. They were ready. Belinda had swallowed her gum because she knew this was for real. The snowflakes clumped together and began howling.

Closing Scene (1963), David Hockney. Oil on canvas, 48" × 48", © David Hockney.

THE SCHOOL PLAY **407**

Robert retied his beard. Belinda, smoothing her skirt, looked at him and said, "If you know what's good for you, you'd better do it right." Robert grew nervous when the curtain parted and his classmates who were assigned to do snow, wind, and hail broke into song.

Alfonso stepped forward with his narrative about a blot on American history that would live with us forever. He looked at the audience, lost for a minute. He continued by saying that if the Donner party could come back, hungry from not eating for over a hundred years, they would be sorry for what they had done.

The play began with some boys in snowshoes shuffling around the stage, muttering that the blizzard would cut them off from civilization. They looked up, held out their hands, and said in unison, "Snow." One stepped center stage and said, "I wish I had never left the prairie." Another one said, "California is just over there." He pointed, and some of the first graders looked in the direction of the piano.

"What are we going to do?" one kid asked, brushing pretend snow off his vest.

"I'm getting pretty hungry," another said, rubbing her stomach.

The audience seemed to be following the play. A ribbon of sweat ran down Robert's face. When his scene came up, he staggered to center stage and dropped to the floor, just as Mrs. Bunnin had said, just as he had seen Robert De Niro do in that movie about a boxer. Belinda, bending over with an "Oh, my," yanked him up so hard that something clicked in his elbow. She boomed, "Is there anything wrong with your eyes?"

Robert rubbed his elbow, then his eyes, and said, "I can see nothing wrong. Wrong is nothing, I can see."

"NOTHING'S WRONG. I CAN SEE."

"How are we going to get through?" she boomed, wringing her hands together at the audience, some of whom had their mouths taped shut because they were known talkers. "My husband needs a doctor." The drama advanced through snow, wind, and hail that sounded like chattering teeth.

Belinda turned to Robert and muttered, "You mess-up. You're gonna hate life."

But Robert thought he'd done okay. At least, he reasoned to himself, I got the words right. Just not in the right order.

With his part of the play done, he joined the snowflakes and trees, chattering his teeth the loudest. He howled wind like a baying hound and snapped his fingers furiously in a snow flurry. He trembled from the cold.

The play ended with Alfonso saying that if they came back to life, the Donner party would be sorry for eating each other. "It's just not right," he argued. "You gotta suck it up in bad times."

Robert figured that Alfonso was right. He remembered how one day his sister had locked him in the closet and he didn't eat or drink for five hours. When he got out, he hit his sister, but not so hard as to leave a bruise. He then ate three sandwiches and felt a whole lot better.

The cast then paraded up the aisle into the audience. Belinda pinched Robert hard, but only once because she was thinking that it could have been worse. As he passed a smiling and relieved Mrs. Bunnin, she patted Robert's shoulder and said, "Almost perfect."

Robert was happy. He'd made it through without passing out from fear. Now the first and second graders were looking at him and clapping. He was sure everyone wondered who the actor was behind that smooth voice and red, red beard. ❖

Connect to the Literature

1. **What Do You Think?**
   What words would you use to describe Robert's feelings at the end of the story?

   Comprehension Check
   • Before the play, why did Robert repeat his line again and again?
   • What happened during the play?

Think Critically

2. Near the end of *The Last Stand,* Alfonso, the play's narrator, says, "You gotta suck it up in bad times." How well do you think Robert lives up to that statement?

   Think About:
   • how he behaves at home
   • what happens to him the day before the performance
   • how he behaves backstage just before the play begins

3. In later years, what do you think Robert would remember most about *The Last Stand*? Why?

4. **ACTIVE READING** **MONITORING READING STRATEGIES**
   Refer to the notes made in your
   READER'S NOTEBOOK. Which reading strategies helped you? Compare with a partner.

Extend Interpretations

5. **What If?** What if Belinda had been the one who forgot her lines? How do you think Robert would have responded? How might the story have ended?

6. **COMPARING TEXTS** The characters of Rachel in "Eleven," on page 26, and Robert in this selection both struggle to express themselves. Compare the way they face their situations. What do you think Robert might say to Rachel about the consequences of a day gone wrong?

7. **Connect to Life** How would you feel if you were in a play and forgot your lines after practicing for many weeks? How would you react during the performance?

Literary Analysis

TONE The writer's attitude toward his or her subject is called **tone.** You can identify the tone by paying attention to the words and images in a story. Consider this example from "The School Play":

Another one said, "California is just over there." He pointed, and some of the first graders looked in the direction of the piano.

This description shows that awkward and humorous things can happen when putting on a play. What attitude toward the subject might this show?

Group Activity In a small group, reread "The School Play." How would you describe the tone of the story? What details, dialogue, and descriptions help create the tone? You might use a web to organize your answer. In the center of the web, state the tone. In the ovals outside, give examples to support your statement.

THE SCHOOL PLAY **409**

Connect to the Literature

1. **What Do You Think?**
   Students may say that Robert is relieved, happy, proud. Their answers should reveal their understanding that even though Robert didn't do a perfect job, he is satisfied with himself.

Comprehension Check
• Robert kept reciting his lines because he was afraid that if he forgot them, Belinda would beat him up and Mrs. Bunnin would be disappointed.
• During the play, Robert mixes up his lines.

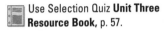 Use Selection Quiz **Unit Three Resource Book,** p. 57.

Think Critically

2. **Possible Responses:** He did not really live up to that statement because he let the pressure of the moment get to him; he did live up to that statement because he tried to take care of his nervousness by rehearsing, and when he messed up he was able to look on the bright side.

3. **Possible Response:** Robert will probably remember that he got through his lines and felt great once the play was over.

4. **Possible Response:** Students' choice of strategies will vary.

Use **Reading and Critical Thinking Transparencies,** p. 1, for additional support.

Literary Analysis

Tone Students' webs should include examples that show that the tone of the story is humorous.

Use **Literary Analysis Transparencies,** p. 25, for additional support.

Extend Interpretations

5. **What If?** Students may say that if Belinda had forgotten her lines, Robert might have felt so good that he would have had a sudden surge of confidence. At the end of the play, he would have felt great. Maybe Belinda would have even apologized for all the threats she made.

6. **Comparing Texts** Students may say that Robert would tell Rachel that just when you think your whole life is terrible, things change. He might tell her that one bad day doesn't mean anything. Everything could change tomorrow, once all the kids see Phyllis Lopez wearing the red sweater.

7. **Connect to Life** Responses will vary. Students may say that they would make up lines that made sense even though they weren't right.

Grammar in Context

WRITING EXERCISE

1. Robert wanted the play to go <u>well</u>.
2. Robert's mother thought he performed as <u>well</u> as Robert De Niro.
3. The pioneers in the play were <u>badly</u> prepared for winter.
4. David played with the grass and thought <u>deeply</u>.
5. Who was the actor whose voice sounded so <u>smooth</u>?

Vocabulary

STANDARDIZED TEST PRACTICE

1. A
2. K
3. A
4. M
5. B

EXERCISE

1. incorrect
2. correct
3. incorrect
4. incorrect
5. incorrect

Sentences will vary.

CHOICES and CHALLENGES

Grammar in Context: Choosing Adjective or Adverb

In "The School Play" Gary Soto describes a moment when Robert is confident:

> He sat up, feeling good because the line came naturally, without much thought.

Notice that Soto used the word *good,* not *well.* *Good* is an **adjective.** In this sentence it modifies the pronoun *he.* The word *well* is an adverb that means "capably" or "in a satisfactory way." The following example shows *well* modifying the verb *performing:*

> Robert dreamed of performing well in the play.

Another tricky pair of words is *bad* and *badly.* *Bad* is an adjective. It is used after linking verbs such as *to be, to feel, to taste,* or *to smell.*

> He felt bad for a minute when he forgot his line.

Vocabulary

STANDARDIZED TEST PRACTICE

Choose the word or group of words that means the same, or nearly the same, as the underlined Word to Know.

1. To <u>quiver</u> in fear
   - **A** cower
   - **B** hide
   - **C** quake
   - **D** whimper
2. An actor's <u>prop</u>
   - **J** script
   - **K** object
   - **L** make-up
   - **M** costume
3. <u>Relentless</u> noise
   - **A** constant
   - **B** frightening
   - **C** deafening
   - **D** random
4. To <u>smirk</u> at someone
   - **J** stare rudely
   - **K** laugh quietly
   - **L** yell loudly
   - **M** smile slyly

Badly is an adverb that means "not capably." Use *badly* after action verbs:

> He flubbed his line badly.

WRITING EXERCISE Rewrite the sentences, choosing the correct adjective or adverb.

Example: *Original* She tried to make Robert feel (bad, badly).

Rewritten She tried to make Robert feel bad.

1. Robert wanted the play to go (good, well).
2. Robert's mother thought he performed as (good, well) as Robert De Niro.
3. The pioneers in the play were (bad, badly) prepared for winter.
4. David played with the grass and thought (deep, deeply).
5. Who was the actor whose voice sounded so (smooth, smoothly)?

Grammar Handbook
See p. R78: Using Modifiers Effectively.

5. Depleted resources
   - **A** disorganized
   - **B** emptied
   - **C** natural
   - **D** extra

EXERCISE: WORD MEANING Decide whether the boldfaced Word to Know is used correctly in each sentence below. On your paper, write "correct" or "incorrect." For each incorrectly used word, write a sentence that uses it correctly.

1. The lead actor said his lines clearly and with a confident **quiver** in his voice.
2. I wanted to **smirk** when my rival messed up.
3. I studied the script to memorize my **prop.**
4. I was glad to see our **depleted** supply of snow, because it meant we had a lot left.
5. The **relentless** applause ended quickly.

Vocabulary Handbook
See p. R20: Context Clues.

Grammar in Context

CHOOSING AN ADJECTIVE OR ADVERB

Instruction Remind students that it isn't only the proper use of *good, well, bad,* and *badly* that can be confusing. It's also easy to get confused about whether to use an adjective or an adverb. Remember: Adjectives tell *which one, what kind,* or *how many* about nouns or pronouns only. Adverbs tell *how, where, when,* or *to what extent* about verbs, adjectives, or other adverbs.

Practice In the sentences below, have students choose the correct word—adjective or adverb—from the suggested pair.

1. Robert's mother felt (<u>proud</u>, proudly) because he had a speaking part in the play.
2. Robert saw Belinda's (<u>angry</u>, angrily) face looking at him.
3. Belinda's gum sat (sad, <u>sadly</u>) on her tongue.
4. *The Last Stand* is a (real, <u>really</u>) good play.

 Use **Unit Three Resource Book,** p. 55,. for more practice.

 For more instruction in choosing an adjective or adverb, see McDougal Littell's **Language Network,** Chapter 5.

For **systematic instruction** in grammar, see:
- **Grammar, Usage, and Mechanics Book**
- pacing chart on p. 315i.

Ode to My Library

by GARY SOTO

Connect to Your Life

Poems that Praise Odes are a writer's way of honoring someone or something that has meaning or power in his or her life. Poets have written odes to their pets, relatives, and even favorite foods such as French fries and watermelons. What might you like to honor in an ode?

Build Background

HISTORY

The speaker of the poem is proud of the Aztec warrior he helped paint in a mural. The Aztecs lived in what is now Mexico and built a great empire that lasted until the Spanish invaded in the 16th century. Some Aztec males were trained to be warriors from the time they were born. At the age of ten, a boy's hair was cut so that a section of hair lay on the back of his neck. He was not allowed to cut this hair until he had brought back from battle at least one live prisoner.

An image of Montezuma II (1466?–1520), Mexico's most famous Aztec emperor.

Focus Your Reading

LITERARY ANALYSIS **IMAGERY**

In his poetry, Gary Soto uses **imagery,** or words and phrases that appeal to his readers' senses. Consider how he describes the warrior in the mural:

> *I made the cuts*
> *Of muscle on*
> *His stomach*
> *And put a boulder*
> *Of strength in each arm.*

This vivid description helps readers to create an image of the warrior in their minds.

ACTIVE READING **VISUALIZING**

When you use your imagination to form a picture of something in your mind, you are **visualizing.** Gary Soto's poetry is a workout for the senses. His language encourages readers to see, hear, touch, smell, and taste as they read.

READER'S NOTEBOOK As you read "Ode to My Library," think about what sense Soto is trying to get you to use with each new description. Write down words and phrases that trigger your senses.

ODE TO MY LIBRARY   **411**

Standards-Based Objectives
• understand and appreciate a **poem**
• understand the author's use of **word choice** and **imagery**
• use **visualizing** to appreciate poet's use of imagery

Summary

In this poem, author Gary Soto writes fondly about the library of his childhood. He fantasizes about bringing his Mexican grandparents to visit the library and showing them the books that he's read, the mural that he helped to paint, and the other things that make his library so special.

Thematic Link

The geographical barrier between the author and his grandparents creates a longing in the author. He wants to break that barrier and bring his grandparents into his world, so that they can experience all the things that make his library an important place.

English Conventions Practice

Daily Language SkillBuilder

Have students **proofread** the display sentences on page 315k and write them correctly. The sentences also appear on Transparency 13 of **Language Transparencies.**

LESSON RESOURCES

UNIT THREE RESOURCE BOOK, pp. 58–59

ASSESSMENT
Formal Assessment, pp. 65–66
Test Generator

SKILLS TRANSPARENCIES AND COPYMASTERS
Reading and Critical Thinking
• Visualizing, TR 4 (pp. 412, 415)
• Cluster Diagram, TR 38 (p. 415)
Language
• Daily Language SkillBuilder, TR 13 (p. 411)
Writing
• Combining Sentences Using Conjunctions, TR 19 (p. 413)

INTEGRATED TECHNOLOGY
Audio Library
Net Activities

Visit our Web site:
www.mcdougallittell.com

For **systematic instruction** in language skills, see:
• **Vocabulary and Spelling Book**
• **Grammar, Usage, and Mechanics Book**
• pacing chart on p. 315i.

Reading Skills and Strategies:
PREVIEW

Have students look through "Ode to My Library." Ask students to think about what the poem might be about.

Active Reading   VISUALIZING

To visualize is to create a mental image. Tell students that sometimes they can better appreciate a story or poem if they visualize what they are reading. Ask students to tell which of the images on page 413 they visualized as they read this part of the poem.

Possible Response: I visualized an old, small library. I focused on the pencil sharpener, with a small piece of crayon stuck inside. Then I saw the librarian with her glasses hanging down instead of on her eyes.

Use **Unit Three Resource Book,** p. 58, for more practice. Use **Reading and Critical Thinking Transparencies,** p. 4, for additional support.

Literary Analysis   IMAGERY

Ask students to identify some of the images that they find especially effective or memorable.

Possible Response: I think the image of the fish making *jeta* is memorable because I can picture it perfectly.

Use **Unit Three Resource Book,** p. 59, for more practice.

Ode TO MY Library

BY GARY SOTO

It's small
With two rooms
Of books, a globe
That I once
5 Dropped, some maps
Of the United States and México,
And a fish tank with
A blue fish that
Is always making *jeta*.[1]
10 There are tables and chairs,
And a pencil sharpener
On the wall: a crayon is stuck
In it, but I didn't do it.

It's funny, but the
15 Water fountain
Is cooled by a motor,
And the librarian reads
Books with her
Glasses hanging

Rainbow,
© Synthia Saint James.

---

1. *jeta* (hĕ'tä) *Spanish:* fat, pouting lips.

Explain to students that free verse is poetry without a regular pattern of rhyme or rhythm. Ask students whether "Ode to My Library" is an example of free verse. Then ask them whether it has a certain rhythm even though it lacks rhyme.

Possible Response: "Ode to My Library" is an example of free verse. The poem does have rhythm, even though it isn't regular, which makes it easy to read.

Literary Analysis: IMAGERY

Tell students that poets use imagery, or sensory details, to appeal to readers' sense of smell, taste, touch, sight, and hearing. Ask students to identify two examples of imagery and to tell to which sense each one appeals.

Possible Response: The detail of the birds talking loudly from the window appeals to the sense of hearing. The detail of his grandparents touching the speaker's hair appeals to the sense of touch.

Reading Skills and Strategies: CONNECT

Ask students to explain how they connected this poem with their own experiences.

Possible Response: I understand how the author feels, because I love my library, too. Although my library is different from the one described in the poem, it is a special place where I spend a lot of time reading and learning.

20   From her neck. If she
      Put them on
      She would see me
      Studying the Incas
      Who lived two steps
25   From heaven, way in the mountains.

      The place says, "Quiet, please,"
      But three birds
      Talk to us
      Loudly from the window.
30   What's best is this:
      A phonograph
      That doesn't work.
      When I put on the headphones,
      I'm the captain of a jet,
35   And my passengers
      Are *mis abuelitos*[2]
      Coming from a dusty ranch
      In Monterrey. I want
      To fly them to California,
40   But then walk
      Them to my library.
      I want to show them
      The thirty books I devoured
      In the summer read-a-thon.

45   I want to show them
      The mural I helped paint.
      In the mural,
      An Aztec warrior
      Is standing on a mountain
50   With a machete[3]
      And a band of feathers
      On his noble head.
      I made the cuts
      Of muscle on
55   His stomach
      And put a boulder
      Of strength in each arm.
      He could gather
      Enough firewood
60   With one fist.
      He could slice
      Open a mountain
      With that machete,
      And with the wave of his arm
65   Send our enemies tumbling.

      If I could fly,
      I would bring
      Mis abuelitos to California.
      They would touch my hair
70   When I showed
      Them my library;
      The fish making *jeta*,
      The globe that I dropped,
      The birds fluttering
75   Their wings at the window.
      They would stand me
      Between them,
      When I showed them
      My thirty books,
80   And the cuts
      On the warrior,
      Our family of people.

---

2. **mis abuelitos** (mēs ä-bwĕ-lē′tôs) *Spanish:* my grandparents.

3. **machete** (mə-shĕt′ē): a large knife with a broad blade.

Cross Curricular Link   Social Studies

THE AZTECS The Aztec empire reached its height under Montezuma II, in the early 1500s. The capital city was Tenochtitlán (tay NOHCH tee TLAHN), located on an island in southern Mexico, where Mexico City stands today. At its peak, the city boasted a population of several hundred thousand. There was a large pyramid temple and an emperor's palace in the city. There were also "floating gardens"—artificial islands made of reed mats and earth on which beans, corn, and squash were raised. They provided the extra farmland needed by the growing population. The Aztecs prayed to many gods, including gods of corn, rain, sun, and war. The Aztec calendar told which month was sacred to each god and goddess. Priests performed ceremonies—including human sacrifice—intended to please these gods.

The Aztecs were a warlike people. They defeated many neighboring towns and cities and then forced the conquered people to give them tribute: food, feathers from tropical birds, gold, and cotton. Many prisoners of war became human sacrifices.

Connect to the Literature

1. What Do You Think?
How does the speaker make you feel about his library?

Comprehension Check
- Who does the speaker pretend to be when he puts on the earphones?
- What would he show to his grandparents?

Think Critically

2. After reading this poem, what image of the library is most vivid for you?

3. Each stanza of this poem is like a different photograph of the library. The last stanza puts them together to create the entire picture. What pictures did each stanza create in your mind as you read the poem?

4. What do you think this poem reveals about the speaker?

   Think About:
   - what the speaker thinks is "best" about the library, and why
   - the aspects of the library that the speaker seems to be most proud of

5. **ACTIVE READING** **VISUALIZING**
   Look back at the words and phrases you listed in your **READER'S NOTEBOOK.** Which sense did you use most while reading this poem? When did you use it?

6. Gary Soto is very active in encouraging children, especially Chicano children, to read. How do you think this poem relates to that goal?

Extend Interpretations

7. **The Writer's Style** Reread the poem, paying attention to how sentences are broken up and where capital letters are used. Then rewrite a stanza as a paragraph, using standard capitalization. How is the effect different?

8. **Connect to Life** Think about a special place that makes you feel safe, happy, or inspired. What words would you use to create a picture of this place?

Literary Analysis

IMAGERY Words and phrases that appeal to the senses are called **imagery.** Imagery helps readers use their imagination to see, feel, hear, taste, or smell what a writer describes. Readers are able to "see" the Aztec warrior when Soto describes him:

. . . standing on a mountain
With a machete
And a band of feathers
On his noble head.

Readers can also "hear" the fluttering of the birds' wings at the window.

Paired Activity With a partner, reread the poem. Pay attention to Soto's use of imagery. Which words and phrases cause you to see, feel, hear, taste, or smell something in your imagination? Describe the mental images the words and phrases created.

Connect to the Literature

1. What Do You Think?
Students might say that the speaker makes them feel that his library is a wonderful place that comes to life when he is there.

Comprehension Check
- He pretends to be the captain of a jet.
- He would show them the thirty books, the fish, the globe, the birds, and the warrior.

Think Critically

2. Responses will vary. Students may mention the phonograph that doesn't work, the mural with the Aztec warrior, the fish making *jeta*.

3. **Possible Responses:** First stanza—the library as inviting, friendly, and full of familiar things; second stanza—what the librarian and the speaker are doing in the present; third stanza—imaginations at work and dreams of going beyond the real world; fourth stanza—a concrete and vivid image of the Aztec warrior.

4. **Possible Responses:** The speaker loves to imagine things; reading thirty books was a big achievement and the speaker is very proud of it; the speaker feels that family and ancestors are important; the speaker is probably of Mexican heritage.

5. Students may say that they used their ability to see the most, envisioning the speaker, the rooms in the library, and the mural.

   Use **Reading and Critical Thinking Transparencies,** p. 4, for additional support.

6. **Possible Responses:** Gary Soto wants his readers to think of libraries as friendly, safe places and as fun and inspirational.

Extend Interpretations

7. **The Writer's Style** Responses will vary, but students should show an understanding of the effect of sentence structure and capitalization on poetry. They should understand how the concise form of a poem enables poets to convey a message in a simple but powerful way. They should understand that the particular words form images that evoke the subject matter of the poem. In rewriting a stanza as a paragraph, students should see that adding words can have a diluting effect, weakening the effect of the poetic images and ideas.

8. **Connect to Life** Students should be able to name several aspects of the place that make it special or pleasant for them. Encourage them to make their images as sharp and clear as possible. Students may find it helpful to use a word web.

   Use **Reading and Critical Thinking Transparencies,** p. 38, for additional support.

Literary Analysis

Imagery Partners will likely discuss the librarian with her glasses dangling, the birds fluttering, the warrior in the mural, and his grandparents visiting.

As they read, students may want to write down who Soto's readers are and how he meets them. After they complete the reading, ask them to discuss how knowing his audience helps Soto write.

Literary Analysis: DESCRIPTION

Soto's writing is vivid and full of humorous description. Ask students to identify some of the sensory words and descriptive phrases that Soto uses in this essay. Ask them to further discuss how the use of these words helps them to comprehend the text.

Possible Responses: *her brow creases deep enough to sow seeds, entirely decorated in red, spinning red lights of a fire engine pulsating on our faces, square head, big ears, spooked eyes*

These phrases help to paint pictures in the mind of the reader. We feel as though we can see exactly the image that Soto is describing.

WHO IS YOUR READER?

by Gary Soto

PREPARING to Read

Focus Your Reading

LITERARY ANALYSIS AUDIENCE

The group of people with whom a writer hopes to share his or her words is the **audience.** A writer thinks about his or her audience when deciding on a **subject,** a **purpose** for writing, and a **tone** in which to write.

In this essay by Gary Soto, he responds to the question "Who are your readers?" In doing so, he describes some of the unusual ways he meets the people who are his audience.

My first book of poems, *The Elements of San Joaquín,* was published in spring 1977 and dedicated in part to *mi abuelita.* My grandmother fled Mexico in 1914, somewhere in the middle of the Mexican Revolution, and like many other early immigrants could read neither Spanish nor English. As a young man of twenty-five, I did my duty by giving her a copy of my book. Grandma's reaction was to smile, and bunch her brow into creases deep enough to sow seeds; she realized an occasion was upon her and fixed me a glorious meal on her four-burner stove—eggs, frijoles, and tortillas. I don't remember what came first, the meal or her hunt for a picture frame into which she fit my book. She placed it on a coffee table in her living room that was entirely decorated in red—sofa, curtains, carpet, and cute ceramic sculptures. In that museum of bad taste, my book was the centerpiece.

Would Grandma be typical of my readership? Would others smile at my book, pat my shoulder for my effort to promote Chicano literacy and literature, and then put it in a picture frame? How do you get people to read your work, I wondered. The agony of writing is a terror in itself, but to build an audience once a book is published?

Unlike most other contemporary poets and writers, I've taken the show on the road and built a name among *la gente,* the people. I have ventured into schools where I have played baseball and basketball with young people, sung songs, acted in skits, delivered commencement speeches, learned three chords on a Mexican guitar to serenade teachers, formed a touring *teatro,* seen that my opera *Nerd-Landia* was mounted in high schools, established scholarships, and given away thousands of dollars to Chicano cultural centers.

My readership is strung from large cities, such as Los Angeles, to dinky Del Rey where peach trees outnumber the population by many thousands. Once,

Courtesy of Gary Soto.

I was a given a parade in Huron, California. The town, nearly all Mexican or Mexican American, numbered four thousand that winter when the mayor proclaimed Gary Soto Day. Because the town was small—three commercial blocks long—we had to start the parade of eight hundred celebrants in the grape vineyards, the spinning red lights of a fire engine pulsating on our faces. I sat in the back of a Chevy convertible while waving to the Spanish-speaking crowd.

© James Prigoff.

Sure, I felt silly, but it had to be done. The crowds watched as we made our way toward the school. There, I premiered my little 16mm film, *The Bike*, which featured the good people from Huron as the principal actors. Why go to the San Francisco Film Festival when a school cafeteria will do? I showed the film on a clean wall but not before a bike was auctioned off and my uncle Shorty, one of the actors, was assigned the duty of judging the Gary Soto portraits done by first graders. I was portrayed with a square head, big ears, spooked eyes—all the body parts of a happy-go-lucky Frankenstein.

Are these my readers? Is this my fame, my earthly reward played out in the grape fields I had wanted so much to escape? That night I had to stack the chairs and later pay for dinner—treating sixteen kids at a Mexican restaurant was an unwise move on my part! Of course, when I speak to college students I put on another face, one that is nearly serene, a college professor's face.

But, teaching is someone else's business. My business is to make readers from non-readers, and if you think it's easy, then join me anytime and see how, where, and why it's done. On the "where" front, I have slept on a lot of floors and couches, and on the "why" front I recall the kinder, gentler America that was proposed several years ago. And where is that America? Because I believe in literature, my task is to start Chicanos reading. If it's my poetry, great. If it's Sandra Cisneros's prose, that's great as well. If Chicanos start with other writers, say Hemingway or Kaye Gibbons, that's fine too. As for me, I start with kindergartners, and move up to college students, not to mention those *abuelitas* who are curious to see how I turned out after all the stupid antics I portrayed in *Living Up the Street*. I'm in their lives and in their hearts. I'm searching for a family whose grandmother, an illiterate, fits a book into a picture frame, the centerpiece for a household that will in time quiet down and throw open the cover. ❖

THINKING *through the* LITERATURE

1. **LITERARY ANALYSIS: AUDIENCE** Now that you have read this essay, how would you answer the question "Who are Gary Soto's readers?"

2. What effect do you think meeting Soto has on his readers?

3. Based on this essay, what advice do you think Soto might give younger writers?

Thinking through the Literature

1. **Possible Response:** Chicano readers, especially children and young people

2. **Possible Response:** Soto's readers are probably amazed to meet such a famous writer who is also a down-to-earth person.

3. **Possible Response:** Soto would probably tell young writers to write about what they know best.

The Jacket

by GARY SOTO

Connect to Your Life

Worn Out Have you ever had to wear a piece of clothing that someone else picked out, or that you thought was uncomfortable or ugly? How did you feel?

Build Background

GEOGRAPHY

The setting for "The Jacket" is Fresno, California, where Gary Soto grew up. Fresno, which means "ash tree" in Spanish, is located in central California. Beginning in the 1920s, farmers needed cheap labor, and Mexican laborers came to work in the fields of cotton, grapes, and beets that surrounded the town. Over time, Fresno's Hispanic and Chicano community grew. Fresno gradually became an industrial city as factories were built to process and market farm produce. Gary Soto's stories are often set in Fresno.

WORDS TO KNOW
Vocabulary Preview

mope	terrorist
profile	vinyl
swoop	

Focus Your Reading

LITERARY ANALYSIS   **HUMOR**

The quality that makes a literary work funny or amusing is called **humor.** One way Gary Soto creates humor in "The Jacket" is by exaggerating, or overstating, things. He also makes surprising comparisons. For example, he describes feeling "bitter as a penny."

ACTIVE READING   **IDENTIFYING THE AUTHOR'S PURPOSE**

Writers usually write for a particular reason or purpose. The **author's purpose** might be to **entertain,** to **inform,** to **express an opinion,** or to **persuade** readers to do or believe something. You can find clues to the author's purpose in the subject and tone of the work, the audience for which it was written, and the effect that it has on readers.

READER'S NOTEBOOK As you read "The Jacket," think about what the author's purpose seems to be. Jot down events, images, or description that suggest Gary Soto's purpose for writing the memoir.

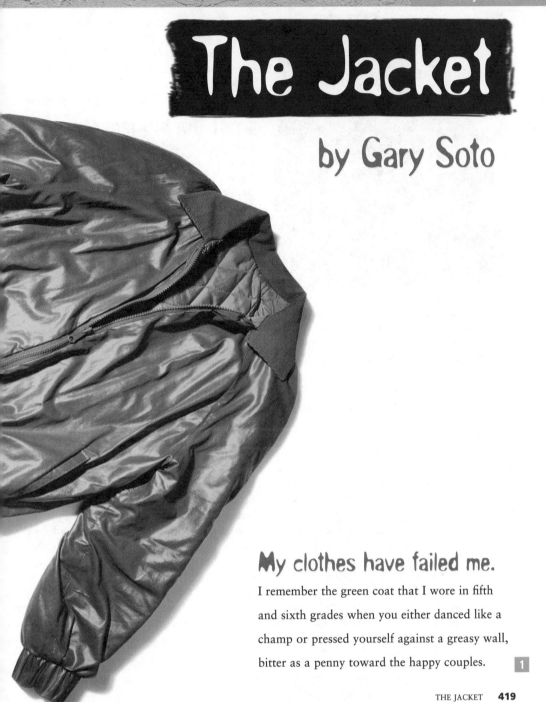

The Jacket

by Gary Soto

My clothes have failed me.

I remember the green coat that I wore in fifth

and sixth grades when you either danced like a

champ or pressed yourself against a greasy wall,

bitter as a penny toward the happy couples.

THE JACKET **419**

Less Proficient Readers
Have students keep these questions in mind as they read:
• Who are the characters in the story? *(The author is the main character. His mother and his schoolmates are the others.)*
• What is the setting of the story? *(Fresno, California)*
• What is the main character's problem or conflict? *(He has to wear an ugly jacket that makes him feel alienated from the other children.)*

English Learners
1 Students may not understand what "bitter as a penny" means. Ask them to suggest a possible definition by looking at the context around the phrase *(unhappy with your situation and yourself).*

Use **Spanish Study Guide,** pp. 88–90, for additional support.

Advanced English
"The Jacket" is rich with figurative language. As students read the story, invite them to keep a running list of metaphors, similes, and personification. Have them write a paragraph discussing the effect of the imagery on the story.

EXPLICIT INSTRUCTION ## Preteaching Vocabulary

WORDS TO KNOW
Call students' attention to the list of WORDS TO KNOW. Tell them that sometimes they can find the meaning of a word in a **clue that defines or restates** the word—that is, uses different words to explain or to say the same thing. Use this model sentence to help students understand how to use restatement clues: Frankie T., the playground *terrorist*, pushed the narrator to the ground and told him to stay there until recess was over.

Teaching Strategy
• Write the model sentence on the board.
• Have a volunteer explain how he or she figured out the meaning of the word *terrorist* by using a restatement clue within the sentence.
• Have students give a definition of the word *terrorist*.
• Ask students to create original sentences using the word *terrorist*.

Practice Have students write original sentences with restatement clues for the rest of the WORDS TO KNOW.

Use **Unit Three Resource Book,** p. 65, for more practice.

For **systematic instruction** in vocabulary, see:
• **Vocabulary and Spelling Book**
• pacing chart on p. 315i.

When I needed a new jacket and my mother asked what kind I wanted, I described something like bikers wear: black leather and silver studs with enough belts to hold down a small town. We were in the kitchen, steam on the windows from her cooking. She listened so long while stirring dinner that I thought she understood for sure the kind I wanted. The next day when I got home from school, I discovered draped on my bedpost a jacket the color of day-old guacamole. I threw my books on the bed and approached the jacket slowly, as if it were a stranger whose hand I had to shake. I touched the <u>vinyl</u> sleeve, the collar, and peeked at the mustard-colored lining.

From the kitchen mother yelled that my jacket was in the closet. I closed the door to her voice and pulled at the rack of clothes in the closet, hoping the jacket on the bedpost wasn't for me but my mean brother. No luck. I gave up. From my bed, I stared at the jacket. I wanted to cry because it was so ugly and so big that I knew I'd have to wear it a long time. I was a small kid, thin as a young tree, and it would be years before I'd have a new one. I stared at the jacket, like an enemy, thinking bad things before I took off my old jacket whose sleeves climbed halfway to my elbow.

I put the big jacket on.

I zipped it up and down several times, and rolled the cuffs up so they didn't cover my hands. I put my hands in the pockets and flapped the jacket like a bird's wings. I stood in front of the mirror, full face, then <u>profile</u>, and then looked over my shoulder as if someone had called me. I sat on the bed, stood against the bed, and combed my hair to see what I would look like doing something natural. I looked ugly. I threw it on my brother's bed and looked at it for a long time before I slipped it on and went out to the backyard, smiling a "thank you" to my mom as I passed her in the kitchen. With my hands in my pockets I kicked a ball against the fence, and then climbed it to sit looking into the alley. I hurled orange peels at the mouth of an open garbage can and when the peels were gone I watched the white puffs of my breath thin to nothing.

I jumped down, hands in my pockets, and in the backyard on my knees I teased my dog, Brownie, by <u>swooping</u> my arms while making bird calls. He jumped at me and missed. He jumped again and again, until a tooth sunk deep, ripping an L-shaped tear on my left sleeve. I pushed Brownie away to study the tear as I would a cut on my arm. There was no blood, only a few loose pieces of fuzz. Dumb dog, I thought, and pushed him away hard when he tried to bite again. I got up from my knees and went to my bedroom to sit with my jacket on my lap, with the lights out.

WORDS	**vinyl** (vī′nəl) *n.* a tough, shiny plastic
TO	**profile** (prō′fīl′) *n.* a side view
KNOW	**swoop** (swŌŌp) *v.* to move in a sudden sweep

420

That was the first afternoon with my new jacket. The next day I wore it to sixth grade and got a D on a math quiz. During the morning recess Frankie T., the playground <u>terrorist</u>, pushed me to the ground and told me to stay there until recess was over. My best friend, Steve Negrete, ate an apple while looking at me, and the girls turned away to whisper on the monkey bars. The teachers were no help: they looked my way and talked about how foolish I looked in my new jacket. I saw their heads bob with laughter, their hands half-covering their mouths.

Even though it was cold, I took off the jacket during lunch and played kickball in a thin shirt, my arms feeling like braille from goose bumps. But when I returned to class I slipped the jacket on and shivered until I was warm. I sat on my hands, heating them up, while my teeth chattered like a cup of crooked dice. Finally warm, I slid out of the jacket but a few minutes later put it back on when the fire bell rang. We paraded out into the yard where we, the sixth graders, walked past all the other grades to stand against the back fence. Everybody saw me. Although they didn't say out loud, "Man, that's ugly," I heard the buzz-buzz of gossip and even laughter that I knew was meant for me.

And so I went, in my guacamole-colored jacket. So embarrassed, so hurt, I couldn't even do my homework. I received Cs on quizzes, and forgot the state capitals and the rivers of South America, our friendly neighbor. Even the girls who had been friendly blew away like loose flowers to follow the boys in neat jackets.

I wore that thing for three years until the sleeves grew short and my forearms stuck out like the necks of turtles. All during that time no love came to me—no little dark

girl in a Sunday dress she wore on Monday. At lunchtime I stayed with the ugly boys who leaned against the chainlink fence and looked around with propellers of grass spinning in our mouths. We saw girls walk by alone, saw couples, hand in hand, their heads like bookends pressing air together. We saw them and spun our propellers so fast our faces were blurs.

I blame that jacket for those bad years. I blame my mother for her bad taste and her cheap ways. It was a sad time for the heart. With a friend I spent my sixth-grade year in a tree in the alley, waiting for something good to happen to me in that jacket, which had become the ugly brother who tagged along wherever I went. And it was about that time that I began to grow. My chest puffed up with muscle and, strangely, a few more ribs. Even my hands, those fleshy hammers, showed bravely through the cuffs, the fingers already hardening for the coming fights. But that L-shaped rip on the left sleeve got bigger, bits

WORDS TO KNOW	**terrorist** (tĕr′ər-ĭst) *n.* one who uses or theatens to use unlawful force

421

Reading and Analyzing

Literary Analysis: MEMOIR

Ask students to tell how they know that "The Jacket" is a memoir—a story about a person's life told by that person.

Possible Responses: The author is remembering a specific time in his life, and that is what a memoir does. He also writes about feelings that only he would know about.

Literary Analysis: EXAGGERATION

A Ask students to find an example of exaggeration—an abnormal or unnatural representation of the truth. Then have students explain why they think the author chose to exaggerate.

Possible Response: The "vicious spelling tests" are an exaggeration. The author probably called the spelling tests *vicious* because he was having such a bad year at school that even the tests he had to take seemed mean.

Reading Skills and Strategies: EVALUATE

Ask students whether they think Soto really hated the jacket and whether he really felt that his mother was to blame for his unhappiness.

Possible Response: The fact that Soto called the jacket his "ugly brother" shows his mixed feelings. He became attached to it even though it wasn't at all what he had wanted. He needed someone or something to blame for his unhappiness, and his mother and the jacket were the easiest targets.

Handball (1939) Ben Shahn. Tempera on paper over composition board, 22¾" × 31¼".
The Museum of Modern Art, New York. Abby Aldrich Rockefeller Fund.
Photograph Copyright © 2001 The Museum of Modern Art, New York.
Copyright © Estate of Ben Shahn/Licensed by VAGA, New York, NY.

of stuffing coughed out from its wound after a hard day of play. I finally Scotch-taped it closed, but in rain or cold weather the tape peeled off like a scab and more stuffing fell out until that sleeve shriveled into a palsied[1] arm. That winter the elbows began to crack and whole chunks of green began to fall off. I showed the cracks to my mother, who always seemed to be at the stove with steamed-up glasses, and she said that there were children in Mexico who would love that jacket. I told her that this was America and yelled that Debbie, my sister, didn't have a jacket like mine. I ran outside, ready to cry, and climbed the tree by the alley to think bad thoughts and watch my breath puff white and disappear.

But whole pieces still casually flew off my jacket when I played hard, read quietly, or took vicious spelling tests at school. When it became so spotted that my brother began to call me "camouflage," I flung it over the fence into the alley. Later, however, I swiped the jacket off the ground and went inside to drape it across my lap and mope.

I was called to dinner: steam silvered my mother's glasses as she said grace; my brother and sister with their heads bowed made ugly faces at their glasses of powdered milk. I gagged too, but eagerly ate big rips of buttered tortilla that held scooped-up beans. Finished, I went outside with my jacket across my arm. It was a cold sky. The faces of clouds were piled up, hurting. I climbed the fence, jumping down with a grunt. I started up the alley and soon slipped into my jacket, that green ugly brother who breathed over my shoulder that day and ever since. ❖

---

1. **palsied** (pôl′zēd): withered by disease.

WORDS
TO
KNOW   **mope** (mōp) v. to be gloomy or in low spirits

423

Connect to the Literature

1. What Do You Think?
Responses will vary but should reflect students' understanding of the author's mixed feelings toward the jacket.

Comprehension Check

• Soto's mother gave him the jacket.
• His friends and teachers ignore him or talk about the jacket in a mean way.
• At the end of the story, the narrator puts the jacket on. He's going to keep it.

 Use Selection Quiz
Unit Three Resource Book, p. 66.

Think Critically

2. Most students will say that the author exaggerated the jacket's role in his life. They may say that he would have been unhappy anyway and that the jacket was just a convenient excuse.

3. **Possible Responses:** He knew that his mother couldn't afford to buy him another one; if he got rid of it, he wouldn't be able to blame it for all his problems; he didn't want to hurt his mother's feelings; he knew his mother would be angry and unsympathetic.

4. Students may say that the author makes this comparison because he has grown fond of the jacket even though it is imperfect.

5. Students' notes will vary. They may say that Gary Soto wanted to share how hard growing up is.

Use **Reading and Critical Thinking Transparencies**, p. 8, for additional support.

Literary Analysis

Humor Students' charts should include examples that contain exaggeration, unlikely comparisons, or funny details. Their explanations should be clear.

Connect to the Literature

1. What Do You Think?
What were your thoughts as you finished reading this selection?

Comprehension Check
• Who gives Soto the jacket?
• How do his friends and teachers react to him in the jacket?
• What does he do with the jacket at the end of the selection?

Think Critically

2. Do you think that the jacket really affected the author's life as much as he claims it did? Explain.

3. Why do you think the author did not get rid of the jacket?

   Think About:
   • his family's circumstances
   • the role the jacket plays in his life while he has it
   • his mother's reaction when he shows her how worn out it is

4. Why do you think Soto compares the jacket to an "ugly brother"?

5. **ACTIVE READING** | **IDENTIFYING THE AUTHOR'S PURPOSE**
   Review the passages you wrote down in your **READER'S NOTEBOOK**. Based on your notes, why do you think Gary Soto wrote this memoir?

Extend Interpretations

6. **What If?** How would this memoir have been different if the author had gotten the jacket he wanted?

7. **Different Perspectives** How do you think the author's mother would have told this story? What might she say about the jacket and why she bought it?

8. **Connect to Life** What would you do if every day you had to wear a jacket that you hated?

Literary Analysis

HUMOR **Humor** is something that amuses readers or makes them laugh. Much of the humor in "The Jacket" comes from Gary Soto's exaggerated descriptions, his choice of funny details, and his comparisons between things that would normally appear to have nothing in common. For example, he compares the new coat to "a stranger whose hand I had to shake." This unlikely comparison between the coat and a stranger is humorous because it exaggerates the author's feeling of discomfort.

Activity Reread "The Jacket," paying close attention to phrases or passages that you find humorous. Make a chart listing at least five examples of humor. Next to each entry, explain briefly why you find it humorous. Compare your chart with that of a classmate.

REVIEW: SIMILE A **simile** is a comparison of two things, using the words *as* or *like*. For example, Soto uses a simile when he says that he was "thin as a young tree."

Extend Interpretations

6. **What If? Possible Responses:** He would have felt more confident and thus been more successful socially; he would still have felt unpopular and would have blamed it on the other jacket; he would have found other excuses for his problems.

7. **Different Perspectives** Responses will vary. Students might say that the author's mother would explain that she bought the jacket because it was inexpensive.

8. **Connect to Life** Responses will vary. Students may discuss finding ways to earn money to buy a new jacket. Or they might say that they could put up with wearing the jacket because they know they wouldn't have to wear it forever.

Grammar in Context: Describing with Prepositional Phrases

In "The Jacket," Gary Soto often uses phrases to add detail rather than single-word adjectives and adverbs. Notice how the highlighted phrases make the following description clear:

> **With my hands clenched I kicked a ball** against the fence.

A **preposition** is a word that shows a relationship between other words. Common prepositions are *at, by, in, of, to, through, like,* and *with.* A **prepositional phrase** is a group of words made up of a preposition, a noun or pronoun, and any modifiers that go with the noun or pronoun. A prepositional phrase may be used as an adjective or adverb. For example, the phrase in red type above is used in place of an adjective to modify the word *I.* The phrase in orange is an adverb phrase, modifying the word *kicked.*

Apply to Your Writing Sometimes a one-word modifier (an adjective or adverb) does not paint a very clear picture of what it is describing. In your writing, look for places where prepositional phrases can pinpoint the exact look or position of something.

WRITING EXERCISE Make up a prepositional phrase to answer the question in parentheses. Rewrite the sentences, including your prepositional phrases.

> **Example: Original** The other students stared. (Where?)
>
> **Rewritten** The other students stared at me.

1. I threw my books. (Where?)
2. I combed my hair. (How?)
3. I wore the jacket. (When?)
4. My mother made me wear the jacket. (What kind?)

Connect to the Literature Find three more prepositional phrases in "The Jacket" that are used as adjectives or adverbs.

Grammar Handbook
See p. R62: Parts of Speech.

Vocabulary

STANDARDIZED TEST PRACTICE

Choose the word or group of words that means the same, or nearly the same, as the underlined Word to Know.

1. My new jacket was made out of <u>vinyl</u>, just like an uncomfortable couch. <u>Vinyl</u> means—
   A soft wool   **B** old denim
   C shiny plastic   **D** smooth leather

2. I tried on the jacket and looked at myself in the mirror, hoping that at least my <u>profile</u> was cool-looking. <u>Profile</u> means—
   F hair   **G** smile
   H front   **J** side

3. When I am feeling unhappy, <u>I swoop</u> down around the <u>dog</u>. Swoop means—
   A hide   **B** lie
   C sit   **D** sweep

4. Frankie T. was the playground <u>terrorist</u>. <u>Terrorist</u> means—
   F guard   **G** athlete
   H bully   **J** tutor

5. The jacket was so ugly that it made me sad; I could only <u>mope</u> around the house. Mope means—
   A sulk   **B** complain
   C march   **D** clean

Vocabulary Handbook
See p. R20: Context Clues.

Grammar in Context

WRITING EXERCISE
Answers will vary. Possible answers are shown.
1. I threw my books onto the sofa in the living room.
2. I combed my hair with an old, broken comb.
3. I wore the jacket through all three years of middle school.
4. My mother made me wear the jacket with the ripped sleeve and the ugly, big zipper.

Connect to the Literature
Three other prepositional phrases that are used as adjectives or adverbs include:
With my hands in my pockets [p. 420]
. . . the first afternoon with my new jacket. [p. 421]
. . . how foolish I looked in my new jacket. [p. 421]

Vocabulary

STANDARDIZED TEST PRACTICE
1. C
2. J
3. D
4. H
5. A

---

^{EXPLICIT INSTRUCTION} Grammar in Context

IDENTIFYING PREPOSITIONS

Instruction Remind students that prepositions are words that show relationships. Some common prepositions are *at, by, in, of, to, through, like, with, on, under,* and *above.* They show how a noun or a pronoun relates to another word. Explain that students should choose their prepositions carefully to make their meaning clear. Changing a preposition can make the meaning of a sentence entirely different. Write the following sentences on the board as examples: Kim is waiting <u>on</u> the stairs. Kim is waiting <u>under</u> the stairs.

Meeting Kim would involve knowing which preposition describes where she is waiting.
Practice In the sentences below, have students underline the prepositions.

1. The narrator's dog jumped <u>onto</u> his jacket and ripped the sleeve <u>with</u> his teeth.
2. <u>On</u> the second day that the narrator wore his jacket, he was pushed <u>by</u> the playground terrorist.
3. <u>During</u> lunchtime, the narrator stood <u>by</u> the fence <u>with</u> the ugly boys.
4. <u>In</u> the cold weather, the pieces <u>of</u> tape that the narrator had put <u>on</u> the rip peeled <u>off</u>.

5. <u>At</u> the end <u>of</u> the story, the narrator puts the jacket <u>on</u>, knowing that it is his <u>for</u> keeps.

 Use **Unit Three Resource Book,** p. 64.

For more instruction in identifying prepositions, see McDougal Littell's **Language Network,** Chapter 6.

For **systematic instruction** in grammar, see:
• **Grammar, Usage, and Mechanics Book**
• pacing chart on p. 315i.

The Author's Style

Soto's writing provides a vivid picture of growing up Chicano and poor. An analysis of his style can help reveal the techniques he uses to write. Students will be made aware of Soto's style through the Key Points and then they will find examples in the three excerpts on the right side of the page.

Key Style Points
First Activity
A Exaggerated Details Soto may use exaggerated details to make sure the reader understands his description. He wants us to really understand that Belinda is tough and that there were a lot of belts on the jacket. He is emphasizing something that he feels is important.

Second Activity
B Unlikely Comparisons By making unlikely comparisons, Soto forces the reader to pay close attention to the text. He helps the reader feel the way he did when he first saw and put on his new jacket.

Third Activity
C Fresh Adjectives Adjectives such as *wormy, frothing, gray,* and *relentless* help add zing to Soto's writing.

The Author's Style

Soto's Dramatic Descriptions
Gary Soto describes himself as "an imagist, that is, someone who paints a vivid picture. . . . I do employ dialogue, but most of my writing is descriptive. You come away with clear pictures of the scene, and hopefully they stay with you for a while." Many of Soto's dramatic descriptions include humor based on exaggeration and unlikely comparisons.

Key Style Points

A Exaggerated Details Soto uses exaggerated details to create memorable images and to emphasize certain points. Why do you think he uses these exaggerations in "The School Play" and "The Jacket"?

B Unlikely Comparisons By using unlikely comparisons, Soto creates humor and vivid images. He points out surprising similarities between things that usually seem unrelated. What effect do the comparisons in this passage from "The Jacket" have?

C Fresh Adjectives To add "zing" to his writing, Soto uses fresh adjectives. What adjectives in the descriptions listed here make them interesting?

Applications

1. **Active Reading** Look back over the selections in this author study. Find two examples for each of the three types of descriptive language listed above. Compare your examples with those of a classmate.

2. **Writing** Recall a humorous experience in your own life. Write a short essay about it, using Soto's descriptive techniques.

3. **Speaking and Listening** With a partner, choose a passage from a Soto selection to read aloud. Use your voice, facial expressions, and gestures to emphasize aspects of Soto's style. Take turns practicing your reading and commenting on each other's performance.

426 UNIT THREE **AUTHOR STUDY**

Exaggerated Details
. . . Belinda was one of the toughest girls since the beginning of the world.
—"The School Play"

. . . I described something like bikers wear: black leather and silver studs with enough belts to hold down a small town.
—"The Jacket"

Unlikely Comparisons
I was a small kid, thin as a young tree, and it would be years before I'd have a new one. I stared at the jacket, like an enemy, thinking bad things . . .
—"The Jacket"

Fresh Adjectives
. . . they bit into chunks of wormy earth.
. . . the janitor's pit bull, who licked his frothing chops. . . .
. . . a ball of gray gum, depleted of sweetness under her relentless chomp.
—"The School Play"

Applications

1. **Active Reading** Answers will vary, but examples should include exaggerated details, unlikely comparisons, and fresh adjectives.

2. **Writing** Answers will vary, but should include the descriptive techniques described on this page.

3. **Speaking and Listening** Suggest that students work together to make up a checklist on which to "grade" each other's performance.

Writing

Embarrassing Moments Gallery
Write an essay describing an embarrassing moment of your own, or one you've heard about. Along with classmates, display your essay on a bulletin board. Also place a copy in your **Working Portfolio.**

Speaking & Listening

Film Review View Gary Soto's short film "The Pool Party." Then present an oral review of the film to the class. Prepare your review by first coming up with a clear statement of your opinion of the film. Did you love it? hate it? feel bored watching it? Next, provide support for your opinion using your own ideas and examples from the film. After rehearsing your oral review a few times, present it to the class.

Speaking and Listening Handbook
See p. R100: Persuasive Presentations.

VIDEO: Literature in Performance

"The Pool Party"

Research & Technology

Justice in the Fields Soto cares about the struggles of farm workers. Do research to learn about the United Farm Workers union. What gains have been made in the last decade? Use books, articles, and the Internet to find information. Present your findings in a poster. Include a list of the sources you used.

Research and Technology Handbook
See p. R106: Navigating the Web.

Author Study Project

On Stage

Now's the chance to bring Gary Soto's vivid descriptions to life! Present a dramatic version of one of the selections in this author study.

❶ **Brainstorm Ideas** With your team, brainstorm about presenting your scene. Decide whether you will use a narrator.

❷ **Create a Script** Rewrite the piece in the form of a script, with a cast of characters, stage directions, and lines of dialogue. Decide whether roles should be deleted or rearranged.

❸ **Build the Scene** Create a background for your scene by drawing scenery or arranging furniture. In addition, gather or make any props and costumes.

❹ **Practice and Perform** Practice your scene. Actors should speak with strong, clear voices and use dramatic gestures. Invite another class to see your production. If equipment is available, you can videotape the performance and watch it together afterward, or share it with family members.

GARY SOTO **427**

Writing

Embarrassing Moments Gallery Keep in mind that some moments are too embarrassing for students to share. You might suggest moments that were embarrassing at the time, but now can be seen with humor.

Use **Writing Transparencies,** pp. 6, 25, for additional support.

Speaking & Listening

Film Review Provide published movie reviews as models for students. To make this activity easier, hold a class discussion of the Soto video before students begin creating their reviews.

Use the **Speaking and Listening Book,** pp. 29, 30, for additional support.

Research & Technology

Justice in the Fields One book on Cesar Chavez that students might enjoy is the bilingual edition (English and Spanish) of *Cesar Chavez: Hope for the People,* by David Goodwin.

Author Study Project

On Stage Make sure that each group includes students who enjoy performing as well as students who can create backgrounds or sets, find music, or collect props.

MULTIMEDIA PROJECT
Students can make a multimedia project of their skits by filming them and arranging them with narration to give a fuller picture of Gary Soto's life. They can also add introductory and background music, as well as sound effects. They could also do this project as a radio play, paying special attention to the music and sound.

The characters in Gary Soto's books grapple with rough kids and bad jobs, tough times and lousy luck. They also find humor in the most unexpected places. In his short stories, novels, and poems, Soto's wise observations touch subjects ranging from baseball and first kisses to racism and poverty.

Baseball in April and Other Stories 1990

ALA Best Book for Young Adults

Set in Soto's hometown of Fresno, California, this award-winning short-story collection focuses on the hopes, dreams, and hardships of young Mexican Americans growing up in the barrio.

Taking Sides 1991

Fourteen-year-old Lincoln Mendoza's world changes when he moves from a San Francisco barrio into a well-to-do suburb. Suddenly, he must struggle to find a place for himself. Among the stresses he deals with are racism at school, his mom's new boyfriend, and a basketball tournament that pits his new school against his old.

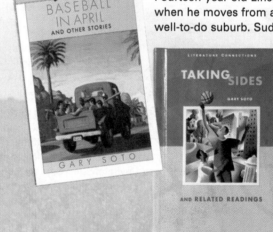

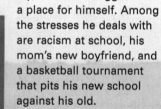

Pacific Crossing 1992

In this sequel to *Taking Sides*, Lincoln is chosen to be a summer exchange student at a small farm in Japan. Living in a different culture gives him a chance to learn about martial arts and meet new friends. It also helps him figure out what being Mexican American really means.

The Pool Party 1993

When Rudy Herrera is invited to a pool party by the rich and popular Tiffany Perez, he discovers that getting ready will be a family affair. It seems like everyone from his sister to his grandfather has already decided how Rudy should behave at the big event.

Local News 1993

One boy tries to save the planet by becoming a vegetarian. Another seeks to blackmail his older brother with pictures taken of him in the shower. These are just two of the funny, believable tales of teenage life in this companion to *Baseball in April*.

A Fire in My Hands 1990

Rich in detail, this poetry collection explores the emotions surrounding first love, family life, and the drama of friendship. Each poem has a brief introduction by the author that tells how he was inspired to write it.

Standards-Based Objectives

- write a 500- to 700-word problem-solution essay
- use a written text as a model for writing
- revise a draft to provide examples
- use the correct comparative adjectives and adverbs
- deliver a presentation on problems and solutions

Introducing the Workshop

Problem-Solution Essay Begin by discussing with students the problem-solution essay form. Tell them that many people write problem-solution essays to help other people who have similar problems, to record how they solved a specific problem, or to persuade someone to solve a problem. Ask them if they have ever read a problem-solution essay, and what it was about.

Ask students to begin thinking about this essay by brainstorming problems that would be worthy of solving. Help focus their discussion on appropriate ideas.

Basics in a Box

Using the Graphic A problem-solution essay begins with a clear and concise explanation of the problem and its significance, proposes a workable solution and includes details that explain and support it, and concludes by restating the problem and the proposed solution. Point out that this graphic organizer helps students to visualize the problem-solution essay.

Presenting the Rubric To help students better understand the assignment, review the Standards for Writing a Successful Problem-Solution Essay. You may also want to share with them the complete rubric, which describes several levels of proficiency.

 See **Unit Three Resource Book**, p. 75.

 For more instruction on essential writing skills, see McDougal Littell's *Language Network,* Chapters 10–17.

 Power Presentation

To engage students visually, use **Power Presentation 2**, Problem-Solution Essay.

Writing Workshop — Problem-Solution Essay

Offering a solution to a problem . . .

From Reading to Writing Life can present difficult problems, from pollution and crime to simply forgetting your homework. Tackling a problem creatively and patiently makes all the difference. Think of Helen Keller. As a child she lost the use of sight, speech, and hearing. Her teacher, Anne Sullivan, helped solve this problem by teaching Helen sign language. Are there problems you would like to solve? Writing a **problem-solution essay** can help you explore a problem and work on solving it.

For Your Portfolio

WRITING PROMPT Identify an important problem and offer a solution.

Purpose: To inform readers about the problem and persuade them to consider your solution

Audience: People who might experience a similar problem, or who can help with the solution

Basics in a Box

Problem-Solution Essay at a Glance

Introduction presents and describes the problem

Body presents and explains possible solutions

Conclusion restates the problem and the benefits of the solution

RUBRIC STANDARDS FOR WRITING

A successful problem-solution essay should

- have an introduction that catches readers' attention
- give a clear picture of the problem
- explore all aspects of the problem, including its causes and effects
- offer a reasonable solution and explain how to put it into effect
- use facts, statistics, examples, opinions, or other details to support the solution
- use logical reasoning to convince the reader
- have a strong conclusion

430 UNIT THREE PART 2: BREAKING BARRIERS

LESSON RESOURCES

USING PRINT RESOURCES
Unit Three Resource Book
- Prewriting, p. 67
- Drafting, p. 68
- Peer Response, p. 69
- Organizational Patterns, p. 70
- Revising, Editing, and Proofreading, p. 71
- Student Models, pp. 72–74
- Rubric, p. 75

Writing
- Structuring the Essay, TR 6 (p. 432)

Speaking and Listening
- Understanding Audience and Purpose, pp. 6–7 (p. 435)
- Developing and Delivering a Presentation, pp. 8–9, 12–13 (p. 435)
- Creating and Analyzing a Problem-Solution Presentation, pp. 31–32 (p. 435)

INTEGRATED TECHNOLOGY
Writing Coach CD-ROM
Visit our Web site:
www.mcdougallittell.com

Analyzing a Student Model

SPEAKING OPPORTUNITY

See the Speaking and Listening Handbook, p. R96 for oral presentation tips.

M. McGoff
St. Clement's Elementary School

A Trip to the Grocery Store

Can you imagine the challenges that people with disabilities face each day? Even simple tasks like grocery shopping can be difficult. Perhaps they can't reach a can of soup on the shelf, or are unable to open a freezer door to get some ice cream. They may not be able to push a cart. They may have vision problems that stop them from reading labels or knowing what choices they have. In cases like these, shopping becomes a real challenge. However, I think grocery stores can do a lot to make shopping easier for people with disabilities.

Because of the different needs of disabled shoppers, I would like to see a shopping assistance program developed in grocery stores. People with disablties would register with the store in advance, letting managers know their needs and problems. The store would then hire an occupational therapist to interview shoppers to find out how the store could support them in becoming more independent. The main purpose of the program would be to find out how each person with a disability needs support and, with the help of an occupational therapist, come up with a plan to help each person shop as independently as possible. This program would also help shoppers feel more supported by the community.

For instance, a shopper might not be able to reach or lift groceries off the shelf but would like the experience of browsing through the aisles. With the help of mechanized devices, this person might tape-record a shopping list or choose things that he or she wants from a store checklist. Then a store assistant could get the items and meet the shopper at the checkout area. The shopper would be able to join the line at the checkout like everyone else. In other cases, a shopper could become perfectly independent with the use of a motorized shopping cart and a long mechanical arm device that could extend to get items from higher places. Still another shopper might require a store employee to walk with him or her to read labels or describe selections.

Despite the program's advantages, store owners might have

RUBRIC
IN ACTION

❶ Introduction presents the problem in the form of a questions

❷ A detailed explanation of the situation helps the reader understand what needs to be done and presents the thesis statement.

❸ The writer presents a realistic and well-defined solution in an organized way.

❹ Supports the main idea of the paragraph with evidence and examples

Other options:
- Support with statistics
- Use description

Teaching the Lesson

Analyzing the Model
A Trip to the Grocery Store
The essay writer describes the challenges faced by disabled people as they attempt the simple task of grocery shopping. The essay explores several support systems and solutions to helping disabled persons have success when grocery shopping.

Have student volunteers read the essay aloud. Discuss the Rubric in Action with students. Point out key words and phrases in the student model that correspond to the elements mentioned in the Rubric in Action.

1. Posing a question is a good way to start a problem-solution essay because it lets the reader know immediately what problem the essay is addressing. Ask students to think of other questions that could be used to begin this essay.
   Possible Response: Have you ever tried to grocery shop on crutches or in a wheelchair?

2. Tell students that giving specific details about the problem helps convince readers of the validity of the problem. Ask them to list some of the details provided in this paragraph.
   Possible Responses: Shoppers can't reach items on shelves, may not be able to push a cart, or can't read labels.

3. Ask students to notice how the writer puts a clear, workable solution early in the essay. Ask students to suggest other workable solutions for this problem.
   Possible Response: The store could hire people to shop for the disabled person and bring the food to his or her home.

4. Point out that the essay continues to add supporting details for the proposed solution. Ask students to select the detail they like most and tell a partner why.

5 Tell students that the writer has pointed out both pros and cons to the proposed solution. Ask them to think of other possible objections to the proposed solution.
Possible Response: Disabled people might feel discriminated against if they were treated differently than other shoppers.

6 The writer has given a clear plan which deals with the possible objections to the proposed solution. Tell students that the more support and explanation the essay provides, the more likely it is to influence the readers. Ask students to discuss what they think of this solution.
Possible Responses: I think the solution is good and well thought out, and I can see some grocery stores trying this. I don't think this is a good plan because grocery stores don't care that much about the people who shop there.

7 The conclusion of the essay should restate the problem, clarify and repeat the solution, and provide the benefits of the proposed solution. Ask students to compare the first and last paragraphs of the essay to see what elements were repeated.
Possible Response: Simple grocery shopping tasks might be difficult or impossible to people with disabilities. Grocery stores could do simple things that would make shopping possible and pleasurable for disabled persons.

objections. They might feel it would cost too much money to hire extra employees to help people with disabilities. They might think that it isn't good business to spend money on a program that won't be profitable. The store owners might also feel there are not enough people who need this service.

> **5** The writer raises possible concerns about the plan.

Contrary to what store owners might believe, solving the problem is easier than it appears. Occupational therapists might be willing to volunteer a couple of hours a week, or the stores could pay therapists only for the number of hours they work. Since customers with disabilities would be shopping at different times, the stores could train employees working on different shifts to assist them. Middle- or high-school students also could volunteer to help disabled shoppers during a few hours after school. This would give the students valuable experience in helping their community.

> **6** The body provides a step-by-step strategy for action to address concerns.

Finally, the stores might also get government or town funding for equipment that would help people with disabilities shop more comfortably. As you can see, it is not just the disabled who would benefit from a program like this. I believe that everyone involved could benefit: store owners, volunteers, therapists, and store employees. The program could also create good publicity for the store. People would know that the store cares about its customers. They would want to shop there because of its reputation as a supportive, caring, community store. More people shopping at the store could help pay for the program.

Buying a pint of ice cream might not seem like a big deal, but to someone who has never had the freedom to do this it is a sign of independence. To get involved, you can contact your local grocery stores and ask them to create programs for the disabled. By doing what you can to solve some of the problems faced by these members of your community, you are helping to create a better world.

> **7** The writer summarizes the problem and tells the reader how to get involved. She restates the benefits of the program to create a strong conclusion.

EXPLICIT INSTRUCTION ## Patterns of Organization

PICTURING TEXT STRUCTURE

Instruction One good way to structure a good problem-solution essay is to think about the main points—stating the problem, offering a solution, and restating the problem and solution—and then to consider the details that support the problem and the solution. Tell students that using a graphic organizer can help them to organize their essay.

Practice Have students analyze the organization of the student model by constructing a diagram similar to the one shown here.

📖 Use **Unit Three Resource Book**, p. 70, to help use order of importance in their problem-solution essays. Use **Writing Transparencies**, p. 6, for additional support.

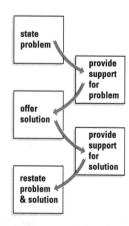

Writing Your Problem-Solution Essay

❶ Prewriting

The best way to escape from a problem is to solve it.
— Alan Saporta, writer

Brainstorm problems that you see around you. **List** school problems, community problems, and world problems. See the **Idea Bank** in the margin for more suggestions. After you have selected a problem, follow these steps.

Planning Your Problem-Solution Essay

1. **Define your problem.** What is the problem you want to solve? If it is too big to explain in one essay, write about one part of the problem. Ask the following questions: How did it start? Who is affected by it? What would happen if it isn't solved? Has anyone else tried to solve it?

2. **Find information.** Research answers to your questions about the problem. Interview people who might be directly affected by it. If you're interested in a world problem, you can do research at the library and on the Internet. This will help you come up with solutions.

3. **Brainstorm solutions.** How might the problem be solved? Write down as many possibilities as you can think of.

4. **Choose the best solution.** Evaluate your solutions. Based on your research, which solutions have been successful in the past? Which might seem too difficult to put into practice? Discuss ideas with classmates, teachers, family members, or people affected by the problem. Then choose the best solution.

---

❷ Drafting

Include as much information as you can in your first draft. Later you can go back and revise your draft.

- In your **introduction,** identify the problem.
- In the **body,** explain the causes and effects of the problem. Describe your solution, and use solid evidence to show that it is realistic.
- In your **conclusion,** summarize the problem and the benefits of your solution.

Ask Your Peer Reader

- Why is solving this problem important?
- Whom does the problem affect?
- Do you think this solution is the best one? Why or why not?
- Which information did you find most and least convincing?

IDEA Bank

1. Your Working Portfolio
Look for ideas in the **Writing** activities you completed earlier.

2. Take a Survey
Ask four or five people to name two problems that they think need solutions. List their answers and choose one of the problems for your essay.

3. Take It Personally
Think of the problems that directly affect you, such as overcrowded classrooms, old gym or lab equipment, or not enough money for class trips. Choose the one you feel most strongly about.

Have a question?

See the **Writing Handbook.**
Problem-Solution, p. R45
Documenting Your Sources, p. R51
See **Language Network.**
Prewriting, p. 264
Drafting, p. 267

Guiding Student Writing

Prewriting
Choosing a Subject
If after reading the Idea Bank, students have difficulty choosing a problem for their problem-solution essay, suggest they try the following:

- go back to their brainstormed lists of problems from the beginning of the lesson
- think about the things in their own lives that trouble them
- talk with a partner about their lives at home, school, and in the community

Planning Your Problem-Solution Essay

1. Students may want to share their problem with a partner as they try to answer the questions posed. The most common error for students is to select a problem that is too big for one essay. Encourage students to help their partners think about how to narrow the problem.

2. Encourage students to talk to family members and others involved with the problem. If it's a school-based problem, allow them time to talk with the personnel involved.

3. Have students do this task individually during a quiet time of freewriting. During this time, students should write down any solution, whether they think it's a good one or not.

4. Once students have generated a list of possible solutions, have them talk with many people to help them get a good feeling for the most probable solution. Remind them that they will have to be able to support this solution in their essay, so they may want to take notes as they talk to other people.

Drafting
Suggest that students jot down the boldfaced key words in the margin where they occur in their first draft. This will help ensure that they get them all, and will make it easier for the peer reader to evaluate. Ask students to read the peer reader question box prior to beginning to write.

Revising
SUPPORTING IDEAS WITH EXAMPLES

Ask students to find a sentence in their essay that could use more details. Ask a volunteer to read one aloud, and help them to see how they can add more examples to support their problem or solution. Remind students to read their entire essay and to revise by adding more examples.

Editing and Proofreading
COMPARING WITH ADJECTIVES AND ADVERBS

Help students to identify comparative adjectives and adverbs in their essays. Check to see if they've used them correctly by asking students to read them aloud.

Reflecting

 Encourage students to be specific in reflecting about their essay writing. Ask them to think about who they might want to read the essay and why.

Option
TEACHING TIP

It is often helpful to pre-select student work to share with the class. As you are reading and conferencing with students on their writing pieces, and you see something you'd like to use in a future lesson, mention it to the students. Have them mark their rough draft, and make a note of it yourself. This way you can be sure to have a student volunteer when you ask. Another way is to ask students for permission to copy their piece and make an overhead transparency of it. You can then use the paper during the appropriate instruction.

Need Revising Help?

Review the **Rubric**, p. 430

Consider **peer reader** comments

Check **Revision Guidelines**, p. R31

SPELLING
From Writing

As you revise your work, look back at the words you misspelled and determine why you made the errors you did. For additional help, refer to the strategies and generalizations in the **Spelling Handbook** on page R26.

Confused about Comparatives and Superlatives?

See the **Grammar Handbook**, p. R62.

SPEAKING
Opportunity

Turn your essay into an oral presentation.

Publishing
IDEAS

- Create a problem-solution bulletin board. Feature one problem and its solution each week.
- Choose essays that address common problems. Submit them to your school newspaper.

● **INTERNET**

Publishing Options
www.mcdougallittell.com

---

❸ Revising
TARGET SKILL ▶ SUPPORTING IDEAS WITH EXAMPLES Supporting your points with examples helps to show that the problem needs to be solved and that your solution is a good one. In the following passage, the writer adds examples to show how her plan might work.

> For instance, if a shopper could not reach or lift groceries on the shelf but would like the experience of browsing through the aisles, he or she might be helped in a couple of ways. tape-record a shopping list or select items from a store checklist.

❹ Editing and Proofreading
TARGET SKILL ▶ COMPARING WITH ADJECTIVES AND ADVERBS When writing a problem-solution essay, you may want to make comparisons between your solution and the existing problem. Words like *better, happier,* and *more* signal a comparison. Most comparative adjectives and adverbs are formed by adding *-er* to short words or by using the word *more* with longer words. After you read the example below, check your essay to see if you have used comparative adjectives and adverbs correctly.

> Contrary to what store owners might believe, solving the problem is more easy *easier* than it appears.

❺ Reflecting
FOR YOUR WORKING PORTFOLIO What did you learn about the problem from writing your problem-solution essay? What did you learn about possible solutions? Attach these answers to your finished essay. Save your problem-solution essay in your Working Portfolio.

EXPLICIT INSTRUCTION   Revision

ORGANIZATION

Instruction Remind students that in a well-organized composition, ideas within the body of the paper need to be supported with examples. In a problem-solution essay, it is even more important to cite examples if you want to persuade people that your proposal is the most effective solution to the problem. Have students review their problem-solution essays to look for examples that support their proposals. Ask them to share those examples with a partner.

Practice Ask students to read each of the paragraphs in the body of their essays to find places where an additional example would make their papers stronger and more convincing.

RUBRIC

3 Full Accomplishment Student supports the description of the problem and the proposed solution with examples. Details, facts, quotations, and anecdotes make his or her reasoning clear.

2 Substantial Accomplishment Student uses several examples throughout the paper to support the description of the problem and the proposed solution. His or her reasoning is clear.

1 Little or Partial Accomplishment Student may use an example or two in support of his or her proposed solution. Reasons are not clearly stated.

See the **Research and Technology Handbook**, pp. R108-109, for information about formatting documents using word processing skills.

Standardized Test Practice

Mixed Review

> Our river, <u>the Hialeah river,</u> <u>is the more polluted river</u> in the state.
> (1)   (2)
> The level of toxic chemicals in the water is high, so the river's fish
> population is <u>not doing good.</u> Many more <u>fish live</u> in the river ten years
>   (3)   (4)
> ago. Not only are there chemicals in the water, <u>but a greater number of</u>
>   (5)
> <u>people</u> use the river as a dumpster than ever before. It makes me sad to
> think that this beautiful <u>Old American river</u> is being destroyed.
>   (6)

Review Your Skills

Use the passage and the questions that follow it to check how well you remember the language conventions you've learned in previous grades.

1. What is the correct capitalization in item 1?
   A. the hialeah river
   B. the hialeah River
   C. the Hialeah River
   D. Correct as is

2. How is item 2 best written?
   A. is the most polluted river
   B. is the most pollutedest river
   C. is the much polluted river
   D. Correct as is

3. How is sentence 3 best written?
   A. not doing more better
   B. not doing well
   C. not doing best
   D. Correct as is

4. What is the correct verb tense in sentence 4?
   A. fish have lived
   B. fish lived
   C. fish are living
   D. Correct as is

5. How is sentence 5 best written?
   A. but a great number of people
   B. but a number of people
   C. but the greatest number of people
   D. Correct as is

6. What is the correct capitalization in sentence 6?
   A. old American River
   B. old American river
   C. Old American River
   D. Correct as is

Self-Assessment

Check your own answers in the **Grammar Handbook.**

Using Verbs Correctly, p. R76

Using Modifiers Effectively, p. R78

Correcting Capitalization, p. R81

Standardized Test Practice

Ask students to read the entire passage prior to correcting the errors. Demonstrate how students can eliminate incorrect choices for the first question. *Hialeah River* is a proper noun, and as such, both words should be capitalized. Therefore choices A and B are incorrect. D is also wrong, because *river* is not capitalized. The correct answer must be C.

Answers:
1. C; 2. A; 3. B, 4. B, 5. D, 6. B

EXPLICIT INSTRUCTION **Speaking Opportunity**

Prepare Once students have written their problem-solution essay, they can present it to an audience. Refer students to page R105 of the Speaking and Listening Handbook at the back of this book for tips on presenting their problem-solution essay.

Present Have students present their problem-solution essays to the class. They should strive to convince audience members that their characterization of the problem and their proposed solutions are logical and reasonable.

RUBRIC

3 Full Accomplishment Student explains the causes and effects of the problem, suggests a workable solution, and offers persuasive evidence that validates the definition of the problem and supports the proposed solution.

2 Substantial Accomplishment Student states the problem but doesn't give much background, suggests a solution, and gives reasons why it will work.

1 Little or Partial Accomplishment Student mentions the problem and proposes solution. He or she gives no background on how the problem developed and little evidence to support the proposed solution.

Use **Speaking and Listening Book,** pp. 6–9, 12–13, 31–32, for additional support in presenting a problem-solution essay.

UNIT THREE *Reflect* and Assess

Standards-Based Objectives
- reflect on and assess student understanding of the unit
- review literary analysis skills introduced in the unit
- assess and build portfolios

Reflecting on Theme

OPTION 1
A successful response will
- identify ten personal qualities which at least three fictional characters or real people in this unit exhibited.
- list the identities of those characters next to their personal traits.
- demonstrate how these traits and qualities helped each character relate to success and/or failure.

OPTION 2
A successful response will
- include thoughtful discussion of the quote from Ibrahima's letter.
- result in interesting role-play with the three story characters identified.
- contain examples from characters' lives which demonstrate their response in struggling towards goals.

OPTION 3
A successful response will
- begin with discussion of the ways people encourage or are encouraged by others.
- evaluate the fictional characters and real people in this selection to discover the ways in which they overcome difficulties and pursue their goals.
- include appropriate quotations from the selections which provide support for tips on the chart.
- reflect the personal goal setting experiences of the student.

Use Unit 3 Resource Book page 76 to provide students a ready-made chart for listing their tips.

Self Assessment
Students should recall all the stories in this unit and think about how both fictional characters and real people behaved when faced with unfairness. The paragraphs should include these ideas, as well as ideas drawn from the student's personal experiences.

A Sense of Fairness

By reading the selections in this unit, you have learned about a wide range of unfair situations and an equally wide range of responses to them. What new thoughts about coping with difficulties have formed in your mind? To explore this question, complete one or more of the options in each of the following sections.

Reflecting on Theme

OPTION 1
Making a Top-Ten List In dealing with life's injustices, which individuals in this unit responded with hope, with wisdom, or with determination? Working in a group, consider how these fictional characters and real people reacted to success or failure. Brainstorm a list of the top ten personal qualities it takes to deal with an unjust situation. Next to each quality, write the name of the characters or people in this unit who displayed it.

OPTION 2
Role-Playing a Response In "Abd al-Rahman Ibrahima," the author says that when Ibrahima wrote a letter asking for help, "he had little faith in the procedure but felt he had nothing to lose." In a group of three, taking the roles of Janet in "The Southpaw," Helen Keller, and Robert in "The School Play," respond to this quote about Ibrahima. What would each individual say about the importance of asking for help? What would each say about the value of struggling toward a goal?

OPTION 3
Finding Inspiration Look over the selections in this unit to find ways in which fictional characters and real people encourage themselves or are encouraged by others. Then create a chart titled "How to Reach Your Goals." List tips for overcoming difficulties and pursuing goals based on the experiences of the individuals. Include any quotes from the selections that you find helpful or inspiring.

Self ASSESSMENT
READER'S NOTEBOOK

After reading the selections in Unit Three, what have you learned about how to deal with unfair situations? Write a paragraph describing how you could use what you have learned in a real-life situation.

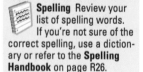

REVIEWING YOUR PERSONAL
WORD List

Vocabulary Review the new words you learned in this unit. If necessary, use a dictionary to check the meaning of each word.

Spelling Review your list of spelling words. If you're not sure of the correct spelling, use a dictionary or refer to the **Spelling Handbook** on page R26.

Reviewing Literary Concepts

OPTION 1

Thinking About Dialogue Choose two selections from this unit that you think have especially effective dialogue. With a partner, read aloud dialogue from each selection in a way that emphasizes the feelings of the characters. How do the spoken lines bring the characters to life? What can you learn about their traits from the words they speak?

OPTION 2

Considering Tone The tone of a story or poem expresses the writer's attitude about the subject. A tone can be serious or humorous; it can be kind, critical, or neutral. Look through these selections to find examples of three or four different tones. Jot down details, word choice, and dialogue that show the writer's attitude. Then, with a few classmates, discuss how the tone of each selection affected your emotions as you read.

Portfolio Building

- **Choices and Challenges—Writing** Several of the writing assignments in this unit asked you to write about autobiographical information. Choose the one that you feel most successfully allows your voice (or the voice of a character) to come through. Write a cover note explaining the reasons for your choice. Then attach the note to the letter and place it in your **Presentation Portfolio.**

- **Writing Workshops** In one Writing Workshop you wrote a comparison-and-contrast essay. In another, you wrote a problem-solution essay. Reread these two pieces and decide which one does a better job of showing your strengths as a writer. Explain your choice in a cover note, attach it to the piece you selected, and place it in your **Presentation Portfolio.**

- **Additional Activities** Think back to the assignments you completed for **Speaking & Listening** and **Research & Technology.** In your portfolio, keep a record of any assignments that you particularly enjoyed, found helpful, or would like to explore further.

Self ASSESSMENT

READER'S NOTEBOOK

Copy down the following literary terms introduced or reviewed in this unit. Put a question mark next to each one that you do not fully understand. Look at the **Glossary of Literary and Reading Terms** (page R116) to clarify the meanings of the terms you've marked.

stage directions	sensory details
dialogue	speaker
narrative poetry	repetition
primary sources	humor
	simile
secondary sources	tone
autobiography	imagery
biography	

Self ASSESSMENT

Compare your choices for your portfolio in Unit Three with the choices you made earlier. Write a note comparing a recent piece with an early one. Point out improvements that the recent piece shows.

Setting GOALS

How well are you working with others in group situations? Are you willing to share your ideas? Do you listen carefully to the ideas of other group members? Write down some practical tips to keep on hand during the next unit.

Reviewing Literary Concepts

OPTION 1

It may be helpful to pair students up according to the two selections they choose. Allow them time to practice reading the dialogue and to discuss their interpretation with their partner. The questions posed in this option might be used to form the basis of this discussion and interpretation.

OPTION 2

A successful response will
- begin with critical analysis of each selection, with individual students identifying several author tones.
- provide examples from the selections of each of the tones chosen.
- include thoughtful discussion of each tone and the effect each had on the reader.

Portfolio Building

Students should evaluate the autobiographical writing in their Working Portfolios and choose the one that represents their best use of voice. Likewise, they should evaluate the two essays and select the one which represents their best work to include in their Presentation Portfolio. As students attach notes to the items they transfer to their Presentation Portfolios, remind them to write the reasoning for their choices clearly so they will understand the notes several months from now.

Self Assessment

It may work well to have students use a different color paper to write the comparison notes. Remind them to be reflective and explicit in the comparison, as this will help them as they work on their writing.

Setting Goals

Help students to focus on the questions, to evaluate themselves honestly, and to set realistic, clear goals.

LITERATURE CONNECTIONS
Maniac Magee

BY JERRY SPINELLI

This Newbery Medal winner tells of homeless wanderer "Maniac" Magee, who can move like no one else the town has ever seen. He intercepts a football on a field of players twice his size, hits a home run without a baseball, and wins a race running backward. But there are two challenges he can't outrun: the strong racial divisions in his hometown, and his need for a loving family.

These thematically related readings are provided along with *Maniac Magee*:

from **Freedom's Children**
BY ELLEN LEVINE

Where the Rainbow Ends
BY RICHARD RIVE

Those Who Don't
BY SANDRA CISNEROS

A Lesson for Kings
BY MARGARET READ MACDONALD

Runner
BY DONNA LUONGO STEIN

Final Curve
BY LANGSTON HUGHES

The Boy with Yellow Eyes
BY GLORIA GONZALEZ

Stormalong
BY MARY POPE OSBORNE

More Choices

Escape to Freedom
BY OSSIE DAVIS
This is the true story of Frederick Douglass, orator, author, diplomat, and former slave.

Martin Luther King: The Peaceful Warrior
BY EDWARD CLAYTON
In this biography, the author describes King's peaceful struggle to break down barriers between the races.

The Miracle Worker
BY WILLIAM GIBSON
This drama focuses on the conflict between blind and deaf Helen Keller and her teacher, Anne Sullivan, as Anne struggles to teach Helen to communicate.
A McDougal Littell *Literature Connection*

Nelda
BY PAT EDWARDS
Eleven-year-old Nelda is tired of being poor, so she leaves her parents to become a friend and companion to the rich Miss Mattie May.

Bullies Are a Pain in the Brain
BY TREVOR ROMAIN
This practical guide on how to deal with bullies is also humorous.

The Secret Garden
BY FRANCES HODGSON BURNETT
Lonely ten-year-old Mary lives in a gloomy manor house in England. When she and her cousin discover a hidden garden, however, their friendship and their imaginations begin to blossom.

The Clay Marble

BY MINFONG HO

This historical novel is set in a Cambodian refugee camp in the early 1980s. Twelve-year-old Dara—with courage, quick thinking, and perseverance—copes with the horrors of war, helped by stories, a good friend, and a "magical" marble.

These thematically related readings are provided along with *The Clay Marble:*

All the People of Khmer Were Very Troubled
BY VEN YEM

My Life Story
BY LAN NGUYEN

Oppression
BY LANGSTON HUGHES

Birthday Box
BY JANE YOLEN

Holes
BY LILLIAN MORRISON

from **Childhood and Poetry**
BY PABLO NERUDA

All-Ball
BY MARY POPE OSBORNE

Dear World, January 17, 1994
BY ALMA LUZ VILLANUEVA

Social Studies Connection

Cry Wolf and Other Aesop Fables
BY BARRY CASTLE AND NAOMI LEWIS
Each fable in this collection ends with a moral or wise saying.

Daedalus and Icarus
BY PENELOPE FARMER
Daedalus and Icarus try to break free from the earth and fly.

A Place in the Sun
BY JILL RUBALCABA
Senmut, a young sculptor in Egypt at the time of Ramses II, is forced to work in the gold mines of Nubia after he accidentally kills a dove.

Joseph's Wardrobe
BY PAUL J. CITRIN
This is the story of the mission to bring Joseph's wardrobe back to his family in Israel after his death in Egypt.

The Golden God: Apollo
BY DORIS GATES
Apollo, the Greek god of medicine and music, had many adventures. In this collection of myths, he fights against Python, loses his son Phaethon, and falls in love with Daphne.

Wondrous Worlds

There are worlds within and worlds without. In Unit Four, students will read about both kinds. Part 1, "Animal Wonders," introduces some animals, both exotic and ordinary, who open people's eyes to the wonders of nature. Part 2, "Imaginary Worlds," takes readers on a journey to the most exciting place of all—their own imaginations!

———— Part 1 ————

Animal Wonders Anyone who has ever loved an animal or wondered how the birds know when it is time to fly south will be enchanted by the selections in Part 1. "Lob's Girl" tells the story of an amazing pet who forever enriches the life of an entire family. These selections take the reader into worlds they may never have known existed.

———— Part 2 ————

Imaginary Worlds The worlds we create inside our heads may be the best of all, because in the imagination, anything is possible! Milo, the main character of the charming drama *The Phantom Tollbooth*, drives through a mysterious tollbooth that takes him to a land where words and numbers are more important than he ever dreamed possible.

UNIT FOUR

WONDROUS WORLDS

In books,

I have traveled not

only to other worlds,

but into my own.

ANNA QUINDLEN
American journalist

Party Animals, Julia Lucich.
Pastel over acrylic, 17" × 22".

440

EXPLICIT INSTRUCTION **Viewing and Representing**

Party Animals
by Julia Lucich

ART APPRECIATION
Instruction Explain that while the giraffes in this painting are very realistic looking in one way, they are fantastic looking in another way. Who has ever seen a blue or red giraffe? The artist explains, "If I had just used brown and tan, it might have been boring. Their astonishing shapes and contours seemed to cry out for a different approach. . . . Sometimes we all wish that the world was more vibrant, filled with more fun and enthusiasm."
Ask: What do you notice about the background of the painting? Why do you think the painter chose to show it this way?
Possible Response: While the giraffes are shown very clearly, the background is hazy. The giraffes appear to be standing in weeds or grass. The background leaves a lot to the imagination.

To help students explore the connections between the art, the quotation, and the unit theme, have them consider the following questions:

Ask: What are some of the wonders of the world that amaze you? Why?
Possible Response: Students' responses will vary, but should provide reasons why they think these wonders are so fascinating.

Ask: How would you paraphrase the quotation by Anna Quindlen on page 440?
Possible Response: Books are a way to learn about the outside world and also a way to learn about yourself.

Ask: What do you think the giraffes in the painting are doing? What might they be looking at?
Possible Response: They may be looking for food or watching to make sure no enemies are nearby.

Ask: What kinds of stories and experiences might you expect to read about in a unit called "Wondrous Worlds"?
Possible Response: You might expect to read about some unusual things that have happened and some strange creatures. You might also read fantasies—stories set in places that exist only in the imagination.

Features and Selections	Literary Analysis	Reading and Critical Thinking	Writing Opportunities		
Wondrous Worlds **Animal Wonders**					
Learning the Language of Literature Plot	Plot, 443				
The Active Reader Skills and Strategies		Recognizing Cause and Effect, 446			
SHORT STORY Lob's Girl **Difficulty Level:** *Challenging*	Foreshadowing, 447, 448, 450, 456, 458, **459** Mood, 452, **459** Details of Setting, 450 Influence of Setting, 451, 452, 454, 458, **459**	Cause and Effect, 447, 448, 450, 452, 456, 458, **459** Thinking About Dialects, 461 Standardized Test Practice, 460 Making Inferences, 455	Newspaper Article, 460 Identifying Prepositions and Their Objects, 461		
Reading for Information Animals to the Rescue		Making Judgments, 462, **463** Making Assertions About a Text, 463			
ESSAY My First Dive with the Dolphins **Difficulty Level:** *Average*	Essay, 465, 466, 473 Specialized Language, 473 Imagery, 468	Making Generalizations, 465, 466, 471, **473** Helping the World, 475	Dolphin Smarts, 474		
POETRY Something Told the Wild Geese Questioning Faces **Difficulty Level:** *Average*	Sound Devices, 476, 478, **479** Rhyme, 477 Repetition and Rhythm, 478	Word Choice, 476, 478, **479**	Field Diary, 480		
SHORT STORY Zlateh the Goat **Difficulty Level:** *Average* **Building Vocabulary** **Related Reading** Chang McTang McQuarter Cat	Climax and Resolution, 481, 482, 486, **488** Author Activity, 490 Details of Setting, 482 Influence of Setting, 483, 485, 487, **488**	Story Mapping, 481, 482, 484, 486, **488**	Dialogue with Zlateh, 489 Art Connection, 489		
Communication Workshop: Process Description **Standardized Test Practice**		Analyzing a Process Description, 501 Patterns of Organization, 501	Creating Your Process Description, 503 Defining Unfamiliar Terms, 509 Revision: Word Choice, 504		

UNIT FOUR
PART 2 SKILLS TRACE

Imaginary Worlds					
Learning the Language of Literature Science Fiction and Fantasy	Science Fiction and Fantasy, 507				
The Active Reader Skills and Strategies		Visualizing, 511			

LEGEND   **DLS – Daily Language SkillBuilder**   **Green type – Teacher's Edition**

Features and Selections	Literary Analysis	Reading and Critical Thinking	Writing Opportunities		
DRAMA **The Phantom Tollbooth** Difficulty Level: *Challenging* **Related Reading** **All That Is Gold**	Fantasy, **512**, 514, 518, 525, 530, 546, **552** Characteristics of Drama, 518, 549 Understanding Theme, 520 Analyzing Plot, 531	Visualizing, **512**, 514, 526, 533, 538, **552** Play vs. Novel, 554	Plot Analysis, 553 Punctuating Prepositional Phrases, 554		
POETRY **The Walrus and the Carpenter** **Fairy Lullaby,** *from* A Midsummer Night's Dream Difficulty Level: *Challenging*	Realistic and Fantastic Details, 555, 556, 561 Review: Rhyme, 561 Tone, 557	Visualizing, 555, 556, 561 Comparing Texts, 561 Clarifying, 559 Read Aloud, 558	Eloquent Speech, 562		
POETRY **Three Limericks** Difficulty Level: *Easy* **Building Vocabulary**	Poetic Form: Limerick, **563**, 564, 566 Review: Rhythm, 566	Reading Aloud, 563, 564, 566 Comparing Texts, 566	Your Own Limericks, 567		
COMPARING LITERATURE **Science Fiction**	Science Fiction, 572	Points of Comparison, 573, 579, 585	Comparison-and-Contrast Essay, 573, 587		
SHORT STORY **The Fun They Had** Difficulty Level: *Easy*	Setting, 574, 576, 579 Evaluating Story Elements, 576	Purposes for Reading, 574, 576, 579			
SHORT STORY **The Sand Castle** Difficulty Level: *Average*	Setting, 580, 582, 585 Understanding Fiction, 582, 584	Purposes for Reading, 580, 582, 585	Futuristic Setting Description, 586		
Comparing Literature: **Standardized Test Practice**		Reading the Prompt, 587	Planning a Comparison-and-Contrast Essay, 587		
Reading for Information **Home on an Icy Planet**		Taking Notes and Outlining Ideas, 588, 589, **589** Preparing Applications, 590			
Writing Workshop: Short Story **Standardized Test Practice**		Analyzing a Student Model, 593 Patterns of Organization, 593	Writing Your Short Story, 595 Maintaining Consistent Point of View, 596 Revision: Organization, 596		
Reflect and Assess	Analyzing Plot Structure, 599 Analyzing Fantasy and Science Fiction Elements, 599	Thinking About Genre, 598	Judging Impact, 598 Analyzing the Theme, 598 Portfolio Building, 599		

	Unit Resource Book	Assessment	Integrated Technology and Media
Lob's Girl *pp. 447–461*	• Summary p. 4 • Active Reading: Cause and Effect p. 5 • Literary Analysis: Foreshadowing p. 6 • Literary Analysis: Influence of Setting p. 7 • Grammar p. 8 • Words to Know p. 9 • Selection Quiz p. 10	• Selection Test, Formal Assessment pp. 79–80 ⊙ Test Generator	⌒ Audio Library
Animals to the Rescue *pp. 462–464*	• Making Judgments p. 11 • Making Assertions p. 12		
My First Dive with the Dolphins *pp. 465–475*	• Summary p. 13 • Active Reading: Making Generalizations p. 14 • Literary Analysis: Essay p. 15 • Literary Analysis: Imagery p. 16 • Grammar p. 17 • Words to Know p. 18 • Selection Quiz p. 19	• Selection Test, Formal Assessment pp. 81–82 ⊙ Test Generator	⌒ Audio Library ⊙ Research Starter www.mcdougallittell.com
Something Told the Wild Geese Questioning Faces *pp. 476–480*	• Active Reading: Word Choice p. 20 • Literary Analysis: Sound Devices p. 21	• Selection Test, Formal Assessment pp. 83–84 ⊙ Test Generator	⌒ Audio Library ⊙ Research Starter www.mcdougallittell.com
Zlateh the Goat *pp. 481–490*	• Summary p. 22 • Active Reading: Story Mapping p. 23 • Literary Analysis: Climax and Resolution p. 24 • Literary Analysis: Influence of Setting p. 25 • Grammar p. 26 • Words to Know p. 27 • Selection Quiz p. 28	• Selection Test, Formal Assessment pp. 85–86 ⊙ Test Generator	⌒ Audio Library

Communication Workshop: Process Description

		Unit Assessment	Unit Technology
Unit Four Resource Book • Planning and Drafting p. 30 • Practicing and Delivering p. 31 • Peer Response Guide p. 32 • Revising Organization and Ideas p. 33 • Refining Your Performance p. 34 • Student Models pp. 35–37 • Rubric for Evaluation p. 38	⊙ **Writing Coach** **Writing Transparencies** TR6 **Speaking and Listening Book** pp. 10, 11, 25, 26	• Unit Four, Part 1 Test, Formal Assessment pp. 87–89 ⊙ Test Generator • Unit Four: Integrated Assessment pp. 19–24	⊙ ClassZone www.mcdougallittell.com ⊙ Electronic Teacher Tools

Additional Support

Literary Analysis Transparencies	Reading and Critical Thinking Transparencies	Language Transparencies	Writing Transparencies	Speaking and Listening Book
• Foreshadowing TR28	• Cause and Effect TR5	• Daily Language SkillBuilder TR14 • Context Clues: Definition and Overview TR53	• Writing Variables TR2 • Transitional Words and Phrases TR9	• Creating a Persuasive Presentation p. 29 • Guidelines: How to Analyze a Persuasive Presentation p. 30
	• Strategies for Reading TR1		• Locating Information Using the Internet I TR47	
	• Making Generalizations TR14 • Main Idea and Supporting Details TR25	• Daily Language SkillBuilder TR15 • Learning and Remembering New Words TR65	• Combining Sentences Using Conjunctions TR19	• Creating a Persuasive Presentation p. 29 • Guidelines: How to Analyze a Persuasive Presentation p. 30
• Poetry: Sound Devices TR20	• Analyzing Word Choice TR15	• Daily Language SkillBuilder TR15	• Sensory Word List TR16 • Locating Information Using Print References TR45	• Choosing Presentation Aids p. 10
	• Summarizing Story Map TR13	• Daily Language SkillBuilder TR16 • Punctuating Elements in a Series TR44 • Context Clues: Compare and Contrast, Cause and Effect, Example TR54	• Dialogue TR24	

ENGLISH LEARNERS / STUDENTS ACQUIRING ENGLISH

The **Spanish Study Guide,** pp. 91–105, includes language support for the following pages:
• Family and Community Involvement (per unit)

• Selection Summaries and Vocabulary
• Active Reading
• Literary Analysis

For **systematic instruction** in language skills, see:
• **Vocabulary and Spelling Book**
• **Grammar, Usage, and Mechanics Book**
• pacing chart on p. 441i

UNIT FOUR
RESOURCE MANAGEMENT GUIDE
PART 2

To introduce the theme of this unit, use transparencies 10–12 in Fine Arts Transparencies.

	Unit Resource Book	Assessment	Integrated Technology and Media
The Phantom Tollbooth *pp. 512–554*	• Summary p. 39 • Active Reading: Visualizing p. 40 • Literary Analysis: Fantasy p. 41 • Literary Analysis: Plot p. 42 • Grammar p. 43 • Words to Know p. 44 • Selection Quiz p. 45	• Selection Test, Formal Assessment pp. 89–90 🖲 Test Generator	🎧 Audio Library
The Walrus and the Carpenter **Fairy Lullaby,** *from* **A Midsummer Night's Dream** *pp. 555–562*	• Active Reading: Visualizing p 46 • Literary Analysis: Realistic and Fantastic Details p. 47	• Selection Test, Formal Assessment pp. 91–92 🖲 Test Generator	🎧 Audio Library
Three Limericks *pp. 563–567*	• Active Reading: Reading Aloud p. 48 • Literary Analysis: Poetic Form: Limerick p. 49	• Selection Test, Formal Assessment pp. 93–94 🖲 Test Generator	🎧 Audio Library
The Fun They Had *pp. 574–579*	• Summary p. 51 • Active Reading: Purposes for Reading p. 52 • Literary Analysis: Setting p. 53 • Active Reading: Evaluating Story Elements p. 54 • Grammar p. 55 • Words to Know p. 56 • Selection Quiz p. 57	• Selection Test, Formal Assessment pp. 95–96 🖲 Test Generator	🎧 Audio Library
The Sand Castle *pp. 580–586*	• Summary p. 58 • Active Reading: Purposes for Reading p 59 • Literary Analysis: Setting p. 60 • Literary Analysis: Forms of Fiction p. 61 • Grammar p. 62 • Words to Know p. 63 • Selection Quiz p. 64	• Selection Test, Formal Assessment pp. 97–98 🖲 Test Generator	🎧 Audio Library
Home on an Icy Planet *pp. 588–591*	• Outlining Ideas p. 66 • Preparing an Application p. 67		

Writing Workshop: Short Story

		Unit Assessment	Unit Technology
Unit Four Resource Book • Prewriting p. 68 • Drafting and Elaboration p. 69 • Peer Response Guide p. 70 • Organizational Patterns: Spatial Order p. 71 • Revising, Editing, and Proofreading p. 72 • Student Models pp. 73–75 • Rubric for Evaluation p. 76	🖲 **Writing Coach** **Writing Transparencies** TR23 **Reading and Critical Thinking Transparencies** TR39 **Speaking and Listening Book** pp. 9, 14, 23–24	• Unit Four, Part 2 Test, Formal Assessment pp. 99–100 🖲 Test Generator • Unit Four: Integrated Assessment pp. 19–24	🔎 ClassZone www.mcdougallittell.com 🖲 Electronic Teacher Tools

Additional Support

Literary Analysis Transparencies	Reading and Critical Thinking Transparencies	Language Transparencies	Writing Transparencies	Speaking and Listening Book
• Drama: Stage Directions TR23	• Visualizing TR4 • Summarizing (Story Map) TR13	• Daily Language SkillBuilder TR16 • Prefixes, Suffixes TR57, TR58	• Locating Information Using Print References TR45	
	• Visualizing TR4	• Daily Language SkillBuilder TR17	• Writing Variables TR2 • Analyzing Word Choice TR15	
• Form in Poetry: Rhyme and Meter TR17		• Daily Language SkillBuilder TR17		
• Setting TR6		• Daily Language SkillBuilder TR18 • Context Clues: Definition and Overview TR53		
• Setting TR6		• Daily Language SkillBuilder TR18 • Word Parts: Roots and Base Words TR56	• Showing, Not Telling TR22 • Comparison and Contrast Essay TR28–29 • Using an Outline TR54	• Conducting Interviews p. 35
	• Note Taking TR46		• Note Taking TR49 • Using an Outline TR54	

ENGLISH LEARNERS / STUDENTS ACQUIRING ENGLISH

The **Spanish Study Guide,** pp. 106–120, includes language support for the following pages:
• Family and Community Involvement (per unit)

• Selection Summaries and Vocabulary
• Active Reading
• Literary Analysis

For **systematic instruction** in language skills, see:
• **Vocabulary and Spelling Book**
• **Grammar, Usage, and Mechanics Book**
• pacing chart on p. 441i

INTEGRATING SKILLS INSTRUCTION PACING CHART

The *Language of Literature* offers several options for integrating language arts instruction and literature.

- Systematic instruction in grammar, vocabulary, and spelling is provided in the *Grammar, Usage, and Mechanics Book* and in the *Vocabulary and Spelling Book.* The pacing chart on the right shows when to use the lessons in these books.
- The Pupil's Edition provides grammar and vocabulary instruction in context. The examples for the grammar feature, *Grammar in Context*, arise from the selections and relate to the grammar focus for each unit. In addition each selection includes vocabulary words called *Words to Know.* Vocabulary practice occurs in *Choices and Challenges* at the end of each selection.
- The Teacher's Edition provides review and reinforcement of the grammar and vocabulary concepts through Explicit Instruction lessons. References to additional support in *Unit Resource Books* and other ancillaries are included at the end of appropriate lessons.

Grammar, Usage and Mechanics
From Grammar, Mechanics, and Usage Book

Chapter 1: Sentence and Its Parts
Chapter 2: Nouns
Chapter 3: Pronouns
Chapter 4: Verbs
Chapter 5: Adjectives and Adverbs

Chapter 6: Prepositions, Conjunctions, and Interjections
- What Is a Preposition?
- Using Prepositional Phrases
- Conjunctions
- Interjections

Chapter 7: Subject-Verb Agreement

For Ongoing Reference
Chapter 8: Capitalization
Chapter 9: Punctuation

Vocabulary
From Vocabulary and Spelling Book

Lesson 1: Context Clues
Lesson 2: Restatement Context Clues
Lesson 3: Contrast ContextClues
Lesson 4: Definition Context Clues
Lesson 5: Comparison Context Clues
Lesson 6: General Context Clues
Lesson 7: Prefixes and Base Words
Lesson 8: Prefixes and Base Words
Lesson 9: Base Words and Suffixes
Lesson 10: Base Words and Suffixes
Lesson 11: Anglo-Saxon Affixes and Base Words
Lesson 12: Roots and Word Families
Lesson 13: Roots and Word Familes
Lesson 14: Analyzing Roots and Affixes
Lesson 15: Analyzing Roots and Affixes
Lesson 16: Foreign Words in English
Lesson 17: Specialized Vocabulary
Lesson 18: Specialized Vocabulary
Lesson 19: Specialized Vocabulary

Lesson 20: Words with Multiple Meanings
Lesson 21: Synonyms
Lesson 22: Antonyms
Lesson 23: Denotation and Connotation
Lesson 24: Using a Thesaurus
Lesson 25: Idioms
Lesson 26: Similes and Metaphors

Lesson 27: Compound Words
Lesson 28: Homonyms
Lesson 29: Homophones and Easily Confused Words
Lesson 30: Homographs
Lesson 31: Analogies
Lesson 32: Using Your Strategies

Spelling
From Vocabulary and Spelling Book

Lesson 1: Silent *e* Words and Suffixes
Lesson 2: The Suffix *ance*
Lesson 3: Plural Words Ending in *o*
Lesson 4: Prefixes and Base Words
Lesson 5: Prefixes and Roots
Lesson 6: Words Ending with *ary*
Lesson 7: Soft and Hard *g*
Lesson 8: Review
Lesson 9: Final *y* words and Suffixes
Lesson 10: The Suffix *able*
Lesson 11: Words Ending with *al + ly*
Lesson 12: The Prefix *com*
Lesson 13: Forms of the Prefix *ad*
Lesson 14: Words Ending with *ory*
Lesson 15: Unstressed Syllables
Lesson 16: Review
Lesson 17: *VAC* Words
Lesson 18: Non-*VAC* Words
Lesson 19: Words Ending with *c + ally*

Lesson 20: The Prefix *ex*
Lesson 21: More Forms of Prefix *ad*
Lesson 22: Base Word Changes
Lesson 23: Words Ending with *cious, cial,* or *cian*
Lesson 24: Review
Lesson 25: Greek Combining Forms
Lesson 26: Compound Words and Contractions

Lesson 27: The Suffix *ible*
Lesson 28: Forms of Prefix *ob + sub*
Lesson 29: Forms of Prefix *in*
Lesson 30: The Suffixes *ence + ent*
Lesson 31: Words Ending with *ize + ise*
Lesson 32: Review

Selection	SkillBuilder Sentences	Suggested Answers
Lob's Girl	**1.** A dog would be a good pet for my brother and I. **2.** Animals can provide protection and love for we.	**1.** A dog would be a good pet for my brother and **me.** **2.** Animals can provide protection and love for **us.**
My First Dive with the Dolphins	**1.** Did you knew that dolphins has distinct personalities? **2.** Researchers have discovers that some dolphins is aggressive, while others are quite playful.	**1.** Did you **know** that dolphins **have** distinct personalities? **2.** Researchers have **discovered** that some dolphins **are** aggressive, while others are quite playful.
Something Told the Wild Geese Questioning Faces	**1.** I've always wondered how birds could fly so good. **2.** I wanted to call the veterinarian, because the baby bird didn't sound so well.	**1.** I've always wondered how birds could fly so **well.** **2.** I wanted to call the veterinarian, because the baby bird didn't sound so **good.**
Zlateh the Goat	**1.** The families goat was named Zlateh **2.** The goats production of milk had become very small.	**1.** The **family's** goat was named Zlateh. **2.** The **goat's** production of milk had become very small.

Selection	SkillBuilder Sentences	Suggested Answers
The Phantom Tollbooth	1. Mom's car gets worser gas mileage than Milo's toy car.	1. Mom's car gets **worse** gas mileage than Milo's toy car.
	2. "The Phantom Tollbooth" is the excitingest and goodest play that I have ever read.	2. "The Phantom Tollbooth" is the **most exciting** and **best** play that I have ever read.
The Walrus and the Carpenter Fairy Lullaby	1. Isn't it funny that the Walrus and the Carpenter wants seven maids with seven mops to sweep away the sand?	1. Isn't it funny that the Walrus and the Carpenter **want** seven maids with seven mops to sweep away the sand?
	2. Do you and your friends like to read poetry that are silly and nonsensical?	2. Do you and your friends like to read poetry that **is** silly and nonsensical?
Three Limericks	1. Even though limericks are silly, them must conform to a definite rhyme scheme.	1. Even though limericks are silly, **they** must conform to a definite rhyme scheme.
	2. Shakespeare wrote poems, but he is best known for him plays.	2. Shakespeare wrote poems, but he is best known for **his** plays.
The Fun They Had	1. We will all be living in the future very soonly.	1. We will all be living in the future very **soon**.
	2. Computers can process information quite rapid.	2. Computers can process information quite **rapidly**.
The Sand Castle	1. "I think it would be great fun to have a computer for a teacher laughed Samuel.	1. "I think it would be great fun to have a computer for a teacher," laughed Samuel.
	2. Some day, said Marianne I'd like to build a time travel machine.	2. "Some day," said Marianne, "I'd like to build a time travel machine."

OVERVIEW

Students explore imaginative worlds and characters by working in small groups to produce and perform original skits for an audience.

Project at a glance Many of the selections in Unit Four focus on fantastic worlds and characters (especially Part 2, Imaginary Worlds). For this project, students will write and act in skits that are set in a futuristic or fantastic world. Skits may be humorous or serious. All skits will be performed in front of a live audience and should be complete with costumes, scenery, and props (insofar as they are practical). This project might be coordinated with a schoolwide Talent Show, or the skits might be scheduled for a time when families can be invited to watch.

SCHEDULING

Skits should take no more than 15 minutes each. You may want to schedule the skits over the course of this unit, or at the end of this unit, depending on your purposes.

PROJECT OBJECTIVES

• To demonstrate the speaking and listening skills introduced in the activity
• To explore the theme of imagination through characters in a dramatic script
• To plan, prepare, and present an original skit
• To develop listening and viewing skills by watching and evaluating the performance of others

SUGGESTED GROUP SIZE

4–6 students per group

▷ Dramatization

Getting Started

Explain that students will be working in groups to plan, write, and act out skits that are set in futuristic or fantastic worlds. You might ask students to make a list of TV shows that deal with science fiction or fantastic characters, worlds, or details.

Use the resources in your school. Invite your school's drama teacher or a volunteer from a local theater group to a few rehearsals. If students will be painting props, make arrangements for materials with your school's art teacher. Also consider borrowing musical instruments from your music department.

If your school has an auditorium, schedule time for each group to hold at least one dress rehearsal. If the skits are to take place in the classroom, arrange for side screens or curtains where students can go "off-stage" during performances.

This project lends itself to everything from a classroom to a schoolwide performance. You may even want to schedule an evening show and sell tickets to give students experience in advertising, sales, and management.

Writing Workshop Connection

As a springboard, students may use the Writing Workshop assignment **Short Story**, p. 592, which they will complete in Part 2 of this unit.

Directing the Project

Preparing (1 class period) Discuss all that is needed in a theatrical production. Remind students that skits should follow the general format of exposition, conflict, and resolution.

▶ Divide students into groups. Each group should brainstorm ideas about the focus of their skit. You may want to have them create main characters who must solve a problem. When they have developed an idea, individual assignments can be made. Encourage everyone to contribute to the writing and acting, as well as to the behind-the-scenes duties. Entrances, exits, and other movements should be indicated in the scripts.

Assigning Roles In addition to individual character roles, you may want to choose a director, stage manager, acting coach, costume designer, and prop person (or people).

▶ After students have done the preliminary planning, they should submit a list and description of characters, and a plot summary. Meet with each group to discuss the scenario before students begin writing. Attend two or more rehearsals for the skit to offer advice and note progress.

▶ You should also work with students to create a set of guidelines for evaluation (i.e.

What Makes a Good Skit) to be filled out after the final performances.

Practicing (1 class period) Have each group read their parts aloud several times to make sure they understand the words and events of the plot. Then stage a walk-through, in which they perform their movements, gestures, and facial expressions as they say their lines. Students should do a final rehearsal using the actual props, lighting, and so on.

▶ Tell students that giving and receiving feedback during the rehearsal stage is crucial. Refer to the tips in the Feedback Center.

Presenting (2–3 class periods) This project could culminate in a Talent Show for the entire student body or just for your class.

▶ To begin, have students take a few deep breaths. Make sure props are in place and that there is adequate seating.

▶ **EVALUATION** Have student audience members complete a brief evaluation after each performance, as well as complete evaluations of their own performances. These should be turned in to you at the end of each performance and can be used for later discussion.

Teaching the Speaking and Listening Skills

The student is expected to:

Analyze the use of aesthetic language for its effects
Teaching Suggestions: Discuss with students how language can be used to create certain effects on an audience. Explain how certain words, phrasings, and rhyme patterns are pleasing to the ear, while others create a sense of disharmony. Also discuss how metaphors, similes, and other forms of figurative language can create pictures in an audience's mind. Have students incorporate these elements into their scripts. For more information, have students turn to the Speaking and Listening Handbook, pages R98–99.

Generate criteria to evaluate presentations of others and generate criteria to evaluate his/her own presentations
Teaching Suggestions: Tell students that before they perform their skits, they must develop a set of guidelines to evaluate their own as well as others' performances. Ask for suggestions about what makes an effective skit—in particular, notes about voice, delivery, pacing, and so on. From this discussion, you can create worksheets for students to use during the final performances. It will also be helpful to have students rate their own performances according to these guidelines.

Compare perceptions with perceptions of others
Teaching Suggestions: After each group has presented and has been evaluated by the class, have students compare their self-evaluations with the evaluations given by others. To do this, you might want to set a list of standards for discussion and explain what is meant by "constructive criticism." This might work best if you act as moderator.

Feedback Center

Students can use the following guidelines when giving and receiving feedback during this project:

Giving Feedback

▶ Provide feedback about the story idea (Does the story make sense?).

▶ Question the characters' tone and motivation (Are they appropriate to the subject?).

▶ Comment on the verbal and nonverbal delivery (pitch, pace, volume, gestures, body language) and its impact on the listener.

Receiving Feedback

▶ Listen to constructive criticism with an open mind.

▶ Use audience feedback and modify the presentation to clarify meaning or organization.

Assessing the Project

The following rubric can be used for group or individual assessment.

3 Full Accomplishment
The group followed directions and produced a creative and engaging skit set in a futuristic or fantastic world. Group used aesthetic language effectively in their skit. Students evaluated their own performance as well as the performance of others and demonstrated thoughtful reflection on strengths and weaknesses. Students demonstrated all three of the Speaking and Listening Skills listed.

2 Substantial Accomplishment
Students produced a skit, but the script was incomplete. It showed some use of futuristic or fantastic elements and some use of aesthetic language. Two out of the three Speaking and Listening Skills were demonstrated.

1 Little Accomplishment
Students' script and skit were incomplete or did not fulfill the requirements of the assignment. Students did not work effectively in a group and demonstrated only one of the Speaking and Listening Skills.

PART 1
Animal
Wonders

Meeting Standards

The Literature You'll Read

The Concepts You'll Study

Vocabulary and Reading Comprehension
Vocabulary Focus: Learning and Remembering
   New Words
Cause and Effect
Making Generalizations
Word Choice
Story Mapping

Writing and Language Conventions
Communication Workshop: Process Description
Using Prepositional Phrases as Transitions
Combining Sentences by Joining Phrases
Appositives and Appositive Phrases

Literary Analysis
Literary Focus: Plot
Foreshadowing
Essay
Sound Devices
Climax and Resolution

Speaking and Listening
Oral Book Review
Opinion Presentation
Multimedia Presentation
Storytelling

442

Plot

> *I have a notebook for plots. . . . If I get the germ of an idea, I scribble it in the notebook. . . . Perhaps after three years, perhaps after seven, there comes a time when I look at it and I see that it is ripe for writing.*
>
> —*Roald Dahl, writer*

Plots are found in all types of stories—fiction, drama, biography, even narrative poetry. The **plot** of a story is the series of events that take place in the story. Most of these events are closely connected to the story's **conflict,** or the problem that the characters face.

The plot usually takes place in four stages, or sections. In the **exposition,** or the beginning stage of a plot, the conflict, characters, and setting are introduced. During the **rising action,** suspense builds as the conflict becomes more complicated for the characters. The story events move toward a **climax,** which is the turning point in the story. Finally, the climax leads to the **falling action** (sometimes called *resolution*), in which loose ends are tied up.

PLOT AT A GLANCE

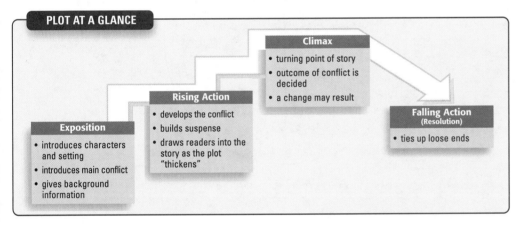

Exposition
- introduces characters and setting
- introduces main conflict
- gives background information

Rising Action
- develops the conflict
- builds suspense
- draws readers into the story as the plot "thickens"

Climax
- turning point of story
- outcome of conflict is decided
- a change may result

Falling Action (Resolution)
- ties up loose ends

OVERVIEW

Standards-Based Objectives
- understand and identify the following literary terms:
  plot
  exposition
  rising action
  climax
  falling action
  resolution
  story structure
  conflict
  sequence of events
  external conflict
  internal conflict
  change
- recognize and analyze story plot, setting, and problem resolution
- analyze characters, including their traits, conflicts, and the changes they undergo

 Use **Literary Analysis Transparencies,** p. 5, for additional support.

Teaching the Lesson

This lesson helps students become more familiar with terms related to plot and shows students how to identify the typical stages in a plot. It also helps students understand the importance of sequence of events, shows them how to recognize how a character changes through a story's plot, and describes the influence of setting on conflict.

Introducing the Concepts
Review with students what they already know about plot. Then have students think of a film they have recently seen or a book they have recently read. Ask them to identify the central conflict of the work, its climax, and the falling action or resolution of the conflict. Using the chart on this page as a model, ask volunteers to chart their responses on the board.

Presenting the Concepts
Sequence of Events

Divide students into small groups. Have each group think of a cause-effect relationship that they could center a story or essay around. Ask them to discuss the possible sequence of events and details surrounding this relationship. Some ideas for a cause-effect relationship might be missing the bus to school, forgetting lunch money, or not doing homework. Have each group share their responses with the class.

Foreshadowing Ask students to think of a movie they have seen that uses the technique of foreshadowing. Then have them think about and discuss the role that foreshadowing played in the movie. What effect did the foreshadowing have on the audience?

YOUR TURN
Answer: Robert fools with his beard during rehearsal.

Sequence of Events

A story moves from beginning to end through a series of events. The order in which these events are presented is called the **sequence of events.** Story events are often presented in the order in which they happen. The story makes sense because the reader can see how one event leads to the next. In addition, the events often have a **cause-and-effect** relationship. The event that happens first is the cause, and the one that follows is the effect.

Sometimes writers interrupt the sequence of events to give clues about what will happen later in the story. This is called **foreshadowing.** The writer may give clues through character dialogue or through descriptions of setting or a character's behavior.

From "The School Play"

YOUR TURN Look at the story wheel below for one scene in "The School Play" by Gary Soto. What event causes Mrs. Bunnin to scold Robert?

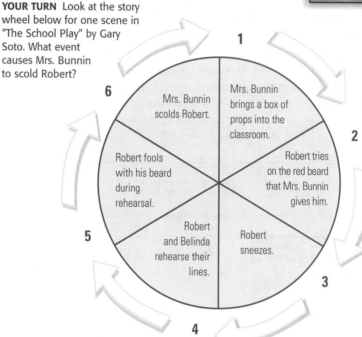

1. Mrs. Bunnin brings a box of props into the classroom.
2. Robert tries on the red beard that Mrs. Bunnin gives him.
3. Robert sneezes.
4. Robert and Belinda rehearse their lines.
5. Robert fools with his beard during rehearsal.
6. Mrs. Bunnin scolds Robert.

444   UNIT FOUR   PART 1: ANIMAL WONDERS

Conflict

Conflict is a struggle or clash between opposing forces. Nearly every story revolves around one main conflict. A conflict may involve something the main character wants and cannot get, or it might center on a problem the main character is trying to solve. Conflict may be **external**—a struggle between a character and an outside force, such as nature or another character. Conflict may also be **internal**—a struggle between opposing desires within a character.

The **setting** of a story is often important to the conflict. For example, if a story is set in a farming community that has had a poor harvest, the main character may have to deal with financial difficulties. As a result of these difficulties, the character may struggle with a difficult decision: he or she may have to sell something valuable or give up a dream in order to have enough money to survive.

Characters also can influence the conflict in a story.

YOUR TURN In the above excerpt, what does Pythias want? What is standing in his way?

CONFLICT

Pythias. I'm worried about what will happen to my mother and my sister when I'm gone.
Damon. I'll take care of them, Pythias, as if they were my own mother and sister.
Pythias. Thank you, Damon. I have money to leave them. But there are other things I must arrange. If only I could go to see them before I die! But they live two days' journey from here, you know.

—Fan Kissen, *Damon and Pythias*

Change

By the end of a story, often a character or a character's situation has changed as a result of an experience. You can learn about the author's perspective and purpose for writing by looking at the **change** that has taken place in a story and determining what events caused the change.

YOUR TURN In this excerpt, how did Helen Keller change? What do you think caused this change?

CHANGE

I left the well-house eager to learn. Everything had a name, and each name gave birth to a new thought. As we returned to the house every object which I touched seemed to quiver with life. That was because I saw everything with the strange, new sight that had come to me. On entering the door I remembered the doll I had broken. I felt my way to the hearth and picked up the pieces. I tried vainly to put them together. Then my eyes filled with tears; for I realized what I had done, and for the first time I felt repentance and sorrow.

—Helen Keller,
The Story of My Life

Conflict
Ask students to discuss examples of internal and external conflicts that story characters might face.

Setting Explain that setting often influences the way conflicts develop because the time and place in which a story takes place may provide hardships that characters must face. A war-torn country, a community in the middle of a drought, and a dangerous road are all details of setting that can influence conflicts or problems. Setting can also influence how conflicts or problems are resolved.

YOUR TURN
Possible Response: Pythias wants to see his mother and sister before he dies, but they live too far away.

Change
Have students think about stories they have read as a class and decide what kinds of changes any of the main characters underwent. Ask them to discuss what they think caused the changes in these characters. Can they determine the author's purpose from the changes the characters experienced? If so, what is it?

YOUR TURN
Possible Response: Helen Keller suddenly realized that things had names and she wanted to learn and understand. She experienced remorse and sorrow for the first time when she realized what she had done to the doll. This change was possibly caused by her new ability to communicate and understand language.

OVERVIEW

Standards-Based Objectives
- develop effective strategies for recognizing cause and effect.
- use the text's structure or progression of ideas such as cause and effect to locate and recall information.
- analyze ways authors organize and present ideas such as through cause and effect.

Teaching the Lesson

The strategies on this page will help students recognize and understand cause and effect in the literature they read.

Presenting the Strategies
Explain to students that the strategies on this page will help them use cause and effect as a way of understanding the events of a story or a work of nonfiction.

SIGNAL WORDS
Help students brainstorm a list of signal words that often indicate a cause and effect relationship: *because, since, therefore, in order that, if/then, so/that,* and *as a result.*

CLARIFY AND QUESTION
Remind students to reread any parts of a selection that are unclear and to ask questions about the sequence of events and about which events were the cause of others.

CONNECT
As a class, discuss cause-effect relationships that happen in daily life.

Use **Reading and Critical Thinking Transparencies,** p. 1, for additional support.

Recognizing Cause and Effect

If you have ever walked into a dark room and turned on a lamp, then you understand cause and effect. Your turning on the lamp caused the room to become bright. The brightness in the room is the effect. The same can be true of events in a story. When something happens that leads to something else, the events are said to be related as cause and effect.

How to Apply the Skill

To **recognize cause and effect,** an active reader will

- Identify signal words that indicate cause and effect, such as *because, therefore, since,* and *so*
- **Clarify** the action by making a cause-effect chart
- **Question** what happened and why
- **Connect** the reading with personal experiences

Try It Now!

Read the excerpt below. Look for cause and effect.

> Jean Pengelly said, "Sandy, your Aunt Rebecca says she's lonesome because Uncle Will Hoskins has gone out trawling, and she wants one of you to go and spend the evening with her. You go, dear; you can take your homework with you."
>
> —Joan Aiken, "Lob's Girl"

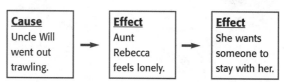

Cause	**Effect**	**Effect**
Uncle Will went out trawling. →	Aunt Rebecca feels lonely. →	She wants someone to stay with her.

Here's how Orlando uses the skill:

*"Looking for **cause-and-effect** relationships helps me to understand what I'm reading. As I read 'Lob's Girl,' I made a cause-effect chart to **clarify** the plot."*

446   UNIT FOUR   PART 1: ANIMAL WONDERS

Lob's Girl

by JOAN AIKEN

This selection is included in the **Grade 6 InterActive Reader.**

Connect to Your Life

Creature Features Have you ever witnessed a pet helping its owner in an extraordinary way? Describe what happened.

Build Background

GEOGRAPHY

The setting of this story is Cornwall, England. Cornwall is a peninsula, bordered by the Atlantic Ocean and the English Channel. The coast of Cornwall is made up of rocky cliffs.

Several of the characters in "Lob's Girl" come from Liverpool, a large city on England's western coast, about 400 miles north of Cornwall.

Focus Your Reading

LITERARY ANALYSIS **FORESHADOWING**

A technique that writers use to hint at future events in a story is called **foreshadowing.** Writers use descriptions of setting, characters, and events to foreshadow future outcomes and to build suspense.

For example, the narrator in "Lob's Girl" describes a "steep, twisting hillroad." This part of the setting will be important to events later in the story. As you read, note words and phrases used to foreshadow events.

ACTIVE READING **CAUSE AND EFFECT**

When one event brings about another, they are said to have a **cause-and-effect** relationship. The event that happens first is the cause. The event that results from the cause is called the effect. One event may cause many things to happen. Some stories have a chain of causes and effects, in which one event causes another, which in turn causes another, and so on.

READER'S NOTEBOOK As you read "Lob's Girl," list cause-and-effect events in a chart like the one shown. Be on the lookout for events that cause more than one effect and for effects that cause other effects.

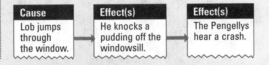

Cause	Effect(s)	Effect(s)
Lob jumps through the window.	He knocks a pudding off the windowsill.	The Pengellys hear a crash.

Standards-Based Objectives

1. understand and appreciate a **short story**
2. understand the author's use of **foreshadowing**
3. understand the use of **mood**
4. recognize **cause and effect** to help understand **foreshadowing**
5. analyze the **influence of setting** on the problem and its resolution

Summary

Sandy is a five-year-old girl living in Cornwall, England, when she first meets the German shepherd, Lob. He soon adopts her and becomes the family pet. When Sandy is a teenager, she is struck by a speeding truck and seriously injured. The doctors are unable to help her and she lies in a coma with not much hope in sight. One day as Sandy's grandmother comes to visit, she sees Lob waiting outside the hospital, and she persuades the hospital staff to let her bring Lob in to see Sandy. Sandy responds to Lob and wakes long enough to rub his head and whisper his name. As Lob runs from the room, Sandy's shocked parents tell the grandmother that Lob had been killed in the accident that injured Sandy.

Thematic Link

Lob stands by Sandy—to the end and perhaps beyond. The author invents a wondrous world in which some events defy explanation.

English Conventions Practice

Daily Language SkillBuilder

Have students **proofread** the display sentences on page 441k and write them correctly. The sentences also appear on Transparency 14 of **Language Transparencies.**

Preteaching Vocabulary

If you would like to preteach the WORDS TO KNOW for this selection, use the Explicit Instruction, page 449.

WORDS TO KNOW **Vocabulary Preview**

agitate	atone	conceal	inquire	rivet
assured	coma	draft	melancholy	transfusion

LESSON RESOURCES

UNIT FOUR RESOURCE BOOK, pp. 4–10

ASSESSMENT
Formal Assessment, pp. 79–80
Test Generator

SKILLS TRANSPARENCIES AND COPYMASTERS
Literary Analysis
• Foreshadowing, TR 28 (pp. 450, 459)
Reading and Critical Thinking
• Cause and Effect, TR 5 (pp. 450, 459)

Language
• Daily Language SkillBuilder, TR 14 (p. 447)
• Context Clues: Definition and Overview, TR 53 (p. 449)

Writing
• Writing Variables, TR 2 (p. 460)
• Transitional Words and Phrases, TR 9 (p. 461)

Speaking and Listening
• Creating a Persuasive Presentation, p. 29 (p. 460)
• Guidelines: How to Analyze a Persuasive Presentation, p. 30 (p. 460)

INTEGRATED TECHNOLOGY
Audio Library

Visit our Web site:
www.mcdougallittell.com

For **systematic instruction** in language skills, see:
• **Vocabulary and Spelling Book**
• **Grammar, Usage, and Mechanics Book**
• pacing chart on p. 441i.

Reading and Analyzing

Literary Analysis FORESHADOWING

Remind students that a hint about an event that will occur later in a story is called foreshadowing. As students read, tell them to look for descriptive words or phrases that the author uses to foreshadow events.

 Use **Unit Four Resource Book**, p. 6, for more practice.

Active Reading CAUSE AND EFFECT

Remind students that when one event brings about another, the events are said to have a cause and effect relationship. Ask students to name the events that are related as cause and effect on page 449. Help them to fill in the chart they began on page 447. Tell students to continue filling in the cause and effect graphic organizer, as they read.

Possible Response: Sandy was named Alexandra *because* she looked like the picture of a queen named Alexandra that hung in her grandmother's kitchen.

 Use **Unit Four Resource Book**, p. 5, for more practice.

Reading Skills and Strategies: PREDICT

Ask students to think ahead to what might happen in the story, and to predict future story events. Remind them to use the information the author has given them along with their own knowledge and experience.

Possible Responses: The story will be about Lob and Sandy because Lob chose Sandy. Lob might have to rescue Sandy from the water because this story takes place near a beach.

EXPLICIT INSTRUCTION **Viewing and Representing**

Maggie
by Judith S. Rubin

ART APPRECIATION This watercolor painting of a German shepherd was done by the artist in 1991.

Instruction Ask students to study the portrait of the dog, noticing the details, which are somewhat blurred by the loose, light strokes of the brush. What kind of animal do they think this dog is—that is, what are his or her traits? How would it make them feel to have a dog like this? *(This dog looks strong and protective, but he/she might also have a soft, loving side. The dog has a kind face. Having a dog like this might make students feel protected and loved.)*

Practice Have students read the description of Lob on page 450. Ask them if this painting is similar to the way they visualized Lob.

Possible Response: Yes, this dog looks the way Lob is described in the story.

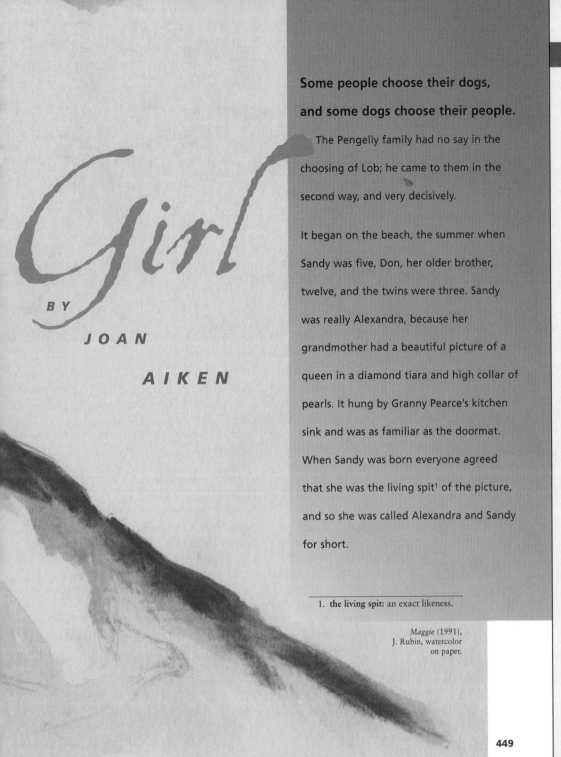

Girl
BY
JOAN AIKEN

Some people choose their dogs,

and some dogs choose their people.

The Pengelly family had no say in the choosing of Lob; he came to them in the second way, and very decisively.

It began on the beach, the summer when Sandy was five, Don, her older brother, twelve, and the twins were three. Sandy was really Alexandra, because her grandmother had a beautiful picture of a queen in a diamond tiara and high collar of pearls. It hung by Granny Pearce's kitchen sink and was as familiar as the doormat. When Sandy was born everyone agreed that she was the living spit[1] of the picture, and so she was called Alexandra and Sandy for short.

---
1. the living spit: an exact likeness.

Maggie (1991),
J. Rubin, watercolor
on paper.

449

Differentiating Instruction

Less Proficient Readers
To help students understand the characters in this story, ask the students whom they have met so far. *(They've met the Pengelly family—Sandy, Don, and the twins; Sandy's Grandmother Pearce; and the dog Lob.)*

Set a Purpose Ask students to read on to find out how Lob affects the lives of the Pengelly family.

English Learners
As students read this story, they will encounter examples of British English, such as "the living spit," "Christmas puddings," and so on. Help them relate these terms and expressions to the American English they are learning.

Use **Spanish Study Guide,** pp. 94–96, for additional support.

Advanced Students
Ask students to discuss how they were named and if their names hold any special meanings. Ask them to think about how that name or meaning has influenced them so far. Have them consider the reason for Sandy's name, and to speculate what effect it might have in this story.

EXPLICIT INSTRUCTION Preteaching Vocabulary

WORDS TO KNOW
Remind students that when they are reading and they come across words they don't know, they can often find clues in the rest of the sentence or paragraph to help explain the meaning of the unfamiliar word. This is called **using context clues.**

Teaching Strategy Ask students to locate the word *tiara* on page 449. Ask them if they can tell what *tiara* means from the context. They

should be able to use the clues "queen" and "diamond" to help them figure out that a tiara is a kind of crown. Explain that not all clues are words. For example, the fact that the word *inquired* is preceded by a question mark on page 451 is a clue to its meaning.

Practice Ask students to preview the selection, looking for the WORDS TO KNOW. Instruct students to cover the definitions provided at the bottom of each page and try to

determine the meaning of the words from their contexts. Have them list the context clues they used.

Use **Unit Four Resource Book,** p. 9, for more practice.

For **systematic instruction** in vocabulary, see:
• **Vocabulary and Spelling Book**
• pacing chart on p. 441i.

Literary Analysis: SETTING

(A) The author uses vivid descriptions of people and places in this section. Ask students to describe the setting.

Possible Response: It is a quiet, warm, summer day. The twins are playing in the seaweed, Father and Don are working on the fishing boat, Mother is making Christmas puddings, and Sandy is lying in the sand.

ACTIVE READER

(B) QUESTION It is the gray-haired man's dog.

Reading Skills and Strategies: VISUALIZE

(C) Ask students to describe the mental image they created as they read about Lob finding Sandy lying on the beach.

Literary Analysis FORESHADOWING

(D) Ask students whether this comment might foreshadow events yet to come. Have them discuss what might happen.

Possible Response: Lob might come to live with Pengellys permanently, so they could play with him every day.

Use **Literary Analysis Transparencies,** p. 28, for additional support.

Active Reading CAUSE AND EFFECT

Remind students to look for cause-and-effect relationships as they read. Ask them to share and record any relationships they found on these pages.

Possible Responses: Lob and his owner live far away from the Pengelly family. As a result, the Pengelly children won't be able to play with Lob in the future.

Use **Reading and Critical Thinking Transparencies,** p. 5, for additional support.

(A) *O*n this summer day she was lying peacefully reading a comic and not keeping an eye on the twins, who didn't need it because they were occupied in seeing which of them could wrap the most seaweed around the other one's legs. Father—Bert Pengelly—and Don were up on the Hard[2] painting the bottom boards of the boat in which Father went fishing for pilchards.[3] And Mother—Jean Pengelly—was getting ahead with making the Christmas puddings because she never felt easy in her mind if they weren't made and safely put away by the end of August. As usual, each member of the family was happily getting on with his or her own affairs. Little did they guess how soon **[1]** this state of things would be changed by the large new member who was going to erupt into their midst.

(C) Sandy rolled onto her back to make sure that the twins were not climbing on slippery rocks or getting cut off by the tide. At the same moment a large body struck her forcibly in the midriff, and she was covered by flying sand. Instinctively she shut her eyes and felt the sand being wiped off her face by something that seemed like a warm, rough, damp flannel. She opened her eyes and looked. It was a tongue. Its owner was a large and bouncy young Alsatian, or German

Breakers at Flood Tide (1909), Frederick Judd Waugh, 35" × 40", The Butler Institute of American Art, Youngstown, Ohio.

shepherd, with topaz eyes, black-tipped prick ears, a thick, soft coat, and a bushy, black-tipped tail.

"Lob!" shouted a man farther up the beach. "Lob, come here!"

But Lob, as if trying to <u>atone</u> for the surprise he had given her, went on licking the sand off Sandy's face, wagging his tail so hard while he kept on knocking up more clouds of sand. His owner, a gray-haired man with a limp, walked over as quickly as he could and seized him by the collar.

"I hope he didn't give you a fright?" the man said to Sandy. "He meant it in play—he's only young."

"Oh, no, I think he's *beautiful*," said Sandy truly. She picked up a bit of driftwood and

(B) **ACTIVE READER**

QUESTION Whose dog is this?

---

2. **Hard:** *British,* a landing place for boats.
3. **pilchards:** small fish, similar to sardines.

WORDS TO KNOW   **atone** (ə-tōn′) *v.* to make amends

450

EXPLICIT INSTRUCTION **Details of Setting**

Instruction Remind students that the setting of a story is the time and place of the action. Explain that sometimes writers give details about a setting early in a story to show readers the importance of the setting to the events that will take place. Ask students what details of setting they noticed on pages 449–451. Then explain that information about setting can include specific factors, such as architecture, weather, transportation, type of landscape (mountains, desert, ocean; hilly, flat), and dis-

tance from other places. Ask students if they learn about any setting details related to distance or landscape. (*Distance—Liverpool is far from Cornwall. Landscape—A narrow and steep road leads into the village. There is a sign warning drivers about the danger of this road.*)

Practice Have students reread pages 449–451 to find and record details about setting.

Possible Responses: summer day; on the beach; fishing village in Cornwall, England; palm trees; rocks; cliffs; beaches and a harbor; white-

washed stone houses; the village is far away from Liverpool; a steep road leads into the village.

Use **Unit Four Resource Book,** p. 7, for more practice.

450   UNIT FOUR   PART 1

threw it. Lob, whisking easily out of his master's grip, was after it like a sand-colored bullet. He came back with the stick, beaming, and gave it to Sandy. At the same time he gave himself, though no one else was aware of this at the time. But with Sandy, too, it was love at first sight, and when, after a lot more stick-throwing, she and the twins joined Father and Don to go home for tea, they cast many a backward glance at Lob being led firmly away by his master.

"I wish we could play with him every day," Tess sighed.

"Why can't we?" said Tim.

Sandy explained. "Because Mr. Dodsworth, who owns him, is from Liverpool, and he is only staying at the Fisherman's Arms till Saturday."

"Is Liverpool a long way off?"

"Right at the other end of England from Cornwall, I'm afraid."

It was a Cornish fishing village where the Pengelly family lived, with rocks and cliffs and a strip of beach and a little round harbor, and palm trees growing in the gardens of the little whitewashed stone houses. The village was approached by a narrow, steep, twisting hillroad and guarded by a notice that said LOW GEAR FOR 1½ MILES, DANGEROUS TO CYCLISTS.

The Pengelly children went home to scones with Cornish cream and jam, thinking they had seen the last of Lob. But they were much mistaken. The whole family was playing cards by the fire in the front room after supper when there was a loud thump and a crash of china in the kitchen.

"My Christmas puddings!" exclaimed Jean, and ran out.

"Did you put TNT[4] in them, then?" her husband said.

But it was Lob, who, finding the front door shut, had gone around to the back and bounced in through the open kitchen window, where the puddings were cooling on the sill.

"I hope he didn't give you a fright?"

Luckily only the smallest was knocked down and broken.

Lob stood on his hind legs and plastered Sandy's face with licks. Then he did the same for the twins, who shrieked with joy.

"Where does this friend of yours come from?" inquired Mr. Pengelly.

"He's staying at the Fisherman's Arms—I mean his owner is."

"Then he must go back there. Find a bit of string, Sandy, to tie to his collar."

"I wonder how he found his way here," Mrs. Pengelly said, when the reluctant Lob had been led whining away and Sandy had explained about their afternoon's game on the beach. "Fisherman's Arms is right round the other side of the harbor."

Lob's owner scolded him and thanked Mr. Pengelly for bringing him back. Jean Pengelly warned the children that they had better not encourage Lob any more if they met him on the beach, or it would only lead to more trouble. So they dutifully took no notice of him the next day until he spoiled their good resolutions by dashing up to them with joyful barks, wagging his tail so hard that he winded Tess and knocked Tim's legs from under him.

---

4. TNT: trinitrotoluene, a powerful explosive.

WORDS TO KNOW **inquire** (ĭn-kwīr') v. to question; ask

451

ACTIVE READER

A **CAUSE AND EFFECT** It makes Sandy feel sad.

Active Reading **CAUSE AND EFFECT**

B Ask students what caused Lob's feet to be worn, dusty, tarry, and cut. Ask them if this effect caused any other events.

Possible Response: Lob's feet are injured *because* he walked all the way from Liverpool to Cornwall—about 400 miles! His injuries cause Sandy and her mother to clean him up and to contact Lob's owner.

Literary Analysis: MOOD

A mood is a feeling that a literary work conveys to readers. Writers carefully choose words and phrases to create moods such as sadness, excitement, and anger. Sometimes writers create several moods in the same story to help readers experience many emotions. Ask students to talk about the various moods in this story and to give examples of what creates each mood.

Possible Response: The author creates a sad mood when Sandy watches Lob leave on the train. Words such as "drooping ears and tail," and "melancholy wail" help create that mood.

They had a happy day, playing on the sand.

The next day was Saturday. Sandy had found out that Mr. Dodsworth was to catch the half-past-nine train. She went out secretly, down to the station, nodded to Mr. Hoskins, the stationmaster, who wouldn't dream of charging any local for a platform ticket, and climbed up on the footbridge that led over the tracks. She didn't want to be seen, but she did want to see. She saw Mr. Dodsworth get on

A **ACTIVE READER**

CAUSE AND EFFECT How does seeing Lob make Sandy feel?

the train, accompanied by an unhappy-looking Lob with drooping ears and tail. Then she saw the train slide away out of sight around the next headland, with a <u>melancholy</u> wail that sounded like Lob's last good-bye.

Sandy wished she hadn't had the idea of coming to the station. She walked home miserably, with her shoulders hunched and her hands in her pockets. For the rest of the day, she was so cross and unlike herself that Tess and Tim were quite surprised, and her mother gave her a dose of senna.[5]

1 A week passed. Then, one evening, Mrs. Pengelly and the younger children were in the front room playing snakes and ladders. Mr. Pengelly and Don had gone fishing on the evening tide. If your father is a fisherman, he will never be home at the same time from one week to the next.

Suddenly, history repeating itself, there was a crash from the kitchen. Jean Pengelly leaped up, crying, "My blackberry jelly!" She and the children had spent the morning picking and the afternoon boiling fruit.

But Sandy was ahead of her mother. With flushed cheeks and eyes like stars she had darted into the kitchen, where she and Lob were hugging one another in a frenzy of joy. About a yard of his tongue was out, and he was licking every part of her that he could reach.

"Good heavens!" exclaimed Jean. "How in the world did *he* get here?"

"He must have walked," said Sandy. "Look at his feet."

They were worn, dusty, and tarry. One had a cut on the pad. **B**

"They ought to be bathed," said Jean Pengelly. "Sandy, run a bowl of warm water while I get the disinfectant."

"What'll we do about him, Mother?" said Sandy anxiously.

Mrs. Pengelly looked at her daughter's pleading eyes and sighed.

"He must go back to his owner, of course," she said, making her voice firm. "Your dad can get the address from the Fisherman's tomorrow, and phone him or send a telegram.

"How in the world did he get here?"

In the meantime he'd better have a long drink and a good meal."

Lob was very grateful for the drink and the meal, and made no objection to having his feet washed. Then he flopped down on the hearth rug and slept in front of the fire they had lit because it was a cold, wet evening, with his head on Sandy's feet. He was a very tired dog. He had walked all the way from Liverpool to

---

5. **senna:** a medicine made from senna leaves.

WORDS
TO   **melancholy** (mĕl'ən-kŏl'ē) *adj.* sad; gloomy
KNOW

452

Instruction Ask students how Sandy and Lob feel as Lob is getting on the train to go back to Liverpool (*very sad*). Ask students to explain how the conflict has changed. (*The conflict is now focused on Lob and Sandy instead of on Lob and the Pengelly children. Lob and Sandy want to be together, but they can't be because they live far away from each other.*) Explain to students that the setting of a story can contribute to the conflict. Remind students that information about setting can include specific factors, such as weather, landscape, and dis-

tance from other places. Review the factor of setting related to distance that students learned about on page 451 (*the great distance between Cornwall and Liverpool*). Then ask students if this setting detail helps bring about the conflict. Discuss students' ideas.

Practice Write these questions on the board: "Is the distance between Cornwall and Liverpool important in the story? How does this factor of setting contribute to the conflict?" Have students work in pairs to write their answers.

Possible Responses: The distance is important in the story. Sandy and Lob love each other from the moment they meet, and they want to be together. Because they live in two places that are far apart from each other, they cannot see each other.

Use **Unit Four Resource Book,** p. 7, for more practice.

Cornwall, which is more than four hundred miles.

The next day Mr. Pengelly phoned Lob's owner, and the following morning Mr. Dodsworth arrived off the night train, decidedly put out, to take his pet home. That parting was worse than the first. Lob whined, Don walked out of the house, the twins burst out crying, and Sandy crept up to her bedroom afterward and lay with her face pressed into the quilt, feeling as if she were bruised all over.

Jean Pengelly took them all into Plymouth to see the circus on the next day and the twins cheered up a little, but even the hour's ride in the train each way and the Liberty horses and performing seals could not cure Sandy's sore heart.

Child in Thought, Francisco Benitez. Courtesy of Chase Gallery, Boston.

She need not have bothered, though. In ten days' time Lob was back—limping this time, with a torn ear and a patch missing out of his furry coat, as if he had met and tangled with an enemy or two in the course of his four-hundred-mile walk.

Bert Pengelly rang up Liverpool again. Mr. Dodsworth, when he answered, sounded weary. He said, "That dog has already cost me two days that I can't spare away from my work—plus endless time in police stations and <u>drafting</u> newspaper advertisements. I'm too old for these ups and downs. I think we'd better face the fact, Mr. Pengelly, that it's your family

he wants to stay with—that is, if you want to have him."

Bert Pengelly gulped. He was not a rich man, and Lob was a pedigreed dog. He said cautiously, "How much would you be asking for him?"

"Good heavens, man, I'm not suggesting I'd *sell* him to you. You must have him as a gift. Think of the train fares I'll be saving. You'll be doing me a good turn."

"Is he a big eater?" Bert asked doubtfully.

By this time the children, breathless in the background listening to one side of

WORDS TO KNOW	**drafting** (drăf'tĭng) *n.* putting into words and writing down; composing **draft** *v.*

453

Differentiating Instruction

Less Proficient Readers

Make sure students understand what is happening with Lob and the Pengelly family by asking the following questions:

- Why does Sandy go to the train station? *(She goes to watch Lob leave for Liverpool with Mr. Dodsworth.)*
- How does Lob get back to Cornwall? *(He walks.)*
- How do the Pengellys get Lob back to Mr. Dodsworth? *(They call Mr. Dodsworth to come and get Lob.)*
- What happens next? *(Lob runs away to Cornwall again. The family contacts Mr. Dodsworth, but he doesn't want to come and get Lob this time.)*

Advanced Students

Ask students to think about whom the painting on this page might represent. What mood does the painting set? Ask students to compare the mood in the story to the mood in the painting. Ask them to discuss why this particular painting may have been included in this story.

Possible Response: The painting may represent Sandy in the story. It shows how sad and gloomy she feels when Lob has to return home to Liverpool. The story has several moods, but the painting seems to capture the sadness the author creates.

English Learners

1 Tell students that *snakes and ladders* is a board game, similar to a U.S. game called Chutes and Ladders.

2 Explain that *rang up* is the British way of saying "called on the phone."

Life in a Fishing Village

Multicultural Link

Life in a fishing village revolves around the sea, and many of the inhabitants make their living from it. Depending on the location, the kind of fish varies, as does the method. People who fish do so with lines, nets, and even spears. Some boats stay out for days, and others set out each morning or evening, depending on the tide. Back on shore, the fish are sold in markets, shipped inland, or canned, frozen, or dried. The people who help maintain the boats, nets, traps, and other equipment have important jobs.

Many fishing villages boast restaurants that spe-cialize in serving up the fresh catch of the day. Some villages attract tourists and artists because of their unspoiled beauty. Tourism has become an important industry in some villages where the fish have become less plentiful, providing a new source of work for the inhabitants. Some formerly "quaint" villages are now overcrowded tourist sites, however.

Fishing is hard, dangerous work, but a love of the sea and the outdoors, coupled with an independent lifestyle, makes it worthwhile.

Ask students to summarize the events leading up to Lob's becoming the Pengelly family pet.

Possible Response: Lob finds Sandy on the beach, and the family plays with him during his visit, but he leaves with his owner on the train for Liverpool. Lob runs away from home to Cornwall, his owner is called, and Lob is returned home. Lob runs away again and comes to Cornwall. Mr. Dodsworth offers to give Lob to the Pengelly family and they accept.

ACTIVE READER

A **EVALUATE** The Pengellys are a loving, close family.

Literary Analysis: RISING AND FALLING ACTION

As a story unfolds, complications usually arise, making the conflict more difficult to resolve. Ask students to tell about the complications so far and to anticipate the action in the rest of the story.

Possible Response: The family meets Lob, then learns he must go away. He comes back and goes away again. Now that he seems to be a permanent part of the family, we can anticipate more events that will lead to the most important event, the climax of the story.

Literary Analysis: CHARACTER TRAITS

Ask students to select one character and write a short description of him or her, sharing their paragraphs with others who have selected the same character.

ACTIVE READER

B **PREDICT** Sandy will probably live, because the story is about her.

---

this conversation, had realized what was in the wind and were dancing up and down with their hands clasped beseechingly.

"Oh, not for his size," Lob's owner <u>assured</u> Bert. "Two or three pounds of meat a day and some vegetables and gravy and biscuits—he does very well on that."

Alexandra's father looked over the telephone at his daughter's swimming eyes and trembling lips. He reached a decision. "Well, then, Mr. Dodsworth," he said briskly, "we'll accept your offer and thank you very much. The children will be overjoyed and you can be sure Lob has come to a good home. They'll look after him and see he gets enough exercise. But I can tell you," he ended firmly, "if he wants to settle in with us, he'll have to learn to eat a lot of fish."

So that was how Lob came to live with the Pengelly family.

> ### ACTIVE READER
> **A** **EVALUATE** What kind of a family are the Pengellys?

Everybody loved him and he loved them all. But there was never any question who came first with him. He was Sandy's dog. He slept by her bed and followed her everywhere he was allowed.

2 Nine years went by, and each summer Mr. Dodsworth came back to stay at the Fisherman's Arms and call on his erstwhile dog. Lob always met him with recognition and dignified pleasure, accompanied him for a walk or two—but showed no signs of wishing **3** to return to Liverpool. His place, he intimated, was definitely with the Pengellys.

In the course of nine years Lob changed less than Sandy. As she went into her teens he became a little slower, a little stiffer, there was

---

a touch of gray on his nose, but he was still a handsome dog. He and Sandy still loved one another devotedly.

In the course of nine years Lob changed less than Sandy.

One evening in October all the summer visitors had left, and the little fishing town looked empty and secretive. It was a wet, windy dusk. When the children came home from school—even the twins were at high school[6] now, and Don was a full-fledged fisherman—Jean Pengelly said, "Sandy, your Aunt Rebecca says she's lonesome because Uncle Will Hoskins has gone out trawling,[7] and she wants one of you to go and spend the evening with her. You go, dear; you can take your homework with you."

Sandy looked far from enthusiastic.

"Can I take Lob with me?"

"You know Aunt Becky doesn't really like dogs—Oh, very well." Mrs. Pengelly sighed. "I suppose she'll have to put up with him as well as you."

Reluctantly Sandy tidied herself, took her schoolbag, put on the damp raincoat she had just taken off, fastened Lob's lead to his collar, and set off to walk through the dusk to Aunt Becky's cottage, which was five minutes' climb up the steep hill.

---

6. **high school:** In Great Britain, students leave elementary school and begin attending high school when they are about 11 years old.

7. **trawling:** fishing with a net pulled behind a boat.

> WORDS
> TO
> KNOW
>
> **assure** (ə-shŏŏr') *v.* to promise or tell positively

Instruction Review the way setting has contributed to the conflict. (*The distance between where Lob lives and where Sandy lives means the two can't see each other.*) Then explain to students that setting can influence not only how conflicts develop but also how they are resolved. Ask what Lob does after he returns to Liverpool. (*He runs away to Cornwall twice.*) Then ask what Mr. Dodsworth does after the second time and how this resolves the conflict. (*He gives Lob to the Pengelly family. Now Lob and Sandy will not be apart.*) Discuss why he does this. (*He tells Mr. Pengelly that he can't*

keep traveling all the way to Cornwall to bring Lob home because it's too far away.) Then ask how this same distance seems to resolve the conflict.

Practice Write these questions on the board: "How does the distance between Cornwall and Liverpool contribute to the resolution of the conflict? How would the story be different if Lob lived in Cornwall, where Sandy lives?" Have students work in pairs to write answers.

Possible Responses: Even though Lob is far away from Cornwall, he is determined to get back to Sandy. Twice he walks from Liverpool to

Cornwall. Each time, Mr. Dodsworth has to come all the way to Cornwall and bring Lob home. Mr. Dodsworth decides that having to travel the distance between Liverpool and Cornwall is too difficult, so he gives the dog to the Pengellys. This resolves the conflict because it means that Lob and Sandy will no longer be apart. If Lob lived in Cornwall, the conflict might not have developed.

 Use **Unit Four Resource Book**, p. 7.

The wind was howling through the shrouds[8] of boats drawn up on the Hard.

"Put some cheerful music on, do," said Jean Pengelly to the nearest twin. "Anything to drown that wretched sound while I make your dad's supper." So Don, who had just come in, put on some rock music, loud. Which was why the Pengellys did not hear the truck hurtle down the hill and crash against the post office wall a few minutes later.

Dr. Travers was driving through Cornwall with his wife, taking a late holiday before patients began coming down with winter colds and flu. He saw the sign that said STEEP HILL. LOW GEAR FOR 1½ MILES. Dutifully he changed into second gear.

"We must be nearly there," said his wife, looking out of her window. "I noticed a sign on the coast road that said the Fisherman's Arms was two miles. What a narrow, dangerous hill! But the cottages are very pretty—Oh, Frank, stop, *stop!* There's a child, I'm sure it's a child—by the wall over there!"

Dr. Travers jammed on his brakes and brought the car to a stop. A little stream ran down by the road in a shallow stone culvert,[9] and half in the water lay something that looked, in the dusk, like a pile of clothes—or was it the body of a child? Mrs. Travers was out of the car in a flash, but her husband was quicker.

"Don't touch her, Emily!" he said sharply. "She's been hit. Can't be more than a few minutes. Remember that truck that overtook us half a mile back, speeding like the devil? Here, quick, go into that cottage and phone for an ambulance. The girl's in a bad way. I'll stay here and do what I can to stop the bleeding. Don't waste a minute."

Doctors are expert at stopping dangerous bleeding, for they know the right places to press. This Dr. Travers was able to do, but he didn't dare do more; the girl was lying in a queerly crumpled heap, and he guessed she had a number of bones broken and that it would be highly dangerous to move her. He watched her with great concentration, wondering where the truck had got to and what other damage it had done.

Mrs. Travers was very quick. She had seen plenty of accident cases and knew the importance of speed. The first cottage she tried had a phone; in four minutes she was back, and in six an ambulance was wailing down the hill.

Its attendants lifted the child onto a stretcher as carefully as if she were made of fine thistledown. The ambulance sped off to Plymouth—for the local cottage hospital did not take serious accident cases—and Dr. Travers went down to the police station to report what he had done.

ACTIVE READER

PREDICT Will Sandy survive? Why or why not?

He found that the police already knew about the speeding truck—which had suffered from loss of brakes and ended up with its radiator halfway through the post-office wall. The driver was concussed[10] and shocked, but the police thought he was the only person injured—until Dr. Travers told his tale.

At half-past nine that night Aunt Rebecca Hoskins was sitting by her fire thinking aggrieved thoughts about the inconsiderateness of nieces who were asked to supper and never turned up, when she was startled by a

---

8. **shrouds:** ropes or cables on a boat's mast.

9. **culvert:** a gutter or tunnel that runs along or under a road.

10. **concussed:** suffering from a concussion, an injury that results from being struck in the head.

Differentiating Instruction

Less Proficient Readers
To ensure that students comprehend the selection, ask them to summarize what happens to Sandy in this section of the story.

Possible Response: Sandy is on her way to her aunt's house when a speeding truck strikes her. Dr. Travers finds her, an ambulance is called, and Sandy is taken to the hospital.

Set a Purpose: Ask students to keep reading to find out what will happen to Sandy and Lob now.

Advanced Students
Ask students to respond to the accident by drawing on their own experiences and to make connections to other texts with similar incidents. Ask them to speculate as a group on how this event may foreshadow the end of the story, and to predict what the end might be.

English Learners
1 Explain to students that *thistledown* is the silky fibers attached to the seeds of a thistle—a kind of prickly weed. Ask students to apply this knowledge by explaining how Sandy was lifted onto the stretcher. (*She was lifted very carefully, as if she might blow away or break easily.*)

You may want to check to see that students know the meanings of the following words:

2 *erstwhile:* in the past, formerly

3 *intimated:* to hint or to make known indirectly

4 *aggrieved:* feeling distress or unease

EXPLICIT INSTRUCTION Making Inferences

Instruction Tell students that an inference is a logical guess based on known facts or evidence. Explain that students make inferences all the time when they read to figure out ideas that are not stated. For example, students make inferences, or logical guesses, about the thoughts and feelings of characters, about causes and effects in a story, and about events in the plot. Continue by explaining that the evidence students use is usually a combination of information from the story along with their own knowledge and experiences.

Practice Write these questions on the board: "What can you infer happened to Lob in the accident? What clues tell you this?" Have students write answers to these questions. Then invite students to share their responses with the class. Remind students that they may receive more information about Lob as they read.

Possible Responses: Lob ran away from the accident and was not hurt because he was not found with Sandy. Or Lob was hurt, but the doctor and his wife only saw Sandy and did not notice Lob.

neighbor, who burst in, exclaiming, "Have you heard about Sandy Pengelly, then, Mrs. Hoskins? Terrible thing, poor little soul, and they don't know if she's likely to live. Police have got the truck driver that hit her—ah, it didn't ought to be allowed, speeding through the place like that at umpty miles an hour, they ought to jail him for life—not that that'd be any comfort to poor Bert and Jean."

Horrified, Aunt Rebecca put on a coat and went down to her brother's house. She found the family with white shocked faces; Bert and Jean were about to drive off to the hospital where Sandy had been taken, and the twins were crying bitterly. Lob was nowhere to be seen. But Aunt Rebecca was not interested in dogs; she did not inquire about him.

"Thank the Lord you've come, Beck," said her brother. "Will you stay the night with Don and the twins? Don's out looking for Lob and heaven knows when we'll be back; we may get a bed with Jean's mother in Plymouth."

"Oh, if only I'd never invited the poor child," wailed Mrs. Hoskins. But Bert and Jean hardly heard her.

That night seemed to last forever. The twins cried themselves to sleep. Don came home very late and grim-faced. Bert and Jean sat in a waiting room of the Western Counties Hospital, but Sandy was unconscious, they were told, and she remained so. All that could be done for her was done. She was given <u>transfusions</u> to replace all the blood she had

Study of a Road Near Rottingdean, Sir Edward Coley Burne-Jones. Courtesy Brighton and Hove Council, The Royal Pavilion Libraries and Museums, Brighton, U.K.

lost. The broken bones were set and put in slings and cradles.

"Is she a healthy girl? Has she a good constitution?"[11] the emergency doctor asked.

"Aye, Doctor, she is that," Bert said hoarsely. The lump in Jean's throat prevented her from answering; she merely nodded.

"Then she ought to have a chance. But I won't <u>conceal</u> from you that her condition is very serious, unless she shows signs of coming out from this <u>coma</u>."

But as hour succeeded hour, Sandy showed no signs of recovering consciousness. Her parents sat in the waiting room with haggard faces; sometimes one of them would go to telephone the family at home, or to try to get a little sleep at the home of Granny Pearce, not far away.

---

11. **constitution:** physical makeup.

WORDS TO KNOW	
transfusion (trăns-fyoo'zhən) *n.* an injection of blood, usually to replace a loss due to bleeding	
conceal (kən-sēl') *v.* to hide	
coma (kō'mə) *n.* a sleeplike state in which a person cannot sense or respond to light, sound, or touch	

At noon next day Dr. and Mrs. Travers went to the Pengelly cottage to inquire how Sandy was doing, but the report was gloomy: "Still in a very serious condition." The twins were miserably unhappy. They forgot that they had sometimes called their elder sister bossy and only remembered how often she had shared her pocket money with them, how she read to them and took them for picnics and helped with their homework. Now there was no Sandy, no Mother and Dad, Don went around with a gray, shuttered face, and worse still, there was no Lob.

The Western Counties Hospital is a large one, with dozens of different departments and five or six connected buildings, each with three or four entrances. By that afternoon it became noticeable that a dog seemed to have taken up position outside the hospital, with the fixed intention of getting in. Patiently he would try first one entrance and then another, all the way around, and then begin again. Sometimes he would get a little way inside, following a visitor, but animals were, of course, forbidden, and he was always kindly but firmly turned out again. Sometimes the guard at the main entrance gave him a pat or offered him a bit of sandwich—he looked so wet and beseeching and desperate. But he never ate the sandwich. No one seemed to own him or to know where he came from; Plymouth is a large city and he might have belonged to anybody.

At tea time Granny Pearce came through the pouring rain to bring a flask of hot tea to her daughter and son-in-law. Just as she reached the main entrance the guard was gently but forcibly shoving out a large, <u>agitated</u>, soaking-wet Alsatian dog.

"No, old fellow, you can *not* come in. Hospitals are for people, not for dogs."

"Why, bless me," exclaimed old Mrs. Pearce. "That's Lob! Here, Lob, Lobby boy!"

Lob ran to her, whining. Mrs. Pearce walked up to the desk.

"I'm sorry, madam, you can't bring that dog in here," the guard said.

Mrs. Pearce was a very determined old lady. She looked the porter in the eye.

"Now, see here, young man. That dog has walked twenty miles from St. Killan to get to my granddaughter. Heaven knows how he knew she was here, but it's plain he knows. And he ought to have his rights! He ought to get to see her! Do you know," she went on, bristling, "that dog has walked the length of England—*twice*—to be with that girl? And you think you can keep him out with your fiddling rules and regulations?"

"I'll have to ask the medical officer," the guard said weakly.

"You do that, young man." Granny Pearce sat down in a determined manner, shutting her umbrella, and Lob sat patiently dripping at her feet. Every now and then he shook his head, as if to dislodge something heavy that was tied around his neck.

That night seemed to last forever.

Presently a tired, thin, intelligent-looking man in a white coat came downstairs, with an impressive, silver-haired man in a dark suit, and there was a low-voiced discussion. Granny Pearce eyed them, biding her time.

"Frankly . . . not much to lose," said the older man. The man in the white coat approached Granny Pearce.

WORDS TO KNOW: **agitated** (ăj′ĭ-tā′tĭd) *adj.* disturbed; upset **agitate** *v.*

Less Proficient Readers
Ask students to explain what they see in the picture on page 456 and how it fits the story. Remind them that they can use illustrations to help them understand what they are reading.
Possible Response: The photograph shows a curvy, hilly road at night, with a small house nearby. It could be the road by Sandy's house or the road where she was walking when she was hit.

English Learners
1 Make sure students understand that the "lump in Jean's throat" does not mean a physical lump. It means that she is so overwhelmed with emotion that she can barely speak.

Advanced Learners
Suggest that students investigate comas. What kinds of events send a person into a coma? What are the physical effects of a coma? How do physicians treat comas? The school library or media center, the Internet, and local medical personnel would all have information about this topic.

Cross Curricular Link Health and Science

HEALTH BENEFITS OF PET OWNERSHIP Owning a pet can bring companionship, pleasure, and protection. But did you know that owning a pet may also be good for your health? Numerous medical studies have been done on the health benefits of pet ownership. Results show that pet owners have significantly lower blood pressure and lower triglycerides than non-pet owners do. In some cases, cholesterol was lowered in new pet owners, and fewer heart problems were reported. Pet owners were found to visit the doctor less often, and reported a significant reduction in minor health problems, such as headaches, backaches, colds and flu, insomnia, and general tiredness. Pet owners also get more exercise than non-owners and seem to experience positive health effects over the long term.

ACTIVE READER

A **CAUSE AND EFFECT** Sandy's condition is so serious that the guard makes an exception.

Literary Analysis: SETTING

As students read the description of Sandy's hospital room, ask them to note the details that the author uses to help the reader visualize the setting. Ask them to identify some of these vivid words.
Possible Response: green-floored corridor; door half-shut; terribly quiet; white-coated man; high, narrow bed; gadgets; very flat; very still.

Active Reading   CAUSE AND EFFECT

B Ask students what causes Sandy to wake from her coma. Remind them to enter this relationship on their chart.
Possible Response: Lob's presence in Sandy's room causes her to wake up, call his name, and touch his head.

Literary Analysis: CLIMAX

Ask students to identify the climax and discuss how they felt when they read the ending. Did the author give them any hints about the twist of events?
Possible Response: The climax is when a dog that looks like Lob visits Sandy in the hospital, helping her to get well.

Literary Analysis   FORESHADOWING

C Now that students know Lob was buried at sea, sunk by a weight on his collar, ask them to think back on details that foreshadowed this ending in the scene where Lob waits at the hospital.
Possible Response: The guard says Lob looked wet; Lob sat dripping at Granny's feet; he shook his head as if trying to dislodge something heavy around his neck.

"It's strictly against every rule, but as it's such a serious case we are making an exception," he said to her quietly. "But only *outside* her bedroom door—and only for a moment or two."

ACTIVE READER

CAUSE AND EFFECT
What caused the guard to allow Lob into the hospital?

Without a word, Granny Pearce rose and stumped upstairs. Lob followed close to her skirts, as if he knew his hope lay with her.

They waited in the green-floored corridor outside Sandy's room. The door was half-shut. Bert and Jean were inside. Everything was terribly quiet. A nurse came out. The white-coated man asked her something and she shook her head. She had left the door ajar and through it could now be seen a high, narrow bed with a lot of gadgets around it. Sandy lay there, very flat under the covers, very still. Her head was turned away. All Lob's attention was <u>riveted</u> on the bed. He strained toward it, but Granny Pearce clasped his collar firmly.

"I've done a lot for you, my boy, now you behave yourself," she whispered grimly. Lob let out a faint whine, anxious and pleading.

At the sound of that whine, Sandy stirred just a little. She sighed and moved her head the least fraction. Lob whined again. And then Sandy turned her head right over. Her eyes opened, looking at the door.

"Lob?" she murmured—no more than a breath of sound. "Lobby, boy?"

The doctor by Granny Pearce drew a quick, sharp breath. Sandy moved her left arm—the one that was not broken—from below the covers and let her hand dangle down, feeling, as she always did in the mornings, for Lob's furry head. The doctor nodded slowly.

"All right," he whispered. "Let him go to the bedside. But keep a hold of him."

Granny Pearce and Lob moved to the bedside. Now she could see Bert and Jean, white-faced and shocked, on the far side of the bed. But she didn't look at them. She looked at the smile on her granddaughter's face as the groping fingers found Lob's wet ears and gently pulled them. "Good boy," whispered Sandy, and fell asleep again.

Granny Pearce led Lob out into the passage again. There she let go of him, and he ran off swiftly down the stairs. She would have followed him, but Bert and Jean had come out into the passage, and she spoke to Bert fiercely.

"*I* don't know why you were so foolish as not to bring the dog before! Leaving him to find the way here himself—"

"But, Mother!" said Jean Pengelly. "That can't have been Lob. What a chance to take! Suppose Sandy hadn't—" She stopped, with her handkerchief pressed to her mouth.

"Not Lob? I've known that dog nine years! I suppose I ought to know my own granddaughter's dog?"

"Listen, Mother," said Bert. "Lob was killed by the same truck that hit Sandy. Don found him—when he went to look for Sandy's schoolbag. He was—he was dead. Ribs all smashed. No question of that. Don told me on the phone—he and Will Hoskins rowed a half mile out to sea and sank the dog with a lump of concrete tied to his collar. Poor old boy. Still—he was getting on. Couldn't have lasted forever."

"*Sank him at sea?* Then what—?"

Slowly old Mrs. Pearce, and then the other two, turned to look at the trail of dripping-wet footprints that led down the hospital stairs.

In the Pengellys' garden they have a stone, under the palm tree. It says: "Lob. Sandy's dog. Buried at sea." ❖

EXPLICIT INSTRUCTION **Influence of Setting**

Instruction Review with students the main conflict of the story. (*Sandy and Lob want to be together but cannot, at first, because of distance.*) Discuss how the original conflict has changed and become more complicated. Ask what is keeping Lob and Sandy apart now. (*an accident—Sandy is unconscious, Lob is missing or dead.*) Remind students that setting details can include specific factors, such as weather, landscape, and distance from other places. Also remind students that on page 451, they learned about these setting details: The road into the village is winding and steep. It is very dangerous. Ask students how this factor of setting helps make the conflict more complicated. Discuss students' ideas.

Practice Have students work in pairs to answer these questions: Is the setting detail about the road important in the story? Why or why not? How does the conflict become more complicated as a result of the road?

Possible Responses: Sandy and Lob were walking down the road when Sandy was hit by a truck. The accident occurs because of the dangerous hillroad that leads into town. The accident complicates the conflict because Sandy is now unconscious and Lob seems to be gone—they are separated again.

Use **Unit Four Resource Book**, p. 7, for more practice.

Connect to the Literature

1. **What Do You Think?**
Did you expect the story to end the way it did? How did you feel about the ending?

Comprehension Check
- How does Lob become the Pengelly family pet?
- What caused the accident that injures Sandy?
- What helps Sandy recover?

Think Critically

2. Why do you think Sandy wishes she had not gone to the train station to see Lob leave?

3. Analyze the plot structure of "Lob's Girl" by identifying the conflict and the climax and then discussing the story's resolution.

4. How does Joan Aiken show the relationship between Lob and Sandy? Use examples from the story to explain your answer.

   Think About:
   - the way Lob and Sandy first meet
   - why Mr. Dodsworth gives Lob away
   - what happens when Granny Pearce visits the hospital

5. Lob is one of the main characters in this story, but he cannot speak. How do his actions show his traits?

6. **ACTIVE READING** **CAUSE AND EFFECT**
   Compare your **READER'S NOTEBOOK** chart on cause and effect with a classmate's. Discuss the causes of key events in the story. Did some events have more than one cause? Did some causes have multiple effects? Explain.

Extend Interpretations

7. **What If?** What if Mrs. Pengelly hadn't let Sandy take Lob with her to Aunt Rebecca's? With a partner, rewrite the end of the story so Lob does not go with Sandy. Tell what happens after Sandy is injured.

8. **Connect to Life** Have you ever experienced or shared with someone the loss of a pet? Discuss with a classmate how you think a pet's death affects its owner.

Literary Analysis

FORESHADOWING
Foreshadowing is a hint about an event or events that will occur later in a story. Writers create foreshadowing with descriptions of setting, characters, or events that often add an element of suspense to a story. Author Joan Aiken uses the technique of foreshadowing in "Lob's Girl." Early in the story, she describes the road where Sandy's accident later will occur. The road is described as "guarded by a notice that said LOW GEAR FOR 1½ MILES, DANGEROUS TO CYCLISTS."
The words *guarded* and *dangerous* suggest that something bad may happen in this place later in the story.

SETTING The **setting** of "Lob's Girl" is important to the conflict. Sandy and Lob love each other from the first time they meet. The fact that Lob and his owner live far away from Sandy means that Sandy and Lob can't see each other very often. This creates a conflict: Sandy and Lob want to be together, but distance keeps them apart.

Paired Activity With a partner, go back through the story and list the words and events that foreshadow Lob coming to live with the Pengellys. Discuss how the author uses descriptions of setting, characters, and events to make you feel that something is going to happen.

Connect to the Literature

1. **What Do You Think?**
Possible Response: The ending was a surprise, but I was happy that Sandy got well.

Comprehension Check
- Lob keeps going to the Pengelly home, so his owner tells the family to keep him.
- A truck that is driving too fast on the hill injures her.
- A dog that looks like Lob visits Sandy at the hospital.

 Use Selection Quiz in **Unit Four Resource Book,** p. 10.

Think Critically

2. **Possible Response:** Watching the train take Lob away makes Sandy realize even more how much she is going to miss him.

3. **Possible Response:** The conflict is that Sandy is injured by a truck. The climax is that a dog who looks like Lob visits Sandy in the hospital, and his presence causes Sandy to get better. The resolution is the revelation that the dog in the hospital could not have been Lob because he died after the truck hit him. The resolution develops the author's theme by showing that Lob's love was so strong that not even death could keep him from Sandy.

4. **Possible Response:** Joan Aiken shows the relationship between Lob and Sandy by making it harder and harder for them to be together but still having Lob find a way to get back to Sandy. Aiken shows Lob's complete devotion to Sandy by having him show up at the hospital to help her out of her coma.

5. **Possible Response:** Lob's actions show that he is enthusiastic, loyal, and devoted. Everything he does is enthusiastic and determined. When he first sees Sandy, he bumps into her and licks her face. Every time his owner takes him away, Lob gets back to Sandy.

6. Responses will vary.

 Use **Reading and Critical Thinking Transparencies,** p. 5, for additional support.

Extend Interpretations

7. **What If?** Accept rewritten endings that have Sandy going alone to her aunt's and that tell what happens after she is hit by the truck.

8. **Connect to Life** Students should draw on their own past experiences, family or friends' experiences, or on books or movies they've read or seen. Encourage them to share descriptions of events.

Literary Analysis

Foreshadowing Students' responses should identify clear examples on pages 449–453 of the author's use of foreshadowing to indicate that Lob will become a member of the Pengelly family.

Use **Literary Analysis Transparencies,** p. 28, for additional support.

Writing

Newspaper Article It would be helpful if students could read several newspaper articles to become familiar with the style of newspaper writing. Remind them to use quotation marks when quoting family members in their article.

 Use **Writing Transparencies,** p. 2, for additional support.

Speaking & Listening

Book Talk You might suggest that students who have similar opinions about "Lob's Girl" pair up to develop and deliver their book talks.

 Use the **Speaking and Listening Book,** pp. 29 and 30, for additional support.

Research & Technology

No More Mystery? Questions will vary. Allow students time to research and write their reports.

Vocabulary

STANDARDIZED TEST PRACTICE

1. D
2. F
3. B
4. H
5. D
6. J
7. A
8. H
9. C
10. G

Writing

Newspaper Article Imagine that you are a newspaper reporter. Write a news story about Lob's mysterious visit to the hospital. Include quotations from members of the Pengelly family, Mr. Dodsworth, the police, and the hospital staff. Place your article in your **Working Portfolio.**

Writing Handbook
See p. R41: Narrative Writing.

This activity asks you to write a news story. To find out about other writing forms you might use when your purpose is to tell about an event, see p. R31: Choosing a Form.

Vocabulary

STANDARDIZED TEST PRACTICE

Choose the word or group of words that means the same, or nearly the same, as the underlined Word to Know.

1. To <u>rivet</u> is to—
   A decorate   B drink
   C slice   D fasten
2. <u>Drafting</u> is another word for—
   F writing   G dodgin
   H blowing   J copying
3. To <u>conceal</u> is to—
   A copy   B hide
   C steal   D collect
4. A <u>coma</u> is a type of—
   F doctor   G medicine
   H blackout   J operation
5. To <u>assure</u> is to—
   A confuse   B endure
   C assign   D promise
6. <u>Agitated</u> means—
   F regretful   G impatient
   H jealous   J disturbed
7. To <u>atone</u> is to—
   A repay   B listen
   C refuse   D betray
8. A <u>transfusion</u> refers to a type of—
   F illness   G machine
   H injection   J hospital
9. To <u>inquire</u> is to—
   A need   B write
   C question   D expect
10. <u>Melancholy</u> means—
    F greedy   G gloomy
    H silly   J mighty

Speaking & Listening

Book Talk Did you enjoy reading "Lob's Girl"? Would you recommend this story to a friend? Create a presentation based on your opinion of this story. Begin with a clear statement of your opinion. Then give reasons and story information to support it. If you decide not to recommend the story, be clear about why you don't like it. Practice delivering your presentation in a strong voice and using gestures and facial expressions. When you are ready, deliver your presentation to the class.

Speaking and Listening Handbook
See p. R100: Persuasive Presentations.

Research & Technology

No More Mystery? Scientists continue to make discoveries about such animal behaviors as why birds sing, and how they can fly hundreds of miles in the dark without getting lost. What questions about animal behavior would you like answered? Create a list of two or three questions. Then use the Internet or library resources to help you answer these questions. Write a short report that includes your questions and the answers you found. Also list the sources you used.

Reading for INFORMATION
Read the magazine article on page 462 before beginning your research.

Grammar in Context: Using Prepositional Phrases as Transitions

In "Lob's Girl" Joan Aiken uses prepositional phrases to make a smooth shift from one paragraph to another:

> **On this summer day** she was lying peacefully, . . .
>
> **By this time** the children, . . . had realized. . . .

The words shown in red are **prepositional phrases.** In the examples above, prepositional phrases set a new scene or show a transition, that is, a change in time.

In the examples, the words *on* and *by* are **prepositions.** A prepositional phrase consists of a preposition, its object, and any modifiers of the object. The **object of the preposition** is the noun or pronoun following the preposition.

WRITING EXERCISE Rewrite each sentence so that a prepositional phrase is used at the beginning to show transition.

Example: *Original* Sandy went to see her Aunt Becky on a lonely October evening.

Rewritten On a lonely October evening, Sandy went to see her Aunt Becky.

1. Dr. Travers discovered at the station that the police knew about the accident.

2. Sandy was unconscious for hour after hour.

3. Dr. and Mrs. Travers went to the cottage at noon the next day.

4. Granny saw the guard at the main entrance refuse to let Lob in.

5. Sandy stirred at the sound of Lob's whine.

Grammar Handbook
See p. R63: The Sentence and Its Parts.

Joan Aiken
born 1924

"I knew from the age of five that I was going to be a writer. . . ."

Photograph by Roy Delroy.

A Young Storyteller Joan Aiken, the daughter of the U.S. poet Conrad Aiken, grew up in England. Because there were no children of her age in the neighborhood, Aiken spent much of her time reading and making up stories to amuse herself and her younger stepbrother. She says, "I knew from the age of five that I was going to be a writer. . . ." Aiken says her writing process involves "a lot of revising and going back and crossing out words." She often gets her story ideas from interesting things she hears or reads, which she records in a notebook.

Tackling an Adult World As an adult, Aiken took jobs at a magazine and an advertising agency to support herself and her young children after she was widowed. To earn extra money, Aiken began writing and publishing short stories. She soon decided to become a full-time writer and has since authored dozens of books for children and adults. Aiken says her books for young people are "concerned with children tackling the problems of an adult world."

AUTHOR ACTIVITY
Thinking About Dialects Joan Aiken often writes in the dialects (different ways of speaking in different regions of a country) of England, her native land. Compare the language in "Lob's Girl" with other stories in this book that use dialects, such as "Cricket in the Road." How do the ways that characters speak help you appreciate a story?

LOB'S GIRL **461**

Grammar in Context
WRITING EXERCISE
Possible Responses:

1. At the station, Dr. Travers discovered that the police knew about the accident.
2. For hour after hour, Sandy was unconscious.
3. At noon the next day, Dr. and Mrs. Travers went to the cottage.
4. At the main entrance, Granny saw the guard refuse to let Lob in.
5. At the sound of Lob's whine, Sandy stirred.

 Use **Writing Transparencies,** p. 9, for additional support.

Joan Aiken

Joan Aiken was born in Rye, Sussex, England in 1924, and claims it is still her favorite place in the world, even though she left it at age three. She says she has haunting and happy memories of that place, and she has set several of her books there. She loves to garden, listen to radio shows, take walks in the countryside, and draw pastel landscapes.

Author Activity

Thinking About Dialects Students may notice that certain words or expressions are unique to each story, which may indicate the region that character lives in. Students should indicate that characters' speech helps form a more complete picture of them for the reader.

EXPLICIT INSTRUCTION ## Grammar in Context

IDENTIFYING PREPOSITIONS AND THEIR OBJECTS Prepositions help to show relationships between nouns and pronouns and other words in a sentence. The noun or pronoun following a preposition is called the object of the preposition.
Instruction Write the following sentence on the board: "Sandy and Lob ran on the beach." Ask students to identify the preposition *(on)* and its object *(beach)*. Help students to see that this phrase helps them to understand the relationship between Sandy, Lob, and the beach.

Practice Ask students to write the prepositions in the following sentences. Beside each preposition, have them write its object.
1. Mrs. Pengelly left the blackberry jelly on the table. *(on, table)*
2. Tess and Tim played tag along the seashore and in the breaking waves. *(along, seashore; in, waves)*
3. Lob showed great courage and endurance when he walked from Liverpool to Cornwall. *(from, Liverpool; to, Cornwall)*

4. Sandy and Lob had a unique relationship, one based upon mutual love. *(upon, love)*

 Use **Unit Four Resource Book,** p. 8.

 For more instruction in identifying prepositions and their objects, see McDougal Littell's *Language Network,* Chapter 6.

For **systematic instruction** in grammar, see:
• **Grammar, Usage, and Mechanics Book**
• pacing chart on p. 441i.

Standards-Based Objectives

• read for information
• read and analyze a magazine article
• use a written text to make judgments
• identify bias in a written text
• make assertions about a text

Connecting to the Literature

This newspaper article is a useful companion piece to the short story "Lob's Girl" because it illustrates how, in real life, dogs have performed feats of great bravery under dangerous conditions in order to save the life of a human.

LESSON RESOURCES

UNIT FOUR RESOURCE BOOK, pp. 11–12

SKILLS TRANSPARENCIES AND COPYMASTERS
Reading and Critical Thinking
• Strategies for Reading, TR 1 (p. 463)
Writing
• Locating Information Using the Internet I, TR 47 (p. 464)

Source: *National Geographic World*

Animals to the Rescue

① Why do animals act to save humans? No one really knows. Until recently scientists believed that animals were only creatures of instinct and training. Now they're not so sure. Some scientists say that animals may have emotions and thoughts like those of humans. Has your cat ever cuddled with you when you were sick in bed? If so, was it concerned and trying to make you feel better, did it want company . . . or was it just looking for a cozy spot? When an animal saves a human from injury, is it inspired by an emotion such as love, or simply acting on instinct? Read on to learn about animals who even risked their lives to help humans. Why did they do it? You be the judge.

Rattle of Terror

② When 8-year-old Teresa Martinez of Loveland, Colorado, was picnicking one day, she accidentally wandered near a den of rattlesnakes. "I heard a rattle and froze. Then I started screaming for help," says Teresa. "Lady (Teresa's dog) raced over and started fighting the five snakes." That gave Teresa a chance to run for safety. Lady suffered three bites but survived thanks to quick medical attention. "Lady knew I was in trouble and wanted to protect me," adds Teresa. "She's a real hero."

Teresa Martinez with Lady, her rescuer.

EXPLICIT INSTRUCTION **Making Judgments**

Instruction Tell students that good readers of nonfiction material make judgments about what they read. Explain that when readers make a judgment, they determine whether the information in an article is accurate and complete. Ask students to come up with questions they might use to make judgments about a nonfiction article. *(Does the article include enough facts about the topic? If the article contains opinions, are these supported with evidence?)* Tell students that when they think an article does not include enough facts and

support for opinions, they can look for this information in other articles or in reference books.

Practice Have students work in pairs to read and complete the numbered activities on the pupil pages.

Possible Responses: See the side columns in the teacher's edition for answers to the activities on the pupil pages.

 Use **Unit Four Resource Book,** p. 11, for more practice.

Danger—Thin Ice

A shortcut across a frozen pond in 1995 could have killed Josh Mitchell, 15, of Indianapolis, Indiana. "There was a whoosh, and I fell through the ice," says Josh. Levi, a mixed golden and Labrador retriever, saw Josh fall. The dog bounded onto the ice and plunged into the cold water. Josh grabbed Levi around the neck and held on. Levi's owners, Denise and George Hamand, rushed to pull out Josh and Levi. Says Josh, "I guess that's why they call a dog 'man's best friend.'"

❸

Levi saved Josh Mitchell from drowning.

4 Possible Responses: There is no support in this section for the viewpoint that animals rescue humans because of instinct. Instead, this section seems to support the viewpoint that animals rescue humans because of emotion. I did not get enough information about the instincts that might have led these dogs to rescue humans. Therefore, I can't "be the judge" about why animals rescue humans.

Identifying Bias
Possible Response: Yes. The writer does try to lead readers to believe that animals rescue humans because animals have emotions like humans. The writer quotes dog owners but not scientists. The people in the article may be biased because they are grateful to the dogs for saving their lives. They see the dogs as special and as more than mere animals.

I think the information in this article is incomplete because the writer does not provide evidence for the idea that animals rescue humans because of instinct.

Reading for Information *continued*

4 Is there support in this section for the viewpoint that animals rescue humans because of instinct? What viewpoint about animal rescues seems to be supported by the information here? Did you get enough information in this article to "be the judge" about why animals rescue humans?

Identifying Bias A writer's viewpoint, or **bias**, can influence his or her choice of what to write about and how to write it. Do you think this writer leads you to believe that animals rescue humans because they have emotions like humans? Support your opinion with evidence from the article. What is your judgment of the information in this article? Is the information accurate and complete? Use the questions at the top of page 463 to help you make a judgment.

Research & Technology
Activity Link: "Lob's Girl," p. 460. What else would you like to know before you judge which explanation of the dogs' behavior is correct? Use library resources to locate two or three more sources that discuss such rescues, as well as instinct, training, emotion, and thought in animals. Then form a judgment based on the facts you find along with your own observations and experience. Record your judgment in a brief essay, citing your sources.

Canine Courage

4 Kelsey, a German shepherd, fought off a rabid raccoon to save Ashley Gillen, of Weymouth, Massachusetts. In 1994, nine-year-old Ashley was playing outside her home when she heard a rustling sound. "A raccoon appeared. It chased me and bit me on the leg," she remembers. The dog ran out of the house and battled the raccoon until Ashley could escape. (Ashley and Kelsey both had follow-up shots to prevent rabies.) Says Ashley, as she gives her pooch a big hug, "Kelsey's a real hero. She saved my life."

Kelsey fought a rabid animal, saving her owner, Ashley.

EXPLICIT INSTRUCTION **Research & Technology**

The Research & Technology activity on this page links to the Research & Technology section of the Choices & Challenges activities following "Lob's Girl."

Instruction Suggest that students be specific in their keyword searches on the Internet and the online systems at the library. Have students write a list of keywords to use, and suggest that they look under topics such as "animal rescues" as well.

Practice Suggest that students construct a chart or graph organizing the information they gather during their research. Once they have analyzed the material, have each student discuss his or her judgment with a partner before starting to write the essay.

Use **Writing Transparencies**, p. 47, for additional support.

My First Dive with the Dolphins

by DON C. REED

Connect to Your Life

What do you know about dolphins? What would you like to learn about them?

Build Background

Dolphins have a streamlined shape, along with fins and flukes to propel and steer them through the water. But in the dark of the ocean, how do dolphins "see"? Using a process called echolocation (ĕk′ō-lō-kā′shən), or sonar, they make clicking noises that travel long distances. These sounds bounce off objects, and dolphins interpret the resulting echo.

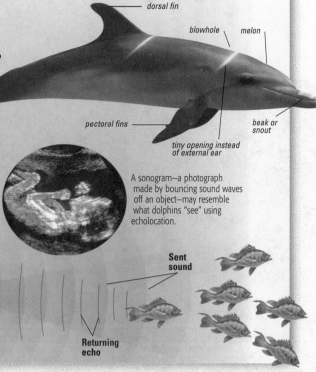

dorsal fin

blowhole   melon

horizontal flukes

keel

pectoral fins

beak or snout

tiny opening instead of external ear

A sonogram–a photograph made by bouncing sound waves off an object–may resemble what dolphins "see" using echolocation.

Melon focuses sound

Sent sound

Returning echo

HOW A DOLPHIN ECHOLOCATES

Focus Your Reading

LITERARY ANALYSIS **ESSAY**

An **essay** is a short work of nonfiction that deals with a single subject. The **purpose** of an essay may be to express feelings, entertain, explain, or persuade.

WORDS TO KNOW **Vocabulary Preview**

aggression	compressed	hurtle	sonar
camouflage	dominant	luminous	
coexistence	elegant	magnification	

ACTIVE READING **MAKING GENERALIZATIONS**

A **generalization** is a conclusion you draw about a whole group of people or things. Example: "Many cities are filled with tall buildings." Be careful not to make a generalization so broad that it is incorrect. For example, the generalization "All apples are red" is too broad. Some apples are green or yellow. As you read, jot down three generalizations about dolphins in your ▭**READER'S NOTEBOOK.** Also note the evidence from the selection that supports your statements.

MY FIRST DIVE WITH THE DOLPHINS   **465**

Standards-Based Objectives

1. understand and appreciate an **essay**
2. understand author's use of **specialized language**
3. **make generalizations** to help understand an essay
4. explain the **effects of imagery**

Summary

The author looks back on his first day as a professional scuba diver. Although he was uncomfortable with the equipment and nervous about getting close to the dolphins, Don Reed plunged in. With courage and curiosity, he survived his first encounter with the fascinating finned creatures that have intrigued us with their intelligence and individuality.

Thematic Link

Reed's essay reveals some of the ways that dolphins, like humans, express their individuality and their intelligence. His writing aims to help himself and others to better understand these fascinating mammals.

English Conventions Practice

Daily Language SkillBuilder

Have students **proofread** the display sentences on page 441k and write them correctly. The sentences also appear on Transparency 15 of **Language Transparencies.**

Preteaching Vocabulary

If you would like to preteach the WORDS TO KNOW for this selection, use the Explicit Instruction, page 466.

LESSON RESOURCES

UNIT FOUR RESOURCE BOOK, pp. 13–19

ASSESSMENT
Formal Assessment, pp. 81–82
Test Generator

SKILLS TRANSPARENCIES AND COPYMASTERS
Reading and Critical Thinking
• Making Generalizations, TR 14 (pp. 466, 473)
• Main Idea and Supporting Details, TR 25 (p. 468)

Language
• Daily Language SkillBuilder, TR 15 (p. 465)
• Learning and Remembering New Words, TR 65 (p. 466)
Writing
• Combining Sentences Using Conjunctions, TR 19 (p. 475)
Speaking and Listening
• Creating a Persuasive Presentation, p. 29 (p. 474)
• Guidlelines: How to Analyze a Persuasive Presentation, p. 30 (p. 474)

INTEGRATED TECHNOLOGY
Audio Library
Teacher's SourceBook, p. 37
Internet: Research Starter

Visit our Web site:
www.mcdougallittell.com

For **systematic instruction** in language skills, see:
• **Vocabulary and Spelling Book**
• **Grammar, Usage, and Mechanics Book**
• pacing chart on p. 441i.

Reading and Analyzing

Reading Skills and Strategies:
PREVIEW

Briefly summarize "My First Dive with the Dolphins." Have students look through the story. Tell them to make a prediction about what it would be like to dive with dolphins.

Literary Analysis   **ESSAY**

Tell students that an essay is a short composition on a single subject. Usually the author of a personal essay conveys his or her view of the subject. Ask students to describe Don Reed's personal view of his work.

Possible Response: The author feels awkward as he embarks on his first day of work as a professional scuba diver.

 Use **Unit Four Resource Book,** p. 15, for more practice.

Active Reading
MAKING GENERALIZATIONS

Remind students that a generalization is a statement that applies to many examples. Have students suggest some of the kinds of generalizations about dolphins that they might encounter in this article. Encourage them to look for generalizations as they read "My First Dive with the Dolphins."

Possible Response: The author might make generalizations about how dolphins act toward people or about why dolphins are so fascinating to people.

 Use **Unit Four Resource Book,** p. 14, for more practice.

 Use **Reading and Critical Thinking Transparencies,** p. 14, for additional support.

MY FIRST DIVE with the Dolphins

by Don C. Reed

EXPLICIT INSTRUCTION   Preteaching Vocabulary

WORDS TO KNOW

Teaching Strategy Call students' attention to the list of WORDS TO KNOW. Remind them that they can learn the meaning of an unfamiliar word by using the dictionary. In order to find the word in the dictionary, students should use the **guide words,** the two words that appear at the top of each page and show the first and last entry word listed on that page. All the entry words are listed in alphabetical order between these words. Say, "If you want to look up the word *compress,* you might find it on a page with the guide words *compound* and *compromise* because *compress* comes between those two words."

Practice Write the word *camouflage* on the board. Then write the following two pairs of guide words. Ask students to identify the pair between which the word *camouflage* would fall.

camel   camera
camel   campaign

Now ask students to select another word from the WORDS TO KNOW list, look it up in the dictionary, and find the two guide words that appear on the page where that word is located.

 Use **Unit Four Resource Book,** p. 18, for more practice.

For **systematic instruction** in vocabulary, see:
- **Vocabulary and Spelling Book**
- pacing chart on p. 441i.

stood on a narrow, red-painted stage above half a million gallons of cold salt water.

A wave slashed foam onto the stage and across my bare feet. I had a black rubber wet suit on but neither a hood nor "booties," those heavy neoprene[1] shoes that divers take for granted nowadays. It didn't occur to me to ask the other divers why we had neither foot nor head protection. I wore what the other folks wore. I wasn't about to complain: if the other divers had jumped off the edge in their underwear, I would have just shrugged and done the same.

That cold, windy March day in 1972 was my first day of work as a professional scuba diver for Marine World, soon to become Marine World/Africa USA, an oceanarium-zoo in northern California. I didn't let on how strange everything felt. I was only six months out of deep-sea-diving school and had almost no idea of what to expect.

The hard rubber mouthpiece still felt foreign clenched between my teeth. It seemed clumsy to breathe through my mouth instead of my nose. Each breath had to be "asked for," pulled in by a conscious lifting of the chest, creating a vacuum to suck in the <u>compressed</u> air.

Not wanting to dangle my legs in the water, I stood awkwardly on one foot at a time as I fumbled into the big, floppy swim fins.

As I pulled the black plastic mask over my face, the strap tugged at my hair. When I opened my eyes, my field of vision was narrowed by the mask. It was like staring through a section of pipe.

I took one giant step forward and fell . . . into another world.

I heard the crash of the surface as it broke apart and thumped shut above me; I felt the massage of pressure and the cold water rushing down my neck and spine. Air bubbles slid ticklingly up my face, heading for the surface, while I headed the opposite way, falling, dragged down by the heavy lead work belt around my waist.

As the bubbles of my entry cleared, my vision returned. My fin tips folded softly underneath me as I landed on the green, algae-covered[2] floor.

Oddly, I didn't spot the dolphins right away. Perhaps their dark/light <u>camouflage</u> patterns broke up their outlines. Then, all at once, there they were—and so much bigger than I had expected. It's only the <u>magnification</u> down here, I told myself, a trick of underwater light. But I knew they

---

1. **neoprene** (nē'ə-prēn'): a weather-resistant synthetic rubber.
2. **algae-covered** (ăl'jē-kŭv'ərd): covered with algae, tiny plantlike organisms that grow in water.

WORDS
TO
KNOW

compressed (kəm-prĕst') *adj.* under greater than normal pressure **compress** *v.*
camouflage (kăm'ə-fläzh') *n.* a disguise produced by blending in with the surroundings
magnification (măg'nə-fĭ-kā'shən) *n.* the causing of objects to appear enlarged

467

Explain that specialized vocabulary tells about a specific topic. Tell students that this essay contains words that tell about scuba diving and words that tell about dolphins. Ask students to identify some of the specialized vocabulary on page 468. Then have them tell which topic the words relate to—scuba diving or dolphins.

Possible Response: Specialized vocabulary such as *air compressor* and *regulator* relate to scuba diving. *Sonar* relates to dolphins.

Reading Skills and Strategies: MAKE INFERENCES

Ⓐ Tell students to reread the paragraph that begins, "I had always thought . . . " Ask them to make an inference about the author's feelings toward the dolphins at this point.

Possible Response: The author seems to be afraid of the dolphins. He's nervous about getting close to Arnie; he's not even sure which dolphin is Arnie.

Reading Skills and Strategies: MAIN IDEA AND DETAILS

Ask students to identify the main idea of the text on page 469. Then tell them to name at least three of the details.

Possible Response: The main idea of the text on this page is that the scuba divers were responsible for scraping the algae off the tank. Some of the details include Ted's instructions to hold the brush upside-down, the reasons why the algae had to be removed, and the author's technique—making a stroke one-inch wide instead of six.

📖 Use **Reading and Critical Thinking Transparencies**, p. 25, for additional support.

---

weighed between 300 and 400 pounds each, as much as a giant professional wrestler or the biggest lineman on a football team.

I tried to remember the one-minute human-dolphin <u>coexistence</u> lesson that head diver Ted Pintarelli had given me.

"Spock—that's the one with the hole in his fin—he won't bother you. Neither will Delbert: he's got a shark scar on his belly that makes him easy to spot. The smallest one's Ernestine; she's okay. Lucky is king bull, the toughest dolphin in the tank. You'll recognize him right away: there's a purple spot on his cheek, and he's big and all scarred up from fights, and . . . well, you'll know him!

"But Arnie, he's the one who'll give you trouble. He thinks he's bad, and he likes to try and scare new guys in the tank. Like he might swim fast at you or something. Just hold still if he does. Don't let him chase you out of the tank, or he'll make a game out of it, and you'll never get any work done. Don't look scared. He'll leave you alone . . . most of the time, anyway," the muscular, red-faced diver had added with a grin.

Ⓐ I had always thought of dolphins as sweet and gentle, like Flipper on the old TV show, who was sort of an oceangoing Lassie, man's best friend in the sea. Now I tried to figure out which one was Arnie. He was supposed to have a lower jaw shaped like a hook, whatever that meant. But it was no use: I couldn't tell the dolphins apart. They all looked like trouble to me.

As the streamlined but massive gray creatures cruised around me, I reminded myself they were not sharks. Their eighty-eight white, needlelike teeth, which I could see so clearly, were meant for snagging swift

herring on the run, not for ripping out a twenty-pound mouthful of flesh, as a white shark's teeth were. Dolphins were mammals, not fish, and the reason for the up-and-down motion of their tails was to bring them back up to the air.

> **"But Arnie, he's the one who'll give you trouble. . . . he likes to try and scare new guys in the tank."**

Some said dolphins were smart like people. Certainly dolphins could do things with <u>sonar</u> that we humans couldn't match. In one experiment I read about, dolphins were able to distinguish between two types of identical-looking plastic-coated wire—one with a lead core, the other with a copper core—just by sending their special clicking sounds inside them.

Well, I wasn't getting a whole lot of work done this way. In the distance I could see the three other divers, already lying down on the floor, their scrub brushes busy. As it was for them, cleaning algae off the underwater floors and walls and windows would be 95 percent of my job. The other 5 percent, the head diver had promised, would be magic.

None of the divers had air tanks. Each diver breathed through a thin yellow air hose leading up to the surface, where it was plugged into a brass outlet on an air compressor. I noticed the strange shape of the bubbles as they left my regulator and wobbled to the surface. They were not round but dome-shaped, flat

WORDS TO KNOW	**coexistence** (kō'ĭg-zĭs'təns) *n.* a state of living together in peace
	sonar (sō'när') *n.* detection of objects by reflected sound waves

468

Instruction Remind students that nonfiction writers also use figurative language and imagery to make their writing interesting and memorable. Review the definition of imagery (*language that appeals to the five senses*). Next, ask a volunteer to read aloud the paragraph that begins at the bottom of page 468 with "As the streamlined but massive gray creatures cruised around me." Other students should listen for words and phrases that help them visualize the description. Ask students to

point out examples of imagery in the paragraph and tell to what senses they appeal. *(sight: needlelike teeth, up-and-down motion of their tails).* Then ask students to tell what feelings the imagery helps convey (*nervousness*).

Practice Have students find other examples of words and phrases that help them see, hear, feel, smell, or taste what the author is describing. For each example, have students identify the sense it appeals to and the mental images it helped create.

Possible Responses: "The hard rubber mouthpiece still felt foreign clenched between my teeth" (p. 467: touch, taste); "His head moved up and down violently, and his tail moved so fast" (p. 470: sight); "It felt smooth, soft, and firm, like the inside surface of a hard-boiled egg" (p. 472: touch). Students' mental images will vary.

📖 Use **Unit Four Resource Book**, p. 16, for more practice.

on the bottom, and they changed as they rose toward the mirrorlike surface twenty feet above.

In my hand was a short iron-handled scrub brush. I held it in the special way Ted had shown me.

"If you hold it the regular way, like a hairbrush, you can't get anything but wrist power behind it," Ted said. "But upside-down, the bristles are next to your palm, and you get your whole body into it. Switch hands every ten or twelve brush strokes, too, so you won't have to stop and rest."

Lying down in a sort of pushup position, I took an experimental scrub stroke at the floor. The brush was neither motorized nor self-operational. My tentative push did not accomplish much. Some scratches appeared in the green algae; that was all. The stuff clung like paint!

The algae has to be taken off, or it grows thicker and thicker and finally rots, breaking off at the roots, clouding the water, clogging the filtration system, and plugging up the windows. There are chemical ways to kill algae, of course, but these cannot be used because they are harmful to the dolphins' eyes.

So we divers scrubbed. Algae was our job security!

I turned the brush on edge, so that the stroke it made would be one inch wide instead of six, and leaned all my shoulder strength behind the stroke. Now the brush bit. There. I had a one-by-twelve-inch piece of clean white

floor. Just eleven more strokes and I'd have one whole square foot finished. And since the tank was 60 by 80 feet, that meant there were only 4,799 more square feet to go.

Suddenly a blur of movement caught my eye. A dolphin was <u>hurtling</u> toward me. Although it was closing the distance between us unbelievably fast, I saw it as if it were in slow motion.

WORDS TO KNOW · **hurtle** (hûr'tl) *v.* to move with great speed

469

Less Proficient Readers
1 Ask students to explain why dolphins must come up for air.
Possible Response: Since dolphins are mammals, they have lungs. Because dolphins need oxygen to breathe, they have to come up for air.

English Learners
2 Point out the phrase *get your whole body into it.* Explain that this phrase means to put all your strength into your actions.
3 Point out the line, *Algae was our job security!* Tell students that job security is knowing that you will keep your job. In this case, algae was the divers' "job security" because they knew that as long as there was algae to scrape off the tank, they would have their jobs.

Advanced Learners
Students might enjoy writing about this encounter from a dolphin's point of view. Have students pick one of the dolphins that the narrator encounters and describe the same series of events from that dolphin's point of view.

The dolphin's lower jaw hooked over its top one: it was Arnie. His head moved up and down violently, and his tail moved so fast that a trail of bubbles formed behind it. As the dolphin charged, I heard a roar of cavitation[3] as the very water tore, breaking into hydrogen and oxygen.

I didn't even have time to flinch properly. It was easy to do just what Ted recommended. I froze.

I knew that if the dolphin ran into me at that speed, whatever he hit would be broken. This was how dolphins were able to kill sharks: they smashed their insides with a high-speed ram.

Whooosh! I felt rather than heard a wash of water like a great wind. I saw the dolphin's

stomach—he had a bellybutton!—then the animal turned like a veering jet.

But not to go away. No more than six feet from me, he stopped. I saw his narrow face, saw his jaws move, heard the *klonk* that I knew signaled aggression. His white teeth gleamed, sharp and clean as if they had been brushed. But dolphins do not fight seriously with their teeth.

In a motion so fast my mind had to reconstruct it afterward, the gristly ridge on the underside of the dolphin's tail flukes suddenly appeared right before my face. It was as if a baseball bat had been swung at my head—and stopped an inch before my face caved in.

Again I did nothing, but not through courage. My reflexes are slow. I had time to tell myself, Hold still; don't do anything to make him think you want to fight. I also had time to feel a wave of anger at this huge animal for picking on me for no reason at all.

Then another dolphin, heavy-bodied with a purple spot on the left side of his beak, eased into my vision, and Arnie casually swam off with him.

When my heart and breathing rates returned to relative normality, I went back to my work. I scrubbed and watched, and watched and scrubbed. My shoulders began to

---

3. **cavitation** (kăv′ĭ-tā′shən): sudden formation of bubbles in a liquid by an object moving rapidly through it.

WORDS TO KNOW

aggression (ə-grĕsh′ən) *n.* threatening behavior; hostility

470

feel pumped full of blood, as they do in weightlifting workouts.

Suddenly something shining caught my attention. I turned my head, and the whirring roar of the regulator seemed to disappear.

 n stillness like the hush in a cathedral, I saw the smallest dolphin move her head just slightly, and from the back of her neck something silvery emerged, as if she were manufacturing a halo.

Naah. Yes! There it was: a glistening, gleaming, silver bubble ring, rising. The dolphin flexed her neck again, and another ring emerged, rising faster, so that it joined its <u>luminous</u> relation and they merged, becoming first a figure eight and then a larger single circle, a Hula-Hoop of light.

After I'd spent nearly two hours in the water, the scrubbed-off algae was rising in darkening clouds, like night closing in.

I kept switching the brush back and forth, from hand to hand, trying not to think about Arnie. Long ago, in India, there was a saying that you should not worry about tigers, lest you bring one to you by the thought.

Still, I couldn't help wondering where he was. My head began to shift back and forth more rapidly as I tried to see but couldn't.

Just then, something touched me!

I rolled, ready to fight, and looked into the red-brown eye and the face of . . . whom?

It was definitely not the hook jaw of Arnie, and the purple spot of Lucky's cheek was not there. Spock was supposed to have a hole in his left pec fin, while Delbert had a shark scar. This must be Ernestine.

I told myself she wasn't really smiling: that happy look was just an accident of jaw formation, indicating nothing more than lines of bone and muscle. But looking at her made me feel happy just the same.

She was so beautiful. From a distance, the dolphins had looked simple, uncomplicated. But up close, everything about Ernestine was astonishing. The black pupil in the center of her red-brown eye seemed to radiate emotion. Six inches back from the eye was a fold of skin with an opening the size of a pinhole in it, the opening to her ear. Even the dolphin's skin was special: not perfectly smooth but textured with the tiniest of lines and colored with subtle gray patterns that were perfectly matched and fitted together, like the interlocking feathers on a hawk.

She was so beautiful. . . . up close, everything about Ernestine was astonishing.

She had pectoral (chest) fins to steer with, tail flukes for power, and a blowhole at the back of her head that could release breath at 200 miles per hour, punching a hole in the ocean spray so the dolphin could inhale relatively dry air and not drown in a storm. From the shape of her beak—the reason for the name "bottlenose"—to the <u>elegant</u> flare of her tail flukes, she was a creature of wonder. I felt I could study her for a thousand years and not see everything.

Ernestine nuzzled in beside me and laid her pectoral fin on my back.

This amazed me. A big animal I had never met before, and it swam up and touched me!

| WORDS TO KNOW | **luminous** (lōō′mə-nəs) *adj.* full of light |
| | **elegant** (ĕl′ĭ-gənt) *adj.* beautiful in shape or style |

471

I couldn't resist her. Without conscious thought, my hand reached up and stroked her side. It felt smooth, soft, and firm, like the inside surface of a hard-boiled egg.

Suddenly the dolphin rolled, bringing the fin on her back into my hand. Then she took off.

 he suddenness of the motion frightened me, and instantly I straightened my fingers, releasing the loose grip I had held so as not to make her feel restrained. Had I offended her?

But she turned and came back, rolling again to place her dorsal fin (the one on her back) in my right hand.

Why fight it? I thought, dropping my scrub brush.

This time, when Ernestine took off, I went along.

I left my human clumsiness behind. For glorious seconds I knew what it was to be the swiftest swimmer in the sea. She towed me, and I tried not to get in the way. I was conscious of my body's shape as an obstruction and tried to narrow myself.

We soared. The water rushed past my face and swirled around my body, and I felt the streaking lines of speed.

Klonk! At the sound, Ernestine flicked out and away from my hand and was gone in an instant. I hung in the water, becoming a sluggish human once again.

Before me "stood" a gray-white dolphin giant. There was no question as to his identity. I knew it was Lucky even before I saw the scars on his face and neck and shoulders and the dark spot on the left side of his jaw.

The <u>dominant</u> dolphin lowered his head slowly. Again I heard the noise of irritation,

threat, or challenge, and for an instant I thought he would give me trouble for getting too friendly with Ernestine. But the *klonk*ing sound was softer now, as if the point had already been made.

I was in the presence of a leader. Whether I labeled him "alpha male" or "dominant dolphin bull" or "king among his own kind" made no difference. This chunk of sea was Lucky's territory, and he was very definitely in charge.

There was depth to Lucky, and intelligence. It was an intelligence different from my own, perhaps, but certainly deserving of respect. He looked like he knew how to live and how to die, like an Apache[4] chieftain living in the wild, who would find hardship and danger at every turn and was content that it should be so.

I was in the presence of a leader.

I did not understand all this at once, of course. I had no words to express what I felt then. There were only raw emotions, ideas, possibilities. My brain felt staggered, like a computer with information overload.

Trying to show neither fear nor aggression (and certainly not disrespect!), I let myself drift down, settling slowly back to the floor of the tank, to my dropped scrub brush, to my work.

Lucky only watched me go and made no move to follow. ❖

---

4. **Apache** (ə-păch′ē): belonging to a Native American people of the southwestern United States and northern Mexico.

WORDS TO KNOW

dominant (dŏm′ə-nənt) *adj.* having the most influence; controlling all others

---

⌒Cross Curricular Link Science

DOLPHIN INTELLIGENCE Dolphins' social behavior and organization is thought to be among the most advanced in the animal kingdom. Because they survive well in captivity, dolphins have been the subject of many studies. Their relatively long life expectancy of 25 years gives scientists and marine biologists ample opportunity to study dolphin behavior.

Dolphins possess a complex communication and detection system. Through use of underwater sonar, dolphins can easily locate food that is 100 meters away. The time it takes for a reflected sound to return indicates how far away the object is from the dolphin.

Dolphins also use their ability to make sounds to communicate with each other. This skill is important in the open ocean, where there can be more than 1,000 dolphins in a living group, or pod.

Connect to the Literature

1. What Do You Think?
How did you react to the author's experience with Lucky?

Comprehension Check
- What is Don C. Reed's job?
- What happens when Reed meets Arnie? Ernestine? Lucky?

Think Critically

2. How do you think Lucky might treat Reed the next time he enters the tank? Explain your response.

3. How do you think Reed feels during his first day on the job?

4. The head diver tells Reed that 95 percent of his job will be cleaning and 5 percent will be fun and excitement. What is exciting about Reed's job?

5. What personality traits does Reed have that you think would be helpful in working with dolphins?

Think About:
- Reed's reaction to the diving gear he receives
- how he deals with the job of removing algae
- his reactions to Arnie, Ernestine, and Lucky

6. **ACTIVE READING** **MAKING GENERALIZATIONS**
Exchange your **READER'S NOTEBOOK** entry with a classmate and discuss the generalizations you each made while reading the essay.

Extend Interpretations

7. The Writer's Style Critics have praised the engaging details in Reed's writing. How does his use of sensory details contribute to your understanding of the selection?

8. Connect to Life On the basis of what you learned from the selection, would you want a job like the author's? Elaborate.

Literary Analysis

ESSAY An **essay** is a short piece of nonfiction that deals with one subject. Like other types of short nonfiction, an essay has an introduction, a body, and a conclusion. Both informal and formal essays are found in magazines and newspapers. An informal essay writer's **purpose** usually is to **entertain** or **persuade** the reader, or to **describe** an incident that is significant to the writer. Writers of **informal essays** often present their own feelings and observations. For example, author Don C. Reed writes that he found Ernestine "beautiful" and "astonishing." **Formal essays** are rarely about personal subjects. They usually are written on scholarly topics.

Activity Look through a magazine or newspaper and find two or three examples of essays. Identify what you consider to be the author's purpose or purposes in each.

SPECIALIZED LANGUAGE
Words or phrases that relate to certain occupations, fields of study, or technology are called **specialized language.** "My First Dive with the Dolphins" contains many examples of specialized—or technical—language. You may wish to revisit unfamiliar terms, such as *alpha male* or *regulator*, and find their definitions in a dictionary.

MY FIRST DIVE WITH THE DOLPHINS **473**

Connect to the Literature

1. What Do You Think?
Encourage students to use specific details from the story to explain their thoughts.

Comprehension Check
- Reed's job is to scrub algae off the walls and floor of the dolphin tank.
- Arnie charges Reed and swings his tail at him. Ernestine puts her fluke in Reed's hand and tows him as she swims. Lucky makes an aggressive sound but leaves Reed alone.

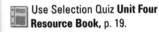 Use Selection Quiz **Unit Four Resource Book,** p. 19.

Think Critically

2. Possible Responses: Lucky would probably be less suspicious of Reed since Reed presented no threat to him; just because Lucky wasn't aggressive on Reed's first day in the tank doesn't mean that he won't be aggressive when Reed returns.

3. Possible Response: Reed has some moments of fear; however, his basic feelings range from excitement to a sense of wonder and respect.

4. Possible Responses: Simply being in the tank with the dolphins is exciting; being in actual contact with the dolphins is exciting.

5. Some students might suggest that Reed's enthusiasm is his most helpful trait. Because Reed wants to do a good job and make contact with the dolphins, he is willing to do the hard work and deal with a degree of risk.

6. Students may say that dolphins are intelligent or that dolphins are physically imposing.

Use **Reading and Critical Thinking Transparencies,** p. 14, for additional support.

Literary Analysis

Essay Encourage students to read some of the essays collected by their classmates. Then lead a discussion about the purposes of the various essays. Ask students if they agree with their classmates on the purposes of the collected essays.

Extend Interpretations

7. The Writer's Style Responses will vary. By describing how swimming with the dolphins affects his senses, Reed makes readers feel as if they are there in the tank with him. For example, Reed describes the way the movement of the water feels when Arnie charges him and how Ernestine's skin feels when he touches it.

8. Connect to Life Some students may respond that Reed's job seems too difficult and dangerous. Other students may say that having a chance to spend time with the dolphins would make the job worthwhile.

Writing

Dolphin Smarts Suggest students reread the article and take notes on information that supports this generalization.

Speaking & Listening

Opinion Presentation After students have developed their presentations, have them work in pairs to practice delivery.

 Use the **Speaking and Listening Book**, pp. 29 and 30, for additional support.

Research & Technology

Science Encourage students to use photos, charts, and illustrations with their posters or presentations to make the information more appealing and more accessible. To make this activity easier, have students work in pairs or small groups, with each student being responsible for a part of the task.

 Use **Writing Transparencies**, p. 47, for additional support.

Vocabulary
EXERCISE

1. compressed
2. coexistence
3. camouflage
4. magnification
5. hurtle
6. aggression
7. sonar
8. luminous
9. elegant
10. dominant

Writing

Dolphin Smarts The author of "My First Dive with the Dolphins" presents this generalization: Dolphins are smart like humans. Write a paragraph using this generalization as your main idea. Use information from the essay to provide examples and supporting information. Place your paragraph in your **Working Portfolio.**

Writing Handbook
See p. R35: Paragraphs.

Speaking & Listening

Opinion Presentation Create a presentation using the writing activity on this page. Use the main idea "Dolphins are smart like humans" to organize your presentation. Practice the way you deliver your presentation. Make sure your voice is loud and strong and that you use facial expressions and gestures. Rehearse your presentation a couple of times. Then deliver it to the class. Afterward, invite classmates to agree or disagree with you.

Speaking and Listening Handbook
See p. R100: Persuasive Presentations.

Research & Technology

SCIENCE

Using the Internet, an encyclopedia, and books about dolphins, find out about the following:

- What areas of the world have dolphin populations?
- How do dolphins interact with other species?
- What do scientists know about dolphin intelligence?

Present your research to the class in the form of an oral presentation or a poster.

INTERNET **Research Starter**
www.mcdougallittell.com

Vocabulary

EXERCISE: CONTEXT CLUES On a sheet of paper, write the Word To Know that best completes each sentence below.

1. While underwater, divers breathe _____ air from a tank or a hose.

2. The _____ of humans and dolphins at the oceanarium was mostly peaceful.

3. The dolphins' _____ makes them difficult to see underwater.

4. The _____ effect of water makes the dolphins look larger than they are.

5. Arnie swam so fast that he seemed to _____ through the water toward me.

6. An angry dolphin makes a special sound, one that is a sign of _____.

7. Dolphins use sounds called _____ to navigate underwater.

8. Ernestine created _____ rings that seemed to shine in the water.

9. From her red-brown eyes to her _____ flukes, Ernestine was beautiful.

10. Lucky was the _____ dolphin in the tank because of his toughness.

Vocabulary Handbook
See p. R20: Context Clues.

WORDS TO KNOW				
aggression	coexistence	dominant	hurtle	magnification
camouflage	compressed	elegant	luminous	sonar

CHOICES and CHALLENGES

Grammar in Context: Combining Sentences by Joining Phrases

In "My First Dive with the Dolphins," Don C. Reed uses smooth, short sentences. For example:

> Again I did nothing, but not through courage.

The word shown in red is a **conjunction,** a word that joins other words or phrases. Common conjunctions include *and, but, for,* and *or.*

Compare the excerpt above to the choppy version below:

> Again I did nothing. My doing nothing was not through courage.

The second example uses too many words to say the same thing as the first. The underlined phrase can be combined with the previous sentence for more drama and a faster pace.

Apply to Your Writing Combining phrases can help you avoid repeating words unnecessarily.

WRITING EXERCISE Combine each pair of sentences using the conjunction in parentheses.

Example: *Original* A wave splashed on the stage. It splashed at my feet. (and)

Rewritten A wave splashed on the stage and at my feet.

1. Clouds of algae spread through the tank. They spread across the surface. (and)
2. I swam away from the shore. I swam into deeper water. (and)
3. Spock will play with you. Spock won't play with other dolphins. (but)

Connect to the Literature Find two examples of sentences in which phrases are joined by conjuctions. Write the sentences, and underline the conjunctions.

Don C. Reed
born 1945

"I want my writing to be a positive force."

Diving In Don C. Reed began his career as a scuba diver in 1972, at Marine World near San Francisco, California. The seaquarium later became Marine World/Africa USA, an oceanarium/zoo, and moved to Vallejo, California. Reed spent 15 years there, eventually becoming head diver.

A Positive Force Reed's adventures with a variety of sea creatures have provided the material for several articles and books. The author views his writing as a way to "help the world." He states, "I want my writing to be a positive force. I will not write empty entertainment. I want my stuff to have . . . value." Although not a scientist, Reed believes humans and sea animals can coexist and may even be able to understand each other. "My First Dive with the Dolphins" is an excerpt from his book *The Dolphins and Me.*

AUTHOR ACTIVITY
Helping the World Read another article or chapter in a book by Don C. Reed. Based on "My First Dive with the Dolphins" and your other reading, evaluate the author's statement that he views his writing as a way to "help the world." Write a paragraph explaining what you think Reed hopes his writing will accomplish. How successful is he in achieving this?

Grammar in Context
WRITING EXERCISE
Possible Responses:

1. Clouds of algae rose in the tank and spread across the surface.
2. I swam away from the shore and into deeper water.
3. Spock will play with you but not with other dolphins.

Connect to the Literature
Answers will vary.

 Use **Writing Transparencies,** p. 19, for additional support.

Don C. Reed

Reed has said that he tries to "listen" to what an animal is thinking. He believes that people and sea animals can communicate their thoughts to each other by means of a yet-to-be discovered form of extrasensory perception.

Author Activity

Helping the World Tell students to consider how Reed's descriptions of his encounters with the dolphins help those people who read his work. Suggest that students also think about what they, themselves, gained from reading "My First Dive with the Dolphins."

EXPLICIT INSTRUCTION ## Grammar in Context

IDENTIFYING CONJUNCTIONS
Instruction Students can make their writing flow more smoothly by using conjunctions. Write the following sentences on the board:
Don C. Reed was nervous about diving into the dolphin tank. He didn't let his fears stop him.
Don C. Reed was nervous about diving into the dolphin tank, but he didn't let his fears stop him.
Point out the way these two thoughts have been merged by using the conjunction *but.*
Practice Tell students to read each pair of sentences and name a conjunction that they could use to combine the two sentences.

1. Reed liked watching Ernestine. He particularly enjoyed swimming with her. (and; but)
2. Reed purposely held still when Arnie approached him. That's what Ted had recommended. (because)
3. Reed sensed that Lucky commanded respect. Reed decided to drift down and return to his work. (so)
4. Ted had given Reed essential information about the dolphins. He knew it would help Reed on his first dive. (because)
5. Reed says he used to think that all dolphins were gentle and sweet. He realizes that each one has a distinct personality. (but)

 Use **Unit Four Resource Book,** p. 17.

 For more instruction in identifying conjunctions, see McDougal Littell's *Language Network,* Chapter 6.

For **systematic instruction** in grammar, see:
- **Grammar, Usage and Mechanics Book**
- pacing chart on p. 441i.

Standards-Based Objectives

1. understand and appreciate **poetry**
2. understand author's use of **sound devices**
3. think about **word choice** to help understand sound devices better
4. understand **influence of rhyme, repetition, and rhythm on meaning**

Summary

Two poets ponder two birds. Rachel Field marvels at how wild geese know when it's time to fly south, while Robert Frost muses about the winter owl, admiring her grace as she veers away from a window.

Thematic Link

Through their poetry, Field and Frost express our desire to understand birds and our ability to appreciate their beauty. These two poems reflect our fascination with bird flight. How is it that these winged creatures know when and where to go?

English Conventions Practice

Daily Language SkillBuilder

Have students **proofread** the display sentences on page 441k and write them correctly. The sentences also appear on Transparency 15 of **Language Transparencies.**

Something Told the Wild Geese

by RACHEL FIELD

Questioning Faces

by ROBERT FROST

Connect to Your Life

Birds of a Feather What have you noticed about the appearance and behavior of birds you see in your community?

Build Background

SCIENCE

In the two poems you are about to read, birds—wild geese and an owl—play important roles. Have you ever asked yourself why birds fly? One explanation is that they need to fly in order to survive. Like most animals, birds have adaptations, or special features, to help them live in certain habitats.

Birds need a steady, yearlong food supply, and many birds need to avoid very cold temperatures. These birds fly to warmer climates in the autumn and return in the spring.

Wild geese have webbed feet for swimming and broad, powerful wings to help them fly south for the winter.

Focus Your Reading

LITERARY ANALYSIS **SOUND DEVICES**

Poets use **sound devices** to make their words more powerful. Common sound devices are rhyme, rhythm, and repetition. Words that end with the same sounds are said to **rhyme.** The pattern of stressed and unstressed syllables that guides your voice when reading is the poem's **rhythm.** The use of sounds, words, or phrases more than once is **repetition.** As you read, look for the patterns of rhyme, rhythm, and repetition.

ACTIVE READING **WORD CHOICE**

The words a poet chooses tell you a lot about his or her message. Specific words about a poem's subject add detail and flavor to a visual image. For example, it can be more interesting and accurate to describe a sky as *azure* instead of *blue.*

In poetry, both the sounds and the meanings of words are important. Well-chosen words help readers understand ideas and visualize images.

READER'S NOTEBOOK As you read each poem, list words and phrases you find especially powerful.

LESSON RESOURCES

UNIT FOUR RESOURCE BOOK, pp. 20–21

ASSESSMENT
Formal Assessment, pp. 83–84
Test Generator

SKILLS TRANSPARENCIES AND COPYMASTERS
Literary Analysis
• Poetry: Sound Devices, TR 20 (p. 479)

Reading and Critical Thinking
• Analyzing Word Choice, TR 15 (p. 479)

Language
• Daily Language SkillBuilder, TR 15 (p. 476)

Writing
• Sensory Words List, TR 16 (p. 480)
• Locating Information Using Print References, TR 45 (p. 480)

Speaking and Listening
• Choosing Presentation Aids, p. 10 (p. 480)

INTEGRATED TECHNOLOGY
Audio Library
Internet: Research Starter

Visit our Web site:
www.mcdougallittell.com

For **systematic instruction** in language skills, see:
• **Vocabulary and Spelling Book**
• **Grammar, Usage, and Mechanics Book**
• pacing chart on p. 441i.

Something Told the Wild Geese

by Rachel Field

Something told the wild geese
   It was time to go.
Though the fields lay golden
   Something whispered,—"Snow."
5 Leaves were green and stirring,
   Berries, luster-glossed,
But beneath warm feathers
   Something cautioned,—"Frost."
All the sagging orchards
10 Steamed with amber spice,
But each wild breast stiffened
   At remembered ice.
Something told the wild geese
   It was time to fly,—
15 Summer sun was on their wings,
   Winter in their cry.

Sunset, Kempenfelt Bay, Lawren Harris.
Collection of Power Corporation of Canada.

THINKING *through the* LITERATURE

1. **Comprehension Check** According to the speaker, what messages does nature send to the geese?
2. What time of year does "Something Told the Wild Geese" describe? What details tell you this?
3. Why might it be necessary for the geese to fly away?

Literary Analysis `SOUND DEVICES`

Ask students to identify the rhymes in "Questioning Faces."

Possible Responses: *pass* and *glass*, *aspread* and *red*, *quill* and *sill*.

Ask students to tap out the rhythm of "Something Told the Wild Geese." Ask how the rhythm emphasizes the idea that something is telling the wild geese to go.

Possible Response: The steady rhythm is like a ticking clock. It reinforces the regular pattern of changing seasons and the idea that it is time for the geese to fly away.

Active Reading `WORD CHOICE`

 A Ask students to consider the word *aspread*. Although they may not find this word in a dictionary, students should have little difficulty figuring out its meaning. Ask them why they think Frost chose this word.

Possible Responses: Frost might have chosen the word *aspread* because it sounds graceful. Because of the rhythm of the poem, a two-syllable word works here.

Use **Unit Four Resource Book**, p. 20, for more practice.

Reading Skills and Strategies:
MAKE INFERENCES

B Ask students to infer what Robert Frost means when he says that the owl's wings "caught color from the last of evening red."

Possible Response: Frost means that the owl's wings were reflecting the setting sun, which looked red.

Questioning Children (1949), Karel Appel. Courtesy of Grand Westin Hotel, Netherlands.

Questioning Faces

by Robert Frost

The winter owl banked just in time to pass

And save herself from breaking window glass.

And her wings straining suddenly aspread   **A**

Caught color from the last of evening red   **B**

In a display of underdown and quill

To glassed-in children at the window sill.

EXPLICIT INSTRUCTION   ## Repetition and Rhythm

Instruction Remind students that poets use sound devices to emphasize meaning. Review repetition (*the repeated use of words, phrases, or lines in a poem*). Ask what word is repeated in "Something Told the Wild Geese" (*something*). Then discuss why the poet chose to repeat this word. Ask if the poet tells what this "something" is (*no*). Explain that the poet may be repeating the words to emphasize her curiosity about what the something is. Point out that this adds a feeling of mystery to the poem. Next, review the definition of alliteration

(*the repetition of consonant sounds at the beginning of words*). Read aloud "Questioning Faces" and ask students to identify examples of alliteration (*straining suddenly, caught color*). Discuss with students where the action in the poem is most dramatic ("*And her wings . . . evening red*"). Ask if the alliteration helps to emphasize the drama of the owl's actions. Discuss responses.

Practice Use the Literary Analysis: Sound Devices note in the green side column to discuss rhyme and rhythm in the poems.

Possible Responses: See the responses in the green side column.

 Use **Unit Four Resource Book**, p. 21, for more practice.

Connect to the Literature

1. **What Do You Think?**
What images formed in your mind after reading Robert Frost's poem?

Comprehension Check
• In "Questioning Faces," why does the owl bank?
• Who is watching the owl?

Think Critically

2. How do you think the children feel about what they've witnessed?

3. How is "Questioning Faces" similar to "Something Told the Wild Geese"? How are these poems different?

   Think About:
   • the image each creates
   • what birds are doing in each poem
   • the presence of humans

4. **ACTIVE READING** **WORD CHOICE**
Look at the list you made in your **READER'S NOTEBOOK**. With a classmate, discuss what these words and phrases add to the poems. Then select one word choice that you think is strong, and complete a web like the one shown.

Extend Interpretations

5. **COMPARING TEXTS**
Compare the poems in this lesson with the three haiku on page 205. How are the ways in which Field and Frost describe nature similar to the way a haiku poet might do so?

6. **Connect to Life** What aspects of nature and wildlife do you find fascinating? Why?

```
Definition        Other Words
   of             Poet Could
  Word              Have
                    Chosen
        \          /
       WORD CHOICE
            |
          My
       Associations
       with the Word
```

Literary Analysis

SOUND DEVICES Poets use **sound devices** such as rhyme, rhythm, and repetition to emphasize certain ideas and images. Words that end with the same sound are said to **rhyme.** Robert Frost's poem is built with rhyming couplets, pairs of lines that end with rhyming words.

When a poem's **rhythm** has a regular beat, it gives the poem a musical quality. Your voice falls into a pattern when you read it aloud. In both of these poems, the rhyme pattern and rhythm stress the final word in each line.

Repeated words can emphasize the poet's ideas. Rachel Field's **repetition** of the word *something* invites you to wonder what that "something" is.

Paired Activity With a classmate, take turns reading the poems aloud. Then make a chart like the one below. Look at the poems again for examples of repetition and rhyme, and list them in your chart. Discuss how your knowledge of rhyme and repetition in the poems helps you hear their rhythms.

Poem Title	Repeated Words	Rhyming Words
"Something Told the Wild Geese"	something	go/snow
"Questioning Faces"		

Connect to the Literature

1. **What Do You Think?**
Students may mention the image of a bird flying straight at them, or that of young children with their faces pressed up against the window.

Comprehension Check
• It banks in order to avoid hitting a window.
• Children are watching the owl.

Think Critically

2. **Possible Response:** They may feel frightened by the bird's flight or worried for its safety, but also excited by the drama they are viewing.

3. **Possible Response:** Both poems are about birds, both concern flight, both marvel at the birds' instinctual knowledge and powerful abilities. "Questioning Faces," however, includes people and the human world, while "Something Told the Wild Geese" does not.

4. Students' answers will vary. Some will be more struck by the rhyming words, others by the sensory words, and still others by the words describing particular bird features.

 Use **Reading and Critical Thinking Transparencies,** p. 15, for additional support.

Literary Analysis

Sound Devices Students' charts should include examples from both poems of words that rhyme. Their examples of repetition should come from "Something Told the Wild Geese."

Use **Literary Analysis Transparencies,** p. 20, for additional support.

SOMETHING TOLD THE WILD GEESE / QUESTIONING FACES **479**

Extend Interpretations

5. **Comparing Texts Possible Response:** All five poets write about nature's wonders in very short, concise ways, but the haiku poets follow a different poetic form than do Field and Frost. The haiku form is shorter, follows a five-seven-five pattern of syllables, and does not rhyme.

6. **Connect to Life** Answers will vary, but should include some reflection on students' feelings and thoughts about the natural world.

Writing

Field Diary Student responses will vary but should include their emotional responses as well as details that appeal to their senses. Tell students to feel free to make drawings of their observations in order to remember details. Students can place their field diaries in their Working Portfolios.

 Use **Writing Transparencies**, p. 16, for additional support.

Speaking & Listening

Multimedia Presentation Give students a few days to prepare their presentations. To make the activity easier, have students work in groups to create presentations.

 Use the **Speaking and Listening Book**, p. 10, for additional support.

Research & Technology

Bird Profile Students could work with partners on this assignment. Tell students it will be easier for them to focus their writing if they keep this writing prompt in mind as they do their research: What makes this type of bird unique?

 Use **Writing Transparencies**, p. 45, for additional support.

Writing

Field Diary Rachel Field and Robert Frost probably got the ideas for their poems by observing nature. Gather details for a poem by watching something in the natural world. Record your observations in a diary or journal entry. Note details that appeal to your senses in a sensory-details chart. Place your notes and your chart in your **Working Portfolio.**

Sight	Hearing	Touch	Taste	Smell

Writing Handbook
See p. R38: Using Language Effectively.

Speaking & Listening

Multimedia Presentation Create a mini-multimedia presentation for the poems. Include music or sound effects and artwork that express the poems' moods and images. Set up the presentation so that the class can see the artwork and hear the music or sound effects at the same time. If possible, include a tape-recorded reading of the poems. Otherwise, you can read aloud the poems as part of your presentation.

Research & Technology

Bird Profile Learn more about wild geese or owls. Conduct research to find out about physical features and adaptations, nesting and feeding habits, typical habitats and migration patterns, and how the birds are affected by humans. Write a short report responding to the question, What makes this type of bird unique? Include a list of the information sources you used.

 Research Starter www.mcdougallittell.com

Rachel Field
1894–1942

"I wasn't one of those children who are remembered . . . as clever and promising."

Newbery Winner Rachel Field overcame severe learning difficulties to become a writer. In 1930, Field received the Newbery Medal for *Hitty: Her First Hundred Years* (1929). *Hitty* combined Field's interests in children's stories and history—particularly the history of pioneer life. Field's 1931 book about pioneers, *Calico Bush,* received a Newbery Honor Award.

Robert Frost
1874–1963

"The poem begins in delight and ends in wisdom."

A New England Poet Robert Frost farmed, taught school, and edited a newspaper before he achieved recognition as a poet. A four-time Pulitzer Prize winner, Frost received the first of these awards in 1924 for his collection *New Hampshire.* Frost more than achieved his life's goal, which he said was to write "a few poems it will be hard to get rid of."

Zlateh the Goat

by ISAAC BASHEVIS SINGER

Connect to Your Life

Working Relationship What roles do animals play in your life? How might you feel about an animal that helped your family to survive?

Build Background

HISTORY

Isaac Bashevis Singer grew up in and near Warsaw, Poland. His father was a rabbi, a scholar trained to interpret Jewish law. Most of Singer's stories for young people are rooted in the traditions of Jewish communities.

"Zlateh the Goat" takes place during Hanukkah. This Jewish religious festival celebrates a long-ago event in which one day's worth of lamp oil burned for eight days. Jews commemorate this miracle by lighting candles for eight nights, eating foods such as potato pancakes that are cooked in oil, and exchanging gifts.

WORDS TO KNOW	Vocabulary Preview		
astonish	dusk	penetrate	thatched
cleft	imp	regain	
content	indicate	splendor	

Focus Your Reading

LITERARY ANALYSIS | **CLIMAX AND RESOLUTION**

Two important parts of a story's plot are climax and resolution. The **climax** is the turning point in a plot and the moment of greatest interest. It usually involves an important decision or event that affects the outcome of the conflict. The **resolution,** or **falling action,** is the part of the story in which the characters' conflicts are often solved and any loose ends in the story are tied up. As you read, identify the main conflict. Then watch for the climax. It's your signal that the resolution is about to begin.

ACTIVE READING | **STORY MAPPING**

Understanding conflict, climax, and resolution can help you understand and enjoy your reading more. Sometimes it's hard to find these elements, however. They may blend into one another. Creating a **story map** can make the key elements and the key events easier to see.

Characters:
Setting:
Conflict:
Key Events:
1.
2.
3.
(add more as needed)
Climax:
Resolution:

READER'S NOTEBOOK

As you read this story, make and fill in a story map similar to the one shown. Describe the main character, setting, and key events. Identify the conflict, climax, and resolution.

ZLATEH THE GOAT   **481**

Standards-Based Objectives

1. understand and appreciate a **short story**
2. understand author's use of **climax and resolution**
3. use **story mapping** to help understand a short story better
4. analyze the **influence of setting** on the problem and its resolution

Summary

Reuven the furrier is having a bad year and decides he must sell the family's goat. He sends his son Aaron to town with the goat, Zlateh. The weather changes as they are on their way to the butcher's. Snow starts to fall. They lose their way and are forced to take shelter in a haystack. There, Zlateh is able to eat the hay, and Aaron drinks the goat's milk for nourishment. They survive the storm and return home, as Aaron has decided he will not sell the goat. Because cold weather has arrived, people need fur coats, so the family's situation is improved. Zlateh, instead of being sold, becomes more beloved to the family than before.

Thematic Link

Zlateh provides enough milk to keep Aaron alive during a blizzard. This interdependence of people and animals has provided endless fascination for writers and readers over the centuries.

English Conventions Practice

Daily Language SkillBuilder

Have students **proofread** the display sentences on page 441k and write them correctly. The sentences also appear on Transparency 16 of **Language Transparencies.**

Preteaching Vocabulary

If you would like to preteach the WORDS TO KNOW for this selection, use the Explicit Instruction, page 484.

LESSON RESOURCES

UNIT FOUR RESOURCE BOOK, pp. 22–28

ASSESSMENT
Formal Assessment, pp. 85–86
Test Generator

SKILLS TRANSPARENCIES AND COPYMASTERS
Reading and Critical Thinking
• Summarizing (Story Map), TR 13 (pp. 484, 488)

Language
• Daily Language SkillBuilder, TR 16 (p. 481)
• Punctuating Elements in a Series, TR 44 (p. 490)
• Context Clues: Compare and Contrast, Cause and Effect, Example, TR 54 (p. 484)

Writing
• Dialogue, TR 24 (p. 489)

INTEGRATED TECHNOLOGY
Audio Library

Visit our Web site:
www.mcdougallittell.com

For **systematic instruction** in language skills, see:
• **Vocabulary and Spelling Book**
• **Grammar, Usage, and Mechanics Book**
• pacing chart on p. 441i.

Zlateh the Goat

by
Isaac Bashevis Singer

At Hanukkah time the road from the village to the town is usually covered with snow, but this year the winter had been a mild one. Hanukkah had almost come, yet little snow had fallen. The sun shone most of the time. The peasants complained that because of the dry weather there would be a poor harvest of winter grain. New grass sprouted, and the peasants sent their cattle out to pasture.

For Reuven the furrier[1] it was a bad year, and after long hesitation he decided to sell Zlateh the goat. She was old and gave little milk. Feyvel the town butcher had offered eight gulden[2] for her. Such a sum would buy Hanukkah candles, potatoes and oil for pancakes, gifts for the children, and other holiday necessaries for the house. Reuven told his oldest boy, Aaron, to take the goat to town.

Aaron understood what taking the goat to Feyvel meant, but he had to obey his father. Leah, his mother, wiped the tears from her eyes when she heard the news. Aaron's younger sisters, Anna and Miriam, cried loudly. Aaron put on his quilted jacket and a cap with earmuffs, bound a rope around Zlateh's neck, and took along two slices of bread

---

1. **furrier:** a person who makes or sells fur garments.
2. **gulden:** gold or silver coins.

The Goat, Pablo Picasso. Musée Picasso, Paris. Copyright © 2001 Estate of Pablo Picasso/Artists Rights Society (ARS), New York. Photo copyright © RMN, Beatrice Hatala.

---

with cheese to eat on the road. Aaron was supposed to deliver the goat by evening, spend the night at the butcher's, and return the next day with the money.

While the family said goodbye to the goat, and Aaron placed the rope around her neck, Zlateh stood as patiently and good-naturedly as ever. She licked Reuven's hand. She shook her small white beard. Zlateh trusted human beings. She knew that they always fed her and never did her any harm.

When Aaron brought her out on the road to town, she seemed somewhat <u>astonished</u>. She'd never been led in that direction before. She looked back at him questioningly, as if to say, "Where are you taking me?" But after a while she seemed to come to the conclusion that a goat shouldn't ask questions. Still, the road was different. They passed new fields, pastures, and huts with <u>thatched</u> roofs. Here and there a dog barked and came running after them, but Aaron chased it away with his stick.

The sun was shining when Aaron left the village. Suddenly the weather changed. A large black cloud with a bluish center appeared in the east and spread itself rapidly over the sky. A cold wind blew in with it. The crows flew low, croaking. At first it looked as if it would rain, but instead it began to hail as in summer. It was early in the day, but it became dark as <u>dusk</u>. After a while the hail turned to snow.

In his twelve years Aaron had seen all kinds of weather, but he had never experienced a snow like this one. It was so dense it shut out the light of the day. In a

I and the Village (1911), Marc Chagall. Oil on canvas, 75 ⅝" × 59 ⅝" (192.1 × 151.4 cm) The Museum of Modern Art, New York. Mrs. Simon Guggenheim Fund. Copyright © 2001 ARS, New York/ADAGP, Paris. Photograph © 2001 The Museum of Modern Art, New York.

WORDS TO KNOW	**astonished** (ə-stŏn′ĭsht) *adj.* surprised; amazed **astonish** *v.*
	thatched (thăcht) *adj.* made of or covered with reeds or straw **thatch** *v.*
	dusk (dŭsk) *n.* the time of day between sunset and complete darkness

483

Reading Skills and Strategies:
VISUALIZE

A Invite students to describe the mental images that descriptions of the storm in the text evoke.

Possible Response: Students might describe the swirling storm or the snow-covered road, goat, and boy.

Reading Skills and Strategies:
PREDICT

B Ask students to predict what will happen next to Zlateh and Aaron.

Possible Responses: Students might predict that someone will appear to save them. Or students might predict that they will ride out the storm in the haystack, warm and safe.

Active Reading STORY MAPPING

Ask students to update their story maps.

Possible Responses: Event 3: They lose their way in a blizzard; Event 4: Aaron finds the haystack and they take shelter in it.

Use **Reading and Critical Thinking Transparencies**, p. 13, for additional support.

short time their path was completely covered. The wind became as cold as ice. The road to town was narrow and winding. Aaron no longer knew where he was. He could not see through the snow. The cold soon <u>penetrated</u> his quilted jacket.

At first Zlateh didn't seem to mind the change in weather. She too was twelve years old and knew what winter meant. But when her legs sank deeper and deeper into the snow, she began to turn her head and look at Aaron in wonderment. Her mild eyes seemed to ask, "Why are we out in such a storm?" Aaron hoped that a peasant would come along with his cart, but no one passed by.

The snow grew thicker, falling to the ground in large, whirling flakes. Beneath it Aaron's boots touched the softness of a plowed field. He realized that he was no longer on the road. He had gone astray. He could no longer figure out which was east or west, which way was the village, the town. The wind whistled, howled, whirled the snow about in eddies. It looked as if white <u>imps</u> were playing tag on the fields. A white dust rose above the ground. Zlateh stopped. She could walk no longer. Stubbornly she anchored her <u>cleft</u> hooves in the earth and bleated as if pleading to be taken home. Icicles hung from her white beard, and her horns were glazed with frost.

Aaron did not want to admit the danger, but he knew just the same that if they did not find shelter, they would freeze to death. This was no ordinary storm. It was a mighty blizzard. The snowfall had reached his knees. His hands were numb, and he could no longer feel his toes. He choked when he breathed. His nose felt

like wood, and he rubbed it with snow. Zlateh's bleating began to sound like crying. Those humans in whom she had so much confidence had dragged her into a trap. Aaron began to pray to God for himself and for the innocent animal.

Suddenly he made out the shape of a hill. He wondered what it could be. Who had piled snow into such a huge heap? He moved toward it, dragging Zlateh after him. When he came near it, he realized that it was a large haystack which the snow had blanketed.

Aaron realized immediately that they were saved. With great effort he dug his way through the snow. He was a village boy and knew what to do. When he reached the hay, he hollowed out a nest for himself and the goat. No matter how cold it may be outside, in the hay it is always warm. And hay was food for Zlateh. The moment she smelled it, she became <u>contented</u> and began to eat. Outside, the snow continued to fall. It quickly covered the passageway Aaron had dug. But a boy and an animal need to breathe, and there was hardly any air in their hide-out. Aaron bored a kind of a window through the hay and snow and carefully kept the passage clear.

Zlateh, having eaten her fill, sat down on her hind legs and seemed to have <u>regained</u> her confidence in man. Aaron ate his two slices of bread and cheese, but after the difficult journey he was still hungry. He looked at Zlateh and noticed her udders were full. He lay down next to her, placing himself so that when he milked her, he could squirt the milk into his mouth. It was rich and sweet. Zlateh was not accustomed to being milked that way, but she did not resist. On the contrary, she

WORDS
TO
KNOW

penetrate (pĕn'ĭ-trāt') v. to pass through or enter into
imp (ĭmp) n. a small demon
cleft (klĕft) adj. divided; split
contented (kən-tĕn'tĭd) adj. happy with things as they are; satisfied
regain (rē-gān') v. to get back; recover

484

EXPLICIT
INSTRUCTION **Preteaching Vocabulary**

WORDS TO KNOW Remind students to draw on their own experiences to bring meaning to words in context.

Teaching Strategy Tell students that sentences often contain clues to help them find a word's meaning. A **comparison clue** compares a word to a similar word or idea and often uses *like* or *as*. Share the following sentence with students:
Zlateh was as <u>astonished</u> as a brand-new lottery winner when they left the yard behind. Because a brand-new lottery winner would probably be surprised, *astonished* must mean

"surprised." **Contrast clues** use the opposite strategy: they compare a word to something very different from it. Look for signal words like *although, but, however,* or *on the other hand.* Share the following sentence:
It seemed like the cold of the storm should <u>penetrate</u> the haystack, but inside it was warm. The second half of the sentence shows that *penetrate* must mean "get through," because of the contrast of the cold on the outside and the warmth inside.

Practice Ask students which sentence gives a comparison clue and which gives a contrast

clue.

1. My brother was <u>content</u> during the car trip, but my sister complained the whole way. (contrast)

2. Thermometers <u>indicate</u> temperature just as clocks show time. (compare)

Use **Unit Four Resource Book**, p. 27, for more practice.

For **systematic instruction** in vocabulary, see:
• **Vocabulary and Spelling Book**
• pacing chart on p. 441i.

January, (1940), Grant Wood. Oil on masonite panel, 18" × 24". Private Collection. Reproduced by permission.
Copyright © Estate of Grant Wood/Licensed by VAGA, New York, NY.

seemed eager to reward Aaron for bringing her to a shelter whose very walls, floor, and ceiling were made of food.

Through the window Aaron could catch a glimpse of the chaos outside. The wind carried before it whole drifts of snow. It was completely dark, and he did not know whether night had already come or whether it was the darkness of the storm. Thank God that in the hay it was not cold. The dried hay, grass, and field flowers exuded the warmth of the summer sun. Zlateh ate frequently; she nibbled from above, below, from the left and right. Her body gave forth an animal warmth, and Aaron cuddled up to her. He had always loved Zlateh, but now she was like a sister. He was alone, cut off from his family, and wanted to talk. He began to talk to Zlateh. "Zlateh, what do you think about what has happened to us?" he asked.

"Maaaa," Zlateh answered.

"If we hadn't found this stack of hay, we would both be frozen stiff by now," Aaron said.

"Maaaa," was the goat's reply.

"If the snow keeps on falling like this, we may have to stay here for days," Aaron explained.

"Maaaa," Zlateh bleated.

"What does 'Maaaa' mean?" Aaron asked. "You'd better speak up clearly."

"Maaaa. Maaaa," Zlateh tried.

"Well, let it be 'Maaaa' then," Aaron said patiently. "You can't speak, but I know you understand. I need you and you need me. Isn't that right?"

"Maaaa."

Literary Analysis
CLIMAX AND RESOLUTION

Ask students to pinpoint the climax.

Possible Response: A peasant gives Aaron and Zlateh directions to get back home. Aaron resolves that he will not sell Zlateh.

Ask students to describe the beginning of the story's resolution.

Possible Response: Aaron and Zlateh arrive home. The family is overjoyed to see them.

Active Reading | STORY MAPPING |

Ask students to complete their story maps.

Possible Response: Resolution: Zlateh, instead of being sold, becomes more beloved than ever.

Aaron became sleepy. He made a pillow out of some hay, leaned his head on it, and dozed off. Zlateh too fell asleep.

When Aaron opened his eyes, he didn't know whether it was morning or night. The snow had blocked up his window. He tried to clear it, but when he had bored through to the length of his arm, he still hadn't reached the outside. Luckily he had his stick with him and was able to break through to the open air. It was still dark outside. The snow continued to fall and the wind wailed, first with one voice and then with many. Sometimes it had the sound of devilish laughter. Zlateh too awoke, and when Aaron greeted her, she answered, "Maaaa." Yes, Zlateh's language consisted of only one word, but it meant many things. Now she was saying, "We must accept all that God gives us—heat, cold, hunger, satisfaction, light, and darkness."

Aaron had awakened hungry. He had eaten up his food, but Zlateh had plenty of milk.

For three days Aaron and Zlateh stayed in the haystack. Aaron had always loved Zlateh, but in these three days he loved her more and more. She fed him with her milk and helped him keep warm. She comforted him with her patience. He told her many stories, and she always cocked her ears and listened. When he patted her, she licked his hand and his face. Then she said, "Maaaa," and he knew it meant, I love you too.

The snow fell for three days, though after the first day it was not as thick and the wind quieted down.

Sometimes Aaron felt that there could never have been a summer, that the snow had always fallen, ever since he could remember. He, Aaron, never had a father or mother or sisters. He was a snow child, born of the snow, and so was Zlateh. It was so quiet in the hay that his ears rang[3] in the stillness. Aaron and Zlateh slept all night and a good part of the day. As for Aaron's dreams, they were all about warm weather. He dreamed of green fields, trees covered with blossoms, clear brooks, and singing birds. By the third night the snow had stopped, but Aaron did not dare to find his way home in the darkness. The sky became clear and the moon shone, casting silvery nets on the snow. Aaron dug his way out and looked at the world. It was all white, quiet, dreaming dreams of heavenly splendor. The stars were large and close. The moon swam in the sky as in a sea.

On the morning of the fourth day, Aaron heard the ringing of sleigh bells. The haystack was not far from the road. The peasant who drove the sleigh pointed out the way to him— not to the town and Feyvel the butcher, but home to the village. Aaron had decided in the haystack that he would never part with Zlateh.

Aaron's family and their neighbors had searched for the boy and the goat but had found no trace of them during the storm. They feared they were lost. Aaron's mother and sisters cried for him; his father remained silent and gloomy. Suddenly one of the neighbors came running to their house with the news that Aaron and Zlateh were coming up the road.

There was great joy in the family. Aaron told them how he had found the stack of hay and how Zlateh had fed him with her milk. Aaron's sisters kissed and hugged Zlateh and gave her a special treat of chopped carrots and potato peels, which Zlateh gobbled up hungrily.

---

3. **his ears rang:** he heard a buzzing or humming sound.

WORDS
TO
KNOW **splendor** (splĕn′dər) *n.* the condition of being brilliant or magnificent

Orion in Winter, Charles Burchfield. Provenance: Museo Thyssen-Bornemisza, Madrid.

Nobody ever again thought of selling Zlateh, and now that the cold weather had finally set in, the villagers needed the services of Reuven the furrier once more. When Hanukkah came, Aaron's mother was able to fry pancakes every evening, and Zlateh got her portion too. Even though Zlateh had her own pen, she often came to the kitchen, knocking on the door with her horns to <u>indicate</u> that she was ready to visit, and she was always admitted. In the evening, Aaron, Miriam, and Anna played dreidel.[4] Zlateh sat near the stove, watching the children and the flickering of the Hanukkah candles.

Once in a while Aaron would ask her, "Zlateh, do you remember the three days we spent together?"

And Zlateh would scratch her neck with a horn, shake her white bearded head, and come out with the single sound which expressed all her thoughts, and all her love. ❖

---

4. **dreidel** (drād′l): a Hanukkah game played by spinning a four-sided top with a different Hebrew letter on each side.

WORDS
TO
KNOW

indicate (ĭn′dĭ-kāt′) *v.* to show or express

487

Advanced Students
Students should complete their lists of figurative language.

Possible Responses:
Personification: "the wind wailed, first with one voice and then with many"; "the moon shone, casting silvery nets on the snow"; "the moon swam in the sky as in a sea" (as well as any mention of the meaning of Zlateh's bleating) Ask students what effect this figurative language has on the reader.

Possible Response: It makes the scenes more vivid and more interesting to read.

Less Proficient Readers
Be sure students understand the ending of the story by asking the following questions:

• What did the family decide to do with Zlateh? *(They kept her.)*
• Why were they able to keep her?
  Possible Response: Because the weather turned cooler, people needed to buy fur coats, and the family's business improved.

English Learners
Have students go back through the story and make a list of the things that were new to them in the tale. Since their experiences are different, their responses will vary, but their list may include details about life in a snowy climate, Jewish holidays, life in a rural area, or survival skills.

EXPLICIT INSTRUCTION **Influence of Setting**

Instruction Ask volunteers to review the way setting has influenced the story so far. (*Poor crops create a lack of money. Reuven decides to sell Zlateh, even though his family loves her. A storm forces Aaron and Zlateh to depend on each other for survival. As a result, Aaron thinks of Zlateh as a sister, and this make selling her even more difficult.*) Then remind students that setting can influence not only how problems develop but how they are resolved. Use the Literary Analysis: Climax and Resolution note in the green side column to discuss the climax and the resolution of the conflict. Ask whether setting had any influence on the climax and resolution. Then ask students how the story might have been different if the snowstorm had not occurred.

Practice Write this question on the board: "How did the snowstorm influence the way Aaron resolved the conflict?" Have students work in pairs to write responses.

Possible Responses: The snowstorm forces Aaron and Zlateh to depend on one another for survival. Aaron realizes that they are almost like equals because they help each other. He begins to think that Zlateh is like a sister, and he decides he cannot sell her. The family also realizes this after Aaron and Zlateh return. They were very worried about Aaron and when they learn that Zlateh helped keep him alive during the storm, they also decide not to sell the goat.

 Use **Unit Four Resource Book**, p. 25, for more practice.

Connect to the Literature

1. What Do You Think?
Most students will be saddened by Zlateh's intended fate and relieved and uplifted by the ending. They may, however, appreciate the family's need to sell Zlateh.

Comprehension Check
• He is taking her to the butcher, because the family needs money.
• They take shelter in a haystack.
• With joy and relief, the family decides to keep Zlateh after all.

 Use Selection Quiz
Unit Four Resource Book, p. 28.

Think Critically

2. Possible Response: Love is the most important because that is what motivates Aaron to keep Zlateh.

3. Most students will recognize that Zlateh is a valued member of the family, both because they need her and because they love her.

4. Possible Response: He is resourceful, strong, confident, and loyal.

5. Possible Response: He matures, learning to make his own decisions about how to survive the snowstorm and about keeping Zlateh.

6. Possible Response: Conflicts: Aaron's desire to save Zlateh and their mutual need to survive the snowstorm; Climax: when Aaron decides he must keep Zlateh; Resolution: Aaron and Zlateh are welcomed home

Use **Reading and Critical Thinking Transparencies,** p. 13, for additional support.

Literary Analysis

Climax and Resolution The conflicts in "Zlateh the Goat" are resolved—the family no longer needs to sell the goat because their income is restored, and Zlateh and Aaron survive their ordeal. The setting influenced both the conflict and the resolution of the conflict. The dry season influenced the father's decision to sell Zlateh and helped bring about the conflict. The snowstorm forced Zlateh and Aaron to help each other survive and influenced Aaron's decision not to sell Zlateh.

Connect to the Literature

1. What Do You Think?
Did you support the family's plan for Zlateh? Why or why not? What was your reaction to the story's ending?

Comprehension Check
• Where is Aaron taking Zlateh, and why?
• How do Aaron and Zlateh save themselves from the storm?
• What does the family do with Zlateh at the end of the story?

Think Critically

2. What emotion do you think is most important in this story? Why?

3. How do you think Aaron and his family feel about Zlateh at the story's beginning? Support your answer.

4. What character traits do you think Aaron has that help him during his journey?

5. How does Aaron change as a result of his experiences with Zlateh?

    Think About:
    • the way he makes decisions
    • his relationship with his father
    • what Zlateh teaches him during the journey

6. | ACTIVE READING | STORY MAPPING |
Look over the story map in your
📖 READER'S NOTEBOOK. Compare with a classmate what you recorded as the **conflict, climax,** and **resolution** of the story.

Extend Interpretations

7. What If? What if the snowstorm had not occurred? What actions might Aaron have taken because of his feelings for Zlateh?

8. The Writer's Style Why do you think Singer set his story during Hanukkah, a festival that celebrates a miracle and a new beginning for the Jewish people?

9. Connect to Life What do you think animals have to offer people? Does this story remind you of any animal-human relationships you've known about?

Literary Analysis

CLIMAX AND RESOLUTION In a story, **climax** is the main turning point. The **resolution,** which usually occurs at the story's conclusion, ties up loose ends and brings the story to a close. Conflicts in the story do not always disappear after the climax. Even if conflicts still are present, something in the story changes after the climax. You might notice a change in the characters or a change in the story's tone.

SETTING AND CONFLICT In "Zlateh the Goat," **setting** is important to the conflict and the resolution. The story's setting is a town that has had a poor harvest. As a result, people are having financial difficulties and Aaron's father decides to sell his family's beloved goat. This creates a conflict for Aaron. Later on, Zlateh and Aaron help each other survive a terrible snowstorm. Aaron decides he cannot sell the goat that helped him live through the storm.

Activity Identify the conflicts in "Zlateh the Goat" and follow them from the time they are introduced until the story's resolution. Are the conflicts resolved or left unresolved at the end? How does setting affect the conflicts?

Extend Interpretations

7. What If? Aaron would probably have tried to find some other way to save Zlateh. However, given his obedience to his father, he'd probably have ended up taking Zlateh to the butcher if no alternative could be found.

8. The Writer's Style It helps suggest the miracle of surviving the snowstorm and the new beginning for Zlateh and the family.

9. Connect to Life Students may say that animals offer companionship, work, and love. They may mention human-animal relationships from films, books, or personal experience.

Writing

Dialogue with Zlateh Imagine that Zlateh really could talk. Reread what Aaron thinks she says to him. Then write your own version of one of their conversations. Place your dialogue in your **Working Portfolio.**

Writing Handbook
See p. R41: Narrative Writing.

Speaking & Listening

Live Storytelling Traditional stories are often shared orally. A good storyteller captures listeners with voice, gesture, and rhythm. Perform a live telling of "Zlateh the Goat." Choose a section of the story that is exciting or dramatic. Work at conveying both suspense and character. Practice using your voice, facial expressions, and gestures to keep your audience entertained.

Speaking and Listening Handbook
See p. R98: Oral Interpretation.

Research & Technology

Poland Today Compare and contrast modern Poland with the village world of "Zlateh the Goat." Write a few paragraphs about how the country has changed. Find information in social studies books or in the library.

Research and Technology Handbook
See p. R107: Library Computer Services.

Art Connection

I and the Village was painted in 1911 by Marc Chagall. His paintings are influenced by dreams and memories. The scenes in *I and the Village* flow together to create a feeling of village life. Write a paragraph describing the colors, scenes, and feelings in this painting. Use sensory details and precise verbs, nouns, and adjectives in your description.

Writing

Dialogue with Zlateh Students can extend the activity by pairing up with another student and reading each of their dialogues aloud.

 Use **Writing Transparencies,** p. 24, for additional support.

Speaking & Listening

Live Storytelling Students may first wish to practice portraying each character to make decisions about how high or low a voice the character speaks in, the speed of his or her speech, and to get used to keeping the character consistent.

Research & Technology

Poland Today Students with an interest in history might also wish to find a map of Poland made just after World War I and compare the borders with the current ones.

Art Connection

Answers will vary, but students should use sensory details and precise language in their descriptions.

Vocabulary and Spelling

EXERCISE: RELATED WORDS On your paper, write the letter of the word that doesn't belong.

1. a) evening b) today c) twilight d) dusk
2. a) astonish b) alarm c) bore d) bewilder
3. a) uneasy b) content c) restless d) jumpy
4. a) rich b) darkness c) splendor d) grand
5. a) giant b) gnome c) imp d) elf
6. a) indicate b) gesture c) point d) observe
7. a) divided b) split c) cleft d) connected
8. a) drill b) penetrate c) leave d) enter
9. a) shed b) lose c) give d) regain
10. a) roofing b) cement c) thatched d) straw

SPELLING STRATEGY: FORMS OF THE PREFIX *IN-* The prefix *in-*, as in the vocabulary word *indicate*, may mean "in or into" or "not or without." The spelling of the prefix depends on the root to which the prefix is joined. For example:

in + adequate = inadequate
im + migrate = immigrate
im + patient = impatient
il + legal = illegal
ir + resistible = irresistible

Make a new word by adding a form of the prefix *in-* to each root word below.

1. regular   3. literate   5. active
2. perfect   4. movable

Spelling Handbook
See p. R26.

Vocabulary and Spelling
EXERCISE: RELATED WORDS

1. b   6. d
2. c   7. d
3. b   8. c
4. b   9. d
5. a   10. b

SPELLING STRATEGY

1. irregular
2. imperfect
3. illiterate
4. immovable
5. inactive

Grammar in Context

Possible Responses:

1. Aaron's father talked of selling Zlateh, the family pet.
2. Feuvel, a butcher from town, had offered eight gulden.
3. Aaron's shelter, a stack of sweet hay, was warm and dry.

Isaac Bashevis Singer

Singer was not the only literary member of his family. His older brother, Israel Joshua, who helped him get out of Poland, was a novelist he both admired and competed with. His sister, Hinde Esther, was also a published novelist.

Author Activity

Fantastic Stories Students can make a chart with two columns—one for realistic details, and one for fantastic details—for each story. When they have logged all three stories, they can decide how realistic or fantastic each story is and how they compare to one another on that scale.

Grammar in Context: Appositives and Appositive Phrases

Isaac Bashevis Singer introduces characters with words that clarify who they are:

> **Leah, his mother, wiped the tears from her eyes. . . . Aaron's younger sisters, Anna and Miriam, cried loudly.**

An **appositive** is a word or phrase that identifies or renames a noun or pronoun that comes right before it. Each phrase in red type above is an **appositive phrase.**

An appositive phrase might be short, or it might be long and descriptive. It might even include a prepositional phrase, as shown here in red, modifying the noun:

> **Aaron, a boy from a small village, learned something. . . .**

Apply to Your Writing Use appositives to
• give your reader clear information
• elaborate quickly and easily
• vary the rhythm of your sentences

WRITING EXERCISE Rewrite the sentences, using some or all of the information in parentheses to make an appositive phrase.

Punctuation Tip: Use a comma before and after an appositive phrase. For a phrase at the beginning or end of a sentence, use one comma.

Example: *Original* Hanukkah held no delight that year. (Hanukkah is a joyful holiday.)
Rewritten Hanukkah, a joyful holiday, held no delight that year.

1. Aaron's father talked of selling Zlateh. (Zlateh was the family pet.)
2. Feuvel had offered eight gulden. (Feuvel was a butcher from town.)
3. Aaron's shelter was warm and dry. (It was a stack of sweet hay.)

Isaac Bashevis Singer
1904–1991

"Children are the best readers of genuine literature. . . ."

Coming to America As the son of a rabbi, Isaac Bashevis Singer received a traditional Jewish education in Poland. In his twenties, Singer decided to become a writer, and in 1935 he followed his older brother to the United States to escape discrimination against Jews in Eastern Europe. After becoming a naturalized citizen, he wrote of his U.S. citizenship, "I would not trade it for all the money in the world."

Just a Storyteller Singer published his first children's book in 1966, noting that "children think about and ponder such matters as justice, the purpose of life, the why of suffering." Singer, a Newbery Honor winner three times, was awarded the Nobel Prize in literature in 1978. The award-winning author maintained, "I am nothing more than a storyteller."

AUTHOR ACTIVITY
Fantastic Stories Some of Singer's stories, like "Zlateh the Goat," are mostly realistic. Other stories are based more on folklore or imagination. Read at least two other stories in the collection *Zlateh the Goat.* Look for realistic and fantastic details.

EXPLICIT INSTRUCTION ## Grammar in Context

PUNCTUATING APPOSITIVES Remind students to punctuate appositive phrases correctly.
Instruction Let students know that an appositive phrase is not necessary for understanding the meaning of a sentence, and it should be set off with a comma or commas. If the phrase is necessary, it should not be set off. Write the following on the board: "Zlateh the goat seemed to understand Aaron. Aaron, a brave and obedient boy, loved Zlateh." Point out that in the first sentence, *the goat* is critical for understanding the meaning. In the second sentence, the

phrase in commas gives additional, nonessential information about Aaron. It could be omitted, and the sentence would still be clear.
Practice Ask students to punctuate the following sentences.

1. Reuven the furrier decided to sell Zlateh. *(no commas)*
2. He asked Aaron his son to take the goat to the butcher. *(Aaron, his son,)*
3. The pair boy and goat lost their way. *(pair, boy and goat,)*

4. Luckily, they found a haystack a big thick mound. *(haystack, a big)*

 Use **Unit Four Resource Book,** p. 26, for more practice.

 For more instruction in punctuating appositives, see McDougal Littell's *Language Network,* Chapter 9.

For **systematic instruction** in grammar, see:
• **Grammar, Usage and Mechanics Book**
• pacing chart on p. 441i.

Building Vocabulary
Learning and Remembering New Words

You have learned several methods of finding the meaning of an unfamiliar word. Using these methods, how would you determine the meaning of *magnification*?

❶ Look for clues in the surrounding text, such as the word bigger and the phrase "trick of underwater light."

❷ Then think of any similar words you know. You might be familiar with magnify, from using a magnifying glass.

❸ Divide the words into parts you recognize. The suffix -tion means "act or state of."

> Then, all at once, there they were—and so much bigger than I had expected. It's only the magnification down here, I told myself, a trick of underwater light.
> —Don C. Reed, "My First Dive with the Dolphins"

You could infer from any or all of these clues that *magnification* roughly means "making things appear larger."

Strategies for Building Vocabulary

Here are some ideas for learning and remembering new words.

❶ **Use Context Clues** Sometimes if you keep reading—or back up and reread a few lines—you'll find clues to the meaning in the text.

❷ **Think of Similar Words** Try to think of other words you know with the same base, or root. Then check whether the definition for that base word makes sense in the context of the sentence. The word *magnification,* for example, might remind you of the word *magnificent,* meaning "grand, stately." From this, you can infer that magnification has to do with making things large.

❸ **Take the Word Apart** If you know definitions of common prefixes, suffixes, and base words, you can often determine a word's meaning by analyzing its parts. For example:

co-	exist	-ence
"together"	"live"	"state of"

Coexistence, we can see, means "the state of living together."

❹ **Consult a Dictionary** After you use context and word parts to figure out a definition, check

your definition in a dictionary. Consider all the definitions listed for the word and choose the one that fits the context. Noting a word's origin will help you connect it to other words.

❺ **Record and Use New Words** Once you learn the meaning of a new word, it's important to remember that word. Record new words and their definitions in your **Personal Word List.** Say each new word aloud and try to use it three or four times in your conversation or writing.

EXERCISE Define each underlined word. Identify the strategy you used to discover the meaning.

1. Pete tried to <u>conceal</u> his black eye by hiding it behind dark glasses.
2. Let's <u>inquire</u> at the lost-and-found office to see if anyone has turned in your watch.
3. The room was pitch dark except for the <u>luminous</u> white glow of the clock.
4. The members of a wolf pack always follow the lead of the <u>dominant</u> male.
5. After tripping over a crack in the ice, the skater struggled to <u>regain</u> her balance.

Standards-Based Objectives
- use context to determine the meaning of unfamiliar words
- apply meanings of roots and base words to comprehend unfamiliar words
- apply meanings of prefixes and suffixes to comprehend unfamiliar words
- use a personal word list to record and remember new words

VOCABULARY EXERCISES
Students' individual decoding strategies will vary.
1. conceal: hide
2. inquire: ask
3. luminous: full of light
4. dominant: having the most influence; controlling all others
5. regain: recover possession of

 Use **Unit Four Resource Book,** p. 29, for more practice.

Standards-Based Objectives

You can use this selection to achieve one or more of the following objectives:

- enjoy independent reading (Option One)
- read and analyze literature with a group (Option Two)
- use the Reader's Notebook to formulate questions about literature (Option Three)
- write in response to literature (Option Three)

Summary

The narrator tells how, while living in Africa for a short time, he and his family were given the responsibility of raising a baby lion rejected by its mother. No one expected it to live, but the family was determined that it would. First, they fed it diluted milk from a baby bottle. It seemed to do all right at first but as it got bigger, it seemed terribly weak. The family finds out that they need to add mutton broth to the lion cub's diet. They also find out that they need to brush its coat in order to make it healthy and clean. They call the cub Sullivan and, as he grows into a healthy young lion, they play with him and teach him how to eat on his own. After studying the lion's behavior, the narrator notes that contrary to popular wisdom, lions are not just big cats: they have a dignity and grace all their own. Then the lion's caretakers have to leave Africa. Those who had doubted that the lion cub would live said that the foursome should take him back to England. The narrator knows, however, that Sullivan would never survive in England's climate and should be left in his homeland of Africa.

HOW TO BRING UP A LION

by Rudyard Kipling

NOW this is a really-truly tale. It all truthfully happened, and I saw it and heard it.

Once there was a mother lion that lived in a cage halfway up a mountain in Africa, behind the house where I was living, and she had two little baby lions. She bit one of them so hard that it died. But the keeper in charge of the cages pulled out the other little lion just in time and carried him down the hill. He put him in an egg box, along with a brindled bulldog puppy, called Budge, to keep him warm.

HOW TO BRING UP A LION **493**

Option Three
Reader's Notebook

- Ask students to read the selection, pausing at the end of the first column on page 493. At that point, ask students to consider the title of the selection and the passage they just read and to predict what they think is going to happen in this story and what its main point might be. Have them write their predictions in their Reader's Notebook. Have them also record any questions they have about the story as they continue to read. At the end of the story, students will return to their predictions and questions. Ask them to note if their predictions were accurate and if their questions were answered. They may want to write down any additional questions they have about the story.

- Ask students to give their impressions of how the narrator and his family felt about Sullivan the lion cub. Have them support their ideas with details from the story.

- Ask students to write a letter, written from the point of view of one of the children, to his or her classmates back home in England describing their adventures in bringing up a lion cub by hand.

When I went to look at the little thing, the keeper said, "This baby lion is going to die. Would you like to bring up this baby lion?" And I said, "Yes," and the keeper said, "Then I will send him to your house at once, because he is certainly going to die here, and you can bring him up by hand."

Then I went home and found Daniel and Una, who were little children, playing. I said, "We are going to bring up a baby lion by hand!" and both children said, "Hurrah! He can sleep in our nursery and not go away for ever and ever."

Then Daniel and Una's mother said to me, "What do you know about bringing up lions?" And I said, "Nothing whatever." And she said, "I thought so," and went into the house to give orders.

Soon the keeper came, carrying the egg box with the baby lion and Budge, the brindled bulldog pup, asleep inside. Behind the keeper walked a man with iron bars and a roll of wire netting and some picks and shovels. The men built a den for the baby lion in the backyard, and they put the box inside and said, "Now you can bring the lion up by hand. He is quite, quite certain to die."

The children's mother came out of the house with a bottle, the kind that you feed very small babies from, and she filled it with milk and warm water. She said, "I am going to bring up this baby lion, and he is *not* going to die."

She pulled out the baby lion (his eyes were all blue and watery and he couldn't see), and she turned him on his back and tilted the bottle into his little mouth. He moved all his four little paws like windmills, but he never let go of the bottle, not once, until it was quite empty and he was quite full.

The children's mother said, "Weigh him on the meat scales," and we did. He weighed four

"WE ARE GOING TO BRING UP A BABY LION BY HAND!"

pounds, three ounces. She said, "He will be weighed once every week, and he will be fed every three hours on warm milk and water—two parts milk and one part water. The bottle will be cleaned after each meal with boiling water."

I said, "What do you know about bringing up lions by hand?" and she said, "Nothing whatever, except that this lion is not going to die. *You* must find out how to bring up lions."

So I said, "The first thing to do is to stop Daniel and Una from hugging and dancing around him because if they hug him too hard or step on him he will surely die."

For ten days the baby lion ate and slept. He didn't say anything; he hardly opened his eyes. We made him a bed of wood shavings (they are better than straw), and we built him a real little house with a thick roof to keep the sun off. And whenever he looked at all hungry, it was time for him to be fed out of the bottle.

Budge tried to make him play, but the little lion wouldn't. When Budge chewed his ears too hard, he would stretch himself all over the puppy and Budge would crawl from under him, half choked.

We said, "It is an easy thing to bring up a lion," and then visitors began to call and give advice.

One man said, "Young lions all die of paralysis[1] of the hindquarters." And another man said, "They perish of rickets,[2] a condition that comes on just as they are cutting their first teeth."

We looked at the baby lion, and his hind legs were very weak indeed. He rolled over when he tried to walk, and his front paws doubled up under him. His eyes were dull and blind.

I went off to find someone who knew about animals' insides. "You must give him broth," I was told. "Milk isn't enough for him. Give him mutton broth at eight in the morning and four in the afternoon. You must also buy a dandy brush, same as they brush horses with, and brush him every day to make up for his own mother not being able to lick him with her tongue."

So we bought a dandy brush (a good hard one) and mutton for broth, and we gave him the broth from the bottle. In two days he was a different lion. His hind legs grew stronger, and his eyes grew lighter, and his furry, woolly skin grew cleaner.

We all said, "Now we must give him a real name of his own." We inquired into his family history and found that his parents were both Matabele[3] lions from the far north and that the Matabele word for lion was "umlibaan." But we called him Sullivan for short, and that very day he knocked a bit of skin off his nose trying to climb the wire fence.

He began to play with Daniel and Una—especially with Una, who walked all around the garden, hugging him till he squeaked.

One day, Una went out as usual and put her hand in Sullivan's house to drag him out, just as usual, and Sullivan flattened his little black-tipped ears back to his thick woolly head and opened his mouth and said "Ough! Ough! Ough!" like a monkey.

Una pulled her hand back and said, "I think

Sullivan has teeth. Come and look." And we saw that he had six or eight very pretty little teeth about a quarter of an inch long, so we said, "Why should we give up our time to feeding this monarch of the jungle every few hours with a bottle? Let him feed himself."

He weighed eight pounds, eight ounces, and he could run and jump and growl and scratch, but he did not like to feed himself.

For two days and two nights, he wouldn't feed himself at all. He sang for his supper, like little Tommy Tucker, and he sang for his breakfast and his dinner, making noises deep in his chest, high noises and low noises and coughing noises. Una ran about saying, "Please let my lion have his bottle!"

Daniel, who didn't speak very plainly, would go off to the lion's den, where poor Sullivan sat looking at a plate of cold broth. He would say, "Tullibun, Tullibun, eat up all your dinner or you'll be hungry."

At last Sullivan made up his mind that bottles would never come again and he put down his little nose and ate for dear life. I was told that the children's mother had been out in the early morning and dipped her finger in mutton broth and coaxed Sullivan to lick it off. She discovered that his tongue was as raspy as a file. Then we were sure he ought to feed himself.

So we weaned Sullivan, and he weighed ten pounds, two ounces, and the truly happy times of his life began. Every morning, Una and Daniel would let him out of the den. He was perfectly polite so long as no one put a hand into his house. He would come out at a steady,

---

1. **paralysis** (pə-răl′ĭ-sĭs): a loss of the ability to move a body part.

2. **rickets:** a disease in which bones fail to grow normally, caused by a lack of calcium, vitamin D, or sunlight.

3. **Matabele** (mä′tä-bĕl′ā): having to do with a people of southwestern Zimbabwe (a country in the southern part of Africa).

Possible Activities

Independent Activities

- Have advanced students skim over the story, noting details, facts, and descriptions about the narrator and the character of the children's mother. Ask them to write in their Reader's Notebook their impressions of these characters and their respective roles in the process of bringing up the lion.
- Have students review the Learning the Language of Literature and Active Reader features, pp. 443–446. Ask them to note which skills and strategies they used while reading this selection.

Discussion Activities

- Use the questions formulated by the students in their Reader's Notebooks as the start of a discussion about this story.
- Ask students if they think the family was right to leave the lion in Africa when they returned to England. What do students think would have happened if the family had taken Sullivan with them?

Assessment Opportunities

- You can assess student comprehension of the story by evaluating the questions they formulate in their Reader's Notebook.
- You can use any of the discussion questions as essay questions.
- You can have students turn any one of their Reader's Notebook entries into an essay.

rocking-horse canter that looked slow but was quicker even than Una's run.

He would be brushed, first on his yellow tummy and then on his yellow back, and then under his yellow chin where he dribbled mutton broth, and then on his dark yellow mane. The mane hair of a baby lion is a little thicker than the rest of his hair, and Sullivan's was tinged with black.

After his brushing, he would go out into the garden to watch Daniel and Una swing. Or he would hoist himself up on the porch to watch their mother sew or he would go into my room and lie under the couch. If I wished to get rid of him I had to call Una, for at her voice he would solemnly trundle out with his head lifted and help her chase butterflies among the hydrangeas. He never took any notice of me.

One of the many queer things about him was the way he matched his backgrounds. He would lie down on the bare tiled porch in the full glare of the sun, and you could step on him before you saw him. He would sit in the shadow of a wall or slide into a garden border, and, till he moved, you could not tell that he was there. That made him difficult to photograph.

Sudden noises, like banging doors, always annoyed him. He would go straight backward almost as fast as he ran forward, till he got his back up against a wall or a shrub. There he would lift one little broad paw and look wicked until he heard Una or Daniel call him.

If he smelled anything in the wind, he would stop quite still and lift his head high into the air, very slowly, until he had quite made up his mind. Then he would slowly steal upwind with his tail twitching a trifle at the very end.

The first time he played with a ball he struck it just as his grandfather must have struck at the big Matabele oxen in the far

ONE DAY I SHALL NEVER FORGET, HE BEGAN TO SEE OUT OF HIS EYES—REALLY SEE.

north—one paw above and one paw below, with a wrench and a twist—and the ball bounced over his shoulder.

He could use his paws as easily as a man can use his arms, and much more quickly. He always turned his back on you when he was examining anything. That was a signal that you were not to interfere with him.

We used to believe that little lions were only big cats, as the books say. But Sullivan taught us that lions are always lions. He would play in his own way at his own games, but he never chased his tail or patted a cork or a string or did any foolish, kitten tricks. He never forgot that he was a lion, not a dog or a cat, but a lion.

When he lay down, he would cross his paws and look like the big carved lions in Trafalgar Square.[4] When he rose and sniffed, he looked like a bronze lion, and when he lifted one paw and opened his mouth and wrinkled up his nose to be angry (as he did when we washed him all over with carbolic and water because of fleas), he looked like the lions the old Assyrians[5] drew on stone.

---

4. **Trafalgar** (trə-făl′gər) **Square:** a plaza in London, England, that is the site of a famous monument (Nelson's Column) surrounded by four large statues of lions.

5. **Assyrians** (ə-sîr′ē-ənz): a people of southwestern Asia whose powerful empire reached its peak from the ninth to the seventh century B.C.

He never did anything funny. He was never silly or amusing (not even when he had been dipped in carbolic and water), and he never behaved as though he were trying to show off. Kittens do.

He kept to himself more and more as he grew older. One day I shall never forget, he began to see out of his eyes—really see. Up till then his eyes had been dull and stupid, just like a young baby's eyes. But that day— I saw them first under the couch—they were grown-up lion's eyes, soft and blazing at the same time, without a wink in them, eyes that seemed to look right through you and out over all Africa.

Though he had been born in captivity, as were his parents, and though the only home he had ever known was on the slopes of the big Table Mountain where Africa ended, we never saw him once look up the hill when he lay down to do his solemn, serious thinking. He always faced squarely to the north, to the great open plains and the ragged, jagged mountains beyond them—looking up and into the big, sunny, dry Africa that had once belonged to his people.

That was curious. He would think and he would sigh, exactly like a man. He was full of curious, half-human noises, grunts and groans and mutters and rumbles.

He grew to weigh more than fifteen pounds when we had to leave him. We were very proud of this, and triumphed over the keeper and the other people who had said we could never bring him up by hand.

"You've certainly won the game," they said. "You can have this lion if you like and take him home and give him to the Zoological Gardens in London."

But we said, "No, Sullivan is one of the family, and if he were taken to a cold, wet, foggy zoo, he'd die. Let him stay here." ❖

Rudyard Kipling
1865–1936

"I write of all matters that lie within my understanding, and of many that do not."

Early Childhood Rudyard Kipling was born to a British family in India, which was a British colony at the time. He spent a great deal of time with his ayah (Indian nanny), who taught him about Indian culture and traditions. When he was five, his parents left him with a foster family in England, so that he could attend school there.

Inspired by India Kipling never forgot the land of his birth. He refused his family's offer to send him to a university, and in 1882 he returned to India. While working as a newspaper reporter, he published many short stories in newspapers and books. Kipling's attachment to India can also be seen in his novel *Kim,* about an Irish orphan who, like the author, finds a home in India.

Fame and Fortune In 1896 Kipling went back to England, where he found himself acclaimed as a great writer. There he wrote one of his best-loved books, *Just So Stories,* a collection of humorous tales that explain how different animals got their physical characteristics. "How to Bring Up a Lion" was inspired by a visit to South Africa in 1900. While in South Africa, Kipling wrote for a newspaper and raised funds for British military veterans. His powers of observation, imagination, and storytelling were recognized in 1907 with the Nobel Prize in literature.

Rudyard Kipling

Kipling's *Jungle Book,* considered to be one of his best works, was written in 1894 while he was living in Vermont with his wife and two baby daughters. The most popular story in the book tells the story of Mowgli, a young boy raised by wolves in the jungle.

In 1899, Kipling's daughter Josephine died from pneumonia, and Kipling coped by losing himself in his work. Two years later he published *Kim,* thought by many to be his finest novel. It tells the story of an orphaned Irish boy who becomes involved in espionage and counterespionage in the hostilities between Great Britain and Russia in late nineteenth-century India.

In 1902 Kipling published the *Just So Stories* which he wrote for his two surviving children, Elsie and John. Written to be read aloud, their language is musical and playful.

The Nantucket Cat, Paul Stagg. From *The Mardi Gras Cat Book* by Paul Stagg and Naomi Lewis, published by Heineman Press. Copyright © The Stephanie Hoppen Picture Archive Ltd., London.

CHANG MCTANG MCQUARTER

by John Ciardi

Chang McTang McQuarter Cat
Is one part this and one part that.
One part is yowl, one part is purr.
One part is scratch, one part is fur.
5   One part, maybe even two,
Is how he sits and stares right through
You and you and you and you.
And when you feel my Chang-Cat stare
You wonder if you're really there.

10   Chang McTang McQuarter Cat
Is one part this and ten parts that.
He's one part saint, and two parts sin.
One part yawn, and three parts grin,
One part sleepy, four parts lightning,
15   One part cuddly, five parts fright'ning,
One part snarl, and six parts play.
One part is how he goes away
Inside himself, somewhere miles back
Behind his eyes, somewhere as black
20   And green and yellow as the night
A jungle makes in full moonlight.

Chang McTang McQuarter Cat
Is one part this and twenty that.
One part is statue, one part tricks—
25   (One part, or six, or thirty-six.)

One part (or twelve, or sixty-three)
Is—Chang McTang belongs to ME!

Don't ask, "How many parts is that?"
Addition's nothing to a cat.

30   If you knew Chang, then you'd know this:
He's one part everything there is.

Standards-Based Objectives
- create a process description
- use a written text as a model for writing
- revise a presentation to include the definitions of unfamiliar terms
- deliver a process description presentation

Introducing the Workshop

Process Description Discuss with students the different kinds of process descriptions that they encounter every day at school, at home, and while pursuing their hobbies. Ask them to think about what makes a process description easy to follow.

Basics in a Box
Presenting the Guidelines and Standards To better understand the assignment, students can refer to the Standards for Writing a Successful Process Description. You may also want to share with them the complete rubric, which describes several levels of proficiency.

 See **Unit Four Resource Book**, p. 35.

 For more instruction on essential writing skills, see McDougal Littell's *Language Network*, Chapters 10–17.

 Power Presentation

To engage students visually, use **Power Presentation 1**, Process Description.

Communication Workshop
Process Description

Explaining one step at a time . . .

From Reading to Presenting When you learned to log on to a computer for the first time, you had to follow step-by-step instructions. If you were given a wrong step, you might have accidentally logged off or retrieved the wrong file. Creating a **process description** is one way you can clarify steps. A process description is a step-by-step explanation of how to do something. You can learn how to do almost anything when the directions are broken down into steps.

For Your Portfolio

WRITING PROMPT Describe how to do something or how something works. Focus on a task or a process that you know well.

Purpose: To inform and explain
Audience: Classmates and others with an interest in your subject

Basics in a Box

GUIDELINES AND STANDARDS	PROCESS DESCRIPTION AT A GLANCE
Content	**Delivery**
A successful process description should	**An effective speaker should**
• focus on a single activity	• have good posture and maintain eye contact with the audience
• begin with a clear statement of the topic and your purpose	• emphasize points in the process with visual aids
• explain how to do something or how something works	• use effective rate, pitch, volume, and tone to sustain audience attention
• present the steps of the process in a logical order	
• give the meaning of terms that may be unfamiliar and provide necessary background information	
• use transitional words to signal the start of each new step	

500   UNIT FOUR   PART 1: ANIMAL WONDERS

LESSON RESOURCES

USING PRINT RESOURCES
Unit Four Resource Book
- Planning and Drafting, p. 30
- Practicing and Delivering, p. 31
- Peer Response Guide, p. 32
- Revising Organization and Ideas, p. 33
- Refining Your Performance, p. 34
- Student Models, pp. 35–37
- Standards for Evaluation, p. 38

Writing
- Structuring the Essay, TR 6 (p. 501)

Speaking and Listening
- Choosing Presentation Aids, p. 10 (p. 505)
- Supporting Opinions with Evidence and Visuals, p. 11 (p. 505)
- Creating and Analyzing an Informative Presentation, pp. 25, 26 (p. 505)

INTEGRATED TECHNOLOGY
Writing Coach CD-ROM
Visit our Web site:
www.mcdougallittell.com

Analyzing a Process Description

Weston Sager
The Paul School

SPEAKING OPPORTUNITY See the Speaking and Listening Handbook, p. R96 for oral presentation tips.

Scrambling for Eggs

There is more to gathering farm-fresh eggs than you might think. Collecting eggs is fun and interesting, believe it or not. Keeping egg-laying hens is rewarding because you get farm-fresh eggs almost every day.

My family owns several six-year-old chickens. They are in good health and lay eggs almost every day. It's unusual to have chickens that are six years old and still lay eggs. My family thinks they are such good layers because in addition to providing them with shelter, and lots of water, we feed them good-quality table scraps and give them special care. As a result, our chickens give us some of the best eggs anywhere, but it isn't easy to gather farm-fresh eggs. Here are the steps you should follow to become a skilled egg-gatherer.

Step 1 First, you need to have a container to carry table scraps and eggs. This container should be able to hold about ten large eggs. A plastic bowl is ideal. <show plastic bowl> You should always use a large container or you might drop some table scraps or eggs. That would be a disaster.

Step 2 Next, you need to have some good table scraps. Hens like stale bread and cake, lettuce stalks, carrot shavings, and other vegetable or grain products. Stay away from pepper, meat, and crustacean shells or they will flavor and color the eggs. Don't use anything too strong-flavored either. You don't want to harm the chickens or make their eggs taste funny. My mother puts leftover food in our table-scrap container every day. This way she never misses an opportunity to feed some scraps to the chickens.

Step 3 After getting the container and the feed ready, make sure you are dressed in the right clothing. The chicken coop is very messy, so always wear sturdy shoes that are easy to clean. Wearing a jacket is a good idea if it is cold outside.

Now it is time to pick up the plastic container with the table scraps and walk outside to the chicken coop. The chicken coop is the shedlike house where the chickens are kept. <show photograph of coop> Our coop is tucked away in a wooded area close to our house. A coop must be well sealed so that predators—animals that kill chickens—cannot get inside and eat the eggs and chickens.

GUIDELINES IN ACTION

❶ Begins with a strong introduction, which includes a clear statement of topic and purpose

❷ Tells about important equipment and includes highlighted notes about when to display equipment and visuals

❸ Explains each step in the order in which it must be done
Another Option:
• Use a storyboard to identify each step.

❹ Defines specific words that may be unfamiliar to the audience

---

Teaching the Lesson

Analyzing the Model
Scrambling for Eggs

The student model is a process description of how to gather farm-fresh eggs. The writer begins by describing the chickens and their environment, and then lays out the steps for gathering the eggs.

Have students think of a situation in which they had to follow written directions. Help students to see how the organization and the use of transitional words make the explanation of the process easy to follow. Then point out the key words and phrases in the student model that correspond to the elements mentioned in the Rubric in Action.

1 Ask students to identify the author's purpose or purposes in this essay.
   Possible Responses: to describe how to gather eggs; to illustrate how the process of gathering eggs can be fun and interesting

2 Have students read the next two paragraphs omitting the transitional words. Ask them how this omission affects the essay.
   Possible Responses: The essay seems less organized and the steps more difficult to follow; the progress from one step to the next is not clearly defined.

3 Ask students to explain how the essay would change if all the steps were combined into one paragraph.
   Possible Responses: The process would be harder to follow and to read. Some of the steps described in the middle of a paragraph might be missed.

4 Ask students to explain why it is important to define unfamiliar or difficult words.
   Possible Response: Understanding the meaning of a sentence or a paragraph might depend upon knowing the definition of the word.

EXPLICIT INSTRUCTION Patterns of Organization

PICTURING TEXT STRUCTURE
Instruction While ideas and word choice play key roles in good writing, the structure of a text—the way in which ideas are organized and events unfold—also contributes to the effectiveness of the work.
Practice Have students analyze the organization of the student model by constructing a diagram or other graphic organizer. The following flow chart is an example.

Use **Writing Transparencies**, p. 6, for additional support.

• **Introduction:** introduces topic of egg gathering and explains that it is fun and interesting

• **Background:** gives information about chickens and describes equipment that is needed and why

• **Directions:** explains the steps involved in gathering eggs and managing chickens

• **Conclusion:** refers back to introduction in order to tie essay together

5/6 Point out that in steps 4, 5, and 6 there are many transitional words that show sequence. Ask students to find some of these words and phrases.

Possible Response: "when you hand out the scraps," "while the chickens are busy," "next," "before," "as you leave."

7 Point out the definition of *mulch* given in the essay.

8 Ask students how the student author connects the last paragraph of this essay to his introduction.

Possible Response: He gives examples of why gathering eggs can be interesting and fun and illustrates why he thinks it is a rewarding task.

Step 4 Once you are at the coop, gently open the door. Make sure you do not scare the chickens. They are very timid and will jump and fly around if you startle them. The chickens know that you are there to feed them, and they will want their food immediately. When you hand out the scraps, be sure to tear up the large pieces so the chickens can eat them easily.

> **⑤** Identifies steps for presenter and makes sequence clear

Step 5 <show photo of eggs in a box> While the chickens are busy eating, look in the egg boxes for the fresh eggs. It is always a surprise. You might find twelve eggs, or, if the chickens have been lazy, you might find only one or two. The eggs are often warm to the touch. You should gather them every day, especially in the winter. If you don't gather them often in the winter, they can freeze and break.

Step 6 Next, collect the eggs and place them carefully in your now-empty container. You don't want the fragile eggs breaking, especially ones of such good quality. Before you leave, check each hen's feet and beak. If the feet and beak are turning bright yellow it means the hens have stopped laying. This is because all of the pigment that colors the egg yolk is being used by the chicken herself.

> **⑥** Uses transitional words to show order of actions

Step 7 As you leave the chicken coop, shut and lock the door securely behind you. Scrape off the bottom of your shoes with a twig or rock. A special brush is also a good idea. Once you are back at your house, wash the eggs. <show photo of eggs covered with mulch> The eggs are often sticky, so they pick up the mulch—ground leaves, straw, or mosses—that is used as cushioning in the egg boxes. You should wash them in cool water with a sponge. The eggs must be clean before you store them.

> **⑦** Defines another unfamiliar word

Step 8 Finally, you can store the eggs. The eggs will last for the longest time if they are put in the refrigerator. They can be stored at room temperature if no more room is available in the refrigerator. We store our eggs in recycled egg cartons. <show carton> This helps the environment and it is free. You might want to give eggs away to friends and relatives because fresh eggs are so delicious. Ask people for extra egg cartons so that you never run out.

No matter what size or color they are, eggs are fun to gather, great tasting, and practically free. Once you have tried a farm-fresh egg, you will become an egghead like me. Just follow these steps and you'll be an expert egg-gatherer in no time.

> **⑧** Ends by restating what audience will be able to do after practicing this process

Creating Your Process Description

❶ Planning Your Presentation

Knowledge advances by steps.
—Thomas Macaulay, 19th-century British writer

One way to find an interesting process to describe is to **list** the tasks that you do from the time you wake up until the time you go to sleep. In the course of the day, you do many things that involve a number of steps. Other people might not know how to do some of the tasks that you do easily. You may instead want to note activities of the people around you and choose one to describe. See the **Idea Bank** in the margin for other suggestions. After you choose a process, follow the steps below.

Steps for Planning and Drafting Your Presentation

▶ 1. **Know your audience.** Think about how much your audience knows about the topic. What background information will they need? Will your description be serious or humorous?

▶ 2. **Gather the information.** List all the steps that are necessary to the process. Then make a note of all the equipment or supplies that you need to demonstrate the process. What background information or details need to be included?

▶ 3. **Organize your information.** Make a numbered list of the steps in chronological order before you begin drafting.

❷ Developing Your Presentation

Begin to draft your process description. **First** tell what you are going to describe and why the process is important or useful. **Next,** describe the steps. Use these points to make your description clear and interesting.

• Include all the steps and describe them using plenty of details. Listeners should be able to use your description to carry out the steps of the process themselves.

• Explain any words your audience might not know.

• Use transitional words such as *first, next, before, during,* or *after* to help your audience know when each step occurs.

• List any supplies or equipment that you will need.

Finally, turn your draft into an outline for your presentation. You can write out your description word for word or just use notes to help you remember what you will say. Include in your outline notes about when you will use any equipment or materials.

IDEA Bank

1. For Your Working Portfolio 🗂
Look for ideas in the **Writing** and **Speaking & Listening** activities that you completed earlier.

2. Equipment Expertise
List pieces of equipment that you know how to operate, like a computer, VCR, or tape recorder. Explain to a partner how to complete a simple function with one of these items.

3. New Horizons
Think about tasks that you've always wanted to be able to do, such as baking bread or building a birdhouse. Interview someone who knows how to do your chosen task. Ask him or her what steps are involved.

Have a question?

See the **Writing Handbook.**
Transitions, p. R36
Elaboration, p. R37

See **Language Network.**
Preparing an Oral Report, p. 489

Guiding Student Writing

Prewriting

Choosing a Subject
If after reading the Idea Bank students have difficulty choosing a subject for their process description, suggest that they try the following:

• Look around and ask yourself how things work—in your house, in nature, in the car. List several processes that you would like to learn more about, such as how a caterpillar turns into a butterfly or how an engine works.

• Think about a hobby or activity you participate in, such as building models or collecting coins. Think about how you can explain this activity to someone who knows nothing about it.

Planning Your Process Description
1. Encourage students to use precise language and vivid descriptions in order to make the process clear and interesting to read.
2. Suggest that students take notes while walking through the process they wish to describe to make sure they include all the steps.
3. Suggest that students use a time line, flow chart, or other diagram to organize their ideas and steps.

Drafting

If students have difficulty getting started, suggest they begin writing about the parts of the process they find most interesting or easiest to describe. Then have them go back and fill in details and missing steps.

Ask Your Peer Reader
Remind students to use the peer reviewer's feedback when revising their drafts.

Practicing and Presenting

Suggest that students become comfortable enough with their material that they won't have to read it exactly as they wrote it. Encourage students to use their written text as a prompt.

Ask Your Peer Reviewer

Suggest that students ask a classmate to view a preliminary run-through of the presentation and give suggestions on ways to improve it.

Refining Your Presentation

DEFINING UNFAMILIAR TERMS

Review the changes made in the sample script with students. Note that in this example the definition is inserted immediately following the unfamiliar term—*mulch.* Suggest that another alternative would be to have an additional sentence to define the word.

Reflecting

As they write their reflections, have students consider what they will be more aware of the next time they learn a new process.

Option

MANAGING THE PAPER LOAD

To cut down on the paper load as you make sure that all students are on track, read only the opening paragraph of each paper. Offer specific written comments rather than meeting with students individually.

Practicing Tip

Have somone videotape a practice delivery so that you can listen and watch for the parts of your presentation that are and are not working.

Need revising help?

Review the **Guidelines and Standards,** p. 500

Consider **peer reader** comments

Check **Revision Guidelines,** p. R31

Publishing IDEAS

- Choose a younger audience for your process description. Simplify the language so that your instructions will be understood.

- Create a do-it-yourself video by narrating your process description and either doing the process at the same time or showing illustrations of each step.

INTERNET

Publishing Options
www.mcdougallittell.com

---

❸ Practicing and Presenting

Practice your presentation several times. This will help you become comfortable with speaking from your outline and handling your equipment.

- Look up at the audience.

- Speak loudly enough to be heard and slowly enough to be understood.

- Vary the tone and pitch of your voice to keep your audience interested.

> **Ask Your Peer Reviewer**
>
> - What did you learn from my presentation?
> - What parts were most effective?
> - What information was confusing?

- Use gestures and facial expressions to emphasize important points.

After rehearsing on your own, deliver your presentation to a friend. Use his or her comments to improve your presentation.

❹ Refining Your Presentation

TARGET SKILL ▷ DEFINING UNFAMILIAR TERMS

As you explain the steps in your process description, look for words or phrases that might be unfamiliar to your audience. If you have used an unfamiliar word, simply include a definition directly after it. For example, in a process description about making fudge, one student explains: *The fudge is done when it congeals, or becomes solid, in cold water.* Explaining the word *congealed* makes the instruction clear.

—ground leaves, straw, or mosses—

The eggs are often sticky, so they pick up the mulch that is used as cushioning in the egg boxes.

❺ Reflecting

FOR YOUR WORKING PORTFOLIO What did you learn about your process by creating a process description? Which part of the description was most difficult to deliver? What other processes or tasks would you like to describe? Attach your answers to your notes. Save your process description in your **Working Portfolio.**

EXPLICIT INSTRUCTION **Revision**

WORD CHOICE

Instruction Remind students that occasionally a technical term will be required to explain a particular process. There is nothing wrong with using the unfamiliar word, but it should be defined for the reader in simple language. The definition can occur within the sentence that uses the technical term, or it can be stated in a separate sentence that occurs just before or just after the sentence with the unfamiliar language. Direct students to look at the definition added to the example on this page to explain the term *mulch.*

Practice Ask students to work with a partner to read the drafts of their process descriptions. Ask each partner to identify any unfamiliar words that keep them from understanding what is happening and to ask the writer to insert a definition before he or she delivers the process description aloud.

See the **Research and Technology Handbook,** pp. R108-109, for information about formatting documents using word processing skills.

Use **Unit Four Resource Book,** p. 33, to help students improve the organization and consistency of ideas in their writing.

Mixed Review

Making fudge can be done <u>real easy</u> if you follow the necessary
₍₁₎
steps. First, you should gather all of the ingredients and supplies. The
recipe calls for the following items: <u>butter, sugar, chocolate, condensed</u>
<u>milk, marshmallows</u>. In addition, you need a pan that will <u>distribute or</u>
₍₂₎   ₍₃₎
<u>spread</u> the heat <u>even</u>. A measuring cup, a tablespoon, <u>a large wooden</u>
₍₄₎   ₍₅₎
<u>spoon, a candy thermometer</u> are also needed. After you collect the
supplies, you can begin to cook. If you follow all the directions, your
fudge will be a <u>success!</u>
₍₆₎

Review Your Skills

Use the passage and the questions that follow it to check how well you remember the language conventions you've learned in previous grades.

1. How is item 1 best written?
   A. really easily
   B. real easily
   C. really easier
   D. Correct as is

2. How is item 2 best written?
   A. butter, sugar, chocolate condensed milk, marshmallows.
   B. butter, sugar, chocolate, condensed milk marshmallows.
   C. butter, sugar, chocolate, condensed, milk marshmallows.
   D. Correct as is

3. How is item 3 best written?
   A. distribute, or spread,
   B. distribute or, spread
   C. distribute but spread
   D. Correct as is

4. How is item 4 best written?
   A. evener
   B. evenly
   C. evenest
   D. Correct as is

5. How is item 5 best written?
   A. a large wooden spoon, or a candy thermometer
   B. a large wooden spoon, and a candy thermometer
   C. a large wooden spoon, but a candy thermometer
   D. Correct as is

6. What is the correct spelling in item 6?
   A. sucess
   B. succes
   C. sucses
   D. Correct as is

Self-Assessment

Check your own answers in the **Grammar Handbook**.

Quick Reference: Parts of Speech, p. R62

Using Modifiers Effectively, p. R78

Correcting Punctuation, p. R86

Demonstrate how students can eliminate incorrect choices for the first question.

A. This choice correctly uses an adverb to modify an adverb.
B. This choice is incorrect because it uses an adjective to modify an adverb.
C. This choice is incorrect because "easier" is an adjective.
D. The original choice is incorrect because the underlined words are adjectives.

Answers:
1. A; 2. D; 3. A; 4. B; 5. B; 6. D.

Use **Speaking and Listening Book,** pp. 10–11, 25–26, for additional support in presenting a process description.

UNIT FOUR
PART 2

PART 2
Imaginary
Worlds

Meeting Standards

The Literature You'll Read

The Concepts You'll Study

Vocabulary and Reading Comprehension
Vocabulary Focus: Understanding Specialized
  Vocabulary
Visualizing
Reading Aloud
Purposes for Reading

Literary Analysis
Genre Focus: Science Fiction and Fantasy
Fantasy
Realistic and Fantastic Details
Poetic Form: Limerick
Setting

Writing and Language Conventions
Writing Workshop: Short Story
Pinpointing with Prepositions

Speaking and Listening
Dramatic Recording
Performance of a Scene
Original Limericks Read-Aloud

506

LEARNING the Language of *Literature*

Science Fiction and Fantasy

Whether writing realism or fantasy, my concerns are the same—how we learn to be . . . human beings.
—*Lloyd Alexander, writer*

Can you imagine building a rocket and traveling to the moon? Writer Jules Verne imagined it. He wrote about it in his book *From Earth to the Moon,* which was published in 1865—almost 100 years before man first set foot on the moon. Today, Jules Verne is considered to be one of the greatest science fiction writers of all time.

Science fiction is a literary genre in which the action of a story usually takes place in the future or in outer space. Imaginary objects and events are based on real or possible science and technology. Science fiction writers have predicted the invention of submarines, cell phones, and computers.

Fantasy is another literary genre that can introduce you to new worlds, unusual characters, and strange events. However, fantasy stories don't have to be based on science and technology. In fact, they are often based on myths and legends. For a story to be considered fantasy, it must include at least one completely unreal or fantastic element, such as elves, fairies, or talking plants.

LEARNING THE LANGUAGE OF LITERATURE **507**

Presenting the Concepts
Science Fiction

Working as a class, have students come up with the opening paragraph for a science fiction story. The paragraph should describe at least one character in detail and should also describe the setting of the story in vivid and specific detail. Remind students that their scientific details should be real or at least possible at some point in the future. Write their paragraph on the chalkboard.

YOUR TURN

Possible Response: "It had been raining for seven years," "A thousand forests had been crushed . . . and grown up a thousand times," "this was the way life was . . . on the planet Venus," "children of the rocket men and women"

Science Fiction

In **science fiction,** the descriptions of setting include details about technology and scientific developments. The technology seems fantastic but also appears to be possible. Science fiction writers use detailed descriptions to help readers visualize **futuristic settings.** In most science fiction stories, vivid details tell you how a place looks, what types of plants are there, what color the sky is, and how the place feels. Characters, too, are described in detail. The details about setting and characters help you compare and contrast the story with what you know about life on earth.

YOUR TURN What details in the excerpt from "All Summer in a Day" create a futuristic setting?

SCIENCE FICTION

It had been raining for seven years; thousands upon thousands of days compounded and filled from one end to the other with rain, with the drum and gush of water, with the sweet crystal fall of showers and the concussion of storms so heavy they were tidal waves come over the islands. A thousand forests had been crushed under the rain and grown up a thousand times to be crushed again. And this was the way life was forever on the planet Venus, and this was the school-room of the children of the rocket men and women who had come to a raining world to set up civilization and live out their lives.

—Ray Bradbury,
"All Summer in a Day"

From "All Summer in a Day"

Fantasy

A work of fiction is **fantasy** if it includes at least one fantastic or unreal element. For example, you may read a fantasy story about a place in which everything seems realistic, except for the fact that the animals can talk. The author of a fantasy makes it possible for you to imagine the impossible. To make this happen, the author will include **imaginative settings, fantastic details, imaginary creatures,** or **impossible events.** For example, an author will try very hard to describe a setting exactly, so that when animal characters start talking, it seems surprising but believable.

YOUR TURN Look at the excerpt from "The Walrus and the Carpenter." Which details and events are possible, and which are not possible?

FANTASY

The sun was shining on the sea,
  Shining with all his might:
He did his very best to make
  The billows smooth and bright—
And this was odd, because it was
  The middle of the night.

The moon was shining sulkily,
  Because she thought the sun
Had got no business to be there
  After the day was done—
"It's very rude of him," she said,
  "To come and spoil the fun!"

—Lewis Carroll,
"The Walrus and the Carpenter"

Comparing
Science Fiction and Fantasy

Science Fiction
- real or possible science data
- often set in the future or in space
- often describes future technology

Both
- imaginative
- new worlds
- unusual characters
- strange events

Fantasy
- unrealistic or fantastic settings
- imaginary creatures
- impossible events
- elements of myths and legends

From "The Walrus and the Carpenter"

Fantasy

Have students working as a group come up with an opening paragraph for a fantasy. Ask students to describe at least one character in detail and to describe the setting of the story in vivid and specific detail. Remind students that either the character or the setting should contain at least one imaginative, unrealistic element. Have them then compare this paragraph to their science fiction paragraph and discuss the similarities and differences between them.

YOUR TURN

Possible Response: The sun shining in the night at the same time as the moon is ordinarily not possible; the moon speaking is not possible.

LEARNING THE LANGUAGE OF LITERATURE **509**

Theme

Theme is the meaning or moral of a story. Writers develop themes in order to express their ideas about life and human nature. Sometimes a theme is stated directly. Usually, however, readers have to make inferences about the theme based on details in a story. You can gather clues to a story's theme by analyzing the characters, the plot, the setting, and the story title.

Many **science fiction** pieces share two common themes:

- the dangers of taking the natural environment for granted
- the effect of technology on our society

In **fantasy** writing, themes often deal with good versus evil, the weak versus the powerful, or characters overcoming odds or completing difficult journeys.

THEME

Milo. But there's so much to learn.

Rhyme. That's true, but it's not just learning that's important. It's learning what to do with what you learn and learning why you learn things that matters.

—Norton Juster and Susan Nanus,
The Phantom Tollbooth

From *The Phantom Tollbooth*

𝒱isualizing

Have you ever listened to someone talk about a great new movie? If so, you probably pictured the people and events as they were described. Whenever you create mental pictures, you are visualizing. You can visualize with literature too. Active readers get the most from what they read by visualizing the settings, characters, and events in a story.

How to Apply the Strategy

To **VISUALIZE,** an active reader will
- Form mental pictures and images
- Look for details and descriptions that appeal to the senses
- Pay attention to the stage directions in a drama
- **Connect** with settings, characters, and events

Try It Now!

Read the excerpt below and visualize the scene.

(LIGHTS UP to reveal MILO'S bedroom. The CLOCK appears to be on a shelf in the room of a young boy—a room filled with books, toys, games, maps, papers, pencils, a bed, and a desk. . . . as well as records, a television, a toy car, and a large box that is wrapped and has an envelope taped to the top. The sound of FOOTSTEPS is heard, and then enter MILO dejectedly. He throws down his books and coat, flops into a chair, and sighs loudly.)

—Norton Juster and Susan Nanus,
The Phantom Tollbooth

Here's how Brittany uses the strategy:

"After I read the stage directions in The Phantom Tollbooth, *I close my eyes and try to picture the scene. I imagine that I see the setting where the action takes place. As I read, I pay attention to how the characters move and speak. I look for details that appeal to my senses. This helps me to **visualize** each description. I feel a **connection** to this piece as I picture Milo coming in. This could almost be my bedroom."*

THE ACTIVE READER **511**

OVERVIEW

Standards-Based Objectives
- develop effective strategies for visualizing
- describe mental images that text descriptions evoke
- respond to text by making connections to prior experiences

Teaching the Lesson

The strategies on this page will help students visualize the settings, characters, and events in the selections they read.

Presenting the Strategies
Help students understand the strategies by asking for volunteers to read them aloud. Emphasize to students that they will be using these strategies as they read the selections in this book.

1 Mental Pictures and Details
Tell students that as they read the excerpt from *The Phantom Tollbooth* they should note details that appeal to the senses as they try to form mental images.

2 Stage Directions
Remind students that since stage directions sometimes tell the actors what to do and where to move, they are a good source of visual information.

3 Connect
As a class, discuss how the material students read is easier to visualize if they relate the descriptions to their own life experiences.

Use **Reading and Critical Thinking Transparencies**, p. 4, for additional support.

Standards-Based Objectives

1. to understand and appreciate **fantasy**
2. to understand and appreciate a **drama**
3. to use **visualizing** to help understand character, setting, and action
4. to understand **theme**
5. to **make reasonable assumptions** about a text
6. to understand and explain **connotation** and **denotation**
7. to analyze **plot**

Summary

Milo is bored until he finds in his room one day a tollbooth. He gets into his toy car and sets off for Dictionopolis. He travels through Expectations and the Doldrums, and joins up with Tock, the Watchdog. In Dictionopolis, they meet the Spelling Bee, Humbug, and King Azaz, the ruler. Azaz and his brother, the Mathemagician, ruler of Digitopolis, banished their sisters, Rhyme and Reason, to the Castle-in-the-Air. Now Azaz wants them back, and Milo finds himself taking on the quest of rescuing the princesses with his friends Tock and Humbug. On their way, they encounter more strange characters. They return to the Land of Wisdom with the princesses, and Milo ends his journey back in his room, having learned many important lessons.

Thematic Link

Milo finds out that there are no limits to what someone can do with a little imagination.

English Conventions Practice

Daily Language SkillBuilder

Have students **proofread** the display sentences on page 441k and write them correctly. The sentences also appear on Transparency 16 of **Language Transparencies.**

Preteaching Vocabulary

If you would like to preteach the WORDS TO KNOW for this selection, use the Explicit Instruction, page 514.

The Phantom Tollbooth

Novel by NORTON JUSTER *dramatized by* SUSAN NANUS

Connect to Your Life

What is the greatest number you can name?

In 1655, the English mathematician John Wallis introduced this symbol to represent infinity.

Build Background

As the main character in *The Phantom Tollbooth* finds out, the series of numbers has no end. No matter how great a number you imagine, you can always add 1 to it. When something has no end, we say that it is *infinite*.

Negative numbers   Positive numbers

−6 −5 −4 −3 −2 −1 0 1 2 3 4 5 6

Numbers are infinite in both "directions." This is why number lines have an arrow on each end. The arrows stand for the infinite progression of numbers on either side of zero.

Focus Your Reading

LITERARY ANALYSIS **FANTASY**

The drama you are about to read is a **fantasy,** a work that contains one or more fantastic or unreal elements. *The Phantom Tollbooth* features fantastic characters and settings. For example, the main character, who is a boy, meets Tock, a talking "watchdog" with an alarm clock in his belly. Together these characters travel to imaginary lands.

ACTIVE READING **VISUALIZING**

Writers of fantasy often provide vivid descriptions of unusual characters and settings. **Visualizing,** or forming pictures in your mind, can help you appreciate and understand a fantasy play, story, or poem. As you read, visualize the places and characters in *The Phantom Tollbooth.*

READER'S NOTEBOOK Jot down key phrases that help create images in your mind.

WORDS TO KNOW **Vocabulary Preview**

acknowledge	deliberately	leisurely	petty
admonishing	destination	mourn	quest
ascend	fanfare	pantomime	vigorously
dejectedly	ignorance	perish	

512   UNIT FOUR   PART 2: IMAGINARY WORLDS

LESSON RESOURCES

UNIT FOUR RESOURCE BOOK, pp. 39–45

ASSESSMENT
Formal Assessment, pp. 89–90
Test Generator

SKILLS TRANSPARENCIES AND COPYMASTERS
Literary Analysis
• Drama: Stage Directions, TR 23 (p. 516)

Reading and Critical Thinking
• Visualizing, TR 4 (pp. 514, 552)
• Summarizing (Story Map), TR 13 (p. 553)
Language
• Daily Language SkillBuilder, TR 16 (p. 512)
• Prefixes, Suffixes, TR 57, TR 58 (p. 514)
Writing
• Locating Information Using Print References, TR 45 (p. 553)

INTEGRATED TECHNOLOGY
Audio Library

Visit our Web site:
www.mcdougallittell.com

For **systematic instruction** in language skills, see:
• **Vocabulary and Spelling Book**
• **Grammar, Usage, and Mechanics Book**
• pacing chart on p. 441i

THE PHANTOM TOLLBOOTH

NOVEL BY

NORTON JUSTER

DRAMATIZED BY

SUSAN NANUS

THE PHANTOM TOLLBOOTH **513**

Differentiating Instruction

Less Proficient Readers
Remind students that drama is meant to be acted out. Review the importance of paying attention to stage directions, which are in italics and describe the appearance, gestures, and movements of the actors and indicate the setting. Tell students that act and scene divisions organize the plot of a play.

English Learners
Help students understand the title by defining *phantom* as "unreal," "something that looks real but isn't," or "ghostlike." Synonyms for *phantom* are *apparition, spirit,* or *illusion.* Then explain that a tollbooth is a place on the roadway where an attendant or machine collects a fee before a car can continue on the road. Ask students to put *phantom* and *tollbooth* together and predict what the story will be about from the title.

Possible Responses: The story will be about an imaginary tollbooth. The story may have a tollbooth that leads to a fantasy world or to some fantastic adventure.

 Use **Spanish Study Guide,** pp. 106–108, for additional support.

Advanced Students
As they read, ask students to consider which of the following quotations from the novel *The Phantom Tollbooth* best describes what Milo learns during his journey. Discuss students' choices and their reasons at the end of their reading of the play.

- "the way you see things depends a great deal on where you look at them from."
- "[time] is our most valuable possession, more precious than diamonds."
- "the most important reason for going from one place to another is to see what's in between."

EXPLICIT INSTRUCTION   Viewing and Representing

Milo and Rhyme and Reason

Instruction Tell students that this photograph is from a production of *The Phantom Tollbooth.* Pictured are Milo, Rhyme, and Reason. Ask students what they might infer about the characters from the picture. (*The costumes of Rhyme and Reason suggest that they are members of royalty. Rhyme and Reason appear as people. This prepares the reader to see other fantastic characters. Milo is young and seems to be looking for something off in the distance.*)

Practice Ask students to react to seeing this image at the beginning of their reading. What does its placement here help them to do?

Possible Responses: Some may find it helpful because they gain an immediate sense of characters; others may say it helps them to form their own mental pictures of a stage production as they read.

Reading and Analyzing

Reading Skills and Strategies:
PREVIEW

Tell students that this is a play about Milo's journey to several destinations. Have students skim the play to get an idea of the characters that Milo meets and the adventures he has. Students should set a purpose before reading each scene.

Literary Analysis [FANTASY]

Remind students that this play contains elements of fantasy. Ask students which settings listed are realistic and which are fantasy settings.

Possible Responses: Milo's bedroom is realistic; the other settings are fantastic.

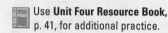 Use **Unit Four Resource Book,** p. 41, for additional practice.

Active Reading [VISUALIZING]

Ⓐ Ask students which details help them to create a mental image of Digitopolis.

Possible Responses: "glittering place without trees or greenery"; "full of shining rocks"; "hundreds of numbers shining"

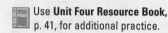 Use **Unit Four Resource Book,** p. 40, for additional practice.
Use **Reading and Critical Thinking Transparencies,** p. 4, for additional support.

Literary Analysis:
CAST OF CHARACTERS

Tell students that many scripts like this one include a list of all the characters in the order in which they appear. Ask students to name the last new character that will be seen.

Answer: Senses Taker

CAST
(in order of appearance)

The Clock
Milo, a boy
The Whether Man
Six Lethargarians
Tock, the Watchdog
  (same as The Clock)
Azaz the Unabridged,
  King of Dictionopolis
The Mathemagician,
  King of Digitopolis
Princess Sweet Rhyme
Princess Pure Reason
Gatekeeper of Dictionopolis
Three Word Merchants
The Letterman
  (Fourth Word Merchant)
Spelling Bee
The Humbug
The Duke of Definition
The Minister of Meaning
The Earl of Essence

The Count of Connotation
The Undersecretary of
  Understanding
A Page
Kakafonous A. Dischord,
  Doctor of Dissonance
The Awful Dynne
The Dodecahedron
Miners of the Numbers Mine
The Everpresent Wordsnatcher
The Terrible Trivium
The Demon of Insincerity
Senses Taker

Preteaching Vocabulary

WORDS TO KNOW
Teaching Strategy Tell students that examining the **prefix** or **suffix** of an unfamiliar word may help them to define it. Display the following prefixes and their meanings: *as, ad* (meanings: to, toward); *de* (meanings: away, from, off, down)

Then tell students that suffixes often determine the word's function in the sentence. Display these suffixes, meanings, and functions: *ly* (meaning: in a way that is; function: adverb); *ation, ion, tion, ance* (meaning: state or condition; function: noun)

Practice Have students analyze the prefixes and suffixes of the WORDS TO KNOW in the right column and match them with the definitions in the left column.

1. to move toward the top   a. dejectedly
2. state of being uneducated   b. ascend
3. in a sad way   c. admonishing
4. done with energy   d. ignorance
5. warning away from   e. vigorously

ANSWERS: 1. b; 2. d; 3. a; 4. e; 5. c

 Use **Unit Four Resource Book,** p. 44, for more practice.

For **systematic instruction** in vocabulary, see:
- **Vocabulary and Spelling Book**
- pacing chart on p. 441i

THE SETS

1. Milo's bedroom

With shelves, pennants, pictures on the wall, as well as suggestions of the characters of the Land of Wisdom.

2. The road to the Land of Wisdom

A forest, from which the Whether Man and the Lethargarians emerge.

3. Dictionopolis

A marketplace full of open-air stalls as well as little shops. Letters and signs should abound. There may be street signs and lampposts in the shapes of large letters (large O's and Q's) and all windows and doors can be in the shape of H's and A's.

4. Digitopolis

A dark, glittering place without trees or greenery, but full of shining rocks and cliffs, with hundreds of numbers shining everywhere. When the scene change is made to the Mathemagician's room, set pieces are simply carried in from the wings.

5. The Land of Ignorance

A gray, gloomy place full of cliffs and caves, with frightening faces. Different levels and heights should be suggested through one or two platforms or risers, with a set of stairs that lead to the castle in the air.

Less Proficient Readers

Put the following chart on the board. Tell students that keeping a chart will help them become familiar with the characters. Remind students that except for Milo's bedroom, all the settings are fantasies.

Act 1	Settings	Characters (introduced)
Scene 1	Milo's bedroom	Clock, Milo
Scene 2	Expectations, Doldrums,	Whether Man, Lethargarians, Tock (Mathemagician and princesses in flashback),
	Dictionopolis	Gatekeeper, Merchants Spelling Bee, Humbug, 5 Ministers, Page, King Azaz

English Learners

Introduce the characters in Act One by reading the names aloud and defining unfamiliar terms:

- *Lethargarians:* from the word "lethargy," which means "drowsiness" or "a state of sluggishness"
- *unabridged:* complete
- *Humbug:* a person who claims to be something other than what he or she is, a fraud, an imposter

Point out that *definition, meaning, essence, connotation,* and *understanding* are all basically synonyms for each other. You might also explain puns such as *whether/weather; be/bee;* and *senses/census.*

Advanced Students

The Phantom Tollbooth was originally a novel. Suggest that interested students read the novel while the rest of the class reads the play, and then share the differences and similarities of the two works with the class.

Reading and Analyzing

Reading Skills and Strategies: EVALUATE

A Have students sit in silence for 30 seconds. Then have students do an activity like copying something for 30 seconds. Ask them if they agree or disagree with the Clock's assessment of time.

Possible Response: Most will agree that when there is much to do, time goes quickly. When there is not much to do, time passes slowly.

Literary Analysis: THEME

B Ask students what important idea is conveyed by the Clock's words.

Possible Response: People should make every minute count and appreciate the time they have. Tell students to look for actions, events, and statements that support this theme as they read.

Literary Analysis: HUMOR

C Tell students that writers can add humor through exaggeration—overemphasis on minor events—or through witty dialogue, sarcasm, or irony. Ask students what device the writer uses here.

Answer: exaggeration

Literary Analysis: STAGE DIRECTIONS

D Tell students that stage directions contain instructions to the performers, director, and stage crew. They are usually italicized and in parentheses. If a play is read instead of viewed, the reader must examine the stage directions for important clues to action and character. Ask students what they learn from the stage directions describing Milo's room.

Possible Response: He has many possessions; he seems to be a typical young boy; images relating to future characters appear on various things in his room.

 Use **Literary Analysis Transparencies,** p. 23, for additional support.

EXPLICIT INSTRUCTION **Viewing and Representing**

Illustration of Milo in his room
by Bruce Roberts

Instruction Remind students that an illustrator's choice of style, elements, and media help to represent or extend the text's meanings. Point out illustrator Bruce Roberts's take on Milo's room. He uses lots of color and loose brush strokes to create a casual, energetic feeling. Ask students how this illustration of Milo compares with the one from page 513, aside from the fact that one is a photograph and one is drawn.

(Milo looks a little older in this illustration. You also get to see him in his own environment—his messy room.)

Practice Tell students to note the various objects in this illustration and to refer back to this page as they meet some of the characters in the course of the play. How are the characters related to what students notice in Milo's room as the play begins?

Possible Responses: Responses will vary.

ACT ONE
SCENE 1

The stage is completely dark and silent. Suddenly the sound of someone winding an alarm clock is heard, and after that, the sound of loud ticking is heard.

Lights up on the Clock, a huge alarm clock. The Clock reads 4:00. The lighting should make it appear that the Clock is suspended in mid-air (if possible). The Clock ticks for 30 seconds.

Clock. See that! Half a minute gone by. Seems like a long time when you're waiting for something to happen, doesn't it? Funny thing is, time can pass very slowly or very fast, and sometimes even both at once. The time now? Oh, a little after four, but what that means should depend on you. Too often, we do something simply because time tells us to. Time for school, time for bed, whoops, 12:00, time to be hungry. It can get a little silly, don't you think? Time is important, but it's what you do with it that makes it so. So my advice to you is to use it. Keep your eyes open and your ears perked. Otherwise it will pass before you know it, and you'll certainly have missed something!

Things have a habit of doing that, you know.

Being here one minute and gone the next.

In the twinkling of an eye.

In a jiffy.

In a flash!

I know a girl who yawned and missed a whole summer vacation. And what about that caveman who took a nap one afternoon, and woke up to find himself completely alone. You see, while he was sleeping, someone had invented the wheel and everyone had moved to the suburbs. And then of course, there is Milo. *(Lights up to reveal Milo's bedroom. The Clock appears to be on a shelf in the room of a young boy—a room filled with books, toys, games, maps, papers, pencils, a bed, a desk. There is a dartboard with numbers and the face of the Mathemagician, a bedspread made from King Azaz's cloak, a kite looking like the Spelling Bee, a punching bag with the Humbug's face, as well as records, a television, a toy car, and a large box that is wrapped and has*

Reading and Analyzing

A **CONNECT** Encourage students to give specific examples of times when they are bored.

Literary Analysis: CHARACTER TRAITS

B Ask students what Milo's speech and tone reveal about him.

Possible Responses: He is discontented and not easily amused; he lacks direction.

Literary Analysis **FANTASY**

Students should be able to recognize the distinguishing features of different genres. Ask students to point out the elements of fantasy in the play to the end of Scene 1.

Possible Responses: the clock speaking, the refunding of wasted time, the mysterious voice, the disappearance of Milo's room

Literary Analysis: SCENE

C Tell students that a scene is a subdivision of an act, which usually indicates a change in setting. Ask students where Scene 2 begins.

Answer: It begins on the road to Dictionopolis

Active Reading: WORD PLAY

D Ask students why Milo is confused by the Whether Man's name.

Possible Response: Because he is carrying an umbrella, Milo assumes that the Whether Man is the weatherman, *weather* being a homophone of *whether*.

Reading Skills and Strategies: MAKE INFERENCES

E Ask students what they think lies beyond Expectations.

Possible Responses: outcomes; results

---

an envelope taped to the top. The sound of footsteps is heard, and then enter Milo dejectedly. He throws down his books and coat, flops into a chair, and sighs loudly.) Who never knows what to do with himself—not just sometimes, but always. When he's in school, he wants to be out, and when he's out, he wants to be in. *(During the following speech, Milo examines the various toys, tools, and other possessions in the room, trying them out and rejecting them.)* Wherever he is, he wants to be somewhere else—and when he gets there, so what. Everything is too much trouble or a waste of time. Books—he's already read them. Games—boring. T.V.—dumb. So what's left? Another long, boring afternoon. Unless he bothers to notice a very large package that happened to arrive today.

[1]

A **CONNECT** Can you picture yourself in Milo's place? When do you feel bored?

Milo. *(Suddenly notices the package. He drags himself over to it, and disinterestedly reads the label.)* "For Milo, who has plenty of time." Well, that's true. *(Sighs and looks at it.)* No. *(Walks away.)* Well . . . *(Comes back. Rips open envelope and reads.)*

Voice. "One genuine turnpike tollbooth, easily assembled at home for use by those who have never traveled in lands beyond."

Milo. Beyond what? *(Continues reading.)*

Voice. "This package contains the following items:" *(Milo pulls the items out of the box and sets them up as they are mentioned.)* "One (1) genuine turnpike tollbooth to be erected according to directions. Three (3) precautionary signs to be used in a precautionary fashion. Assorted coins for paying tolls. One (1) map, strictly up to date, showing how to get from here to there. One (1) book of rules and traffic regulations which may not be bent or broken. Warning! Results are not guaranteed. If not perfectly satisfied, your wasted time will be refunded."

Milo. *(Skeptically.)* Come off it, who do you think you're kidding? *(Walks around and examines tollbooth.)* What am I supposed to do with this? *(The ticking of the Clock grows loud and impatient.)* Well . . . what else do I have to do. *(Milo gets into his toy car and drives up to the first sign. NOTE: The car may be an actual toy propelled by pedals or a small motor, or simply a cardboard imitation that Milo can fit into, and move by walking.)*

Voice. "Have your destination in mind."

Milo. *(Pulls out the map.)* Now, let's see. That's funny. I never heard of any of these places. Well, it doesn't matter anyway. Dictionopolis.[1] That's a weird name. I might as well go there. *(Begins to move, following map. Drives off.)*

Clock. See what I mean? You never know how things are going to get started. But when you're bored, what you need more than anything is a rude awakening.

(The alarm goes off very loudly as the stage darkens. The sound of the alarm is transformed into the honking of a car horn, and then is joined by the blasts, bleeps, roars and growls of heavy highway traffic. When the lights come up, Milo's bedroom is gone and we see a lonely road in the middle of nowhere.)

---

1. **Dictionopolis** (dĭk´shə-nŏp´ə-lĭs): an imaginary place name, formed from *dictionary* (an alphabetical listing of the words of a language) and the root *–polis*, meaning "city or state."

WORDS TO KNOW	**dejectedly** (dĭ-jĕk´tĭd-lē) *adv.* in a depressed manner
	destination (dĕs´tə-nā´shən) *n.* the place to which one intends to go

---

EXPLICIT INSTRUCTION **Characteristics of Drama**

Instruction Review drama as stories acted out on stage for an audience. Explain that a drama is presented in parts, called acts, that are broken down into smaller parts, called scenes. Stage directions describe for the actors and technical crew the setting, the props that should be used, and any necessary sound effects. Stage directions also tell actors when to enter and exit the stage, how they should move, and what their tone of voice should be as they deliver their lines. Ask, "What information do the stage directions on page 517 give?" *(They describe sound effects and lighting. They also describe the props, such as the big clock, and the things that are in Milo's bedroom.)*

Practice Have students find examples of stage directions on page 518 that do the following:

1 tell an actor how to move
2 tell an actor how to speak
3 tell about props
4 describe sound effects
5 describe setting

Possible Responses: 1 "flops into a chair"; **2** "skeptically"; **3** "toys, tools, and other possessions in the room"; **4** "The sound of footsteps is heard"; **5** "we see a lonely road in the middle of nowhere"

SCENE 2

THE ROAD TO
DICTIONOPOLIS

*Enter Milo in
his car.*

Milo. This is weird! I don't recognize any of this scenery at all. *(A sign is held up before Milo, startling him.)* Huh? *(Reads.)* Welcome to Expectations. Information, predictions and advice cheerfully offered. Park here and blow horn. *(Milo blows horn.)*

Whether Man. *(A little man wearing a long coat and carrying an umbrella pops up from behind the sign that he was holding. He speaks very fast and excitedly.)* My, my, my, my, my, welcome, welcome, welcome, welcome to the Land of Expectations, Expectations, Expectations! We don't get many travelers these days; we certainly don't get many travelers. Now what can I do for you? I'm the Whether Man.

Milo. *(Referring to map.)* Uh . . . is this the right road to Dictionopolis?

Whether Man. Well now, well now, well now, I don't know of any wrong road to Dictionopolis, so if this road goes to Dictionopolis at all, it must be the right road, and if it doesn't, it must be the right road to somewhere else, because there are no wrong roads to anywhere. Do you think it will rain?

Milo. I thought you were the Weather Man.

Whether Man. Oh, no, I'm the Whether Man, not the weather man. *(Pulls out a sign or opens a flap of his coat, which reads: "Whether.")* After all, it's more important to know whether there will be weather than what the weather will be.

Milo. What kind of place is Expectations?

Whether Man. Good question, good question! Expectations is the place you must always go to before you get where you are going. Of course, some people never go beyond Expectations, but my job is to hurry them along whether they like it or not. Now what else can I do for you? *(Opens his umbrella.)*

Milo. I think I can find my own way.

Whether Man. Splendid, splendid, splendid! Whether or not you find your own way, you're bound to find some way. If you happen to find my way, please return it. I lost it years ago. I imagine by now it must be quite rusty. You did say it was going to rain, didn't you? *(Escorts Milo to the car under the open umbrella.)* I'm glad you made your own decision. I do so hate to make up my mind about anything, whether it's good or bad, up or down, rain or shine. Expect everything, I always say, and the unexpected never happens. Goodbye, goodbye, goodbye, good . . . *(A loud clap of thunder is heard.)* Oh dear! *(He looks up at the sky, puts out his hand to feel for rain and runs away. Milo watches puzzledly, and drives on.)*

Milo. I'd better get out of Expectations, but fast. Talking to a guy like that all day would get me nowhere for sure. *(He tries to speed up, but finds instead that he is moving slower and slower.)* Oh, oh, now what? *(He can

THE PHANTOM TOLLBOOTH **519**

Differentiating Instruction

Less Proficient Readers
Ask students the following questions:
- Why does Milo unwrap the package and follow the directions?
  Possible Response: He has nothing better to do.
- What destination does Milo decide on? *(Dictionopolis)*

Set a Purpose Have students read to find out what Milo's next obstacle is and who rescues him.

English Learners
1 Tell students that in this sentence, *dumb* means "stupid" or "senseless." Ask students to point out anything in the text that they find humorous. Point out to students that the sentences *"If you happen to find my way, please return it. I lost it years ago. I imagine by now it must be quite rusty"* are —supposed to be humorous. The sentences turn an abstract expression, "find one's way," into something tangible that might rust.

Advanced Students
Milo begins his journey in the Land of Expectations. By the end of his stay, he wants to leave because talking will get him "nowhere for sure." Ask students to discuss the significance of this statement.

Possible Response: People always have expectations when starting new experiences or journeys. However, if people only have expectations and never act on them, they will accomplish nothing and go nowhere. Also, many people talk but never do anything, and Milo realizes that talking is not the same as doing, and things will never change if all he does is talk about them.

EXPLICIT INSTRUCTION **Viewing and Representing**

Illustration of Milo in his car
by Jules Feiffer

ART APPRECIATION

Jules Feiffer (b. 1929) has been interested in art all his life. He began drawing cartoons after high school, and since then, his cartoons have been syndicated internationally. He illustrated the novel *The Phantom Tollbooth* in the early part of his career.

Instruction Tell students to notice Feiffer's style of drawing, which uses loose, sparse pen strokes. Although there is not a great deal of detail, a definite impression of the character is created. Ask students what the portrait of Milo suggests about his character. *(uncertainty; anxiety; wondering alertness as he moves into the unknown)*

Practice Ask students whether this cartoon image of Milo matches their mental image. Have them explain why or why not.

Possible Responses: Some students may think the cartoon shows a more mature and older Milo than the text depicts. Others may see the artist's portrayal as just the sort of wide-eyed, curious boy they imagine.

A VISUALIZE Possible Responses: "carry small pillows that look like rocks"; "colored in the same colors of the trees or the road"; "move very slowly"; "stop to rest"

Reading Skills and Strategies: CAUSE AND EFFECT

B Ask students to locate the reason Milo is stuck in the Doldrums. What will he have to do to get out?

Possible Response: He stopped thinking. He'll have to start thinking again.

Active Reading: WORD PLAY

C Ask what the two meanings of "watchdog" are in the play.

Possible Responses: The first is literally a dog that contains a watch. The second is someone who tracks what others are doing or a guard dog.

Literary Analysis: IDIOM

D Ask students what effect the use of the idiom *killing time* has on their perception of time.

Possible Response: Time seems to be alive, so *killing* it becomes a terrible thing.

Literary Analysis: CHARACTERIZATION

E Ask students what the Watchdog's words and actions show about the kind of influence he will be on Milo.

Possible Response: He will be a positive influence.

barely move. Behind Milo, the Lethargarians[2] begin to enter from all parts of the stage. They are dressed to blend in with the scenery and carry small pillows that look like rocks. Whenever they fall asleep, they rest on the pillows.) Now I really am getting nowhere. I hope I didn't take a wrong turn. *(The car stops. He tries to start it. It won't move. He gets out and begins to tinker with it.)* I wonder where I am.

Lethargarian 1. You're . . . in . . . the . . . Dol . . . drums[3] . . . (Milo looks around.)

Lethargarian 2. Yes . . . in . . . the . . . Dol . . . drums . . . (A yawn is heard.)

Milo. *(Yelling.)* What are the Doldrums?

Lethargarian 3. The Doldrums, my friend, are where nothing ever happens and nothing ever changes. *(Parts of the scenery stand up or six people come out of the scenery colored in the same colors of the trees or the road. They move very slowly and as soon as they move, they stop to rest again.)* Allow me to introduce all of us. We are the Lethargarians at your service.

ACTIVE READER

VISUALIZE Picture the Lethargarians. What words or phrases help you?

A

Milo. *(Uncertainly.)* Very pleased to meet you. I think I'm lost. Can you help me?

Lethargarian 4. Don't say think. *(He yawns.)* It's against the law.

Lethargarian 1. No one's allowed to think in the Doldrums. *(He falls asleep.)*

Lethargarian 2. Don't you have a rule book? It's local ordinance 175389-J. *(He falls asleep.)*

Milo. *(Pulls out rule book and reads.)* Ordinance 175389-J: "It shall be unlawful, illegal and unethical to think, think of thinking, surmise, presume, reason, meditate or speculate while in the Doldrums. Anyone breaking this law shall be severely punished." That's a ridiculous law! Everybody thinks.

All the Lethargarians. We don't!

Lethargarian 2. And the most of the time, you don't, that's why you're here. You weren't thinking and you weren't paying attention either. People who don't pay attention often get stuck in the Doldrums. Face it, most of the time, you're just like us. *(Falls, snoring, to the ground. Milo laughs.)*

Lethargarian 5. Stop that at once. Laughing is against the law. Don't you have a rule book? It's local ordinance 574381-W.

Milo. *(Opens the rule book and reads.)* "In the Doldrums, laughter is frowned upon and smiling is permitted only on alternate Thursdays." Well, if you can't laugh or think, what can you do?

Lethargarian 6. Anything as long as it's nothing, and everything as long as it isn't anything. There's lots to do. We have a very busy schedule . . .

Lethargarian 1. At 8:00 we get up and then we spend from 8 to 9 daydreaming.

Lethargarian 2. From 9:00 to 9:30 we take our early midmorning nap . . .

Lethargarian 3. From 9:30 to 10:30 we dawdle and delay . . .

Lethargarian 4. From 10:30 to 11:30 we take our late early morning nap . . .

Lethargarian 5. From 11:30 to 12:00 we bide our time and then we eat our lunch.

---

2. **Lethargarians** (lĕth′ər-jâr′ē-anz): a made-up name based on the word *lethargy*. A *Lethargarian* would thus be dull, inactive, or uncaring.

3. **in the doldrums** (dōl′drəmz′): the condition of being depressed or listless; here, *the Doldrums* refers to an imaginary land.

EXPLICIT INSTRUCTION Understanding Theme

Instruction Remind students that theme is the meaning or moral of a story. It is a message about life or human nature that the writer wants to share with the reader. Also remind students that in order to figure out the theme of a story, they must pay attention to story details. Next, write this statement on the board: "People who waste time and do not use their minds go nowhere in life." Briefly discuss information on pages 520–521 that supports this theme.

Practice Have pairs of students work together to find and list information on pages 520–521 that supports this theme. Remind them to consider the characters and events and to read the stage directions and the characters' lines.

Possible Responses: The Lethargarians are characters who never think and who live in the Doldrums. They spend their days napping, eating, daydreaming, dawdling, and delaying. Because of these time-wasting activities, they never go anyplace. They tell Milo that because he wasn't thinking or paying attention, he ended up in the Doldrums. The Watchdog tells Milo that since he got there by not thinking, he can get out by using his head. Milo starts to think, and he and the Watchdog begin to move.

Lethargarian 6. From 1:00 to 2:00 we linger and loiter . . .

Lethargarian 1. From 2:00 to 2:30 we take our early afternoon nap . . .

Lethargarian 2. From 2:30 to 3:30 we put off for tomorrow what we could have done today . . .

Lethargarian 3. From 3:30 to 4:00 we take our early late afternoon nap . . .

Lethargarian 4. From 4:00 to 5:00 we loaf and lounge until dinner . . .

Lethargarian 5. From 6:00 to 7:00 we dilly-dally . . .

Lethargarian 6. From 7:00 to 8:00 we take our early evening nap and then for an hour before we go to bed, we waste time.

Lethargarian 1. *(Yawning.)* You see, it's really quite strenuous doing nothing all day long, and so once a week, we take a holiday and go nowhere.

Lethargarian 5. Which is just where we were going when you came along. Would you care to join us?

Milo. *(Yawning.)* That's where I seem to be going, anyway. *(Stretching.)* Tell me, does everyone here do nothing?

Lethargarian 3. Everyone but the terrible Watchdog. He's always sniffing around to see that nobody wastes time. A most unpleasant character.

Milo. The Watchdog?

Lethargarian 6. The Watchdog!

All the Lethargarians. *(Yelling at once.)* Run! Wake up! Run! Here he comes! The Watchdog! *(They all run off. Enter a large dog with the head, feet, and tail of a dog, and the body of a clock, having the same face as the character The Clock.)*

Watchdog. What are you doing here?

Milo. Nothing much. Just killing time. You see . . .

Watchdog. Killing time! *(His alarm rings in fury.)* It's bad enough wasting time without killing it. What are you doing in the Doldrums, anyway? Don't you have anywhere to go?

Milo. I think I was on my way to Dictionopolis when I got stuck here. Can you help me?

Watchdog. Help you! You've got to help yourself. I suppose you know why you got stuck.

Milo. I guess I just wasn't thinking.

Watchdog. Precisely. Now you're on your way.

Milo. I am?

Watchdog. Of course. Since you got here by not thinking, it seems reasonable that in order to get out, you must start thinking. Do you mind if I get in? I love automobile rides. *(He gets in. They wait.)* Well?

Milo. All right. I'll try. *(Screws up his face and thinks.)* Are we moving?

Watchdog. Not yet. Think harder.

Milo. I'm thinking as hard as I can.

Watchdog. Well, think just a little harder than that. Come on, you can do it.

Milo. All right, all right. . . . I'm thinking of all the planets in the solar system, and why water expands when it turns to ice, and all the words that begin with "q," and . . . *(The wheels begin to move.)* We're moving! We're moving!

Watchdog. Keep thinking.

Milo. *(Thinking.)* How a steam engine works and how to bake a pie and the difference between Fahrenheit and centigrade[4] . . .

---

4. **Fahrenheit** (făr′ən-hīt′) **and centigrade** (sĕn′tĭ-grād′): *Fahrenheit* is a temperature scale on which water freezes at 32 and boils at 212 degrees. On the centigrade (Celsius) scale, water freezes at 0 and boils at 100 degrees.

THE PHANTOM TOLLBOOTH **521**

A **PREDICT** Possible Responses: There will be words and letters scattered about, piled up, and arranged on shelves. Buildings might look like pages of a dictionary.

Literary Analysis: CHARACTER

B Ask students to explain what is suggested by the names of the two kings. **Possible Responses:** *Azaz* suggests the alphabet, the letters from A to Z; *Mathemagician* suggests that he can work magic with numbers.

Literary Analysis: FLASHBACK

C Explain to students that a flashback is a literary device in which a scene that took place at an earlier time is presented. Writers use flashback to provide background information. Ask students what they learn from this flashback. **Possible Responses:** Azaz and the Mathemagician don't agree on anything; the two princesses were banished because their brothers did not like the way they settled their argument.

Reading Skills and Strategies: WORD PLAY

D Have students explain the two meanings of *count* in this sentence. **Possible Response:** *Count* means numbers "are important" and "show numerical value."

Literary Analysis: PROPS

E Tell students that props are objects used on stage. They may be functional or symbolic. Ask students what the significance of the tollbooth is. **Possible Response:** It links back to the tollbooth found in Milo's room and indicates that another stage of Milo's journey is about to begin.

Watchdog. Dictionopolis, here we come.

Milo. Hey, Watchdog, are you coming along?

1 **Watchdog.** You can call me Tock, and keep your eyes on the road.

Milo. What kind of place is Dictionopolis, anyway?

A **PREDICT** What do you think Dictionopolis will look like?

Tock. It's where all the words in the world come from. It used to be a marvelous place, but ever since Rhyme and Reason[5] left, it hasn't been the same.

Milo. Rhyme and Reason?

Tock. The two princesses. They used to settle all the arguments between their two brothers who rule over the Land of Wisdom. You see, Azaz is the king of Dictionopolis and the Mathemagician is the king of Digitopolis[6] and they almost never see eye to eye on anything. It was the job of the Princesses Sweet Rhyme and Pure Reason to solve the differences between the two kings, and they always did so well that both sides usually went home feeling very satisfied. But then, **2** one day, the kings had an argument to end all arguments. . . .

C *(The lights dim on Tock and Milo, and come up on King Azaz of Dictionopolis on another part of the stage. Azaz has a great stomach, a gray beard reaching to his waist, a small crown and a long robe with the letters of the alphabet written all over it.)*

Act One, Scene 2. Milo and Tock on the road to Dictionopolis.

Azaz. Of course, I'll abide by the decision of Rhyme and Reason, though I have no doubt as to what it will be. They will choose words, of course. Everyone knows that words are more important than numbers any day of the week.

---

5. **Rhyme and Reason:** sense or explanation. The princesses try to establish order. When they disappear, there is "neither Rhyme nor Reason in this kingdom."

6. **Digitopolis** (dĭj′ə-tŏp′ə-lĭs): another made-up place name, this uses *digit* (any of the numbers 0–9) and the root *–polis* ("city or state") to describe a land of numbers.

EXPLICIT INSTRUCTION ## Viewing and Representing

Milo and Tock on the road to Dictionopolis

Instruction Tell students that this photograph from a production of *The Phantom Tollbooth* illustrates how directors have their own visions of characters. In this image, Tock appears quite a bit larger than Milo. Ask students how this affects their impression of the relationship between the two characters. *(Tock is seen as a protector of Milo and as a character whose wisdom and experience can help guide Milo.)*

Ask students to describe the look on Milo's face in this photograph. *(He appears interested and happy.)*

Practice Ask students if they agree with this director's portrayal of Tock and why or why not. **Possible Response:** Many will agree that Tock's actions show him to be more mature and knowledgeable than Milo. This is shown when he leads Milo out of the Doldrums and fills him in on the background of Rhyme and Reason.

(The Mathemagician appears opposite Azaz. The Mathemagician wears a long flowing robe covered entirely with complex mathematical equations, and a tall pointed hat. He carries a long staff with a pencil point at one end and a large rubber eraser at the other.)

Mathemagician. That's what you think, Azaz. People wouldn't even know what day of the week it is without numbers. Haven't you ever looked at a calendar? Face it, Azaz. It's numbers that count.

Azaz. Don't be ridiculous. *(To audience, as if leading a cheer.)* Let's hear it for words!

Mathemagician. *(To audience, in the same manner.)* Cast your vote for numbers!

Azaz. A, B, C's!

Mathemagician. 1, 2, 3's! *(A fanfare is heard.)*

Azaz and Mathemagician. *(To each other.)* Quiet! Rhyme and Reason are about to announce their decision.

(Rhyme and Reason appear.)

Rhyme. Ladies and gentlemen, letters and numerals, fractions and punctuation marks—may we have your attention, please. After careful consideration of the problem set before us by King Azaz of Dictionopolis *(Azaz bows.)* and the Mathemagician of Digitopolis *(Mathemagician raises his hands in a victory salute.)* we have come to the following conclusion:

Reason. Words and numbers are of equal value, for in the cloak of knowledge, one is the warp and the other is the woof.[7]

Rhyme. It is no more important to count the sands than it is to name the stars.

Rhyme and Reason. Therefore, let both

kingdoms, Dictionopolis and Digitopolis, live in peace.

(The sound of cheering is heard.)

Azaz. Boo! is what I say. Boo and Bah and Hiss!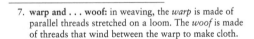

Mathemagician. What good are these girls if they can't even settle an argument in anyone's favor? I think I have come to a decision of my own.

Azaz. So have I.

Azaz and Mathemagician. *(To the Princesses.)* You are hereby banished from this land to the Castle-in-the-Air. *(To each other.)* And as for you, keep out of my way! *(They stalk off in opposite directions.)*

(During this time, the set has been changed to the Market Square of Dictionopolis. Lights come up on a deserted square.)

Tock. And ever since then, there has been neither Rhyme nor Reason in this kingdom. Words are misused and numbers mismanaged. The argument between the two kings has divided everyone and the real value of both words and numbers has been forgotten. What a waste!

Milo. Why doesn't somebody rescue the princesses and set everything straight again?

Tock. That is easier said than done. The Castle-in-the-Air is very far from here, and the one path which leads to it is guarded by ferocious demons. But hold on, here we are. *(A man appears, carrying a gate and a small tollbooth.)* **E**

---

7. **warp and . . . woof:** in weaving, the *warp* is made of parallel threads stretched on a loom. The *woof* is made of threads that wind between the warp to make cloth.

WORDS TO KNOW **fanfare** (făn′fâr′) *n.* a loud blast of trumpets

523

sidebar

Differentiating Instruction

Less Proficient Readers
Ask students the following questions:
- Who are Rhyme and Reason?
  Possible Response: They are princesses, sisters of Azaz and the Mathemagician. The princesses gave order to the kingdoms of Dictionopolis and Digitopolis.
- Why did they leave Dictionopolis?
  Possible Response: They were banished by their brothers, who didn't like the way they settled an argument.
- Where did Rhyme and Reason go? *(The went to the Castle-in-the-Air.)*

Set a Purpose Have students read to find out what Dictionopolis looks like and whom Milo meets there.

English Learners
1 Have students figure out why the Watchdog is called Tock. (It is one of the sounds that a clock makes—*tick, tock.*)
2 Explain that "an argument to end all arguments" means "an especially bad quarrel."
3 Tell students that the sounds that Azaz makes show his unhappiness with the decision of Rhyme and Reason.

Advanced Students
Both Azaz and the Mathemagician have strong opinions about letters and numbers. Azaz believes letters are more important and the Mathemagician believes the world would not run without numbers. Have students discuss and decide for themselves what they think is more important to everyday life.

Cross Curricular Link **History**

CASTLES Over the centuries, changes were made in both the design and material of castles. The first castles, built in northwest Europe in the ninth century, were made mostly of earth and wood. By the end of the twelfth century, however, stone was replacing timber, as more sophisticated designs spread to western Europe from the Holy Land. Castle construction reached its golden age by the thirteenth century, particularly in Great Britain. Several lines of defense had to be penetrated in the castles of the late thirteenth century before the invaders could reach the inner living quarters.

Although the invention of gunpowder is considered a primary reason for the decline of the importance of the castle by the fifteenth century, economic and domestic factors also contributed. Central governments could afford to pay a large mercenary army with the money raised by merchant taxes, and people no longer wanted to live in damp, uncomfortable castles. Many times, castles were left to decay while new residences or palaces were built next to them.

THE PHANTOM TOLLBOOTH **523**

Reading and Analyzing

Literary Analysis: REALISTIC AND FANTASTIC DETAILS

A Ask students what is realistic about the setting described here. What is fantastic?

Possible Response: The marketplace, with its merchants and vendors, is realistic. The sudden appearance of the market and the selling of words and letters are fantastic.

Ask students if a lack of realistic details would have changed the play's effect.

Possible Response: The play would have been more difficult to relate to and comprehend.

ACTIVE READER

B **VISUALIZE** **Possible Response:** The marketplace is a square filled with movement, crowds, and voices. Tock and Milo can be seen looking around.

Reading Skills and Strategies: CLARIFY

C Ask why it makes sense that *A* and *I* are more popular than *X* and *Z*.

Possible Response: They are tastier.

Literary Analysis: STAGE DIRECTIONS

D Ask students what impression of Humbug the stage directions create.

Possible Response: He seems dapper and perhaps vain; his actions of swinging his cane and clicking his heels attract attention.

Literary Analysis: CHARACTER TRAITS

E Ask what the Spelling Bee's reaction to Humbug reveals about Humbug's stories.

Possible Response: Humbug is not always truthful.

Gatekeeper. AHHHHREMMMM! This is Dictionopolis, a happy kingdom, advantageously located in the foothills of Confusion and caressed by gentle breezes from the Sea of Knowledge. Today, by royal proclamation, is Market Day. Have you come to buy or sell?

Milo. I beg your pardon?

Gatekeeper. Buy or sell, buy or sell. Which is it? You must have come here for a reason.

Milo. Well, I . . .

Gatekeeper. Come now, if you don't have a reason, you must at least have an explanation or certainly an excuse.

Milo. *(Meekly.)* Uh . . . no.

Gatekeeper. *(Shaking his head.)* Very serious. You can't get in without a reason. *(Thoughtfully.)* Wait a minute. Maybe I have an old one you can use. *(Pulls out an old suitcase from the tollbooth and rummages through it.)* No . . . no . . . no . . . this won't do . . . hmmm . . .

Milo. *(To Tock.)* What's he looking for? *(Tock shrugs.)*

Gatekeeper. Ah! This is fine. *(Pulls out a medallion on a chain. Engraved in the medallion is: "Why not?")* Why not. That's a good reason for almost anything . . . a bit used, perhaps, but still quite serviceable. There you are, sir. Now I can truly say: Welcome to Dictionopolis.

A *(He opens the gate and walks off. Citizens and merchants appear on all levels of the stage, and Milo and Tock find themselves in the middle of a noisy marketplace. As some people buy and sell their wares, others hang a large banner which reads: Welcome to the Word Market.)*

Milo. Tock! Look!

Merchant 1. Hey-ya, hey-ya, hey-ya, step right up and take your pick. Juicy tempting words for sale. Get your fresh-picked "if's," "and's" and "but's"! Just take a look at these nice ripe "where's" and "when's."

Merchant 2. Step right up, step right up, fancy, best-quality words here for sale. Enrich your vocabulary and expand your speech with such elegant items as "quagmire," "flabbergast," or "upholstery."

Merchant 3. Words by the bag, buy them over here. Words by the bag for the more talkative customer. A pound of "happy's" at a very reasonable price . . . very useful for "Happy Birthday," "Happy New Year," "happy days," or "happy-go-lucky." Or how about a package of "good's," always handy for "good morning," "good afternoon," "good evening," and "goodbye."

Milo. I can't believe it. Did you ever see so many words?

Tock. They're fine if you have something to say. *(They come to a Do-It-Yourself Bin.)*

Milo. *(To Merchant 4 at the bin.)* Excuse me, but what are these?

Merchant 4. These are for people who like to

ACTIVE READER

VISUALIZE Close your eyes and picture the Word Market. Note details. **B**

make up their own words. You can pick any assortment you like or buy a special box complete with all the letters and a book of instructions. Here, taste an "A." They're very good. *(He pops one into Milo's mouth.)*

Milo. *(Tastes it hesitantly.)* It's sweet! *(He eats it.)*

Merchant 4. I knew you'd like it. "A" is one of our best-sellers. All of them aren't that good, you know. The "Z," for instance—very dry and sawdusty. And the "X?" Tastes like a trunkful of stale air. But most of the others aren't bad at all. Here, try the "I."

Milo. *(Tasting.)* Cool! It tastes icy.

Merchant 4. *(To Tock.)* How about the "C" for you? It's as crunchy as a bone. Most people are just too lazy to make their own words, but take it from me, not only is it more fun, but it's also *de*-lightful, *(Holds up a "D.")* e-lating, *(Holds up an "E.")* and extremely useful! *(Holds up a "U.")*

Milo. But isn't it difficult? I'm not very good at making words.

(The Spelling Bee, a large colorful bee, comes up from behind.)

Spelling Bee. Perhaps I can be of some assistance . . . a-s-s-i-s-t-a-n-c-e. *(The Three turn around and see him.)* Don't be alarmed . . . a-l-a-r-m-e-d. I am the Spelling Bee. I can spell anything. Anything. A-n-y-t-h-i-n-g. Try me. Try me.

Milo. *(Backing off, Tock on his guard.)* Can you spell goodbye?

Spelling Bee. Perhaps you are under the misapprehension[8] . . . m-i-s-a-p-p-r-e-h-e-n-s-i-o-n that I am dangerous. Let me assure you that I am quite peaceful. Now, think of the most difficult word you can, and I'll spell it.

Milo. Uh . . . o.k. *(At this point, Milo may turn to the audience and ask them to help him chose a word or he may think of one on his own.)* How about . . . "Curiosity?"

Spelling Bee. *(Winking.)* Let's see now . . . uh . . . how much time do I have?

Milo. Just ten seconds. Count them off, Tock.

Spelling Bee. *(As Tock counts.)* Oh dear, oh dear. *(Just at the last moment, quickly.)* C-u-r-i-o-s-i-t-y.

Merchant 4. Correct! *(All cheer.)*

Milo. Can you spell anything?

Spelling Bee. *(Proudly.)* Just about. You see, years ago, I was an ordinary bee minding my own business, smelling flowers all day, occasionally picking up part-time work in people's bonnets. Then one day, I realized that I'd never amount to anything without an education, so I decided that . . .

Humbug. *(Coming up in a booming voice.)* Balderdash! *(He wears a lavish coat, striped pants, checked vest, spats and a derby hat.)* Let me repeat . . . Balderdash! *(Swings his cane and clicks his heels in the air.)* Well, well, what have we here? Isn't someone going to introduce me to the little boy?

Spelling Bee. *(Disdainfully.)* This is the Humbug. You can't trust a word he says.

Humbug. Nonsense! Everyone can trust a Humbug. As I was saying to the king just the other day . . .

Spelling Bee. You've never met the king. *(To Milo.)* Don't believe a thing he tells you.

Humbug. Bosh, my boy, pure bosh. The Humbugs are an old and noble family, honorable to the core. Why, we fought in the Crusades with Richard the Lion-hearted,[9] crossed the Atlantic with Columbus, blazed trails with the pioneers. History is full of Humbugs.

Spelling Bee. A very pretty speech . . . s-p-e-e-c-h. Now, why don't you go away? I

---

8. **misapprehension** (mĭs-ăp′rĭ-hĕn′shən): the misunderstanding of something.

9. **fought in the Crusades with Richard the Lion-hearted:** the Crusades were journeys undertaken by European Christians in the eleventh through thirteenth centuries to fight the Muslims for control of the Holy Land. Richard the Lion-hearted was an English king who led the Third Crusade (1190–1192).

Differentiating Instruction

Less Proficient Readers
Ask students the following questions:
- What do the merchants sell on Market Day in Dictionopolis?
  Possible Response: They sell words and letters.
- What options does the letter merchant offer?
  Possible Response: Customers may buy an assortment or a box complete with all the letters and instructions.
- Whom does Milo meet in Dictionopolis?
  Possible Response: He meets the Spelling Bee and Humbug.

Set a Purpose Have students read to find out who the five gentlemen are who appear in the marketplace.

English Learners
1 Read Merchant 1's speech aloud to students. Use your tone of voice to show how *hey-ya* is used to attract people's attention.
2 Tell students that *having a bee in your bonnet* is an idiom that means "being upset or worked up about something."
3 Explain that *Balderdash* means nonsense.
4 *Bosh* is also a slang word for nonsense.

EXPLICIT INSTRUCTION **Understanding Fantasy**

Instruction Remind students that a fantasy is a work of fiction that includes at least one unrealistic element. It may contain many realistic elements and just one fantastic element, or it may contain many fantastic elements. Ask students to name fantastic details from earlier in the story.

Practice Use the Literary Analysis: Realistic and Fantastic Details note in the green side column to give students practice in noticing and differentiating these details.
Possible Responses: See the responses given in the side column.

Active Reading VISUALIZING

A Ask students to describe the mental image evoked by this passage of the text.

Possible Response: The Ministers, who are almost identical, stand in a line, reading or speaking one after the other. They all have very stuffy expressions.

Literary Analysis: HUMOR

B Ask students how the author's style makes this bit of dialogue humorous.

Possible Response: The author uses exaggeration. Five ministers saying essentially the same thing in different words several times is humorous.

Reading Skills and Strategies: EVALUATE

C Ask students whether they think the minister's comment that "one word is as good as another" is valid.

Possible Response: No; one word is not as good as another. Words have different dictionary definitions and different connotations.

---

was just advising the lad of the importance of proper spelling.

Humbug. Bah! As soon as you learn to spell one word, they ask you to spell another. You can never catch up, so why bother? (*Puts his arm around Milo.*) Take my advice, boy, and forget about it. As my great-great-great-grandfather George Washington Humbug used to say . . .

Spelling Bee. You, sir, are an impostor i-m-p-o-s-t-o-r who can't even spell his own name!

Humbug. What? You dare to doubt my word? The word of a Humbug? The word of a Humbug who has direct access to the ear of a king? And the king shall hear of this, I promise you . . .

1 **Voice 1.** Did someone call for the king?

Voice 2. Did you mention the monarch?

Voice 3. Speak of the sovereign?

Voice 4. Entreat the emperor?

Voice 5. Hail his highness?

A (*Five tall, thin gentlemen regally dressed in silks and satins, plumed hats and buckled shoes appear as they speak.*)

Milo. Who are they?

Spelling Bee. The king's advisors. Or in more formal terms, his cabinet.

Minister 1. Greetings!

Minister 2. Salutations!

Minister 3. Welcome!

Minister 4. Good afternoon!

B **Minister 5.** Hello!

Milo. Uh . . . Hi.

(*All the Ministers, from here on called by their numbers, unfold their scrolls and read in order.*)

Minister 1. By the order of Azaz the Unabridged . . .

Minister 2. King of Dictionopolis . . .

Minister 3. Monarch of letters . . .

Minister 4. Emperor of phrases, sentences, and miscellaneous figures of speech . . .

Minister 5. We offer you the hospitality of our kingdom . . .

Minister 1. Country

Minister 2. Nation

Minister 3. State

Minister 4. Commonwealth

Minister 5. Realm

Minister 1. Empire

Minister 2. Palatinate

Minister 3. Principality.

Milo. Do all those words mean the same thing?

Minister 1. Of course.

Minister 2. Certainly.

Minister 3. Precisely.

Minister 4. Exactly.

Minister 5. Yes.

Milo. Then why don't you just use one? Wouldn't that make a lot more sense?

Minister 1. Nonsense!

Minister 2. Ridiculous!

Minister 3. Fantastic!

Minister 4. Absurd!

Minister 5. Bosh!

Minister 1. We're not interested in making sense. It's not our job.

Minister 2. Besides, one word is as good as another, so why not use them all?

Minister 3. Then you don't have to choose which one is right.

Minister 4. Besides, if one is right, then ten are ten times as right.

EXPLICIT INSTRUCTION ## Denotation and Connotation

Instruction Tell students that the dictionary definition of a word is its denotation. The attitudes and shades of meaning associated with a word are its connotations. Say, "A good writer chooses a word for its connotation as well as for its dictionary definition." Write the following sentence on the board: The details of the story are *fantastic*.

Ask a volunteer to rewrite the sentence on the board, substituting *absurd* for *fantastic*. Discuss the differences between the two sentences. Help students understand that although the words share similar meanings, *absurd* has a connotation of "silly," while *fantastic* has a more positive connotation.

Practice Write the following sentences on the board and have students explain how replacing the underlined word with the word in parentheses affects the meaning of each sentence:

- Milo walked up to the door timidly. (cautiously)
- Humbug compliments the king. (flatters)
- The Lethargarian knew how to relax. (loaf)

Possible Responses: *Timidly* implies being afraid. *Cautiously* implies being careful. *Compliments* implies saying something nice because someone has done something nice. *Flatters* implies false compliments. *Relax* implies taking time off. *Loaf* implies being lazy.

VIEW AND COMPARE

These images show Milo, Tock, and the Spelling Bee meeting the Humbug in the Word Market.

The animated musical film *The Phantom Tollbooth* was co-directed by Chuck Jones, well-known animator of popular characters from Bugs Bunny to the Grinch.

THE PHANTOM TOLLBOOTH ©1969 Turner Entertainment Co. A Time Warner Company. All rights reserved.

OperaDelaware ventured into new territory with *The Phantom Tollbooth* adapted and performed as an opera, a drama set to music.

What are the advantages and disadvantages of using animation, compared with live actors, to tell the story **?**

Reading and Analyzing

A **PREDICT** Possible Responses: alphabet soup; foods served in alphabetical order, ranging from asparagus to zucchini; juggling letters; singing the A B C's

**Reading Skills and Strategies:
WORD PLAY**

B Call on volunteers to explain the word play with *light*.
Possible Response: Milo means something not too filling, or heavy; Azaz literally serves light.

C Ask students to explain the play on the word *square*.
Possible Response: Milo means a well-balanced, nutritionally sound meal; Azaz serves squares.

**Reading Skills and Strategies:
AUTHOR'S PURPOSE**

Ask students to identify the author's purpose for including the banquet scene.
Possible Response: The author includes it to entertain the reader but also to show how words can be played with, manipulated, and interpreted in different ways.

Minister 5. Obviously, you don't know who we are. *(Each presents himself and Milo acknowledges the introduction.)*

Minister 1. The Duke of Definition.

Minister 2. The Minister of Meaning.

Minister 3. The Earl of Essence.

Minister 4. The Count of Connotation.

Minister 5. The Undersecretary of Understanding.

A **PREDICT** What sorts of food and entertainment might be offered at the banquet?

All Five. And we have come to invite you to the Royal Banquet.

Spelling Bee. The banquet! That's quite an honor, my boy. A real h-o-n-o-r.

Humbug. Don't be ridiculous! Everybody goes to the Royal Banquet these days.

Spelling Bee. *(To the Humbug.)* True, everybody does go. But some people are invited and others simply push their way in where they aren't wanted.

Humbug. How dare you? You buzzing little upstart, I'll show you who's not wanted . . . *(Raises his cane threateningly.)*

Spelling Bee. You just watch it! I'm warning w-a-r-n-i-n-g you! *(At that moment, an earshattering blast of trumpets, entirely off-key, is heard, and a Page appears.)*

Page. King Azaz the Unabridged is about to begin the Royal Banquet. All guests who do not appear promptly at the table will automatically lose their place. *(A huge table is carried out with King Azaz sitting in a large chair, carried out at the head of the table.)*

Azaz. Places. Everyone take your places. *(All the characters, including the Humbug and the Spelling Bee, who forget their quarrel, rush to take their places at the table. Milo and Tock sit near the King. Azaz looks at Milo.)* And just who is this?

Milo. Your Highness, my name is Milo and this is Tock. Thank you very much for inviting us to your banquet, and I think your palace is beautiful!

Minister 1. Exquisite.

Minister 2. Lovely.

Minister 3. Handsome.

Minister 4. Pretty.

Minister 5. Charming.

Azaz. Silence! Now tell me, young man, what can you do to entertain us? Sing songs? Tell stories? Juggle plates? Do tumbling tricks? Which is it?

Milo. I can't do any of those things.

Azaz. What an ordinary little boy. Can't you do anything at all?

Milo. Well . . . I can count to a thousand.

Azaz. AARGH, numbers! Never mention numbers here. Only use them when we absolutely have to. Now, why don't we change the subject and have some dinner? Since you are the guest of honor, you may pick the menu.

Milo. Me? Well, uh . . . I'm not very hungry. Can we just have a light snack?

Azaz. A light snack it shall be!

(Azaz claps his hands. Waiters rush in with covered trays. When they are uncovered, shafts of light pour out. The light may be created through the use of battery-operated flashlights which are secured in the trays and covered with a false bottom. The guests help themselves.)

WORDS
TO
KNOW

acknowledge (ăk-nŏl'ĭj) *v.* to admit or to value the existence of

Humbug. Not a very substantial meal. Maybe you can suggest something a little more filling.

Milo. Well, in that case, I think we ought to have a square meal . . .

Azaz. (Claps his hands.) A square meal it is! (Waiters serve trays of colored squares of all sizes. People serve themselves.)

Spelling Bee. These are awful. (Humbug coughs and all the guests do not care for the food.)

Azaz. (Claps his hands and the trays are (removed.) Time for speeches. (To Milo.) You first.

Milo. (Hesitantly.) Your Majesty, ladies and gentlemen, I would like to take this opportunity to say that . . .

Azaz. That's quite enough. Musn't talk all day.

Milo. But I just started to . . .

Azaz. Next!

Humbug. (Quickly.) Roast turkey, mashed potatoes, vanilla ice cream.

Spelling Bee. Hamburgers, corn on the cob, chocolate pudding p-u-d-d-i-n-g. (Each guest names two dishes and a dessert.)

Azaz. (The last.) Pâté de fois gras, soupe a l'oignon, salade endives, fromage et fruits et demitasse.[11] (He claps his hands. Waiters serve each guest his words.) Dig on. (To Milo.) Though I can't say I think much of your choice.

Milo. I didn't know I was going to have to eat my words. **[1]**

Azaz. Of course, of course, everybody here does. Your speech should have been in better taste.

Minister 1. Here, try some somersault. It improves the flavor.

Minister 2. Have a rigamarole. (Offers breadbasket.) **[2]**

Minister 3. Or a ragamuffin.

Minister 4. Perhaps you'd care for a synonym bun.

Minister 5. Why not wait for your just desserts?

Azaz. Ah yes, the dessert. We're having a special treat today . . . freshly made at the half-bakery.

Milo. The half-bakery?

Azaz. Of course, the half-bakery! Where do you think half-baked ideas come from? Now, please don't interrupt. By royal command, the pastry chefs have . . . **[3]**

Milo. What's a half-baked idea?

(Azaz gives up the idea of speaking as a cart is wheeled in and the guests help themselves.)

Humbug. They're very tasty, but they don't always agree with you. Here's a good one. (Humbug hands one to Milo.)

Milo. (Reads.) "The earth is flat."

Spelling Bee. People swallowed that one for years. (Picks up one and reads.) "The moon is made of green cheese." Now, there's a half-baked idea.

---

11. pâté de foie gras . . . demi-tasse French: pâté de foie gras (pâ-tä′ də fwä grä): a paste made from goose liver; soupe a l'oignon (sōōp ä lô′nyôn): onion soup; salade endives (sä′läd än′dĕv): lettuce salad; fromage et fruits (frô′mäzh ā frwē): cheese and fruit; demitasse (dĕmē′täs): a small cup of strong, black coffee.

Differentiating Instruction

Less Proficient Readers
Ask students the following questions to check comprehension:
• What is the first meal Milo orders? How is it served?
  Possible Response: He orders a light snack. It turns out to be trays with rays of light coming from them.
• What is Milo's second request? How is it served?
  Possible Response: His second request is for a square meal, which consists of trays filled with colored squares.
• What happens after the guests make speeches?
  Possible Response: They eat their words.

Set a Purpose Have students read to find out what journey Milo and his friends are going to make and what obstacles they can anticipate.

English Learners
To help students appreciate the humor in the banquet scene, be sure they understand the figurative interpretations of the idioms.

[1] Explain to students that "eating your words" is having to take back what you've said.

[2] Help students to appreciate the humor created by using words unrelated to food but having the name of a food item in them or suggesting a food by their sound. somersault – salt; rigamarole – roll; ragamuffin – muffin; synonym bun – cinnamon bun

[3] Explain that a "half-baked idea" is an idea that is not very sensible or well thought out.

Advanced Students
The Ministers of Dictionopolis are speaking in synonyms. Have students sit in a circle. Give them a word and then have each student try to come up with a synonym like the Ministers do in the play.

Multicultural Link Idioms Borrowed From Other Languages

Although many idioms seem as "American as apple pie," their origins may reach back as far as the ancient civilizations. Some of the best known expressions have been translated from other languages to take the form in which we know them.

"Without rhyme or reason" was borrowed from the French of the late Middle Ages, who said "na Ryme ne Raison." The modern French phrase is "ni rime ni raison." English speakers have been using the phrase "without rhyme or reason" since the sixteenth century.

The English language has included the phrase "a castle in the air" since the late 1500s. The French, however, have used "a castle in Spain," to mean roughly the same thing since the 1300s, "un château en Espagne."

Over four hundred years ago, the Dutch gave English speakers the idiom "in a pretty pickle." Their saying was "in de pekel zitten," which meant to literally sit in the salty liquid used to pickle. Anyone sitting in that liquid for too long would be in trouble!

Reading and Analyzing

Reading Skills and Strategies:
CLARIFY

(A) Ask students why there is confusion in King Azaz's kingdom.

Possible Response: There is no Rhyme or Reason.

Literary Analysis:
CHARACTER TRAITS

(B) Students should be able to analyze characters, including their traits, by using the characters' words and actions. Ask students what is revealed about Humbug's character through his comments.

Possible Response: Humbug is easily influenced and wants to be on whichever side appears to be in favor.

Literary Analysis FANTASY

(C) Ask students to identify fantastic details in this account.

Possible Responses: entering the Mountains of Ignorance; climbing a two-thousand-foot staircase without railings; fighting off frightening fiends

Literary Analysis: QUEST

Tell students that a quest is a journey of discovery, often motivated by a noble purpose. Ask students what is noble about Milo's quest.

Possible Response: His goal is to rescue the princesses.

What might Milo discover along the way?

Possible Responses: He might discover his own inner qualities. He might learn more about ignorance and obstacles on the path to success

---

(Everyone chooses one and eats. They include: "It Never Rains but Pours," "Night Air Is Bad Air," "Everything Happens for the Best," "Coffee Stunts Your Growth.")

Azaz. And now for a few closing words. Attention! Let me have your attention! *(Everyone leaps up and exits, except for Milo, Tock and the Humbug.)* Loyal subjects and friends, once again on this gala occasion, we have . . .

Milo. Excuse me, but everybody left.

Azaz. *(Sadly.)* I was hoping no one would notice. It happens every time.

Humbug. They've gone to dinner, and as soon as I finish this last bite, I shall join them.

Milo. That's ridiculous. How can they eat dinner right after a banquet?

Azaz. Scandalous! We'll put a stop to it at once. From now on, by royal command, everyone must eat dinner before the banquet.

Milo. But that's just as bad.

Humbug. Or just as good. Things which are equally bad are also equally good. Try to look at the bright side of things.

(A) **Milo.** I don't know which side of anything to look at. Everything is so confusing, and all your words only make things worse.

Azaz. How true. There must be something we can do about it.

Humbug. Pass a law.

Azaz. We have almost as many laws as words.

Humbug. Offer a reward. *(Azaz shakes his head and looks madder at each suggestion.)* Send for help? Drive a bargain? Pull the switch? Lower the boom? Toe the line? *(As Azaz continues to scowl, the Humbug loses confidence and finally gives up.)*

Milo. Maybe you should let Rhyme and Reason return.

Azaz. How nice that would be. Even if they were a bother at times, things always went so well when they were here. But I'm afraid it can't be done.

Humbug. Certainly not. Can't be done.

Milo. Why not?

Humbug. *(Now siding with Milo.)* Why not, indeed?

Azaz. Much too difficult.

Humbug. Of course, much too difficult.

Milo. You could, if you really wanted to.

Humbug. By all means, if you really wanted to, you could.

Azaz. *(To Humbug.)* How?

Milo. *(Also to Humbug.)* Yeah, how?

Humbug. Why . . . uh, it's a simple task for a brave boy with a stout heart, a steadfast dog and a serviceable small automobile.

Azaz. Go on.

Humbug. Well, all that he would have to do is cross the dangerous, unknown countryside between here and Digitopolis, where he would have to persuade the Mathemagician to release the princesses, which we know to be impossible because the Mathemagician will never agree with Azaz about anything. Once achieving that, it's a simple matter of entering the Mountains of <u>Ignorance</u> from where no one has ever returned alive, an effortless climb up a two-thousand-foot stairway without railings in a high wind at night to the Castle-in-the-Air. After a pleasant chat with the princesses, all that remains is a <u>leisurely</u> ride back through those chaotic crags where the frightening fiends

---

WORDS TO KNOW	
	ignorance (ĭg′nər-əns) *n.* the state of being uneducated or unaware
	leisurely (lē′zhər-lē) *adj.* unhurried

530

have sworn to tear any intruder from limb to limb and devour him down to his belt buckle. And finally after doing all that, a triumphal parade! If, of course, there is anything left to parade . . . followed by hot chocolate and cookies for everyone.

Azaz. I never realized it would be so simple.

Milo. It sounds dangerous to me.

Tock. And just who is supposed to make that journey?

Azaz. A very good question. But there is one far more serious problem.

Milo. What's that?

Azaz. I'm afraid I can't tell you that until you return.

Milo. But wait a minute, I didn't . . .

Azaz. Dictionopolis will always be grateful to you, my boy and your dog. *(Azaz pats Tock and Milo.)*

Tock. Now, just one moment, sire . . .

Azaz. You will face many dangers on your journey, but fear not, for I can give you something for your protection. *(Azaz gives Milo a box.)* In this box are the letters of the alphabet. With them you can form all the words you will ever need to help you overcome the obstacles that may stand in your path. All you must do is use them well and in the right places.

Milo. *(Miserably.)* Thanks a lot.

Azaz. You will need a guide, of course, and since he knows the obstacles so well, the Humbug has cheerfully volunteered to accompany you.

Humbug. Now, see here . . . !

Azaz. You will find him dependable, brave, resourceful and loyal.

Humbug. *(Flattered.)* Oh, Your Majesty.

Milo. I'm sure he'll be a great help. *(They approach the car.)*

Tock. I hope so. It looks like we're going to need it.

(The lights darken and the King fades from view.)

Azaz. Good luck! Drive carefully! *(The three get into the car and begin to move. Suddenly a thunderously loud noise is heard. They slow down the car.)*

Milo. What was that?

Tock. It came from up ahead.

Humbug. It's something terrible. I just know it. Oh, no. Something dreadful is going to happen to us. I can feel it in my bones. *(The noise is repeated. They all look at each other fearfully as the lights fade.)*

END of ACT ONE

THINKING through the LITERATURE

1. **Comprehension Check**
   • How does Milo escape the Doldrums?
   • What caused Azaz and the Mathemagician to quarrel?

2. How does Milo change during Act One?
   Think About:
   • his reason for going on this journey
   • his experiences in the Doldrums
   • how he "volunteers" for the rescue

3. On page 526, the Ministers list synonyms for *country, certainly,* and *nonsense.* Using a thesaurus, how many other synonyms can you find for these words?

4. *The Phantom Tollbooth* is also a novel and an animated film. How do you think watching theater—a live performance of a literary work—is different from reading a book or watching a movie?

Less Proficient Readers
Ask students the following questions:
• Where is Milo going next?
   Possible Response: first to Digitopolis, then to the Castle-in-the-Air
• What does Humbug warn Milo to expect on his journey?
   Possible Response: Milo will have to enter the Mountains of Ignorance, climb a two-thousand-foot stairway without railings in a high wind, and fight off dangerous fiends.
Set a Purpose Have students read to find out what produces the loud noise.

Thinking through the Literature

1. **Comprehension Check**
   • He is able to move his car by thinking.
   • Azaz thinks words are more important than numbers, and the Mathemagician thinks numbers are more important.

2. **Possible Response:** At the beginning, Milo doesn't know what to do with himself, and he goes through the tollbooth because he doesn't have anything better to do. In the Doldrums, Milo realizes that he will be stuck in one place forever unless he starts thinking. At the end, Milo challenges Azaz to let Rhyme and Reason return. At first Milo is reluctant to take on the task of rescuing the princesses, but then he accepts it, which shows how he has started to change from someone with no purpose or goals to someone who has them.

3. **Possible Responses:** government, fatherland, kingdom, state; unquestionably, without fail, undeniably, surely; absurdity, folly, Baloney, silliness, fantasy

4. **Answers will vary.** Students may say that watching a live performance makes them feel as if they are part of the action.

EXPLICIT INSTRUCTION Plot

Instruction Review elements of plot with the class. Have volunteers explain what happens during the exposition, rising action, climax, and falling action/resolution stages of plot. *(The setting, characters, and initial conflict are revealed in the exposition; plot complications occur in the rising action; the climax is the point of greatest tension; the resolution ties up loose ends.)* Ask students to identify the conflicts in Act One. *(conflict between Milo's intelligence and his boredom; conflict between words and numbers, between Azaz and Mathemagician, between Azaz/Mathemagician and Rhyme and Reason, between the Spelling Bee and Humbug, between Milo and the forces of ignorance)*

Practice Ask students to list the important events in Act One that move the plot along.
Possible Response: Milo goes through tollbooth; he meets the Whether Man and sets off for Dictionopolis; he gets stuck in the Doldrums; he meets Tock and thinks his way out of the Doldrums; in Dictionopolis, Milo and Tock meet the Spelling Bee, Humbug, and King Azaz; Milo learns that Azaz and his brother, the Mathemagician, banished their sisters, Rhyme and Reason, to the Castle-in-the-Air; Milo decides to rescue the sisters.

Use **Unit Four Resource Book,** p. 42, for more practice.

Reading Skills and Strategies:
MONITOR

Have students pause to monitor their own comprehension by reviewing the major events of Act One, rereading portions of the text if necessary. Discuss ways in which they might adjust their reading strategy in Act Two.

Literary Analysis: ACT

A Tell students that longer plays are divided into acts. An act is a major unit of action. Ask students what they anticipate happening during the second act.
Possible Responses: They might mention Milo visiting Digitopolis and meeting the Mathemagician or Milo's attempt to rescue the princesses.

Literary Analysis: HUMOR

B Ask students why Humbug's remark is humorous.
Possible Response: He literally will be standing behind Milo for protection.

Literary Analysis:
CHARACTER TRAITS

C Ask students to analyze the difference in the character traits of Milo as compared to Humbug.
Possible Response: Milo shows more courage and leadership than Humbug.

ACTIVE READER

D **VISUALIZE** Possible Responses: The dishes would crash noisily; the ant would be silent; and the octopus would snap and crinkle.

EXPLICIT INSTRUCTION Viewing and Representing

Illustration of Dr. Dischord
by Bruce Roberts
Instruction Point out the exuberance illustrator Bruce Roberts captures in this drawing of Dr. Dischord. Everything seems to be noisy and chaotic—just the way the scene is described. Objects fly everywhere, there seem to be explosions. Even the colors are loud and clashing! Ask students what noises Dr. Dischord might be mixing with his mortar and pestle. (*car horns,*

explosions, popcorn, fireworks, screeching brakes, crashing cymbals)
Practice Have students refer back to the illustration as they read the description of Dr. Dischord and his activities. Ask which of Dr. Dischord's noises they find particularly appealing—or particularly unappealing. What other noises would they add to his collection?
Possible Responses: Responses will vary.

Ⓐ ACT TWO

SCENE 1

The set of Digitopolis glitters in the background, while upstage right near the road, a small colorful wagon sits, looking quite deserted. On its side in large letters, a sign reads:

"KAKAFONOUS A. DISCHORD

Doctor of Dissonance"[12]

Enter Milo, Tock, and Humbug, fearfully. They look at the wagon.

Tock. There's no doubt about it. That's where the noise was coming from.

Humbug. *(To Milo.)* Well, go on.

Milo. Go on what?

Humbug. Go on and see who's making all that noise in there. We can't just ignore a creature like that.

Milo. Creature? What kind of creature? Do you think he's dangerous?

Ⓑ Humbug. Go on, Milo. Knock on the door. We'll be right behind you.

Milo. O.K. Maybe he can tell us how much further it is to Digitopolis.

Ⓒ *(Milo tiptoes up to the wagon door and knocks timidly. The moment he knocks, a terrible crash is heard inside the wagon, and Milo and the others jump back in fright. At the same time,* the door flies open and from the dark interior, a hoarse Voice inquires.)

Voice. Have you ever heard a whole set of dishes dropped from the ceiling onto a hard stone floor? *(The others are speechless with fright. Milo shakes his head. Voice happily.)* Have you ever heard an ant wearing fur slippers walk across a thick wool carpet? *(Milo shakes his head again.)* Have you ever heard a blindfolded octopus unwrap a cellophane-covered bathtub? *(Milo shakes his head a third time.)* Ha! I knew it. *(He hops out, a little man, wearing a white coat, with a stethoscope around his neck, and a small mirror attached to his forehead, and with very huge ears,*

Ⓓ

ACTIVE READER

VISUALIZE What would these events sound, feel, and look like?

---

12. **Kakafonous A. Dischord, Doctor of Dissonance:** the doctor's first name is a playful spelling of *cacophonous* (kə-kŏf′ə-nəs), which means having a loud, harsh, sound. *Dischord* (dĭs′ kôrd′) is an intentional misspelling of *discord*, which, along with *dissonance* (dĭs′ə-nəns), means clashing sounds.

---

and a mortar and pestle[13] in his hands. He stares at Milo, Tock and Humbug.) None of you looks well at all! Tsk, tsk, not at all. *(He opens the top or side of his wagon, revealing a dusty interior resembling an old apothecary shop, with shelves lined with jars and boxes, a table, books, test tubes and bottles and measuring spoons.)*

Milo. *(Timidly.)* Are you a doctor?

(A) **Dischord.** *(Voice.)* I am Kakafonous A. Dischord, Doctor of Dissonance! *(Several small explosions and a grinding crash are heard.)*

Humbug. *(Stuttering with fear.)* What does the "A" stand for?

Dischord. AS LOUD AS POSSIBLE! *(Two screeches and a bump are heard.)* Now, step a little closer and stick out your tongues. *(Dischord examines them.)* Just as I expected. *(He opens a large dusty book and thumbs through the pages.)* You're all suffering from a severe lack of noise. *(Dischord begins running around, collecting bottles, reading the labels to himself as he goes along.)* "Loud Cries." "Soft Cries." "Bangs, Bongs, Swishes, Swooshes." "Snaps and Crackles." "Whistles and Gongs." "Squeeks, Squacks, and Miscellaneous Uproar." *(As he reads them off, he pours a little of each into a large glass beaker and stirs the mixture with a wooden spoon. The concoction smokes and bubbles.)* Be ready in just a moment.

Milo. *(Suspiciously.)* Just what kind of doctor are you?

Dischord. Well, you might say, I'm a specialist. I specialize in noises, from the loudest to the softest, and from the slightly annoying to the terribly unpleasant. For instance, have you ever heard a square-wheeled steamroller ride over a street full of hard-boiled eggs? *(Very loud crunching sounds are heard.)*

Milo. *(Holding his ears.)* But who would want all those terrible noises?

Dischord. *(Surprised at the question.)* Everybody does. Why, I'm so busy I can hardly fill all the orders for noise pills, racket lotion, clamor salve and hubbub tonic.[14] That's all people seem to want these days. Years ago, everyone wanted pleasant sounds and business was terrible. But then the cities were built and there was a great need for honking horns, screeching trains, clanging bells and all the rest of those wonderfully unpleasant sounds we use so much today. I've been working overtime ever since and my medicine here is in great demand. All you have to do is take one spoonful every day, and you'll never have to hear another beautiful sound again. Here, try some.

Humbug. *(Backing away.)* If it's all the same to you, I'd rather not.

Milo. I don't want to be cured of beautiful sounds.

Tock. Besides, there's no such sickness as a lack of noise.

Dischord. How true. That's what makes it so difficult to cure. *(Takes a large glass bottle from the shelf.)* Very well, if you want to go all through life suffering from a noise deficiency, I'll just give this to Dynne for his lunch. *(Uncorks the bottle and pours the liquid into it. There is a rumbling and then a loud explosion accompanied by smoke, out of*

---

13. **mortar** (môr′tər) **and pestle** (pĕs′əl): a mortar is a container in which substances are ground with a hand-held tool (a pestle).

14. **clamor** (klăm′ər) **salve** (săv) **and hubbub** (hŭb′ŭb) **tonic:** a clamor is a loud outcry, and hubbub is noisy confusion. Salve is a healing cream, and tonic can also be a kind of medicine.

which *Dynne*,[15] *a smog-like creature with yellow eyes and a frowning mouth, appears.*)

Dynne. *(Smacking his lips.)* Ahhh, that was good, Master. I thought you'd never let me out. It was really cramped in there.

Dischord. This is my assistant, the awful Dynne. You must forgive his appearance, for he really doesn't have any.

Milo. What is a Dynne?

Dischord. You mean you've never heard of the awful Dynne? When you're playing in your room and making a great amount of noise, what do they tell you to stop?

Milo. That awful din.

Dischord. When the neighbors are playing their radio too loud late at night, what do you wish they'd turn down?

Tock. That awful din.

Dischord. And when the street on your block is being repaired and the drills are working all day, what does everyone complain of?

Humbug. *(Brightly.)* The dreadful row.[16]

Dynne. The Dreadful Rauw was my grandfather. He perished in the great silence epidemic of 1712. I certainly can't understand why you don't like noise. Why, I heard an explosion last week that was so lovely, I groaned with appreciation for two days. *(He gives a loud groan at the memory.)*

Dischord. He's right, you know. Noise is the most valuable thing in the world.

Milo. King Azaz says words are.

Dischord. Nonsense! Why, when a baby wants food, how does he ask?

Dynne. *(Happily.)* He screams!

Dischord. And when a racing car wants gas?

Dynne. *(Jumping for joy.)* It chokes!

Dischord. And what happens to the dawn when a new day begins?

Dynne. *(Delighted.)* It breaks!

Dischord. You see how simple it is? *(To Dynne.)* Isn't it time for us to go?

Milo. Where to? Maybe we're going the same way.

Dynne. I doubt it. *(Picking up empty sacks from the table.)* We're going on our collection rounds. Once a day, I travel throughout the kingdom and collect all the wonderfully horrible and beautifully unpleasant sounds I can find and bring them back to the doctor to use in his medicine.

Dischord. Where are you going?

Milo. To Digitopolis.

Dischord. Oh, there are a number of ways to get to Digitopolis, if you know how to follow directions. Just take a look at the sign at the fork in the road. Though why you'd ever want to go there, I'll never know.

Milo. We want to talk to the Mathemagician.

Humbug. About the release of the Princesses Rhyme and Reason.

Dischord. Rhyme and Reason? I remember them. Very nice girls, but a little too quiet for my taste. In fact, I've been meaning to send them something that Dynne brought home by mistake and which I have absolutely no use for. *(He rummages through the wagon.)* Ah, here it is . . . or maybe you'd like it for yourself. *(Hands Milo a package.)*

Milo. What is it?

---

15. **Dynne** (dĭn): this name is a play on the word *din*, a jumble of loud, confusing noises.

16. **row** (rou): a noisy disturbance.

WORDS TO KNOW   **perish** (pĕr´ĭsh) *v.* to die, perhaps in an untimely or painful way

535

Differentiating Instruction

Less Proficient Readers
Ask students the following questions to check comprehension:
- What is Dr. Dischord's occupation?
  Possible Response: He is a specialist in unpleasant and annoying noises.
- What does Dynne look like?
  Possible Response: He is a smog-like creature with yellow eyes and a frowning mouth.
- What are Dynne and Dr. Dischord setting off to do?
  Possible Response: They are going to collect horrible sounds.

Set a Purpose Have students read to find out what Dr. Dischord gives Milo and who the Dodecahedron is.

English Learners
1 Be sure students know that the labels describe the kinds of noises found in the bottles.

Advanced Students
Dr. Discord mentions that "Years ago, everyone wanted pleasant sounds" but today people want the loud sounds of cities and other modern things. Ask students, "Why does it seem to Dr. Discord that people do not want pleasant sounds anymore?"

Possible Responses: People moved from farms and quiet country life to noisy cities. Or, people created modern technologies that made more noise in the world than before.

Reading Skills and Strategies: CONNECT

A Ask students how Humbug's comment affects their view of him. Have students talk about times when they have been hungry at an inopportune time.
Possible Response: Humbug seems more human.

Literary Analysis: CHARACTER

B Ask students why they think the author included the character of Dodecahedron.
Possible Response: He is an introduction to the world of mathematics; he illustrates an otherwise difficult idea to visualize.

ACTIVE READER

C VISUALIZE **Possible Responses:** confusing; unsettling; unusual

---

Dischord. The sounds of laughter. They're so unpleasant to hear, it's almost unbearable. All those giggles and snickers and happy shouts of joy, I don't know what Dynne was thinking of when he collected them. Here, take them to the princesses or keep them for yourselves, I don't care. Well, time to move on. Goodbye now and good luck! *(He has shut the wagon by now and gets in. Loud noises begin to erupt as Dynne pulls the wagon offstage.)*

1 Milo. *(Calling after them.)* But wait! The fork in the road . . . you didn't tell us where it is . . .

Tock. It's too late. He can't hear a thing.

A Humbug. I could use a fork of my own, at the moment. And a knife and a spoon to go with it. All of a sudden, I feel very hungry.

Milo. So do I, but it's no use thinking about it. There won't be anything to eat until we reach Digitopolis. *(They get into the car.)*

Humbug. *(Rubbing his stomach.)* Well, the sooner the better is what I say.

(A sign suddenly appears.)

Voice. *(A strange voice from nowhere.)* But which way will get you there sooner? That is the question.

Tock. Did you hear something?

Milo. Look! The fork in the road and a signpost to Digitopolis! *(They read the sign.)*

DIGITOPOLIS

5	Miles
1,600	Rods
8,800	Yards
26,400	Feet
316,800	Inches
633,600	Half Inches

AND THEN SOME

Humbug. Let's travel by miles, it's shorter.

Milo. Let's travel by half inches. It's quicker.

Tock. But which road should we take? It must make a difference.

Milo. Do you think so?

Tock. Well, I'm not sure, but . . .

Humbug. He could be right. On the other hand, he could also be wrong. Does it make a difference or not?

Voice. Yes, indeed, indeed it does, certainly, my yes, it does make a difference.

(The Dodecahedron appears, a 12-sided figure with a different face on each side, and with all the edges labeled with a small letter and all the angles labeled with a large letter. He wears a beret and peers at the others with a serious face. He doffs his cap and recites:)

Dodecahedron. My angles are many.
My sides are not few.
I'm the Dodecahedron.
Who are you?

Milo. What's a Dodecahedron?

Dodecahedron. *(Turning around slowly.)* See for yourself. A Dodecahedron is a mathematical shape with 12 faces. *(All his faces appear as he turns, each face with a different expression. He points to them.)* I usually use one at a time. It saves wear and tear. What are you called?

ACTIVE READER

VISUALIZE What would it be like to talk to a creature with 12 faces?

C

Milo. Milo.

Dodecahedron. That's an odd name. *(Changing his smiling face to a frowning one.)* And you have only one face.

Milo. *(Making sure it is still there.)* Is that bad?

Dodecahedron. You'll soon wear it out using it for everything. Is everyone with one face called Milo?

VIEW AND COMPARE

Which image of Tock the watchdog do you like best? Why?

Tock in OperaDelaware's production sings his lines. ▼

Children from The Cambridgeport School created this Tock costume. ▶

The original Tock, illustrated by Jules Feiffer for his friend Norton Juster's novel. ▼

Tock, from the Chuck Jones animated film, keeps his clock under his fur. ▶

THE PHANTOM TOLLBOOTH
©1969 Turner Entertainment Co.
A Time Warner Company. All rights reserved.

Describe the costume you would design for Tock. What features would be most important ?

Differentiating Instruction

Less Proficient Students
Ask students the following questions to check comprehension:
- What does Dr. Dischord give Milo to take to the princesses?
  Possible Response: He gives him the sounds of laughter.
- How does he describe the sounds?
  Possible Response: He finds them unpleasant to hear.
- Who is Dodecahedron?
  Possible Response: He is a twelve-sided figure who appears as the three travelers are deciding which road to take to Digitopolis.

Set a Purpose Have students read to find out how numbers are obtained.

English Learners
1 Many words in English have more than one meaning. *Fork* is a good example. In this section it refers to a place where the road splits, as well as to a utensil used for eating. See if students can figure out how the two meanings are related.
Possible Response: The road has the shape of a fork. It is going in one direction and then breaks off into different directions at one intersection like the tines of a fork.

Advanced Students
Have students consider the sign mentioned on page 536 of the pupil's edition. Why are Humbug's comment, "Let's travel by miles, it's shorter," and Milo's comment, "Let's travel by half inches. It's quicker," illogical?
Possible Response: All of the measurements are the same, they are just in different forms. 316,800 inches is the same as 5 miles. No matter what road is taken, everyone would have the same distance to travel to Digitopolis.

VIEW AND COMPARE
Have students work in pairs to discuss their answers to the questions on page 537. Students should work independently to write their answers. Remind them to support their ideas.
Possible Responses: (question at top of page) Students' preferences will vary, but they should explain what they like about their first choice. (question at bottom of page) Students' descriptions of the costumes they would design should be consistent with the description of this character presented in the text.

Reading and Analyzing

Reading Skills and Strategies:
CLARIFY

(A) Ask students to eliminate all the details that do not relate to the problem.
Possible Responses: size of car; time of day; time of year; occupants of car
Ask students what becomes clear when the extra details have been omitted.
Possible Response: All cars will arrive at the same time.

Literary Analysis: IDIOM

(B) Ask students to think of other expressions that incorporate numbers.
Possible Responses: "six of one, half a dozen of the other," "high noon," "four corners," "two to tango," "three bears," "half and half," "fifty-fifty."

Active Reading VISUALIZING

(C) Ask students to pick out details that enable them to imagine the sounds in the mine.
Possible Responses: "digging and chopping"; "shoveling and scraping"; "His voice echoes and reverberates."

Literary Analysis: STAGE DIRECTIONS

(D) Ask students how the actor playing Humbug might show the feeling of being intimidated.
Possible Response: He would back away, speak softly, and smile uncertainly.

ACTIVE READER

(E) **EVALUATE: Possible Response** The author is saying that numbers are very precious.

Milo. Oh, no. Some are called Billy or Jeffery or Sally or Lisa or lots of other things.

Dodecahedron. How confusing. Here everything is called exactly what it is. The triangles are called triangles, the circles are called circles, and even the same numbers have the same name. Can you imagine what would happen if we named all the twos Billy or Jeffery or Sally or Lisa or lots of other things? You'd have to say Robert plus John equals four, and if the fours were named Albert, things would be hopeless.

Milo. I never thought of it that way.

Dodecahedron. *(With an admonishing face.)* Then I suggest you begin at once, for in Digitopolis, everything is quite precise.

Milo. Then perhaps you can help us decide which road we should take.

Dodecahedron. *(Happily.)* By all means. There's nothing to it. *(As he talks, the three others try to solve the problem on a large blackboard that is wheeled onstage for the occasion.)* Now, if a small car carrying three people at 30 miles an hour for 10 minutes along a road 5 miles long at 11:35 in the morning starts at the same time as 3 people who have been traveling in a little automobile at 20 miles an hour for 15 minutes on another road exactly twice as long as half the distance of the other, while a dog, a bug, and a boy travel an equal distance in the same time or the same distance in an equal time along a third road in mid-October, then which one arrives first and which is the best way to go?

Humbug. Seventeen!

Milo. *(Still figuring frantically.)* I'm not sure, but . . .

Dodecahedron. You'll have to do better than that.

Milo. I'm not very good at problems.

Dodecahedron. What a shame. They're so very useful. Why, did you know that if a beaver 2 feet long with a tail a foot and a half long can build a dam 12 feet high and 6 feet wide in 2 days, all you would need to build Boulder Dam is a beaver 68 feet long with a 51-foot tail?

Humbug. *(Grumbling as his pencil snaps.)* Where would you find a beaver that big?

Dodecahedron. I don't know, but if you did, you'd certainly know what to do with him.

Milo. That's crazy.

Dodecahedron. That may be true, but it's completely accurate, and as long as the answer is right, who cares if the question is wrong?

Tock. *(Who has been patiently doing the first problem.)* All three roads arrive at the same place at the same time.

Dodecahedron. Correct! And I'll take you there myself. *(The blackboard rolls off, and all four get into the car and drive off.)* Now you see how important problems are. If you hadn't done this one properly, you might have gone the wrong way.

Milo. But if all the roads arrive at the same place at the same time, then aren't they all the right road?

Dodecahedron. *(Glaring from his upset face.)* Certainly not! They're all the wrong way! Just because you have a choice, it doesn't mean that any of them has to be right. *(Pointing in another direction.)* That's the way to Digitopolis and we'll be there any moment. *(Suddenly the lighting grows*

WORDS TO KNOW

admonishing (ăd-mŏn′ĭsh-ĭng) *adj.* issuing a gentle warning   **admonish** *v.*

538

Multicultural Link   ## The Abacus

The abacus is most commonly thought of as the Chinese device consisting of a small wooden frame with beads on wires. However, a similar device was developed in the West. The ancient Greeks and Romans most commonly did their calculations by moving counters, known to the Romans as "calculi," on a sanded table, wooden board, or a stone or marble tablet. The calculi were usually under an inch in diameter and were made of bone, ivory, or glass.

The abacus, or counting table, had symbols representing the significant numerical values in the counting system. Counters would be placed next to the symbols. Subtraction, addition, multiplication, or other calculations could be done quite easily by adding to or subtracting from the original counters. For example, 1,252 would have one counter next to the 1,000 mark, two on the 100 line, one on the 50 line, and two on the 1 line. To subtract 1100 would mean removing the counter next to the 1000 and 1 of the counters from the 100 line. The remaining total could be easily figured out from the counters left on the table.

dimmer.) In fact, we're here. Welcome to the Land of Numbers.

Humbug. *(Looking around at the barren landscape.)* It doesn't look very inviting.

Milo. Is this the place where numbers are made?

Dodecahedron. They're not made. You have to dig for them. Don't you know anything at all about numbers?

Milo. Well, I never really thought they were very important.

Dodecahedron. Not important! Could you have tea for two without the 2? Or three blind mice without the 3? And how would you sail the seven seas without the 7?

Milo. All I meant was . . .

Dodecahedron. *(Continues shouting angrily.)* If you had high hopes, how would you know how high they were? And did you know that narrow escapes come in different widths? Would you travel the whole wide world without ever knowing how wide it was? And how could you do anything at long last without knowing how long the last was? Why, numbers are the most beautiful and valuable things in the world. Just follow me and I'll show you. *(He motions to them and pantomimes walking through rocky terrain with the others in tow. A doorway similar to the tollbooth appears and the Dodecahedron opens it and motions the others to follow him through.)* Come along, come along. I can't wait for you all day. *(They enter the doorway and the lights are dimmed very low, as to simulate the interior of a cave. The sounds of scrapings and tapping, scuffling and digging are heard all around them. He hands them helmets with flashlights attached.)* Put these on.

Milo. *(Whispering.)* Where are we going?

Dodecahedron. We're here. This is the numbers mine. *(Lights up a little, revealing little men digging and chopping, shoveling and scraping.)* Right this way and watch your step. *(His voice echoes and reverberates. Iridescent and glittery numbers seem to sparkle from everywhere.)*

Milo. *(Awed.)* Whose mine is it?

Voice of Mathemagician. By the four million eight hundred and twenty-seven thousand six hundred and fifty-nine hairs on my head, it's mine, of course! *(Enter the Mathemagician, carrying his long staff which looks like a giant pencil.)*

Humbug. *(Already intimidated.)* It's a lovely mine, really it is.

Mathemagician. *(Proudly.)* The biggest number mine in the kingdom.

Milo. *(Excitedly.)* Are there any precious stones in it?

Mathemagician. Precious stones! *(Then softly.)* By the eight million two hundred and forty-seven thousand three hundred and twelve threads in my robe, I'll say there are. Look here. *(Reaches in a cart, pulls out a small object, polishes it vigorously and holds it to the light, where it sparkles.)*

Milo. But that's a five.

Mathemagician. Exactly. As valuable a jewel as you'll find anywhere. Look at some of the others. *(Scoops up others and pours them into Milo's arms. They include all numbers from 1 to 9 and an assortment of zeroes.)*

> **ACTIVE READER**
>
> **EVALUATE** What is the author saying about numbers by comparing them to jewels?

WORDS
TO
KNOW

pantomime (păn′tə-mīm′) *v.* to express oneself using only gestures and facial expressions

vigorously (vĭg′ər-əs-lē) *adv.* done with force and energy

539

Differentiating Instruction

Less Proficient Readers
Ask students these questions to check comprehension:
- Where do the numbers come from? *(They come from the number mines.)*
- What does the Mathemagician say when Milo drops some numbers? *(He says that the broken ones will be used for fractions.)*

Set a Purpose Have students read to find out the effect of lunch on Milo and his friends and what Milo learns about the number of greatest magnitude.

English Learners
1 Explain to students that the Dodecahedron is illustrating the importance of numbers by mentioning titles and idiomatic expressions with references to quantities or measurements in them.

Advanced Students
Ask students to consider the word problems in this part of the play from a mathematical point of view. Which problems can be solved, and which are just silly? Have students discuss the following lines and see if they agree or disagree with what is said:
- "As long as the answer is right, who cares if the question is wrong?"
- "Just because you have a choice, it doesn't mean that any of them has to be right."

Reading and Analyzing

Literary Analysis: SCENERY

A Tell students that although not all plays use scenery to produce mood and create setting, in many plays, scenery is important. Point out how specific the instructions about scenery are in these stage directions. Ask students what ideas the scenery reinforces.

Possible Response: Mathematics enters into many aspects of life and is very important.

Reading Skills and Strategies: AUTHOR'S PURPOSE

B Ask students what the author accomplishes by emphasizing the power of math through the character of the Mathemagician.

Possible Response: The Mathemagician helps to persuade the reader that math is fun and nothing to be afraid of.

Reading Skills and Strategies: MAKE INFERENCES

C Ask students to draw an inference about Milo's math ability and support it with evidence from the text.

Possible Response: He has gained confidence in his mathematical ability; he has improved his math skills.

Dodecahedron. We dig them and polish them right here, and then send them all over the world. Marvelous, aren't they?

Tock. They are beautiful. *(He holds them up to compare them to the numbers on his clock body.)*

Milo. So that's where they come from. *(Looks at them and carefully hands them back, but drops a few which smash and break in half.)* Oh, I'm sorry!

Mathemagician. *(Scooping them up.)* Oh, don't worry about that. We use the broken ones for fractions. How about some lunch?

(Takes out a little whistle and blows it. Two miners rush in carrying an immense cauldron which is bubbling and steaming. The workers put down their tools and gather around to eat.)

Humbug. That looks delicious! *(Tock and Milo also look hungrily at the pot.)*

Mathemagician. Perhaps you'd care for something to eat?

Milo. Oh, yes, sir!

Tock. Thank you.

Humbug *(Already eating.)* Ummm . . . delicious! *(All finish their bowls immediately.)*

Mathemagician. Please have another portion. *(They eat and finish. Mathemagician serves them again.)* Don't stop now. *(They finish.)* Come on, no need to be bashful. *(Serves them again.)*

Milo. *(To Tock and Humbug as he finishes again.)* Do you want to hear something strange? Each one I eat makes me a little hungrier than before.

Mathemagician. Do have some more. *(He serves them again. They eat frantically, until the Mathemagician blows his whistle again and the pot is removed.)*

Humbug. *(Holding his stomach.)* Uggghhh! I think I'm starving.

Milo. Me, too, and I ate so much.

Dodecahedron. *(Wiping the gravy from several of his mouths.)* Yes, it was delicious, wasn't it? It's the specialty of the kingdom . . . subtraction stew.

Tock. *(Weak from hunger.)* I have more of an appetite than when I began.

Mathemagician. Certainly, what did you expect? The more you eat, the hungrier you get, everyone knows that.

Milo. They do? Then how do you get enough?

Mathemagician. Enough? Here in Digitopolis, we have our meals when we're full and eat until we're hungry. That way, when you don't have anything at all, you have more than enough. It's a very economical system. You must have been stuffed to have eaten so much.

Dodecahedron. It's completely logical. The more you want, the less you get, and the less you get, the more you have. Simple arithmetic, that's all. *(Tock, Milo and Humbug look at him blankly.)* Now, look, suppose you had something and added nothing to it. What would you have?

Milo. The same.

Dodecahedron. Splendid! And suppose you had something and added less than nothing to it? What would you have then?

Humbug. Starvation! Oh, I'm so hungry.

Dodecahedron. Now, now, it's not as bad as all that. In a few hours, you'll be nice and full again . . . just in time for dinner.

Milo. But I only eat when I'm hungry.

Mathemagician. *(Waving the eraser of his staff.)* What a curious idea. The next thing you'll have us believe is that you only sleep when you're tired.

(The mine has disappeared as well as the miners. This may be done by dropping a curtain in front of the mine, through a blackout[17] on the stage, while a single spotlight remains on the Mathemagician and the others, or through the use of multi-level platforms. The miners may fall behind the platforms, as two-dimensional props which depict the Mathemagician's room are dropped down or raised up.)

Humbug. Where did everyone go?

Mathemagician. Oh, they're still in the mine. I often find that the best way to get from one place to another is to erase everything and start again. Please make yourself at home.

(They find themselves in a very unique room, in which all the walls, tables, chairs, desks, cabinets and blackboards are labeled to show their heights, widths, depths and distances to and from each other. To one side is a gigantic notepad on an artist's easel, and from hooks and strings hang a collection of rulers, measures, weights and tapes, and all other measuring devices.)

Milo. Do you always travel that way? *(He looks around in wonder.)*

Mathemagician. No, indeed! *(He pulls a plumb line[18] from a hook and walks.)* Most of the time I take the shortest distance between any two points. And of course, when I have to be in several places at once . . . *(He writes $3 \times 1 = 3$ on the notepad with his staff.)* I simply multiply. *(Three figures looking like the Mathemagician appear on a platform above.)*

Milo. How did you do that?

Mathemagician and the Three. There's nothing

Act Two, Scene 1. The Mathemagician asks Milo to name the greatest number he can think of.

to it, if you have a magic staff. *(The Three cancel themselves out and disappear.)*

Humbug. That's nothing but a big pencil.

Mathemagician. True enough, but once you learn to use it, there's no end to what you can do.

Milo. Can you make things disappear?

Mathemagician. Just step a little closer and watch this. *(Shows them that there is nothing up his sleeve or in his hat. He writes:)* $4 + 9 - 2 \times 16 + 1 = 3 \times 6 - 67 + 8 \times 2 - 3 + 26 - 1 - 34 + 3 - 7 + 2 - 5 =$ *(He looks up expectantly.)*

Humbug. Seventeen?

Milo. It all comes to zero.

Mathemagician. Precisely. *(Makes a theatrical bow and rips off paper from notepad.)* Now, is there anything else you'd like to see? *(At*

---

17. **blackout:** the switching off of stage lights to mark the end of an act or scene.
18. **plumb line** (plŭm līn): a line from which a weight is hung to determine distance.

THE PHANTOM TOLLBOOTH **541**

Literary Analysis: HUMOR

(A) Students should be able to recognize how tone and mood contribute to the effect of the text. Ask why the Mathemagician's reaction is humorous.

Possible Response: No one could possibly understand his letter; yet he thinks he is being friendly and generous by writing it to his brother.

Literary Analysis: CHARACTER TRAITS

(B) Ask students how Milo's interaction with the Mathemagician differs from what he would have done at the beginning of the play.

Possible Response: Milo doesn't give up or lose interest in the situation. He uses his reason to solve the problem.

Active Reading: PREDICT

(C) Ask students what the obstacle might be.

Possible Responses: The obstacle might be something that will trap them upon their return; the impossibility of getting back to the Land of Wisdom once they have left it; or becoming trapped in the castle.

---

this point, an appeal to the audience to see if anyone would like a problem solved.)

Milo. Well . . . can you show me the biggest number there is?

Mathemagician. Why, I'd be delighted. *(Opening a closet door.)* We keep it right here. It took four miners to dig it out. *(He shows them a huge "3" twice as high as the Mathemagician.)*

Milo. No, that's not what I mean. Can you show me the longest number there is?

Mathemagician. Sure. *(Opens another door.)* Here it is. It took three carts to carry it here. *(Door reveals an "8" that is wide as the "3" was high.)*

Milo. No, no, that's not what I meant either. *(Looks helplessly at Tock.)*

Tock. I think what you would like to see is the number of the greatest possible magnitude.

Mathemagician. Well, why didn't you say so? *(He busily measures them and all other things as he speaks, and marks it down.)* What's the greatest number you can think of? *(Here, an appeal can also be made to the audience or Milo may think of his own answers.)*

Milo. Uh . . . nine trillion, nine hundred and ninety-nine billion, nine hundred ninety-nine million, nine-hundred ninety-nine thousand, nine hundred and ninety-nine. *(He puffs.)*

Mathemagician. *(Writes that on the pad.)* Very good. Now add one to it. *(Milo or audience does.)* Now add one again. *(Milo or audience does so.)* Now add one again. Now add one again. Now add . . .

Milo. But when can I stop?

Mathemagician. Never. Because the number you want is always at least one more than the number you have, and it's so large that if you started saying it yesterday, you wouldn't finish tomorrow.

Humbug. Where could you ever find a number so big?

Mathemagician. In the same place they have the smallest number there is, and you know what that is?

Milo. The smallest number . . . let's see . . . one one-millionth?

Mathemagician. Almost. Now all you have to do is divide that in half and then divide that in half and then divide that in half and then divide that . . .

Milo. Doesn't that ever stop either?

Mathemagician. How can it when you can always take half of what you have and divide it in half again? Look. *(Pointing offstage.)* You see that line?

Milo. You mean that long one out there?

Mathemagician. That's it. Now, if you just follow that line forever, and when you reach the end, turn left, you will find the Land of Infinity. That's where the tallest, the shortest, the biggest, the smallest and the most and the least of everything are kept.

Milo. But how can you follow anything forever? You know, I get the feeling that everything in Digitopolis is very difficult.

Mathemagician. But on the other hand, I think you'll find that the only thing you can do easily is be wrong, and that's hardly worth the effort.

Milo. But . . . what bothers me is . . . well, why is it that even when things are correct, they don't really seem to be right?

Mathemagician. *(Grows sad and quiet.)* How true. It's been that way ever since Rhyme and Reason were banished. *(Sadness turns to fury.)* And all because of that stubborn wretch Azaz! It's all his fault.

Milo. Maybe if you discussed it with him . . .

Mathemagician. He's just too unreasonable! Why just last month, I sent him a very friendly letter, which he never had the courtesy to answer. See for yourself. (*Puts the letter on the easel. The letter reads:*)
4738 1919,
667 394107 5841 62589
85371 14 39588 7190434 203
27689 57131 481206.
5864 98053,
62179875073

Milo. But maybe he doesn't understand numbers.

Mathemagician. Nonsense! Everybody understands numbers. No matter what language you speak, they always mean the same thing. A seven is a seven everywhere in the world.

Milo. (*To Tock and Humbug.*) Everyone is so sensitive about what he knows best.

Tock. With your permission, sir, we'd like to rescue Rhyme and Reason.

Mathemagician. Has Azaz agreed to it?

Tock. Yes, sir.

Mathemagician. Then I don't! Ever since they've been banished, we've never agreed on anything, and we never will.

Milo. Never?

Mathemagician. Never! And if you can prove otherwise, you have my permission to go.

Milo. Well then, with whatever Azaz agrees, you disagree.

Mathemagician. Correct.

Milo. And whatever Azaz disagrees, you agree.

Mathemagician. (*Yawning, cleaning his nails.*) Also correct.

Milo. Then, each of you agree that he will disagree with whatever each of you agrees with, and if you both disagree with the same thing, aren't you really in agreement?

Mathemagician. I've been tricked! (*Figures it over, but comes up with the same answer.*)

Tock. And now may we go?

Mathemagician. (*Nods weakly.*) It's a long and dangerous journey. Long before you find them, the demons will know you're there. Watch out for them, because if you ever come face to face, it will be too late. But there is one other obstacle even more serious than that.

Milo. (*Terrified.*) What is it?

Mathemagician. I'm afraid I can't tell you until you return. But maybe I can give you something to help you out. (*Claps hands. Enter the Dodecahedron, carrying something on a pillow. The Mathemagician takes it.*) Here is your own magic staff. Use it well and there is nothing it can't do for you. (*Puts a small, gleaming pencil in Milo's breast pocket.*)

Humbug. Are you sure you can't tell about that serious obstacle?

Mathemagician. Only when you return. And now the Dodecahedron will escort you to the road that leads to the Castle-in-the-Air. Farewell, my friends, and good luck to you. (*They shake hands, say goodbye, and the Dodecahedron leads them off.*) Good luck to you! (*To himself.*) Because you're sure going to need it. (*He watches them through a telescope and marks down the calculations.*)

Dodecahedron. (*He re-enters.*) Well, they're on their way.

Mathemagician. So I see. (*Dodecahedron stands waiting.*) Well, what is it?

Dodecahedron. I was just wondering myself, your Numbership. What actually *is* the serious obstacle you were talking about?

Mathemagician. (*Looks at him in surprise.*) You mean you really don't know?

BLACKOUT

INFINITY The Mathemagician makes the concept of infinity seem easy. That is part of his magic. In reality, though, the theory of infinity took centuries to explore and formulate. Galileo, in the 17th century, was one of the first to advance mathematical ideas about infinity. Multiplying a number by itself equals a number called a square. For example, the square of 2 is 4, the square of 4 is 16, the square of 16 is 256. Galileo said that for every number, there is a square. Since numbers go on to infinity, then there must also be an infinite number of squares. Furthermore, every number has a square so there are as many squares as there are numbers. Galileo did not want to use the word *equal* to describe the relationship between the numbers and their squares. He didn't think that infinite quantities could be proven to be equal, greater, or lesser. However, Georg Cantor, in the late 19th century, proved that those terms could be used in connection with infinity. He said that if two sets of numbers, like whole numbers and their squares, could be paired into infinity, then the sets had equal numbers of members.

THE PHANTOM TOLLBOOTH **543**

Differentiating Instruction

Less Proficient Readers
Ask the following questions to check students' comprehension:

- What is the challenge that the Mathemagician issues to Milo?
  Possible Response: If Milo can prove that the Mathemagician agrees with Azaz about anything, then Milo has his permission to rescue the princesses.

- How does Milo win the challenge?
  Possible Response: He proves that the Mathemagician agrees with Azaz because they both disagree with what each other agrees.

Set a Purpose Have students read to find out what jobs Milo and his friends undertake as they travel into the Land of Ignorance.

Advanced Students
Ask students to decide whether they think the Castle-in-the-Air symbolizes goals and dreams or a prison. Have students interpret the significance of the demons according to their view.

Possible Responses: If the Castle-in-the-Air symbolizes dreams or goals, the demons represent all of the obstacles that keep people from reaching their ideals by obscuring the truth, distracting them, or substituting false goals for real ones. Because Rhyme and Reason are trapped in the castle, it might be seen as a prison. Trying to reach the Castle-in-the-Air condemns a person to traveling through a life filled with pitfalls and traps and prevents him or her from living fully in the present.

Literary Analysis: COUPLET

A Define a couplet as two successive lines of poetry with the same end rhyme. Ask students to identify the rhyme in these four lines.

Answers: smart/heart; dreams/schemes

ACTIVE READER

B **CLARIFY** Possible Response: Rhyme speaks in rhyme. Reason is cool and logical.

Literary Analysis: SETTING

C Ask students what they learn about the Land of Ignorance from Milo's words.

Possible Response: It is very dark. Ask students to explain the significance of the dark setting.

Possible Response: People who are ignorant are figuratively "in the dark" because there is so much of which they are unaware or unknowing.

Reading Skills and Strategies: WORD PLAY

D Ask students to point out the homophones and homonyms that the Bird uses to play on Milo's words.

Possible Responses: morning/mourning; spend; sense/cents; mean/mean; weight/wait

ACTIVE READER

E **RECALL** Possible Response: Milo has received the tollbooth, some signs and coins, a map, a rule book, a box with letters of the alphabet, and the sound of laughter.

SCENE 2

THE LAND OF IGNORANCE

Lights up on Rhyme and Reason, in their castle, looking out two windows.

Rhyme. I'm worried sick, I
        must confess
    I wonder if they'll have
        success
    All the others tried in vain,
    And were never seen or heard again.

Reason. Now, Rhyme, there's no need to be so pessimistic. Milo, Tock, and Humbug have just as much chance of succeeding as they do of failing.

A **Rhyme.** But the demons are so deadly smart
    They'll stuff your brain and fill your heart
    With <u>petty</u> thoughts and selfish dreams
    And trap you with their nasty schemes.

ACTIVE READER

CLARIFY How is the manner in which each princess speaks appropriate to her name?

B **Reason.** Now, Rhyme, be reasonable, won't you? And calm down, you always talk in couplets when you get nervous. Milo has learned a lot from his journey. I think he's a match for the demons and that he might soon be knocking at our door. Now come on, cheer up, won't you?

Rhyme. I'll try.

(Lights fade on the Princesses and come up on the little car, traveling slowly.)

C **Milo.** So this is the Land of Ignorance. It's so dark. I can hardly see a thing. Maybe we should wait until morning.

Voice. They'll be <u>mourning</u> for you soon enough. *(They look up and see a large, soiled, ugly bird with a dangerous beak and a malicious expression.)*

Milo. I don't think you understand. We're looking for a place to spend the night.

Bird. *(Shrieking.)* It's not yours to spend!

Milo. That doesn't make any sense, you see . . .

Bird. Dollars or cents, it's still not yours to spend.

Milo. But I don't mean . . .

Bird. Of course you're mean. Anybody who'd spend a night that doesn't belong to him is very mean.

Tock. Must you interrupt like that?

Bird. Naturally, it's my job. I take the words right out of your mouth. Haven't we met before? I'm the Everpresent Wordsnatcher.

Milo. Are you a demon?

Bird. I'm afraid not. I've tried, but the best I can manage to be is a nuisance. *(Suddenly gets nervous as he looks beyond the three.)* And I don't have time to waste with you. *(Starts to leave.)*

Tock. What is it? What's the matter?

Milo. Hey, don't leave. I wanted to ask you some questions. . . . Wait!

Bird. Weight? Twenty-seven pounds. Bye-bye. *(Disappears.)*

Milo. Well, he was no help.

Man. Perhaps I can be of some assistance to you? *(There appears a beautifully dressed man, very polished and clean.)* Hello, little boy. *(Shakes Milo's hand.)* And how's the faithful dog? *(Pats Tock.)* And who is this handsome creature? *(Tips his hat to Humbug.)*

WORDS TO KNOW	**petty** (pĕt′ē) *adj.* narrow-minded; shallow
	mourn (môrn) *v.* to feel or express grief or sorrow

544

Humbug. *(To others.)* What a pleasant surprise to meet someone so nice in a place like this.

Man. But before I help you out, I wonder if first you could spare me a little of your time, and help me with a few small jobs?

Humbug. Why, certainly.

Tock. Gladly.

Milo. Sure, we'd be happy to.

Man. Splendid, for there are just three tasks. First, I would like to move this pile of sand from here to there. *(Indicates through pantomime a large pile of sand.)* But I'm afraid that all I have is this tiny tweezers. *(Hands it to Milo, who begins moving the sand one grain at a time.)* Second, I would like to empty this well and fill that other, but I have no bucket, so you'll have to use this eyedropper. *(Hands it to Tock, who begins to work.)* And finally, I must have a hole in this cliff, and here is a needle to dig it. *(Humbug eagerly begins. The man leans against a tree and stares vacantly off into space. The lights indicate the passage of time.)*

Milo. You know something? I've been working steadily for a long time, now, and I don't feel the least bit tired or hungry. I could go right on the same way forever.

Man. Maybe you will. *(He yawns.)*

Milo. *(Whispers to Tock.)* Well, I wish I knew how long it was going to take.

Tock. Why don't you use your magic staff and find out?

ACTIVE READER

RECALL Can you remember what other gifts Milo has received on his journey?

Milo. *(Takes out pencil and calculates to Man.)* Pardon me, sir, but it's going to take 837 years to finish these jobs.

Man. Is that so? What a shame. Well, then, you'd better get on with them.

Milo. But . . . it hardly seems worthwhile.

Man. Worthwhile! Of course they're not worthwhile. I wouldn't ask you to do anything that was worthwhile.

Tock. Then why bother?

Man. Because, my friends, what could be more important than doing unimportant things? If you stop to do enough of them, you'll never get where you are going. *(Laughs villainously.)*

Milo. *(Gasps.)* Oh, no. You must be . . .

Man. Quite correct! I am the Terrible Trivium,[19] demon of petty tasks and worthless jobs, ogre of wasted effort and monster of habit. *(They start to back away from him.)* Don't try to leave, there's so much to do, and you still have 837 years to go on the first job.

Milo. But why do unimportant things?

Man. Think of all the trouble it saves. If you spend all your time doing only the easy and useless jobs, you'll never have time to worry about the important ones which are so difficult. *(Walks toward them, whispering.)* Now do come and stay with me. We'll have such fun together. There are things to fill and things to empty, things to take away and things to bring back, things to pick up and things to put down . . . *(They are transfixed by his soothing voice. He is about to embrace them when a Voice screams.)*

Voice. Run! Run! *(They all wake up and run with the Trivium behind. As the Voice continues to call out directions, they follow until they lose the Trivium.)* Run! Run! This way! Over here! Over here! Up here! Down there! Quick, hurry up!

Tock. *(Panting.)* I think we lost him.

---

19. **Trivium** (trĭv′ē-əm): a made-up name, this uses the same root as *trivial*, which means utterly unimportant.

Reading and Analyzing

Literary Analysis: SYMBOL

(A) Ask students to interpret the symbolism of the attractive appearances of the Terrible Trivium and the demon of Insincerity.

Possible Response: Sometimes evil is disguised as good and appears attractive and tempting, not frightening or repulsive. This deceptive appearance makes it more dangerous.

Reading Skills and Strategies: CAUSE AND EFFECT

Ask students what results when people are discovered to be insincere.

Possible Response: They are no longer trusted because a person can never be sure when they are telling the truth.

Literary Analysis: REALISTIC AND FANTASTIC DETAILS

Ask students to identify what is realistic and what is fantastic about the sequence where the three run from the demons.

Possible Responses: Their reactions are realistic; the demons and the location of the castle are fantastic.

Literary Analysis **FANTASY**

Ask students to analyze the effect of the fantasy setting of the Land of Ignorance.

Possible Response: It allows the writer to incorporate symbolic demons and create a frightening atmosphere without instilling real fear in the reader.

Voice. Keep going straight! Keep going straight! Now step up! Now step up!

Milo. Look out! *(They all fall into a trap.)* But he said "up!"

Voice. Well, I hope you didn't expect to get anywhere by listening to me.

Humbug. We're in a deep pit! We'll never get out of here.

Voice. That is quite an accurate evaluation of the situation.

Milo. *(Shouting angrily.)* Then why did you help us at all?

(A) **Voice.** Oh, I'd do as much for anybody. Bad advice is my specialty. *(A little furry creature appears.)* I'm the demon of insincerity. I don't mean what I say; I don't mean what I do; and I don't mean what I am.

Milo. Then why don't you go away and leave us alone!

Insincerity. *(Voice.)* Now, there's no need to get angry. You're a very clever boy and I have complete confidence in you. You can certainly climb out of that pit . . . come on, try . . .

Milo. I'm not listening to one word you say! You're just telling me what you think I'd like to hear, and not what is important.

Insincerity. Well, if that's the way you feel about it . . .

Milo. That's the way I feel about it. We will manage by ourselves without any unnecessary advice from you.

Insincerity. *(Stamping his foot.)* Well, all right for you! Most people listen to what I say, but if that's the way you feel, then I'll just go home. *(Exits in a huff.)*

Humbug. *(Who has been quivering with fright.)* And don't you ever come back! Well, I guess we showed him, didn't we?

Milo. You know something? This place is a lot more dangerous than I ever imagined.

Tock. *(Who's been surveying the situation.)* I think I figured a way to get out. Here, hop on my back. *(Milo does so.)* Now you, Humbug, on top of Milo. *(He does so.)* Now hook your umbrella onto that tree and hold on. *(They climb over Humbug, then pull him up.)*

Humbug. *(As they climb.)* Watch it! Watch it, now. Ow, be careful of my back! My back! Easy, easy . . . oh, this is so difficult. Aren't you finished yet?

Tock. *(As he pulls up Humbug.)* There. Now, I'll lead for a while. Follow me, and we'll stay out of trouble. *(They walk and climb higher and higher.)*

Humbug. Can't we slow down a little?

Tock. Something tells me we better reach the Castle-in-the-Air as soon as possible, and not stop to rest for a single moment. *(They speed up.)*

Milo. What is it, Tock? Did you see something?

Tock. Just keep walking and don't look back.

Milo. You did see something!

Humbug. What is it? Another demon?

Tock. Not just one, I'm afraid. If you want to see what I'm talking about, then turn around.

546 UNIT FOUR   PART 2: IMAGINARY WORLDS

EXPLICIT INSTRUCTION **Understanding Fantasy**

Instruction Ask students to explain how they might distinguish a fantastic selection from a realistic selection. *(A fantasy has one or more unreal elements.)* Ask students to identify some of the unrealistic elements in Scene 1 of Act Two. *(the characters of Dischord, Dynne, Dodecahedron; the numbers mine, the subtraction stew, and the magic staff)*

Practice Use the Literary Analysis: Realistic and Fantastic Details note in the green side column to give students more practice in identifying details of fantasy.

Possible Responses: See the responses in the side column note.

546   UNIT FOUR   PART 2

(They turn around. The stage darkens and hundreds of Yellow Gleaming Eyes can be seen.)

Humbug. Good grief! Do you see how many there are? Hundreds! The Overbearing Know-it-all,[20] the Gross Exaggeration,[21] the Horrible Hopping Hindsight,[22] . . . and look over there! The Triple Demons of Compromise! Let's get out of here! *(Starts to scurry.)* Hurry up, you two! Must you be so slow about everything?

Milo. Look! There it is, up ahead! The Castle-in-the-Air! *(They all run.)*

Humbug. They're gaining!

Milo. But there it is!

Humbug. I see it! I see it!

(They reach the first step and are stopped by a little man in a frock coat, sleeping on a worn ledger. He has a long quill pen and a bottle of ink at his side. He is covered with ink stains over his clothes and wears spectacles.)

Tock. Shh! Be very careful. *(They try to step over him but he wakes up.)*

1

Senses Taker.[23] *(From sleeping position.)* Names? *(He sits up.)*

Humbug. Well, I . . .

Senses Taker. Names? *(He opens book and begins to write, splattering himself with ink.)*

Humbug. Uh . . . Humbug, Tock and this is Milo.

Senses Taker. Splendid, splendid. I haven't had an "M" in ages.

Milo. What do you want our names for? We're sort of in a hurry.

Senses Taker. Oh, this won't take along. I'm the official Senses Taker and I must have some information before I can take your sense. Now if you'll just tell me: *(Handing them a form to fill. Speaking slowly and <u>deliberately</u>.)* When you were born, where you were born, why you were born, how old you are now, how old you were then, how old you'll be in a little while . . .

Milo. I wish he'd hurry up. At this rate, the demons will be here before we know it!

Senses Taker. . . . Your mother's name, your father's name, where you live, how long you've lived there, the schools you've attended, the schools you haven't attended . . .

Humbug. I'm getting writer's cramp. **2**

Tock. I smell something very evil and it's getting stronger every second. *(To Senses Taker.)* May we go now?

Senses Taker. Just as soon as you tell me your height, your weight, the number of books you've read this year . . .

Milo. We have to go!

Senses Taker. All right, all right, I'll give you the short form. *(Pulls out a small piece of paper.)* Destination?

Milo. But we have to . . .

Senses Taker. Destination?

Milo, Tock and Humbug. The Castle-in-the-Air! *(They throw down their papers and run past him up the first few stairs.)*

Senses Taker. Stop! I'm sure you'd rather see

---

20. **Overbearing Know-it-all:** *overbearing* means pushy and arrogant.
21. **Gross Exaggeration:** a *gross* exaggeration is one that is obvious and overstated.
22. **Hindsight** (hīnd′sīt′): to view an event in hindsight means to consider its meaning after it has already occurred.
23. **Senses Taker:** A play on words: a *census taker* makes an official count of a population.

> **WORDS TO KNOW**
> **deliberately** (dĭ-lĭb′ər-ĭt-lē) *adv.* done in a slow, purposeful manner

547

Differentiating Instruction

Less Proficient Readers
Ask students the following questions to check comprehension:
- Who is the man with the jobs? *(the Terrible Trivium)*
- How do they escape from the pit into which the demon of insincerity leads them?
  Possible Response: Humbug climbs over Tock and Milo and hooks his umbrella on the tree to hold himself. Then Milo and Tock climb over him and pull him up.
- Who are some of the other demons?
  Possible Responses: Overbearing Know-it-all; the Gross Exaggeration; Horrible Hopping Hindsight; Triple Demons of Compromise

Set a Purpose Have students read to find out how Milo uses the gifts of Dr. Dischord and Azaz to help rescue the princesses.

English Learners
1 Explain to students that the senses are sight, hearing, touch, smell, and taste, and that "Senses Taker" is a pun on the title "Census Taker," someone who counts the people who live in a particular place.
2 Tell students that *writer's cramp* refers to the stiffness of the fingers or hand of someone who has written a lot.

EXPLICIT INSTRUCTION ## Viewing and Representing

Illustration of Tock, Milo, and Humbug
by Jules Feiffer

Instruction Students will notice that this illustration has more background detail than those previously seen. Ask students how the artist uses this background to convey the difficulty of the escape from the pit. *(It is shown as very deep, and the walls are smooth, meaning that there is nothing to give the characters a foothold. The ground looks rocky, which would make a fall very uncomfortable.)*

Practice Ask students why Humbug, who is portrayed as the biggest of the three, is on top.
Possible Response: As the biggest, Humbug will have the most strength to hold on as the other two characters climb over him to reach the top. The illustration emphasizes that the characters have learned to work as a team to solve problems. Each one is willing to help the others. Also ask students what the illustration emphasizes about the relationship of the three characters.

Reading and Analyzing

Reading Skills and Strategies: CLARIFY

A Ask students why a particular image is shown to each character.
Possible Response: The Senses Taker shows each character an image of something that particularly appeals to him. The Senses Taker seems to know what each character likes or wants.

Reading Skills and Strategies: CONNECT

B Have students use their knowledge and experience to comprehend what the Senses Taker is saying.

Reading Skills and Strategies: STORY MAPPING

Tell students that mapping this scene will help them review the events leading up to the climax. Have them design a flow chart and fill in events.
Possible Responses: Major conflict: rescuers vs. demons
Event 1: Rescuers enter Ignorance and encounter the Wordsnatcher; Event 2: Rescuers escape from the Terrible Trivium's trap; Event 3: Rescuers follow the demon of Insincerity and fall into a pit; Event 4: They escape from the pit and make it past the Senses Taker

ACTIVE READER

C VISUALIZE **Possible Responses:** The castle is rising out of the clouds; it has a moat, drawbridge, and several towers

ACTIVE READER

D PREDICT **Possible Responses:** Time goes quickly or in this situation, time literally flies. The rescuers and princesses will hang on to Tock and reach the ground.

A what I have to show you. *(Snaps his fingers; they freeze.)* A circus of your very own. *(Circus music is heard. Milo seems to go into a trance.)* And wouldn't you enjoy this most wonderful smell? *(Tock sniffs and goes into a trance.)* And here's something I know you'll enjoy hearing . . . *(To Humbug. The sound of cheers and applause for Humbug is heard, and he goes into a trance.)* There we are. And now, I'll just sit back and let the demons catch up with you.

Act Two, Scene 2. The demons of insincerity pursue Milo, Tock, and the Humbug.

(Milo accidentally drops his package of gifts. The Package of Laughter from Dr. Dischord opens, and the Sounds of Laughter are heard. After a moment, Milo, Tock and Humbug join in laughing and the spells are broken.)

Milo. There was no circus.

Tock. There were no smells.

Humbug. The applause is gone.

B **Senses Taker.** I warned you I was the Senses Taker. I'll steal your sense of purpose, your sense of duty, destroy your sense of proportion—and but for one thing, you'd be helpless yet.

Milo. What's that?

Senses Taker. As long as you have the sound of laughter, I cannot take your sense of humor. Agh! That horrible sense of humor.

Humbug. Here they come! Let's get out of here!

(The demons appear in nasty slithering hordes, running through the audience and up onto the stage, trying to attack Tock, Milo and Humbug. The three heroes run past the Senses Taker up the stairs toward the Castle-in-the-Air with the demons snarling behind them.)

ACTIVE READER

VISUALIZE Picture the Castle-in-the-Air. Think about size, color, and shape.

C

Milo. Don't look back! Just keep going! *(They reach the castle. The two Princesses appear in the windows.)*

Princesses. Hurry! Hurry! We've been expecting you.

Milo. You must be the princesses. We've come to rescue you.

Humbug. And the demons are close behind!

Tock. We should leave right away.

Princesses. We're ready anytime you are.

Milo. Good, now if you'll just come out. But wait a minute—there's no door! How can we rescue you from the Castle-in-the-Air if there's no way to get in or out?

Humbug. Hurry, Milo! They're gaining on us.

Reason. Take your time, Milo, and think about it.

Milo. Ummm, all right . . . just give me a second or two. *(He thinks hard.)*

Humbug. I think I feel sick.

Milo. I've got it! Where's that package of presents? *(Opens the package of letters.)* Ah, here it is. *(Takes out the letters and sticks them on the door, spelling:)* E-N-T-R-A-N-C-E. Entrance. Now let's see. *(Rummages through and spells in smaller letters:)* P-u-s-h. Push. *(He pushes and a door opens. The Princesses come out of the castle. Slowly, the demons ascend the stairway.)*

Humbug. Oh, it's too late. They're coming up and there's no other way down!

Milo. Unless . . . *(Looks at Tock.)* Well . . . Time flies, doesn't it?

ACTIVE READER

PREDICT What are the two meanings of "time flies"? Predict what will happen next.

Tock. Quite often. Hold on, everyone, and I'll take you down.

Humbug. Can you carry us all?

Tock. We'll soon find out. Ready or not, here we go!

(His alarm begins to ring. They jump off the platform and disappear. The demons, howling with rage, reach the top and find no one there. They see the Princesses and the heroes running across the stage and bound down the stairs after them and into the audience. There is a mad chase scene until they reach the stage again.)

Humbug. I'm exhausted! I can't run another step.

Milo. We can't stop now . . .

Tock. Milo! Look out there! *(The armies of Azaz and Mathemagician appear at the back of the theatre, with the kings at their heads.)*

Azaz. *(As they march toward the stage.)* Don't worry, Milo, we'll take over now.

Mathemagician. Those demons may not know it, but their days are numbered!

Spelling Bee. Charge! C-H-A-R-G-E! Charge! *(They rush at the demons and battle until the demons run off howling. Everyone cheers. The Five Ministers of Azaz appear and shake Milo's hand.)*

Minister 1. Well done.

Minister 2. Fine job.

Minister 3. Good work!

Minister 4. Congratulations!

Minister 5. Cheers! *(Everyone cheers again. A fanfare interrupts. A page steps forward and reads from a large scroll:)*

Page. Henceforth, and forthwith,
Let it be known by one and all,
That Rhyme and Reason
Reign once more in Wisdom.
(The Princesses bow gratefully and kiss their brothers, the kings.)
And furthermore,
The boy named Milo,
The dog known as Tock,
And the insect hereinafter referred to as
   the Humbug

WORDS TO KNOW   **ascend** (ə-sĕnd′) *v.* to move upward

Differentiating Instruction

Less Proficient Readers
Ask students the following questions to check comprehension:

- How does their gift from Dr. Dischord save the trio from the Senses Taker?
  Possible Response: As long as people have their sense of humor, the Senses Taker can't destroy their sense of duty, purpose, and proportion.
- How does Azaz's gift help the trio?
  Possible Response: Milo can create an entrance to the Castle-in-the-Air.
- How does Tock help them escape from the mountain?
  Possible Response: They hold onto him and fly down.

Set a Purpose Have students read to find out what Azaz and the Mathemagician couldn't tell Milo before he set off.

English Learners
The author makes plays on words, uses puns, takes things that are figurative and treats them as if they are literal, and uses homophones. Have students brainstorm examples from the text for each of the author's devices.

EXPLICIT INSTRUCTION ## Characteristics of Drama

Instruction Help students identify differences between reading a drama and reading a short story. Write the differences on the board. *(A short story is meant to be read, a drama is meant to be acted out; a short story gives descriptions of characters and settings in a narrator's or a character's words; a drama gives this information largely through stage directions.)*

Practice Ask students to write a paragraph that tells which activity they enjoy most—reading a drama or reading a short story—and why.

Possible Responses: Some students may link reading a drama with watching a movie and like drama better for this reason. Some may suggest that reading a drama is more fun because the reader can imagine different actors in the different roles. Others may suggest that when reading a short story, they can use their imaginations to develop the character instead of relying on the stage directions for the information. They may say that reading a drama is more difficult because of the stage directions.

Literary Analysis: HERO

A Ask students what characteristics of a hero they would associate with Milo.

Possible Responses: He showed courage; he didn't give up; he overcame obstacles; he accomplished his quest; he became a better person.

Literary Analysis: QUEST

B Ask students what broader purpose besides rescuing the princesses they see Milo's quest fulfilling.

Possible Response: It showed him that there was no limit to what he could accomplish if he tried.

ACTIVE READER

C **EVALUATE** **Possible Response:** Rhyme speaks in rhyme. Reason states everything clearly.

Literary Analysis: THEME

D Ask students what major idea of the play Reason's words support and reinforce.

Possible Response: Learning opens many roads into the future and prepares a person to overcome obstacles in his or her life. Learning is valuable if it is used to help others.

A   Are hereby declared to be Heroes of the Realm. *(All bow and salute the heroes.)*

Milo. But we never could have done it without a lot of help.

Reason. That may be true, but you had the courage to try, and what you can do is often a matter of what you will do.

Azaz. That's why there was one very important thing about your <u>quest</u> we couldn't discuss until you returned.

Milo. I remember. What was it?

Azaz. Very simple. It was impossible!

Mathemagician. Completely impossible!

Humbug. Do you mean . . . ? *(Feeling faint.)* Oh, . . . I think I need to sit down.

Azaz. Yes, indeed, but if we'd told you then, you might not have gone.

B   **Mathemagician.** And, as you discovered, many things are possible just as long as you don't know they're impossible.

Milo. I think I understand.

Rhyme. I'm afraid it's time to go now.

Reason. And you must say goodbye.

Milo. To everyone? *(Looks around at the crowd. To Tock and Humbug.)* Can't you two come with me?

Humbug. I'm afraid not, old man. I'd like to, but I've arranged for a lecture tour which will keep me occupied for years.

Tock. And they do need a watchdog here.

Milo. Well, O.K., then. *(Milo hugs the Humbug.)*

1   **Humbug.** *(Sadly.)* Oh, bah.

Milo. *(He hugs Tock, and then faces everyone.)* Well, goodbye. We all spent so much time together, I know I'm going to miss you. *(To Princesses.)* I guess we would have reached you a lot sooner if I hadn't made so many mistakes.

Reason. You must never feel badly about making mistakes, Milo, as long as you take the trouble to learn from them. Very often you learn more by being wrong for the right reasons than you do by being right for the wrong ones.

ACTIVE READER

EVALUATE What types of aesthetic, or pleasing, language do the princesses use?

C   **Milo.** But there's so much to learn.

Rhyme. That's true, but it's not just learning that's important. It's learning what to do with what you learn and learning why you learn things that matters.

Milo. I think I know what you mean, Princess. At least, I hope I do. *(The car is rolled forward and Milo climbs in.)* Goodbye! Goodbye! I'll be back someday! I will! Anyway, I'll try. *(As Milo drives, the set of the Land of Ignorance begins to move offstage.)*

Azaz. Goodbye! Always remember. Words! Words! Words!

Mathemagician. And numbers!

Azaz. Now, don't tell me you think numbers are as important as words?

Mathemagician. Is that so? Why I'll have you know . . . *(The set disappears, and Milo's room is seen onstage.)*

Milo. *(As he drives on.)* Oh, oh, I hope they don't start all over again. Because I don't think I'll have much time in the near future to help them out. *(The sound of loud ticking is heard. Milo finds himself in his room. He gets out of the car and looks around.)*

WORDS TO KNOW   **quest** (kwĕst) *n.* a journey in search of adventure or to perform a task

Clock. Did someone mention time?

Milo. Boy, I must have been gone for an awful long time. I wonder what time it is. *(Looks at Clock.)* Five o'clock. I wonder what day it is. *(Looks at calendar.)* It's still today! I've only been gone for an hour! *(He continues to look at his calendar, and then begins to look at his books and toys and maps and chemistry set with great interest.)*

Clock. An hour. Sixty minutes. How long it really lasts depends on what you do with it. For some people, an hour seems to last forever. For others, just a moment, and so full of things to do.

Milo. *(Looks at clock.)* Six o'clock already?

Clock. In an instant. In a trice. Before you have time to blink. *(The stage goes black in less than no time at all.)* ❖

END

All That Is Gold

by J. R. R. Tolkien

All that is gold does not glitter,

Not all those who wander are lost;

The old that is strong does not wither,

Deep roots are not reached by the frost.

From the ashes a fire shall be woken,

A light from the shadows shall spring;

Renewed shall be blade that was broken:

The crownless again shall be king.

Differentiating Instruction

Less Proficient Readers
Ask students what Milo couldn't be told about his quest. *(It was impossible.)*

English Learners
1 Explain to students that there is a well-known expression, "Bah, humbug!" taken from a story by Charles Dickens.
2 Tell students that *Boy* expresses Milo's surprise, like the word "Wow" might.

Advanced Students
Have students consider whether Milo's adventure could have been a dream. They should support their views with evidence from the text. Ask students whether the theme would be altered if the adventure were actually a dream.
Possible Response: Yes, it might be a dream. The length of time, the objects in Milo's room, which resemble the characters he meets, and the fact that he returns to his room support this view. The lessons he learned remain the same, even if the experience is a dream.

RELATED READING

J.R.R. Tolkien, who died in 1973, was the author of *The Hobbit* and *The Lord of the Rings* trilogy. This poem is taken from the trilogy's first book, *The Fellowship of the Ring*. It is spoken by Bilbo, who, like Milo, has returned from a successful quest from which he learned a great deal. Ask students to read the poem and compare the lessons that Bilbo and Milo have both learned.
Possible Responses: They have both learned that things are not always what they seem; that a defeat is not the end, it is only temporary; that imagination makes even the dullest things valuable.

Connect to the Literature

1. What Do You Think?
Answers will vary. Students should support their responses with selection details.

Comprehension Check
- Both take the same amount of time.
- He meets the Everpresent Wordsnatcher, the Terrible Trivium, the demon of Insincerity, and the Senses Taker.
- Using the letters that King Azaz gave him, Milo creates a doorway in the Castle-in-the-Air.

 Use Selection Quiz
Unit Four Resource Book, p. 45.

Think Critically

2. Possible Response: If Milo had known the quest was impossible, his expectations for success would have been very low. He might have been too discouraged to even try.

3. Possible Response: At first, Milo doesn't like school, and he gets bored easily, as do many children. He finds the situations that he encounters in the land beyond "weird" and is reluctant to try to rescue the princesses. His questions and reactions are much like the reader's would be in similar situations. The author made the main character realistic so that the reader could identify with him.

4. Possible Response: Milo becomes much more interested in learning and participating. In the beginning, he doesn't know what to do with himself and feels he has "plenty of time." He doesn't think he is very good at making words or solving problems. However, when Milo has reasons to work with words and numbers, he successfully does so. By the end of the play, Milo feels that time is too short to do everything that he wants to do.

5. Possible Responses: word market, the banquet, the armies fighting the demons

 Use **Reading and Critical Thinking Transparencies,** p. 4.

Connect to the Literature

1. What Do You Think?
Which scene or incident in the play did you find the most exciting? Why?

Comprehension Check
- Which route to Digitopolis is faster, 5 miles or 633,600 half inches?
- What creatures does Milo meet in the Land of Ignorance?
- How does Milo rescue the princesses?

Think Critically

2. How might Milo's quest have been affected if Azaz and the Mathemagician had told him ahead of time that it was impossible? Elaborate.

3. In what ways does Milo behave as an ordinary boy might? Why do you think the author chose to make the main character in this fantasy realistic?

4. How does Milo change over the course of the play?

> **Think About:**
> - the questions he asks in Act Two
> - his approach to problem-solving in Act Two
> - what he says about learning at the end

5. ACTIVE READING VISUALIZING
Share with a classmate the notes you made in your READER'S NOTEBOOK. Discuss the images you each pictured as you read the play. Which images do you think would make good scenes in a film of *The Phantom Tollbooth*?

Extend Interpretations

6. The Writer's Style Much of Norton Juster's word play is based on idioms. An idiom is a phrase whose meaning cannot be understood from the literal meanings of the words. "To eat your words" is an example of an idiom. It means to admit that you were wrong. How does Juster use idioms to add to the humor of the play?

7. Connect to Life On page 538, the Dodecahedron says it is a shame that Milo is "not good at problems," because "they're so very useful." Is mathematics useful in your life? When and how?

Literary Analysis

FANTASY A work of fiction that contains one or more fantastic, or unreal, elements is called a **fantasy.** The **setting** of a fantasy might be a totally imaginary world—like the "lands beyond" in *The Phantom Tollbooth*—or a realistic place where unrealistic things happen. The **plot** of a fantasy often involves magic or characters with extraordinary abilities, such as the Mathemagician in *The Phantom Tollbooth*. Although the play is a fantasy, the fanciful creatures that Milo meets often behave much the same way humans might.

An author's **purpose** in writing fantasy may be to entertain or to make a serious comment on reality. While Norton Juster's main purpose is to entertain, he also uses fantasy and humor to make a point about the importance of learning.

Activity In the center of a sheet of paper, draw one of the characters or settings from the play. Leave space around your drawing for labels. On the left side of the paper, label fantastic details of this creature or place, and on the right side, label the realistic details.

Extend Interpretations

6. The Writer's Style Milo encounters many idioms in the land beyond. They add humor because they often turn out to be literally true. For example, Milo really does have to eat his words at the banquet, and time really does fly when Tock helps Milo and the others escape from the demons.

7. Connect to Life Answers will vary.

Literary Analysis

Fantasy Have students choose a significant character, such as Humbug, or a major setting, such as Digitopolis. Students should review the text for realistic and fantastic details for their labels.

Writing

Plot Analysis To help you understand *The Phantom Tollbooth,* fill in a story map similar to the one below. Identify the play's main conflict, climax, and resolution. Then use your chart to write a summary of the plot. Place the summary in your **Working Portfolio.**

The Phantom Tollbooth	
Characters:	**Setting:**
Conflict:	
Event 1: *Milo receives a tollbooth.* **Event 2:** **Event 3:** (more key events)	
Climax:	**Resolution:**

Speaking & Listening

Dramatic Recording Make a dramatic recording of part or all of the play. Assign roles and find ways to produce sound effects. Before you begin recording, rehearse a few times to make sure your voice is strong and clear. Also, if you are using a video recorder, practice incorporating facial expressions and gestures in your performance. If a video or audio recorder is not available, present your performance live.

Speaking and Listening Handbook
See p. R98: Oral Interpretation.

Research & Technology

MATHEMATICS

Research a counting system, such as roman numerals or the system you use today—arabic numerals. Use an encyclopedia to find out about the origins of these symbols and how they have changed over time. Create a poster or time line to present your findings.

Research and Technology Handbook
See p. R107: Library Computer Services.

Vocabulary and Spelling

EXERCISE: LEARNING AND REMEMBERING NEW WORDS Use a dictionary to look up the entire definition of each of the Words to Know. In your own words, paraphrase the definition in just one sentence. Then write another sentence that helps you remember the word in context.

The more imaginative your sentences are, the more they will help you remember new words. For example: *The talking tree gave me an **admonishing** look when I picked one of its apples.*

SPELLING STRATEGY: THE SUFFIX -*ANCE* The suffix -*ance* is often added to words to form nouns or adjectives. For example, the vocabulary word *ignorance* is formed by adding -*ance* to the word *ignore*. *Ignore* ends with a silent *e*; always drop a silent *e* before adding -*ance*.

1. Add -*ance* to the following words:
   guide   perform   insure
2. Find two other words in *The Phantom Tollbooth* that end with -*ance*. Write each word along with its base word.

Spelling Handbook
See p. R26.

WORDS TO KNOW	acknowledge admonishing ascend	dejectedly deliberately destination	fanfare ignorance leisurely	mourn pantomime perish	petty quest vigorously

THE PHANTOM TOLLBOOTH **553**

Writing

Plot Analysis Remind students that a summary includes the main ideas. To make this assignment easier, have students divide into groups, with each group working on a story map for one scene.

Use **Reading and Critical Thinking Transparencies,** p. 13, for additional support.

Speaking & Listening

Dramatic Recording To get students started on this assignment, have them choose part of a scene with lively dialogue and distinguishing sound effects. They should experiment with sound effects.

Research & Technology

Mathematics Students may find that the appendices of a dictionary are a good starting point. Some students may wish to generate slides on the computer for their presentation.

Use **Writing Transparencies,** p. 45, for additional support.

Vocabulary and Spelling
EXERCISE: LEARNING AND REMEMBERING NEW WORDS

Accept reasonable responses.

SPELLING STRATEGY
1. guidance; performance; insurance
2. Possible responses include:

appearance	root: appear
assistance	root: assist
importance	root: import
dissonance	root: dissonant

Grammar in Context

WRITING EXERCISE

Possible Responses:

1. Castle in the Air – A tower surrounded by jagged rocks
2. Dischord (Listens through a stethoscope)
3. The Marketplace – A mixture of colors and sounds

Connect to the Literature

Possible Response: at Tock (adverb), in surprise (adverb), on a pillow (adjective)

Author Activity

Play vs. Novel To extend this activity, assign each student a scene from the novel that was not in the play. Have students present their summaries in the order in which the scenes occur. To make this assignment more challenging, have students compare and contrast elements of the novel and the play and present their findings to the class.

Grammar in Context: Pinpointing with Prepositions

Notice how the settings in *The Phantom Tollbooth* are described. What words or phrases provide the details?

Milo's bedroom—with shelves, pennants, pictures on the wall. . . .
Digitopolis—a dark, glittering place without trees or greenery. . . .

The words shown in red are **prepositions,** words that show the relationship between a noun or a pronoun and some other word in the sentence. In each example above, the underlined words are the **object of the preposition.** Together, each preposition and its object form a **prepositional phrase,** which works as an **adjective** to modify a noun or a pronoun.

A prepositional phrase can also work as an **adverb** to modify a verb, an adjective, or an adverb. The phrase in the following stage direction is functioning as an adverb:

(His alarm rings in fury.)

The phrase "in fury" modifies the verb *rings.*

WRITING EXERCISE Expand each setting or stage direction by completing the prepositional phrase.

Example: *Original* The Doldrums—A gloomy land of . . .

Rewritten The Doldrums—A gloomy land of mist and shadow

1. Castle in the Air—A tower surrounded by . . .
2. **Dischord** (*Listens through . . .*).
3. The Marketplace—A mixture of . . .

Connect to the Literature Read some of the stage directions in *The Phantom Tollbooth.* Find and list three prepositional phrases, telling whether each phrase is used as an adjective or an adverb.

Norton Juster
born 1929

"In many ways I came to writing by accident."

From the City to the Country Norton Juster grew up in Brooklyn, New York. He studied architecture at the University of Pennsylvania and city planning at the University of Liverpool in England. After teaching at the Pratt Institute and practicing architecture in New York City, Juster and his family moved to a farm in western Massachusetts. There he is a partner in an architectural firm and teaches architectural design at Hampshire College.

Author and Architect Juster considers himself primarily an architect rather than a writer, but finds that the two vocations complement each other. He began writing *The Phantom Tollbooth,* his first book, in 1959 as a way to relax from the pressures of an architectural project. He has written several other books for children, including *Alberic the Wise* and *Silly as Knees, Busy as Bees: An Astounding Assortment of Similes,* as well as books for adults.

AUTHOR ACTIVITY

Play vs. Novel Find a copy of the novel *The Phantom Tollbooth,* on which the play is based. Locate a scene in the novel that was not included in the play. Write a brief summary of the scene and share it with the class.

EXPLICIT INSTRUCTION Grammar in Context

PUNCTUATING PREPOSITIONAL PHRASES

Instruction Tell students that most prepositional phrases are not set off by commas. However, introductory phrases and phrases that break the flow of thought in a sentence must be set off by commas. Display the following sentence: At the end of his quest, Milo was surprised at his accomplishments.

Practice Ask students to rewrite each of the sentences using the correct punctuation.

1. Throughout the journey Milo kept up his hopes. (*journey,*)
2. Reason inside the castle never doubted the success of the rescuers. (*, inside the castle,*)
3. With the magic pencil Milo and his friends escaped the Terrible Trivium's trap. (*pencil,*)
4. After the subtraction stew they were hungrier than ever. (*stew,*)

 Use **Unit Four Resource Book,** p. 43.

For more instruction in punctuating prepositional phrases, see McDougal Littell's *Language Network,* Chapter 9.

For **systematic instruction** in grammar, see:
• **Grammar, Usage, and Mechanics Book**
• pacing chart on p. 441i

The Walrus and the Carpenter

by LEWIS CARROLL

Fairy Lullaby

from **A Midsummer Night's Dream**

by WILLIAM SHAKESPEARE

Connect to Your Life

Tricky Tales Have you ever had a trick played on you, or have you ever read a story about someone who was tricked? What happened?

This illustration of Alice was created in 1865 by Sir John Tenniel, the first and most famous illustrator of *Alice's Adventures in Wonderland*, by Lewis Carroll.

Build Background

Fantasy in Poem and Song "The Walrus and the Carpenter," by Lewis Carroll, and "Fairy Lullaby," by William Shakespeare, are examples of fantasy written in verse.

In England in the 1800s, when Lewis Carroll lived, schoolchildren were often asked to memorize long, dull poems meant to teach proper behavior. "The Walrus and the Carpenter" makes fun of this approach to education.

"Fairy Lullaby" appears in Shakespeare's play *A Midsummer Night's Dream*. In the play, Oberon, the king of the fairies, decides to play a trick on Titania, his queen. While Titania sleeps, Oberon plans to put drops in her eyes that will make her fall in love with the first thing she sees when she awakes. As Titania prepares for bed, her fairy attendants sing "Fairy Lullaby" to protect her from harm as she sleeps.

Focus Your Reading

LITERARY ANALYSIS | **REALISTIC AND FANTASTIC DETAILS**

These two poems are works of **fantasy.** A fantasy contains at least one fantastic, or unreal, element. In "The Walrus and the Carpenter," some of the **characters** are fantastic. The Walrus and the Oysters have the ability to speak, and the Oysters walk, as if they had legs. At the same time, some elements of the poem are realistic, such as the **setting** and the character of the Carpenter. As you read the poems, look for other examples of **realistic and fantastic details.**

ACTIVE READING | **VISUALIZING**

When you **visualize** something, you use your imagination to form a picture of it in your mind. To appreciate the realistic and fantastic details in the two poems, try to visualize the **setting** and the **characters.**

📖 **READER'S NOTEBOOK** As you read the poems, pay attention to the realistic and fantastic details that help you visualize. Use a chart like the one shown here to record the details that you notice.

Title	Realistic Details	Fantastic Details
"The Walrus and the Carpenter"	sandy shore	sun at midnight
"Fairy Lullaby"		

THE WALRUS AND THE CARPENTER / FAIRY LULLABY **555**

📖 This selection appears in Spanish in the **Spanish Study Guide.**

Standards-Based Objectives

1. understand and appreciate a **narrative poem and a song**
2. understand author's use of **realistic and fantastic details**
3. use **visualizing** to help understand realistic and fantastic details.
4. define how **tone** is conveyed in poetry

Summary

Lewis Carroll's poem tells the tale of a walrus and a carpenter who invite a group of oysters to join them for a walk on a sunny beach in the middle of the night. The walk turns out to be a cruel trick, as every one of the oysters gets eaten. In "Fairy Lullaby," a group of fairies attends the fairy queen. Their soothing song is used to protect the queen from a variety of creepy creatures.

Thematic Link

Both selections take the reader into worlds that live only in the imagination. A land where walruses talk to oysters? One with tiny fairy creatures? Why not? Use your imagination! These writers did.

English Conventions Practice

Daily Language SkillBuilder

Have students **proofread** the display sentences on page 441k and write them correctly. The sentences also appear on Transparency 17 of **Language Transparencies.**

LESSON RESOURCES

UNIT FOUR RESOURCE BOOK, pp. 46–47

ASSESSMENT
Formal Assessment, p. 91–92
Test Generator

SKILLS TRANSPARENCIES AND COPYMASTERS
Reading and Critical Thinking
• Visualizing, TR 4 (pp. 556, 561)

Language
• Daily Language SkillBuilder, TR 17 (p. 555)
Writing
• Writing Variables, TR 2 (p. 562)
• Analyzing Word Choice, TR 15 (p. 562)

INTEGRATED TECHNOLOGY
Audio Library

Visit our Web site:
www.mcdougallittell.com

For **systematic instruction** in language skills, see:
• **Vocabulary and Spelling Book**
• **Grammar, Usage, and Mechanics Book**
• pacing chart on p. 441i

REALISTIC AND FANTASTIC DETAILS

Ask students to identify two realistic details and two fantastic details.

Possible Response: Two realistic details: "The sea was wet," and "The sands were dry as dry." Two fantastic details are the sun shining in the middle of the night and the moon thinking.

 Use **Unit Four Resource Book**, p. 47, for more practice.

Active Reading VISUALIZING

Have students describe the mental images they picture as they read.

Possible Response: I imagine a beautiful beach, but the lighting is strange because the moon and the sun are both out. The Walrus and the Carpenter are walking side by side. The Walrus is walking on his back flipper.

 Use **Reading and Critical Thinking Transparencies**, p. 4, for additional support.

ACTIVE READER

A VISUALIZE Students might say that the beach is realistic but the talking walrus and the talking moon are fantasy.

B CLARIFY The Walrus wants no more than four, so that he and the Carpenter can each hold two.

C QUESTION Perhaps he's afraid. He knows he shouldn't walk with strangers.

D VISUALIZE Students might say that the Oysters seem like eager toddlers; "eager," "hopping," "scrambling"

The Walrus and the Carpenter
by Lewis Carroll

The sun was shining on the sea,
    Shining with all his might:
He did his very best to make
    The billows smooth and bright—
5 And this was odd, because it was
    The middle of the night.

The moon was shining sulkily,
    Because she thought the sun
Had got no business to be there
10   After the day was done—
"It's very rude of him," she said,
    "To come and spoil the fun!"

The sea was wet as wet could be,
    The sands were dry as dry.
15 You could not see a cloud because
    No cloud was in the sky:
No birds were flying overhead—
    There were no birds to fly.

The Walrus and the Carpenter
20   Were walking close at hand:
They wept like anything to see
    Such quantities of sand:
"If this were only cleared away,"
    They said, "it *would* be grand!"

GUIDE FOR READING

4 billows: large waves.

7 sulkily (sŭl′kə-lē): in a gloomy, pouting way.

13–24 Picture the scene that Carroll describes. What parts are realistic? What parts are fantastic? **A**

EXPLICIT INSTRUCTION Visualizing

Instruction Remind students that when they read a poem, they should picture in their minds, or visualize, the descriptions, characters, and events. Also remind students that poets usually use imagery and figurative language to create memorable and interesting images in readers' minds. Tell students that visualizing may be especially helpful with "The Walrus and the Carpenter" because this poem is full of fantastic details. Visualizing these details will help students check their understanding.

Practice Have students list four or five words, phras or images on this page that helped them visualize a character, setting, or action in "The Walrus and the Carpenter." Ask them to describe what they visualize with each word or image. Then ask volunteers to share their choices with the class.

Possible Responses: Responses will vary but shoul indicate that students recognize visual language and details.

 Use **Unit Four Resource Book**, p. 46, for more practice.

25   "If seven maids with seven mops
        Swept it for half a year,
     Do you suppose," the Walrus said,
        "That they could get it clear?"
     "I doubt it," said the Carpenter,
30   And shed a bitter tear.

     "O Oysters, come and walk with us!"
        The Walrus did beseech.
     "A pleasant walk, a pleasant talk,
        Along the briny beach:
35   We cannot do with more than four,
        To give a hand to each."

     The eldest Oyster looked at him,
        But never a word he said:
     The eldest Oyster winked his eye,
40   And shook his heavy head—
     Meaning to say he did not choose
        To leave the oyster-bed.

     But four young Oysters hurried up,
        All eager for the treat:
45   Their coats were brushed, their faces washed,
        Their shoes were clean and neat—
     And this was odd, because, you know,
        They hadn't any feet.

     Four other Oysters followed them,
50   And yet another four;
     And thick and fast they came at last,
        And more, and more, and more—
     All hopping through the frothy waves,
        And scrambling to the shore.

35–36 Why does the Walrus say he wants only four Oysters to walk with him and the Carpenter? **B**

37–42 Why do you think the eldest Oyster doesn't want to join the Walrus and the Carpenter? **C**

51–54 What images does Carroll's description of the Oysters bring to your mind? What words in this description make it especially vivid? **D**

THE WALRUS AND THE CARPENTER   **557**

EXPLICIT INSTRUCTION   Tone

Instruction Remind students that the tone of a work is the author's attitude toward the subject. For example, a tone may be sad or amused, humorous or serious, admiring or angry. Students can determine tone by examining the poet's word choice and the images the poet creates. Have students reread the poem. Then ask students to describe the tone of "The Walrus and the Carpenter." *(humorous, silly, joking)*

Practice Have pairs of students write a description of the tone of "The Walrus and the Carpenter" and identify words and images in the poem that convey the tone. Ask volunteers to share their responses with the class. Compare the descriptions of tone.

Possible Responses: Students might describe the tone as humorous, comical, silly. There are many images that show this tone.

Reading and Analyzing

Literary Analysis: IMAGERY

Ask students to read page 558 and name an image that they find especially easy to visualize, or create a mental image of, and explain why.

Possible Response: I think the image of the Oysters turning blue is easy to visualize, because they're frightened that they're about to be eaten. In literature, and in real life, creatures and people feeling fearful become cold, turn bluish, and shiver. Also colors are easy to visualize.

ACTIVE READER

A **VISUALIZE** Students might say they see slimy creatures scurrying or slithering over the forest floor, possibly a green snake, an orange newt, a pink worm.

55　The Walrus and the Carpenter
　　　Walked on a mile or so,
　And then they rested on a rock
　　　Conveniently low:
　And all the little Oysters stood
60　　And waited in a row.

　"The time has come," the Walrus said,
　　　"To talk of many things:
　Of shoes—and ships—and sealing-wax—
　　　Of cabbages—and kings—
65　And why the sea is boiling hot—
　　　And whether pigs have wings."

　"But wait a bit," the Oysters cried,
　　　"Before we have our chat;
　For some of us are out of breath,
70　　And all of us are fat!"
　"No hurry!" said the Carpenter.
　　　They thanked him much for that.

　"A loaf of bread," the Walrus said,
　　　"Is what we chiefly need:
75　Pepper and vinegar besides
　　　Are very good indeed—
　Now, if you're ready, Oysters dear,
　　　We can begin to feed."

　"But not on us!" the Oysters cried,
80　　Turning a little blue.
　"After such kindness, that would be
　　　A dismal thing to do!"
　"The night is fine," the Walrus said.
　　　"Do you admire the view?

85　"It was so kind of you to come!
　　　And you are very nice!"
　The Carpenter said nothing but
　　　"Cut us another slice.
　I wish you were not quite so deaf—
90　　I've had to ask you twice!"

　"It seems a shame," the Walrus said,
　　　"To play them such a trick.
　After we've brought them out so far,
　　　And made them trot so quick!"
95　The Carpenter said nothing but
　　　"The butter's spread too thick!"

　"I weep for you," the Walrus said:
　　　"I deeply sympathize."
　With sobs and tears he sorted out
100　　Those of the largest size,
　Holding his pocket-handkerchief
　　　Before his streaming eyes.

　"O Oysters," said the Carpenter,
　　　"You've had a pleasant run!
105　Shall we be trotting home again?"
　　　But answer came there none—
　And this was scarcely odd, because
　　　They'd eaten every one.

EXPLICIT INSTRUCTION **Read Aloud**

Instruction Read aloud a passage from the poem. Model how to read effectively by reading expressively and with appropriate intonation and pacing. You may wish to model using different voices for the different characters. Tell students that they should pay attention to the rhymes and the rhythm in the poem as they read. Caution students that they may want to read quickly because of the regular rhyme and rhythm, but that doing so will make understanding difficult for listeners. Remind students to look up unfamiliar words in a dictionary to see how they are pronounced.

Practice Have students work in pairs. Direct partners to each choose a section of the poem to read aloud. Have them practice reading aloud, with one another as the audience. Partners can evaluate and offer suggestions for improving their readings. When students are ready, have them read their sections to the class.

Fairy Lullaby

from A Midsummer Night's Dream
by William Shakespeare

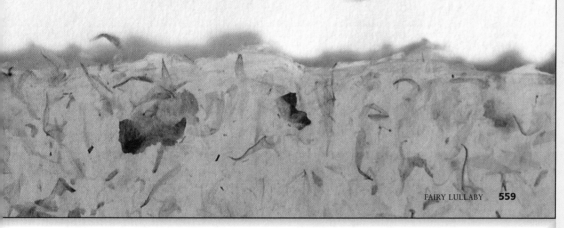

First Fairy. You spotted snakes with double tongue,
Thorny hedgehogs, be not seen,
Newts and blind-worms, do not wrong,
Come not near our fairy queen.

5 **Chorus.** Philomele, with melody,
Sing in our sweet lullaby,
Lulla, lulla, lullaby, lulla, lulla, lullaby.
Never harm,
Nor spell, nor charm,
10 Come our lovely lady nigh.
So good night, with lullaby.

GUIDE FOR READING

1–3 Close your eyes and picture the
animals described in the song.
What do you see? **A**

5 Philomele (fĭl′ə-mē′lə): in Greek
mythology, a princess from Athens
who was turned into a nightingale.

Differentiating Instruction

Less Proficient Readers
Some of the words in "Fairy Lullaby"
may look strange to students. Tell
students that *nigh* means "nearby,"
hence means "away from here," and
aloof means "distant physically or
emotionally."

English Learners
Explain that because this poem was
written almost 400 years ago, the language and the syntax, or word order,
are different from the way we speak
today. Tell students to focus on the
meaning of the poem and not to worry
about the unusual word order. You
might also explain archaic or unfamiliar
words, such as those listed above
under Less Proficient Readers.

Advanced Students
Encourage students to read more by
William Shakespeare, and to see as
many of his plays as they can. Many
Shakespearean plays have been made
into popular movies. Students might
enjoy comparing two versions, such as
the classic version of *Romeo and Juliet*
and the modern adaptation of the
same play.

EXPLICIT INSTRUCTION **Clarifying**

Instruction Tell students that the poem "Fairy
Lullaby" may be hard to understand because of
the many unusual words and the style of the
language. Remind students that they can help
themselves understand this poem by clarifying
as they read. Say, "When you pause while reading to review events and ideas or unfamiliar
words, you are clarifying."

Practice After reading the complete poem, have
students list the words or phrases they need

clarified. Point out the Guide for Reading notes
in the right margin and tell students to use them
to clarify. Remind students that they can also
use a dictionary to clarify unfamiliar words.
Have students work in pairs to clarify the difficult
events and words in this poem. Then ask
students to share the difficulties they were able
to clarify and the ideas that are still unclear.

Possible Responses: Responses will vary.

Reading and Analyzing

Literary Analysis: POETIC LANGUAGE

Tell students to look for poetic language as they read "Fairy Lullaby." Ask them to cite two examples. Then ask them to think about how this language sounds.

Possible Response: One example of poetic language is "Come our lovely lady nigh." Another example is the last two lines of the poem, "Hence, away! now all is well. One aloof stand sentinel." I think this language sounds old-fashioned, but beautiful.

Reading Skills and Strategies: CLARIFY

Ask students whether they understood the meaning of the last line—"One aloof stand sentinel." Ask them how they figured it out.

Possible Response: I wasn't sure what the word *sentinel* meant, so I looked it up in the dictionary. Once I knew that it meant "to guard," I understood the line.

ACTIVE READER

A EVALUATE The rhythm and repetition create a soothing, musical, lulling effect.

First Fairy. Weaving spiders, come not here;
    Hence, you long-legg'd spinners, hence!
    Beetles black, approach not near;
15 Worm nor snail, do no offense.

Chorus. Philomele, with melody,
    Sing in our sweet lullaby,
    Lulla, lulla, lullaby, lulla, lulla, lullaby.
    Never harm,
20 Nor spell, nor charm,
    Come our lovely lady nigh.
    So good night, with lullaby.

Second Fairy (spoken). Hence, away! now all is well.
    One aloof stand sentinel.

16–22 What effect does Shakespeare create through repetition and rhyme?

A

Connect to the Literature

1. **What Do You Think?**
   What was your reaction to the song? Explain.

   Comprehension Check
   • Who are the fairies trying to protect?
   • What dangers do they fear?

Think Critically

2. Why do the fairies list particular animals? What do you think these creatures have in common?

3. Do you think that Carroll intends for you to feel sorry for the Oysters in "The Walrus and the Carpenter"? Support your answer.

4. "The Walrus and the Carpenter" and "Fairy Lullaby" are both fantasies, but they create very different effects. How would you describe the mood of the poem and the song?

   Think About:
   • sound devices
   • word choice
   • word play

5. **ACTIVE READING** **VISUALIZING**
   Look over the chart you made in your **READER'S NOTEBOOK**. With a partner, discuss which images in "The Walrus and the Carpenter" and "Fairy Lullaby" you enjoyed the most. Which did you respond to more strongly, realistic details or fantastic details? Why?

Extend Interpretations

6. **COMPARING TEXTS** Compare and contrast the humor in "The Walrus and the Carpenter" with the humor in *The Phantom Tollbooth* (page 512). What similarities do you see between the two works?

7. **Connect to Life** What kind of tricks do you think are mean? Are there tricks that you think are acceptable to play on people? Elaborate.

Literary Analysis

REALISTIC AND FANTASTIC DETAILS

"The Walrus and the Carpenter" and "Fairy Lullaby" are both examples of **fantasy**. Each contains fantastic, or unreal, elements. A fantasy may have a totally imaginary setting, or the setting may be a realistic place where impossible things happen, as in these two works.

As in most fantasies, this poem and song blend realistic **details** with imaginary ones. For example, the animals mentioned in Shakespeare's song actually exist. The characters singing the song, however, are fairies—imaginary beings.

Paired Activity For each fantastic detail in "The Walrus and the Carpenter," suggest a realistic alternative. For example, what if the main characters were not a walrus and a carpenter, but a pair of chefs?

With a partner, discuss how the poem would be different if these details were realistic. How would these changes affect the poem's humor?

REVIEW: RHYME **Rhyme** is the repetition of similar sounds at the ends of words. The poems you just read contain rhyming words at the ends of the lines. Poets use rhyme to link words, ideas, and feelings in poems. Rhyme can also add to the humor or absurdity of poems like "The Walrus and the Carpenter."

Connect to the Literature

1. **What Do You Think?**
   Accept all reasonable responses.

   Comprehension Check
   • The fairies are trying to protect the fairy queen.
   • They fear snakes, hedgehogs, newts, spells, charms, spiders, beetles, worms, and snails.

Think Critically

2. The fairies name these particular animals because all of them are scary, slimy, or capable of causing injury.

3. **Possible Responses:** Yes, because the Walrus cries for the Oysters. No, because the poem is humorous, not serious.

4. **Possible Responses:** The regular rhythm and rhyme scheme of the poem give it a singsong quality, like a nursery rhyme. The stiff, formal way that the Walrus and the Oysters speak makes them sound silly. The poem has a humorous mood. The song has a more serious mood. The repetition of "lullaby" gives it a dreamy quality.

5. Accept responses that include supporting details from the selection.

   Use **Reading and Critical Thinking Transparencies,** p. 4, for additional support.

Literary Analysis

Realistic and Fantastic Details Students' discussions should show a clear understanding of the difference between reality and fantasy and of how fantasy adds to the humor of the poem.

Extend Interpretations

6. **Comparing Texts** **Possible Response:** The humor in the two selections is similar. Both works contain fantastic characters, such as talking animals. Both works feature characters who play tricks on other characters. For example, in the "The Walrus and the Carpenter," the Walrus invites the Oysters to go for a walk, and then he and the Carpenter eat them. In "The Phantom Tollbooth," Milo orders a light snack at the banquet, and he is served actual light on a plate. In the Land of Ignorance, Milo meets the Everpresent Wordsnatcher, who deliberately misunderstands everything that Milo says.

7. **Connect to Life** Responses will vary.

Writing

Eloquent Speech Students' speeches should be clear and well-written. They should have strong arguments that would dissuade the Walrus and the Carpenter from eating the Oyster.

 Use **Writing Transparencies,** pp. 2, 15, for additional support.

Speaking & Listening

Dramatic Reading Encourage students to work in small groups as they prepare the dramatic reading.

Research & Technology

Comparing Performances Tell students to pay close attention to details such as sets, costumes, and the individual performances of the actors. Have them carefully consider why they prefer one performance over another.

More About the Authors

In Lewis Carroll's *Through the Looking Glass,* everything seems backward. For example, Alice must walk away from a place in order to reach it and must run fast in order to remain where she is!

William Shakespeare is probably the English language's most quoted writer. In his plays and poetry, Shakespeare expressed deep thoughts and feelings in beautiful and powerful words. His mastery of the technical aspects of poetry—rhythm, image, metaphor—is considered unrivaled.

Writing

Eloquent Speech Suppose that one of the Oysters wants to avoid being eaten. Help the Oyster by writing an eloquent speech to persuade the Walrus and the Carpenter to spare him or her. Place your speech in your **Working Portfolio.**

Writing Handbook
See p. R47: Persuasive Writing.

> This activity asks you to use the speech form. To find out about other writing forms you might use when your purpose is to persuade, see p. R31: Choosing a Form.

Speaking & Listening

Dramatic Reading Read a modern retelling of *A Midsummer Night's Dream,* such as Bruce Coville's illustrated version or Charles and Mary Lamb's *Tales from Shakespeare.* Present a dramatic reading of one scene. Rehearse using gestures and facial expressions as you read. Then perform the reading for the class.

Speaking and Listening Handbook
See p. R98: Oral Interpretation.

Research & Technology

Comparing Performances Your school library or a public library may have performances of *Through the Looking Glass* and *A Midsummer Night's Dream* on videotape. Choose either work and view at least two different performances of it. Compare interpretations of "The Walrus and the Carpenter" or "Fairy Lullaby" in the different productions. Which performance do you prefer? Why? Be sure to support your opinions with facts and examples.

Lewis Carroll
1832–1898

"Curiouser and curiouser!"

Fun and Games Lewis Carroll was the pen name of the writer and mathematician Charles Lutwidge Dodgson. Although very intelligent, he was shy as a child and stammered when he spoke to adults. Throughout his life, Dodgson felt more comfortable around children and enjoyed making up puzzles and stories to entertain them. He invented "Alice's Adventures Underground" to amuse a ten-year-old friend, Alice Liddell. The story was published in 1865 as *Alice's Adventures in Wonderland.*

William Shakespeare
1564–1616

"All the world's a stage, And all the men and women merely players: . . ."

Actor, Playwright, Poet William Shakespeare is probably the best-known English writer of all time. The son of a businessman, Shakespeare grew up in Stratford-upon-Avon, a town to which he returned periodically throughout his life. As a young man, he acted on the London stage and helped found the famous theater, the Globe. By his late twenties, Shakespeare had begun to write plays. He is equally famous for his comedies, such as *A Midsummer Night's Dream,* and his tragedies, like *Hamlet* and *Macbeth.* Shakespeare is also well-known for his poetry, especially his sonnets.

Three Limericks

by EDWARD LEAR, OGDEN NASH, *and* JACK PRELUTSKY

Connect to Your Life

Ever Get the Giggles? You probably can think of many times when something made you smile or chuckle or even laugh out loud. Maybe you were riding a roller coaster, watching a cartoon, or simply making a silly face. What makes you laugh? Try describing it in one sentence. Now try describing it in two lines that rhyme.

Build Background

HISTORY

The limerick is a form of poetry that first appeared in England in the early 1800s. Limericks were made popular by Edward Lear, who said he first saw the limerick form used in a nursery rhyme. Lear paired his poetry with his own humorous illustrations, as shown below, and published them in *A Book of Nonsense* in 1846.

There was an Old Man who said, "Hush! I perceive a young bird in this bush!"
When they said, "Is it small?" he replied, "Not at all!
It is four times as big as the bush!"

Focus Your Reading

LITERARY ANALYSIS POETIC FORM: LIMERICK

Limericks are a form of nonsense verse. A typical limerick has five lines and follows the **rhyme scheme** *aabba*. Like other types of poetry, limericks often are meant to be read aloud.

ACTIVE READING READING ALOUD

Reading aloud makes it easier to hear the careful arrangement of sounds and syllables in a limerick. To enjoy these poems fully, read them aloud, first to yourself and then to a partner. As you read, don't let yourself be hurried by the sing-song rhythm. Reading at a normal pace often better conveys the poem's humor.

📖 **READER'S NOTEBOOK** As you read these poems, jot down words or lines that you find funny. Then note examples of the poems' sound devices, such as rhythm, rhyme, and repetition.

Standards-Based Objectives
1. understand and appreciate **poetry**
2. understand the poetic form **limerick**
3. use **reading aloud** to help understand and enjoy a limerick

Summary
In limericks by three of the masters of this form, we meet a young boy who swallows his watch, a very frugal bugler, and an old man whose beard grows out of control. There are hilarious results for each predicament.

Thematic Link
Strange and improbable things happen in limericks. People of all ages enjoy them for their sheer silliness and clever word play.

English Conventions Practice

Daily Language SkillBuilder

Have students **proofread** the display sentences on page 441k and write them correctly. The sentences also appear on Transparency 17 of **Language Transparencies.**

THREE LIMERICKS **563**

LESSON RESOURCES

UNIT FOUR RESOURCE BOOK, pp. 48–49

ASSESSMENT
Formal Assessment, pp. 93–94
Test Generator

SKILLS TRANSPARENCIES AND COPYMASTERS
Literary Analysis
• Form in Poetry: Rhyme and Meter, TR 17 (pp. 564, 566)
Language
• Daily Language SkillBuilder, TR 17 (p. 563)

INTEGRATED TECHNOLOGY
Audio Library

Visit our Web site:
www.mcdougallittell.com

For **systematic instruction** in language skills, see:
• **Vocabulary and Spelling Book**
• **Grammar, Usage, and Mechanics Book**
• pacing chart on p. 441i

Literary Analysis
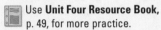
POETIC FORM: LIMERICK

In addition to the AABBA rhyme scheme, a limerick has other distinguishing features and structural requirements. Each line has a definite number of stressed syllables. Ask students to count the stressed syllables in each line to figure out the pattern.

Possible Response: The lines that rhyme have the same number of stressed syllables. For example, in Ogden Nash's limerick, lines 1, 2, and 5 all have three stressed syllables. Lines 3 and 4 contain two stressed syllables apiece.

Use **Unit Four Resource Book,** p. 49, for more practice.

Use **Literary Analysis Transparencies,** p. 17, for additional support.

Active Reading   READING ALOUD

After partners read the limericks aloud, ask them whether they knew which words to stress the first time they read, and whether their reading improved with each successive try.

Possible Response: The first time I read the limericks aloud, I wasn't sure which words to emphasize. With practice, though, I got to know the poems and I understood where to place the stress.

Use **Unit Four Resource Book,** p. 48, for more practice.

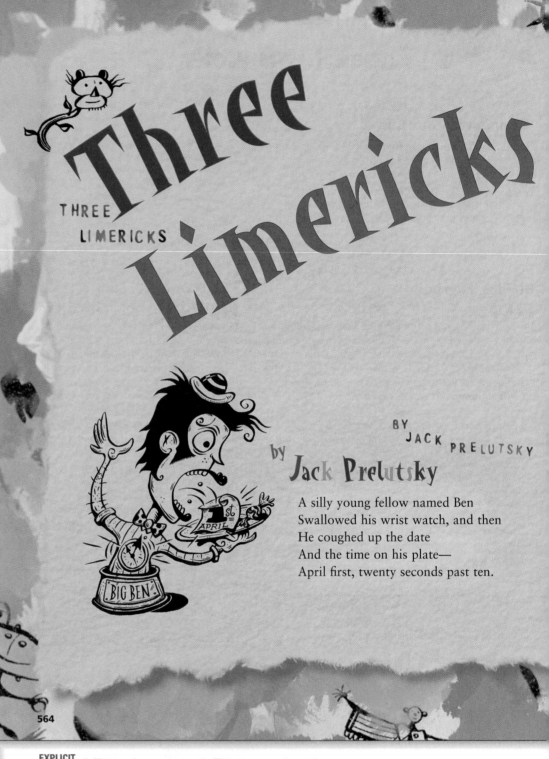

Three Limericks

by Jack Prelutsky

A silly young fellow named Ben
Swallowed his wrist watch, and then
He coughed up the date
And the time on his plate—
April first, twenty seconds past ten.

564

EXPLICIT INSTRUCTION   Viewing and Representing

VIEW AND CREATE YOUR OWN ILLUSTRATIONS

Instruction Point out that the illustrations provided are all humorous character sketches. The artist has started with a human face and then altered it to fit the limerick.

Practice Tell students to make their own pen and ink illustrations for the three limericks on pages 564–565. They should start with a pencil sketch, working into it with the eraser and the pencil until it becomes very exaggerated and expressive. Then have them use black felt-tipped pens to finish the cartoon drawing. When the illustrations are complete, hang them up around the classroom. Invite volunteers to discuss their artwork.

by Ogden Nash

A bugler named Dougal MacDougal
Found ingenious ways to be frugal.
He learned how to sneeze
In various keys,
Thus saving the price of a bugle.

by Edward Lear

There was an old man with a beard,
Who said, "It is just as I feared!—
Two owls and a hen, four larks and a wren,
Have all built their nests in my beard!"

Less Proficient Readers
Help students work out the rhythm of limericks by using nonsense syllables to chant the rhythm or by tapping with a pencil on a desk to beat out the rhythm.

English Learners
Point out the word *ingenious* in Ogden Nash's limerick. Tell students that this is another word for "clever." Ask them whether they could figure out the meaning of *ingenious* by using context clues. Now, see if students can understand the meaning of *frugal* using context clues. Tell them that the word *price*, in the last line of the limerick, is a clue. (*A frugal person is thrifty and wants to save money as much as possible.*)

Use **Spanish Study Guide**, pp. 112–114, for additional support.

Advanced Students
Encourage students to write their own limericks. Suggest that they use the trio of limericks as models. Tell them that they can think of an idea first and then begin writing, or they might start with one line and see how it develops.

Connect to the Literature

1. What Do You Think?
Answers will vary but should be clearly explained. Most students will say that the limericks are funny in a silly sort of way.

Think Critically

2. A number of birds make nests in the old man's beard.

3. Possible Response: Dougal McDougal is a cheapskate and is willing to do anything to save money. But he is also tricky and clever, and especially talented. He is probably a happy-go-lucky guy.

4. Possible Response: A boy with a wristwatch is realistic, but swallowing it is less so. Coughing up the time and date is complete fantasy. A musician being frugal could be realistic, but playing music by sneezing is fantastic. An old man with a long beard is realistic, but birds nesting in a beard is fantastic.

5. Students' answers will vary.

Literary Analysis

Limericks Students' evaluations of the three limericks should be detailed and include an examination of rhythm, rhyme, and humor.

 Use **Literary Analysis Transparencies,** p. 17, for additional support.

Connect to the Literature

1. What Do You Think? Did you find these poems funny? Why or why not?

Think Critically

2. Explain what happens to the old man in Edward Lear's poem.

3. What kind of a person is Dougal MacDougal?

Think About:
• what the word *frugal* means
• what Dougal teaches himself, and why

4. In each poem, decide which details are realistic and which are fantastic. Which details came as a complete surprise to you?

5. **ACTIVE READING   READING ALOUD**
Look back at the words and lines you recorded in your **READER'S NOTEBOOK**. Then talk with a classmate about the parts of the poems each of you found to be funniest. Compare different ways of reading the poems to convey their humor.

Extend Interpretations

6. **COMPARING TEXTS** Compare and contrast the three limericks with "The Walrus and the Carpenter" (page 555). Consider structure, rhyme scheme, and rhythm. Also think about the humor in the poems.

7. Connect to Life Think back to the Connect to Your Life discussion on page 563. After reading these poems, can you add limericks to the list of things that make you laugh? Use details to explain why or why not.

Literary Analysis

LIMERICKS Limericks are humorous nonsense poems—the ideas in them may not make any sense. Limericks usually contain five lines, have a sing-song **rhythm,** and **rhyme.** The rhyme scheme or pattern consists of two rhyming couplets (pairs of lines that end with rhyming words) and a fifth line that rhymes with the first couplet. As you read, consider the way in which rhythm and rhyme add to the humor of these poems.

REVIEW: RHYTHM **Rhythm** is the pattern of stressed and unstressed syllables in a poem. It guides your voice to emphasize certain words and sounds. In these poems, the rhythm has a musical, sing-song quality.

Paired Activity Working with a partner, study each limerick. Identify parts of the poem that are nonsense. Examine the rhyme scheme to identify the rhyming words. When you are finished, rate each poem for **humor, rhythm,** and **rhyme.** Which limerick works best? Why?

Extend Interpretations

6. Comparing Texts   Possible Response: Both the limericks and "The Walrus and the Carpenter" use humor and fantasy. The limericks are very short and fit the standard limerick form and rhyme scheme. "Walrus" is a longer poem with several stanzas of rhyming lines.

7. Connect to Life Answers will vary, but students should be able to explain their opinions.

Writing

Your Own Limericks Write three limericks of your own. Start by thinking of rhyming words. You might try a limerick about something clumsy you did, or about sports, or an animal friend. Put your limericks in your **Working Portfolio.**

Speaking & Listening

Limericks Out Loud Read aloud to the class the limericks you wrote for the activity above. Practice reading them aloud. You may feel you want to read them quickly because of the rhythm. Try not to do this. Instead, practice reading at a slower pace.

Ogden Nash
1902–1971

"I've been in love with words all my life."

Not for Grownups During Ogden Nash's childhood, his family divided its time between Savannah, Georgia, and a New York City suburb. He tried different jobs after college, including becoming a bond trader on Wall Street. When Nash tried to sell the poetry he had written for adults, he got absolutely nowhere. But when he began to write light verse intended for children, he found success. Nash has also edited a magazine, written film screenplays, and helped create a successful Broadway musical.

Edward Lear
1812–1888

"There was an Old Derry down Derry, / who loved to see little folks merry . . ."

An Artist and Traveler Edward Lear was born in England, the second youngest of 21 children. He was raised by two older sisters who read him poetry and encouraged him to draw. Although he is best known for his nonsense verse, Lear first worked as an artist illustrating books about animals. He also gave art lessons. Queen Victoria of England was one of his students. Later he began writing light verse to entertain his employer's children. His *Book of Nonsense* made him famous in England. Lear traveled often, for pleasure and for his health. He wrote and sketched wherever he went.

Jack Prelutsky
born 1940

"Poetry is . . . one way a human being can tell another human being what's going on inside."

Try, Try Again Jack Prelutsky's first love was music; at one point, he trained to be an opera singer. Then he became a folk singer, combining his love of music with an interest in storytelling. However, once he began writing poetry for children, he never stopped. Prelutsky writes poems often—once he wrote six poems in one day. He also visits many schools, where, he says, "I try to tell kids that poetry is not boring or a chore. . . . It is one way a human being can tell another human being what's going on inside."

THREE LIMERICKS **567**

Writing

Your Own Limericks Students' limericks will vary, but should have the AABBA rhyme scheme, a discernible rhythm, and humor. If possible, provide students with rhyming dictionaries.

Speaking & Listening

Limericks Out Loud You might suggest students exchange limericks with a partner and read each other's work aloud.

Standards-Based Objectives
- expand vocabulary through wide reading
- use context to determine the meaning of specialized vocabulary
- use reference tools to determine word meanings

VOCABULARY EXERCISE

1. **sector:** part; (Computer Science): A bit or set of bits on a magnetic storage system that makes up the smallest addressable unit of information.
2. **ozone layer:** A region of the upper atmosphere, between ten and twenty miles in altitude, containing a relatively high concentration of ozone that absorbs solar ultraviolet radiation in a wavelength range not screened by other atmospheric components.
3. **stimulus:** something that causes a response.
4. **altimeter:** An instrument for determining the elevation of an aircraft.
5. **dorsal:** Of or toward the back or upper surface.

 Use **Unit Four Resource Book,** p.50.

Building Vocabulary
Understanding Specialized Vocabulary

When you watch a weather report, you may not know all the technical terms the meteorologist, or weather forecaster, uses. Still, you can understand the forecast. That's because you understand the context, the words around the technical or **specialized vocabulary.** You can do the same thing when you read.

> Mrs. Pavloff reached for her protective sun goggles that covered most of her face. It screened all ultraviolet light from the once life-giving sun; now, it, the sun, scorched the Earth, killing whatever it touched.
>
> —Alma Luz Villanueva, "The Sand Castle"

You can tell from the clues in the surrounding text that the sun produces **ultraviolet light** and that ultraviolet light can cause harm.

Strategies for Building Vocabulary

Professionals in many fields use and understand their own specialized vocabulary. The following strategies can help you understand the technical meanings of specialized vocabulary:

❶ **Use Context Clues** Often the **context,** or surrounding text, gives clues that help you infer the meaning of an unfamiliar term. Let's consider the following example.

> "Our television screen must have had a million books on it and it's good for plenty more. . . ."
> "Same with mine," said Margie. She was eleven and hadn't seen as many telebooks as Tommy had.
>
> —Isaac Asimov, "The Fun They Had"

In this example, the author invented the term *telebook.* The context helps us understand that a telebook is a book that appears on a television screen.

❷ **Use a Reference Tool** Sometimes context clues aren't enough to clarify the meaning. Textbooks often define a special term when it is first introduced. Look for definitions or restatement clues in parentheses. Also you can try to find definitions in footnotes, a glossary, or even a dictionary. If you still need more information, you can refer to a specialized reference, such as

- an encyclopedia
- a field guide
- an atlas
- a user's manual
- a technical dictionary (such as a medical dictionary)

EXERCISE Use context clues to make a guess at the meaning of each underlined term. Then check a dictionary and revise your definition.

1. I can't run this software because my hard drive has a damaged <u>sector</u>. At least all my files aren't lost.
2. Holes in the <u>ozone layer</u>, that atmospheric layer of protection, may contribute to global warming.
3. The victim did not respond to any <u>stimulus</u>; she appeared to be in a coma.
4. The plane's <u>altimeter</u> indicated that it had climbed to 30,000 feet.
5. The dolphin slipped its <u>dorsal</u> fin into a ring that was floating on the water.

Where the Sidewalk **Ends**

by Shel Silverstein

There is a place where the sidewalk ends
And before the street begins,
And there the grass grows soft and white,
And there the sun burns crimson bright,
5 And there the moon-bird rests from his flight
To cool in the peppermint wind.

Let us leave this place where the smoke blows black
And the dark street winds and bends.
Past the pits where the asphalt flowers grow
10 We shall walk with a walk that is measured and slow,
And watch where the chalk-white arrows go
To the place where the sidewalk ends.

Yes we'll walk with a walk that is measured and slow,
And we'll go where the chalk-white arrows go,
15 For the children, they mark, and the children, they know
The place where the sidewalk ends.

WHERE THE SIDEWALK ENDS **569**

Possible Objectives
- enjoy independent reading (Option One)
- read and analyze poetry with a group (Option Two)
- use the Reader's Notebook to formulate questions about poetry (Option Three)
- write in response to poetry (Option Three)

Summary
Shel Silverstein's poem "Where the Sidewalk Ends" describes a place that young children might imagine exists at the end of the entire length of the world's sidewalks. He describes the grass as being soft and white, the sun as especially bright, and the wind as cool as peppermint. In the poem, this special place offers refuge from the scariness of the real world. Similarly, Virginia Hamilton's poem "Under the Back Porch" describes a place of refuge for a child. In this case, it is a secret hiding place underneath the back porch of her white house. This is her special place where she can be alone, away from her brothers and sisters. She describes this space as being shaded and damp with the sunlight filtering through the slats of wood and the smell of damp, green moss.

Reading the Selections

Option One
Independent Reading
You might set aside time each week for independent reading to help your students approach the goal of reading 1 million words a year. During this time, you and your students would read for enjoyment. The poems can be read independently in 15 minutes or so. To encourage students to read for pleasure, consider making no assignments related to this selection. However, Options Two and Three offer suggestions in case you do want to make assignments.

SHEL SILVERSTEIN
Shel Silverstein's varied and numerous creative abilities earned him the title of "Renaissance Man," or man of many talents, during his lifetime. As well as writing poetry and stories for children, which he illustrated himself, Silverstein also wrote and performed music. In 1969 he wrote a number one hit for country music star Johnny Cash, called "A Boy Named Sue." Eleven years later, he recorded an album of country music himself, called *The Great Conch Train Robbery.* Following on the heels of his recording successes, Silverstein branched out into theater work. In the eighties he wrote several hit plays and screenplays for movies.

UNDER THE BACK
by Virginia Hamilton

Option Two
Group Reading

You may assign students to groups or allow them to choose their own. Students can read the selections together, alternately reading sections aloud, or they can read independently and meet to cooperate in a project that portrays some element of the poems.

Possible Projects

• Using the descriptions from the poems, students could create illustrations for each poem by drawing or painting their own illustrations, or by finding art or photographs that represent their vision of the places in the poems.

• Students can memorize the poems and present them to the class, taking turns within each group so that all students get a chance to recite.

Option Three
Reader's Notebook

• Ask students to read the selections and to analyze their initial reactions to the special places that are described in these poems. Have them write their reactions in their Reader's Notebooks. Have them also write any questions they have about the poems or their meanings.

After reading the selections a second time, students will return to their initial reactions and questions. Ask them to note if their impressions remained the same after rereading the poems and if their questions were answered. They may want to write down any additional questions.

• Ask students to note which descriptions in the poems seem most vivid to them and to explain why.

• Ask students to write a passage or a poem describing a special place where they go to be alone.

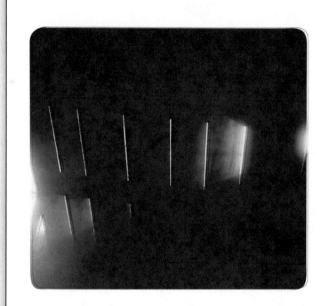

Our house is two stories high
shaped like a white box.
There is a yard stretched around it
and in back
5   a wooden porch.

Under the back porch is my place.
I rest there.
I go there when I have to be alone.
It is always shaded and damp.
10 Sunlight only slants through the slats
in long strips of light,
and the smell of the damp
is moist green,
like the moss that grows here.

PORCH

```
15    My sisters and brothers
      can stand on the back porch
      and never know
      I am here
      underneath.
20    It is my place.
      All mine.
```

Shel Silverstein
1932–1999

"I have ideas, and ideas are too good not to share."

An Adult Who Thinks Like a Child Shel Silverstein started writing and drawing when he was around 12, although, he has said, "I would much rather have been a good baseball player." In addition to writing and illustrating poetry and stories, Silverstein was a songwriter. One of his songs, "A Boy Named Sue," became a hit when it was recorded by Johnny Cash in 1969. A critic once called Silverstein "that rare adult who can still think like a child." Perhaps because of this quality, Silverstein's work appeals to people of all ages. His books include *The Giving Tree* and *A Light in the Attic.*

Virginia Hamilton
born 1936

"I write books because I love chasing after a good story. . . ."

Writing from Roots As a child Virginia Hamilton loved to listen to her parents tell her family history, such as the story of her grandfather's escape from slavery. She knew then that she wanted to be a writer. Hamilton attended college in Ohio and then studied writing in New York. There she published her first book, *Zeely,* in 1967. Later, she moved back to her family's Ohio farm, where she has lived ever since. Hamilton's work has received, among many awards, the Newbery Medal, the National Book Award, and the Coretta Scott King Award.

UNDER THE BACK PORCH **571**

Possible Activities

Independent Activities

- Have advanced students skim over the selections, noting the rhythm and rhyming patterns in the poems. Ask them to write in their Reader's Notebooks their analysis of the effect of the rhythm and rhyming patterns on the poems in general.
- Have students review the Learning the Language of Literature and Active Reader pages, pp. 507–511. Ask them to note which skills and strategies they used while reading these selections and to explain how a particular strategy helped.

Discussion Activities

- Use the questions formulated by the students in their Reader's Notebooks as the start of a discussion about these poems.
- Ask students if they found the descriptions of the special places in the poems effective. Have the poets managed to convince the students that these places are special and wonderful? Have them discuss why or why not.

Assessment Opportunities

- You can assess student comprehension of the story by evaluating the questions they formulate in their Reader's Notebooks.
- You can use one of the discussion questions as an essay question.
- You can have the students turn any one of their Reader's Notebook entries into an essay.

VIRGINIA HAMILTON

Storytelling was such a part of Virginia Hamilton's childhood that as she grew up, she "learned to think and to manage feelings in terms of stories." Many of the stories she heard as a child centered on her mother's ancestor, Levi Perry, a fugitive slave who eventually settled in the Ohio town of Yellow Springs. Virginia's fascination with her own history and culture is evident in the fiction she writes for children, but she has also written factual, historical accounts of African Americans. Her book *Many Thousand Gone: African-Americans from Slavery to Freedom* tells fascinating tales of famous and not so famous African American slaves from the beginning of slavery until the end of the Civil War.

This feature gives students an opportunity to compare, evaluate, and form opinions about two short science fiction selections. The focus of this comparison is on the settings of the stories.

Teaching Option
Because each work of science fiction is accompanied by its own introductory and response pages, teachers have the option of pairing the stories or teaching them individually. Used in conjunction with the Comparing Literature. Standardized Test Practice on page 587, the selections may also be used to help students prepare for literature-based writing assessments.

Science Fiction

You are about to read two works of short fiction that take place in the future. Each of them tells a type of story known as **science fiction**—an imaginary look at how science and technology could change people's lives in surprising ways. "The Fun They Had" predicts the way students might learn in the year 2157, while "The Sand Castle" envisions the kind of environment that people might face in the future.

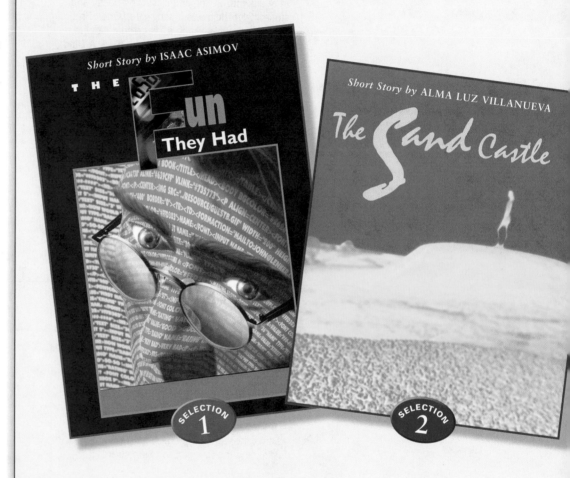

Short Story by ISAAC ASIMOV

THE
Fun
They Had

SELECTION
1

Short Story by ALMA LUZ VILLANUEVA

The *Sand* Castle

SELECTION
2

572   UNIT FOUR   PART 2: IMAGINARY WORLDS

Connect to Your Life

What Does the Future Hold?

Think of the ways that scientific advances have made your life different from the lives of your great-grandparents.

◆ How has technology affected communication?

◆ What effects have technology had on the environment?

◆ Which of these changes do you think are good ones, and which do you think are bad?

Discuss your responses with a small group of classmates.

POINTS OF COMPARISON

The most important difference between science fiction and other types of fiction is the **setting.** Science fiction is usually set in the future and often includes technology that doesn't exist today. In the pages that follow, you will compare and contrast the settings of two short works of science fiction. To help you note similarities and differences, keep these **Points of Comparison questions** in mind as you read:

◆ What is the **time** and **place** of each story?

◆ In what ways are the **settings** of the stories similar to and different from each other?

◆ How do the settings compare to our world today?

"The Fun They Had"	"The Sand Castle"
Details of Setting	**Details of Setting**
• takes place on May 17, 2157	
• set in the future	

Take notes on the settings in a **Points of Comparison diagram** like the one shown above. As you read each selection, fill in the Details of Setting columns. After you have read *both* stories, complete the Venn diagram to help you compare and contrast the settings.

Assessment Option: Comparison-and-Contrast Essay

Writing After you have read "The Fun They Had" and "The Sand Castle," you will have the option of writing a comparison-and-contrast essay. Your diagram will help you plan and write the essay.

Connect to Your Life

Students may benefit from a whole class brainstorming session, listing scientific and technological advances that have occurred in the last fifty years. Students could then use this list to respond to the questions. Allow students time to rehearse prior to meeting with their small group.

Possible Responses: Students may suggest these forms of communication: cordless telephones, cellular phones, fax machines, pagers, high speed computer modems, interactive online Web sites and chat rooms, email. Their responses should include effects of these technological advances as well as which ones they think are good or bad and why.

Points of Comparison

Students will compare the setting across both stories. Have them copy the comparison chart in their notebooks, and remind them to add details as often as they want, making sure they come back to the chart at the end of each selection.

Assessment Option: Comparison-and-Contrast Essay

Students should complete the points of comparison chart carefully, as this information will serve as the basis for their essay.

This selection is included in the **Grade 6 InterActive Reader.**

Standards-Based Objectives

1. understand and appreciate a **short story**
2. understand author's use of **setting in science fiction**
3. understand a short story better by identifying the **purposes for reading**
4. evaluate **story elements**

Summary

In this futuristic story, set in 2157, two friends learn about schools of the past. When Tommy finds an old-fashioned book, one with real pages, he and Margie eagerly read it to find out about schools of long ago. When Margie compares those schools to her room at home with a mechanical teacher and her punch code assignments, she wishes she could have attended one of those old-fashioned schools. Students may delight in the irony that the *old-fashioned* schools sound like our current day schools.

Thematic Link

One imaginary world is the world of the future. Science fiction writers, like Isaac Asimov, are experts at imagining what technologies may develop and change, and how those changes might affect society as we know it.

English Conventions Practice

Daily Language SkillBuilder

Have students **proofread** the display sentences on page 441k and write them correctly. The sentences also appear on Transparency 18 of **Language Transparencies.**

Preteaching Vocabulary

If you would like to preteach the WORDS TO KNOW for this selection, use the Explicit Instruction, page 575.

SELECTION 1

The Fun They Had

by ISAAC ASIMOV

Build Background

TECHNOLOGY

Isaac Asimov wrote "The Fun They Had" in 1951. Back then, computers were huge machines that had to be kept in refrigerated buildings. They were not user-friendly, and only a computer expert could operate them. Specialists stored information in computers by punching patterns of holes into cards or tape. (Notice that a character in the story uses this "punch code" method instead of a keyboard.) It was only after the invention of the silicon chip in the 1960s that computers became smaller, easier to use, and less expensive. In 1977, the first personal computers became available for home use.

Focus Your Reading

LITERARY ANALYSIS | **SETTING**

The time and place in which the action of a story happens is called the **setting.** In science fiction, setting is a key element. Almost all science fiction is set in the future. Many science fiction writers create settings that combine realistic details with elements of fantasy. In futuristic settings, imagined technological advances are often an important part of the landscape.

ACTIVE READING | **PURPOSES FOR READING**

People read for many different purposes. Two of the most common purposes are entertainment and understanding. Your purpose in reading "The Fun They Had" is to understand the story's setting so that you can compare it with the setting of the next selection, "The Sand Castle." Paying attention to the details of setting will help you understand how setting affects a story.

WORDS TO KNOW
Vocabulary Preview
dispute   scornful
loftily   sector
nonchalantly

READER'S NOTEBOOK As you read, keep your purpose in mind. Jot down notes to help you answer the Points of Comparison questions on page 573.

574   UNIT FOUR   PART 2: IMAGINARY WORLDS

LESSON RESOURCES

UNIT FOUR RESOURCE BOOK, pp. 51–57

ASSESSMENT
Formal Assessment, pp. 95–96
Test Generator

SKILLS TRANSPARENCIES AND COPYMASTERS
Literary Analysis
• Setting, TR 6 (pp. 576, 579)

Language
• Daily Language SkillBuilder, TR 18 (p. 574)
• Context Clues: Definition and Overview, TR 53 (p. 575)

INTEGRATED TECHNOLOGY
Audio Library

Visit our Web site:
www.mcdougallittell.com

For **systematic instruction** in language skills, see:
• **Vocabulary and Spelling Book**
• **Grammar, Usage, and Mechanics Book**
• pacing chart on p. 441i

THE **Fun** They Had

BY ISAAC ASIMOV

M argie even wrote about it that night in her diary. On the page headed May 17, 2157, she wrote, "Today Tommy found a real book!"

It was a very old book. Margie's grandfather once said that when he was a little boy, his grandfather told him that there was a time when all stories were printed on paper.

They turned the pages, which were yellow and crinkly, and it was awfully funny to read words that stood still instead of moving the way they were supposed to—on a screen, you know. And then, when they turned back to the page before, it had the same words on it that it had when they read it the first time.

Reading and Analyzing

Literary Analysis `SETTING`

A Remind students to look for details that give information about the setting in this story and to record that information in the Points of Comparison charts they began earlier. Although many aspects of the setting are different from the present, some things may be the same. Ask students which elements of the setting are similar to those of today.

Possible Responses: The children live in houses with their parents. Tommy's house has an attic.

Use **Unit Four Resource Book**, p. 53, for more practice. Use **Literary Analysis Transparencies**, p. 6, for additional support.

Active Reading
`PURPOSES FOR READING`

Remind students that they are reading this selection for information. In particular they are looking for details that describe the setting of the story. Encourage them to look for descriptions of setting as they read, and to take notes.

Use **Unit Four Resource Book**, p. 52, for more practice.

Reading Skills and Strategies: CONNECT

B Ask students to reflect on the discussion Tommy and Margie have about their teachers and to discuss how this compares with experiences they have had with their own teachers.

Possible Responses: Students should talk about the obvious difference—human versus machine—but also the class size idea, the individualized curriculum, and the process for submitting homework.

"Gee," said Tommy, "what a waste. When you're through with the book, you just throw it away, I guess. Our television screen must have had a million books on it and it's good for plenty more. I wouldn't throw it away."

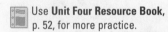

"**A** man can't know as much as a teacher."

"Same with mine," said Margie. She was eleven and hadn't seen as many telebooks[1] as Tommy had. He was thirteen.

She said, "Where did you find it?"

"In my house." He pointed without looking, because he was busy reading. "In the attic."

"What's it about?"

"School."

Margie was <u>scornful</u>. "School? What's there to write about school? I hate school." Margie always hated school, but now she hated it more than ever. The mechanical teacher[2] had been giving her test after test in geography, and she had been doing worse and worse until her mother had shaken her head sorrowfully and sent for the county inspector.

He was a round little man with a red face and a whole box of tools with dials and wires. He smiled at her and gave her an apple, then took the teacher apart. Margie had hoped he wouldn't know how to put it together again, but he knew how all right, and after an hour or so, there it was again, large and ugly, with a big screen on which all the lessons were shown and the questions were asked. That wasn't so bad. The part she hated most was the slot where she had to put homework and test papers. She always had to write them out in a punch code they made her learn when she was six years old, and the mechanical teacher calculated the mark in no time.

The inspector had smiled after he was finished and patted her head. He said to her mother, "It's not the little girl's fault, Mrs. Jones. I think the geography <u>sector</u> was geared a little too quick. Those things happen sometimes. I've slowed it up to an average ten-year level. Actually, the overall pattern of her progress is quite satisfactory." And he patted Margie's head again.

Margie was disappointed. She had been hoping they would take the teacher away altogether. They had once taken Tommy's teacher away for nearly a month because the history sector had blanked out completely.

So she said to Tommy, "Why would anyone write about school?"

---

1. **telebooks** (tĕl'ə-bŏŏks): books presented on a television screen.
2. **mechanical teacher:** a machine or computer that serves as a teacher.

WORDS TO KNOW	**scornful** (skôrn'fəl) *adj.* having an attitude of contempt; disdainful **sector** (sĕk'tər) *n.* a part or division

576

EXPLICIT INSTRUCTION ## Evaluating Story Elements

Instruction Remind students that to evaluate or critique a story means to make judgments about the story. Explain that when readers evaluate a story, they judge how well the writing measures up to their expectations or standards. Then they make specific statements that summarize their judgments. Tell students that the first step in evaluating a story is to examine the characters, setting, and plot. Say, "You should examine these elements to evaluate how realistic the characters are, whether the details of setting are accurate and believable, and whether the plot is believable." Tell students that their evaluations should be specific statements that can be supported with facts and examples.

Practice Write these questions on the board and have students write answers: How realistic are the characters? Would real people act and speak that way? Ask students to share their responses with the class.

Possible Responses: Responses will vary but should be supported by reasons.

For more practice with evaluating, use **Unit Four Resource Book**, p. 54.

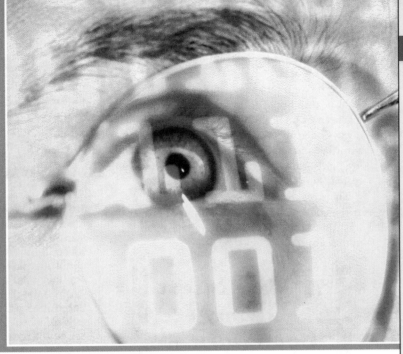

Tommy looked at her with very superior eyes, "Because it's not our kind of school, stupid. This is the old kind of school that they had hundreds and hundreds of years ago." He added <u>loftily</u>, pronouncing the word carefully, "*Centuries* ago."

Margie was hurt. "Well, I don't know what kind of school they had all that time ago." She read the book over his shoulder for a while, then said, "Anyway, they had a teacher."

"Sure they had a teacher, but it wasn't a regular teacher. It was a man."

"A man? How could a man be a teacher?"

"Well, he just told the boys and girls things and gave them homework and asked them questions."

"A man isn't smart enough."

"Sure he is. My father knows as much as my teacher."

"He can't. A man can't know as much as a teacher."

"He knows almost as much I betcha."

Margie wasn't prepared to <u>dispute</u> that. She said, "I wouldn't want a strange man in my house to teach me."

Tommy screamed with laughter. "You don't know much, Margie. The teachers didn't live in the house. They had a special building and all the kids went there."

"And all the kids learned the same thing?"

"Sure, if they were all the same age."

"But my mother says a teacher has to be adjusted to fit the mind of each boy and girl it teaches and that each kid has to be taught differently."

"Just the same, they didn't do it that way then. If you don't like it, you don't have to read the book."

"I didn't say I didn't like it," Margie said quickly. She wanted to read about those funny schools.

They weren't even half finished when Margie's mother called, "Margie! School!"

Margie looked up. "Not yet, Mamma."

"Now," said Mrs. Jones. "And it's probably time for Tommy, too."

Margie said to Tommy, "Can I read the book some more with you after school?"

"Maybe," he said, <u>nonchalantly</u>. He walked

B

WORDS TO KNOW	**loftily** (lôf'tĭ-lē) *adv.* in a grand or pompous way
	dispute (dĭ-spyōōt') *v.* to argue about; debate
	nonchalantly (nŏn'shə-länt'lē) *adv.* in a casual, unconcerned way

577

away whistling, the dusty old book tucked beneath his arm.

Margie went into the schoolroom. It was right next to her bedroom, and the mechanical teacher was on and waiting for her. It was always on at the same time every day except Saturday and Sunday, because her mother said little girls learned better if they learned at regular hours.

The screen was lit up, and it said: "Today's arithmetic lesson is on the addition of proper fractions. Please insert yesterday's homework in the proper slot."

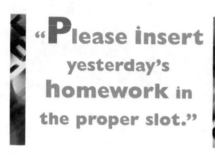

> "Please insert yesterday's homework in the proper slot."

Margie did so with a sigh. She was thinking about the old schools they had when her grandfather's grandfather was a little boy. All the kids from the whole neighborhood came, laughing and shouting in the schoolyard, sitting together in the schoolroom, going home together at the end of the day. They learned the same things so they could help one another on the homework and talk about it.

And the teachers were people. . . .

The mechanical teacher was flashing on the screen: "When we add the fractions $\frac{1}{2}$ and $\frac{1}{4}$—"

Margie was thinking about how the kids must have loved it in the old days. She was thinking about the fun they had. ❖

Isaac Asimov
1920–1992

"I do not fear computers. I fear the lack of them."

The Hardest-Working Writer The *New York Times* once called Isaac Asimov a "writing machine." Over his lifetime this acclaimed science fiction author wrote or edited more than 470 books—more than any other American writer. Asimov was born in Russia. When he was three years old he came to the United States with his parents. When he grew older he received an advanced science degree and served as a professor of biochemistry for several years before becoming a full-time writer at the age of 38.

A Little Story About School In the first volume of his autobiography, Asimov explains how he came to write "The Fun They Had." A friend had asked him to write a story for young readers. "I thought about it and decided to write a little story about school," Asimov says. "What could interest children more? It would be about a school of the future, by way of teaching machines, with children longing for the good old days when there were old-fashioned schools that children loved. I thought the kids would get a bang out of the irony."

Connect to the Literature

1. What Do You Think?
What was your reaction to the end of the story?

Think Critically

2. [ACTIVE READING | PURPOSES FOR READING]
Share the notes that you made in your **READER'S NOTEBOOK** with a classmate. Discuss how the author shows the reader that the setting is important.

3. What If? If Margie were to visit a school like yours, what might be her reaction? Do you think she would like it as much as she thinks she would in the story? Explain your answer.

4. Connect to Life Think of the tasks for which you use a computer. Make a list of these activities. With the class, share your opinions about the advantages and disadvantages of using computers for these purposes.

Comprehension Check
• What made Tommy think the book was "a waste"?
• Why did Margie do badly in geography?
• Where was Margie's "schoolroom"?

Literary Analysis

[SETTING] The world that Isaac Asimov presents in "The Fun They Had" is very different from our own. Imagine what it would be like to be taught by a mechanical teacher, the way Margie is, instead of by a human teacher. Although there are many differences between Asimov's earth in 2157 and our world today, there are also many similarities. For example, in the future, children still have homework (although they must write it in punch code) and they still complain about it.

POINTS OF COMPARISON

Fill in the Details of Setting column for "The Fun They Had" in your Points of Comparison diagram. Several details are already listed for you.

Paired Activity Share the notes you made in your **READER'S NOTEBOOK** with a classmate. Together, discuss which details of the setting indicate that you are reading a science fiction story. In what ways might the setting be different if the story were not science fiction?

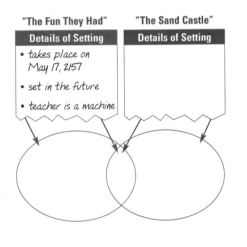

"The Fun They Had"
Details of Setting
• takes place on May 17, 2157
• set in the future
• teacher is a machine

"The Sand Castle"
Details of Setting

Connect to the Literature

1. What Do You Think?
Accept all reasonable answers.

Comprehension Check
• Tommy thought the book was a waste because it could only tell one story as opposed to a computer, which can contain many books.
• Margie did poorly in geography because the geography sector of her mechanical teacher was set to a level too advanced for Margie.
• Margie's schoolroom was in her house, in the room next to her bedroom.

 Use Selection Quiz
Unit Four Resource Book, p. 57.

Think Critically

2. Possible Responses: Students should discuss the futuristic setting, using specific examples drawn from the story.

3. What If? Answers will vary, but should be supported by evidence from the story.

4. Connect to Life Students may wish to make a graphic organizer to keep track of the pros and cons they come up with.

Literary Analysis

Setting Ask students to discuss with a partner some of the similarities and differences found between the setting of Asimov's story and the world today. Students can use this discussion to help them complete the Points of Comparison activity.

 Use **Literary Analysis Transparencies**, p. 6, for additional support.

Points of Comparison

Ask students to refer to the diagram they drew at the beginning of the selection. Ask them to fill in the details about the setting in this story. Remind them to draw on the information discussed with a partner earlier.

The Sand Castle

by ALMA LUZ VILLANUEVA

Build Background

SCIENCE

In recent decades, many scientists have been concerned that the earth could be in danger from the sun's rays, due to a thinning of the ozone layer. Ozone is a form of oxygen high up in the atmosphere that normally absorbs harmful ultraviolet rays from the sun before they reach the earth. Chemicals called CFCs—used in air conditioners, aerosol sprays, and other products—may have eaten away at the ozone layer, allowing an increase in harmful ultraviolet radiation at the earth's surface. The long-term effects of ozone depletion could be deadly for marine life, birds, and even people.

Focus Your Reading

LITERARY ANALYSIS SETTING

Almost all science fiction is set in the future, but writers often focus on different aspects of life in the future. In "The Fun They Had," Isaac Asimov focuses on how changes in technology affect people's lives. Ray Bradbury's "All Summer in a Day" (page 209) is an example of science fiction that emphasizes the impact of environment—in this case, the weather on Venus—on people. As you read "The Sand Castle," consider how both technology and environment affect the characters.

ACTIVE READING PURPOSES FOR READING

Your purpose for reading "The Sand Castle" is to understand the story's setting so that you can **compare and contrast** it with the setting of "The Fun They Had." You can understand the setting and how it affects a story by paying attention to details of setting.

WORDS TO KNOW
Vocabulary Preview
cumbersome   listlessly
forlorn   ultraviolet
hostile

READER'S NOTEBOOK As you read, refer to the Points of Comparison questions on page 573. Note the details of setting in this story.

LESSON RESOURCES

The Sand Castle

by Alma Luz Villanueva

"**H**AVE YOU DRESSED YET?" their grandmother called. "Once a month in the sun and they must almost be forced," she muttered. "Well, poor things, they've forgotten the warmth of the sun on their little bodies, what it is to play in the sea, yes. . . ." Mrs. Pavloff reached for her protective sun goggles that covered most of her face. It screened all <u>ultraviolet</u> light from the once life-giving sun; now, it, the sun, scorched the Earth, killing whatever it touched. The sea, the continents, had changed. The weather, as they'd called it in the last century, was entirely predictable now: warming.

Mrs. Pavloff slipped on the thick, metallic gloves, listening to her grandchildren squabble and she heard her mother's voice calling her, "Masha, put your bathing suit under your clothes. It's so much easier that way without having to go to the bathhouse first. Hurry! Father's waiting!" She remembered the ride to the sea, the silence when the first shimmers of water became visible. Her father had always been first into the chilly water. "Good for the health!" he'd yell as he dove into it, swimming as far as he could, then back. Then he'd lie exhausted

WORDS
TO   **ultraviolet** (ŭl′trə-vī′ə-lĭt) *adj.* consisting of invisible radiation wavelengths
KNOW

Less Proficient Readers
Tell students that the author is using a literary device called *flashback* in this story. Help them to see that the story is taking place with Masha (Mrs. Pavloff) and her grandchildren as they prepare for a trip to the beach. However, Masha is *flashing back* to her own childhood when her mother and father took her to the beach.

Set a Purpose Ask students to read to find out what happens to Mrs. Pavloff and her grandchildren.

English Learners
Give students extra help with the technical and scientific terms in this selection.

 Use **Spanish Study Guide,** pp. 118–120, for additional support.

Advanced Students
Ask students to think of a trip they've taken with their family, to the beach or somewhere else. Ask them to rehearse telling the story of that trip with a partner. Encourage them to recall specific details of the trip, and to add them to their stories. Remind students that making connections to their own lives can help them understand the stories they read.

EXPLICIT INSTRUCTION **Preteaching Vocabulary**

WORDS TO KNOW
Remind students that many words we use are actually made up of other words, called *root* or **base words,** and **affixes** (prefixes and suffixes).

Teaching Strategy Write the following word on the chalkboard, and ask students to look at it to see if they can recognize its parts:

ineffective

Help them to see a prefix (*in-*), a base word (*effect*), and a suffix (*-ive*). Tell them they can use the meanings of each part to help figure

out the entire word. In this example, *in-* means "not," so *ineffective* means "not effective." If students need further help, suggest they look up the meanings of *effect* and *-ive,* or of *effective.*

Practice Ask students to locate the WORDS TO KNOW and to break each word into its parts and give a definition. Students may need to use a dictionary if some of the parts are unfamiliar. Then have them write each word in a sentence.

 Use **Unit Four Resource Book,** p. 63, for more practice.

For **systematic instruction** in vocabulary, see:
• **Vocabulary and Spelling Book**
• pacing chart on p. 441i

Reading and Analyzing

Literary Analysis `SETTING`

Tell students that there are actually two settings described here, one in the present time, and one in Mrs. Pavloff's memories. Ask them to compare and contrast the two settings, perhaps by making a two-column chart.

Possible Responses: The current setting is hot, barren, and unsafe to go outside without protection. Most people go out only at night, so it is usually dark when they see the outside. In Masha's memories the sun is warm, the sea is refreshing, and people walk outside during the day without protective clothing.

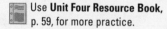
Use **Unit Four Resource Book**, p. 60, for more practice.
Use **Literary Analysis Transparencies**, p. 6, for additional support.

Active Reading
`PURPOSES FOR READING`

Remind students that they are reading for information. Encourage them to pay attention to the details of the setting so they can compare and contrast them with the setting of "The Fun They Had."

Use **Unit Four Resource Book**, p. 59, for more practice.

on the sand, stretched to the sun. Such happiness to be warmed by the sun.

Then the picnic. She could hear her mother's voice, "Stay to your knees, Masha! Only to your knees!" To herself: "She'd be a mermaid if I didn't watch," and she'd laugh. Masha would lie belly down, facing the sea, and let the last of the waves roll over her. She hadn't even been aware of the sun, only that she'd been warm or, if a cloud covered it, cold. It was always there, the sun: its light, its warmth. But the sea—they travelled to it. So, she'd given all of her attention to the beautiful sea.

She saw her father kneeling next to her, building the sand castle they always built when they went to the sea. Her job was to find seashells, bird feathers, and strips of seaweed to decorate it. How proud she'd felt as she placed her seashells where she chose, where they seemed most beautiful. Only then was the sand castle complete. She heard her father's voice, "The Princess's castle is ready, now, for her Prince! Come and look, Anna! What do you think?" She saw herself beaming with pride, and she heard her mother's laugh. "Fit for a queen, I'd say! Can I live in your castle, too, Masha? Please, Princess Masha?" "Of course, Mother! You can live with me always. . . ." She remembered her mother's laughing face, her auburn hair lit up by the sun, making her look bright and beautiful.

The sun, the sun, the sun. The scientists were saying that with the remedies they were employing now and the remedies begun twenty years ago—they'd stopped all nuclear testing[1] and all manufacturing of ozone-depleting[2] chemicals was banned worldwide—the scientists were saying that the sun, the global problem, would begin to get better. Perhaps for her grandchildren's children. Perhaps they would feel the sun on their unprotected bodies.

Perhaps they would feel the delicious warmth of the sun.

All vehicles were solar powered. The populations took buses when they needed transportation and people emerged mainly at night. So, most human activity was conducted after the sun was gone from the sky. Those who emerged during the day wore protective clothing. Everything was built to screen the sun's light. Sometimes she missed the natural light of her childhood streaming through the windows so intensely the urge to just run outside would overtake her. She missed the birds, the wild birds.

But today, they were going out, outside in the daytime, when the sun was still in the sky. Masha knew they were squabbling because they hated to dress up to go outside. The clothing, the gloves, the goggles, were uncomfortable and <u>cumbersome</u>. She sighed,

---

1. **nuclear testing:** experimental explosions of nuclear bombs.
2. **ozone-depleting** (ō′zōn′ dĭ-plē′tĭng) **chemicals:** substances that can damage the atmosphere's ozone layer, which helps to protect living things from the harmful ultraviolet radiation in sunlight.

WORDS TO KNOW   **cumbersome** (kŭm′bər-səm) *adj.* uncomfortably heavy or bulky

582

EXPLICIT INSTRUCTION **Understanding Fiction**

Instruction Tell students that literature comes in many different varieties. Write the following terms on the board: *science fiction, fantasy, realistic fiction.* Ask students to name characteristics of each type of fiction. Note students' ideas next to each term. Use the following chart to help you discuss these types of fiction.

Types of Fiction			
	Fantasy	**Realistic F.**	**Science F.**
Characters	Characters may be imaginary creatures	Characters are modern people	Characters are usually realistic
Setting	May be imaginary	Modern world as we know it	Futuristic or space settings
Plot	A series of fantastic or impossible events	Modern problems solved through human abilities	Problems based on real or possible science and technology

Practice Ask students to name and describe stories they have read that are examples of these types of fiction.
Possible Responses: Responses will vary.

Use **Unit Four Resource Book**, p. 61, for more practice.

tears coming to her eyes. Well, they're coming, Masha decided. They can remove their goggles and gloves on the bus.

The sea was closer now and the bus ride was comfortable within the temperature controlled interior. Those with memories of the sea signed up, bringing grandchildren, children, friends, or just went alone. Masha had taken her grandchildren before, but they'd sat on the sand, listlessly, sifting it through their gloved hands with bored little faces. She'd tried to interest them in the sea with stories of her father's swimming in it as far as he could. But they couldn't touch it, so it, the sea, didn't seem real to them. What was it: a mass of undrinkable, hostile water. Hostile like the sun. They'd taken no delight, no pleasure, in their journey to the sea.

But today, yes, today we will build a sand castle. Masha smiled at her secret. She'd packed everything late last night to surprise them at the sea.

Why haven't I thought of it before? Masha asked herself, and then she remembered the dream, months ago, of building a sand castle with her father at the sea. It made her want to weep because she'd forgotten. She'd actually forgotten one of the most joyful times of her girlhood. When the sea was still alive with life.

Today we build a sand castle.

They trudged on the thick, dense sand toward the hiss of pale blue. Only the older people picked up their step, excited by the smell of salt in the air. Masha's grandchildren knew they'd be here for two hours and then trudge all the way back to the bus. The darkened goggles made the sunlight bearable. They hated this forlorn place where the sun had obviously drained the life out of everything. They were too young to express it, but they felt it as they walked, with bored effort, beside their grandmother.

"We're going to build a sand castle today— what do you think of that?" Masha beamed, squinting to see their faces.

"What's a sand castle?" the boy mumbled.

"You'll see, I'll show you. . . ."

"Is it fun Grandmama?" the girl smiled, taking her grandmother's hand.

"Yes, it's so much fun. I've brought different sized containers to mold the sand, and, oh, you'll see!"

The boy gave an awkward skip and nearly shouted, "Show us, Grandmama, show us what you mean!"

Masha laughed, sounding almost like a girl. "We're almost there, yes, we're almost there!"

The first circle of sandy shapes was complete, and the children were so excited by what they were building they forgot about their protective gloves.

"Now, we'll put a pile of wet sand in the middle and build it up with our hands and then we'll do another circle, yes, children?"

The children rushed back and forth from the tide line carrying the dark, wet sand. They only had an hour left. Their eyes, beneath the goggles, darted with excitement.

"Just don't get your gloves in the water, a little wet sand won't hurt, don't worry, children. When I was a girl there were so many birds at the sea we'd scare them off because they'd try to steal our food. Seagulls, they were, big white birds that liked to scream at the sea, they sounded like eagles to me. . . ."

WORDS TO KNOW	**listlessly** (lĭst′lĭs-lē) *adv.* without energy or interest; sluggishly
	hostile (hŏs′təl) *adj.* unfavorable to health or well-being; dangerous
	forlorn (fər-lôrn′) *adj.* miserable and lonely; desolate

583

Cross Curricular Link Science

EFFECTS OF THE SUN'S RAYS It seems we all like to work or play in the warm sunshine, but are we actually harming ourselves by doing so? Scientists are becoming increasingly concerned that we are. How did this happen? The sun's rays have always been dangerous for humans, but most of the sun's rays never reached us. The ozone in the earth's atmosphere filters most of the sun's ultraviolet rays, but in recent years, the ozone layer has eroded, and more dangerous rays are getting to earth. There are several reasons why the ozone is being depleted, but one major cause is the common use of certain chemicals, such as those in air conditioners, refrigerators, and aerosol sprays. Since 1987, leaders from over 160 countries have signed a treaty banning ozone depleting substances. The Environmental Protection Agency (EPA) works to enforce the bans in the United States. The EPA also educates people on the link between ultraviolet radiation and skin cancer, and promotes the following action steps: avoid midday sun; seek shade; wear SPF 15 or higher sunblock, a hat, full-length clothing, and 99–100% UV blocking glasses.

Reading Skills and Strategies
EVALUATE

Ask students to think about Mrs. Pavloff and her reasons for taking her grandchildren to the beach to build a sand castle. Ask students to evaluate her actions by discussing these questions. Do they agree or disagree with her? Why? Would they do the same in her place?

Possible Responses: Students may agree or disagree with Masha's decision. In either case they should be able to support their choices and to put themselves in a similar situation.

Literary Analysis:
AUTHOR'S PURPOSE

Many authors write stories to teach their readers something, or to cause them to think about issues and ideas. Ask students to discuss what purpose the author, Alma Luz Villanueva, may have had in writing this story.

Possible Response: She may have written this story so we would all think about what might happen to the earth if we don't stop depleting the ozone layer.

Author Activity

Allow students time to practice reciting the poems. They may want to do some of the poems with a partner, in a choral reading.

"You used to eat at the sea, Grandmama?" the girl asked incredulously.

"We used to call them picnics. . . ."

"What are eagles, Grandmama?" the boy wanted to know, shaping the dark sand with his gloved hands.

"They used to be one of the largest, most beautiful wild birds in the world. My grandfather pointed them out to me once. . . ." Until that moment, she'd forgotten that memory of nearly sixty years ago. They'd gone on a train, then a bus, to the village where he'd been born. She remembered her grandfather looking up toward a shrill, piercing cry that seemed to come from the sky. She'd seen the tears in her grandfather's eyes and on his cheeks. He'd pointed up to a large, dark flying-thing in the summer blue sky: "That's an eagle, my girl, the spirit of the people."

Sadness overtook Masha, but she refused to acknowledge its presence. The sand castle, Masha told herself sternly—the sand castle is what is important now. "I've brought a wonderful surprise, something to decorate the castle with when we're through building it."

"Show us Grandmama, please?"

"Yes, please, please show us now!"

Masha sighed with a terrible, sudden happiness as she brought out the plastic bag. Quickly, she removed each precious seashell from its protective cotton: eight perfect shells from all over the world.

"But grandmama, these are your special shells! You said the sea doesn't make them anymore. . . ."

"It will, Anna, it will." Masha hugged her granddaughter and made her voice brighten with laughter. "Today we will decorate our sand castle with the most beautiful shells in the world, yes!" ❖

Alma Luz Villanueva
born 1944

"Writing takes all your courage. . . ."

Villanueva's Themes Alma Luz Villanueva is a Mexican-American writer known for both her poetry and her prose. Two aspects of Villanueva's life have had a strong influence on her writing. One was her Mexican grandmother, with whom she lived until she was 11 years old and who taught her many stories and poems. The other was a stay in the Sierra Nevada mountains. Both of these influences—the role women play in passing along tradition, and the importance of our environment—are key themes in the story you have just read.

Poetry and Prose Villanueva grew up in the Mission district of San Francisco. After her grandmother died, she lived as an adolescent with her young mother and an aunt. In the late 1960s, Villanueva began writing poetry based largely on her childhood experiences. She has published a number of poetry books, novels, and a collection of short stories, from which this selection was taken.

AUTHOR ACTIVITY
Poem Search Go to the library and choose a book of poetry by the author. Select your favorite poem and share it with a group.

EXPLICIT INSTRUCTION ## Forms of Fiction

Instruction Draw a Venn diagram on the board with the following three labels: short story, novel, both. Remind students that novel and short story are two forms of fiction. Ask students to name characteristics that are shared by these two forms and record them in the middle section of the Venn diagram. *(Both contain elements of setting, character, plot, and theme.)* Next, ask students to name characteristics that are unique to each form. Record these in the appropriate sections of the diagram.

(Novel—longer than a short story; more complex; elements of setting, character, conflict, and plot are developed in greater detail; Short story—short enough to be read in one sitting; usually tells about one main conflict, one main character, and one set of events)

Practice Say, "Imagine this short story is a 200-page novel. What new information would the author include in a novel that she couldn't include in a short story?" Have partners choose a character, setting detail, or story event from

"The Sand Castle." Then have them work together to brainstorm how their story element would be developed in a novel. To help students get started, ask, "What more would you learn about the character, setting detail, or event?"

Possible Responses: Responses will vary.

Use **Unit Four Resource Book,** p. 61, for more practice.

THINKING through the LITERATURE

Connect to the Literature

1. What Do You Think?
Did you enjoy "The Sand Castle" more or less than "The Fun They Had"? Explain.

Comprehension Check
- Why do the characters need to wear protective clothing to go outside during the day?
- Where does Mrs. Pavloff take her grandchildren?
- What are Mrs. Pavloff and her grandchildren going to use to decorate their sand castle?

Think Critically

2. ACTIVE READING PURPOSES FOR READING
Did you find any clues that suggest how far into the future this story might be set? What about place? How do time and place compare between these two stories?

3. Connect to Life In what ways might your own grandparents' memories of sunning at the beach or just spending time outside be different from your experiences?

Literary Analysis

SETTING A science fiction writer's descriptions of the future often contain a message, or even a warning, about what the future might hold. Science fiction writers like to speculate, or guess, about how changes in technology or the environment might affect people. Sometimes the effects they envision are produced by people's actions today. In "The Sand Castle," Alma Luz Villanueva describes how damage to the earth's ozone layer affects the environment, and how the resulting environmental changes might affect people in the future.

POINTS OF COMPARISON

Fill in the Details of Setting column for "The Sand Castle" in your Points of Comparison diagram. Remember to consider the time and place of the story, and how it is similar to and different from our world today. Then fill in the Venn diagram for the two stories. In the center, write what the settings of the stories have in common. Then write details of the settings that are unique to one selection or the other in the spaces on either side.

Paired Activity With a partner, discuss the ways in which the setting of "The Sand Castle" is different from the world you know. Does the setting of "The Sand Castle" seem more or less unusual than the setting of "The Fun They Had"? Why?

"The Fun They Had"
Details of Setting
- takes place on May 17, 2157
- set in the future
- teacher is a machine
- set on earth

"The Sand Castle"
Details of Setting
- takes place two generations in the future
- set on earth
- sun is dangerous to people

Venn diagram:
- May 17, 2157 / machine for a teacher
- future earth
- two generations into the future / sun is dangerous

THE SAND CASTLE **585**

Points of Comparison

Ask students to complete the chart with the details about the setting in "The Sand Castle." Remind them to fill in the center of the Venn diagram with those elements of the setting that are common to both stories.

Connect to the Literature

1. What Do You Think?
Accept all reasonable responses.

Comprehension Check
- There is too much ultraviolet light in the sunlight that reaches the earth, and people have to wear protective gear so that they aren't harmed by it.
- Mrs. Pavloff takes her grandchildren to the beach.
- Mrs. Pavloff and her grandchildren will decorate their sand castle with her special seashells.

Use Selection Quiz
Unit Four Resource Book, p. 64.

Think Critically

2. Possible Response: Mrs. Pavloff's memories of her childhood (going to the shore, taking trains and busses, seeing birds) seem a lot like my childhood today, so this story could be set about two generations into the future.

3. Possible Response: My grandparents didn't use sunscreen or worry too much about getting sunburned because they didn't know that the sun could be bad for you. Also sun exposure was less dangerous then, when the ozone layer was thicker. "The Fun They Had" is set in the future, on a particular day and year. The setting details are focused on changes in the way students read and learn. "The Sand Castle" is also set in the future, but we don't know exactly when. The environment is damaged. In both stories, the young characters seem to think the past is silly or less efficient than the present.

Literary Analysis

Setting Provide students with time to meet with partners and discuss the questions posed in the paired activity. It might be helpful for them to consult their Reader's Notebook.

Use **Literary Analysis Transparencies**, p. 6, for additional support.

THE SAND CASTLE **585**

Writing

Futuristic Setting Description Encourage students to revisit their comparison charts of the settings in these two stories. They may be able to draw on some of the ideas presented there.

 Use **Writing Transparencies**, p. 22, for additional support.

Speaking & Listening

Technology Interview Encourage students to write their questions prior to conducting the interviews. It would be appropriate to develop the questions as a whole class activity, and each pair could then individualize the list of questions for their own interview.

 Use the **Speaking and Listening Book**, p. 35, for additional support.

Research & Technology

Future Perfect The school librarian or media specialist may be able to recommend some older science fiction titles that would be appropriate.

Writing

Futuristic Setting Description If you were to write a science fiction story with a strong message, what would the setting be like? Imagine and write a description of a futuristic setting. Consider the time and place and how this futuristic world is different from our world today. How do changes in technology or the environment affect your setting? Place the description in your **Working Portfolio.**

Writing Handbook
See p. R38: Using Language Effectively.

Speaking & Listening

Technology Interview With a partner, plan and conduct an interview with an older relative or friend to learn about technology in the past. Before the interview, create a list of questions to ask. Your questions might focus on changes in technology that have occurred in his or her lifetime, changes in the ways people communicate, or changes in the environment. Use the information you gather to create a Venn diagram that compares past and present technology. Share your diagram and your interview notes with the class.

Speaking and Listening Handbook
See p. R105: Conducting Interviews.

Research & Technology

Future Perfect Research old science fiction stories for descriptions of the future. You might want to find an anthology of science fiction stories in the library. Choose two stories from the anthology to read. Then set up a chart like the one shown here to keep track of the descriptions you find and whether or not they are accurate today.

Story Name and Description	Today's Reality

Reading for INFORMATION
Read "Home on an Icy Planet" on pages 588–591 before filling in your chart of descriptions.

586   UNIT FOUR   PART 2: IMAGINARY WORLDS

586   UNIT FOUR   PART 2

Standardized Test Practice

Comparing Literature

PART 1 Reading the Prompt

On tests you are often asked to respond to a writing prompt like the one below. A writing prompt gives you a topic for an essay and often explains how to focus your writing. When you come across a writing prompt, first read the entire prompt carefully. Then read it again, looking for key words that can help you identify the purpose of the essay.

> **Write a Comparison-and-Contrast Essay**
>
> "The Fun They Had" and "The Sand Castle" both present visions of what the future might be like. In an essay, <u>compare and contrast</u> the settings of the two stories. Use examples from the stories to support your points. Conclude your essay by explaining <u>which setting you think is more frightening and why.</u> **❶** **❷** **❸**

> **STRATEGIES**
> IN ACTION
>
> **❶** I have to **compare and contrast** the settings of two stories about the future.
>
> **❷** I need to use **examples** from the stories.
>
> **❸** I have to tell **which future** I think is scarier, and why.

PART 2 Planning a Comparison-and-Contrast Essay

- Review the Points of Comparison questions on page 573.
- Use your Points of Comparison diagram to find examples of similarities and differences in the two stories' settings.

- Create an outline with headings for "Introduction," "Body," and "Conclusion."

> I. Introduction
> II. Body
>   A. Time
>   1. "The Fun They Had": 2157
>   2. "The Sand Castle": two generations into the future
>   B.
>   C.
> III. Conclusion

PART 3 Drafting Your Essay

Introduction Clearly state your essay's purpose—to compare and contrast two science fiction settings. Briefly describe your understanding of a science fiction setting.

Body Decide how to organize your essay. One way is to use a separate paragraph to discuss each aspect of setting (time, place, what is similar to today's world, what is different from today's world). Start each paragraph with a topic sentence. Include examples from the stories. As you write, refer to your Points of Comparison diagram.

Conclusion Your conclusion should be your most lasting idea, such as which future you find more frightening.

Revising Reread your essay to make certain that it is free of mistakes. Check to make sure that your ideas are clear and well-organized and that the reader always knows which story you are discussing.

Writing Handbook

See p. R43: Compare and Contrast.

PART 1 Reading the Prompt

Model the process of reading a prompt.

- Read through the prompt in its entirety.
- Point out key words of the assignment (*compare, contrast, settings, examples, frightening*)
- Clarify the key words using the Strategies in Action to show how students can restate the prompts in their own words.

PART 2 Planning a Comparison-and-Contrast Essay

- Students can use the charts referenced on pages 573, 579, and 585.
- Have students use the outline on this page as a model for their own outline.
- Students may wish to fill in the outline with details about the setting of one story and then the other story, using the information from their Venn diagrams.

> Use **Unit Four Resource Book,** p. 65, for more practice. Use **Writing Transparencies,** p. 54, for additional support.

PART 3 Drafting Your Essay

Introduction Students should include the titles of the two selections they are comparing. They should also clearly explain that they will be comparing the two stories to each other, as well as to today's world.

Body Another way to organize would be to discuss all the elements of one story in one paragraph, all the elements of the other story in the next paragraph, and then write two more paragraphs comparing each story to today's world.

Conclusion Encourage students to not only tell which setting was more frightening, but to tell why. This will create a more powerful essay.

Revising Have students check each paragraph in the body for strong topic sentences. A strong topic sentence will help them to maintain their organization and will make the order of their comparison clear.

> Use **Writing Transparencies,** pp. 28–29, for additional support.

Standards-Based Objectives

- read and analyze a magazine article
- understand how main idea and supporting details are presented
- use the skills of note taking, paraphrasing, summarizing, and outlining
- learn about how some students have connected their own ideas and their school studies to create a realistic project

Connecting to the Literature

An article such as "Home on an Icy Planet" can help students make connections to stories such as "The Sand Castle" and "The Fun They Had." As students read, ask them to think about how the students in this article took ideas from science and from their imaginations and turned them into a realistic model.

LESSON RESOURCES

UNIT FOUR RESOURCE BOOK, pp. 66-67

SKILLS TRANSPARENCIES AND COPYMASTERS

Reading and Critical Thinking
- Note Taking, TR 46 (p. 591)

Writing
- Note Taking, TR 49 (p. 591)
- Using an Outline, TR 54 (p. 591)

Source: *Time for Kids*

HOME on an Icy Planet

From left to right, engineer Craig Smith, Adam Patinkin, Brian Freedman, alternate Dan Dresner, Matt Keenan, and teacher Barbara Janes with the winning model.

588 UNIT FOUR PART 2: IMAGINARY WORLDS

EXPLICIT INSTRUCTION Taking Notes

Instruction Explain that taking notes on articles and books will help students remember the important ideas they read. Taking notes can also help students prepare for tests and conduct research. Ask volunteers to explain how they take notes. How do they make sure they will understand their notes later? Tell students that in order to take notes, they need to identify main ideas and supporting details. Ask volunteers to explain how to do this.

Practice Have students read and complete the numbered activities on pupil page 589.

Possible Responses: See the side column on page 589 in the teacher's edition for responses to the activities on the pupil pages.

Kids design a winning city for the future

①
②
    It all began with a frozen planet named Hoth in the movie *The Empire Strikes Back*. What a cool place for a human colony! Four seventh-grade boys from Central School in Illinois decided to design a city on such a planet. Their city, Seolforis (See-*ol*-for-ees), won the $5,000 prize in the Future City Competition in Washington, D.C. The contest is held each February during National Engineers Week.

    "The biggest challenge was balancing the atmosphere so that the ice wouldn't melt," says Adam Patinkin, 13. The boys decided to build the city near geothermal vents—deep cracks that let heat escape from a planet's hot core. The surface there would be warmest and most livable.

    The boys built a model with plastic cups, boxes and Petri dishes. They could not spend more than $100.

    Matt Keenan, 12, explains that humans would have come to Seolforis (early English for "silver ice") to mine rich pockets of silver. He planned the mines and a hydroponics system—a way to grow plants with water and nutrients but no soil.

Reading for Information

As a student, you often need to find the important ideas in a text and write them down. You may need to do this when you are conducting research for a report or when you are preparing for a test. Two methods you can use to record and understand important information in a text are **taking notes** and **outlining.**

Taking Notes and Outlining Ideas
When you take notes about an article, you find the important information and record it in a form that's easier to understand and remember. You can write your notes in whole sentences, phrases, or key words. Just make sure you will be able to understand your notes when you read them later.

    To take notes, you need to first read the entire article. Then go back and find **main ideas** and **supporting details** in the individual paragraphs.

YOUR TURN *Use the questions and activities below to help you take notes on this article.*

① The main idea of a paragraph may be stated or unstated. If a main idea is unstated, use all the details in the paragraph to determine the main idea. Then write a sentence in your own words that tells the main idea. What is the main idea of the first paragraph?

② What important details in this paragraph support the main idea? Write down these details under the main idea. Indent each supporting detail so you won't confuse it with the main idea. Remember to write down only the most important information. Continue to take notes on the rest of the article. Your notes should look like the example below.

> *The boys had to plan for the planet's atmosphere.*
>
> *—built the city near cracks that let heat escape from planet's core*
>
> *—built city on planet's surface because it would be warmer and more livable*

Reading for Information

Tell students that this magazine article appeared in *Time for Kids*. As they read through the article, have them use the material in the right hand column as a guide to reading. The following are possible responses to the three numbered activities.

1. Remind students that the main idea should be a simple sentence that tells what most of the sentences in the paragraph are about.
Possible Response: Four seventh grade boys won the Future City competition.

2. Encourage students to list several supporting details for the main idea.
Possible Response: Details might include the inspiration for the project, its name (Seolforis), the prize the boys won, and information about where and when the contest was held.

Students' notes will vary but should include main ideas and details noted in a way that distinguishes them. Students' notes should make sense to them.

EXPLICIT INSTRUCTION **Outlining Ideas**

Instruction Tell students that the organization and main points of an article will become clear when they outline an article. Introduce outlining to the class as a more formal organization of their notes. Draw the following diagram on the board:

I. (main topic or idea)
    A. (supporting detail)
    B. (supporting detail)
        1. (less important detail)

Then say, "To outline, find the main ideas or topics and label each main topic with a roman numeral. Under the main topic, indent and label subtopics or supporting details with capital letters. Under supporting details, indent and label less important but useful details with numbers."

Practice Have students read and complete the activity labeled "Outlining" on pupil page 591.

Possible Responses: See the side column on page 591 of the teacher's edition for responses to the outlining activity on the pupil page.

 Use **Unit Four Resource Book**, p. 66, for additional practice.

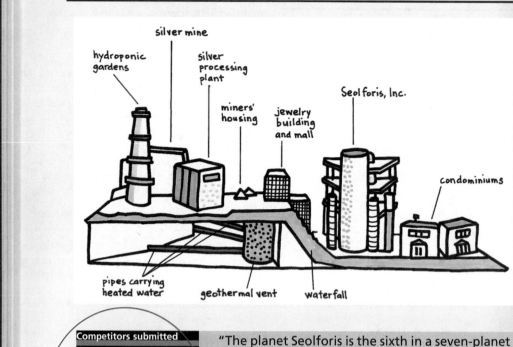

silver mine

hydroponic gardens

silver processing plant

miners' housing

jewelry building and mall

Seolforis, Inc.

condominiums

pipes carrying heated water

geothermal vent

waterfall

Competitors submitted diagrams, like the one above, and essays describing their future cities. Here's an excerpt from Matthew Ryan Keenan's essay, "Seolforis."

"The planet Seolforis is the sixth in a seven-planet system. Since it is a barren world with a three-mile thick layer of ice, the first colonists of the city Seolforis faced two major problems. First, where could they get fresh fruit and vegetables? Second, how could they utilize the planet's geothermal resources? Engineers found the answers in hydroponics, the science of growing plants without soil, and in using geothermal steam to heat buildings and create energy. Drawing on past experiences, the engineers designed hydroponic systems, and the geothermal pipe networks that provide heat for the planet's buildings."

Preparing Applications

Instruction Tell students that the boys who entered and won the Future City Contest had to fill out an application for the contest first. Ask volunteers to identify situations that require applications to be filled out. Jot responses on the board. *(library membership, summer recreation/swimming program membership, forms for school activities and sports teams)* Next, ask students what steps they should take to make sure they fill out

applications accurately and completely. Review the steps for completing an application on page R18 of the Reading Handbook (located in the back of this book).
Practice Distribute page 64 of the **Unit Four Resource Book,** which provides an application for students to fill in.
Possible Responses: The application includes sections for students to fill in and sections that should be completed by others. Students'

responses will vary, but they should recognize and circle areas that are to be filled in by someone else—a parents or another adult.

 Unit **Four Resource Book,** p. 67.

Brian Freedman, 13, was the city planner who made sure Seolforis would have everything its people might need, including education, jobs, recycling, food and lots of fun.

"Where we come from, a really small town, there isn't anything to do within 20 miles," says Brian, who built the city model with Dan Dresner. Lucky citizens could watch the Seolforis Miners play baseball on climate-controlled Koufax Field. They could also check out 3-D holographic movies.

Science teacher Barbara Janes and engineer Craig Smith helped the team. But the boys had to nail down tricky scientific details. "If we had it to do over, we would not put the city on an ice planet," says Adam. "It took us so long to figure everything out."

The Future City Competition Handbook contains the rules, regulations, and entry form for the contest.

Reading for Information *continued*

Outlining Outlining is a more organized kind of note taking. When you outline an article, you use a system of letters and numbers to arrange main ideas and supporting details.

- Use **roman numerals** for main ideas.
- Use **indented capital letters** for supporting details.
- Use **indented numbers** for less important details.

Below is an example of how the first paragraph of this article could be outlined. Use your notes to create an outline for the rest of the article. Remember to include only key information in your outline. Don't try to copy every word; paraphrase or summarize information.

I. Four seventh-grade boys won the Future City Competition.
  A. They designed a human city on a frozen planet.
    1. Competition is held every year in Washington, D. C.
    2. The prize is #5,000
  B. The boys got the idea for their city from watching The Empire Strikes Back.
    1. The city is called Seolforis

Research & Technology
Activity Link: "The Fun They Had" and "The Sand Castle," p. 586. Suppose you decide to enter the Future City Competition and want to create a city based on either "The Fun They Had" or "The Sand Castle." Use information from the story, as well as your own imagination, to create an outline that will help you plan, build, and prepare your model. Your outline may include your city's name, its location, the names of your advisors and team members and their roles or tasks, and the materials you will need to build your model.

Possible Response for outline:

II. The planet's atmosphere presented challenges for creating the city.
  A. The city needed to be warm enough for people to live in it.
  B. The boys had to make sure the city's heat wouldn't melt the planet's ice.
    1. They built Seolforis near geothermal vents.
    2. The vents let heat escape from the planet's core.
III. The boys made sure the city would meet its citizens' needs.
  A. The planet has a rich silvermine.
  B. People able to grow plants without soil, using water.
  C. Citizens would also have a baseball team and 3-D holographic movies.
IV. The boys did most of the work themselves.
  A. They could only spend $100 to build their model.
    1. They used paper cups, boxes, and Petri dishes.
  B. They learned a lot from the experience.

Use **Writing Transparencies,** pp. 49, 54, for additional support. Use **Reading and Critical Thinking Transparencies,** p. 46, for additional support.

Research & Technology

The Research & Technology activity on this page links to the Research & Technology activity on page 586 from the Choices & Challenges page following "The Fun They Had" and "The Sand Castle." **Instruction** Lead a discussion reviewing the main ideas of the two selections, with a focus on the settings. Ask students to compare these settings with those given for the city created in the Future City Contest. Remind students of the guidelines for outlining. Help them create an outline for their own Future City entry by modeling one of your own, or from data gathered from the class. Focus the discussion on the setting of this Future City entry. Encourage students to be creative and to use past personal experiences as well as the material in the selections and the magazine article. **Practice** As students work on their outlines, provide opportunities for them to share with peers and to revise and adjust their outlines as appropriate.

Writing Workshop
Short Story

Standards-Based Objectives
- write a 500- to 700-word short story
- use a written text as a model for writing
- revise a draft to maintain a consistent point of view
- use appositive phrases correctly
- deliver a narrative presentation

Introducing the Workshop

Short Story Discuss with students short stories they have previously read as a class. Have them consider which stories are most memorable and ask them to explain why.

Basics in a Box
Using the Graphic The graphic on this page shows the three main parts of a short story. Point out that the graphic suggests elements for each part that students should include when they draft their stories.

Presenting the Rubric To better understand the assignment, students can refer to the standards for writing a successful short story. You may also want to share with them the complete rubric, which describes several levels of proficiency.

 See **Unit Four Resource Book,** p. 73.

 For more instruction on essential writing skills, see McDougal Littell's *Language Network,* Chapters 10–17.

 Power Presentation

To engage students visually, use **Power Presentation 2,** Short Story.

Writing Workshop — Short Story

Developing plot and setting . . .

From Reading to Writing What will the world be like in a hundred years? Isaac Asimov answers this question in the futuristic story "The Fun They Had." Even though the setting of the story is imaginary, it seems real because of the vivid details and realistic dialogue between characters. As the writer of a **short story,** you, too, can create your own setting and the characters who live within it.

For Your Portfolio

WRITING PROMPT Write a short story set in an imaginary world or in a place that interests you.

Purpose: To entertain
Audience: Your classmates, family, or general readers

Basics in a Box

Short Story at a Glance

Introduction
Sets the stage by
- introducing the **characters**
- describing the **setting**

Body
Develops the plot by
- introducing the conflict
- telling a sequence of **events**
- developing **characters** through words and actions
- building toward a **climax**

Conclusion
Finishes the story by
- resolving the **conflict**
- telling the **last event**

RUBRIC STANDARDS FOR WRITING

A successful short story should
- have a strong beginning and ending
- use the elements of character, setting, and plot to create a convincing world
- use techniques such as vivid sensory language, concrete details, and dialogue to create believable characters and setting
- have a main conflict
- present a clear sequence of events
- maintain a consistent point of view

592 UNIT FOUR PART 2: IMAGINARY WORLDS

LESSON RESOURCES

USING PRINT RESOURCES
Unit Four Resource Book
- Prewriting, p. 68
- Drafting and Elaboration, p. 69
- Peer Response Guide, p. 70
- Organizational Patterns, p. 71
- Revising, Editing, and Proofreading, p. 72
- Student Models, pp. 73–75
- Rubric for Evaluation, p. 76

Writing
- Point of View, TR 23 (p. 596)

Reading and Critical Thinking
- Sequence Chain, TR 39 (p. 593)

Speaking and Listening
- Emphasizing Points for the Listener, p. 9 (p. 597)
- Evaluating Reading Aloud, p. 14 (p. 597)

- Creating and Analyzing a Narrative Presentation, pp. 23–24 (p. 597)

INTEGRATED TECHNOLOGY
Writing Coach CD-ROM
Visit our Web site:
www.mcdougallittell.com

Analyzing a Student Model

Ben Wright
Somerville Charter School

SPEAKING OPPORTUNITY
See the Speaking and Listening Handbook, p. R96 for oral presentation tips.

A World of Color

"Clones! Awaken!" The Leader's booming voice echoed through the city. Bleary-eyed, Zolak sat up in bed and looked at the digital display on his wall. 6:00 A.M. He shook the dreams from his mind and quickly reviewed his day. Again, he would have to work hard with the other clones to maintain the city. He scanned the shelves of his cubicle for all of his necessities: a food-pellet processor, a single blue uniform, and a one-way communication unit that broadcasted his daily directives. He had everything he needed, but life on his planet was not easy. Each day his normal routine drew him out of the room and down to the work lines where all the clones stood together, building, repairing, and ripping down power lines and bridges, walls and gutters.

Zolak looked like all the others, but he had never quite fit in. Years ago, he had had fantastic dreams about a world of colors—a world of trees and flowers and birds—things you only saw in books. And of course there was the letter he still carried with him from his mother. "You are not a clone. You must never believe the Leader's lies." She had been terminated because of her strange ideas.

Zolak had kept quiet about the letter. He was lucky to be alive. Most plant and animal life had been destroyed during the Great War, so the Leaders had to clone people and animals to maintain life on the planet. The human clones were "born" at the age of fifteen, possessing all the knowledge they would need to work for the Leaders. Their lives would be terminated at age thirty by an electrical pulse sent through the bracelets they all wore. The world the Leaders had designed was extremely efficient and full of constant work.

As he swallowed his morning food pellet, he noticed for the first time that it was bland. Was something happening to him? Then the loud voice of the Leader interrupted him. "Zolak, today you are assigned to drill air holes in Sector Twenty-one." Zolak quickly walked out of his cubicle to join the other clones.

The clones moved in silent lines like ants. Every now and then, they would pass through the oxygen booths that provided a quick dose of pure oxygen. Without this oxygen, they would tire rapidly and couldn't work in the polluted subterranean atmosphere. The air holes that they were going to drill in Sector Twenty-one were the first step in constructing new oxygen booths. Zolak imagined that the world above

RUBRIC IN ACTION

1 Captures reader's attention with dialogue
Other Options:
· Begin with action
· Begin with a description

2 Precise sensory details establish setting.

3 Develops central conflict that was hinted at in the introduction

4 Concrete language helps develop plot and character.

5 Background information is ordered chronologically.

Analyzing a Student Model
A World of Color
The student model is a short story about a clone who lives in a colorless and restricted world but longs to live in a world of color and freedom. The student author uses vivid details and descriptions to help the reader visualize the setting and the characters.

Have students think of a short story they have read in which the setting is particularly memorable and easy to visualize. Help students to see how vivid details and sensory descriptions bring a story to life. Then point out the key words and phrases in the student model that correspond to the elements mentioned in the rubric in action.

1 Have students think of an alternative opening sentence.
Possible Responses: Zolak opened his eyes and looked around his gray, colorless surroundings; Zolak leaped out of bed as the Leader's voice boomed over the city.

2 Ask students what impression they get of Zolak's life from this description.
Possible Responses: Zolak's life is tedious and his days are filled with hard labor; the tasks that make up his daily life are never-ending and always the same.

3 Ask students to summarize the central conflict in their own words.
Possible Response: Since most plant and animal life had been wiped out in the Great War, clones—like Zolak—that "live" for 15 years do all the work of the society.

4 Ask students to comment on the importance of describing the bracelets.
Possible Response: The writer states that this world is efficient; the electrical pulse delivered through the bracelets emphasizes that point.

5 Ask students why this background information is important to the story.
Possible Responses: Because it reveals more about Zolak's life and his character; because it moves the story ahead to the ending events.

EXPLICIT INSTRUCTION
Patterns of Organization

PICTURING TEXT STRUCTURE
Instruction While word choice and ideas play key roles in good writing, the structure of a text—the way in which ideas are organized and events unfold—also contributes to the effectiveness of the work.

Practice Have students analyze the organization of the student model by constructing a diagram or other graphic organizer. The following flow chart is an example.

Use **Reading and Critical Thinking Transparencies**, p. 39, for additional support.

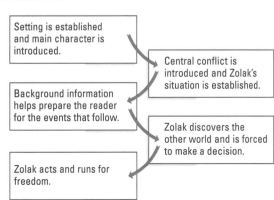

Setting is established and main character is introduced.

Central conflict is introduced and Zolak's situation is established.

Background information helps prepare the reader for the events that follow.

Zolak discovers the other world and is forced to make a decision.

Zolak acts and runs for freedom.

6 Ask students to describe the effect that is created by the third-person point of view.
Possible Responses: Suspense and tension is heightened because neither the reader nor the narrator knows what is going to happen; the reader has a sense of being outside Zolak's world, looking in.

7 Discuss the color images in this paragraph and how they contrast with Zolak's world.
Possible Responses: Zolak never saw green or blue, let alone *shades* of these colors, except in dreams. The color was the most important thing missing from his world.

8 Ask students to discuss how the student author creates tension and suspense in this paragraph.
Possible Responses: By including dialogue that increases the action; by using strong, active verbs; by emphasizing the strangeness of Zolak's situation.

9 Ask students to discuss the effectiveness of the dialogue.
Possible Responses: The voice lets the reader know that Zolak has been discovered and that he will have to die.

10 Ask students to explain how the student author ties the conclusion of the story into the opening paragraphs.
Possible Response: The author places Zolak in the world of bright colors that he longed for in the beginning of the story.

had oxygen. He wondered what else it it might have? He stopped himself from wondering why none of the other clones had questions.

Zolak's bracelet beeped. While he had been lost in thought, the other clones had finished and were back in their cubicles. Zolak spoke into his bracelet. "I have one more hole to drill."

The piercing voice answered him. "You have thirty minutes to finish."

Zolak was alone. He tried to concentrate on his drilling. He finally finished the hole. Suddenly the area around it began to crack and crumble around him. He looked up. He was face to face with a pair of sparkling aqua eyes. He had never seen such a creature.

A high, singing voice said, "Zolak, we have been waiting a long time for you." Zolak was astonished. The creature had yellow hair and red lips. It motioned for him to come forward through the opening. Zolak looked through. All the shades of green, blue, yellow, pink, and other colors that he had only seen in his dreams washed over him. Hundreds of creatures, all shapes and sizes with high singing voices, surrounded him. They repeated his name. The creature, the one with the aqua eyes, took his hand and laughed. "You are one of us. This is your home." Zolak experienced joy for the first time in his life, but he had no word for it.

Just then, fear seized him. He looked at his bracelet. The piercing voice cut in, "Where are you, Zolak? Why is your heart beating so quickly?" Zolak tried to answer in his usual voice but couldn't. He was dizzy from all of the pure air he had breathed. It was difficult to think, and soon he was running back from the hole. The piercing voice demanded, "You are trying to escape."

"No, I'm coming. It took longer than I expected," Zolak gasped.

"That is a lie, Zolak. You must be terminated."

It was now or never. Zolak could die in the middle of this cold tunnel or he could try to escape to the world of colors. The voice began counting down: "10 . . . 9 . . . 8." Zolak turned back and sprinted with every ounce of strength he could muster. He could see the light now. "6 . . . 5 . . . ." The tunnel was beginning to get warmer. "4! . . . 3! . . . 2!" The voice was crazy, angry. But he was almost there. "1!" He leaped for the hole as the voice screamed "ZERO!" The glowing bracelet flashed and went dark. As he entered his new world, Zolak felt his bracelet rip from his wrist. Surrounded by singing and laughter under a deep blue sky, Zolak was finally free.

6 Uses third-person point of view throughout the story

7 Sensory details contrast the world above with Zolak's world below.

8 Character's reactions make him seem believable.

9 Uses dialogue to further the narrative

10 Conflict is resolved in the conclusion

Writing Your Short Story

❶ Prewriting

Stories are like fairy gold. The more you give away, the more you have.
— Polly McGuire

Write down familiar places and people and **imagine** how they would be different in a future or past world. **Listen** for stories or unusual happenings. **Read** information on the kind of space travel that is possible now. See the **Idea Bank** in the margin for more suggestions. After you select an idea, follow the steps below.

Planning Your Short Story

1. **Plan the major parts of your story.**
   - **Characters.** You'll probably have one or more main characters plus some minor ones. Decide what background information is necessary to include.
   - **Setting.** Where will the story take place and when? Does the setting affect the characters and plot in any way?
   - **Plot.** Work out the major events of your story. What is the conflict? Decide what will happen at the beginning, middle, and end of the story.

2. **Choose a narrator.** Who will tell your story? Do you want one of the characters to tell the story in the first person, or would you like your narrator to be outside of the action?

3. **Create a mood.** Do you want your story to be sad, frightening, mysterious, humorous, or serious? How will you create that feeling through your characters and setting?

❷ Drafting

Begin writing your short story by introducing the **setting, characters,** or first event in your **plot.** Include **dialogue** that will help your reader get to know the characters and see the action unfolding. Also use **sensory details** to make your story come alive. For example, "The Fun They Had" gives readers the sensation of how antique pages look and feel: "They turned the pages, which were yellow and crinkly. . . ."

IDEA Bank

1. Your Working Portfolio 🗂
Look for ideas in the **Writing** activities you completed earlier.

2. Sequels
Think of stories that you've enjoyed. Imagine how you might go about writing a sequel, or follow-up story, to one of them, using the same characters but a different plot and setting.

3. Puzzle Pieces
Fold a piece of paper into nine squares. Write down three names of people, three feeling words, and three events—anything from a birthday party to a natural disaster. Then cut out the squares and turn them, face down. Choose two squares from the names section, one from the feeling section, and one from events. Put the words together and use them as a starting point for your story.

Have a question?

See the **Writing Handbook**
Using Language Effectively, p. R38
Descriptive Writing, p. R39
Narrative Writing, p. R41

Ask Your Peer Reader

- Which characters were most interesting? Which were least interesting?
- Which parts of the plot were most interesting? Which parts needed to be clearer?
- How would you describe the mood of the story?

Guiding Student Writing

Prewriting

Choosing a Subject
If after reading the Idea Bank students have difficulty choosing a subject for their short stories, suggest that they try the following:

- Think of a setting that would be ideal for a scary story or for a fairy tale. Describe the setting in detail and then decide what kinds of characters would fit in with the setting. Build your story around the setting and the characters.
- Pick a wild animal whose habits you know something about, such as a rabbit or a squirrel, and write an imaginative story about how that animal might spend its day.

Planning Your Short Story
1. Encourage students to brainstorm possible characters, plots, and settings.
2. Suggest that students write two versions of an introductory paragraph from two different points of view, and then decide which one is more interesting and suitable for the story topic.
3. Suggest that students write a list of words that they think evoke the mood they wish to create. They can use these words as a starting point.

Drafting

Suggest that student volunteers read the dialogue and descriptions they've written to the class. Ask students to discuss ways to make the dialogue natural and exciting, and to add vivid and precise language in order to enhance the descriptions.

Ask Your Peer Reader
Remind students to use the peer reviewer's feedback when revising their drafts.

Revising

MAINTAINING A CONSISTENT POINT OF VIEW

Review the change in the sample with students. To help students practice maintaining a consistent point of view, have them share their drafts with a partner who will check the essay for inconsistencies.

 Use **Writing Transparencies**, p. 23, for additional support.

Editing and Proofreading

APPOSITIVE PHRASES

Remind students that appositive phrases usually follow a noun or pronoun and identify or explain it. Have students explain the change in the sample.

Reflecting

As they write their reflections, have students consider what aspects of short stories they will be more aware of in the future.

Option

MANAGING THE PAPER LOAD

To reduce grading time, try reading students' stories quickly for enjoyment and then respond by using a check, a plus, or a minus sign rather than formal letter or number grades.

SPELLING From Writing

 As you revise your work, look back at the words you misspelled and determine why you made the errors you did. For additional help, refer to the strategies and generalizations in the **Spelling Handbook** on page R26.

Need revising help?

Review the **Rubric**, p. 592
Consider **peer reader** comments
Check **Revision Guidelines**, p. R31

Frantic about phrases?

See the **Grammar Handbook**, p. R62.

SPEAKING Opportunity

Turn your story into an oral presentation.

Publishing IDEAS

- Organize your stories and those of your classmates into a short-story collection. Use a computer to print out copies for friends and family.
- Host a Read-Aloud Month. Invite students from other classes to come in and listen to various short stories being read out loud.

▶ INTERNET

Publishing Options
www.mcdougallittell.com

❸ Revising

TARGET SKILL ▶ **MAINTAINING CONSISTENT POINT OF VIEW** Because you do not want your readers to be confused, you must maintain a consistent point of view throughout your story. You may choose to use a first-person narrator who is one of the characters. When the narrator is a participant in the story and refers to himself or herself as *I*, this indicates first-person point of view. When events are told by a narrator outside the story, using the pronouns *he, she, it*, and *they*, this indicates third-person point of view. Whichever point of view you choose, stay with it throughout your story.

> Zolak spoke into his bracelet. "I have one more hole to
> drill." The piercing voice answered me. ~~of him~~

❹ Editing and Proofreading

TARGET SKILL ▶ **APPOSITIVE PHRASES** An appositive phrase renames something. It is used to give more details or information about a person, idea, or thing. For example, the appositive phrase in the following sentence gives added detail about the subject: *Ellen, a hard-working student, finished the book report before going out to play.* Make sure that you set off appositive phrases with commas.

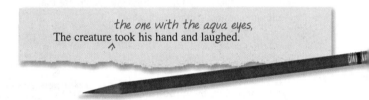

> the one with the aqua eyes,
> The creature took his hand and laughed.
> ^

❺ Reflecting

FOR YOUR WORKING PORTFOLIO Which parts of the writing process did you find most difficult? What did you learn about short stories from writing your own? Attach your answers to your finished work. Save your short story in your **Working Portfolio**.

EXPLICIT INSTRUCTION **Revision**

ORGANIZATION

Instruction Remind students that a well-organized short story maintains a consistent point of view. If the writer of the story uses a first-person narrator, all narration has to be done with the words *I, me, my*, and *mine*. If the narrator refers to himself or herself along with others in the story, words like *we, our, ours*, and *us* would be used. A short story may be told by a third-person narrator instead. As long as the narrator stays consistently with first-person or third-person, there is no problem.

Practice Ask students to reread their short stories to look for inconsistencies in the narrator's voice.

See the **Research and Technology Handbook,** pp. R108-109, for information about formatting documents using word processing skills.

 Use **Unit Four Resource Book,** p. 71, to help students understand and use spatial order.

Standardized Test Practice

Mixed Review

Sand stretched across the horizon. The egyptian princess began to
<u>(1)</u>
panic. She wondered aloud, "Were are we?" Her camels and most of her
<u>(2)</u>
water supply had been stolen by soldiers of her enemy; Prince Neto.
<u>(3)</u>
The princess walked alongside her loyal servants and guards. <u>Trudged</u>
<u>(4)</u>
<u>in the heat for several hours.</u> Suddenly, clouds on the horizon signaled
the approach of other <u>travlers.</u> <u>The princess watched, frozen with fear,</u>
<u>(5)</u> <u>(6)</u>
<u>nervously.</u> Then she recognized the king coming to assist her.

Review Your Skills

Use the passage and the questions that follow it to check how well you remember the language conventions you've learned in previous grades.

1. What is the correct capitalization in sentence 1?
   A. The Egyptian princess
   B. The Egyptian Princess
   C. The egyptian Princess
   D. Correct as is

2. What is the correct spelling in sentence 2?
   A. "Ware are we?"
   B. "Wear are we?"
   C. "Where are we?"
   D. Correct as is

3. How is sentence 3 best written?
   A. by soldiers of her enemy.
      Prince Neto.
   B. by soldiers of her enemy:
      Prince Neto.
   C. by soldiers of her enemy,
      Prince Neto.
   D. Correct as is

4. How is sentence 4 best written?
   A. Trudging in the heat for
      several hours.
   B. They trudged in the heat for
      several hours.
   C. They, trudging in the heat for
      several hours.
   D. Correct as is

5. What is the correct spelling in sentence 5?
   A. travlerrs
   B. travvelers
   C. travelers
   D. Correct as is

6. How is sentence 6 best written?
   A. The princess watched
      nervously frozen, with fear.
   B. The princess frozen with fear
      watched nervously.
   C. The princess, frozen with fear,
      watched nervously.
   D. Correct as is

Self-Assessment

Check your own answers in the **Grammar Handbook**

Quick Reference: Punctuation, p. R64

Quick Reference: Capitalization, p. R66

Standardized Test Practice

Demonstrate how students can eliminate incorrect choices for the first question.

A. This choice correctly capitalizes Egyptian, which is a proper adjective.

B. This choice incorrectly capitalizes princess.

C. This choice is incorrect because Egyptian should be capitalized.

D. The original choice is incorrect because Egyptian should be capitalized.

Answers:
1. A; **2.** C; **3.** C; **4.** B; **5.** C; **6.** C.

EXPLICIT INSTRUCTION **Speaking Opportunity**

Prepare Once students have written their short story, they can read it aloud to an audience. Refer students to pages R102–103 of the Speaking and Listening Handbook at the back of this book for tips on presenting their short story.

Present Have students present their short stories to the class. They should strive to have an interesting plot, a consistent point of view, and a range of narrative devices.

RUBRIC

3 Full Accomplishment Student uses precise language and concrete details in support of an interesting plot. He or she includes narrative devices like dialogue or suspense and speaks clearly and expressively.

2 Substantial Accomplishment Student includes some details and creates an interesting plot. He or she uses some dialogue and occasionally delivers the story with expression.

1 Little or Partial Accomplishment Student tells a confusing story, lapsing into different points of view, using few, if any, details, and speaking with little expression.

Use **Speaking and Listening Book,** pp. 9, 14, 23–24 for additional support in presenting a short story.

Standards-Based Objectives

- reflect on and assess student understanding of the unit and its theme
- review literary concepts and skills introduced in the unit
- assess and build portfolios

Reflecting on Theme

OPTION 1

A successful response will

- include a chosen selection from the unit and an explanation for its choice
- provide support for selection choice with examples of the "wondrous" elements each contains
- evaluate the author's craft in creating a "wondrous world"

OPTION 2

A successful response will

- begin with a detailed list of animals and the traits that make each animal wondrous
- include thoughtful writing with examples of the wondrous animals from each list
- conclude with a paragraph of summary, using ideas from each animal and its traits, to make a generalization about animals and their wondrous nature

OPTION 3

A successful response will

- include reflective discussion of the fantasy and science fiction genres, and the elements that make them unique
- provide specific examples from the selections in the unit to support that discussion
- compare these genres to realistic fiction and offer a concluding statement that reflects the theme of the unit

Self Assessment

It may be helpful for students to discuss the quotation with a partner or small group prior to the writing portion of the assessment. Encourage students to reflect on their peer discussion, the stories in this unit, and their own personal experiences, thoughts, and feelings.

Wondrous Worlds

In the selections in this unit, you've seen that wondrous worlds are found not just in imaginary lands and made-up adventures, but in the everyday behavior of animals around us. How have these stories changed the way you view the world around you? Explore this question by completing one or more of the options in each of the following sections.

Party Animals, Julia Lucich.

Reflecting on Theme

OPTION 1

Judging Impact   Which works of literature in this unit inspire awe, surprise, or admiration? Choose the selection that made the biggest impression on you, and write two or three paragraphs about its "wondrous" elements. How do you think the author of the work achieves this impact?

OPTION 2

Analyzing the Theme   Make a list of all the animals in Part One of this unit. Think about the part theme, "Animal Wonders." Next to each animal's name, make notes about how the animal relates to the theme. What about each animal or its behavior is wondrous or remarkable? Read over your list, and then write a paragraph answering this question: What makes an animal a "wonder"? Support your explanation with examples from the selections.

OPTION 3

Thinking About Genre   Why do you think some writers choose to write in the genres of fantasy and science fiction? What do these types of literature allow a writer to do that he or she cannot do in realistic fiction? Write a few paragraphs in response to these questions. As you write your response, keep in mind the elements of science fiction and fantasy and the theme of this unit.

Self ASSESSMENT

Reconsider the quotation at the beginning of the unit: "In books, I have traveled not only to other worlds, but into my own." Write a paragraph explaining how reading the selections in this unit has given you a better understanding of the quotation's meaning.

REVIEWING YOUR PERSONAL WORD List

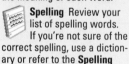

Vocabulary   Review the new words you learned in this unit. If necessary, use a dictionary to check the meaning of each word.

Spelling   Review your list of spelling words. If you're not sure of the correct spelling, use a dictionary or refer to the **Spelling Handbook** on page R26.

Reviewing Literary Concepts

OPTION 1

Analyzing Plot Structure Make a chart like the one shown to analyze the climax and resolution of each fiction selection you have read in this unit. Also note how a character or situation is changed by the events of each story's climax.

Story	Climax	Resolution	What Changes
Lob's Girl	Sandy comes out of a coma.	Granny finds out that Lob is dead.	The family understands Lob's love for Sandy.

OPTION 2

Analyzing Fantasy and Science Fiction Elements Create a fantasy and science fiction spectrum. Draw a horizontal line. Label one end of the line "Fantasy" and the other "Science Fiction." For each selection in Part Two of this unit, decide whether the selection is fantasy, science fiction, or a combination, and write its title on the line where you think it belongs. Discuss with the class where you placed each selection on the spectrum and why.

Portfolio Building

- **Choices and Challenges—Writing** Some of the writing assignments in this unit asked you to write forms of poetry. Choose the one that you feel best expresses a sense of wonder. Write a note explaining the reasons for your choice. Then attach the note to the poem and place it in your **Presentation Portfolio.**

- **Writing Workshops** In this unit you wrote and presented a process description and wrote a short story. Reread these two pieces and decide which you think is a stronger piece of writing. Write a cover note explaining the reasons for your choice, attach it to the piece, and place it in your **Presentation Portfolio.**

- **Additional Activities** Think back to any of the assignments you completed under **Speaking & Listening** and **Research & Technology.** Keep a record of the assignments that you especially enjoyed, found helpful, or would like to do further work on.

Self ASSESSMENT

READER'S NOTEBOOK

On a sheet of paper, copy the following literary terms introduced in this unit, listing them in order of difficulty. Write down the concepts you find easiest to understand first, and put at the bottom of the list the concepts you're not sure of. Use the **Glossary of Literary Terms** on page R116 to look up the terms in the lower half of your list.

story structure
foreshadowing
climax
essay
sound devices
resolution

realistic and fantastic details
fantasy
futuristic settings
mood

Self ASSESSMENT

Look over and compare the earliest work in your **Presentation Portfolio** with your more recent work. Write a note to yourself, describing what you now see as the strengths and weaknesses in your writing skills.

Setting GOALS

What reading or writing strategies do you want to work on as you complete the next unit? Write at least three goals on a sheet of paper. Exchange papers with a classmate and discuss ways that each of you might achieve your goals.

Reviewing Literary Concepts

OPTION 1

Use the Unit 4 Resource Book, page 77, to provide students with a ready-made chart for analyzing plot structure. Have students complete the chart, including information about the climax and resolution of each selection. Make sure they analyze these elements of the plot carefully and thoughtfully and include discussion of how these events impacted the characters and situations in each story.

OPTION 2

Students should work independently on the spectrum, reflecting carefully before making each placement on the line. Encourage them to think of the evidence they will provide their classmates to support each placement. Students may want to share their spectrums with a small group prior to the whole class to allow them time to practice and reconsider each placement.

Portfolio Building

Students should evaluate the items in their Working Portfolios and choose pieces that represent their highest quality work for their Presentation Portfolio. As they attach notes to the items they transfer to their Presentation Portfolios, remind them to write the reasoning for their choices clearly so they will understand the notes several months from now.

REFLECT AND ASSESS **599**

LITERATURE CONNECTIONS
The Call of the Wild

BY JACK LONDON

Buck, a beloved family pet, is stolen and shipped to Alaska during the 1890s Gold Rush. Mistreated, he learns to survive as a member of a dog sled team. Becoming more like a wolf and less like a domestic dog, Buck encounters many dangers. Jack London used his own experiences in the Klondike to write this classic tale of survival and adventure.

These thematically related readings are provided along with *The Call of the Wild*:

The Wolf and the Dog
BY MARIE DE FRANCE

from **The Hidden Life of Dogs**
BY ELIZABETH MARSHALL THOMAS

The Wolf Said to Francis
BY A. G. ROCHELLE

The Man Who Was a Horse
BY JULIUS LESTER

Unsentimental Mother
BY SALLY CARRIGHAR

Long Duel
BY ROBERT MURPHY

More Choices

The Animal Family
BY RANDALL JARRELL
When a lonely hunter meets a singing mermaid, they quickly become friends. They learn each others' languages and even adopt a baby bear cub into their home.

The Elephant's Child
BY RUDYARD KIPLING
This is the story of a curious young elephant who asks a lot of questions. His teacher, the crocodile, gives him knowledge and grants him a trunk.

The Hobbit
BY J. R. R. TOLKIEN
Comfort-loving hobbit Bilbo Baggins ventures out to hunt a dragon.

James and the Giant Peach
BY ROALD DAHL
James is happy to roll away from his two unkind aunts in a magical giant peach. He meets many animal friends along the way.

My Friend Flicka
BY MARY O'HARA
After Kennie convinces his father to give him a colt, he proves his devotion.

The Wind in the Willows
BY KENNETH GRAHAME
Mr. Mole enjoys sharing his life near the river with Water Rat and Toad of Toad Hall.

LITERATURE CONNECTIONS
A Wrinkle in Time

BY MADELEINE L'ENGLE

A science fiction novel about the struggle between good and evil, this absorbing story relates how Meg, her brother Charles Wallace, and her friend Calvin become involved with supernatural beings, inhabitants of distant planets, and a daring rescue.

These thematically related readings are provided along with _A Wrinkle in Time_:

Odd Jobs
BY JUDITH GOROG

Reversible
BY OCTAVIO PAZ

Behind Bars
BY FADWA TUQAN

from **World of the Brain**
BY ALVIN AND VIRGINIA SILVERSTEIN

from **It's Our World, Too!**
BY PHILLIP HOOSE

The Dark Princess
BY RICHARD KENNEDY

The Sparrow
BY IVAN TURGENEV

Colony
BY RICK WERNLI

Social Studies Connection

A Chinese Zoo
BY DEMI
In this collection of ancient Chinese fables, each story teaches a lesson about life.

The Golden Swan: An East Indian Tale of Love from the Mahabharata
BY MARIANNA MAYER
In this fantastic love story, Damayanti and Nala need the help of different gods in order to find each other.

Jataka Tales
EDITED BY NANCY DeROIN
This is a collection of ancient Indian tales and fables. The stories describe the different forms Buddha took on earth, including many animal forms.

Yeh-Shen: A Cinderella Story from China
BY AI-LING LOUIE
In this Chinese telling of the classic Cinderella story, the young Yeh-Shen ends up marrying a handsome prince.

Weaving of a Dream: A Chinese Folktale
BY MARILEE HEYER
In this retelling of the traditional Chinese tale, an old woman weaves a beautiful tapestry that is soon stolen by fairies. Only her sons can make the magical trip and bring it back to her.

This feature provides more practice in taking standardized tests. As students work through this lesson, they will have an opportunity to practice strategies for reading comprehension questions, multiple-choice questions, and essay and short-answer questions. Boxed strategies located alongside the text will help guide students through the activities. These strategies model processes for students to follow when taking standardized tests.

STANDARDS-BASED OBJECTIVES

- understand and apply strategies for reading a test selection
- recognize and answer questions about tone in a test selection
- analyze a literary excerpt included in a test selection
- understand and apply strategies for answering multiple-choice questions about a test selection
- respond to a prompt by extracting information from the text and presenting it in a written answer
- understand and apply strategies for revising and proofreading a test response

Standardized Test Practice

Reading and Writing for Assessment

When you studied the test-taking strategies on pages 308-313, you learned helpful new techniques. The following pages will give you practice using these strategies and more.

PART 1 **How to Read the Test Selection**

Listed below are some basic reading strategies. By applying these strategies and by taking notes, you can identify the information you need in answering test questions.

STRATEGIES FOR READING A TEST SELECTION

▸ **Before you begin reading, skim the questions that follow the passage.** These can help focus your reading.

▸ **Think about the title and message.** What does the title suggest about the overall message or theme of the selection?

▸ **Use active reading strategies such as analyzing, predicting, and questioning.** If the test directions allow you to mark on the test itself, make notes in the margin as you read.

▸ **Look for main ideas.** These are often stated at the beginning or end of paragraphs. Sometimes they are implied, not stated. After reading each paragraph, ask, What was this passage about?

▸ **Note the literary elements and techniques used by the writer.** Consider the effects of word choice, figurative language, and mood.

▸ **Evaluate the organization.** For a comparison-and-contrast essay, how well does the use of feature-by-feature or subject-by-subject organization work in the piece?

▸ **Look for expert testimony.** What supporting evidence or sources of information does the writer use? Why are these sources appropriate to the subject?

▸ **Make judgments about the writer's purpose.** Does the writer have a bias or use a particular tone? How does this affect the message and presentation of information?

Reading Selection

STRATEGIES
IN ACTION

❶ Moving On

by Asher Owens

1   For as long as I can remember, I've been falling asleep to the chirping of crickets. That is because I grew up on a farm that has been in our family for generations. Last year, when my dad's brother was old enough, he decided to take over the farm so that we could move into the city. **❷ I didn't know then that leaving the country behind me would take some adjusting.**

2   **The first thing I noticed about the city was the lack of open space.** Growing up on a farm with the nearest house three miles away, I got used to the open landscape. I remember climbing the chestnut tree at the edge of our cornfield and looking out over **❸ a huge quilt of green and gold.** Every day after school, I'd climb to my post and look out. After the crops were harvested and the fields were completely empty, it was easy to imagine I was the only one left on the planet. In a city, you have to look harder to find that freedom. When I take the elevator up to the rooftop of my apartment building, I stare out across the blazing sky, swollen with buildings. The skyline looks as though it is on fire when the sun goes down.

3   The busy landscape isn't the only thing I've had to get used to since leaving the **❹ rustic life.** On a farm, things pretty much wind down when the sun sets. In the city, it is harder to find peace and quiet. For the first few months, sleeping was difficult because the traffic outside my window never stops. I had to learn how to tune out the blaring horns. Now I can just close my eyes and imagine I hear the wind rustling in the oaks outside. Sometimes I can even hear the crickets chirping, and this almost always puts me to sleep.

4   Some people think that life on a farm is boring, that there is nothing to do, but this is not the case. **❺ Actually, I have more free time now that I live in the city.** On the farm, I rarely stayed up too long after dinner because I had to get up early to do chores. As soon as I grew strong enough to carry the buckets of corn to the hogs, chores took up much of my daily life. Chores meant feeding the pigs, cleaning out their pens, and fixing whatever needed

❶ Think about the title.
One Student's Thoughts
"I wonder who is moving and what they are moving on from."

❷ Make judgments about the writer's purpose.
"The writer seems less complimentary about city life, at least at the beginning."
YOUR TURN
Determine the writer's purpose.

❸ Note literary elements like the use of figurative language.
"The writer uses a metaphor, a 'quilt of green and gold,' to refer to the crops."
YOUR TURN
Why do you think the writer uses metaphor here?

❹ Use context clues to understand vocabulary.
"It seems like *rustic* is the opposite of city life."

❺ Read actively—analyze.
"If country life is so peaceful, why does the writer have more free time in the city?"

Teaching the Lesson

Begin by previewing the text. Note the title and ask students to identify the subject. Read through the questions and prompts at the end of the text. Discuss with students what they should look for as they read the selection.

1 Point out the dual meanings of *moving on*— "physical movement" and "moving on to a new stage of life." Suggest to students that the title of a test selection is likely to give important clues that will help them answer the test questions. The tone set by the title is often a clue to the tone of the selection.

2 Point out that the author is setting up a compare-and-contrast situation between city and country. So far, the writer seems to have a more positive attitude about the country.

YOUR TURN By setting up this compare-and-contrast situation, the writer is letting readers know that he is going to tell things he likes about both city and country, as well as the things he dislikes.

3 Ask students what other metaphor or simile the writer uses in this paragraph. *(He says the skyline looks as if it is on fire when the sun goes down.)*

YOUR TURN The metaphor "a quilt of green and gold" makes the country sound appealing and beautiful.

4 Remind students to use various kinds of context clues as they try to figure out unfamiliar words. They can search the words and sentences around the unfamiliar word for definition or restatement clues. They can look for comparisons and contrasts. They can also look for word parts, such as prefixes, suffixes, and roots, to give them clues to a word's meaning.

5 In order to analyze, remind students to ask questions as they read. For example, they might ask, "Is the writer starting to find good things about city living? What evidence in this paragraph points to that?" *(The writer has far fewer chores to do and can sleep later in the morning; he can also stay up later because he's not as tired from getting up early to do chores.)*

fixing. I rarely slept in on weekends. Now that I live in the city, I go to sleep later and get up later. My chores consist of taking out the trash on Wednesday and sweeping off the front step. This leaves me much more time to hang out with my friends and relax.

5   Because we are not as busy doing chores, you'd think my family and I would see more of each other, but this is not the case. ❻ On the farm, no matter what you were doing during the day, dinnertime was sacred. Everyone had to be at the dinner table each night, no excuses. Now my siblings are involved in different activities and we rarely have dinner together. My two younger brothers are involved in sports, my sister is in the drama club, and my mother has enrolled in night classes. ❼ She has also taken a part-time job teaching nursery school. This is something she had always wanted to do but couldn't because running the farm took so much of her time. We still spend some time together as a family, though. Every Sunday we take turns making a breakfast. When it is my turn, I make waffles with lots of whipped cream and, when they are in season, fresh blueberries or strawberries. We sit around the big kitchen table, the same one we had at our farm, and we laugh and take turns sharing stories about what has happened during our week.

6   Moving was a big change for all of us, but I have come to appreciate city life. I have also come to appreciate those things that have stayed the same. My mother still makes apple pies from scratch. We still have fresh squash and tomatoes in the summer; now they come from my father's rooftop garden. I still ride my bike a lot, and it is easier now because I don't have to ride on rocky dirt roads. The most important thing I have learned is that it really doesn't matter where you live as long as you have your family. In this respect, the farm and the city are exactly the same.

---

6 Ask students, What are the writer's feelings about mealtimes together? Where the family always ate dinner together on the farm, they are less likely to do so in the city where there are more activities competing for their time. Discuss the purpose of this comparison.

YOUR TURN Comparing this one feature allows the writer to tell in more depth how this change in mealtime togetherness affects the family.

7 Point out that skimming the questions will help students find the information they need as they look back at the text.

Check Your Understanding

Have students use the following questions to test their understanding of the selection before they answer the questions in their texts.

• What were the main ideas of the selection?

• How does the author use comparison and contrast to support his main ideas?

• What structure does the writer use in his comparison-and-contrast essay—feature by feature or subject by subject?

• What conclusion does the writer come to after comparing country and city life?

---

❻ **Evaluate the writer's use of comparison and contrast.**

"One feature—dinnertime—is compared within a paragraph."

YOUR TURN

How well does the use of feature-by-feature organization work in the essay?

❼ **Skim the questions that follow the passage.**

"There's a question about his mother's part-time job. The selection says that she could never have had this opportunity when they lived on the farm."

PART 2 **How to Answer Multiple-Choice Questions**

Use the strategies in the box and notes in the side column to
help you answer the questions below and on the following pages.

Based on the selection you have just read, choose the best
answer for each of the following questions.

1. Why do you think the essay is titled "Moving On"?
   A. People move faster in the city.
   B. The writer has moved on to a new life in the city.
   C. Everything on a farm is constantly moving.
   D. The writer's family needed help moving to the city.

2. Why does the writer begin with crickets chirping?
   A. He wants the reader to appreciate crickets and
   their contribution to the world.
   B. He wants to hook the reader with a statement that
   appeals to the senses.
   C. The thesis of the paper has to do with noise levels.
   D. He never has trouble sleeping.

3. What main idea does the writer support by mentioning
   that he saw a "quilt of green and gold" from the
   treetops?
   A. You rarely see those colors in the city.
   B. Tree climbing is excellent exercise and helps
   develop the muscles.
   C. There is much more open land in the country.
   D. Everything looks better when viewed from up high.

4. Why does the writer mention his mother's part-time job?
   A. To show that his mother has no time for the family.
   B. To show that everyone in his family is doing more
   meaningful work.
   C. To show that his family members see less of each
   other now.
   D. All of the above.

5. What is the writer's tone at the end of the essay?
   A. His attitude toward country life changes from
   positive to negative.
   B. His attitude toward the move has not changed at all.
   C. He appreciates both country and city life.
   D. He regrets the life he has lost.

STRATEGIES FOR ANSWERING
MULTIPLE-CHOICE QUESTIONS

▶ **Ask questions** that help you
eliminate some of the choices.
▶ **Pay attention to choices such
as "all of the above" or "none
of the above."** To eliminate
them, all you need to find is one
answer that does not fit.
▶ **Choose the one best answer.**
More than one choice may be
true, but only one will be true and
answer the question completely.

STRATEGIES
IN ACTION

Choose the one best answer.

One Student's Thoughts
"All these answers might be true, but
this essay doesn't deal with exercise,
so I can eliminate choice B."

YOUR TURN
*What other choices can you
eliminate?*

**Pay attention to choices such as
"all of the above."**

One Student's Thoughts
"I don't think the writer feels that
his mother has no time for the
family. He even says that she still
makes apple pies from scratch. So
I can eliminate choice A. That
means that choice D—all of the
above—can't be right either."

YOUR TURN
*Which of the remaining choices
makes the most sense?*

YOUR TURN This essay is about the
comparison between city and country
life, not about how things look better
from up high, so Choice D can be eliminated, as well.

4. C

YOUR TURN Choice C makes the most
sense, because the writer says that the
family sees less of each other now, and
his mother's job is one of the examples
he uses to explain what he means.

5. C

Short-Answer Question

The writer's purpose in comparing city and country life is to explain how he made the adjustment from one to the other. He concludes that both have advantages, but that being with the family counts the most.

YOUR TURN One clue is that the writer says the move took some adjusting on his part. He begins by thinking he won't like city life, but as he goes on, he sees some advantages that put the change in perspective.

Essay Question

City life differs from country life in several ways. First of all, there is the look of the city. In the country, there are vast, open spaces to see and explore. The city is more crowded, with buildings as far as the eye can see. The city is also noisy, with the sounds of traffic replacing the quiet country sound of crickets chirping. Life on a farm provides less leisure time, since there are always chores to be done and animals to tend. In the city, chores are fewer, so there is more time to relax and hang out. Finally, the busier pace and greater variety of activities mean that the family spends less time together. What time they do spend, though, might tend to be appreciated more, since they are spending it together by choice, not by necessity.

YOUR TURN Important points to include are the differences in the following: landscape, noise level, leisure time, and family time.

Check Your Understanding

Have students reread their own responses to the short-answer and essay questions. Then have them ask themselves the following questions as they revise and edit their own work.

- Have I responded directly to the direction words in the writing prompt?
- Have I covered the points I wanted to make?
- Do I have an introductory sentence?
- Have I supported my ideas with evidence?
- Have I written a conclusion?
- Have I used correct grammar?

PART 3 **How to Respond in Writing**

You may be asked to write answers to questions about a reading passage. **Short-answer questions** often ask you to answer in a sentence or two. **Essay questions** require a fully developed piece of writing.

Short-Answer Question

STRATEGIES FOR RESPONDING TO SHORT-ANSWER QUESTIONS

▸ **Identify key words** in the writing prompt that tell you the ideas to discuss. Make sure you know what each word means.
▸ **State your response directly** and to the point.
▸ **Support your ideas** by using evidence from the selection.
▸ **Use correct grammar.**

Sample Question

Answer the following question in one or two sentences.

Explain what you think the writer's purpose was in comparing and contrasting country and city life.

Essay Question

STRATEGIES FOR ANSWERING ESSAY QUESTIONS

▸ **Look for direction words** in the writing prompt such as *essay, analyze, describe,* or *compare and contrast.*
▸ **List the points** you want to make before beginning to write.
▸ **Writing an interesting introduction** that presents your main point.
▸ **Develop your ideas** by using evidence from the selection that supports the statements you make. Present the ideas in a logical order.
▸ **Write a conclusion** that summarizes your points.
▸ **Check your work** for correct grammar.

Sample Prompt

The writer of this selection sees many differences between life in the city and life in the country. Write an essay in which you summarize these differences.

STRATEGIES IN ACTION

Identify key words.

One Student's Thoughts
"The key words are *explain* and *purpose*. This means that I'll have to decide why the writer wrote the article and tell why I think that way."

YOUR TURN
What clues to the writer's purpose can you find in the selection?

Look for direction words.

One Student's Thoughts
"The important words are *essay* and *summarize*. This means that I'll have to discuss the differences in a fully developed piece of writing."

YOUR TURN
What important points you will have to include in your essay?

Here is a student's first draft in response to the writing prompt at the bottom of page 606. Read the paragraph and answer the multiple-choice questions that follow.

1	The writer says that city life differs from country life. He
2	mentions four major ways. First, the city landscape is
3	littered with buildings instead of being open and vast.
4	Second, there is more noise living in the city. Which the
5	writer has had to get used to. The amount of time he has is
6	also a difference. He spends less time with his family.
7	However, at least once a week the family shares a meal
8	together. Sunday breakfasts are special. He never misses it.

1. What is the BEST way to combine the sentences in lines 1–2 (The writer says . . . four major ways.)?

   A. The writer says that city life differs from country life; four major ways.

   B. The writer says that city life differs from country life, but he mentions four major ways.

   C. The writer says that city life differs from country life, though he mentions four major ways.

   D. The writer says that city life differs from country life in four major ways.

2. What is the BEST way to revise the sentences in lines 4–5 (Second, there is . . . used to.)?

   A. Second, there is more noise living in the city of which the writer has had to get used to.

   B. Second, there is more noise living in the city: which the writer has had to get used to.

   C. Second, there is more noise and the writer has had to get used to it living in the city.

   D. Second, living in the city, the writer has had to get used to more noise.

3. What is the BEST way to revise the sentence in line 8 (He never misses it.)?

   A. They never miss it.

   B. They never miss him.

   C. He never misses them.

   D. They never misses it.

STRATEGIES FOR REVISING, EDITING, AND PROOFREADING

▸ **Read the passage carefully.**
▸ **Note the parts that are confusing** or don't make sense. What kinds of errors would that signal?
▸ **Look for errors** in grammar, usage, spelling, and capitalization. Common errors include
   • run-on sentences
   • sentence fragments
   • lack of subject-verb agreement
   • unclear pronoun antecedents
   • lack of transition words

Making Your Mark

In Unit Five, students will read about how people have left their stamp on the world, both in the modern world and in ancient times. The selections in this unit may prompt students to consider how they can make their own marks in life.

——————— **Part 1** ———————

Finding Your Voice In order to make your mark, you first have to find your voice—the way in which you can best express who you are. In *Words on a Page,* a young girl discovers that through her writing she is able to bring together the two parts of her life that she holds most dear.

——————— **Part 2** ———————

Voices from the Past The voice of history is never stilled. Things that happened thousands of years ago still have an impact on today's world. In "The Dog of Pompeii," we get a glimpse of ordinary life almost 2,000 years ago and find how little some things have changed.

Making Your Mark

Not for power,

not for money,

but simply to say

"I was here for a

little while;

I left this mark."

**WILLIAM FAULKNER
AMERICAN WRITER**

608

Philip and Karen Smith, © Tony Stone Images.

EXPLICIT INSTRUCTION Viewing and Representing

Photograph of Cave Painting,
Cuevos Los Manos, Argentina

ART APPRECIATION

Instruction Ask if students remember when they were little and made tracings of their hands, impressions of their hands in clay, or other artworks using the shape of their hands. This ancient cave painting is a little bit like that, but the hands are many and of different shapes and colors. It seems like people have always wanted to make their mark, no matter how far back in history you go!

Ask: What do the hands in the painting appear to be doing?

Possible Response: Some of the hands look as if they may be reaching for something. Some look as if they want to touch each other.

Ask: Do you think everyone wants to leave a mark on the world? Why?

Possible Response: Yes, because everybody wants to be remembered for something.

To help students explore the connections between the art, the quotation, and the unit theme, have them consider the following questions:

Ask: What would you want the mark you make to say about you?
Possible Response: Students' responses will vary, but should involve things they would like to be remembered for, either by people they know or by future generations.

Ask: What question do you think William Faulkner might have been responding to in his quotation on page 608?
Possible Response: Faulkner might have been responding to a question about why he is a writer.

Ask: If you were to choose a title for this ancient cave painting, what would it be?
Possible Responses: "Making Your Mark"; "Hands On"; "Striving"

Ask: What kinds of stories and experiences might you expect to read about in a unit called "Making Your Mark"?
Possible Response: You might expect to read about some people who left their mark on the world, for better or for worse. You might also read about some historical events and archaeological discoveries.

609

Features and Selections	Literary Analysis	Reading and Critical Thinking	Writing Opportunities
Making Your Mark **Finding Your Voice**			
Learning the Language of Literature Theme	Theme, 611		
The Active Reader Skills and Strategies		Drawing Conclusions, 613	
DRAMA Words on a Page Difficulty Level: *Average* **Related Reading** Bringing the Prairie Home	Theme, 614, 616, 618, 619, 620, 623, 624, 627, 630, 631, 633	Drawing Conclusions, 614, 616, 620, 622, 625, 626, 630, 633 Comparing Texts, 633 Reading Films, 635 Read Aloud, 632	Character Comparison, 634
ESSAY *from* All I Really Need to Know I Learned in Kindergarten Difficulty Level: *Average*	Personal Essay, 636, 638, 640 Author's Purpose, 640 Small Wonders, 642	Identifying Main Idea and Details, 636, 638, 640 Standardized Test Practice, 641 Examining Persuasion, 638 Noting Propaganda, 639	Personal Credo, 641
POETRY You Sing (Sonnet 52)/Soneto 52 How to Paint the Portrait of a Bird Difficulty Level: *Challenging*	Personification, 643, 644, 648 Punctuation in Poetry, 647 Onomatopoeia, 648	Noting Sensory Details, 643, 644, 646, 648 Comparing Texts, 648	Sensory Description, 649
Reading for Information Flip Out!		Following Complex Directions, 651, 651 Preparing an Application, 650	
SHORT STORY The Scribe Difficulty Level: *Easy* **Building Vocabulary**	Character Traits, 653, 654, 655, 656, 657, 658, 660, 661	Making Inferences About Characters, 653, 654, 656, 658, 660, 661 New Views, 662	Letter to the Editor, 662
AUTHOR STUDY Lois Lowry			
SHORT STORY Crow Call Difficulty Level: *Average*	Symbol, 668, 670, 674 Plot, 673	Recognizing Cause and Effect, 668, 670, 672, 674	
SPEECH Newbery Acceptance Speech		Identifying the Author's Purpose, 676	
MEMOIR *from* Looking Back Difficulty Level: *Easy*	Voice, 678, 680, 682, 684	Identifying Effects of Author's Perspective, 678, 680, 684 Comparing Texts, 684 Connecting, 681	
The Author's Style Author Study Project	Key Style Points, 686	Active Reading, 686	Writing, 686 Photo Essay, 687 Author Study Project, 687

LEGEND   DLS – Daily Language SkillBuilder   Green type – Teacher's Edition

Speaking and Listening Viewing and Representing	Research and Technology	Grammar, Usage, and Mechanics	Vocabulary
Art Appreciation, 608			
Video Critic, 634 Art Appreciation, 617 Loon Poster, 629 Read Aloud, 632	Research Project, 634	Sentence Fragments and Run-on Sentences, 635 DLS, 614 Examples as Fragments, 635	Context Clues, 634 Using Context Clues, 615
Credo Speech, 641		Sentence Variety Using Colons, 642 DLS, 636 Using Colons Correctly, 642	Standardized Test Practice, 641 Using a Thesaurus, 637
Sharing Your Description, 649	Something New, 649	DLS, 643	
	Research and Technology-Activity Link, 652, 652		
Read Aloud, 662	Spreading the Word, 662	DLS, 653	Researching Word Origins, 663 Dictionary, 654
Art Appreciation, 671		Subjects in Unusual Order, 675, 675 DLS, 668	Standardized Test Practice, 675 Analogies, 669
Read Aloud, 683		Combining Sentences, 685, 685 DLS, 678	Hard and Soft *g*, 685 Meaning Clues, 679, 685
Speaking and Listening, 686 Book Talk, 687	Photo Features, 687		

Features and Selections	Literary Analysis	Reading and Critical Thinking	Writing Opportunities	
Writing Workshop: Opinion Statement **Standardized Test Practice**		Analyzing a Student Model, 691 Patterns of Organization, 691	Writing Your Opinion Statement, 693 Making Weak Endings Stronger, 694 Revision: Organization, 694	

Voice From the Past				
Learning the Language of Literature Reading History Through Historical Fiction	Reading History Through Literature, 697			
The Active Reader Skills and Strategies		Distinguishing Fact from Opinion, 699		
SHORT STORY The Dog of Pompeii **Difficulty Level:** *Average*	Historical Fiction, 700, 702, 704, 706, 708, 710, 711 Review: Conflict, 711 Evaluating Story Elements, 705, 709 Point of View, 707 Influence of Setting, 710	Distinguishing Fact from Nonfact, 700, 702, 706, 708, 710, 711 Comparing Texts, 711	Facts from Fiction, 712 Informative Images, 712 Poetic Works, 713	
Reading for Information A 9,500-Year-Old Summer Home		Reading a Newspaper Article, 714, 715 Using Databases, 715		
INFORMATIVE NONFICTION Tutankhamen, *from* Lost Worlds **Difficulty Level:** *Challenging* **Related Reading** Ancestors	Informative Nonfiction, 718, 720, 725 Review: Sources of Information, 725 Activity, 725 Imagery, 723 Forms of Fiction, 724	Patterns of Organization, 718, 720, 725 Summarizing, 721	Archaeological Catalog, 726	
INFORMATIVE NONFICTION The First Emperor, *from* The Tomb Robbers **Difficulty Level:** *Challenging*	Informative Nonfiction, 728, 730, 734	Main Idea and Details, 728, 730, 734 Comparing Texts, 730, 734 Text Organization: Comparison-Contrast Order, 730 Summarizing, 731 Connecting Main Ideas, 732	The Emperor's Traits, 735 Amazing Burials, 736	
POETRY Barbara Frietchie **Difficulty Level:** *Average* **Building Vocabulary**	Poetic Form: Couplet, 737, 738, 740 Review: Sound Devices, 740 Narrative Poetry, 739	Clarifying, 737, 738, 740 Author Activity, 741	Frietchie Interview, 741	
Writing Workshop: Research Report **Standardized Test Practice**		Analyzing a Student Model, 755 Patterns of Organization, 756	Writing Your Research Report, 759 Focusing Your Report, 760 Revision: Organization, 760	
Reflect and Assess	Looking at Symbols, 763 Thinking About History, 763	Comparing Qualities, 762	Predicting Outcomes, 762 Portfolio Building, 763	

LEGEND   DLS – Daily Language SkillBuilder   **Green type – Teacher's Edition**

UNIT FIVE
RESOURCE MANAGEMENT GUIDE
PART 1

To introduce the theme of this unit, use transparencies 13–15 in Fine Arts Transparencies.

	Unit Resource Book	Assessment	Integrated Technology and Media
Words on a Page *pp. 614–635*	• Summary p. 4 • Active Reading: Conclusions p. 5 • Literary Analysis: Theme p. 6 • Literary Analysis: Theme and Character p. 7 • Grammar p. 8 • Words to Know p. 9 • Selection Quiz p. 10	• Selection Test, Formal Assessment pp. 101–102 ○ Test Generator	○ Audio Library ▬ Video: Literature in Performance, Video Resource Book pp. 25–30 ○ Research Starter www.mcdougallittell.com
from **All I Really Need to Know I Learned in Kindergarten** *pp. 636–642*	• Summary p. 11 • Active Reading: Identifying Main Idea and Details p. 12 • Literary Analysis: Personal Essay p. 13 • Active Reading: Identifying Propaganda and Persuasion p. 14 • Grammar p. 15 • Words to Know p. 16 • Selection Quiz p. 17	• Selection Test, Formal Assessment pp. 103–104 ○ Test Generator	○ Audio Library
You Sing (Sonnet 52) How to Paint the Portrait of a Bird *pp. 643–649*	• Active Reading: Noting Sensory Details p. 18 • Literary Analysis: Personification p. 19	• Selection Test, Formal Assessment pp. 105–106 ○ Test Generator	○ Audio Library
Flip Out *pp. 650–652*	• Following Complex Directions p. 20 • Preparing an Application p. 21		
The Scribe *pp. 653–662*	• Summary p. 22 • Active Reading: Making Inferences p. 23 • Literary Analysis: Character Traits p. 24 • Literary Analysis: Traits and Plot p. 25 • Grammar p. 26 • Words to Know p. 27 • Selection Quiz p. 28	• Selection Test, Formal Assessment pp. 107–108 ○ Test Generator	○ Audio Library
Crow Call *pp. 668–675*	• Summary p. 30 • Active Reading: Cause-Effect p. 31 • Literary Analysis: Symbol p. 32 • Literary Analysis: Plot p. 33 • Grammar p. 34 • Words to Know p. 35 • Selection Quiz p. 36	• Selection Test, Formal Assessment pp. 109–110 ○ Test Generator	○ Audio Library ○ More Online: Author Link www.mcdougallittell.com ○ NetActivities
from **Looking Back** *pp. 678–685*	• Summary p. 37 • Active Reading: Author's Perspective p. 38 • Literary Analysis: Voice p. 39 • Active Reading: Connecting p. 40 • Grammar p. 41 • Words to Know p. 42 • Selection Quiz p. 43	• Selection Test, Formal Assessment pp. 111–112 ○ Test Generator	○ Audio Library ○ Research Starter www.mcdougallittell.com ○ NetActivities

Writing Workshop: Opinion Statement

		Unit Assessment	Unit Technology
Unit Five Resource Book • Prewriting p. 44 • Drafting and Elaboration p. 45 • Peer Response Guide p. 46 • Organizational Patterns: Order of Importance p. 47 • Revising, Editing, and Proofreading p. 48 • Student Models pp. 49–51 • Rubric for Evaluation p. 52	○ **Writing Coach** **Reading and Critical Thinking Transparencies** TR25 **Speaking and Listening Book** pp. 6–9, 12–13, 19–22, 29–30	• Unit Five, Part 1 Test, Formal Assessment pp. 113–114 ○ Test Generator • Unit Five: Integrated Assessment pp. 25–30	○ ClassZone www.mcdougallittell.com ○ Electronic Teacher Tools

Additional Support

Literary Analysis Transparencies	Reading and Critical Thinking Transparencies	Language Transparencies	Writing Transparencies	Speaking and Listening Book
• Theme TR7	• Drawing Conclusions TR18	• Daily Language SkillBuilder TR19 • Sentence Fragments TR32 • Context Clues: Overview and Definition TR53	• Transitional Words List TR10	• Creating a Persuasive Presentation p. 29 • Guidelines: How to Analyze a Persuasive Presentation p. 30
	• Main Idea and Supporting Details TR25	• Daily Language SkillBuilder TR19 • Synonyms TR60	• Writing Variables TR2 • Elaboration TR13	• Matching Your Message with Purpose and Audience p. 6
• Poetry: Figurative Language TR19	• Noting Sensory Details TR11	• Daily Language SkillBuilder TR20	• Sensory Words List TR16	• Evaluating Reading Aloud p. 14
	• Making Inferences TR10 • Venn Diagram TR35	• Daily Language SkillBuilder TR20 • Learning and Remembering New Words TR65		• Evaluating Reading Aloud p. 14
	• Cause and Effect TR5	• Daily Language SkillBuilder TR21 • Subject-Verb Agreement TR37 • Analogies TR64	• Varying Sentence Openers and Closers TR18	
• Author's Style TR9	• Author's Purpose and Audience TR8	• Daily Language SkillBuilder TR21 • Context Clues: Compare and Contrast, Cause and Effect, Example TR54	• Personal Experience Essay TR25	• Creating a Persuasive Presentation p. 29 • Guidelines: How to Analyze a Persuasive Presentation p. 30

ENGLISH LEARNERS / STUDENTS ACQUIRING ENGLISH

The **Spanish Study Guide,** pp. 121–141, includes language support for the following pages:
• Family and Community Involvement (per unit)
• Selection Summaries and Vocabulary
• Active Reading
• Literary Analysis

For **systematic instruction** in language skills, see:
• **Vocabulary and Spelling Book**
• **Grammar, Usage, and Mechanics Book**
• pacing chart on p. 609i

UNIT FIVE
RESOURCE MANAGEMENT GUIDE
PART 2

To introduce the theme of this unit, use transparencies 13–15 in Fine Arts Transparencies.

	Unit Resource Book	Assessment	Integrated Technology and Media
The Dog of Pompeii *pp. 700–713*	• Summary p. 53 • Active Reading: Distinguishing Fact from Nonfact p. 54 • Literary Analysis: Historical Fiction p. 55 • Active Reading: Evaluating Story Elements p. 56 • Grammar p. 57 • Words to Know p. 58 • Selection Quiz p. 59	• Selection Test, Formal Assessment pp. 115–116 ◉ Test Generator	🎧 Audio Library
500 Year Old Summer Home *pp. 714–717*	• Reading a Newspaper Article p. 60 • Organizational Features p. 61		
Tutankhamen, *from* **Lost Worlds** *pp. 718–727*	• Summary p. 62 • Active Reading: Patterns of Organization p. 63 • Literary Analysis: Informative Nonfiction p. 64 • Literary Analysis: Fiction and Nonfiction p. 65 • Grammar p. 66 • Words to Know p. 67 • Selection Quiz p. 68	• Selection Test, Formal Assessment pp. 117–118 ◉ Test Generator	🎧 Audio Library 🖱 Research Starter www.mcdougallittell.com
The First Emperor, *from* **The Tomb Robbers** *pp. 728–736*	• Summary p. 69 • Active Reading: Main Idea and Supporting Details p. 70 • Literary Analysis: Informative Nonfiction p. 71 • Active Reading: Connecting Main Ideas p. 72 • Grammar p. 73 • Words to Know p. 74 • Selection Quiz p. 75	• Selection Test, Formal Assessment pp. 119–120 ◉ Test Generator	🎧 Audio Library 🖱 Research Starter www.mcdougallittell.com
Barbara Frietchie *pp. 737–741*	• Active Reading: Clarifying p. 76 • Literary Analysis: Poetic Form: Couplet p. 77	• Selection Test, Formal Assessment pp. 121–122 ◉ Test Generator	🎧 Audio Library 🖱 Research Starter www.mcdougallittell.com

Writing Workshop: Research Report

		Unit Assessment	**Unit Technology**
Unit Five Resource Book • Prewriting p. 79 • Drafting and Elaboration p. 80 • Peer Response Guide p. 81 • Organizational Patterns: Organization by Category p. 82 • Revising, Editing, and Proofreading p. 83 • Student Models pp. 84–86 • Rubric for Evaluation p. 87	◉ **Writing Coach** **Writing Transparencies** TR7, TR12, TR41, TR53, TR54, TR56 **Reading and Critical Thinking Transparencies** TR37 **Speaking and Listening Book** pp. 10, 11, 25–26	• Unit Five, Part 2 Test, Formal Assessment pp. 123–124 ◉ Test Generator • Unit Five Integrated Test, Integrated Assessment pp. 25–30	🖱 ClassZone www.mcdougallittell.com ◉ Electronic Teacher Tools

Additional Support

Literary Analysis Transparencies	Reading and Critical Thinking Transparencies	Language Transparencies	Writing Transparencies	Speaking and Listening Book
• Conflict TR8	• Distinguishing Fact from Opinion TR26	• Daily Language SkillBuilder TR22 • Subject-Verb Agreement TR37 • Synonyms and Antonyms TR60–61	• Sensory Words List TR16 • Using Periodical Indexes TR44	
			• Using the Library Catalog TR42	
	• Patterns of Organization (Text Structure) TR24	• Daily Language SkillBuilder TR22 • Context Clues: Definition and Overview TR53	• Writing Variables TR2	
	• Main Idea and Supporting Details TR25	• Daily Language SkillBuilder TR23 • Word Parts: Roots and Base Words TR56	• Effective Language TR15	
• Form in Poetry: Rhyme and Meter TR17	• Strategies for Reading TR1	• Daily Language SkillBuilder TR23		

ENGLISH LEARNERS / STUDENTS ACQUIRING ENGLISH

The **Spanish Study Guide,** pp. 142–153, includes language support for the following pages:
• Family and Community Involvement (per unit)
• Selection Summaries and Vocabulary
• Active Reading
• Literary Analysis

For **systematic instruction** in language skills, see:
• **Vocabulary and Spelling Book**
• **Grammar, Usage, and Mechanics Book**
• pacing chart on p. 609i

INTEGRATING SKILLS INSTRUCTION PACING CHART

The *Language of Literature* offers several options for integrating language arts instruction and literature.

- Systematic instruction in grammar, vocabulary, and spelling is provided in the *Grammar, Usage, and Mechanics Book* and in the *Vocabulary and Spelling Book*. The pacing chart on the right shows when to use the lessons in these books.
- The Pupil's Edition provides grammar and vocabulary instruction in context. The examples for the grammar feature, *Grammar in Context*, arise from the selections and relate to the grammar focus for each unit. In addition each selection includes vocabulary words called *Words to Know*. Vocabulary practice occurs in *Choices and Challenges* at the end of each selection.
- The Teacher's Edition provides review and reinforcement of the grammar and vocabulary concepts through Explicit Instruction lessons. References to additional support in *Unit Resource Books* and other ancillaries are included at the end of appropriate lessons.

Grammar, Usage and Mechanics
From Grammar, Mechanics, and Usage Book

Chapter 1: Sentence and Its Parts
Chapter 2: Nouns
Chapter 3: Pronouns
Chapter 4: Verbs
Chapter 5: Adjectives and Adverbs
Chapter 6: Prepositions, Conjunctions, and Interjections

Chapter 7: Subject-Verb Agreement
- Agreement in Number
- Compound Subjects
- Phrases Between Subjects and Verbs
- Indefinite Pronouns as Subject
- Subjects in Unusual Positions

For Ongoing Reference
Chapter 8: Capitalization
Chapter 9: Punctuation

Vocabulary
From Vocabulary and Spelling Book

Lesson 1: Context Clues
Lesson 2: Restatement Context Clues
Lesson 3: Contrast ContextClues
Lesson 4: Definition Context Clues
Lesson 5: Comparison Context Clues
Lesson 6: General Context Clues
Lesson 7: Prefixes and Base Words
Lesson 8: Prefixes and Base Words
Lesson 9: Base Words and Suffixes
Lesson 10: Base Words and Suffixes
Lesson 11: Anglo-Saxon Affixes and Base Words
Lesson 12: Roots and Word Families
Lesson 13: Roots and Word Familes
Lesson 14: Analyzing Roots and Affixes
Lesson 15: Analyzing Roots and Affixes
Lesson 16: Foreign Words in English
Lesson 17: Specialized Vocabulary
Lesson 18: Specialized Vocabulary
Lesson 19: Specialized Vocabulary
Lesson 20: Words with Multiple Meanings
Lesson 21: Synonyms
Lesson 22: Antonyms
Lesson 23: Denotation and Connotation
Lesson 24: Using a Thesaurus
Lesson 25: Idioms
Lesson 26: Similes and Metaphors

Lesson 27: Compound Words
Lesson 28: Homonyms
Lesson 29: Homophones and Easily Confused Words
Lesson 30: Homographs
Lesson 31: Analogies
Lesson 32: Using Your Strategies

Spelling
From Vocabulary and Spelling Book

Lesson 1: Silent *e* Words and Suffixes
Lesson 2: The Suffix *ance*
Lesson 3: Plural Words Ending in *o*
Lesson 4: Prefixes and Base Words
Lesson 5: Prefixes and Roots
Lesson 6: Words Ending with *ary*
Lesson 7: Soft and Hard *g*
Lesson 8: Review
Lesson 9: Final *y* words and Suffixes
Lesson 10: The Suffix *able*
Lesson 11: Words Ending with *al + ly*
Lesson 12: The Prefix *com*
Lesson 13: Forms of the Prefix *ad*
Lesson 14: Words Ending with *ory*
Lesson 15: Unstressed Syllables
Lesson 16: Review
Lesson 17: *VAC* Words
Lesson 18: Non-*VAC* Words
Lesson 19: Words Ending with *c + ally*
Lesson 20: The Prefix *ex*
Lesson 21: More Forms of the Prefix *ad*
Lesson 22: Base Word Changes
Lesson 23: Words Ending with *cious, cial,* or *cian*
Lesson 24: Review
Lesson 25: Greek Combining Forms
Lesson 26: Compound Words and Contractions

Lesson 27: The Suffix *ible*
Lesson 28: Forms of Prefix *ob + sub*
Lesson 29: Forms of Prefix *in*
Lesson 30: The Suffixes *ence + ent*
Lesson 31: Words Ending with *ize + ise*
Lesson 32: Review

Selection	SkillBuilder Sentences	Suggested Answers
Words on a Page	1. Some stories is wonderful to read out loud.	1. Some stories **are** wonderful to read out loud.
	2. Can you give me an idea of how long this play last?	2. Can you give me an idea of how long this play **lasts**?
from All I Really Need to Know . . .	1. When he was young, his personal statements was lengthy.	1. When he was young, his personal statements **were** lengthy.
	2. He and I shares some of the same beliefs.	2. He and I **share** some of the same beliefs.
You Sing (Sonnet 52)/Soneto 52	1. It might be a women's voice that is being described in the first poem.	1. It might be a **woman's** voice that is being described in the first poem.
How to Paint the Portrait of a Bird	2. One of the poet's is well known as a playwright also.	2. One of the **poets** is well known as a playwright also.
The Scribe	1. Like the boy in the story, my parents and me live in a city.	1. Like the boy in the story, my parents and **I** live in a city.
	2. The people in the story were like people in mine neighborhood.	2. The people in the story were like people in **my** neighborhood.
Crow Call	1. Lois Lowry loves to garden cook play Bridge watch movies and read.	1. Lois Lowry loves to garden, cook, play Bridge, watch movies, and read.
	2. Lowry's dog Bandit is a Tibetan terrier and brings her great joy.	2. Lowry's dog, Bandit, is a Tibetan terrier and brings her great joy.
from Looking Back	1. "My brother Jon was younger than I said Lois, and yet we had a lot in common."	1. "My brother Jon was younger than I," said Lois, "and yet we had a lot in common."
	2. I wanted to write something for his daughter to remember him by, Lois replied when asked about the book she wrote about her son.	2. "I wanted to write something for his daughter to remember him by," Lois replied when asked about the book she wrote about her son.

Selection	SkillBuilder Sentences	Suggested Answers
The Dog of Pompeii	**1.** The eruption of Mount Vesuvius completely buried the city of Pompeii in ashs.	**1.** The eruption of Mount Vesuvius completely buried the city of Pompeii in **ashes**.
	2. Because of this, we now know how mens and woman of that time dressed and lived.	**2.** Because of this, we now know how **men** and **women** of that time dressed and lived.
Tutankhamen	**1.** Lord Carnarvon the man who paid for Howard Carter's archaeological work.	**1.** Lord Carnarvon **was** the man who paid for Howard Carter's archaeological work.
	2. Carter insisted that his team.	**2.** Carter insisted that his team **cover the entire area.**
The First Emperor	**1.** Ch'in Shih Huang Ti's tomb is one of the greatest archaeological finds ever it contains thousands of clay figures and covers a vast area.	**1.** Ch'in Shih Huang Ti's tomb is one of the greatest archaeological finds ever. **It** contains thousands of clay figures and covers a vast area.
	2. The first emperor used his power to build the Great Wall. As well as a tomb for himself.	**2.** The first emperor used his power to build the Great Wall, **as** well as a tomb for himself.
Barbara Frietchie	**1.** Its a tragedy that so many soldiers died in the Civil War.	**1.** **It's** a tragedy that so many soldiers died in the Civil War.
	2. I think that this womans courage is truly admirable.	**2.** I think that this **woman's** courage is truly admirable.

OVERVIEW

Students work with partners to present staged interviews with historical figures.

Project at a glance Many of the selections in Unit Five, Part 2, focus on historical topics or people. For this project, each partnered team will choose a historical figure from the unit (or another figure that interests them) and deliver a staged interview session. Students will research the life of the historical figure, gather information, and prepare an interview. Both partners will share responsibilities for researching and writing. Students might present the interviews in a "History Day."

SCHEDULING

Partners should take no more than ten minutes to present their interview. You may want to schedule the interviews over the course of 2–3 class periods and/or align them with one of your social studies units, if it is practical.

PROJECT OBJECTIVES

- To demonstrate the speaking and listening skills introduced in the activity
- To research the life and accomplishments of a historical figure
- To play the role of a historical figure and give an interview
- To demonstrate interviewing skills
- To answer questions from the audience

SUGGESTED GROUP SIZE
Partners

Historical Interview

 ## 1 Getting Started

Explain that students will be working with partners to present an interview with a historical figure. See the Selections Overview for summaries of the stories in this unit.

Before students begin, do a little research yourself to see if your school library has sufficient information (biographies, autobiographies) on historical figures. If it does not, arrange with a local library for these materials to be available to students.

You might also locate a collection of films or videos on historical figures of your choice. Students should be encouraged to "get into character," which might involve dressing up as the historical figure, with the appropriate costumes, props, makeup, and so on. You should make arrangements for these items to

be available, either from your school's drama department or from some other source.

This project should only require rearranging a bit of furniture in your classroom on the appropriate day. There should be two chairs in the front of the room, as well as seating for audience members. If you think students are ready for a real audience, you might create a History Day and invite other classes, parents, or teachers to act as judges or audience members.

Writing Workshop Connection

As a springboard, students may use the Writing Workshop assignment **Research Report**, p. 754.

 ## 2 Directing the Project

Preparing As a class, briefly discuss the historical topics featured in this unit, as well as any other topics you might be covering in a social studies unit or another related unit.

▶ Divide students into pairs. Tell students that each team will write and present an interview with a historical figure. Have students choose a figure from the unit or another figure. They should decide who will act as the figure and the interviewer.

Assigning Roles Have students divide the work up evenly within each team. Roles might include writer, interviewer, researcher, and so on. You might want to choose one student to write and present an introduction and conclusion for the entire class presentation (or you could fill this position yourself).

▶ After teams have chosen their historical figure, they should begin researching. Meet with them to make sure there are no duplications. Students should collect information using multiple sources (films, videos, books, and so on) and choose an important event in their subject's life. They should then write an interview script based on that event. Or they may simply choose to focus on their subject's life in general.

▶ Later, meet with each team to refine the interview, offer help, or make suggestions. Before the presentation, students should check

to make sure all the main points are supported with facts and examples. Review with students the Speaking and Listening Strategies found in the Speaking and Listening Handbook, page R105.

Practicing You should allow time for teams to rehearse their interviews. The interviewer should go over his or her notes, and the historical figure should be well prepared to answer questions.

▶ For this stage, both students may use notes to help prepare; however, this should be discouraged during the final presentation. Remind students to stay in character during the interview in order to make the presentation convincing.

▶ Tell students that giving and receiving feedback during the rehearsal stage is crucial. Refer to the tips in the Feedback Center.

Presenting This project could culminate in a History Day for the entire student body or just for your class.

▶ To begin, have students take a few deep breaths and focus on what they want to communicate. Students should take their places in front of the audience. After the initial interview, you might open the forum to questions from the audience. The historical figure could then answer in character and provide further insights.

Teaching the Speaking and Listening Skills

The student is expected to:

Adapt spoken language such as word choice, diction, and usage to the purpose, audience and occasion

Teaching Suggestions: Tell students that "getting into character" means learning about the culture and context of their historical figure. This will require research. Perhaps students can watch films set in their speaker's era. Students should adjust their message to fit their audience's knowledge and expectations, and adjust their speech and delivery to fit the occasion (formal vs. informal). Students should also try to match their language to the purpose of their message. Have students identify their purposes and discuss with them ways in which they might adjust their language to best suit those purposes.

Interpret a speaker's verbal and nonverbal message, purpose, and perspective

Teaching Suggestions: Discuss with students how body language can reflect a speaker's message. Ask students for suggestions as to the types of signals that indicate nonverbal messages (for instance, arms folded across one's chest might mean that the person is not open to new information). During the interview, have student audience members pay particular attention to the historical figure's verbal and nonverbal message. Decide how it reflects their purpose and perspective.

Listen to learn by taking notes, organizing ideas, and summarizing ideas

Teaching Suggestions: Have student audience members take notes during the interviews so that they are prepared to ask questions afterward. Briefly outline note-taking techniques and the use of outline form. Tell students that they don't need to write down everything that is said during an interview or speech; they need only the major ideas and perhaps a word or phrase that will jog their memory when it is time to ask questions. They should also jot down questions to be asked later. When asking a question, students should briefly summarize the character's point of view (for example, "Beethoven, I know your father was a singer. What did you learn about music from him?").

Feedback Center

Students can use the following guidelines when giving and receiving feedback during this project:

Giving Feedback

▶ Ask questions concerning content, delivery, purpose and point of view (for example, is tone appropriate to purpose?).

▶ Provide feedback about the coherence and logic of the content, delivery, and overall impact on the listener.

▶ Comment on the verbal and nonverbal delivery (pitch, pace, volume, gestures, body language) and its impact on the listener.

▶ Respond to persuasive messages with questions, challenges, or affirmations.

▶ Question the evidence to support the speaker's claims and conclusions.

Receiving Feedback

▶ Listen to constructive criticism with an open mind.

▶ Use audience feedback and modify the presentation to clarify meaning or organization.

 Assessing the Project

The following rubric can be used for group or individual assessment.

3 Full Accomplishment

Students followed directions and presented a coherent interview based on solid research and investigation. The ideas discussed were well supported with evidence and examples. Students worked effectively with partners and demonstrated all of the Speaking and Listening Skills listed.

2 Substantial Accomplishment

Students presented a coherent interview based on adequate research. There was some supporting evidence. Students worked adequately with partners, and the presentation, however lacking in originality or insight, met most of the Speaking and Listening points.

1 Little Accomplishment

Partners' interviews were incomplete or did not fulfill the requirements of the assignment. There was inadequate research, points were not supported with evidence, and the interview lacked a convincing tone.

UNIT FIVE
PART 1

PART 1
Finding
Your Voice
Meeting Standards

The Literature You'll Read

The Concepts You'll Study

Vocabulary and Reading Comprehension
Vocabulary Focus: Researching Word Origins
Drawing Conclusions
Identifying Main Idea and Details
Noting Sensory Details
Making Inferences About Characters
Recognizing Cause and Effect
Identifying the Author's Purpose
Identifying Effects of an Author's Perspective

Writing and Language Conventions
Writing Workshop: Opinion Statement
Sentence Fragments and Run-on Sentences
Sentence Variety Using Colons
Subjects in Different Positions
Combining Sentences

Literary Analysis
Literary Focus: Theme
Theme
Personal Essay
Personification
Character Traits
Symbol
Voice

Speaking and Listening
Video Review
Short Speech
Original Description Read-Aloud
Story Read-Aloud
Favorite Book Presentation

610

LEARNING the Language of *Literature*

Theme

> *To produce a mighty book, you must choose a mighty theme.*
> —Herman Melville, author of Moby Dick

Theme is the meaning or moral of a story. It is a message about life or human nature that the writer shares with the reader. A typical theme statement might be "You'll never know what you can accomplish until you try" or "True friendship is more important than popularity." In folktales, themes may be stated directly. For example, in "The Wolf and the House Dog," there is a lesson about freedom stated at the end of the story. Most themes, however, are unstated. You must figure them out by paying attention to what happens in a story. A story may have more than one theme, but usually there is one theme that is central.

The Difference Between Subject and Theme

The **subject** of a story is what the story is about—the characters and the important events. The **theme** is the meaning behind the story. For example, the subject of *The Phantom Tollbooth* is a young boy's adventure in a land of words and numbers. The central theme, or meaning of the play, might be stated as "With courage and caring, nothing is impossible." The dialogue in the passage to the right helps convey this theme.

THEME

(All bow and salute the heroes.)

Milo. But we never could have done it without a lot of help.

Reason. That may be true, but you had the courage to try, and what you can do is often a matter of what you will do.

—Norton Juster and Susan Nanus,
The Phantom Tollbooth

From *The Phantom Tollbooth*

611

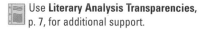

Identifying Theme

Have students reread a short story they've previously read as a class. Ask them to discuss their interpretation of the title after reading the story. Then ask them to describe the setting of the story, the main character, and the central conflict that the main character experiences.

Examining Characters

Focusing on the story you had students reread, ask students "What lesson does the main character learn as a result of the conflict? How might that lesson apply to other people?"

Identifying Theme

You can gather clues to the theme of a piece of literature by looking at the **characters,** the **plot,** the **setting,** and the **story title.** Read a story all the way through before you begin to look for the theme. Then reread the story and use the questions in the chart to help you record important story information. Use your answers to help you figure out the theme of the story, or the author's message.

One of the themes of "The Scribe" is "People can use their talents to make positive changes in the world." Some of the clues to the theme are shown in the chart.

Examining Characters

Pay special attention to the actions, thoughts, and words of the important characters. Theme is often conveyed through these elements. Also notice how the important characters change in a story.

When you are trying to determine theme, ask yourself these questions: What is the message behind the actions, thoughts, and words of the characters? What message is the writer trying to give me?

IDENTIFYING THEMES	
What to think about	**Questions to answer**
Characters	• Who is the main character? *a 13-year-old boy named James* • Who are the other important characters? *the people James reads for, James's parents, Mr. Silver and Mr. Dollar* • How does the main character change during the story? *He changes from being angry about what is happening to being a problem-solver.* • What does the main character learn? *He learns that he can make important changes and that he should not give up.*
Plot	• What conflict does the main character face? *James is in conflict about how some people in his neighborhood are being treated.* • What is the climax of the story? • How is the conflict resolved?
Setting	• What is the setting? • How does it affect the conflict?
Title	• What in the story does the title refer to?

From "The Scribe"

*D*rawing Conclusions

Have you ever walked inside a house and smelled something cooking? If you were able to guess what it was, you were drawing a conclusion based on past experiences and common sense. In life, drawing conclusions helps you understand the world. In literature, drawing conclusions gives you a fuller understanding of what you are reading.

How to Apply the Skill

To **draw conclusions,** an active reader will
- Look for facts and details
- Consider experience and knowledge
- Make logical guesses
- **Evaluate** information
- **Connect** personally

Try It Now!

Read and draw conclusions from the excerpt below.

> **Miss Walker** *(quietly)*. Lenore, that was beautiful! *(Lenore gives a shy, tentative smile.)* . . .
>
> **Girl #2.** It was just like a book. *(There is a silent moment after this pronouncement. Lenore looks at the other students, trying to suppress her excitement.)* . . .
>
> **Miss Walker.** I'm really very impressed, Lenore. Leave your story on my desk. There are some people I'd like to show it to.
> —Keith Leckie, *Words on a Page*

Here's how Talisa uses the skill:

*"I can **connect** to the happiness and pride that Lenore feels from getting so many compliments. After **evaluating** the class's reaction and Miss Walker's decision to show Lenore's story to other people, I **conclude** that Lenore will continue writing. She probably feels that writing is one of the most important things in her life."*

OVERVIEW

Standards-Based Objectives
- draw conclusions
- support responses by referring to text evidence and one's own experiences

Teaching the Lesson

The strategies on this page will help students learn how to draw conclusions about plot, character, setting, and theme in a story.

Presenting the Strategies
To help students understand the strategies, ask for volunteers to read them aloud. Emphasize to students that they will be using these strategies as they read the selections in this book. Ask them to follow the strategies outlined on this page as they do the following:

Draw Conclusions
Choose a selection from this unit to read, and divide the class into small groups. Ask each group to use the strategies outlined on this page and to list the significant facts and details in the story. Then have students discuss the inferences that they are able to draw from these facts and details.

Evaluate
Ask a volunteer from each group to share the group's conclusions and explain how the group arrived at them.

Connect
As a class, discuss connections that students could make between the elements in the story and their own life experiences. How does connecting help them draw conclusions?

Use **Reading and Critical Thinking Transparencies,** p. 1, for additional support.

Standards-Based Objectives

1. understand and appreciate **drama**
2. understand and appreciate **theme**
3. use the reading skill of **drawing conclusions**

Summary

Lenore Green, an Ojibway teenager, is a promising writer. Her teacher enters Lenore's writing in the District Writing Competitions, giving Lenore the chance to appear before a panel of judges and win a scholarship. Lenore's father, a loving but somewhat bitter man, refuses to allow his daughter to participate, fearing that her encounters with the outside world will take her away from her home and Ojibway heritage and subject her to the same kind of humiliations he has suffered at the hands of white people. The deep understanding between father and daughter, even with all its conflicts, eventually solves the problem.

Thematic Link

Lenore Green has found her voice, but will it fall on deaf ears? Or will her message be so powerful that it cannot fail to make its mark?

English Conventions Practice

Daily Language SkillBuilder

Have students **proofread** the display sentences on page 609k and write them correctly. The sentences also appear on Transparency 19 of **Language Transparencies.**

Words on a Page

by KEITH LECKIE

Traditionally, the Ojibway lived in wigwams, dome-shaped wooden frame houses covered in bark or animal skins.

Connect to Your Life

What traditions have been handed down in your own family?

Build Background

The main characters in this drama are Native Americans of the Ojibway (or Ojibwa or Chippewa) people. Before European settlement in North America, the Ojibway were one of the largest native groups. Like Pete in this drama, they were hunters and fishers. Like Lenore, they wrote about their history, recording important events in pictures drawn on birch bark.

The Ojibway were also known as warriors. They fought in the French and Indian War and with the British in the American Revolution. Like other Native Americans, they lost most of their land to the U.S. government. Today, they live primarily on reservations in the Upper Great Lakes region of the United States and Canada.

Focus Your Reading

LITERARY ANALYSIS   THEME

In a work of literature, the **theme** is a message about life or human nature the writer wishes to share. A work may have more than one theme. As you read this drama, think about its message and the lessons you might learn from it.

WORDS TO KNOW **Vocabulary Preview**

abundance	expertise	gesture	tentative
anticipation	foliage	hover	
collective	foreground	momentum	

ACTIVE READING   DRAWING CONCLUSIONS

When you pay attention to details as you are reading and make guesses about what they mean, you are **drawing conclusions.** In drawing conclusions, you use information from your reading as well as from your own experiences.

📖 **READER'S NOTEBOOK**   As you read, note words or phrases that point to a larger message or meaning, that state beliefs, or that comment on life. Use this information and your own prior knowledge to draw conclusions about the theme of the story.

LESSON RESOURCES

For **systematic instruction** in language skills, see:
• **Vocabulary and Spelling Book**
• **Grammar, Usage, and Mechanics Book**
• pacing chart on p. 609i

Words on a Page
by Keith Leckie

Characters

Lenore Green, an Ojibway teenager

Pete Green, Lenore's father, a fisherman and trapper

Connie Green, Lenore's mother

Sadie Green, Lenore's younger sister

Miss Walker, Lenore's grade ten teacher

The Principal of Lenore's high school

Various Students

Driver

Man

Reading Skills and Strategies:
PREVIEW

Have students look through the selection and note how it differs from the stories they've read. You might point out that this is not just a drama, but a teleplay, or a drama meant to be presented on television or film. Tell students to notice how the selection is divided and how the stage directions are shown.

Literary Analysis THEME

Remind students that the theme is an important statement the author makes about life. What statement is Lenore making about life in the piece she reads on this page?

Possible Response: She is saying that her home is important to her.

Use **Literary Analysis Transparencies,** p. 7, for additional support.

Active Reading
DRAWING CONCLUSIONS

Ask students what inference or conclusion they can draw about what Girl #2 means when she says, "It was just like a book."

Possible Response: She means it was as well written as a published book.

Use **Unit Five Resource Book,** p. 5, for more practice. Use **Reading and Critical Thinking Transparencies,** p. 18, for additional support.

Literary Analysis: TELEPLAY

Explain to students that a teleplay is a drama written for television. Ask them to note several words on this page that indicate this is a teleplay.

Possible Responses: camera, panning, holding, cuts, pulls focus

Scene 1 Interior. Classroom. Day.

It is a sunny fall afternoon in Lenore's grade ten English class. Sunrays through dust particles in the air. There are a dozen classmates, a mixture of white and native, listening as Lenore reads a story she has written.

Lenore. . . . So on that morning before she left, they went by canoe one last time to those favorite places. It was at first light, when the water is a mirror and the trees are still, as if nature is holding her breath.

(A variety of young faces listen, all enthralled with her story. Camera moves slowly, panning across the classroom, holding on different faces.)

And there was the beaver and the loon and the hawk circling above the treetops. And below the trout and the sturgeon slipped silently through the black water.

(Camera stops on one Girl, listening intently, then moves again. Camera holds on two Boys slouching close together, almost touching, but their eyes and attention are on Lenore at the front of the class.)

Creatures as powerful as the great moose, as small as a minnow. She and her father took their place among them.

(Camera cuts to Miss Walker, the native teacher. She sits to one side of Lenore listening as intently as the rest. She is very impressed.)

Camera pans and pulls focus to hold finally on Lenore as she finishes the story. She has memorized most of it and hardly has to look at the page. She speaks very well with skilled emphasis and a personal passion for her words.)

And in this world there was a peace and harmony that she knew no matter how far she traveled, she would never find again. She understood now why her father had brought her here. She felt the morning sun on her face and the gentle rocking of the canoe and smiled because she knew that here would always be her home.

(Lenore stops speaking, holds the few pages against her chest with both arms and looks at Miss Walker a little anxiously. There is a hushed silence for a moment.)

Miss Walker *(quietly).* Lenore, that was beautiful!

(Lenore gives a shy, <u>tentative</u> smile.)

What did you think, class?

(The class gives a <u>collective</u> chatter of positive response, then . . .)

Girl #1. It was real sad.

Boy #1. It reminded me of . . . like around Shadow River.

Girl #2. It was just like a book.

(There is a silent moment after this pronouncement. Lenore looks at the other students, trying to suppress her excitement.)

(The bell rings signaling the end of class and the students quickly exit the classroom. When the wave of students has passed, Lenore is left still standing there. Miss Walker puts a hand on her shoulder.)

Miss Walker. I'm really very impressed, Lenore. Leave your story on my desk. There are some people I'd like to show it to.

(Miss Walker then exits, leaving Lenore alone. She takes a deep breath then allows herself a beaming smile as she hugs her story against herself.)

| WORDS TO KNOW | **tentative** (těn′tə-tǐv) *adj.* uncertain; hesitant |
| | **collective** (kə-lěk′tǐv) *adj.* done by a number of people acting as a group |

616

EXPLICIT INSTRUCTION ## Understanding Theme

Instruction Ask a volunteer to explain what theme is. (*the meaning or moral of a story; a message from the writer to the reader*) Then ask students what they know about how to identify the theme of a story. Remind students that the theme of a story is usually unstated and that they must pay attention to story details in order to figure out the theme. Next, write the word *characters* on the board and remind students that examining characters is important to figuring out the theme. Ask students to name things about characters that can give clues to a theme. Note suggestions on the board and make sure

they include these ideas: *what characters say and think, how they feel and act, the conflicts they have, what they learn, how they change.* Tell students that many of the characters in this drama are storytellers. Explain that some of the clues to the theme will come from the stories the characters tell. Students should pay special attention to the stories.

Practice Use the Literary Analysis: Theme note in the green side column to give students practice in understanding characters' stories. First, have students create a chart with five columns in their notebooks. They should label

the columns with these headings: *characters' stories, characters' words, characters' actions, characters' thoughts or feelings, characters' conflicts.* Tell students to record in their charts their answers to the question in the side column. Also tell them to continue taking notes as they read this drama.

Possible Responses: See the possible responses given with the note in the side column.

Use **Unit Five Resource Book,** p. 6, for more practice.

Good Afternoon #1, Alex Katz. Oil on canvas, 71½" × 96", Private Collection, Paris. Courtesy of Colby College Museum of Art.
Copyright © Alex Katz/Licensed by VAGA, New York, NY/Marlborough Gallery, NY.

Less Proficient Readers

Help students understand that while the setting of this scene—Lenore's classroom—does not change, the images that would be seen on camera do change. Point out that each set of stage directions in italics indicates a different camera shot that a viewer would see on the screen. You may want to make sure students know what beavers, loons, hawks, trout, sturgeon, moose, and minnows look like. Point out that when Lenore says, "And there was the beaver and the loon and the hawk circling above the treetops," that the phrase "circling above the treetops" does not apply to the beaver.

English Learners

1 Point out that *native* here refers to Native Americans. The Ojibway are a Native American people.

2 Explain that in film terminology, *to pan* is to move a camera so that it follows an object.

3 In movie terms, *to cut to* something means to move abruptly from one thing to another.

4 *To pull focus* means to stop and focus on a particular subject.

Advanced Students

Have students research where the term *pan* comes from and why it is used to mean "to move a camera so that it follows an object."

Viewing and Representing

EXPLICIT
INSTRUCTION

Good Afternoon #1
by Alex Katz

ART APPRECIATION Alex Katz, born in Brooklyn, New York, in 1927, studied art in Skowhegan, Maine. He has donated hundreds of his works to Colby College's museum in Waterville, Maine.

Instruction This painting is one of a series of four paintings the artist created in 1974, depicting Coleman Lake, near his summer home in Maine, at different times of the day. The woman is paddling right toward the viewer. A feeling of calm pervades the painting. Point out that the canoe is made from birch bark, a material that the Ojibway used to record their history in drawings.

Practice Ask students how they think this painting may be related to the setting of this teleplay.

Possible Response: Lenore and her family might live in a place that looks like this. Since they fish, they may do so from canoes like this one, made out of birch bark.

Reading and Analyzing

Literary Analysis: TELEPLAY

(A) Point out that the term *stock shot* means a camera shot that is taken from stock, or from what is already on hand. Ask why filmmakers might use a stock shot of a beaver swimming rather than go out and shoot a new image.

Possible Responses: Any shot of a beaver swimming would work here; it's often easier and cheaper to use stock shots in situations that do not include characters or important action.

Literary Analysis **THEME**

(B) In order to make a point, many times people tell stories like the one Lenore's father tells. What theme does her father seem to be getting at with his story about the beaver?

Possible Response: He might be saying that if you do things for the wrong reason, they will backfire on you.

ACTIVE READER

(C) CONCLUSIONS They seem to be close and are able to talk about a lot of things.

Literary Analysis: CONFLICT

(D) Ask what conflict the father's question might introduce.

Possible Response: He doesn't seem to like the idea of Lenore's spending so much time on her schoolwork; Lenore, on the other hand, loves school and writing.

Literary Analysis: CHARACTER TRAITS

(E) What does Lenore's comment about Pauline Johnson's having had a hard time getting gas for her outboard reveal about Lenore's character traits?

Possible Response: It shows that Lenore has a good sense of humor. Obviously, there were no outboard motors for boats a hundred years ago.

Scene 2A Exterior. Stream. Afternoon.

The prow of a cedar canoe cuts through the calm water. Lenore and her father Pete, in the stern, are canoeing their way up a quiet stream. It is late in the afternoon. The shadows are lengthening, and the sunlight retains the shimmering intensity of this time of day as it filters through the autumn <u>foliage</u>.

1 **Pete.** Good here for beaver. Heavy willow growth. Lots of food. *(Lenore notices a beaver swimming. She points.)*

2 **Lenore.** Look, Baba.

(A) *(Shot of beaver swimming. He suddenly slaps his tail loudly and dives—stock shot.)*

He's warning his friends about us.

Pete *(seriously).* You know that a long time ago the beaver only had a little skinny tail.

Lenore. Oh yeah?

(Lenore looks back smiling expectantly. She knows this is the opening to one of her father's crazy stories.)

3 **Pete** *(storytelling tone).* You see, one day Nanabozho was out paddling his big canoe. He's pretty lazy so he decided if he gave the beaver a big paddle tail, he could tie them on the back and they would push his canoe. But once he had given the beaver a paddle tail, the beaver was too quick to catch. So he didn't get a chance to try it.

(B) **Lenore** *(only half serious).* D'you think it would work?

Pete. Cheemo and I tried it once.

Lenore. Really?

Pete. Sure! Roped a couple 70 pound beavers on the back of this canoe.

Lenore. What happened?

Pete. Well, they chewed a hole in the canoe and we all sank and they got away!

(Lenore laughs at this image and turns to look back at her father.)

Lenore. Serves you right.

(Pete laughs too. They continue paddling slowly, quietly.)

Scene 2B Exterior. Beaver pond. Day.

They canoe near a bubbling beaver dam with more beaver houses visible.

Pete. You said you had a dream to tell.

Lenore. Yes. *(She turns around in the canoe, facing him.)* It's pretty simple, I guess. I'm standing in the woods. There's a raven flying just above my head. It <u>hovers</u> there. It has something to tell me. *(pause, thinking)* It wants to land . . . but it can't. It only hovers there. It never lands.

(Pete thinks about the dream very seriously for a moment.)

(C) **ACTIVE READER**

CONCLUSIONS What can you conclude about Lenore's relationship with Pete?

Pete. Sounds like a good dream. Can't tell you what it means. Maybe it isn't finished with you yet. *(Lenore smiles. Pause)* You know Cheemo had the same dream for five nights in a row. He dreamed he was swimming underwater.

Lenore. Yeah?

Pete. Every night, same thing. Swimming underwater!

Lenore. Yeah?

Pete. On the sixth day, he couldn't stand it anymore. He jumped into the lake! And no more dream.

WORDS TO KNOW
foliage (fō′lē-ĭj) *n.* plant leaves, especially tree leaves, considered as a group
hover (hŭv′ər) *v.* to remain floating or suspended nearby

618

EXPLICIT INSTRUCTION **Understanding Theme**

Instruction Remind students that in order to identify the theme of a selection, readers must pay attention to the important characters and the ways in which they act and change. Ask, "Who is the main character of this screenplay?" *(Lenore)* "Do any other characters seem important?" *(Lenore's father, Pete)* Discuss with students what they learn about each of these characters and their relationship on page 618.

Practice Have students work in pairs to discuss what they know so far about Pete and Lenore and to add this information to the appropriate

columns in the charts they created. Remind students that they will need to continue adding information to this chart as they read.

Possible Responses: Lenore, the main character, is a good writer. She is observant of the natural world and seems to love it. Lenore and Pete have a good sense of humor. Both seem to have a close relationship and talk easily.

Use **Unit Five Resource Book**, p. 6, for more practice.

(They both laugh again.)

We'll go upstream to the next pond and . . .

Lenore *(hesitant)*. Baba, I . . .

Pete. What?

Lenore *(feeling bad)*. I've got all kinds of homework to do. We've got a lot of tests coming up . . .

Pete. Isn't it enough they have you all day at that school?

Lenore. I'm sorry, Baba.

Pete *(gruffly)*. Never mind.

(Pete quickly backpaddles to turn the canoe around and they head back the way they came. Lenore looks unhappy.)

Scene 3 Exterior. Schoolyard. Day.

It is lunch break at school. A number of students are sitting around on the grass and walls eating lunch. Some play volleyball nearby. Lenore is sitting on a bench reading some poetry to a Classmate. Sadie, Lenore's sister, is listening in. Lenore reads with feeling from the book.

Lenore. "Up on the hill against the sky,
A fir tree rocking its lullaby,
Swings, swings,
Its emerald wings,
Swelling the song that my paddle sings."

Classmate #1. That's neat!

Lenore. Yeah. Pauline Johnson. She's a native poet who traveled all around these lakes almost 100 years ago. Musta been hard to get gas for her outboard then, eh? *(They laugh. Miss Walker comes up behind them with a letter in her hand. She crouches behind them.)*

Miss Walker *(excited, smiling)*. Lenore? I've got some news for you. I sent your story in to the District Writing Competitions. You have been accepted as a finalist!

(She shows Lenore the letter. Lenore and Sadie read it together. Lenore is both excited and disbelieving.)

Next week you go down to Thunder Bay to read your story to the judges!

(Lenore and Sadie look at each other in amazement.)

This is wonderful! If you do well there, they could send you to a special high school in the south. Then maybe to study English at university!

Lenore *(mixed emotions)*. University!

Miss Walker. Well, let's see how Thunder Bay goes. We just need a letter of permission from your parents and we're all set!

(Lenore looks at the letter again, confused and excited. Miss Walker smiles at her, then leans forward and gives her a little hug.)

I'm proud of you.

(Miss Walker gets up and leaves them. Again Sadie and Lenore look at each other.)

Sadie. Nice going!

Lenore *(grinning)*. Yeah! I can't believe it! *(frowning)* I just wonder what Baba is going to say.

Scene 4 Interior. Kitchen (Lenore's home). Evening.

Lenore, Sadie, their mother Connie, and Pete are having fish dinner. Pete eats his food hungrily. Lenore looks up at him once, then again. Then she notices Sadie staring at her impatiently. Lenore glares at Sadie and they both resume eating.

Pete *(to all)*. Good trout, eh? We caught them way north of Mulligan Bay. Cold and deep.

(He takes another huge mouthful.)

Connie. We should have enough in the freezer to last until Christmas.

Literary Analysis: STAGE DIRECTIONS

(A) What is Pete doing as Sadie is telling him Lenore has something to tell him? How do you know that?

Possible Response: He is eating fish for dinner and acting rather uninterested. The stage directions tell the reader that this is what is going on.

Active Reading

DRAWING CONCLUSIONS

(B) Ask students to draw a conclusion about what Pete means when he says, "'Want' and 'Can' are not always the same thing"?

Possible Response: He means that you can't always have everything just because you want it.

(C) In her story, Lenore's character is talking to her father about why he won't let her go to the city to visit her aunt. What do you think Leonore is really thinking about when she reads this?

Possible Response: She is probably thinking of the fact that her father won't let her go to Thunder Bay to read her story.

ACTIVE READER

(D) MAKE INFERENCES Possible Response: There are different ways of solving the same problem.

Untitled (1960), Henri Michaux. Copyright © 2001 Artists Rights Society (ARS), New York/ADAGP, Paris. Collections du Centre Georges Pompidou/Musée National d'Art Moderne, Paris.

Pete. The King of France never ate better than this.

(There is a moment of silence. Sadie can wait no longer.)

Sadie. Baba, Lenore has something to ask you.

(Pete and Connie look up. Lenore glares at Sadie.)

Pete. Uh huh?

Lenore. Well . . . I've been doing some work at school . . .

Pete. Yeah. So?

Lenore. You know . . . like writing.

(A) *(Pete takes another large bite of fish, only vaguely interested.)*

Anyway . . . the new teacher, Miss Walker, said I've been doing real well . . . and there was a story I wrote . . .

Pete. A what?

Lenore *(hesitating).* Well, a story . . . and they, ah . . .

Sadie *(interrupting).* The story won a contest and now she has to go to Thunder Bay to read it and then they'll send her away to university!

(Lenore "looks daggers" at Sadie. Both Pete and Connie look at Lenore in surprise.)

Lenore. Can't you shut up!

Pete. University!

(Lenore passes Pete the letter.)

Lenore. Well, no! It's only if I win, but . . .

(Pete glances at the letter then pushes it away.)

Pete. That's crazy! You're only a young girl! You can forget about going to Thunder Bay.

Lenore. But I have to! I'm representing the school!

EXPLICIT INSTRUCTION **Understanding Theme**

Instruction Encourage students to discuss the complications that occur on pages 620 and 621. Ask, "How does the conflict between Lenore and her father become more complicated here?" *(Lenore wants to go to the city as a representative of her school. Her father forbids the trip.)* Have a volunteer read aloud Lenore's story in Scene 5. Then ask students to think about how this story is tied to the conflict between Lenore and her father. Ask, "Whose feelings is Lenore expressing in this story?" Also ask whether the story contributes to students' understanding of what the theme of this drama might be.

Practice Have students add information about the complications to the conflict and about Lenore's story to their charts. Also have students reread the story that Connie tells Lenore and note the message of the story in their charts. After students have made their notes, ask volunteers if they can identify any themes yet.

Possible Response: Students might suggest these themes: A child sometimes has to set his or her own goals. Children and parents may have different goals.

Use **Unit Five Resource Book,** p. 6, for more practice.

Pete. They can find someone else.

Lenore. But they want my story!

Pete. Then send the story to Thunder Bay.

Lenore *(approaching tears).* But I want to go!!

Pete. "Want" and "Can" are not always the same thing.

(Pete goes back to his dinner.)

Lenore. You never . . . !

(Lenore is about to continue her argument but her mother is signaling her not to continue along these lines. Lenore stands up and quickly exits the kitchen.)

Scene 5 Interior. Classroom. Day.

The classroom is empty except for Lenore standing at the front and Miss Walker sitting at a desk several rows back. Lenore is practicing reading her story with a compelling intensity.

Lenore. She found her father out behind the shed laying the steaming cedar strips across the frame of a new canoe, his strong hands molding the soft wood. "Baba," she said, "Why can't I visit Aunt Doreen for the summer? I'm not a child anymore. I want to ride a subway, Baba! I want to climb to the top of a skyscraper, and see a museum and go to a play. I want to see the world!" But her father turned away and would not look at her.

(Lenore stops and thinks about her father for a moment.)

Miss Walker *(quietly).* Yes. Go on.

(Suddenly all of Lenore's <u>momentum</u> *is gone. She appears weary.)*

Lenore. Can we stop now?

D

Miss Walker. Sure. Sure, that's fine. It's coming along really well, Lenore. Parents' Night will be a good rehearsal for the finals.

(Pause, looking at Lenore who appears distracted)

Is everything all right?

Lenore. Yes, I'm just tired.

Miss Walker. Good. You get a good sleep. I'll see you tomorrow.

(Lenore gives her a half-hearted smile and leaves the classroom. Miss Walker looks after her, wondering if there is anything wrong.)

3

Scene 6 Interior. Kitchen (Lenore's house). Day.

Lenore comes into the kitchen, tosses down her books and flops down at the table. Her mother is making bannock bread. They are alone. Her mother notices her unhappiness.

Connie. How was school?

Lenore. Okay. *(pause)* Actually it was lousy. *(sudden anger)* I just don't understand! Why won't he let me go?!

(Connie stops work and sits down across from her.)

Connie *(after a moment).* He's afraid of what will happen to you.

Lenore. He wants to trap me!

Connie. It might seem like that, but he believes he's protecting you.

Lenore *(deflated).* What am I going to do, Mom?

Connie. He's stubborn. The harder you push, the more he digs in his heels. *(pause)* D'you remember the story of the Sun and the Wind, how they had a contest to see who could get the coat off a passing man? The Wind blew as hard as he could, but the man held the coat on tightly. When the Sun had his

ACTIVE READER

MAKE INFERENCES

What is the theme or message of Connie's story?

WORDS
TO
KNOW

momentum (mō-měn′təm) *n.* the energy of an object or idea

621

Differentiating Instruction

Less Proficient Readers

Help students summarize what has happened in Scene 4 by asking the following questions:

- Why is Lenore uneasy about telling her father about the writing contest?
  Possible Response: She thinks that he won't let her go to Thunder Bay.
- Why is Lenore angry with her sister?
  Possible Response: Lenore wants to tell her father in her own way, not just blurt it out as Sadie does.
- Why does Lenore stop arguing with her father?
  Possible Response: Her mother signals Lenore to stop because she won't convince her father by arguing.

English Learners

1 Explain that the phrase *looks daggers* means "gives someone a look that is sharp and angry."

2 Make sure students understand the stage directions just before Scene 5: "Lenore is about to continue her argument but her mother is signaling her not to continue along those lines." Two phrases in this sentence may be difficult to understand. "Signaling her" means that Lenore's mother was trying to tell Lenore to do something without actually speaking to her. "Along those lines" refers to the argument Lenore was making, which Lenore's mother did not think was a good approach for Lenore to use with her father.

3 Demonstrate a "half-hearted smile," one that involves only your mouth, not your eyes. Explain that such a smile indicates that the person isn't genuinely feeling the happiness that usually accompanies a smile.

Literary Analysis: CONFLICT

Ⓐ Ask students what conflict Lenore's excitement, followed by her subdued answer, indicates. Is this an internal conflict or an external one?

Possible Response: Lenore wants to please her father and enjoys being with him, but she doesn't want to miss school. The conflict is internal because it's inside Lenore's own mind.

Literary Analysis: TELEPLAY

Ⓑ Point out the description of the scene under the heading "Scene 8." Ask students which direction tells how the scene is to be photographed, and why they think the filmmaker would want it to be seen that way.

Possible Response: The description says "Camera at stream level." By placing the camera at stream level, the film maker would be able to show both Lenore's and Pete's expressions.

Ⓒ Point out the description of the scene under the heading "Scene 9." How does it indicate the dream sequence is to be shot? Why do you think the filmmaker would do this?

Possible Response: It says, "Shot in slightly slow motion." This could make it look dreamy and would also differentiate it from the rest of the film.

ACTIVE READER

Ⓓ VISUALIZE Possible Response: The birds may look like the hawk in Lenore's story.

Active Reading

DRAWING CONCLUSIONS

Ⓔ What conclusion might you draw from the driver's having to turn the bill right side up for Pete?

Possible Response: Pete can't read.

---

turn, he shone warm and bright and the man just took off his coat.

Lenore. I should be the sun?

(Connie nods.)

Connie. Maybe you could read your story to him.

Lenore. I have to read it on Parents' Night. But he'll never come.

Connie. Maybe this time, if you ask, he will.

(Lenore looks suddenly hopeful.)

Lenore. You think so?

Connie *(smiling).* Maybe.

(Lenore smiles happily.)

Scene 7   Exterior. Woods. Day.

A small cedar tree crashes to the ground near the banks of a stream. Pete stands beside the stump, axe in hand. He wipes a sleeve across his sweating forehead, then quickly begins to trim the branches.

1
2
With a smaller axe Lenore competently trims the branches of another downed cedar in the foreground. In the background we see a sturdy lean-to, three-quarters completed, large enough to sleep two or three people with provisions— side walls, open front, firepit. Lenore lifts her ten-foot cedar pole, takes it to the structure and fits it in place, resting on the center beam nailed between two trees.

Pete is suddenly beside her and places his pole beside hers which almost completes the superstructure of the roof. He smiles at her.

Pete. Now the tarp, a good layer of cedar boughs and one snowfall will make it warm and dry. Ron and I'll live here a week for trapping. *(looking at her)* What do you think? You want to come?

Lenore. Where?

Pete. Out on the new trapline in November with Ron and me?

Lenore *(excited).* Yeah! *(then subdued)* But I've got school.

(Pete turns away to adjust the crosspiece.)

(hopefully) But maybe I can get off for a couple of days.

Pete *(not looking at her).* You think about it.

Scene 8   Exterior. Rocky stream bed. Day.

Lenore kneels down on a flat rock. Holding her hair back she drinks from the surface of the black, bubbling stream. Camera at stream level. She looks up, satisfied, her face wet. She watches her father who puts his face right down in the water and shakes his head, splashing and blowing bubbles. He looks up at her and they both laugh, water dripping off their faces.

Pete cups some water in his hand and brings it to his lips to drink. Lenore watches him a moment.

Lenore. Sometimes I wish I could be a son for you, Baba.

(Pete looks up at her curiously at this statement out of the blue.)

Pete. A son?

Lenore. Yes. I know every father wants a son.

(Pete considers this as he fills a canteen with water.)

Pete. I would like a son. Maybe someday . . . *(pause)* but the first time I saw you and you smiled at me, I wouldn't have traded you for ten sons!

(Lenore smiles at this, watching him fill the canteen.)

Lenore. Baba?

WORDS
TO   **foreground** (fôr'ground) *n.* the part of a scene or picture that is nearest to the viewer
KNOW

Pete. Hummm?

Lenore. Parents' Night is on Wednesday.

Pete (distastefully). Parents' Night?

Lenore. Yeah. I'm going to read something. Be real nice if you were there.

Pete. I don't have anything to say to those teachers.

Lenore. You don't have to say anything.

Pete (resisting). And we're fishing next day. We'll be outfitting the boat.

Lenore. Just for a little while? Maybe? (pause) Please?

Pete. Okay. I'm not promising but I'll try.

(Lenore smiles, her eyes sparkling.)

Scene 9 Exterior. Open sky (dream). Day.

In slow motion against a blue sky background a single bird comes into frame. Shot in slightly slow motion. It hovers above the camera. After a moment it is joined by other birds . . . two, three, four, all hover in frame above the camera. It is not a threatening image. The motion is beautiful to watch. The sound of wings becomes steadily louder.

ACTIVE READER

VISUALIZE Imagine Lenore's dream. What do you think the birds look like?

Scene 10A Interior. Lenore's bedroom. Night.

Lenore, with a little gasp, suddenly sits up in bed, staring out in front of her. Her tense body relaxes. She thinks for a moment about the images of the dream. She lies down again and rolls over, her face toward camera. She smiles with excitement and anticipation.

Scene 10B Exterior. Spirit Bay docks. Late day.

A pick-up truck stops beside the docks. Pete is waiting. The Driver gets out and opens the tailgate.

Driver. Got your new nets, Pete.

(Pete inspects the three bundles of nets as the Driver drops them to the ground.)

Pete. Hey, they don't have floats!

(The Driver hands him the bill.)

Driver. See? Nothing about floats.

(Pete looks at the bill. The Driver looks at him, then turns the bill right side up for him to read. Pete glances at it and stuffs it into his pocket.) **E**

Pete. Gonna take me all night to sew floats on these nets.

Driver. You want 'em or not?

(Pete nods. The Driver drops the last net on the ground, gets back in the truck and drives off. As the truck drives away, Pete checks his watch, looks unhappy, then carries the first bundle toward the boat.)

Scene 11 Interior. School auditorium. Evening.

It's Parents' Night in the small auditorium. There are about two dozen parents present, native and white. Tables display artwork of various kinds and highly graded tests and essays. There is a coffee and pastry table where parents stand in small groups talking with four or five teachers.

There is a podium[1] at the front of the auditorium. Lenore stands near it anxiously watching the doorway, holding the pages of her story.

---

1. **podium** (pō′dē-əm): an elevated platform or stand, as for a public speaker.

WORDS TO KNOW — **anticipation** (ăn-tĭs′ə-pā′shən) n. the feeling of expecting something

623

Differentiating Instruction

Less Proficient Students

1 Help students use context to figure out the meaning of *tarp*. Walk them through picturing the lean-to that is described in the stage directions (side walls, open front, poles, roof, firepit). Then ask students to think about what they might put over this frame in order to protect themselves from the weather. Students should infer that tarp is a waterproof cloth used to cover things.

English Learners

2 Explain out that a *lean-to* is a kind of temporary shelter. One side usually consists of a building or other solid area, such as a line of trees. A slanting roof is propped up on poles so it leans against the solid wall. Sometimes the sides are also covered, but the front is usually open.

On these two pages, the author uses the terms *trapping, trapline,* and *nets with floats*. Ask students what the men are doing to provide food for their families.

Possible Response: They are setting traps along a line and then camping out in the lean-to. They check the traps periodically to see if anything has been caught. They also fish with nets. The floats are small, plastic bubbles, filled with air, that are attached to the nets to keep them from sinking to the bottom and getting caught in the weeds. Floats also allow fishermen to find their nets in the water more easily.

Advanced Students

3 Have students think of another dream sequence they have read in a book or seen in a movie. How did that sequence help them predict what happened next in the book or movie? What kind of prediction can this sequence help them make?

EXPLICIT INSTRUCTION Understanding Theme

Instruction Use the Literary Analysis: Conflict note in the green side column to discuss the development of the conflict between Lenore and her father. Next, ask a volunteer to read aloud the stage directions on page 623 that begin, "Pete looks at the bill." Then use the Active Reading: Drawing Conclusions note in the green column to discuss the significance of the information in these stage directions. Ask students how Pete might feel about his daughter's talent as a writer when he cannot read. (He might feel ashamed that he is unable to read.

He might be afraid to tell Lenore because she might be ashamed of him. He might feel that Lenore's reading and writing will take her away from him.) Have students share some of the information they have recorded so far in their charts. Students should explain why they think the information is important.

Practice Have students add information to their charts about the story conflict and about Pete. Then ask students if they can identify any themes yet.

Possible Responses Responses will vary. Students may identify these themes: The harder you push someone, the more he or she will resist. Secrets can come between people.

Use **Unit Five Resource Book**, p. 6, for more practice.

Ask students to summarize the theme of the play thus far.

Possible Response: Parents and children do not always see eye to eye.

A What is the theme of the Principal's speech?

Possible Response: There is so much to know in the modern world that a good education is even more important than ever.

Reading Skills and Strategies: VISUALIZE

B Ask students to picture and then describe what the scene looks like after Lenore runs from the room.

Possible Response: The people probably sit quietly for a while; then they might start to talk among themselves and look outside the room to see what is going on. Some of them probably stare at Mrs. Green.

Reading Skills and Strategies: PREDICT

Ask students to predict whether they think Lenore will give up the chance to go to Thunder Bay and win the contest.

ACTIVE READER

C CONCLUSIONS **Possible Response:** Lenore feels that if her father did not even come to hear her read at Parents' Night, he'll never allow her to go to Thunder Bay to compete, so there's no point in reading her story.

---

1 **Sadie.** Betcha he doesn't come.

Lenore. He'll come.

(Miss Walker approaches them.)

Miss Walker. Hi Lenore. Are you ready?

Lenore *(anxious).* I think so.

Miss Walker. You'll do great! Are your parents here yet? I was looking forward to meeting them.

2 **Lenore** *(eyeing the doorway).* They'll be here any minute.

(The Principal moves behind the podium to address those present. Conversation dwindles.)

Principal. Good evening, and welcome to the first Parents' Night of the year at Nipigon District Junior High School. Glad you could come out. In a moment I'll ask one of our students to come up and read a prize-winning story she's written . . .

(Principal's talk continues over dialogue between Lenore and Miss Walker, below.)

But first I would like to say a few words about the challenges facing us in the coming year. Never before has there been such an <u>abundance</u> of information and communication in our world . . .

(Lenore whispers anxiously to Miss Walker.)

Lenore. Wait! I can't do it yet!

Miss Walker. Don't worry. I'll stall him if necessary. *(smiling)* Mr. Crankhurst goes on forever, anyway.

(Lenore tries to smile. She looks at the Principal.)

A **Principal.** It is almost overwhelming when you consider it. In the face of this, a sound education has never been more important. And so, our goal will remain a high standard of academic achievement and individual excellence in all our endeavors. We are deeply aware of our responsibility here at Beardmore to mold the bright minds of young men and women who will in a few short years forge the destiny of our world!

(Connie comes through the door into the auditorium. She is alone. Lenore watches her. Connie stops, looks around the room and sees Lenore. She looks at her and shakes her head sadly. Pete is not coming. Lenore appears as if she's about to cry. Sadie takes this all in.)

So now let me introduce one of those bright young minds, to read her story that has been selected for the finals of the District Writing Competition . . . Lenore Green.

(There is polite applause. Lenore turns to Miss Walker in anger and frustration.)

Lenore. I'm not going to do it.

Miss Walker *(sudden alarm).* What!?

Lenore. Why bother!

(The applause dies out. The Principal and all others are looking expectantly at Lenore. With story in hand, Lenore turns and exits the auditorium. There are whispered comments in the audience of parents. Miss Walker quickly follows Lenore.)

Scene 12 Interior. Hallway (school). Evening.

The hallway is deserted. Lenore walks determinedly away from the auditorium. Miss Walker comes out the door and calls after her.

Miss Walker. Lenore! Lenore!

(Lenore stops and turns back. Miss Walker comes up to her.)

Miss Walker. What's wrong!? I don't understand.

Lenore. I don't want to read my story. And I don't want to go to Thunder Bay!

WORDS
TO
KNOW   **abundance** (ə-bŭn′dəns) *n.* a great amount

624

Afternoon Light #6, © Lee Wallat Illustration. 8¼" × 11" pastel.

Miss Walker. But Lenore! This is a great opportunity! This is the first big step in your career.

Lenore. What career?!

Miss Walker. You could do anything—go to university, become a journalist or an English professor or a playwright. You've been given a talent. You can't turn your back on it!

Lenore. It's only a stupid story. I'm sorry I even wrote it.

ACTIVE READER

CONCLUSIONS Why do you think Lenore won't read her story?

(Lenore throws the story down on the floor, turns and walks away. After a beat Miss Walker reaches down and picks up the spilled pages. She looks at them, then watches Lenore walking away from her.)

Scene 13A Interior. Classroom. Morning.

Miss Walker is sitting at her desk marking tests in the empty classroom. She works quickly for a moment, but then her momentum slows, her eyes leave her work, and brows knitted she begins to think again about Lenore. She can't figure it out.

3

Sadie and Connie enter the room behind her. Connie is intimidated by a woman of her own generation with a university education. She looks uncomfortably around the room.

Sadie. Miss Walker?

Miss Walker *(turns around and stands).* Hi Sadie . . . and Mrs. Green. How are you?

(Connie nods shyly. It takes a moment to find the words, but she speaks them with determination.)

WORDS ON A PAGE **625**

Differentiating Instruction

English Learners
1 Point out that *betcha* is slang for "I bet you." Sadie is so sure that her father will not come that she is willing to bet on it.
2 Help students figure out the meaning of *eyeing* by asking, "What do you do with your eyes?"
3 Demonstrate a face with *brows knitted.* Ask students what such an expression might indicate.
Possible Response: It might indicate concern, worry, or deep thought.

Less Proficient Readers
Help students understand that Scene 12 occurs outside the room where Scene 11 takes place. The people are still in the auditorium, wondering what might have caused Lenore to run out of the room as she did.
Ask students how much time has passed since the end of Scene 12 and the beginning of Scene 13A *(one night).*
When writers switch back and forth between settings, they need to do it without confusing their readers. How does the author make transitions between school and home settings, and between the main story and the one Lenore is writing, without confusing the reader?
Possible Responses: Each new scene is marked with a scene number and tells the location and time of day. The use of italics describes the new setting and the action that will take place there.

Advanced Learners
Many excellent writers have been inspired by their Native American heritage. Encourage students to ask their school or community librarian to recommend authors and stories that feature, or draw their inspiration from, Native American cultures.

EXPLICIT INSTRUCTION **Drawing Conclusions**

Instruction Tell students that when they use the information from a story and from their own knowledge and experience to make a logical guess about what is happening in a story, they are drawing conclusions. Say, "For example, when you read Pete's actions and words at the beginning of the play, even though Pete never says so, you can draw the conclusion that he is unhappy about Lenore's love of school, and he feels sad that she does not want to lead the same kind of life he has led." Have students discuss what happened at the auditorium and what Miss Walker says to Lenore on page 625. Ask, "What conclusions can you draw about why Lenore refuses to read her story?"

Practice Have students write their conclusions and list any details from the story and from their own experience that helped them draw such conclusions.

Possible Responses: Lenore does not read her story because she feels she will not be allowed to become a writer or a university student. If that is so, she does not want to pretend, by reading her story in public, that she will have a writing career or a chance of going to college. The details that support this conclusion are Pete's absence in the auditorium and the importance that Lenore places on Pete's approval. I know how it feels to want something but feel I won't be able to have it.

Literary Analysis: TELEPLAY

How many scenes are on these two pages?

Answer: five (or four and a half—13B only, 14, 15, 16, 17)

Literary Analysis: STAGE DIRECTIONS

A How is Connie feeling as she begins to talk to Miss Walker? How do you know?

Possible Response: She feels a little ashamed. The stage directions tell the reader that is how she's feeling.

Literary Analysis: CONFLICT

B The stage directions say that Pete feels bad. What internal conflict is making him feel that way?

Possible Response: He loves Lenore and wants to make her happy, but he is afraid to let her out into the world and away from the community.

Active Reading

DRAWING CONCLUSIONS

C Have students draw a conclusion about why Connie wants so much for Lenore to go to university.

Possible Response: Connie was a good student herself, but never took the opportunity to go to university, so now she really wants her daughter to go.

Connie. There is something you should know. Lenore loves to write more than anything. And she wants to go to Thunder Bay. But my husband . . . *(a little ashamed)* he won't let her.

A

Sadie. Baba doesn't believe in schools and books and stuff.

Miss Walker *(reflectively).* I see. Please sit.

(Miss Walker gestures to a chair for Connie and another for Sadie.)

Scene 13B Exterior. Spirit Bay docks. Afternoon.

Pete is unloading his catch after a good day's fishing. He is on the dock. A Crewman hands him a tub full of ice and fish from the deck on the boat. There are several tubs on the dock.

Pete *(feigning pain).* Uhhh! The only trouble with a good catch is it's bad for my back!

(The Crewman laughs. Pete lifts the tub of fish and walks a few steps to the other tubs when he notices Lenore. Lenore stands—with school books—at the far end of the dock watching Pete from a distance. Other students pass by behind her on their way home. Lenore and Pete look at each other a moment. Pete puts the tub down with the others and wiping his hands with a rag takes a step toward her. Lenore turns and quickly walks away. Pete stops and watches her, feeling bad.)

B

Scene 14 Interior. Classroom. Afternoon.

Connie and Sadie are talking to Miss Walker. Connie is more relaxed now. She is reflective.

C

Connie. When I was Lenore's age, I was real good at school too. Top of my class. I might have gone on to university, even! But I couldn't decide . . . and then I met Pete . . . *(pause, then with conviction)* I want this for Lenore!

Miss Walker. So do I.

Connie. We're having a roast Sunday. Why don't you come by?

(Connie and Miss Walker and Sadie share a conspiratorial smile.)

Miss Walker. Good! I will.

Scene 15 Exterior. Lenore's house. Day.

Establishing shot/time passage. A car and a pickup truck are parked outside.

Scene 16 Interior. Kitchen (Lenore's house). Day.

The table is nicely laid out with flowers and a bright, plastic tablecloth and a variety of food—fish, slices of moose, potatoes and other vegetables, and bannock bread. Miss Walker sits at one end of the table, Pete at the other. Sadie and Connie sit on one side, Lenore on the other.

Lenore is very quiet. She is angry at her father and embarrassed by Miss Walker being there. She is uncomfortable to be at the table with both of them.

Miss Walker takes a platter of meat from Lenore.

Miss Walker. Thanks, Lenore.

(Pete is eating his food hungrily, eyes on his plate. Miss Walker is talking mostly to Connie, although she watches Pete for any response.)

. . . and we're getting in a new portable classroom and adding to the library . . .

(Pete, without looking up, grunts his disfavor over this.)

And what I'm hoping for by the end of the year is a computer terminal for the students to use . . .

Pete *(grunts again).* Pass the moose.

(Miss Walker finds the platter of moose beside her and passes it. Pete piles moose meat on his

WORDS TO KNOW **gesture** (jĕs′chər) v. make a motion to express thought or emphasize words

626

Cross Curricular Link **Social Studies**

OJIBWAY ART

If you go to Thunder Bay, Ontario, you can visit the Thunder Bay Museum, which features exhibits of Ojibway art. Among them are the stunning traditional beadwork for which the Ojibway are known.

Modern Ojibway have brought their art into the contemporary world, as well. Among the best-known artists is Norval Morrisseau. He is the founder of the school of art called "Legend" or "Woodland." Morrisseau was born on Sand Point Reserve, near Beardmore, Ontario, in 1932. He was fascinated by the ancient rock art of his people, and when he began to paint, his style echoed some of what he had seen there. When he attempted to paint his dreams, thoughts, and visions, he was criticized by some Ojibway for revealing their legends and beliefs. He maintained that he wanted to restore cultural pride to his people, and has donated paintings to raise money for Ojibway causes. Other Ojibway artists include Patrick DesJarlait, Francis Kaegig, and Daphne Odjig.

plate. Miss Walker looks at him, is about to say something to him, then thinks better of it.)

Miss Walker. One thing I'm excited about *(She looks at Pete.)* . . . and Mr. Crankhurst seems open to it . . . is an Ojibway Studies course.

(Pete looks up at this.)

Pete *(with disdain).* Ojibway Studies?

Miss Walker. Yes. The language and customs and history . . .

Pete. Like one of them dead civilizations in a museum.

Miss Walker. No! Not at all. In fact, you trap and fish. Maybe you'd come in and give demonstrations of your <u>expertise</u>?

Pete. Expertise! If you get paid by the word, that's a ten dollar one for sure!

(Sadie giggles at this. Miss Walker is angry. The gloves are off.)

Miss Walker. I can see you don't think much of education, but it can give all kinds of things to a girl like Lenore.

Pete. You mean like a one-way ticket out of here.

(Miss Walker takes out the folded pages of Lenore's story and unfolds them.)

Miss Walker. Have you read this?

Pete. No.

(Connie looks worried.)

Miss Walker. Well I think you should read it!

Pete *(suddenly awkward).* I will . . . later.

Miss Walker. Read it now! Just the first page.

(She stands up, reaches over and puts the manuscript² down in front of him. Pete moves it away. Miss Walker stays standing.)

Pete. No.

Miss Walker. Well if you don't care enough to even read . . .

(Pete stands up angrily.)

Pete. You saying I don't care about my daughter?!

Miss Walker. She has talent and imagination and desire! You can't imprison her here!

Pete. Prison!

Miss Walker. There's a whole world waiting for her out there!

(Lenore sits there becoming angry and frustrated listening to this.)

Pete. In that world she'll be an outsider! She'll be alone and unhappy and forget who she is!

(Lenore stands up and looks at Pete.)

Lenore. You don't know who I am! *(then at Miss Walker)* Neither of you! No one even cares what I want!

(Lenore turns away and exits the house. Pete and Miss Walker look at each other, now sorry that they have been so insensitive.)

Scene 17 Exterior. End of dock (Sunset Lodge). Day.

Lenore crouches on the end of the dock. She looks down at her reflection in the black water. She holds out a pebble and lets it drop into the reflection. When it clears a moment later, her father's reflection can be seen behind. He stands there a moment.

Lenore *(residual³ anger).* Why won't you read my story?

---

2. **manuscript** (măn′yə-skrĭpt′): an unpublished version of a book or other work.

3. **residual** (rĭ-zĭj′ō͞o-əl): remaining after the feeling has mostly passed.

627

Differentiating Instruction

Less Proficient Readers
The many scene changes on these two pages may be difficult for students to follow. Help students note or chart the changes and tell what happens in each location in their own words.

English Learners
1 Explain that a *roast* is a gathering at which some kind of food—usually fish or meat—is cooked over an open fire.

Ask students to consider Pete's thinking when he says, "In that world she'll be an outsider! She'll be alone and unhappy and forget who she is!" What do you think he means by this?
Possible Responses: He is afraid she will lose her Ojibway customs and feel a loss of identity. He may be afraid that she will be changed or be negatively influenced by other cultures. Pete may also be worried that Lenore will move away and never come home to visit her family.

Advanced Students
Have students work in pairs to write new dialogue for Scene 16, in which both Miss Walker and Pete say what they really mean to each other. Have students discuss whether this straight-forward approach might have prevented an argument.

EXPLICIT INSTRUCTION ## Understanding Theme

Instruction Review the conflict with students. *(Lenore badly wants to go to Thunder Bay to represent her school and read her story. Her father will not let her go.)* Remind students that the climax occurs when the conflict is most intense. Have students identify the climax on page 627. *(The climax occurs when Pete and Miss Walker reach a breaking point in their argument about what is best for Lenore, and Lenore runs away from the table.)* Invite volunteers to read aloud the lines in the play where the climax occurs.

Practice Have students record additional information about the characters and their conflicts in their charts. Tell students to continue to add information as they read about the resolution of the conflict and the resulting feelings of the main characters.
Possible Responses: Notes about Climax—Miss Walker and Pete want different things for Lenore. Each thinks he or she knows what is best for Lenore. They forget Lenore in their anger at each other. Lenore is torn. Notes about Resolution—Pete tells Lenore he can't read and

that the reason he doesn't encourage her at school is that he's afraid she will go away and never come back. Lenore tells her father that she wants to become a better writer so she can write about her people.

Use **Unit Five Resource Book**, p. 6, for more practice.

Reading and Analyzing

Literary Analysis: CONFLICT

Ⓐ Ask students what conflict Pete faces here.

Possible Response: He has to either tell Lenore he can't read or let her think he doesn't care enough to read her story.

Literary Analysis: STAGE DIRECTIONS

Ⓑ What adverb tells how Pete feels as he says these words?

Answer: bitterly

ACTIVE READER

Ⓒ CONCLUSIONS **Possible Response:** They probably feel peaceful and as if they can talk about anything.

Literary Analysis: SYMBOLISM

Ⓓ Students should be able to recognize and interpret literary devices such as symbolism. What do the birds in Lenore's dream symbolize?

Possible Response: They symbolize her dreams of becoming a writer.

(Pete crouches down beside her and looks out at the water a moment. He doesn't look at her as he speaks.)

Ⓐ **Pete.** Because. . . I can't.

(Lenore looks at him in surprise.)

I never learned to read so good. You never knew, eh?

Ⓑ *(Lenore shakes her head; pause, then bitterly)*

When I went to school there was a teacher. . . If I didn't learn my lessons or talked Indian, he'd beat me with a switch and call me names. One day I took the switch away from him and never went back. Never been in school since.

(Lenore watches her father, her expression softening.)

Lenore. Come for a walk?

(Pete looks up at her for the first time, smiles and nods.)

Scene 18 A Exterior. Spirit Bay Field. Day.

A telephoto lens shows Pete and Lenore walking side by side toward camera. The background shows the picturesque village of Spirit Bay on the edge of the lake. They walk in silence for a moment.

1

Pete. I'm afraid. *(pause)* Afraid that you'll go away and become a stranger to us.

Lenore. How could I do that?!

Pete. If you go south to school. It's very different there.

Scene 18 B Exterior. Spirit Bay Road. Day.

Pete and Lenore walk toward camera, telephoto lens.

Lenore. I'll always be Nishnabe, Baba. And Spirit Bay is my home.

Pete. Others have said that and not come back.

Lenore. I'll come back! I want to learn to write

---

better so I can live here and tell about our people! That's why I want to write!

(Pete thinks about this hard as they walk along. They fall silent again.)

Scene 19 Exterior. Dreamer's Rock. Afternoon.

Pete and Lenore sit atop Dreamer's Rock facing the lake that stretches out before them to the horizon. The village can be seen below, and distant islands in the lake.

ACTIVE READER

CONCLUSIONS How do you think this setting makes Pete and Lenore feel?

Lenore. I've been waiting to tell you the last of the dreams. The dreams of the bird that wants to land.

Pete *(very interested)*. Yes! Is it finished?

Lenore. It's finished.

Pete. How did it end?

Lenore. Remember I told you the bird was hovering and trying to land? *(Pete nods.)* Well then each night there were more birds— a few and then dozens . . . then hundreds of birds! *(pause, remembering)* And there was a wide open field of snow! And there they began to land, black against the white snow.

(Pete is listening intently.)

Pete. They all landed?

Lenore. Yes! And as each bird landed it became a letter. And the snow was like a page. And the bird-letters formed words. And the words sentences. *(looking at him)* They were my words, Baba! They were the words I wrote!

(Lenore stops, thinking about the images. Pete smiles at her, excited by the dream, but saddened by its meaning.)

Pete. Sounds like you were meant to be a writer. I won't stop you.

(Lenore is not satisfied.)

Courtesy of Christopher Pullman, WGBH, Boston.

Differentiating Instruction

English Learners

1 Ask students to find the root word in *picturesque (picture)*. Tell them that if a village is described as being *picturesque,* it is like something they might see in a picture or postcard of a village. Ask them how they think the village looks and to explain why.
Possible Response: It is probably attractive, quaint, or charming because most things tend to be represented in their best light in pictures.

Less Proficient Readers

Ask students to think about the names of places in this story: Thunder Bay, Spirit Bay, Dreamer's Rock, and Lakehead University. How do these names help us understand the story? What meaning might each name have?
Possible Responses: Thunder Bay is the place where Lenore will go to read her story. It sounds ominous—like a storm about to break. Spirit Bay is the home of the Ojibway people; the name implies health and energy, as well as a resting place for the spirits of deceased Ojibways. Dreamer's Rock is where Lenore tells her father her dream and her hopes for the future. Lakehead University must be at the head of the lake. The name could imply a new beginning.

Advanced Students

Some people claim to be able to interpret dreams. Have your students describe a dream they have had and write what they think it means. Tell them there are no right or wrong answers. Alternatively, you might encourage students to keep a personal dream journal. They should write their dreams down when they awake in the morning.

EXPLICIT INSTRUCTION Viewing and Representing

LOON POSTER

Instruction The image shown on this page was used as a poster to advertise a morning radio music program. The central figure of this poster is the loon. This bird has a strange cry that mimics human laughter. Many people find it a haunting, lonely sound. Ask students what things about the image make them think of morning. *(The pink sky and shadowy hills look like morning. The feeling is very peaceful and quiet, like this time of day.)*

Practice Why do you think this poster was chosen to accompany *Words on a Page?*
Possible Responses: It looks like the place where Pete and Lenore might sit and talk. The birds in the sky remind me of the birds in Lenore's dream.

Literary Analysis THEME

Ask students to elaborate on their earlier thoughts about the theme of this play.
Possible Response: The theme still has to do with a conflict between the generations. It also says that people must find their own way in the world, and having a strong sense of "home" gives them a better chance of finding who they really are.

ACTIVE READER

A CONCLUSIONS Possible Response: Lenore feels home and harmony with nature are the most important parts of her life.

Active Reading
DRAWING CONCLUSIONS

B Ask students if they think the behavior of the audience at the university in any way changed Pete's feelings about how his people are treated by outsiders.

Possible Responses: No, the people didn't seem to act very warmly toward Lenore and her story; Yes, after a while, everybody started to applaud for Lenore.

Lenore. But I need more, Baba. I don't know if I can do it alone. I need your help.

Pete. My help? I can't even read!

Lenore. Not that kind. I need your . . . *(pause, finding right word)* courage. Will you come to Thunder Bay and hear me read my story?

Pete *(unhappily).* At the university?

(Lenore nods. Pete hesitates, then answers.)

I'll come.

(Lenore takes his hand and smiles at him happily.)

Scene 20A Exterior. Lakehead University. Day.

Establishing shot of university with an identifying sign.

Scene 20B Interior. University. Day.

Pete, Lenore, Sadie, Connie and Miss Walker approach a Man in a suit outside the lecture room doors. Pete looks around uncomfortably.

Miss Walker *(to Man).* Is this the District Writing Finals?

Man *(officious).* Yes. They're about to begin.

(Lenore is excited and scared. She hesitates at the door.)

Lenore. I . . . I don't think . . .

(Pete puts a hand on her shoulder. She looks up at him.)

Pete *(smiling).* Read it to me. Just to me.

(Lenore takes heart in these instructions. She smiles and goes quickly inside followed by the others.)

Scene 21 Interior. Lecture hall. Day.

The lecture hall is quite full of people. A panel of six judges sits at a table at the front listening as Lenore reads her story.

Lenore. So on that morning before she left, they went by canoe one last time to those favorite places. It was at first light, when the water is

---

a mirror and the trees are still, as if nature is holding her breath.

(Near the front rows sit Miss Walker, Pete, Connie and Sadie listening. Lenore reads directly to her father, inspired by his presence. Pete listens intently.)

And there was the beaver and the loon and the hawk circling above the treetops. And below, the trout and the sturgeon slipped silently through the black water.

Creatures as powerful as the great moose, as small as the minnow. She and her father took their place among them.

(Pete, in his solemn features, reveals amazement at his daughter's ability and the touching sentiments of the story.)

And in this world there was a peace and harmony that she knew no matter how far she traveled, she would never find again.

She understood now why her father had brought her here. She felt the morning sun on her face and the gentle rocking of the canoe and smiled because she knew that here would always be her home.

ACTIVE READER

A CONCLUSIONS

What conclusions can you draw about what is most important to Lenore?

(When Lenore finishes, the hall is silent. Pete, very moved by his daughter's story, rises immediately to his feet. He begins to applaud loudly—the only one in the hall. The Judges look at him with disfavor. But then Sadie applauds and stands and Connie and Miss Walker stand applauding and then others and finally the whole hall is on its feet applauding. Even two of the Judges give polite applause. Connie, Miss Walker and Sadie smile at Pete. Pete looks only at Lenore.)

(Pete and Lenore, with tears in her eyes, look at each other and smile meaningfully at one another.) ❖

Theme and Character

Instruction Have students review the information they recorded in their charts and discuss the additions they've made. Then write the following questions on the board and tell students to use their answers to the questions to figure out themes. *What does the main character want? What must she overcome to get it? What lessons do the important characters learn in the process?*

Practice Have students work in pairs to answer the questions. Then have partners use their answers and the information they record-

ed in their charts to identify themes. Have students share their answers and themes with the class. Ask them which story details support their themes.

Possible responses: Lenore wants to represent her school in a writing contest in Thunder Bay. She must overcome her father's objections to this trip. She learns that she cannot force her father to see her point of view. Instead, she must help him understand her. Pete learns that he must let Lenore be free to explore her life and her talents, and that he

mustn't let his fears ruin their relationship.
Possible Themes: People who love each other should try to accept each other's differences. When people really love each other, they must find a way to work out their differences. Parents should allow their children to find their own way in the world.

📖 Use **Unit Five Resource Book,** p. 7, for more practice in finding and supporting themes.

BRINGING THE PRAIRIE HOME

by Patricia MacLachlan

Place.

This is one of my favorite words, and I am a writer
because of it.
Place.

I remember vividly the place where I was born: the smell of
the earth, the look of the skies when storms came through;
the softness of my mother's hollyhock blooms that grew by
the back fence.
When I was ten years old, I fell in love with place. My
parents and I drove through the prairie, great stretches of
land between small towns named wonderful names like
Spotted Horse, Rattlesnake, Sunrise. We stopped once for
drinks that we fished out of cold-water lift-top tanks, and my
mother and I walked out onto the prairie. Then my mother
said something that changed my life forever. She took a step,
looked down at her footprint, and said, "Someone long ago
may have walked here, or maybe no one ever has. Either way
it's history."

Cross Curricular Link Geography

THE PRAIRIE

The great central plains of Canada and the
United States are covered by prairie—flat, rolling
grasslands. Rainfall averages 12 to 40 inches (30
to 51 cm) per year in this temperate land.
Weather on the prairie can be harsh. Winter
storms often blow across this open land, and
hot summers can bring drought. However, some
of the richest farmland in the world is in the
North American prairie, giving it the nickname,
"the nation's breadbasket."

Native Americans lived on the prairie for thousands of years, but in the 1800s, their land was
taken by the U.S. government and given away to
settlers who agreed to farm it. They toiled to
plow through the prairie sod, the top layer of
soil, which was held together by the thick, mat-
ted roots of the prairie grasses. The sod was so
firm that it could be cut into brick-like pieces and
used to build homes. But the rich soil was fertile
for farming.

In the 1930s, many Great Plains farms were dev-
astated by a severe drought. Without the prairie
grass roots to hold the soil together, winds created great dust storms. The area most affected
became known as the Dust Bowl, and thousands
of farm families were forced from their land.

×××××××××××××××

I thought of those who might have come before me and those who might come after, but mostly I was face-to-face with the important, hopeful permanence of place, place that I knew was there long before I walked there, and would be there long after I was gone. I realized, in that moment, that the Earth is history. The Earth is like a character who has secrets; the Earth holds important clues to who we are, who we've been; who we will be. We are connected to the land and to those secrets.

It was after this event that I bought a diary and began writing all sorts of truths about myself, as if I, too, might leave clues about myself behind. I was becoming a writer. All because of place. Now I cannot write a story unless I know the place, the landscape that shapes the story and the people in the story. And to remind myself of the place that changed me, I have carried a small bag of prairie dirt with me for years.

I took that bag of prairie dirt with me once to a class of fourth graders, and I found that those children are connected to place, too. Some had moved from place to place many times: One boy's house had burned in a fire recently; another was about to move to a place he had never been.

"Maybe," I said, "I should toss this out onto my New England yard. I'll probably never live on the prairie again."

"No!" cried a boy, horrified. "It might blow away!"

And then a girl had a suggestion.

"Maybe you should put that prairie dirt in a glass on your windowsill, so you can see it when you write. It would be like bringing the prairie home."

And that is where that little piece of my prairie is today; my place, my past, my landscape; in a glass on my windowsill. I have brought the prairie home so that I can look at it every day; write about it, write about me, and remind myself that the land is the connection that links us all.

Read Aloud

Instruction Read aloud the first two paragraphs of "Bringing the Prairie Home" to students. Model how to read effectively by using punctuation marks as guides and by reading expressively and with appropriate intonation and pacing. When you come to the mother's words, read them as you feel she would say them. Ask students how they might prepare for a reader's theater presentation. How could they be sure to avoid stumbling over unfamiliar words? *(look up the words in a dictionary ahead of time to see how they are pronounced, so that the reading will be fluent)*

Practice Have each student choose a partner. Direct pairs to choose a passage from the selection to read aloud. Have them practice and evaluate each other's reading. When students are ready, have each pair read their passages to the class.

Connect to the Literature

1. What Do You Think?
How did you feel about Lenore's writing?

Comprehension Check
• Why is Lenore invited to Thunder Bay?
• What is her father's reaction to the invitation?
• What secret does Pete share with Lenore at the end of the drama?

Think Critically

2. How does Lenore feel about her father and her community? What **conflict** do these feelings create for her?

3. Why do you think Lenore is angry at both Miss Walker and her father?

Think About:
• how they have treated Lenore
• what each wants from Lenore
• Lenore's wishes for her future

4. What does Pete want for Lenore's future? Why is he worried about her?

5. ACTIVE READING DRAWING CONCLUSIONS
What are some of the conclusions you noted in your READER'S NOTEBOOK? Compare your notes with those of a classmate. How were your conclusions different? Would you change any of them now that you have finished reading the drama?

Extend Interpretations

6. COMPARING TEXTS Look back at "Aaron's Gift" on page 248. Both Aaron and Lenore seem to have a special bond with their family elders. How would you compare their feelings about family history? How do they show their feelings?

7. Connect to Life Pete hides the fact that he cannot read behind an attitude that school is not important. Why do you think it can be hard for a person to admit he or she cannot do something?

Literary Analysis

 THEME **Theme** is the meaning or moral of a piece of literature. Often the theme is a message about life or human nature that the writer wants to share with readers. Themes are usually unstated. The words, thoughts, and actions of **characters** offer clues to the theme. Clues can also be found in the **plot,** the **setting,** and the **story title.** One of the themes of "Words on a Page" is stated below.

People shouldn't try to change others.

This theme is conveyed through
• the stories Lenore and her father tell
• the conflict between Lenore and her father
• the ways that Lenore and her father change and what they learn about each other

Group Activity In a small group, discuss the theme stated above. List story events that show this theme. Then list other themes and the story information that reveals them. Compare your list with that of another group.

• Support from others can help you find your voice.

WORDS ON A PAGE **633**

Connect to the Literature

1. What Do You Think?
Answers will vary, but students should support their opinions with information from the selection.

Comprehension Check
• She is invited to read her story at a contest.
• Her father forbids her to go.
• He finally tells her that he never learned to read.

Use Selection Quiz
Unit Five Resource Book, p. 10.

Think Critically

2. Possible Responses: Lenore loves her father and her community very much. She also loves to read, write, and learn. She wants to explore the world. This creates a conflict between her two sets of wishes and between her wishes and those of her father.

3. Answers will vary, but should note that both adults are planning Lenore's future based on their needs and wants. They are arguing with each other and ignoring Lenore as if she were a child too young to discuss her own future.

4. Possible Response: Pete wants her to stay in the Native American community. He thinks she'll be treated badly outside the community and she won't return home.

5. Students' conclusions will vary, but should be reasonable and based on the information presented.

Use **Reading and Critical Thinking Transparencies,** p. 18, for additional support.

Literary Analysis

Theme Students' responses will vary but should show an understanding of the story and its characters and how they convey themes.

 Use **Literary Analysis Transparencies,** p. 7, for additional support.

Extend Interpretations

6. Comparing Texts Both Lenore and Aaron understand that prejudice has had an impact on their families. Aaron is especially sad for what his grandmother had to go through in her youth because of prejudice against the Jews. In "Words on a Page," Lenore is better able to understand her father's sometimes harsh attitude toward the outside world after she learns what is behind Pete's feelings.

7. Connect to Life Possible Response: The person is embarrassed. The person may believe that others will think less of him or her for not knowing how to do something.

Writing

Character Comparison To get students started, draw a Venn diagram on the board and hold a class discussion about Pete and Lenore. Have volunteers record the similarities and differences between the characters. Students can use the diagram to write their paragraphs.

 Use **Writing Transpancies**, p. 10, for additional support.

Speaking & Listening

Video Critic Encourage students to provide constructive criticism of the presentations. Demonstrate how to be courteous and encouraging when offering someone suggestions for improvement.

 Use the **Speaking and Listening Book**, pp. 29 and 30, for additional support.

Research & Technology

Research Project Tell students that they may also find information about the Ojibway under these spellings: Ojibwe, Ojibwa, and Chippewa. To make this activity easier, suggest that students work in pairs or small groups.

Vocabulary

EXERCISE

1. foliage
2. hover
3. momentum
4. foreground
5. anticipation
6. abundance
7. expertise
8. gesture
9. tentative
10. collective

Writing

Character Comparison What values, traditions, experiences, and talents do Pete and Lenore share? What makes them different? Use a Venn diagram to explore your thoughts. Then write a paragraph comparing the two characters. Place your draft in your **Working Portfolio**.

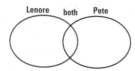

Speaking & Listening

Video Critic View the video version of *Words on a Page*. How does the setting compare with the way you visualized it as you read? Do Lenore and Pete perform their roles as you imagined?

VIDEO: Literature in Performance

"Words on a Page"

Create a presentation that compares the video with the play. Choose two or three main points of comparison to discuss. End your presentation with a statement about which version of the story you liked better and why. Be sure to support your opinion with specific reasons and examples.

Speaking and Listening Handbook
See p. R100: Persuasive Presentations.

Research & Technology

SOCIAL STUDIES

Research Project What are today's Ojibway communities like? What kinds of work do Ojibway adults do? How many people leave the community for school or work? Gather information from encyclopedias and the Internet. Then make a poster that presents your findings to the class.

INTERNET Research Starter
www.mcdougallittell.com

Vocabulary

EXERCISE: CONTEXT CLUES On your paper, write the Word to Know that best completes each sentence.

1. The fall _____ dazzled Lenore with its shades of gold and crimson.
2. A gull can _____ as though it is suspended in midair.
3. Lenore slumped over her desk, her _____ gone.
4. The photograph showed a raven perched in the _____, while water gleamed in the background.
5. Backstage, Lenore clutched her essay, filled with eager _____.
6. Lenore's mother was amazed by the university's _____ of information.
7. The class listened as Pete shared his fishing _____.
8. The teacher began to _____ for Lenore to speak more loudly.
9. Lenore accepted Miss Walker's compliment with a shy, _____ smile.
10. At Parents' Night, Lenore's reading inspired _____ shouts of joy.

Vocabulary Handbook
See p. R20: Context Clues.

WORDS TO KNOW	abundance anticipation	collective expertise	foliage foreground	gesture hover	momentum tentative

Grammar in Context: Sentence Fragments and Run-on Sentences

A sentence contains a subject and a predicate, and it expresses a complete thought. Keith Leckie's characters often use phrases that do not express complete thoughts. Sometimes a writer will use this technique to mimic actual speech.

> Good here for beaver. Lots of food.

A **sentence fragment** is a part of a sentence that is written as if it were a complete sentence. You can fix a sentence fragment by adding the words that will complete the thought.

A **run-on sentence** has the opposite problem. It is two or more sentences written as one.

> The story won a contest now she has to go to Thunder Bay to read it then they'll send her away to university!

You can fix a run-on sentence by making it two or more sentences, or by adding a comma and a **coordinating conjunction.**

> The story won a contest, and now she has to go to Thunder Bay to read it. Then they'll send her away to university!

Apply to Your Writing Use sentence fragments and run-on sentences only when you are trying to show casual or broken speech.

WRITING EXERCISE Rewrite the sentences to fix fragments and run-ons.

Example: *Original* Sunrays through dust particles.

Rewritten Sunrays fell through dust particles.

1. Be really nice if you were there.
2. Your parents aren't here I was looking forward to meeting them.
3. Can't tell you what it means.
4. I'm excited about the course Mr. Crankhurst is open to it.

Grammar Handbook
See p. R67: Writing Complete Sentences.

Keith Leckie
born 1952

"Most of all, I want to write a good love story."

Behind the Scenes Keith Leckie is a lifelong resident of Toronto, Ontario. He has worked in Canadian filmmaking since the mid-1970s. He started as part of a production crew, working with the many people who film scenes. Later he became a scriptwriter and director for both television and film.

Working for Change Leckie served as a volunteer for groups sending aid to Central America. Later, he researched that region's political history for a book. He has also written about the struggle for freedom by people in Afghanistan. Leckie enjoys creating fiction about lighter subjects as well. His other works include *The Seventh Gate* and *The Coco River*.

AUTHOR ACTIVITY
Reading Films Many popular film and TV dramas have been published. With a partner, read a key scene in a script for a film you enjoyed. How could the scene have been performed or filmed differently? Discuss.

Grammar in Context
WRITING EXERCISE
Possible Responses:

1. It would be really nice if you were there.
2. Your parents aren't here. I was looking forward to meeting them.
3. I can't tell you what it means.
4. I'm excited about the course, and Mr. Crankhurst is open to it.

Keith Leckie

Keith Leckie (b. 1952) wrote the screenplay for the acclaimed movie *Where the Spirit Lives*. It tells the story of a Blackfoot girl who is taken from her people to be educated in a white school. The movie was directed by Bruce Pittman.

Author Activity

Reading Films Students will need time to find and read film and TV scripts. Interested students might show a scene from a film or TV show to the class, and then present their own ideas about how the scene could have been done differently.

EXPLICIT INSTRUCTION **Grammar in Context**

EXAMPLES AS FRAGMENTS
When you use examples in your writing, it is easy to write a fragment unintentionally.
Instruction Display the following sentences: *Canada has produced many famous writers. Such as Keith Leckie and Margaret Atwood.* Point out that the first sentence is complete; the line beginning with "Such as" is a fragment. Sometimes fragments can be attached to the sentence before them to make a complete sentence: Canada has produced many famous writers<u>, such as</u> Keith Leckie and

Margaret Atwood. Sometimes, however, it is necessary to turn the fragment into a new sentence: *Writers should use a variety of sources. For example, looking on the Internet and interviewing experts.*
The writer could correct the fragment by adding a subject and changing the verbals *looking* and *interviewing* to verbs: For example, <u>they should look</u> on the Internet and <u>interview</u> experts.
Practice Have students correct the fragment that follows. Lenore wanted to learn more

about the world outside Spirit Bay. Especially the big cities to the south. *(Bay, especially)*

 Use **Unit Five Resource Book**, p. 8.

 For more instruction in correcting sentence fragments, see McDougal Littell's *Language Network*, Chapter 1.

For **systematic instruction** in grammar, see:
- **Grammar, Usage, and Mechanics Book**
- pacing chart on p. 609i

Standards-Based Objectives

1. understand and appreciate **nonfiction**
2. understand and appreciate a **personal essay**
3. use the reading skill of **identifying main idea and details**
4. examine **evidence for author's conclusions**
5. note **propaganda and persuasion** in text

Summary

In this personal essay, Robert Fulghum tells how each spring, he writes a statement of personal belief. When he was young, his credo filled many pages as he tried to cover every eventuality. As he grew older, his statements became more abbreviated. Recently, he decided to condense his personal beliefs into one page. Upon reflection, he realized that the precepts he learned at a young age have been the foundation of his personal beliefs all along. Kindergarten taught him the importance of sharing, caring for others and the world's resources, appreciating the wonder around him, living a balanced life, and remembering that death comes to all. He concludes by observing that the world would be a better place if everyone lived by these principles.

Thematic Link

For Robert Fulghum, finding his voice means looking at the lessons he has learned in the past that have helped him to become who he is today.

English Conventions Practice

Daily Language SkillBuilder

Have students **proofread** the display sentences on page 609k and write them correctly. The sentences also appear on Transparency 19 of **Language Transparencies.**

from All I Really Need to Know I Learned in Kindergarten

by ROBERT FULGHUM (fŏŏl′jŭm)

Connect to Your Life

Doing Your Best In the selection you are about to read, Robert Fulghum lists what he thinks a person needs to know in order to live a meaningful life. List three things you think everyone "needs to know" about life. Share your list with a partner.

Build Background

HISTORY

Many people set aside time once a year to think about how to improve their lives and make the world a better place. January 1 is a traditional time to do this. January was named for Janus, the Roman god of gates and doorways, who is usually depicted with two faces: one looking back into the past and one looking forward into the future. For centuries, the beginning of January has been a popular time to think about the past and plan for the future.

> WORDS TO KNOW
> **Vocabulary Preview**
> bland   idealism   sanitation
> cynical   naive

Focus Your Reading

LITERARY ANALYSIS **PERSONAL ESSAY**

A **personal essay**, or informal essay, is a short work of nonfiction in which a writer expresses his or her thoughts, feelings, and opinions about a subject. Usually, personal essays include anecdotes or personal experiences. The writer of a personal essay may seek to express his or her ideas. The writer may also wish to entertain, to inform, or to persuade readers to think or feel a particular way. As you read, think about why Robert Fulghum wrote this essay.

ACTIVE READING **IDENTIFYING MAIN IDEA AND DETAILS**

Most nonfiction writing is organized around a **main idea.** The main idea may appear as a statement, or it may be developed throughout the work. The main idea is supported by strong, well-chosen details. Identifying the main idea and supporting **details** can help you understand what you read.

READER'S NOTEBOOK As you read, think about what the author's main idea seems to be. Jot down details you think support this main idea.

LESSON RESOURCES

UNIT FIVE RESOURCE BOOK, pp. 11–17

ASSESSMENT
Formal Assessment, pp. 103–104
Test Generator

SKILLS TRANSPARENCIES AND COPYMASTERS
Reading and Critical Thinking
• Main Idea and Supporting Details, TR 25 (pp. 638, 640)

Language
• Daily Language SkillBuilder, TR 19 (p. 636)
• Synonyms, TR 60 (p. 637)
Writing
• Writing Variables, TR 2 (p. 641)
• Elaboration, TR 13 (p. 641)
Speaking and Listening
• Matching Your Message with Purpose and Audience, p. 6 (p. 641)

INTEGRATED TECHNOLOGY
Audio Library

Visit our Web site:
www.mcdougallittell.com

For **systematic instruction** in language skills, see:
• **Vocabulary and Spelling Book**
• **Grammar, Usage, and Mechanics Book**
• pacing chart on p. 609i

All I Really Need to Know I Learned in Kindergarten
by Robert Fulghum

Illustrations, by students of the Harlem School of the Arts, copyright © 1994 by Oxford University Press, Inc.

Each spring for many years, I have set myself the task of writing a personal statement of belief: a Credo. When I was younger, the statement ran for many pages, trying to cover every base, with no loose ends. It sounded like a Supreme Court brief, as if words could resolve all conflicts about the meaning of existence.

The Credo has grown shorter in recent years—sometimes <u>cynical</u>, sometimes comical, sometimes <u>bland</u>—but I keep working at it. Recently I set out to get the statement of personal belief down to one page in simple terms, fully understanding the <u>naive</u> <u>idealism</u> that implied.

WORDS TO KNOW	**cynical** (sĭn′ĭ-kəl) *adj.* expressing scorn and mockery
	bland (blănd) *adj.* dull
	naive (nä-ēv′) *adj.* as simple and believing as a young child
	idealism (ī-dē′ə-lĭz′əm) *n.* the practice of imagining that things could be absolutely perfect

637

Reading and Analyzing

Literary Analysis | PERSONAL ESSAY

Ask students how Robert Fulghum achieves an informal style and how it contributes to the effect of the text.

Possible Responses: He uses sentence fragments, colloquial language, anecdotes, and direct address of the reader for a friendly, conversational tone.

Use **Unit Five Resource Book,** p. 13 for more practice.

Active Reading | IDENTIFYING MAIN IDEA AND DETAILS

Remind students that a main idea is developed through several types of details. Ask students what kinds of supporting details they find in this essay.

Possible Response: examples and incidents

Use **Unit Five Resource Book,** p. 12 for more practice.

Use **Reading and Critical Thinking Transparencies,** p. 25, for additional support.

Literary Analysis: METAPHOR

A Ask students what the author compares himself to when he has trouble making an important decision.

Possible Response: He compares himself to his old car stalling.

Ask students what larger metaphor is implied through the car comparison.

Possible Response: Life is a journey.

Reading Skills and Strategies: ANALYZE COMMON PERSUASIVE TECHNIQUES

B Ask students how this conclusion reinforces the author's purpose.

Possible Response: The author's purpose is to persuade readers to live by the rules they learned in kindergarten. He offers specific examples and finishes by reiterating, in a memorable way, the most important point.

The inspiration for brevity[1] came to me at a gasoline station. I managed to fill an old car's tank with super-deluxe high-octane go-juice. My old hoopy couldn't handle it and got the willies—kept sputtering out at intersections and belching going downhill. I understood. My mind and my spirit get like that from time to time. Too much high-content information, and I get the existential[2] willies—keep sputtering out at intersections where life choices must be made and I either know too much or not enough. The examined life is no picnic.

All I really need to know about how to live and what to do and how to be I learned in kindergarten. Wisdom was not at the top of the graduate-school mountain, but there in a sand pile at Sunday school. These are the things I learned:

Share everything.

Play fair.

Don't hit people.

Put things back where you found them.

Clean up your own mess.

Don't take things that aren't yours.

Say you're sorry when you hurt somebody.

Wash your hands before you eat.

Flush.

Warm cookies and cold milk are good for you.

Live a balanced life—learn some and think some and draw and paint and sing and dance and play and work every day some.

Take a nap every afternoon.

When you go out into the world, watch out for traffic, hold hands and stick together.

Be aware of wonder. Remember the little seed in the Styrofoam cup: The roots go down and the plant goes up and nobody really knows how or why, but we are all like that.

Goldfish and hamsters and white mice and even little seeds in the Styrofoam cup—they all die. So do we.

And then remember the Dick-and-Jane books and the first word you learned—the biggest word of all—LOOK.

Everything you need to know is in there somewhere. The Golden Rule and love and basic <u>sanitation</u>. Ecology and politics and equality and sane living.

Take any one of those items and extrapolate[3] it into sophisticated adult terms and apply it to your family life or your work or your government or your world and it holds true and clear and firm. Think what a better world it would be if we all—the whole world—had cookies and milk about three o'clock every afternoon and then lay down with our blankies for a nap. Or if all governments had a basic policy to always put things back where they found them and to clean up their own mess.

And it is still true, no matter how old you are—when you go out into the world, it is best to hold hands and stick together. ❖

---

1. **brevity** (brĕv′ĭ-tē): being brief and to the point.
2. **existential** (ĕg′zĭ-stĕn′shəl): of or relating to existence.
3. **extrapolate** (ĭk-străp′ə-lāt′): to make predictions based on limited information.

WORDS TO KNOW | **sanitation** (săn′ĭ-tā′shən) *n.* the creation of rules designed to protect public health

638

Examining Persuasion

EXPLICIT INSTRUCTION

Instruction Ask volunteers to identify the major purposes for writing. *(to inform, to entertain, to express, and to persuade)* Tell the class that an author may have more than one purpose for writing. Ask students to describe Fulghum's purpose or purposes. Then ask if the author wants to persuade readers to do or believe something. *(Fulghum's purposes are to inform, entertain, and persuade. He wants to convince readers to live by the rules they learned in kindergarten.)* Use the Reading Skills and Strategies: Analyzing

Common Persuasive Techniques note in the green side column to extend this discussion.

Practice After students read the selection, have them work in pairs to paraphrase the examples Fulghum gives in the last two paragraphs to support his opinion that people can live by the rules they learned in kindergarten.

Possible Responses: The rules you learn in kindergarten can be applied to family life, work, the government, and the world. We would all be better for taking a nap every

afternoon. Governments should be responsible for any problems they cause and should try to correct them. We should all stick together as we make our way through life.

The Gifted Boy, Paul Klee. Super Stock. Copyright © 2001 Artists Rights Society (ARS), New York/VG Bild-Kunst, Bonn.

Differentiating Instruction

Less Proficient Readers
Ask students the following questions in order to check their comprehension:
- What did Robert Fulghum learn in kindergarten about how to treat other people?
  Possible Response: He learned to treat others well and to be considerate of them.
- What did he learn to include in his life every day?
  Possible Response: some work, some play, some relaxation, some learning, and some happiness
- What does he think would happen if all adults lived by these rules?
  Possible Response: The world would be a better place.

English Learners
1 Explain that *old hoopy* refers to Fulghum's old car and *the willies* means "feelings of uneasiness or fear."
2 Have students take turns reading the rules aloud. Pause to discuss those that might be less familiar to students.

Advanced Students
Challenge students to write one of the following essays, or to suggest one of their own to write:
- Everything I Need to Know I Learned in the Library
- Everything I Need to Know I Learned at Camp
- Everything I Need to Know I Taught Myself
- Everything I Need to Know I Learned from My Grandmother

EXPLICIT INSTRUCTION Noting Propaganda

Instruction Review the section titled Persuasive Appeals in the Reading Handbook, pages R13–R14. Ask, "Does Robert Fulghum use any of these propaganda techniques in his essay?" (*No, he does not call anyone names, he does not try to appeal to people's sense of being better than others, and he does not use overgeneralizations.*) Point out that Fulghum supports his statements with examples and appeals to his readers through respect, not snob appeal. Remind students to watch for examples of propaganda, which makes a writer's opinion less believable.

Practice Write the following statements on the board and have students identify the one that is an opinion and the two that are propaganda.
- Any person with half a brain knows that nothing lives forever.
- Facing a scary world is easier if you have a friend with you.
- If you are not hopelessly ignorant, you will realize that washing your hands before eating helps prevent the spread of disease.

Answers: The first and third statements are examples of propaganda. The second statement is an opinion.

Use the **Unit Five Resource Book**, p. 14, for more practice in understanding propaganda.

Connect to the Literature

1. What Do You Think?
Responses will vary. Students may think that the list makes sense. Others may find the list overly simple or too light-hearted to be practical.

Comprehension Check
- He was at the gas station.
- Don't hit people or take things that aren't yours.
- Governments should put things back where they find them and clean up their own mess.

 Use Selection Quiz, **Unit Five Resource Book,** p. 17.

Think Critically

2. Possible Responses: Sharing, playing fair, cleaning up after yourself, saying you're sorry, and sticking together are the most important. Following these rules will prevent conflicts and injustices that cause unhappiness.

3. Possible Responses: Fulghum means that life choices can be difficult, particularly when it seems that there are so many factors to consider in making them. It is easy to lose sight of the basics, such as those he lists in this essay, and become overwhelmed by too much complex information.

4. Possible Response: Writing a credo each year helps Fulghum keep the important things in mind. This helps him face conflicts and work to make his own life meaningful.

5. Possible Response: The main idea is that we already know all that we need to know in order to have a meaningful life and make good decisions. Fulghum supports this idea with his list of the most basic rules for social conduct, and by asking the reader to imagine what the world would be like if everyone followed these rules.

Use **Reading and Critical Thinking Transparencies,** p. 25, for additional support.

Literary Analysis

Author's Purpose Encourage students to list direct and indirect lessons that Fulghum shares, such as the importance of taking stock of one's life. Students will probably conclude that he wrote the essay to inform and persuade.

640 UNIT FIVE PART 1

Connect to the Literature

1. What Do You Think? How did you react to Robert Fulghum's list of important things to know?

Comprehension Check
- Where was Fulghum when he was inspired to write his list?
- What are the two things he says not to do?
- What basic policy does he think governments should follow?

Think Critically

2. Look again at Fulghum's list of what he learned in kindergarten. Which five things do you think are most important? Explain.

3. Fulghum says the "examined life is no picnic." What do you think he means by this statement?

   Think About:
   - why he writes a credo
   - how he feels when facing life choices
   - how the credo relates to his life

4. Fulghum believes that words cannot resolve the conflicts about the meaning of life. If this is true, why do you think he continues to write a credo every year?

5. **ACTIVE READING** **IDENTIFYING MAIN IDEA AND DETAILS** Look back through the notes you made in your **READER'S NOTEBOOK.** What do you think is the main idea of the essay? What details support it? Compare your thoughts with those of a partner.

Extend Interpretations

6. Critic's Corner One critic has said that Fulghum "specializes in the celebration of the everyday event." Do you think this is true of this selection? Why?

7. Connect to Life Do you agree with Fulghum's belief that all we need to know we learned in kindergarten? Explain your opinion.

640 UNIT FIVE PART 1: FINDING YOUR VOICE

Extend Interpretations

6. Critic's Corner Possible Response: This is true because Fulghum says that little things, such as taking a nap and learning to share, should be appreciated because they are so important that they could even help to create world peace.

7. Connect to Life Possible Responses: I do agree, because if all the countries of the world followed these rules, there would not be war; I do not agree, because real-world decisions can be very complex and require advanced education and mature thought. For example, "playing fair" can be a complicated thing to define.

Literary Analysis

PERSONAL ESSAY A **personal essay** is a short work of nonfiction about one subject. Personal essays are usually **autobiographical.** They focus on the author's own experiences and the lessons he or she has learned.

AUTHOR'S PURPOSE A writer usually writes for one or more purposes. To express oneself, to inform or explain, to persuade, and to entertain, may all be purposes for writing.

Activity Review Fulghum's essay. Then jot down ideas about what he learned from his experiences and why he wrote the essay. Compare your notes with those of a partner.

What Fulghum learned:

His purpose for writing:

Writing

Personal Credo Look back through Fulghum's statements of personal belief. Then make a list of your own strongest beliefs about life. Write a paragraph or two on one of these beliefs, describing why you feel this way and when this belief became important to you. Place it in your **Working Portfolio.**

Writing Handbook
See p. R35: Paragraphs.

> This activity asks you to describe your important beliefs. To find out about writing forms you might use when your purpose is to describe, see p. R31: Choosing a Form.

Strongest Beliefs
1. Everyone should be treated equally

Speaking & Listening

Credo Speech Fulghum first shared much of his writing as a public speaker. Share the description you wrote for the Writing activity by turning it into a speech. Practice presenting your speech in a clear, strong voice. Use facial expressions and gestures as you speak to help your audience understand and enjoy your presentation. Entertain your audience by relating an incident or story that supports your statement. Present your speech to the class.

Speaking and Listening Handbook
See p. R96: Organization and Delivery.

Writing

Personal Credo Have students develop their explanation of why this belief is important by offering several examples of how it affects their lives and could affect the lives of others.

 Use **Writing Transparencies,** pp. 2 and 13, for additional support.

Speaking & Listening

Credo Speech To get students started on this assignment, have them review the personal credo they wrote. Encourage them to brainstorm incidents that led them to this belief or that taught them the validity of the rule. Have students rehearse their speeches with a partner.

Use the **Speaking and Listening Book,** p. 6, for additional support.

Vocabulary

STANDARDIZED TEST PRACTICE

Choose the word or group of words that means the same, or nearly the same, as the underlined Word to Know.

1. A <u>cynical</u> comedian
   - **A** successful
   - **B** scornful
   - **C** respectful
   - **D** playful

2. A <u>bland</u> book
   - **J** long
   - **K** borrowed
   - **L** dull
   - **M** little

3. A strong <u>idealism</u>
   - **A** hopefulness
   - **B** intention
   - **C** attitude
   - **D** stubbornness

4. A <u>naive</u> child
   - **J** friendly
   - **K** moody
   - **L** suspicious
   - **M** simple

5. A city's <u>sanitation</u>
   - **A** public health rules
   - **B** traffic rules
   - **C** construction rules
   - **D** government meeting rules

EXERCISE For each of the Words to Know, write a new sentence that correctly uses the word. Then rewrite your sentences on a new sheet of paper and leave a blank where the Word to Know should be. Exchange papers with a classmate and fill in the correct vocabulary words for each other's sentences.

Vocabulary

STANDARDIZED TEST PRACTICE

1. B
2. L
3. A
4. M
5. A

EXERCISE
Sentences will vary.

Grammar in Context

1. Live a balanced life: learn, think, draw, paint, sing, dance, play, and work.
2. This advice is good: watch for traffic, hold hands, and stick together.
3. There is one thing politicians do not know: clean up your mess.
4. All things die: goldfish, hamsters, white mice, and everything else.

Author Activity

Small Wonders To extend this assignment, have students discuss lessons that they might draw from the world around them.

Grammar in Context: Sentence Variety Using Colons

Robert Fulghum uses a **colon** to let us know that he's going to list the lessons he learned in kindergarten:

> These are the things I learned: Share everything. Play fair. . . .

A colon can be used to introduce a list of items in a sentence. It can also be used between two sentences when the second sentence explains the first sentence.

> Here is my most important belief: always try to be kind.

Punctuation Tip: Use a colon after the salutation of a business letter and between hours and minutes in an expression of time. In a play or a script, a colon may appear between a speaker's name and what the speaker says.

WRITING EXERCISE Punctuate each sentence with a colon.

Example: ***Original*** Here's my credo all you really need to know you learn in kindergarten.

Rewritten Here's my credo: all you really need to know you learn in kindergarten.

1. Live a balanced life learn, think, draw, paint, sing, dance, play, and work.
2. This advice is good watch for traffic, hold hands, and stick together.
3. There is one thing politicians do not know clean up your mess.
4. All things die goldfish, hamsters, white mice, and everything else.

Grammar Handbook
See p. R64: Quick Reference Punctuation.

Robert Fulghum
born 1937

"I've always made a clear distinction between making a life and making a living."

Artist and Orator Before becoming a world-famous author, Robert Fulghum created motel art, taught folk music, and worked as a singing cowboy and amateur rodeo performer. Fulghum grew up in Waco, Texas, and left home after high school to explore the world. Eventually, he went to college and became a minister.

Popular Wisdom Most of Fulghum's best-selling 1988 book *All I Really Need to Know I Learned in Kindergarten: Uncommon Thoughts on Common Things* was originally written for his sermons and church newsletters. It has been published in 93 countries and in 27 languages.

The Importance of Fun Fulghum's books have sold more than 15 million copies. However, he does not take fame and fortune too seriously. "Any fool can make enough money to survive," Fulghum says. "It's another thing to keep yourself consistently entertained." His books include *It Was on Fire When I Lay Down on It* and *Uh-Oh: Some Observations from Both Sides of the Refrigerator Door.*

AUTHOR ACTIVITY

Small Wonders In his writing, Fulghum often examines what seems like a simple subject and finds great meaning in it. Look for some of these everyday subjects in Fulghum's other essays. Share your findings with the class.

EXPLICIT INSTRUCTION Grammar in Context

USING COLONS CORRECTLY

Instruction Remind students of these two uses of the colon: to introduce a list of items and to introduce a sentence of explanation. Tell students that there are situations when a colon might seem correct, but isn't. One error that many writers make is to use a colon after the word *because*. Write the following sentence on the board: *I eat ice cream often because: I really like it.*

Ask a volunteer to rewrite the sentence correctly, with or without the colon. (*I eat ice cream often because I really like it.* OR *This is why I eat ice cream often: I really like it.*)

Practice Have students look for and correct missing or misused colons in the following sentences. If the sentence is correct, have them write *correct.*

1. Sharing is important because: it will help you get along with others.
2. These are my favorite foods ice cream, pizza, and broccoli.

3. I shared my ice cream with my brother because I know he likes ice cream.

 Use **Unit Five Resource Book,** p. 15.

 For more instruction in using colons, see McDougal Littell's ***Language Network,*** Chapter 9.

For **systematic instruction** in grammar, see:
- **Grammar, Usage, and Mechanics Book**
- pacing chart on p. 609i

You Sing (Sonnet 52)

by PABLO NERUDA

How to Paint the Portrait of a Bird

by JACQUES PRÉVERT (zhäk prā′vĕr)

Connect to Your Life

What Inspires You? Something makes you sit up and take notice. Maybe it's a song on the radio or a beautiful sunrise. What stirs your feelings and your imagination? Discuss with a partner.

Build Background

Artistic Inspiration Pablo Neruda once said that in the area where he grew up, "Nature . . . went to my head . . . I was barely ten at the time, but already a poet." As a writer and an artist, Jacques Prévert was inspired to create poems, plays, songs, and children's books, as well as pictures. In the poems that follow, Neruda and Prévert use poetry to capture sounds and images that move them.

Focus Your Reading

LITERARY ANALYSIS **PERSONIFICATION**

When a poet or writer gives human qualities to an animal, object, or idea, the technique is called **personification.** Poets use personification to create strong images that help readers visualize and understand the ideas in a poem. As you read these poems, look for examples of personification and other kinds of figurative language.

ACTIVE READING **NOTING SENSORY DETAILS**

Words and phrases that help the reader see, hear, taste, smell, and feel what the writer is describing are called **imagery,** or **sensory details.** Noting sensory details helps you share the writer's experience.

READER'S NOTEBOOK As you read, jot down sensory details in a chart like the one shown.

Sound	Sight	Touch	Taste	Smell
creaking wheels				

Standards-Based Objectives

1. understand and appreciate **poetry**

2. understand and appreciate **onomatopoeia**
3. identify and understand **personification** as one type of figurative language
4. note **sensory details**

Summary

The poem "You Sing" by Pablo Neruda describes a voice that keeps company with the moving forces of nature and soars above the clamor of tools and machinery and bells that toll the passage of time. To the speaker the voice is powerful, gentle, and life-giving.

The poem "How to Paint the Portrait of a Bird" by Jacques Prévert metaphorically describes the creative process. The artist must first paint a cage and leave the door open, wait for the bird to fly in, close the door, paint out the bars of the cage, create a scene of beauty for the bird, and then wait to see if the bird sings. If the bird sings, then the artist's ideal has indeed come to life.

Thematic Link

Pablo Neruda and Jacques Prévert write about the joys and challenges of self-expression.

English Conventions Practice

Daily Language SkillBuilder

Have students **proofread** the display sentences on page 609k and write them correctly. The sentences also appear on Transparency 20 of **Language Transparencies.**

YOU SING (SONNET 52) / HOW TO PAINT THE PORTRAIT OF A BIRD **643**

LESSON RESOURCES

UNIT FIVE RESOURCE BOOK, pp. 18–19

ASSESSMENT
Formal Assessment, pp. 105–106
Test Generator

SKILLS TRANSPARENCIES AND COPYMASTERS
Literary Analysis
• Poetry: Figurative Language, TR 19 (pp. 644, 648)

Reading and Critical Thinking
• Noting Sensory Details, TR 11, (p. 644, 648)
Language
• Daily Language SkillBuilder, TR 20 (p. 643)
Writing
• Sensory Words List, TR 16 (p. 649)
Speaking and Listening
• Evaluating Reading Aloud, p. 14 (p. 649)

INTEGRATED TECHNOLOGY
Audio Library

Visit our Web site:
www.mcdougallittell.com

For **systematic instruction** in language skills, see:
• **Vocabulary and Spelling Book**
• **Grammar, Usage, and Mechanics Book**
• pacing chart on p. 609i

Ask students what object is given human characteristics in the first stanza.

Possible Response: The pine trees are personified.

 Use **Literary Analysis Transparencies,** p. 19, for additional support.

Active Reading

NOTING SENSORY DETAILS

Ask students to describe the sounds in the second stanza.

Possible Response: The sounds created by the sensory details are clanging, harsh, painful, and metallic.

Ask students how these sounds are related to the sound of the voice.

Possible Response: The voice is in contrast to these noises and soars above them.

 Use **Unit Five Resource Book,** p. 18, for more practice.
Use **Reading and Critical Thinking Transparencies,** p. 11, for additional support.

Literary Analysis ONOMATOPOEIA

Ask students what effect the word *zing* in line 10 creates.

Possible Response: *Zing* suggests speed and the sound of the arrow's release from the bow.

Reading Skills and Strategies: MAKING INFERENCES

Ask students to infer from the last line the speaker's feelings toward the person whose voice is the subject of the poem.

Possible Response: It is the voice of someone he loves.

Your Sing (Sonnet 52)

by Pablo Neruda

You sing, and your voice peels the husk
of the day's grain, your song with the sun and sky,
the pine trees speak with their green tongue:
all the birds of the winter whistle.

5 The sea fills its cellar with footfalls,
with bells, chains, whimpers,
the tools and the metals jangle,
wheels of the caravan creak.

But I hear only your voice, your voice
10 soars with the zing and precision of an arrow,
it drops with the gravity of rain,

your voice scatters the highest swords
and returns with its cargo of violets:
it accompanies me through the sky.

translated by Stephen Tapscott

EXPLICIT INSTRUCTION Personification

Instruction Remind students that poets use figurative language to convey meaning in their poems. Ask students, "What example of figurative language is used in this image: *The angry wind screamed as it tore down the buildings*"? (*personification*) "What is the definition of personification?" (*Personification is giving human qualities to an animal, object, or idea.*) Ask students find examples of personification in the poem above. (*your voice peels the husk of the day's grain, pine trees speak, sea fills its cellar*)

Practice Have students choose an example of personification from "You Sing" to examine. Tell students to identify the human qualities given to the object in the example. Then have them describe what the poet is saying about the object by giving it human qualities.

Possible Response: Example of Personification: "the pine trees speak with their green tongue." Human Qualities: speech. The image helps readers visualize a part of nature making its own statement about the joy of life.

 Use **Unit Five Resource Book,** p. 19, for more practice.

Soneto 52

Cantas, y a sol y a cielo con tu canto
tu voz desgrana el cereal del día,
hablan los pinos con su lengua verde:
trinan todas las aves del invierno.

5 El mar llena sus sótanos de pasos,
de campanas, cadenas y gemidos,
tintinean metales y utensilios,
suenan las ruedas de la caravana.

Pero sólo tu voz escucho y sube
10 tu voz con vuelo y precisión de flecha,
baja tu voz con gravedad de lluvia,

tu voz esparce altísimas espadas,
vuelve tu voz cargada de violetas
y luego me acompaña por el cielo.

THINKING through the LITERATURE

1. **Comprehension Check** What does the speaker say is the only thing he hears?

2. How would you describe the speaker's feelings about the voice in this poem?

3. How does the speaker use comparison and contrast to explain his feelings? Refer to lines in the poem that support your answer.

Differentiating Instruction

Less Proficient Readers
Read the poem aloud to students before they read it silently. Then check their understanding by asking the following questions:
- What does the poet associate with the voice in the first stanza?
  Possible Response: forces of nature
- What does the last line of the poem mean?
  Possible Response: The voice lives in the speaker's memory and heart.

Set a Purpose Have students read the next poem to find out the steps involved in painting the portrait of a bird.

English Learners
Have a Spanish-speaking volunteer read the poem in the original Spanish. Follow up by reading it to students in English and comparing the rhythm of the poem in each language. Focus on a few images, such as those in the first and fourth stanzas, that express specific ideas about the voice.

 Use **Spanish Study Guide**, pp. 130–132, for additional support.

Thinking through the Literature

1. **Comprehension Check** He hears only "your voice."
2. **Possible Response:** The speaker loves the voice and feels that it keeps him going through the day.
3. **Possible Response:** In line 10, the speaker compares the voice to the *zing* of an arrow.

Nobel Prize for Literature

Multicultural Link

Pablo Neruda was the recipient of the Nobel Prize for Literature in 1971. This prize is given annually by the Swedish Academy for achievements in literature, language, or areas of general culture. Candidates for the prize cannot apply but must be nominated by members of the Swedish Academy or similar academies, former Nobel laureates, or others eminent in the fields of language and literature. The money for the prize comes from a fund created by the fortune left by Alfred Nobel, who died in 1896. The fund is managed by the Nobel Foundation.

Pablo Neruda was awarded the prize "for a poetry that, with the action of an elemental force, brings alive a continent's destiny and dreams." In his Nobel lecture, Neruda speaks about his decision to be politically active. He says that he saw his task "to join the extensive forces of the organized masses of the people," even if his actions led to criticism. He believes a poet's responsibilities "involve friendship not only with the rose . . . with exalted love . . . but also with unrelenting human occupations . . . "

Reading and Analyzing

Reading Skills and Strategies:
VISUALIZE

A Ask students to describe the mental images evoked by the text description.
Possible Response: A person is crouching behind a tree in absolute silence and stillness.

Literary Analysis: SYMBOLISM

B Ask students to interpret the symbolism of the bird.
Possible Response: inspiration

Active Reading

NOTING SENSORY DETAILS

C Point out to students that this poem creates a picture within a picture. Ask students to pick out the details that appeal to the senses in this description.
Possible Responses: The images "green leaves" and "dust in the sun" appeal to sight; "freshness of the wind" appeals to touch; "sound of the insects in the summer grass" appeals to hearing.

Literary Analysis: METAPHOR

Ask students what the process of capturing and painting the portrait of the bird metaphorically represents.
Possible Response: The process describes the creation of a work of art.

Reading Skills and Strategies:
MAKE INFERENCES

Ask students what they can infer from the painter's action of signing the canvas.
Possible Response: He or she is pleased with and proud of the painting.

How to Paint the Portrait of a Bird

by Jacques Prévert ❧ translated by Paul Dehn

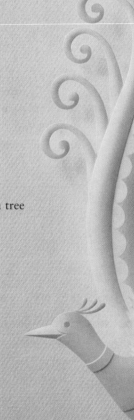

First paint a cage
with an open door
then paint
something pretty
5   something simple
something fine
something useful
for the bird
next place the canvas against a tree
10   in a garden
in a wood
or in a forest
hide behind the tree
A without speaking
15   without moving . . .

Sometimes the bird comes quickly
but it can also take many years
before making up its mind
Don't be discouraged
20 wait
     wait if necessary for years
     the quickness or the slowness of the coming
     of the bird having no relation
     to the success of the picture
25 When the bird comes
     if it comes
     observe the deepest silence
     wait for the bird to enter the cage
     and when it has entered
30 gently close the door with the paint-brush
     then
     one by one paint out all the bars
     taking care not to touch one feather of the bird
     Next make a portrait of the tree
35 choosing the finest of its branches
     for the bird
     paint also the green leaves and the freshness of the wind
     dust in the sun
     and the sound of the insects in the summer grass
40 and wait for the bird to decide to sing
     If the bird does not sing
     it is a bad sign
     a sign that the picture is bad
     but if it sings it is a good sign
45 a sign that you are ready to sign
     so then you pluck very gently
     one of the quills[1] of the bird
     and you write your name in a corner of the picture.

---

1. **quill** (kwĭl): any of the larger feathers of a bird; also, a
   writing pen made from such a feather.

Less Proficient Readers
Ask students to list the steps that someone must follow to paint the portrait of a bird, according to the poem.
Possible Response: First paint a cage with an open door. Then place the picture of the cage in a natural setting and wait. When the bird enters the cage, push the door shut and paint out the bars. Paint a tree and a beautiful scene for the bird. If the bird sings, sign the painting.

English Learners
1 Be sure students understand the two meanings of the word *sign* as it is used in this line. The first *sign* is an indication or signal; the second one means to write one's name.

Advanced Students
To further the discussion of "You Sing," point out the contradictions in the images used by the poet to describe the voice, and ask students to consider what these paradoxes suggest.
Possible Response: The speaker's appreciation of the voice is profound.

As students read "How to Paint the Portrait of a Bird," ask them how this poem might express Prévert's credo, or statement of belief, about being a poet.
Possible Response: Prévert's credo might be that inspiration is essential to write poetry. If a poet is fortunate enough to receive inspiration, he or she must nurture it and show it off to its best advantage. If the finished poem is not authentic, or does not "sing," he or she has failed.

EXPLICIT INSTRUCTION Punctuation in Poetry

Instruction Ask students what they know about punctuation in poetry. (*Poets may use traditional punctuation, nontraditional punctuation, or no punctuation at all to emphasize ideas and feelings.*) Then have students read "How to Paint the Portrait of a Bird" and tell which punctuation technique the poet has used. (*The poet uses almost no punctuation.*) Ask students how the absence of punctuation affects their reading of the poem. How can they tell when to pause? (*Read each line as a single thought, with a pause afterward.*) Ask

students to note the ellipsis at the bottom of the first page.
Practice Have students identify the effect of the ellipsis in the poem. Then have them compare the lines before the ellipsis with those that follow it. Have students suggest reasons why the poet might have varied his poem in this way.
Possible Responses: The ellipsis provides a pause in the poem and breaks it into two sections. The lines before the ellipsis describe cre-

ating a cage for the bird and waiting for the bird to come. The lines after the ellipsis describe waiting and what to do when the bird arrives.

Connect to the Literature

1. What Do You Think?
Possible Response: The image of an open birdcage waiting for a bird to enter is a very strong image that stays in my mind.

Comprehension Check
- First, paint a cage with an open door.
- You should pause quietly when the bird comes, and then close the cage door and paint out its bars.
- The painting is good.

Think Critically

2. Possible Response: Sight is most important, as is appropriate to a poem about the visual medium of painting.

Use **Reading and Critical Thinking Transparencies,** p. 11, for additional support.

3. Possible Response: The bird represents creativity. Sometimes creative inspiration takes a long time to come.

4. Possible Responses: Be open to life and its beauties; wait patiently for inspiration; seize creative opportunity when it comes; erase traces of your effort to make it look easy; strive to create art that seems alive.

Literary Analysis

Personification **Responses will vary.** Examples of personification from "You Sing" include: "the pine trees speak with their green tongues" (human quality: speech).

Use **Literary Analysis Transparencies,** p. 19, for additional support.

Connect to the Literature

1. What Do You Think?
What image does this poem leave in your mind?

Comprehension Check
- How does the speaker say to begin painting?
- What does the speaker say you should do if the bird comes?
- What does it mean if the bird sings?

Think Critically

2. **ACTIVE READING** **NOTING SENSORY DETAILS**
Which sense does this poem appeal to most? With a partner, use your  **READER'S NOTEBOOK** chart to discuss how sensory details bring the poem to life.

3. What do you think the bird represents? Why must the painter wait so patiently for the bird to come?

4. What advice do you think the speaker of this poem offers to readers?

Extend Interpretations

5. **COMPARING TEXTS** Compare the two poems. How are they similar and different? How would you describe the mood created by each poem?

6. Critic's Corner One critic has said that Neruda "does not describe, he glorifies." Do you think this is true of "You Sing"? Explain.

7. Connect to Life Recall your prereading discussion about finding inspiration. What experiences do you think inspire strong feelings in these two poets?

Literary Analysis

PERSONIFICATION The use of human qualities to describe an object, animal, or idea is called **personification.** For example, Neruda describes trees that "speak with their green tongue." Poets use personification and other kinds of figurative language to create vivid mental pictures in readers' minds. These pictures help readers understand the thoughts, feelings, and ideas the poet is writing about.

Activity With a small group, make a list of the items in the poems that are described using personification. Next to each item, write the human qualities each item is given. Discuss how the use of personification helped you understand and visualize each poet's ideas. Share your list with another group.

ONOMATOPOEIA Words such as *hiss* and *bang* that sound like what they mean are examples of **onomatopoeia.** These words are a kind of sensory language that helps writers create vivid images. Onomatopoeic words often describe movement, such as the *zing* of the arrow in "You Sing."

Extend Interpretations

5. Comparing Texts **Possible Responses:** In "You Sing," the speaker is telling the person he addresses how that person brightens his life. In "How to Paint the Portrait of a Bird," the speaker is giving advice about how to be creative and about how to live life.

6. Critic's Corner **Possible Response:** Yes, because Neruda praises the good qualities of the person to whom the poem is addressed.

7. Connect to Life **Possible Responses:** The sound of a beloved person's voice inspires Neruda. Prévert is inspired by the beauty of nature. The fact that it is hard to capture seems to make it even more beautiful to him.

Writing

Sensory Description Recall a vivid sound or image you have experienced, such as a clap of thunder, breaking glass, a sunset, or the ocean. How did you feel? Write a description, using sensory language and personification. Include precise verbs, nouns, and adjectives in your description. Place it in your **Working Portfolio.**

Writing Handbook
See p. R38: Using Language Effectively.

Speaking & Listening

Sharing Your Description Read aloud the description you wrote for the Writing activity on this page. Practice reading slowly, with a loud, clear voice. Add facial expressions and gestures to make your reading more interesting. After reading aloud, invite classmates to share their reactions with you.

Speaking and Listening Handbook
See p. R98: Oral Interpretation.

Research & Technology

Something New What sport, hobby, or other activity have you always been curious about? List activities you want to learn about, such as field hockey, painting, juggling, or photography. Then choose one activity and find books or articles that explain the basics of the activity. Write a short report that tells about what you learned.

Reading for INFORMATION
Before beginning your work, read "Flip Out!" on pages 650–652.

Writing

Sensory Description To help students choose a subject for this assignment, have them jot down, for two or three days, the sights, sounds, and other sensations that they experience at a particular time of day.

 Use **Writing Transparencies,** p. 16, for additional support.

Speaking & Listening

Sharing Your Description Students might enjoy guessing what their classmates have described. Invite students to keep the subjects of their descriptions secret. After each student reads aloud, ask the class to identify the sound or image described.

 Use the **Speaking and Listening Book,** p. 14, for additional support.

Research & Technology

Something New To make this assignment easier, have students brainstorm activities in small groups. Students may wish to research some of the activities mentioned by other students in their group.

Pablo Neruda
1904–1973

"What could I ever say without my roots?"

Born a Poet When Pablo Neruda was growing up in a small Chilean village, poetry seemed an unlikely career. But as a child, Neruda would say, "I'm going out hunting poems." First published when he was 15, by his college years Neruda was a well-known poet.

Freedom and Fame Declaring himself a poet of the people, Neruda wrote poems and prose supporting social change. In 1971 he received the Nobel Prize in literature. Neruda's work has been translated into dozens of languages. Collections of his poems include *Elementary Odes* and *Residence on Earth.*

Jacques Prévert
1900–1977

"Don't joke about humor— humor is serious!"

On Page and Screen Born in a small town in France, Jacques Prévert was educated in Paris, where he spent much of his adult life. A very popular poet, he is also regarded as one of his country's greatest screenwriters. He also wrote plays, song lyrics, and children's books.

Loved and Hated Critics are divided about Prévert's poetry. Some find his work moving; others claim he is often driven by anger. In "How to Paint the Portrait of a Bird," he seems to reveal at least part of his true nature. Prévert tells artists to seize life with gusto—yet still be patient.

Standards-Based Objectives

- read to be informed
- use study strategies to understand and follow complex directions
- monitor and adjust strategies to improve comprehension
- find out how to make a flipbook

Connecting to the Literature

"Flip Out!" is a nonfiction article that complements the poem "How to Paint the Portrait of a Bird" because it outlines the process for arriving at an end result. Both the article and the poem rely on the reader's ability to follow directions exactly and in order. Because it is obvious that omitting steps or doing them in the wrong sequence would sabotage the success of the flipbook, students can more easily understand the importance of following the steps in the poem to arrive at the full literal and metaphorical meaning.

LESSON RESOURCES

UNIT FIVE RESOURCE BOOK, pp. 20–21

Flip Out!

Without film or camera you can make simple cartoons jump to life. Even animators of big-budget, computer-rendered cartoons still test their pencil drawings in flipbooks before developing them for the big screen.

The pages of a flipbook show a series of drawings. Each page has one drawing that is changed in some small way from the previous drawing. By flipping the pages, you make the character or designs in the drawings appear to bounce, bend, change, or fly away. Below are instructions on how to make your own flipbook. Read the directions carefully before you begin.

❶

Step 1. You'll need a small, blank, white stationery pad. A pad about 6" x 4" is a good size. The pad should contain about 100 sheets of paper.

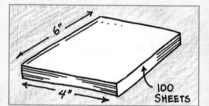

Step 2. First, secure the top of the pad with small binder clips or masking tape. This will ensure that the pad does not fall apart as you use it and will keep your drawings in order.

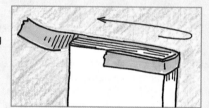

650 UNIT FIVE   PART 1: FINDING YOUR VOICE

EXPLICIT INSTRUCTION Preparing an Application

Instruction Tell students that the article they are about to read is a set of directions for creating a flipbook. Ask how following these directions might be similar to following instructions in order to fill out an application. Remind students that in both situations, they need to read carefully and make sure they understand each step. Ask volunteers to identify situations that require applications to be filled out. Jot their responses on the board. *(library membership, summer recreation/swimming programs, forms for school activities and sports teams)* Review the steps for completing applica-

tions on page R18 of the Reading Handbook, located at the back of this book.

Practice Distribute page 21 of the **Unit Five Resource Book,** which provides an application for students to fill out.

Possible Responses Responses will vary but should indicate that students read the application carefully and understood which sections to fill out.

 Use **Unit Five Resource Book,** p. 21.

(LEAVE ABOUT A ¼" AROUND)

3" x 3½"

START HERE

(BOTTOM)

Step 3. Next, open the pad to the last page. With a pencil, lightly mark a 3" x 3½" rectangle at the bottom of the page, leaving about a ¼" space from the edges. This is your work area, where you will create your drawings. Drawings too close to the bound edge of your pad will not be visible when you flip them.

START HERE

Step 4. Decide what sort of movement you want to illustrate. It takes about 24 drawings to animate one second of movement, so keep it simple! Don't start by drawing a running horse or a baseball slugger. Instead, try something like a floating balloon, a hatching egg, or a sprouting seed. It is also fun to begin with a simple shape and "morph," or transform, it into a completely different shape.

Step 5. Using a pencil, place your first simple line drawing within the frame, or work area, on the last page. Make the drawing dark enough so that you will be able to see it through the second page of the pad. (You may not be able to see all the details, but its location should be clearly visible.)

Some people have careers that not only help pay their bills but also give great pleasure, allowing them to make full use of their talents. Yet no matter how exciting a particular job may seem, there is usually some part of it that is difficult or time consuming. In order to make a difficult task easier, it pays to follow directions.

Following Complex Directions

The first and most important step in trying a new or complicated activity is to read through the directions.

Good directions are clear, complete, and in the correct order. Numbers or letters make the steps easy to follow. Look for words such as *first, second, next,* and *finally.* Read the steps in the given order.

Complex directions often include illustrations that make it easier for the reader to complete the activity. Make sure you examine any diagrams or illustrations, including their labels and captions.

Remember, if you don't understand the directions the first time, try rereading or asking for help. When you are sure you understand the directions, collect the materials and carry out the steps in order.

YOUR TURN *Use the questions and activities below to follow the directions.*

❶ What is the first step in following any set of directions? Why do you think it is important?

❷ What features of a good set of directions are used here?

As you go through the article with students, have them use the material in the right-hand column as a guide to reading complex sets of instructions. The following are possible responses to the four questions and activities:

1 The first step is to read through the directions completely. This will help you to find out what supplies you need before you can begin, to estimate how long the activity will take you, and to figure out answers to questions that you may have about the process.

2 An illustration with captions is included. The step is numbered, and the transitional word *next* is used.

EXPLICIT INSTRUCTION **Following Complex Directions**

Instruction Ask students to think of situations when they have to follow directions. List students' suggestions on the board. *(making a recipe, building something from a kit, playing a new game, using certain products, fixing something, reading directions for finding a place)* Then ask students what steps they take to make sure they are following the directions correctly. Tell students that whenever they have to follow directions, they should do the following:

• Read through the directions completely and make sure they understand them.

• Look at any illustrations or diagrams that will help them follow the directions.

• Gather any materials they will need before they begin following the steps included in the directions.

Practice Have students complete the numbered questions and activities on the pupil pages.

Possible Responses See the responses in the side columns in the teacher's edition.

 Use **Unit Five Resource Book,** p. 20, for more practice.

3 The illustration shows that the drawings on each page are very similar and that you work from the back to the front. If this step were completed before Step 2, you would not be able to keep the pages in the correct order or keep them together to trace the drawings accurately.

4 Responses will vary. Step 10 might be paraphrased to read as follows: Draw until every page is filled or until you have finished the sketch. Adding a little more detail to each drawing will make the end result more eye-catching.

Activity

Students may suggest the following: that all the necessary supplies be listed under a separate heading at the beginning of the directions, instead of integrated with the steps; that the additional explanations of why something must be done a certain way be simplified; that more diagrams be included. For example, an illustration for Step 10 would be helpful to show how to make each drawing more complex.

Reading for Information *continued*

3 How does this illustration help make the directions easier to follow? What do you think might happen if you carried out this step before you did Step 2?

4 Remember to apply your study skills when you read new or complex material. If you still don't understand something after reading through all the directions, try paraphrasing. Choose one of the flipbook steps and paraphrase it.

When you have finished reading the directions, collect your materials and make your own flipbook. Note any steps that you had difficulty understanding or completing. How would you change the directions to make them easier to follow?

Research & Technology
Activity Link: "You Sing (Sonnet 52),"
"How to Paint the Portrait of a Bird,"
p. 649. Write directions for an activity that was once new to you. You may choose to describe how to write a poem or how to carry out some other activity that you had difficulty learning or particularly enjoyed—a new sport, or your first part in a play, for example. Make sure your guidelines are clear, complete, and in the correct order.

3

Step 6. Turn to the second page, the next-to-last page of your flipbook. Re-draw or trace your first drawing with some small change. For example, a hatching egg might begin to show a small crack.

Step 7. Repeat Step 6 until you have about 12 drawings.

Step 8. Check your drawings to see how they "move." Hold the top of the pad in one hand with the bottom of the pad against your palm and your fingers curled over the top. Hold the free edge of the pad with your other hand. Put your fingers on top and your thumb under the bottom page.

Step 9. Let pages flip down past your thumb so that you view them in the order in which you drew them, from bottom to top. Try it several times at different speeds. If your animation does not flow smoothly, adjust your drawings. If necessary, remove a page, but try not to do this often or the action will skip or "jump."

Step 10. Continue drawing on each remaining page until you have either drawn on every sheet in the pad or completed your cartoon. You may want to let your drawings get more complex, leading up to a big finish.

4

EXPLICIT INSTRUCTION **Research & Technology**

The Research & Technology activity on this page links to the Research & Technology section of Choices and Challenges on page 649.

Instruction Suggest that students choose an activity with which they are familiar or one that they have researched thoroughly. Have students brainstorm the steps necessary to complete the activity. Performing the activity may help refresh their memories.

Practice Have students write each step on a separate index card. The order of the steps can then be changed easily or the step rewritten in more concise language. Each card should refer to the diagram or illustration that will accompany the step; students may prefer to attach the diagram to the card. Encourage students to check the accuracy of their directions and the clarity of their language by reading the instructions aloud to a partner.

The Scribe

by KRISTIN HUNTER

Connect to Your Life

Part of a Solution What problems or needs do you see in your community? What can you do to help? Working in a small group, identify local problems and brainstorm ways that you and other young people can help solve those problems. Use a chart like the one shown to record your ideas.

Problems	Solutions
1. Litter in the streets	1. Organize Saturday street cleanup

Build Background

SOCIAL STUDIES

One problem that exists in many communities is illiteracy. A person who is illiterate has not learned to read and write. In the United States, it is estimated that between 40 million and 44 million adults are functionally illiterate. This means they cannot read or write well enough to fill out a job application or address a letter so that it will reach its destination. Although many of these people have enrolled in school at some time in their lives, for various reasons they did not learn to read and write well.

Many communities have literacy volunteer groups. Volunteers help illiterate or low-literate adults learn to read and write. Some workplaces also offer classes to help employees improve their literacy skills.

Focus Your Reading

LITERARY ANALYSIS   CHARACTER TRAITS

A few of the many words that might name a character's **traits**, or **qualities**, include *generosity, determination,* and *kindness.* You can learn about a character's traits through

- the character's speech, thoughts, feeling, and actions
- the speech, thoughts, and actions of other characters
- the writer's statements about the character

As you read "The Scribe," look for information that will help you determine the main character's traits. Also think about how these traits influence the actions he takes and the decisions he makes.

ACTIVE READING   MAKING INFERENCES ABOUT CHARACTERS

An inference is a logical guess based on evidence. A good reader **makes inferences about characters** in a story. You can make an inference about a character's traits, emotions, or motivations, for example, or about the changes he or she might undergo.

📖 **READER'S NOTEBOOK**   As you read, notice how James responds to events. Why does he act as he does? Use your observations to write down inferences about James's character. Next to each inference, note evidence from the story that supports it.

LESSON RESOURCES

UNIT FIVE RESOURCE BOOK, p. 22–28

ASSESSMENT
Formal Assessment, pp. 107–108
Test Generator

SKILLS TRANSPARENCIES AND COPYMASTERS
Reading and Critical Thinking
- Making Inferences, TR 10 (pp. 654, 661)
- Venn Diagram, TR 35 (p. 662)

Language
- Daily Language SkillBuilder, TR 20 (p. 653)
- Learning and Remembering New Words, TR 65 (p. 654)
Speaking and Listening
- Evaluating Reading Aloud, p. 14 (p. 662)

INTEGRATED TECHNOLOGY
Audio Library

Visit our Web site:
www.mcdougallittell.com

For **systematic instruction** in language skills, see:
- **Vocabulary and Spelling Book**
- **Grammar, Usage, and Mechanics Book**
- pacing chart on p. 609i

Standards-Based Objectives

1. understand and appreciate a **short story**
2. understand the role of **characterization** in fiction
3. analyze the **effect of a character's qualities** on the plot and its resolution
4. use the reading skill of **making inferences** to understand the characters in the story

Summary

Thirteen-year-old James and his family live in an apartment above the Silver Dollar Check Cashing Service. James becomes angry when he learns how this shop makes money—by charging customers for services such as cashing checks and filling out forms. Many of the Silver Dollar's customers need these services because they cannot read or write. James decides to help these customers by reading and writing for them, just like the scribes in the Bible. When James sets up his free service in front of the Silver Dollar, people flock to his table, until a police officer arrives, threatening to shut him down for not having a business license. Still determined to help, James reappears in front of the Silver Dollar the next day. This time, he tries to guide customers to a nearby bank that cashes checks for free. Only one person accepts, an elderly woman who proudly opens her first bank account. She inspires James to think about applying for a business license, so that he can continue to be a scribe.

Thematic Link

James discovers that he can have a voice in his community, first as a scribe and then as a friendly guide. He helps others and in turn is helped by them.

Note: Point out that slang, such as "Man!" and other dated expressions, can help readers identify the setting (mid-twentieth century). Encourage students to suggest modern equivalents.

English Conventions Practice

Daily Language SkillBuilder

Have students **proofread** the display sentences on page 609k and write them correctly. The sentences also appear on Transparency 20 of **Language Transparencies.**

Reading and Analyzing

Literary Analysis
CHARACTER TRAITS

A Remind students that a story's narrator may be a character in the story. When the narrator is a character, readers learn his or her thoughts. This information can help them analyze characters and their traits, motivations, and conflicts. Ask students to describe what James thinks about the people who come into the Silver Dollar.

Possible Responses: They are in bad shape; they are treated badly.

Active Reading
MAKING INFERENCES ABOUT CHARACTERS

B To help students make inferences and support them with text evidence and experience, ask students what evidence in the story suggests that the narrator does not like the way Mr. Silver treats customers.

Possible Responses: He takes their picture "like they're some kind of criminal"; he yells at them; he calls them by their first names.

C Why might the old man not want someone to know that he can't fill in forms himself?

Possible Responses: He is embarrassed; he does not want to be yelled at.

Use **Unit Five Resource Book,** p. 23, for more practice. Use **Reading and Critical Thinking Transparencies,** p. 10, for additional support.

The Scribe
by Kristin Hunter

Copyright © Michael Paraskevas.

EXPLICIT INSTRUCTION **Preteaching Vocabulary**

WORDS TO KNOW

Teaching Strategy Remind students that in some cases they will not be able to figure out the meaning of a word through context when the context does not provide adequate clues. In such cases they should look up the unfamiliar word in a **dictionary.** Have the class read the paragraph in the second column on page 655 that begins, "Look, Marie." When they come to the word *dignified,* ask, "Are there any context clues that help you understand this word?" *(no)* Have them look up the word

in a dictionary, and ask a volunteer to write the definition on the board. *(noble, stately, having a proud manner)* Ask students if knowing the meaning of the word *dignified* helps them know more about the woman in the check-cashing service.

Practice Have students work in pairs to find dictionary definitions of the following WORDS TO KNOW: *class, disgrace, license, scribe.* Encourage students to write the definition of each word on a sheet of paper and then use the word in a sentence. Ask volunteer pairs to

share their words and sentences with the rest of the class. Have student pairs write a descriptive paragraph using as many of the words, including *dignified,* as possible.

Use **Unit Five Resource Book,** p. 27, for more practice.

For **systematic instruction** in vocabulary, see:
- **Vocabulary and Spelling Book**
- pacing chart on p. 609i

*W*e been living in the apartment over the Silver Dollar Check Cashing Service five years. But I never had any reason to go in there till two days ago, when Mom had to go to the Wash-a-Mat and asked me to get some change.

And man! Are those people who come in there in some bad shape.

Old man Silver and old man Dollar, who own the place, have signs tacked up everywhere:

NO LOUNGING, NO LOITERING[1]
THIS IS NOT A WAITING ROOM
and
MINIMUM CHECK CASHING FEE, 50¢
and
LETTERS ADDRESSED, 50¢
and
LETTERS READ, 75¢
and
LETTERS WRITTEN, ONE DOLLAR

And everybody who comes in there to cash a check gets their picture taken like they're some kind of criminal.

After I got my change, I stood around for a while digging the action. First comes an old lady with some kind of long form to fill out. The mean old man behind the counter points to the "One Dollar" sign. She nods. So he starts to fill it out for her.

"Name?"

"Muskogee Marie Lawson."

"SPELL it!" he hollers.

"M, m, u, s—well, I don't exactly know, sir."

"I'll put down 'Marie,' then. Age?"

"Sixty-three my last birthday."

"Date of birth?"

"March twenty-third"—a pause—"I think, 1900."

"Look, Marie," he says, which makes me mad, hearing him first-name a dignified old gray-haired lady like that, "if you'd been born in 1900, you'd be seventy-two. Either I put that down, or I put 1910."

"Whatever you think best, sir," she says timidly.

He sighs, rolls his eyes to the ceiling, and bangs his fist on the form angrily. Then he fills out the rest.

"One dollar," he says when he's finished. She pays like she's grateful to him for taking the trouble.

Next is a man with a cane, a veteran who has to let the government know he moved. He wants old man Silver to do this for him, but he doesn't want him to know he can't do it himself.

"My eyes are kind of bad, sir. Will you fill this thing out for me? Tell them I moved from 121 South 15th Street to 203 North Decatur Street."

Old man Silver doesn't blink an eye. Just fills out the form, and charges the crippled man a dollar.

And it goes on like that. People who can't read or write or count their change. People who don't know how to pay their gas bills, don't know how to fill out forms, don't know how to address envelopes. And old man Silver

---

1. **loitering** (loi′tər-ĭng): staying around without purpose.

Less Proficient Readers
Explain the title to students by saying that a *scribe* is someone who writes or copies words. They will learn more about scribes as they read this story.
Set a Purpose Have students read to find out who the scribe is in this story and why that person is a scribe.

English Learners
Students may have difficulty with some of the idioms, regional dialect, and other examples of informal English.
1 Explain that *digging the action* means "enjoying what's going on."
2 When the narrator says, "Old man Silver doesn't blink an eye," it means that he shows no reaction or emotion.

Use **Spanish Study Guide**, pp. 133–135, for additional support.

Advanced Students
Point out to students that the problem of illiteracy in the United States has still not been solved. Many state and local agencies offer courses for adults who cannot read. Additional courses are often directed toward immigrants and other people who have difficulty reading and writing in English. Have students discuss how these agencies might publicize information about such courses to potential students who are unable to read about them.

EXPLICIT INSTRUCTION **Character Traits**

Instruction Remind students that such words as *polite, courageous,* and *cowardly* can be used to describe a character's traits. Also remind them that identifying a character's traits helps a reader understand the character's actions and the plot. Say, "In this story, people who are not highly educated need the services of a check-cashing business. What kinds of traits do you see in the characters of Marie Lawson and the veteran?" (*They are unsure of themselves when dealing with numbers and words. They are also polite and dignified.*)

"Which of these characters' words, actions, or thoughts reveal that they are polite and dignified?" (*They call the old men "sir" even though the men are rude.*) "What traits do the Silver and Dollar have?" (*impatience, rudeness, disrespect*) "What words or actions show these traits?" (*They are extremely rude and unkind to their customers.*)
Practice Ask students to determine James's traits. Have students list these traits and the information that reveals them.

Possible Responses: sensitive and sympathetic—he's upset by way customers are treated; observant—he notices that one man is a veteran; polite—he thinks the men should not call an older woman by her first name.

Use **Unit Five Resource Book**, p. 24, for more practice.

Literary Analysis

CHARACTER TRAITS

A Ask students what this speech reveals about James's mother. Have them analyze her traits.

Possible Response: She doesn't want her son to judge people; she sympathizes with people who can't read.

Active Reading | **MAKING INFERENCES ABOUT CHARACTERS**

B Ask students what they can infer about Mom's religious beliefs. Have them make inferences and support them with text evidence and their own experience.

Possible Response: She is religious; she knows the Bible and has certificates.

Active Reading | **MAKING INFERENCES ABOUT CHARACTERS**

C Ask students what inferences they can make about James from his sign.

Possible Response: He wants to help; he does not care about money.

Literary Analysis

CHARACTER TRAITS

D Ask students what James's silence reveals about his character.

Possible Response: He is kind; he does not want to embarrass the woman.

Literary Analysis

CHARACTER TRAITS

E Ask what James's action reveals about him.

Possible Response: He does not want to take money from people; he just wants to help.

> "There was a time in history when nobody could read or write except a special class of people."

and old man Dollar cleaning up on all of them. It's pitiful. It's disgusting. Makes me so mad I want to yell.

And I do, but mostly at Mom. "Mom, did you know there are hundreds of people in this city who can't read and write?"

Mom isn't upset. She's a wise woman. "Of course, James," she says. "A lot of the older people around here haven't had your advantages. They came from down South, and they had to quit school very young to go to work.

A "In the old days, nobody cared whether our people got an education. They were only interested in getting the crops in." She sighed. "Sometimes I think they *still* don't care. If we hadn't gotten you into that good school, you might not be able to read so well either. A lot of boys and girls your age can't, you know."

"But that's awful!" I say. "How do they expect us to make it in a big city? You can't even cross the streets if you can't read the 'Walk' and 'Don't Walk' signs."

"It's hard," Mom says, "but the important thing to remember is it's no disgrace. There was a time in history when nobody could read or write except a special class of people."

B And Mom takes down her Bible. She has three Bible study certificates and is always giving me lessons from Bible history. I don't

656   UNIT FIVE   PART 1: FINDING YOUR VOICE

exactly go for all the stuff she believes in, but sometimes it *is* interesting.

"In ancient times," she says, "no one could read or write except a special class of people known as scribes. It was their job to write down the laws given by the rabbis and the judges.[2] No one else could do it.

"Jesus criticized the scribes," she goes on, "because they were so proud of themselves. But he needed them to write down his teachings."

"Man," I said when she finished, "that's something."

My mind was working double time. I'm the best reader and writer in our class. Also it was summertime. I had nothing much to do except go to the park or hang around the library and read till my eyeballs were ready to fall out, and I was tired of doing both.

So the next morning, after my parents went to work, I took Mom's card table and a folding chair down to the sidewalk. I lettered a sign with a Magic Marker, and I was in business. My sign said:

PUBLIC SCRIBE—ALL SERVICES FREE

I set my table up in front of the Silver Dollar and waited for business. Only one thing bothered me. If the people couldn't read, how would they know what I was there for?

But five minutes had hardly passed when an old lady stopped and asked me to read her grandson's letter. She explained that she had just broken her glasses. I knew she was fibbing, but I kept quiet.

---

2. **the rabbis and the judges:** the teachers and rulers of the ancient Hebrews.

EXPLICIT INSTRUCTION Character Traits

Instruction Write the word *sympathetic* on the board and tell students that someone who is sympathetic feels unhappy when he or she sees others who are mistreated or unhappy. Ask students if James is sympathetic. *(yes)* Ask them to point out James's words, feelings, or actions on these pages that reveal this trait. (*In his conversation with his mother, James is shocked and angry to learn that so many people can't read and must put up with people like Mr. Silver and Mr. Dollar.*) Ask volunteers to read aloud

examples in the story that show this trait. Ask students what conflict is revealed on page 656. (*James is in conflict with the check-cashing service. They take advantage of people who can't read and James wants to offer the people an alternative.*) Ask what character traits are revealed by the conflict James feels. Does this conflict show that he is sympathetic? What else does it show?

Practice Have students list more of James's traits and the information on page 656 that reveals them.

Possible Responses: passionate and sympathetic—he thinks it's awful that people can't read; thoughtful—he listens to his mother and thinks about what she says; clever and creative—he figures out a way to deal with the problem of illiteracy

 Use **Unit Five Resource Book**, p. 24, for more practice.

Afternoon Glare—Main Street (1991), Carl J. Dalio. Collection of the artist. Copyright © 1991 Carl J. Dalio.

I read the grandson's letter. It said he was having a fine time in California but was a little short. He would send her some money as soon as he made another payday. I handed the letter back to her.

"Thank you, son," she said, and gave me a quarter.

I handed that back to her too.

The word got around. By noontime I had a whole crowd of customers around my table. I was kept busy writing letters, addressing envelopes, filling out forms, and explaining official-looking letters that scared people half to death.

I didn't blame them. The language in some of those letters—"Establish whether your disability is one-fourth, one-third, one-half, or total, and substantiate[3] in paragraph 3 (b) below"— would upset anybody. I mean, why can't the government write English like everybody else?

Most of my customers were old, but there were a few young ones too. Like the girl who had gotten a letter about her baby from the Health Service and didn't know what "immunization"[4] meant.

At noontime one old lady brought me some iced tea and a peach, and another gave me

---

3. **substantiate** (səb-stăn'shē-āt): to give evidence to prove a claim.

4. **immunization** (ĭm'yə-nĭ-zā'shən): medicine given to protect against disease.

Active Reading | **MAKING INFERENCES ABOUT CHARACTERS**

A Ask students to infer how the narrator feels. Have them support their answer with text evidence and experience.

Possible Response: He's scared. His knees are knocking; people shiver when they are scared.

Reading Skills and Strategies: CAUSE AND EFFECT

B Ask students why the narrator closes his business. Have them use the text's structure or progression of ideas such as cause and effect to recall information.

Possible Response: The policeman told him that he should charge money, but then he would be breaking the law unless he had a license.

Active Reading | **MAKING INFERENCES ABOUT CHARACTERS**

C Ask students to infer who the mother means by "our people."

Possible Response: She means African-American people; she says that some think that banks are only for white people.

some fried chicken wings. I was really having a good time when the shade of all the people standing around me suddenly vanished. The sun hit me like a ton of hot bricks.

1 Only one long shadow fell across my table. The shadow of a tall, heavy, blue-eyed cop. In our neighborhood, when they see a cop, people scatter. That was why the back of my neck was burning.

"What are you trying to do here, sonny?" the cop asks.

A "Help people out," I tell him calmly, though my knees are knocking together under the table.

"Well, you know," he says, "Mr. Silver and Mr. Dollar have been in business a long time on this corner. They are very respected men in this neighborhood. Are you trying to run them out of business?"

"I'm not charging anybody," I pointed out.

"That," the cop says, "is exactly what they don't like. Mr. Silver says he is glad to have some help with the letter writing. Mr. Dollar says it's only a nuisance to them anyway and takes up too much time. But if you don't charge for your services, it's unfair competition."

Well, why not? I thought. After all, I could use a little profit.

"All right," I tell him. "I'll charge a quarter."

"Then it is my duty to warn you," the cop says, "that it's against the law to conduct a business without a license. The first time you accept a fee, I'll close you up and run you off this corner."

> He really had me there. What did I know about licenses? I'm only thirteen, after all.

He really had me there. What did I know about licenses? I'm only thirteen, after all. Suddenly I didn't feel like the big black businessman anymore. I felt like a little kid who wanted to holler for his mother. But she was at work, and so was Daddy.

"I'll leave," I said, and did, with all the cool I could muster. But inside I was burning up, and not from the sun.

One little old lady hollered "You big bully!" and shook her umbrella at the cop. But the rest of those people were so beaten down they didn't say anything. Just shuffled back on inside to give Mr. Silver and Mr. Dollar their hard-earned money like they always did.

I was so mad I didn't know what to do with myself that afternoon. I couldn't watch TV. It was all soap operas anyway, and they seemed dumber than ever. The library didn't appeal to me either. It's not air-conditioned, and the day was hot and muggy.

Finally I went to the park and threw stones at the swans in the lake. I was careful not to hit them, but they made good targets because they were so fat and white. Then after a while the sun got lower. I kind of cooled off and came to my senses. They were just big, dumb, beautiful birds and not my enemies. I threw them some crumbs from my sandwich and went home.

EXPLICIT INSTRUCTION Traits and Conflict

Instruction Ask students to identify how the conflict develops on this page and what actions James takes as a result. *(James is confronted by a policeman who tells him he cannot continue offering a scribe service. Suddenly James has no way to offer an alternative to the unfair check-cashing service. James is angry and depressed. He watches boring television and then throws rocks at the swans in the park. Finally he realizes he is being cruel and throws them some bread.)*

Practice Have students describe in writing an action on this page that shows James's sensitivity and another action that shows his determination.

Possible Responses: Sensitivity—he stops throwing rocks at the birds and gives them crumbs instead; he calls the birds beautiful. Determination—he thinks of another way to help people.

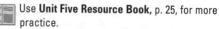 Use **Unit Five Resource Book**, p. 25, for more practice.

"Daddy," I asked that night, "how come you and Mom never cash checks downstairs in the Silver Dollar?"

"Because," he said, "we have an account at the bank, where they cash our checks free."

"Well, why doesn't everybody do that?" I wanted to know.

"Because some people want all their money right away," he said. "The bank insists that you leave them a minimum balance."

"How much?" I asked him.

"Only five dollars."

"But that five dollars still belongs to you after you leave it there?"

"Sure," he says. "And if it's in a savings account, it earns interest."

"So why can't people see they lose money when they *pay* to have their checks cashed?"

"A lot of *our* people," Mom said, "are scared of banks, period. Some of them remember the Depression,⁵ when all the banks closed and the people couldn't get their money out. And others think banks are only for white people. They think they'll be insulted, or maybe even arrested, if they go in there."

Wow. The more I learned, the more pitiful it was. "Are there any black people working at our bank?"

"There didn't use to be," Mom said, "but now they have Mr. Lovejoy and Mrs. Adams. You know Mrs. Adams, she's nice. She has a daughter your age."

"Hmmm," I said, and shut up before my folks started to wonder why I was asking all those questions.

The next morning, when the Silver Dollar opened, I was right there. I hung around near the door, pretending to read a copy of *Jet* magazine.

"Psst," I said to each person who came in. "I know where you can cash checks *free*."

It wasn't easy convincing them. A man blinked his red eyes at me like he didn't believe he had heard right. A carpenter with tools hanging all around his belt said he was on his lunch hour and didn't have time. And a big fat lady with two shopping bags pushed past me and almost knocked me down, she was in such a hurry to give Mr. Silver and Mr. Dollar her money.

But finally I had a little group who were interested. It wasn't much. Just three people. Two men—one young, one old—and the little old lady who'd asked me to read her the letter from California. Seemed the grandson had made his payday and sent her a money order.

"How far is this place?" asked the young man.

"Not far. Just six blocks," I told him.

"Aw shoot. I ain't walking all that way just to save fifty cents."

So then I only had two. I was careful not to tell them where we were going. When we finally got to the Establishment Trust National Bank, I said, "This is the place."

"I ain't goin' in there," said the old man. "No sir. Not me. You ain't gettin' me in *there*." And he walked away quickly, going back in the direction where we had come.

To tell the truth, the bank did look kind of scary. It was a big building with tall white marble pillars. A lot of Brink's armored trucks and Cadillacs were parked out front. Uniformed guards walked back and forth inside with guns. It might as well have a "Colored Keep Out" sign.

Whereas the Silver Dollar is small and dark and funky and dirty. It has trash on the floors and tape across the broken windows.

---

5. **Depression:** the Great Depression, a period of slow business activity and high unemployment from 1929 through the 1930s, before bank deposits were insured.

Differentiating Instruction

Less Proficient Readers

1 Encourage students to visualize the scene between the policeman and the narrator and to describe the mental images the descriptions evoke. How do students picture the police officer?

Possible Responses: big, serious, uniformed

2 Ask students to summarize what happened when the policeman spoke to the narrator.

Possible Response: The officer tells James that he has to charge money, but if he does charge money it is against the law unless he has a license. James doesn't know what else to do, so he leaves.

Set a Purpose Encourage students to continue reading to find out what the narrator does next to help people.

English Learners

You may need to help students understand the following idioms:

- *He really had me there:* I could not think of a good response.
- *I kind of cooled off and came to my senses:* I grew calmer and less angry.
- *shut up:* stopped talking
- *Aw shoot:* an expression of disappointment
- *colored:* a term once used for African Americans, now considered offensive

Advanced Students

3 Ask students if James might be referring to something besides birds when he says, "They were just big, dumb, beautiful birds and not my enemies."

Possible Responses: The birds could represent all of the unsympathetic people that James has encountered. He may be feeling that rather than getting angry, he should assume their problem is ignorance. Rather than attack the people, should do something constructive to find another way to set things right.

Active Reading | MAKING INFERENCES ABOUT CHARACTERS

A Ask students to infer why Mrs. Adams and the narrator wink at each other.

Possible Responses: They know that glasses are not the problem; they know that the woman cannot read.

Literary Analysis
CHARACTER TRAITS

B Ask students what they learn about Mrs. Franklin's traits when she winks at the narrator and then talks to him.

Possible Responses: She is bright and lively; she has the courage to try new things.

Literary Analysis
CHARACTER TRAITS

C To help students analyze characters and the changes they undergo, ask how the narrator changes by the end of the story. What is different about him?

Possible Responses: He is more determined to help; he knows what to do.

I looked at the little old lady. She smiled back bravely. "Well, we've come this far, son," she said. "Let's not turn back now."

So I took her inside. Fortunately Mrs. Adams's window was near the front.

"Hi, James," she said.

"I've brought you a customer," I told her.

Mrs. Adams took the old lady to a desk to fill out some forms. They were gone a long time, but finally they came back.

"Now, when you have more business with the bank, Mrs. Franklin, just bring it to me," Mrs. Adams said.

"I'll do that," the old lady said. She held out her shiny new bankbook. "Son, do me a favor and read that to me."

"Mrs. Minnie Franklin," I read aloud. "July 9, 1972. Thirty-seven dollars."

"That sounds real nice," Mrs. Franklin said. "I guess now I have a bankbook, I'll have to get me some glasses."

A Mrs. Adams winked at me over the old lady's head, and I winked back.

> "Well, we've come this far, son," she said. "Let's not turn back now."

"Do you want me to walk you home?" I asked Mrs. Franklin.

"No thank you, son," she said. "I can cross streets by myself all right. I know red from green."

And then she winked at both of us, letting us know she knew what was happening.

"Son," she went on, "don't ever be afraid to try a thing just because you've never done it before. I took a bus up here from Alabama by myself forty-four years ago. I ain't thought once about going back. But I've stayed too long in one neighborhood since I've been in this city. Now I think I'll go out and take a look at *this* part of town."

Then she was gone. But she had really started me thinking. If an old lady like that wasn't afraid to go in a bank and open an account for the first time in her life, why should I be afraid to go up to City Hall and apply for a license?

Wonder how much they charge you to be a scribe? ❖

EXPLICIT INSTRUCTION **Traits and Resolution**

Instruction Tell students that a character's traits affect the way he or she resolves conflicts in the story. Ask a volunteer to tell the class how James resolves his conflict. *(James decides to help people open accounts at a bank, where they will not be charged for cashing a check. This will lessen their dependence on the check-cashing service.)* Have students look at the list of traits they made. Ask them to name the traits that are supported by the way James solved the conflict. Ask students how

the story might have ended differently if James had the trait of hopelessness instead of determination.

Practice Write these traits on the board: *hopeless, cruel, rude.* Ask students to write how James might have resolved the conflict if these were his traits. Ask students to read their responses aloud. Then ask how they think a character's traits can affect the plot of a story. Discuss students' responses.

Possible Responses: If James had these traits, he would have given up his idea of helping people. He might have continued to throw rocks at the swans until he hit them. He might have been rude to the police officer and to his parents.

Use **Unit Five Resource Book**, p. 25, for more practice.

Connect to the Literature

1. **What Do You Think?** Does anything about James remind you of yourself? Explain.

Comprehension Check
- What services do the owners of the Silver Dollar offer?
- Why don't James's parents cash checks at the Silver Dollar?
- Why does the police officer shut down James's business?

Think Critically

2. Why do you think James wants to help people?

3. What does James learn from Mrs. Franklin?

4. In your opinion, what effects do James's efforts to help others have on his community?

   Think About:
   - the people he helps with reading and writing
   - the people he tries to take to the bank
   - the owners of the Silver Dollar

5. **ACTIVE READING** MAKING INFERENCES ABOUT CHARACTERS
   What does James's behavior toward his parents and toward the customers of the Silver Dollar tell you about him? Refer to the notes you made in your **READER'S NOTEBOOK**.

6. What do you think James will do after the story ends? Make a prediction based on James's character traits and the clues at the end of the story.

Extend Interpretations

7. **Different Perspectives** Imagine how this story would be different if it had been told by Mr. Silver. How might he view James's efforts?

8. **Connect to Life** Think about an unfair situation you have seen or experienced. How did you respond? What might you do differently now?

Literary Analysis

CHARACTER TRAITS

Readers can learn about a character's **traits,** or qualities, by paying attention to
- the character's speech, thoughts, feelings, and actions
- the speech, thoughts, and actions of other characters
- the writer's direct statements about the character
- descriptions of the character's physical appearance

One of James's character traits—determination—is shown through his unwillingness to stop trying to help the people in his neighborhood. How do you think the story would be different if James did not have this trait?

Paired Activity Working with a partner, go through the story again and look for details that help you understand James's character traits. Make a chart to organize these details.

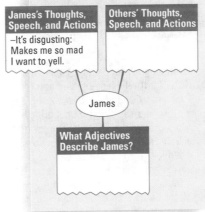

James's Thoughts, Speech, and Actions
–It's disgusting: Makes me so mad I want to yell.

Others' Thoughts, Speech, and Actions

James

What Adjectives Describe James?

THE SCRIBE **661**

Connect to the Literature

1. **What Do You Think?** Students' answers will vary, but should explain why they think James is or is not like them.

Comprehension Check
- They cash checks; they read, write, and address letters for customers.
- They have an account at the bank.
- The Silver Dollar's owners have complained to the police that James is taking away business by helping people for free. James needs a license to operate legally.

 Use Selection Quiz, **Unit Five Resource Book,** p. 28.

Think Critically

2. **Possible Response:** Answers will vary but should mention that James cares about people.

3. **Possible Response:** Her example gives him the courage to consider applying for a license.

4. **Possible Response:** He makes people feel better about themselves, and they now know that the bank is an option. He has also shown the owners of the Silver Dollar that they may have competition.

5. **Possible Response:** James has a good relationship with his parents; he empathizes with other people and likes to help them.

Use **Reading and Critical Thinking Transparencies,** p. 10, for additional support.

6. **Possible Response:** James will get a license and continue his work, or he will find another way to help people.

Literary Analysis

Character Traits Students' charts should contain specific details that reveal character traits, such as James's kindness when he returns the old lady's quarter. The words that students select might include the following: *kind, brave, nice, polite,* or *honest.*

Extend Interpretations

7. **Different Perspectives** Students' responses should show an appreciation of the fact that Mr. Silver is likely to view James's activities as a nuisance or a threat.

8. **Connect to Life** Responses will vary. Some students will say that today they would behave just as they did then; others will say they would behave differently. Encourage students to give reasons for their responses.

Writing

Letter to the Editor Remind students that a letter to the editor should contain a statement of opinion and reasons that support it. To make this activity easier, have students work in pairs or small groups to brainstorm details of what they want to write about James.

Speaking & Listening

Read Aloud Remind students that in a dramatization, gestures and expressions can be as important as words.

 Use the **Speaking and Listening Book**, p. 14, for additional support.

Research & Technology

Spreading the Word The first printed book appeared in China about 1000 A.D. Some centuries later—in 1438—Johann Gutenberg pioneered a movable-type printing press. Students may enjoy working cooperatively and presenting their research by means of a class time line.

Kristin Hunter

In one interview, Hunter said, "I have tried to show some of the positive values existing in the so-called ghetto—the closeness and warmth of family life, the willingness to extend help to strangers in trouble. . . . and the strong tradition of religious faith."

Author Activity

New Views When they compare details with those in the story, encourage students to think about the writer's home, her upbringing, and her occupation. Even if students cannot find additional details about the author, the ones on the pupil page will allow them to recognize that the character is in some ways like the writer.

Use **Reading and Critical Thinking Transparencies,** p. 35, for additional support.

Writing

Letter to the Editor Imagine you live in James's city. Write a letter to the local paper about James and his efforts to help people. In your letter, describe James' traits and use examples from the story that show these traits. Also describe how life might have been different for the people James helped if he did not have these traits. Place your letter in your **Working Portfolio.**

Writing Handbook
See p. R43: Expository Writing.

Speaking & Listening

Read Aloud Choose a section of "The Scribe" to read aloud to the class. Practice several times to make sure you know how to read any difficult words. Also make sure that your voice is strong and clear and that you are not reading too fast. Add facial expressions and gestures as you read to keep your audience interested. When you are ready, read the section to the class.

Speaking and Listening Handbook
See p. R98: Oral Interpretation.

Research & Technology

Spreading the Word After the invention of the printing press by Johannes Gutenberg in 1450, literacy greatly increased in Europe. Use of the press gradually spread to other areas as well. Research the impact and development of the printing press, and present your findings to the class.

Research and Technology Handbook
See p. R106: Getting Information Electronically.

Kristin Hunter
born 1931

"I really cannot say when I didn't want to be a writer."

A Lifelong Writer At age 14, Hunter was a writer for the Philadelphia edition of the *Pittsburgh Courier.* On the job, she spent time in Philadelphia's South Street area, an African-American cultural center that inspired her fiction. Her writing includes novels, short stories, poems, and magazine articles for adults, young adults, and children. She has received numerous awards, including the Children's Prize of the Council on Interracial Books for Children, the Lewis Carroll Shelf Award for *Soul Brothers* *and Sister Lou,* and the *Chicago Tribune* Book World Prize for *Guests in the Promised Land.*

A Message of Hope Hunter says, "The bulk of my work has dealt—imaginatively, I hope—with relations between the white and black races in America." Her stories about urban life suggest that individuals can change their lives and improve their circumstances, however difficult, by believing in themselves and their ability to make a difference.

AUTHOR ACTIVITY
New Views Hunter had a middle-class upbringing, but came to know people who grew up with fewer advantages. Read more about Hunter and her childhood. Then create a Venn diagram comparing her upbringing with details about the character of James.

Building Vocabulary
Researching Word Origins

The English language is like a collage made of words from different languages and periods in history.

Most English words can be traced to Greek, Latin, Old English, or another historical language.

> And in this world there was a peace and harmony that she knew no matter how far she traveled, she would never find again. She understood now why her father had brought her here.
>
> —Keith Leckie, *Words on a Page*

Latin *pax,* peace

| **Old English** *faeder,* from the **Latin** *pater,* father. | **Greek** *harmos,* joint, something shared, a place where things come together. |

Strategies for Building Vocabulary

When you study a word's history and origin, it's like going behind the scenes at a play. You find out when, where, and sometimes how it came to be. This information can help you see how the spelling and meaning of words are related. Use the following strategies to discover more about word origins.

❶ **Read Dictionary Entries** A complete dictionary includes each word's history and origin. Notice the highlighted part of this entry for *drama.*

dra•ma (drä′ma) *n.* **1.** A work that is meant to be performed by actors. **2.** Theatrical works of a certain type or period in history. [Late Latin *drama, dramat-,* from Greek *dran,* to do or perform.]

This entry shows that the earliest form of the word *drama* was the Greek word *dran.* In many dictionaries, an appendix at the back of the book lists common word parts and their origins.

❷ **Discover How Words Begin** Many words have interesting histories. Some come from the names of people and places. A German engineer named Rudolf Diesel invented the type of engine now called a *diesel* engine.

Other words, like *mailbox, bookkeeping,* and *eggshell,* were created by joining two existing words.

❸ **Look for Word Families** Words with the same history often have meanings that are connected. For example, the words *remember, memory,* and *memorial* all grew from the Latin word *memor,* which means "mindful." Read the chart below to see other words related to each other by origin.

Latin Root:	*senus,* to sense or feel	Greek Root:	*aster,* star
English:	**sensory** perceived through one of the senses	**English:**	**asteroid** a small object in outer space
	sensitive responds to senses or feelings		**asterisk** a star-shaped punctuation mark
	sensation a perception or feeling		**astronomy** the study of outer space

EXERCISE Use a dictionary to find information about the history or origin of each of the following words. Paraphrase any information about roots and their meanings.

Example:
   cry: from Latin *quiritare,* to cry out

1. happy
2. sandwich
3. boardwalk
4. dairy
5. potato
6. captain
7. grammar
8. battle
9. klutz
10. tofu

BUILDING VOCABULARY **663**

Standards-Based Objectives
- research and use word origins as an aid to understanding meanings
- research word origins as an aid to spelling
- apply meanings of word roots and affixes to determine the meanings of unfamiliar words
- use a personal word list to record and remember new words

VOCABULARY EXERCISE
1. from Middle English *hap,* "luck"
2. food named after John Montagu, the Fourth Earl of Sandwich
3. a walk made of planks or boards: combines the words *board* and *walk*
4. from Middle English *daie,* "dairymaid," from Old English *dæge,* "bread kneader"
5. from Spanish *patata* and Taino *batata,* "sweet potato"
6. from Latin *caput,* "head"
7. from Greek *gramma,* "letter"
8. from Latin *battuere,* "to beat"
9. from Yiddish *klotz,* from Middle High German *kloz,* "block, lump"
10. from Japanese *tofu,* from Chinese *doufu,* "curdled bean"

Use **Unit Five Resource Book,** p. 29, for more practice.

Standards-Based Objectives

- appreciate the works of a contemporary author
- interpret the possible influences of personal events in Lowry's life on her writing
- gain information on the genres of short story, speech, and memoir
- look at the lively language techniques used by Lowry

The Author Study offers a special opportunity for students to focus on the work of a popular contemporary author. Students will be exposed to information about Lowry's life, which will give them insight into the person behind the stories. They will explore some of the lively language techniques used by Lowry and apply these to their own writing.

Author Study Lois Lowry

Through a Child's Eyes

"That is how I write—I go back to the child I was and see things through those eyes."

born 1937

A YOUNG TRAVELER, A YOUNG READER

Lois Lowry was born Cena Hammersberg on March 20, 1937, in Honolulu, Hawaii. She was named for her grandmother, who was not pleased by the gesture and insisted that her granddaughter be given a more common name. The baby was soon renamed Lois. Because Lowry's father was an army dentist, the family moved often, rarely settling in one place for more than a few years. Reading and imagination were always an important part of Lowry's life. "I was a solitary child who lived in the world of books and my own imagination," she says. By the time Lowry was three, she was able to read—an ability that set her apart from the rest of her nursery school class.

Her LIFE and TIMES

1937 Born on March 20 in Honolulu, Hawaii

1948 Moves to Japan

1956 Leaves Brown University to marry Donald Lowry

1962 Sister Helen's death from cancer

1940   **1950**   **1960**

1941 United States enters World War II.

1945–1946 Nazi leaders are tried and sentenced at Nuremberg trials.

1950 Korean War begins.

Sculpture from Korean War Memorial in Washington, D.C.

WAR AND SEPARATION In December 1941, the Japanese bombed Pearl Harbor in Hawaii. When the attack ended, over 2,300 Americans had been killed and the United States was at war. More than 50 years later, Lowry still remembered "the fear in Mother's voice when she hear[d] the news on the radio." Lowry's father left home to fight in the war, and the rest of the family moved to Pennsylvania. In 1948 they rejoined Lowry's father, who was stationed in Japan. Lowry was overjoyed to be with her father again and viewed life in Japan as a grand adventure. Already filled with a writer's curiosity, she often sneaked out of the American compound to explore the neighborhoods of Tokyo. There she saw the tragedy and destruction of war. Entire families lived in packing crates because their houses had been destroyed by bombs. Two years later, when war broke out in nearby Korea, Lowry returned to the states with her mother, sister Helen, and brother Jon while her father remained in Japan.

Did You Know?

- For years Lowry made a living as a portrait photographer.
- She appeared on *Jeopardy!*
- She took the cover photographs on the first editions of *Number the Stars* and *The Giver*.
- She has traveled to Fiji, Antarctica, and the Serengeti.
- She didn't care if her children cleaned their rooms or ate their vegetables.
- She grows yellow helenium flowers in memory of her sister, Helen.

Books

A Lowry describes herself as an introvert, a kid who hung out with books because she wasn't really comfortable with people. She wasn't an athlete, so when most kids were out on a ball field, she was curled up with a good book. It is in these books that she learned about language and the way to put together a story. Lowry says that reading brilliant paragraphs makes her want to write brilliant paragraphs. She is still an avid reader today and has an extensive personal library, which she has organized in her own eclectic way.

A Transient Life

B After Lowry's birth in Hawaii, Lois's family moved to New York. When her father was called to World War II, her mother and siblings moved to her mother's hometown in Pennsylvania. After the war, the family moved to Japan to be with her father. Several years later, Lois, her brother, sister, and mother moved back to the United States, while her father stayed in Japan. Lois attended high school in New York City. She attended college for two years at Brown University in Rhode Island, where she met and married her husband, Donald Lowry. He was also a military man, and they lived in California, Connecticut, Florida, South Carolina, Massachusetts, and Maine, where she raised her four children. Today she lives in Cambridge, Massachusetts.

Family

C Lois's father was a dentist in the military, and her mother was a homemaker. Lois's older sister Helen was much like their mother, gentle and eager to please. Her younger brother, Jon, was always playing with electric trains and construction sets, and when he was older, tinkering with cars with their father.

1972 Receives college degree after four years of part-time study

1977 Publishes *A Summer to Die*

1990 Wins Newbery Medal for *Number the Stars*

1994 Wins Newbery Medal for *The Giver*

1970 — 1980 — 1990 — 2000

1975 Vietnam War ends.

1976 Jimmy Carter is elected president.

1997 Madeleine Albright is sworn in as U.S. secretary of state.

1999 Computer experts prepare for the year 2000 ("Y2K").

LOIS LOWRY **665**

Author Study Lois Lowry

A Writer's Beginnings

D Lowry didn't begin writing professionally until she was in her mid-thirties, even though as a child she had scribbled endless stories and poems in notebooks. She says her books have one general theme: the importance of human connections. Most of her stories come about because of people she knows and stories she's heard. She believes that all of her experiences have an influence on her writing and that eventually they end up in one of her books.

Emotional Healing

E When confronted with tough situations, Lowry finds comfort and healing in writing. Writing has become so much a part of her that it is what she turns to constantly. Some of her books have resulted from tragedy, as did *A Summer to Die*, a fictionalized account of her sister's death from cancer. One of her daughters has become disabled as a result of a disease of the central nervous system, and Lowry says since that time her books have reflected a new and passionate awareness of the importance of human connections that transcend physical differences. Her father, who prior to his death had poor health and a failing memory, prompted images for *The Giver*, as she thought about how without memory there is no pain. And when her son, an Air Force pilot, was killed during a take-off, she wrote a sort of newsletter so that everyone would know the treasure she had lost.

Anastasia Krupnik

F Lowry created the character of Anastasia Krupnik in 1978, when Jimmy Carter was president of the United States. Lowry gives credit for the character of Anastasia Krupnik to Amy Carter, the president's daughter. Amy Carter's physical appearance and her behavior in public while her father was in office prompted Lowry to model the character of Anastasia after her.

FAMILY YEARS The family reunited in New York City just as Lowry was beginning the tenth grade. They lived on an army base on an island in the city's harbor, and Lowry traveled to school by ferry. Reading and writing were her favorite pursuits. Lowry's teachers encouraged her literary talent, and her classmates decorated her yearbook picture **D** with the caption "Future Novelist." Brown University in Rhode Island granted her a scholarship to its creative writing program. After her second year there, however, she left college to marry Donald Lowry, a naval officer. For the next 15 years, Lowry put aside her dreams of writing while she raised their four children. The family moved often before settling in Maine. Lowry later said, "My children grew up in Maine. So did I."

FINALLY A WRITER "Now, when I write," says Lowry, "I draw a great deal from my own past." In the early 1970s, she finished her college degree and began writing stories based on her childhood. In 1977 she **E** published her first novel, *A Summer to Die*, which was inspired by her sister Helen's death from cancer 15 years earlier. Lowry says the novel brought together "details and fragments that accompanied a time of saying good-bye in the lives of two sisters." In that same year, her marriage ended and she started a new life on her own. Since then she has written about two dozen novels, including two Newbery Medal winners, *Number the Stars* and *The Giver*, and the popular Anastasia Krupnik series. Lowry has earned the devotion of a **F** generation of young readers. She lives and writes in Cambridge, Massachusetts, where she shares her home with a shaggy Tibetan terrier named Bandit.

666

TALKING WITH LOIS LOWRY

When Lois Lowry meets with her readers, she often is asked about her reading and writing habits. Here, she responds to some of these questions.

Q: What's your favorite place to sit and read?

A: Depends whether it is summer or winter. In summer I read in a hammock on the screened porch of my house in the country. I watch the birds come and go as I read. In winter I mostly read in the city house. My favorite spot is a pale yellow couch by the fireplace. That's my dog's favorite spot, too, so sometimes I have to fight him for it. I'm bigger than he is, so I always win.

Q: You have written about the impact that *The Yearling* had on you when you were young. What other stories or writers have influenced you?

A: I loved the book *A Tree Grows in Brooklyn*. I encountered it first when I was 11 years old, living in Pennsylvania. I had lived in Brooklyn as a small child, so the title attracted me to the book—then when I read it, I discovered a whole world unlike mine: a crowded, noisy, exuberant world of immigrant life. I moved right into it and lived there for the length of the book. A good book lets you do that.

Q: You used to work as a photographer. Do you still like to make photographs? What kinds of things are interesting to photograph?

A: I love photographing people, especially children. Mostly I photograph my grandchildren now—not the one who's almost 16, though. He's tired of having Grandma torment him with a camera. The little ones still don't mind.

Q: Are you glad you became a writer? Why?

A: I feel very fortunate because I make my living doing what I love most. A lot of people work at jobs that they dislike, or that bore them. Not me. Even before I was a Writer, I was a writer. It has always been a part of my life: my favorite part.

Q: What do you like most about yourself? Why?

A: I suppose what I like best is that I have always had an eager curiosity. That means that I am never bored. I don't understand boredom, really. There is so much to learn, to observe, to think about. What a waste of time to shrug and turn away from it all. I don't like people who do that. I want to poke them.

INTERNET Author Link
www.mcdougallittell.com

CD ROM NetActivities: Author Exploration

Other Favorites

Besides reading, there are other activities that occupy Lois Lowry's time. She enjoys gardening in the spring and summer and knitting in the winter. She has remained faithful to photography over the years, taking the pictures on the covers of *Number the Stars* and *The Giver*. She loves watching movies, eating Mexican food, and cooking. In fact, she has an extensive library of cookbooks. She also likes to play bridge, travel, and spend time with her children, grandchildren, and her dog Bandit.

Writing Today

Most mornings you can find Lowry at her computer and working by eight o'clock. She works all morning, sometimes stopping for a short lunch break. She works into the afternoon as well, usually stopping for the day in mid-afternoon. She has written novels, short stories, and essays. Mostly she writes for young people, but she also writes for herself and for members of her family. She varies the point-of-view of her stories, but says it's not a conscious decision. It just seems that some books need to be told from an omniscient, third-person viewpoint and others need the first person voice in all its uniqueness. She also says she doesn't set out to place a moral in each story, but that a message usually works its way into each story. Her goal when she sits down to write a story, though, is just to tell her readers a good story.

Crow Call

by LOIS LOWRY

Standards-Based Objectives

1. understand and appreciate a **short story**
2. understand and appreciate a **symbol**
3. use the reading skill of **recognizing cause and effect**
4. understand **plot structure**

Summary

In this short story, the narrator tells of a hunting trip she took with her father. She was nine years old, and her father had recently returned from the war. Before the trip, her father had bought her a large, plaid, man's hunting shirt, which she now wears proudly. When her father stops for breakfast, cherry pie is ordered for both, as it is her favorite food. When they get to the hunting ground, they traipse through the woods, talking about what in life scares them, until her father finds the spot. The narrator's job is to blow the crow call to get the crows awake and flying so her father can shoot. But the joy and fun that blowing the crow call brings the young girl also brings joy to her father, and they conclude their hunting trip without firing a single shot.

Thematic Link

Learning about yourself can often be sparked by unusual situations. The narrator and her father share such a situation in this story. In living through it, the narrator learns about herself and maybe a little about who she will become.

English Conventions Practice

Daily Language SkillBuilder

Have students **proofread** the display sentences on page 609k and write them correctly. The sentences also appear on Transparency 21 of **Language Transparencies.**

Connect to Your Life

Life Lessons Think about a time in your life when you shared an experience with someone special and, in the process, learned something about the person. Share your memory with a partner.

Build Background

BIOLOGY

In this story, the narrator and her father set off to hunt crows.

Crows are omnivorous, meaning that they will eat just about anything. They eat berries, grains, insects, the eggs of other birds, and even the meat of dead animals. Farmers consider them pests because they eat crops in the fields.

Common crows are abundant, adaptable, and considered to be very intelligent. Some crows in captivity have been trained to "speak" and count.

WORDS TO KNOW
Vocabulary Preview

arrogantly	mannequin	ruddy
condescending	marred	subside
decoy	poised	
disgruntled	practical	

Focus Your Reading

LITERARY ANALYSIS SYMBOL

A **symbol** is a person, a place, or an object that stands for something else. In literature, objects and images may be used to symbolize things that cannot be seen, such as ideas or feelings. In "Crow Call," a reader might see the narrator's hunting shirt as representing her desire for closeness with her father. As you read, look for other symbols.

ACTIVE READING RECOGNIZING CAUSE AND EFFECT

A story usually is based on a chain of events, with one event causing another. Events in this chain are said to be related as **cause and effect.** Recognizing causes and their effects can help you understand the meaning of a story as it unfolds. It can also help you make predictions.

READER'S NOTEBOOK Use a chart like the one below to help recognize causes and their effects within the story. As you read, make a chart for each cause and effect that you find.

Cause
Narrator pauses by shop window.

↓

Effect
Father buys hunting shirt.

LESSON RESOURCES

UNIT FIVE RESOURCE BOOK, pp. 30–36

ASSESSMENT
Formal Assessment, pp. 109–110
Test Generator

SKILLS TRANSPARENCIES AND COPYMASTERS
Reading and Critical Thinking
• Cause and Effect, TR 5 (pp. 670, 674)

Language
• Daily Language SkillBuilder, TR 21 (p. 668)
• Subject-Verb Agreement, TR 37 (p. 675)
• Analogies, TR 64 (p. 669)
Writing
• Varying Sentence Openers and Closers, TR 18 (p. 675)

INTEGRATED TECHNOLOGY
Audio Library
More Online: Author Link

Visit our Web site:
www.mcdougallittell.com

For **systematic instruction** in language skills, see:
• **Vocabulary and Spelling Book**
• **Grammar, Usage, and Mechanics Book**
• pacing chart on p. 609i

CROW CALL

by Lois Lowry

Crow, Lucy White. Dye, resin, dishcloth on wood, 23″ × 23″ × 2″. Courtesy of the Bernard Toale Gallery.

 was morning, early, barely light, cold for November. I was nine and the war was over. At home, in the bed next to mine, my older sister still slept, adolescent, her blond hair streaming over the edge of the sheet. I sat shyly in the front seat of the car next to the stranger who was my father, my blue-jeaned legs pulled up under the too-large wool shirt I was wearing, making a bosom of my knees.

"Daddy," I said, the title coming uncertainly, "I've never gone hunting before. What if I don't know what to do?"

"Well," he said, "I've been thinking about that, and I've decided to put you in charge of the crow call. Have you ever operated a crow call?"

I shook my head. "No."

"It's an art," he said. "No doubt about that. But I'm pretty sure you can handle it. Some people will blow and blow on a crow call and not a single crow will even wake up or bother to listen, much less answer. But I really think you can do it. Of course," he added, chuckling, "having that shirt will help."

CROW CALL　**669**

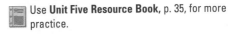

Reading and Analyzing

Active Reading

RECOGNIZING CAUSE AND EFFECT

A Ask students what two events occurred in this section. Which one was the cause, and which was the effect?

Possible Response: The narrator's pigtails being tucked in her shirt caused the waitress to think she was a boy.

Set a Purpose Remind students to look for cause-and-effect relationships as they read. They should fill in the chart in their Reader's Notebook each time they find a cause-and-effect relationship.

📖 Use **Unit Five Resource Book,** p. 31, for more practice. Use **Reading and Critical Thinking Transparencies,** p. 5, for additional support.

Literary Analysis   SYMBOL

B Remind students that sometimes objects or events in stories can stand for something else. Ordering cherry pie for breakfast is certainly unusual. Ask students to think about what the cherry pie for breakfast may symbolize.

Possible Response: Cherry pie for breakfast might symbolize the special occasion of the narrator and her father's getting to know each other again.

📖 Use **Unit Five Resource Book,** p. 32, for more practice.

Reading Skills and Strategies: PREDICT

C Ask students to think about what might happen as the narrator and her father finally reach the hills for the hunt.

Possible Responses: They will be successful and shoot a crow; there will be an accident with her father's gun, and someone will get hurt; they will not hunt at all, but talk and rebuild their relationship.

I glanced over quickly to see if he was laughing at me, but his smile was inclusive; I chuckled too, hugging my shirt around me.

My father had bought the shirt for me. In town to buy groceries, he had noticed my hesitating in front of Kronenberg's window. The plaid hunting shirts had been in the store window for a month—the popular red-and-black and green-and-black ones toward the front, clothing ruddy mannequins holding guns and duck decoys; but my shirt, the rainbow plaid, hung separately on a wooden hanger toward the back of the display. I had lingered in front of Kronenberg's window every chance I had since the hunting shirts had appeared.

My sister had rolled her eyes in disdain. "Daddy," she pointed out to him as we entered Kronenberg's, "that's a *man's* shirt."

The salesman had smiled and said dubiously, "I don't quite think . . ."

"You know," my father had said to me as the salesman wrapped the shirt, "buying this shirt is probably a very practical thing to do. You will never *ever* outgrow this shirt."

Now, as I got out of the car in front of the diner where we were going to have breakfast, the shirt unfolded itself downward until the bottom of it reached my knees; from the bulky thickness of rolled-back cuffs my hands were exposed. I felt totally surrounded by shirt.

My father ordered coffee for himself. The waitress, middle-aged and dawn-sleepy, asked, "What about your boy? What does he want?"

My father winked at me, and I hoped that my pigtails would stay hidden inside the plaid wool collar. Holding my head very still, I looked at the menu. At home my usual breakfast was cereal with honey and milk.

> "What's your favorite thing to eat in the whole world?" asked my father...

My mother kept honey in a covered silver pitcher. The diner's menu, grease-spotted and marred with penciled notations and paper-clipped addenda,[1] seemed not to include honey.

"What's your favorite thing to eat in the whole world?" asked my father.

I smiled at him. If he hadn't been away for so long, he would have known. It was a family joke in a family that hadn't included him. "Cherry pie," I admitted.

My father handed back both menus to the waitress. "Three pieces of cherry pie," he told her.

"Three?" She looked at him sleepily, not writing the order down. "You mean two?"

"No," he said, "I mean three. One for me, with black coffee, and two for my hunting companion, with a large glass of milk."

She shrugged.

We ate quickly, watching the sun rise now across the Pennsylvania farm lands. Back in the car, I flipped my pigtails out from under my shirt collar and giggled.

"Hey, boy," my father said to me in an imitation of the groggy waitress's voice, "you sure you can eat all that cherry pie, boy?"

---

1. **addenda** (ə-dĕn′də): things that have been added, especially a supplement to a book.

	WORDS TO KNOW	
	ruddy (rŭd′ē) *adj.* reddish; rosy	
	mannequin (măn′ĭ-kĭn) *n.* a model of the human body, used for displaying clothes	
	decoy (dē′-koi′) *n.* an artificial bird used to attract live birds within shooting range	
	practical (prăk′tĭ-kəl) *adj.* useful	
	marred (märd) *adj.* damaged; marked **mar** *v.*	

670

Cherry Pie (1962), Roy Lichtenstein. Oil on canvas,
20" × 24". Collection of Sydney and Frances Lewis. Photograph
courtesy of the Virginia Museum of Fine Arts, Richmond.

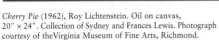

... "Cherry pie," I admitted.

"Just you watch me, lady," I answered in a deep, I thought boyish, voice, pulling my face into stern, serious lines. We laughed again, driving out into the graygreen hills of the early morning.

Grass, frozen after its summer softness, crunched under our feet; the air was sharp and supremely clear, free from the floating pollens of summer, and our words seemed etched and breakable on the brittle stillness. I felt the smooth wood of the crow call in my pocket, moving my fingers against it for warmth, memorizing its ridges and shape. I stamped my feet hard against the ground now and then as my father did. I wanted to scamper ahead of him like a puppy, kicking the dead leaves and

reaching the unknown places first, but there was an uneasy feeling along the edge of my back at the thought of walking in front of someone carrying a gun. Carefully I stayed by his side.

It was quieter than summer. There were no animal sounds, no bird-waking noises; even the occasional leaf that fell within our vision did so in silence, spiraling slowly down to blend in brownly with the others. But most leaves were already gone from the trees; those that remained seemed caught there by accident, waiting for the wind that would free them. Our breath was steam.

"Daddy," I asked shyly, "were you scared in the war?"

C

Less Proficient Readers

1 Help students understand that this section of the story is a flashback to another time in the narrator's life. She is telling the story to help us understand the importance of the hunting shirt. Students may be confused as to what is happening now, and what has happened in the past.

Set a Purpose Have students read to find out what happens on the hunting trip.

2 Have students listen to the descriptive language in this section as you read it aloud. Ask them to identify which words in the description are most effective in helping them create their mental images.

Possible Responses: frozen, crunched, sharp, supremely clear, etched, brittle stillness, smooth, stamped, scamper, uneasy feeling

English Learners

This story is easier to understand if the reader knows something about hunting. If students are unfamiliar with this activity, you may want to have a class discussion about why people hunt *(for food, for sport, and to rid the area of dangerous, pesky, or sick animals).* Plaid shirts are common among hunters, not only because they are generally made of warm wool or flannel, but also because another hunter can easily mistake a plain brown, green, or black shirt for an animal.

Advanced Learners

Many good stories raise unanswered questions in the reader's mind. Ask students what questions come to mind when they read this story. What questions would they like to ask the author? The characters?

EXPLICIT INSTRUCTION   Viewing and Representing

Cherry Pie
by Roy Lichtenstein

ART APPRECIATION Roy Lichtenstein (1923–1997) was a teacher and artist who did much of his work in commercial art and design. He is considered a part of the Pop Art movement; his best known works from the 1960s are based on comic strip and advertising images.

Instruction Ask students to think about the senses to which this painting appeals, and to jot them down. Ask them to use descriptive words

that help them experience each sense. *(smell: warm, cherry, sweet, baking crust, yummy; taste: sweet, juicy, tart, hot, delicious; sight: fresh, steaming, red, ripe berries, flaky crust)*

Practice Ask students to recall these sensory words as they reread the restaurant scene on page 670. Have students write a short paragraph describing the same scene, using their descriptions and their own experiences. Have them share their paragraphs with a partner.

Possible Responses: Responses will vary.

Literary Analysis: DIALOGUE

A Authors often use dialogue to move the plot forward and to reveal the personalities of the characters. Ask students to think about what this section of dialogue reveals about the narrator and her father.

Possible Responses: The narrator is afraid of her father's gun, she doesn't like death and killing, and she doesn't want to hunt the crows; her father knows what fear is and he didn't like the thought of killing anyone in the war; they both have a sense of humor and are learning to enjoy each other's company again.

Active Reading

RECOGNIZING
CAUSE AND EFFECT

B Remind students to fill in their cause-and-effect charts. In this section, the crows begin to stir, flutter, and call. Ask students to identify the cause of this action.

Possible Response: The narrator blew on the crow call and it caused the crows to wake up.

READING SKILLS AND STRATEGIES: CONNECT

C Ask students to recall a meaningful experience they shared with a parent or other adult. Have them share their experiences with each other and talk about how the narrator's hunting trip might impact the relationship she has with her father.

Possible Response: Because the narrator had such a good time with her father, she will probably be able to share other happy times with him, and their relationship will get stronger.

"Listen, Daddy!
Do you hear them?

He looked ahead, up the hill, and rubbed the stock of his gun thoughtfully with one hand and said after a moment, "Yes. I was scared."

"Of what?"

"Lots of things. Of being alone. Of being hurt. Of hurting someone else."

"Are you still?"

He glanced down. "I don't think so. Those kind of scares go away."

"I'm scared sometimes," I confided.

He nodded, unsurprised. "I know," he said. "Are you scared now?"

I started to say no, and then answered, "Maybe of your gun, a little."

I looked quickly at his gun, his polished, waxed prize, and then at him. He nodded, not saying anything. We walked on.

"Daddy?"

"Mmmmmm?" He was watching the sky, the trees.

"I wish the crows didn't eat the crops."

"They don't know any better," he said. "Even people do bad things without meaning to."

"Yes, but . . ." I paused and then told him what I'd been thinking. "They might have babies to take care of. Baby crows."

"Not now, not this time of year," he said. "By now their babies are grown. It's a strange thing, but by now they don't even know who their babies are." He put his free arm over my shoulders for a moment.

"And their babies grow up and eat the crops too," I said, and sighed, knowing it to be true and unchangeable.

"It's too bad," he acknowledged. We began to climb the hill.

"Can you call anything else, Daddy? Or just crows?"

"Sure," he said. "Listen. *Moooooooo.* That's a cow call."

"Guess the cows didn't hear it," I teased him when we encountered silence.

"Well, of course, sometimes they choose not to answer. I can do tigers too. *Rrrrrrrrrrr.*"

"Ha. So can I. And bears. Better watch out, now. Bears might come out of the woods on this one. *Grrrrrrrrr.*"

He looked at me arrogantly. "You think you're so smart, doing bears. Listen to this. Giraffe call." He stood with his neck stretched out, soundless.

I tried not to laugh, wanting to do rabbits next, but couldn't keep from it. He looked so funny, with his neck pulled away from his shirt collar and a condescending, poised, giraffe look on his face. I giggled at him and we kept walking to the top of the hill.

From where we stood we could see almost back to town. We could look down on our car and follow the ribbon of road through the farm lands until it was lost in trees. Dark roofs of houses lay scattered, separated by pastures.

"Okay," said my father, "you can do the crow call now. This is a good place."

WORDS	**arrogantly** (ăr′ə-gənt-lē) *adv.* with excessive and often undeserved pride in oneself
TO	**condescending** (kŏn′dĭ-sĕn′dĭng) *adj.* displaying an attitude of patronizing superiority **condescend** *v.*
KNOW	**poised** (poizd) *adj.* seeming calm and well balanced **poise** *v.*

"They think I'm their friend!"

I saw no crows. For a moment the fear of disappointing him struggled with my desire to blow into the smooth, polished tip of the crow call. But he was waiting, and I took it from my pocket, held it against my lips and blew softly.

The harsh, muted sound of a sleepy crow came as a surprise to me, and I smiled at it, at the delight of having made that sound myself. I did it again, softly.

From a grove of trees on another hill came an answer from a waking bird. Just one, and then silence.

Tentatively I called again, more loudly. The branches of a nearby tree rustled, and crows answered, fluttering and calling crossly. They flew briefly into the air and then settled on a branch—three of them.

"Look, Daddy," I whispered. "Do you see them? They think I'm a crow!"

He nodded, watching them.

I moved away from him with confidence and stood on a rock at the top of the hill and blew loudly several times. From all the trees rose crows. They screamed with harsh voices and I responded, blowing again and again as they flew from the hillside in circles, dipping and soaring; landing speculatively, lurching from the limbs in afterthought and then settling again with resolute and <u>disgruntled</u> shrieks.

"Listen, Daddy! Do you hear them? They think I'm their friend! Maybe their baby, all grown up!"

I ran about the top of the hill and then down, through the frozen grass, blowing the crow call over and over. The crows called back at me, and from all the trees they rose, from all the hills. They circled and circled, and the morning was filled with the patterns of calling crows as I looked back, still running. I could see my father sitting on a rock, his gun leaning against him, and I could see he was smiling.

My crow calling came in shorter and shorter spurts as I became breathless; finally I stopped and stood laughing at the foot of the hill, and the noise from the crows <u>subsided</u> as they circled irritably and settled back in the trees. They were waiting for me.

My father came down the hill to meet me coming up. He carried his gun carefully; and though I was grateful to him for not using it, I felt that there was no need to say thank you, for I felt that he knew. The crows would always be there and they would always eat the crops; and some other morning, on some other hill, he would shoot them.

I blew the crow call once more, to say good morning and good-by and everything that goes in between. Then I put it into the pocket of my shirt and reached over out of my enormous cuffs and took my father's hand. We stood there, he and I, halfway up the November hillside, and the newly up sun was a pink wash across the Pennsylvania sky. The brown grass and curled leaves were thick around our feet, and above our heads the air was filled with the answering sound of the circling crows. ❖

| WORDS TO KNOW | **disgruntled** (dĭs-grŭn′tld) *adj.* not happy |
| | **subside** (səb-sīd′) *v.* to sink or settle down to a lower or normal level |

673

Differentiating Instruction

Advanced Students

1 Ask students to brainstorm how this story would have been different if the narrator's father had not been smiling as he watched and listened. What other emotions could he have exhibited here, and how would the story change as a result? Students may want to suggest alternate endings for the story based on one of their suggestions.
Possible Response: The narrator's father might have been angry and upset. He could have yelled at her and gone home right then.

Less Proficient Readers
To ensure that students have understood the story, ask the following questions:
• What happens when the narrator and her father get to the top of the hill?
Possible Response: She begins to blow the crow call over and over, running and laughing.
• How does the hunting trip end?
Possible Response: They go home without firing a single shot.

English Learners
Have students find at least one synonym for each of the following words and phrases used in the story: harsh *(abrasive, coarse, discordant)*; muted *(hushed, soft, muffled)*; speculatively *(hypothetically, thoughtfully)*; resolute *(firm, stubborn)*; irritably *(angrily)*; a pink wash *(a pink stain, tint, coating, or film)*.

EXPLICIT INSTRUCTION Plot

Instruction Tell students that the main elements of a plot are the exposition (introduction of characters, setting, and conflict), rising action (complications, increasing tension), climax (turning point, or point of greatest tension), and resolution of conflict. Ask, "What is a conflict in a story?" (*a struggle between opposing forces, or opposing characters*)
Practice Have students outline the plot of "Crow Call." Ask them to identify any conflicts in the story and explain how they are resolved.

Possible Response: Exposition—The setting is a November day in a Pennsylvania woodland community; the characters are the narrator and her father. The conflict is between the father, who is hunting for crows, and the narrator, who doesn't want the crows to be killed. The rising action begins when the narrator talks about crow babies and her father says there aren't any this time of year; the two characters imitate other animals; the narrator blows the crow call and many crows settle

nearby. The climax happens when the narrator tells her father the crows think she is their friend, or maybe even their baby. In the resolution, the father does not kill any crows.

Use **Unit Five Resource Book,** p. 33, for more practice.

Connect to the Literature

1. What Do You Think?
Possible Response: She is happy because she and her father enjoyed themselves and got to know each other again, and because she was successful at doing the crow call.

Comprehension Check
- The narrator has two pieces of cherry pie, and her father has one.
- The crows answer back and start to fly out of the trees.
- The crows think she's their friend or one of their babies that has grown up.

 Use Selection Quiz,
Unit Five Resource Book, p. 36.

Think Critically

2. Possible Responses: The narrator's father wants to get reacquainted with her. He has just returned from war and knows that he has to readjust to family life and that the family has to readjust to him. He realizes that there is a lot he no longer knows about his children, so he sets time aside to be with them individually. The narrator's sister would obviously not be interested in this type of activity, and her presence would have spoiled it.

3. Possible Response: She thinks about breaking up the crows' families.

4. Possible Response: He knows that his daughter doesn't want to see the crows killed. This shows sensitivity, understanding, and the ability to be flexible.

5. Possible Response: The most important result was the renewed closeness with her father. The special treatment her father showed her caused this closeness to return.

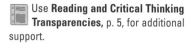 Use **Reading and Critical Thinking Transparencies,** p. 5, for additional support.

Literary Analysis

Symbol Students' charts will vary, but students should support their choice of symbols with evidence from the selection.

Connect to the Literature

1. What Do You Think?
What do you think the narrator is feeling as she walks down the hill with her father?

Comprehension Check
- What do the narrator and her father have for breakfast?
- What happens when the narrator blows the crow call?
- What does the narrator say the crows think she is?

Think Critically

2. Why do you think the narrator's father takes her on this hunting trip?

Think About:
- the narrator's feelings about her father at the beginning of the story
- the fact that her sister isn't with them
- her father's recent experience

3. What thoughts does the narrator have about the crows as she climbs the hill?

4. Why do you think the narrator's father doesn't shoot the crows? What might this reveal about him?

5. **ACTIVE READING** **RECOGNIZING CAUSE AND EFFECT**
Look back at the chart in your **READER'S NOTEBOOK**. What do you think was the most important result of this trip for the narrator? What caused this effect?

Extend Interpretations

6. Different Perspectives Imagine that this story was told by the father. What might he have been thinking as he looked at his daughter sitting next to him in the car?

7. Connect to Life Think about the narrator's experience of blowing the crow call. Was there ever a time when a simple act, such as riding a bicycle, gave you a feeling of power? Explain.

Literary Analysis

SYMBOL Writers use **symbols**—people, places, or objects that stand for something other than themselves—to represent ideas or feelings. Some symbols represent the same ideas in many literary works. For example, a rising sun often symbolizes a beginning or a fresh start. As the narrator and her father stand on the hill in "Crow Call," the sun has just risen. This might symbolize that the narrator's relationship with her father is entering a new stage. Other symbols—such as the hunting shirt—have meaning only within a particular story.

Paired Activity With a partner, reread "Crow Call," looking for symbols. Discuss what each symbol represents and how it adds to the meaning of the story. Organize your ideas in a chart like the one shown.

Symbol	What It Represents	Its Importance in the Story
hunting shirt	the narrator's father	When her father buys it, it shows he understands his daughter.

Extend Interpretations

6. Different Perspectives The father might have felt concerned and anxious about the success of the day. He may have felt that he didn't know his daughter very well. He might have been eager to spend some time alone with his daughter, without other distractions.

7. Connect to Life Encourage students to list activities that are meaningful to them, that foster partnership or cooperation, or that provide opportunities for quiet conversation. Students should provide specific reasons for their choices.

Grammar in Context: Subjects in Unusual Order

Lois Lowry varies her sentences by not always placing the **subject** at the beginning.

> At home, in the bed next to mine, my older sister still slept. . . .
>
> Holding my head very still, I looked at the menu.
>
> Carefully I stayed by his side.

Subjects usually appear at the beginning of a sentence. Sometimes, however, a sentence begins with a phrase or word that adds important information.

Apply to Your Writing Varying your sentences by using a phrase or descriptive word before the subject will make your writing more interesting.

Vocabulary

STANDARDIZED TEST PRACTICE

Determine the relationship between the first pair of words. Then decide which Word to Know best completes the analogy. The first sentence may be restated as *"Whitish* is to *pale* as *reddish* is to _____."

1. WHITISH : PALE :: reddish : _____
2. MOVIE : FILM :: model : _____
3. HUMAN : DOLL :: bird : _____
4. USELESS : FUNCTIONAL :: silly : _____
5. INJURED : HURT :: damaged : _____
6. PLEASED : UNHAPPY :: satisfied : _____
7. INCREASE : RISE :: decrease : _____
8. BOLDLY : BRAVELY :: proudly : _____
9. TRUTHFUL : HONEST :: graceful : _____
10. CRANKY : GRUMPY :: patronizing : _____

WRITING EXERCISE Rewrite each sentence, moving the subject from the beginning.

Example: *Original* The leaf fell silently, spiraling slowly to the ground.

Rewritten Spiraling slowly to the ground, the leaf fell silently.

1. The grass crunched softly under our feet.
2. He stood with his neck stretched out, soundless.
3. The crows arose from the trees and the hills.
4. My father smiled as he watched me.

Connect to the Literature Skim "Crow Call." Find another example of a sentence that does not begin with its subject.

Grammar Handbook

See p. R86: Correcting Punctuation.

EXERCISE Write a sample page for a catalog of sportswear or camping equipment, using all the Words to Know. Add illustrations if you like.

Vocabulary Handbook

See p. R24: Analogies.

WORDS TO KNOW	arrogantly condescending	decoy disgruntled	mannequin marred	poised practical	ruddy subside

Grammar in Context

WRITING EXERCISE
Possible Responses:

1. Under our feet, the grass crunched softly.
2. Soundless, he stood with his neck stretched out.
3. From the trees and the hills, the crows arose.
4. As he watched me, my father smiled.

Connect to the Literature
Possible Response: Back in the car, I flipped my pigtails out.

 Use **Writing Transparencies,** p. 18, for additional support.

Vocabulary
STANDARDIZED TEST PRACTICE

1. ruddy
2. mannequin
3. decoy
4. practical
5. marred
6. disgruntled
7. subside
8. arrogantly
9. poised
10. condescending

EXERCISE

Accept pages that use all the Words to Know.

EXPLICIT INSTRUCTION Grammar in Context

SUBJECTS IN UNUSUAL ORDER
Remind students that in interrogative and exclamatory sentences, the subject sometimes can be hard to identify because it may come after, rather than before, the verb.

Instruction To find the subject of an interrogative or exclamatory sentence, first change it to a declarative sentence; then ask *who?* or *what?*

Interrogative: Does Lois like hunting?
Declarative: Lois does like hunting.

Who likes hunting? *Lois* does. *Lois* is the subject of the sentence.

Exclamatory: Was that a great day!
Declarative: That was a great day.

What was? *That* was. *That* is the subject of the sentence.

Exercises Ask students to find the subject in each sentence.

1. Here come the crows! *(crows)*
2. Are the crows afraid of us? *(crows)*
3. Do they think we're other crows? *(they)*
4. Isn't that cherry pie delicious? *(cherry pie)*
5. Do you want another piece? *(you)*

 Use **Unit Five Resource Book,** p. 34.

 For more instruction in subjects in unusual order, see McDougal Littell's *Language Network,* Chapter 1.

For **systematic instruction** in grammar, see:
• **Grammar, Usage, and Mechanics Book**
• pacing chart on p. 609i

Teaching the Literature

Active Reading: IDENTIFYING AUTHOR'S PURPOSE

In this acceptance speech for *The Giver*'s Newbery Award, Lois Lowry explains some of her purposes for writing that book. Her speech also had a purpose. Ask students to think about the message the speech conveys and the reasons why they think she wrote the speech this way. Ask them to cite specific examples from the speech to validate their stance. They may be able to get these examples from the notes they made in their Reader's Notebook as they read.

Use **Reading and Critical Thinking Transparencies,** p. 8, for additional support.

Literary Analysis: FLASHBACK

In her speech, Lowry looks back on several times in her life and uses examples to describe where she got her inspiration. Ask students to think about the use of flashback in her speech. Was it effective? Ask them to discuss what impact these examples had on the speech as a whole.

Possible Response: The use of flashback was effective because it showed how events in Lowry's life impacted the writing of *The Giver*. Specific examples, such as the time when she rode her bike out of the safe community again and again, show the audience how this idea of going beyond the comfortable ended up in *The Giver*.

PREPARING to *Read*

Focus Your Reading

ACTIVE READING | **IDENTIFYING THE AUTHOR'S PURPOSE**

Authors write for many reasons: to entertain, to explain or inform, to express opinions, to persuade readers. Often a writer has more than one purpose for creating a piece. As you read, think about what Lois Lowry wants to share with her audience and why.

READER'S NOTEBOOK

Lowry gave this speech to accept an award. But it is clear from reading it that she also had other purposes in mind. Jot down phrases or sentences that hint at these other purposes.

This evening it feels right to start by quoting a passage from *The Giver*, a scene set during the days in which the boy, Jonas, is beginning to look more deeply into the life that has been very superficial, beginning to see that his own past goes back further than he had ever known and has greater implications than he had ever suspected.

Now he saw the familiar wide river beside the path differently. He saw all of the light and color and history it contained and carried in its slow-moving water; and he knew that there was an Elsewhere from which it came, and an Elsewhere to which it was going.

Every author is asked again and again the question we probably each have come to dread the most: HOW DID YOU GET THIS IDEA?

I'd like, tonight, to try to tell you the origins of this book. It is a little like Jonas looking into the river and realizing that it carries with it everything that has come from an Elsewhere. A spring, perhaps, at the beginning, bubbling up from the earth; then a trickle from a glacier; a mountain stream entering farther along; and each tributary bringing with it the collected bits and pieces from the past, from the distant, from the countless Elsewheres: all of it moving, mingled, in the current.

For me, the tributaries are memories, and I've selected only a few. I'll tell them to you chronologically. I have to go way back. I'm starting forty-six years ago.

In 1948, I am eleven years old. I have gone with my mother, sister, and brother, to join my father, who has been in Tokyo for two years and will be there for several more.

We live there, in the center of that huge Japanese city, in a small American enclave with a very American name: Washington Heights. We live in an American-style house, with American neighbors, and our little community has its own movie theater, which shows American movies; and a small church, a tiny library, and an elementary school; and in many ways it is an odd replica of a United States village.

(In later, adult years I was to ask my mother why we had lived there instead of taking advantage of the opportunity to live within the Japanese community and to learn and experience a different way of life. But she

seemed surprised by my question. She said that we lived where we did because it was comfortable. It was familiar. It was safe.)

I have a bicycle. Again and again—countless times—without my parents' knowledge, I ride my bicycle out the back gate of the fence that surrounds our comfortable, familiar, safe, American community. I ride down a hill because I am curious and I enter, riding down that hill, an unfamiliar, slightly uncomfortable, perhaps even unsafe—though I never feel it to be—area of Tokyo that throbs with life.

It is a district called Shibuya.

I remember, still, after all these years, the smells: fish and fertilizer and charcoal; the sounds: music and shouting and the clatter of wooden shoes and wooden sticks and wooden wheels; and the colors: I remember the babies and toddlers dressed in bright pink and orange and red, most of all; but I remember, too, the dark blue uniforms of the schoolchildren: the strangers who are my own age.

I wander through Shibuya day after day during those years when I am eleven, twelve, and thirteen. I love the feel of it, the vigor, and the garish brightness and the noise: all of such a contrast to my own life.

But I never talk to anyone. I am not frightened of the people, who are so different from me, but I am shy. I watch the children shouting and playing around a school, and they are children my age, and they watch me

in return; but we never speak to one another.

1991. I am in an auditorium somewhere. I have spoken at length about my book, *Number the Stars*, which has been honored with the 1990 Newbery Medal. A woman raises her hand. When the turn for her question comes, she sighs very loudly and says, "Why do we have to tell this Holocaust thing over and over? Is it really *necessary?*"

I answer her as well as I can—quoting, in fact, my German daughter-in-law, who has said to me, "No one knows better than we Germans that we must tell this again and again."

But I think about her question—and my answer—a great deal. Wouldn't it, I think, playing Devil's Advocate to myself, make for a more comfortable world to forget the Holocaust? And I remember once again how comfortable, familiar, and safe my parents had sought to make my childhood by shielding me from Elsewhere. But I remember, too, that my response had been to open the gate again and again. ❖

THINKING *through the* LITERATURE

1. According to Lowry's mother, why did the family live in the American community in Japan?

2. **ACTIVE READING** **AUTHOR'S PURPOSE**
   With a partner, share the information you noted in your 📖 **READER'S NOTEBOOK**. Decide what purposes Lowry accomplishes with her speech.

Thinking through the Literature

1. They lived in the American community because it was safe, familiar, and comfortable.

2. **Possible Response:** Lowry's main purpose was to describe how her memories flow together to create ideas for her writing. She used *The Giver* as a specific example because she is being honored for that book.

PREPARING to Read

MEMOIR

from Looking Back

by LOIS LOWRY

Connect to Your Life

I Remember When In her book *Looking Back: A Book of Memories,* Lois Lowry shares photographs and memories of her family. She recalls funny moments, embarrassing incidents, and important experiences. What events in your life have been captured in photographs? Describe some of these moments.

Build Background

HISTORY

When she started to write *Looking Back,* Lois Lowry prompted her memories by looking at old photographs. The art of photography started in the 1830s in France with the daguerreotype (də-gâr′ə-tīp), an image that was created on a silver-covered copper plate. In the 1800s, millions of people who could not afford to have portraits painted relied on the daguerreotype to preserve images of important people in their lives. Now, in the age of instant photography, most families have albums full of pictures.

> WORDS TO KNOW
> **Vocabulary Preview**
> modest   obnoxious   vigil
> mortification   peer

Focus Your Reading

LITERARY ANALYSIS **VOICE**

A writer's **voice** is his or her style or way of writing. Voice is shaped by the writer's choice of words, the way he or she puts them together, and the incidents or ideas he or she chooses to write about. As you read, listen for Lois Lowry's voice. In *Looking Back* she writes as if she is talking to the reader. She even asks the reader questions.

ACTIVE READING **IDENTIFYING EFFECTS OF AUTHOR'S PERSPECTIVE**
Every writer looks at the world differently. A writer's **perspective** is influenced by his or her experiences, feelings, and beliefs. This perspective is communicated to the reader through the **tone** that the writer takes toward the subject and through concrete details. For example, Lowry's sister would provide different details than Lowry herself does.

Notice that one effect of the author's perspective is that the anecdotes are not presented chronologically. Instead, they emerge and fade like memories. The effect is that of a scrapbook or family album.

READER'S NOTEBOOK As you read, think about how Lowry's experience as a photographer may have led her to write a memoir based on looking at photographs. Note each place in which Lowry refers to details in photographic images.

LOOKING BACK

BY LOIS LOWRY

✾1941✾

When I was very young, about four, I had a friend named <u>Modest</u> Storewrecker. That didn't seem unusual to me at the time, because when you are four, nothing seems unusual.

But later, when I was grown up, more literate, and living in a different place, I thought occasionally about Modest Storewrecker. I wondered if she was still at it. I pictured her blushing shyly (an immodest storewrecker would have been boastful and <u>obnoxious</u>) and explaining, "Ah, shucks, it was nothing. I just took my baseball bat and went into Woolworth's and bashed everything."

Then, visiting my elderly parents, I was looking at old photograph albums and came across a picture of three children: me, another little girl, named Betty June, and Modest Storewrecker, taken fifty years before. It had come loose from the page. I picked it up and smiled at the little girls staring self-consciously at the camera.

"Remember her?" I asked my mother. She <u>peered</u> through her bifocals at the picture.

"That's you," she said.

"No, I mean the *other* one."

"Betty June Rose."

"No, Mom, the other one."

She peered more closely. "Of course," she told me. "She lived just down the street. A nice little girl. Her name was Mardis Storacker."

WORDS TO KNOW	**modest** (mŏd'ĭst) *adj.* not likely to call attention to oneself **obnoxious** (ŏb-nŏk'shəs) *adj.* worthy of disapproval or dislike **peer** (pîr) *v.* to look intently

679

Differentiating Instruction

Less Proficient Readers
To help students understand the format of this autobiography, explain that each photograph and section are accompanied by a date, and the text is boxed in with the photograph. Tell them that each boxed set is one memory, and that, taken together, they help us learn about Lois Lowry as a child.

Set a Purpose Ask students to read one memory at a time and discuss each with a partner before reading the next one.

1 Help students understand why the name *Modest Storewrecker* is humorous, and how this memory is built upon that misconception. Help them see that Lois's friend didn't really destroy the store, and that it is a play on words.

English Learners
Students may not be familiar with some of the cultural references in this selection, such as Woolworth's and *The Yearling*.

Use **Spanish Study Guide**, pp. 139–141, for additional support.

Advanced Students
Students may want to bring in a favorite photograph from their own early childhood. Encourage them to select one for which there is a story to tell. Ask them to write a short paragraph describing the memory. Have them think about the language Lowry uses to write her memories, and suggest they use similarly informal language.

EXPLICIT INSTRUCTION **Preteaching Vocabulary**

WORDS TO KNOW
Remind students that using **context clues** is one strategy for determining unknown words. One type of context clue is called a **meaning clue.**
Teaching Strategy Write the following sentence on the board or read it aloud:
I knew Carrie to be a modest person, never calling attention to herself.
Ask students what *modest* means and how they figured out the definition. Point out that the phrase "never calling attention to herself" gives a meaning clue.

Practice Ask students to look up each of the WORDS TO KNOW in a dictionary. Have them write each word in a sentence, using a meaning clue to help readers understand the word's meaning.

 Use **Unit Five Resource Book**, p. 42, for more practice.

For **systematic instruction** in vocabulary, see:
• **Vocabulary and Spelling Book**
• pacing chart on p. 609i

Reading and Analyzing

❧1942❧

Helen and I were probably five and eight in this snapshot. Her bathing suit was blue; mine was white, with blue polka dots. The photograph is black and white, as most photos were in those days. But I remember the colors, as well as the textures and smells. My bathing suit had a shiny quality to it, and when it was damp, an odor of mildew and pond scum.

I can't imagine that my mother, a kind woman, went into a store and said to a salesperson, "Please find me the two most hideous bathing suits in the world for my daughters."

So how did she end up buying these two wretched bathing suits? I have no idea.

❧1945❧

Having a little brother was, on the whole, an enjoyable thing. Sometimes, when he was little, Jon was a pest. Most of the time we got along pretty well, although I have never entirely forgiven him for the time he broke the china head of an antique doll that I loved.

But sometimes, when he was little, I was a bully and a torturer. When we lived in Japan, Jonny accumulated a collection of fireworks, which were plentiful, available, and legal there. He was seven when we returned to Pennsylvania, and he says that I told him he would be arrested if they caught him trying to bring Japanese fireworks into the United States. So as we crossed the Pacific, he says, he went out to the stern of the ship, all alone, and very solemnly and sadly threw his beloved fireworks into the sea.

I don't remember that at all. And Jon says he doesn't remember smashing the head of my doll.

Isn't it amazing how we forget the things we are ashamed of?

(But isn't it amazing, too, how we forgive each other?)

Jon and I looked somewhat alike; I didn't know that then, but I can see it now, looking back. When I was eight and he was two, I wore glasses and he didn't. When I was nine and he was three, he wore glasses and I didn't. Now we both wear glasses. But now he has a beard, and I don't. So we are never *exactly* in sync; but still, we look somewhat alike.

❧1946❧

My mother read *The Yearling* to Helen and me. I was nine; Helen was twelve. Mother sat in the hall outside our bedrooms and read aloud.

I thought *The Yearling* was the most wonderful book I'd ever encountered. It made me want to be a boy; I wanted to be poor and live in a swamp, where I would have animals as friends.

There was a picture in our copy of *The Yearling* which showed Jody sitting on the floor beside his father's bed. His father— Pa—had been bitten by a rattlesnake. "Snakebit," they said in the book.

In the picture, you can see Pa's face, looking almost dead because that was how you looked if you got snakebit. Jody looked very sad and beautiful, leaning against the patchwork quilt.

Sometimes I would sit on the floor beside my own bed, pretending to be Jody. I leaned my head the way he did, and tried to look sad and beautiful.

The caption under the picture was "The Vigil." I didn't know what a vigil was. But a few pages earlier in the book, it said, of Jody: "The vigil was in his hands."

In the picture, Jody's right hand was clearly empty. So the vigil had to be in his left, which was sort of in shadows. A vigil had to be something fairly small, to fit into one left hand.

I put a crayon in my left hand and sat on the floor beside my bed. I leaned my head and closed my eyes and looked mournful. "The vigil was in her hands," I said to myself, even though secretly I knew it was only a crayon. I sighed, clasping the vigil tightly, and prayed for my snakebit Pa to get well.

My sister walked past my room, looked in, and groaned. "Mom," she called loudly down to the kitchen, "Lois is doing that weird thing by her bed again."

Reprinted with permission of Atheneum Books for Young Readers, an imprint of Simon & Schuster Children's Publishing Division, from THE YEAR-LING by Marjorie Kinnan Rawlings, illustrated by N.C. Wyeth. Illustrations copyright 1939 Charles Scribner's Sons; copyright renewed © 1967 Charles Scribner's Sons.

WORDS
TO
KNOW
vigil (vĭj′əl) *n.* a watch kept during normal sleeping hours

681

English Learners

1 Ask students if they themselves or other members of their family have made the journey from another country to the United States. How did they travel? Invite students to share their stories about such travel, their understanding of customs checks, and the rules about what can and cannot be brought into a country. Fluent English speakers may have travel stories to share as well.

Advanced Students

2 Ask students to think about the word *vigil*, and to discuss how Lowry constructed the meaning she did for it. Have them suggest ways in which she could have discovered the word's real meaning as a child. Ask them to speculate whether knowing the correct meaning was important to Lowry, and if it would have changed her attachment to *The Yearling*.

Less Proficient Readers

3 Ask students what they think the word "vigil" means, and whether or not it is something that you can hold in your hand. Make sure students understand that *vigil* means "a watch kept during hours when people normally sleep," and therefore is not a tangible thing that can be held in one's hand.

EXPLICIT INSTRUCTION **Connecting**

Instruction Remind students that when they read a story, they may be reminded of their own thoughts and feelings or of events in their own lives. Explain that paying attention to these connections between themselves and the story can help them understand what they read. Ask, "Do you connect with any of the experiences, feelings, or thoughts that Lois Lowry describes in this selection? For example, have you ever heard someone's name incorrectly and continued to pronounce it that way for many years? Have you worn clothing that embarrassed you? Have you

teased your brother or your sister?" Ask volunteers to describe such connections.

Practice Ask students to write a paragraph about something in this selection that they have thought, felt, or experienced. Ask volunteers to read their paragraphs to the class.

Possible Responses: Paragraphs will vary but should show students' understanding of the details of Lois Lowry's life.

Use **Unit Five Resource Book**, p. 40, for more practice.

Ask students to identify what Lowry's voice sounds like in this section, and how she presents it to us.

Possible Response: At the beginning of the section, Lowry's voice is reflective as she thinks about her mother. Near the end, her voice becomes sarcastic; we read her sarcasm when she uses italics to emphasize important words, like *clothes* and *Not*.

Use **Literary Analysis Transparencies**, p. 9, for additional support.

Literary Analysis: POINT OF VIEW

B This section is told from Lowry's point of view. Ask students to discuss how this photograph might be explained from Lowry's mother's point of view.

Possible Response: Lowry's mother probably thought Lois looked cute in it.

Reading Skills and Strategies: EVALUATE

C Ask students to think about Lowry's game and to evaluate the kind of person they think Lowry is to have devised such a game. Do they think this game would be fun to play? Why or why not?

Possible Response: Lowry is obviously a well-read person who enjoys books and thinking. She is also clever. I think this game would be fun because I love to read books too.

❧1928❧

A

Long before she was married, back when she had just finished college, my mother had traveled in Europe. I have her passport, dated 1928; it shows a pretty young woman and tells me that she had a scar on her right eyelid (something I never knew, never noticed), and that she visited Germany, Italy, France, Belgium, Switzerland, and England that summer, when she was twenty-two years old.

Now that I am grown, and now that she has been dead for several years, I feel glad on Mother's behalf that she had that opportunity when she was young. But when I was young, when I was seven and eight and nine years old, I wished that my mother had never ever visited any foreign country in her life.

She had, you see, brought back *clothes*. Children's clothes. I suppose even then, when she was twenty-two, she had looked forward to one day having children. Probably she had expected that her children would one day enjoy wearing the little foreign outfits she had brought back from several European countries.

Not, as my grandson would say today.

❧1945❧

B

Here I am in my little boy's (okay, so she didn't know, when she was twenty-two, that she would have *girls*) lederhosen from Switzerland. Observe the socks, which were wool and itched. Observe the pants, which were leather and wouldn't bend. Observe the hat, which had a feather of the most embarrassing sort.

Observe the look on the little girl's face. Many words would describe that look. I choose *mortification*.

WORDS TO KNOW

mortification (môr'tə-fĭ-kā'shən) *n.* a feeling of shame or humiliation

⌒Cross Curricular Link **Social Studies**

JAPAN AFTER WORLD WAR II Lowry moved to Japan with her family in 1948, approximately three years after World War II had ended. During World War II, the Japanese had suffered heavy losses of buildings and people. The atomic bombs dropped on Hiroshima and Nagasaki took many lives. After the war, Americans occupied much of the country and were involved in some of the rebuilding efforts. As Japan began to rebuild its war-damaged cities and industries, it became a strong and stable country once again. Only eight years after the war ended, Japan was producing more goods than it had been producing before the war began.

After the war, Japan established a new constitution and a new style of government. They began to have a prime minister as the head of their government and a legislative body called the Diet. The members of the Diet are elected by the people. This is very different from the imperial system Japan had in place before World War II. Japan kept its emperor, but he does not lead the government.

❧ 1945 ❧

Bobby Hobaugh, who lived next door, lent me his football uniform the Halloween that I was eight. I wanted to wear it forever. It made me feel powerful and brave, two things that I had never been.

I walked around the house wearing my football uniform and Bobby Hobaugh's sneakers, which were much too big, saying footbally sounding things like "Hike!" and "Hup!" in as masculine a voice as I could fake.

My brother, Jon, who was three, was scared of me when I turned into a football player. He whimpered when he saw me coming in those big sneakers.

My eleven-year-old sister, who was being a very serious ballerina, ignored me completely.

❧ 1984 ❧

Here's a game I like to play with my children, who are all grown up, and with my grandchildren, who are growing up very quickly, and with my friends, who are all ages. Age doesn't matter with this game. The only thing that matters is loving books.

The game is simply this. When you see a certain scene, you say, "What book does this remind you of?" and everybody who loves books will answer. Some will answer very quickly, and some will think a while and answer after a moment has passed.

There are no wrong answers.

For example, suppose you are walking through a meadow on a breezy day, with three friends. Suppose you stop walking, look around, and say, "What book does this remind you of?"

One friend (maybe he will be an elderly man wearing a tweed vest) will say, *"Wind in the Willows."* He will be right.

Another friend (maybe a tall, thin lady with sunglasses and a straw hat) will say, *"Gone with the Wind."* She will be right, too.

Maybe the third friend will be a very small boy with a freckled nose. Maybe he will say, after a moment of serious thinking, *"Where the Wild Things Are."* And of course—you guessed it— he, too, will be right. ❖

Connect to the
Literature

1. What Do You Think?
Answers will vary, but students should refer to one incident and offer reasons for their choice.

Comprehension Check
• The children are Helen, Lois, and Jon.
• Lowry remembers the football uniform, the Swiss outfit (lederhosen and hat), and the white bathing suit with blue polka dots.

 Use Selection Quiz,
Unit Five Resource Book, p. 43.

Think Critically

2. Possible Response: Young Lois is imaginative, dramatic, self-conscious, mischievous, and forgiving.

3. Possible Response: It reveals her love of books and her fondness for sharing this love with her family.

4. Possible Response: Lowry's tone is mostly humorous. The details that she chooses highlight the humor in many situations and create a vivid sense of the people in her life. Lowry looks at her past with affection for the child she was and a sense of gratitude for the people who influenced her development and created a happy childhood for her.

Use **Reading and Critical Thinking Transparencies,** p. 8, for additional support.

5. Possible Responses: Lowry may have chosen to write this book to relive some happy times in her life; to make sure that she remembered people no longer with her; or to preserve her family's history for other family members.

Literary Analysis

Voice Encourage students to work together to generate the list of words or phrases that depict Lowry's childlike voice.

Use **Literary Analysis Transparencies,** p. 9, for additional support.

THINKING through the LITERATURE

Connect to the Literature

1. What Do You Think?
Which of Lois Lowry's memories is your favorite? Why?

Comprehension Check
• List the children in Lois Lowry's family from oldest to youngest.
• What outfits does Lowry vividly remember from her childhood?

Think Critically

2. What words would you use to describe the young Lois Lowry?

Think About:
• her reaction to *The Yearling*
• her feelings about the clothes her mother made her wear
• her relationships with her brother and sister

3. What does the game that Lowry enjoys playing with her children and grandchildren reveal about her?

4. **ACTIVE READING** **IDENTIFYING EFFECTS OF AUTHOR'S PERSPECTIVE**

Look back at the notes you made in your **READER'S NOTEBOOK.** What effect do you think Lowry's experiences might have on her ability to "see through a child's eyes"?

5. Lowry wrote *Looking Back* after her son was killed in an accident. What are some reasons she may have decided to write this kind of book?

Extend Interpretations

6. **COMPARING TEXTS** Compare the narrator's attitude toward clothing in "Crow Call" on page 668 with Lowry's attitude as revealed in *Looking Back.*

7. Connect to Life Think about your own memories. Which ones are most important to you? What people do you most want to remember? Why?

Literary Analysis

VOICE A writer's unique manner of expression is his or her **voice.** In *Looking Back,* Lowry has a friendly and conversational voice. One way she creates this voice is through a detailed description of her movements during each incident.

I put a crayon in my left hand and sat on the floor beside my bed. I leaned my head and closed my eyes and looked mournful.

Lowry carefully chooses words, such as *mournful,* that might have been in her head at the time. Her choice of incidents and details also helps to create her voice.

Paired Activity With a partner, look through the selection to see how Lowry captures a childlike voice by choosing particular words. Make a list of words that were spoken when she was young and words that she might have liked to use at the time.

"sad and beautiful"

Extend Interpretations

6. Comparing Texts Both the narrator in "Crow Call" and Lowry see certain clothes as symbols of identities that they want to assume. For the narrator, the oversized hunting shirt gives her a sense of security and is a symbol of the adult world. For Lowry, the football uniform empowers her and gives her confidence that she does not otherwise possess.

7. Connect to Life Memories will vary, but students should be able to explain why each is important to them.

Grammar in Context: Combining Sentences

Notice that Lois Lowry often combines two sentences that have closely related ideas into one longer sentence by using a **comma** and a **coordinating conjunction.**

> He was seven when we returned to Pennsylvania, and he says that I told him he would be arrested if they caught him trying to bring Japanese fireworks into the United States.

You may combine two closely related sentences by connecting them with a comma followed by a coordinating conjunction such as *and, or,* or *but.*

Another way of combining closely related sentences is to use a **semicolon** and no coordinating conjunction.

> My Mother read *The Yearling* to Helen and me. I was nine; Helen was twelve.

Vocabulary and Spelling

EXERCISE: MEANING CLUES Read the following newspaper headlines. Then, on your paper, write the Word to Know that would be most likely to appear in the article that goes with each headline.

1. Brother Repeats Everything Sister Says
2. Prize Winner Describes Self as "Ordinary"
3. Boy Stays Awake All Night with Sick Puppy
4. Girl Spills Grape Juice on Friend
5. Judges Look Closely to Examine Photos

WRITING EXERCISE Combine the sentences with a comma and a coordinating conjunction or with a semicolon.

Example: ***Original*** Many words could describe her look. I choose *mortification.*

Rewritten Many words could describe her look, but I choose *mortification.*

1. I don't remember about his fireworks. Jon doesn't remember smashing my doll.
2. Helen's bathing suit was blue. Mine was white, with blue polka dots.
3. I was eight. Jon was two.
4. Jon and I looked alike. I didn't know it then.

Grammar Handbook
See p. R83: Phrases and Clauses.

SPELLING STRATEGY: THE HARD AND SOFT *G* SOUNDS The letter *g* can have a soft sound or a hard sound. Notice the difference between the two sounds:

Soft *g* *vigil*
Hard *g* *legal*

Read aloud the following words from this selection: *photograph, page, living, college, Germany, glad.* Which words use a soft *g* sound? Which words use a hard *g*? Find ten other words that have hard and soft *g* sounds, either in your own writing or in this book. Make a list of these words. Indicate after each one whether it uses a hard or soft *g* sound.

Spelling Handbook
See p. R26.

WORDS TO KNOW	modest	mortification	obnoxious	peer	vigil

Grammar in Context
WRITING EXERCISE
Possible Responses:

1. I don't remember about his fireworks, and Jon doesn't remember smashing my doll.
2. Helen's bathing suit was blue; mine was white, with blue polka dots.
3. I was eight, and Jon was two.
4. Jon and I looked alike, but I didn't know it then.

Vocabulary and Spelling
EXERCISE: MEANING CLUES

1. obnoxious
2. modest
3. vigil
4. mortification
5. peer

SPELLING STRATEGY
Hard *g*: *photograph, glad*
Soft *g*: *page, living, college, Germany*
Students should make a chart, listing both hard and soft *g* words from their own writing, and/or the stories in this book.

EXPLICIT INSTRUCTION **Grammar in Context**

COMBINING SENTENCES
Remind students that when two sentences are closely related, they can be joined by adding a comma followed by a conjunction such as *and, or,* or *but.*
Instruction Ask volunteers to suggest two related sentences. Write them on the board, and demonstrate how to combine them.
Practice Have students work with a partner.

Each student should write five pairs of related sentences, using information about Lois Lowry or topics from her stories and memoirs. After students have written their individual sentences, have them trade papers and combine the pairs into five complete sentences. Ask partners to share their new sentences with the class.

 Use **Unit Five Resource Book,** p. 41.

 For more instruction in combining sentences, see McDougal Littell's *Language Network,* Chapter 11.

For **systematic instruction** in grammar, see:
- **Grammar, Usage, and Mechanics Book**
- pacing chart on p. 609i

Lowry's writings provide insight into her life and the events and people who have influenced her. An analysis of her style can help reveal the techniques she uses to write. Students will be made aware of Lowry's style through the Key Style Points and examples.

Key Style Points

First Activity
Varied Sentence Length and Type
The short sentence adds emphasis and draws attention to the idea that is expressed.

Second Activity
Realistic Dialogue He is encouraging and sensitive.

Third Activity
Word Choice: Sound and Image
Words that create sound include *screamed, harsh,* and *resolute* and *disgruntled shrieks.* Words that evoke visual images include *circles, dipping and soaring, landing speculatively,* and *lurching.*

The Author's Style

Lowry's Lively Language

When she was very young, Lois Lowry was thrilled to discover the power of language. "I remember the feeling of excitement that I had, the first time that I realized each letter had a sound and the sounds went together to make words, and the words became sentences and the sentences became stories. . . ." As a writer, Lowry reveals the power of words by choosing them skillfully.

Key Style Points

Varied Sentence Length and Type Lois Lowry uses a combination of sentence lengths and types to hold the reader's interest. What is the effect of the short sentence among the longer ones in this passage from *Looking Back?*

Realistic Dialogue Dialogue can move the action forward and reveal character traits. What do you learn about the narrator's father from his words to his daughter in this passage from "Crow Call"?

Word Choice: Sound and Image Lively writing doesn't tell the reader what he or she should hear or see. Instead, authors like Lois Lowry choose nouns, verbs, adjectives, and adverbs that re-create sounds and paint strong visual images. Which words in the third passage at the right evoke images or sounds?

> ### Varied Sentences
> When I was eight and he was two, I wore glasses and he didn't. When I was nine and he was three, he wore glasses and I didn't. Now we both wear glasses. But now he has a beard, and I don't.
> —*Looking Back*

> ### Realistic Dialogue
> "Well," he said, "I've been thinking about that, and I've decided to put you in charge of the crow call. Have you ever operated a crow call?"
> I shook my head. "No."
> "It's an art," he said. "No doubt about that. But I'm pretty sure you can handle it. Some people will blow and blow on a crow call and not a single crow will even wake up or bother to listen, much less answer. But I really think you can do it. . . ."
> —*"Crow Call"*

> ### Word Choice
> From all the trees rose crows. They screamed with harsh voices and I responded, blowing again and again as they flew from the hillside in circles, dipping and soaring; landing speculatively, lurching from the limbs in afterthought and then settling again with resolute and disgruntled shrieks.
> —*"Crow Call"*

Applications

1. **Active Reading** Look back through the stories and personal memories in this author study to find examples of these three elements of Lowry's style.

2. **Writing** Recall a time in your childhood when you learned a new skill. Describe the experience in a few paragraphs. Choose words that evoke images and sounds.

3. **Speaking and Listening** With a partner, find a paragraph from one of the selections that uses a variety of sentence types and lengths. Rewrite it in short statements. Read each aloud. How is the effect different?

Applications

1. **Active Reading** Encourage students to draw from all of the selections to answer this question. Students should be able to defend their choices by explaining the effect of the varying sentence lengths, discussing what certain lines of dialogue reveal, and pointing out specific words that they feel are descriptive.

2. **Writing** To help students get started on this assignment, ask them to brainstorm incidents and choose the one they think is the most humorous. Allow the students to break into pairs and tell their stories to each other before writing them.

3. **Speaking and Listening** Students should hear the differences between the two versions. With a variety of sentence lengths and types, the writer keeps the reader interested and adds emphasis to important ideas. If all the sentences are uniformly simple and short, the writing sounds choppy, ideas are equally emphasized, and there is less unity in the paragraph.

Writing

Photo Essay Find an old photograph of yourself. In an essay, recall what you were like at that age. Include funny or interesting stories about yourself. Use sensory details and precise verbs, nouns, and adjectives to help readers visualize the details you describe. Place the essay in your **Working Portfolio.**

Writing Handbook
See p. R38: Using Language Effectively.

Speaking & Listening

Book Talk What is the best book you've ever read? What made you like it so much? Create a presentation to share this book with classmates. In your presentation, explain why you like and recommend the book. If possible, bring in a copy of the book to pass around as you speak.

Speaking and Listening Handbook
See p. R99: Informative Presentations.

Research & Technology

Photo Features Using nonfiction books, the Internet, and other media, find out what careers today use photography. Pick one career and write a brief report explaining why photography is important to it.

Research and Technology Handbook
See p. R107: Library Computer Services.

 INTERNET **Research Starter**
www.mcdougallittell.com

Writing

Photo Essay Students should locate several photographs and freewrite about them to see what they remember about each occasion and themselves at that age. Students should then choose the photograph that evokes the most complete memories and use their freewriting to help them shape their essays.

Use **Writing Transparencies,** p. 25, for additional support

Speaking & Listening

Book Talk To help students develop a sense of audience, encourage them to think of reasons that their classmates also might like the books and to conclude their presentations by listing the reasons.

Use the **Speaking and Listening Book,** pp. 29 and 30, for additional support.

Research & Technology

Photo Features Encourage students to ask a librarian to lead them to Web sites that might be helpful.

Author Study Project
Class Yearbook

When you look back on this year in school, what will you most want to remember? Create a yearbook that preserves your class's memories.

❶ **Create a List** In a small group, brainstorm a list of people and events you would like to remember. Choose the memories you will include and decide how you will organize them.

❷ **Find the Illustrations** Which memories will you illustrate? Gather photographs and make your own art.

❸ **Write the Descriptions** Write paragraphs that include lively descriptions of each memory. Match them with your illustrations.

❹ **Assemble the Book** Glue your illustrations and descriptions into a scrapbook. If you like, make a label for the cover. Invite other students to read your yearbook.

LOIS LOWRY **687**

Author Study Project

CLASS YEARBOOK
Encourage students to assign each member of the group a specific role, such as collecting photographs and organizing them. All students in the group should be involved in writing descriptions of the events. Have them read their paragraphs aloud before making a final copy so that they can make adjustments in content and style.

As an alternative, students might want to do a Video Yearbook, in which video recordings of various events, as well as interviews with students and teachers, are included.

Other Works by Lois Lowry

Lois Lowry's readers are drawn to the voice they find in her books, a voice that seems to know their own hearts and minds. It's no wonder Lowry's books are so believable. Many of the emotions she describes come from her own vivid memories. Whether exploring the world of family or the world at war, Lowry brings to life the challenges and discoveries that shape the years of becoming an adult.

The Giver 1994
Newbery Medal

This disturbing novel is set in a futuristic community that appears to have solved all of the world's problems. Because 12-year-old Jonas has special talents, he is chosen for a unique honor—to be an apprentice to the Giver, the society's keeper of all of its memories, both good and bad. Not until his apprenticeship begins does Jonas understand the true meaning of the Giver's work. With this new knowledge, he begins to doubt the deepest values of his community.

Number the Stars 1990
Newbery Medal

To young Annemarie Johansen, it feels as if war is all anyone can talk about since the Nazis occupied her home city in Denmark. But food shortages and soldiers in the streets seem like petty matters after Annemarie becomes part of a secret and dangerous plot. As tensions build, Annemarie and her family risk their lives to help their Jewish friends to safety in Sweden. This gripping novel was inspired by real-life events of World War II.

A Summer to Die 1977

International Reading Association's Children's Literature Award
Everything seems new the summer that Meg's family moves to the
country. The change brings 13-year-old Meg new neighbors, new
friends, and, unfortunately, a new room she has to share with her
beautiful and popular 15-year-old sister, Molly. But when Molly falls
ill, Meg finds she will need new strength more than anything.

Anastasia Krupnik 1979

Anastasia Krupnik is always in crisis. Her grandmother can't recall
her name, her teacher doesn't understand her poetry, and a certain
sixth-grade boy doesn't seem to know she exists. Worse, her parents
have provided her with yet one more item for her "things I hate"
list: they're adding a new baby to the family, and without consulting
Anastasia first. This is the first novel in Lowry's popular and
hilarious Anastasia Krupnik series.

Rabble Starkey 1987

Boston Globe–Horn Book Award, Golden Kite Award
Twelve-year-old Parable Ann "Rabble" Starkey and her mother have
never had it easy. Her mother had Rabble when she was only 14,
and struggles to support them by cleaning houses in their small
mountain town. When they move in with Rabble's best friend,
Veronica Bigelow, while Mrs. Bigelow is in the hospital, Rabble feels
like she's found her dream home. How will Rabble cope when it's
time to return to her old life?

Standards-Based Objectives

- write a 500- to 700-word opinion statement
- use a written text as a model for writing
- revise a draft to make weak endings stronger
- correct sentence fragments
- deliver a persuasive presentation

Introducing the Workshop

Opinion Statement Locate and share with the class several short opinion statements, such as editorials and letters to the editor in newspapers and magazines. A student newspaper might be a good source for examples. Have them think about how successful the authors were at convincing their readers of their opinions. Ask them to consider what factors made some of the authors more successful than others.

Basics in a Box

Using the Graphic The graphic on this page illustrates how an opinion statement should be organized. Point out that the graphic suggests elements that students should include when they draft their own statements.

Presenting the Rubric To better understand the assignment, students can refer to the Standards for Writing a Successful Opinion Statement. You may also want to share with them the complete rubric, which describes several levels of proficiency.

 See **Unit Five Resource Book,** p. 52.

 For more instruction on essential writing skills, see McDougal Littell's *Language Network,* Chapters 10–17.

 Power Presentation

To engage students visually, use **Power Presentation 1,** Opinion Statement.

Writing Workshop — Opinion Statement

Expressing your opinion . . .

From Reading to Writing Can you remember what you learned in kindergarten? Do you believe the lessons you learned can guide you through the rest of your life? Robert Fulghum does. In his book *All I Really Need to Know I Learned in Kindergarten,* he gives reasons and examples to support his opinion. Writing an **opinion statement** is one way to make your voice heard. Backing up your statement with facts and evidence can help you convince others to see things your way.

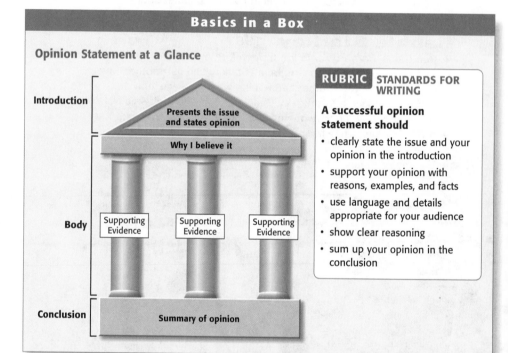

For Your Portfolio

WRITING PROMPT Write an opinion statement about an issue that you care about.

Purpose: To share your opinion and support it with evidence
Audience: Anyone interested in the same issue

Basics in a Box

Opinion Statement at a Glance

Introduction — Presents the issue and states opinion

Why I believe it

Body — Supporting Evidence | Supporting Evidence | Supporting Evidence

Conclusion — Summary of opinion

RUBRIC STANDARDS FOR WRITING

A successful opinion statement should

- clearly state the issue and your opinion in the introduction
- support your opinion with reasons, examples, and facts
- use language and details appropriate for your audience
- show clear reasoning
- sum up your opinion in the conclusion

LESSON RESOURCES

USING PRINT RESOURCES
Unit Five Resource Book
- Prewriting, p. 44
- Drafting, p. 45
- Peer Response, p. 46
- Organizational Patterns, p. 47
- Revising, Editing, and Proofreading, p. 48
- Student Models, pp. 49–51
- Rubric for Evaluation, p. 52

Reading and Critical Thinking
- Main Idea and Supporting Details, TR 25 (p. 691)

Speaking and Listening
- Matching Your Message with Purpose and Knowing Your Audience, p. 6–7 (p. 695)
- Writing Your Speech, p. 8 (p. 695)
- Emphasizing Points for the Listener, p. 9 (p. 695)
- Sustaining Audience Interest and Attention, p. 12 (p. 695)
- Nonverbal Strategies, p. 13 (p. 695)

- Analyzing, Identifying, and Evaluating Rhetorical Devices, pp. 19–20 (p. 695)
- Recognizing Persuasive Techniques and Propaganda, pp. 21–22 (p. 695)
- Creating and Analyzing a Persuasive Presentation, pp. 29–30 (p. 695)

INTEGRATED TECHNOLOGY

Writing Coach CD-ROM

Visit our Web site:
www.mcdougallittell.com

Analyzing a Student Model

SPEAKING OPPORTUNITY

See the Speaking and Listening Handbook, p. R96 for oral presentation tips.

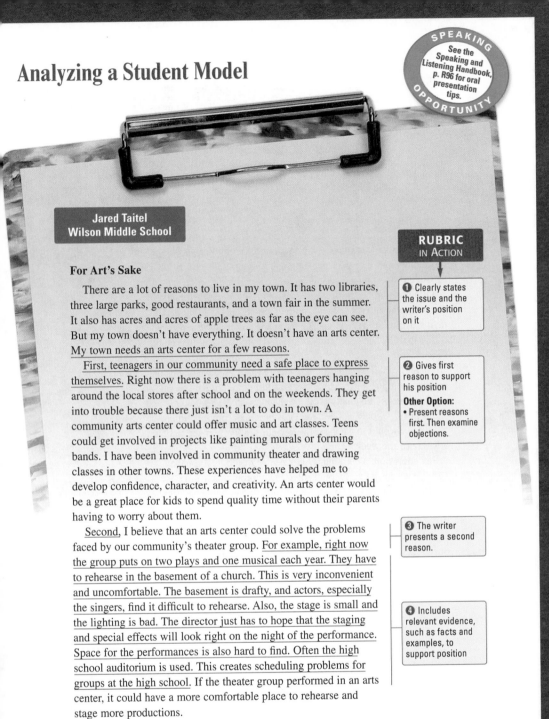

**Jared Taitel
Wilson Middle School**

For Art's Sake

There are a lot of reasons to live in my town. It has two libraries, three large parks, good restaurants, and a town fair in the summer. It also has acres and acres of apple trees as far as the eye can see. But my town doesn't have everything. It doesn't have an arts center. My town needs an arts center for a few reasons.

First, teenagers in our community need a safe place to express themselves. Right now there is a problem with teenagers hanging around the local stores after school and on the weekends. They get into trouble because there just isn't a lot to do in town. A community arts center could offer music and art classes. Teens could get involved in projects like painting murals or forming bands. I have been involved in community theater and drawing classes in other towns. These experiences have helped me to develop confidence, character, and creativity. An arts center would be a great place for kids to spend quality time without their parents having to worry about them.

Second, I believe that an arts center could solve the problems faced by our community's theater group. For example, right now the group puts on two plays and one musical each year. They have to rehearse in the basement of a church. This is very inconvenient and uncomfortable. The basement is drafty, and actors, especially the singers, find it difficult to rehearse. Also, the stage is small and the lighting is bad. The director just has to hope that the staging and special effects will look right on the night of the performance. Space for the performances is also hard to find. Often the high school auditorium is used. This creates scheduling problems for groups at the high school. If the theater group performed in an arts center, it could have a more comfortable place to rehearse and stage more productions.

RUBRIC IN ACTION

❶ Clearly states the issue and the writer's position on it

❷ Gives first reason to support his position
Other Option:
• Present reasons first. Then examine objections.

❸ The writer presents a second reason.

❹ Includes relevant evidence, such as facts and examples, to support position

---

Teaching the Lesson

Analyzing the Model
For Art's Sake

The student model is an opinion statement about the need for an arts center in the writer's town. The student writer states his opinion that his town needs to provide an alternative meeting place for teenagers and those interested in the arts. He supports his assertions with examples and facts.

Have students think of a problem or issue about which they have a strong opinion. Help students see how supporting an argument with examples and details helps to clarify the argument and convince the readers. Then point out the key words and phrases in the student model that correspond to the elements mentioned in the Rubric in Action.

1 Ask students why they think the writer starts off with this description of his town.
   Possible Response: It starts the essay off on a positive note; it shows that the writer is able to see the good in the town as well as the problems.

2 Ask students to consider why the writer addresses the problems of the teens in the town first.
   Possible Responses: It is the most immediate and visible problem; it is a concern of all the town residents.

3 Point out that the student author uses a transitional word at the beginning of this paragraph to signal that he is moving on to another idea.

4 Ask students what impression is created by the facts and examples included in this paragraph.
   Possible Responses: The writer knows his facts and has thought his plan through; the situation of the theater group needs to be remedied.

EXPLICIT INSTRUCTION Patterns of Organization

PICTURING TEXT STRUCTURE

Instruction The effectiveness of a written text depends on word choice, ideas, and the structure of the text—the way in which ideas are organized and events unfold.

Practice Have students analyze the organization of the student model by listing the main idea and supporting details of the essay in a chart similar to the one shown here.

Use **Reading and Critical Thinking Transparencies**, p. 25, for additional support.

Title:	For Art's Sake
Main Idea:	writer's town needs an arts center
Detail:	Teens need activities and a safe place in which to do them.
Detail:	The community theater group needs new facilities.
Detail:	The community already has a building that could be used as an arts center—the old Town Hall.

5 Ask students why they think the writer's third reason is significant to the essay.

Possible Responses: It provides a practical solution to the problem of where the center would go; it takes care of the problem of having a vacant building in the middle of the town; it anticipates the objections that it would be too expensive or complicated to create an arts center.

6 Ask students why the writer mentions building more office space.

Possible Responses: The writer wants to get this suggestion out in the open in order to refute it. He thinks an art center is a better idea and wants to show why.

7 Ask students what effect this conclusion has on the reader.

Possible Responses: It reinforces the arguments that the author made; offers an easy way for the reader to get involved; makes the arts center seem logical and fairly easy to achieve.

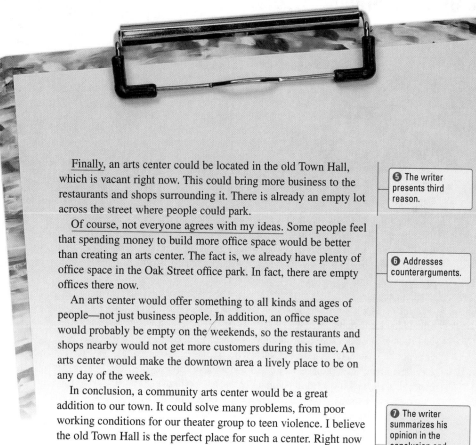

Finally, an arts center could be located in the old Town Hall, which is vacant right now. This could bring more business to the restaurants and shops surrounding it. There is already an empty lot across the street where people could park.

❺ The writer presents third reason.

Of course, not everyone agrees with my ideas. Some people feel that spending money to build more office space would be better than creating an arts center. The fact is, we already have plenty of office space in the Oak Street office park. In fact, there are empty offices there now.

❻ Addresses counterarguments.

An arts center would offer something to all kinds and ages of people—not just business people. In addition, an office space would probably be empty on the weekends, so the restaurants and shops nearby would not get more customers during this time. An arts center would make the downtown area a lively place to be on any day of the week.

In conclusion, a community arts center would be a great addition to our town. It could solve many problems, from poor working conditions for our theater group to teen violence. I believe the old Town Hall is the perfect place for such a center. Right now many volunteers for the arts center have begun sending letters out to citizens asking for their support. Why not get involved and make our great town even greater? By working together, we can solve our community's problems.

❼ The writer summarizes his opinion in the conclusion and ends on a positive note, with a specific request for action.

Writing Your Opinion Statement

❶ Prewriting

Writing comes more easily if you have something to say.
—Sholem Asch, novelist

To find a subject for your opinion statement, **list** topics in your school or community about which you feel strongly. **Write down** changes you think need to be made or things that strike you as unfair. See the **Idea Bank** in the margin for more suggestions. After you have decided on an issue, follow the steps below.

Planning Your Opinion Statement

▶ 1. **Decide on your focus.** Make sure you understand the issue. Is there one specific part you want to focus on? Can you state your opinion clearly in one sentence?

▶ 2. **Think about the reasons for your opinion.** Why do you have this opinion? Which of your reasons are the most convincing?

▶ 3. **Find the facts.** What facts or examples support your reasons? Go to the library or talk to an expert to find as much relevant evidence as you can about your position.

▶ 4. **Identify your audience.** Who will read your opinion statement? Which of your arguments will work best with the people reading your statement? How much background information do you need to give your readers? Can you anticipate what their concerns and counterarguments might be?

❷ Drafting

Begin writing your opinion statement. Keep in mind that you can revise and rewrite it later, but remember that every reason for your opinion must be supported. When you write a reason, follow it up with the **facts** or **examples** that support it. You will probably want to put your reasons in order from weakest to strongest so that your evidence is well organized. Cover a different reason in each paragraph. Be sure to state your opinion in the **introduction** and summarize it in the **conclusion.**

IDEA Bank

1. Your Working Portfolio 📁
Look for ideas in the **Writing** activities you completed earlier.

2. If I ruled the world . . .
Use the sentence starter above to come up with ideas to improve life for people in your school, home, city, state, or country.

3. Debate!
With a partner, decide on a topic that both of you are familiar with, such as a sport, a current event, or a local community issue. Choose opposite sides to create a debate. Take notes and use the information for your paper.

Have a question?

See the **Writing Handbook**
Prewriting, R30
See **Language Network**
Opinion Statement, p. 398

Ask Your Peer Reader

- What is my opinion about this issue?
- Which reasons were most convincing?
- Where do I need more supporting evidence?
- What information was not convincing?
- How did you feel about the issue after reading my essay?

Prewriting

Choosing a Subject
If after reading the Idea Bank students have difficulty choosing a subject for their opinion statements, suggest that they try the following:

- Read through the local newspaper and find an issue that interests you and that seems to have sparked some debate or controversy in your town, such as curfews for students, or the closing of a popular park.
- Find out what the central issues are for local elections in your town. Research one issue and state your opinion in your essay.

Planning Your Opinion Statement
1. Remind students that they can break a complicated issue into components and focus on only one element of the larger issue in order to make it manageable for discussion.
2. Suggest that students make a list of their reasons and arrange them according to priority.
3. Encourage students to research possible objections to their suggestions so they can address these in their statements.
4. Have students think about how much knowledge their intended audience has about the issue being discussed so they can tailor their essays.

Drafting
If students have difficulty starting their essays, suggest that they begin writing the parts of the essay that they are most comfortable with or have the most ideas about, and then go back and fill in their statement and details. Some students may find that writing their statement of opinion helps them to focus their argument as they draft.

Ask Your Peer Reader
Remind students to use the peer reviewer's feedback when revising their drafts.

Revising

MAKING WEAK ENDINGS STRONGER

Review the changes in the sample with students. To help students practice writing strong endings, ask volunteers to share the conclusions from their drafts. Have the rest of the class suggest ways to make the conclusion stronger and more effective.

Editing and Proofreading

CORRECTING SENTENCE FRAGMENTS

Remind students always to express themselves in complete thoughts so that their readers are able to understand the argument. Have students explain the change in the sample. For more practice, see the Grammar Mini Lesson at the bottom of the next page.

Reflecting

 As they write their reflections, have students think about what they will look for in the editorials and letters to the editor that they read in the future.

Option

MANAGING THE PAPER LOAD

In order to decrease your grading time, tape-record your comments and reactions to students' papers rather than writing them down. Then have students listen to your remarks and make any changes in their essays.

Need revising help?

Review the **Rubric**, p. 690

Consider **peer reader** comments

Check **Revision Guidelines,** p. R31

See **Language Network,** Writing the Conclusion, p. 319

SPELLING From Writing

As you revise your work, look back at the words you misspelled and determine why you made the errors you did. For additional help, refer to the strategies and generalizations in the **Spelling Handbook** on page R26.

Wondering what sentence part is missing?

See the **Grammar Handbook,** p. R62.

SPEAKING Opportunity

Turn your essay into a speech to convince others to think and feel the way that you do.

Publishing IDEAS

• Submit your opinion statement to your school or community newspaper.

> INTERNET
> Publishing Options
> www.mcdougallittell.com

---

❸ Revising

TARGET SKILL ▶ MAKING WEAK ENDINGS STRONGER

The ending of your paper is often the part that readers will remember most. That is why it is important to restate your opinion and your strongest supporting arguments in your conclusion.

> *a community arts center would be a great addition*
> In conclusion, ~~I think a community arts center is a good~~ to our town. It would solve many problems, from poor ~~idea. That is the end of my essay. I hope you agree!~~ working conditions for our theater group to teen violence.

❹ Editing and Proofreading

TARGET SKILL ▶ CORRECTING SENTENCE FRAGMENTS

A sentence fragment is a group of words that does not express a complete thought. It may be confusing to the reader because it is not a complete sentence. It may be lacking a subject, a predicate, or some final phrase that completes the thought. Avoid sentence fragments in order to make your writing more easily understood.

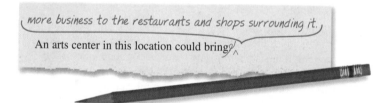

> *more business to the restaurants and shops surrounding it.*
> An arts center in this location could bring

❺ Reflecting

FOR YOUR WORKING PORTFOLIO How did your opinion change or develop as you wrote your opinion statement? What did you learn about writing an opinion statement? What other issues would you like to write about? Attach your answers to your finished essay. Save your opinion statement in your **Working Portfolio.**

ORGANIZATION

Instruction Remind students that an important part of a well-organized composition is a strong conclusion. Discuss with students what qualities make a conclusion strong. *(summarizing the strongest arguments; restating the opinion; ending with an interesting quotation, prediction, or action that can be taken)*

Practice Have students work in pairs to read each other's conclusions. Can the partner who is reading the conclusion restate the opinion? Can he or she think of any counterarguments?

The writer can then revise the opinion statement to include answers to the counterarguments and to more clearly state the opinion.

RUBRIC

3 Full Accomplishment Student restates the opinion forcefully, summarizes the arguments effectively, and has an unforgettable last sentence.

2 Substantial Accomplishment Student restates the opinion, recaps the arguments, and concludes with a catchy last line.

1 Little or Partial Accomplishment Student reasserts opinion without summarizing the arguments and trails off weakly.

See the **Research and Technology Handbook,** pp. R108-109, for information about formatting documents using word processing skills.

Use **Unit Five Resource Book,** p. 47, to help students understand and use order of importance.

Standardized Test Practice

Mixed Review

> Our principal, Mr. Dolinger, says we don't need to have dances at
> our school. He said "There are already too many activities here" It is
> true that some students are involved in sports, while others participate
> in the newspaper and yearbook. However, only 40 percent of our
> students. That statistic shows that a lot of us aren't doing anything
> with people in our school. Having dances on Valentine's day, the first
> day of Spring, or on other special occasions would help to build school
> spirit, to create a sense of friendship among students. One school
> activity that everyone could enjoy.
>
> (1) our school. (2) activities here" (3) only 40 percent of our students. (4) Valentine's day, the first day of Spring, (5) spirit, to create a sense of friendship (6) One school activity

Review Your Skills

Use the passage and the questions that follow it to check how well you remember the language conventions you've learned in previous grades.

1. What is the correct capitalization in item 1?

  A. Our Principal, Mr. Dolinger

  B. Our Principal, mr. dolinger,

  C. Our principal, mr. Dolinger,

  D. Correct as is

2. How is item 2 best written?

  A. He said "There are already too many activities here.

  B. He said, "There are already too many activities here."

  C. He said, There are already too many activities here.

  D. Correct as is

3. What is the correct punctuation in item 3?

  A. only 40 percent of our students participate at all.

  B. only 40 percent of our students:

  C. only 40 percent.

  D. Correct as is

4. How is item 4 best written?

  A. Valentine's Day, the first day of spring,

  B. valentine's day, the first day of spring,

  C. Valentine's Day, the first day of Spring,

  D. Correct as is

5. How is item 5 best written?

  A. to build school spirit and to create a sense of friendship

  B. to build school spirit: to create a sense of friendship

  C. to build school spirit to create a sense of friendship

  D. Correct as is

6. How is item 6 best written?

  A. Dances are one school activity

  B. Are one activity

  C. School activity

  D. Correct as is

Self-Assessment

Check your own answers in the **Grammar Handbook.**

Writing Complete Sentences, p. R67

Correcting Capitalization, p. R81

Correcting Punctuation, p. R86

Demonstrate how students can eliminate incorrect choices for the first question.

A. This choice incorrectly capitalizes *principal.*

B. This choice incorrectly capitalizes *principal* and does not capitalize the first letters of the proper name.

C. This choice is incorrect because the title *Mr.* is not capitalized.

D. The original sentence is correct.

Answers:
1. D; **2.** B; **3.** A; **4.** A; **5.** A; **6.** A.

EXPLICIT INSTRUCTION   Speaking Opportunity

Prepare Once students have written their opinion statement, they can plan to present it to an audience. Refer students to pages R104–105 of the Speaking and Listening Handbook at the back of this book for tips on presenting their opinion statement.

Present Have students present their opinion statements to the class. They should strive to be clear, convincing, and logical and to capture the interest of their audience members.

RUBRIC

3 Full Accomplishment Student clearly states a position on a well-defined issue or proposal and uses convincing evidence.

2 Substantial Accomplishment Student defines and issue or proposal and uses convincing evidence.

1 Little or Partial Accomplishment Student states a positions but has little evidence to support it.

Use **Speaking and Listening Book,** pp. 6–9, 12–13, 19–22, 29–30 for additional support in preparing an opinion statement.

UNIT FIVE
PART 2

PART 2
Voices From
the Past

Meeting Standards

The Literature You'll Read

The Concepts You'll Study

Vocabulary and Reading Comprehension
Vocabulary Focus: Denotative and Connotative
Meanings
Distinguishing Fact from Nonfact
Patterns of Organization
Main Idea and Details
Clarifying

Writing and Language Conventions
Writing Workshop: Research Report
Indpendent and Dependent Clauses
Complex Sentences
Compound-Complex Sentences

Literary Analysis
Genre Focus: Historical Fiction
Historical Fiction
Informative Nonfiction
Poetic Form: Couplet

Speaking and Listening
Live News Report
Radio Drama
Research Questions Presentation
Choral Reading

696

LEARNING the Language of *Literature*

*R*eading History Through Literature

> *Young readers write to me, "How did you learn about Indians?" or about life in colonial times? The answer of course, is research. . . . To me, it is an ever-fascinating game which I have likened to a scavenger hunt.*
> —Elizabeth George Speare, novelist

What would it have been like to be a young person in ancient Egypt, colonial America, or the Roman Empire? What kinds of clothes did kids wear? What games did they play? What did they learn in school? You can explore the past by reading historical fiction and informative nonfiction.

Informative nonfiction that is focused on history gives factual information about real events, places, and people from the past. You can also learn about history by reading **historical fiction.** This kind of fiction combines historical facts with details from the writer's imagination to tell a story. Historical fiction can give you a sense of how people thought and felt at a particular time in history.

Standards-Based Objectives
• understand and identify the following literary terms:
  historical fiction
  informative nonfiction
  real characters
  setting
  plot
• appreciate the writer's craft
• recognize the distinguishing features of historical fiction

Teaching the Lesson

This lesson analyzes the elements of plot, character, and setting in historical fiction. In addition, it compares the elements and purposes of historical fiction with informative nonfiction that has a historical focus.

Introducing the Concepts
Ask students to think of a book they've recently read or a film they've recently seen that is based on a realistic story set in an earlier time. As a class, discuss what makes these works interesting and what students learned from reading or seeing them.

697

Presenting the Concepts

History in Informative Nonfiction

Have students name works of informative nonfiction they have recently read, such as newspaper and magazine articles and reference books. Then ask them if any of these works told about people, places, or events from history. Ask students to explain why they read these works (e.g. to be entertained, to learn new facts, to conduct research for a project).

Discuss with students where they might go to find information about the life of George Washington, about World War II, or about life in New York City in the 1800's. Explain that these could all be topics of informative nonfiction articles.

History in Fiction

Tell students that the informative nonfiction topics they discussed—the life of George Washington, World War II, and life in New York City in the 1800's—could also be subjects of historical fiction narratives. Ask students how an informative article on George Washington and a short story about him might be similar and different.

Characters Have students choose a historical figure they would like to center a story around. Ask what imaginary characters might interact with the historical figure.

Setting Tell students that an important feature of historical fiction is its setting in a past time and place. Tell students to imagine that they are to write a work of historical fiction. Ask them to describe the setting they would choose, including the time period and appropriate details.

 Use **Literary Analysis Transparencies**, p. 6, for additional support.

Plot Ask students to think about what historical event they would weave into a work of historical fiction. What role would the event have in the story? Ask volunteers to share their ideas with the rest of the class.

History in Informative Nonfiction

Informative nonfiction about history presents factual information about people, places, and events from the past. Writers of informative nonfiction try to present information as accurately as possible so that readers will have a clear understanding of the past. Their main purpose for writing is to inform.

History in Fiction

Historical fiction includes all the elements of fiction: character, setting, plot, and theme. Writers of historical fiction weave historical facts, actual events, and imaginary details into stories. Their purposes for writing are to entertain and to inform.

- **Characters** Historical fiction includes real characters from history as well as made-up ones. The characters often face problems that real people faced at that time in history. The dialogue, thoughts, and feelings of the characters are usually made up.

- **Setting** Writers use their imaginations to describe settings, but they try to be accurate in the way they show daily life, details about technology and transportation, and people's thoughts and feelings.

- **Plot** In historical fiction, plot is often strongly influenced by the setting. This is because characters are influenced by the events of their time.

> **INFORMATIVE NONFICTION**
>
> In the spring of 1974 a peasant plowing a field near Mount Li uncovered a life-sized clay statue of a warrior. Further digging indicated that there was an entire army of statues beneath the ground.
>
> —Daniel Cohen, "The First Emperor"

> **SETTING**
>
> The forum was the favorite promenade for rich and poor. What with the priests arguing with the politicians, servants doing the day's shopping, tradesmen crying their wares, women displaying the latest fashions from Greece and Egypt, children playing hide-and-seek among the marble columns, knots of soldiers, sailors, peasants from the provinces—to say nothing of those who merely came to lounge and look on—the square was crowded to its last inch.
>
> —Louis Untermeyer, "The Dog of Pompeii"

The Active Reader: Skills and Strategies

Distinguishing Fact from Opinion

Suppose someone tells you, "*Star Wars* is the best movie ever made! It has an exciting plot, great actors, and terrific special effects." Someone else says, "*Star Wars* was released in 1977. It starred Mark Hamill, Carrie Fisher, and Harrison Ford." Can you tell which is fact and which is opinion? Being able to tell the difference will help you win arguments, defend your own opinions, and evaluate what you read.

How to Apply the Skill

To **distinguish fact from opinion,** an active reader will:
- **Clarify** statements of fact as true or false
- Look for words or phrases that signal opinions
- **Evaluate** and analyze ideas and reasoning
- Look for supporting evidence

Try It Now!

Read and distinguish fact from opinion in the excerpt below.

In November 1922, Carter and his crew began uncovering the area near the tomb of Rameses VI—the only section that had not been dug up in the Valley of the Kings. . . . To the eyes of most people their undertaking seemed absurd. Nearly everybody was convinced that Tutankhamen's tomb had already been found.
—Anne Terry White, "Tutankhamen"

Here's how Chris uses the strategies:

*"The first statement about Carter is a fact because I can check the month and year the excavation began in a history book. Judgment words such as terrible, great, always, never, probably, all, most, and none, and phrases—I think, I feel, I believe, it seems—help me to recognize an opinion. I **evaluate** the last sentences, to see that this part is an opinion. The words* most *and* seemed *and the phrase* nearly everybody was convinced *can't be proved."*

Standards-Based Objectives
- distinguish fact from opinion in various texts
- support responses by referring to relevant aspects of text

Teaching the Lesson

The strategies on this page will help students understand how to tell the difference between facts and opinions in written texts.

Presenting the Strategies
Help students understand the strategies by asking for volunteers to read them aloud. Emphasize to students that they will be using these strategies as they read the selections in this book.

Divide students into small groups. Choose a selection from this unit to read and divide it into sections. Assign one section to each group of students. Ask each group to use the strategies outlined on this page to identify the facts and opinions in their section.

CLARIFY
Have the students construct a chart listing the statements that are fact and those that are opinion. Suggest they also note words that signal opinions in the text.

EVALUATE
Ask for a volunteer from each group to draw the chart on the board and explain their conclusions.

As a class, discuss with students additional ways of determining what is fact and what is opinion in written texts.

This selection is included in the **Grade 6 InterActive Reader.**

This selection appears in Spanish in the **Spanish Study Guide.**

Standards-Based Objectives

1. understand and appreciate a **short story**
2. understand and appreciate **historical fiction**
3. use details in the text to **distinguish fact from nonfact**
4. evaluate **credibility of characterization and plot**
5. identify **point of view**
6. analyze **influence of setting**

Summary

In the ancient Roman city of Pompeii, the blind boy Tito and his dog Bimbo live a simple life together. Three times a day, Bimbo slips away to steal raisin cakes and scraps of food for them to live on. Together they roam Pompeii, exploring its smells and sounds. One night the city's people are especially merry as they celebrate the birthday of the Roman emperor. Afterward, Tito sleeps soundly, exhausted from the excitement. Early the next morning his dog pulls him awake and drags him toward the Forum. The ground trembles and volcanic ash fills the air—the nearby volcano, Mount Vesuvius, is erupting! Pompeiians crowd the street as buildings burn and pumice falls. Confused and frightened, Tito tries to head toward the center of town, but Bimbo forces him toward the sea. There someone lifts Tito safely into a boat, leaving Bimbo behind in the commotion. Centuries later, scientists find the skeleton of a dog in a Pompeiian bakery, a raisin cake still in its mouth.

Thematic Link

Although the physical voices of those from the past may be stilled, the artifacts that people leave behind speak for them.

English Conventions Practice

Daily Language SkillBuilder

Have students **proofread** the display sentences on page 609k and write them correctly. The sentences also appear on Transparency 22 of **Language Transparencies.**

The Dog of Pompeii

by LOUIS UNTERMEYER

Connect to Your Life

What do you know about the ancient city of Pompeii? In a chart like the one shown, record what you already know about this city, and what you would like to learn.

What I Know	What I Want to Learn	What I Learned
It was buried by a volcanic eruption.		

Build Background

HISTORY

In A.D. 79, the volcanic mountain Vesuvius in southern Italy erupted. It poured tons of burning lava and ashes over the countryside and buried Pompeii, a nearby city, under about 20 feet of ash and cinders. The blast was as strong as a nuclear explosion. Out of the estimated population of 20,000, nearly 2,000 were killed, many of them trapped in their homes. Other victims died trying to escape by boat.

Later eruptions continued to cover the ruins, and Pompeii lay undisturbed under lava deposits for almost 1,700 years. The ruins were first discovered in the late 1500s, but excavation did not begin until 1748. The excavations that followed uncovered Pompeii. The remains of the city, well preserved by the ashes, present a clear picture of what life was like in the ancient Roman Empire. We now know how people dressed, how children were taught, and even how foods were prepared.

> WORDS TO KNOW **Vocabulary Preview**
> dislodging   eruption   restore   shrine   vapor

Focus Your Reading

LITERARY ANALYSIS **HISTORICAL FICTION**

When a writer bases all or part of a story on real people or events from the past, the result is called **historical fiction.** The writer may blend factual information about a time, a place, and historical persons with imaginary characters, dialogue, and events.

ACTIVE READING **DISTINGUISHING FACT FROM NONFACT**

A **fact** is a statement that can be proven to be true. Fiction tells about imaginary people, places, and events. As you read, try to decide which elements are true and which are made up. Record facts and fictional details (nonfacts) in a two-column chart in your 📖 READER'S NOTEBOOK.

Fact	Nonfact
"Once a year the Caesar visited the pleasure city."	"The sacrifices in the forum were better than a show."

LESSON RESOURCES

UNIT FIVE RESOURCE BOOK
pp. 53–59

ASSESSMENT
Formal Assessment,
pp. 115–116
Test Generator

SKILLS TRANSPARENCIES AND COPYMASTERS
Literary Analysis
• Conflict, TR 8 (p. 711)
Reading and Critical Thinking
• Distinguishing Fact from Opinion, TR 26 (p. 702)

Language
• Daily Language SkillBuilder, TR 22 (p. 700)
• Subject-Verb Agreement TR 37 (p. 713)
• Synonyms and Antonyms TR 60–61 (p. 701)
Writing
• Sensory Words List, TR 16 (p. 712)
• Using Periodical Indexes, TR 44 (p. 712)

INTEGRATED TECHNOLOGY
Audio Library

Visit our Web site:
www.mcdougallittell.com

For **systematic instruction** in language skills, see:
• **Vocabulary and Spelling Book**
• **Grammar, Usage, and Mechanics Book**
• pacing chart on p. 609i

THE DOG OF POMPEII

by Louis Untermeyer

Cave Canem [Beware of dog], Roman mosaic. Museo Archeologico Nazionale, Naples, Italy. Scala/Art Resource, New York.

Tito and his dog Bimbo lived (if you could call it living) under the wall where it joined the inner gate. They really didn't live there; they just slept there. They lived anywhere. Pompeii was one of the gayest of the old Latin towns, but although Tito was never an unhappy boy, he was not exactly a merry one. The streets were always lively with shining chariots and bright red trappings; the open-air

701

Differentiating Instruction

Less Proficient Readers
Ask students if they have ever had a pet. What was the pet's relationship with their family? Ask if they think that people in ancient times had the same types of relationships with their pets.
Set a Purpose Have students read to find out about Tito's relationship with his dog, Bimbo.

English Learners
Be sure to have students read the background notes on page 700. This will help them understand that Roman towns were built with walls around them. These walls served as protection, and it is under the gate in the wall around the city of Pompeii that Bimbo and Tito slept.

Use **Spanish Study Guide,** pp. 142–144, for additional support.

Advanced Students
Point out to students that animals are commonly depicted in fiction as faithful companions and helpers. Encourage them to recall other literary works that deal with similar relationships. Have students identify details in these works that address the theme of loyalty between humans and animals.

EXPLICIT INSTRUCTION   Preteaching Vocabulary

WORDS TO KNOW
Teaching Strategy Call students' attention to the WORDS TO KNOW. Remind them that **synonyms** and **antonyms** near an unfamiliar word can provide context clues to help them understand its meaning.
Practice Have students identify the word or phrase that is a synonym or antonym of the underlined WORD TO KNOW in each item.

1. We visited several <u>shrines</u>, and one temple looked very familiar. *(temple, synonym)*

2. Something keeps <u>dislodging</u> this step, so I have to keep replacing it. *(replacing, antonym)*

3. At first, we worried about the fumes, but the <u>vapor</u> was harmless. *(fumes, synonym)*

4. I will repair the gate, which should <u>restore</u> it. *(repair, synonym)*

5. Most people were unprepared for the <u>eruption</u>, because of the prevailing calm beforehand. *(calm, antonym)*

Use **Unit Five Resource Book,** p. 58, for more practice.

For **systematic instruction** in vocabulary, see:
• **Vocabulary and Spelling Book**
• pacing chart on p. 609i

(A) theaters rocked with laughing crowds; sham battles and athletic sports were free for the asking in the great stadium. Once a year the Caesar[1] visited the pleasure city, and the fireworks lasted for days; the sacrifices[2] in the forum were better than a show. But Tito saw none of these things. He was blind—had been blind from birth. He was known to everyone in the poorer quarters. But no one could say how old he was; no one remembered his parents; no one could tell where he came from. Bimbo was another mystery. As long as people could remember seeing Tito—about twelve or thirteen years—they had seen Bimbo. Bimbo had never left his side. He was not only dog but nurse, pillow, playmate, mother, and father to Tito.

Did I say Bimbo never left his master? (Perhaps I had better say comrade, for if anyone was the master, it was Bimbo.) I was wrong. Bimbo did trust Tito alone exactly three times a day. It was a fixed routine, a custom understood between boy and dog since the beginning of their friendship, and the way it worked was this: Early in the morning, shortly after dawn, while Tito was still dreaming, Bimbo would disappear. When Tito woke, Bimbo would be sitting quietly at his side, his ears cocked, his stump of a tail tapping the ground, and a fresh-baked bread—more like a large round roll—at his feet. Tito would stretch himself; Bimbo would yawn; then they would breakfast. At noon, no matter where they happened to be, Bimbo would put his paw on Tito's knee, and the two of them would return to the inner gate. Tito would curl up in the corner (almost like a dog) and go to sleep, while Bimbo, looking quite important (almost like a boy), would disappear again. In

(B)

1

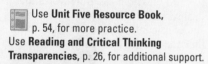

THERE WAS PLENTY OF EVERYTHING IN POMPEII IF YOU KNEW WHERE TO FIND IT—AND IF YOU HAD A DOG LIKE BIMBO.

half an hour he'd be back with their lunch. Sometimes it would be a piece of fruit or a scrap of meat; often it was nothing but a dry crust. But sometimes there would be one of those flat, rich cakes, sprinkled with raisins and sugar, that Tito liked so much. At suppertime the same thing happened, although there was a little less of everything, for things were hard to snatch in the evening with the streets full of people. Besides, Bimbo didn't approve of too much food before going to sleep. A heavy supper made boys too restless and dogs too stodgy—and it was the business of a dog to sleep lightly with one ear open and muscles ready for action.

But whether there was much or little, hot or cold, fresh or dry, food was always there. Tito never asked where it came from, and Bimbo never told him. There was plenty of rainwater in the hollows of soft stones; the old egg-woman at the corner sometimes gave him a cupful of strong goat's milk; in the grape season the fat winemaker let him have drippings of the mild juice. So there was no danger of going hungry or thirsty. There was plenty of everything in Pompeii if you knew where to find it—and if you had a dog like Bimbo.

ACTIVE READER

(C)
SUMMARIZE How does Bimbo care for Tito?

As I said before, Tito was not the merriest boy in Pompeii. He could not romp with the other youngsters and play hare and hounds and I spy and follow-your-master and ball-against-the-building and

---

1. **the Caesar** (sē′zər): the Roman emperor.
2. **sacrifices:** offerings of animals or objects to the gods.

jackstones and kings and robbers with them. But that did not make him sorry for himself. If he could not see the sights that delighted the lads of Pompeii, he could hear and smell things they never noticed. He could really see more with his ears and nose than they could with their eyes. When he and Bimbo went out walking, he knew just where they were going and exactly what was happening.

"Ah," he'd sniff and say as they passed a handsome villa, "Glaucus Pansa is giving a grand dinner tonight. They're going to have three kinds of bread, and roast pigling, and stuffed goose, and a great stew—I think bear stew—and a fig pie." And Bimbo would note that this would be a good place to visit tomorrow.

Or, "H'm," Tito would murmur, half through his lips, half through his nostrils. "The wife of Marcus Lucretius is expecting her

2

The Sorceress and the Traveler. Mosaic from Pompeii, House of the Dioscuri. Museo Archeologico Nazionale, Naples, Italy. Scala/Art Resource, New York.

Advanced Students
Encourage students to think about Tito's blindness and whether it is represented as a handicap or not. What characteristics does Tito have that compensate for his blindness?
Possible Responses: The author does not dwell on Tito's blindness as a handicap. He presents Tito as a person who possesses skills that help him live his life fully. His senses of smell and hearing are acute, which is an advantage for a boy living on the streets without anyone to care for him but a dog.

Less Proficient Readers
1 Help students recognize that the narrator is being humorous here, suggesting that Tito is behaving like a dog and Bimbo like a boy.
Set a Purpose Have students read to find out what a typical day is like for this boy. Encourage students to create story webs to record details about the characters, setting, and plot of this story.

English Learners
2 Explain that the suffix *-ling* means "small," so a pigling is a small pig. Ask what the more common word *duckling* means.
   Ask students to consider how Bimbo the dog is like a person. What details in the story show his "human" characteristics?
Possible Responses: Bimbo has a regular schedule. He shares his food with Tito. He seems to understand what Tito is saying when Tito talks about the food at Glaucus Pansa's grand dinner.

EXPLICIT INSTRUCTION ## Viewing and Representing

The Sorceress and the Traveler,
Mosaic from Pompeii

ART APPRECIATION Explain that many of Pompeii's walls were preserved by the ash that covered them. The art and writing on those walls give modern viewers a glimpse into the society of Pompeii.
Instruction Use the following questions to help students compare and contrast the art with the story.
• How can you tell that dogs existed in Pompeii? *(A dog is shown in the mosaic.)*

• What can you learn about what the characters in the story might have worn? *(They likely wore tunics or robes and wide, shade-giving hats.)*
• What can you infer from the traveler's staff? *(He has been walking.)*
Practice Ask students what this illustration adds to their understanding of the story.
Possible Response: It shows what characters may have looked like, including Bimbo, the dog.

A **FACT AND OPINION** **Possible Responses:** Students might mention the following as true: There were no private houses, and buildings were replaced after the earthquake. Opinions might include the following: everything glittered, and citizens were ambitious.

ACTIVE READER

B **FACT AND NONFACT** **Possible Responses:** Imaginary parts of the conversation might include bath master Rufus's opinion that there will be no more earthquakes. Parts based on fact include the statement that two towns were destroyed three times in 15 years by earthquakes.

Literary Analysis
HISTORICAL FICTION

Remind students that historical fiction is like any other fiction in many ways. Discuss what students already know about the elements of fiction. Have them identify the setting and characters and predict what the central conflict might be, based on story clues.

Possible Responses: The setting is ancient Pompeii; the characters include Tito and Bimbo; the central conflict will probably center around the eruption of Mount Vesuvius.

---

mother. She's shaking out every piece of goods in the house; she's going to use the best clothes—the ones she's been keeping in pine needles and camphor[3]—and there's an extra girl in the kitchen. Come, Bimbo, let's get out of the dust!"

Or, as they passed a small but elegant dwelling opposite the public baths, "Too bad! The tragic poet is ill again. It must be a bad fever this time, for they're trying smoke fumes instead of medicine. Whew! I'm glad I'm not a tragic poet!"

Or, as they neared the forum, "Mm-m! What good things they have in the macellum today!" (It really was a sort of butcher-grocer-marketplace, but Tito didn't know any better. He called it the macellum.) "Dates from Africa, and salt oysters from sea caves, and cuttlefish, and new honey, and sweet onions, and—ugh!—water-buffalo steaks. Come, let's see what's what in the forum." And Bimbo, just as curious as his comrade, hurried on. Being a dog, he trusted his ears and nose (like Tito) more than his eyes. And so the two of them entered the center of Pompeii.

The forum was the part of the town to which everybody came at least once during each day. It was the central square, and everything happened here. There were no private houses; all was public—the chief temples, the gold and red bazaars, the silk shops, the town hall, the booths belonging to the weavers and jewel merchants, the wealthy woolen market, the <u>shrine</u> of the household gods. Everything glittered here. The buildings looked as if they were new—which, in a sense, they were. The earthquake of twelve years ago had brought down all the old structures, and since the citizens of Pompeii were ambitious to

ACTIVE READER

FACT AND OPINION
Which parts of this description of the buildings could be proved to be true? Which are opinion?

rival Naples and even Rome, they had seized the opportunity to rebuild the whole town. And they had done it all within a dozen years. There was scarcely a building that was older than Tito.

Tito had heard a great deal about the earthquake, though being about a year old at the time, he could scarcely remember it. This particular quake had been a light one—as earthquakes go. The weaker houses had been shaken down; parts of the outworn wall had been wrecked; but there was little loss of life, and the brilliant new Pompeii had taken the place of the old. No one knew what caused these earthquakes. Records showed they had happened in the neighborhood since the beginning of time. Sailors said that it was to teach the lazy city folk a lesson and make them appreciate those who risked the dangers of the sea to bring them luxuries and protect their town from invaders. The priests said that the gods took this way of showing their anger to those who refused to worship properly and who failed to bring enough sacrifices to the altars and (though they didn't say it in so many words) presents to the priests. The tradesmen said that the foreign merchants had corrupted the ground and it was no longer safe to traffic in imported goods that came from strange places and carried a curse with them. Everyone had a different explanation—and everyone's explanation was louder and sillier than his neighbor's.

They were talking about it this afternoon as Tito and Bimbo came out of the side street

---

3. **camphor** (kăm′fər): a strong-smelling substance used as a moth repellent.

WORDS
TO
KNOW

shrine (shrīn) *n.* a place of worship

704

Cross Curricular Link **Science**

VOLCANOES Although Italy has seen some terrible eruptions, including the one that buried Pompeii, most active volcanoes form in a region called The Ring of Fire, an area that rims the Pacific Ocean. Here plates, or huge sections of the earth's crust, lying beneath the Pacific Ocean meet plates that lie beneath surrounding land forms. Many volcanoes form where plates meet. Two famous Indonesian eruptions were said to be even more powerful than that of Vesuvius:

• In 1815, Mt. Tambora blew its top and created devastating tidal waves and storms. The ash from the eruption affected weather around the globe. Approximately 90,000 people died, either during the eruption itself or afterward.

• In 1883, Mt. Krakatoa exploded with a noise that could be heard thousands of miles away. The ash and tidal waves wiped out 36,000 people.

into the public square. The forum was the favorite promenade⁴ for rich and poor. What with the priests arguing with the politicians, servants doing the day's shopping, tradesmen crying their wares, women displaying the latest fashions from Greece and Egypt, children playing hide-and-seek among the marble columns, knots of soldiers, sailors, peasants from the provinces⁵—to say nothing of those who merely came to lounge and look on—the square was crowded to its last inch. His ears even more than his nose guided Tito to the place where the talk was loudest. It was in front of the shrine of the household gods that, naturally enough, the householders were arguing.

"I tell you," rumbled a voice which Tito recognized as bath master Rufus's, "there won't be another earthquake in my lifetime or yours. There may be a tremble or two, but earthquakes, like lightnings, never strike twice in the same place."

"Do they not?" asked a thin voice Tito had never heard. It had a high, sharp ring to it, and Tito knew it as the accent of a stranger. "How about the two towns of Sicily that have been ruined three times within fifteen years by the eruptions of Mount Etna? And were they not warned? And does that column of smoke above Vesuvius mean nothing?"

"That?" Tito could hear the grunt with which one question answered another. "That's always there. We use it for our weather guide. When the smoke stands up

> IT WAS THE CENTRAL SQUARE, AND EVERYTHING HAPPENED HERE. . . . EVERYTHING GLITTERED HERE.

straight, we know we'll have fair weather; when it flattens out, it's sure to be foggy; when it drifts to the east—"

"Yes, yes," cut in the edged voice. "I've heard about your mountain barometer. But the column of smoke seems hundreds of feet higher than usual, and it's thickening and spreading like a shadowy tree. They say in Naples—"

"Oh, Naples!" Tito knew this voice by the little squeak that went with it. It was Attilio, the cameo⁶ cutter. "*They* talk while we suffer. Little help we got from them last time. Naples commits the crimes, and Pompeii pays the price. It's become a proverb with us. Let them mind their own business."

"Yes," grumbled Rufus, "and others, too."

"Very well, my confident friends," responded the thin voice, which now sounded curiously flat. "We also have a proverb—and it is this: Those who will not listen to men must be taught by the gods. I say no more. But I leave a last warning. Remember the holy ones. Look to your temples. And when the smoke tree above Vesuvius grows to the shape of an umbrella pine, look to your lives."

Tito could hear the air whistle as the speaker drew his toga about him, and the

---

4. **promenade** (prŏm′ə-nād′): a public place for leisurely walking.
5. **provinces:** areas of a country that are far from the capital.
6. **cameo** (kăm′ē-ō′): a gem or shell with a picture carved on it.

ACTIVE READER

FACT AND NONFACT In your opinion, which elements of this conversation are imaginary? Which are based on fact?

WORDS TO KNOW — **eruption** (ĭ-rŭp′shən) *n.* an outburst or throwing forth of lava, water, steam, and other materials

705

2

Differentiating Instruction

English Learners

1 Be sure students understand that *Mm-m!* represents the sound Tito makes to indicate his appreciation of the smell of food. Model the appropriate intonation of "Mm-m!" and the exclamation "What good things they have in the macellum today!" Explain the sound *ugh* two sentences later. Suggest to students that it is likely that the dog is reacting to expressive sounds such as *mm-m* and *ugh* rather than to Tito's actual words.

Less Proficient Readers

Ask the following questions to make sure students understand the story so far:

- How does Tito know what is going on inside the houses?
  Possible Response: He uses his sense of smell and knows how to interpret the odors.
- Why was Pompeii rebuilt?
  Possible Response: An earthquake had destroyed many buildings.
- What are the bath master and the stranger talking about?
  Possible Response: They are talking about whether to worry about the smoke above Vesuvius or not—the sign of another possible eruption or earthquake.

Set a Purpose Have students read to find out if the stranger or the local people are correct.

Advanced Students

2 Challenge students to explain why hot smoke rises straight up in good weather, but flattens out in foggy weather. See if they can relate their answer to weather patterns.

EXPLICIT INSTRUCTION ## Evaluating Story Elements

Instruction Tell students that to evaluate or critique a story means to make judgments about the story. Explain that when readers evaluate a story, they judge how well the writing measures up to their expectations or standards. Then they make specific statements that summarize their judgments. Explain that the first step in evaluating a short story is to examine and judge its parts—its characters, setting, and plot. List the following questions on the board and tell students to use them to help them evaluate characters and setting:

1. How realistic are the characters, including animals?
2. Would real people act and speak this way?
3. Are the details about the setting accurate and believable?

Tell students that when they state or write evaluations, they should make specific statements that are supported with facts and examples.

Practice Have students write answers to the questions you wrote on the board. Invite students to share their responses.

Possible Responses: Responses will vary. Students might say that Bimbo's loyalty and Tito's use of his senses of sound and smell seem realistic. They might say that Bimbo seems too human, but that the setting is believable because of all the details the writer uses. All responses should be supported.

Use **Unit Five Resource Book,** p. 56, for more practice.

A Ask students what they learn here about the activities in ancient Pompeii.
Possible Response: Caesar's birthday is celebrated with food and theater.

ACTIVE READER

B **VISUALIZE Possible Responses:** "The air was hot. And heavy", "[it] turned to . . . warm powder that stung his nostrils and burned his . . . eyes"; "Peculiar sounds"; "Hissings and groanings and muffled cries. . . ."

Active Reading
DISTINGUISHING FACT FROM NONFACT

Ask students which elements of this day are probably imaginary and which are based on fact. Discuss with students how writers might discover facts about something that happened long ago.
Possible Responses: The heat and heaviness of the air, the burning powder, the sounds, and the hot water are probably based on fact. The people's cries and movements are probably from the writer's imagination. Writers could learn the factual information through research.

---

quick shuffle of feet told him the stranger had gone.

"Now what," said the cameo cutter, "did he mean by that?"

"I wonder," grunted Rufus. "I wonder."

Tito wondered, too. And Bimbo, his head at a thoughtful angle, looked as if he had been doing a heavy piece of pondering. By nightfall the argument had been forgotten. If the smoke had increased, no one saw it in the dark. Besides, it was Caesar's birthday, and the town was in holiday mood. Tito and Bimbo were among the merrymakers, dodging the charioteers who shouted at them. A dozen times they almost upset baskets of sweets and jars of Vesuvian wine, said to be as fiery as the streams inside the volcano, and a dozen times they were cursed and cuffed. But Tito never missed his footing. **A** He was thankful for his keen ears and quick instinct—most thankful of all for Bimbo.

They visited the uncovered theater, and though Tito could not see the faces of the actors, he could follow the play better than most of the audience, for their attention wandered—they were distracted by the scenery, the costumes, the by-play, even by themselves—while Tito's whole attention was centered in what he heard. Then to the city walls, where the people of Pompeii watched a mock naval battle in which the city was attacked by the sea and saved after thousands of flaming arrows **1** had been exchanged and countless colored torches had been burned. Though the thrill of flaring ships and lighted skies was lost to Tito, the shouts and cheers excited him as much as any, and he cried out with the loudest of them.

> THE NOISES CAME FROM UNDERNEATH. HE NOT ONLY HEARD THEM—HE COULD FEEL THEM.

The next morning there were *two* of the beloved raisin and sugar cakes for his breakfast. Bimbo was unusually active and thumped his bit of a tail until Tito was afraid he would wear it out. The boy could not imagine whether Bimbo was urging him to some sort of game or was trying to tell him something. After a while, he ceased to notice Bimbo. He felt drowsy. Last night's late hours had tired him. Besides, there was a heavy mist in the air—no, a thick fog rather than a mist—a fog that got into his throat and scraped it and made him cough. He walked as far as the marine gate[7] to get a breath of the sea. But the blanket of haze had spread all over the bay, and even the salt air seemed smoky.

He went to bed before dusk and slept. But he did not sleep well. He had too many dreams— dreams of ships lurching in the forum, of losing his way in a screaming crowd, of armies marching across his chest, of being pulled over every rough pavement of Pompeii.

He woke early. Or, rather, he was pulled awake. Bimbo was doing the pulling. The dog had dragged Tito to his feet and was urging the boy along. Somewhere. Where, Tito did not know. His feet stumbled uncertainly; he was still half asleep. For a while he noticed nothing except the fact that it was hard to breathe. The air was hot. And heavy. So heavy that he could taste it. The air, it seemed, had turned

ACTIVE READER

B **VISUALIZE** What sensory details help you to visualize this description?

---

7. **marine gate:** a gate in the city wall, leading to the sea.

Cross Curricular Link History

POMPEII In A.D. 62, seventeen years before Vesuvius erupted, a strong earthquake had damaged Pompeii and the neighboring city of Herculaneum. Scientists now believe that Vesuvius was trying to erupt then, but that people did not understand the warning.
The blast that occurred in A.D. 79 was 10 times more powerful than the 1980 eruption of Mount St. Helens in the state of Washington.

Mount Vesuvius in Eruption (1817), Joseph Mallord William Turner. Watercolor on paper. Yale Center for British Art, Paul Mellon Collection, USA/Bridgeman Art Library.

to powder, a warm powder that stung his nostrils and burned his sightless eyes.

Then he began to hear sounds. Peculiar sounds. Like animals under the earth. Hissings and groanings and muffled cries that a dying creature might make <u>dislodging</u> the stones of his underground cave. There was no doubt of it now. The noises came from underneath. He not only heard them—he could feel them. The earth twitched; the twitching changed to an uneven shrugging of the soil. Then, as Bimbo half pulled, half coaxed him across, the ground

jerked away from his feet and he was thrown against a stone fountain.

The water—hot water—splashing in his face revived him. He got to his feet, Bimbo steadying him, helping him on again. The noises grew louder; they came closer. The cries were even more animal-like than before, but now they came from human throats. A few people, quicker of foot and more hurried by fear, began to rush by. A family or two—then a section—then, it seemed, an army broken out of bounds. Tito, bewildered though he

> WORDS
> TO
> KNOW
>
> **dislodging** (dĭs-lŏj′ĭng) *adj.* moving from a settled position **dislodge** *v.*

707

Less Proficient Students

1 Have students summarize in their own words what Tito does on this night. *(He celebrates Caesar's birthday with other townspeople and goes to the theater, where he listens to the performance.)*

To help students follow the story, ask the following questions:

- What was Pompeii celebrating? *(Caesar's birthday)*
- Why weren't people paying attention to the increasing smoke?
  Possible Response: They were too busy having fun.
- What does Bimbo do in the morning, and what does Tito notice?
  Possible Responses: Bimbo gives Tito two cakes and pulls the boy along. Tito notices that the air has warm powder in it. He hears underground noises and people yelling.
- What is causing the hot air, the rumbling noises, and the hot water in the fountain? *(Vesuvius is erupting.)*

Set a Purpose Instruct students to pay attention to what happens to Tito during the volcanic eruption.

Advanced Students

2 Many people believe that animals are sensitive to seismic activity, such as earthquakes and volcanic eruptions. Have students do research to find out the kinds of things animals might be sensitive to that humans are not.

EXPLICIT INSTRUCTION **Point of View**

Instruction Remind students that the person who tells a story is called the narrator or speaker. Explain that in a short story, the writer might choose either the first-person or the third-person point of view to tell the story. In the first-person point of view, the story is told by a character in the story. The narrator uses the pronouns *I, me,* and *we.* The reader learns only as much as the narrator knows. A story told by an outsider—someone who is not a story character—is told from the third-person point of view using pronouns such as *he, she,* and *they.* A third-person narrator can depict the thoughts of many characters. Ask students to determine the point of view of this story.

Practice Have students rewrite the paragraph on page 707 that begins "Then he began to hear sounds." Students should change the point of view from third-person to first-person. Remind them to include information about Tito's thoughts and feelings. Have students read their paragraphs aloud.

Possible Responses: Responses will vary.

The volcanic ash that covered victims of the Pompeii disaster hardened over time. Archaeologists used the resulting "shells" as molds for body casts. © Krafft/Explorer, Photo Researchers.

ACTIVE READER

CONNECT Do you recall
a personal experience in
which time seemed to
"stand still"? What
caused this feeling?

was, could recognize
Rufus as he bellowed
past him, like a water
buffalo gone mad. Time
was lost in a nightmare.

It was then the
crashing began. First a
sharp crackling, like a monstrous snapping
of twigs; then a roar like the fall of a whole
forest of trees; then an explosion that tore
earth and sky. The heavens, though Tito
could not see them, were shot through with
continual flickerings of fire. Lightnings above
were answered by thunders beneath. A house
fell. Then another. By a miracle the two
companions had escaped the dangerous side

streets and were in a more open space. It was
the forum. They rested here awhile—how long
he did not know.

Tito had no idea of the time of day. He
could *feel* it was black—an unnatural
blackness. Something inside—perhaps the lack
of breakfast and lunch—told him it was past
noon. But it didn't matter. Nothing seemed to
matter. He was getting drowsy, too drowsy to
walk. But walk he must. He knew it. And
Bimbo knew it; the sharp tugs told him so.
Nor was it a moment too soon. The sacred
ground of the forum was safe no longer. It was
beginning to rock, then to pitch, then to split.
As they stumbled out of the square, the earth
wriggled like a caught snake, and all the

columns of the temple of Jupiter[8] came down. It was the end of the world—or so it seemed.

To walk was not enough now. They must run. Tito was too frightened to know what to do or where to go. He had lost all sense of direction. He started to go back to the inner gate; but Bimbo, straining his back to the last inch, almost pulled his clothes from him. What did the creature want? Had the dog gone mad?

Then, suddenly, he understood. Bimbo was telling him the way out—urging him there. The sea gate, of course. The sea gate—and then the sea. Far from falling buildings, heaving ground. He turned, Bimbo guiding him across open pits and dangerous pools of bubbling mud, away from buildings that had caught fire and were dropping their burning beams. Tito could no longer tell whether the noises were made by the shrieking sky or the agonized people. He and Bimbo ran on—the only silent beings in a howling world.

New dangers threatened. All Pompeii seemed to be thronging toward the marine gate; and, squeezing among the crowds, there was the chance of being trampled to death. But the chance had to be taken. It was growing harder and harder to breathe. What air there was choked him. It was all dust now—dust and pebbles, pebbles as large as beans. They fell on his head, his hands—pumice[9] stones from the black heart of Vesuvius. The mountain was turning itself inside out. Tito remembered a phrase that the

stranger had said in the forum two days ago: "Those who will not listen to men must be taught by the gods." The people of Pompeii had refused to heed the warnings; they were being taught now—if it was not too late.

Suddenly it seemed too late for Tito. The red hot ashes blistered his skin; the stinging vapors tore his throat. He could not go on. He staggered toward a small tree at the side of the road and fell. In a moment Bimbo was beside him. He coaxed. But there was no answer. He licked Tito's hands, his feet, his face. The boy did not stir. Then Bimbo did the last thing he could— the last thing he wanted to do. He bit his comrade, bit him deep in the arm. With a cry of pain, Tito jumped to his feet, Bimbo after him. Tito was in despair, but Bimbo was determined. He drove the boy on, snapping at his heels, worrying his way through the crowd; barking, baring his teeth, heedless of kicks or falling stones. Sick with hunger, half dead with fear and sulphur[10] fumes, Tito pounded on, pursued by Bimbo. How long he never knew. At last he staggered through the marine gate and felt soft sand under him. Then Tito fainted. . . .

Someone was dashing seawater over him. Someone was carrying him toward a boat.

"Bimbo," he called. And then louder, "Bimbo!" But Bimbo had disappeared.

> ALL POMPEII SEEMED TO BE THRONGING TOWARD THE MARINE GATE . . . . THERE WAS THE CHANCE OF BEING TRAMPLED TO DEATH.

C

---

8. **Jupiter:** the supreme god in Roman mythology.
9. **pumice** (pŭm'ĭs): a light rock formed from lava.
10. **sulphur** (sŭl'fər): a pale yellow chemical element that produces a choking fume when burned.

WORDS TO KNOW **vapor** (vā'per) *n.* fumes, mist, or smoke

Reading and Analyzing

Voices jarred against each other. "Hurry—hurry!" "To the boats!" "Can't you see the child's frightened and starving!" "He keeps calling for someone!" "Poor boy, he's out of his mind." "Here, child—take this!"

They tucked him in among them. The oarlocks creaked; the oars splashed; the boat rode over toppling waves. Tito was safe. But he wept continually.

"Bimbo!" he wailed. "Bimbo! Bimbo!" He could not be comforted.

Petrified bread from Pompeii. Museo Archeologico Nazionale, Naples, Italy. Alinari/Art Resource, New York.

Eighteen hundred years passed. Scientists were <u>restoring</u> the ancient city; excavators were working their way through the stones and trash that had buried the entire town. Much had already been brought to light—statues, bronze instruments, bright mosaics,[11] household articles; even delicate paintings had been preserved by the fall of ashes that had taken over two thousand lives. Columns were dug up, and the forum was beginning to emerge.

It was at a place where the ruins lay deepest that the director paused.

"Come here," he called to his assistant. "I think we've discovered the remains of a building in good shape. Here are four huge millstones that were most likely turned by slaves or mules—and here is a whole wall standing with shelves inside it. Why! It must have been a bakery. And here's a curious thing. What do you think I found under this heap where the ashes were thickest? The skeleton of a dog!"

"Amazing!" gasped his assistant. "You'd think a dog would have had sense enough to run away at the time. And what is that flat thing he's holding between his teeth? It can't be a stone."

"No. It must have come from this bakery. You know it looks to me like some sort of cake hardened with the years. And, bless me, if those little black pebbles aren't raisins. A raisin cake almost two thousand years old! I wonder what made him want it at such a moment."

"I wonder," murmured the assistant. ❖

---

11. **mosaics** (mō-zā′ĭks): pictures or designs made by setting small colored stones or tiles into surfaces.

WORDS TO KNOW

restore (rĭ-stôr′) v. to bring back to an original condition

710

710   UNIT FIVE   PART 2

Connect to the Literature

1. What Do You Think?
How did you feel after reading the story?

Comprehension Check
- How does Tito get the food he eats?
- Why does Bimbo pull Tito awake the morning after the emperor's birthday?
- How does Tito manage to escape?

Think Critically

2. Louis Untermeyer ends the story of the disaster 1,800 years later. Why do you think he does this?

3. Do you think Bimbo is a realistic character? Defend your answer with evidence from the story.

Think About:
- Bimbo's role in Tito's everyday life
- how Bimbo responds to the volcanic eruption

4. **ACTIVE READING** **DISTINGUISHING FACT FROM NONFACT**
With a partner, go over the chart you made in your **READER'S NOTEBOOK**. Does the story seem more like history or more like fiction? Explain.

Extend Interpretations

5. **COMPARING TEXTS** Think back to Lob's relationship with Sandy in "Lob's Girl" (page 447). How is it similar to Bimbo's relationship with Tito? How do both dogs show courage and loyalty to their people?

6. Critic's Corner One critic believes that the role of historical fiction is to help readers see the "similarities and differences in people from other times and places." What similarities do you see between life in ancient Pompeii and the United States today?

7. Connect to Life What did you learn about the city of Pompeii that you didn't know before? Record any new information in the last column of the chart you made for the Connect to Your Life activity.

Literary Analysis

HISTORICAL FICTION Fiction that brings a period of history to life through a writer's imagination is called **historical fiction.** From such literature you learn not only the facts about historical events but also the feelings people may have had. In reading "The Dog of Pompeii," what did you learn about how people may have felt when Mt. Vesuvius erupted?

REVIEW: CONFLICT Most stories revolve around a central **conflict**—a struggle between opposing forces. An **external conflict** is a struggle between a character and an outside force, such as a natural disaster or a rival character. An **internal conflict** occurs within a character's mind. It may be the opposing ideas or feelings that when a character tries to make a tough decision.

Group Activity In a small group, discuss how Louis Untermeyer uses the elements of fiction in "The Dog of Pompeii." Who are the main characters? What events lead to a climax, or turning point? How is the setting important? What do you think is the theme?

Connect to the Literature

1. What Do You Think?
Responses will vary. Students may feel wonder, surprise, or confusion about whether to believe the last scene.

Comprehension Check
- Bimbo steals raisin cakes and food scraps three times a day.
- Bimbo wakes Tito because the volcano has begun to erupt.
- Tito boards a boat and goes out to sea.

 Use Selection Quiz, **Unit Five Resource Book,** p. 59.

Think Critically

2. Possible Response: The ending reveals what happened to Bimbo after Tito left the city. In addition, it shows Bimbo's loyalty and heroism because the raisin cake found in his mouth shows that he died trying to take care of Tito. It's as if Bimbo's loyalty and heroism have been preserved for all time.

3. Possible Responses: He is realistic, because he acts like a loyal dog, caring for and protecting Tito. He is not realistic, because he shows too many human qualities.

4. Possible Responses: It has so many facts that it seems more like history. It has such a good plot that it seems more like a story.

Literary Analysis

Historical Fiction Students should mention as the main characters Bimbo and Tito. The events leading up to the climax might include overhearing the conversation on the street and awakening to the hot and heavy air. The setting is crucial because it creates the story's main conflict and affects the characters' actions. The theme might be a dog's loyalty, or that people need to show respect for nature's powers.

Use **Literary Analysis Transparencies,** p. 8, for additional support.

Extend Interpretations

5. Comparing Texts Both relationships are based on a deep bond that is revealed through daily interaction. Both dogs demonstrate their devotion in ways that seem amazing, touching, and even puzzling.

6. Critic's Corner Possible Responses: Pompeii and cities in the United States both have lively urban streets, crowding, and traffic. Both have theaters, athletic events, bakeries, public places, new buildings, and various foods for sale. Both have wealthy citizens and people who live in the streets.

7. Connect to Life Responses will vary. Some students may be surprised that the eruption occurred so quickly that people could not escape. They may be interested that such a complex city existed so long ago. They may be surprised at some of the details about volcanic eruptions. To extend this activity, suggest that students do more research on one aspect that they recorded.

Writing

Facts from Fiction To help students get started, have them go through the story and list information about daily life in Pompeii. Students can use this list to help them write their descriptions.

 Use **Writing Transparencies**, p. 16, for additional support.

Speaking & Listening

Live News Report Students may enjoy working in teams, as many news professionals do. One announcer can provide certain details and then switch to another announcer.

Research & Technology

Dig It Many times, archaeological discoveries are made during public works projects that include new highways and subway excavation.

 Use **Writing Transparencies**, p. 44, for additional support.

Art Connection

Informative Images Encourage students to focus on the animal's posture and expression and its being leashed.

Vocabulary

EXERCISE A

1. synonym
2. antonym
3. synonym
4. synonym
5. antonym

EXERCISE B

Students might enjoy making some of their drawings mosaic style, using graph paper to help them.

Writing

Facts from Fiction This story includes information about daily life in Pompeii, including details about food, jobs, games, and entertainment. Using this information, write a description of how you might spend your day as a young person from Pompeii. Include details about what you might see and do in a day. If you have trouble getting started, use this beginning: "I start my day with a delicious breakfast of raisin and sugar cakes. Afterwards, I wander down to the forum to watch . . . ." You fill in the rest. Place your description in your **Working Portfolio.**

Speaking & Listening

Live News Report Naples and Pompeii lie on opposite sides of a large bay. Imagine you are safely in Naples on the day Vesuvius erupts. Write a live news report of what you see happening in Pompeii. Reread parts of the story to help you imagine what you would see. Use sensory details to help listeners see, hear, smell, and feel what is happening. Present your news report to your class.

Research & Technology

Dig It Archaeological discoveries have been made just about everywhere people have lived. Using the library or the Internet, find a newspaper or magazine article describing an archaeological discovery in your state. Write a summary of your findings and list the information source you used.

Reading *for* INFORMATION
Before beginning your research, read "A 9,500-Year-Old Summer Home" on page 714.

Art Connection

Informative Images In Pompeii, homeowners warned off robbers by placing mosaics like the one above at the entrance of their homes. On some of these mosaics, the words *Cave canem* (kä'wā kä'něm), meaning "Beware of Dog," appear. Even without this message, how can you tell that the mosaic serves as a warning? Use precise verbs, nouns, and adjectives to describe the mosaic.

Vocabulary

EXERCISE A: SYNONYMS AND ANTONYMS Identify each pair of words as synonyms or antonyms by writing *synonym* or *antonym* next to each on your paper. Then write a new synonym for each Word to Know.

1. **vapor**—fume
2. **restore**—destroy
3. **eruption**—explosion
4. **shrine**—temple
5. **dislodging**—replacing

EXERCISE B Draw pictures that show the meaning of each Word to Know. Hang them on a bulletin board and invite your classmates to guess which word each picture illustrates.

Vocabulary Handbook
See p. R22: Synonyms and Antonyms.

WORDS TO KNOW				
vapor	restore	eruption	shrine	dislodging

Grammar in Context: Independent and Dependent Clauses

Look at this sentence describing characters from Louis Untermeyer's "The Dog of Pompeii."

When Tito woke, Bimbo would be sitting quietly at his side.

The sentence is made up of two clauses—an **independent clause** and a **dependent clause.** The independent clause expresses a complete thought and can stand alone as a sentence. The dependent clause does not express a complete thought, so it cannot stand alone. Dependent clauses often begin with words such as *when, after, although,* and *if.* A dependent clause may come at the beginning or the end of a sentence.

WRITING EXERCISE Write these sentences on a sheet of paper. Underline each independent clause once and each dependent clause twice.

Example: *Original* After Tito fell asleep, Bimbo went off to find food.

Rewritten After Tito fell asleep, Bimbo went off to find food.

1. When the Caesar visited, the fireworks lasted for days.
2. Although Tito did not have a family, his dog took care of him.
3. Bimbo looked for food while Tito slept.
4. After Tito took a nap, he walked with Bimbo in the forum.
5. The volcano was ready to erupt when the smoke became very thick.

Grammar Handbook
See p. R83: Phrases and Clauses.

Louis Untermeyer
1885–1977

"Fantasy was the most important part of my boyhood—at least it is the only part I remember. "

Dreaming Days As a boy, Louis Untermeyer disliked school but read constantly. A storyteller at an early age, at bedtime he would tell his brother fantastic tales of his own creation.

From Goldsmith to Wordsmith While working successfully in the jewelry business for more than 20 years, Untermeyer spent much of his free time writing poems. After publishing a book of poems, he decided to devote all his time to writing.

Making Poets Popular Untermeyer made a name for himself as a poet, critic, and novelist. He is best known, however, as an editor of major poetry collections, many of which have been used to teach the art of poetry. He edited 56 collections and is credited with introducing the works of Robert Frost to a large audience.

AUTHOR ACTIVITY
Poetic Works Browse through one of Louis Untermeyer's poetry anthologies, such as *The Paths of Poetry: Twenty-Five Poets and Their Poems.* Choose one poem and explain in a paragraph why you like it.

Grammar in Context

WRITING EXERCISE
Answers:

1. When the Caesar visited, the fireworks lasted for days.
2. Although Tito did not have a family, his dog took care of him.
3. Bimbo looked for food while Tito slept.
4. After Tito took a nap, he walked with Bimbo in the forum.
5. The volcano was ready to erupt when the smoke became very thick.

Louis Untermeyer

Untermeyer lived and wrote into his nineties. On his ninetieth birthday, he announced that he was writing his third autobiography. "The other two were premature," he explained.

Author Activity

Poetic Works Students' choices will vary, but they should be able to explain what appeals to them about the poem.

EXPLICIT INSTRUCTION ## Grammar in Context

INDEPENDENT AND DEPENDENT CLAUSES
Instruction Explain that a clause is a group of words containing a verb and its subject. An independent clause can stand alone as a sentence. A dependent clause cannot stand alone as a sentence. Dependent clauses often begin with subordinate conjunctions such as *when, although, after, while,* and *if.* Write the following sentence on the board and identify the dependent and independent clauses: *Tito was never an unhappy boy, although he was not exactly a merry one.*

Practice Have students identify the independent and dependent clause in each sentence below.

1. After Tito ate breakfast, he went back to sleep.
2. Tito knew something was wrong when he felt the earth shake.
3. After Bimbo pulled Tito to the harbor, the dog disappeared.
4. When the scientists excavated the bakery, they found the skeleton of a dog.

 Use **Unit Five Resource Book,** p.57, for more practice.

For **systematic instruction** in grammar, see:
• **Grammar, Usage, and Mechanics Book**
• pacing chart on p. 609i

Reading *for* INFORMATION
NEWSPAPER ARTICLE
Real World Link to "The Dog of Pompeii"

Standards-Based Objectives

You can use this selection to achieve one or more of the following objectives:
- read to be informed
- use text organizers to locate and organize information, including headings
- determine a text's main ideas and how those ideas are supported with details
- paraphrase and summarize informational text

Connecting to the Literature

This newspaper article, "A 9,500-Year-Old Summer Home," is a companion piece to "The Dog of Pompeii" because it deals with a similar situation: the discovery of a site that had been buried by a volcanic eruption. However, unlike the historical fiction story, which takes place half a world away, this site is in the United States, and it was found recently. The article explains how the buried site was discovered in October of 1998, what the "house" contained, and what researchers learned from the buried artifacts.

Use **Writing Transparencies**, p. 42, for additional support.

LESSON RESOURCES

UNIT FIVE RESOURCE BOOK, pp. 60–61

SKILLS TRANSPARENCIES AND COPYMASTERS

Writing
- Using the Library Catalog, TR 42 (p. 714)

---

① LOS ANGELES TIMES • OCTOBER 10, 1998

Science

Excavators work on the floor of a 9,500-year-old house in Oregon that was preserved by a layer of volcanic ash.

A 9,500-Year-Old Summer Home

by Thomas H. Maugh II

② Researchers in Oregon have found the remains of what appears to be the oldest house ever discovered in the United States, a 9,500-year-old lakeside dwelling that is providing new insights into the lives of some of the continent's earliest inhabitants.

The structural remains were unearthed in central Oregon by construction workers enlarging a road into the Newberry National Volcanic Monument, archaeologist[1] Tom Connolly of the University of Oregon will report today at the Great Basin Archaeology Conference in Eugene.

---

1. **archaeologist** (är′kē-ŏl′ə-jĭst): a scientist who studies the material evidence—such as buildings, tools, and pottery—remaining from past cultures.

EXPLICIT INSTRUCTION **Reading a Newspaper Article**

Instruction Tell students that they can get information from newspaper articles not only by reading the text but also by looking closely at special features, such as pictures, captions, graphs, and maps. Tell them that specific features of newspapers, such as datelines, bylines, and headlines, are also important sources of information. Ask volunteers to identify the features in this article. Then have students read and examine the various features and explain what they think the article will be about.

Practice Have students work in pairs to read and complete the numbered activities on the pupil pages.

Possible Responses: See the side columns in the teacher's edition for possible responses to the activities on the pupil pages.

Use **Unit Five Resource Book,** p. 60, for more practice.

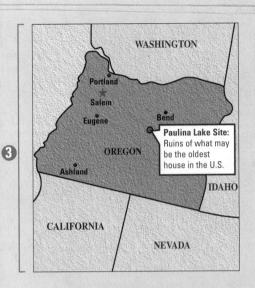

Paulina Lake Site: Ruins of what may be the oldest house in the U.S.

His team has discovered not only the remains of the house, but a variety of tools, food remnants and other artifacts that paint the most comprehensive picture available of everyday life not long after humans first arrived on this continent.

"This find adds a great deal of detail to our understanding of how these people lived their lives," Connolly said. "Our ideas were previously based on small bits of information gathered here and there—a kind of conjectural[2] view. Now we have lots of solid evidence."

Connolly has tentatively identified what appear to be the remains from several other dwellings nearby, suggesting that the site was a summer encampment on the shores of Paulina Lake in Newberry Crater.

"The site is unique . . . and the oldest in the United States as far as I know," said archaeologist Kenneth Ames of Portland State University. "The next oldest one dates from only 7,500 years before the present."

---

2. **conjectural** (kən-jĕk′chər-əl): based on partial evidence and logical guesswork.

Reading for Information

Newspaper articles can be good sources of current information. Like other kinds of informative nonfiction, newspaper articles present factual information about real people, places, and events. They also include pictures and other structural features and text organizers to provide information and clarify ideas.

Reading a Newspaper Article

When you look at a newspaper article, you will usually find at least some of the features listed below. These features give basic information about the article, such as who wrote it and where it takes place.

- **Headline** a short, attention-getting title
- **Byline** the name of the reporter who wrote the article
- **Dateline** where the article takes place

Another feature found on almost every page of a newspaper is the **folio.** The folio is a line at the top of the page that shows the name of the newspaper, the date, and, sometimes, the page number. You should record this information if you plan to use a newspaper article as a source for a research report.

YOUR TURN *Use the questions and activities below to get the most from reading a newspaper article.*

❶ What newspaper did this article come from? On what day was the article published?

❷ What is the article's headline? Who wrote the article? What do you think this article is about?

❸ Newspaper articles may contain a variety of informational features, such as maps, charts, and diagrams. These are called **infographics.** When you look at an infographic, you can get information quickly. What do you learn from the map?

Reading for Information

As you go through the article with students, suggest that they use the material in the right-hand column as a guide to reading newspaper articles effectively. The following are possible responses to the questions and activities:

1. Los Angeles Times; October 10, 1998
2. Headline: A 9,500-Year-Old Summer Home; Writer: Thomas H. Maugh II; students might say this article will be about a very old house.
3. I learn that the house referred to in the title may be the oldest house in the U.S. I also learn exactly where it is located.

EXPLICIT INSTRUCTION Using Databases: The Computer Library Catalog

Instruction Ask how many students have used a library's computer catalog to find materials. Have a volunteer explain how he or she uses the catalog. Tell students that the library catalog contains information about all of the items the library owns, including books, periodicals, maps, and audiovisual materials. In order to find materials, students need to know how to use the search features of the catalog. Explain that students can search the computer catalog using an author's name, a title, or a subject. Say, "Searching by subject is often the easiest way to find materials on a research topic." Ask students to name keywords they might use to find books on archaeological sites in the U.S. *(archaeology United States; U.S. archaeology sites; ruins United States)*

Practice Have groups of students list the steps involved in conducting a computer catalog search and locating a book on the shelf after finding its title through the catalog. Have groups present their steps.

Possible Responses: (1) Develop a list of keyterms for searching. (2) Enter keyterms in catalog. (3) Look at the results and write down the author, title, and call number of useful books. (4) Use the call number to find the book on the shelf.

Use **Unit Five Resource Book,** p. 61, for more practice.

LOS ANGELES TIMES • OCTOBER 10, 1998

The site is fairly well preserved because it was buried in the massive eruption of Mt. Mazama about 7,500 years ago. That eruption, several times larger than the 1980 explosion at Mt. St. Helens, formed what is now Crater Lake. Although Newberry Crater is about 50 miles away from Mt. Mazama, it was nonetheless buried in at least two feet of volcanic ash, protecting the remains of the dwelling.

The burial also aided dating because anything below the ash has to be at least 7,500 years old, Connolly said.

Newberry Crater is a volcanic caldera,[3] formed from a massive eruption about 200,000 years ago. Researchers have found traces of 25 small eruptions in the caldera over the last 10,000 years, the most recent occurring about 1,300 years ago.

Alerted by construction workers, Connolly discovered a large fire hearth and the remains of structural posts enclosing an oval area about 14 feet across and 18 feet wide. Radiocarbon dating[4] of the posts indicates an age of about 9,490 years.

Charred fragments from the hearth are a few hundred years older, Connolly said, but the residents may have been burning fuel that had been dead for many years.

The dating indicates that the residents belonged to the Windust group of Native Americans, named after earlier discoveries in the Windust caves along the Columbia River. The Windust people, mobile tribes of hunter-gatherers, were in the region as early as 11,000 years ago. They did not settle down into permanent villages until about 4,000 to 5,000 years ago, according to Ames, which supports the idea that the newly discovered house was part of a temporary summer settlement.

Other scientists had previously unearthed about 70 pairs of sandals made of sagebrush bark, dating from the same period as the new Paulina Lake discovery, at Fort Rock Cave, about 25 miles away from the Paulina site.

Connolly's group also found chipped-stone and obsidian cutting, grinding and abrading tools, as well as a stone pestle that could have been used for pulping roots, breaking up bones and other purposes. The obsidian was traced to a site more than 60 miles away, indicating that the people "had a pretty substantial range" of movement, he said.

> **The Windust people, . . . were in the region as early as 11,000 years ago.**

Dr. Dennis Jenkins examines stone tools that may have been used for cutting meat and grinding food.

---

3. **caldera** (kăl-dâr′ə): a crater formed by a volcanic explosion.

4. **radiocarbon dating:** a method to tell the approximate age of an ancient object by the amount of carbon 14 that it contains.

4. **Possible Response:** The pulled quotation says that the Windust people were in the region as early as 11,000 years ago. This might be an important clue about who lived in the 9,500-year-old house.

5. The first picture shows excavators digging up the house. The caption gives details about what part of the house they are digging in and what the soil is like. The second picture shows a man digging up something small. The caption tells me that the man is a doctor—probably a scientist—and that he is looking at stone tools that might have been used with food. The third picture shows another angle of the dig. The caption tells me that a very large volcanic explosion covered the house with ash.

The remains of the house were buried under at least two feet of ash from a volcanic explosion several times larger than the Mt. St. Helens eruption of 1980.

⑤

Blood traces on the tools suggest that the dwelling's residents hunted bison, rabbit, bear, sheep and deer or elk—all of which would have been abundant.

Remnants in the hearth indicate that they ate chokeberries, hazelnuts, blackberries and other fruits and nuts. They also processed hardwood bark, bulrushes and other plants to make baskets, clothing, and floor and roof coverings.

They kept warm and cooked with fires from lodgepole pine, ponderosa pine and sagebrush. The region was probably a ponderosa pine forest at the time, Connolly said, but destruction of the forest by Mazama's eruption allowed lodgepole pine to displace it.

Connolly has found another central hearth nearby and traces of other houses, but no other structural remains. "We have one house that we are sure of, and suggestions of others," he said.

And the modern road? That underwent "significant design changes" to protect the site, he said.

Reading for Information *continued*

④ Both magazine and newspaper articles may take a quotation from a story and show it in large type. This is called a **pulled quotation;** it usually shows an important or interesting piece of information from the story. What information is given in this pulled quotation? How might this information be important to the story?

⑤ A **caption** gives information about a photograph or an illustration. Look at the photographs in this article and read the captions. What do you learn about the article from these features?

Research & Technology
Activity Link: "The Dog of Pompeii,"
p. 712. Locate a newspaper article about an archaeologist or an archaeological discovery. Take notes on the headline, byline, and other features you just learned about. Present your notes and a summary of the article to the class.

EXPLICIT INSTRUCTION **Research & Technology**

The Research & Technology activity on this page links to the Research & Technology activity in the Choices & Challenges section on page 712.

Instruction Explain that before students read the article they have chosen, they should examine the structural features, such as headlines, maps, photos, and captions, to gather information. Remind them that reporters need to find answers to the following questions: *Who? What? Where? When? Why? How?* Explain that such questions usually cover most of the important details and can be used to help students write a summary.

Practice After students have found articles about archaeologists (or discoveries), have them survey the features of the articles. Then have students begin their analysis by asking questions that begin with *Who, What, Where, When, Why,* and *How.* After they have asked and answered these questions, they can write their summaries.

This selection is included in the **Grade 6 InterActive Reader.**

Standards-Based Objectives

1. understand and appreciate **informative nonfiction**
2. **analyze patterns of organization**
3. clarify an understanding of a text by **creating a summary**

Summary

The archaeologist who led the team that discovered King Tut's tomb reaped the rewards after many years of hard work. The story of Howard Carter's fantastic find is fascinating, not only for the riches he unearthed, but also for the tale it tells about the value of persistence and thoroughness.

Thematic Link

The work of Howard Carter and other archaeologists reveals much about how ancient peoples lived—their beliefs, their food, their clothing, and even their furniture.

English Conventions Practice

Daily Language SkillBuilder

Have students **proofread** the display sentences on page 609k and write them correctly. The sentences also appear on Transparency 22 of **Language Transparencies.**

Preteaching Vocabulary

If you would like to preteach the WORDS TO KNOW for this selection, use the Explicit Instruction, page 720.

PREPARING to *Read*

Across the Curriculum
Social Studies

INFORMATIVE NONFICTION

Tutankhamen
from Lost Worlds
by ANNE TERRY WHITE

Connect to Your Life

What do you know about burial practices in ancient Egypt?

Build Background

For more than 1,000 years, ancient Egyptians built great pyramids as tombs for their kings, or pharaohs (fâr′ōs). The treasures of these tombs were often stolen by grave robbers. By the 15th century B.C., pharaohs were no longer buried in pyramids. Instead, their tombs were hidden underground. More than 60 tombs have been discovered in what became known as the Valley of the Kings.

The Great Pyramid
king's burial chamber

The most famous pyramids, now thousands of years old, are near Cairo.

passageway

The jackal-headed god Anubis was believed to accompany the pharaohs after death.

Focus Your Reading

LITERARY ANALYSIS INFORMATIVE NONFICTION
Writing that provides factual information is called **informative nonfiction.** Forms of informative nonfiction include science and history textbooks, encyclopedias, and most of the articles in magazines and newspapers.

> **WORDS TO KNOW Vocabulary Preview**
> dissuade intact sentinel systematically tedious

ACTIVE READING PATTERNS OF ORGANIZATION
If you know how facts are organized it is easier to recall them later. Informative nonfiction may be organized in many ways, such as **cause and effect, comparison and contrast, chronological order,** or **spatial order.** As you read, ask yourself how the piece is organized. How would you describe the organization? Make note in your ▯ READER'S NOTEBOOK of the most important idea or fact in each paragraph.

718 UNIT FIVE PART 2: VOICES FROM THE PAST

LESSON RESOURCES

UNIT FIVE RESOURCE BOOK, pp. 62–68

ASSESSMENT
Formal Assessment, pp. 117–118
Test Generator

SKILLS TRANSPARENCIES AND COPYMASTERS
Reading and Critical Thinking
• Text Structure (Organization) TR 24 (pp. 720, 725)
Language
• Daily Language SkillBuilder, TR 22 (p. 718)
• Context Clues: Definition and Overview, TR 53 (p. 720)
Writing
• Writing Variables, TR 2 (p. 726)

INTEGRATED TECHNOLOGY
Audio Library
Internet: Research Starter

Visit our Web site:
www.mcdougallittell.com

For **systematic instruction** in language skills, see:
• **Vocabulary and Spelling Book**
• **Grammar, Usage, and Mechanics Book**
• pacing chart on p. 609i

TUTANKHAMEN

FROM

LOST

WORLDS

BY

ANNE TERRY WHITE

One of the four miniature coffins that
contained Tutankhamen's internal organs.
Copyright © Boltin Picture Library.

719

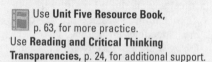
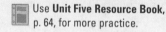
*Five seasons had passed and the British
archaeologist Howard Carter and his financial
supporter, Lord Carnarvon, had failed in their
search for the tomb of Pharaoh Tutankh-amen.
Howard Carter remained convinced that he
was close to the 3,200-year-old tomb. Carter
persuaded Lord Carnarvon that the tomb most
likely lay in the center of the Valley of the
Kings. In November 1922, Carter and his crew
began uncovering the area near the tomb of
Rameses VI—the only section that had not
been dug up in the Valley of the Kings.*

Now Carnarvon and Carter were not
planning to dig at random in the
Valley of the Tombs of the Kings.
They were on the lookout for a particular
tomb, the tomb of the Pharaoh Tutankhamen,
and they believed they had worked out the
location where it lay. To the eyes of most
people their undertaking seemed absurd.
Nearly everybody was convinced that
Tutankhamen's tomb had already been found.
But Lord Carnarvon and Mr. Carter were not
to be <u>dissuaded</u>, for they believed that the pit-
tomb containing the fragments bearing the
figures and names of Tutankhamen and his
queen was far too small and insignificant for a
king's burial. In their opinion the things had
been placed there at some later time and did
not indicate that the Pharaoh himself had been
buried on the spot. They were convinced that
the tomb of Tutankhamen was still to be
found, and that the place they had chosen—
the center of the Valley—was the best place to
look for it. In that vicinity had been unearthed
something which they considered very good
evidence—two jars containing broken bits of

things that had been used at the funeral
ceremonies of King Tutankhamen.

Nevertheless, when in the autumn of 1917
the excavators came out to look over the spot
they had chosen and to begin their Valley
campaign in earnest, even they thought it was
a desperate undertaking. The site was piled
high with refuse thrown out by former
excavators. They would have to remove all
that before they could begin excavating in
virgin soil.[1] But they had made up their minds
and meant to go through with it; even though
it took many seasons, they would go
<u>systematically</u> over every inch of ground.

In the years that followed, they did. They
went over every inch, with the exception of a
small area covered with the ruins of stone
huts that had once sheltered workmen
probably employed in building the tomb of
Rameses VI.[2] These huts lay very near the
tomb of the Pharaoh on a spot which Carter
and Carnarvon had not touched for reasons of
courtesy. The tomb of Rameses VI was a
popular show place in the valley, and digging
in the area of the huts would have cut off
visitors to the tomb. They let it be, and
turned instead to another site which they felt
had possibilities.

The new ground proved, however, no better
than the old, and now Lord Carnarvon began
to wonder whether with so little to show for
six seasons' work they were justified in going
on. But Carter was firm. So long as a single
area of unturned ground remained, he said,
they ought to risk it. There was still the area

 1

---

1. **virgin soil:** ground that has not been dug up or explored.
2. **Rameses** (răm′ĭ-sēz′) **VI:** a Pharaoh whose tomb was
   built higher on the hill, above Tutankhamen's.

WORDS
TO
KNOW

dissuade (dĭ-swād′) *v.* to persuade someone not to do something; discourage
systematically (sĭs′tə-măt′ĭk-lē) *adv.* in an orderly, thorough manner

720

Howard Carter (left) and Lord Carnarvon at the entrance to Pharoah Tutankhamen's tomb, February 1923.

The Griffith Institute, Ashmolean Museum, Oxford, England.

of the huts. He insisted on going back to it. On November first, 1922, he had his diggers back in the old spot.

And now things happened with such suddenness that Carter afterward declared they left him in a dazed condition. Coming to work on the fourth day after the digging on the little area had started, he saw at once that something extraordinary had happened. Things were too quiet; nobody was digging and hardly anybody was talking. He hurried forward, and there before him was a shallow step cut in the rock beneath the very first hut attacked! He could hardly believe his eyes. After all the disappointments of the past six seasons, was it possible that he was actually on the threshold[3] of a great discovery? He gave the command to dig, and the diggers fell to work with a will. By the next afternoon Carter was able to see the upper edges of a stairway on all its four sides, and before very long there stood revealed twelve steps, and at the level of the twelfth the upper part of a sealed and plastered doorway.

Carter's excitement was fast reaching fever **[2]** pitch. Anything, literally anything, might lie beyond. It needed all his self-control to keep from breaking the doorway down and satisfying his curiosity then and there. But was it fair to see what lay beyond that door alone? Although Lord Carnarvon was in England, was it not his discovery as much as Carter's? To the astonishment of the workmen, the excavator gave orders to fill the stairway in again, and then he sent the following cable off to Carnarvon: "At last have made wonderful discovery in Valley. A magnificent tomb with seals <u>intact</u>. Recovered same for **[3]** your arrival. Congratulations."

---

3. **threshold:** an entrance or beginning.

WORDS
TO
KNOW **intact** (ĭn-tăkt′) *adj.* whole and undamaged

721

Ask students to tell what they learn from skimming these two pages—getting an overview by moving their eyes rapidly over the text and illustration. Then ask them to scan—to look for a specific fact by sweeping their eyes over each page—to find out where the golden couches and other riches lay.

Possible Response: By skimming, I can tell that these two pages are about what Carter and Carnarvon found after the workers broke down the door. By scanning, I learned that these riches are in an antechamber, a small room leading to a larger room.

Reading Skills and Strategies:
CLARIFY

Ask students to explain how they keep track of the various doors and rooms that are mentioned in this part of the selection.

Possible Response: I was a little confused by all the doors, so I reread this part to clarify the layout in my mind.

Literary Analysis: MAIN IDEA AND DETAILS

A Ask students to identify the main idea of this paragraph on page 723. Then have them identify two details.

Possible Response: The main idea of this paragraph is that Carter and Carnarvon have made an amazing discovery of riches. Two of the details are the golden couches and inlaid caskets.

Some of the artifacts discovered in Tutankhamen's tomb. Note the numbered labels used to catalogue the objects.
Valley of the Kings antechamber, west side with numbers (Egyptian Dynasty XVIII, Thebes). Photo by Egyptian Expedition, The Metropolitan Museum of Art. Copyright © The Metropolitan Museum of Art, all rights reserved.

As he waited for Lord Carnarvon to come, Carter found it hard to persuade himself at times that the whole episode had not been a dream. The entrance to the tomb was only thirteen feet below the entrance to the tomb of Rameses VI. No one would have suspected the presence of a tomb so near the other. Had he actually found a flight of steps? Was it really there under the sand, waiting to conduct him to the great mystery?

1 In two weeks' time Lord Carnarvon and his daughter were on the spot. Carter now ordered his men to clear the stairway once more, and there on the lower part of the sealed doorway the explorers beheld what almost took their breath away—the seal of the Pharaoh Tutankhamen. Now they knew. Beyond this doorway lay either the Pharaoh's secret treasure store or else the very tomb for which they were searching. Yet one thing made them uneasy. They noticed that part of the door was patched up and that in the patched-up part there stood out clearly the seal of the cemetery. It was evident that the door had been partly broken down—by robbers, of course—and then patched up again by cemetery officials. Had the robbers been caught in time? Did at least some of Tutankhamen's glory yet remain behind that twice-sealed doorway? Or would perhaps only barren walls reward their years of <u>tedious</u> toil?

WORDS TO KNOW   **tedious** (tē′dē-əs) *adj.* long, tiring, and boring

722

Cross Curricular Link Social Studies

KING TUTANKHAMEN AND LATER DISCOVERIES

King Tutankhamen, known as the Boy Pharaoh, ruled Egypt for about ten years in the mid-14th century B.C. Historians are uncertain how he died or who his parents were. Tutankhamen, encouraged by his minister of state, Ay, restored the ancient religion of Egypt, which recognized many gods and goddesses. After the Pharaoh's death, Ay directed his burial in the Valley of the Kings, and then he ruled briefly as king. Tutankhamen's tomb may be the most spectacular of the Egyptian tombs unearthed, but it was not the last. In 1996, archaeologists discovered a 2,000 year old cemetery at the Bahariya Oasis. The discovery was made after a donkey slipped into an opening to one of the tombs. More than 100 mummies of men, women, and children have been found. Perhaps the most amazing fact of all is that looters had never found this site, and therefore, it contains a wealth of well-preserved artifacts. It may take archaeologists a decade to examine everything.

With pounding hearts they broke down the door. Beyond lay only another obstacle to their progress—a passage filled with stone. Had the robbers got beyond that? They began slowly to clear away the stone, and on the following day—"the day of days," Carter called it, "and one whose like I can never hope to see again"—they came upon a second sealed doorway, almost exactly like the first and also bearing distinct signs of opening and reclosing.

His hands trembling so that he could scarcely hold a tool, Carter managed to make a tiny hole in the door and to pass a candle through it. At first he could see nothing, but as his eyes grew accustomed to the light, "details of the room slowly emerged from the mist, strange animals, statues, and gold—everywhere the glint of gold."

"Can you see anything?" Carnarvon asked anxiously as Carter stood there dumb with amazement.

"Yes, wonderful things!" was all the explorer could get out.

And no wonder. What he saw was one of the most amazing sights anybody has ever been privileged to see. It seemed as if a whole museumful of objects was in that room. Three gilt[4] couches, their sides carved in the form of monstrous animals, and two statues of a king, facing each other like two <u>sentinels</u>, were the most prominent things in the room, but all around and between were hosts of other things—inlaid caskets, alabaster vases, shrines, beds, chairs, a golden inlaid throne, a heap of white boxes (which they later found were filled with trussed ducks and other food offerings), and a glistening pile of overturned chariots. When Carter and Carnarvon got their senses together again, they realized all at once that there was no coffin in the room. Was this then merely a hiding place for treasure? They

examined the room very intently once again, and now they saw that the two statues stood one on either side of a sealed doorway. Gradually the truth dawned on them. They were but on the threshold of their discovery. What they saw was just an antechamber.[5] Behind the guarded door there would be other rooms, perhaps a whole series of them, and in one of them, beyond any shadow of doubt they would find the Pharaoh lying.

But as they thought the thing over, the explorers were by no means certain that their first wild expectations would actually come to pass. Perhaps that sealed doorway, like the two before it, had also been re-opened. In that case there was no telling what lay behind it.

On the following day they took down the door through which they had been peeping, and just as soon as the electric connections had been made and they could see things clearly, they rushed over to the doubtful door between the royal sentinels. From a distance it had looked untouched, but when they examined it more closely, they saw that here again the robbers had been before them; near the bottom was distinct evidence that a small hole had been made and filled up and resealed. The robbers had indeed been stopped, but not before they had got into the inner chamber.

It took almost as much self-command not to break down that door and see how much damage the robbers had done as to have filled in the staircase after it had once been cleared. But Carter and Carnarvon were not treasure-seekers; they were archaeologists, and they

---

4. **gilt:** covered with a layer of gold.
5. **antechamber** (ăn′tē-chām′bər): a small room leading to a larger one.

WORDS TO KNOW

sentinel (sĕn′tə-nəl) *n.* one who keeps watch; guard

723

English Learners

1 Point out the word *beheld.* Tell students that *beheld* is the past tense of *behold,* which means "to look upon; gaze at."

2 Point out the word *dumb.* Tell students that in this context *dumb* means "unable to speak." Explain that Carter knew how to talk, but that he was so amazed by what he saw that he was speechless.

Less Proficient Readers

Encourage students to make a diagram showing the path that the excavators took. Their diagrams should show the stairway, the various doors, the rooms between the doors, and some of the contents of the rooms. Students can refer to their diagrams as they read to keep track of the workers' progress and to help visualize what they are reading.

Advanced Students

This selection offers an example of great discoveries that were made after a painstaking effort. Ask students to name other discoveries that required such effort.

Possible Responses: Thomas Edison went through dozens of possible filaments before he found the right one; Marie Curie went through large quantities of rock to isolate a tiny amount of radium; the men and women of NASA went through many years of innovation, bravery, and hard work to put a human on the moon.

EXPLICIT INSTRUCTION **Effects of Imagery**

Instruction Tell students that nonfiction writers use imagery—words that appeal to readers' five senses—to help readers visualize what is being described and to make factual accounts interesting. Read aloud the paragraph on page 723 that begins, "And no wonder. What he saw was one of the most amazing sights." Have students read along silently.

Practice Have students work in small groups to identify imagery in the paragraph that you read aloud. Have students list the examples of imagery and describe the mental picture they

created as they read the paragraph. Ask students if the writer's use of imagery made the facts more interesting.

Possible Responses: "It seemed as if a whole museumful of objects was in that room: gilt couches, their sides carved in the form of monstrous animals;" "two statues of a king, facing each other like two sentinels;" "a heap of white boxes; a glistening pile of overturned chariots." The imagery helped me imagine what the men found and how excited they must have been.

Ask students to describe the order of events chronologically, beginning with the discovery of the first step.

Possible Response: On November 1, 1922, workers found the step. The next day, they unearthed the stairway and the upper part of a sealed doorway. Then Carter told the workers to fill in the stairway, and he sent a cable to Carnarvon. Two weeks later, Carnarvon and his daughter arrived. Workers cleared the stairway, revealing the doorway with Tutankhamen's seal. Workers broke down the doorway, revealing a passage filled with stones. They cleared the stones, then found a second sealed doorway. Carter made a small hole in the door and passed a candle through it, seeing many precious objects, but no coffin. The next day, workers removed the doorway to the antechamber. After entering the antechamber, the crew found another doorway that had been resealed. Then they discovered a small hole, looked through it, and saw another chamber filled with even more objects.

RELATED READING

Reading Skills and Strategies: CLARIFY

Have students read "Ancestors," paraphrase the questions that Dudley Randall poses, and explain their meaning.

Possible Response: Randall asks why history pays so much attention to royalty and so little to everyday people. He wonders whether everyone was a king. The questions posed by this poem say that history books make it seem as if only kings and princes were important.

would not take the chance of injuring the objects within the antechamber just to satisfy their curiosity. For the moment they let that go and turned their attention to the things already before them.

There was enough there to leave them altogether bewildered. But while they were yet going crazily from one object to another and calling excitedly to each other, they stumbled on yet another discovery. In the wall, hidden behind one of the monstrous couches, was a small, irregular hole, unquestionably made by the plunderers[6] and never re-sealed. They dragged their powerful electric light to the hole and looked in. Another chamber, smaller than the one they were in, but even more crowded with objects! And everything was in the most amazing mess they had ever seen. The cemetery officials had made some attempt to clean up the antechamber after the robbers and to pile up the funeral furniture in some sort of order, but in the annex they had left things just as they were, and the robbers had done their work "about as thoroughly as an earthquake." Not a single inch of floor space remained unlittered.

Carter and Carnarvon drew a long breath and sobered down. They realized now that the job before them was going to take months and months. It would be a monumental task to photograph, label, mend, pack, and ship all this furniture, clothing, food, these chariots, weapons, walking sticks, jewels—this museumful of treasures. ❖

---

6. **plunderers:** people who invade a place to rob and destroy it.

ANCESTORS

BY DUDLEY RANDALL

Why are our ancestors
always kings or princes
and never the common people?

Was the Old Country a democracy
where every man was a king?
Or did the slavecatchers
take only the aristocracy[1]
and leave the fieldhands
laborers
streetcleaners
garbage collectors
dishwashers
cooks
and maids
behind?

My own ancestor
(research reveals)
was a swineherd
who tended the pigs
in the Royal Pigstye
and slept in the mud
among the hogs.

Yet I'm as proud of him
as of any king or prince
dreamed up in fantasies
of bygone glory.

---

1. **aristocracy** (ăr′ĭ-stŏk′rə-sē): nobility; rulers.

Forms of Fiction

Instruction Discuss with students the differences between fiction and nonfiction. Then ask students how they might use the information in this selection to write a piece of historical fiction. Who would be the main characters? How many different settings would there be? What dramatic events would take place? Discuss students' ideas. Then remind students that there are different forms of fiction, such as short story and novel. Ask students to name the similarities and differences between these forms. *(Both contain elements of setting, character, plot, and theme.*

Novel—longer than a short story; more complex; elements of setting, character, conflict, and plot are developed in greater detail. Short story—short enough to be read in one sitting; usually tells about one main conflict and one set of events.)

Practice Ask students which form they would use to write the historical fiction piece on the discovery of Tutankhamen's tomb. Have students write a paragraph about their ideas and the reasons for their choice. Invite students to share their paragraphs.

Possible Responses: Responses will vary.

Use **Unit Five Resource Book,** p. 65, to give students more practice in understanding forms of fiction.

Connect to the Literature

1. **What Do You Think?**
   How did you react to this account of the discovery of Tutankhamen's tomb?

   Comprehension Check
   • Why did people think Carter's search for the tomb was "absurd"?
   • What did Carter hope to find in the tomb?
   • What was behind each of the three sealed doors?

Think Critically

2. What traits do you think Carnarvon and Carter show in their efforts to locate the tomb?

3. Why did Carter feel it was important to find the king's coffin, even though they had already found so much?

4. Tutankhamen was not a particularly important ruler. Why is his tomb so interesting to historians?

   Think About:
   • the condition of other tombs
   • what might be learned from the objects found in the tomb

5. Based on the artifacts found in the tomb, what can you say about the beliefs of the ancient Egyptians? Give reasons for your answer.

6. **ACTIVE READING** **PATTERNS OF ORGANIZATION**

   Look at your notes in your **READER'S NOTEBOOK**. How would you describe the organization of this piece? How did the **organization** help you to find or to remember the facts in the Comprehension Check questions above?

Extend Interpretations

7. **The Writer's Style** Recall that suspense is the feeling of tension and excitement that makes a reader curious about what happens next in a story. Reread the last page of the selection. What words and phrases help create suspense?

8. **Connect to Life** Dry air and sand preserved the buried treasures of Egyptian tombs for thousands of years. Do you think these artifacts should be left untouched, or made available for public viewing in museums? Explain your opinion.

Literary Analysis

INFORMATIVE NONFICTION Writing that provides factual information about real people, places, or events is called **informative nonfiction.** Because its main purpose is to inform, writing of this kind requires a great deal of research by the author to make sure the information is correct. Writers of informative nonfiction study materials such as reference books, diaries, and other sources to gather information.

REVIEW: SOURCES OF INFORMATION Writers of informative nonfiction use both primary and secondary sources to find out about historical subjects. A **primary source,** such as a journal, diary, or letter, presents firsthand knowledge. This means that the person who wrote the primary source actually witnessed the event he or she is writing about. A **secondary source,** such as a biography or reference book, presents indirect, secondhand information that is based on other people's experiences. If you were going to write a report on Carter's discoveries, what types of sources might you use?

Activity Look back through the selection. What are some sources Anne Terry White might have consulted before she wrote this account?

Connect to the Literature

1. **What Do You Think?**
   Students may have been curious throughout about what would happen next.

Comprehension Check
• People called the search "absurd," because they thought that the tomb had already been found.
• Carter hoped to find the coffin and mummy of the king and many important artifacts.
• Behind the first door lay a passage filled with stone; behind the second door lay a room with statues and gold objects, but no coffin; behind the third door lay another chamber, which contained objects in "the most amazing mess."

 Use Selection Quiz, **Unit Five Resource Book,** p. 68.

Think Critically

2. **Possible Response:** Carnarvon and Carter were persistent, enthusiastic, considerate, and energetic.

3. **Possible Response:** It was important to find the king's coffin because it would prove that the king had been buried there.

4. **Possible Response:** Tutankhamen's tomb was important because it was one of the very few to be discovered intact, and all the objects in it revealed valuable information about the lives of the ancient Egyptians.

5. **Possible Response:** The ancient Egyptians believed in a life after death in which the spirit needed all the usual earthly comforts.

6. Responses will vary. Students may say that the piece is organized in both chronological and spatial order. Knowing the latter would help them answer the third Comprehension Check question in particular.

Use **Reading and Critical Thinking Transparencies,** p. 24, for additional support.

Extend Interpretations

7. **The Writer's Style Possible Response:** Words and phrases that help create suspense include *going crazily, calling excitedly.*

8. **Connect to Life** Possible Responses: Artifacts should be made available for public viewing in museums because museums work hard to preserve and protect the artifacts. *Or:* Artifacts should be left untouched because the people who enclosed them in the tombs wished for them to remain that way.

Literary Analysis

Sources of Information **Possible Responses:** She would probably use primary sources, such as diaries or logs kept by Carter, Carnarvon, and others involved in the dig. She might also use secondary sources, such as museum catalogs and books about Carter.

Writing

Archaeological Catalog Students' descriptions will vary but should reflect some thought on the value of the objects chosen. As students compare their descriptions, remind them that some objects may have served several purposes.

 Use **Writing Transparencies,** p. 2, for additional support.

Speaking & Listening

Radio Drama Students' scenes should show their knowledge of King Tutankhamen, as well as their insight into the methods and approach taken by Carter and Carnarvon.

Research & Technology

Hieroglyphics Students could work in pairs or small groups to make this assignment easier. Tell students that hieroglyphs can be read from left to right, right to left, or even top to bottom in vertical columns. Hieroglyphs are used to tell a person's name and what he or she did. Sometimes they express prayers for the owner.

Vocabulary and Spelling

EXERCISE: CONTEXT CLUES

1. tedious
2. sentinel
3. dissuade
4. systematically
5. intact

SPELLING STRATEGY

1. historically
2. logically
3. systematically
4. basically

Writing

Archaeological Catalog Choose several items found in the tomb and write a description of each. Tell why each item was important and what it revealed. Compare your catalog with that of a classmate. Then place it in your **Working Portfolio.**

Writing Handbook

See p. R38: Using Language Effectively.

> This writing activity asks you to use a catalog form. To find out about other writing forms you might use when your purpose is to inform, see p. R31: Choosing a Form.

Speaking & Listening

Radio Drama Adapt the events in the selection into a radio drama. With a partner, improvise a scene in which Carter and Carnarvon unearth the pharaoh's long-buried tomb. Tape-record your drama and play it for the class or perform it live. Use the tone of your voice to show the excitement and the emotions the men felt.

Speaking and Listening Handbook

See p. R98: Oral Interpretation.

Research & Technology

HIEROGLYPHICS

An archaeological discovery in 1799 made it possible to read some hieroglyphics. Use encyclopedias and other reference materials to learn about this ancient form of Egyptian writing. Make a poster showing some common hieroglyphics and what they mean.

INTERNET **Research Starter**
www.mcdougallittell.com

Vocabulary and Spelling

EXERCISE: CONTEXT CLUES Write the Words to Know that best fill the blanks.

Those months in Egypt were the most exhausting of my life. Every day I spent long, __1__ hours digging under the hot sun. On the nights when I was the __2__, I stayed awake until dawn to guard our precious tools. My family wanted to __3__ me from this seemingly fruitless work, but I was too excited by the possibility of finding the tomb. Then one day, after we had __4__ examined miles of the valley, my shovel struck a buried door! My hands trembled as I scraped away the sand to reveal the beautiful gold seals, still __5__, that held it shut. Could the legendary tomb lie within?

Vocabulary Handbook

See p. R20: Context Clues.

SPELLING STRATEGY: WORDS ENDING IN -ALLY When forming an adverb with a word ending in the letter *c*, you should use the ending *-ally*, not *-ly*. For example, the correct form is *magically*, not *magicly*.

Rewrite each sentence using the correct form of the boldfaced word.

1. A selection such as "Tutankhamen" should be **historic** accurate.
2. Lord Carnarvon felt the tomb would **logic** be found in the center of the valley.
3. They **systematic** investigated the desert, inch by inch.
4. You might think that different parts of the valley looked **basic** the same.

Spelling Handbook

See p. R26.

> WORDS TO KNOW   dissuade   intact   sentinel   systematically   tedious

Grammar in Context: Complex Sentences

Anne Terry White varies her sentence structure in "Tutankhamen." One way she adds variety is by using **complex sentences.**

> **After Lord Carnarvon arrived,** the workers cleared the stairway.

A complex sentence contains one independent clause and one or more **dependent clauses.** In the sentence above, the words *the workers cleared the stairway* form an independent clause because these words can stand alone as a sentence. The words *After Lord Carnarvon arrived* form a dependent clause. These words cannot stand alone. Dependent clauses often begin with such words as *after, although, because, if, since,* and *when.*

Apply to Your Writing Add variety to your writing by using different types of sentences, such as simple, compound, and complex. In a complex sentence, you can place the dependent clause at the beginning or the end of the sentence.

WRITING EXERCISE Combine each pair of sentences into one complex sentence. Use the word in parentheses to turn one sentence in each pair into a dependent clause.

Example: *Original* (When) Carter made a small hole for a candle. The workers found another doorway.

Rewritten Carter made a small hole for a candle <u>when</u> the workers found another doorway.

1. (When) Carter started the project. Most people thought he would not find the tomb.
2. (Although) Carter would not give up his search. Lord Carnarvon started to lose hope.
3. (Because) Carter was determined. The tomb was finally found.
4. (Because) Some of Tutankhamen's treasures were missing. Robbers had stolen them.
5. (When) The archaeologists found many artifacts. They opened the chambers of the tomb.

Grammar Handbook
See p. R84: The Structure of Sentences.

Anne Terry White
1896–1980

"[Archaeology] has the fascination of the detective story, the charm of the jigsaw puzzle."

Sharing the Classics The first book by Anne Terry White was about Hebrew Bible figures; her second book was about William Shakespeare. She wrote the books to introduce her daughters to great works of literature in a way that would be both entertaining and easy to understand.

Amazing True Stories "Tutankhamen" is an excerpt from White's book *Lost Worlds: The Romance of Archaeology.* Considered one of the foremost writers of nonfiction for young people, she retold myths, legends, and folktales. Her other works include *Prehistoric America* and *Odysseus Comes Home from the Sea.*

AUTHOR ACTIVITY
Long-Lost Worlds Find out what other ancient subjects White has explored in her books. In an oral report, tell which one of these topics you would most like to learn about and why.

Grammar in Context
WRITING EXERCISE
Possible Responses:

1. When Carter started the project, most people thought he would not find the tomb.
2. Carter would not give up his search, although Lord Carnarvon started to lose hope.
3. Because Carter was determined, the tomb was finally found.
4. Some of Tutankhamen's treasures were missing because robbers had stolen them.
5. The archaeologists found many artifacts when they opened the chambers of the tomb.

Anne Terry White

Anne Terry White came to the United States from the Ukraine when she was eight years old. Her interest in her background is reflected in her book of Russian folktales.

Author Activity

Long-Lost Worlds Anne Terry White also wrote books about the underground railroad, the Atlantic slave trade, and the forced removal of the Cherokees from Georgia. Her wide-ranging interests were expressed in her many books.

EXPLICIT INSTRUCTION Grammar in Context

COMPLEX SENTENCES
Instruction Remind students that a complex sentence contains an independent clause (one that can stand alone as a sentence) and one or more dependent clauses (clauses that cannot stand alone as sentences). Dependent clauses are introduced by subordinating conjunctions, such as *when, although, while, until, after,* and *if.* Write the following complex sentence on the board: *Carter saw many treasures when he looked in the tomb.* Explain that it is a complex sentence because

it contains a dependent clause *(when he looked in the tomb)* and an independent clause *(Carter saw many treasures).* Point out the subordinating conjunction *when.*

Practice Have students underline each independent clause once and each dependent clause twice in the sentences below.

1. <u>The workers removed debris</u> <u>before they began to dig.</u>
2. <u>Carter thought he would find the tomb</u> <u>if he looked in the right place.</u>
3. <u>When the workers started digging,</u> <u>they</u>

didn't know the project would go on for years.

 Use **Unit Five Resource Book,** p. 66, for more practice.

For **systematic instruction** in grammar, see:
- **Grammar, Usage, and Mechanics Book**
- pacing chart on p. 609i

Summary

Ch'in Shih Huang Ti, the first emperor of China, had an obsessive fear of his own death. Although he searched for the secret of immortality, he also had the foresight to begin construction on his own tomb, which took 30 years to complete. According to legend, the tomb's incredible contents included miniature reproductions of Shih Huang Ti's 270 palaces, a solid copper burial chamber, and loaded crossbows poised to shoot intruders. The tomb lay covered with earth for many centuries until 1974, when a peasant plowing a nearby field uncovered a life-sized clay statue of a warrior. Further excavations revealed thousands of similar statues, all part of the emperor's "spirit army," who were meant to serve the dead ruler in the next world. Whether the tomb has been robbed or still holds the legendary treasures remains to be seen, as Chinese archaeologists are still slowly and carefully working their way toward the tomb site.

Thematic Link

In this selection, the voices from the past appear in the guise of the thousands of sculptures that embody the wishes of the emperor, the skill of his sculptors, and offer a picture of people from long ago.

The First Emperor
from The Tomb Robbers

by DANIEL COHEN

Connect to Your Life

Life Without End In the selection you are about to read, an early Chinese ruler searches for a secret that would let him live forever. What would be the advantages of living forever? What would be the disadvantages?

Build Background

HISTORY

Three dynasties, or ruling families, controlled ancient China from about 2000 to 256 B.C. In 256 B.C., the feudal state of Ch'in defeated the ruler of the Zhou (jō) dynasty. Ten years later a man named Cheng, the subject of this selection, became king of Ch'in. By 221 B.C., he had united all of China under the Ch'in dynasty.

Believing that he would live forever, and that his family's reign would last 10,000 generations, the new ruler created a new title. He added *shih* (shē), meaning "first," to *huang ti* (hwäng dē), meaning "emperor," and called himself Ch'in Shih Huang Ti. The Ch'in dynasty survived only 15 years, but it began 2,000 years of rule by emperors. Throughout the following seven major dynasties, Chinese emperors were called *huang ti.* Imperial rule lasted until 1912, when China became a republic.

WORDS TO KNOW
Vocabulary Preview

consolidate	preservation	tyrant
immortality	proclaim	unparalleled
insignificant	reproduction	
intricate	surpass	

Focus Your Reading

LITERARY ANALYSIS **INFORMATIVE NONFICTION**

The selection you are about to read is another example of **informative nonfiction.** It provides factual information about a historical figure—the first emperor of China. As you read, look for facts about the first emperor and his tomb.

ACTIVE READING **MAIN IDEA AND DETAILS**

In informative nonfiction, you can figure out the writer's most important points by identifying the **main idea** of each paragraph. The main idea may be stated at the beginning, middle, or end of the paragraph. It may also be unstated but suggested by **details.** As you read, note the main ideas and supporting details in at least five different paragraphs. Jot down this information in your
READER'S NOTEBOOK.

AMBITION 志

DESTINY 命

ETERNITY 求

LOYALTY 忠

The First EMPEROR

from *The Tomb Robbers* by Daniel Cohen

729

Less Proficient Readers
Tell students that this selection is about a powerful ruler who lived in China more than two thousand years ago.
Set a Purpose Ask students to read to learn about the many accomplishments of the first emperor of China.

English Learners
Because much of this selection is speculative, words and phrases such as *may, it is said, according to legend,* and *authorities believe* are sprinkled throughout. List them on the chalkboard, and explain to students that these words signal that whatever follows is a likely conclusion, but is not a hard fact.

 Use **Spanish Study Guide,** pp. 148–150, for additional support.

Advanced Students
Tell students that there are different systems for translating ancient Chinese names into English. They will find the dynasty name of *Ch* is written also as *Qin,* and *Shih Huang Ti* is also written *She Huangdi.* If students are studying ancient civilizations in social studies, they may have covered the policies and achievements of Emperor Shih Huang Ti in unifying Northern China. Encourage them to read more from *The Tomb Robbers,* and to find other accounts of the archaeological digs at this fascinating site.

Preteaching Vocabulary

WORDS TO KNOW
Remind students that they can infer meanings of unfamiliar words by applying their knowledge of **root words, prefixes,** and **suffixes.**
Teaching Strategy Write *consolidate* on the chalkboard. Draw lines before and after the root *solid.* Explain that a prefix and a suffix have been added to a root word to form this derivative word. Knowing that *solid* means "firm or compact" gives a clue to the meaning of *consolidate,* "to bring together, to make strong or secure." If students also know that *con-* means "together or with," and

-ate means "become, cause, or make," they have a good idea of the word's meaning.
Practice Have students look up each of the other WORDS TO KNOW in a dictionary and list the roots, prefixes, and suffixes that make up each one. Then have them write a sentence using each word.

Use **Unit Five Resource Book,** p. 74, for more practice.

For **systematic instruction** in vocabulary, see:
• **Vocabulary and Spelling Book**
• pacing chart on p. 609i

Active Reading

MAIN IDEA AND DETAILS

Ask students to identify the main idea of the opening paragraph. Then ask them to list several details that support the main idea.

Possible Response: Main idea—The tomb of the emperor Ch'in Shih Huang Ti may be the greatest archeological find of all times. Details—Unlike Tutankhamen, Ch'in was enormously important in Chinese history. In some ways, he was the founder of China.

 Use **Unit Five Resource Book,** p. 70, for more practice. Use **Reading and Critical Thinking Transparencies**, p. 25, for additional support.

Literary Analysis

INFORMATIVE NONFICTION

Remind students that many of the articles they read in newspapers and magazines are informative nonfiction. As students read this selection, have them keep a list of 5 pieces of factual information.

Use **Unit Five Resource Book,** p. 71, for more practice.

Literary Analysis: AUTHOR'S PURPOSE

Guide students to recall the different purposes of various types of texts such as to inform, to influence, to express, or to entertain. Ask students what the author's primary purpose seems to be for this selection.

Possible Response: The author's primary purpose is to inform.

Terra cotta statues from the tomb of Ch'in Shih Huang Ti.
Copyright © An Keren/PPS/Photo Researchers.

There is what may turn out to be the greatest archaeological find of modern times, one that may ultimately outshine even the discovery of the tomb of Tutankhamen. It is the tomb of the emperor Ch'in Shih Huang Ti. Now admittedly the name Ch'in Shih Huang Ti is not exactly a household word in the West. But then neither was Tutankhamen until 1922. The major difference is that while Tutankhamen himself was historically <u>insignificant</u>, Ch'in Shih Huang Ti was enormously important in Chinese history. In many respects he was really the founder of China.

The future emperor started out as the king of the small state Ch'in. At the time, the land was divided up among a number of small states, all constantly warring with one another. Ch'in was one of the smallest and weakest. Yet the king of Ch'in managed to overcome all his

WORDS
TO
KNOW

insignificant (ĭn′sĭg-nĭf′ĭ-kənt) *adj.* having little or no importance

730

Text Organization: Comparison-Contrast Order

Instruction Remind students that writers choose patterns of organization to help them present information. Writers may use one pattern of organization, such as chronological order, comparison and contrast, or cause and effect, or they may use several patterns in one piece of writing. Ask which pattern a writer would use to tell about events in the order in which they happened (*chronological order*). Explain that when writers want to describe how two ideas, people, or objects are similar and different, they use comparison-and-contrast order. Have students reread the first paragraph of this selection. Ask if the paragraph uses comparison-and-contrast order. (*yes*) Then ask what two subjects the author is comparing and contrasting. (*the discovery of the tomb of Tutankhamen and the discovery of the tomb of the emperor of China*)

Practice Draw a Venn diagram on the board with the following three labels: *Tutankhamen's tomb, Emperor's tomb, Both.* Have students copy the diagram and fill it in using the information in the first paragraph.

Possible Responses: Tutankhamen's tomb: important discovery, well-known discovery, Tutankhamen himself was historically insignificant. Emperor's tomb: more important discovery; emperor not well-known, emperor important in Chinese history. Both: neither ruler was well-known until recently, tombs discovered in 20th century.

rivals, and in the year 221 B.C. he proclaimed himself emperor of the land that we now know as China. From that date until the revolution of 1912, China was always ruled by an emperor. The name China itself comes from the name Ch'in.

Shih Huang Ti ruled his empire with ferocious efficiency. He had the Great Wall of China built to keep out the northern barbarians. The Great Wall, which stretches some fifteen hundred miles, is a building project that rivals and perhaps surpasses the Great Pyramid.[1] The Great Wall took thirty years to build and cost the lives of countless thousands of laborers. Today the Great Wall remains China's number one tourist attraction.

As he grew older, Shih Huang Ti became obsessed with the prospect of his own death. He had survived several assassination attempts and was terrified of another. He traveled constantly between his 270 different palaces, so that no one could ever be sure where he was going to be. He never slept in the same room for two nights in a row. Anyone who revealed the emperor's whereabouts was put to death along with his entire family.

Shih Huang Ti searched constantly for the secret of immortality. He became prey to a host of phony magicians and other fakers who promised much but could deliver nothing.

The emperor heard that there were immortals living on some far-off islands, so he sent a huge fleet to find them. The commander of the fleet knew that if he failed in his mission, the emperor would put him to death. So the fleet simply never returned. It is said that the fleet found the island of Japan and stayed there to become the ancestors of the modern Japanese.

In his desire to stay alive, Shih Huang Ti did not neglect the probability that he would die someday. He began construction of an immense tomb in the Black Horse hills near one of his favorite summer palaces. The tomb's construction took as long as the construction of the Great Wall—thirty years.

The emperor, of course, did die. Death came while he was visiting the eastern provinces. But his life had become so secretive that only a few high officials were aware of his death. They contrived to keep it a secret until they could consolidate their own power. The imperial procession headed back for the capital. Unfortunately, it was midsummer and the emperor's body began to rot and stink. So one of the plotters arranged to have a cart of fish follow the immense imperial chariot to hide the odor of the decomposing corpse. Finally, news of the emperor's death was made public. The body, or what was left of it, was buried in the tomb that he had been building for so long.

---

1. **Great Pyramid:** one of the largest pyramids built by the ancient Egyptians. It is made of more than 2 million stone blocks, each weighing about two tons. Each side of its base is longer than two football fields.

WORDS
TO
KNOW

proclaim (prō-klām') v. to announce officially; declare
surpass (sər-păs') v. to be better or greater than
immortality (ĭm'ôr-tăl'ĭ-tē) n. endless life or existence
consolidate (kən-sŏl'ĭ-dāt') v. to make strong or secure

731

Reading and Analyzing

A soldier and his horse, two of many remarkable statues found in the tomb of the Emperor Shih Huang Ti.
Copyright © Laurie Platt Winfrey, Inc.

Stories about that tomb sound absolutely incredible. It was said to contain miniature reproductions of all the emperor's 270 palaces. A map of the entire empire with all the major rivers reproduced in mercury, which by some mechanical means was made to flow into a miniature ocean, was also part of the interior of the tomb. So was a reproduction of the stars and planets. According to legend, the burial chamber itself was filled with molten copper so that the emperor's remains were sealed inside a gigantic ingot.[2]

It was also said that loaded crossbows were set up all around the inside of the tomb and that anyone who did manage to penetrate the inner chambers would be shot full of arrows. But just to make sure that no one got that far, the pallbearers who had placed Shih Huang Ti's remains in the tomb were sealed inside with it. They were supposed to be the only ones who knew exactly how to get in and out of the intricate tomb. All of this was done to preserve the emperor's remains from the hands of tomb robbers. Did it work? We don't really know yet.

---

2. **ingot** (ĭng´gət): a mass of metal shaped as a bar or block.

WORDS
TO
KNOW

reproduction (rē´prə-dŭk´shən) *n.* a copy; an imitation
intricate (ĭn´-trĭ-kĭt) *adj.* full of complicated details

732

EXPLICIT INSTRUCTION Connecting Main Ideas

There are two contradictory stories about the tomb of Ch'in Shih Huang Ti. The first says that it was covered up with earth to make it resemble an ordinary hill and that its location has remained unknown for centuries.

But a more accurate legend holds that there never was any attempt to disguise the existence of the tomb. Ch'in Shih Huang Ti had been building it for years, and everybody knew where it was. After his death the tomb was surrounded by walls enclosing an area of about five hundred acres. This was to be the emperor's "spirit city." Inside the spirit city were temples and all sorts of other sacred buildings and objects dedicated to the dead emperor.

Over the centuries the walls, the temples, indeed everything above ground was carried away by vandals. The top of the tomb was covered with earth and eventually came to resemble a large hill. Locally the hill is called Mount Li. But still the farmers who lived in the area had heard stories that Mount Li contained the tomb of Ch'in Shih Huang Ti or of some other important person.

In the spring of 1974 a peasant plowing a field near Mount Li uncovered a life-sized clay statue of a warrior. Further digging indicated that there was an entire army of statues beneath the ground. Though excavations are not yet complete, Chinese authorities believe that there are some six thousand life-sized clay statues of warriors, plus scores of life-sized statues of horses. Most of the statues are broken, but some are in an absolutely remarkable state of <u>preservation</u>. Each statue is finely made, and each shows a distinct individual, different from all the others.

This incredible collection is Shih Huang Ti's "spirit army." At one time Chinese kings practiced human sacrifice so that the victims could serve the dead king in the next world. Shih Huang Ti was willing to make do with the models. Men and horses were arranged in a military fashion in a three-acre underground chamber. The chamber may have been entered at some point. The roof certainly collapsed. But still the delicate figures have survived surprisingly well. Most of the damage was done when the roof caved in. That is why the Chinese archaeologists are so hopeful that when the tomb itself is excavated, it too will be found to have survived surprisingly well.

The Chinese are not rushing the excavations. They have only a limited number of trained people to do the job. After all, the tomb has been there for over two thousand years. A few more years won't make much difference.

Though once denounced as a <u>tyrant</u>, Ch'in Shih Huang Ti is now regarded as a national hero. His name is a household word in China. The Chinese government knows that it may have an <u>unparalleled</u> ancient treasure on its hands, and it wants to do the job well. Over the next few years we should be hearing much more about this truly remarkable find. ❖

B

WORDS	**preservation** (prĕz′ər-vā′shən) *n.* the condition of being kept perfect or unchanged
TO	**tyrant** (tī′rənt) *n.* a cruel, unjust ruler
KNOW	**unparalleled** (ŭn-păr′ə-lĕld′) *adj.* having no equal; unmatched

733

Cross Curricular Link Social Studies

THE FIRST EMPEROR Ch'in Shih Huang Ti came to power in 246 B.C., at the age of 13. He gained control of much territory and divided the empire into 36 provinces, each with two officials—one governor and one defender. This brought unity to the empire and allowed the emperor to establish standard systems of money, measurement, and writing. Taking the land away from thousands of noble families, he put an end to the feudal system and allowed anyone who could pay taxes to own land.

To protect his empire from possible invasion from the north, Shih Huang Ti used a forced-labor crew of hundreds of thousands to build the Great Wall of China. Lengthened and repaired over the centuries, this massive wall stretched for 4,000 miles by the time of the Ming Dynasty (1368–1644).

Much of the emperor's burial site still remains to be uncovered. In addition to the clay army, archaeologists have found chariots, iron farm tools, objects of silk, linen, jade, and bone, and weapons such as spears and swords that remain sharp and shiny to this day.

Connect to the Literature

1. What Do You Think?
Students may say that they are amazed by the contents of the emperor's tomb, by the power he exercised, or by his dramatic efforts to live forever.

Comprehension Check
- Shih Huang Ti was the first to rule over all the land, which was divided into small states.
- The Great Wall and his tomb were both constructed during his rule.
- The tomb was discovered in 1974 by a farmer who was plowing a field.

 Use Selection Quiz,
Unit Five Resource Book, p. 75.

Think Critically

2. Possible Response: Shih Huang Ti accomplished important things such as unifying the country and protecting the people from northern invaders. However, he was also cruel. Working conditions on his projects were so bad that thousands of people died, and he killed anyone who revealed his whereabouts.

3. Responses will vary, but details given should support the main idea.

4. Possible Response: Archaeologists have learned about the clothing and weapons used by the emperor's soldiers and the artistic achievements of the people who made the statues.

5. Possible Response: Archaeologists might want to learn more about the past, to find interesting and valuable objects, and to become famous. Opinions will vary.

Literary Analysis

Informative Nonfiction Answers will vary but should show students' ability to discern facts.

Connect to the Literature

1. What Do You Think?
What were your thoughts as you finished reading this selection?

Comprehension Check
- Why is Shih Huang Ti called the first emperor of China?
- What two large-scale construction projects were carried out during his rule?
- When and how was the emperor's tomb discovered?

Think Critically

2. How would you describe Shih Huang Ti?

Think About:
- his attempts to achieve immortality
- his accomplishments
- his effects on those he ruled

3. **ACTIVE READING** **MAIN IDEA AND DETAILS**
Look at the main ideas and supporting details you noted in your **READER'S NOTEBOOK.** How do the details support the main ideas?

4. What kinds of information about Chinese history have archaeologists learned from the tomb so far?

5. Some archaeologists spend their lives searching for the remains of past civilizations. What do you think motivates them? In your opinion, do the time and effort equal the rewards?

Extend Interpretations

6. **COMPARING TEXTS** Now that you have read "The First Emperor," think back to "The Dog of Pompeii" (page 700) and "Tutankhamen" (page 718). Compare the ancient cultures of Pompeii, Egypt, and China as revealed by the artifacts described in each selection.

7. Connect to Life Many people would like to achieve a certain kind of immortality—that of having their names and achievements live on after their deaths. If you could choose one thing to be remembered by, centuries from now, what would it be?

Literary Analysis

INFORMATIVE NONFICTION
Magazine articles, newspaper articles, textbooks, and reference books are all types of **informative nonfiction**— writing that contains factual information. Informative nonfiction that is focused on **history** provides factual information about real events, places, and people from the past. The main purpose of informative nonfiction is to inform readers. In this selection, Daniel Cohen's main purpose is to inform readers about the first emperor of China and the excavation of his tomb.

Paired Activity What amazed you most about the first Chinese emperor? With a partner, go back through the selection and look for five facts that you think are interesting. Record these facts and share them with the class.

Extend Interpretations

6. Comparing Texts Responses will vary. Students should skim the other two selections and note similarities and differences among such areas as forms of government, interest in the arts, and belief in life after death.

7. Connect to Life Responses will vary. Students may wish to be remembered for their hobbies or concerns, from painting to baseball to caring for animals.

Writing

The Emperor's Traits Based on what you read about Ch'in Shih Huang Ti, write a description of this historical figure's character traits. What words describe him? Look back through the selection to find information that will help you answer this question. Begin your description with a clear statement about the emperor's traits. Support this statement with information from the selection. Place your description in your **Working Portfolio.**

Speaking & Listening

Asking Questions What questions do you have about the excavation of the emperor's tomb or about the life of the first emperor? Write a list of five open-ended questions—questions that can't be answered with a simple yes or no. Then read your questions to the class.

Research & Technology

Finding Answers Choose one of the questions you wrote for the Speaking & Listening activity and conduct research to find the answer. Use articles, books, and the Internet to find the information you need. Take notes and present your findings to the class. Be sure to note the sources you used to find the information.

Research and Technology Handbook
See p. R106: Getting Information Electronically.

 INTERNET Research Starter
www.mcdougallittell.com

Art Connection

Amazing Individuals The terra cotta soldier and horse shown on page 732 were among the more than 6,000 statues discovered in the tomb. No two are alike. Look carefully at the figures on page 732. Write a description of the details you observe.

Vocabulary

EXERCISE: RELATED WORDS On your paper, write the letter of the phrase that best explains the meaning of the boldfaced Word to Know.

1. A historically **insignificant** ruler was (a) important, (b) cruel, (c) not important.

2. The **intricate** security system of the tomb is thought to be (a) easy to get inside, (b) filled with cement, (c) complicated.

3. When Shih Huang Ti chose to **proclaim** himself emperor, he (a) was voted into the position, (b) won the title in a contest, (c) made himself emperor.

4. Obsessed with the thought of his death, the emperor sought **immortality,** (a) wanting to live forever, (b) needing more money, (c) hoping to die painlessly.

5. When officials **consolidate** power, each (a) gets a new job, (b) gets more power, (c) gets elected.

6. A small **reproduction** of the palace would look like (a) a miniature palace, (b) a blueprint, (c) a door key.

7. If the Great Wall did **surpass** all other monuments in its amount of stone, then it (a) used less stone, (b) used more stone, (c) used stone efficiently.

8. The **preservation** of the artifacts is amazing; they are (a) in terrific condition, (b) crumbling, (c) in a heap.

9. He was considered a **tyrant** because he could be (a) cruel, (b) lazy, (c) fair.

10. If the tomb is an **unparalleled** Chinese treasure, it is (a) unique in the world, (b) the oldest known, (c) a great treasure.

THE FIRST EMPEROR **735**

Writing

The Emperor's Traits To help students get started, have them brainstorm with a partner a list of the unusual things they read about the emperor.

Use **Writing Transparencies**, p. 15, for additional support.

Speaking & Listening

Asking Questions List the following terms on the board: people, places, objects, historical periods, events, occupations. Tell students to use these topics to help them remember and think about subjects from the article they might like to explore. You might suggest they use these terms as headings in a chart. They can jot down notes about the article under the headings.

Research & Technology

Finding Answers Allow students time to conduct their research. Tell students that if their question is too broad, and they are finding too much information, they can revise the question.

Art Connection

Amazing Individuals Responses will vary. Students may point out the armor on the soldier's chest, the covering on the back of the horse, the stiffness of the horse's mane, and other details.

Vocabulary

1. c
2. c
3. c
4. a
5. b
6. a
7. b
8. a
9. a
10. a

Grammar in Context

WRITING EXERCISE
Possible Responses:
1. complex
2. compound-complex
3. compound-complex
4. complex

Daniel Cohen

Though Cohen has written about many different subjects, there are some subjects he says he can't or won't write about, including mathematics and disciplining children. But that still leaves him plenty of room, and as he says, he's "turned out books on an alarming number of subjects."

Amazing Burials Students might wish to compare the different ways Ch'in Shih Huang Ti and others tried to protect their graves from robbery.

Grammar in Context: Compound-Complex Sentences

The sentence below uses information from Daniel Cohen's "The First Emperor." It is a **compound-complex sentence.**

> **While the emperor was in power,** he had the Great Wall built, and he looked for a way to live forever.

A compound-complex sentence contains **two or more independent clauses** and **one or more dependent clauses.** In the sentence above, the words *he had the Great Wall built* and the words *he looked for a way to live forever* are both independent clauses—they can stand alone as sentences. The words *While the emperor was in power* is a dependent clause because it cannot stand alone.

A **complex sentence** has one independent clause and one or more dependent clauses.

> **While the emperor was in power,** he had the Great Wall built.

WRITING EXERCISE Identify each sentence as complex or compound-complex.

1. Because the emperor's tomb was covered with earth, some people called it Mount Li.
2. When a farmer found a clay statue of a soldier, archaeologists began digging, and they found a whole army of clay soldiers.
3. The statues are finely made, and each one looks different, although most of them are broken.
4. The emperor was buried with six thousand clay soldiers after he died.

Grammar Handbook

See p. R84: The Structure of Sentences.

Daniel Cohen
born 1936

". . . eccentric beliefs not only add spice to life, they can stimulate the mind."

A Rapid Writer Daniel Cohen has written more than 130 books, most of which are young-adult nonfiction. A Chicago native, Cohen earned a degree in journalism from the University of Illinois. After a decade in the magazine business, he became a freelance writer. His best-known works include *Young and Famous: Sports' Newest Superstars, Phantom Animals,* and *Prophets of Doom.*

Spooky Subjects Research for his popular books on ghost stories and superstitions led Cohen to creep around houses believed to be haunted and to spend "a damp and chilly night in an English churchyard." One of his most popular books is *The Body Snatchers,* a history of grave robbing. About his choice of spooky material, he says, "I don't really 'believe in' most of the subjects I write about, and I don't pretend to." With his wife, Susan Cohen, he has cowritten several popular books for teenagers on subjects ranging from movies to dinosaurs.

AUTHOR ACTIVITY
Amazing Burials Read a chapter from *The Tomb Robbers* to find out about another famous tomb. Share your findings in a report.

EXPLICIT INSTRUCTION Grammar in Context

COMPOUND-COMPLEX SENTENCES
Instruction Define a compound-complex sentence as one that contains two or more independent clauses and one or more dependent clauses. Write the following sentence on the board, underlining the independent clauses once and the dependent clause twice, as shown:

While Natalie mowed the lawn, her brother raked the leaves, and her father painted the fence.

Explain that a compound-complex sentence can be formed by adding another independent clause to a complex sentence. Remind students that a dependent clause often begins with *although, when, since,* or *because.*
Practice Have students work in pairs to combine the three sentences below into one compound-complex sentence.

The movie was about an ancient emperor.
The movie was very interesting.
I fell asleep watching it.

(The movie was about an ancient emperor, and it was very interesting, but I fell asleep watching it.)

 Use **Unit Five Resource Book,** p. 73, for more practice.

For **systematic instruction** in grammar, see:
• **Grammar, Usage, and Mechanics Book**
• pacing chart on p. 609i

Barbara Frietchie

by JOHN GREENLEAF WHITTIER

This selection is included in the **Grade 6 InterActive Reader.**

Connect to Your Life

Bravest of All Just what is bravery? Is bravery simply a willingness to fight? Consider acts of bravery you have heard about or seen. Then write your own definition of bravery. Give an example with your definition.

Standards-Based Objectives

1. understand and appreciate **poetry**
2. understand and appreciate the **couplet** as an element of poetic form
3. use **reading aloud** to help with **clarifying**

Build Background

HISTORY

John Greenleaf Whittier wrote this poem to honor a legendary act of courage. On September 10, 1862, General Robert E. Lee, commander of the Confederate Army of Northern Virginia, and General Thomas J. "Stonewall" Jackson led almost 40,000 soldiers through Frederick, Maryland. They were on their way to Sharpsburg and to defeat in a battle—the battle of Antietam—that would include the bloodiest single day of the war.

One citizen of Frederick was Barbara Frietchie, an elderly widow who was fiercely loyal to the Union. According to legend, as Jackson's troops marched through the town she defiantly waved a Union flag at the Confederate troops.

Focus Your Reading

LITERARY ANALYSIS   POETIC FORM: COUPLET

A rhymed pair of lines in a poem is called a **couplet.** Here is a couplet from the poem you are about to read:

> *Bravest of all in Frederick town,*
> *She took up the flag the men hauled down*

"Barbara Frietchie" is a narrative poem—a poem that tells a story—written entirely in couplets.

ACTIVE READING   CLARIFYING

When you stop while you are reading to quickly review or figure out what has happened, you are **clarifying.** Clarifying can help you find answers for any questions you might have. Reading aloud can also help you clarify why a story or poem unfolds as it does.

READER'S NOTEBOOK As you read "Barbara Frietchie," you may come across confusing lines or sentences. Sometimes this is because the words were arranged to fit the rhythm of the poem. You may want to pause at the end of every few couplets to clarify what you have just read. Jot down key events in the narrative, using your own words.

Summary

An elderly woman's loyalty proves to be an effective protest to a coming attack during the Civil War. Barbara Frietchie's act of courage is honored in this narrative poem.

Thematic Link

Barbara Frietchie's show of courage serves as a symbol of the power of the individual in American life. Her act of bravery echoes throughout American history as one of many voices from the past that express the freedom that is the best of America.

English Conventions Practice

Daily Language SkillBuilder

Have students **proofread** the display sentences on page 609k and write them correctly. The sentences also appear on Transparency 23 of **Language Transparencies.**

BARBARA FRIETCHIE   **737**

LESSON RESOURCES

UNIT FIVE RESOURCE BOOK, pp. 76–77

ASSESSMENT
Formal Assessment, pp. 121–122
Test Generator

SKILLS TRANSPARENCIES AND COPYMASTERS
Literary Analysis
• Form in Poetry: Rhyme and Meter, TR 17 (pp. 738, 740)
Reading and Critical Thinking
• Strategies for Reading, TR 1 (p. 740)
Language
• Daily Language SkillBuilders, TR 23 (p. 737)

INTEGRATED TECHNOLOGY
Audio Library
Internet: Research Starter

Visit our Web site:
www.mcdougallittell.com

For **systematic instruction** in language skills, see:
• **Vocabulary and Spelling Book**
• **Grammar, Usage, and Mechanics Book**
• pacing chart on p. 609i

POETIC FORM: COUPLET

Ask students to identify and read aloud three couplets. Then have them explain what makes each one a couplet.

Possible Response: Students' answers will vary, but should reflect an understanding of the definition of a couplet—a pair of lines with end rhymes.

 Use **Unit Five Resource Book,** p. 77, for more practice. Use **Literary Analysis Transparencies,** p. 17, for more support.

Active Reading **CLARIFYING**

Ask students to clarify the meaning of lines 13–16.

Possible Response: In the morning there were forty Union flags flying. By noon, there were none.

 Use **Unit Five Resource Book,** p. 76, for more practice.

Literary Analysis: SOUND DEVICES

Ask students to name some of the sound devices used in this poem.

Possible Response: The poet uses repetition in lines 13 and 14. He also uses alliteration in line 32, in the phrase "snatched the silken scarf," and in line 39, in the phrase "nobler nature."

Reading Skills and Strategies: PARAPHRASE NARRATIVE POETRY

Ask students to use their own words to express the meaning of the poem by paraphrasing every 6 lines as they read.

Possible Response: (for first six lines) On a cool September morning in Frederick, Maryland, when the orchards and fields were full of ripe fruit, . . .

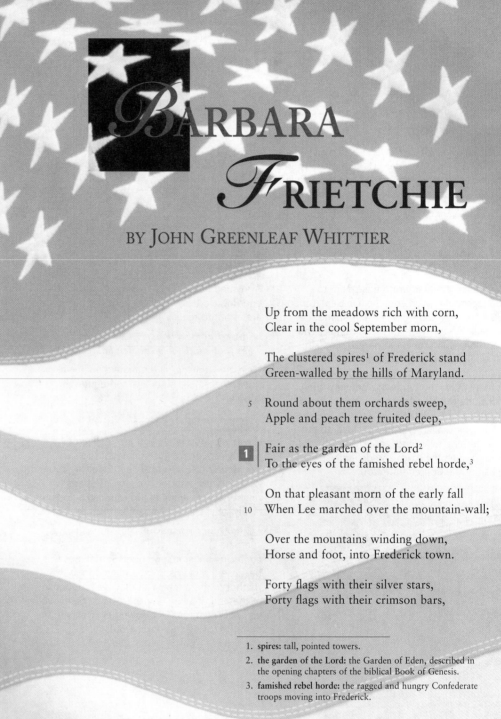

BARBARA FRIETCHIE

BY JOHN GREENLEAF WHITTIER

Up from the meadows rich with corn,
Clear in the cool September morn,

The clustered spires[1] of Frederick stand
Green-walled by the hills of Maryland.

5   Round about them orchards sweep,
Apple and peach tree fruited deep,

Fair as the garden of the Lord[2]
To the eyes of the famished rebel horde,[3]

On that pleasant morn of the early fall
10   When Lee marched over the mountain-wall;

Over the mountains winding down,
Horse and foot, into Frederick town.

Forty flags with their silver stars,
Forty flags with their crimson bars,

---

1. **spires:** tall, pointed towers.
2. **the garden of the Lord:** the Garden of Eden, described in the opening chapters of the biblical Book of Genesis.
3. **famished rebel horde:** the ragged and hungry Confederate troops moving into Frederick.

Cross Curricular Link   Social Studies

THE EVOLUTION OF THE AMERICAN FLAG As the nation has changed, so has its flag. The first flag was created by Congress in 1777. It had 13 red and white stripes and 13 white stars in a field of blue. The 13 stripes and stars represented the 13 colonies that originally constituted the U.S. In 1795, after Vermont and Kentucky had joined the Union, Congress adopted a flag of 15 stripes and 15 stars. By 1817, there were 20 states in the Union. It was decided that adding more stripes to the flag would ruin its shape.

Congress voted to return to the original design of 13 stripes and to represent each state with one star. In 1912, President Taft decided that there should be 6 even rows of 8 stars each. Previously, the flag makers determined the placement of the 48 stars. Of course, today there are 50 stars because of the addition of Alaska and Hawaii as states.

There are fascinating stories about the making of our country's early flags. Encourage interested students to research the first flags and report back to the class on their findings.

15 Flapped in the morning wind; the sun
    Of noon looked down and saw not one.

2 Up rose old Barbara Frietchie then,
    Bowed with her fourscore years and ten;

    Bravest of all in Frederick town,
20 She took up the flag the men hauled down;

    In her attic window the staff[4] she set,
    To show that one heart was loyal yet.

    Up the street came the rebel tread,
    Stonewall Jackson riding ahead.

25 Under his slouched hat[5] left and right
    He glanced; the old flag met his sight.

    "Halt!"—the dust-brown ranks stood fast.
    "Fire!"—out blazed the rifle-blast.

    It shivered[6] the window, pane and sash;
30 It rent[7] the banner with seam and gash.

    Quick, as it fell, from the broken staff
    Dame Barbara snatched the silken scarf.

    She leaned far out on the window-sill,
    And shook it forth with a royal will.

35 "Shoot, if you must, this old gray head,
    But spare your country's flag," she said.

    A shade of sadness, a blush of shame,
    Over the face of the leader came;

    The nobler nature within him stirred
40 To life at that woman's deed and word;

    "Who touches a hair of yon gray head
    Dies like a dog! March on!" he said.

    All day long through Frederick street
    Sounded the tread of marching feet:

45 All day long that free flag tossed
    Over the heads of the rebel host.

    Ever its torn folds rose and fell
    On the loyal winds that loved it well;

    And through the hill-gaps sunset light
50 Shone over it with a warm good-night.

    Barbara Frietchie's work is o'er,
    And the Rebel rides on his raids no more.

    Honor to her! and let a tear
    Fall, for her sake, on Stonewall's bier.[8]

55 Over Barbara Frietchie's grave,
    Flag of Freedom and Union, wave!

    Peace and order and beauty draw
    Round that symbol of light and law;

    And ever the stars above look down
60 On thy stars below in Frederick town!

---

4. **staff:** a pole on which a flag is displayed.
5. **slouched hat:** a soft hat with a wide brim.
6. **shivered:** caused to break into pieces.
7. **rent:** tore or split apart.
8. **bier** (bîr): a coffin and its stand.

BARBARA FRIETCHIE   **739**

EXPLICIT INSTRUCTION **Narrative Poetry**

Instruction Read aloud the poem and discuss what it is about. Invite students to point out any confusing parts and help them with their understanding. Then tell students that a poem that tells a story is called a narrative poem. Explain that a narrative poem has features of both a story and a poem: a narrative poem has characters, a setting, and a plot and it may have patterns of rhyme and rhythm. Tell students that when they read a narrative poem, they should try to picture the setting and the characters. Also tell students to make sure they understand what is happening as the plot unfolds.

Practice Have students identify the characters and the setting of the poem. Then have them identify important events in the plot of the poem.

Possible Responses: Characters: Barbara Frietchie, Stonewall Jackson, soldiers. Setting: Frederick, Maryland, during the Civil War. Events: an elderly woman waves a Union flag as Confederate soldiers approach her town.

Connect to the Literature

1. What Do You Think?
Responses will vary. Students may admire the bravery of an unarmed elderly woman who stands up to armed soldiers. They may find her patriotism moving. Others may say that she was foolish to have taken such a risk.

Comprehension Check
• Frietchie challenges Jackson to shoot her instead of the flag.
• It symbolizes light and law.

Think Critically

2. Possible Responses: Whittier might have been sympathetic to the Union, moved by Frietchie's bravery, or impressed by Jackson's fair response.

3. Possible Responses: The Confederate army marched into Frederick, Maryland, tearing down the Union flag. An old woman hung the fallen flag out her window and challenged the soldiers to shoot her instead of the flag. The Confederate general was so impressed with her character and loyalty that he let the flag fly all day.

📖 Use **Reading and Critical Thinking Transparencies,** p. 1, for additional support.

4. Responses will vary. Students may say that bravery can mean a willingness to sacrifice for great ideals.

5. Possible Responses: The lines are "'Shoot, if you must, this old gray head,/But spare your country's flag,' she said." These line's show the woman's courage and patriotism— her character, with her own words.

Literary Analysis

Poetic Form: Couplet Students should find several examples of unusual syntax and poetic words, such as: "Over the face of the leader came"; *o'er, yon, thy;* "the staff she set"

📖 Use **Literary Analysis Transparencies,** p. 17, for additional support.

Connect to the Literature

1. What Do You Think? What is your reaction to the character of Barbara Frietchie?

Comprehension Check
• What challenge does Frietchie call out to Jackson?
• What does the speaker say that the American flag symbolizes?

Think Critically

2. In your opinion, why might John Greenleaf Whittier have been inspired to write this narrative poem about Barbara Frietchie?

> **Think About:**
> • how Whittier seems to feel about the war
> • Frietchie's age and actions
> • Stonewall Jackson's reaction

3. **ACTIVE READING** **CLARIFYING** Look at the notes you made in your 📖 **READER'S NOTEBOOK.** Briefly retell the sequence of events in the poem.

4. Reread the definition of bravery you wrote before reading this poem. Do Barbara Frietchie's actions fit your definition? Would you revise your definition on the basis of your reading of the poem? Explain.

5. A pair of lines in "Barbara Frietchie" have become famous. Some people can recite these lines from memory, even if they cannot remember one other word from the poem. Which two lines do you think should be famous and why?

Extend Interpretations

6. Writer's Style In a group, reread "Barbara Frietchie." How does Whittier reveal the personalities and beliefs of Frietchie and Jackson? Make a chart like the one shown, noting the results of your discussion.

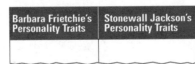

Barbara Frietchie's Personality Traits	Stonewall Jackson's Personality Traits

7. Connect to Life A flag is only a piece of fabric. Yet many men and women have acted with courage to protect their national flags. Why do you think flags can be so important to people? Explain.

Extend Interpretations

6. Writer's Style Students' charts will differ, but should include some basic personality traits. Students might say that Barbara Frietchie was brave, loyal, and committed to the Union. They might say that Stonewall Jackson was compassionate, wise, sensitive, and a strong leader.

7. Connect to Life Students may say that flags are valued not because they are decorated pieces of fabric but because they are symbols of a country's distinct identity. Flags are held high when diplomats from different countries convene, when athletes compete at the Olympics, and when school children begin the day by reciting the "Pledge of Allegiance." The flag of the United States is a source of pride and a symbol that is treated with respect, because it represents values that most people in this country cherish, such as liberty and justice.

Literary Analysis

POETIC FORM: COUPLET "Barbara Frietchie" is divided into pairs of rhymed lines, or **couplets.** Many readers find reading this poem aloud to be fun, because the structure and rhythm allow the reader to move along quickly. Note the brisk pace of this couplet:

> *Up the street came the rebel tread*
> *Stonewall Jackson riding ahead.*

Activity In order to make couplets rhyme, poets may arrange words in a way different from the word order that people generally use in conversation. In addition, they may use unusual words, such as *morn* rather than *morning,* to fit the rhyming pattern. Look back through the poem. What examples of these techniques can you find?

REVIEW: SOUND DEVICES Poets use sound devices such as **rhyme, rhythm,** and **repetition** to emphasize ideas and feelings in their poems. How do sound devices in "Barbara Frietchie" contribute to the feeling of the poem?

Writing

Frietchie Interview Imagine that the Civil War has just ended. You have been sent to interview Barbara Frietchie. What would your first five questions be? Place them in your **Working Portfolio.**

Speaking and Listening Handbook
See p. R105: Preparing for the Interview.

Speaking & Listening

Choral Reading With a group of classmates, develop and present a choral reading of "Barbara Frietchie" for the rest of the class or for another class in your school.

Speaking and Listening Handbook
See p. R98: Oral Interpretation.

Research & Technology

Comparison Flags Barbara Frietchie waved a Union flag out her window at the approaching troops. How does the U.S. flag of the early 1860s compare with the flag of today? Research how the flag has changed. Present your findings in a series of drawings of the flag at various times.

INTERNET Research Starter
www.mcdougallittell.com

John Greenleaf Whittier
1807–1892

". . . duty hath no place for fear."

A Poet with a Passion The son of Quaker farmers, John Greenleaf Whittier was born in Haverhill, Massachusetts. At 14, he began to write poetry. However, Whittier found the greatest meaning in his life through the abolitionist cause, a movement of people who demanded freedom for slaves. He worked tirelessly as an abolitionist, speaking publicly and publishing his writings on the subject.

Riches of Many Kinds Whittier's first book was published in 1831. In 1846 he published a collection of antislavery poems, *Voices of Freedom.* After the Civil War, he turned to writing poetry about his youth, his family, and the New England countryside, as in his best-known work, *Snow-Bound.* When Whittier died at 85, he was a famous and well-loved poet as well as a wealthy one. He left money to the Hampton Institute, a school in Virginia for African Americans and Native Americans.

AUTHOR ACTIVITY

Voicing Values Whittier often wrote poems about moral issues or about heroes he admired. Find one of these poems. What do you think it reveals about Whittier's character?

Writing

Frietchie Interview Students' responses will vary but should reflect their understanding of Barbara Frietchie's position. Students might ask her why she risked putting out her flag, how she reacted to Stonewall Jackson's response, or what life is like in Maryland now that the war is over.

Speaking & Listening

Choral Reading As groups prepare their reading, encourage them to make notes to remind themselves of which words to stress, which phrases to read with particular enthusiasm, and which to read more quietly, so as to express sadness.

Research & Technology

Comparison Flags Suggest that students research not only the various designs but also the reasons behind the design changes. Encourage students to make a presentation in which they explain the evolution of the flag.

John Greenleaf Whittier

In addition to being a poet, Whittier was also a journalist and a leading abolitionist. As such, he endorsed the presidential candidacy of Abraham Lincoln.

Author Activity

Voicing Values Choices of poems will vary, but many will reflect the author's commitment to the abolition of slavery.

Building Vocabulary
Denotative and Connotative Meanings

Standards-Based Objectives
- understand the differences between denotation and connotation of words
- use reference materials such as a dictionary or thesaurus to determine connotations of words
- identify relation of word meanings in connotations

VOCABULARY EXERCISE
Possible Responses:

1. Cats snoop in places they do not belong.
   Cats like to investigate their surroundings carefully.
2. I admire her unique style of dress.
   Her odd clothing makes her stand out like a sore thumb.
3. Because Malik is so assertive, he is a good salesperson.
   I think that salespeople are a bit too pushy when they call our home.
4. His fussy rules make us feel nervous and trapped.
   We admire his careful way of organizing the class.
5. Her reckless behavior is dangerous.
   Everyone is in awe of her daring feats.

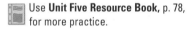 Use **Unit Five Resource Book,** p. 78, for more practice.

Good writers choose just the right word to communicate specific meaning. Louis Untermeyer could have chosen any of the following words to describe the crowded theaters. Why did he instead choose *rocked*?

moved
made some kind of motion

stirred
began to move from a resting position

burst
broke free, or broke open

> The streets were always lively with shining chariots and bright red trappings; the open-air theaters rocked with laughing crowds; sham battles and athletic sports were free for the asking in the great stadium.
>
> —Louis Untermeyer, "The Dog of Pompeii"

In this passage, **rocked** implies strong, rhythmic, dramatic motion.

Strategies for Building Vocabulary

A word's dictionary meaning or definition is called its **denotation.** The images and feelings you connect to a word give it finer shades of meaning, called **connotation.** Connotative meaning stretches beyond a word's most basic, dictionary definition. In fact, it is possible for two synonyms to have different connotations. The strategies below should help you understand the connotations of words.

❶ **Look for Positive or Negative Connotations**
Writers use the connotations of words to communicate positive or negative feelings. Read the passage below, noticing how the word *obsessed* is used.

> As he grew older, Shih Huang Ti became obsessed with the prospect of his own death. He had survived several assassination attempts and was terrified of another. He traveled constantly between his 270 different palaces, so that no one could ever be sure where he was going to be.
>
> —Daniel Cohen, "The First Emperor"

The word *obsessed* refers to someone who is concerned with a single idea or feeling to the point of being irrational. Although the words *concerned* or *involved* have similar denotations, they do not have the same negative connotation that *obsessed* does. *Obsessed* gives the best impression of the dark quality of the emperor's situation.

❷ **Think About Connotations When You Write**
Always consider the connotations of the words you use in your own writing. Think about images and feelings connected to certain words. Some examples are listed in the chart below.

Positive Connotations	Negative Connotations
thrifty	cheap
young	immature
slim	scrawny

EXERCISE The words in the following pairs have similar denotations but different connotations. Think about how they differ, using a dictionary if necessary. Then write a sentence using each word. Make sure your sentence reveals the word's connotation.

1. snoop / investigate
2. unique / odd
3. assertive / pushy
4. fussy / careful
5. reckless / daring

Beethoven, Lucien Levy Dhurmer. Ville
de Paris Musée du Petit Palais.

Beethoven
Lives Upstairs

BY BARBARA NICHOL

On Thursday, March 29, 1827, the people of Vienna flooded
into the streets. They came to pay their respects to Ludwig van
Beethoven, the great composer, who had died three days earlier.

743

You can use this selection to achieve
one or more of the following objectives:

Possible Objectives
• enjoy independent reading (Option
One)
• read and analyze literature with a
group (Option Two)
• use the Reader's Notebook to formulate questions about literature (Option
Three)
• write in response to literature (Option
Three)

Summary
This story, set in Austria in the 1820s, is
a series of letters written between a
young boy, Christoph, who lives in
Vienna and his uncle, a music student
who lives in Salzburg. In the letters,
Christoph tells his uncle of the strange
gentleman who has rented a room in
the boy's home. This gentleman's name
is Ludwig van Beethoven. According to
Christoph's early letters, Mr. Beethoven
is a serious disruption to the household,
and Christoph thinks that he may be
mad. The uncle replies to the boy's
letters with information about the
famous Mr. Beethoven. As the boy
begins to know Mr. Beethoven, he
understands that it is Beethoven's deafness which makes him create so much
noise upstairs. Christoph begins to
appreciate the genius of the strange
house guest. When Beethoven's famous
Ninth Symphony is ready to be performed, Christoph informs his uncle that
he and his mother are invited to be in
the audience. In the letter that follows
the performance, Christoph reports the
outstanding success of the symphony,
and his sympathy and appreciation for
the composer are evident.

Reading the Selection

Option One
Independent Reading

You might set aside time each week for independent reading to help your students approach the goal of reading 1 million words a year. During this time, you and all of your students would read for enjoyment. "Beethoven Lives Upstairs" will appeal to many students and can be read independently in about thirty minutes. If you want to encourage students to read for pleasure, you might forego any assignments related to this selection. Should you want to make assignments, Options Two and Three offer suggestions.

Option Two
Group Reading

You may assign students to groups or allow them to choose their own. Students can read this selection together, alternately reading sections aloud, or they can read independently and meet to cooperate in a project that portrays some element of the story.

Possible Projects

- Using elements from the story, students can create a short play based on the possible interaction of the young boy Christoph and Beethoven after the performance of the Ninth Symphony. They can focus on Christoph's appreciation of Beethoven's talent and his change of feeling for his strange neighbor. They can perform this play for the rest of the class.

- Students can create a setting for the performance of the play, choosing one of the locations described in the story.

 At three o'clock in the afternoon nine priests blessed the coffin, and the funeral procession left Mr. Beethoven's house for the church. So dense were the crowds that the one-block journey took an hour and a half.

I wasn't in Vienna on that famous day. I was a student of music in Salzburg at the time. But if you had looked carefully, you might have spotted in the crowd a little boy with a serious face. He is Christoph, my nephew, and there was a time when he came to know Mr. Beethoven quite well.

It was not a happy time in Christoph's life. He was only ten years old, and his father had recently died.

The first of Christoph's letters arrived at my door in the autumn of 1822. I was surprised that he had written. I had not seen my nephew for some years. . . .

7 September 1822

Dear Uncle,

I hope you will remember me. It is Christoph, your nephew, who writes. As to the reasons, I will not keep you in suspense. I write, Uncle, because something terrible has happened. A madman has moved into our house.

Do you remember that when Father died, Mother decided to rent out his office upstairs? Well, she has done it, and Ludwig van Beethoven has moved in.

Every morning at dawn Mr. Beethoven begins to make his dreadful noise upstairs. Loud poundings and howlings come through the floor. They are like the sounds of an injured beast. All morning Mr. Beethoven carries on this way. After lunch he storms into the street. He comes home, sometimes long after the house is quiet for the night, tracking mud and stamping his way up the stairs above our heads.

Mother says I mustn't blame him. He's deaf and can't hear the noise he makes. But he wakes up the twins, and they start their crying. They cry all day.

Uncle, I must make this one request. I beg you to tell my mother to send Mr. Beethoven away.

Your nephew, Christoph

10 October 1822

My dear Christoph,

I arrived home last night to find your letter on the table in the hall. Do I remember you? Of course I do!

I should tell you that I have received a letter from your mother as well. As you know, she is concerned about you and wants you to be happy. She assures me that Mr. Beethoven is peculiar perhaps, but certainly not mad.

Christoph, Mr. Beethoven will settle in soon, I'm sure. I know that life will be more peaceful before long.

Your uncle, Karl

Having answered my nephew's letter, I left Salzburg for some weeks on matters related to my studies. In truth, I expected no further messages. The three letters that follow arrived in my absence.

22 October 1822

Dear Uncle,

I hope you will forgive my troubling you, but I am sure that you will want to hear this news. Our family is now the laughingstock of Vienna.

I opened the door this morning to find a crowd in front of our house. They were looking up at Mr. Beethoven's window and laughing, so I looked up too. There was

744   UNIT FIVE   PART 2: VOICES FROM THE PAST

Mr. Beethoven, staring at a sheet of music. And Uncle, he had no clothes on at all! It was a dreadful sight!

You should see him setting out for the afternoon. He hums to himself. He growls out tunes. He waves his arms. His pockets bulge with papers and pencils. On the street the children run and call him names.

Mr. Beethoven is so famous that sometimes people stop outside our house, hoping they will see him. But if anyone asks, I say he has moved away.

Your nephew, Christoph

29 October 1822

Dear Uncle,

I have now seen with my own eyes that Mr. Beethoven is mad. I will tell you the story in the hope that you will do something at last.

Last night, when I was getting ready for bed, I happened to look up. There were beads of water collecting on the ceiling above my head.

As usual, Mother was busy with the twins, so I climbed the stairs and crept along the hall to Mr. Beethoven's room. I looked in. He was standing there with no shirt on. He had a jug of water in his hands. He was pouring the water over his head, right there in the middle of the room, and all this time stamping his feet like he was marching or listening to a song.

A madman has moved into our house.

You should see my father's study! Do you remember how tidy he was? Well, now there are papers lying everywhere—on the floor, on the chairs, on the bed that isn't made. There are dirty dishes stacked up and clothing crumpled on the floor. And another thing, he has been writing on the wall with a pencil!

I said nothing to Mr. Beethoven, of course. Luckily, he did not see me, and I ran back down the stairs.

Uncle, if you are thinking of coming to our aid, there could be no better time than now.

Christoph

5 November 1822

Dear Uncle,

Another week has passed, but life is no calmer here.

I've been thinking. If Mr. Beethoven were to leave, surely we could find someone nice to live upstairs. The rooms are large, and Father's patients always talked about the view of the river. Father used to carry me down to the riverbank on his shoulders, even down the steep part right behind the house.

I think that of all the places in the house, I like the outside best. I can be alone there and get away from all the noise inside. But on this day even the stray dog outside was making his pitiful voice heard.

Yours truly, Christoph

22 November 1822

My dear Christoph,

Today I have returned home from a visit away to find three of your letters waiting. Christoph, I will admit that Mr. Beethoven does not seem to be an easy guest.

Perhaps I can help, though, by saying that as strange as Mr. Beethoven seems, there are reasons for the way he acts.

Option Three
Reader's Notebook

- Ask students what impression they initially get of Beethoven and then ask them to explain how their perceptions of him as a character change by the end of the story.
- Ask students to read the selection, pausing at the end of the letter dated 10 March, 1823, on page 748. At that point, ask students to predict what they think is going to happen during the rest of the story. Have them write their predictions in their Reader's Notebook. Have them also write any questions they have so far about the story or the characters.
  At the end of the story, students can return to their predictions and questions. Ask them to note if their predictions were accurate and if their questions were answered. They may want to write down any additional questions they have about the story or the characters.
- Ask students to write a note from Christoph to an ailing Mr. Beethoven, explaining how knowing Beethoven impacted his childhood and changed his life.

Possible Activities

Independent Activities

- Have advanced students skim over the story, noting details, facts, and descriptions about the character of Christoph. Ask them to write in their Reader's Notebook their analysis of the ways in which his character develops throughout the selection. Remind them to support their responses with evidence from the selection.

- Have students review the Learning the Language of Literature and Active Reader pages, pp. 697–699. Ask them what elements of historical fiction they noticed while reading this selection.

Discussion Activities

- Use the questions formulated by the students in their Reader's Notebooks as the start of a discussion about this story.

- Ask students what role they think the dog has in the story and to explain why they think the author included the details about the dog.

Assessment Opportunities

- You can assess student comprehension of the story by evaluating the questions students formulate in their Reader's Notebook.

- You can use any of the discussion questions as essay questions.

- You can have students turn any one of their Reader's Notebook entries into an essay.

They say he is working on a symphony. And so, all day long, he is hearing his music in his head. He doesn't think, perhaps, how very strange he sometimes seems to us.

Tomorrow I am leaving Salzburg again and traveling with friends to Bonn, the city where Mr. Beethoven was born. I know I will find something to tell you about and I will be sure to write on my return.

Uncle Karl

10 December 1822

Dear Uncle,

It has now been a full three months since Mr. Beethoven moved in, but our household has not yet become like any sort of ordinary place.

Mr. Beethoven has a friend named Mr. Schindler who visits almost every day. He always says, "Poor Mr. Beethoven. He is a lonely man."

You know that Mr. Beethoven is deaf. When he has visitors, they write what they want to say in a book. He reads their message and answers them out loud. He has a low and fuzzy voice.

Mr. Beethoven's eyes are weak as well. When he works too long by candlelight, his eyes begin to ache. He sometimes sits alone, with a cloth wrapped around his head to keep out the light. He sits, not seeing and not hearing, in his chair.

Uncle, there is no hour of the day when I forget that Mr. Beethoven is in the house.

Your nephew, Christoph

© Joseph Daniel Fiedler.

I returned to Salzburg in late January of 1823.

22 January 1823

Dear Christoph,

I have this very day returned from the place where Mr. Beethoven was born. It seems his family is well remembered there.

They say Mr. Beethoven's grandfather was a musician, in charge of all the music at the palace. And Mr. Beethoven's father was a musician, too. But Christoph, this father was an unhappy man who took to drink. Mr. Beethoven was not a happy child.

People who lived near their house remember hearing music coming from the attic late at night. Sometimes Mr. Beethoven's father would come home long after dark and get the young boy out of bed. He would make him practice his piano until dawn.

The little Beethoven would play all night, tired and cold, his face awash with tears. Finally, as the sun came up, he would go to bed to the sound of morning bells.

I will send this letter right away, in the hope that you will answer soon.

Affectionately, Uncle

4 February 1823

Dear Uncle,

This afternoon a messenger arrived, bearing a note for Mr. Beethoven.

The messenger said to me, "This is from Prince Karl Lichnowsky. But the prince says that if Mr. Beethoven's door is closed, he is not to be disturbed."

Mr. Beethoven must be a terrible man if even a prince is afraid of him.

Your nephew,
Christoph

15 February 1823

Dear Christoph,

I've been thinking of your story about the prince. Christoph, I don't think the prince is afraid of Mr. Beethoven. I believe he is showing him respect. In Vienna, music is so loved that even a prince will tread carefully around a composer.

Alas, Mr. Beethoven has not returned their kindness. He has not been gentle with the fine people of Vienna, and they have done everything they can to please him. Mr. Beethoven has always had rough manners. He turns down their invitations, dresses carelessly to visit, and arrives late for their dinners.

He sits, not seeing and not hearing, in his chair.

Sometimes he is very angry if he is asked to play his music. There is one famous story of a grand lady who got down on her knees one evening to beg Mr. Beethoven to play. He refused.

And there is another tale about a prince who teased Mr. Beethoven for not playing at dinner. Mr. Beethoven flew into a rage. "There are many princes," he said, "but there is only one Beethoven."

My belief, Christoph, is that a prince has more to fear from Mr. Beethoven than has a little boy.

Affectionately, Uncle

26 February 1823

Dear Uncle,

No news today but this—do you remember I once told you about a stray dog who was whining on the street? He is a small and spotted dog, and I have found a way to make him stop his crying.

Today he seemed quite pleased to share my sugar cake from lunch.

Christoph

2 March 1823

Dear Christoph,

I write again so soon because I have been making inquiries on your behalf.

I spoke today with a man who once worked for Mr. Beethoven, copying out music for the players. He told me that Mr. Beethoven never stays in one home very long. He moves often—as often as three times a year.

Sometimes Mr. Beethoven wants a sunnier home, sometimes shadier. Sometimes he says he cannot live on the ground floor; then he cannot live on the top. And I hear he has been asked to leave from time to time as well.

He has a restless nature, so perhaps before too long you will have your wish and quieter people will be living upstairs.

But in the meantime, tell me . . . is it true, as I have also heard, that Mr. Beethoven has three pianos in his room?

Your uncle

10 March 1823

Dear Uncle,

No, it is not true that Mr. Beethoven has three pianos. He has four! And you should see them! To begin with, some of his pianos have no legs. He takes the legs off to move them and so that he can play them when he is sitting on the floor. That way he can feel his playing through the floorboards, which he must do because, of course, he cannot hear.

But it's surprising that his pianos can be played at all. Many of the strings are broken and curled up. They look like birds' nests made of wire. And the pianos are stained inside from the times he's knocked the inkwell with his sleeve.

And Mr. Beethoven has all sorts of bells on his desk, and four ear trumpets to help him hear, and something called a metronome as well. It's a little box with a stick on it. The stick goes back and forth and back and forth and tells musicians how fast they should play.

Mr. Beethoven has a name for me. He calls me "the little gatekeeper" because I am always sitting outside on the step.

Yours truly,
Christoph
Gatekeeper

When he laughs, he sounds like a lion.

2 April 1823

Dear Christoph,

Your letter about Mr. Beethoven's piano has reminded me that there was a time when Mr. Beethoven was more famous for his playing than his composing.

When Mr. Beethoven first lived in Vienna, he would sit down with orchestras to play his music, without a single note written out. It was all in his head.

And the music he played! His music was so beautiful that sometimes people who were listening would start to cry. But Mr. Beethoven would laugh at them and say, "Composers do not cry. Composers are made of fire."

Now that Mr. Beethoven is deaf, of course, he plays the piano with the bumps and crashes you hear upstairs all day.

And I have another story for you, a story people tell about his deafness. One afternoon Mr. Beethoven was out walking in the woods with a friend. A shepherd was playing a flute nearby. Mr. Beethoven's friend said, "Listen!" and stopped to hear the flute. But Mr. Beethoven heard nothing. And so he knew, that day, that he was going deaf.

When Mr. Beethoven was still a young man, he began to hear humming and buzzing in his ears. At first he couldn't hear high notes. Then he couldn't hear soft voices. How frightening it must have been for him, Christoph, and how alone that man who lives upstairs must feel.

To hear Mr. Beethoven's story convinces me that I am the most fortunate man alive.

Your uncle

21 April 1823

Dear Uncle,

Do you remember my telling you that Mr. Beethoven leaves each afternoon for a walk? Did you wonder where he goes? Well, now I know, and I will tell you the story.

Mother sometimes says that instead of just staying on the front steps it would be nice if I'd spend some time inside. I used to believe she meant it until this morning.

Beethoven's Room at the Time of His Death (1827), Johann Nepomuk Hoechle. Historisches Museum der Stadt, Vienna, Austria/Bridgeman Art Library.

I thought of something to play with the twins. I rolled up a bit of cardboard like an ear trumpet and put one end in little Teresa's ear. I said, "GOOD MORNING, BABY!" very loudly, and she started to scream. Mother said it hurt her. So I went outside again and sat in my usual place on the step.

Then Mr. Schindler came downstairs. He said to me, "The master needs new pencils," and off I went to the shop.

When I came back, Mr. Schindler was gone. No one was upstairs but Mr. Beethoven, and he was writing at his desk. I stamped my feet on the floor to get his attention and when he didn't notice I stamped harder until at last I was stamping as hard as I could. Then suddenly he turned around and saw me. When he laughs, he sounds like a lion.

So today I went along with him on his walk. At times Mr. Beethoven forgot that I was with him. He would hum and sometimes wave his arms. He took out his papers and made some little notes.

We walked outside Vienna into the tall woods and then past the woods and into the fields. Uncle, if you were to come to visit me, I would show you today.

Christoph

In July of 1823 the following note arrived, unfinished and unsigned. Christoph was preoccupied, I suspect, by the pleasures of summertime and was too busy for letter writing. The note was sent to me by his mother, included in a letter of her own.

30 June 1823

Dear Uncle,

Spring has come and gone, and now it is summer. The house is quiet because tonight Mr. Beethoven has gone to Baden, where he will spend the hottest months. He will finish his symphony and then he will come back.

Tonight as I write you it is evening, but I cannot sleep with the sun still shining through the shutters. From my room I can hear Mother playing piano as she used to when I was small.

I have been sitting here thinking about something Mr. Schindler said. He said, "Mr. Beethoven works so hard because he believes that music can change the world."

In the autumn of 1823 Mr. Beethoven returned to Vienna from his summer lodgings.

29 October 1823

Dear Uncle,

Mr. Beethoven has come home, and so our house is in an uproar again. Someone has

Oratorio Performance at the Drury Lane Theatre (part two of a triptych, 1814) John Nixon/Private Collection/Bridgeman Art Library

given him another piano, and there was a lot of trouble getting it up the stairs.

And then last night he had a party. A lot of people went in and out very late, and the more cheerful they became upstairs, the noisier it was for us.

Finally, it was impossible to sleep. I could hear two ladies singing. I had seen them earlier, laughing on the stairs. They are called sopranos because they are singers who can sing very high.

Mr. Beethoven has a housekeeper. She says that when the sopranos come up the stairs, Mr. Beethoven rushes like a schoolboy to change his coat. And he won't let her make the coffee for them. It must be perfect, with exactly sixty beans for every cup. He counts them himself.

Uncle, I have asked Mother if you can come to visit. She said she would be delighted if you would. She thinks you would enjoy the goings-on.

Christoph

4 January 1824

Dear Christoph,

How glad I was to receive your letter. I hope you will forgive my very late reply. Did you know that your mother has written to me as well? She tells me there's a steady stream of great musicians up and down your stairs.

Since Mr. Beethoven is writing his Ninth Symphony in your very house, perhaps you will be interested in the things I have heard. According to the stories, Mr. Beethoven has felt that he is not appreciated in Vienna. He almost agreed to perform his new symphony in Berlin! I'm happy to say, though, that so many people begged Mr. Beethoven to change his mind that, luckily, he did.

And there is other news: they say the orchestra members are complaining about their parts. The bass players say their instruments aren't nimble enough for Mr. Beethoven's quick notes. The sopranos say their notes are just too high. All over Vienna the musicians are struggling with their tasks.

His symphony will put to music the poem "Ode to Joy."

I hear as well that because Mr. Beethoven is deaf, he will lead the orchestra with another conductor—one who can hear—conducting alongside him.

Amid these great events, little gatekeeper, how is life at home? Do your twin sisters still torment you with their terrible shouts? Perhaps before too long I shall hear them for myself.

Uncle Karl

27 March 1824

Dear Uncle,

I know this will come as a surprise, but this time I write you with good news.

I was standing on the upstairs landing today when my favorite soprano came by to get tickets for the concert. At least she is now my favorite.

She had something to ask of Mr. Beethoven and she wrote her request in his book. Then she wrote another request, handed him the book, and winked at me.

He read her words and said, "Certainly. The boy and his mother will have tickets as well."

And so Mother and I will be going to the Ninth Symphony. I wrote "thank you" as neatly as I could in his book.

As for the twins, Uncle, of course they still torment me. It is what they were put on earth to do.

Now I have a new name for my sisters. I call them the sopranos.

Now I have a new name for my sisters. I call them "the sopranos." It makes my mother laugh.

Yours truly, Christoph

20 April 1824

Dear Uncle,

I know now that all of us have been quite happy of late. And the way I know it is that in the past few days our happiness has vanished once again. With the symphony just two weeks away, Mr. Beethoven's moods are fierce.

Caroline, his housekeeper, is going to leave to marry the baker next door. She told Mr. Beethoven today, and he became very angry. He picked up an egg and threw it at her.

Then Mr. Schindler came rushing down the stairs like a scalded cat. He had told Mr. Beethoven that his new coat won't be ready for the concert in time. He tried to talk to Mr. Beethoven about another coat but, as Mr. Schindler said, "The master is in no mood for details."

And I have not helped matters. Today, when I was in his room, I disturbed some of his papers as I was passing by his desk. They fluttered to the floor. I am afraid these papers had been ordered in some very special way because Mr. Beethoven said, "Now I must do work again that I have already done."

Uncle, just when life was getting better, I have ruined things again.

Your nephew

28 April 1824

My dearest Christoph,

How shall I console you? Perhaps by telling you that Mr. Beethoven is famous for his temper and that his moods are not your fault.

Imagine how frustrating his life must be. Imagine how lonely to hear no voices. Imagine hearing no birds sing, no wind in the trees, no pealing of bells. Imagine: he hears no music played, not even his own!

So Mr. Beethoven has a great temper. How could he not? But if you listen to his music, you will hear that his heart is great as well, too great to be angry for long at an innocent boy.

You write me that, for the moment, your happiness has vanished. I can give you my promise, Christoph, that unhappiness has a way of vanishing as well.

Your uncle and friend, Karl

The unsigned and undated note below was written in May of 1824, on the eve of the first performance of the Ninth Symphony. It arrived tucked into the letter that follows it.

Dear Uncle,

Mr. Beethoven has forgotten the incident with the papers. He squeezed my shoulder in a friendly way when he passed me in the hall this afternoon.

Now the house is quiet, and I am alone. The concert is tomorrow night, and so, of course, I cannot sleep. I think of Mr. Beethoven alone upstairs. I have not heard him stir for quite some time. I wonder what he's thinking about. I wonder if he's awake tonight like me.

Perhaps he is hearing something beautiful in his head.

Perhaps he is hearing something beautiful in his head.

7 May 1824

Dear Uncle,

Tonight I have been to the Ninth Symphony. It is very late. I have already tried to sleep, but it seems I cannot do so before I describe this night to you.

The concert looked as I expected. There was Mr. Beethoven on the stage, waving his arms as I have seen him do so many times upstairs. And there were the singers. I had seen them often too, tramping up and down our halls. And there were the musicians scowling at their charts. These sights were so familiar.

It was the music, Uncle, that took me by surprise.

And when the music ended, the audience was on its feet. Everyone was standing and cheering and clapping and waving scarves and crying and trying to make Mr. Beethoven hear them.

But he couldn't hear us and he didn't know that we were cheering until one of the sopranos took his sleeve and turned him to face the crowd. Four times the audience finished their clapping and then began to clap and cheer again. Up on the stage Mr. Beethoven bowed and bowed.

As the carriage took us home, I could hear the music in my head. But my thoughts kept turning back to Mr. Beethoven himself.

He has so many troubles, how can he have a heart so full of joy?

I cannot describe the music, Uncle. I can only tell you what the music made me think.

Uncle, how difficult Mr. Beethoven's life must be. To feel so much inside, even so much joy, must be almost more than he can bear.

Christoph

In June of 1824 I finally paid a visit to Vienna, to the home of my sister, her twin girls, and Christoph. It was Christoph, of course, who took the most delight in explaining the many eccentricities of the genius up the stairs. This letter, the final portion of which is now missing, is the last in which my nephew mentions Mr. Beethoven. It arrived at my home in Salzburg almost a year after my visit to Vienna.

31 March 1825

Dear Uncle,

As you know, Mr. Beethoven moved away soon after your visit. But I have seen him again and thought you might like to hear about it.

It was on the street. I saw him rushing by, humming to himself as always. I ran up and caught him by the sleeve. He looked confused at first, but then he recognized me. He said, "It's the little gatekeeper," and took my hands in his.

I took his book and asked if he was well. He had hoped his health would be better living away from the river. He told me his health has not improved. I wrote in his book that when I grow up I'm going to be a doctor like my father and then I will make him better.

He asked about Mother and the twins, and he was glad to hear that Mother is teaching piano again. And then I told him that we miss him. He squeezed my hands and looked down at the ground.

And as for other news, the twins have finally stopped their screaming. I know, however, that our good luck will not hold. I have seen them exchanging looks in their carriage and can see that they are hatching some new plan.

But Uncle! Best of all! Mother has agreed to let me keep the spotted dog.

I have named him Metronome, because of his wagging tail. ❖

Barbara Nichol
born 1954

"I liked the experience of making [fiction] believable."

Hardworking Humorist A comedy writer for television and radio in Toronto, Barbara Nichol is known for her "mockumentary" projects. These include the award-winning television special *The Home for Blind Women* and radio's *The Lying Down*, about a fictional disease that causes people to appear dead but awaken after burial.

Nichol and her two sisters all have had successful media careers. "I think there was a feeling in our family that you have to get out there and roll up your sleeves," she says.

Creative Pursuits Nichol's best-selling first book, *Beethoven Lives Upstairs*, made its debut in audio form but soon gained fame on page and video. Her second book, *Dippers*, caused a stir when it came out on April Fool's Day in 1997. This fantasy about winged, doglike beasts who infest Cabbagetown, Toronto, in 1912 has caused some readers to ask, "Is it real?"—high praise for this inventive writer. Recently, Nichol published a book of poems about dogs and their feelings.

Standards-Based Objectives

- write a research report
- use a written text as a model for writing
- revise a draft to focus on one topic
- use compound subjects correctly
- deliver a research report

Introducing the Workshop

Research Report Tell students that a research report is an informational piece that explores one topic in detail. Discuss with students any research reports they may have read for science or social studies class. Have them think about what kinds of topics are usually written about in research reports. Lead the class in brainstorming a list of topics that might be appropriate for a research report.

Basics in a Box

Using the Graphic The elements that make up a research report—introduction, body, conclusion, and works cited list—are shown in the graphic. These elements are combined to form a cohesive report. Help students to understand the term *thesis* as a statement made about a topic. Point out that the graphic contains the elements that students will be asked to include when they draft their report.

Presenting the Rubric To help students better understand the assignment, review the Standards for Writing a Successful Research Report. You may also want to share with them the complete rubric, which describes several levels of proficiency.

 See **Unit Five Resource Book,** p. 86.

 For more instruction on essential writing skills, see McDougal Littell's *Language Network,* Chapters 10–17.

 Power Presentation

To engage students visually, use **Power Presentation 1,** Research Report.

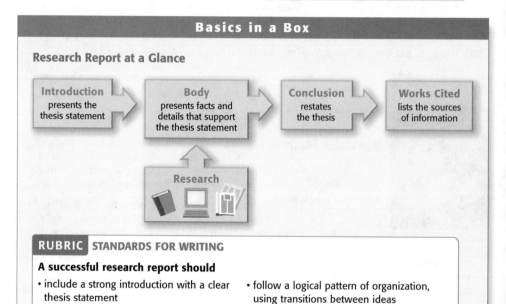

Writing Workshop

Research Report

Sharing Information . . .

From Reading to Writing Do the places you read about in historical fiction exist? One way to find the answer is to write a **research report.** This will help you learn to organize and share information from a variety of sources, including reference books, the Internet, and materials from certain organizations. When you set out to write a research report, you embark on a mystery and you are the detective.

For Your Portfolio

WRITING PROMPT Write a research report on a topic that interests you.

Purpose: To learn about the subject and share information with others

Audience: Your classmates, your teacher, or anyone who shares your interest in the topic

Basics in a Box

Research Report at a Glance

```
Introduction          Body              Conclusion         Works Cited
presents the          presents facts and restates           lists the sources
thesis statement      details that support the thesis        of information
                      the thesis statement

                      Research
```

RUBRIC STANDARDS FOR WRITING

A successful research report should

- include a strong introduction with a clear thesis statement
- use evidence from primary or secondary sources to develop and support ideas
- credit sources of information
- follow a logical pattern of organization, using transitions between ideas
- use information from more than one source
- summarize ideas in the conclusion
- include a correctly formatted Works Cited list at the end of the report

754 UNIT FIVE PART 2: VOICES FROM THE PAST

LESSON RESOURCES

Analyzing a Student Model

SPEAKING OPPORTUNITY

See the Speaking and Listening Handbook, p. R96 for oral presentation tips.

Helming 1

Katherine Helming
English, Grade 6
Mrs. Ruby
April 11

Perseus: Not Just Any Old Star

Have you ever looked up into the northern sky at night and seen the constellation Perseus? A constellation is a group of stars that form a design. Perseus was a hero of Greek mythology, famous for cutting off the head of the terrible Medusa. His character traits of courage, strength, kindness, compassion, and wisdom were important to the Greek people.

The story of Perseus dates back to the mid-400s B.C. in Athens. In Greek myth, Perseus was the son of Zeus, father of the gods, and Danaë, a mortal woman (D'Aulaire 115). Danaë's father, King Acrisius, had been warned that her son would bring him death (Felson-Rubin 295). Acrisius sent them both out to sea. Luckily, they were rescued.

Perseus grew up to be a strong athlete. He could jump higher, run faster, and use a sword better than all others in the kingdom. To the Greeks these traits were important. The Greeks held games (the Olympics!) in which athletes competed against each other. The Greeks believed their efforts pleased the gods (Paul 754, 760). It is easy to see why the Greeks valued Perseus.

Courage and wisdom were other qualities that the Greek people admired. Perseus first showed courage when he agreed to kill Medusa— "a snake-haired monster called a Gorgon whose horrible face turned all who looked at her to stone" (Felson-Rubin 295). Perseus was determined to succeed.

During his travels he met three sisters who told him that he would need both wisdom and strength to accomplish his task. He would also need a magic helmet, winged sandals, a sword, and a shield. The sisters gave him the helmet and sandals that would make him fly. The god Hermes and the goddess Athena gave him the sword and shield and told him where Medusa lived. Clever Perseus looked only at Medusa's reflection in his shield as he hovered above her and chopped off her head (Burn 63).

RUBRIC IN ACTION

❶ Uses a question to catch readers' attention

Another option:
· Begin with a quotation.

❷ States the subject and focus of the report (thesis statement)

❸ Supports main ideas of the report with details and explanations paraphrased from more than one authoritative source

❹ Uses transitions between ideas and follows a logical pattern of organization

Teaching the Lesson

Analyzing the Model

Perseus: Not Just Any Old Star
This research report recounts the story of Perseus from Greek mythology, for whom a constellation was named. Point out the Rubric in Action and discuss its use. Help students to see that the underlined sections correspond to the elements mentioned in the Rubric in Action. Ask students to read the report with a partner, discussing the Rubric in Action elements as they read.

1 Ask students to think about what kind of quotation might open this report. How would they go about selecting an appropriate quotation for their research report?

Possible Response: The quotation should be powerful and explicit so that the reader is drawn into the report right away. To select a good quotation, you should read carefully through the sources you have collected, looking for something intriguing.

2 Remind students that a thesis statement should clearly state the focus of the report. Ask them to suggest an alternative thesis statement.

Possible Response: Perseus was an important figure in Greek mythology, performing many heroic acts in his lifetime.

3 Ask students to identify the sources quoted in this section. Help them to see how different sources of information can be used to weave together a coherent report.

Answer: D'Aulaire, Felson-Rubin and Paul (both writing for the *World Book Encyclopedia)* are the sources quoted in this section.

4 Ask students to describe how this transition sentence helps the report flow smoothly and easily into the next paragraph.

Possible Response: In the thesis statement, several character traits are mentioned. The paragraphs that follow it discuss some of those traits. This transition sentence lets the reader know that more of the traits will be discussed in the next section.

5 Ask students what the number next to the name in parentheses represents.
Answer: the page number on which the quote can be found in the source material

Explain to students that a research report would need to continue on for several more paragraphs in order to be complete. Remind them that an important part of a research report is a strong conclusion that restates the thesis. Ask students how they might word a concluding statement for this research topic.
Possible Response: It is easy to see why such a noble hero was so important to the Greek people.

Works Cited: Ask students to look at the list of works cited and to decide which word in each entry was used for alphabetizing the list.
Possible Response: All the resources are alphabetized by the first letter in the first listed author's last name, even if the articles are in an encyclopedia.

Helming 2

Perseus needed compassion and strength in his next adventure. One day he found a beautiful girl chained to a rock. She explained that in her land there was a fierce sea monster. The monster had eaten many people and would stop only if she gave up her life. Perseus' heart filled with compassion for the girl (Burn 65).

Her name was Andromeda, the daughter of the king. The king told Perseus that if he could save Andromeda, he could have her hand in marriage (Burn 65). As the sea monster came toward Andromeda, Perseus jumped on its back. After a struggle, turned it to stone by showing it Medusa's head. Perseus and Andromeda were married that very night.

Though Perseus did not know it, the greatest test of his wisdom, strength, and compassion was upon him. Perseus returned home with Andromeda and found Danaë. Together they traveled to her native kingdom, Argos (D'Aulaire 120). On the way, Danaë told Perseus the story of his grandfather, King Acrisius. When they met, Acrisius could tell that Perseus was kind and would never try to harm him. Acrisius called all the people of the kingdom to come and listen to Perseus' adventures. He offered Perseus a discus and asked him to show the people how far he could throw it. When Perseus threw it, it hit the king. Perseus apologized over and over again. The king said that it wasn't his fault because what the gods predicted always came true. After telling Perseus to rule wisely

5 Credits source of each fact or quotation

Helming 4

Works Cited

Burn, Lucilla. Greek Myths. Austin: U of Texas P, 1990.

D'Aulaire, Ingri, and Edgar Parin D'Aulaire. Ingri and Edgar Parin D'Aulaire's Book of Greek Myths. Garden City: Doubleday, 1962.

Felson-Rubin, Nancy. "Perseus." The World Book Encyclopedia. 1990 ed.

Hunter, James. "Perseus." The Encyclopedia Mythica. Ed. M. F. Lindemans. 22 Mar. 1999. <http://www.pantheon.org/mythica/articles/p/perseus.html>.

Paul, C. Robert, Jr. "Olympic Games." The World Book Encyclopedia. 1990 ed.

Works Cited

The writer
• includes a biography, or list of the works used as sources for the report.
• arranges sources alphabetically by the authors' last names or the first words of the titles.

EXPLICIT INSTRUCTION ## Patterns of Organization

PICTURING TEXT STRUCTURE
Instruction One way to structure a good research report is to have students identify the focus or thesis of the report, then think of the main ideas of the focus. Finally, students list the details that support each main idea. In other words, each detail supports each main idea, and the main ideas taken together form the thesis statement. Discuss the sample graphic at the right with students.

Practice Have students analyze the organization of the student model by constructing a similar concept web.

Use **Reading and Critical Thinking Transparencies**, p. 37, for additional support.
Use **Writing Transparencies**, p. 7, for additional support.

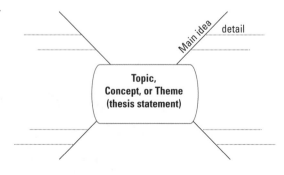

Writing Your Research Report

❶ Prewriting and Exploring

As a general rule, the most successful man in life is the man who has the best information.
—Benjamin Disraeli, 19th-century British prime minister

To find a topic that interests you, **list** the places mentioned in the Unit Five selections. **Write down** actions, beliefs, or discoveries that the stories deal with. **Name** people about whom you would like to know more. See the **Idea Bank** in the margin for more suggestions. After choosing your subject, follow the steps below.

Planning Your Research Report

▶ **1. Find a focus.** You can't cover everything about your topic in one report. To find your focus, create a web diagram of ideas. Ask questions about your topic that you will be able to answer in your research. Reading a general encyclopedia article about your topic can also help you choose one aspect to focus on.

▶ **2. Identify your audience.** How much background information will your readers need to know about your subject? What information will be most useful or interesting to them?

▶ **3. Set a purpose.** Think about why you are writing this report. Try to write your purpose in one sentence. Later, you will use this sentence to help you write your **thesis statement**. This is the sentence that states the subject and purpose of your report. A clear purpose will guide you in your research.

❷ Researching

Researching is the stage where you find facts about your topic. First read a few general articles. Then make a list of questions you want answered. Let your search for answers guide your research.

Remember there are two types of sources—primary and secondary. **Primary sources** provide firsthand information. They include letters, diaries, journals, and historical documents. **Secondary sources** provide explanations and comments on other sources. Encyclopedias, newspapers, magazines, and textbooks are examples of secondary sources. These resources provide different types of information.

IDEA Bank

1. Research and Technology
Look for ideas in the **Research and Technology** activities you completed in this unit and in earlier units.

2. Current Events
Watch the news or read a newspaper to find a country that interests you. Research current events in that country. Your report might also explore that country's history.

3. Get in the Know
Ask friends or relatives to list subjects about which they have some knowledge. Choose a subject that you'd like to know more about.

Need help with your report?

See Forming and Revising Research Questions, pp. 388–390.

See the **Writing Handbook,** pp. R49–R53.

See **Language Network,** Research Report, p.418 Finding Information, p.437

Guiding Student Writing

Prewriting and Exploring
Choosing a Subject
If after reading the Idea Bank students have difficulty choosing a subject for their research report, suggest they try the following:

- Go back to the brainstormed lists of possible topics from the beginning of the lesson.
- Think about the topics they are currently studying in social studies and science.
- Talk with a partner about possible topics on their list.

Planning Your Research Report
1. Students may want to share their topic with a partner and brainstorm ideas about a focus for that topic. The most common error for students is to select a topic that is too big for one report. Encourage students to help their partners think about how to narrow the subject into one strong focus.
2. Remind students that depending on who will be reading the report, specific background information will have to be provided. Encourage them to identify an audience prior to moving on to the next step.
3. Have students do this task individually. It should reflect their personal reasons for writing this research report. Stress the idea that having one strong sentence—rather than a paragraph of explanation that wanders around the topic—will make it easier for them later.

Researching
It may be helpful for students to spend a class period in the library gathering their resources. A place to start is with the examples listed in this section under primary and secondary sources. A librarian or media specialist could be of benefit during this first source-gathering session.

After students have had a chance to look at the sources selected, they may need additional trips to the library as their topic becomes more focused.

📋 Use **Writing Transparencies,** p. 41, for additional support.

Evaluate Your Sources

Encourage students to use the questions included in this section to evaluate each of their potential sources. Remind them that it is okay to not use every source they find initially and to keep looking if their questions are not being answered. Engage the support of your school librarian again for helping students in identifying reliable and current source material.

 Use **Writing Transparencies**, p. 53, for additional support.

Make Source Cards

Ask a student to volunteer to help you model a source card. Have the student provide you with the information needed as you create a large class model. This will give students a visual reminder of how to complete their own source cards. Remind them to number the source cards as they complete them.

Take Notes

Remind students that they should not copy any material directly from a source unless it is a short excerpt to be used as a direct quotation. In such cases they should include quotation marks in their notes. Review summarizing and paraphrasing as necessary. Use another large class model card to demonstrate how to take information from a source and paraphrase it for a note card. Tell students to number the note card with the source card number and page number, as this will be important should they need to look up this information later.

RESEARCH Tip

Check the list of sources at the end of books or articles and investigate some of the sources that the author of your source used.

INTERNET Tip

Ask your librarian to help you carefully choose keywords to do an Internet search.

Need help organizing your note cards?

See the **Writing Handbook** Making Source Cards, p. R50.

You may want to explore the computerized card catalog in your local library to help you locate sources. To see if a **book** contains the information you need, look at its table of contents. **Periodicals, newspapers,** and **magazines** can be found by using your library's periodical index, which lists magazine articles by subject. This source may also be online in your library. The **Internet** is also a source of many types of information.

Evaluate Your Sources

Remember, you cannot believe everything you read. Checking several sources to see if the facts are the same will help you decide if a source is reliable. Especially when using the Internet, ask these questions.

- **What are the qualifications of the author?** Is the author from a respected institution? Is he or she a professional? Does the author have a bias that affects the way the information is presented?

- **Is the information up-to-date and accurate?** Use the most recent information you can find.

Make Source Cards

Using index cards, create source cards for the sources that you use. Write the relevant information for each source on a separate index card, and number each card. The cards will help you to create your Works Cited list. Follow the format shown on the right.

Take Notes

Use index cards to record information. Write the main idea of each note at the top of the card, along with the number that you assigned the source on the source card. Write just one piece of information on each card.

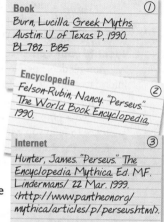

Book ①
Burn, Lucilla. *Greek Myths.* Austin: U of Texas P, 1990. BL782 .B85

Encyclopedia ②
Felson-Rubin, Nancy. "Perseus." *The World Book Encyclopedia.* 1990.

Internet ③
Hunter, James. "Perseus." *The Encyclopedia Mythica.* Ed. M.F. Lindermans/ 22 Mar. 1999. <http://www.pantheon.org/mythica/articles/p/perseus.html>.

Perseus and Medusa
Perseus agreed to kill Medusa. Medusa was a "snake-haired monster called a Gorgon whose horrible face turned all who looked at her into stone." 295
(Paraphrase and Quotation)

Source Number

Paraphrase. Restate ideas in your own words to avoid plagiarism, which is using someone else's original words without giving credit to the author.

Quotation. Write the quote exactly as it appears in the source. Use quotation marks to show where it begins and ends.

Page Number

Organize Your Material

Now group the cards by similar main points. Think about the order of ideas. You might choose a **chronological, cause-and-effect, comparison-and-contrast,** or **problem-solution** pattern of organization. Once you write down your main headings, think about **subheadings,** specific points to cover.

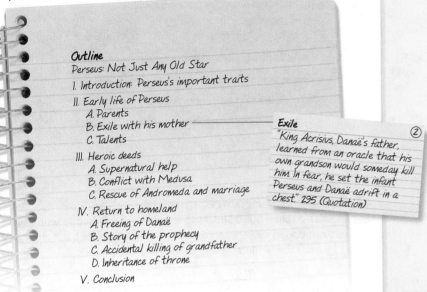

Outline
Perseus: Not Just Any Old Star
I. Introduction: Perseus's important traits
II. Early life of Perseus
   A. Parents
   B. Exile with his mother
   C. Talents
III. Heroic deeds
   A. Supernatural help
   B. Conflict with Medusa
   C. Rescue of Andromeda and marriage
IV. Return to homeland
   A. Freeing of Danaë
   B. Story of the prophecy
   C. Accidental killing of grandfather
   D. Inheritance of throne
V. Conclusion

Exile   ②
"King Acrisius, Danaë's father, learned from an oracle that his own grandson would someday kill him. In fear, he set the infant Perseus and Danaë adrift in a chest." 295 (Quotation)

❸ Drafting

Using your outline as your guide, begin to write your first draft.

- In your **introduction,** capture the attention of your readers with a quotation, an anecdote, or an explanation of why the subject interests you. State the topic and purpose of your report in one sentence if you can. This is your **thesis statement.**

- The **body** of your report presents the main ideas, supporting facts, and the other details that you discovered in your research. However, this doesn't mean that you should only restate facts or retell events. You will need to make inferences and draw conclusions based on the information you have uncovered.

- **Conclude** by summarizing the focus of your report and what you've learned.

DRAFTING Tip

Begin a new body paragraph for each new subheading in your outline.

Ask Your Peer Reader: EVALUATING

- Did you understand my topic?
- Were any parts confusing?
- Where do I need more facts, examples, and explanations?

Organize Your Material

It may be helpful to students to review the organizational methods listed here. Providing them with graphic organizers of each method would also help. Encourage students to select an organizational method that matches the content of their report.

After selecting the organizational format, model the outlining process as shown on this page. Again, making a large outline for the model will provide students with a mental and physical image of the process they need to follow as they organize and outline their own reports.

Use **Writing Transparencies,** p. 54, for additional support.

Drafting

Tell students that they may want to refer back to the Standards for Writing a Successful Research Report on page 754 as they begin their first draft. A quick reminder of the rubric will focus students' writing on the key elements.

Ask Your Peer Reader

Asking a peer reviewer to read the draft of the research report will focus on some of the key elements. Encourage peer readers to read critically and to take notes for the writer. As students conference about each report, remind them to be respectful of the author's work, yet constructive in their suggestions for revisions.

Revising
FOCUSING YOUR REPORT

Remind students that their peer reader may have suggestions about what to eliminate in order to keep the report focused on one topic. Ask students to reread their reports and to carefully reconsider each sentence.

 Use **Writing Transparencies**, p. 12, for additional support.

Editing and Proofreading
COMPOUND SUBJECTS

Tell students that using compound subjects in some of their sentences can make their writing smoother. Ask them to think about which short or choppy sentences could be rewritten with compound subjects to make a new, smoother sentence. Ask for student volunteers to share cases from their own writing, and model how to create a new sentence.

Making a Works Cited List

Tell students to take their source cards and highlight the key word by which they will alphabetize. Then they can sort the cards into alphabetical order by the highlighted words. It is then an easy step to copy the information from the source cards into a Works Cited List.

 Use **Writing Transparencies**, p. 56, for additional support.

Reflecting

Encourage students to be specific as they identify the part of the research process they learned the most from. Ask them to think about why this part helped them. Have them list several other topics they may wish to research at another time.

Option
TEACHING TIP

Research reports can have a tendency to become dry and boring. Help students to choose engaging topics, use interesting words and descriptions, and have fun with language and information throughout their report.

Need revising help?

Review the **Rubric**, p. 754.
Consider **peer reader** comments.
Check **Revision Guidelines**, p. R31.

Questioning compound subjects?

See the **Grammar Handbook**, p. R68.

SPELLING From Writing

As you revise your work, look back at the words you misspelled and determine why you made the errors you did. For additional help, refer to the strategies and generalizations in the **Spelling Handbook** on page R26.

Speaking OPPORTUNITY

Turn your research report into an oral presentation.

Publishing IDEAS

- Create a multimedia presentation that presents the most important ideas about your topic. Use visual aids to make your report more interesting.
- Find students who chose topics related to yours. Combine your reports into a booklet that gives in-depth information about the topic.

INTERNET
Publishing Options
www.mcdougallittell.com

---

❹ Revising
TARGET SKILL ▸ FOCUSING YOUR REPORT Your researching process will sometimes lead you to information on other subjects connected to your topic. Because you can't include everything in one report, however, you need to keep your focus on one topic. Always ask yourself whether a fact, an example, or a detail develops the main idea you have chosen. Check your report for unrelated details or poor organization.

> In Greek mythology, Perseus was the son of Zeus, father of
> the gods, and Danaë, a mortal woman. ~~Zeus had many~~ *(D'Aulaire 115).*
> ~~children that were half god and half mortal. Another~~
> ~~famous Greek hero Hercules also had Zeus as his father.~~
> Danaë's father, King Acrisius, had been warned that her
> son would bring him death.

❺ Editing and Proofreading
TARGET SKILL ▸ COMPOUND SUBJECTS Get rid of short, choppy sentences by using compound subjects. A **compound subject** whose parts are joined by *and* takes a plural verb.

> *and Zeus were*
> Athena ~~was~~ about to ask him to fly over the mountains
> until he came to the sea.

❻ Making a Works Cited List
When you have finished revising your report, make an alphabetical list of the sources that you used. See page R52 in the **Writing Handbook** for the correct format.

❼ Reflecting
FOR YOUR WORKING PORTFOLIO What did you learn about the research process from writing your report? What other topics would you like to research? Attach your answers to your finished report. Save your research report in your **Working Portfolio**.

EXPLICIT INSTRUCTION **Revision**

ORGANIZATION

Instruction Remind students that in a well-organized research report, using facts, examples, and details to support main ideas strengthens their reports and provides focus. Unnecessary information, however, can confuse or annoy the reader. Unrelated details or interesting information that is not particularly on the point can detract from the main focus.

Practice Ask students to read their essays looking for extraneous or unnecessary facts, details, and examples. They should delete any information that does not contribute to the focus of their essay.

> See the **Research and Technology Handbook**, pp. R108–109, for information about formatting documents using word processing skills.

Use **Unit Five Resource Book**, p. 82, to help students understand and use organization by categories.

Standardized Test Practice

Mixed Review

The gods Odin in Norse mythology and Zeus in Greek mythology
<u>is very different</u> from each other. <u>Odin does not never eat</u> with the other
(1)   (3)
gods and goddesses. He sits quietly, thinking about the advice of his two
ravens, whose names are Thought and Memory. <u>Odin is willing</u> to
pursue wisdom even if he has to suffer. <u>He go to the Well of Wisdom.</u>
(5)
Mimir the wise tells him that he has to give up one of his eyes to gain
the knowledge. <u>Odin hardly doesn't mind at all.</u>
(6)

1. How is item 1 best written?

A. The Gods Odin in norse mythology and Zeus in Greek

B. The gods Odin in Norse mythology and zeus in Greek

C. The gods Odin in norse mythology and Zeus in greek

D. Correct as is

2. How is item 2 best written?

A. are very different

B. is very differently

C. are being very different

D. Correct as is

3. How is item 3 best written?

A. Odin never eats

B. Odin don't ever eat

C. Odin does hardly not eat

D. Correct as is

4. How is item 4 best written?

A. Odin was willing

B. Odin would have been willing

C. Odin will be willing

D. Correct as is

5. How is sentence 5 best written?

A. He is gone to the Well of Wisdom.

B. He goes to the Well of Wisdom.

C. He is going to the Well of Wisdom.

D. Correct as is

6. How is sentence 6 best written?

A. Odin hardly minds at all.

B. Odin barely doesn't mind at all.

C. Odin doesn't scarcely mind.

D. Correct as is

Review Your Skills

Use the passage and the questions that follow it to check how well you remember the language conventions you've learned in previous grades.

Self-Assessment

Check your own answers in the **Grammar Handbook.**

Using Verbs Correctly, p. R76

Using Modifiers Effectively, p. R78

Correcting Capitalization, p. R81

Ask students to read the entire passage prior to correcting the errors. Demonstrate how students can eliminate incorrect choices for the first question. The words Norse and Greek are both proper adjectives and should be capitalized. Therefore A and C are not correct choices. In choice B, the name Zeus is not capitalized. The sentence is correct as it is, so D is the correct answer.

Answers:
1. D; **2.** A; **3.** A, **4.** D, **5.** B, **6.** A

EXPLICIT INSTRUCTION Speaking Opportunity

Prepare Once students have written their research report, they can plan to present it to an audience. Refer students to pages R103–104 of the Speaking and Listening Handbook at the back of this book for tips on presenting their research report.

Present Have students present their reports to the class. They should strive to gather evidence from a variety of sources and to present information in a way that is clear and accurate.

RUBRIC

3 Full Accomplishment Student poses a relevant question about a topic, includes pertinent evidence in support of the topic, and cites reference sources appropriately, including multimedia items.

2 Substantial Accomplishment Student poses a question about a topic, has some evidence in support of the topic, and cites reference sources appropriately.

1 Little or Partial Accomplishment Student has a topic, but does not provide much support for that topic. Sources are cited in incorrect form.

Use **Speaking and Listening Book,** pp. 10–11, 25–26, for additional support in presenting a research report.

UNIT FIVE *Reflect* and Assess

Standards-Based Objectives

- reflect on unit themes
- review literary analysis skills used in the unit
- paraphrase and summarize text to recall, inform, or organize ideas
- recognize how style, tone, and mood contribute to the effect of the text
- assess and build portfolios

Reflecting on Theme

OPTION 1

A successful response will

- compare and contrast the younger character with the older character
- display an understanding of the character and her/his voice
- support responses by referring to relevant aspects of text
- discuss reasons for opinions in brief written form

OPTION 2

A successful response will

- creatively illustrate the uniqueness of the culture
- show an understanding of the culture and the text through the chosen quotes
- use multiple sources, including electronic texts, experts, and print resources, to locate information relevant to research

OPTION 3

A successful response will

- demonstrate effective communication skills while providing information
- clarify and support spoken ideas with evidence, elaborations, and examples
- illustrate an understanding of the character or person under discussion and the ways in which that character or person developed

Self Assessment

In order to help students organize their ideas, have them create a chart that lists the ways people in this unit made their mark. Suggest that students then look at this list and make a connection based on their own life experiences.

Making Your Mark

By reading the selections in this unit, you have seen that there are many ways to make your mark. A person might develop a particular talent, give an extra effort, or just see where his or her interests lead. There are as many ways to leave an impression as there are people in the world. Use the following options to reflect on what you've learned.

Reflecting on Theme

OPTION 1

Predicting Outcomes What impact can early experiences have on a person's future? Imagine that ten years have passed in the lives of Lenore in *Words on a Page*, the narrator in "Crow Call," and James in "The Scribe." Draft a brief description of each character's new situation. Share opinions about how their experiences might have affected the way each found their voice.

OPTION 2

Remembering the Past In her "Newbery Acceptance Speech," Lois Lowry spoke of the character Jonas discovering that "his own past goes back further than he had ever known." What do you think people can gain from learning about the far past? Think about the ancient cultures you read about in this unit. Choose one and make a poster that celebrates it. Include quotes from the selection, drawings of artifacts, and facts you find surprising.

OPTION 3

Comparing Qualities What qualities do you think make it possible for a person to make his or her mark? Make a list of the strongest qualities shown by different characters and real people in the selections in this unit. Use the list to evaluate four of these characters or real people. In your opinion, which one had the greatest impact on his or her world? Consider each one's situation. Which one made the biggest breakthrough? Discuss your choices with a partner.

Self ASSESSMENT

READER'S NOTEBOOK

After reading the selections in Unit Five, what have you learned about the many ways people can make their marks? Which of these ways might you like to pursue? Write a paragraph explaining your response.

REVIEWING YOUR PERSONAL WORD List

Vocabulary Review the new words you learned in this unit. If necessary, use a dictionary to check the meaning of each word.

Spelling Review your list of spelling words. If you're not sure of the correct spelling, use a dictionary or refer to the **Spelling Handbook** on page R26.

Reviewing Literary Concepts

Looking at Symbols As you know, objects and images are sometimes used in literature to symbolize things—such as ideas or feelings—that cannot be seen. Copy this diagram and work with a partner to identify a symbol in each of the selections listed. Discuss what you think each symbol stands for.

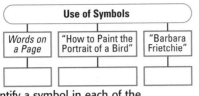

Use of Symbols

Words on a Page	"How to Paint the Portrait of a Bird"	"Barbara Frietchie"

Thinking About History You have learned about two important sources you can use to find out about history: historical fiction and informative nonfiction. Look through the selections in this unit to find examples of each type. Make a chart like the one shown, and use it to record your examples. Beneath the examples, list the strengths of each type.

Historical Fiction	Informative Nonfiction

📁 Portfolio Building

- **Choices and Challenges—Writing** Several of the Writing assignments in this unit asked you to describe someone or something. Choose the description that makes you most proud. Write a cover note telling what you like about your work. Then add your description and note to your **Presentation Portfolio.** 📁

- **Writing Workshops** In one Writing Workshop, you wrote an opinion statement. In another, you wrote a research report. Review these two pieces. Which one better shows your strengths? Write a note explaining your choice and place it with the piece in your **Presentation Portfolio.** 📁

- **Additional Activities** Think back to the assignments you completed for **Speaking & Listening** and **Research & Technology.** Keep a record in your portfolio of assignments you particularly enjoyed, found helpful, or would like to explore further.

Self ASSESSMENT

📖 READER'S NOTEBOOK

Copy the following list of literary terms introduced or reviewed in this unit. Put a check mark next to each one you do not fully understand. Look at the **Glossary of Literary and Reading Terms** (p. R116) to clarify the meanings of the terms you marked.

theme
personal essay
onomatopoeia
symbol
voice
historical fiction
conflict
informative
 nonfiction

primary
 source
secondary
 source
couplet
sound
 devices

Self ASSESSMENT

Compare the recent additions to your portfolio with earlier pieces. How has your writing improved? Write down your three strongest improvements as a writer and reader.

Setting GOALS

By now you have completed a number of research-based projects. In doing them, what did you discover to be your greatest strength? Write a note describing how that strength can help you with future research projects.

Reviewing Literary Concepts

Students should choose the symbol that they feel is most significant for each story. Ask for volunteers to share their ideas with the rest of the class.

A successful response will:

- recognize the distinguishing features of historical fiction and informative nonfiction
- provide appropriate examples of the strengths of each genre.

📁 Portfolio Building

Students should evaluate the items in their Working Portfolios and choose pieces that represent their highest quality work for their Presentation Portfolios.

LITERATURE CONNECTIONS
I, Juan de Pareja

BY ELIZABETH BORTON DE TREVIÑO

This Newbery Award–winning historical novel, set in 17th-century Spain, is based on the life of a young black slave inherited by master painter Diego Velázquez. Juan de Pareja begins secretly indulging his own love of painting, an activity forbidden to slaves.

These thematically related readings are provided along with *I, Juan de Pareja*:

How to Paint the Portrait of a Bird
BY JACQUES PRÉVERT

Mi Maestro
BY ANA CASTILLO

The Magical Horse
BY LAURENCE YEP

from **The American Eye**
BY JAN GREENBERG AND SANDRA JORDAN

The Jade Stone
BY CARYN YACOWITZ AND AARON SHEPARD

A Work of Art
BY MARGARET MAHY

To Look at Any Thing
BY JOHN MOFFITT

Aunt Zurletha
BY RUBY DEE

More Choices

Black Star, Bright Dawn
BY SCOTT O'DELL
In this story, a girl takes her father's place in a 1,000 mile dogsled race. She must depend on her lead dog for survival.

Roller Skates
BY RUTH SAWYER
When her parents go to Europe, tomboy Lucinda sets out to explore New York City on her roller skates.

Sequoyah
BY ROBERT CWIKLIK
Cherokee leader Sequoyah worked for many years to create a written version of the Cherokee language. His work gave his people a voice.

Shadow of a Bull
BY MAIA WOJCIECHOWSKA
Eleven-year-old Manolo is terrified of bulls but he must follow in the footsteps of his father, who was one of the greatest bullfighters in Spain.

Sojourner Truth and the Struggle for Freedom
BY EDWARD BEECHER CLAFLIN
Sojourner Truth, a freed slave, helped other slaves escape the South. She went on to give her voice to the abolitionist and women's rights movements.

LITERATURE CONNECTIONS
Across Five Aprils

BY IRENE HUNT

A family is divided by the Civil War when the three oldest boys go off to battle and the youngest, Jethro Creighton, is left to run the farm. Over five years, Jethro grows up with the fears, sorrows, and horrors of war as experienced from the home front. This historical novel is a Newbery Honor Book.

These thematically related readings are provided along with *Across Five Aprils*:

from **The Boys' War**
BY JIM MURPHY

**The Mysterious
Mr. Lincoln**
BY RUSSELL FREEDMAN

**The Gettysburg
Address**
BY ABRAHAM LINCOLN

**The Drummer Boy
of Shiloh**
BY RAY BRADBURY

Around the Campfire
BY ANDREW HUDGINS

The Huts at Esquimaux
BY NORMAN DUBIE

The Sniper
BY LIAM O'FLAHERTY

from **Voices from the
Battlefield**
BY MILTON MELTZER

Social Studies Connection

The Roman News
BY ANDREW LANGLEY, PHILIP
DE SOUZA
Here is life in ancient Rome, presented in newspaper form.

The Bronze Bow
BY ELIZABETH SPEARE
A young man seeks vengeance against Roman conquerors for the deaths of his father, uncle, and brother.

Detectives in Togas
BY HENRY WINTERFELD
A group of young friends living in ancient Rome set out to solve a crime involving graffiti scrawled on the temple wall.

Julius Caesar
EDITED BY DIANE DAVIDSON
This 40-minute version of the classic Shakespearean play set in Roman times introduces the play and preserves Shakespeare's language.

Song for a Dark Queen
BY ROSEMARY SUTCLIFF
Boudicca was a warrior queen in the first century A.D. This is the story of her fight against Roman rule of her people.

Pompeii
BY TIMOTHY LEVI BIEL
This is the story of the city of Pompeii before, during, and after the volcano Mt. Vesuvius erupted and destroyed it.

Unit Overview

In Unit Six, "The Oral Tradition: Tales from the Ancient World to Today," students will explore folk tales, fables, myths, and legends from around the world. The selections in Unit Six are grouped in "links" that correspond thematically to the previous units. The selections may be read separately, or each grouping of "links" may be read with the selections of the corresponding thematic unit.

Links to Unit One: Tests of Courage
- The Boy Who Flew
- Arachne
- Ceres and Proserpina

Links to Unit Two: Growth and Change
- The Disobedient Child
- The Bamboo Beads

Links to Unit Three: A Sense of Fairness
- In the Land of Small Dragon
- King Thrushbeard

Links to Unit Four: Wondrous Worlds
- Why Monkeys Live in Trees
- The Legend of the Hummingbird
- The Living Kuan-yin

Links to Unit Five: Making Your Mark
- The Frog Who Wanted to Be a Singer
- Where the Girl Rescued Her Brother

UNIT SIX

The Oral Tradition

Tales from the Ancient World to Today

"You can learn through the laughter. You can learn through the tears."

Diane Ferlatte
storyteller

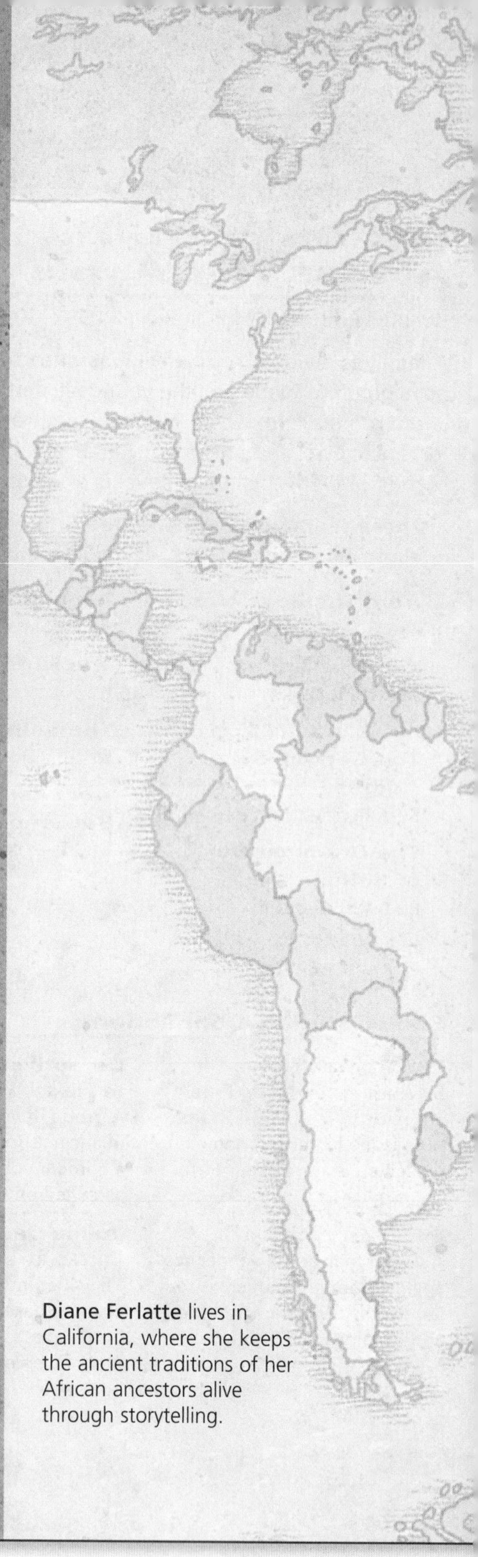

Diane Ferlatte lives in California, where she keeps the ancient traditions of her African ancestors alive through storytelling.

767

Discussion Questions
Discovering the Oral Tradition

Have students read the quotation on page 766 by storyteller Diane Ferlatte, whose photograph appears on page 767. Then ask the following discussion questions:

1. What do you think Diane Ferlatte means by "the laughter" and "the tears"?
   Possible Response: She means the happiness and sorrow that come into everybody's life.
2. What might a storyteller learn through the laughter and tears?
   Possible Responses: She might learn how to tell a story that moves people; she might learn how to be in touch with and express her own joys and sorrows.
3. What stories have you read or seen in movies or television shows that made you laugh or cry?

Introducing Storytelling

Use the following activity to help students experience how a story takes shape and changes as it is passed around. Divide the class into four or five groups. Have the first group make up or relate a true story about a childhood experience to tell the second group. Groups may wish to appoint one person as storyteller or take turns telling parts of the story. Have the second group tell the story to the third group and so on until all groups have heard it. Have the last group tell the story to the whole class.

Then have students compare and contrast the story that the last group told and the story that other groups told or heard. Challenge students to make a generalization about what happens to a story as it is passed along orally.

Possible Responses: The words change. Details may be added or subtracted. They may become exaggerated. Sometimes the meaning changes, too.

EXPLICIT INSTRUCTION ## Speaking and Listening

STORYTELLING IN THE CLASSROOM

Students can help create an atmosphere for storytelling by being attentive listeners. Consider having them sit quietly for a moment before beginning a story. Some students might try listening with their eyes closed or try helping the storyteller by adding sound effects.

Features and Selections	Literary Analysis	Reading and Critical Thinking	Writing Opportunities	
The Oral Tradition **Storytellers Past and Present** **Keeping the Past Alive**				
Links to Unit 1	As You Read, 773 Setting, 787	Summary, 777		
Links to Unit 2	As You Read, 789 Plot and Theme, 793			
Links to Unit 3	As You Read, 801	Comparing a Video with a Story, 813 Persuasive Devices, 810		
Links to Unit 4	As You Read, 817	Cause-and-Effect Relationships, 821		
Links to Unit 5	As You Read, 831	Summary, 840		
Writing Workshop: Multimedia Presentation **Standardized Test Practice**		Analyzing a Multimedia Presentation, 845 Standardized Test Practice, 849	Creating Your Presentation, 846	
Building Your Portfolio **Across Cultures: The Oral Tradition**		Studying Heroes, 850 Self Assessment, 850	Building your Portfolio, 850	

LEGEND   DLS – Daily Language SkillBuilder   Green type – Teacher's Edition

Speaking and Listening Viewing and Representing	Research and Technology	Grammar, Usage, and Mechanics	Vocabulary	
Storytelling, 767, 769 Listening to a Story, 768				
Art Appreciation, 775 Read Aloud, 776 Illustration, 778 Interviewing, 781 Drama Performance, 785		Daily Language Skillbuilder, 772		
Viewing and Representing, 790, 797 Art Appreciation, 797 Dialect, 794		Daily Language Skillbuilder, 788		
Choral Reading, 803 Interviews, 806 Storytelling, 811		Daily Language Skillbuilder, 800		
Art Appreciation, 822 Viewing and Representing, 818, 827 Choral Reading, 825		Daily Language Skillbuilder, 816		
Art Appreciation, 832, 837 Rhythm and Blues, 836		Daily Language Skillbuilder, 830		
Practicing and Presenting, 847		Consistent Form, 848		

	Unit Resource Book	Assessment	Integrated Technology and Media
Links to Unit 1 *pp. 770–787*	• Summaries p. 4 • Active Reading: Summarize p. 5 • Literary Analysis: Myth p. 6 • Words to Know p. 7 • Selection Quiz p. 8	• Selection Test, Formal Assessment pp. 125–126 🖸 Test Generator	🎧 Audio Library 📼 Video: Literature in Performance, Video Resource Book pp. 31–38 🖱 Research Starter www.mcdougallittell.com
Links to Unit 2 *pp. 788–799*	• Summaries p. 9 • Active Reading: Story Mapping p. 10 • Literary Analysis: Setting p. 11 • Words to Know p. 12 • Selection Quiz p. 13	• Selection Test, Formal Assessment pp. 127–128 🖸 Test Generator	🎧 Audio Library 🖱 Research Starter www.mcdougallittell.com
Links to Unit 3 *pp. 800–815*	• Summaries p. 14 • Active Reading: Using Text Organizers p. 15 • Literary Analysis: Figurative Language p. 16 • Words to Know p. 17 • Selection Quiz p. 18	• Selection Test, Formal Assessment pp. 129–130 🖸 Test Generator	🎧 Audio Library 🖱 Research Starter www.mcdougallittell.com
Links to Unit 4 *pp. 816–829*	• Summaries p. 19 • Active Reading: Connecting p. 20 • Literary Analysis: Characterization p. 21 • Words to Know p. 22 • Selection Quiz p. 23	• Selection Test, Formal Assessment pp. 131–132 🖸 Test Generator	🎧 Audio Library
Links to Unit 5 *pp. 830–841*	• Summaries p. 24 • Active Reading: Making Inferences p. 25 • Literary Analysis: Fantasy p. 26 • Words to Know p. 27 • Selection Quiz p. 28	• Selection Test, Formal Assessment pp. 133–134 🖸 Test Generator	🎧 Audio Library

Communication Workshop: Multimedia Presentation

		Unit Assessment	*Unit Technology*
Unit Six Resource Book • Planning Your Presentation p. 29 • Developing, Practicing, and Presenting p. 30 • Peer Response Guide pp. 31–32 • Refining, Editing, and Proofreading p. 33 • Rubric for Evaluation p. 34	🖸 **Writing Coach** **Writing Transparencies** TR18 🖸 **Speaking and Listening Book** pp. 8–13	• Unit Test, Formal Assessment pp. 135–136 🖸 Test Generator • Unit Six: Integrated Assessment pp. 13–18	🖱 ClassZone www.mcdougallittell.com 🖸 Electronic Teacher Tools

Additional Support

Literary Analysis Transparencies	Reading and Critical Thinking Transparencies	Language Transparencies	Writing Transparencies	Speaking and Listening Book
• Fables, Myths, and Legends TR30 • Major Greek and Roman Deities TR31	• Summarizing (Story Map) TR13 • 5W's and How Question Frame TR45	• Daily Language SkillBuilder TR24		• Evaluating Reading Aloud p. 14 • Creating a Narrative Presentation p. 23 • Guidelines: How to Analyze a Narrative Presentation p. 24
• Setting TR6	• Summarizing (Story Map) TR13	• Daily Language SkillBuilder TR24		
• Characterization TR4		• Daily Language SkillBuilder TR25		• Evaluating Reading Aloud p. 14 • Conducting Interviews p. 35 • Guidelines: How to Analyze an Interview p. 36
• Characterization TR4	• Connecting TR2	• Daily Language SkillBuilder TR25		• Evaluating Reading Aloud p. 14
	• Predicting TR7 • Making Inferences TR10	• Daily Language SkillBuilder TR26		

ENGLISH LEARNERS / STUDENTS ACQUIRING ENGLISH

The **Spanish Study Guide,** pp. 166–171, includes language support for the following pages:
• Family and Community Involvement (per unit)

• Selection Summaries and Vocabulary
• Active Reading
• Literary Analysis

For **systematic instruction** in language skills, see:
• **Vocabulary and Spelling Book**
• **Grammar, Usage, and Mechanics Book**
• pacing chart on p. 767e

INTEGRATING SKILLS INSTRUCTION PACING CHART

The *Language of Literature* offers several options for integrating language arts instruction and literature.

- Systematic instruction in grammar, vocabulary, and spelling is provided in the *Grammar, Usage, and Mechanics Book* and in the *Vocabulary and Spelling Book*. The pacing chart on the right shows when to use the lessons in these books.
- The Pupil's Edition provides grammar and vocabulary instruction in context. The examples for the grammar feature, *Grammar in Context*, arise from the selections and relate to the grammar focus for each unit. In addition each selection includes vocabulary words called *Words to Know*. Vocabulary practice occurs in *Choices and Challenges* at the end of each selection.
- The Teacher's Edition provides review and reinforcement of the grammar and vocabulary concepts through Explicit Instruction lessons. References to additional support in *Unit Resource Books* and other ancillaries are included at the end of appropriate lessons.

Grammar, Usage and Mechanics
From Grammar, Mechanics, and Usage Book

Chapter 1: Sentence and Its Parts
Chapter 2: Nouns
Chapter 3: Pronouns
Chapter 4: Verbs
Chapter 5: Adjectives and Adverbs
Chapter 6: Prepositions, Conjunctions, and Interjections
Chapter 7: Subject-Verb Agreement
Chapter 8: Capitalization
Chapter 9: Punctuation

Vocabulary
From Vocabulary and Spelling Book

Lesson 1:   Context Clues
Lesson 2:   Restatement Context Clues
Lesson 3:   Contrast ContextClues
Lesson 4:   Definition Context Clues
Lesson 5:   Comparison Context Clues
Lesson 6:   General Context Clues
Lesson 7:   Prefixes and Base Words
Lesson 8:   Prefixes and Base Words
Lesson 9:   Base Words and Suffixes
Lesson 10: Base Words and Suffixes
Lesson 11: Anglo-Saxon Affixes and Base Words
Lesson 12: Roots and Word Families
Lesson 13: Roots and Word Familes
Lesson 14: Analyzing Roots and Affixes
Lesson 15: Analyzing Roots and Affixes
Lesson 16: Foreign Words in English
Lesson 17: Specialized Vocabulary
Lesson 18: Specialized Vocabulary
Lesson 19: Specialized Vocabulary
Lesson 20: Words with Multiple Meanings
Lesson 21: Synonyms
Lesson 22: Antonyms
Lesson 23: Denotation and Connotation
Lesson 24: Using a Thesaurus
Lesson 25: Idioms
Lesson 26: Similes and Metaphors
Lesson 27: Compound Words
Lesson 28: Homonyms
Lesson 29: Homophones and Easily Confused Words
Lesson 30: Homographs
Lesson 31: Analogies
Lesson 32: Using Your Strategies

Spelling
From Vocabulary and Spelling Book

Lesson 1:   Silent *e* Words and Suffixes
Lesson 2:   The Suffix *ance*
Lesson 3:   Plural Words Ending in *o*
Lesson 4:   Prefixes and Base Words
Lesson 5:   Prefixes and Roots
Lesson 6:   Words Ending with *ary*
Lesson 7:   Soft and Hard *g*
Lesson 8:   Review
Lesson 9:   Final *y* words and Suffixes
Lesson 10: The Suffix *able*
Lesson 11: Words Ending with *al + ly*
Lesson 12: The Prefix *com*
Lesson 13: Forms of the Prefix *ad*
Lesson 14: Words Ending with *ory*
Lesson 15: Unstressed Syllables
Lesson 16: Review
Lesson 17: *VAC* Words
Lesson 18: Non-*VAC* Words
Lesson 19: Words Ending with *c + ally*
Lesson 20: The Prefix *ex*
Lesson 21: More Forms of the Prefix *ad*
Lesson 22: Base Word Changes
Lesson 23: Words Ending with *cious, cial,* or *cian*
Lesson 24: Review
Lesson 25: Greek Combining Forms
Lesson 26: Compound Words and Contractions
Lesson 27: The Suffix *ible*
Lesson 28: Forms of Prefix *ob + sub*
Lesson 29: Forms of Prefix *in*
Lesson 30: The Suffixes *ence + ent*
Lesson 31: Words Ending with *ize + ise*
Lesson 32: Review

Selection	SkillBuilder Sentences	Suggested Answers
Links to Unit One	**1.** Daedalus and Icarus wants to learn how to fly. **2.** The gods looks down on people and meddles in their lives.	**1.** Daedalus and Icarus **want** to learn how to fly. **2.** The gods **look** down on people and **meddle** in their lives.
Links to Unit Two	**1.** Papa Bois did'nt tell anyone who he was. **2.** She cant' figure out where those beads came from.	**1.** Papa Bois **didn't** tell anyone who he was. **2.** She **can't** figure out where those beads came from.
Links to Unit Three	**1.** The Princess didn't want to marry king thrushbeard. **2.** This story took place a long time ago in germany, a Country in europe.	**1.** The **princess** didn't want to marry **King Thrushbeard**. **2.** This story took place a long time ago in **Germany**, a **country** in **Europe**.

Selection	SkillBuilder Sentences	Suggested Answers
Links to Unit Four	1. King Gorilla was mean to the animals and tried to play a joke on their. 2. A nasty old King Gorilla was him!	1. King Gorilla was mean to the animals and tried to play a joke on **them.** 2. A nasty old King Gorilla was **he**!
Links to Unit Five	1. Frog had the most deepest voice of all the animals. 2. The show on Friday night was interestinger than usual.	1. Frog had the **deepest** voice of all the animals. 2. The show on Friday night was **more interesting** than usual.

OVERVIEW

Students plan a program of stories to be told during a storytelling festival.

Project at a glance The selections in Unit Six emphasize how storytelling acts as a means of preserving cultural heritage and passes on oral histories and traditions. For this project, students will work in small groups to plan a Storytelling Festival, in which each member of the group will tell a story which relates to a theme or culture assigned to the group. Groups will collaborate on the selection of stories as well as the props and/or costumes, rehearsing together so others can help with the interpretation of the story and characterization for the narrator. The stories will be told either in a festival or in front of the class.

SCHEDULING
Individual stories should take about five minutes. You may want to schedule the presentations over the course of 2–3 class periods, or at the end of the unit depending on your purposes.

PROJECT OBJECTIVES
- To demonstrate the speaking and listening skills introduced in the activity
- To learn about the importance and use of folklore and storytelling
- To work collaboratively with a small group to prepare a program of stories
- To develop storytelling skills by recognizing what keeps an audience interested
- To develop listening and speaking skills by participating in a storytelling festival

SUGGESTED GROUP SIZE
5–6 students per group

Storytelling Festival

 # Getting Started

If you are going to create an actual festival with an invited audience, reserve a date in the auditorium or other appropriate room, as well as some rehearsal time for the groups. If you plan to decorate, start gathering sheets for backdrops that groups can paint. Decide if you will get costumes or if they will be the responsibility of individual groups. Invite not only other students but administrators and families as well.

If you are using your classroom as a stage, consider arranging the audience's seats in a large semicircle, in order to give the storyteller adequate room to move around and, perhaps, to interact with the audience.

If you would like to invite a storyteller to talk to the class, now is the time to locate one and schedule a time. You should also make available different types of books about the cultures students will be focusing on.

You might want to record the storytellers on video to preserve the performances for other classes and for your own review. Arrange for a school media person or volunteer parent to assist with the taping.

Communication Workshop Connection

As a springboard, students may use the Communication Workshop assignment **Multimedia Presentation,** p. 844.

 # Directing the Project

Preparing Divide students into groups. Tell students that they will be working cooperatively to plan and present a program of stories. Each group member will tell a story. Stories should be no longer than five minutes, so group members may have to edit their stories for length.

▶ Select a culture or theme for each group. Have students research the culture before creating their presentation. Groups will decide together which stories will be told and should help one another edit stories. At this time, explain exactly what you expect in the way of props, costumes, and setting. You might also review with students the Speaking and Listening Skills on the next page.

▶ When groups have finalized their list of stories, meet with them to check for coherency in theme or culture. As groups work to edit the stories, meet again to offer suggestions and help them decide which elements of each story are necessary and which are expendable. Stress that the oral tradition entails personal interpretation each time the tale is retold, so students can add their own touches as long as the basic story and lesson remain intact. Tell students there is no one "correct" interpretation. Encourage them to imagine how they would feel if they were the actual characters in the situations they are depicting.

▶ You should discuss what makes a story interesting to an audience. You might point out that the character of the narrator has a great deal of influence on how the audience responds to the story.

▶ Students should be aware of the guidelines for working in a group, found on pages R104–105 in the Speaking and Listening Handbook.

Practicing Groups should determine the order in which they would like to tell the stories. They should rehearse as a group, relying on one another to help with interpretation and to give suggestions. Tell students that giving and receiving feedback during the rehearsal stage is crucial. Refer to the tips in the Feedback Center.

▶ Remind students that there is a time limit. If each story is five minutes, give them a cumulative amount of time for the entire group.

Presenting Before the performances, have students focus on the strategies listed in the Speaking and Listening Handbook on pages R98–99. Share with them this quotation by storyteller Brenda Wong Aoki: ". . . I sculpt a story until I get to the emotional truth, the human truth. It is this truth that makes a bridge of understanding between peoples." Tell them that one of their primary goals is to communicate this truth both verbally and nonverbally.

▶ If you are able to videotape the storytelling, you can share the performance by circulating the tapes around school.

Teaching the Speaking and Listening Skills

The student is expected to:

Identify how language use—for instance, labels (terms) and sayings (idioms)—reflects regions and cultures

Teaching Suggestions: Have students explore and discuss the culture from which their story originates. If they are unfamiliar with the culture, have them research the country of origin and relevant points that might affect language, such as history, climate, and so on. Then you might have them read through the story and pick out language that reflects this culture. For example, the speaker in the story "The Bamboo Beads" uses the idiom "When I was in my bare feet still" to mean "When I was a child." This reflects the warm climate of the islands of Trinidad and Tobago, and the fact that in the speaker's day, many young children did not wear shoes.

Compare oral traditions across regions and cultures

Teaching Suggestions: After students have a solid basis of understanding about the culture they are focusing on, ask them to discuss the key points of the culture's oral tradition. One way to do this might be to ask, "What values of the society are revealed through the stories?" You may want to bring the class together and create a chart on the board comparing the various cultures they are studying. Ask students to hypothesize:

- why the values and traditions of these cultures may be different.
- what factors may have influenced these differences.
- how they might have changed over time. For example, the Greek myth "Arachne" illustrates how treating others fairly and with kindness was important to the ancient Greeks.

Analyze oral interpretations of literature for effects on the listener

Teaching Suggestions: Discuss with students how nonverbal gestures, body language, and tone of voice affect the message. Encourage them to imagine how they would feel if they were making the same gestures and facial expressions. Have students rehearse their stories for one another and provide feedback as to how well the interpretation is working. You may want to have students fill out a brief evaluation sheet to be discussed at the end of each presentation.

Feedback Center

Students can use the following guidelines when giving and receiving feedback during this project:

Giving Feedback

▶ Ask questions concerning content, purpose, and point of view.

▶ Provide feedback about the interpretation (for instance, the overall impact on the listener).

▶ Comment on the verbal delivery (pitch, pace, volume) and its impact on the listener.

▶ Comment on the nonverbal delivery (body language, including facial expressions and gestures) and its impact on the listener.

Receiving Feedback

▶ Listen to constructive criticism with an open mind.

▶ Use audience feedback in order to modify the presentation to clarify meaning or organization.

 ## Assessing the Project

The following rubric can be used for group or individual assessment.

3 Full Accomplishment

Students followed directions and performed successful oral interpretations that demonstrated an understanding of the content and cultural backdrop of their stories. Students used appropriate body language and tone to enhance the stories, and the audience easily followed their presentations.

2 Substantial Accomplishment

Students selected, edited, and performed oral interpretations for an audience, but the selections were unrelated or not easily followed by the audience. The presentations may have lacked a strong delivery and appropriate body language. Some of the Speaking and Listening Skills were demonstrated.

1 Little Accomplishment

Students did not fully complete the project to the point of performing, or the performance did not fulfill the requirements of the assignment.

Standards-Based Objectives
Through an article and a diagram, students discover the past influences that shaped a modern-day storyteller and her views about why the oral tradition endures.
• To understand and appreciate the richness of oral storytelling
• To apply and practice skills learned in previous selections

Reading and Analyzing

Reading Skills and Strategies:
MAKE JUDGMENTS

Have students assess Diane Ferlatte's statement that "the best way to learn about a people and a culture is to know their stories." Then invite volunteers to give examples from their experience of how knowing someone else's life story can make a difference in a personal relationship.
Possible Response: Knowing something about how my parents grew up helped me better understand their values.

Reading Skills and Strategies:
MAKE INFERENCES

Ask students to study the figure of the Xhosa Storyteller by Hubert Shuptrine and to think about why contemporary storytellers might wear traditional dress.
Possible Response: They probably feel more authentic when they are dressed this way and think their listeners will pay more attention to what they say.

STORYTELLERS PAST AND PRESENT

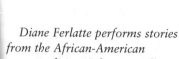

DIANE FERLATTE

A Present-Day Storyteller Speaks

Diane Ferlatte performs stories from the African-American tradition. Like storytellers from ancient times, she uses gestures, props, and facial expressions to engage listeners in the drama of the story.

When I was 10, my parents moved to California, looking for work. Every summer they drove me back to New Orleans. I would complain, "Why won't you take me back to Disneyland?" But my parents knew what they were doing. They took me back to my roots. They took me back to Grandpa and Grandma, to homemade biscuits, singing on the porch, and stories when there was no TV or video. I heard many stories at my grandparents' home. Sitting on the big porch in a swing, that's what we'd do. The old folks would always be talking about family, about fishing, about true stories, about ghost stories, or about something that happened at church. As a little kid, I heard lots of stuff. If I had known I was going to be a storyteller, I sure would have listened more carefully.

My stories come from anywhere and everywhere. Most of the African stories I tell are from West Africa. In the old days, stories served to pass along information. That was part of the job of the *griots* (grē-ōz′) who kept alive the oral tradition of a village or family. They could tell you about your whole family line—where your mother came from, who your father was, what they did. It's important to keep alive the history of where you come from and what you are about.

Stories also told about people's adventures, their fears, their hopes.

EXPLICIT INSTRUCTION Speaking and Listening

LISTENING TO A STORY
Instruction Remind students that to enjoy the performance of a storyteller, they must listen carefully. Review with them these elements of being a good listener:
• Don't whisper or talk while the story is being told.
• Watch the storyteller as you listen to him or her. This will keep your attention on the story.
• Don't interrupt if you hear something you don't understand. Wait to see if the next part of the story makes it clear.

• Keep in mind any questions that arise as you listen. After the story has finished, ask your questions.
Practice Have students watch the performance of "The Cow Tail Switch," shown on the accompanying videotape. Afterwards, have them write brief summaries of the story.

An Ancient Storyteller
For over 500 years the Xhosa (kō′sä) people have lived and shared their stories in southern Africa.

Stories were a way of answering questions. That's where a lot of our "why" and "how" stories come from—how the lion got his roar, for example. People were curious. In African cultures, storytelling is not pure narration, or speaking. There is also music and dance and singing and religion connected with storytelling. All the arts are connected.

Stories come from the conditions in which people live. When the Africans came here as slaves, they weren't allowed to speak their own language, to play their drums, even to learn to read or write. But they could still tell their stories. The oral tradition was very strong in the world of the slaves because that was all they had. A lot of African-American stories have humor in them too. Life was so brutal for the slaves they had to laugh to keep from crying.

That's the power of communication, of the oral tradition. Once you hear somebody else's problem, it makes you think, "I'm not alone in this. Somebody else is going through the same thing." When you hear a story, you can see more of a common thread that goes through all of us. With so many cultures in this country today, we need to talk to each other. And the best way to learn about a people and a culture is to know their stories.

VIDEO: Literature in Performance

An *umnqwazi* (ŏŏm-ən-kwä′zē), a headdress made of many pieces of cloth, was worn by Xhosa women.

A Xhosa storyteller might begin with a phrase that means "Now for a tale."

The hands are nearly as important as the voice in the telling of a tale, or *ntsomi* (ən-tsō′mē). Hands act out major actions, express emotions, and stress ideas.

STORYTELLERS **769**

STORYTELLER
"The Cow Tail Switch," performed here by professional storyteller Diane Ferlatte, is a typical West African folk tale. It is a story that is closely tied to the culture and ancestry of Africa. "Stories come out from the folk," says Ferlatte. "The stories reflect the world in which the people live—their struggles and the conditions of their lives." Ferlatte explains, "The theme of this story shows how important ancestors are in the African culture." She adds, "This story tells us about where Africans come from."

"I tell this story because it has a good message," Ferlatte says. "You are not dead until you are forgotten. Understanding yourself and your family comes from knowing the stories in your life, from your family's stories. The stories you tell come out of who you are and where you're from."

EXPLICIT INSTRUCTION Speaking and Listening

STORYTELLING
Instruction Point out that different families have their stories, too. You may wish to provide students with an example of a "family folk tale"—a story that is told over and over again in one's own family.

Practice Have students work in small groups. Have each group member tell a story either from his or her home culture or family. Then have the group identify the stories' similarities and differences. If time permits, call on one volunteer from each group to summarize group members' stories for the class.

Standards-Based Objectives
- To understand the history of oral traditions around the world
- To understand and appreciate types of literature in the oral tradition

Reading and Analyzing

Reading Skills and Strategies:
CHRONOLOGICAL ORDER

Point out to students that a time line allows students to see a sequence of events in a visual way. Explain that this time line shows the places where stories in this unit originated and historic events that occurred there.

Ask which event took place first, the reign of the First Emperor or the first Olympic Games in Greece.

Answer: the first Olympic Games

Reading Skills and Strategies:
MAKE INFERENCES

Direct students' attention to the pictures of the Sphinx and the Great Wall. Ask what such structures might tell about the rulers who had them built.

Possible Response: They were very powerful, commanding a huge force to do this work.

Literary Analysis: ORAL TRADITION

Ask students to review the box diagram on page 770 and compare and contrast the four kinds of literature. What are their similarities and differences?

Possible Response: Students may point out the different purposes, characters, or settings in the types. They should be able to point out as similarities the "Common Elements" that all four types share.

KEEPING THE PAST ALIVE

For nearly as long as words have been spoken, there have been tellers of stories and listeners eager to hear them. When they told stories well, they inspired others to retell them. From generation to generation, stories were passed within families, villages, and cultures. The tellers and listeners were taking part in what came to be called the **oral tradition.** The types of stories in the oral tradition appear in the chart below.

The stories of the oral tradition are a major part of folklore. Folklore brings the past to life for tellers, listeners, and readers of today. Like thread connecting pieces of cloth, folklore connects people's lives across time and place. The time line at the right presents important events of the past in cultures around the world. The legendary tales in this unit reflect those cultures. By reading them, you can discover for yourself how the oral tradition links people and keeps the past alive.

AFRICA

Why Monkeys Live in Trees 818

. . .

2600–2100 B.C. *First Egyptian pyramid and Great Sphinx of Giza built.*

THE AMERICAS

The Disobedient Child 790

The Frog Who Wanted to Be a Singer 832

Where the Girl Rescued Her Brother 837

. . .

2750–2000 B.C. *Farmers begin to settle in region between modern-day Mexico and Nicaragua.*

MYTHS
- *attempt to answer basic questions about the world*
- *are considered truthful by their originators*

FOLK TALES
- *are told primarily for entertainment*
- *feature humans or humanlike animals*

COMMON ELEMENTS
- keep the past alive
- teach lessons about human behavior
- reveal the values of the society

FABLES
- *are short tales that illustrate morals*
- *often have characters that are animals*

ORAL HISTORY
- *is based on real events*
- *is considered factual by the teller*
- *passes along information*

770 UNIT SIX THE ORAL TRADITION

Cross Curricular Link **History**

THE GREAT PYRAMID The Great Pyramid, resting place of King Khufu, is one of the wonders of architecture. It was originally 480 feet high (146 meters), yet it was built without cranes, pulleys, or lifting tackle.

How did the ancient Egyptians manage to build such a huge structure without these machines? Even today, architects remain unsure of how they did it.

The Great Pyramid is located in Giza, near the modern city of Cairo, Egypt.

700s B.C. *First recorded Olympic Games in Greece; Founding of Rome*

215 B.C. *Reign of Ch'in Shih Huang Ti (The First Emperor); Construction of Great Wall begins*

A.D. 1492 *Carib Indians on various Caribbean islands have first contact with Europeans after the arrival of Christopher Columbus.*

A.D. 1547 *Holy Roman Emperor Charles V defeats Protestant princes of Germany.*

INTERNET

Social Studies Connection
www.mcdougallittell.com

Differentiating Instruction

Less Proficient Readers

To help students use the time line, point out that it organizes events in chronological order. Make sure that students understand the difference between B.C. and A.D. Then discuss the following questions to make sure that students understand the graphic:

• Which way do you read this time line to see the events and stories in order from beginning to end? *(Start at the upper left and read down, then move back up and to the right.)*

• What was happening in the Americas between 2750 and 2000 B.C.? **Possible Response:** Farmers were beginning to settle in the area between modern-day Mexico and Nicaragua.

• Which story in this unit comes from Europe? *(King Thrushbeard)*

English Learners

Have students study a globe or a map of the world to see where these ancient civilizations were located. Point out to students that early cultures grew up in temperate climates. They settled where water was plentiful enough to support agriculture, transportation, and trade. In order to introduce the unit, ask students to summarize any folk tales or myths that they know.

Advanced Students

Tell students that as they read this unit they should think about the significance of mythology to everyday life. Have them keep track of how Greek mythology continues to permeate literature and language today.

Cross Curricular Link History

THE ROMAN EMPIRE The area controlled by Rome extended so far that Julius Caesar and Tacitus both describe encounters with Germanic and Celtic tribes. The Romans controlled southern and western Europe during the second century B.C. to the fifth century A.D. Around 50 B.C., Julius Caesar conquered tribes west of the Rhine River in Gaul, an area that is modern-day France. The Romans then tried to extend their rule north of the Elbe River in what is modern Germany, but they failed.

The Romans built thousands of miles of roads in order to connect their growing empire. These roads allowed them to trade with people in distant lands and to exchange ideas with other cultures. The roads were so well constructed that portions of them remain to this day.

Standards-Based Objectives

1. To understand and appreciate three myths
2. To understand and appreciate the values and customs of ancient Greece and Rome
3. To extend understanding of the myths through a variety of activities

Reading Pathways

- Select one or several students to read each story aloud to the entire class or to small groups of students. Assign this reading in advance so that students have time to become familiar with the story—the characters, vocabulary, conflicts, and so on. Have the audience listen carefully to the stories without following along in their texts.
- Read the stories aloud to the class, pausing at key points to discuss how elements of the story inform students about the customs, values, or beliefs of ancient Greece and Rome.
- After students have read the stories once, they can reread them to identify structural elements such as main character, minor characters, conflict, setting, and plot. Then have students identify similarities and differences between these stories and the selections in Unit One.

 Use **Unit Six Resource Book,** p. 7, for work with Words to Know.

English Conventions Practice

Daily Language SkillBuilder

Have students **proofread** the display sentences on page 767g and write them correctly. The sentences also appear on Transparency 24 of **Language Transparencies.**

LINKS TO UNIT ONE

Tests of Courage

The selections in Unit One describe challenges that force people to find their inner courage. Some of these challenges come from relationships with people, and others are found in struggles with forces of nature. In each of the tales that follow, a mythical character responds to a challenge—and must face the consequences.

ANCIENT ROME

The Story of Ceres and Proserpina

retold by Mary Pope Osborne

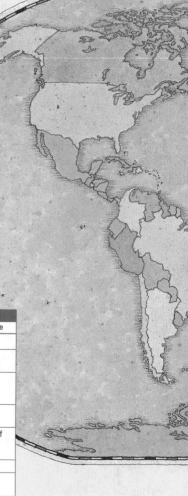

The ancient Romans had the same gods and goddesses as the ancient Greeks, but called them by different names. Ceres (sîr′ēz) is the Roman name for Demeter dĭ-mēt′ər), goddess of the harvest. Her daughter is Proserpina (prō-sûr′pə-nə), the Roman name for Persephone, goddess of the dead and of the fertility of the earth. Pluto, Proserpina's husband, is called Hades (hā′dēz) in Greek mythology. In this **myth** Pluto kidnaps Proserpina, and Ceres seeks her daughter's return.

MAJOR GREEK AND ROMAN DEITIES		
	Greek Name	Roman Name
Goddess of love	Aphrodite	Venus
God of medicine and music	Apollo	Apollo
Goddess of wisdom, war, and the arts	Athena	Minerva
God of the underworld	Hades	Pluto
Goddess of marriage and women	Hera (wife of Zeus)	Juno (wife of Jupiter)
God of the sea	Poseidon	Neptune
Ruler of the gods, god of the sky	Zeus	Jupiter

LESSON RESOURCES

UNIT SIX RESOURCE BOOK pp. 4–8

ASSESSMENT
Formal Assessment, pp. 125–126
Test Generator

SKILLS TRANSPARENCIES AND COPYMASTERS
Literary Analysis
- Fables/Myths/Legends, TR 30 (p. 774)
- Greek/Roman Deities Chart, TR 31 (p. 780)

Reading and Critical Thinking
- Summarizing (Story Map), TR 13 (p. 774)
- 5 W's and How Question Frame, TR 45 (p. 781)
Language
- Daily Language SkillBuilder, TR 24 (p. 772)
Speaking and Listening
- Evaluating Reading Aloud, p. 14 (p. 776)
- Creating a Narrative Presentation, p. 23 (p. 785)
- Guidelines: How to Analyze a Narrative Presentation, p. 24 (p. 785)

INTEGRATED TECHNOLOGY
Audio Library
Video: Literature in Performance
- Icarus. See **Video Resource Book,** pp. 31–38
Internet: Research Starter

Visit our Web site: www.mcdougallittell.com

For **systematic instruction** in language skills, see:
- **Vocabulary and Spelling Book**
- **Grammar, Usage, and Mechanics Book**
- pacing chart on p. 767e.

ANCIENT GREECE

The Boy Who Flew

retold by Anne Rockwell

Many Greek **myths** focus on individuals who suffer for their prideful or disobedient behavior. The ancient Greeks placed a great deal of importance on showing respect for human rulers as well as for gods and goddesses. Set mainly on the island of Crete in the Aegean (ĭ-jē′ən) Sea, "The Boy Who Flew" retells the Greek myth of Daedalus (dĕd′l-əs) and Icarus (ĭk′ər-əs). Daedalus was a brilliant inventor who disobeyed the rulers of Crete; his son, Icarus, disobeyed him. Both suffered for their actions.

ITALY

GREECE

ANCIENT GREECE

Arachne

retold by Olivia E. Coolidge

In ancient Greece, the rule of the gods and goddesses was not to be questioned. Many Greek **myths** are about characters who do not stay within limits set by the gods or who ignore their warnings. In this myth a weaver, Arachne (ə-răk′nē), pits herself against Athena (ə-thē′nə), the goddess of wisdom and of all crafts, particularly weaving.

AS YOU READ . . .

Make note of what lessons about human behavior the myths teach.

Keep track of characters' choices and the way conflicts are resolved.

Find out what mysteries of nature are explained.

Summary

In "The Boy Who Flew," Daedalus, a brilliant inventor, is called upon to create a structure to confine the Minotaur, a monster with a bull's head and a man's body. When Daedalus defies King Minos and has the Minotaur murdered, Daedalus and his son, Icarus, become prisoners on the island of Crete. Their effort to escape by means of flight results in Icarus's death when he flies too near the sun, and his wax wings melt.

Reading and Analyzing

Literary Analysis: DISTINGUISH LITERARY FORMS: MYTH

Ask students to describe some of the features that make "The Boy Who Flew" a myth.

Possible Response: This story is a myth because it is set in ancient Greece. Some of the characters, such as the Minotaur, are not realistic.

Use **Unit Six Resource Book**, p. 6, for more practice. Use **Literary Analysis Transparencies**, p. 30, for additional support.

Active Reader: SUMMARIZE

A Students are expected to paraphrase and summarize text. Ask students to tell what has happened up to this point since Daedalus came to Crete.

Possible Response: Daedalus built a maze to contain the Minotaur, but upon learning that the monster killed 12 youths a year, he helped to kill the Minotaur. King Minos imprisoned Daedalus and his son.

Use **Unit Six Resource Book**, p. 5, for more practice. Use **Reading and Critical Thinking Transparencies**, p. 13, for additional support.

THE BOY WHO Flew

by Anne Rockwell

ONE of Athene's[1] pupils was a man called Daedalus.[2] Even though he was mortal, he was almost as remarkable an inventor and craftsman as the god Hephaestus.[3] He became famous throughout the world.

In the island kingdom of Crete, there was a monster that belonged to King Minos[4] and Queen Pasiphae.[5] This monster had the head of a bull and the body of a man. It was cruel and dangerous, and it was called the Minotaur.[6] Worse yet, it was the child of the queen. King Minos asked Daedalus to come to his kingdom and build something that would imprison the Minotaur within the palace walls.

Daedalus came to Crete, bringing his young son, Icarus,[7] with him. Inside the palace walls,

he built a marvelous <u>maze</u>. This maze had such complicated passageways that the monster could not find its way out.

But Daedalus soon discovered that, each year, the Minotaur needed to kill twelve youths and maidens from the city of Athens. Each year, twelve fine young men and women from

---

1. **Athene** (ə-thē′nē): the Greek goddess of wisdom, also known as Athena.

2. **Daedalus** (dĕd′l-əs).

3. **Hephaestus** (hĭ-fĕs′təs): the Greek god of fire and metalworking.

4. **Minos** (mī′nəs).

5. **Pasiphae** (pə-sĭf′ə-ē′).

6. **Minotaur** (mĭn′ə-tôr′).

7. **Icarus** (ĭk′ər-əs).

WORDS TO KNOW   **maze** (māz) *n.* a confusing network of winding paths or passageways

Minotaur (1958), Pablo Picasso. Mayor Gallery, London UK/Bridgeman Art Library
Copyright © 2001 Estate of Pablo Picasso/Artists Rights Society (ARS), New York.

Athens were sent to Crete to die in the maze. Daedalus did not want his work to be used for murder, so he helped one of the young men who came to die to save himself and his companions and to kill the Minotaur.

Queen Pasiphae was very angry because, as its mother, she loved the Minotaur, terrible as it had been. Her husband, in order to soothe her, decided to punish Daedalus. He made Daedalus and his son prisoners.

No captain of any ship that sailed to Crete dared take them away because the king had decreed that the inventor and his son could never leave the island. They lived in an <u>isolated</u> tower, where Daedalus had a simple workshop. They had only the seagulls for company. How Daedalus <u>yearned</u> to show Icarus the world beyond their island prison!

One day as Daedalus was watching the gulls <u>wheeling</u> and circling above the surf, he had

WORDS TO KNOW	**isolated** (ī'sə-lā'tĭd) *adj.* away from others; lonely **isolate** *v.*
	yearn (yûrn) *v.* to desire strongly
	wheeling (hwē'lĭng) *adj.* flying in curves or circles **wheel** *v.*

775

EXPLICIT INSTRUCTION Viewing and Representing

Minotaur
by Pablo Picasso

ART APPRECIATION Pablo Picasso (1881–1973) is considered by many to have been one of the 20th century's most creative and most prolific artists. Picasso, originally from Spain, produced thousands of paintings, sculptures, drawings, and ceramics. Although his earlier works show things in a realistic way, Picasso is best known for his many works of cubist art. Cubist art breaks down its subject matter into fragments, sometimes presenting parts from various angles, or perspectives.

Instruction Point out some of the facial features of the creature depicted in *Minotaur*.

Practice Ask students to consider how Picasso succeeds in creating the look of a monstrous and imposing creature while also conveying a sense of the minotaur's monstrous and imposing confinement.

Possible Response: This painting is not a realistic depiction of a bull. You can tell from the horns, the large nostrils, and the big teeth that this is a monstrous and frightening sort of bull. The composition pushes toward the center and many of the lines suggest a maze.

Ask students to tell whether they had predicted that Icarus would disregard his father's warning.

Possible Response: I had a feeling that Icarus might get carried away with himself and try to fly too high, especially when he started to swoop and soar like a gull.

Reading Skills and Strategies:
MAKE INFERENCES

Ask students to make an inference about the message of this myth.

Possible Response: I think that the message of "The Boy Who Flew" is that young people should heed the advice of their elders, because older people have more experience and wisdom. Even though young people have more physical energy, they don't always have the knowledge and experience needed to make good decisions.

Daedalus and Icarus (15th c.) Private Collection/Bridgeman Art Library.

an inspiration. He shouted down to his son, who was gathering shells on the lonely beach, "Minos may rule the sea, but he does not rule the air!"

Daedalus had observed how the gulls' wings were shaped, and how they worked. No mortal had ever before figured out how a bird could fly, but Daedalus thought he understood.

He and Icarus began to collect all the gull feathers they could find along the beach. They gathered the large, stiff ones and the tiny, light, downy ones that floated in the breeze. They saved the wax that honeybees made. Then Daedalus made wings of the seagull feathers and the beeswax for himself and Icarus. He worked long and patiently, and Icarus helped him,

always doing what his father told him to do.

After they had made two pairs of long, curved wings, Daedalus made two harnesses[8] of leather. He showed Icarus how to place the wings on his shoulders. Then showed him how to run along the beach until he caught the wind and, like a seagull, flew up into the air.

Father and son practiced together until, one day, Daedalus decided it was time for them to leave the island. As they rose into the air and headed away from their island prison toward the sea, Daedalus called out to Icarus, "Follow me! Do not fly too low, or you will lose the air

---

8. **harnesses:** arrangements of straps (for attaching the wings to their bodies).

EXPLICIT INSTRUCTION Speaking and Listening

READ ALOUD
Tell students that one way to visualize the events in a story is by acting them out. Although there is not a lot of dialogue on these two pages, students can write a dialogue based on the narrative.
Prepare Tell students to spend some time rereading this part of the story. Then have them write a scene based on the events that happen on these two pages. Suggest that the scene include a narrator, Daedalus, and Icarus.

Present Give students time to rehearse the dialogue. Let students take turns reading the dialogue aloud fluently and accurately.

Tell the class to listen carefully and provide constructive feedback when each group is finished with its reading.

Use **Speaking and Listening Book**, p. 14, for additional support.

and sink into the waves. But do not fly too high, or the heat from the sun will melt the beeswax."

"Yes, Father," shouted Icarus above the sea noises and the wailing of the seagulls who flew beside him.

Higher and higher they flew. At last, Daedalus said, "We will stay at this level all the way. Remember what I told you— follow me!"

As they flew by, fishermen dropped their nets in wonder and farmers stopped at their plows. They thought they were seeing two gods in flight, for surely only gods could fly.

Icarus began to feel more and more sure of himself. He flew upward, then downward. He swooped and soared like a gull, laughing joyously as he did so. He cried out, "Look at me, Father!" and soared upward.

Daedalus beckoned him down, but Icarus thought, He is old and timid while I am young and strong. Surely I can fly a little better than he. Suddenly the boy disappeared into a cloud and flew up and up and up, higher and higher.

Too late, he saw feathers begin to fall from his wings. As the hot sun melted the wax, more and more feathers dropped away. Frantically, the boy flapped his arms in the air, but he could not fly without the wings. Instead, he dropped down and down until he fell into the sea and drowned.

Daedalus flew up in search of his son, calling as he went, "Icarus! Come down to me!"

Then he saw the telltale feathers drifting past him, and he heard the distant splash as Icarus fell into the sea. The old man cried as he continued on his journey, but he flew to freedom. He never made wings for anyone again. ❖

Anne Rockwell
born 1934

". . . I acquired a love for stories about the Greek gods and goddesses that lasted all my life."

A Love of Reading Anne Rockwell has been creating books for more than 30 years. Trained as an artist, she originally worked in an advertising agency. After starting a family, she wanted to write for children in order to share her love of reading. She began her writing career with retellings of folk tales from different cultures. More recently, she has focused on picture books and informative nonfiction for young children.

Writing and Illustrating Rockwell has written and illustrated more than 70 books and has collaborated with other authors and illustrators on many more. Where do all her ideas come from? "I get ideas walking on the beach with my dog," she says, "or traveling in a country where the language is unfamiliar." She keeps a sketchbook to record ideas for stories and illustrations, and she finds classical music very inspiring. "The Boy Who Flew" comes from her book *The Robber Baby: Stories from the Greek Myths.*

English Learners

1 Help students understand the meaning of the word *beckoned* by explaining that Daedalus is very worried about Icarus. He is urging him to come down, because he knows what will happen if Icarus flies too close to the sun.

2 Define the word *telltale* by telling students that the flying feathers "tell a tale" about what happened to Icarus. They are evidence of his tragic end.

Less Proficient Readers

Ask students to explain why Icarus doesn't listen to his father's warning.

Possible Response: Icarus thinks that because he is younger and stronger, he can fly higher. Ironically, it is the inexperience of youth that brings about Icarus's death.

Advanced Students

Humans have always been fascinated with the idea of flying. Have students brainstorm all the ways in which humans experience flight.

Possible Responses: helicopters; airplanes; blimps; gliders; hang gliders; skydiving; hot air balloons

---

EXPLICIT INSTRUCTION **Summary**

Instruction Students should be able to clearly summarize the plot of the story in a few paragraphs.

Practice Have students reread the story. Then have them close their books and summarize the story in their own words. Use the following rubric to evaluate their responses.

RUBRIC

3 Full Accomplishment Summary reflects a full understanding of the events in the story and of the characters of Daedalus and Icarus.

2 Substantial Accomplishment Summary shows a general grasp of the events but only a partial understanding of Daedalus or Icarus.

1 Little or Partial Accomplishment Summary shows little understanding of the events or of the main characters.

Summary

The Greek maiden Arachne boasts that her weaving is as beautiful as that of the goddess Athena. When an old woman warns Arachne to take back her claim, Arachne refuses. The old woman reveals herself to be Athena. The two women then have a weaving contest. Although they are equally skilled, Athena is quicker. Her cloth shows mortals challenging the gods and suffering, but Arachne pays no attention. Her weaving shows the gods' crimes. Athena is insulted, and she rips the cloth in two and hits Arachne. In the end, Athena turns Arachne into a spider as a reminder to all Greeks not to compete with the gods.

Reading and Analyzing

Literary Analysis: SETTING

Ask students to describe the setting of the story.

Possible Response: The setting is ancient Greece, inside a modest cottage in a small town.

Literary Analysis: FORESHADOWING

Ask students to think about how the beginning of the story may foreshadow events to come.

Possible Response: Everything sounds a little too perfect. The description of Arachne as such a gifted weaver makes the reader think that something bad is going to happen to her.

ARACHNE

Illustration by Arvis Stewart, from *The Macmillan Book of Greek Gods and Heroes* by Alice Low. Copyright © 1985 Macmillan Publishing Company, reprinted with the permission of Simon & Schuster Books for Young Readers, an imprint of Simon & Schuster Children's Publishing Division.

RETOLD BY OLIVIA E. COOLIDGE

EXPLICIT INSTRUCTION **Viewing and Representing**

Illustration
by Arvis Stewart

Instruction Direct students to the illustration on page 778, explaining that Arvis Stewart creates many illustrations for books, such as the one this is taken from. Ask students to identify the rectangular structure in the background.

Practice Ask students to describe what is being made.

Possible Response: The thing in the background is a loom. It is used to weave cloth. It looks like a cloth of many different colors is being woven. Ask students to identify the characters in the illustration.

Possible Response: The large figure of a woman is probably Arachne, but I'm not sure about the others. Maybe if I read on, I'll figure out who they are.

*A*rachne[1] was a maiden who became famous throughout Greece, though she was neither wellborn[2] nor beautiful and came from no great city. She lived in an <u>obscure</u> little village, and her father was a humble dyer of wool. In this he was very skillful, producing many varied shades, while above all he was famous for the clear, bright scarlet which is made from shellfish and which was the most glorious of all the colors used in ancient Greece. Even more skillful than her father was Arachne. It was her task to spin the fleecy wool into a fine, soft thread and to weave it into cloth on the high-standing loom[3]

within the cottage. Arachne was small and pale from much working. Her eyes were light and her hair was a dusty brown, yet she was quick and graceful, and her fingers, roughened as they were, went so fast that it was hard to follow their flickering movements. So soft and even was her thread, so fine her cloth, so gorgeous her embroidery, that soon her products were known all over Greece. No one had ever seen the like of them before.

---

1. **Arachne** (ə-răk′nē).
2. **wellborn:** of a high social class.
3. **high-standing loom:** a tall frame used to hold threads in a vertical position as other threads are woven through horizontally.

WORDS
TO
KNOW   **obscure** (ŏb-skyŏŏr′) *adj.* not well-known or important

779

Differentiating Instruction

English Learners

1 Explain the meaning of the word *humble* by telling students that Arachne's father does not have a lot of money or material possessions. He is modest in his behavior and not overly proud of his work.

2 Point out the phrase *the like* in the last sentence on page 779. Tell students that the sentence could be rewritten as "No one had ever seen anything like her woven products."

Less Proficient Readers

Point out to students that the unusual syntax of some of the sentences and the use of negatives may make some sentences difficult to understand. In the first sentence the author uses both "neither" and "no." Have students find the simple subject of each of these sentences, and rewrite the sentences to put the subject first and to make them simpler.

- "Even more skillful than her father was Arachne." (***Arachne*** *was even more skillful than her father.*)
- "So soft and even was her thread, so fine her cloth, so gorgeous her embroidery, that soon her products were known all over Greece." (*Her* ***products*** *were known all over Greece because her thread was soft and even, her cloth was fine, and her embroidery was gorgeous.*)

Active Reader

A EVALUATE Possible Responses: Arachne's pride is justified because she is the best weaver anyone has ever seen; her pride is excessive because her talent as a weaver is god-given.

Reading Skills and Strategies:
MAKE JUDGMENTS

Ask students to judge Arachne's character and to tell whether or not they like her, and why.

Possible Responses: She isn't very likeable because she is vain, proud, and rude; she is highly skilled at weaving and therefore is justified in her impatience with others.

Active Reader

B PREDICT Possible Response: It seems that a goddess would have to win the contest over a mortal.

*A*t last Arachne's fame became so great that people used to come from far and wide to watch her working. Even the graceful nymphs[4] would steal in from stream or forest and peep shyly through the dark doorway, watching in wonder the white arms of Arachne as she stood at the loom and threw the shuttle[5] from hand to hand between the hanging threads or drew out the long wool, fine as a hair, from the distaff[6] as she sat spinning. "Surely Athena herself must have taught her," people would murmur to one another. "Who else could know the secret of such marvelous skill?"

ACTIVE READER

A

EVALUATE What do you think of Arachne's pride?

Arachne was used to being wondered at, and she was immensely proud of the skill that had brought so many to look on her. Praise was all she lived for, and it displeased her greatly that people should think anyone, even a goddess, could teach her anything. Therefore, when she heard them murmur, she would stop her work and turn round indignantly to say, "With my own ten fingers I gained this skill, and by hard practice from early morning till night. I never had time to stand looking as you people do while another maiden worked. Nor if I had, would I give Athena credit because the girl was more skillful than I. As for Athena's weaving, how could there be finer cloth or more beautiful embroidery than mine? If Athena herself were to come down and compete with me, she could do no better than I."

One day when Arachne turned round with such words, an old woman answered her, a grey old woman, bent and very poor, who stood leaning on a staff and peering at Arachne amid the crowd of onlookers.

"Reckless girl," she said, "how dare you claim to be equal to the immortal gods themselves? I am an old woman and have seen much. Take my advice and ask pardon of Athena for your words. Rest content with your fame of being the best spinner and weaver that mortal eyes have ever beheld."

"Stupid old woman," said Arachne indignantly, "who gave you a right to speak in this way to me? It is easy to see that you were never good for anything in your day, or you would not come here in poverty and rags to gaze at my skill. If Athena resents my words, let her answer them herself. I have challenged

"STUPID OLD WOMAN," SAID ARACHNE INDIGNANTLY, "WHO GAVE YOU A RIGHT TO SPEAK IN THIS WAY TO ME?"

---

4. **nymphs** (nĭmfs): in Greek mythology, minor goddesses of nature.

5. **shuttle:** a piece of wood holding the thread that is to be woven horizontally through the vertical threads on a loom.

6. **distaff:** a short rod for holding wool that is to be spun into thread.

WORDS TO KNOW
indignantly (ĭn-dĭg′nənt-lē) *adv.* in a way that is angry, because of an insult or an attack on one's self-respect
immortal (ĭ-môr′tl) *adj.* living or lasting forever

780

Multicultural Link   Greek Mythology

Greek mythology is the collection of stories told about the gods, goddesses, and legendary humans worshiped or revered by the ancient Greeks. Twelve chief gods and goddesses lived on Mount Olympus, and there were many lesser ones. Zeus ruled the sky and was ruler of all the Olympians. Poseidon ruled the seas and rivers, while Hades oversaw the underworld. The Romans worshiped many of the same deities but called them by different names.

Athena was one of the most important goddesses. She sprang fully grown from the forehead of Zeus and was his favorite child. Athena's major temple, the Parthenon, was in Athens. According to legend, the temple became hers when she won a contest with Poseidon by giving the Athenians the olive tree.

Use **Literary Analysis Transparencies,** p. 31, for additional support.

MAJOR GREEK AND ROMAN DEITIES		
	Greek Name	**Roman Name**
Goddess of love	Aphrodite	Venus
God of medicine and music	Apollo	Apollo
Goddess of wisdom, war, and the arts	Athena	Minerva
God of the underworld	Hades	Pluto
Goddess of marriage and women	Hera (wife of Zeus)	Juno (wife of Jupiter)
God of the sea	Poseidon	Neptune
Ruler of the gods, god of the sky	Zeus	Jupiter

her to a contest, but she, of course, will not come. It is easy for the gods to avoid matching their skill with that of men."

At these words the old woman threw down her staff and stood <u>erect</u>. The wondering onlookers saw her grow tall and fair and stand clad in long robes of dazzling white. They were terribly afraid as they realized that they stood in the presence of Athena. Arachne herself flushed red for a moment, for she had never really believed that the goddess would hear her. Before the group that was gathered there she would not give in; so pressing her pale lips together in <u>obstinacy</u> and pride, she led the goddess to one of the great looms and set herself before the other. Without a word both began to thread the long woolen strands that hung from the rollers and between which the shuttle would move back and forth. Many skeins[7] lay heaped beside them to use, bleached white, and gold, and scarlet, and other shades, varied as the rainbow. Arachne had never thought of giving credit for her success to her father's skill in dyeing, though in actual truth the colors were as remarkable as the cloth itself.

 oon there was no sound in the room but the breathing of the onlookers, the whirring of the shuttles, and the creaking of the wooden frames as each pressed the thread up into place or tightened the pegs by which the whole was held straight. The excited crowd in the doorway began to see that the skill of both in truth was very nearly equal but that, however the cloth might turn out, the goddess was the quicker of the two. A pattern

of many pictures was growing on her loom. There was a border of twined branches of the olive, Athena's favorite tree, while in the middle, figures began to appear. As they looked at the glowing colors, the spectators realized that Athena was weaving into her pattern a last warning to Arachne. The central figure was the goddess herself, competing with Poseidon[8] for possession of the city of Athens; but in the four corners were mortals who had tried to strive with gods and pictures of the awful <u>fate</u> that had overtaken them. The goddess ended a little before Arachne and stood back from her marvelous work to see what the maiden was doing.

ACTIVE READER

PREDICT How do you think the weaving contest will end?

Never before had Arachne been matched against anyone whose skill was equal, or even nearly equal, to her own. As she stole glances from time to time at Athena and saw the goddess working swiftly, calmly, and always a little faster than herself, she became angry instead of frightened, and an evil thought came into her head. Thus, as Athena stepped back a pace to watch Arachne finishing her work, she saw that the maiden had taken for her design a pattern of scenes which showed evil or unworthy actions of the gods, how they had deceived fair maidens, resorted to trickery, and appeared on earth from time to time in the form of poor and humble people. When the goddess saw this insult glowing in bright colors on Arachne's loom, she did not wait while the cloth was judged but stepped

---

7. **skeins** (skānz): rolls of thread or yarn.
8. **Poseidon** (pō-sīd′n): in Greek mythology, the god of the sea.

WORDS
TO
KNOW
erect (ĭ-rĕkt′) *adj.* firmly straight in posture; not bending or slumping
obstinacy (ŏb′stə-nə-sē) *n.* unreasonable stubbornness
fate (fāt) *n.* a final outcome that cannot be avoided

781

Differentiating Instruction

English Learners
1 Explain the meaning of the word *clad* by telling students that it is the past tense of the verb to *clothe*.

2 Tell students that the word *before*, as used here, means "in the presence of."

3 Point out that *whirring* and *creaking* are two examples of onomatopoeia, words that imitate sounds, in this case, the sound of the looms.

Less Proficient Readers
4 Ask students why Arachne is weaving a scene that shows the gods tricking people.

Possible Response: Arachne is using her weaving to express her anger at Athena for disguising herself as an old woman and tricking Arachne.

Advanced Students
Have students work in groups to brainstorm ideas for myths that would explain the habits of other insects, such as bees, moths, butterflies, flies, or ants.

EXPLICIT INSTRUCTION ## Speaking and Listening

INTERVIEWING
Prepare Explain to students that investigative reporters gather information by asking questions. Tell students about the five W's and one H question that reporters ask: *who, what, where, when, why,* and *how.* Suggest that students investigate the events of "Arachne" by asking these questions: Where and when does the story take place? Who are the main characters? What happens to them? What is the conflict? How is the conflict resolved?

Present Suggest that students work in small groups of three or four. One member of each group plays the role of an investigative reporter doing a story on Arachne and Athena. Other group members can play the roles of Arachne, Athena, and the onlookers watching the weaving contest. Before the role-playing begins, groups should brainstorm a list of questions—five W's and one H. Have groups present their role-playing for the class.

Use **Reading and Critical Thinking Transparencies**, p. 45, for additional support.

Active Reader: SUMMARIZE

Ask students to summarize the ending of the story.

Possible Response: In the end, Arachne is so humiliated by Athena's actions that she attempts to end her life by hanging herself. Athena intervenes and transforms Arachne into a small spider. Athena's action serves as a warning to other humans not to challenge the gods.

Reading Skills and Strategies:
MAKE INFERENCES

Have students infer from this myth what the ancient Greeks thought about human pride.

Possible Response: The ancient Greeks believed that human pride was a fault that could cause terrible things to happen.

---

forward, her grey eyes blazing with anger, and tore Arachne's work across. Then she struck Arachne across the face. Arachne stood there a moment, struggling with anger, fear, and pride. "I will not live under this insult," she cried, and seizing a rope from the wall, she made a noose and would have hanged herself.

The goddess touched the rope and touched the maiden. "Live on, wicked girl," she said. "Live on and spin, both you and your descendants. When men look at you, they may remember that it is not wise to strive with Athena." At that the body of Arachne shriveled up; and her legs grew tiny, spindly, and <u>distorted</u>. There before the eyes of the spectators hung a little dusty brown spider on a slender thread.

All spiders descend from Arachne, and as the Greeks watched them spinning their thread wonderfully fine, they remembered the contest with Athena and thought that it was not right for even the best of men to claim equality with the gods. ❖

Olivia E. Coolidge
born 1908

"The more facts I have to work with, the freer I am. . . ."

Across the Atlantic Olivia E. Coolidge grew up in England, where her father was a journalist and historian. After completing her studies at Oxford University, Coolidge came to the United States and taught English for several years.

Careful Researcher Coolidge has written a number of biographies for young people in which she needed to carefully separate facts from opinions. As Coolidge says, "Facts are the bricks with which a biographer builds. . . . The more facts I have to work with, the freer I am to design my own book." Coolidge carefully researches her subjects and then forms her own opinions.

Ancient to Modern Coolidge's first book was *Greek Myths,* which she wrote using ancient Greek sources. Since then she has written of other ancient legends, and of daily life in ancient cultures. More recently, her biographical accounts, such as *Gandhi* (1971), have won her awards and a wide readership.

WORDS
TO
KNOW

distorted (dĭ-stôr′tĭd) *adj.* twisted out of shape **distort** *v.*

EXPLICIT INSTRUCTION **Point of View**

Instruction Tell students that one way to indicate their understanding of a story is to tell it from the point of view of one of the characters.

Practice Have students write or speak about the story from Arachne's point of view. Use the following rubric to evaluate their work. Remind students to use the proper pronouns to reflect the first-person point of view. Suggest that students include comments that would accurately reveal Arachne's feelings about her encounter with Athena.

RUBRIC

3 Full Accomplishment Response reflects a full understanding of the events of the story and the character of Arachne.

2 Substantial Accomplishment Response shows a partial understanding of the events but may not fully reflect the character of Arachne.

1 Little or Partial Accomplishment Response shows little understanding of the story and of Arachne's character.

THE STORY OF
CERES AND PROSERPINA
retold by M A R Y   P O P E   O S B O R N E

Bourrasque (Gust of Wind), Levy Dhurmer. Private Collection/Bulloz.

One day Proserpina, the young maiden of spring, was picking wildflowers with her mother, Ceres, the goddess of grain. Entering the cool moist woods, Proserpina filled her basket with lilies and violets. But when she spied the white petals of the narcissus flower, she strayed far from her mother.

Summary
While picking flowers one day, Proserpina, the maiden of spring, is kidnapped by Pluto, the god of the underworld. Ceres, Proserpina's mother and the goddess of grain, discovers that Proserpina has been taken by Pluto. Ceres transforms herself into an old woman and is taken in by a family of princesses. While there, Ceres decides to turn the family's baby boy into a god. When the boy's mother realizes who Ceres is, she builds a temple in her honor in exchange for learning the secret rites to make the corn grow. Even after the temple is built, Ceres' sadness continues, causing everything on earth to stop growing. Ceres agrees to make the earth fertile again if her daughter is returned. In the end, Proserpina spends each fall and winter in the underworld with Pluto and returns to earth every spring and summer.

Differentiating Instruction

Less Proficient Readers
Have students keep these questions in mind as they read:
• Who are the characters in the story?
• What is the setting of the story?
• What is the main problem in the story?

English Learners
Tell students to pay close attention to the footnotes. They supply pronunciations of names as well as definitions of some of the unfamiliar words.

Advanced Students
Encourage students to research some of the gods mentioned in this story—Ceres, Hecate, Helios, Pluto, Jupiter, and Mercury.

Jo Whaley/The Image Bank. © Copyright 2000.

Just as Proserpina picked a beautiful narcissus, the earth began to rumble. Suddenly the ground cracked open, splitting fern beds and ripping flowers and trees from their roots. Then out of the dark depths sprang Pluto, god of the underworld.[1]

Standing up in his black chariot,[2] Pluto ferociously drove his stallions toward Proserpina. The maiden screamed for her mother, but Ceres was far away and could not save her.

Pluto grabbed Proserpina and drove his chariot back into the earth. Then the ground closed up again, leaving not even a seam.

When the mountains echoed with Proserpina's screams, her mother rushed into the woods, but it was too late—her daughter had disappeared.

Beside herself with grief, Ceres began searching for her kidnapped daughter in every land. For nine days the goddess did not rest, but carried two torches through the cold nights, searching for Proserpina.

On the tenth day, Hecate,[3] goddess of the dark of the moon, came to Ceres. Holding up a lantern, the shrouded[4] goddess said, "I also heard your daughter's screams, but I didn't see her. Let us fly to Helios,[5] the sun god, and ask him what happened."

Ceres and Hecate flew to Helios, the sun god; and weeping, Ceres asked Helios if he'd seen her daughter while he was shining down upon the woods.

"I pity you, Ceres," said Helios, "for I know what it is to lose a child. But I know the truth. Pluto wanted Proserpina for his wife, so he asked his brother, Jupiter, to give him

---

1. **underworld:** the world of the dead, believed by the Greeks and Romans to be located underground.
2. **chariot** (chăr′ē-ət): a horse-drawn two-wheeled vehicle used in ancient times.
3. **Hecate** (hĕk′ə-tē).
4. **shrouded:** hidden by wrappings; veiled.
5. **Helios** (hē′lē-ŏs′).

In Greek and Roman mythology, the pomegranate—a fruit containing many seeds—is a symbol of the underworld.

permission to kidnap her. Jupiter gave his consent, and now your daughter <u>reigns</u> over the land of the dead with Pluto."

Ceres screamed in rage and thrust her fist toward Mount Olympus, cursing Jupiter for aiding in the kidnapping of his own daughter. Then she returned to earth, disguised as an old woman, and began wandering from town to town.

One day as she rested by a well, Ceres watched four princesses gathering water. Remembering her own daughter, she began to weep.

"Where are you from, old woman?" one princess asked.

"I was kidnapped by pirates, and I escaped," said Ceres. "Now I know not where I am."

Feeling pity for her, the princesses brought Ceres home to their palace. At the palace, their mother, the queen, took an immediate liking to Ceres when she noticed how good she was with her baby son the prince. When she asked Ceres if she would live with them and be his nurse, the goddess gladly consented.

Ceres grew deeply fond of the child. The thought that he would someday grow old and die was too much for her to bear. So she decided to change him from a mortal to a god. Every night, when everyone else was asleep, she poured a magic liquid on the body of the baby prince and held him in a fire. Soon the prince began to look like a god; everyone was amazed at his beauty and strength. The queen, disturbed by the changes in her child, hid in the nursery and watched Ceres and the boy. And when she saw Ceres place the child into the fire, she screamed for help.

"Stupid woman!" shouted Ceres, snatching the baby from the fire. "I was going to make your son a god! He would have lived forever! Now he'll be a mere mortal and die like the rest of you!"

The king and queen then realized that the boy's nurse was Ceres, the powerful goddess of grain, and they were terrified.

WORDS TO KNOW	**reign** (rān) *v.* to rule as a king or queen

785

Less Proficient Readers
Use the following questions to discuss what happens after Ceres realizes that Proserpina is missing:

- How does Ceres discover what happened to Proserpina?
  Possible Response: Ceres and Hecate fly to Helios, the sun god. Helios tells them that Pluto kidnapped Proserpina and took her to the underworld.
- What does Ceres do after learning that her daughter is living with Pluto in the underworld?
  Possible Response: Ceres returns to earth, disguised as an old woman, and moves in with a king and queen and their four daughters and infant son.
- Why does Ceres decide to turn the baby boy into a god?
  Possible Response: She becomes attached to the baby and realizes that he is mortal and will die one day. She thinks that if she transforms him into a god, she will never have to mourn for him the way she has mourned for Proserpina.

English Learners
This story gives students the opportunity to review nouns commonly found in fairy tales: *prince, princess, god, goddess, palace, temple, throne, queen,* and *king.* Have students write a paragraph using these nouns.

Advanced Students
Students might notice that Pluto and Jupiter are the names of two planets in our solar system. Have students find a list of the planets in a science book and see how many of them are named after Greek or Roman gods and goddesses. *(Mercury, Venus, Mars, Jupiter, Saturn, Neptune, Uranus, Pluto)* Then have students discuss why these planets were given these names.

EXPLICIT INSTRUCTION ## Speaking and Listening

DRAMA PERFORMANCE

Prepare Explain that writing and performing a play helps to get inside of the characters' minds and really understand their thoughts and actions. Tell students that they are going to dramatize "The Story of Ceres and Proserpina."

Divide the class into small groups. Have each group write a scene based on one part of the story. Tell students not to limit themselves to the dialogue from this story. They should feel free to write additional yet appropriate dialogue to tell the story.

Present Give groups time to rehearse their scene. Then have the groups perform their scenes in sequential order. Afterward, encourage students to discuss how acting out their scenes helped them better understand the myth.

 Use **Speaking and Listening Book,** pp. 23–24, for additional support.

Literary Analysis: SETTING

Ask students to describe the setting of the underworld.

Possible Response: The underworld is a grim, dark place. It is smoky and filled with creepy ghosts. It is devoid of color—everything looks gray and old.

Reading Skills and Strategies: PREDICT

Have students make predictions about whether Proserpina will return to earth.

Possible Responses: I don't think Proserpina will return, because she has gotten used to living in the underworld; I think Proserpina will go back, because even though she's grown accustomed to life in the underworld, she still misses her mother.

Literary Analysis: CHARACTER

Ask students to describe the character of Proserpina.

Possible Response: I think Proserpina is brave, because she chooses to leave Pluto, who is a powerful god. She is devoted to her mother, and even though she hasn't seen her mother in a long time, she remembers how much she loved her.

"I will only forgive you," said Ceres, "if you build a great temple in my honor. Then I will teach your people the secret rites[6] to help the corn grow."

At dawn the king ordered a great temple be built for the goddess. But after the temple was completed, Ceres did not reveal the secret rites. Instead she sat by herself all day, grieving for her kidnapped daughter. She was in such deep mourning that everything on earth stopped growing. It was a terrible year—there was no food, and people and animals began to starve.

Jupiter grew worried—if Ceres caused the people on earth to die, there would be no more gifts and offerings for him. Finally he sent gods from Mount Olympus to speak with her.

The gods came to Ceres and offered her gifts and pleaded with her to make the earth <u>fertile</u> again.

1 "I never will," she said, "not unless my daughter is returned safely to me."

Jupiter had no choice but to bid his son, Mercury, the messenger god, to return Proserpina to her mother.

2 Wandering the underworld, Mercury passed through dark smoky caverns filled with ghosts and phantoms, until he came to the misty throne room of Pluto and Proserpina. Though the maiden was still frightened, she had grown accustomed to her new home and had almost forgotten her life on earth.

"Your brother, Jupiter, has ordered you to return Proserpina to her mother," Mercury told Pluto. "Otherwise, Ceres will destroy the earth."

Pluto knew he could not disobey Jupiter, but he didn't want his wife to leave forever, so he said, "She can go. But first, we must be alone."

When Mercury left, Pluto spoke softly to Proserpina: "If you stay, you'll be queen of the underworld, and the dead will give you great honors."

As Proserpina stared into the eyes of the king of the dead, she dimly remembered the joy of her mother's love. She remembered wildflowers in the woods and open sunlit meadows. "I would rather return," she whispered.

Pluto sighed, then said, "All right, go. But before you leave, eat this small seed of the pomegranate[7] fruit. It is the food of the underworld—it will bring you good luck."

Proserpina ate the tiny seed. Then Pluto's black chariot carried her and Mercury away. The two stallions burst through the dry ground of earth—then galloped over the <u>barren</u> countryside to the temple where Ceres mourned for her daughter.

When Ceres saw her daughter coming, she ran down the hillside, and Proserpina sprang from the chariot into her mother's arms. All day the two talked excitedly of what had

---

6. **rites:** religious ceremonies.
7. **pomegranate** (pŏm′grăn′ĭt).

WORDS TO KNOW	**fertile** (fûr′tl) *adj.* rich in vegetation; fruitful
	barren (băr′ən) *adj.* lacking vegetation

Cross Curricular Link Science

THE POMEGRANATE Because of its many seeds, the pomegranate has long been a symbol of fertility. Its large scarlet leaves and spherical shape have also made it a symbol of beauty. For these reasons, there are many references to pomegranates in both literature and art.

The pomegranate grows wild in Iran and other neighboring countries. It is cultivated in the tropics and subtropics. In Iran and Jamaica,

the juice from the pomegranate is used in soups, sauces, and jellies.

It takes work to eat a pomegranate. You must pull apart the various chambers and either pick the seeds out, one at a time, or bite into it one section at a time. Despite the effort it takes to eat a pomegranate, many people enjoy this sweet, juicy fruit.

happened during their separation, but when Proserpina told Ceres about eating the pomegranate seed, the goddess hid her face and moaned in <u>anguish</u>.

"What have I done?" cried Proserpina.

"You have eaten the sacred food of the underworld," said Ceres. "Now you must return for half of every year to live with Pluto, your husband."

And this is how the seasons began—for when fall and winter come, the earth grows cold and barren because Proserpina lives in the underworld with Pluto, and her mother mourns. But when her daughter comes back to her, Ceres, goddess of grain, turns the world to spring and summer: The corn grows, and everything flowers again. ❖

Mary Pope Osborne
born 1949

". . . I've been able to channel so many different interests into books. . . ."

A Nomadic Life Mary Pope Osborne's experiences have provided her with a wealth of material. Her father was in the military, so the family moved often. She found it difficult to settle in one place for long, even as an adult. After studying drama and religion at the University of North Carolina, she traveled extensively in Asia and lived in a cave on the Greek island of Crete. She worked as a window dresser and a travel agent before becoming a full-time writer.

Travels with Books Many of Osborne's books transport readers to different places and times. Along with retellings of ancient myths and legends, she has written the Magic Tree House series of books. In these stories, a tree house is filled with books that involve two young readers in adventures with dinosaurs, knights, and other historical creatures and characters. Osborne has won many awards and honors for her writing. Her books *American Tall Tales* and *Mermaid Tales from Around the World* have been recognized by the National Council for the Social Studies/Children's Book Council.

WORDS TO KNOW

anguish (ăng'gwĭsh) *n.* severe mental pain

787

Standards-Based Objectives

1. To understand and appreciate a fable and a folk tale that explore a period of growth and change in a young person's life

2. To appreciate the folklore and cultures of Trinidad and Tobago and Guatemala

3. To extend understanding of the selections through a variety of activities

Reading Pathways

• Select one or several students to read each story aloud to the entire class or to small groups of students. Assign this reading in advance so that the readers can incorporate into their presentations some of the techniques used by professional storytellers. Have the audience listen carefully to the stories without following along in their texts.

• Read the stories aloud to the class, pausing at key points to discuss how elements of the stories inform students about the folklore and cultures of Trinidad and Tobago or Guatemala. Have students compare these cultures to their own.

• After students have read the stories once, have them read them again to identify structural elements such as main characters, minor characters, conflict, setting, and plot. Then have students identify similarities and differences between these stories and the selections in Unit Two. Students can compare the way the young characters in "Aaron's Gift" and "The Bamboo Beads" grow and change as a result of the stories their older relatives tell.

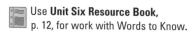 Use **Unit Six Resource Book,** p. 12, for work with Words to Know.

English Conventions Practice

Daily Language SkillBuilder

Have students **proofread** the display sentences on page 767g and write them correctly. The sentences also appear on Transparency 24 of **Language Transparencies.**

LINKS TO UNIT TWO

Growth and Change

What does it mean to belong? How do our home and heritage affect the way we grow? These and other questions are raised in the selections in Unit Two. Many folk tales have also explored these issues. Both of the folk tales you are about to read describe periods of growth and change in the lives of young people.

GUATEMALA

TRINIDAD AND TOBAGO

TRINIDAD AND TOBAGO

The Bamboo Beads

retold by Lynn Joseph

This **folk tale** comes from Trinidad and Tobago, a country made up of two islands off the coast of Venezuela. The islands were first inhabited by native Caribbean peoples. Over the years, the islands were claimed by Spain, Great Britain, and the Netherlands. Many French people also settled there to run sugar-cane farms, and Africans were brought as slaves to work on these plantations. After slavery was abolished, plantations employed workers from India.

By the time Trinidad and Tobago achieved independence in 1962, it was a country with a diverse heritage. Although English is the official language, the influences of many languages can be heard.

This tale features Papa Bois (pä-pä-bwä'), one of the islands' popular folklore characters. His duty is to protect trees and woodland animals, which include the scarlet ibis, the iguana, and many poisonous snakes.

788   UNIT SIX   THE ORAL TRADITION

LESSON RESOURCES

UNIT SIX RESOURCE BOOK
pp. 9–13

ASSESSMENT
Formal Assessment,
pp. 127–128
Test Generator

SKILLS TRANSPARENCIES AND COPYMASTERS
Literary Analysis
• Setting, TR 6 (p. 790)
Reading and Critical Thinking
• Summarizing (Story Map),
  TR 13 (p. 790)
Language
• Daily Language SkillBuilder,
  TR 24 (p. 788)

INTEGRATED TECHNOLOGY
Audio Library
Internet: Research Starter

Visit our Web site:
www.mcdougallittell.com

For **systematic instruction** in language skills, see:
• **Vocabulary and Spelling Book**
• **Grammar, Usage, and Mechanics Book**
• pacing chart on p. 767e.

GUATEMALA

The Disobedient Child

retold by Victor Montejo (mōn-tā′hō)

Guatemala is one of the seven countries that form Central America, the narrow land bridge that connects North and South America. One of the first civilizations in the Americas, the Mayan Empire, thrived in Central America from about A.D. 250 to 900. Mayan cities occupied the Yucatán Peninsula, southern Mexico, Honduras, and Belize, as well as Guatemala.

Today, about half of Guatemala's population is descended from the Maya. Many Guatemalans speak Mayan languages and follow traditional ways of life. Ancient Mayan culture is reflected in this Guatemalan **fable** about a boy who ignores warnings. The boy seems unwilling to listen until he is put to the test by someone with supernatural powers.

AS YOU READ . . .

See how the values of family and community are portrayed in different cultures.

Find out which elements of nature and which imagined forces are feared.

See how consequences of characters' choices unfold.

Less Proficient Readers

In both of these stories, the main characters' actions have a strong bearing on what happens to them. Ask students to read these stories paying special attention to what the main character does and what results from this action.

English Learners

Have students locate the countries of Guatemala and Trinidad and Tobago on the map, or use a larger map that shows the surrounding countries. Encourage students to share what they know of these areas of the world. You also might want them to locate Spain, France, Great Britain, and the Netherlands on the map so that they can better understand the background notes on these two pages.

Use **Spanish Study Guide,** pp. 160–162, for additional support.

Advanced Students

Ask students to pay particular attention to the character in each story who has special powers, and to consider how each story would change without such a character.

home. He takes shelter with an old man, who asks him to cook 13 beans in a pot. When the boy disobeys, the old man next forbids him to open a little door in the house. The boy opens the door, finding three capes and three jars, one of which he opens. When huge clouds spring out of the jar, the boy puts on one of the capes. He is then turned into thunder and lifted into the stormy sky. Hearing the thunder, the old man rushes home, rescues the boy, and restores the sky. The old man then reveals that he is Qich Mam, a powerful rain spirit. The boy feels guilty and promises Qich Mam never again to disobey his parents.

Reading and Analyzing

Literary Analysis: SETTING

Ask students where this story is set.

Possible Response: It is set in a lonely little house in the Guatemalan woods.

Use **Unit Six Resource Book,** p. 11, for more practice. Use **Literary Analysis Transparencies,** p. 6, for additional support.

Active Reader: STORY MAPPING

Ask students to use a story map like the one shown to represent the story. What parts can they fill in at this point?

Setting: little house in the woods	Characters: boy and old man
Problem: boy is disobedient	
Events:	
Resolution:	

Use **Unit Six Resource Book,** p. 10, for more practice. Use **Reading and Critical Thinking Transparencies,** p. 13, for additional support.

Effigy vessel (about A.D. 1000–1250), unknown Mayan artist. Ceramic, painted red, blue, and white, 31.7 cm in height, Museo Nacional de Antropología, Mexico. Photograph copyright © Stuart Rome. Reproduction authorized by the National Institute of Anthropology and History.

EXPLICIT INSTRUCTION **Viewing and Representing**

Effigy Vessel
by an unknown Mayan artist

This hand-painted ceramic pot was made about A.D. 1000–1250.

Instruction Tell students that an effigy vessel is a pot with a human or animal form. This vessel was found in a cave near Chichén Itzá in Mexico and was probably used in Mayan cave rituals. For the ancient Mayas, caves were the source of rain and fertility and embodied the mysteries of life and death.

Practice Ask students to describe the expression on the vessel's face.

Possible Response: Students may say the face appears determined, serious, or even angry.

Practice Ask how they can relate the face to the fable of the disobedient boy.

Possible Response: It may relate to the jars in the story, or anger directed at the child.

THE DISOBEDIENT CHILD

RETOLD BY VICTOR MONTEJO

In old times in *Xaqla'* Jacaltenango[1] there was a very disobedient child who often disappointed his parents. No matter how hard they tried to teach him, he never changed.

One afternoon the boy ran away from home, looking for someone who would tolerate his mischief. Walking through the woods he discovered a lonely little house and ran up to it. On the porch of the straw-covered house sat an old man, smoking peacefully. The boy stood before him without saying hello or any other word of greeting.

When the old man noticed the boy's presence, he stopped smoking and asked him, "Where do you want to go, boy?"

"I am looking for someone who can give me something to eat," the boy answered.

The wise old man, who already knew the boy's story, said, "No one will love you if you continue being so bad."

The boy did not respond except to laugh.

1. ***Xaqla'* Jacaltenango** (chäk-lä' häk'äl-tĕ-nän'gô): town in the mountains of Guatemala.

WORDS TO KNOW **tolerate** (tŏl'ə-rāt') *v.* to put up with

Differentiating Instruction

Less Proficient Readers
Invite volunteers to share stories about times when their curiosity caused them to get into trouble.

Set a Purpose Have students read to find out the real identity of the man who takes in the runaway child.

English Learners
Preview the Words to Know and the footnotes at the bottom of the page with students before they read. Then they should try to read the story, using their knowledge of word parts and context clues to figure out the meanings of unfamiliar words. After students have read the story, have them look up the meanings of any words they can't figure out or don't know.

Advanced Students
Ask students to think about how fables not only explain natural phenomena but also help to teach people to behave in socially acceptable ways.

A Students can answer different types and levels of questions such as open-ended, literal, and interpretive. Ask students to interpret why they think the old man offers to let the boy stay with him.

Possible Responses: The old man takes in the disobedient child because he wants to teach him a lesson. The old man has some magical powers, as shown by the knowledge of the boy's story. The old man is lonely and wants the boy's company, despite the boy's disobedient nature.

Reading Skills and Strategies:
MONITOR

B Students can monitor their own comprehension and make modifications when understanding breaks down, such as by rereading a portion aloud, using reference aids, searching for clues, and asking questions. Discuss the questions or comments students have about the old man's actions at this point. You may wish to model thinking through the story by saying something like the following: "I wonder what the old man is up to. Why does he give the boy this strange warning? How could it possibly matter whether the boy puts 13—or 10 or 11 or even 20—beans into the pot? I think the old man is testing the boy to see if the boy will obey his instructions."

Active Reader: STORY MAPPING

Have students continue filling in the story maps they began earlier.

A Then the old man smiled and said, "You can stay with me. We will eat together."

The boy accepted his offer and stayed in the old man's house. On the following day before going to work, the old man told the boy: "You should stay in the house, and the only duty **B** you will have is to put the beans to cook during the afternoon. But listen well. You should only throw thirteen beans in the pot and no more. Do you understand?"

The boy nodded that he understood the directions very well. Later, when the time arrived to cook the beans, the boy put the clay pot on the fire and threw in thirteen beans as he had been directed. But once he had done that, he began to think that thirteen beans weren't very many for such a big pot. So, disobeying his orders, he threw in several more little fistfuls.

When the beans began to boil over the fire, the pot started to fill up, and it filled up until it overflowed. Very surprised, the boy quickly took an empty pot and divided the beans between the two pots. But the beans overflowed the new pot, too. Beans were pouring out of both pots.

When the old man returned home, he found piles of beans, and the two clay pots lay broken on the floor.

"Why did you disobey my orders and cook more than I told you to?" the old man asked angrily.

1 The boy hung his head and said nothing. The old man then gave him instructions for the next day. "Tomorrow you will again cook the beans as I have told you. What's more, I <u>forbid</u> you to open that little door over there. Do you understand?"

The boy indicated that he understood very well.

The next day the old man left the house after warning the boy to take care to do exactly what he had been told. During the afternoon the boy put the beans on the fire to cook. Then he was filled with curiosity. What was behind the little door he had been forbidden to open?

Without any fear, the boy opened the door and discovered in the room three enormous covered water jars. Then he found three capes inside a large trunk. There was one green cape, one yellow cape and one red cape. Not satisfied with these discoveries, the boy took the top off the first water jar to see what it contained.

Immediately the water jar began to <u>emit</u> great clouds that quickly hid the sky. Frightened and shivering with cold, the boy opened the trunk and put on the red cape. At that instant a clap of thunder exploded in the house. The boy was turned into thunder and lifted to the sky, where he unleashed a great storm.

When the old man heard the thunder, he guessed that something extraordinary had happened at home, and he hurried in that direction. There he discovered that the forbidden door was open and the top was

IMMEDIATELY THE WATER JAR BEGAN TO EMIT GREAT CLOUDS THAT QUICKLY HID THE SKY.

WORDS TO KNOW	
forbid (fôr-bĭd′) v. to command someone not to do something	
emit (ĭ-mĭt′) v. to send out; give forth, usually with force	

off the jar of clouds, from which churning mists still rose toward the sky. The old man covered the jar and then approached the trunk with the capes. The red cape, the cape of storms, was missing. Quickly the old man put on the green cape and regained control over the sky, calming the great storm. Little by little the storm subsided, and soon the man returned to the house, carrying the unconscious boy in his arms.

A little while later the old man uncapped the same jar, and the clouds which had blackened the sky returned to their resting place, leaving the heavens bright and blue again. When he had done this, the old man capped the jar again and put away the red and green capes.

Through all of this the boy remained stunned and soaked with the rains until the kind old man restored his spirit and brought him back to normal. When the boy was alert again and his fear had left, the old man said, "Your disobedience has almost killed you. You were lucky that I heard the storm and came to help. Otherwise you would have been lost forever among the clouds."

The boy was quiet and the old man continued.

"I am Qich Mam,[2] the first father of all people and founder of *Xaqla'*, he who controls the rain, and waters the community's fields when they are dry. Understand, then, that I wish you no harm and I forgive what you have done. Promise me that in the future you will not disobey your parents."

The boy smiled happily and answered, "I promise, Qich Mam, I promise." Qich Mam patted him gently and said, "Then return to your home and be useful to your parents and to your people."

From that time on the boy behaved differently. He was very grateful for the kindness of the old man who held the secret of the clouds, the rains, the wind and the storms in his hands. ❖

---

2. **Qich Mam** (kĕch′ mäm′): a thunder spirit of the Mayan people.

Victor Montejo
born 1951

"I want to . . . preserve the history of the Mayan oral tradition."

Far from Home Victor Montejo was born and raised in Guatemala and later taught primary school in Jacaltenango, the setting of "The Disobedient Child." Unfortunately, because of the political climate in Guatemala, Montejo was forced to flee to the United States in 1982.

Success in the States Since then, he has published a number of stories, fables, and poems and has worked as a writer-in-residence at Bucknell University in Pennsylvania. He has also done doctoral work in anthropology at the University of Connecticut. "The Disobedient Child" is from Montejo's book *The Bird Who Cleans the World.*

Summary

The Trinidadian narrator of this tale listens as her great-aunt explains the origin of a string of beads she wears. Tantie describes how, as a young girl at the market, she gave bread to a ragged old man with hooves instead of feet. In return he gave her a piece of string, which she wore as a necklace. Thereafter, colorful bamboo beads began to turn up everywhere, and Tantie added each one to her necklace. Tantie's mother understood that they had come from the forest spirit Papa Bois. When Tantie encountered Papa Bois again at the market, she learned that the beads represented the number of children she would have someday—who turned out actually to be her grandnieces and grandnephews. After telling this story, Tantie entrusts the necklace to her grandniece—the narrator.

Reading and Analyzing

Literary Analysis: SIMILE

A Tell students that it is useful to identify literary terms across a variety of literary forms. Remind them that a simile is a comparison using *like* or *as*. Ask students to identify the two similes that appear in this passage.

Answer: Her mother's flowers were "red as the evening sun," "the moon was round and white as my Sunday hat."

The Bamboo Beads

by Lynn Joseph

Illustration Copyright © 1991 Brian Pinkney. From *A Wave in Her Pocket* by Lynn Joseph, reprinted by permission of Clarion Books/Houghton Mifflin Co. All rights reserved.

EXPLICIT INSTRUCTION Speaking and Listening

DIALECT

Students can identify how language use reflects regions and cultures.

Instruction Explain that a dialect is the language spoken by a group of people from a specific region. It might differ from the standard language in the way it is pronounced, its grammar, or its vocabulary. The characters in "The Bamboo Beads" speak an island dialect.

Practice Invite volunteers to select and read aloud from the story a passage featuring a Trinidad dialect. To help students get a better sense of this dialect, play vocal music from Trinidad or other West Indian islands. Discuss the ways in which this dialect differs from the English they are familiar with. Ask whether there are any sayings that are unfamiliar to them.

Possible Response: Students may note use of *de, yuh,* or *chile,* they may notice that a verb is omitted ("This de same string, Tantie?"), or they may be unfamiliar with an expression like "when I was in my bare feet still" to refer to being a child.

Last year during the planting season, I helped Mama plant seeds on our hill. "One seed for each of my brothers and sisters," she said, and she covered up seven seeds with dark dirt. Mama's family lives on the other side of the island, so we hardly ever see them.

Each day I watched Mama water the dark mounds of dirt and weed around them. Soon, flowers grew up. They were red as the evening sun. But one day the floods came and swept them to the sea.

"Poor Mama," I said.

"They'll grow again," she replied.

She looked at her gardening gloves hanging on a nail. "If they don't grow back, we'll plant some more." And she smiled.

That night the moon was round and white as my Sunday hat. I told Daddy how Mama's flowers had drowned in the flood rains. He said, "Did I ever show you how *I* count my brothers and sisters?"

"No," I answered.

Then Daddy showed me the fisherman stars. "They point fishermen to the way home," he said. "There are eight of them. I named one each for my brothers and sisters."

"How do you know which is which?" I asked.

Daddy pointed again to the bright stars. "Well, there's Rupert and Hazel, Anthony and Derek, Peter, Janet, and Neil."

"You forgot Auntie Sonia," I said.

Daddy smiled and pointed to a tiny star. "That one's her."

I nodded my head as Daddy moved his finger around, although I couldn't tell which star was who.

After that, Daddy and I looked for the fisherman stars each night. Some nights when the sea breezes blew dark clouds in the sky, we couldn't see them. But Daddy would say, "They'll come back." And he'd smile.

"I wish I had brothers and sisters to plant flowers for or to count stars on," I told Mama and Daddy one day. "I'm tired of having only myself."

"What about all your cousins?" asked Mama.

"You can count them on something," said Daddy.

"What can I count them on?" I wondered.

"Maybe Tantie can help find you something," said Mama. "She's the one who keeps track of all yuh."

So, the next time Tantie came to visit, I said, "Tantie, Mama said you keep track of me and my cousins."

"That's right, chile," said Tantie. "And is plenty of all yuh to keep track of, too." **1**

"I know," I said, "but how you do it? I want something that I can name after each one of my cousins. Something I can count them on. Like Mama has flowers and Daddy has his fisherman stars."

Well, Tantie looked me in the eye for a long time. Then from underneath the neck of her dress she pulled out a brown string full of bright, colorful beads.

"Tantie, where you get those pretty beads from?" I asked.

"These, my dear, is a story by itself, and if you have de time to listen, I'll tell it to you."

I nodded and sat down on the porch swing next to Tantie. As Tantie told her story, I kept trying to push the swing with my foot. But

English Learners

1 Point out that the spelling *chile* for "child" represents Tantie's island accent. Invite students to use context clues to infer what standard English word the spelling *yuh* represents. *(you)*

Less Proficient Readers

Have students describe the sequence of events that leads to Tantie's telling a story.

Possible Response: The narrator watches her mother plant flower seeds for each of her siblings and her father count his siblings by the stars. The narrator, an only child, asks for a way to count her cousins. Her parents suggest that she consult Tantie. In response to the request, Tantie scrutinizes the narrator and begins a story.

Advanced Students

Have students read this story and summarize it in 150 words or less. Then have them compare their summaries with the work of fellow classmates and with the summary on page 794.

Literary Analysis: CHARACTERIZATION

A Students can analyze characters, including their traits, motivations, conflicts, points of view, relationships and changes they undergo. Although the reader does not realize it at this point in the narrative, this initial meeting between the old man and Tantie is an important one. Have students describe what they learn about Tantie's character from her behavior in this passage.

Possible Response: Tantie doesn't stare at the man's unusual feet and she gives him food. These acts show that she is kind, generous, and thoughtful.

Reading Skills and Strategies: PREDICT

B Have students predict where the beads have come from. Which clues and details in the story help them make their predictions?

Possible Response: Students may predict that the beads are from the poor man, since he gave Tantie the string.

Tantie was too heavy. The swing sat quiet. The only sound was Tantie's voice.

"A long, long time ago," she began, "when I was in my bare feet still, I went to market with a basket of bread and red-currant buns to sell. Market day was de busiest time. There was plenty to see as I set up my little stall and tucked cloths around de bread and buns so de flies wouldn't get them.

"I hadn't sold one thing yet when an old man came up. His clothes were ragged and he didn't have on no shoes. His feet didn't look like no ordinary feet. They looked like cow hooves. I didn't stare, though, because it rude to do that.

A "He asked for a piece of bread. Well, I remember Mama telling me that morning to get good prices for de bread, but I was sure Mama hadn't meant from this man too. So, I cut off a hunk of bread, wrapped it in brown paper, and handed it to him. He looked so hungry that I reached for a bun and gave him that too. De man smiled and bowed his head at me. Then he went his way.

"After that I was busy selling bread. De buns went even faster. By afternoon, I had sold them all. Then I saw de old man coming over again. He didn't look so ragged anymore. His hair was combed and he had on a new shirt.

2 "'I'm sorry,' I said. 'No more bread left.'

"He didn't answer. Instead he handed me something. It was a piece of brown string. It looked like an ordinary old string, but I didn't tell him that.

"'Thank you for de bread, child,' he said. Then he shuffled off and was gone.

"I looked at de string for a while. I could use it to tie up my bread cloths, I thought. Or

I could use it as a hair ribbon. But I decided I would put de string around my neck and wear it like a necklace."

"This de same string, Tantie?" I asked, fingering Tantie's bead necklace.

"De very same," she answered.

"Well, that evening, Mama was so proud I had sold all de bread that she gave me a treat. It was a small blue bamboo bead. It was de exact color of Mama's best blue head scarf.

"'Where you get this bead, Mama?' I asked.

"'Found it in de yard,' she replied.

"I wondered how it got there, but it didn't matter. I pulled out my brown string and untied it. Then I slipped de blue bead on and tied it around my neck again. It looked like a real necklace now that it had Mama's bead on it."

"Is this your mama's bead?" I asked, touching a bright blue bead on Tantie's string.

"Yes, that's it, chile," said Tantie. "And it shines more now than de day I got it.

"Two days later, Daddy found a smooth black bead down by de sea. He brought it home in his pocket.

"'I thought you might like this,' he said, and handed it to me. It sparkled like a black sun. I untied my necklace and slipped it on next to de blue bead. Now my string was beautiful with Mama's and Daddy's bamboo beads on it.

"During de next few days, Mama and Daddy and I kept finding shiny bamboo beads

> Then I slipped de blue bead on and tied it around my neck again.

Multicultural Link **Trinidad Languages**

The official language of Trinidad is English, but islanders also speak French, Spanish, and Hindi. This mixture of languages reflects Trinidad's history as a colonized island. Christopher Columbus claimed Trinidad for Spain in 1498. The island was at that time inhabited by the Arawak and Carib tribes. Haitian planters of French ancestry settled in Trinidad and established a profitable sugar cane industry using African slave labor. The British gained possession of the island in 1802. Trinidad, along with the nearby island Tobago,

gained independence in 1962. The Trinidad English that Tantie speaks here is a reflection of these many influences. For instance, her name derives from the French word for aunt, *tante*. *Bois* is the French word for woods, a fitting name for the wood spirit Papa Bois. Words from native Caribbean languages have also been incorporated into the English language. *Hurricane, tobacco, canoe,* and *hammock* all come from words originating in native Caribbean languages.

in de strangest places. I found a red one under de bed. Mama found a green one in de garden, and Daddy found a yellow one in his shoe. Mama and Daddy didn't think nothing of it, but as I added each new bead to my necklace, I got a strange, trembly feeling.

"De next week when I took Mama's bread and currant buns to market, I saw de old man who had given me my string. His clothes were still ragged and he clumped around on his hooves.

"'Hello, mister,' I said when he came over. I wrapped up a chunk of bread and two buns this time and gave them to him. He smiled and shuffled off.

"Again my day of selling flew by. Before lunchtime I had sold everything. Mama hugged me hard when I got home. But then she sat down at de kitchen table and looked serious.

"'What's wrong?' I asked.

"'Look,' she said, pointing to a bowl on the table. I looked inside and there were de most beautiful, shiny bamboo beads I'd ever seen. Lots and lots of them. I put my hand in and touched de smooth wood.

"'Where they come from?' I asked.

"'Don't know,' said Mama. 'They were here when I turned around from de sink this morning. I thought you might know something about them, since you're collecting beads.'

"'No,' I said. 'I don't know about these.'

Illustration Copyright © 1991 Brian Pinkney. From *A Wave in Her Pocket* by Lynn Joseph, reprinted by permission of Clarion Books/Houghton Mifflin Co. All rights reserved.

"Then Mama said, 'Let me see that string of beads around your neck, girl.'

"I showed it to Mama. She looked and looked at de beads and tugged on de string until I thought she'd break it. Then she looked at me and said, 'You've met Papa Bois.'[1]

"'Papa who?'

"'Papa Bois,' she murmured. 'He lives in de

---

1. Papa Bois (pä pä bwä') *French:* Father Forest.

WORDS TO KNOW

murmur (mûr′mər) *v.* to speak so quietly that the words are difficult to make out

EXPLICIT INSTRUCTION **Viewing and Representing**

Illustration by Brian Pinkney

ART APPRECIATION This illustration, done especially for "The Bamboo Beads," uses a scratchboard technique.

Instruction To create a scratchboard drawing, a specially prepared surface is covered with black ink. The artist then uses a fine, sharp instrument to scratch the delicate lines of the drawing.

Practice Ask students if this illustration matches their ideas about how the characters look and act. Why or why not?

Possible Response: Answers will vary but should be supported by details from the story.

Practice Ask students to choose a scene from the story to illustrate. To make a scratchboard-like drawing, they can color a heavy white paper completely with black crayon, then use a sharp instrument—such as the end of a compass—to scratch the drawing.

Literary Analysis: FOLK TALE

Students can recognize the distinguishing features of various genres. Remind students that a folk tale is a story that is handed down, usually by word of mouth, among the people of a region. Like fables, folk tales often teach lessons. Ask students to describe the characteristics of this story that make it a folk tale.

Possible Response: It is being told aloud to another character, it comes from the region of Trinidad, it is about ordinary people, it contains a supernatural being, and it seems to be teaching the value of kindness.

forest and protects de trees and forest animals from hunters. He spends his time <u>whittling</u> bamboo beads from fallen bamboo shoots. He's de only one who could make these beads. They're priceless.'

"Mama looked at me and gave me back de necklace. 'Have you met an old man without any feet?' she asked.

"I immediately thought of de old man from de market. 'Yes, Mama, I met him last week at de market. An old man in ragged clothes and no feet. He had cow hooves instead.'

"Mama closed her eyes and nodded her head. 'That's Papa Bois,' she said. 'He can be dangerous. Once he meets someone, he keeps track of them by counting their sins, their blessings, even their teeth, on his whittled beads. You never know with Papa Bois just what he's counting for you. The last time Papa Bois gave someone beads, the beads represented de number of days he had left to live. These beads on de table must be for you. He's counting something for you.'"

"'What?' I whispered, almost too frightened to speak.

"'We won't know till he's ready to say. Were you kind or mean to him?'

"'I gave him some bread to eat because he looked hungry,' I said.

"'Good,' said Mama, and she pulled me into her arms. 'That was very kind. Now you might as well put de beads on de string and wait until Papa Bois comes back and tells you what he's counting.'

"I put de pretty beads on de string. I didn't think they would all fit, but no matter how many I put on, de string never filled up. When every bead was on, I counted thirty-three beads. Then I tied it around my neck once more. It wasn't any heavier than when I wore de string empty.

"As de days passed, Mama, Daddy, and I kept our eyes open for Papa Bois. We thought he might come by any time. I wondered over and over what Papa Bois could be counting on my beads."

"Were you scared, Tantie?" I interrupted.

"A little," she answered. "But I knew I had been kind to Papa Bois, and that was all that mattered.

"De next time I went to market for Mama, she wanted to come with me. I told her Papa Bois might not come to our stall if she was there.

"At the stall I laid de bread and buns out nicely and covered them with cloths. I saw de old man shuffling up to my table.

"'*Bonjour, vieux Papa,*'[2] I said. Mama had told me that to say hello in French was de polite way to greet Papa Bois. She also said not to look at his feet no matter what.

"'*Bonjour,*' said de old man.

"'Would you like some bread?' I asked. Papa Bois nodded.

"As I cut him a chunk of bread, I said, 'Thank you for de pretty necklace.'

"'It's for you to wear always,' he said. 'Until you find someone who should wear it instead.'

> "That was de last time I ever see Papa Bois."

---

2. ***Bonjour, vieux Papa*** (bôn-zhoor' vyœ' pä-pä') *French:* Hello, old Father.

WORDS
TO
KNOW
    whittling (hwĭt'lĭng) *adj.* carving by shaving away bits of wood with a knife **whittle** *v.*

"Papa Bois's eyes looked kind in his wrinkled face. I decided I go ask him what de beads were for.

"'De beads,' he answered, 'are for all de little children you'll one day have.'

"'Thirty-three children?' I asked.

"'Yes, they'll be yours, but they won't be yours,' he said mysteriously. But then he smiled a big smile.

"'All right,' I said, and I handed him de bread and buns.

"That was de last time I ever see Papa Bois. Mama said he only comes out of his forest when he's lonely for human company. Otherwise his friends are de deer, de squirrels, and de trees. The first person he meets when he leaves his forest early in de morning is de one who counts. If that person stares at his feet or laughs at him—watch out!"

"But Tantie, what happen to de thirty-three children?" I asked.

"You're one of them," she said. "Ever since your oldest cousin Jarise was born, I been de one helping to take care of all yuh. I have thirty grandnieces and nephews now. That mean three more to come. And all yuh are my children, just like Papa Bois said."

Tantie reached up and unhooked her bamboo bead necklace. Then she laid it in my hands.

"Oh," I said, looking at Tantie's necklace again. "I'd like to be de red bead."

Tantie took the necklace out of my hands and put it around my neck. She tied the string. The necklace felt cool and smooth against my skin.

"I wish I had a mirror," I said.

"It looking beautiful," said Tantie. "And it for you now. You can count your cousins on them beads."

"You're giving this to me, Tantie?" I asked, not believing what I had heard.

"Papa Bois said I go find someone who should wear it."

"Thank you," I said. I ran my fingers over the bamboo smoothness of the beads and admired the pretty colors.

"And since you wear Papa Bois's beads, you can start helping me tell these stories," said Tantie. "I been doing de work alone for too long."

Tantie reached over and adjusted the bead string on my neck.

I looked down at the shiny red bead that was me and smiled and smiled. ❖

Lynn Joseph

". . . I've never forgotten the smells, sounds, and foods of my island."

My Beautiful Island Lynn Joseph recalls: "When I was a little girl in Trinidad, I could not imagine anywhere else but my beautiful island, with its tall coconut trees, sandy beaches, and happy sounds of steel-band music. I've lived in many other places since then, but I've never forgotten the smells, sounds, and foods of my island." Joseph moved to the United States with her family and graduated from the University of Colorado. She currently lives in New York City. Joseph says she remembers listening to stories like "The Bamboo Beads" when she was growing up. Joseph is best known for her books of poetry *Coconut Kind of Day: Island Poems* and *A Wave in Her Pocket*. She recently published a well-received biography of Bessie Coleman, *Fly, Bessie, Fly*.

THE BAMBOO BEADS   **799**

- To understand and appreciate two folk tales that illustrate a lesson in justice
- To appreciate the folklore and cultural history of Germany and Vietnam
- To extend understanding of the selection through a variety of activities

Reading Pathways

- Select one or several students to read each story aloud to the entire class or to small groups of students. Assign this reading in advance so that the readers can incorporate into their presentations some of the techniques used by professional storytellers. Have the audience listen carefully to the stories without following along in their texts.
- Read the stories aloud to the class, pausing at key points to discuss how elements of the stories inform students about the folklore and cultures of Vietnam and Germany. Have students compare these cultures to their own.
- After students have read the stories once, have them read them again to identify structural elements such as main characters, minor characters, conflict, setting, and plot. Then have students identify similarities and differences between these stories and the selections in the Unit 3. Students can compare the treatment received by the king's daughter in "King Thrushbeard" with that of Selo in "Cricket in the Road."

 Use **Unit Six Resource Book,** p. 17, for work with Words to Know.

English Conventions Practice

Daily Language SkillBuilder

Have students **proofread** the display sentences on page 767g and write them correctly. The sentences also appear on Transparency 25 of **Language Transparencies.**

PREPARING to *Read*

The Oral Tradition

LINKS TO UNIT THREE

A Sense of Fairness

Do two wrongs make a right? How can you resolve an injustice? What is just and what is unjust? These questions are raised in the selections in Unit Three. Folk tales from many different cultures have also explored these issues. Each of the tales you are about to read illustrates a lesson in justice.

GERMANY

King Thrushbeard

retold by the Brothers Grimm

This tale was recorded by the famous Brothers Grimm, whose stories are still told to children today. In the early 1800s, the brothers collected and wrote down stories that had been told in Germany for generations. Their **fairy tales** include "Cinderella," "The Frog Prince," "Rumpelstiltskin," "Hansel and Gretel," and "Snow White." In this lesser-known story, a princess who finds fault with almost everyone learns a lesson about pride.

The story takes place in medieval Germany, in the days of nobles, knights, and peasants. Although those days are long gone, many German castles from this period of history still stand. Some are open to visitors as museums. Like the Grimms' fairy tales, they help people remember and learn from the past.

LESSON RESOURCES

UNIT SIX RESOURCE BOOK
pp. 14–18

ASSESSMENT
Formal Assessment,
pp. 129–130
Test Generator

SKILLS TRANSPARENCIES AND COPYMASTERS
Literary Analysis
- Characterization, TR 4 (p. 804)

Language
- Daily Language SkillBuilder, TR 25 (p. 800)

Speaking and Listening
- Evaluating Reading Aloud, p. 14 (p. 803)
- Conducting Interviews, p. 35 (p. 806)
- Guidelines: How to Analyze an Interview, p. 36 (p. 806)

INTEGRATED TECHNOLOGY
Audio Library
Internet: Research Starter

Visit our Web site:
www.mcdougallittell.com

For **systematic instruction** in language skills, see:
- **Vocabulary and Spelling Book**
- **Grammar, Usage, and Mechanics Book**
- pacing chart on p. 767e.

English Learners
Read the story aloud and have students follow along in their texts to connect spoken and written language.

 Use **Spanish Study Guide,** pp. 163–165, for additional support.

Less Proficient Readers
As students read each story, pause to ask questions to confirm that students are keeping track of critical events in the story.

Advanced Students
Challenge students to consider questions such as the following as they read:
• What purpose have folk tales served?
• Do they still serve that purpose today?
• Are there any modern folk tales?
• Do these two tales offer lessons we are still in need of learning?

GERMANY

VIETNAM

AS YOU READ . . .

Think about similar stories you may have read in the folklore of other cultures.

Identify traits that vary from one culture to another.

Think about why certain values endure.

VIETNAM

In the Land of Small Dragon

told by Dang Manh Kha (däng′-män′kä) to Ann Nolan Clark

Different versions of the same story may appear in many cultures. Usually these stories focus on values that the cultures hold in common. For example, many versions of the Cinderella story can be found, from Canada to Africa to Japan. This **Cinderella tale** told in verse comes from Vietnam, a country in Southeast Asia.

Vietnam was governed for long periods by China and then by France. Yet the Vietnamese have retained much of their own folklore and cultural identity. Today Vietnam is an independent nation. This version of the Cinderella story includes a jealous stepmother, a fairy godmother, and a magical fish.

LINKS TO UNIT THREE **801**

Summary

In a Vietnamese folk tale similar to "Cinderella," the beautiful T'âm is mistreated by her jealous stepmother and her stepsister, Cám. When the girls' father holds a fishing contest to see who will be his Number One Daughter, Cám cheats T'âm out of the title by stealing all but one of her fish. T'âm feels sorry for her little remaining fish and becomes its friend and caretaker—until Cám eats it. A fairy tells the grieving T'âm to bury her fish's bones; later she digs them up and discovers in their place a silk dress and two jeweled shoes. After she loses one shoe in a rice paddy, a bird carries it to the emperor's garden. There the emperor's son picks it up and proclaims that its owner will be his wife. Although Cám's mother does her best to keep T'âm from going with her stepsister to the palace, T'âm does go. The prince easily slips the shoe onto T'âm's foot and declares that she will be his wife.

Reading and Analyzing

Active Reader:
USING TEXT ORGANIZERS

Students can represent text information in different ways such as in outlines, time lines, or graphic organizers. Invite them to use a family tree to help them identify relationships among characters. Have students copy the family tree into their Reader's Notebooks and refer to it as they follow the emerging family conflict in the story.

Father's first wife — Father — Father's second wife

T'âm   Cám

Use **Unit Six Resource Book,** p. 15, for more practice.

Multicultural Link   Years of the Chinese Calendar

The Chinese assign an animal, real or mythical, to each year. There are 12 different animals in the cycle, which is sometimes referred to as the Chinese Zodiac. Like a person's astrological sign, a person's birth year is believed to give the person certain characteristics. For example, people born in the Year of the Rooster (or Chicken, as it is called in the story) are supposed to be loners who are less adventurous than they appear to be. They are supposed to be most compatible with people born in the year of the Dragon, Snake, or Ox. Each year begins some time in either January or February. The cycle of animals is as follows:

2000	Dragon	2006	Dog
2001	Snake	2007	Pig
2002	Horse	2008	Rat
2003	Sheep	2009	Ox
2004	Monkey	2010	Tiger
2005	Rooster	2011	Rabbit

Students can count backward (1999 was also year of the Rabbit) to find their own birth year.

In the LAND of SMALL DRAGON

As told by
Dang Manh Kha
to Ann Nolan Clark

1

Man cannot know the whole world,
But can know his own small part.

In the Land of Small Dragon,
In the Year of the Chicken,[1]
In a Village of No-Name,
In the bend of the river,
There were many small houses
Tied together by walkways.
Mulberry and apricot,
Pear tree and flowering vine
Dropped their delicate blossoms
On a carpet of new grass.

---

1. **Year of the Chicken:** the name of a year in the old
Chinese calendar; commonly called Year of the
Rooster. Every year in the Chinese calendar has
1 of 12 animal names. For example, 1911 was a
Year of the Pig, which next occurred 12 years
later, in 1923.

Literary Analysis: CHARACTERIZATION

 A Students can analyze characters, including their traits, motivations, conflicts, points of view, relationships and changes they undergo, as they read. Ask students to interpret the italicized words. How do they apply to Cám?

Possible Response: If a person is bad inside, it shows on his or her face. Cám's ugly face reflects her mean spirit.

📑 Use **Literary Analysis Transparencies,** p. 4, for additional support.

Reading Skills and Strategies: ANALYZE

B Have students identify the things in this passage that come in twos and ones. Ask students what the narrator communicates by giving Cám's mother a single-minded purpose and a heart with a single door.

Possible Response: The narrator communicates disharmony. If Cám's mother could find room in her mind and heart for two daughters, all would be well.

Literary Analysis: POINT OF VIEW

Remind students that point of view refers to how a writer tells a story. Ask what point of view this story is told from.

Answer: third-person point of view Ask how students can tell.

Possible Response: The narrator is outside the story and uses third-person pronouns such as *he, she,* and *they.*

In a Village of No-Name
Lived a man and two daughters.
T'âm[2] was the elder daughter;
Her mother died at her birth.

A jewel box of gold and jade
Holds only jewels of great price.

T'âm's face was a golden moon,
Her eyes dark as a storm cloud,
Her feet delicate flowers
Stepping lightly on the wind.
No envy lived in her heart,
Nor bitterness in her tears.
Cám[3] was the younger daughter,
Child of Number Two Wife.
Cám's face was long and ugly,
Scowling and discontented,
Frowning in deep displeasure.
Indolent, slow and idle,
Her heart was filled with hatred
For her beautiful sister.

A *An evil heart keeps records*
On the face of its owner.

The father loved both daughters,
One not more than the other.
He did not permit his heart
To call one name more dearly.

He lived his days in justice,
Standing strong against the wind.

B Father had a little land,
A house made of mats and clay,
A grove of mulberry trees
Enclosed by growing bamboo,
A garden and rice paddy,[4]

Two great water buffalo,[5]
A well for drinking water,
And twin fish ponds for the fish.
Cám's mother, Number Two Wife,
Cared only for her own child.
Her mind had only one thought:
What would give pleasure to Cám.

Her heart had only one door
And only Cám could enter.

Number Two Wife was jealous
of T'âm, the elder daughter,
Who was beautiful and good,
So the mother planned revenge
On the good, beautiful child.
To Cám she gave everything,
But nothing but work to T'âm.
T'âm carried water buckets,
Hanging from her bamboo pole.
T'âm carried forest fagots[6]
To burn in the kitchen fire.
T'âm transplanted young rice plants
From seed bed to rice paddy.
T'âm flailed[7] the rice on a rock,
Then she winnowed and gleaned it.[8]
T'âm's body ached with tiredness,

---

2. **T'âm** (täm).
3. **Cám** (cäm).
4. **rice paddy:** flooded field used for growing rice.
5. **water buffalo:** slow, powerful, oxlike animals used for pulling loads.
6. **fagots** (făg′əts): bundles of sticks or twigs; also spelled *faggots.*
7. **flailed:** beat out grain from its husk, or dry outer casing.
8. **winnowed and gleaned it:** separated out the useless parts of the rice and collected the remaining good parts.

WORDS
TO
KNOW   **indolent** (ĭn′də-lənt) *adj.* lazy

Her heart was heavy and sad.
She said, "Wise Father, listen!
I am your elder daughter;
Therefore why may I not be
Number One Daughter, also?
A Number One Daughter works,
But she works with dignity.
If I were your Number One
The honor would ease my pain.
As it is, I am a slave,
Without honor or dignity."
Waiting for wisdom to come,
Father was slow to give answer.
"Both of my daughters share my heart.
I cannot choose between them.
One of you must earn the right
To be my Number One child."

*A man's worth is what he does,
Not what he says he can do.*

"Go, Daughters, to the fish pond;
Take your fish baskets with you.
Fish until night moon-mist comes.
Bring your fish catch back to me.
She who brings a full basket
Is my Number One Daughter.
Your work, not my heart, decides
Your place in your father's house."
T´âm listened to her father
And was quick to obey him.
With her basket, she waded
In the mud of the fish pond.
With quick-moving, graceful hands
She caught the quick-darting fish.
Slowly the long hours went by.
Slowly her fish basket filled.
Cám sat on the high, dry bank
Trying to think of some plan,

Illustration Copyright © 1982 Vo-Dinh Mai. From *The Brocaded Slipper and Other Vietnamese Tales* by Lynette Dyer Vuong. Reprinted by permission of HarperCollins Publishers.

Differentiating Instruction

English Learners
1 In this story, the father will pick a "number one" and a "number two" daughter according to who works the hardest. In some cultures, birth order determines a child's role in the family. Invite students to discuss what they think about these cultural traditions.

English Learners
2 Remind students that there are many words in English that can be used as nouns, verbs, and adjectives, and that the context usually makes clear what meaning is intended. Point out that the word *fish* is used in each of these three ways in this section and invite students to identify each type of use.

Less Proficient Readers
Help students review the tale thus far by asking the following questions:
• Which sister works hard? Which does no work?
 Possible Responses: T´âm works hard; Cám does nothing.
• Who makes T´âm work hard?
 Possible Responses: her stepmother
• What does T´âm want from her father?
 Possible Responses: to be Number One Daughter

Set a Purpose Have students read to find out how a dead fish brings beauty into T´âm's life.

Advanced Students
Ask students what they think is meant by the saying, "A man's worth is what he does, not what he says he can do." Have them think of other common sayings that mean something similar.
Possible Responses: The saying means it only matters what you do, not what you say you can or will do in the future. The following common sayings also convey the same meaning:
• "Actions speak louder than words."
• "Talk is cheap."
• "Put your money where your mouth is."

Reading Skills and Strategies: QUESTION

 Remind students to offer observations, make connections, react, speculate, interpret, and raise questions in response to texts. Discuss questions or comments students have as the devious Cám addresses T'âm. You may wish to model your own process of thinking:

I wonder what Cám is up to. I don't trust her. If she is so concerned about Father, why doesn't she sing to him herself?

Active Reader: USING TEXT ORGANIZERS

Remind students that they can remember and review a selection by classifying its various elements, including genre, setting, and theme, in a graphic organizer.

Have students classify or identify various elements of the story by completing a graphic organizer such as the one shown.

Genre	folk tale
Theme	the need to belong
Conflict	person vs. person: T'âm vs. her stepmother and stepsister
Setting	a small village in Vietnam
Main Characters	T'âm, her stepmother, Cám, Father

Her basket empty of fish,
But her mind full of cunning.
"I, wade in that mud?" she thought.
"There must be some better way."
At last she knew what to do
To be Number One Daughter.
"T'âm," she called, "elder sister,
Our father needs a bright flower,
A flower to gladden his heart.
Get it for him, dear sister."
T'âm, the good, gentle sister,
Set her fish basket aside
And ran into the forest
To pick the night-blooming flowers.
Cám crept to T'âm's fish basket,
Emptied it into her own.

"Little fish, dear little fish, I will put you in the well."

Now her fish basket was full.
T'âm's held only one small fish.
Quickly Cám ran to Father,
Calling, "See my full basket!"
T'âm ran back to the fish pond
With an armload of bright flowers.
"Cám," she called, "what has happened?
What has happened to my fish?"
Slowly T'âm went to Father
Bringing him the flowers and fish.
Father looked at both baskets.

Speaking slowly, he told them,
"The test was a full basket,
Not flowers and one small fish.
Take your fish, Elder Daughter.
It is much too small to eat.
Cám has earned the right to be
Honorable Number One."

2

T'âm looked at the little fish.
Her heart was filled with pity
At its loneliness and fright.
"Little fish, dear little fish,
I will put you in the well."
At night T'âm brought her rice bowl,
Sharing her food with the fish—
Talked to the thin fish, saying,
"Little fish, come eat with me"—
Stayed at the well at nighttime
With the stars for company.
The fish grew big and trustful.
It grew fat and not afraid.
It knew T'âm's voice and answered,
Swimming to her outstretched hand.
Cám sat in the dark shadows,
Her heart full of jealousy,
Her mind full of wicked thoughts.
Sweetly she called, "T'âm, sister.
Our father is overtired.
Come sing him a pretty song
That will bring sweet dreams to him."
Quickly T'âm ran to her father,
Singing him a nightbird song.
Cám was hiding near the well,
Watching, waiting and watching.
When she heard T'âm's pretty song
She crept closer to the fish,
Whispering, "Dear little fish,
Come to me! Come eat with me."

EXPLICIT INSTRUCTION **Speaking and Listening**

INTERVIEWING

Students can demonstrate effective communication skills that reflect such demands as interviewing, reporting, requesting, and providing information.

Prepare Tell students that before an interview, the interviewer should contact the potential interviewee, learn all he or she can about the subject, prepare questions, and organize supplies. The person being interviewed should think about questions that are likely to be asked and prepare answers, especially to tough questions. At the actual interview, he or she should answer as fully as possible, but not offer more information than he or she is asked for.

Present Select students to portray the stepmother, Cám, and Father. Have other students act as journalists, interviewing the characters about their roles in creating a household in which a member was ill-treated. After the interviews, discuss as a class what information interviewers elicited about the characters and how the characters handled uncomfortable questions.

Use **Speaking and Listening Book**, pp. 35–36, for additional support.

The fish came, and greedy Cám
Touched it, caught it and ate it!
T'âm returned. Her fish was gone.
"Little fish, dear little fish,
Come to me! Come eat with me!"

2 Bitterly she cried for it.

The stars looked down in pity;
The clouds shed teardrops of rain.

3

T'âm's tears falling in the well
Made the water rise higher.
And from it rose Nang Tien,
A lovely cloud-dressed fairy.
Her voice was a silver bell
Ringing clear in the moonlight.
"My child, why are you crying?"
"My dear little fish is gone!
He does not come when I call."
"Ask Red Rooster to help you.
His hens will find Little Fish."
Soon the hens came in a line
Sadly bringing the fish bones.
T'âm cried, holding the fish bones.
"Your dear fish will not forget.
Place his bones in a clay pot
Safe beneath your sleeping mat.
Those we love never leave us.
Cherished bones keep love alive."
In her treasured clay pot, T'âm
Made a bed of flower petals
For the bones of Little Fish
And put him away with love.
But she did not forget him;
When the moon was full again,
T'âm, so lonely for her fish,
Dug up the buried clay pot.
T'âm found, instead of fish bones,

A silken dress and two jeweled *hai*.[9]
Her Nang Tien spoke again.
"Your dear little fish loves you.
Clothe yourself in the garments
His love has given you."
T'âm put on the small jeweled *hai*.
They fit like a velvet skin
Made of moonlight and stardust
And the love of Little Fish.
T'âm heard music in her heart
That sent her small feet dancing,
Flitting like two butterflies,
Skimming like two flying birds,
Dancing by the twin fish ponds,
Dancing in the rice paddy.
But the mud in the rice paddy
Kept one jeweled *hai* for its own.
Night Wind brought the *hai* to T'âm.
"What is yours I bring to you."
Water in the well bubbled,
"I will wash your *hai* for you."
Water buffalo came by.
"Dry your *hai* on my sharp horn."
A blackbird flew by singing,
"I know where this *hai* belongs.
In a garden far away
I will take this *hai* for you."

4

What is to be must happen
As day follows after night.

In the Emperor's garden,
Sweet with perfume of roses,
The Emperor's son, the Prince,
Walked alone in the moonlight.
A bird, black against the moon,

---

9. *hai* (hi): shoes.

English Learners

1 Explain that *elder* is a more formal synonym for "older" and that the word refers only to people.

2 Call students' attention to *Bitterly she cried for it* and remind them that adverbs in English usually follow the verb, but may precede the verb for literary effect. Rephrase the passage to *She cried bitterly for it* and discuss whether it has the same power.

Less Proficient Readers

Ask students how a dead fish brings beauty into T'âm's life.

Possible Response: The fish, which T'âm buried lovingly, according to a fairy's instructions, makes a silk dress and two jeweled *hai* out of its bones and its love for T'âm.

Set a Purpose Have students read to find out the sequence of events through which T'âm escapes her step-mother's clutches.

Advanced Students

Ask students how this fable might be adapted to be a short story, puppet show, or a play. What would be gained or lost by changing genres?

Flew along the garden path,
Dropping a star in its flight.
"Look! A star!" exclaimed the Prince.
Carefully he picked it up
And found it was the small jeweled *hai.*
"Only a beautiful maid
Can wear this beautiful *hai.*"
The Prince whispered to his heart,
And his heart answered, "Find her."

In truth, beauty seeks goodness:
What is beautiful is good.

The Prince went to his father:
"A bird dropped this at my feet.
Surely it must come as truth,
Good and fair the maid it fits.
Sire,[10] if it is your pleasure
I would take this maid for wife."
The Great Emperor was pleased
With the wishes of his son.
He called his servants to him,
His drummers and his crier,[11]
Proclaiming a Festival
To find one who owned the *hai.*
In the Village of No-Name
The Emperor's subjects heard—
They heard the Royal Command.
There was praise and rejoicing.
They were pleased the Royal Son
Would wed one of their daughters.

5

Father's house was filled with clothes,
Embroidered *áo-dài*[12] and *hai*
Of heavy silks and rich colors.
Father went outside to sit.

Cám and her mother whispered
Their hopes, their dreams and their plans.
Cám, Number One Daughter, asked,
"Mother, will the Prince choose me?"
Mother said, "Of course he will.
You will be the fairest there!
When you curtsy to the Prince
His heart will go out to you."
Tâm, Daughter Number Two, said,
"May I go with you and Cám?"
Cám's mother answered <u>curtly</u>,
"Yes, if you have done this task:
Separating rice and husks
From one basket into two."

"Stay at home, you Number Two!"

Tâm knew Cám's mother had mixed
The cleaned rice with rice unhusked.
She looked at the big basket

---

10. **Sire:** title of respect for a superior, in this case, an emperor.

11. **crier:** person who makes public announcements in the streets of a village or town.

12. **embroidered *áo-dài*** (ou′dī): robes decorated with fancy needlework.

WORDS
TO
KNOW
curtly (kûrt′lē) *adv.* in a way that uses so few words it is either rude or almost rude

Full to brim with rice and husks.
Separating the cleaned rice
From that of rice unhusked
Would take all harvest moon time,
When the Festival would end.
A cloud passed over the moon.
Whirring wings outsung the wind.
A flock of blackbirds lighted
On the pile of leaves and grain.
Picking the grain from the leaves,
They dropped clean rice at T´âm's feet.
T´âm could almost not believe
That the endless task was done.
T´âm, the elder daughter, said,
"May I go? May I go, too,
Now that all my work is done?"
Cám taunted, "How could you go?
You have nothing fit to wear."
"If I had a dress to wear
Could I go to the Palace?"
"If wishes were dresses, yes,
But wishes are not dresses."
When Mother left she said,
"Our dear Cám is ravishing.
Stay at home, you Number Two!
Cám will be the one to wed."
T´âm dug up the big clay pot.
The dress and one *hai* were there—
As soft as misty moon clouds,
Delicate as rose perfume.
T´âm washed her face in the well,
Combed her hair by the fish pond.
She smoothed down the silken dress,
Tied one *hai* unto her belt
And, though her feet were bare,
Hurried, scurried, ran and ran.
She ran to the Festival
In the King's Royal Garden.
At the Palace gates the guards

Bowed before her, very low.
Pretty girls stood in a line
With their mothers standing near;
One by one they tried to fit
A foot into a small, jeweled *hai*.
Cám stood beside her mother,
By the gilded[13] throne-room door.
Her face was dark and angry
Like a brooding monsoon[14] wind.
Cám, wiping her tears away,
Sobbed and whimpered and complained,
"My small foot fits his old shoe—
Everything but my big toe."
T´âm stood shyly by the door
Looking in great wonderment
While trumpeters and drummers
Made music for her entrance.
People looked at gentle T´âm.
Everyone was whispering,
"Oh! She is so beautiful!
She must be a Princess fair
From some distant foreign land."
Then the Prince looked up and saw
A lady walking toward him.
Stepping from his Royal Throne,
He quickly went to meet her,
And taking her hand led her
To His Majesty the King.
What is to be must happen
As day happens after night.

Real beauty mirrors goodness.
What is one is the other.

---

13. **gilded:** covered with a thin layer of gold.
14. **monsoon:** in south Asia, a wind that begins the rainy season.

WORDS TO KNOW   **ravishing** (răv´ĭ-shĭng) *adj.* unusually beautiful; delightfully pleasing

809

English Learners

1 Make sure that students know the meaning of the word "maid" as it is used on page 808. It is used to refer to an unmarried young woman, and is short for maiden. Ask students what other words have the word "maid" within them.

Possible Responses: handmaid; milk-maid; old maid; maiden name; maidenly

Less Proficient Readers

Have students describe the sequence of events through which T´âm escapes her stepmother's clutches.

Possible Response: A raven carries one of T´âm's *hai* to the prince. With the Great Emperor's approval, the prince decides that the owner of the *hai* will be his wife.

Set a Purpose Ask students to read on to find out what happens to T´âm.

Possible Response: Her foot slips into the *hai*, proving that she is the owner. T´âm is deemed Wife Number One.

Advanced Students

Ask students to finish reading the story and write a brief essay in response to its final lines. Ask them if they believe a person's fate or destiny is set at birth and cannot be changed. Remind students to support their opinions with examples, either from the story or from their own experiences.

Possible Response: Students may agree or disagree, but should back up their response with examples.

Literary Analysis: RHYTHM

Remind students that rhythm is the pattern of stressed and unstressed syllables in a piece of writing, such as a poem or a folk tale. A selection can have a regular or an irregular rhythm. Call on students to read aloud different sections of "In the Land of Small Dragon." Have listeners describe the effect of the line breaks on the rhythm. Then read aloud to students one section of the tale, heeding end punctuation but ignoring line breaks. Ask students to compare and contrast the readings.

"We will

have a

Wedding

feast."

Kneeling, the Prince placed the *hai*
On Tấm's dainty little foot.
Tấm untied the *hai* she wore
And slid her bare foot in it.

Beauty is not painted on.
It is the spirit showing.

The Prince spoke to his father.
"I would take this maid for wife."
His Royal Highness nodded.
"We will have a Wedding feast."
All the birds in all the trees
Sang a song of happiness:
"Tấm, the Number Two Daughter,
Is to be Wife Number One."

What is written in the stars
Cannot be changed or altered.

Dang Manh Kha

"Man cannot know the whole world, but can know his own small part."

Teacher and Storyteller Dang Manh Kha was born in Vietnam. After attending St. John's University in Minnesota, he taught school in El Paso, Texas, for four years. In 1975 he worked for the Southeast Asian Resettlement Program to aid Vietnamese refugees. Dang Manh Kha now lives in Tucson, Arizona.

Ann Nolan Clark
1896–1995

"All of my books are based upon actual experiences. . . ."

Teacher and Writer Born in New Mexico, Ann Nolan Clark served for many years as a teacher and writer for the Bureau of Indian Affairs and the U.S. Department of Education in Latin America. Clark wrote numerous books about children in various countries, including *Secret of the Andes,* set in Peru, which won the Newbery Medal in 1953.

Writing from Experience Clark once said, "All of my books are based upon actual experiences, knowing the people and places I write about, having been there." She spent her final years near Tucson, Arizona. Her other works include *In My Mother's House, To Stand Against the Wind, Little Navajo Bluebird, Santiago,* and *Tia Maria's Garden.*

EXPLICIT INSTRUCTION Persuasive Devices

Instruction Sometimes students are asked questions to see if they can recognize when they are being persuaded to think or feel a certain way.

Practice Work through the process of deciding which of the following passages from the story is meant to persuade, rather than to inform or entertain:

A. He lived his days in justice, standing strong against the wind.

B. Tấm, sister. Our father is overtired. Come sing him a pretty song that will bring sweet dreams to him.

C. A flock of blackbirds lighted on the pile of leaves and grain.

D. We will have a Wedding feast.

A is not persuasive; it is a poetic description of a just person, and is meant to inform and to entertain. In *B,* Cám is trying to convince Tấm to sing (so she can eat Tấm's fish). You can see the use of appeal and flattery in the words *pretty* and *sweet,* so *B* is the correct answer. *C* and *D* are statements of fact and are informative, not persuasive, so both are incorrect.

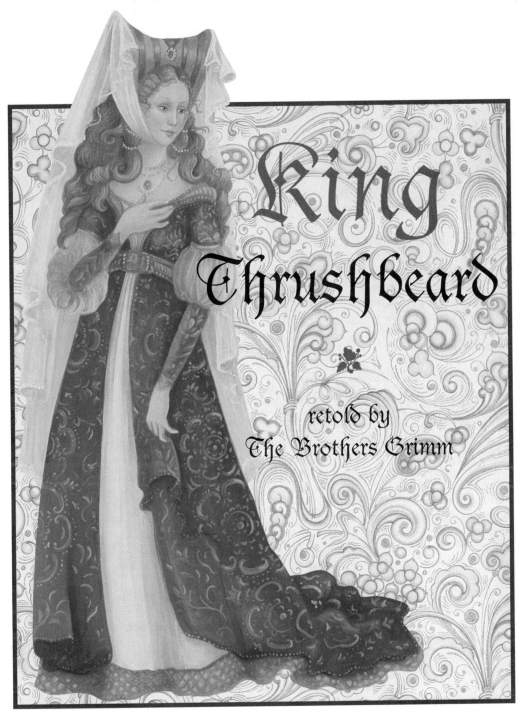

King Thrushbeard

‧

retold by
The Brothers Grimm

Copyright © Joyce Patti.

Summary

A furious king swears to make his overly particular daughter marry the first beggar who comes to his door. Thus, she winds up marrying a poor minstrel and living with him in extreme poverty. To make ends meet, she unsuccessfully tries weaving baskets, spinning, and selling pots. Finally, she gets a job as kitchen maid in another king's palace. At the wedding feast of the king's eldest son, she fills her pockets with scraps of food. Suddenly the king's son appears and asks her to dance. To her horror, he is King Thrushbeard—the rejected suitor whose chin she compared to a thrush's beak. She runs away in humiliation but is stopped by Thrushbeard, who explains that he masqueraded as her minstrel husband out of love and to teach her humility. Her lesson well learned, the king's daughter and Thrushbeard celebrate their wedding.

Differentiating Instruction

English Learners

Explain that this story contains figurative language, in which the words mean more than their literal meanings. Encourage students to point out phrases they don't understand and ask for clarification.

Less Proficient Readers

Set a Purpose Tell students that this story is a folk tale with a king's daughter as the main character. Ask them what kinds of plot elements they would expect to find in such a story. As students read the beginning of the tale, have them note how the king's daughter treats her suitors and what this reveals about her character.

EXPLICIT INSTRUCTION ## Speaking and Listening

STORYTELLING

Students should understand that it is important to adapt spoken language such as word choice, diction, and usage to the audience, purpose, and occasion. Tell students that when they are thinking about a young audience, they should pay particular attention to their word choice. They may also wish to simplify the plot.

Prepare Have students work in groups of three or four. Tell students to imagine that their group will be presenting "King Thrushbeard" to young children. Have groups decide how they would revise the story to interest this age group. Ask them what storytelling techniques they might use most effectively. Have a recorder for each group keep track of group decisions.

Present Ask each group to present and compare their plans.

You may wish to extend this activity by having groups perform a revised version of "King Thrushbeard" for a first- or second-grade audience.

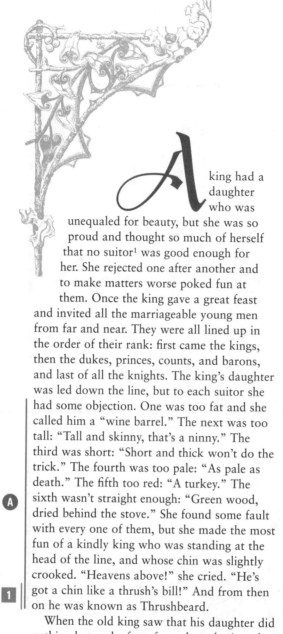

A king had a daughter who was
unequaled for beauty, but she was so
proud and thought so much of herself
that no suitor[1] was good enough for
her. She rejected one after another and
to make matters worse poked fun at
them. Once the king gave a great feast
and invited all the marriageable young men
from far and near. They were all lined up in
the order of their rank: first came the kings,
then the dukes, princes, counts, and barons,
and last of all the knights. The king's daughter
was led down the line, but to each suitor she
had some objection. One was too fat and she
called him a "wine barrel." The next was too
tall: "Tall and skinny, that's a ninny." The
third was short: "Short and thick won't do the
trick." The fourth was too pale: "As pale as
death." The fifth too red: "A turkey." The
sixth wasn't straight enough: "Green wood,
dried behind the stove." She found some fault
with every one of them, but she made the most
fun of a kindly king who was standing at the
head of the line, and whose chin was slightly
crooked. "Heavens above!" she cried. "He's
got a chin like a thrush's bill!" And from then
on he was known as Thrushbeard.

When the old king saw that his daughter did
nothing but make fun of people and rejected
all the suitors who had come to the feast, he
flew into a rage and swore to make her marry
the first beggar who came to his door. A few
days later a wandering minstrel[2] came and
sang under the window in the hope of earning
a few coins. When the king heard him, he said:
"Send him up." The minstrel appeared in his
ragged, dirty clothes, sang for the king and his
daughter, and asked for a gift when he had
finished. The king said: "Your singing has
pleased me so well that I'll give you my
daughter for your wife." The princess was
horrified, but the king said: "I swore I'd give
you to the first beggar who came by, and I'm
going to abide by my oath."

All her pleading was in vain; the priest was
called, and she was married to the minstrel
then and there. After the ceremony the king
said: "Now that you're a beggar woman, I
can't have you living in my palace. You can
just go away with your husband."

The beggar took her by the hand and led
her out of the palace, and she had to go with
him on foot. They came to a large forest, and
she asked:

"Who does that lovely forest belong to?"
"That forest belongs to King
Thrushbeard.
If you'd taken him, you could call it
your own."
"Alas, poor me, if I'd only known,
If only I'd taken King Thrushbeard!"
Next they came to a meadow, and
she asked:
"Who does that lovely green meadow
belong to?"
"That meadow belongs to King
Thrushbeard.
If you'd taken him, you could call it
your own."
"Alas, poor me, if I'd only known,

---

1. **suitor:** a man seeking to marry a woman.
2. **minstrel** (mĭn′strəl): traveling poet or singer.

Cross Curricular Link Social Studies

MINSTRELS Though the minstrel in this story
never performs to earn his keep, this was certainly not true of real minstrels, who lived in Europe
between the 12th and 17th centuries. They were
wandering entertainers, especially musicians, who
went from place to place, stopping when there
was a chance of being paid to perform. Because
much of their music was improvised, and since
most of them could not write their music down,
little of it survives, but the quality of the best of it
was probably quite high. Over time, minstrel
guilds developed. This brought minstrels further
into the mainstream of town life. The guilds saw
to it that people found apprenticeships to learn
their craft and helped trained minstrels find work.
The distinction that existed between musicians
who played sacred (religious) music and who
could read music, and minstrels, who played sec-
ular, improvised music and could not read music,
began breaking down in the 1500s. The rise in
written compositions and decline of improvisation
was the beginning of the end for minstrels. They
continued to exist, but slowly vanished as a distinct part of the musical scene.

If only I'd taken King Thrushbeard!"

Then they passed through a big city, and she asked:

"Who does this beautiful city belong to?"

"This city belongs to King Thrushbeard.
If you'd taken him, you could call it
your own."

"Alas, poor me, if only I'd known,
If only I'd taken King Thrushbeard!"

"You give me a pain," said the minstrel, "always wishing for another husband. I suppose I'm not good enough for you!" At last they came to a tiny little house, and she said:

"Heavens, this shack is a disgrace!
Who could own such a wretched place?"

"If you want something done, you'll have to do it for yourself."

The minstrel answered, "It's my house and yours, where we shall live together." The king's daughter had to bend down to get through the low doorway. "Where are the servants?" she asked. "Servants, my foot!" answered the beggar. "If you want something done, you'll have to do it for yourself. And now make a fire and put on water for my supper because I'm dead tired." But the king's daughter didn't know the first thing about fires or cooking, and the beggar had to help her

or he wouldn't have had any supper at all. When they had eaten what little there was, they went to bed. But bright and early the next morning he made her get up and clean the house.

They worried along for a few days, but then their provisions were gone, and the man said: "Wife, we can't go on like this, eating and drinking and earning nothing. You'll have to weave baskets." He went out and cut willow withes[3] and brought them home. She began to weave but the hard withes bruised her tender hands. "I see that won't do," said the man. "Try spinning; maybe you'll be better at it." She sat down and tried to spin, but the hard thread soon cut her soft fingers and drew blood. "Well, well!" said the man. "You're no good for any work. I've made a bad bargain. But now I think I'll buy up some earthenware pots and dishes. All you'll have to do is sit in the marketplace and sell them." **B**

"Goodness gracious!" she thought. "If somebody from my father's kingdom goes to the marketplace and sees me sitting there selling pots, how they'll laugh at me!" But there was no help for it; she had to give in or they would have starved.

The first day, all went well: people were glad to buy her wares because she was beautiful; they paid whatever she asked, and some didn't even trouble to take the pots they had paid for. The two of them lived on the proceeds as long as the stock held out, and then the husband

---

3. **withes** (wĭths): tough, bendable twigs.

Differentiating Instruction

English Learners
1 Lead students to understand that a *bill* is a bird's beak and that a *thrush* is a kind of bird.

2 Point out that *my foot* is an exclamation of disbelief.

Less Proficient Readers
Ask students to describe how the king's daughter treats the men who want to marry her.

Possible Response: She makes fun of them; she rejects them.

Then ask what her treatment of the men reveals about her character.

Possible Response: She is spoiled, vain, cruel, and proud.

Set a Purpose Have students read to learn what the king's daughter's new life is like.

Advanced Students
As students read, ask how this story and other tales they may have read present a narrow role for women.

Possible Responses: They are usually portrayed as daughters and/or wives. The heroines are usually beautiful and sometimes clever while the villains are usually ugly. Generally their only aspiration is to marry a handsome prince and to live without responsibility and in splendor.

EXPLICIT INSTRUCTION ## Speaking and Listening

COMPARE VIDEO WITH A STORY
Students can compare and contrast print, visual, and electronic media such as film with a written story.

Prepare Tell students that when they watch a video, it is doing the visualizing for them. Ask how they have to visualize when they read a story.

Possible Response: They need to use their imaginations and written descriptions.

There are many different video versions of Grimm's fairy tales. One excellent series, put

together by actress/producer Shelley Duvall, is *Faerie Tale Theatre* (Playhouse Video).

Present Invite students to watch a video of one or more well-known Grimm's fairy tales that they have also read. Ask them to describe how the version they watched was similar to or different from the way they had visualized it. Then discuss how people today might find aspects of these stories strange. For instance, ask if they think members of royalty would be able to disguise themselves as beggars.

Literary Analysis: CHARACTER

A Ask students how they think the princess has changed.

Possible Response: She has lost her pride and arrogance, as shown by the fact that she now gratefully accepts the leftover food. She has learned a lesson in humility.

Literary Analysis: SENSORY DETAILS

B Remind students that sensory details appeal to a reader's sense of touch, taste, smell, sight, and hearing. Ask students to note the senses to which this description of the King's celebration appeals.

Possible Response: touch—putting scraps in a jar;—taste and smell—succulent dishes; sight—lit candles, courtiers' dress, the King's son's clothing and jewelry

Literary Analysis CONFLICT

Students should analyze characters, including their traits, motivations, conflicts, points of view, relationships and changes they undergo when reading. Remind students that plots are usually built around a conflict—a problem or struggle between two or more opposing forces. Conflicts can range from a life-or-death struggle to a disagreement between friends, and can be internal or external. Have students identify the main conflict in this story.

Possible Response: The conflict is an internal one as the king's daughter deals with the consequences of her own pride and arrogance.

bought up a fresh supply of crockery. She took a place at the edge of the market, set out her wares around her and offered them for sale. All of a sudden a drunken hussar[4] came galloping through, upset her pots and smashed them all into a thousand pieces. She began to cry; she was worried sick. "Oh!" she wailed. "What will become of me? What will my husband say!" She ran home and told him what had happened. "What did you expect?" he said. "Setting out earthenware pots at the edge of the market! But stop crying. I can see you're no good for any sensible work. Today I was at our king's palace. I asked if they could use a kitchen maid, and they said they'd take you. They'll give you your meals."

So the king's daughter became a kitchen maid and had to help the cook and do the most disagreeable work. She carried little jars in both her pockets, to take home the leftovers they gave her, and that's what she and her husband lived on.

It so happened that the marriage of the king's eldest son was about to be celebrated. The poor woman went upstairs and stood in the doorway of the great hall, looking on. When the candles were lit and the courtiers[5] began coming in, each more magnificent than the last, and everything was so bright and full of splendor, she was sad at heart. She thought of her miserable life and cursed the pride and arrogance that had brought her so low and made her so poor.

Succulent dishes were being carried in and out, and the smell drifted over to her. Now and then a servant tossed her a few scraps, and she put them into her little jars to take home.

"I can see you're no good for any sensible work."

And then the king's son appeared; he was dressed in silk and velvet and had gold chains around his neck. When he saw the beautiful woman in the doorway, he took her by the hand and asked her to dance with him, but she refused. She was terrified, for she saw it was King Thrushbeard, who had courted her and whom she had laughed at and rejected. She tried to resist, but he drew her into the hall. Then the string that kept her pockets in place snapped, the jars fell to the floor, the soup

---

4. **hussar** (hə-zär′): a cavalry soldier—that is, a soldier who fights on horseback.

5. **courtiers** (kôr′tē-ərz): attendants at a royal palace.

WORDS TO KNOW   **succulent** (sŭk′yə-lənt) *adj.* tasty; delicious

spilled and the scraps came tumbling out. The courtiers all began to laugh and jeer, and she would sooner have been a hundred fathoms[6] under the earth. She bounded through the door and tried to escape, but on the stairs a man caught her and brought her back, and when she looked at him, she saw it was King Thrushbeard again. He spoke kindly to her and said: "Don't be afraid. I am the minstrel you've been living with in that wretched shack; I disguised myself for love of you, and I was also the hussar who rode in and smashed your crockery. I did all that to humble your pride and punish you for the <u>insolent</u> way you laughed at me." Then she wept bitterly and said: "I've been very wicked and I'm not

worthy to be your wife." But he said: "Don't cry; the hard days are over; now we shall celebrate our wedding." The maids came and dressed her magnificently, her father arrived with his whole court and congratulated her on her marriage to King Thrushbeard, and it was then that the feast became really joyful. I wish you and I had been there. ❖

---

6. **fathoms** (făth′əmz): units of measurement, each equal to six feet.

Jakob Grimm
1785–1863

Wilhelm Grimm
1786–1859

"Up to the very end, we worked in two rooms next to each other, . . ."

A Passion for the Past The brothers Grimm, born in Hanau, Germany, trained to be lawyers. However, an early exposure to old German romantic poems eventually led them to become interested in the language and literature of the

German past. Jakob wrote, "It is high time that these old traditions were collected and rescued before they perish like dew in the hot sun."

A Team Effort Happier collecting local folk tales than practicing law, the brothers began a search for folk tales, particularly ones passed along orally to children, that was to become their lifelong commitment. They were always very close; according to Jakob, "Up to the very end, we worked in two rooms next to each other, always under one roof." *Grimm's Fairy Tales* has remained popular to this day.

English Learners

1 Point out that *worried sick* is a common expression that means "extremely worried." You may want to preview the meanings of the following words with students:

• *wares:* something put out to be sold by a merchant in a marketplace
• *wailed:* cried loudly; screamed out in anguish
• *rejected:* refused to accept or give attention to
• *courtiers:* attendants at the court of a king, queen, or other monarch
• *bounded:* leapt forward
• *wretched:* in a lowly, deplorable state of being

Less Proficient Readers
Ask students questions such as the following to check that they are understanding the main ideas of the story:

• How is the king's daughter treated by her new husband?
Possible Response: He treats her harshly. He makes her work hard to support them.
• How does she react to her new life?
Possible Response: She is humiliated but thinks she has no choice but to go along with her husband's demands.

Set a Purpose Ask students to read the end of the folk tale and think about whether the ending is what they expected.

Advanced Students
Challenge students to make a connection between King Thrushbeard's name and the disguise he adopts.

Possible Response: The princess says the king's chin is the bill of a thrush, a kind of songbird. He disguises himself as a minstrel, a kind of singer.

Standards-Based Objectives

- To understand and appreciate three folk tales from different cultures that explore the mysteries of nature through oral language tradition
- To appreciate the cultures of China, Puerto Rico, and West Africa
- To extend understanding of the stories through a variety of activities

Reading Pathways

- Select one or several students to read each story aloud to the entire class or to small groups of students. Assign this reading in advance so readers can incorporate into their presentations some of the techniques used by professional storytellers. Have the audience listen carefully to the tales without following along in their texts.
- Read the stories aloud to the class, pausing at key points to discuss how elements of each tale inform students about the customs, values, or beliefs of people in Puerto Rico, China, and West Africa. Have students record their responses and observations in their notebooks.
- After students have read the stories once, they can read them again to identify structural elements such as main characters, minor characters, conflict, setting, and plot. Then have students identify similarities and differences between these tales and selections in Unit 4. For example, students might compare and contrast the relationships between Taroo and Alida in "The Legend of the Hummingbird" with the relationship between Sandy and Lob in "Lob's Girl."

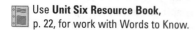 Use **Unit Six Resource Book,** p. 22, for work with Words to Know.

English Conventions Practice

Daily Language SkillBuilder

Have students **proofread** the display sentences on page 767g and write them correctly. The sentences also appear on Transparency 25 of **Language Transparencies.**

LINKS TO UNIT FOUR

Wondrous Worlds

The selections in Unit Four demonstrate the wonder that is to be found in the natural world—and in the imagination. The oral tradition often combines these two worlds within a "long ago and far away" setting, as seen in these tales from different cultures.

PUERTO RICO

PUERTO RICO

The Legend of the Hummingbird

retold by Pura Belpré (pōō′rä běl-prä′)

Puerto Rico, an island in the Caribbean Sea, is a commonwealth of the United States. Although the U.S. Congress is responsible for the overall government of Puerto Rico, the local Puerto Rican governance generally makes its own decisions. The folklore of Puerto Rico reflects a mixture of cultures, with strong roots in Spain, West Africa, and Asia as well as native Caribbean cultures such as the Taino. Set in a world where people become animals and animals behave in decidedly human ways, this **legend** explains the origin and habits of the hummingbird. Many species of hummingbird thrive on the islands of the Caribbean.

LESSON RESOURCES

UNIT SIX RESOURCE BOOK, pp. 19–23

ASSESSMENT
Formal Assessment, pp. 131–132
Test Generator

SKILLS TRANSPARENCIES AND COPYMASTERS

Literary Analysis
- Characterization, TR 4 (p. 818)

Reading and Critical Thinking
- Connecting, TR 2 (p. 820)

Language
- Daily Language SkillBuilder, TR 25 (p. 816)

Speaking and Listening
- Evaluating Reading Aloud, p. 14 (p. 825)

INTEGRATED TECHNOLOGY
Audio Library

Visit our Web site:
www.mcdougallittell.com

For **systematic instruction** in language skills, see:
- **Vocabulary and Spelling Book**
- **Grammar, Usage, and Mechanics Book**
- pacing chart on p. 767e.

CHINA

The Living Kuan-yin

retold by Carol Kendall and Yao-wen Li (you'wən'lē)

China is bounded on every side by mountains, desert, or ocean. These geographical features have helped to preserve a civilization that dates back nearly 4,000 years. Buddhism, one of the world's major religions, arrived in China before A.D. 100. Kuan-yin (gwän' yǐn') is the Buddhist deity of mercy, who works to save people from their faults and failures. In this **legend,** a man named Chin Po-wan journeys to see Kuan-yin. People ask him for help along the way, and Po-wan's generosity gets him into trouble.

WEST AFRICA

Why Monkeys Live in Trees

retold by Julius Lester

The continent of Africa is home to a rich variety of cultures, each with a wealth of folklore. Many traditional West African tales feature animal characters. This folk tale recounts Monkey's attempt to outwit other animals, and, typical of a **"trickster tale,"** the trickster's cleverness only lands him in trouble. The story also attempts to explain why monkeys behave the way they do. Stories that answer the question *why?* are called **"pourquoi tales."**

AS YOU READ . . .

See how mysteries of nature are explained in various cultures.

Notice which human traits are seen as weaknesses and which are admired.

Notice common images, themes, and other literary devices used in the oral tradition across cultures.

LINKS TO UNIT FOUR **817**

Less Proficient Readers
Tell students that folk tales can teach us about various cultures. In these three tales, they will learn something about the cultures of Puerto Rico, China, and West Africa.

Set a Purpose Ask students to think about what they learn about the cultures of Puerto Rico, China, and West Africa as they read the three folk tales.

English Learners
Ask students to share any stories or tales from their own cultures that have similar characters or situations to those in the folk tales here. Ask them to think about how they first heard the story and to tell what it teaches about their culture.

Use **Spanish Study Guide,** pp. 166–168, for additional support.

Advanced Students
Ask students to think about the geography of the places in these tales. As they read each story, have them locate the country and region on a map. Encourage students to discuss the climate, resources, and land forms found there and to speculate about what those factors tell them about the culture of each place.

egy, it seems, is to swallow a mouthful of the black dust, which is really pepper, rest in some tall grass, and then repeat the process. Leopard, astonished by Monkey's success, climbs onto a tree limb to get a better view. What he sees—a hundred identical monkeys hiding in the tall grass—angers him so much that he jumps into the grass to punish their trickery just as Monkey wins the pot of gold. The only way the monkeys can escape is to climb to the top of the tallest trees, where they still live today.

Reading and Analyzing

Literary Analysis: CHARACTERIZATION

A Ask students to name Leopard's main character trait. Ask what the beginning of the folk tale reveals about Leopard.

Possible Response: The folk tale's opening says that gazing at his own reflection is Leopard's favorite activity. This suggests that Leopard is vain.

Use **Unit Six Resource Book,** p. 21, for more practice.
Use **Literary Analysis Transparencies,** p. 4, for additional support.

Reading Skills and Strategies: PREDICT

B Ask students to predict what kind of contest they think King Gorilla will have.

Possible Responses: Students may predict that the contest will involve running, jumping, climbing trees, or eating fruit.

Exotic Landscape (1910), Henri Rousseau. Oil on canvas, 51¼" × 64". The Norton Simon Foundation, Pasadena, California.

818 UNIT SIX THE ORAL TRADITION

EXPLICIT INSTRUCTION Viewing and Representing

Exotic Landscape
by Henri Rousseau

ART APPRECIATION

Rousseau (1844–1910), today celebrated as a pioneer in modern art, was unappreciated during his lifetime and was buried in a pauper's grave.

Instruction Rousseau's paintings combine the brilliant colors and decorative patterns of the Impressionists with precise detail and highly polished surfaces of his own devising. In addition to

subjects from French middle-class life, such as weddings and patriotic celebrations, Rousseau painted realistic figures in fantastical settings.

Practice Ask students, "What aspects of this painting look realistic? What aspects do not? How does the painting relate to this selection?"

Possible Responses: The trees, grass, and monkeys look realistic. The painting relates to the selection because it is about monkeys living in trees, and both monkeys and trees are pictured here.

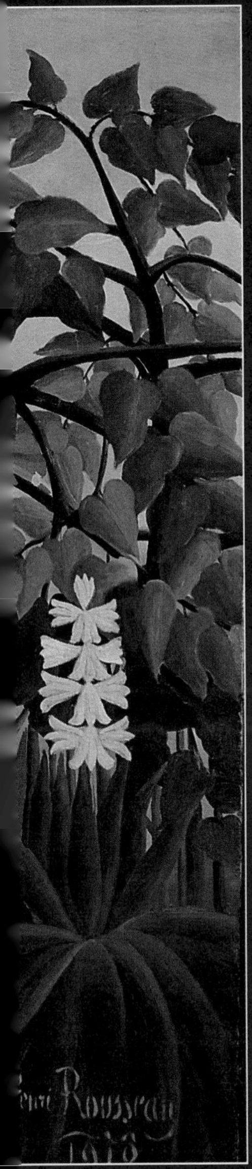

Why Monkeys Live in TREES

retold by **Julius Lester**

One day Leopard was looking at his reflection in a pool of water. Looking at himself was Leopard's favorite thing in the world to do. Leopard gazed, wanting to be sure that every hair was straight and that all his spots were where they were **A** supposed to be. This took many hours of looking at his reflection, which Leopard did not mind at all.

Finally he was satisfied that nothing was **1** disturbing his handsomeness, and he turned away from the pool of water. At that exact moment, one of Leopard's children ran up to him.

"Daddy! Daddy! Are you going to be in the contest?"

"What contest?" Leopard wanted to know. If it was a beauty contest, of course he was going to be in it.

"I don't know. Crow the Messenger just flew by. **B** She said that King Gorilla said there was going to be a contest."

Differentiating Instruction

Less Proficient Readers
Tell students that the animals in this story will be involved in a contest. Ask them to tell about any contests in which they have participated.

Advanced Students
Ask students to think about the three animals mentioned on this page. What do the names of Crow the Messenger and King Gorilla say about these characters? Ask students to predict what kind of characters they might be and to brainstorm other jungle animals and give them names that would hint at their personality and character.
Possible Response: Crow probably carries messages, talks, or gossips a lot. The gorilla is in charge; he's the king.

English Learners
1 Point out that the suffix *-ness* is often added to adjectives in order to form nouns. *Handsomeness,* therefore, refers to the leopards' quality of being handsome. Ask volunteers to form similar nouns from the adjectives *kind, dry, wild,* and *slow.*

Active Reader: CONNECTING

Ask students to think about "The Walrus and The Carpenter" and to recall the trick these characters played on the oysters. How was that similar to or different from the trick in "Why Monkeys Live in Trees"?

Possible Response: The walrus and carpenter tricked the oysters so they could eat them. King Gorilla tricked the animals, and the monkeys tried to trick King Gorilla, but he found them out.

📖 Use **Unit Six Resource Book,** p. 20, for more practice.
Use **Reading and Critical Thinking Transparencies,** p. 2, for additional support.

Reading Skills and Strategies: CLARIFY

Ⓐ Ask students what else is explained in this folk tale other than why monkeys live in trees.
Answer: why chickens have no ears

Reading Skills and Strategies: EVALUATE

Have students evaluate the attitudes of the animals who are happy because they still have a chance to win the gold, despite having seen the effects of the dust on Hippopotamus. Ask students what effect the thought of the gold is having on the animals.
Possible Response: The gold is making the animals greedy.

Literary Analysis: CHARACTERIZATION

Ⓑ Ask students to think about how the monkeys are described in this section. What have we learned about the character of the monkeys?
Possible Responses: Because the monkeys are clever and smart, they are able to outwit the other animals.

Without another word, Leopard set off. He went north-by-northeast, made a right turn at the mulberry bush and traveled east-by-south-by-west until he came to a hole in the ground. He went around in a circle five times and headed north-by-somersault until he came to a big clearing in the middle of the jungle, and that's where King Gorilla was.

King Gorilla sat at one end of the clearing on his throne. Opposite him, at the other side of the clearing, all the animals sat in a semicircle. In the middle, between King Gorilla and the animals, was a huge mound of what looked like black dust.

Leopard looked around with calm dignity. Then he strode regally[1] over to his friend, Lion.

"What's that?" he asked, pointing to the mound of black dust.

1 "Don't know," Lion replied. "King Gorilla said he will give a pot of gold to whoever can eat it in one day. I can eat it in an hour."

Leopard laughed. "I'll eat it in a half hour."

It was Hippopotamus's turn to laugh. "As big as my mouth is, I'll eat that mound in one gulp."

The time came for the contest. King Gorilla had the animals pick numbers to see who would go in what order. To everybody's dismay, Hippopotamus drew Number 1.

Hippopotamus walked over to the mound of black dust. It was bigger than he had thought. It was much too big to eat in one gulp. Nonetheless, Hippopotamus opened his mouth as wide as he could, and that was very wide indeed, and took a mouthful of the black dust.

He started chewing. Suddenly he leaped straight into the air and screamed. He

---

1. **strode regally:** walked in a grand manner, like a king or queen.

Hippopotamus **roared** and Hippopotamus bellowed. Then he started **sneezing** and **crying,** . . .

screamed so loudly that it knocked the ears off the chickens, and that's why to this day chickens don't have ears.

Hippopotamus screamed and Hippopotamus yelled. Hippopotamus roared and Hippopotamus bellowed. Then he started sneezing and crying, and tears rolled down his face like he was standing in the shower. Hippopotamus ran to the river and drank as much water as he could, and that was very much, indeed, to cool his mouth and tongue and throat.

The animals didn't understand what had happened to Hippopotamus, but they didn't care. They were happy because they still had a chance to win the pot of gold. Of course, if they had known that the mound of black dust was really a mound of black pepper, maybe they wouldn't have wanted the gold.

Nobody was more happy than Leopard because he had drawn Number 2. He walked up to the black mound and sniffed at it.

"AAAAAAAAACHOOOOOOO!" Leopard didn't like that, but then he remembered the pot of gold. He opened his mouth wide, took a mouthful and started chewing and swallowing.

Leopard leaped straight into the air, did a back double flip and screamed. He yelled and he roared and he bellowed and, finally, he started sneezing and crying, tears rolling down

---

Ⓒ **Multicultural Link**   ## African Animals

The jungles and deserts of Africa are rich with animal life. Hippopotamus, leopard, lion, monkey, and gorilla—all of which we meet in this story—are just a few of them. There are also rhinoceros, elephant, zebra, antelope, cheetah, gazelle, hyena, and many more. Large numbers of tourists go on safari to observe and photograph these beautiful animals in their natural habitats.

One particularly interesting animal is the rhino. There are five species of rhinoceros in the world. Two of them live in Africa, the black rhino

and the white rhino. Despite their names, both are gray! The white rhino's name comes from the Afrikaans word describing its mouth, *weit,* which means "wide." The white rhino has a mouth that measures two feet across. It's a grass eater and needs that mouth for "mowing" the grass down. The black rhino has a smaller, triangular-shaped mouth, which it uses for feeding from trees and shrubs. It is probably called "black" because it wallows in the dark local soil and becomes covered with mud, as well as to differentiate it from the white rhino.

his face like a waterfall. Leopard ran to the river and washed out his mouth and throat and tongue.

Lion was next, and the same thing happened to him as it did to all the animals. Finally only Monkey remained.

Monkey approached King Gorilla. "I know I can eat all of whatever that is, but after each mouthful, I'll need to lie down in the tall grasses and rest."

King Gorilla said that was okay.

Monkey went to the mound, took a tiny bit of pepper on his tongue, swallowed, and went into the tall grasses. A few minutes later, Monkey came out, took a little more, swallowed it, and went into the tall grasses.

Soon the pile was almost gone. The animals were astonished to see Monkey doing what they had not been able to do. Leopard couldn't believe it either. He climbed a tree and stretched out on a sturdy limb to get a better view. From his limb high in the tree Leopard could see into the tall grasses where Monkey went to rest. Wait a minute! Leopard thought something was suddenly wrong with his eyes because he thought he saw a hundred monkeys hiding in the tall grasses.

He rubbed his eyes and looked another look. There wasn't anything wrong with his eyes. There were a hundred monkeys in the tall grasses, and they all looked alike!

Just then, there was the sound of loud applause. King Gorilla announced that Monkey had won the contest and the pot of gold.

Leopard growled a growl so scary that even King Gorilla was frightened. Leopard wasn't thinking about anybody except the monkeys. He took a long and beautiful leap from the tree right smack into the middle of the tall grasses where the monkeys were hiding.

The monkeys ran in all directions. When the other animals saw monkeys running from the grasses, they realized that the monkeys had tricked them, and started chasing them. Even King Gorilla joined in the chase. He wanted his gold back.

The only way the monkeys could escape was to climb to the very tops of the tallest trees where no one else, not even Leopard, could climb.

And that's why monkeys live in trees to this very day. ❖

Julius Lester
born 1939

"I have found writing for children of all ages more rewarding than writing for adults, . . ."

Fascinated by Folklore Julius Lester connects his interest in folklore to his father, who was a minister and a good storyteller. Lester says, "As a child, I loved it when my father got together with other ministers on a summer evening, because I knew that I would be treated to stories for as long as I was allowed to stay up, which was never long enough."

It's an Honor Lester's work has received numerous awards, including a 1969 Newbery Honor award for *To Be a Slave.* "Why Monkeys Live in Trees" is from the book *How Many Spots Does a Leopard Have?,* which contains tales that reflect both African and Jewish story traditions. Lester currently divides his time between writing and serving as a professor at the University of Massachusetts.

WHY MONKEYS LIVE IN TREES **821**

EXPLICIT INSTRUCTION **Cause-and-Effect Relationships**

Instruction Remind students that an event can cause another event, or it can be related in some other way. Two events can occur together coincidentally, or two events may happen in sequence but not be linked causally.
Practice Write the following question on the board or read it aloud:
What event caused the animals in this story to attempt to eat a large pile of black dust?
A. The animals discussed how long it would take to eat the dust.
B. The animals liked eating pepper.
C. King Gorilla offered a pot of gold to whoever could eat all the black dust.
D. The animals decided to have a contest.

Guide students through the process of selecting the correct answer. *A* is a true statement, but is not the event that caused the animals to attempt to eat the dust. *B* is not a true statement; in fact the animals did not even know that the black dust was pepper. *D* is not true. Although there was a contest in this story, the animals did not decide to have it themselves: King Gorilla did. *C* is the correct answer.

Summary

This Puerto Rican legend explains how the hummingbird came to be. Alida, the daughter of an Indian chief, falls in love with Taroo, a young man from an enemy tribe. The young lovers meet secretly at a pool surrounded by pomarosa trees. When Alida's father learns of their meetings, he arranges for her to marry someone else. Alida begs the god Yukiyú to spare her from marrying a man she doesn't love, so the god turns her into a delicate red flower. Taroo, knowing nothing of Alida's fate, waits for her by the pool until the moon tells him what has happened. Taroo begs Yukiyú to help him find Alida, and the god responds by turning Taroo into a hummingbird. Ever since, the hummingbird flies from flower to flower looking for his lost love.

Reading and Analyzing

Active Reader: CONNECTING

Ask students to think about hummingbirds. Have them share what they know about hummingbirds with a partner.

Active Reader: SET A PURPOSE

Ask students to read to find out what the legend of the hummingbird is and to connect the ideas in the story to what they just talked about.

Reading Skills and Strategies: VISUALIZE

After students have read the opening on page 823, ask them to close their eyes and listen as you read it to them. Ask them to visualize the scene that is described there. Have them share with the class what things they see in the scene, and what it reminds them of.

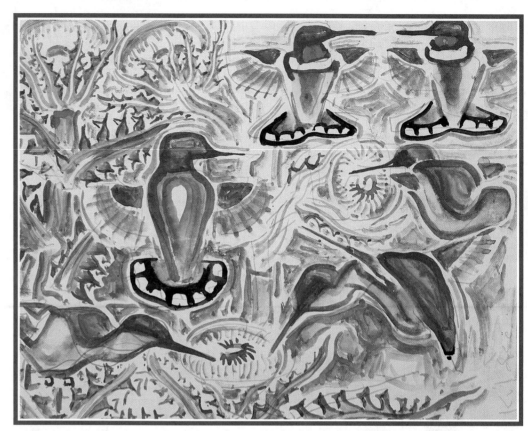

Hummingbirds in Thistle (1955), Walter Anderson. Watercolor. Walter Anderson Museum of Art, Ocean Springs, Mississippi, courtesy of the family of Walter Anderson.

EXPLICIT INSTRUCTION Viewing and Representing

Hummingbirds in Thistle
by Walter Anderson

ART APPRECIATION

Walter Anderson made hundreds of wood block prints and thousands of watercolors. He also illustrated fairy tales and classics. Anderson is best known for his depictions of the flora and fauna of the Gulf Coast, which he captured in lush watercolors.

Instruction Ask students to brainstorm everything they know about how hummingbirds move.

Practice Ask students the following questions: How many hummingbirds can you find in the picture? What are the hummingbirds doing? How does the artist convey the hummingbirds' rapid wing movement?

Possible Responses: There are at least six hummingbirds in the picture. It appears that they are drinking the nectar from flowers. The movement of their wings is shown through a series of soft, blended lines which, taken together, simulate movement.

The Legend of the Hummingbird

retold by Pura Belpré

Between the towns of Cayey and Cidra,[1] far up in the hills, there was once a small pool fed by a waterfall that tumbled down the side of the mountain. The pool was surrounded by pomarosa trees,[2] and the Indians used to call it Pomarosa Pool. It was the favorite place of Alida, the daughter of an Indian chief, a man of power and wealth among the people of the hills.

1

---

1. **Cayey** (kä-yā′) . . . **Cidra** (sē′drä): towns in Puerto Rico.
2. **pomarosa** (pô-mä-rô′sä) **trees:** trees, found in the West Indies, that bear an applelike fruit; also spelled *poma rosa*.

Reading and Analyzing

Literary Analysis: CHARACTERIZATION

Ask students to list the character traits of both Alida and Taroo. Ask them to compare the two lists and to think about what it was that drew the two to each other and helped form their friendship.

Possible Responses: Alida was lonely and fond of nature. Taroo also liked the outdoors, and he was honest, lonely, and courageous. They were probably drawn together because they were both lonely and liked to be outside with nature.

Active Reader: CONNECTING

Ask students whether they have ever been in a situation like Alida's, in which their parents forbade them to be friends with someone they liked. Ask how this made them feel. Ask how they handled the situation with their parents and their friend and what they think Alida might do in this situation.

Possible Responses: Students should share personal memories, prompted by this section of the story. Alida probably felt upset, sad, and angry. She might not listen to her father and try to see Taroo anyway.

Reading Skills and Strategies: IDENTIFY CAUSE-AND-EFFECT RELATIONSHIPS

Ask students to describe what events caused Taroo to be turned into a small, many-colored bird.

Answer: Taroo fell in love with Alida, but Alida was forbidden to see Taroo. Alida asked the god Yukiyú for help, and he changed her into a delicate red flower. Taroo missed her desperately, the moon told Taroo what had happened, and Taroo asked Yukiyú to help him find Alida.

One day, when Alida had come to the pool to rest after a long walk, a young Indian came there to pick some fruit from the trees. Alida was surprised, for he was not of her tribe. Yet he said he was no stranger to the pool. This was where he had first seen Alida, and he had often returned since then to pick fruit, hoping to see her again.

And the great god Yukiyú took pity on her and changed her into a delicate red flower.

He told her about himself to make her feel at home. He confessed, with honesty and frankness, that he was a member of the dreaded Carib[3] tribe that had so often attacked the island of Boriquen.[4] As a young boy, he had been left behind after one of those raids, and he had stayed on the island ever since.

Alida listened closely to his story, and the two became friends. They met again in the days that followed, and their friendship grew stronger. Alida admired the young man's courage in living among his enemies. She learned to call him by his Carib name, Taroo, and he called her Alida, just as her own people did. Before long, their friendship had turned into love.

Their meetings by the pool were always brief. Alida was afraid their secret might be discovered, and careful though she was, there came a day when someone saw them and told her father. Alida was forbidden to visit the Pomarosa Pool, and to put an end to her romance with the stranger, her father decided to marry her to a man of his own choosing. Preparations for the wedding started at once.

Alida was torn with grief, and one evening she cried out to her god: "O *Yukiyú*,[5] help me! Kill me or do what you will with me, but do not let me marry this man whom I do not love!"

And the great god Yukiyú took pity on her and changed her into a delicate red flower.

Meanwhile Taroo, knowing nothing of Alida's sorrow, still waited for her by the Pomarosa Pool. Day after day he waited. Sometimes he stayed there until a mantle[6] of stars was spread across the sky.

One night the moon took pity on him. "Taroo," she called from her place high above the stars. "O Taroo, wait no longer for Alida! Your secret was made known, and Alida was to be married to a man of her father's choosing. In her grief she called to her god, Yukiyú; he heard her plea for help and changed her into a red flower."

"Ahee, ahee!" cried Taroo. "O moon, what is the name of the red flower?"

---

3. **Carib** (kăr′ĭb): a Native American people of the West Indies.
4. **Boriquen** (bô-rē′kěn): an early name for Puerto Rico.
5. *Yukiyú* (yōō-kē-yōō′).
6. **mantle:** covering.

"Only Yukiyú knows that," the moon replied.

Then Taroo called out: "O Yukiyú, god of my Alida, help me too! Help me to find her!"

And just as the great god had heard Alida's plea, he listened now to Taroo and decided to help him. There by the Pomarosa Pool, before the moon and the silent stars, the great god changed Taroo into a small many-colored bird.

"Fly, *Colibrí*,[7] and find your love among the flowers," he said.

Off went the Colibrí, flying swiftly, and as he flew, his wings made a sweet humming sound.

In the morning the Indians saw a new bird darting about among the flowers, swift as an arrow and brilliant as a jewel. They heard the humming of its wings, and in amazement they saw it hover in the air over every blossom, kissing the petals of the flowers with its long slender bill. They liked the new bird with the music in its wings, and they called it Hummingbird.

Ever since then the little many-colored bird has hovered over every flower he finds, but returns most often to the flowers that are red. He is still looking, always looking, for the one red flower that will be his lost Alida. He has not found her yet. ❖

---

7. *Colibrí* (kô-lē-brē′).

Pura Belpré
1899–1982

"My vivid imagination . . . kept scenes that impressed me as a child very alive."

Filling a Need Pura Belpré, author and puppeteer-storyteller, was born in Puerto Rico and came to the United States in the 1920s. Beginning in 1921, she worked in the New York Public Library as that library's first Hispanic librarian. Belpré realized there were no books of folklore from Puerto Rico on the shelves. She set about expanding the library's Puerto Rican folklore programs.

Honored Storyteller Belpré grew up in a family of storytellers and was fluent in Spanish, English, and French. She incorporated her Spanish ancestry into her puppet shows as well as her books to provide young people with a way of learning more about Puerto Rican culture. Her other works include *Juan Bobo and the Queen's Necklace: A Puerto Rican Folk Tale,* and *Once in Puerto Rico.* In 1978 Belpré was honored for her distinguished contribution in Spanish literature by the Bay Area Bilingual Education League and the University of San Francisco.

THE LEGEND OF THE HUMMINGBIRD **825**

Summary

Chin Po-wan begins life as a wealthy person, but he gives all his money away to the needy. He undertakes a journey to ask the Living Kuan-yin, a goddess who allows each visitor to ask her three questions, why his fortune has run out. On the way, a snake helps Po-wan cross a river, an innkeeper feeds him a delightful meal, and a rich man lets him sleep in his beautiful home. Each requests that Po-wan ask the Living Kuan-yin a question for him. When Po-wan reaches the Living Kuan-yin, he asks their three questions instead of his own. The goddess tells him the answers. When Po-wan delivers the messages, he becomes a wealthy man again.

Reading and Analyzing

Reading Skills and Strategies:
EVALUATE

Have students give possible answers to Po-wan's question, "Why am I so poor?"

Possible Response: You have overestimated the money you inherited—no one has a "never-ending" supply.

Reading Skills and Strategies:
CLARIFY

Ask what has happened to Po-wan.

Possible Response: Po-wan has given away his fortune to needy, hungry people and become needy himself.

Literary Analysis: FORESHADOWING

A Ask students to think about the line "he had but one of his own to ask" and remind them that authors often foreshadow future events. Ask them to think about what else might happen in the story related to this line.

Possible Response: Po-wan will meet more people who want him to ask questions, and he won't get to ask his own question.

THE LIVING KUAN-YIN

RETOLD BY

CAROL KENDALL AND YAO-WEN LI

Even though the family name of Chin means "gold," it does not signify that everyone of that name is rich. Long ago, in the province of Chekiang,[1] however, there was a certain wealthy Chin family of whom it was popularly said that its fortune was as great as its name. It seemed quite fitting, then, when a son was born to the family, that he should be called Po-wan, "Million," for he was certain to be worth a million pieces of gold when he came of age.

With such a happy circumstance of names, Po-wan himself never doubted that he would have a never-ending supply of money chinking through his fingers, and he spent it accordingly—not on himself, but on any unfortunate who came to his attention. He had a deep sense of compassion for anyone in distress of body or spirit: a poor man had only to hold out his hand, and Po-wan poured gold into it; if a destitute widow and her brood of starvelings[2] but lifted sorrowful eyes to his, he provided them with food and lodging and friendship for the rest of their days.

In such wise did he live that even a million gold pieces were not enough to support him.

His resources so dwindled that finally he scarcely had enough food for himself, his clothes flapped threadbare[3] on his wasted frame, and the cold seeped into his bone marrow[4] for lack of a fire. Still he gave away the little money that came to him.

One day, as he scraped out half of his bowl of rice for a beggar even hungrier than he, he began to ponder on his destitute state.

"Why am I so poor?" he wondered. "I have never spent extravagantly. I have never, from the day of my birth, done an evil deed. Why, then, am I, whose very name is A Million Pieces of Gold, no longer able to find even a copper[5] to give this unfortunate creature, and have only a bowl of rice to share with him?"

He thought long about his situation and at last determined to go without delay to the South Sea. Therein, it was told, dwelt the all-merciful goddess, the Living Kuan-yin, who could tell the

---

1. **province of Chekiang** (chŭ'kyäng'): a region on the eastern coast of China.
2. **brood of starvelings** (stärv'lĭngz): starving children.
3. **threadbare:** so worn down that the threads show.
4. **marrow:** the soft tissue that fills the middle of most bones.
5. **copper:** a coin of little value.

WORDS
TO
KNOW
compassion (kəm-păsh'ən) *n.* sympathy for the suffering of others; pity
destitute (dĕs'tĭ-tōōt') *adj.* living in complete poverty; extremely poor
extravagantly (ĭk-străv'ə-gənt-lē) *adv.* excessively; too much

826

past and future. He would put his question to her, and she would tell him the answer.

Soon he had left his home country behind and traveled for many weeks in unfamiliar lands. One day he found his way barred by a wide and furiously flowing river. As he stood first on one foot and then on the other, wondering how he could possibly get across, he heard a commanding voice calling from the top of an overhanging cliff.

"Chin Po-wan!" the voice said. "If you are going to the South Sea, please ask the Living Kuan-yin a question for me!"

"Yes, yes, of course," Po-wan agreed at once, for he had never in his life refused a request made of him. In any case, the Living Kuan-yin permitted each person who approached her three questions, and he had but one of his own to ask.

Craning his head towards the voice coming from above, he suddenly began to tremble, for the speaker was a gigantic snake with a body as large as a temple column. Po-wan was glad he had agreed so readily to the request.

"Ask her, then," said the snake, "why I am not yet a dragon, even though I have practiced self-denial[6] for more than one thousand years."

"That I will do, and gl-gladly," stammered Po-wan, hoping that the snake would continue to practice self-denial just a bit longer. "But, your . . . your Snakery . . . or your Serpentry, perhaps I should say . . . that is . . . you see, don't you . . . first I must cross this raging river, and I know not how."

"That is no problem at all," said the snake. "I shall carry you across, of course."

Bodhisattva Guanyin (Song Dynasty, 960–1279), unknown Chinese artist. Wood, 30" × 36" × 64", Eugene Fuller Memorial Collection, Seattle (Washington) Art Museum. Photo by Paul Macapia.

"Of course," Po-wan echoed weakly. Overcoming his fear and his reluctance to touch the slippery-slithery scales, Chin Po-wan climbed onto the snake's back and rode across quite safely. Politely, and just a bit hurriedly, he thanked the self-denying serpent and bade him good-bye. Then he continued on his way to the South Sea.

By noon he was very hungry. Fortunately, a nearby inn offered meals at a price he could afford. While waiting for his bowl of rice, he chatted with the innkeeper and told him of the

---

6. **self-denial:** the giving up of desires or pleasures.

Reading Skills and Strategies:
QUESTION

A Have students think about Po-wan's journey so far and what he has encountered. Ask them to create a list of questions they have about the events surrounding the journey.

Set a Purpose Ask students to read to find out if any of their questions are answered.

Reading Skills and Strategies:
PREDICT

B Ask students which question they think Po-wan will leave out and to tell why they think so.

Literary Analysis: THEME

Ask students what they think the theme of this story, or its message about life, is.
Possible Response: Generosity and kindness will always be rewarded.

Snake of the Cliff, which the innkeeper knew well and respected, for the serpent always denied bandits the crossing of the river. <u>Inadvertently</u>, during the exchange of stories, Po-wan revealed the purpose of his journey.

"Why, then," cried the innkeeper, "let me prevail upon your generosity to ask a word for me." He laid an appealing hand on Po-wan's ragged sleeve. "I have a beautiful daughter," he said, "wonderfully <u>amiable</u> and pleasing of disposition. But although she is in her twentieth year, she has never in all her life uttered a single word. I should be very much obliged if you would ask the Living Kuan-yin why she is unable to speak."

Po-wan, much moved by the innkeeper's plea for his mute daughter, of course promised to do so. For after all, the Living Kuan-yin allowed each person three questions, and he had but one of his own to ask.

Nightfall found him far from any inn, but there were houses in the neighborhood, and he asked for lodging at the largest. The owner, a man obviously of great wealth, was pleased to offer him a bed in a fine chamber but first begged him to partake of a hot meal and good drink. Po-wan ate well, slept soundly, and, much refreshed, was about to depart the following morning when his good host, having learned that Po-wan was journeying to the South Sea, asked if he would be kind enough to put a question for him to the Living Kuan-yin.

"For twenty years," he said, "from the time this house was built, my garden has been cultivated with the utmost care; yet in all those years, not one tree, not one small plant, has bloomed or borne fruit, and because of this, no bird comes to sing, nor bee to gather nectar. I don't like to put you to a bother, Chin Po-wan, but as you are going to the South Sea

anyway, perhaps you would not mind seeking out the Living Kuan-yin and asking her why the plants in my garden don't bloom."

"I shall be delighted to put the question to her," said Po-wan. For after all, the Living Kuan-yin allowed each person three questions, and he had but . . .

Traveling onward, Po-wan examined the quandary[7] in which he found himself. The Living Kuan-yin allowed but three questions, and he had somehow, without quite knowing how, accumulated four questions. One of them would have to go unasked, but which? If he left out his own question, his whole journey would have been in vain.[8] If, on the other hand, he left out the question of the snake, or the innkeeper, or the kind host, he would break his promise and betray their faith in him.

"A promise should never be made if it cannot be kept," he told himself. "I made the promises and therefore I must keep them. Besides, the journey will not be in vain, for at least some of these problems will be solved by the Living Kuan-yin. Furthermore, assisting others must certainly be counted as a good deed, and the more good deeds abroad in the land, the better for everyone, including me."

At last he came into the presence of the Living Kuan-yin.

First, he asked the serpent's question: "Why is the Snake of the Cliff not yet a dragon, although he has practiced self-denial for more than one thousand years?"

And the Living Kuan-yin answered: "On his head are seven bright pearls. If he removes six of them, he can become a dragon."

---

7. **quandary** (kwŏn'də-rē): confusing situation.

8. **in vain:** useless.

| WORDS TO KNOW | **inadvertently** (ĭn'əd-vûr'tnt-lē) *adv.* by mistake or without meaning to; not deliberately |
| | **amiable** (ā'mē-ə-bəl) *adj.* good-natured and likable |

Multicultural Link **Folk Tales**

Instruction Many cultures have folk tales, like this one, in which a hero is rewarded for his or her unselfishness. Folk tales are a part of the oral tradition and share the characteristics shown on the word web.

Practice Have students copy the web shown. Then have them add to their web details about this tale's characters, lessons, and the values it reveals to their webs.

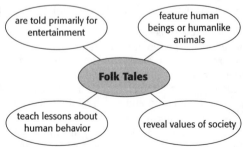

are told primarily for entertainment

feature human beings or humanlike animals

Folk Tales

teach lessons about human behavior

reveal values of society

Next, Po-wan asked the innkeeper's question: "Why is the innkeeper's daughter unable to speak, although she is in the twentieth year of her life?"

And the Living Kuan-yin answered: "It is her fate to remain mute until she sees the man destined[9] to be her husband."

Last, Po-wan asked the kind host's question: "Why are there never blossoms in the rich man's garden, although it has been carefully cultivated for twenty years?"

And the Living Kuan-yin answered: "Buried in the garden are seven big jars filled with silver and gold. The flowers will bloom if the owner will rid himself of half the treasure."

Then Chin Po-wan thanked the Living Kuan-yin and bade her good-bye.

On his return journey, he stopped first at the rich man's house to give him the Living Kuan-yin's answer. In gratitude the rich man gave him half the buried treasure.

Next, Po-wan went to the inn. As he approached, the innkeeper's daughter saw him from the window and called out, "Chin Po-wan! Back already! What did the Living Kuan-yin say?"

Upon hearing his daughter speak at long last, the joyful innkeeper gave her in marriage to Chin Po-wan.

Lastly, Po-wan went to the cliffs by the furiously flowing river to tell the snake what the Living Kuan-yin had said. The grateful snake immediately gave him six of the bright pearls and promptly turned into a magnificent dragon, the remaining pearl in his forehead lighting the headland[10] like a great beacon.[11]

And so it was that Chin Po-wan, that generous and good man, was once more worth a million pieces of gold. ❖

---

9. **destined** (dĕs′tĭnd): determined beforehand, as by fate.

10. **headland:** a point of land reaching out into the water.

11. **beacon:** a light for signaling or guiding.

Carol Kendall
born 1917

"My life and writing have always been inextricably entangled."

Born Climber Carol Kendall says the things she likes to do best are writing, reading, studying Chinese, and "climbing to the tops of things." Kendall is best known for *The Gammage Cup*, a 1960 Newbery Honor Book, which was adapted as an animated film for television in 1987. Kendall now lives in Lawrence, Kansas, where she met Yao-Wen Li.

Yao-wen Li
born 1924

"It just happened, and I found myself a writer."

True "Brilliance" "The Living Kuan-yin" is from *Sweet and Sour,* a collection of Chinese folk tales that Yao-wen Li coauthored with Carol Kendall. Born and raised in Canton, China, Li has lived in the United States since 1947. A return visit to China in 1973 inspired Li (whose first name means "literary brilliance") to begin collecting traditional Chinese tales.

THE LIVING KUAN-YIN **829**

Standards-Based Objectives

- To understand and appreciate a folk tale
- To understand and appreciate an oral history
- To understand and appreciate the values and customs of historical and contemporary America

Reading Pathways

- Select one or several students to read each story aloud to the entire class or to small groups of students. Assign this reading in advance so the readers can incorporate into their presentations some of the techniques used by professional storytellers. Have the audience listen carefully to the stories without following along in their texts.
- Read the stories aloud to the class, pausing at key points to discuss how elements of the story inform students about the purpose of a "pourquoi" tale or the history of the Cheyenne people.
- After students have read the stories once, they can read them again to identify structural elements such as main character, minor characters, conflict, setting, and plot. Then have students identify similarities and differences between these two stories and the stories in Unit 5.

 Use **Unit Six Resource Book,** p. 27, for work with Words to Know.

English Conventions Practice

Daily Language SkillBuilder

Have students **proofread** the display sentences on page 767g and write them correctly. The sentences also appear on Transparency 26 of **Language Transparencies.**

PREPARING to Read

The Oral Tradition

LINKS TO UNIT FIVE

Making Your Mark

The selections you read in Unit Five are about characters and historical figures who find ways to express themselves. In so doing, they leave their imprints, or marks, on the world. Likewise, each tale you're about to read contains a message about the impact that one person can have on his or her community.

UNITED STATES

GREAT PLAINS

UNITED STATES

The Frog Who Wanted to Be a Singer

by Linda Goss

There is a folklore tradition, stretching across all cultures, that uses storytelling to explain how things came to be. "The Frog Who Wanted to Be a Singer" is another example of a "why story" or a **"pourquoi tale."**

Many traditional pourquoi tales have animals as main characters. This contemporary American **folk tale,** which takes place "in the days when the animals talked and walked upon the earth," was inspired by traditional African tales. The story offers one explanation of the way a certain type of music was first created. In it, Frog encounters some serious challenges as he pursues his dream of being a singer.

830   UNIT SIX   THE ORAL TRADITION

LESSON RESOURCES

UNIT SIX RESOURCE BOOK, pp. 24–28

ASSESSMENT
Formal Assessment, pp. 133–134
Test Generator

SKILLS TRANSPARENCIES AND COPYMASTERS
Reading and Critical Thinking
- Predicting, TR 7 (p. 832)
- Making Inferences, TR 10 (p. 838)
Language
- Daily Language SkillBuilder, TR 26 (p. 830)

INTEGRATED TECHNOLOGY
Audio Library

Visit our Web site:
www.mcdougallittell.com

For **systematic instruction** in language skills, see:
- **Vocabulary and Spelling Book**
- **Grammar, Usage, and Mechanics Book**
- pacing chart on p. 767e.

Where the Girl Rescued Her Brother

retold by Joseph Bruchac (broo'chăk')

This selection is an **oral history**—an account of an event that actually happened, handed down by word of mouth. The Cheyenne (shī-ĕn') are Native Americans whose homeland in the 19th century was the Great Plains, the grassland stretching through the central United States. With the Indian Removal Act of 1830, the U.S. government established land west of the Mississippi River as a reservation for Native Americans.

Western settlement increased in the 1850s, however, and the government began to make treaties with Plains tribes to restrict them to smaller areas. Settlers claimed more and more land. The government changed the terms of some treaties without permission or made treaties with Native Americans who did not represent their tribes. Soon, fighting broke out between Native Americans and government troops. This oral history tells of one such battle, in which a young Cheyenne woman makes her mark.

AS YOU READ . . .

See how the values and customs of the cultures are presented.

Discover what lessons about human behavior are taught.

Think about the conflicts that arise and how they are resolved.

Summary

A frog desperately wants to sing, but all the animals in the forest insist that only birds can sing. This frog doesn't give up easily, though. He convinces the fox, who organizes the Friday night concert series, to give him a chance. When Friday night arrives, the frog tentatively approaches the microphone. The audience makes fun of him and pelts him with fruit, but he is not discouraged. The frog stands up to the sly fox and makes his way back on stage. The other animals find that they can't resist the frog's singing, and soon they are all dancing. The frog is the originator of a new style of music, rhythm and blues.

Reading and Analyzing

Literary Analysis: FANTASY

Students should be able to recognize the distinguishing features of genres, including fantasy. Ask students to tell whether this story is fantastic or realistic and explain what details tell them this.

Possible Response: This story is fantasy, because animals don't really talk and frogs can't sing.

 Use **Unit Six Resource Book,** p. 26, for more practice.

Reading Skills and Strategies: PREDICT

Have students make predictions about the story. Ask them whether they think the frog's goal will be met and how he might go about accomplishing it.

Use **Reading and Critical Thinking Transparencies,** p. 7, for additional support.

The FROG Who Wanted to Be a...

Pine Barren Tree Frog, Andy Warhol, (1928–1987). Endangered Species Series, 1983. One from a portfolio of ten screenprints and colophon, 38" × 38". Printed on Lenox Museum Board. Copyright © 2001 The Andy Warhol Foundation for the Visual Arts/ARS, New York

832

EXPLICIT INSTRUCTION **Viewing and Representing**

Pine Barren Tree Frog
by Andy Warhol

ART APPRECIATION The late Andy Warhol made several series of prints. He made prints of celebrities, including Marilyn Monroe, Jacqueline Kennedy Onassis, and Mao Tse-tung. Warhol is perhaps best known for his contributions to Pop Art, a style in which everyday consumer items, such as soup cans, are used as subject matter for art.
Instruction Point out the use of primary colors.

Practice Ask students what effect is produced by the colors of the frog and the background.
Possible Response: The bright colors make the frog stand out against the dark blue background. The frog looks vibrant and alive, as though he might jump out of the picture.
Practice Tell students to read the caption and discuss why Warhol chose to represent this particular kind of frog.
Possible Response: Warhol chose the pine barren tree frog because he wanted to call attention to its endangered status.

SINGER

by Linda Goss

Well, friends, I got a question for you. Have you ever been frustrated? That's right. I said *frustrated*. Tell the truth now. Everybody in this room should be screaming, "Yeah, I've been frustrated," because you know you have, at least once in your lives. And some of us here are frustrated every single day.

How do you tell when you are frustrated? Do you feel angry? Do you feel depressed? Are you full of anxiety? Are you tense? Are you nervous? Confused? Sometimes you can't stop eating. Sometimes you don't want to eat at all. Sometimes you can't sleep. And sometimes you don't want to wake up. *You are frustrated!*

Well, friends, let's go back. Back to the forest. Back to the motherland. Back to the days when the animals talked and walked upon the earth, as folks do now.

Let's examine a little creature who is feeling mighty bad, mighty sad, mighty mad, and mighty frustrated. We call him the frog. There's nothing wrong in being a frog. But this particular frog feels that he has talent. You see, he wants to be a singer. And there's nothing wrong in wanting to be a singer except that in this particular forest where this particular frog lives, frogs don't sing. Only the birds are allowed to sing. The birds are considered the most beautiful singers in the forest.

So, for a while, the frog is cool. He's quiet. He stays to himself and practices on his lily pad, jumping up and down, singing to himself.

But one day all of this frustration begins to swell inside him. He becomes so swollen that frustration bubbles start popping from his mouth, his ears, his nose, even from his eyes, and he says to himself (in a froglike voice): "You know, I'm tired of feeling this way. I'm tired of holding all this inside me. I've got talent. I want to be a singer."

The little frog decides to share his <u>ambitions</u> with his parents. His parents are somewhat worried about his desires, but since he is their son, they encourage him and say: "Son, we're behind you one hundred percent. If that's what you want to be, then go right ahead. You'll make us very proud."

This makes the frog feel better. It gives him some confidence, so much so that he decides to share the good news with his friends. He jumps over to the other side of the pond and says, "Fellows, I want to share something with you."

"Good!" they reply. "You got some flies we can eat."

"No, not flies. I got talent. I want to be a singer."

"Fool, are you crazy?" says one friend. "Frogs don't sing in this place. You'd better keep your big mouth shut."

They laugh at the frog, so he jumps back over to his lily pad.

WORDS TO KNOW

ambition (ăm-bĭsh′ən) *n.* a goal that is strongly desired

833

Literary Analysis: TONE

Ask students to take a close look at the language of this story. Tell them to think about how the author uses particular words and phrases to set the tone. Then ask them to describe the tone.

Possible Response: The author sets the tone by using certain phrases such as, ". . . the frog is cool," the frog is going to "do his thing," and "Boo, you jive turkey." The slang gives the story a conversational feel. It's easy to imagine hearing the story told out loud.

Literary Analysis: CHARACTER

Ask students to use adjectives to describe the frog's character. Then have them characterize the fox.

Possible Response: Frog is determined, confident, persistent, and fair-minded. The fox is deceptive, dishonest, and untrustworthy.

Literary Analysis: FANTASY

Describe a scene from these two pages that could only take place in a fantasy.

Possible Response: Only in a fantasy could there be a concert with foxes, lions, elephants, and other animals in the audience.

He rocks back and forth, meditating and <u>contemplating</u> his situation, and begins to realize that perhaps he should go and talk with the birds. They seem reasonable enough; maybe they will allow him to join their singing group.

He gathers up his confidence, jumps over to their tree house, and knocks on their trunk. The head bird flies to the window, looks down on the frog's head, and says: "Oh, it's the frog. How may we help you?"

"Can I come up? I got something to ask you," says the frog.

"Very well, Frog. Do jump up."

Frog enters the tree house, and hundreds of birds begin fluttering around him.

"Come on in, Frog. Why don't you sit over there in the corner," says the head bird. Frog sits down but he feels a little shy. He begins to chew on his tongue.

"Frog, how may we help you?"

"Uh, well, uh, you see," says Frog, "I would like to become a part of your group."

"That's wonderful," says the head bird.

"Yes, wonderful," echo the other birds.

"Frog, you may help us carry our worms," said the head bird.

"That's not what I had in mind," says Frog.

"Well, what do you have in mind?"

Frog begins to stutter: "I-I-I-I-I want to-to-to sing wi-wi-with your group."

"What! You must be joking, of course. An ugly green frog who is full of warts sing with us delicate creatures. You would cause us great embarrassment."

"B-b-but . . ." Frog tries to plead his case, but the head bird becomes angry.

"Out! Out! Out of our house you go." He kicks the frog from the house. Frog rolls like a ball down the jungle path.

When he returns home, he feels very sad. The frog wants to cry but doesn't, even though he aches deep inside his gut. He wants to give up, but he doesn't. Instead he practices and practices and practices and practices.

Then he begins to think again and realizes that even though the birds sing every Friday night at the Big Time Weekly Concert, they don't control it. The fox is in charge. The frog jumps over to the fox's place and knocks on his cave.

"Brother Fox, Brother Fox, it's me, Frog. I want to talk to you."

The fox is a fast talker and a busy worker, and really doesn't want to be bothered with the frog.

"Quick, quick, quick, what do you want?" says the fox.

"I want to be in the concert this Friday night."

"Quick, quick, what do you want to do?"

"I want to sing," says the frog.

"Sing? Get out of here, quick, quick, quick!"

"Please, Brother Fox. Please give me a chance."

"Hmmm," says the fox, shifting his eyes. "Uh, you know something, Froggie? Maybe I could use you. Why don't you show up Friday, at eight o'clock sharp, OK?"

"You mean I can do it?"

"That's what I said. Now, get out of here. Quick, quick, quick!"

Oh, the frog is happy. He is going to "do his thing." He is going to present himself to the world.

Meanwhile, the fox goes around to the animals in the forest and tells them about the frog's plans. Each animal promises to be there and give the frog a "little present" for his singing debut.

And so Monday rolls around, Tuesday rolls around, Wednesday rolls around, Thursday

WORDS TO KNOW **contemplating** (kŏn′təm-plā′tĭng) *adj.* considering carefully; pondering
contemplate *v.*

rolls around, and it is Friday. The frog is so excited, he bathes all day. He combs his little green hair, parts it in the middle, and slicks down the sides. He scrubs his little green fingers and his little green toes. He looks at his little reflection in the pond, smiles, and says, "Um, um, um, I am *beauuuutiful!* And I am going to 'do my thing' tonight." And soon it is seven o'clock, and then it is seven thirty, and then it is seven forty-five, and there is the frog trembling, holding on to the edge of the curtain.

He looks out at the audience and sees all the animals gathering in their seats. The frog is scared, so scared that his legs won't stop trembling and his eyes won't stop twitching. Brother Fox strolls out onstage and the show begins.

"Thank you, thank you, thank you. Ladies and gentlemen, we have a wonderful show for you tonight. Presenting, for your entertainment, the frog who thinks he's a singer. Come on, let's clap. Come on out here, Frog, come on, come on. Let's give him a big hand." The animals clap and roar with laughter. The frog jumps out and slowly goes up to the microphone.

"For-for-for-for my first number, I-I-I-I—"

Now, before that frog can put the period at the end of that sentence, the elephant stands up, pulls down a pineapple, and throws it right at the frog's head.

"Ow!" cries the frog. And the lion pulls down a banana, throws it, and hits that frog right in the mouth. "Oh," gulps the frog. Other animals join in the act of throwing things at the frog. Some of them shout and yell at him, "Boo! Boo! Get off the stage. You stink! You're ugly. We don't want to hear a frog sing. Boo, you jive turkey!"

The poor little frog has to leap off the stage and run for his life. He hides underneath the stage. Brother Fox rushes back on the stage.

"OK, OK, OK, calm down—just trying out our comic routine. We have some real talent for your enjoyment. Presenting the birds, who really can sing. Let's hear it for the birds." The audience claps loudly. The birds fly onto the stage, their heads held up high. Their wings slowly strike a stiff, <u>hypnotic</u> pose as if they are statues. Their stage presence demands great respect from the audience. They chirp, tweet, and whistle, causing the audience to fall into a soft, peaceful nod.

Everyone is resting quietly except the frog, who is tired of being pushed around. The frog is tired of feeling frustrated. He leaps over the fox. He grabs him, shakes him, puts his hands around the fox's throat, and says, "You tricked me. You tried to make a fool out of me."

"Leave me alone," says the fox. "If you want to go back out there and make a fool of yourself, go right ahead."

"Hmph," says the frog. "That's just what I'm going to do."

Now that little green frog hippity-hops back onto the stage. He is shaking but determined to sing his song.

"I don't care if you are asleep. I'm gonna wake you up. I came here to sing a song tonight, and that's what I'm going to do."

In the style of what we call boogie-woogie, the frog begins to "do his thing":

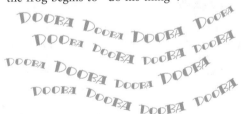

DOOBA DOOBA DOOBA DOOBA
DOOBA DOOBA DOOBA DOOBA
DOOBA DOOBA DOOBA DOOBA
DOOBA DOOBA DOOBA DOOBA

WORDS TO KNOW **hypnotic** (hĭp-nŏt′ĭk) *adj.* trance-inducing **hypnotize** *v.*

835

Multicultural Link Boogie-Woogie

Tell students that "boogie-woogie" is a style of piano that was later adapted for band performance. While the left hand plays repeated patterns of blues chords, the right hand plays syncopated melodies. In order to play boogie-woogie, a pianist's hands must play independently of each other.

The term "boogie-woogie" was first used in the late 1920s, and it may have originally been used to describe a dance that was accompanied by this lively piano music.

Boogie-woogie was most popular during the Swing Era of the 1930s and 1940s. Musicians like Tommy Dorsey, Count Basie, and the Andrews Sisters all played boogie-woogie.

Bring in some recordings of boogie-woogie music. Ask students to listen to the music and then discuss how it makes them feel. Can they understand how this music affected the animals in the frog's audience?

Literary Analysis: AUTHOR'S PURPOSE

Ask students why they think Linda Goss wrote this story and whether they think she succeeds at her purpose.

Possible Responses: She wrote this story to entertain readers, and she succeeds, because this story is funny—not a serious explanation of the birth of rhythm and blues; She may have wanted to inspire readers to "go for" their dreams.

Literary Analysis: UNCONVENTIONAL TEXT

Lead a discussion about the "wavy" text that describes the frog's singing on pages 849–850. Ask students why they think the words are styled this way. Then ask them whether they like this technique, and why or why not.

Possible Response: The wavy words give you a feeling for the rhythm of the music that the frog is playing. Printed this way, the words make the page look lively and fun.

The frog bops his head about as though it were a jazzy saxophone. His fingers move as though they were playing a funky bass fiddle.

The elephant opens one eye. He roars "Uuumphf!" He jumps from his seat. He flings his hips from side to side, doing a dance we now call the "bump." The lion is the next animal to jump up from his seat. He shouts: "I love it! I love it!" He shakes his body thisaway and thataway and every whichaway, doing a dance we now call the "twist." Soon the snakes are boogalooing and the giraffes are doing the jerk. The hyenas do the "slop" and

the fox does the "mashed potato." The birds also want to join in: "We want to do Dooba Dooba, too." They chirp and sway through the trees.

The whole forest is rocking. The joint is jumping. The animals are snapping their fingers. They are *dancing*, doing something that they have never done before.

The fox runs back on the stage, grabs the mike, and shouts: "Wow, Frog, you are a genius. You have given us something new."

From then on, the frog is allowed to sing every Friday night at the Big Time Weekly Concert.

And, as my granddaddy used to say, that is how Rhythm and Blues was born.

Linda Goss
born 1942

"I have always been a talker."

A Storyteller's Beginnings Linda Goss was born in Alcoa, Tennessee. When asked how she became a storyteller, she has said, "I have always been a talker. When I was in the first grade, my teacher wrote on my report card, 'Linda talks too much.' As I grew older, I decided

to put my talking to good use." She attended Howard University, where she studied drama.

Doing Her Own Thing When Goss was young, few people considered storytelling to be a possible career. She worked as a teacher and then decided to become a full-time professional storyteller, despite the difficulties. "Frog needed to do his own thing, and so do I," she says.

Career Success With her husband, Clay Goss, Goss has edited two collections of African-American stories and written two children's books. She is the official storyteller of Philadelphia, where she now resides.

Multicultural Link Rhythm and Blues

Prepare Explain that rhythm and blues is a kind of music that combines elements of blues and jazz. Rhythm and blues, also known as R&B, was developed by African Americans and is characterized by a strong backbeat and repeated variations on instrumental phrases. Most authorities agree that it is a precursor to rock and roll. Bring in some examples of rhythm and blues recordings. Tell students to listen for some of the instruments mentioned in the story, such as the saxophone, bass, and fiddle.

Present Lead a discussion about this kind of music. Ask students whether they have ever heard this kind of music before, and if so, where. Have students think about whether this type of music sounds difficult to play. Students who play instruments might enjoy sharing with the class any knowledge they have about playing R&B. Then discuss how this kind of music makes them feel.

WHERE THE GIRL RESCUED HER BROTHER

retold by **Joseph Bruchac**

>>>

I t was the moon when the chokecherries were ripe. A young woman rode out of a Cheyenne camp with her husband and her brother. The young woman's name was Buffalo Calf Road Woman.

Cheyenne Young Woman,
Edward S. Curtis. Plate #64 from
"The North American Indians."
Philadelphia Museum of Art:
Funds from the American
Museum of Photography.

Summary
Buffalo Calf Road Woman, together with her husband, who is a Cheyenne chief, and her brother ride with a group of Cheyenne to meet their allies, the Lakota. The Native Americans are on their way to engage the white men in battle. Their goal is to drive the whites off Native American lands. During the fierce battle, Buffalo Calf Road Woman sees that her brother is unhorsed and fighting for his life. She rides into the fray on her pony and carries her brother to safety. Both Native Americans and whites pause to cheer her bravery. Her act of courage inspires the Native American warriors to victory.

Differentiating Instruction

English Learners
Tell students that *chokecherries* are a fruit from a shrub or small tree in the rose family. The fruit is dark red or almost black and has a strong flavor.

Discuss the name "Buffalo Calf Road Woman." Ask students whether they are familiar with other Native American names. If students can't think of any names, mention Sitting Bull, a Sioux leader who led his people to victory over General Custer at the Battle of the Little Bighorn in 1876. Lead a discussion about the significance of Native American names.

Less Proficient Readers
If students know something about the life of Native Americans in earlier times, they will better understand this story. Ask students to share what they know, and to find details of the daily life of the Cheyenne from the story.

EXPLICIT INSTRUCTION ## Viewing and Representing

Cheyenne Young Woman
by Edward S. Curtis

ART APPRECIATION Edward Curtis was a portrait photographer based in Seattle who devoted himself to documenting Native Americans.
Instruction Between 1907 and 1937, Edward Curtis produced 20 volumes of text and 20 volumes of portraits under the title *The North American Indian.* President Theodore Roosevelt wrote the foreword to the series.

Curtis felt that it was important to record the customs of Native Americans before their tradi-tions disappeared. Because of his feeling that some of these tribes were dying out or would soon become modernized, Curtis sometimes had his subjects pose in the dress of their ancestors so that future generations would have a record of their elders.

Practice Ask students to write a paragraph describing the portrait. Encourage them to tell what they know and feel about this woman from studying the photograph.

er husband, Black Coyote, was one of the chiefs of the Cheyenne, the people of the plains who call themselves Tsis-tsis-tas, meaning simply "The People." Buffalo Calf Road Woman's brother, Comes-in-Sight, was also one of the Cheyenne chiefs, and it was well-known how close he was to his sister.

Like many of the other young women of the Cheyenne, Buffalo Calf Road Woman was respected for her honorable nature. Although it was the men who most often went to war to defend the people—as they were doing on this day— women would accompany their husbands when they went to battle. If a man held an important position among the Cheyenne, such as the keeper of the Sacred Arrows, then his wife, too, would have to be of the highest moral character, for she shared the weight of his responsibility.

Buffalo Calf Road Woman was well aware of this, and as she rode by her husband she did so with pride. She knew that today they were on their way to meet their old <u>allies</u>, the Lakota.[1] They were going out to try to drive back the *veho*, the spider people who were trying to claim all the lands of the Native peoples.

The Cheyenne had been worried about the *veho*, the white people, for a long time. They had given them that name because, like the black widow spider, they were very beautiful but it was dangerous to get close to them. And unlike the Cheyenne, they seemed to follow a practice of making promises and not keeping them. Although their soldier chief Custer had promised to be friendly with the Cheyenne, now he and the others had come into their lands to make war upon them.

Early Moonlight, Little Horn, Montana, Joseph Henry Sharp. Watercolor on paper. Stark Museum of Art, Orange, Texas.

Buffalo Calf Road Woman wore a robe embroidered with porcupine quills. The clothing of her brother and her husband, Black Coyote, was also beautifully decorated with those quills, which had been flattened, dyed in different colors, folded, and sewed on in patterns. Buffalo Calf Road Woman was proud that she belonged to the Society of Quilters. As with the men's societies, only a few women—those of the best character— could join. Like the men, the women had to be

---
1. **Lakota** (lə-kō′tə).

WORDS TO KNOW

ally (ă-lī′) *n.* a person, group, or nation that works with another to achieve shared goals

strong, honorable, and brave. Buffalo Calf Road Woman had grown up hearing stories of how Cheyenne women would defend their families when the men were away. The women of the Cheyenne were brave, and those in the Society of Quilters were the bravest of all.

Buffalo Calf Road Woman smiled as she remembered one day when the women of the Society of Quilters showed such bravery. It was during the Moon of Falling Leaves. A big hunt had been planned. The men who acted as scouts had gone out and located the great buffalo herd. They had seen, too, that there were no human enemies anywhere near their camp. So almost none of the men remained behind.

On that day, when all the men were away, a great grizzly bear came into the camp. Such things seldom happened, but this bear was one that had been wounded in the leg by a white fur-trapper's bullet. It could no longer hunt as it had before, and hunger brought it to the Cheyenne camp, where it smelled food cooking.

When the huge bear came walking into the camp, almost everyone scattered. Some women grabbed their little children. Old people shut the door flaps of their tepees, and the boys ran to find their bows and arrows. Only a group of seven women who had been working on the embroidery of an elk-skin robe did not run. They were members of the Society of Quilters, and Buffalo Calf Road Woman was among them. The seven women put down their work, picked up the weapons they had close to hand, and stood to face the grizzly bear.

Now of all of the animals of the plains, the only one fierce enough and powerful enough to attack a human was the grizzly. But confronted by that determined group of women, the grizzly bear stopped in its tracks. It had come to steal food, not fight. The head of the Society of Quilters stepped forward a pace and spoke to the bear.

"Grandfather," she said, her voice low and firm, "we do not wish to harm you, but we will protect our camp. Go back to your own home."

The grizzly shook its head and then turned and walked out of the camp. The women stood and watched it as it went down through the cottonwoods and was lost from sight along the bend of the stream.

Buffalo Calf Road Woman turned her mind away from her memories. They were close to Rosebud Creek. The scouts had told them that a great number of the *veho* soldiers would be there and that the Gray Fox, General George Crook, was in command. The Cheyenne had joined up now with the Oglala,[2] led by Crazy Horse. The Lakota people were always friends to the Cheyenne, but this man, Crazy Horse, was the best friend of all. Some even said that he was one of their chiefs, too, as well as being a war leader of his Oglala.

There were Crow and Shoshone scouts with Crook, and the *veho* had many cannons. The Lakota and the Cheyenne were outnumbered by the two thousand men in Crook's command. But they were prepared to fight. They had put on their finest clothes, for no man should risk his life without being dressed well enough so that if he died, the enemy would know a great warrior had fallen. Some of the men raised their headdresses three times, calling out their names and the deeds they had done. Those headdresses of eagle feathers were thought to give magical protection to a warrior. Other men busied themselves painting designs on their war ponies.

Now they could hear Crook's army approaching. The rumble of the horses' hooves echoed down the valley, and there was the

---

2. Oglala (ō-glä′lə).

Differentiating Instruction

Less Proficient Readers

1 Ask students to explain why the Cheyenne refer to the white people as the "spider people."

Possible Response: The Cheyenne call white people "the spider people" because they think that, like a black widow spider, the white people are beautiful but dangerous.

2 Have students identify the season during which the Moon of Falling Leaves takes place.

Possible Response: The Moon of Falling Leaves takes place in the autumn, because that's when leaves fall.

English Learners

Cultures differ in the roles that are deemed traditional for women and men. Have students describe what this story tells them about the roles of men and women in the Cheyenne culture, citing specific details from the text.

Advanced Students

Ask students what they know about the relationship between humans and grizzly bears. Encourage them to find out if grizzlies attack people, and how common it is for them to try to steal food from humans. Two sources of information are our national park service and the park's individual Web sites.

Possible Responses: Bear attacks and sightings have increased in recent years as bears increasingly associate humans with food. Some humans make the mistake of feeding the bears, or leaving food for them, which increases the dependency of bears on humans. With the expanding population, more land is needed for humans. This is an encroachment on the bears' territory and they have close interaction with humans as a result.

Multicultural Link — Native American Beliefs

Although there are many different Native American tribes, each with its own traditions and history, most tribes share some common beliefs. For example, most Native Americans believe in a unity among the earth's people, animals, and other living things. They believe that each living thing contains a spirit and that any two living things can make spiritual contact.

Native American buffalo hunters gave thanks to the buffalo for giving its life so that people could eat and live. This reverence for life is one of the reasons why Native Americans used every part of the buffalo—nothing went to waste after the buffalo had given its life.

Reading and Analyzing

Literary Analysis: SETTING

Ask students to describe the setting of this part of the story.

Possible Response: This part of the story takes place at Rosebud Creek, the site of a battle between the Cheyenne people and the white soldiers. The Lakota tribe is helping the Cheyenne in their fight against the white people, who are getting help from members of the Crow and the Shoshone tribes.

Reading Skills and Strategies: SUMMARIZE

Have students summarize the reason why this battle is taking place.

Possible Response: This battle is taking place because the white people are trying to claim the land of the native peoples.

Reading Skills and Strategies: ANALYZE

Ask students why they think this story about Buffalo Calf Road Woman has particular significance to the Cheyenne people.

Possible Response: This story is probably important to the Cheyenne people because it is an impressive example of the strength and bravery not only of Buffalo Calf Road Woman but also of the Cheyenne people as a whole.

The Battle of the Rosebud, which the Cheyenne call "Where the Girl Rescued Her Brother," was fought on June 17, 1876, on the banks of the Rosebud Creek in southeastern Montana.

sound of trumpets. War ponies reared up and stomped their feet. Many of the Cheyenne men found it hard to put on the last of their paint as their hands shook from the excitement of the coming battle.

Crazy Horse <u>vaulted</u> onto his horse and held up one arm. "*Hoka Hey,*" he cried. "It is a good day to die."

Buffalo Calf Road Woman watched from a hill as the two lines of men—the blue soldiers to one side, and the Lakota and Cheyenne to the other—raced toward each other. The battle began. It was not a quick fight or an easy one. There were brave men on both sides. Two Moons, Little Hawk, Yellow Eagle, Sitting Bull, and Crazy Horse were only a few of the great warriors who fought for the Cheyenne and the Lakota. And Crook, the Gray Fox general of the whites, was known to be a tough fighter and a worthy enemy.

Buffalo Calf Road Woman's husband, Black Coyote, and her brother, Comes-in-Sight, were in the thick of the fight. The odds in the battle were almost even. Although the whites had more soldiers and guns, the Lakota and the Cheyenne were better shots and better

horsemen. Had it not been for the Crow and Shoshone scouts helping Crook, the white soldiers might have broken quickly from the ferocity of the attack.

From one side to the other, groups of men attacked and retreated as the guns cracked, cannons boomed, and smoke filled the air. The war shouts of the Lakota and the Cheyenne were almost as loud as the rumble of the guns. The sun moved across the sky as the fight went on, hour after hour, while the confusion of battle swirled below.

Then Buffalo Calf Road Woman saw something that horrified her. Her brother had been drawn off to one side, surrounded by Crow scouts. He tried to ride free of them, but his pony went down, struck by a rifle bullet and killed. Now he was on foot, still fighting. The Crow warriors were trying to get close, to count coup[3] on him. It was more of an honor to touch a living enemy, so they were not firing

_____

3. **count coup** (ko͞o): to touch an enemy in battle with a rod called a coup stick, considered an act of bravery by some Native American peoples.

WORDS TO KNOW   **vault** (vôlt) *v.* to jump or to leap with the use of the hands

840

their rifles at him. And he was able to keep them away with his bow and arrows. But it was clear that soon he would be out of ammunition and would fall to the enemy.

Buffalo Calf Road Woman waited no longer. She dug her heels into her pony's sides and galloped down the hill. Her head low, her braids streaming behind her, she rode into the heart of the fight. Some men moved aside as they saw her coming, for there was a determined look in her eyes. She made the long howling cry that Cheyenne women used to urge on the warriors. This time, however, she was the one going into the fight. Her voice was as strong as an eagle's. Her horse scattered the ponies of the Crow scouts who were closing in on her brother, Comes-in-Sight. She held out a hand; her brother grabbed it and vaulted onto the pony behind her. Then she wheeled, ducking the arrows of the Crow scouts, and heading back up the hill.

That was when it happened. For a moment, it seemed as if all the shooting stopped. The Cheyenne and the Lakota, and even the *veho* soldiers, lowered their guns to watch this act of great bravery. A shout went up, not from one side but from both, as Buffalo Calf Road Woman reached the safety of the hilltop again, her brother safe behind her on her horse. White men and Indians cheered her.

So it was that Buffalo Calf Road Woman performed the act for which the people would always remember her. Inspired by her courage, the Cheyenne and Lakota drove back the Gray Fox—Crook made a strategic withdrawal.[4]

"Even the *veho* general was impressed," said the Cheyenne people. "He saw that if our women were that brave, he would stand no chance against us in battle."

So it is that to this day, the Cheyenne and the Lakota people do not refer to the fight as the Battle of the Rosebud. Instead, they honor Buffalo Calf Road Woman by calling the fight Where the Girl Rescued Her Brother. ❖

---

4. **strategic withdrawal:** retreat.

Joseph Bruchac
born 1942

"Have pride in what you are and recognize that we as human beings make ourselves."

Sharing the "Good Paths" The poet, novelist, and storyteller Joseph Bruchac began hearing Native American legends as a small child. A descendant of Abenaki Native Americans, Bruchac says he likes to share stories from Native American traditions because "they have messages, sometimes very subtle, which can help show young people the good paths to follow." Born in the Adirondack Mountains, Bruchac has also drawn upon the legends of those mountains for his stories.

Award-Winning Author Before becoming a writer and a scholar, Joseph Bruchac taught English and literature in Ghana, West Africa, and creative writing and African-American literature at Skidmore College in New York. The author of more than 60 books, Bruchac has received numerous awards for his writing, including a fellowship from the National Endowment for the Arts and a Rockefeller Foundation Humanities Fellowship. "Where the Girl Rescued Her Brother" appears in Bruchac's collection *The Girl Who Married the Moon: Tales from Native North America.*

English Learners

1 Point out the phrase "in the thick of the fight." Explain to students that this phrase means "in the middle of the fight."

2 Point out the word *ferocity*. Tell students that this noun has the same root found in the word *ferocious*. If necessary, explain that *ferocious* means "extremely savage, fierce."

Less Proficient Readers

Ask students to draw a diagram in order to gain a clearer understanding of the battle. Ask students to represent all the factions involved—the Cheyenne and the Lakota, the white soldiers, the Crow, and the Shoshone—as well as the various leaders.

Advanced Students

Ask students to tell the battle story from another point of view. Some possibilities are from the point of view of Comes in Sight, Black Coyote, or the United States army.

Literature Connection

Dramatize a Tale As students divide the tasks of preparing the storyboard and drafting the script, they should also assign someone the job of editor to review the storyboard for accuracy and continuity. The editor should also review the script to make sure it follows the storyboard before the actors begin to learn their lines.

RUBRIC

3 Full Accomplishment The dramatization grows out of the storyboard. Both depict significant scenes. Dialogue is meaningful and true to character.

2 Substantial Accomplishment The relationship between the storyboard and dramatization is sometimes unclear. Scenes are well played but not always significant enough to merit treatment. Dialogue, while entertaining, shows lapses in understanding of character.

1 Little or Partial Accomplishment Storyboard and dramatization do not reflect careful thought or preparation. The tale would not be intelligible to an audience member who had not heard it already.

Literature Connection

Hold a Storytelling Festival Suggest that students choose a theme for their festival so that the stories all share a common thread.

RUBRIC

3 Full Accomplishment Students present stories in a clear and effective manner. Their flyers and invitations are neat, legible, and convey the necessary information.

2 Substantial Accomplishment Students present stories clearly, but their flyers and invitations could be neater and more complete.

1 Little or Partial Accomplishment Students do not clearly convey the stories, and their flyers and invitations are carelessly done or contain incorrect information.

Interdisciplinary Projects

LITERATURE CONNECTION

Dramatize a Tale Dramatize and perform one of the tales you have read in this unit. Form teams to carry out the following tasks: creating a storyboard; writing the script; and working as costumers, set designers, actors, and technical crew. Use the following steps as a guide.

Step 1: Storyboard Design and make a storyboard, a series of drawings that illustrate the tale's events. Use the storyboard to determine which events from the tale to include and what they will look like. Include props, costumes, and sound effects.

Step 2: Script Write a script for a narrator and dialogue for the characters.

Step 3: Performance Rehearse and perform your dramatization with lighting and sound effects. If equipment is available, videotape or photograph the performance to share with another class or with family members.

LITERATURE CONNECTION

Hold a Storytelling Festival Work with your classmates to present a storytelling festival for other classes in your grade or for a group of younger students. First, decide which stories from the unit and which other tales from world folklore to include in the festival. Then, form groups to carry out the following steps.

Step 1: Rehearsals Rehearse each story in front of friends. Practice using gestures and tones of voice that make the stories come alive.

Step 2: Advertisements Create flyers to advertise the festival. Create and distribute invitations containing the date, time, and location. Produce illustrated programs to hand out at the festival.

Step 3: Props and Costumes Locate or construct appropriate props, and provide costumes for the storytellers.

Step 4: Performance Borrow the school's equipment or equipment loaned by the community. Make an audio or video recording of the performance, or take pictures of the festival. You may also want to locate videotapes of professional storytellers for viewing in a separate area of the festival.

SOCIAL STUDIES CONNECTION

Update a Folk tale Often, similar folk tales appear in different cultures, each version flavored with details that reflect the setting. Reread one of these tales to find details that reflect the culture of long-ago Vietnam or of medieval Germany. Record your findings in a chart like the one shown. Think about how those details might be different if the story were set in your culture today, and record your ideas. Then write your own version of the story, reflecting the new setting.

Details of Culture	In (name of tale)	In My Community
Valued Possessions		
Valued Traits		
Important Social Events		

Social Studies Connection

Update a Folk Tale If students need help with the chart, ask them more direct questions, such as, What is T'em's strongest character trait? or What event was the climax of "King Thrushbeard"?

RUBRIC

3 Full Accomplishment Entries are clear and accurate; new story retains basic theme and has been updated in imaginative yet believable manner.

2 Substantial Accomplishment Entries are complete but not entirely clear; new story retains basic theme but update could be more imaginative.

1 Little or Partial Accomplishment Entries are incomplete or inaccurate; new story does not retain important elements and does not reflect students' culture.

SCIENCE CONNECTION

Research Flight From watching birds fly, Daedalus got the idea for building wings that could help humans fly. Use an encyclopedia and books about flight to research what makes flight possible. Create a display that presents a basic explanation of the physics of bird flight and several modes of human flight (planes, helicopters, dirigibles, and so on).

RUBRIC

3 Full Accomplishment Students' displays are clear, complete, and attractively presented.

2 Substantial Accomplishment Students' displays are generally clear, give an adequate amount of information, and are relatively well presented.

1 Little or Partial Accomplishment Students' displays are unclear, give little information, and are poorly presented.

Across Cultures

COMPARING TEXTS **Compare Myths** Look in collections of myths and tales from several cultures. Find stories that teach similar lessons or explain the origins of similar things. For example, there are many stories in the oral tradition about the creation of the world, the origin of the seasons, and the reasons that animals behave the ways they do. Using a chart like the one shown, compare the stories you find.

Stories that explain		
Title		
Culture		
Explanation		

Compare Versions Find versions of the Cinderella tale from as many cultures as you can. Compare "In the Land of Small Dragon" with Cinderella-like tales from other cultures, such as China, Egypt, Germany, and Native American groups. Get together with classmates and take turns sharing your findings. Arrange a display of any picture-book versions you find.

Find the Trickster Almost every culture has trickster tales that have been passed from one generation to the next through the oral tradition. Find out more about tricksters in world folklore. Then create a "Wanted" poster for your favorite trickster. Include an illustration, a description of the suspect, the charges against him or her, and any reward offered.

Across Cultures
COMPARING TEXTS

Compare Myths As students are comparing the myths, suggest that they think about the similarities and differences between myths that teach similar lessons. Encourage them to consider possible reasons for the difference. Tell them to consider how the differences might reflect the differences between the cultures.

Compare Versions Students can use a school or public library to find Cinderella-like tales from other cultures. Effective displays will enable viewers to compare the tales easily.

Find the Trickster Since trickster characters are often animals, suggest that students look in books of animal tales for ideas for trickster characters. Aesop's fables are one source of trickster tales, as are many Native American tales, particularly those by Paul Goble.

Standards-Based Objectives
- create a multimedia presentation
- use a written text as a model for writing
- refine a presentation by varying the types of materials
- use consistent form

Introducing the Workshop

Multimedia Presentation Discuss with students multimedia presentations that they have participated in or experienced as members of the audience. Have them think about what types of sounds and visuals these presentations used, and how effective these tools were in creating interest and activity.

Basics in a Box
Presenting the Guidelines and Standards To better understand the assignment, students can refer to the Guidelines and Standards for a successful multimedia presentation. You may also want to share with them the complete guidelines and standards, which describe several levels of proficiency.

 See **Unit Six Resource Book,** p. 34.

 For more instruction on essential communication skills, see McDougal Littell's *Language Network,* Chapter 29.

 Power Presentation

To engage students visually, use **Power Presentation 2,** Multimedia Presentation.

Communication Workshop — Multimedia Presentation

Using text, pictures, and sounds to inform . . .

From Reading to Presenting Wouldn't it be thrilling to explore the island of Crete in the Aegean Sea or the Mayan cities in Guatemala? Geographical explorations can teach us a lot about our history and the people who lived before us. One exciting way to bring this information to an audience is to create a **multimedia presentation** that combines sound and visuals with text. Professors, businesspeople, and others use multimedia presentations with audiences of all kinds.

For Your Portfolio

WRITING PROMPT Create a multimedia presentation about a topic in history or any other topic that interests you.

Purpose: To inform and entertain
Audience: Classmates, family, friends

Basics in a Box

GUIDELINES AND STANDARDS | MULTIMEDIA PRESENTATION

Content

A successful multimedia presentation should

- capture the audience's attention with a strong beginning
- clearly and logically present information
- use media appropriate to the content
- use media from different sources
- end by summarizing the topic and the points made

Delivery

An effective presenter should

- have good posture and maintain eye contact with the audience
- speak so that the audience can hear and understand
- use gestures and body language to get the point across
- use visual aids effectively to help the audience understand the topic

---

LESSON RESOURCES

USING PRINT RESOURCES
Unit Five Resource Book
- Planning and Drafting, p. 29
- Practicing and Delivering, p. 30
- Peer Response Guide, pp. 31–32
- Refining Your Performance, p. 33
- Rubric for Evaluation, p. 34

Writing
- Varying Sentence Openers and Closers, TR 18 (p. 847)

Speaking and Listening
- Writing Your Speech, p. 8 (p. 849)
- Strategies for Delivery, pp. 9, 12–13 (p. 847)
- Using Visuals, pp. 10–11 (pp. 847, 849)

INTEGRATED TECHNOLOGY
Writing Coach CD-ROM
Visit our Web site:
www.mcdougallittell.com

Analyzing a Multimedia Presentation

SPEAKING OPPORTUNITY See the Speaking and Listening Handbook, p. R96 for oral presentation tips.

\<show first visual: clip of Cleopatra movie>

Cleopatra—The Queen, Queen of the Nile, Queen of Kings, New Goddess, Daughter of the Sun-God—these titles only begin to describe the woman who was the last in a long line of Greek royalty to rule Egypt.

\<show second visual: map of Egypt>

Cleopatra was not Egyptian, but she spent her life trying to keep peace within Egypt and trying to stop Egypt from becoming part of the Roman Republic. Although some of her ancestors expanded Egypt's borders and wealth, Egypt was in a terrible state by the time she came to power.

\<show third visual: time line of Cleopatra>

Born around 70 B.C., Cleopatra was in her late teens when her father, the king, died. She reigned from 51 B.C. to her death in 30 B.C. During that time, she shared the throne with two brothers and her son, one after the other. However, Cleopatra was the one in control. Her strength and intelligence protected Egypt from the Romans for 20 years.

\<show fourth visual: picture of Julius Caesar; play cued audiotape of Shakespeare's *Julius Caesar*>

To keep her country safe, she made friends with Roman rulers such as Julius Caesar. He became Cleopatra's ally and helped her regain her throne after a rebellion led by her brother. Then the Roman leader Mark Antony joined forces with Cleopatra. She would eventually marry him. It was Mark Antony who continued to help her keep Egypt independent. Mark Antony, however, lost power in Rome. A man named Octavian then rose to power. He wanted to conquer Egypt. He did not fall for Cleopatra's charm and he took over Egypt in 30 B.C.

Many people don't think of Cleopatra as an important ruler. However, historians say that she was able to do what many of her male ancestors could not. She won the loyalty of Egyptians and gave Egypt peace and independence for 20 years.

\<play cued audiotape of quotation from Shakespeare's play>

Map of Ancient Egypt

GUIDELINES IN ACTION

1 Captures audience attention with interesting video clip

Other Option:
• Begin with a question.

2 Script includes notes about when to include media elements.

3 Visuals help the audience understand the background of the topic.

4 Effectively combines media elements to reinforce the information

5 Details develop and support the main idea.

6 The conclusion reinforces main idea.

7 Leaves audience with a memorable quote

COMMUNICATION WORKSHOP **845**

Teaching the Lesson

Analyzing the Model

Cleopatra Presentation

The student model is the written text for a multimedia presentation on Cleopatra. Notes in the text indicate where the student intends to use visuals and sound effects to enhance and expand the oral presentation. Have students think of a presentation or book report they have given in the past and to consider how they could make it into a multimedia presentation. Then point out the key elements in the student model that correspond to the elements mentioned in the Guidelines in Action.

1 Ask students to think of alternative ways to open the presentation.

Possible Response: They might begin with a question for the audience or with a quote about Cleopatra from an historian or from literature.

2 Tell students that these reminders to yourself can help you feel well-organized and, therefore, less nervous.

3 Ask students to analyze the benefits of having a map of Egypt included in the presentation.

Possible Response: It enables the audience to see where Egypt is; it could help the audience to see Egypt's proximity to the Roman Empire.

4 Point out that the student author uses visuals or sound to reinforce all new information that is discussed.

5 Point out that the use of visuals and sound builds on the facts and details in the presentation.

6 Ask students what effect the conclusion has on the audience.

Possible Response: The paraphrasing of historians lends the conclusion credibility; it reinforces the main idea of the presentation with a statement of fact.

7 Ask why the student might choose to end the presentation this way.

Possible Response: This would allow the presentation to end on a dramatic note as well as with a kind of epitaph.

Planning Your Presentation

Choosing a Subject

If after reading the Idea Bank students have difficulty choosing a subject for their multimedia presentations, suggest they try the following:

- Think of a hobby or sport that you are interested in. Trace its origins and its development into what it is today.
- Research your family history and prepare a multimedia presentation on the story of your family and how they came to be in America.

Planning Your Multimedia Presentation

1 Suggest that, if possible, students talk to an expert on their subject.

2 Encourage students to include unusual or little-known facts about their subject to make it more interesting.

3 Have students talk their subject over with a partner who can help decide what elements need more or less explanation.

4 Suggest that students construct a graph or chart to help them organize the material in a logical manner.

5 Encourage students to brainstorm possible uses for media in their presentations, and then pursue the ideas that seem most available and most effective.

IDEA Bank

1. Your Working Portfolio
Look for ideas in the **Writing** activities that you completed earlier.

2. Be Inventive
Think about inventions that affect your life today. Choose one that you think is important and trace the history of its creation.

3. Go Global
Choose a culture or country that interests you. Dig into the history of the people or place and choose an event, a person, or an era as the topic of your presentation.

Have a question?

See the **Speaking and Listening Handbook.**
Using Visuals, p. R111

Creating Your Multimedia Presentation

❶ Planning Your Presentation

Brainstorm a list of historical figures that fascinate you. **Interview** your relatives to see what important historical events they remember or have witnessed. See the **Idea Bank** in the margin for more suggestions. After you have chosen your topic, follow the steps below.

Steps for Planning Your Multimedia Presentation

▶ **1. Get to know your subject.** Do some general research about your topic by reading an encyclopedia article, searching the Internet, or finding information in a history book.

▶ **2. Narrow your focus.** Ask, What will my audience find most interesting? What is most important about my topic? Once you've decided what part of your subject to focus on, find more facts and details. Check other sources to make sure your facts are correct.

▶ **3. Think about your audience.** How much background information will the audience need to understand your topic? What do they already know about it? How will you capture their interest in the beginning?

▶ **4. Organize your information.** What are some ways you can group the information? In what order should you present it? You might use chronological order, or you might use order of importance.

▶ **5. Decide which media to use in your presentation.** What types of resources are available? Which will help your audience remember the information? Consider the following:

- **Audiotapes and compact discs** add memorable sound effects, such as music and voices.

- **Charts, time lines, posters, slides, and graphs** give the audience a clear way to understand information and to see a visual representation of the ideas you are presenting.

- **Videos** provide both sound and visual effects.

- **Computer programs** can create effective visual aids such as graphs, charts, and drawings. You can also project a slide show, or even project text and graphics, from a computer.

❷ Developing Your Presentation

Once you have gathered your facts and other information, begin putting your media elements into your presentation.

Steps for Developing Your Multimedia Presentation

▷ **1. Write your script.** Include all of the facts you wish to present. Choose the best order for your details. Note where to show visuals or include other media. Write out an explanation for each element if necessary.

▷ **2. Create a strong introduction and conclusion.** Capture your audience's attention in the beginning with a question, an anecdote, or a quotation. You can also begin with music or a powerful image. Reinforce your main idea in your conclusion.

▷ **3. Gather or create your media elements.** Prepare your media elements and find the equipment that you will need. Make sure that charts, time lines, and other visuals are large enough to see from the back of the room and that audiotapes or videos are loud enough.

▷ **4. Look over your media choices.** Be sure that you have chosen the best media for the kind of information you want to give. Lists, charts, and graphs are good for organizing a lot of facts; slides and videos can show powerful images.

❸ Practicing and Presenting

Practice your presentation several times. You should be familiar with your script and feel comfortable handling the media elements.

- **Look at your audience often** during your presentation.
- **Speak loudly and slowly** so that your audience understands what you are saying.
- **Include gestures** to emphasize important points.
- **Work on showing your media elements. Practice with the equipment.**

After rehearsing on your own, invite some friends and family to view your presentation. Use their comments to help you improve your program.

TECH Tool

Use a computer with graphics software to help you create a time line. Add images to show important events for some of the years listed. If you need help, see your school's technology adviser.

Ask Your Peer Reviewers

- What did you learn from my presentation?
- What parts of my presentation did you find most interesting?
- What information was confusing? Why?
- Which media elements added the most to the presentation? Which ones seemed unnecessary?

Developing Your Presentation

1. Suggest that students keep the language in their written texts as natural as possible, since the text will be listened to, not read, by the audience.
2. Encourage students to be creative in their introductions and conclusions.
3. Encourage students to look into all kinds of media resources for their presentations and not to eliminate any ideas until they have explored them.
4. Have students consider the effect that they want their presentations to have. Ask them to look critically at the media choices they have made to make sure they achieve this effect.

 Use **Writing Transparencies,** p. 18, for additional support.

Practicing and Presenting

Suggest that students become familiar enough with their material that they don't have to read it or recite it from memory. Encourage students to use their written text as a prompt and not rely on it completely for information.

Ask Your Peer Reviewer

Suggest that students ask a classmate to view a preliminary run-through of the presentation and give suggestions on ways to improve it. Remind students to use the peer reviewer's feedback when refining their presentations.

 Use the **Speaking and Listening Book,** pp. 9–13, for additional support.

Refining Your Presentation
VARYING THE TYPES OF MATERIALS

Review the changes made in the sample script with students. To help students practice varying the types of materials they use in their presentations, ask volunteers to share portions of their presentations with the class. Have the rest of the class suggest other media choices that would create more variety in the presentation.

Editing and Proofreading
CONSISTENT FORM

Remind students that consistency in the way information is presented helps the audience stay focused on the topic and helps them to understand the material more fully. Have the students explain the changes in the sample.

Reflecting

As they write their reflections, have students consider what they will be more aware of the next time they are part of the audience for a multimedia presentation.

Option
MANAGING THE PAPER LOAD

If students do their initial drafts on a computer, you may wish to consider typing your comments right into their drafts. Students will find typed comments easier to read.

Need revising help?

Review the **Guidelines and Standards**, p. 844

Consider **peer reviewer** comments

Check **Revision Guidelines**, p. R31

SPELLING From Writing

 As you revise your work, look back at the words you misspelled and determine why you made the errors you did. For additional help, refer to the strategies and generalizations in the **Spelling Handbook** on page R26.

Publishing IDEAS

- Dress up as a figure from history. Give your presentation from this figure's point of view.
- Working with your technology adviser or teacher, put your presentation on the computer. Then, with your classmates, set up a tour through history in which the programs are arranged to run chronologically.

🌐 **INTERNET**

Publishing Options
www.mcdougallittell.com

---

❹ Refining Your Presentation

TARGET SKILL ▶ VARYING THE TYPES OF MATERIALS To keep your audience interested, use visuals and audio material to support your main points and to create a balance between your speaking and your presenting.

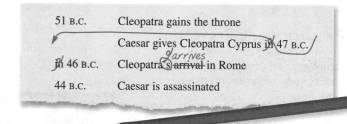

⟨show fourth visual: picture of Julius Caesar; play cued
 To keep her country safe, she made friends with
 audiotape of Shakespeare's Julius Caesar⟩
 Roman rulers such as Julius Caesar. He became

Cleopatra's ally and helped her to regain her throne after

a rebellion led by her brother.

❺ Editing and Proofreading

TARGET SKILL ▶ CONSISTENT FORM When you create a visual, it is very important to present the information consistently. Things like using different formats, changing the order in which dates are presented, and having inconsistent punctuation will confuse the audience. Before you use your visuals, hang them up and look at them from a distance. Ask yourself, Can I read the words? Do I understand the information being presented?

51 B.C.	Cleopatra gains the throne
	Caesar gives Cleopatra Cyprus in 47 B.C.
in 46 B.C.	Cleopatra's ~~arrival~~ arrives in Rome
44 B.C.	Caesar is assassinated

❻ Reflecting

FOR YOUR WORKING PORTFOLIO What did you learn about your topic from doing this multimedia presentation? Which parts of your presentation did you like the most? What would you do differently for your next multimedia presentation? Attach your answers to your script. Save your script in your **Working Portfolio**.

EXPLICIT INSTRUCTION **Revision**

CONSISTENT FORM

Instruction Tell students that inconsistencies in their visuals will distract the audience and weaken the impact of their presentations. Remind them that visuals should enhance a presentation by illustrating information clearly and effectively, and they should help the audience understand the material and make connections more quickly and easily.

Practice Have students find the inconsistencies in the following visual and suggest ways to make it more uniform and understandable.

The City of Pompeii

- Pompeii buried under 12 to 15 feet of ash from Vesuvius—A.D. 79
- nearly 10% of the population perished
- undisturbed by lava deposits for almost 1,700 years

In 1748, the accidental discovery of a buried wall led to the excavation of Pompeii.

Standardized Test Practice

Mixed Review

The Anglo-Saxon culture <u>Ruled England until A.D. 1066.</u> Poems
₍₁₎ from that time period describe the life of the Anglo-Saxons. <u>Some people</u>
<u>thought, the poets</u> had made up details about the way of life. Then in
₍₂₎ 1939 a farmer <u>plowed his field but found clues</u> that hinted at something
₍₃₎ exciting buried in the ground. When archaeologists completed <u>they're</u>
₍₄₎ work they found the remains of a huge ship containing many treasures
that were more than 1,300 years old. It was probably the burial ship of
a king because the center of the ship had <u>many valuable objects: a</u>
<u>sword, a scepter, a harp,</u> gold buckles, silver drinking cups, and a
₍₅₎ helmet. This ship proved that the <u>storys</u> told by the poets truly
₍₆₎ described the Anglo-Saxon culture.

1. How is sentence 1 best written?
   A. ruled England until A.D. 1066
   B. ruled England until a.d. 1066.
   C. ruled england until a.d. 1066.
   D. Correct as is

2. How is sentence 2 best written?
   A. Some people, thought the poets,
   B. Some, people thought the poets
   C. Some people thought the poets
   D. Correct as is

3. How is sentence 3 best written?
   A. plowed his field and found clues
   B. plowed his field then found clues
   C. plowed his field or found clues
   D. Correct as is

4. What is the correct spelling in sentence 4?
   A. there
   B. there're
   C. their
   D. Correct as is

5. How is sentence 5 best written?
   A. many valuable objects a sword, a scepter, a harp,
   B. many valuable objects; a sword, a scepter, a harp,
   C. many valuable objects. A sword, a scepter, a harp,
   D. Correct as is

6. What is the correct spelling in sentence 6?
   A. story's
   B. stories
   C. storyes
   D. Correct as is

Review Your Skills

Use the passage and the questions that follow it to check how well you remember the language conventions you've learned in previous grades.

Self-Assessment

Check your own answers in the **Grammar Handbook.**

Correcting Capitalization, p. R81

Correcting Punctuation, p. R86

Demonstrate how students can eliminate incorrect choices for the first question.

A. This choice uses capitalization correctly for *England* and *A.D.*
B. This choice incorrectly uses lowercase letters for *A.D.*
C. This choice incorrectly uses lowercase letters for *England* and for *A.D.*
D. The original sentence incorrectly capitalizes *ruled.*

Answers:
1. A; 2. C; 3. A; 4. C; 5. D; 6. B

Use **Speaking and Listening Book,** pp. 8–10, for additional support in presenting a multimedia presentation.

UNIT SIX *Reflect* **and Assess**

Objectives
• reflect on and assess student understanding of the unit
• assess and build portfolios

Reflecting on Theme

The Oral Tradition: Tales from the Ancient World to To[

In this unit, you discovered that tales from the past explore universal themes. Across cultures and generations, these stories continue to delight, inspire, and teach readers and listeners. To show what you have learned, complete one or more of the following options.

Reflecting on Theme

OPTION 1

A successful response will
• identify at least five heroic characters from the folk tales in this unit.
• include a web showing the qualities and actions of the most heroic character.
• present a brief essay explaining why the student chose the character he or she did.

OPTION 1

Studying Heroes With a partner, identify at least five characters who act as heroes in the folklore you have read. Then choose the character who you think displays the most heroic qualities. Make a web like the one shown. On one side, list this character's heroic traits. On the other side of the web, list the actions taken by the character that demonstrate these qualities. Use your web to help you write a brief essay explaining why you chose the character you did.

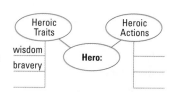

OPTION 2

A successful response will
• identify themes evident in the folk tales in this unit.
• explore one lesson from the unit and explain why the student thinks it stands out the most.

OPTION 2

Self Assessment Use the **Table of Contents** for Unit Six on pages 770–771 to recall what themes are present in the folklore you've read. What one lesson in the tales stands out the most? Why? Respond in your **READER'S NOTEBOOK.**

Portfolio Building

Literature Connections
Students should evaluate the pieces in their Working Portfolios and choose one that represents their highest quality work for their Presentation Portfolios.

As students write the note to attach to the item, remind them to respond to the literature that inspired the writing and express their reasons for selecting this piece.

Portfolio Building

• **Making Connections** Select an example of the work you did for the Interdisciplinary Projects on pages 842–843. In a note, comment on what you enjoyed about creating the work. Explain how the literature you read inspired you. Add the example and the note to your **Presentation Portfolio.**

• **Setting Goals** As you completed the activities in this unit, you probably found certain selections that you really liked. Which author's work would you like to find out more about? Which cultures are you curious about? Which would you like to continue to explore? Write your goals for further reading and research in your **READER'S NOTEBOOK.**

Setting Goals
Students may wish to look back through the unit to help them identify the authors and cultures they want to learn more about.

Introduction to Mythology

The gods and goddesses, warriors, and heroes of world mythology appear and reappear in literature and films. Here are their origins—presented by scholars and storytellers, from Bullfinch to San Souci. This volume begins with Greek and Roman myths, and travels the globe. Maps, diagrams, and time lines add context. Part of the *NexText* series from McDougal Littell, the book comes with online activities at **www.nextext.com.**

Other Collections

Cinderella
COLLECTED BY JUDY SIERRA
Cinderella in many different cultures
(*Links to* **In the Land of Small Dragon**)

Moon Was Tired of Walking on Air
RETOLD BY NATALIA M. BELTING
Origin myths of South America
(*Links to* **The Disobedient Child**)

Fairy Tales from the Brothers Grimm
COLLECTED BY NEIL PHILLIP
An illustrated edition of these classic tales
(*Links to* **King Thrushbeard**)

The Girl Who Married the Moon
TOLD BY JOSEPH BRUCHAC & GAYLE ROSS
Legends of Native American heroines
(*Links to* **Where the Girl Rescued Her Brother**)

A Ring of Tricksters
RETOLD BY VIRGINIA HAMILTON
Tales of wit and cunning
(*Links to* **Why Monkeys Live in Trees** and
The Frog Who Wanted to Be a Singer)

Informative Nonfiction

Trinidad and Tobago
BY PATTI UROSEVICH
(*Links to* **The Bamboo Beads**)

The Puerto Ricans
BY JEROME J. ALIOTTA
(*Links to* **The Legend of Hummingbird**)

Ancient China
BY BRIAN WILLIAMS
(*Links to* **The Living Kuan-yin**)

Be a Friend: The Story of African American Music in Song, Words, and Pictures
BY LEOTHA STANLEY
(*Links to* **The Frog Who Wanted to Be a Singer**)

The Cheyennes
BY VIRGINIA DRIVING HAWK SNEVE
(*Links to* **Where the Girl Rescued Her Brother**)

Other Media

American Fairy Tales
From Rip Van Winkle to the Rootabaga Stories
Audio Bookshelf (AUDIOCASSETTE)

Jim Henson's The Storyteller
A storyteller recounts legendary tales.
Jim Henson Productions (VIDEO SERIES)

Legends of the Americas
Illustrated legends of the Maya, Aztec, and Inca
Troll Associates (CD-ROM)

Just So Stories
Kipling's pourquoi tales
Blackstone Audio Books (AUDIOCASSETTE)

My Land Sings: Stories from the Rio Grande
RETOLD BY RUDOLFO ANAYA
Folk tales of the Southwestern United States

The Language of Literature
Student Resource Bank

Reading for Different Purposes

Having a clear purpose for reading can help you better remember and understand what you read. You may be reading for relaxation and pleasure. Perhaps you need to read for information so you can pass a test. Maybe you need to read directions to program your VCR or to fill out an application. You will need specific reading strategies for every type of reading you do. This Reading Handbook will help you become a better reader of all kinds of materials.

Reading Literature

Forms: stories, plays, poems, memoirs, biographies, some nonfiction

Purpose for reading: for pleasure, for increased understanding

Strategies for Reading

- **Predict**
- **Visualize**
- **Connect**
- **Question**
- **Clarify**
- **Evaluate**

See page S3 for details about each strategy.

Reading for Information

Forms: newspapers, magazines, reference works, online information, textbooks

Purpose for reading: to be informed

Strategies for Reading

- **Look for text organizers such as titles, subheads, graphics, and charts.**
- **Notice the organization of the text.**
- **Look for connections to something you already know.**
- **Read, reread, and answer questions to increase your understanding.**

See pages R4–R11 for help with these strategies.

Critical Reading

I'm not a very good athlete. I would usually rather read a book than hit a ball around. Even so, I believe that it would be a terrible mistake for the Board of Education to cut the physical education program at our school.

Gym class is a good way for students to burn off energy. Even though I'm not the greatest at sports, I like to get outside and run around. After gym, I'm relaxed and can concentrate better on my classes.

Forms: newspaper editorials, opinion statements, advertisements, political ads, letters

Purpose for reading: to be informed, to make a decision

Strategies for Reading

- **Look for the author's opinion on the issue.**
- **Examine the supporting evidence the author uses.**
- **Ask yourself: does the author use enough evidence? Is the evidence reliable?**

See pages R12–R16 for detailed examples.

Functional Reading

Forms: applications, instruction manuals, schedules, product information, technical directions

Purpose for reading: to make decisions and solve problems

Strategies for Reading

- **Skim the whole piece.**
- **Read the information in the order presented.**
- **Look carefully at any drawings or pictures.**
- **Reread when the meaning is unclear.**

See pages R17–R19 for examples.

Methods of Reading

When you read something for the first time, review material for a test, or search for specific information, you use different methods of reading. The following techniques are useful with all kinds of reading materials.

Skimming When you run your eyes quickly over a text to look at headings, graphic features, and highlighted words, you are skimming. Skimming is particularly useful for reading and understanding informational materials.

Scanning To find a specific piece of information in a text, such as the date of a battle, use scanning. Place a card under the first line of a page and move it down slowly. Look for key words and phrases in each line.

In-Depth Reading In-depth reading involves asking questions, taking notes, looking for main ideas, and drawing conclusions as you read slowly and carefully. Use this type of reading for literary works and textbooks.

Reading for Information

Informational materials such as textbooks, magazine articles, newspaper articles, and online text, use special features to show information. These features include headings, charts, and special type. When you read informational materials you need to know how to use these features to get information. Listed below are strategies that will help you read and understand any kind of informational text.

Text Organizers

Writers use special features, such as headings, large or dark type, pictures and captions, or drawings, to show you the most important information. The pages here show how these features might appear in a textbook. You can find these features in all kinds of informational materials. Use them to help you understand and remember what you read.

Strategies for Reading

A First, look at the **title** and any **subheads**. These will tell you the main idea of the lesson.

B Many textbooks have one or more **objectives** or **key terms** at the beginning of each lesson. Keep these in mind as you read. They will help you identify the most important details. You may also want to read any **questions** at the end of the lesson to find out what you'll need to learn.

B.C. A.D.

4000   3000   2000   1000

LESSON 1

A The Gift of the Nile

B THINKING FOCUS

What did the ancient Egyptians accomplish because of the "gifts of the Nile"?

D Key Terms

- cataract
- delta
- papyrus
- dynasty

➤ *In this scene at Aswan in south Egypt, the fertile riverbank contrasts sharply with the barren desert.*

186

Grain was scarce, and fruit was dried up. People robbed their neighbors. Babies were crying, and old men were sad as they sat on the ground with their legs bent and their arms folded.

So begins an ancient legend about the Nile River. The Egyptians depended on the flooding of the Nile to water their fields. Some years there were "high Niles," when crops grew well and people had plenty to eat. Other years there were "low Niles," when the fields became dry, baked by the sun, and few had enough food.

The legend tells of a time of low Niles, when Egypt had seven years of famine. This time fell during the reign of King Zoser in the 2600s B.C. The king watched the crops withering, and he saw his people starving. He turned to his

chief advisor, Imhotep, fo... The answer was to learn t... of the god of the Nile so t... pray to him, said Imhotep... he told the king that the N... in two caverns below a te... Egypt's southern border. ... Khnum (*kuh NOOM*) cor... the floodgates and let the ... toward Egypt.

Later that night, Zose... dreamed that Khnum spo... him: "I am Khnum. I kno... Nile. When it covers the f... gives them life. Now the N... pour over the land withou... ping. Plants will grow, bo... down with fruit. The years... vation will be over."

When the king awoke,... the people to honor Khnu... ing him a portion of each ... harvest. The "high Niles"... and the years of hunger e...

Chapter 7

Instruction Ask students to describe what they see on the textbook spread above besides the text of the chapter. (*map, photographs, captions, key terms*) Explain that these are features used in many informational materials—such as textbooks, magazine and newspaper articles, and online articles—to give readers additional information. Say, "The text of an article or book is an important source of information, but special features are also

important. These features can help you preview an article and better understand the main text of an article." Read aloud the lettered Strategies for Reading. After each, ask a volunteer to identify or read aloud that feature in the textbook spread. Explain that some of these features, such as objectives, key terms, and questions, are not usually found in newspaper, magazine, or Internet articles, but most of the other features are.

Practice Have pairs of students choose one of the features you discussed and write a short description of its purpose.

Possible Responses: Responses will vary but should show an understanding of the features found in the textbook spread.

C Look at the **visuals**—photographs, illustrations, maps, timelines, or other graphics—and read their **captions**. These will help you understand what you are about to read.

D Don't forget about the **key terms**. These are often boldfaced or underlined where they appear in the text. Be sure you understand what they mean.

E Examine **maps**. Read their **titles**, **captions**, and **legends**. Make certain you know what the map shows and how it relates to the text.

Geography of the Nile **A**

...ypt is on the northeastern ...of Africa. Look at the map ...and locate Egypt on the ...in the inset. Now ...e Nile River on ...ge map. ...e Nile is Egypt's ...e. Without it, the ...ould be mostly ...It is the longest ...n the world, trav- ...over 4,000 miles ...ts source in the ...and marshes of central ...to its outlet in the Mediter- ...a Sea.

...six places along the Nile's ...g course, stone cliffs and ...ers force its waters through ...w channels. The rushing ...forms waterfalls and rapids ...**cataracts.** The first cataract ...d the southern boundary of ...t Egypt. Find it on the map. ...om the first cataract, the Nile ...north for about 600 miles. ...ost of this journey, it flows as ...e river. But just south of ...s today Cairo *(KY roh)*, it di- ...nto many small channels and ...s. This triangle of marshy ...ds is called the **delta.** **D**

...hts and Floods
...om the air much of the Nile ...ike a brown snake wriggling ...across a vast desert. Its nar- ...anks are green with crops ...alms. Abruptly they turn into ...—red stones and hot sands. ...eople who lived there 4,000 ...ago called their fertile, dark- ...valley the Black Land. The ...was the Red Land. ...ypt gets almost no rain. The ...s on the east and west are

parts of the Sahara, the desert that covers much of northern Africa. Desert on two sides, mountains on the south, and the Mediterranean Sea on the north—all of these natural barriers iso- lated ancient Egypt and thus protected it from invaders.

In this desert land, Egyptians depended on the Nile for water and for life. The amount of water the Nile carried on its journey to

◄ *The Egyptians used stone nilometers like this one to measure the yearly flood level of the Nile.*

▼ *Some have compared the shape of Egypt with that of a lotus flower. Can you see the flower's blos- som and stem?*

Ancient Egypt

ASIA MINOR
CYPRUS
Mediterranean Sea
Dead Sea
LOWER EGYPT
Memphis
SINAI PENINSULA
UPPER EGYPT
ARABIA
LIBYAN DESERT
Thebes
Red Sea
First Cataract
Tropic of Cancer
Second Cataract
NUBIA
NUBIAN DESERT
Third Cataract
Napata
KUSH
Fourth Cataract
Fifth Cataract
Meroe
Sixth Cataract

Fertile area
Desert
Cataract

0   50   100 mi.
0 50 100 km
Mercator Projection

187

More Examples

To learn how to gather information by using special features in other kinds of informational materials, see the pages listed below.

For examples of **newspaper articles**, see pages 201, 340, and 714.

For examples of **magazine articles**, see pages 48, 145, 388, 462, and 588.

For an example of an **Internet article**, see page 260.

Patterns of Organization

Reading any type of writing is easier if you understand how it is organized. A writer organizes ideas in a structure, or pattern, that helps the reader see how the ideas are related. The following are four important structures:

• main idea and supporting details
• chronological order
• comparison and contrast
• cause and effect

This page contains an overview of the four structures, which you will learn about in more detail on pages R7–R11. Each structure has been drawn as a map, or graphic organizer, to help you see how the ideas are related.

Main Idea and Supporting Details
The main idea of a paragraph or a longer piece of writing is its most important point. Supporting details give more information about the main idea.

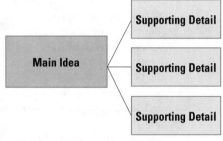

Chronological Order
Writing that is organized in chronological order presents events in the order in which they happened.

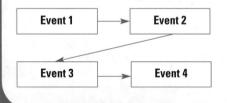

Comparison and Contrast
Comparison-and-contrast writing explains how two or more subjects are similar and how they are different.

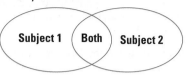

Cause and Effect
Cause-and-effect writing explains the relationship between events. The cause is the first event. The effect happens as a result of the cause. A cause may have more than one effect, and an effect may have more than one cause.

Single Cause with Multiple Effects

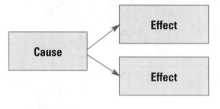

Multiple Causes with Single Effect

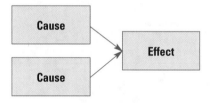

Cause-and-Effect Chain

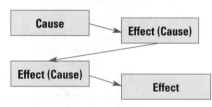

Main Idea and Supporting Details

The **main idea** of a paragraph is the basic point you should remember from your reading. The **supporting details** in the paragraph tell more about the main idea. The main idea is often the first or last sentence of a paragraph, but it can appear anywhere in a paragraph. Sometimes, the main idea is not stated directly but is suggested by the details that are provided. This is called an **implied main idea.**

Strategies for Reading

- To find the **main idea**, ask, "What is this paragraph about?"
- To find **supporting details**, ask, "What details in the paragraph tell me more about the main idea?"

MODEL

Main Idea as the First Sentence

Main Idea

The ancient Egyptians originally buried their kings, or pharaohs, in huge pyramids. **The preserved body of the pharaoh was buried in a special room in the pyramid. The pyramid was filled with food, clothing, and other items the pharaoh might need in the afterlife.**

Supporting Details

MODEL

Main Idea as the Last Sentence

Supporting Details

The Egyptians had special reasons for believing that the god Osiris would weigh their hearts when they died. People who had committed many sins would have heavy hearts. Any heart that was heavier than a feather would be eaten up by a fierce beast. To have a light heart, a person would have to live a good life. **The Egyptians took weighing of hearts seriously because it determined whether they would have eternal life.**

Main Idea

MODEL

Implied Main Idea

Implied main idea: The Egyptians gave the world many important inventions.

The Egyptians developed a writing system called hieroglyphics. In this system, pictures stood for ideas. They also invented papyrus, which was a new and better writing surface than stone. The Egyptians created a number system and a way of using numbers to make calculations. They developed a very accurate calendar for measuring time. Finally, they discovered a scientific way of treating diseases.

PRACTICE AND APPLY

MODEL

In 1352 B.C., the young Egyptian pharoah Tutankhamen was buried in a tomb filled with splendid golden objects. In one of the mysteries of history, the tomb lay hidden until November 26, 1922. On that date archaeologist Howard Carter and his wealthy employer, Lord Carnarvon, finally succeeded in locating the tomb after years of failure. Their discovery is one of the greatest events of modern archaeology.

Read the model above and do the following activities.

1. Identify the main idea of the paragraph. Is it stated or implied? If it is stated, where does it appear in the paragraph?
2. List three details that support the main idea.
3. Show the structure of this paragraph using a main idea chart like the one on page R6.

Practice and Apply
Possible Responses:

1. Their discovery is one of the greatest events of modern archaeology. It is a stated main idea that appears as the last sentence in the paragraph.
2. Tutankhamen was buried in 1352 B.C. Tomb was hidden until 1922. Carter and Carnarvon succeeded in finding the tomb after years of failure.
3. See below.

3.

Main idea
Their discovery is one of the greatest events of modern archaeology.

Supporting detail
Tutankhamen was buried in 1352 B.C.

Supporting detail
The tomb was hidden until 1922

Supporting detail
Tomb found after years of looking.

Practice and Apply
Possible Responses:

1. later, after 2,500 years, in 479, 100 years later, in 289 B.C., in 221 B.C.

2. 551 B.C.: Confucius born

   548 B.C.: father dies

   536 B.C.: heart set on learning

   479 B.C.: Confucius dies

   c. 379 B.C.: Mencius spreads Confucius's ideas

   289 B.C.: Mencius dies

   289 B.C.: Hsun-tzu carries on Confucius's ideas

   221 B.C.: Ch'in Dynasty begins

3. See below.

Chronological Order

Chronological, or time, order presents ideas in the order in which they happened. Historical events are usually presented in chronological order. The steps of a process may also be presented in time order.

Strategies for Reading

- Look for the individual events that are described. These will often be presented in separate paragraphs.

- Look for words and phrases that show **time,** such as *a year ago, next week, in 1717 B.C.,* and *later.*

- Look for words that signal **order,** such as *first, afterward, then, before, finally,* and *next.*

Events

Time phrases

The great Chinese teacher, Confucius, was born in 551 B.C. His father died when he was three years old. Although Confucius came from a very poor family, he studied hard and became well-educated.

By the time he was 15, in 536 B.C., Confucius's heart was set on learning. In his 30s, Confucius started his teaching career. He later became one of the most important teachers in history. One of his teachings was that people should treat each other the way they would like to be treated. His teachings still seem wise after 2,500 years.

When Confucius died in 479 B.C., he had many followers. About 100 years later, one of those followers, Mencius, began spreading Confucius' ideas. Mencius extended these ideas and added some of his own. He taught that people are basically good and that everyone has equal value. For that reason, he

believed that rulers are no better than their subjects. A good king, he said, must treat his people well.

After Mencius died in 289 B.C., Hsun-tzu carried on Confucius' teachings. Hsun-tzu lived from about 300 to 230 B.C. He did not agree with Mencius that people were basically good. Instead, he taught that human nature was evil. He did believe that education and strong laws and governments could help people become good. Some people say that Hsun-tzu's teachings about strong government later helped the dictator Shih Huang Ti to conquer China and set up the Ch'in Dynasty in 221 B.C.

PRACTICE AND APPLY

After reading the model, do the following activities.

1. Look at the time phrases that are highlighted in the model. Then list three other words or phrases in the model that signal time.

2. List all the events in the history of Confucius and his followers that are mentioned in the model.

3. Create a time line on your paper. The first event should be the birth of Confucius in 551 B.C. The last event should be the beginning of the Ch'in Dynasty in 221 B.C. Add each of the other events you listed in question 2 to your time line.

3.

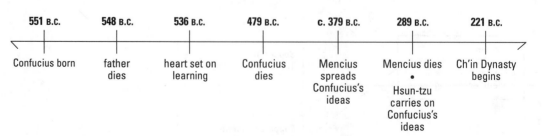

551 B.C.	548 B.C.	536 B.C.	479 B.C.	c. 379 B.C.	289 B.C.	221 B.C.
Confucius born	father dies	heart set on learning	Confucius dies	Mencius spreads Confucius's ideas	Mencius dies • Hsun-tzu carries on Confucius's ideas	Ch'in Dynasty begins

Cause and Effect

Cause-and-effect writing explains how events are related. A **cause** is an event that brings about another event. An **effect** is something that happens as a result of the first event. Cause-and-effect writing usually has one of three organizations:

1. starting with a cause and explaining the effect

2. starting with the effect and explaining the cause

3. describing a chain of causes and effects

Strategies for Reading

- To find the **effect** or **effects**, ask, "What happened?"

- To find the **cause** or **causes**, ask, "Why did it happen?"

- Look for **signal words** such as *cause, effect, because, consequently, as a result, for that reason, so,* and *since.*

MODEL

Cause

We are all affected by the weather in one way or another. Certainly we complain about it often enough. Our early human ancestors were affected even more than we are today. Around 2.5 million years ago, the earth entered the Ice Age, which lasted until 12,000 years ago. During that time, temperatures on the earth went through great changes. Periods of extreme cold alternated with warmer times.

Signal words

Effects

Early human beings did not have an easy time adjusting to these extreme changes in temperature. Because they did not have fur to protect them from the cold, they had to learn ways to stay warm. Over thousands of years, early people discovered how to create fire. Later, they learned how to sew animal skins together to make clothes.

The Ice Age had other effects on early humans, too. When the glaciers formed, they took water away from the oceans. As the level of the water dropped, land was uncovered. Some of this land connected continents that had been separated for hundreds of thousands of years. One of these land bridges connected Asia with North America. Others connected Australia and the islands in Southwest Asia. Consequently, people used these land bridges to reach and settle new parts of the world.

Scientists think that something even more dramatic may have resulted from the Ice Age. They say that facing the challenges of huge temperature changes caused the brains of humans to grow larger and more complex. With these big brains, our ancestors were able to develop language. Once people had language, they began to develop societies and cultures. So, if the Ice Age hadn't happened, we wouldn't be the human beings we are, and we certainly wouldn't be able to complain about the weather.

PRACTICE AND APPLY

Read the model on this page and then do the following activities.

1. List four effects on human beings that resulted from the Ice Age.

2. Two words that signal causes and effects already have been highlighted in the passage. Find and list three more.

3. Create a chart on your paper that shows a single cause with multiple effects, similar to the chart on page R6. Fill in the cause and the effects described in the model.

Practice and Apply
Possible Responses:

1. discovered fire
   learned to sew clothes
   used land bridges to settle new lands
   developed larger brains
   developed language

2. consequently, resulted, caused, so

3.

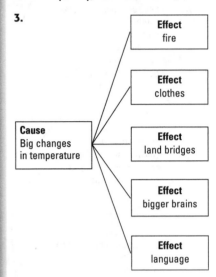

Practice and Apply

A. Possible Responses:

1. Sparta and Athens
2. unlike, like, both, in contrast,
3. education, military service
4.

Sparta
- unhealthy babies left to die
- boys sent away to school at age 7
- both boys and girls trained in physical education
- all men serve in military
- girls marry by age 15 and stay at home

Both
- boys are educated
- military service for men
- girls marry by age 15 and stay at home

Athens
- only wealthy boys get an education
- girls sometimes left to die
- girls kept at home
- men serve two years in army
- girls marry by age 15

Reading Handbook

Comparison and Contrast

Comparison-and-contrast writing explains how two different subjects are alike and different. There are two main ways in which this type of writing is organized. In a **subject-by-subject** organization, the writer describes all the features of one subject and then all the features of the other subject.

Subject by Subject
Subject A: Toads
Feature 1: Where they live
Feature 2: How they look
Subject B: Frogs
Feature 1: Where they live
Feature 2: How they look

In a **feature-by-feature** organization, the writer describes the features one by one, first in one subject and then in the other.

Feature by Feature
Feature 1: Where they live
Subject A: Toads
Subject B: Frogs
Feature 2: How they look
Subject A: Toads
Subject B: Frogs

Strategies for Reading

1. Look for one or two sentences that explain exactly what subjects are being compared.

2. Look for words and phrases that signal **comparison**, such as *like, similarly, both, also,* and *in the same way.*

3. Look for words and phrases that signal **contrast**, such as *unlike, on the other hand, in contrast,* and *however.*

4. As you read, ask yourself these questions: What subjects are being compared? Why are they being compared? How are these subjects alike and different?

MODEL

Subjects
Comparison Words

Sparta and **Athens** were the two biggest city-states in ancient Greece. Although **both** were Greek, life in the two cities was very different.

Every Spartan baby was checked over by a government official right after it was born. If the baby was healthy, it went home with its parents. If not, it was taken to a cave and left there to die.

Spartan boys were sent away from their homes to be educated when they were 7 years old. Both girls and boys were trained in physical education. Boys also had military training.

When they became adults at age 18, Spartan boys entered the army. They served there until they were 30. At that time, they became full citizens of Sparta. Girls usually got married by the time they were 15. They then raised children and took care of their homes.

Contrast Words

Babies born in Athens, **on the other hand**, were luckier. At least boys were. They were not left to die. Girls were not as valuable as boys to the Athenians. Many of them were left at the city gates. Sometimes, people who passed by rescued the baby girls and raised them.

Unlike Spartan children, not all Athenian young people got an education. Only wealthy boys went to school. There, like Spartan boys, they studied physical education. They also learned the arts, reading, writing, and mathematics, something that did not happen in Sparta. Girls stayed home and learned skills and poetry from their mothers. As in Sparta, many Athenian girls married by age 15.

EXPLICIT INSTRUCTION Comparison and Contrast

Instruction Hold up two different books, two different shoes, or two other items that are both similar and different. Ask students to tell how the two items are similar and different. Then tell the class that writers compare and contrast ideas, people, and events in their writing to highlight similarities and differences. Tell students that recognizing this pattern of organization when they read will help them better understand the writer's ideas. Go over the "Comparison and Contrast" lesson. Then have

pairs of students copy blank subject-by-subject and feature-by-feature charts in their notebooks and fill them in by comparing two objects, such as their shirts, sweaters, or shoes. Invite pairs to share their charts.

Practice Have students work in pairs to complete the Practice and Apply section on page R11.

Possible Responses: See the side column on page R11 for possible responses.

Both Spartan and Athenian men served in the army. In contrast to Spartans, though, Athenians served for only two years. Women in both societies devoted themselves to their homes and families.

PRACTICE AND APPLY

A. Read the model and then do the following activities.

1. What two subjects are being compared?

2. Several words and phrases that signal similarities and differences have been highlighted. List at least three more from the last part of the model.

3. One of the features discussed in this model is the fate of a baby in Sparta and in Athens. List the two other features that are discussed.

4. Create a Venn diagram like the one on page R6. Fill in the similarities and differences between young people growing up in Sparta and Athens.

B. Read the model below and then do the activities that follow.

MODEL

Limericks are a lot of fun to read. Two of my favorites are by Ogden Nash and Edward Lear. They are on page 565 of this book.

Both limericks are short poems. They have different numbers of lines, though. Ogden Nash's limerick about Dougal MacDougal has five lines. On the other hand, Edward Lear's limerick about the old man with a beard has only four lines.

The limericks have similar rhyme schemes, though. The first, second, and last lines of each limerick rhyme. In Nash's poem, the third and fourth lines rhyme. If you split the third line of Lear's limerick in half, those two lines also rhyme.

Another similarity between the limericks is that each one is about a man who is sort of strange. The man in Nash's poem makes music through his nose. The one in Lear's limerick has birds living in his beard.

The characters in the two limericks have some differences, though. Dougal MacDougal in Nash's poem is a real go-getter. He discovers how to save money by making musical sneezes. The man with the beard in Lear's poem, however, is just plain lazy. He is so lazy that he just sits there while birds settle down under his chin.

One basic thing about these two limericks is exactly the same, though. They both made me laugh.

1. What two subjects are being compared?

2. List all the words and phrases in the model that signal similarities and differences.

3. Below are two ways that comparison-and-contrast writing can be organized. After studying these organizational patterns, choose the one that fits this model. Copy the correct chart on your paper and fill in the details of the model's subjects and features.

Subject-by-Subject Organization	Feature-by-Feature Organization
Subject 1 _____	Feature 1 _____
Feature 1	Subject 1
Feature 2	Subject 2
Subject 2 _____	Feature 2 _____
Feature 1	Subject 1
Feature 2	Subject 2

4. Compare this model with the one on the previous page. Are they organized the same way or differently? Which one is organized by subject? Which is organized by feature?

Practice and Apply
B. Possible Responses:

1. Limericks by Ogden Nash and Edward Lear

2. both, different, similar, similarity, differences, however

3.

Feature-by-Feature Organization
Feature 1: Numbers of lines
Subject 1: Ogden Nash
Subject 2: Edward Lear
Feature 2: Rhyme schemes
Subject 1: Ogden Nash
Subject 2: Edward Lear
Feature 3: Subject
Subject 1: Ogden Nash
Subject 2: Edward Lear
Feature 4: Differences in the characters
Subject 1: Ogden Nash
Subject 2: Edward Lear

4. No. They are organized differently. The model about Sparta and Athens is organized by subject. The model about Nash and Lear is organized by feature.

Critical Reading: Persuasion

Everyday you encounter writing whose purpose is to inform and persuade you. This writing can take many forms, such as speeches, newspaper editorials, advertisements, and billboards. Good readers read critically, or question what they read. They make sure the details presented are accurate and truly support the author's main ideas.

What Is an Argument?

Much of the information you read is designed to persuade you to think a certain way. This type of writing presents an **argument** for believing or doing something.

An effective argument clearly states a position on an issue and supports it with good evidence and logical reasoning. It also presents opposing views and explains their weaknesses.

Strategies for Reading

Keep these questions in mind when you are trying to tell the difference between an effective argument and a poor one.

- Does the author state an **opinion** clearly?
- Does the author **support** that opinion with **evidence**—reasons, examples, facts, and the opinions of experts?
- Does the author discuss the **concerns** of the **audience** (his or her readers)?

MODEL

Author's position — I'm not a very good athlete. I would usually rather read a book than hit a ball around. Even so, I believe that it would be a terrible mistake for the Board of Education to cut the physical education program at our school.

Reason — Gym class is a good way for students to burn off energy. Even though I'm not the greatest at sports, I like to get outside and run around. After gym, I'm relaxed and can concentrate better on my classes.

Reason — The exercise that we get in gym class also helps keep us healthy. My pediatrician, Dr. Alice Abrahams, says, "Preteens need regular exercise to develop strong, healthy bodies. If young people establish good exercise habits early, they'll establish a positive pattern for the rest of their lives."

Evidence supporting the author's position

Audience's concern — Some parents and teachers believe that gym classes should be cut so students have more time for math, science, and reading.

Author's response — However, it makes no sense to take away one subject that students need—physical education—to add more time for other needed subjects. Instead, the school should consider offering before-school or after-school tutoring for students who are falling behind.

Physical education has a long history as a part of an educational system. The Greeks knew that a good education develops both the body and the mind. The basis of a Greek child's schooling was strict physical training. The Greeks gave us many great thinkers, but they also gave us the Olympic Games. The fact that we still hold the Olympic Games shows that sports and physical fitness are valuable.

Restatement of the author's position — Our schools teach history, so they should learn from it, too. Cutting out physical education would be a huge step backward.

Critical Reading: Persuasion

Instruction Ask students, "If you wanted to persuade a friend to go with you to the movies, what evidence or reasons would you give to make your friend want to go?" Explain that writing that presents evidence and logical reasoning to convince readers to hold a certain opinion or come to a particular conclusion is called persuasive writing. Explain that in persuasive writing, an argument is the evidence and logic the writer uses to persuade readers. A good argument includes sound reasons,

examples, and facts. A poor argument does not present evidence, or presents evidence that is weak, untrustworthy, or inaccurate. Say, "It is the reader's job to evaluate a writer's evidence in order to decide whether to agree or disagree with the writer's opinion." Go over the "What Is an Argument?" lesson with students.

Practice Have students answer the following questions about the model in their own words.

What is the author's position? What evidence is presented to support the position? Does the writer present a good argument? Tell students to support their last answer with evidence from the model.

Possible Responses: Students' responses should be clearly based on the model and be written in their own words. Their assertions about the model should be supported with examples.

Evaluating Evidence

Reasons, facts, examples, and expert opinions are all types of **evidence** an author might use for support. You must **evaluate,** or carefully think about, the evidence an author presents. Use these questions to help you evaluate evidence.

- **Where are the facts?** Make sure you know the difference between facts and opinions. The facts should support the author's statement or opinion.

- **Is the information accurate?** The facts and examples should be up-to-date. The information should come from a reliable source, such as a reference book or a government agency.

- **Does the writer include expert opinions if needed?** An expert is someone who has closely studied a certain topic. A school nurse is an expert on children's nutrition and health. A friend who uses computers is not necessarily a computer expert.

- **Is the evidence adequate?** There should be adequate, or enough, evidence to support what the author is trying to say.

- **Is the evidence appropriate?** To be appropriate, the evidence should relate to the topic and not include poor reasoning or misleading information.

Examples of Poor Evidence
In these examples the evidence lacks specific, up-to-date, reliable facts and reasons.

> Unsupported opinion:
> **Staying in shape is really important.**
>
> Outdated information:
> **A study from 1982 shows that most American children get little exercise.**
>
> Nonexpert opinion:
> **My aunt is very smart, and she says physical education classes are needed.**

Examples of Effective Evidence
These examples show evidence that is

> Reliable source:
> **According to the President's Council on Physical Fitness and Sports, people of all ages and abilities should participate in sports and physical activities.**
>
> Recent information:
> **In October 2000, the Centers for Disease Control said that obesity is one of the 10 biggest health threats of the next 100 years.**
>
> Expert opinion:
> **Nutrition professor Marion Nestle says it is vital that physical education programs get enough money.**

Persuasive Appeals

appropriate and reliable.

Some authors try to persuade you to agree with them by using misleading techniques and false information instead of reliable evidence. They try to make you respond with your emotions instead of with clear thinking. This kind of persuasion is called **propaganda.** The following emotional appeals are all forms of propaganda.

Name-Calling
Name-calling involves attacking a person's character or personality instead of focusing

> Name-calling:
> **Only an idiot would suggest that we get rid of our school's physical education program.**
>
> Balanced statement:
> **Eliminating our school's physical education program could be bad for students' health because they would exercise less often.**

EXPLICIT INSTRUCTION **Evaluating Evidence**

Instruction Remind students that a sound or good argument is made up of solid evidence, such as reasons, facts, examples, and the opinions of experts. A poor argument includes no evidence, information that is inaccurate or out of date, or opinions from people who are not experts. Explain that in order to decide whether an argument includes solid evidence, readers must evaluate the evidence. Go over the lesson titled "Evaluating Evidence." Remind students that a good argument uses enough evidence—not just one fact but several—and evidence that is strong.

Practice List the following phrases on the board: a receptionist at a kennel, a veterinarian, a dog owner. Ask students which person would be the most reliable source of information on dog behavior. Discuss students' responses. Then ask students whether the evidence in the model on page R12 seems adequate and appropriate.

Possible Responses: Students should say that a veterinarian would have the best scientific background in dog behavior. They should recognize that the evidence in the model on page R12 includes facts, reasons, and expert opinions; as a result, the evidence is both adequate and appropriate.

Snob Appeal

A writer who uses snob appeal tries to convince readers that if they agree with the stated opinion, they are smarter or otherwise better than people who disagree with it.

> **Snob appeal:**
> I'm sure that intelligent people will agree with me and fight to preserve physical education.
>
> **Balanced statement:**
> Doctors and nutritionists agree that everyone needs regular exercise. Gym classes are an effective way to make sure that students get enough physical activity.

Bandwagon Appeal

Unlike snob appeal, bandwagon appeal pressures readers to think as others are thinking. A bandwagon appeal basically says, "Everyone else believes this, so why don't you?"

> **Bandwagon appeal:**
> Everyone knows that gym classes are essential for students' health.
>
> **Balanced statement:**
> Cutting physical education classes could cause more problems than it solves because it would reduce students' opportunities to exercise.

Evaluating Reasoning

Some arguments seem strong at first but are based on *fallacious*, or false, reasoning. Here are some examples to watch out for.

Overgeneralization

An overgeneralization is a statement that is so broad that it cannot possibly be true. Overgeneralizations often include the words *all, none, everyone, no one, any,* and *anyone.*

> **Overgeneralization:**
> All kids love gym class.
>
> **Logical statement:**
> Most kids enjoy exercising, even if they're not good at team sports.

Unsupported Inference

An **inference** is a logical guess or conclusion. Authors and other people, including you, make inferences by combining what they know with new information. For example, if you see an unfamiliar adult sitting at your teacher's desk, you might infer that that person is your substitute teacher. Watch out for an author's unsupported inferences. An **unsupported inference** is a guess that is not supported by the information available.

> **Unsupported inference:**
> My science teacher believes that physical education classes should be cut. She must not care about whether we stay healthy.
>
> **Reasonable inference:**
> My science teacher believes that physical education classes should be cut. She may think that we are not spending enough time learning about science.

Either-Or Thinking

Either-or thinking states that there are only two possible solutions to a problem. Many situations have a number of solutions.

> **Either-or thinking:**
> Either the school keeps teaching physical education, or kids will grow up to be weak and sickly.
>
> **Clear thinking:**
> Without gym classes, kids will lose a chance to train their bodies and develop healthy habits that will last their whole lives.

EXPLICIT INSTRUCTION Persuasive Appeals

Instruction Explain that some persuasive writing uses emotional appeals instead of sound reasoning. A writer who uses propaganda tries to make a reader feel an emotion in order to change the reader's opinion. This is different from presenting sound evidence that will allow a reader to use logic to come to a conclusion. Say, "A writer who uses persuasive appeals might try to make you feel happy, sad, angry, important, or insecure." Go over the lesson called "Persuasive Appeals," which begins on page R13.

Practice Write the following statements on the board. (1) Every sixth grader knows that Jennifer will make the best class president. (2) Jennifer understands the concerns of students because she has volunteered as a peer mediator for two years. (3) Jennifer is a goody-goody—is this someone you want for class president?

Ask students to identify each statement as an example of name calling, snob appeal, bandwagon appeal, or a well-supported opinion. Have students compare their answers.

Answers: (1) bandwagon appeal; (2) well-supported opinion; (3) name-calling

Circular Reasoning

Circular reasoning is a way of supporting a statement by just repeating it using different words. Statements like these offer no solid facts or reasons.

> Circular reasoning:
>
> Physical education is important because it is needed.
>
> Clear reasoning:
>
> Physical education is important because it helps students become healthy.

PRACTICE AND APPLY

A. Read the model and then do the activities that follow.

MODEL

The Springfield Board of Education recently announced that all schools in our community will be open year around. Classes will be in session for three months, followed by a one-month break. This means that the breaks will be in April, August, and December with school in session the other nine months. I believe the board is making a mistake.

One of the first things to be affected is our school's sports program. We will not be able to participate in league sports. Our school will be on break just when teams from other schools are in the final part of the season. Only a mean person would want to take league sports away from our school.

Families will also be affected. Finding child care for younger children will be more difficult. Now older children are at home during summer vacations and can help with child care. If these kids are in school during the summer, they will not be available to help care for their younger brothers and sisters. Parents may also have trouble getting vacation time from work at odd times of the year.

The heat in July and August will make concentrating on classes difficult. The school will need air conditioning, and that will take money away from other programs, such as purchasing new computers. Either we go back to our regular school schedule, or students in Springfield will not learn to use computers.

People in favor of year-around school say that students will learn more because the class periods can be longer, with more chances to learn subjects in depth. The one-month break is short enough so students will not forget what they learned.

Those arguments may make sense, but the effect on the lives of all the families in Springfield will just not make the change worthwhile. The issues involving child care, schedules for sports and other activities, and family time together are too important to ignore. The adjustment would be so difficult that students would learn less, not more. Every intelligent person knows I'm right.

I hope the school board will think again about their decision to change to a year-around school schedule.

1. State the author's position on the issue.

2. List two pieces of evidence the author gives to support his or her position.

3. One example of propaganda—name-calling—begins with the words "Only a mean person . . . ." Rewrite this statement to remove the propaganda.

4. Find another example of propaganda in this model. What kind of propaganda is it?

5. Find an example of either-or thinking in the model, and write it on your paper. Then rewrite it to eliminate the problem.

Practice and Apply
A. Possible Responses:

1. The author is opposed to a year-around school schedule in Springfield.

2. Participation in league sports will not be possible. Child care for families will be harder. Summer classes will require air conditioning the school.

3. "Some people will be deeply disappointed if our school cannot participate in league sports."

4. "Every intelligent person knows I'm right." Snob appeal.

5. "Either we go back to our regular school schedule, or students in Springfield will not learn to use computers." *Rewritten:* "If we go back to our regular school schedule, we may have more money to purchase computers."

EXPLICIT INSTRUCTION Evaluating Reasoning

Instruction Explain that errors in reasoning can confuse readers and lead to false conclusions and unsupported inferences. Tell students that in addition to evaluating a writer's evidence, they should also evaluate the writer's reasoning. Write these statements on the board: *Mrs. Carrick almost always wears the color yellow. She must hate all other colors.* Ask students if the second statement is a reasonable inference about Mrs. Carrick, based on the information given in the first statement. Why or why not? *(No, the information in the first sentence does not support the inference. A more reasonable inference would be that Mrs. Carrick must love the color yellow.)* Review the "Evaluating Reasoning" lesson on page R14 with students.

Practice Write these statements on the board or read them aloud and have students identify each type of false reasoning. (1) If students don't stop watching so much television, they will never be able to think for themselves. (2) Every student in sixth grade loves to watch television. (3) Television is entertaining because it is fun. (4) I know that Jen watches basketball games on television and plays for the school basketball team. She must not care about anything but basketball.

Answers: (1) either-or; (2) overgeneralization; (3) circular reasoning (4) unsupported inference

Practice and Apply
B. Possible responses:

1. "We must find a way to stop teenagers from smoking before they damage their health."

2. "Teen smoking has to stop right now because it just can't go on." *Rewritten:* "Smoking is a very serious health risk for teenagers."

3. A recent study reported by Reuters Health Information shows that teenagers who smoke have "more physical and mental health problems . . . "
"A recent study by the Surgeon General found that 22 percent of 13-year-old smokers bought cigarettes from vending machines."

4. "You would have to be stupid not to agree with me." Name calling.

B. Read the model on this page and do the activities that follow.

MODEL

Smoking is one of the worst things young people can do to their bodies. The government needs to do more to stop them from smoking.

Every day, about 3,000 American teenagers start smoking. A recent study reported by Reuter's Health Information shows that teenagers who smoke have "more physical and mental health problems, including headaches, neck pain, muscle and joint pain, stomach problems, hearing problems, nervousness, and sleep difficulties" than teens who don't smoke. Either someone will find a way to stop them, or they'll totally ruin their lives.

The government has already taken some steps to solve the problem. For example, it banned cigarette ads from television. However, tobacco companies still find ways to get their message to teenagers. They run ads in magazines read by teens—ads that show smoking as a way to be attractive, independent, and fun. Some tobacco companies have even used cartoon characters in their ads to appeal to children.

The government has also passed laws against selling cigarettes to minors. In many places, teenagers can get around those laws. A recent study by the Surgeon General found that 22 percent of 13-year-old smokers bought cigarettes from vending machines. Teens can also borrow cigarettes from adults or get adults to buy cigarettes for them.

Some people say that cracking down on teen smoking will only make it more attractive to rebellious teens. However, studies show that 80 to 90 percent of smokers begin the habit in their teens. Therefore, it makes sense to target teenagers in campaigns to prevent smoking. Experts at the Centers for Disease Control and Prevention say that a variety of approaches are needed to prevent people from ever starting to smoke.

There is no one way to solve the smoking problem, but here are some things the government should do now: 1) strictly enforce the laws against selling cigarettes to minors, 2) ban cigarette vending machines, 3) stop tobacco companies from advertising cigarettes, and 4) support antismoking groups. Teen smoking has to stop right now because it just can't go on. You would have to be stupid not to agree with me.

1. An example of either-or thinking begins with the words "Either someone will find a way to stop them, or . . . ." Rewrite this statement to make it logical.

2. Find another example of faulty reasoning in the model, and rewrite it to make it logical.

3. Write down two pieces of evidence from the model that you judge to be both adequate and appropriate support for the author's position.

4. Find an example of propaganda and identify what kind it is.

Functional Reading

It takes some special strategies to read the many different kinds of materials you need in order to function effectively in your everyday life. After studying the real-life examples in this section, you will be better able to fill out an application; understand product labels, public notices, and workplace documents; and follow various kinds of instructions. Look at each example as you read the strategies.

Practice and Apply
1. 8
2. Saturated fat
3. 2,000
4. Carbohydrate

Product Information: Food Label

Strategies for Reading

A Check the serving size carefully. The serving size listed may be smaller than the serving most people eat.

B The "% Daily Value" tells you the percentage of the recommended daily amount of a nutrient that is in one serving.

C This section shows the amounts and percent of daily values of such nutrients as fat and sodium. Amounts are measured in grams (g) and milligrams (mg).

D The U.S. Food and Drug Administration has not come up with a percent of a daily value for added sugars or protein.

E This section shows the percent of daily values of nutrients such as vitamins and minerals.

F Read the small print at the bottom of the label to understand what the numbers mean.

A

Nutrition Facts
Serving Size 4 cookies (31g)
Servings per Container about 9

Amount Per Serving

Calories 160	Calories from Fat 80

B **% Daily Value***

Total Fat 9 g	13%
Saturated Fat 6 g	28%
Cholesterol 0m g	0%

C

Sodium 140 mg	6%
Total Carbohydrate 20 g	7%
Dietary Fiber 1 g	5%
Sugars 11 g **D**	
Protein 1 g	

E

Vitamin A 0%	•	Vitamin C 0%
Calcium 0%	•	Iron 2%

F * Percent Daily Values are based on a 2,000-calorie diet. Your daily values may be higher or lower depending on your calorie needs.

PRACTICE AND APPLY

Reread the food label and answer the questions.

1. How many cookies are in two servings?
2. Which nutrient has the highest percent daily value?
3. The percent daily values are based on a diet of how many calories?
4. Saturated fat is a kind of fat. What kind of nutrient is sugar?

Practice and Apply

1. To be responsible for all materials.
2. When the applicant is 14 years old or under
3. The last section

Application

Strategies for Reading

A **Begin at the top.** Skim the application to see what the different sections are.

B Watch for **sections you don't have to fill in** or **questions you don't have to answer.**

C Notice any **special markings** such as dividing lines, boxes, or boldface type.

D Pay special attention to any part of an application that calls for **your signature.**

PRACTICE AND APPLY

Reread the application and answer the questions.

1. What promise do you make to the library when you sign this application?
2. When is a parent or guardian required to sign this application?
3. When you fill out the application, what parts should you skip?

A MILLWOOD PUBLIC LIBRARY CARD APPLICATION

(for office use only) CARD NO._____ **B**

Please print clearly.

NAME_____
          Last   First   Middle

LOCAL ADDRESS _____

CITY _____ STATE _____ ZIP CODE _____

HOME PHONE (____)_____ WORK PHONE (____)_____

SEX _____ _____   BIRTH DATE _____ / _____ / _____
    Male   Female   Month Day Year

I agree to be responsible for all materials borrowed from the Millwood Public Library in my name.

D SIGNATURE_____ DATE _____

C If applicant is 14 years old or under, parent or guardian must sign and supply printed name.

I agree to be responsible for all materials borrowed from the Millwood Public Library in my child's name.

Parent Signature _____ Date _____

Parent's Printed Name _____

for office use only
STAFF INITIALS _____ REGISTRATION CLASS _____
MI CH NS   OTHER FEE STAFF   ISU   KE   NL   TE

Technical Directions

Strategies for Reading

A Read the **instructions** all the way through at least once.

B Look for **numbers** or **letters** that give the steps in sequence.

C Look for **words that tell you what to do,** for example, *press, close, select.*

D Look at **pictures** or **visuals** to help you understand and follow steps.

E Watch for **warnings** or **notes** with more information.

A **Loading the Film**

B **1.** **Slide the back cover release upward to open the back cover.**

E Note: Do not touch the inside of the camera, especially the lens. If there is dust or dirt on the lens, remove it with a blower brush.

D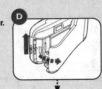

C **2.** **Insert the film cartridge, making sure the film is lying flat.**

Correct
The film should be lying flat before you close the back cover.

Incorrect
If the film is not lying flat, the film cartridge will not load properly.

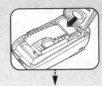

3. **Make sure the film leader is lined up with the red mark.**

Close the back cover and wait for the film to automatically load to the first frame.

4. **Press the power switch button. The exposure counter should read "1."**

If "E" blinks in the counter, as shown, the film is not loaded properly. Follow steps 1–4 again and reload the film.

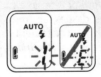

PRACTICE AND APPLY

Reread the directions and answer the questions.

1. What is the first thing you must do when you load film into a camera?

2. What do the instructions recommend you use to remove dust or dirt from the lens?

3. What should you do before you close the back cover?

4. What does it mean when the exposure counter blinks "E"?

Practice and Apply

1. Slide the back cover release upward to open the back cover.
2. A blower brush
3. Make sure the film leader is lined up with the red mark.
4. The film is not loaded properly.

Vocabulary Handbook

1 Context Clues

One way to figure out the meaning of a word you don't know is by using context clues. The context of a word is made up of the punctuation marks, other words, sentences, and paragraphs that surround the word.

1.1 General Context Sometimes you need to infer the meaning of an unfamiliar word by reading all the information in the sentence or paragraph.

> Kevin set out the broom, a dustpan, dusting rag, vacuum cleaner, and three trash bags before beginning the **monumental** task of cleaning his room.

1.2 Definition Clue Often a difficult word will be followed by a definition of its meaning. Commas, dashes, or other punctuation marks can signal a definition.

> Sometimes the explorers encountered **leads**—open channels of water—and were forced to wait until the ice formed before going on.

1.3 Restatement Clues Sometimes a writer restates a word or term in easier language. Commas, dashes, or other punctuation can signal restatement clues as well as expressions such as *that is, in other words,* and *or.*

> The boy put together a **hand-collated** set of trading cards; in other words, he put together a set of trading cards by hand.

1.4 Example Clues Sometimes writers suggest the meanings of words with one or two examples.

> The cabin had several **annoyances,** including a leak in the roof, mildew in the shower, and a family of mice.

1.5 Comparison Clues Sometimes a word's meaning is suggested by a comparison to something similar. *Like* or *as* are words that signal comparison clues.

> The twins **barreled** through the living room like a tornado.

1.6 Contrast Clues Sometimes writers point out differences between things or ideas. Contrast clues are often signaled by words like *although, but, however, unlike,* or *in contrast to.*

> The student was usually **bold,** but he became **hesitant** when he had to present a report to the class.

1.7 Idiom and Slang An idiom is an expression whose overall meaning is different than the meaning of the individual words. Slang is informal language in which made-up words and ordinary words are used to mean something different than in formal English. Use context clues to figure out the meaning of idioms and slang.

> The mosquitoes **drove us crazy** on our hike through the woods. (idiom)

> That's a really **cool** backpack that you are wearing. (slang)

For more about context clues, see page 79.

❷ Word Parts

If you know roots, base words, and affixes, you can figure out the meanings of many new words.

2.1 *Base Words* A base word is a complete word that can stand alone. Other words or word parts can be added to base words to form new words.

2.2 *Roots* Many English words contain roots that come from older languages, such as Latin, Greek, or Anglo-Saxon. A root is a base word that contains the core meaning of the word. Knowing the meaning of a word's root can help you tell the word's meaning.

root	meanings	example
cooperire	to cover	discover
tourner	to turn	return
gradus	step, degree	graduate

2.3 *Prefixes* A prefix is a word part that appears at the beginning of a root or base word to form a new word. A prefix usually changes the meaning of a root or a base word.

prefix	meanings	example
ex-	out, from	export
in-	in, into, not	incite
pre-	before	preface
pro-	forward, favoring	propose
re-	again, back	rebound
un-	not, opposite	unhappy

2.4 *Suffixes* A suffix is a word part that appears at the end of a root or base word to form a new word. Some suffixes do not change word meaning.

These suffixes are
- added to nouns to change the number
- added to verbs to change the tense
- added to adjectives to change the degree of comparison
- added to adverbs to show how.

suffix	meanings	example
-s, -es	to change the number of a noun	snack + s, snacks
-ed, -ing	to change verb tense	walk + ed, walked walk + ing, walking
-er, -est	to change the degree of comparison in modifiers	wild + er, wilder wild + est, wildest

Other suffixes are added to a root or base word to change the word's meaning. These suffixes can also be used to change the word's part of speech

	suffix	meanings	example
Noun	-age	action or process	pilgrim + age, pilgrimage
Adjective	-able	ability	remark + able, remarkable
Verb	-ize	to make	public + ize, publicize

TIP To find the meaning of an unfamiliar word, divide the word into parts. Think about the meaning of the prefix, the suffix, and the base or root word. Use what you know to figure out the meaning of the word. Then check to see if the word makes sense in context.

For more about root words and base words, see page 149; about prefixes and suffixes, see page 397.

❸ Word Origins

When you study a word's history and origin, you find out when, where, and how the word came to be. A complete dictionary entry includes each word's history.

> **dra•ma** (drä′ma) *n.* **1.** A work that is meant to be performed by actors. **2.** Theatrical works of a certain type or period in history. [Late Latin *drama, dramat-*, from Greek *dran,* to do or perform.]

This entry shows you that the earliest form of the word *drama* was the Greek word *dran.*

3.1 *Word Families* Words that have the same root make up a word family and have related meanings. The charts below show common Greek and Latin roots. Notice how the meanings of the example words are related to the meanings of their roots.

Latin Root: *senus,* to sense or feel

English:	**sensory** perceived through one of the senses
	sensitive responds to senses or feelings
	sensation a perception or feeling

Greek Root: *aster,* star

English:	**asteroid** a small object in outer space
	asterisk a star-shaped punctuation mark
	astronomy the study of outer space

TIP Once you recognize a root in one English word, you will notice the same root in other words. Because these words developed from the same root, all the words in the word family are similar in meaning.

3.2 *Foreign Words* Some words come into the English language and stay the way they were in their original language.

French	Dutch	Spanish	Italian
beret	cookie	taco	spaghetti
ballet	snoop	tornado	macaroni
vague	hook	rodeo	ravioli
mirage	caboose	bronco	

For more about about researching word origins, see page 663.

❹ Synonyms and Antonyms

When you read, pay attention to the precise words a writer uses.

4.1 *Synonyms* A synonym is a word that has the same or almost the same meaning as another word. Read each set of synonyms listed below.

occasionally/sometimes parcel/package

pledge/vow satisfy/please

rob/steal schedule/agenda

TIP You can find synonyms in a thesaurus or dictionary. In a dictionary, synonyms are often given as part of the definition of a word. Although synonyms have similar meanings, the words do not mean the same thing.

4.2 *Antonyms* An antonym is a word with a meaning opposite of that of another word. Read each set of antonyms listed below.

accurate/incorrect   similar/different

reveal/conceal   rigid/flexible

fresh/stale   unusual/ordinary

Sometimes an antonym is formed by adding the negative prefixes *anti-, in-, un-,* and *ex-* to a word as in the chart below.

word	prefix	suffix
climax	*anti-*	anticlimax
kind	*un-*	unkind
change	*ex-*	exchange

TIP Dictionaries of synonyms and antonyms, as well as some thesauruses, can help you find antonyms.

TIP After a dictionary entry, some dictionaries contain notes that discuss synonyms and antonyms for specific words. These notes often include sentences that illustrate the relationships between the words.

For more about synonyms and antonyms, see page 230.

⑤ Connotative and Denotative Meaning

Good writers choose just the right word to communicate specific meaning.

5.1 *Denotative Meaning* A word's dictionary meaning is called its denotation. For example, the denotative meaning of the word *thin* is "having little flesh; spare; lean."

5.2 *Connotative Meaning* The images or feelings you connect to a word give it finer **shades of meaning,** called connotation. Connotative meaning stretches beyond a word's most basic, dictionary definition. Writers use connotations of words to communicate positive or negative feelings. Some examples are listed below.

Positive Connotations	Negative Connotations
thin	scrawny
careful	cowardly
delicious	edible
thrifty	cheap
young	immature

TIP After a dictionary entry, some dictionaries contain notes that discuss connotative meanings of the words.

For more information about denotative and connotative meanings, see page 742.

6 Homonyms, Homophones, and Words with Multiple Meaning

Homonyms, multiple-meaning words, and homophones can be confusing to readers, and can plague writers.

6.1 Homonyms Words that have the same spelling and pronunciation but different meaning and origin (usually) are called homonyms. Consider this example:

The boy had to **stoop** to find his ball under the **stoop**.

Stoop can mean "a small porch," but it can also mean "to bend down." Because the words have different origins, each word has its own dictionary entry.

6.2 Words with Multiple-Meanings Multiple-meaning words are ones that have acquired additional meanings over time based on the original meaning. Consider these examples:

Thinking of the horror movie made my skin **creep.**

I saw my little brother **creep** around the corner.

Creep and *creep* have different meanings, but all of the meanings have developed from the original meaning. You will find all the meanings for *creep* listed under one entry in the dictionary.

6.3 Homophones Words that sound alike but have different meanings and spellings are called homophones. Consider this example:

Paul heard his mother say on the phone, "I **hear** you as well as I would if you were **here** talking to me."

Homophones don't usually cause problems for readers, but they can be problems for writers. Many common words with Anglo-Saxon origins (*there, their; write, right*) have homophones. Be sure to check your writing for misspelled homophones.

For more about homonyms and multiple-meaning words, see page 289.

7 Analogies

7.1 Analogy An analogy is a statement that compares two pairs of words. The relationship between the first pair of words is the same as the relationship between the second pair of words. In the example below, each pair of words shows a relationship of an item to a category.

TRACTOR : VEHICLE :: wrench : tool

A tractor is a type of vehicle, just as a wrench is a type of tool.

The sign : stands for "is to." The sign :: stands for "as." The analogy is read like this:

"tractor is to vehicle as wrench is to tool."

7.2 Types of Analogies Here are some common word relationships.

type of analogy	example	relationship
Part to Whole	STAGE : THEATER	is a part of
Synonyms	SWEET : THOUGHTFUL	is similar in meaning
Antonyms	FANTASTIC : AWFUL	is different in meaning
Degree of Intensity	SATISFACTORY : EXCELLENT	is less (or more) intense than
Characteristics to Object	ROUGHNESS : SANDPAPER	is a quality of
Item to Category	ANT : INSECT	is a type of

For more about analogies, see page 348.

8 Specialized Vocabulary

Professionals who work in fields such as law, science, or sports use their own technical or specialized vocabulary. Use these strategies to help you figure out the meanings of specialized vocabulary.

8.1 *Use Context Clues* Often the surrounding text gives clues that help you infer the meaning of an unfamiliar term.

8.2 *Use Reference Tools* Textbooks often define a special term when it is first introduced. Look for definitions or restatement clues in parentheses. Also you can try to find definitions in footnotes, a glossary, or a dictionary. If you need more information, refer to a specialized reference, such as

- an encyclopedia,
- a field guide,
- an atlas,
- a user's manual, or
- a technical dictionary.

For more about specialized vocabulary, see page 568.

9 Decoding Multisyllabic Words

Many words are familiar to you when you speak them or hear them. Sometimes these same words may be unfamiliar to you when you see them in print. When you come across a word unfamiliar in print, first try to pronounce it to see if you might recognize it. Use these syllabication generalizations to help you figure out a word's pronunciation.

Generalization 1: **VCCV**

When there are two consonants between two vowels, divide between the two consonants, unless they are a blend or a digraph.

    pic/ture   a/brupt   feath/er

Generalization 2: **VCCCV**

When there are three consonants between two vowels, divide between the blend or the digraph and the other consonant.

    an/gler   mer/chant   tum/bler

Generalization 3: **VCCV**

When there are two consonants between two vowels, divide between the consonants, unless they are a blend or a digraph. The first syllable is a closed syllable, and the vowel is short.

    lath/er   ush/er   ten/der

Generalization 4: **Common Vowel Clusters**

Do not split common vowel clusters, such as long vowel digraphs, r-controlled vowels, and vowel diphthongs.

    par/ty   poi/son   fea/ture

Generalization 5: **VCV**

When you see a VCV pattern in the middle of a word, divide the word either before or after the consonant. If you divide the word after the consonant, the first vowel sound will be short. If you divide the word before the consonant, the first vowel sound will be long.

    mod/el   ro/bot   cra/zy

Generalization 6: **Compound Words**

Divide compound words between the individual words.

    grape/vine   life/guard

Generalization 7: **Affixes**

When a word includes an affix, divide between the base word and the affix.

    re/bound   rest/less

Spelling Handbook

1 Improving Your Spelling

Like hitting a fastball or mastering the backstroke, becoming a spelling whiz takes planning and practice. By following these tips and basic rules, you can become a better speller.

Spelling Tips

1. **Identify your own spelling demons.** Make a list of the words you have misspelled in your writing.

2. **Pronounce words carefully.** Sometimes people misspell words because they say them incorrectly. For example, if you say the word *library* correctly, you will not misspell it *l-i-b-e-r-r-y.*

3. **Make a habit of seeing the letters in a word.** Pay attention to every letter of a new or difficult word. For example, when you come upon a word like *library,* look at each letter to fix the spelling in your mind.

4. **Invent memory devices for problem words.** Here are some examples:

   princi**pal** (pal)   The princi**pal** is my **pal.**

   trage**dy** (age)   Every **age** has its trage**dy.**

   emba**rr**a**ss** (rr, ss)   I turned **r**eally **r**ed and felt **s**o **s**illy.

5. **Proofread what you write.** Reread your work word for word so that you catch incorrectly spelled words.

Steps for Mastering Difficult Words

1. Look at the word and say it one syllable at a time.
2. Look at the letters and say each one.
3. Picture the word in your mind as you write it.
4. Check to see that you have spelled the word correctly. If you misspelled the word, notice what the mistake was and repeat steps 1–3.

One of the best ways to improve your spelling is to learn the following rules.

Words Ending in a Silent e

Before adding a suffix beginning with a vowel to a word ending in a silent e, drop the e (with some exceptions).

love + -able = lovable
improve + -ing = improving

The following words are exceptions:
dye + -ing = dyeing
mile + -age = mileage

When adding a suffix beginning with a consonant to a word ending in a silent e, keep the e (with some exceptions).

hate + -ful = hateful
excite + -ment = excitement

The following words are exceptions:
true + -ly = truly
argue + -ment = argument

Words Ending in y

When adding a suffix to a word that ends in a y preceded by a consonant, change the y to i.

noisy + -ly = noisily
nutty + -est = nuttiest

However, when adding *-ing,* do not change the y.

cry + -ing = crying
deny + -ing = denying

When a suffix is added to a word that ends in a *y* preceded by a vowel, the *y* usually does not change.

play + -ing = playing
enjoy + -ment = enjoyment

Words Ending in a Consonant

If a one-syllable word ends in one consonant preceded by one vowel, double the final consonant before adding a suffix beginning with a vowel, such as *-ing* or *-ed.* (Such a word is sometimes called a 1 + 1 + 1 word.)

sit + -ing = sitting
red + -est = reddest

The rule does not apply to words of one syllable that end in a consonant preceded by two vowels.

meet + -ing = meeting
dream + -er = dreamer

For a word of more than one syllable, double the final consonant when the word ends in one consonant preceded by one vowel *and* the word is accented on the last syllable.

ad•mit′   be•gin′   pre•fer′

In these examples, note that after the suffix is added, the accent remains on the same syllable.

ad•mit′ + -ed = ad•mit′ted
be•gin′ + -ing = be•gin′ning

In this example, the accent does not remain on the same syllable; thus, the final consonant is not doubled.

pre•fer′ + -able = pref′er•a•ble

The Suffixes -ly and -ness

When adding *-ly* to a word ending in *l,* keep both *l*'s. When adding *-ness* to a word ending in *n,* keep both *n*'s.

practical + -ly = practically
mean + -ness = meanness

Prefixes

When adding a prefix to a word, do not change the spelling of the base word.

un- + known = unknown
mis- + spell = misspell

Words with the Seed Sound

One English word ends in *-sede:* *supersede.* Three words end in *-ceed: exceed, proceed,* and *succeed.* All other words ending in the sound *seed* are spelled with *-cede.*

concede   precede   recede   secede

Words with ie *and* ei

When choosing between *ie* and *ei,* if the sound is long *e* (ē), you should usually spell the word with *ie* except after *c.*

i before *e*		except after *c*	
belief	niece	conceit	deceive
shield	field	receive	receipt
yield		ceiling	

Exceptions: *either, neither, weird, leisure, seize*

---

❷ Using the Right Word

The following words are commonly misused or misspelled. Some of these words are **homonyms,** *or words that have similar sounds but are spelled differently and have different meanings. Study this section to make sure you are using words correctly in your writing. Try using memory devices to help you associate words and meanings.*

accept, except *Accept* means "to agree to" or "to receive willingly." *Except* usually means "not including."

My brother will *accept* the job at the grocery store.

Luis likes every flavor of yogurt *except* lemon.

EXPLICIT INSTRUCTION ## Commonly Confused Words

Instruction Write the following sentence with answer choices on the board: *Last night I ate strawberry shortcake for (dessert, desert).* Have students identify the word that correctly completes the sentence. Circle the correct answer and point out that these two words are commonly confused and misused because they look similar. Explain that almost everyone has at least some problems with spelling, but there are strategies students can use to avoid spelling problems. Using memory devices for

words like *dessert* and *desert* is one strategy that will help students correctly spell words that are commonly confused.

Using the sentence on the board, circle the *ss* in the word *dessert,* the *s* at the beginning of *strawberry,* and the *s* at the beginning of *shortcake.* Say, "If you remember that the *ss* in *dessert* stands for "strawberry shortcake"— a kind of dessert—you will always remember how to spell this word correctly."

Share these other spelling strategies with students: (1) Proofread everything you write. (2) Look up difficult words in a dictionary. (3) Keep a list of the words that you often misspell.

Practice Have partners choose a set of commonly misspelled words from the spelling handbook and create a memory device to help them spell these words correctly in the future.
Possible Responses: Responses will vary. Ask partners to share their devices.

all ready, already *All ready* means "all are ready" or "completely prepared." *Already* means "previously."

> Janet was all ready to pitch in the big game.

a lot *A lot* is informal. Do not use it in formal writing. *Alot* is always incorrect.

borrow, lend *Borrow* means "to receive on loan." *Lend* means "to give temporarily."

> I *borrowed* my sister's watch.

> Please *lend* me your eraser.

capital, capitol, the Capitol *Capital* means "very serious" or "very important." It also means "seat of government." A *capitol* is a building in which a state legislature meets. *The Capitol* is the building in Washington, D.C., in which the U.S. Congress meets.

> The *capital* of Illinois is the city of Springfield.

> The Illinois *capitol* is a stately building in Springfield.

> The senator arrived at the *Capitol* in time to vote.

desert, dessert *Desert* (dĕz′ərt) means "a dry, sandy, barren region." *Desert* (dĭ-zûrt′) means "to abandon." *Dessert* (dĭ-zûrt′) is a sweet food, such as pie.

> Tall cactus plants grow in the *desert*.

> The crane would not *desert* his injured mate.

> Jake loves ice cream for *dessert*.

good, well *Good* is always an adjective. *Well* is usually an adverb that modifies an action verb. *Well* can also be an adjective meaning "in good health."

> That dress looks *good* on you.

> Anne performed her skating routine *well*.

> Nikki didn't feel *well* today.

hear, here *Hear* means "to listen to." *Here* means "in this place."

> Every time I *hear* this song, I feel happy.

> The mayor's family has lived *here* for generations.

its, it's *Its* is a possessive pronoun. *It's* is a contraction of *it is* or *it has*.

> The boat lost *its* sail during the storm.

> *It's* nearly midnight.

lay, lie *Lay* is a verb that means "to place." It takes a direct object. *Lie* is a verb that means "to recline" or "to be in a certain place." *Lie* never takes a direct object.

> Don't *lay* your coat on the couch.

> The terrier likes to *lie* under the swing.

> The island *lies* in the path of the hurricane.

lead, led *Lead* can be a noun that means "a heavy metal" or a verb that means "to show the way." *Led* is the past tense form of the verb.

> These pellets contain *lead*.

> Ask the lieutenant to *lead* her troops.

> He *led* a group of explorers out of the jungle.

learn, teach *Learn* means "to gain knowledge." *Teach* means "to instruct."

> In social studies we are *learning* about frontier life.

> He is *teaching* us to use a computer.

like, as, as if *Like* is a preposition. Use *as* or *as if* to introduce a clause.

> He ran the pass pattern *as* he should.

loose, lose *Loose* means "free" or "not fastened." *Lose* means "to mislay or suffer the loss of."

> The rider kept the horse's reins *loose*.

> If you *lose* your book, tell the librarian right away.

of Use *have*, not *of*, in phrases such as could *have*, should *have*, and must *have*.

> We should *have* invited her to our party.

passed, past *Passed* is the past tense of *pass* and means "went by." *Past* is an adjective that means "of a former time." *Past* is also a noun that means "the time gone by."

> A car that was driving too fast *passed* us on the highway.

Past problems at the parade have included littering.

It is important to remember the mistakes of the *past.*

peace, piece *Peace* means "calm" or "quiet." *Piece* means "a section or part."

After two years of war came *peace.*

The statue was carved from a *piece* of jade.

principal, principle *Principal* means "of chief or central importance" or "the head of a school." *Principle* means "basic truth," "standard," or "rule of behavior."

The *principal* export of Brazil is coffee.

The *principal* of our school organized a safety council.

One *principle* of science is that all matter occupies space.

quiet, quite *Quiet* means "free from noise or disturbance." *Quite* means "truly" or "almost completely."

The library is *quiet* in the afternoon.

The aquarium tank is *quite* full.

raise, rise *Raise* means "to lift" or "to cause to go up." It takes a direct object. *Rise* means "to go upward." It does not take a direct object.

Can you *raise* the sail by yourself?

The jury will *rise* when the judge enters the courtroom.

set, sit *Set* means "to place." It takes a direct object. *Sit* means "to occupy a seat or a place." It does not take a direct object.

I *set* the bag of groceries inside the door.

Sit still while we take your picture.

stationary, stationery *Stationary* means "fixed or unmoving." *Stationery* means "fine paper for writing letters."

Robin rode a *stationary* bicycle for exercise when the weather was bad.

Use your best *stationery* when you write to your grandmother.

than, then *Than* is used to introduce the second part of a comparison. *Then* means "next in order."

I like mysteries better *than* science fiction stories.

Jane put the spaghetti on a serving dish and *then* grated cheese over it.

their, there, they're *Their* means "belonging to them." *There* means "in that place." *They're* is a contraction of *they are.*

Our neighbors sold *their* house and moved to a farm.

Please play with the squirt guns over *there.*

My sisters don't swim, but *they're* eager to learn.

to, too, two *To* means "toward" or "in the direction of." *Too* means "also" or "very." *Two* is the number 2.

The surgeon dashed *to* the emergency room.

It was *too* hot to run a race.

Only *two* of the six lifeboats reached shore.

weather, whether *Weather* refers to conditions such as temperature or cloudiness. *Whether* expresses a choice.

The *weather* is perfect for a picnic.

Whether we drive or take the train, we will arrive late.

whose, who's *Whose* is the possessive form of *who.* *Who's* is a contraction of *who is* or *who has.*

Whose wallet is lying under the chair?

Who's been chosen the student of the month?

your, you're *Your* is the possessive form of *you.* *You're* is a contraction of *you are.*

Please bring *your* cameras to the assembly.

You're doing much better this semester than last.

① The Writing Process

The writing process consists of four stages: prewriting, drafting, revising and editing, and publishing and reflecting. As the graphic shows, these stages are not followed rigidly. You may return to any stage of the process at any point.

Prewriting
Drafting
Peer Response
Revising and Editing
Publishing and Reflecting

①.① Prewriting

In the prewriting stage, you explore your ideas and discover what you want to write about.

Finding Ideas for Writing

Try one or more of the following techniques to help you find a writing topic.

Personal Techniques

- Practice imaging, or trying to remember mainly sensory details about a subject—its look, sound, feel, taste, and smell.

- Complete a knowledge inventory to discover what you already know about a subject.

- Browse through magazines, newspapers, and on-line bulletin boards for ideas.

- Start a clip file of articles that you want to save for future reference. Be sure to label each clip with source information.

Sharing Techniques

- With a group, brainstorm a topic. Try to come up with as many ideas as you can without stopping to critique or examine them.

- Interview someone who knows a great deal about your topic.

Writing Techniques

- After freewriting on a topic, try looping, or choosing your best idea for more freewriting. Repeat the loop at least once.

- Make a list to help you organize ideas, examine them, or identify areas for further research.

Graphic Techniques

- Create a pro-and-con chart to compare the positive and negative aspects of an idea or a course of action.

- Use a cluster map or tree diagram to explore subordinate ideas that relate to your general topic or central idea.

LINK TO LITERATURE Some of the best ideas for writing can come from your own experiences. Isaac Bashevis Singer, author of "Zlateh the Goat," on page 481, says, "I write about the things where I grew up, and where I feel completely at home."

Determining Your Purpose

Your purpose for writing may be to express yourself, to entertain, to describe, to explain, to analyze, or to persuade. To clarify your purpose, ask questions like these:

- Why did I choose to write about my topic?

- What aspects of the topic mean the most to me?

- What do I want others to think or feel after they read my writing?

Identifying Your Audience

Knowing who will read your writing can help you focus your topic and choose relevant details. As you think about your readers, ask yourself questions like these:

- What does my audience already know about my topic?
- What will they be most interested in?
- What language is most appropriate for this audience?

Choosing a Form

A form of writing is a particular shape or structure that the writing takes. The chart below shows some common forms. To figure out what form you should use, think about your purpose for writing, your topic, and your audience.

If my purpose is to. . .	A possible form might be . . .
• tell about a specific event (funny or serious)	• short story, play, personal letter or e-mail, news article
• describe an intense feeling, memory, or experience	• poem, personal narrative, personal letter, memoir, or autobiography
• explain how to do something	• how-to essay, set of directions
• inform readers about a particular subject	• research report, expository essay, interview
• persuade readers to believe or do something or to express an opinion	• persuasive essay, editorial, speech letter to the editor
• describe a book, movie, or performance	• review, interpretive essay

1.2 Drafting

In the drafting stage, you put your ideas on paper and allow them to develop and change as you write.

Two broad approaches in this stage are discovery drafting and planned drafting.

Discovery drafting is a good approach when you are not quite sure what you think about your subject. You just plunge into your draft and let your feelings and ideas lead you where they will. After finishing a discovery draft, you may decide to start another draft, do more prewriting, or revise your first draft.

Planned drafting may work better for research reports, critical reviews, and other kinds of formal writing. Try making a writing plan or a scratch outline before you begin drafting. Then, as you write, you can fill in the details.

LINK TO LITERATURE Some writers plan and outline. Others write in a great flurry, without much previous planning, as ideas occur to them; of course, the ideas have been developing within them before they begin to write. Walter Dean Myers, who wrote "Abd al-Rahman Ibrahima," on page 365, had to gather many notes about his subject's life before he could begin to write Ibrahima's biography.

1.3 Revision Guidelines

The changes you make in your writing during this stage usually fall into three categories: revising for content, revising for structure, and proofreading to correct mistakes in mechanics.

Use the questions that follow to assess problems and determine what changes would improve your work.

Revising for Content

- Does my writing have a main idea or central focus? Is my thesis clear?
- Have I incorporated adequate detail? Where might I include a telling detail, revealing statistic, or vivid example?
- Is any material unnecessary, irrelevant, or confusing?

Revising for Structure

- Is my writing unified? Do all ideas and supporting details pertain to my main idea or advance my thesis?
- Is my writing clear and coherent? Is the flow of sentences and paragraphs smooth and logical?

EXPLICIT INSTRUCTION Choosing a Form

Instruction Tell students that after they choose the topic they plan to write about, they are ready to select the form for their writing. Explain that writing assignments often specify a form. For example, an assignment might ask students to write a short story, a persuasive essay, or a poem. Say, "Sometimes, however, you must choose the form. To do this, you should think about your purpose for writing." Explain that there are many reasons why people write. They may want to explain something, share informa-tion, persuade readers to see their point of view, or describe feelings, places, or people. Say, "You may want to use the essay form if your purpose is to explain, use poetry to express feelings, and use a short story to enter-tain." Go over the section called "Choosing a Form" on the pupil page above.

Practice List or read the following purposes and have students choose a form from the chart that suits the purpose: (1) to describe how you felt when your best friend moved away, (2) to get others to understand that being kind to each other is important, (3) to explain how to create a Web site, (4) to compare two books that you have read, (5) to describe a new science fiction movie.
Possible Responses: (1) poem, (2) editorial, (3) how-to essay, (4) expository essay, (5) review

- Do I need to add transitional words, phrases, or sentences to make the relationships among ideas clearer?
- Are my sentences well constructed? What sentences might I combine to improve the grace and rhythm of my writing?

WRITING TIP Be sure to consider the needs of your audience as you answer the questions under Revising for Content and Revising for Structure. For example, before you can determine whether any of your material is unnecessary or irrelevant, you need to identify what your audience already knows.

Proofreading to Correct Mistakes in Grammar, Usage, and Mechanics

When you are satisfied with your revision, proofread your paper, looking for mistakes in grammar, usage, and mechanics. You may want to use the checklist below several times, looking for different types of mistakes each time.

Sentence Structure and Agreement
- Are there any run-on sentences or sentence fragments?
- Do all verbs agree with their subjects?
- Do all pronouns agree with their antecedents?
- Are verb tenses correct and consistent?

Forms of Words
- Do adverbs and adjectives modify the appropriate words?
- Are all forms of *be* and other irregular verbs used correctly?
- Are pronouns used correctly?
- Are comparative and superlative forms of adjectives correct?

Capitalization, Punctuation, and Spelling
- Is any punctuation mark missing or not needed?
- Are all words spelled correctly?
- Are all proper nouns and adjectives capitalized?

WRITING TIP For help identifying and correcting problems that are listed in the Proofreading Checklist, see the Grammar Handbook, pages R62–R95. You might wish to mark changes on your paper by using proofreading symbols.

Proofreading Symbols

∧	Add letters or words.	/	Make a capital letter lowercase.
⊙	Add a period.	¶	Begin a new paragraph.
≡	Capitalize a letter.	ℐ	Delete letters or words.
⌒	Close up a space.	∿	Switch the positions of letters or words.
⋏	Add a comma.		

1.4 Publishing and Reflecting

Always consider sharing your finished writing with an audience. Reflecting on your writing is another good way to bring closure to a project.

Creative Publishing Ideas
Following are some ideas for publishing and sharing your writing.

- Post your writing on an electronic bulletin board or send it to others via email.
- Create a multimedia presentation and share it with classmates.
- Publish your writing in a school newspaper or literary magazine.
- Present your work orally in a report, a speech, a reading, or a dramatic performance.
- Submit your writing to a local newspaper or a magazine that publishes student writing.
- Form a writing exchange group with other students.

WRITING TIP You might work with other students to publish an anthology of class writing. Then exchange your anthology with another class or another school. Reading the work of other student writers will help you get ideas for new writing projects and find ways to improve your work.

Reflecting on Your Writing

Think about your writing process and whether you would like to add what you have written to your portfolio. You might attach a note in which you answer questions like these:

- What did I learn about myself and my subject through this writing project?

- Which parts of the writing process did I most and least enjoy?

- As I wrote, what was my biggest problem? How did I solve it?

- What did I learn about my own process that I can use the next time I write?

1.5 Using Peer Response

Peer response consists of the suggestions and comments your peers or classmates make about your writing.

You can ask a peer reader for help at any point in the writing process. For example, your peers can help you brainstorm a topic, narrow your focus, notice confusing words or passages, or think of a structure for your writing.

Questions for Your Peer Readers

You can help your peer readers provide you with the most useful feedback by following these guidelines:

- Tell readers where you are in the writing process. Are you still trying out ideas, or have you completed a draft?

- Ask pointed but open-ended questions that will help you get specific information about your writing. Questions that require more than yes-or-no answers are more likely to give you information you can use.

- Give your readers plenty of time to respond thoughtfully to your writing.

- Encourage your readers to be honest when they respond to your work. It's OK if you don't agree with them—you always get to decide which changes to make.

Tips for Being a Peer Reader

Follow these guidelines when you respond to someone else's work:

- Respect the writer's feelings.

- Make sure you understand what kind of feedback the writer is looking for, and then respond accordingly.

- Use "I" statements, such as "I like . . . ," "I think . . . ," or "It would help me if . . . ." Remember that your impressions and opinions are your own. They won't be the same as everyone's.

WRITING TIP Writers are better able to absorb criticism of their work if they first receive positive feedback. When you act as a peer reader, try to start your review by telling something you like about the piece. The chart below explains different peer response techniques.

Peer Response Techniques

Sharing Use this when you are just exploring ideas or when you want to celebrate the completion of a piece of writing.

- *Will you please read or listen to my writing without criticizing or making suggestions afterward?*

Summarizing Use this when you want to know if your main idea or goals are clear.

- *What do you think I'm saying? What's my main idea or message?*

Replying Use this strategy when you want to make your writing richer by adding new ideas.

- *What are your ideas about my topic? What do you think about what I have said in my piece?*

Responding to Specific Features Use this when you want a quick overview of the strengths and weaknesses of your writing.

- *Are the ideas supported with enough examples? Did I persuade you? Is the organization clear enough for you to follow the ideas?*

Telling Use this to find out which parts of your writing are affecting readers the way you want and which parts are confusing.

- *What did you think or feel as you read my words? Would you show me which passage you were reading when you had that response?*

---

② Building Blocks of Good Writing

Whatever your purpose in writing, you need to capture your readers' interest, organize your ideas well, and present your thoughts clearly. Giving special attention to particular parts of a story or an essay can make your writing more enjoyable and more effective.

2.1 Introductions

When you flip through a magazine trying to decide which articles to read, the opening paragraph is often critical. If it does not grab your attention, you are likely to turn the page.

Kinds of Introductions

Here are some introduction techniques that can capture a reader's interest.

- Make a surprising statement
- Provide a description
- Pose a question
- Relate an anecdote
- Address the reader directly
- Begin with a thesis statement

Make a Surprising Statement Beginning with a startling statement or an interesting fact can capture your reader's curiosity about the subject, as in the model below.

> MODEL
> A male Kodiak bear may weigh 1,500 pounds, measure ten feet long, and run 35 miles an hour. Protected within Alaska's Kodiak National Wildlife Refuge, nearly 3,000 of these bears share 100-mile-long Kodiak Island, where they feast on fish, berries, and whale and seal carcasses.

Provide a Description A vivid description sets a mood and brings a scene to life for your reader. Here, details about running on a track set the tone for a narrative about a foot race.

> MODEL
> In the pale morning light, the shadowy track was still. Rounding the curve, the athlete locked her eyes on the single floodlight at the far end of the track, her every muscle straining toward it.

Pose a Question Beginning with a question can make your reader want to read on to find out the answer. The following introduction asks a question about the importance of a particular person to a sport.

> MODEL
> Why does Danielle Del Ferraro hold a special place in the history of the Soap Box Derby? Since the Derby began in 1934, she has been the only participant ever to win twice. Her success is also noteworthy because girls were not allowed to enter the gravity-powered car race until 1970.

Relate an Anecdote Beginning with a brief anecdote, or story, can hook readers. The anecdote below introduces a firsthand account of an important family event.

> MODEL
> Dressed in my best clothes, I rushed outside, late for my sister's wedding. I waited impatiently for the light to change at the corner. Then, from out of nowhere came an out-of-control in-line skater. The result was a head-on collision.

Address the Reader Directly Speaking directly to readers establishes a friendly, informal tone and involves them in your topic.

> MODEL
> Find out how you can get in shape and have fun at the same time. Come to a free demonstration of Fit for Life on Friday night at 7:00 P.M.

Begin with a Thesis Statement A thesis statement expressing a paper's main idea may be woven into both the beginning and the end of nonfiction writing. The following is a thesis statement that introduces a response to literature.

> MODEL
> In "The Circuit," Francisco Jiménez shows how migrant farmwork affects the children of families that work in the fields.

WRITING TIP You may want to try more than one kind of introduction and then decide which is the most effective.

 ## 2.2 Paragraphs

A paragraph is made up of sentences that work together to develop an idea or accomplish a purpose. Whether or not it contains a topic sentence stating the main idea, a good paragraph must have unity and coherence.

Unity

A paragraph has unity when all the sentences support and develop the main idea. Use the following techniques to create unity.

Write a Topic Sentence A topic sentence states the main ideas of the paragraph; all other sentences in the paragraph provide supporting details. A topic sentence is often the first sentence in a paragraph. However, it may also appear later in the paragraph or at the end, to summarize or reinforce the main idea.

> MODEL
> The most important rule for a beginning photographer is this: check before you click. Is the film loaded? Is your subject well lighted or will you need a flash? Have you framed your picture carefully? Are you holding the camera still? Checking the basics will go a long way toward making your snapshots memorable.

Relate All Sentences to an Implied Main Idea A paragraph can be unified without a topic sentence as long as every sentence supports the implied, or unstated, main idea.

> MODEL
> The chef carefully poured in the mixture of freshly sliced apples, sugar, flour, and cinnamon. Then she floured her hands again before adding strips of pastry in crisscrosses across the top. She dotted some butter all along the top. Finally she placed the masterpiece in the oven.

Coherence

A paragraph is coherent when all its sentences are related to one another and flow logically from one to the next. The following techniques will help you achieve coherence in paragraphs.

- Present your ideas in the most logical order.
- Use pronouns, synonyms, and repeated words to connect ideas.
- Use transitional devices to show the relationships among ideas.

> MODEL
> Most scientists believe that all of the earth's land once formed one super continent. About 200 million years ago, this supercontinent began to break into two large masses of land. Since that time the plates on which continents rest have continued to move.

2.3 Transitions

Transitions are words and phrases that show the connections between details. Clear transitions help show how your ideas relate to each other.

Kinds of Transitions

Transitions can help readers understand several kinds of relationships:

- Time or sequence
- Spatial relationships
- Degree of importance
- Compare and contrast
- Cause and effect

Time or Sequence Some transitions help to clarify the sequence of events over time. When you are telling a story or describing a process, you can connect ideas with such transitional words as *first, second, always, then, next, later, soon, before, finally, after, earlier, afterward,* and *tomorrow.*

> **MODEL**
> During the Revolutionary War, many of the colonists who remained loyal to the British monarchy lost their houses and land by force. After the war, between 80,000 and 100,000 of these Loyalists went to England or emigrated elsewhere.

Spatial Relationships Transitional words and phrases such as *in front, behind, next to, along, nearest, lowest, above, below, underneath, on the left,* and *in the middle* can help readers visualize a scene.

> **MODEL**
> As I waited, I stared at the bleachers across the rink. My family was lined up in the front row. Behind this group and to the right were friends from school, and next to my friends were three of my teachers.

Degree of Importance Transitional words such as *mainly, strongest, weakest, first, second, most important, least important, worst,* and *best* may be used to rank ideas or to show degree of importance.

> **MODEL**
> Why do I read mysteries? Mainly because I enjoy suspense. Second, I like meeting characters who are different from anybody I know in real life. Least important, but still a reason, is that I enjoy reading about interesting places.

WRITING TIP When you begin a sentence with a transition such as *most important, therefore, nevertheless, still,* or *instead,* set off the transition with a comma.

Compare and Contrast Words and phrases such as *similarly, likewise, also, like, as, neither . . . nor,* and *either . . . or* show similarity between details. *However, by contrast, yet, but, unlike, instead, whereas,* and *while* show difference.

> **MODEL**
> Matthew Henson was not recognized as the codiscoverer of the North Pole until 1944, although he and Robert Peary had reached it on April 6, 1909. By contrast, the achievement of Roald Amundsen's team, which made it to the South Pole in December 1911, was recognized almost immediately.

Cause and Effect When you are writing about a cause-and-effect relationship, use transitional words and phrases such as *since, because, thus, therefore, so, due to, for this reason,* and *as a result* to help clarify that relationship.

> **MODEL**
> Because a tree fell across the electric wires Monday night, we lost our electricity for four hours.

2.4 Conclusions

A conclusion should leave readers with a strong final impression. Try any of these approaches.

Kinds of Conclusions

Here are some effective methods for bringing your writing to a conclusion:

- Restate your thesis
- Ask a question
- Make a recommendation
- Make a prediction
- Summarize your information

Restate Your Thesis A good way to conclude an essay is by restating your thesis, or main idea, in different words. The conclusion below restates the thesis introduced on page R35.

> MODEL
> As these examples from "The Circuit" show, Francisco Jiménez succeeds in making the reader understand the effects of the migrant farmworker's way of life on children.

Ask a Question Try asking a question that sums up what you have said and gives readers something new to think about. The question below concludes a persuasive essay on the need for bike lanes in the writer's community.

> MODEL
> More and more people are biking to school and to work and are riding for exercise. Doesn't it make sense to create safe bike lanes throughout our city?

Make a Recommendation When you are persuading your audience to take a position on an issue, you can conclude by recommending a specific course of action.

> MODEL
> You can make your research easier by taking advantage of the Internet. Develop a list of key words that will help you narrow your search.

Make a Prediction Readers are concerned about matters that may affect them and therefore are moved by a conclusion that predicts the future.

> MODEL
> If landowners continue to drain wetlands, we will see a tremendous decline in the number and variety of wildlife.

Summarize Your Information Summarizing reinforces the writer's main ideas, leaving a strong, lasting impression.

> MODEL
> At 64, Denise St. Aubyn Hubbard sailed alone across the Atlantic. Bill Pinkney was in his 50s when he sailed around the world by himself. And Tristan Jones, in his 60s and having lost a leg, sailed solo from California to Thailand. Don't ever think that courage belongs only to the young.

2.5 Elaboration

Elaboration is the process of developing a writing idea by providing supporting details. Choose details that are appropriate to the purpose and form of your writing.

Facts and Statistics A fact is a statement that can be verified, while a statistic is a fact stated in numbers. Make sure the facts and statistics you supply are from a reliable, up-to-date source. As in the model below, the facts and statistics you use should strongly support the statements you make.

MODEL

Women have aided the United States' military efforts for more than a century. Since the 1860s, more than 11 million women have served in or assisted the armed forces. Today approximately 200,000 women are on active duty.

Sensory Details Details that show how something looks, sounds, tastes, smells, or feels can enliven a description.

MODEL

Anna Hawk got off her bike and sat beside the muddy road. The rain on her poncho made the only sound, and nothing on the prairie moved. Anna took a sip of warm, sweet cocoa from her thermos bottle.

Incidents From our earliest years, we are interested in hearing stories. One way to illustrate a point powerfully is to relate an incident or tell a story.

MODEL

Some of our most valuable sources of historical knowledge come from tragic events. The eruption of the volcano Vesuvius in A.D. 79 was a nightmare for the people of Pompeii. About 2,000 inhabitants died, and their homes were buried under tons of volcanic ash.

Examples An example can help make an abstract or a complex idea concrete or can provide evidence to clarify a point.

MODEL

Throughout history, people have used observations of nature to predict the weather. For example, you may have heard that "red skies at night are a sailor's delight."

Quotations Choose quotations that clearly support your points and be sure that you copy each quotation word for word. Remember always to credit the source.

MODEL

The use of dialect in fiction makes the characters and setting seem more real to the reader. In "The Bamboo Beads," the character speaks a dialect of English found in Trinidad and Tobago. Dialogue such as "I put de pretty beads on de string," helps readers hear in their minds just how Tantie sounds.

2.6 Using Language Effectively

Effective use of language can help readers to recognize the significance of an issue, to visualize a scene, or to understand a character. The specific words and phrases that you use have everything to do with how effectively you communicate meaning. Keep these particular points in mind.

Specific Nouns Nouns are specific when they refer to individual or particular things. If you refer to a city, you are being general. If you refer to London, you are being specific. Specific nouns help readers identify the who, what, and where of your message.

Specific Verbs Verbs are the most powerful words in sentences. They convey the action, the movement, and sometimes the drama of thoughts and observations. Verbs such as *trudged, skipped,* and *sauntered* provide a more vivid picture of the action than the verb *walked.*

Specific Modifiers Use modifiers sparingly, but when you use them, make them count. Is the building big or towering? Are your poodle's paws small or toylike? Once again, it is the more specific word that carries the greater impact.

Descriptive Writing

Descriptive writing allows you to paint word pictures about anything and everything in the world, from events of global importance to the most personal feelings. It is an essential part of almost every piece of writing, including essays, poems, letters, field notes, newspaper reports, and videos.

RUBRIC **STANDARDS FOR WRITING**

A successful description should

- have a clear focus and sense of purpose
- use sensory details and precise words to create a vivid image, establish a mood, or express emotion
- present details in a logical order

3.1 Key Techniques

Consider Your Goals What do you want to accomplish in writing your description? Do you want to show why something is important to you? Do you want to make a person or scene more memorable? Do you want to explain an event?

Identify Your Audience Who will read your description? How familiar are they with your subject? What background information will they need? Which details will they find most interesting?

Think Figuratively What figures of speech might help make your description vivid and interesting? What simile or metaphor comes to mind? What imaginative comparisons can you make? What living thing does an inanimate object remind you of?

MODEL

The sun burned in the sky like a bare light bulb. When I squinted, it looked as if butterflies were dancing on the desert's horizon, though I knew it was really only currents of heat rising from the sand. The plain water in the canteen that I held to my lips tasted sweeter than any soda I could remember.

Gather Sensory Details Which sights, smells, tastes, sounds, and textures make your subject come alive? Which details stick in your mind when you observe or recall your subject? Which senses does it most strongly affect?

MODEL

Andrew slumped against the wall outside the gym. His calves ached more than his stomach, empty and tense. In his mind, he replayed the last minutes of the game— tasting sweat, hearing cheers, feeling the seams of the basketball under his fingers— but he couldn't visualize missing the shot.

You might want to use a chart like the one shown here to collect sensory details about your subject.

Sights	Sounds	Textures	Smells	Tastes

Create a Mood What feelings do you want to evoke in your readers? Do you want to soothe them with comforting images? Do you want to build tension with ominous details? Do you want to evoke sadness or joy?

MODEL

The Condors were one run ahead. Just one more strike by the Cranes' batter would end the game. The crowd stood. Orange and white streamers waved desperately on one side of the stadium while blue and gold ones mimicked them on the other side. One more strike—just one. The pitcher wound up. The batter poised. Here came the ball.

3.2 Options for Organization

Spatial Order Choose one of these options to show the spatial order of a scene.

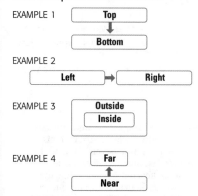

EXAMPLE 1
Top → Bottom

EXAMPLE 2
Left → Right

EXAMPLE 3
Outside / Inside

EXAMPLE 4
Far ← Near

MODEL
Arthur and Chantal came to the bicycle race to cheer for their friends. As the first group of cyclists approached the finish line, Arthur and Chantal cheered wildly when they saw their friend Lindsay leading the pack. Another friend, Charles, was just behind her. Far off in the distance, they could just make out their friend Georgia's red bike.

WRITING TIP Use transitions that help the reader picture the relationship among the objects you describe. Some useful transitions for showing spatial relationships are *behind, below, here, in the distance, on the left, over,* and *on top.*

Order of Impression Order of impression is how you notice details.

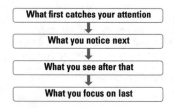

What first catches your attention
↓
What you notice next
↓
What you see after that
↓
What you focus on last

MODEL
Mike descended the stairs slowly, so we saw his shoes first—polished to a gleaming black so that they looked almost like patent leather. Then, the satin stripe on each trouser leg told us he was dressed for a formal event. Finally, we saw the white bow tie, just below the grin.

WRITING TIP Use transitions that help readers understand the order of the impressions you are describing. Some useful transitions are *after, next, during, first, before, finally,* and *then.*

Order of Importance (Climactic Order)
You might want to use order of importance as the organizing structure for your description.

Least important
↓
More important
↓
Most important

MODEL
Most impressionist paintings were created outdoors. The paintings feature bright colors and loose brushwork. The painters used these techniques to portray the effects of sunlight on objects. The goal of the impressionists was to capture their immediate "impression" of a brief moment in time.

WRITING TIP Use transitions that help the reader understand the order of importance that you attach to the elements of your description. Some useful transitions are *first, second, mainly, more important, most important,* and *more to the point.*

④ Narrative Writing

Narrative writing tells a story. A story from your imagination is a fictional narrative. A true story about actual events is a nonfictional narrative. Narrative writing can be found in short stories, novels, news articles, and biographies.

RUBRIC STANDARDS FOR WRITING

A successful narrative should

- include descriptive details and dialogue to develop the characters, setting, and plot
- have a clear beginning, middle, and end
- have a logical organization with clues and transitions to help the reader understand the order of events
- maintain a consistent tone and point of view
- use language that is appropriate for the audience
- demonstrate the significance of events or ideas

④.1 Key Techniques

Identify the Main Events What are the most important events in your narrative? Is each event part of the chain of events needed to tell the story? In a fictional narrative, this series of events is the story's plot.

MODEL

Event 1	Danielle receives a gift—a horse to train—from Aunt Jessica.
Event 2	Danielle and the horse do not get along. The horse seems to be unable to learn anything.
Event 3	Danielle accepts that the horse is proud and spirited and that she may never train him.
Event 4	Danielle adjusts her training methods, and the horse begins to respond to her.

Describe the Setting When do the events occur? Where do they take place? How can you use setting to create mood and to set the stage for the characters and their actions?

MODEL

At first, Danielle just sat on the weathered split-rail fence and watched the horse canter. When the sun shone hot on her back, she slid off the fence and walked toward him through the overgrown pasture.

Depict Characters Vividly What do your characters look like? What do they think and say? How do they act? What vivid details can show readers what the characters are like?

MODEL

Danielle let her long blond hair fall around her face to hide the tears in her eyes, and forced herself to smile.

WRITING TIP Dialogue is an effective way of developing characters in a narrative. Choose words that express your characters' personalities and show how the characters feel about one another and about the events in the plot.

MODEL

"I know he's not your favorite horse, but he needs training," said Aunt Jessica.

Danielle tried to keep disappointment out of her voice as she replied, "Thanks, Aunt Jessica. I know I can train him like you taught me."

"You can do anything you set your mind to," Aunt Jessica said.

4.2 Options for Organization

Option 1: Chronological Order One way to organize a piece of narrative writing is to arrange the events in chronological order, as shown below.

	MODEL
Introduction *characters and setting*	Aunt Jessica gives Danielle her first horse to train.
Event 1	He's a horse Danielle doesn't like; he's stubborn, and when Danielle tries to train him, nothing happens.
Event 2	Danielle sees the horse running in the field; he looks proud and independent.
End *perhaps show the significance of the events*	Aunt Jessica asks Danielle if she would like a different horse to train. Danielle says she wants to keep the horse she has. Aunt Jessica smiles warmly at her.

Option 2: Focus on Character You may prefer to focus on characters, especially if a change in character—the way someone thinks, feels, or behaves—is important to the outcome of the story.

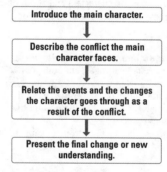

> Introduce the main character.
>
> Describe the conflict the main character faces.
>
> Relate the events and the changes the character goes through as a result of the conflict.
>
> Present the final change or new understanding.

Option 3: Focus on Conflict When the telling of a fictional narrative focuses on a central conflict, the story's plot may follow the model shown below.

	MODEL
Describe the main characters and setting.	Danielle lives on the Kansas prairie near her Aunt Jessica, who raises horses. Danielle excels at everything she does and is a little spoiled; she looks up to her aunt, who is quiet and thoughtful.
Present the conflict.	When Danielle asks for a horse to train, Jessica deliberately gives her a horse that will be hard to train.
Relate the events that make the conflict complex and cause the characters to change.	• Danielle is hurt that her aunt has given her a horse she dislikes. • Danielle wants to train the horse quickly so that she can ride him in a competition. • Danielle and Aunt Jessica have always been very close.
Present the resolution or outcome of the conflict.	By dealing with the challenge of training a difficult horse, Danielle becomes more mature. She and her aunt are brought closer together.

Explanatory Writing

Explanatory, or expository, writing informs and explains. For example, you can use it to explain how to cook spaghetti or to compare two pieces of literature. The rubric on the left shows you the basics of successful explanatory writing.

RUBRIC STANDARDS FOR WRITING

Successful explanatory writing should

- engage the interest of the reader
- state a clear purpose
- develop the topic with supporting details
- create a visual image for the reader by using precise verbs, nouns, and adjectives
- conclude with a detailed summary linked to the purpose of the composition

Types of Explanatory Writing

There are many types of explanatory writing. Select the type that presents your topic most clearly.

Compare and Contrast How are two or more subjects alike? How are they different?

> MODEL
> **The narrator and her grandfather have different ideas about beauty.**

Cause and Effect How does one event cause something else to happen? What are the results of an action or a condition?

> MODEL
> **Because she wears freckle remover in the sun, the narrator's freckles grow darker.**

Analysis/Classification How does something work? How can it be defined? What are its parts? How can it be classified into categories?

> MODEL
> **Unlike the narrator, I believe beauty is made up of a good appearance, self-confidence, and character.**

Problem-Solution How can you identify and state a problem? How would you analyze the problem and its causes? How can it be solved?

> MODEL
> **Some people, like the narrator, wish they could look like someone else. The best solution is learning to appreciate your appearance as it is.**

5.2 Compare and Contrast

Compare-and-contrast writing examines the similarities and differences between two or more subjects.

RUBRIC STANDARDS FOR WRITING

Successful compare-and-contrast writing should

- clearly identify the subjects that are being compared and contrasted
- include specific, relevant details
- follow a clear plan of organization dealing with the same features of both subjects under discussion
- use language and details appropriate to the audience
- use transitional words and phrases to clarify similarities and differences

Options for Organization

Compare-and-contrast writing can be organized in different ways. The examples that follow demonstrate feature-by-feature organization and subject-by-subject organization.

Option 1: Feature-by-Feature Organization

MODEL

Feature 1
I. The characters' standards of beauty

Subject A. The narrator's standard of beauty is based on her cousin's appearance.

Subject B. The grandfather thinks beauty takes many forms.

Feature 2
II. The characters' ideas about attaining beauty

Subject A. The narrator thinks she will be beautiful if she loses her freckles.

Subject B. The grandfather thinks the narrator is already beautiful.

Option 2: Subject-by-Subject Organization

MODEL

Subject A
I. The narrator

Feature 1. The narrator's standard of beauty is based on her cousin's appearance.

Feature 2. The narrator thinks she will be beautiful if she loses her freckles.

II. The grandfather

Subject B
Feature 1. The grandfather thinks beauty takes many forms.

Feature 2. The grandfather thinks the narrator is already beautiful.

WRITING TIP Support your comparison and contrast with expressive language and specific details.

5.3 Cause and Effect

Cause-and-effect writing explains why something happened, why certain conditions exist, or what resulted from an action or a condition.

RUBRIC STANDARDS FOR WRITING

Successful cause-and-effect writing should

- clearly state the cause-and-effect relationship
- show clear connections between causes and effects
- present causes and effects in a logical order and use transitions effectively
- use facts, examples, and other details to illustrate each cause and effect
- use language and details appropriate to the audience

Options for Organization

Your organization will depend on your topic and purpose for writing.

Option 1: Effect-to-Cause Organization

- To explain the causes of an event, such as the closing of a factory, you might first state the effect and then examine its causes.

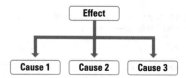

Option 2: Cause-to-Effect Organization

- To explain the effects of an event, such as the passage of a law, you might first state the cause and then explain the effects.

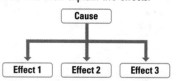

Option 3: Cause-and-Effect Chain Organization

- Sometimes you'll want to describe a chain of cause-and-effect relationships to explore a topic, such as the disappearance of tropical rain forests or the development of home computers.

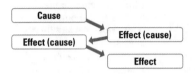

5.4 Problem-Solution

Problem-solution writing clearly states a problem, analyzes the problem, and proposes a solution to the problem. It can be used to identify and solve a conflict between characters, analyze a chemistry experiment, or explain why the home team keeps losing.

RUBRIC STANDARDS FOR WRITING

Successful problem-solution writing should

- identify the problem and help the reader understand the issues involved
- analyze the causes and effects of the problem
- integrate quotations, facts, and statistics into the text
- explore possible solutions to the problem and recommend the best one(s)
- use language, tone, and details appropriate to the audience

Options for Organization

Your organization will depend on the goal of your problem-solution piece, your intended audience, and the specific problem you choose to address. The organizational methods that follow are effective for different kinds of problem-solution writing.

Option 1: Simple Problem-Solution

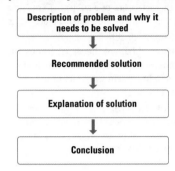

Option 2: Deciding Between Solutions

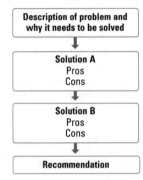

WRITING TIP Have a classmate read and respond to your problem-solution writing. Ask your peer reader: Is the problem clearly stated? Is the organization easy to follow? Do the proposed solutions seem logical?

5.5 Analysis/Classification

In writing an analysis or classification, you explain how something works, how it is defined, or what its parts are. The details you include will depend upon the kind of analysis you write.

Process Analysis What are the major steps or stages in a process? What background information is needed to understand each step? You might use process analysis to explain how to program a VCR.

Definition Analysis What are the most important characteristics of a subject? To define a rain forest, you might include such characteristics as rainfall, vegetation, and animal life.

Parts Analysis What are the parts, groups, or types that make up a subject? Parts analysis could be used to explain the parts of the human brain.

Classification How can one or more items be classified into categories? For example, you might use classification to explain how honey bees may be drones, workers, or queens.

RUBRIC STANDARDS FOR WRITING

A successful analysis should

- hook readers with a strong introduction
- clearly state the subject and its parts
- use a specific organizing structure to provide a logical flow of information
- show connections among facts and ideas through transitional words and phrases
- use language and details appropriate for the audience

Options for Organization

Organize your details in a logical order.

Option 1: Process Analysis A process analysis is usually organized chronologically, with steps or stages in the order they occur.

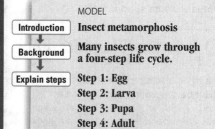

MODEL

Insect metamorphosis

Many insects grow through a four-step life cycle.

Step 1: Egg
Step 2: Larva
Step 3: Pupa
Step 4: Adult

Option 2: Definition Analysis You can organize the details in a definition or parts analysis in order of importance or impression.

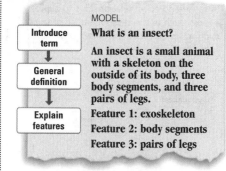

MODEL

What is an insect?

An insect is a small animal with a skeleton on the outside of its body, three body segments, and three pairs of legs.

Feature 1: exoskeleton
Feature 2: body segments
Feature 3: pairs of legs

Option 3: Parts Analysis The following parts analysis describes the parts of an insect's body.

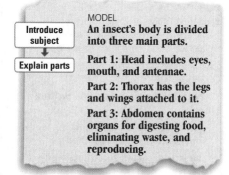

MODEL

An insect's body is divided into three main parts.

Part 1: Head includes eyes, mouth, and antennae.

Part 2: Thorax has the legs and wings attached to it.

Part 3: Abdomen contains organs for digesting food, eliminating waste, and reproducing.

Option 4: Classification The following model groups things based on characteristics.

MODEL

One way that scientists classify insects is by dividing them into species that are social and those that are not. Most insects are nonsocial. They meet one another only to reproduce. The female lays her eggs near a food source and then leaves them. Social insects, on the other hand, live in organized communities and depend on one another. Social insects have specific roles within their communities. Examples of social insects include termites, ants, many bees, and some wasps.

⑥ Persuasive Writing

Persuasive writing allows you to use the power of language to inform and influence others. It can take many forms, including speeches, newspaper editorials, billboards, advertisements, and critical reviews.

RUBRIC · STANDARDS FOR WRITING

Successful persuasive writing should

- state the issue and the writer's position
- give opinions and support them with facts or reasons
- have a reasonable and respectful tone
- answer opposing views
- use sound logic and effective language
- conclude by summing up reasons or calling for action

6.1 Key Techniques

Clarify Your Position What do you believe about the issue? How can you express your opinion most clearly?

> MODEL
> Our city should create bike lanes on all major streets to increase safety.

Know Your Audience Who will read your writing? What do they already know and believe about the issue? What objections to your position might they have? What additional information might they need? What tone and approach would be most effective?

> MODEL
> The popularity of bike riding for fun and exercise has greatly increased over the last five years. Unfortunately, there has also been an increase in injuries during this period. I believe the creation of bike lanes is necessary for public safety.

Support Your Opinion Why do you feel the way you do about the issue? What facts, statistics, examples, quotations, anecdotes, or opinions of authorities support your view? What reasons will convince your readers? What evidence can answer their objections?

> MODEL
> According to the National Safe Kids Campaign, in 1997 more than 350,000 children ages 14 and under were treated in hospital emergency rooms for bicycle-related injuries.

Begin and End with a Bang How can you hook your readers and make a lasting impression? What memorable quotation, anecdote, or statistic will catch their attention at the beginning or stick in their minds at the end? What strong summary or call to action can you conclude with?

> BEGINNING
> Whether you are a bicyclist, a driver, or even a pedestrian, chances are you've been put in a dangerous situation because bikes must use the same lanes as cars.
> CONCLUSION
> Please help improve safety for everyone in our community by supporting the creation of bike lanes on all major streets.

6.2 Options for Organization

In a two-sided persuasive essay, you want to show the weaknesses of other opinions as you explain the strengths of your own.

The example below demonstrates one method of organizing your persuasive essay to convince your audience.

Option 1: Reasons for Your Opinion

MODEL
Our city should create bike lanes on all major streets to encourage safety.

Reason 1 **Bicycle accidents often result in serious injuries.**

Reason 2 **Bicycle lanes would separate bike traffic from car traffic, making travel safer for everyone.**

Reason 3 **Safe bike paths would encourage people to ride bicycles for recreation and transportation.**

WRITING TIP Starting a persuasive piece with a question, a surprising fact, or an anecdote will capture your readers' interest and make them want to keep reading.

The ending of a persuasive piece is often the part that sticks in a reader's mind. Your conclusion might summarize the two sides of an issue or call for some action.

Depending on the purpose and form of your writing, you may want to show the weaknesses of other opinions as you explain the strength of your own. Two options for organizing writing that includes more than just your side of the issue are shown below.

Option 2: Why Your Opinion Is Stronger

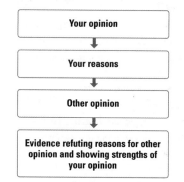

Option 3: Why Another Opinion Is Weaker

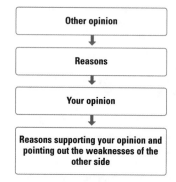

Research Report Writing

In research report writing, you can find answers to questions about a topic in which you're interested. Your writing organizes information from various sources and presents it to your readers as a unified and coherent whole.

RUBRIC STANDARDS FOR WRITING

An effective research report should

- clearly state the purpose of the report in a thesis statement
- use evidence and details from a variety of sources to support the thesis
- contain only accurate and relevant information
- document sources correctly
- develop the topic logically and include appropriate transitions
- include a properly formatted Works Cited list

7.1 Key Techniques

Develop Relevant, Interesting, and Researchable Questions Asking thoughtful questions is an ongoing part of the research process. You might begin with a list of basic questions that are relevant to your topic. These would focus on getting basic facts that answer the questions *who, what, where, when, how,* and *why* about your topic. If you were researching dragons in world folklore, you might develop a set of questions similar to these.

> MODEL
> **What cultures have dragons in their folklore?**
>
> **How are stories of dragons around the world similar and different?**

As you become more familiar with your topic, think of questions that might provide an interesting perspective that makes readers think.

> MODEL
> **What do dragons symbolize in different cultures?**

Check that your questions are researchable. Ask questions that will uncover facts, statistics, case studies, and other documentable evidence.

Clarify Your Thesis A thesis statement is one or two sentences clearly stating the main idea that you will develop in your report. A thesis may also indicate the organizational pattern you will follow and reflect your tone and point of view.

> MODEL
> **Folk tales and myths about dragons exist in cultures all over the world, but dragons symbolize good in some cultures and bad in others.**

Document Your Sources You need to document, or credit, the sources where you find your evidence. In the example below, the writer paraphrases and documents a passage from David Passes's book about dragons.

> MODEL
> **In Mordiford, England, people tell the legend of a wyvern, a two-legged dragon with wings. The wyvern terrorized the village until a prisoner named Garstone gave his life saving the community from the fire-breathing monster (Passes 30–31).**

Support Your Ideas You should support your ideas with relevant evidence—facts, anecdotes, and statistics—from reliable sources. In the example below, the writer supports the idea that dragon images still exist in cultures today.

MODEL

During the Chinese New Year, the elaborate dragon dance is used in the celebrations to drive away bad luck and bring people good luck for the coming year.

7.2 Finding and Evaluating Sources

Begin your research by looking for information about your topic in books, magazines, newspapers, and computer databases. In addition to using your library's card or computer catalog, look up your subject in indexes, such as the *Readers' Guide to Periodical Literature* or the *New York Times Index.* The bibliographies in books you find during your research may also lead to additional sources. The following checklist will help you evaluate the reliability of the sources you find.

Checklist for Evaluating Your Sources	
Authoritative	Someone who has written several books or articles on your subject or whose work has been published in a well-respected newspaper or journal may be considered an authority.
Up-to-date	Check the publication date to see if the source reflects the most current research on your subject.
Respected	In general, tabloid newspapers and popular-interest magazines are not reliable sources. If you have questions about whether you are using a respected source, ask your librarian.

WRITING TIP Your reading can inspire ideas for research topics. The title of the story "In the Land of Small Dragon," on page 804, might lead you to explore the importance of dragons in Vietnamese traditions as well as in other cultures.

7.3 Making Source Cards

For each source you find, record the bibliographic information on a separate index card. You will need this information to give credit to the sources in your paper. The samples below show how to make source cards for encyclopedia entries, magazine articles, and books. You will use the source number on each card to identify the notes you take during your research.

Encyclopedia Article

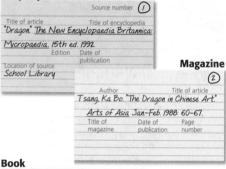

Magazine

Book

7.4 Taking Notes

As you find material that suits the purpose of your report, record each piece of information on a separate note card. You will probably use all three of the note-taking methods listed below.

Paraphrase Restate the passage in your own words. Start by finding the main idea and rewriting it in your own words. Then find and list the details that support the idea. As you restate the passage, try to use simpler language. Remember to note the source of the passage.

Summarize, or rephrase the passage in fewer words. Restate only the main ideas, using your own words. Leave out details. As a final step, check to make sure that your summary is accurate and that it does not include unnecessary information.

Quote Copy the original text word for word if you think the author's own words best clarify a particular point. Use quotation marks to signal the beginning and the end of the quotation.

For more details on making source cards and taking notes, see the Research Report Workshop on pages 754–761.

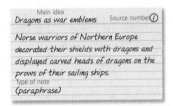

Main idea
Dragons as war emblems   Source number ①

Norse warriors of Northern Europe
decorated their shields with dragons and
displayed carved heads of dragons on the
prows of their sailing ships.
Type of note
(paraphrase)

7.5 Writing a Thesis Statement

A thesis statement in a research report defines the main idea, or overall purpose, of your report. A clear one-sentence answer to your main question will result in a good thesis statement.

Question How are stories of dragons around the world similar and different?

Thesis Statement Folk tales and myths about dragons exist in cultures all over the world, but dragons symbolize good in some cultures and bad in others.

Dragons Around the World
Thesis Statement Dragons
symbolize good and bad.
I. Origin of dragon stories
II. Dragon stories around the world
    A. Asia
    B. Europe
        1. Beowulf and the fire dragon
        2. The Mordiford wyvern
    C. North America
III. Dragon images in cultures today

7.6 Making an Outline

To organize your report, group your note cards according to their main ideas and arrange them in a logical order. With your notes, make a topic outline, beginning with a shortened version of your thesis statement. Key ideas are listed after Roman numerals, and subpoints are listed after uppercase letters and Arabic numerals.

7.7 Documenting Your Sources

When you quote one of your sources or write in your own words information you have found in a source, you need to credit that source. You can do this by using parenthetical documentation. Electronic sources, such as CD-ROMs and Web sites, must be credited just as you would credit print sources.

USING TABLES OF CONTENTS Some students may not realize that the quickest way of finding information in a reference or nonfiction book is with the table of contents. Point out that a table of contents lists the chapters and sections of a book, giving the page numbers on which each begins. Sometimes a brief chapter summary or bulleted list of main ideas appears with each entry.

Locating Information on a Topic In any research that students perform it will be helpful to scan tables of contents. For example, ask students to suppose they have begun researching ways in which horses were important to the Sioux. Ask students: Through use of a library catalog, you have found 30 books about horses and 30 books on the Sioux; how will you know which books contain information on your topic? If they narrow their catalog searches, they might miss some books. Instead they need to go to the library shelves and begin to check the books' tables of contents. If a table of contents has interesting headings, it might even suggest a new or revised research question.

Organizing Information As students compile research reports they might wish to organize them into sections with topic headings. This is also useful with group projects that combine the focused reports of several students under one broader topic. A table of contents for such a project should list the title and author(s) of each section with the page number on which it begins. You might ask students to save their outlines as they draft their research reports and to consider using their outline headings as section or chapter headings.

Guidelines for Parenthetical Documentation

Work by One Author	Put the author's last name and, if appropriate, the page reference in parentheses: (**Passes 19**). If you mention the author's name in the sentence, put only the page reference in parentheses: (**19**). For electronic sources, which usually have no page numbers, give the author's name in parentheses unless the name is already included in the text. (**Frieb**)
Work by Two or Three Authors	Put the last names of the authors and the page reference in parentheses: (**Guise, Gushwa, and Donnelly 99**).
Work by More Than Three Authors	Give the first author's last name followed by et al. and the page reference: (**Park et al. 233**).
Work with No Author Given	Give the title or a shortened version and, if appropriate, the page reference: (**"Dragon"**). Electronic sources usually have no page numbers. No page number is necessary for documentation of an encyclopedia article.
One of Two or More Works by Same Author	Give the author's last name, the title or a shortened version, and the page reference: (**Guccione, "On Dragons' Wings" 71**).

WRITING TIP Presenting someone else's writing or ideas as your own is plagiarism. To avoid plagiarism, you need to credit sources as noted above. However, if a piece of information is common knowledge—available in several sources—you do not need to credit the source. To see an example of parenthetical documentation, see the essay on page 755.

7.8 Creating a Works Cited Page

At the end of your research report, you need to include a Works Cited page. All the sources that you have cited in your report should be listed alphabetically by the authors' last names. If no author is given for a work, use the editor's last name or the title of the work. Note the guidelines for spacing and punctuation on the model page. Works Cited entries for electronic sources require slightly more information than those for print sources.

Internet Sources A Works Cited entry for an Internet source includes the same information as one for a print source. It also includes the date you accessed the information and the electronic address of the information. Some of the information about the source may be unavailable. Include as much as you can.

CD-ROMs A Works Cited entry for a CD-ROM includes the publication medium (CD-ROM), the company that distributes it, and the date of publication. Some of this information may not be available. Include as much as you can.

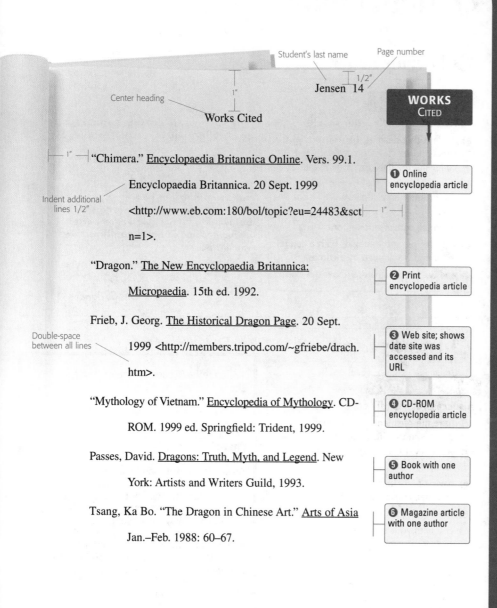

Student's last name   Page number

Jensen 14   1/2"

Center heading

Works Cited

1"

WORKS CITED

Indent additional lines 1/2"

"Chimera." <u>Encyclopaedia Britannica Online</u>. Vers. 99.1.

Encyclopaedia Britannica. 20 Sept. 1999

<http://www.eb.com:180/bol/topic?eu=24483&sct

n=1>.

1"

❶ Online encyclopedia article

"Dragon." <u>The New Encyclopaedia Britannica:</u>

<u>Micropaedia</u>. 15th ed. 1992.

❷ Print encyclopedia article

Double-space between all lines

Frieb, J. Georg. <u>The Historical Dragon Page</u>. 20 Sept.

1999 <http://members.tripod.com/~gfriebe/drach.

htm>.

❸ Web site; shows date site was accessed and its URL

"Mythology of Vietnam." <u>Encyclopedia of Mythology</u>. CD-

ROM. 1999 ed. Springfield: Trident, 1999.

❹ CD-ROM encyclopedia article

Passes, David. <u>Dragons: Truth, Myth, and Legend</u>. New

York: Artists and Writers Guild, 1993.

❺ Book with one author

Tsang, Ka Bo. "The Dragon in Chinese Art." <u>Arts of Asia</u>

Jan.–Feb. 1988: 60–67.

❻ Magazine article with one author

⑧ Model Bank

8.1 Friendly Letter

Model 1: Friendly Letter

BASICS IN A BOX

A successful friendly letter should

❶ begin with a heading that contains your street address, town or city, state and ZIP code, and the date you write the letter

❷ have a salutation that begins with a capital letter and is followed by a comma

❸ have a body that is written in an informal, conversational tone

❹ have a closing that begins with a capital letter and is followed by a comma

❺ end with your signature under the closing

> 309 Mayo Street ❶
> Tallahassee, Florida 33333
> July 29, 2000
>
> Dear Tova, ❷
>   It was great to get your postcard. I can't believe you are in Alaska! How are you doing?
>   Last night my mom and I made pizza. We used peppers, sausage, and asparagus to make a cat face. It was really fun, but I would rather be where you are. We don't have so many mosquitoes here, but we don't have glaciers or horseback riding nearby, either. I can't wait until you get back. ❸
>   Write again and tell me everything!
>
>   Love, ❹
>   Carlendra ❺

8.2 Friendly Email

Model 2: Friendly Email

BASICS IN A BOX

A successful friendly email should

❶ have the recipient's exact email address in the "To:" line

❷ state the subject of the email in the "Subject" line

❸ have a body that is written in an informal, conversational tone

❹ close with your name

❺ end with your exact email address after your name

Tips on "Netiquette"
- Always end with your name and email address.
- Always include a subject heading.
- Take as much care with spelling and punctuation as you would in a letter.
- Don't write in all capitals or it will look as if you are shouting.

> To: cmitchell@speedy.net ❶
> cc:
> bcc:
> Subject: Hungry in Alaska ❷
>
> I'm sorry I didn't write back sooner. I have been very busy having the best time ever! This place is awesome. Alaska is beautiful and the people here are really nice. I have been canoeing three times, horseback riding once, and I have plans to go rock climbing. My parents are way into hiking, so we're going up a glacier tomorrow. I wish you could visit. I miss you and I miss having pizza. Can you believe, my parents ate reindeer sausage? (yuck!) ❸
>
> See you in ten days!
> :-)
>
> Tova Goodman ❹
> tovagood@root.net ❺

8.3 Book Review

BASICS IN A BOX

A successful book review should

1. have an introduction that gives the title, author, and some information about the book
2. summarize the work without giving away the ending
3. explain why you admire or dislike the work
4. if the work is fiction, discuss the plot, setting, characters, and theme
5. support your reactions with details from the work
6. conclude with a strong statement of your opinion or a recommendation

Model 5: Book Review

Lyddie: A Book with Heart

Reviewed by Nadette Wallis

Can you imagine leaving your family to go to work somewhere you've never been? In Katherine Paterson's book *Lyddie*, that's exactly what happens. In the 1840s, a Vermont farm girl named Lyddie leaves home for a factory job in the big city of Lowell, Massachusetts. This amazing book not only holds you in suspense, it tells you what life was really like in the first American factories.

I admire Lyddie because she is a tough but caring person. She faces a bear who crashes into her family cottage on the farm. She even pushes a stagecoach out of the mud while three men just stand there. But Lyddie also shows she cares about her friends and family—and strangers too.

She shows the most courage at the factory, where every day is hard. The factory has tall, cracking ceilings, dusty windows, and deafening noises. The workers feel powerless to improve this life, but later Lyddie surprises everyone with her bold actions. Throughout the book, Lyddie cares about other people, like when she helps the runaway slave rather than collecting a reward. My favorite part is when she stands up for her friend Brigid against Mr. Marsden, the overseer, and dumps a full bucket over his head.

What will happen when she gets her boss angry? As you can tell, this book is full of taking chances and facing danger. Lyddie doesn't want to leave home, but in her adventures she becomes a hero. I recommend *Lyddie* to anyone who would like to read a fast-paced novel about a girl who never lets life get her down.

8.4 Oral Response to Literature (personal)

BASICS IN A BOX

Content

A successful oral response to literature should:

1. give the author and the title of the work
2. clearly express a personal reaction and a judgment about the writing
3. tell enough about the work for readers to understand the response
4. contain reasons for the response
5. draw an overall conclusion

Delivery

An effective speaker should:

- express enthusiasm and confidence
- stand with good but relaxed posture
- speak in a loud, clear voice
- make eye contact with the audience
- use expressive gestures and body language

Model 4: Oral Response to Literature

Responding to "The Circuit"   (intro)

by Vanessa Ramirez

When I read and reread "The Circuit" by Francisco Jiménez, I didn't understand why it made me feel sad, but then I realized at the end that it reminded me of when I was small, when I first started school.

In the story a boy named Panchito can't go to school because he has to work in the fields to help his family. When he finally goes to school in November, he forgets how to speak in English.

(body 1)

Panchito says that when he entered the school office, he heard a voice say, "May I help you?" Then he says, "I had not heard English for months. For a few seconds I remained speechless." I put myself in Panchito's place when I read this, because I had already experienced it before. When I first started school, I spoke only Spanish, but my parents spoke for me. So that was a great relief.

The reason I say it was a great relief is because in my situation my parents spoke for me in order to enroll me

❹

(body 2)

and in his situation Panchito had to speak for himself to enroll in school. This part of the story hit my heart.

When people are used to talking in one language, it is very hard when they realize they're being told something in another language. It must be sad because they don't understand, or maybe they do, but they are embarrassed because they don't know how to speak the other language well. That's how Panchito felt when he went to enroll in school and when the teacher asked him to read in class.

❹

(conclusion)

I liked writing about this story because as I was writing, I was imagining that I was there in the story and because it kind of has to do with what happened to me. I think that my response shows that Francisco Jiménez is a good writer. His writing is very realistic, and he really made me feel what Panchito was going through.

❺

Classification Essay

BASICS IN A BOX

A successful classification essay should:

❶ introduce topic and reason for classifying

❷ clearly present two or more main categories or aspects of the topic

❸ provide one or more main ideas about each category

❹ use details to help develop main ideas

❺ show the bigger picture in a clear conclusion

Model 5: Classification Essay

The Basics of a Smashing Soccer Team

by Tianna Reyes

A soccer team sometimes looks disorganized to people who don't play. It's just eleven players running around the field doing whatever they want, right? Wrong! People don't realize the huge amount of planning and strategy involved. A soccer team can be broken down into three main parts, the offense, the midfield players, and the defense.

The offense is an extremely important part of the team. There are usually three players on offense—the right wing, the left wing, and the center forward. The job of the offense is to score goals! Usually they do this by getting the ball from their midfielders and shooting the ball towards the goal. These players must be fast and good at shooting.

Midfield players are part offense and part defense. These three players are like a bridge between the offense and defense. They are responsible for passing the ball up the field to the offense players so they can try to score goals. Because they play farther back on the field they see more of the game than the offense does. So midfielders help their offense players see the weak spots in the opponent's defense. Midfield players also help their team's defense to keep the other team from scoring goals. These players do the most running, so they have to have endurance. Good passing skills are also very important for midfielders.

Classification Essay at a Glance

Introduction
- states reason for classifying
- establishes categories

Body
- presents main ideas for each category
- develops main ideas with details

Conclusion
- shows importance of classification

The defense is key, in more ways than one. **The defense is the team's "security system."** They are there to keep the opposing team from getting the ball and especially from scoring goals. These players are usually four, plus the goalie. They try to take the ball from the other offense and give it back to their own team's offense. "Goalie" is a special defensive position. This player blocks kicks. A good goalie keeps the other team from scoring. She or he is the team's last line of defense. When the ball is shot at the goal, the goalkeeper must do everything he or she can to keep it out of there. Defensive players must be quick and fierce. They must also be sneaky at stealing the ball.

❸

❹

Now you know a soccer team is not just a bunch of people who are good at running and kicking. A soccer team is a group of individuals who have many talents. They are placed in positions that are best for their skills, and they must work together in an overall strategy.

❺

8.6 Persuasive Essay

BASICS IN A BOX

A successful persuasive essay should:

❶ open with a dramatic statement of the issue and your opinion
❷ address the audience you are trying to persuade
❸ provide facts, examples, and reasons to support your opinion
❹ answer opposing views
❺ show clear reasoning
❻ include strategies such as frequent summaries to help readers remember your message
❼ end with a strong position statement or call to action

Model 6: Persuasive Essay

Preserve the Past for the Future

by Brendan Keough

How will we know what it was like to live without electricity or highways? What was it like to watch the first American walk on the moon? The only ones who know the answers are those who lived through these times. But since we pay very little attention to old people, whole chapters of history are being erased. We can stop this great loss by taking the time to interview older relatives. ❶

Hearing people you actually know tell their stories makes history a lot more interesting. Writing down these stories means that others can learn from them, too. Think about how quickly the world changed in the 20th century. ❸ When your grandfather or grandmother was a little kid, television hadn't even been invented yet. Your own parents may not have grown up with VCRs, CDs, PCs, or MP3s. ❷ What did they do for fun? What were their biggest worries? How was life different for them?

Most of the kids I know don't want to hear their parents talk about "When I was your age. . ." But, if you don't get started recording your family history right now, you'll probably wish you had. My parents are sad that they didn't write down the stories their grandparents told. ❹

Persuasive Essay at a Glance

Introduction
- presents the issue dramatically

Body
- addresses target audience
- gives evidence: facts, examples, reasons

Conclusion
- summary and call to action

And, because they didn't record those stories I never got to hear them. ─❺

Some kids our age probably think that old people's stories are boring. I used to think that, but then when I interviewed my great-uncle, Milton, I found out that he lived a pretty exciting life. For example, he was a well-digger, which is a job I had never heard of before. Even during the Great Depression, when most people lost their jobs and money, he always had work. Later, technology advanced so machines could do his job much faster and cheaper. When everyone else was back working and earning money, he was out of work. Luckily he had nine grown-up kids to help him pull through. ─❸

I believe that learning about people's lives from the past can help you set goals for your own life. When you hear about how hard your grandparents had to work or what people went through in wars and in the Depression, it really can change the way you look at life's little everyday problems. Don't wait until it's too late! Talk to your relatives and older friends now, and help to preserve the past for the future. ─❻ ─❼

Grammar Handbook

❶ Quick Reference: Parts of Speech

Part of Speech	Definition	Examples
Noun	Names a person, place, thing, idea, quality, or action.	Icarus, Greece, boat, freedom, joy, sailing
Pronoun	Takes the place of a noun or another pronoun.	
Personal	Refers to the one speaking, spoken to, or spoken about.	I, me, my, mine, we, us, our, ours, you, your, yours, she, he, it, her, him, hers, his, its, they, them, their, theirs
Reflexive	Follows a verb or preposition and refers to a preceding noun or pronoun.	myself, yourself, herself, himself, itself, ourselves, yourselves, themselves
Intensive	Emphasizes a noun or another pronoun.	(Same as reflexives)
Demonstrative	Points to specific persons or things.	this, that, these, those
Interrogative	Signals questions.	who, whom, whose, which, what
Indefinite	Refers to person(s) or thing(s) not specifically mentioned.	both, all, most, many, anyone, everybody, several, none, some
Relative	Introduces subordinate clauses and relates them to words in the main clause.	who, whom, whose, which, that
Verb	Expresses action, condition, or state of being.	
Action	Tells what the subject does or did, physically or mentally.	run, reaches, listened, consider, decides, dreamt
Linking	Connects subjects to that which identifies or describes them.	am, is, are, was, were, sound, taste, appear, feel, become, remain, seem
Auxiliary	Precedes and introduces main verbs.	be, have, do, can, could, will, would, may, might
Adjective	Modifies nouns or pronouns.	**strong** women, **two** poems, **lucky** me
Adverb	Modifies verbs, adjectives, or other adverbs.	walked **out**, **really** funny, **far away**
Preposition	Relates one word to another (following) word.	at, by, for, from, in, of, on, to, with
Conjunction	Joins words or word groups.	
Coordinating	Joins words or word groups used the same way.	and, but, or, for, so, yet, nor
Correlative	Joins words or word groups used the same way and used in pairs.	both . . . and, either . . . or, neither . . . nor
Subordinating	Joins word groups not used the same way.	although, after, as, before, because, when, if, unless
Interjection	Expresses emotion.	wow, ouch, hurrah

❷ Quick Reference: The Sentence and Its Parts

The diagrams that follow will give you a brief review of the essentials of the sentence—subjects and predicates—and of some of its parts.

Milo's **car** **stalled** in the Doldrums.

The **complete subject** includes all the words that identify the person, place, thing, or idea that the sentence is about.

The **complete predicate** includes all the words that tell or ask something about the subject.

car

stalled

The **simple subject** tells exactly whom or what the sentence is about. It may be one word or a group of words, but it does not include modifiers.

The **simple predicate**, or **verb**, tells what the subject does or is. It may be one word or several, but it does not include modifiers.

At school, an understanding teacher **had given** Panchito English lessons.

A **prepositional phrase** consists of a preposition, its object, and any modifiers of the object. In this phrase, *at* is the preposition and *school* is its object.

The **subject** tells who or what the sentence is about.

Verbs often have more than one part. They may be made up of a **main verb**, like *given,* and one or more **auxiliary,** or **helping verbs,** like *had.*

A direct object is a word or group of words that tells who or what receives the action of the verb in the sentence.

An indirect object is a word or group of words that tells *to whom* or *for whom* or *to what* or *for what* about the verb. A sentence can have an indirect object only if it has a direct object. The indirect object always comes before the direct object in a sentence.

❸ Quick Reference: Punctuation

Punctuation	Function	Examples
End Marks period, question mark, exclamation point	to end sentences	We can start now. When would you like to leave? What a fantastic hit!
	initials and other abbreviations	Mr. Gary Soto, J. K. Rowling, McDougal Littell Inc., P.M., A.D., lbs., oz., Blvd., Dr.

	items in outlines	I. Volcanoes
		  A. Central-vent
		    1. Shield

	exception: postal abbreviations	NE (Nebraska), NV (Nevada)
Commas	before a conjunction in a compound sentence	I have never disliked poetry, but now I really love it.
	items in a series	She is brave, loyal, and kind. The slow, easy route is best.
	words of address	Maria, how can I help you? You must do something, soldier.
	parenthetical expressions	Well, what if we can't? Hard workers, as you know, don't quit. I'm not a quitter, believe me.
	introductory phrases and clauses	In the beginning of the day, I feel fresh. While she was out, I was here. Having finished my chores, I went out.
	nonessential phrases and clauses	Ed Pawn, captain of the chess team, won. Ed Pawn, who is the captain, won. The two leading runners, sprinting toward the finish line, ended in a tie.
	in dates and addresses	September 21, 2001. Mail it by May 14, 2000, to Hauptman Company, 321 Market Street, Memphis, Tennessee.
	in letter parts	Dear Jim, Sincerely yours,
	for clarity, or to avoid confusion	By noon, time had run out. What the minister does, does matter. While cooking, Jim burned his hand.
Semicolons	in compound sentences that are not joined by coordinators *and,* etc.	I went to Houston in January; in June I'm going to Seattle. I read science fiction; however, I don't like fantasy stories.
	with items in series that contain commas	We invited my sister, Jan; her friend, Don; my uncle, Jack; and Mary Dodd.
	in compound sentences that contain commas	After I ran out of money, I called my parents; but only my sister was home, unfortunately.

Punctuation	Function	Examples
Colons	to introduce lists	**Correct:** Those we wrote were the following: Dana, John, and Will. **Incorrect:** Those we wrote were: Dana, John, and Will.
	before a long quotation	Abraham Lincoln wrote: "Four score and seven years ago, our fathers brought forth on this continent a new nation. . . ."
	after the salutation of a business letter	To whom it may concern: Dear Leonard Atole:
	with certain numbers	1:28 P.M., Genesis 2:3–5
Dashes	to indicate an abrupt break in thought	I was thinking of my mother—who is arriving tomorrow—just as you walked in.
Parentheses	to enclose less important material	It was so unlike him (John is always on time) that I began to worry. The last World Series game (Did you see it?) was fun.
Hyphens	with a compound adjective before nouns	The not-so-rich taxpayer won't stand for this!
	in compounds with *all-, ex-, self-, -elect*	The ex-firefighter helped rescue him. Our president-elect is self-conscious.
	in compound numbers (to ninety-nine)	Today, I turn twenty-one.
	in fractions used as adjectives	My cup is one-third full.
	between prefixes and words beginning with capital letters	Which pre-Raphaelite painter do you like best? It snowed in mid-October.
	when dividing words at the end of a line	How could you have any reasonable expec-tations of getting a new computer?
Apostrophes	to form possessives of nouns and indefinite pronouns	my friend's book, my friends' book, anyone's guess, somebody else's problem
	for omitted letters in numbers/contractions	don't (omitted *o*); he'd (omitted *woul*) the class of '99 (omitted *19*)
	to form plurals of letters and numbers	I had two A's and no 2's on my report card.
Quotation Marks	to set off a speaker's exact words	Sara said, "I'm finally ready." "I'm ready," Sara said, "finally." Did Sara say, "I'm ready"? Sara said, "I'm ready!"
	for titles of stories, short poems, essays, songs, book chapters	I liked Paulsen's "Older Run" and Roethke's "Night Journey." I like Cole Porter's "You're the Top."
Ellipses	for material omitted from a quotation	"When in the course of human events . . . and to assume among the powers of the earth. . . ."
Italics	for titles of books, plays, magazines, long poems, operas, films, TV series, names of ships	*The House on Mango Street, Hamlet, Newsweek, The Odyssey, Madame Butterfly, Gone with the Wind, Seinfeld, U.S.S. Constitution*

❹ Quick Reference: Capitalization

Category/Rule	Examples
People and Titles	
Names and initials of people	Sandra Cisneros, J. R. R. Tolkien
Titles with names or in place of them	Dr. Rodriguez, Senator Long, the Senator
Deities and members of religious groups	God, Allah, the Lord, Zeus; Baptists, Roman Catholics
Names of ethnic and national groups	Asians, African Americans, Navajos, Armenians
Geographical Names	
Cities, states, countries, continents, planets	Philadelphia, Kansas, Japan, Europe, Jupiter, Pluto
Regions, bodies of water, mountains	the South, Colorado River, the Rockies
Geographic features, parks	Great Basin, Yellowstone National Park
Streets and roads	East Sutton Drive, Kings Highway, 125th Street
Organizations and Events	
Companies, organizations, teams	Boy Scouts of America, St. Louis Cardinals
Buildings, bridges, monuments	Empire State Building, Eads Bridge, Washington Monument
Documents, awards	the Declaration of Independence, Stanley Cup
Special named events	Mardi Gras, World Series
Governmental bodies, historical periods and events	U.S. Senate, House of Representatives, Middle Ages, Vietnam War
Days and months, holidays	Thursday, March, Thanksgiving, Labor Day
Specific cars, boats, trains, planes	Edsel, Mississippi Queen, Orient Express, Concorde
Proper Adjectives	
Adjectives formed from proper nouns	French cooking, Shakespearian theater, Atlantic coast
First Words and the Pronoun *I*	
The first word in a sentence or quotation	They thanked him. Then he said, "Let's go."
Complete sentence in parentheses	(Consult the previous chapter.)
Salutation and closing of letters	Dear Sir or Madam, To all concerned, Very truly yours,
First letters in lines of most poetry and the personal pronoun, *I*	Then am I A happy fly If I live Or if I die.
First, last, and all important words in titles	*The Call of the Wild,* "Life Doesn't Frighten Me"

⑤ Writing Complete Sentences

5.1 Sentence Fragments A sentence fragment is a group of words that does not express a complete thought. It may be missing a subject, a predicate, or both. A sentence fragment makes you wonder *What is this about?* or *What happened?*

Missing Subject or Predicate You can correct a sentence fragment by adding the missing subject or predicate to complete the thought.

> **FRAGMENTS:** *Rehearsed their parts for three weeks. Even then some students.*
> **CORRECTED:** *The students rehearsed their parts for three weeks. Even then some students forgot their lines.*

Phrase and Dependent-Clause Fragments When the fragment is a phrase or a dependent (subordinate) clause, you may join the fragment to an existing sentence.

> **EXAMPLE:** *Under normal circumstances, the conflicts neighbors have are easy to ignore; however, these unresolved problems can suddenly become huge when a crisis threatens.*

GRAMMAR PRACTICE

Rewrite this paragraph, correcting the sentence fragments.

1) The play in the story. **2)** Is based on a tragedy of the winter of 1846–1847. **3)** Late in October, George and Jacob Donner. **4)** Led a party through the Sierra Nevada in California. **5)** A terrible snowstorm. **6)** Blocked the pass. **7)** By April almost half of the 82 members of the original party. **8)** Had died of starvation. **9)** Some of the survivors. **10)** Resorted to eating the corpses of those who had died.

5.2 Run-on Sentences A run-on sentence consists of two or more sentences written incorrectly as one. A run-on sentence occurs because the writer either used no end mark or used a comma instead of a period to end the first complete thought. A run-on sentence may confuse readers because it does not show where one thought ends and the next begins.

Forming Separate Sentences One way to correct a run-on sentence is to form two separate sentences. Use a period or other end punctuation after the first sentence, and capitalize the first letter of the next sentence.

> **RUN-ON:** Damon and Pythias *retells an ancient Greek legend this version is in the form of a play.*
> **MAKE TWO SENTENCES:** Damon and Pythias *retells an ancient Greek legend. This version is in the form of a play.*

Forming Compound Sentences You can also correct a run-on sentence by rewriting it to form a compound sentence. One way to do this is by using a comma and a coordinating conjunction.

Never join simple sentences with a comma alone, or a run-on sentence will result. You need a comma followed by a conjunction such as *and, but,* or *or* to hold the sentences together.

> **RUN-ON:** *The king was cruel no one dared to criticize him.*
> **ADD A CONJUNCTION:** *The king was cruel, but no one dared to criticize him.*

You may use a semicolon to join two ideas that are closely related.

In addition, you can correct a run-on sentence by using a semicolon and a conjunctive adverb. Commonly used conjunctive adverbs are *however, therefore, nevertheless,* and *besides.*

> **RUN-ON:** *Damon would have taken Pythias' punishment Pythias returned just in time.*
> **ADD A SEMICOLON AND A CONJUNCTIVE ADVERB:** *Damon would have taken Pythias' punishment; however, Pythias returned just in time.*

Grammar Practice Answers

The play in the story "The School Play" is based on a tragedy of the winter of 1846–1847. Late in October, George and Jacob Donner led a party through the Sierra Nevada in California. A terrible snowstorm blocked the pass. By April almost half of the 82 members of the original party had died of starvation. Some of the survivors resorted to eating the corpses of those who had died.

In *Damon and Pythias,* the friendship of two young men helps them face death. Another story about friends is found in the Bible. David and Jonathan were friends who protected each other and warned each other of danger. David was a musician whose songs soothed Saul, the king of Israel. Jonathan was the son of Saul. He also remained David's closest friend throughout his life. David's brave acts made him a hero, and Saul became jealous of him. On more than one occasion Jonathan warned David of Saul's plots. Saul tried to kill David with a dagger. David had opportunities to kill Saul, but he always refused to do bad things. Such honorable conduct shamed Saul. Jonathan defended David even against his own father.

6.1

1. tells
2. take
3. excites
4. seems
5. thinks
6. wonder
7. dates
8. suggests
9. forms
10. measure

Grammar Handbook

Rewrite this paragraph, correcting the run-on sentences.

1) In *Damon and Pythias* the friendship of two young men helps them face death another story about friends is found in the Bible. **2)** David and Jonathan were friends who protected each other they warned each other of danger. **3)** David was a musician his songs soothed Saul, the king of Israel. **4)** Jonathan was the son of Saul he remained David's closest friend throughout his life. **5)** David's brave acts made him a hero Saul became jealous of him. **6)** On more than one occasion Jonathan warned David of Saul's plots Saul tried to kill David with a dagger. **7)** David had opportunities to kill Saul he always refused to do bad things. **8)** Such honorable conduct shamed Saul Jonathan defended David even against his own father.

❻ Making Subjects and Verbs Agree

6.1 *Simple and Compound Subjects* A verb must agree in number with its subject. When a word refers to more than one thing, it is plural.

Agreement with Simple Subjects Use a singular verb with a singular subject.

When the subject is a singular noun, you use the singular form of the verb. The present-tense singular form of a regular verb usually ends in *-s* or *-es.*

> **INCORRECT:** *"Tutankhamen" tell of a famous archaeological discovery.*
> **CORRECT:** *"Tutankhamen" tells of a famous archaeological discovery.*

USAGE TIP To find the subject of a sentence, first find the verb. Then ask *who* or *what* performs the action of the verb. Say the subject and the verb together to see if they agree.

Use a plural verb with a plural subject.

> **INCORRECT:** *Two determined men looks for the tomb of Pharaoh Tutankhamen.*
> **CORRECT:** *Two determined men look for the tomb of Pharaoh Tutankhamen.*

Agreement with Compound Subjects Use a plural verb with a compound subject whose parts are joined by *and,* regardless of the number of each part.

> **INCORRECT:** *Carter and Carnarvon exclaims when they find "wonderful things."*
> **CORRECT:** *Carter and Carnarvon exclaim when they find "wonderful things."*

When the parts of a compound subject are joined by *or* or *nor,* make the verb agree in number with the part that is closer to it.

Usually *or* and *nor* appear with their correlatives *either* and *neither.*

> **EXAMPLE:** *Neither Carnarvon nor the Egyptians know where to look for the rich tomb. A frequent problem for archaeologists is that grave robbers or time causes great damage.*

Write the correct form of the verb given in parentheses.

1. "Tutankhamen" (tell, tells) of a great archaeological discovery in Egypt.

2. Many wonderful discoveries also (take, takes) place in our part of the world.

3. A recent discovery (excite, excites) archaeologists in Mexico.

4. The city (seems, seem) to have been abandoned suddenly about A.D. 1000.

5. One archaeologist (think, thinks) that this city hit its peak in the Classic Period, from A.D. 300 to A.D. 600.

6. Sarah Goodman and other archaeologists (wonder, wonders) what brought about such growth.

7. Several smaller settlements (date, dates) from about that time.

8. Research (suggest, suggests) that El Pital was a center of trade and culture.

9. Earth or stone (form, forms) more than a hundred dwellings, ball courts, temples, and long platforms.

10. Some buildings (measure, measures) 130 feet in height.

6.2 *Pronoun Subjects* When a pronoun is used as a subject, the verb must agree with it in number.

Agreement with Personal Pronouns
When the subject is a singular personal pronoun, use a singular verb. When the subject is a plural personal pronoun, use a plural verb.

Even though *I* and *you* are singular, they take the plural form of the verb.

> **INCORRECT**: *I believes that "Abd al-Rahman Ibrahima" is a true story.*
> **CORRECT**: *I believe that "Abd al-Rahman Ibrahima" is a true story.*

When *he, she,* or *it* is the part of the subject closer to the verb in a compound subject containing *or* or *nor*, use a singular verb. When a pronoun is a part of a compound subject containing *and*, use a plural verb.

> **INCORRECT**: *Neither the other captives nor he expect treachery.*
> **CORRECT**: *Neither the other captives nor he expects treachery.*

Agreement with Indefinite Pronouns
When the subject is a singular indefinite pronoun, use the singular form of the verb.

The following are singular indefinite pronouns: *another, either, nobody, anybody, everybody, somebody, no one, anyone, everyone, someone, one, nothing, anything, everything, something, each,* and *neither.*

> **INCORRECT**: *During Ibrahima's time with Dr. Cox, everything go well.*
> **CORRECT**: *During Ibrahima's time with Dr. Cox, everything goes well.*

When the subject is a plural indefinite pronoun *(both, few, many,* or *several)*, use the plural form of the verb.

> **INCORRECT**: *Ibrahima learns that many deceives or betrays others.*
> **CORRECT**: *Ibrahima learns that many deceive or betray others.*

The indefinite pronouns *some, all, any, none,* and *most* can be either singular or plural. When the pronoun refers to one thing, use a singular verb.

When the pronoun refers to several things, use a plural verb.

> **INCORRECT**: *Of the captives Ibrahima meets, many dies on the trip, and most suffers on landing.*
> **CORRECT**: *Of the captives Ibrahima meets, many die on the trip, and most suffer on landing.*

GRAMMAR PRACTICE

Write the correct form of the verb given in parentheses.

1. Of the people in the world, many (live, lives) on the huge continent of Africa.

2. Some (appear, appears) in the selection "Abd al-Rahman Ibrahima."

3. Each group (speak, speaks) its own language or dialect.

4. Ibrahima speaks Fulani because he (belong, belongs) to the Fula people.

5. Most Fula (wear, wears) their hair long.

6. They are a pastoral people, so many (raise, raises) livestock.

7. In the selection, we (meet, meets) the Mandingo, enemies of the Fula.

8. They (come, comes) from West Africa and belong to many independent kingdoms.

9. One (trace, traces) its dynasty back 13 centuries with hardly a break.

Grammar Practice Answers

1. live
2. appear
3. speaks
4. belongs
5. wear
6. raise
7. meet
8. come
9. traces

6.3 Common Agreement Problems

Several other situations can cause problems in subject-verb agreement.

Agreement with Irregular Verbs Use the singular forms of the irregular verbs *do, be,* and *have* with singular subjects. Use the plural forms of these verbs with plural subjects.

WATCH OUT! Look carefully at words that come before the subject. Remember that the subject may not be the noun or pronoun closest to the verb.

	Do	Be	Have
Singular Subjects	I do	I am/was	I have
	you do	you are/were	you have
	the dog does	Joe is/was	Pat hasn't
	it does	he isn't/wasn't	she has
	each doesn't	either is/was	anybody has
Plural Subjects	we do	we are/were	we have
	dogs do	boys are/were	girls have
	they do	they are/were	they haven't
	many don't	both are/were	few have

> **INCORRECT:** *"The All-American Slurp" do a good job of describing manners. The story have examples of Chinese and American mistakes. They is both funny.*
> **CORRECT:** *"The All-American Slurp" does a good job of describing manners. The story has examples of Chinese and American mistakes. They are both funny.*

Interrupting Words Be sure the verb agrees with its subject when a word or words come between them.

Sometimes one or more words come between the subject and the verb. The interrupter does not affect the number of the subject.

> **INCORRECT:** *Many of the girls in the group feels embarrassed. A dip of sour cream and onion flakes cause a problem.*
> **CORRECT:** *Many of the girls in the group feel embarrassed. A dip of sour cream and onion flakes causes a problem.*

Interrupting Phrases Be certain that the verb agrees with its subject when a phrase comes between them.

The subject of a verb is never found in a prepositional phrase, which may follow the subject and come before the verb.

> **INCORRECT:** *The members of the Gleason family offers snacks to the Lins. A cooked vegetable, according to many Chinese people, taste better than a raw one.*
> **CORRECT:** *The members of the Gleason family offer snacks to the Lins. A cooked vegetable, according to many Chinese people, tastes better than a raw one.*

Phrases beginning with *including, as well as, along with,* and *in addition to* are not part of the subject.

> **INCORRECT:** *The Lins learn that celery, as well as radishes and carrots, count as a finger food. Each guest, including the parents and the children, skip the dip.*
> **CORRECT:** *The Lins learn that celery, as well as radishes and carrots, counts as a finger food. Each guest, including the parents and the children, skips the dip.*

The subject of the verb is never found in an appositive, which may follow the subject and come before the verb.

> **INCORRECT:** *Meg, daughter of the Gleasons, struggle to eat a traditional Chinese meal. Pot stickers, a Chinese delicacy, is enjoyed by almost everyone.*
> **CORRECT:** *Meg, daughter of the Gleasons, struggles to eat a traditional Chinese meal. Pot stickers, a Chinese delicacy, are enjoyed by almost everyone.*

Inverted Sentences When the subject comes after the verb, be sure the verb agrees with the subject in number.

A sentence in which the subject follows the verb is called an inverted sentence. Questions are usually in inverted form, as are sentences beginning with *here, there,* and *where. (Where are the reporters? There are two press conferences today.)*

INCORRECT: *From knowing the rules of courtesy come confidence. From breaking them, however, come the most fun and laughter.*

CORRECT: *From knowing the rules of courtesy comes confidence. From breaking them, however, comes the most fun and laughter.*

USAGE TIP To check subject-verb agreement in inverted sentences, place the subject before the verb. For example, to check agreement, change *There are many people* to *Many people are there.*

GRAMMAR PRACTICE

Write the correct form of each verb given in parentheses.

1. The story "The All-American Slurp" (does, do) readers a favor; it helps us not take ourselves too seriously.

2. Most of us, at some time or another, (has, have) wondered about etiquette.

3. What (is, are) the right things to do?

4. Raw food, including things like celery, (was, were) difficult for the Lins.

5. (Does, Do) you handle similar problems in another country as well as the Lins do?

6. The difficulties for a traveler (is, are) often embarrassing.

7. (Is, Are) there a gracious way to deal with a disgusting dish? Here (is, are) some ways.

8. Swallowing fast and telling yourself that it "tastes just like chicken" (is, are) a good way.

9. Some people, to disguise the texture of a food, (slice, slices) the item thinly.

❼ Using Nouns and Pronouns

7.1 *Plural and Possessive Nouns* Nouns refer to people, places, things, and ideas. Nouns are plural when they refer to more than one person, place, thing, or idea. Possessive nouns show who or what owns something.

Plural Nouns Follow these guidelines to form noun plurals.

Nouns	To Form Plural	Examples
Most nouns	add -*s*	jaw—jaws
Most nouns that end in *s, sh, ch, x,* or *z*	add -*es*	fox—foxes flash—flashes
Most nouns that end in *ay, ey, oy,* or *uy*	add -*s*	delay—delays valley—valleys
Most nouns that end in a consonant and *y*	change *y* to *i* and add -*es*	cavalry—cavalries casualty—casualties
Most nouns that end in *o*	add -*s*	alto—altos arroyo—arroyos soprano—sopranos
Some nouns that end in a consonant and *o*	add -*es*	echo—echoes hero—heroes tomato—tomatoes
Most nouns that end in *f* or *fe*	change *f* to *v,* add -*es* or -*s*	sheaf—sheaves knife—knives *but* belief—beliefs

WATCH OUT! The plurals of many musical terms that end in *o* preceded by a consonant are formed by adding -*s*. These nouns include *tempos* and *concertos.*

Grammar Practice Answers

1. does
2. have
3. are
4. was
5. Do
6. are
7. Is, are
8. is
9. slice

1. world's
2. family's
3. holidays
4. signs
5. emotions
6. People, messages
7. symphonies, compositions
8. years, extremes
9. songs, melodies, critic's
10. heroes
11. critics, Beethoven's

Grammar Handbook

Some nouns use the same spelling in both singular and plural: *series, fish, sheep, deer.* Some noun plurals use irregular forms that don't follow any rule: *teeth, geese, feet, mice, people, children, women, men.*

> **INCORRECT:** *In "Beethoven Lives Upstairs," Beethoven disrupts the lifes of his neighbors. When writing his symphonys, he plays piano with loud bumps and crashs.*
>
> **CORRECT:** *In "Beethoven Lives Upstairs," Beethoven disrupts the lives of his neighbors. When writing his symphonies, he plays piano with loud bumps and crashes.*

USAGE TIP The dictionary usually lists the plural form of a noun if the plural form is irregular or if there is more than one plural form. Dictionary listings are especially helpful for nouns that end in *o, f,* and *fe.*

Possessive Nouns Follow these guidelines to form possessive nouns.

Nouns	To Form Possessive	Examples
Singular nouns	add apostrophe and -*s*	league—league's
Plural nouns ending in *s*	add apostrophe	fields—fields' brigades—brigades'
Plural nouns not ending in *s*	add apostrophe and -*s*	children—children's oxen—oxen's

> **INCORRECT:** *The sopranos voices echoed throughout Christophs house.*
>
> **CORRECT:** *The sopranos' voices echoed throughout Christoph's house.*

WATCH OUT! Be careful when placing apostrophes in possessive nouns. A misplaced apostrophe changes the meaning. For example, *boy's* refers to possession by one boy, but *boys'* refers to possession by two or more boys.

GRAMMAR PRACTICE

Write the correct form given in parentheses.

1. Many people consider Ludwig van Beethoven the (world's, worlds') greatest composer.

2. His (family's, familys') many musicians included his father and grandfather.

3. Born in Germany, Beethoven, as a young man, settled in Vienna, thereafter leaving only for summer (holidays, holidaies, holiday's).

4. Before he was 30, he began to notice (sign, signs) of deafness.

5. After experiencing a range of (emotions, emotiones), he swore to "seize fate by the throat" and went on to compose groundbreaking works.

6. (People, peoples) wrote (messages, messages') in "conversation books" to communicate with him.

7. His nine (symphonys, symphonies) and many other (composition's, compositions) show great achievement.

8. Particularly in earlier (year, years), his music leaned toward (extreme's, extremes) of piano and forte.

9. His passionate (songs, songs') and simple folk (melodys, melodies) moved many a (critics, critic's) heart.

10. His powerful work and personality made some musicians call him one of the artist (heros, heroes) of modern times.

11. Many music (critics, critic's) of the 19th century found (Beethoven's, Beethovens') music impossible to understand.

7.2 *Pronoun Case* A personal pronoun is a pronoun that can be used in the first, second, or third person. A personal pronoun has three forms: the subject form, the object form, and the possessive form.

Subject Pronouns Use the subject form of a pronoun when it is the subject of a sentence or the subject of a clause. *I, you, he, she, it, we,* and *they* are subject pronouns.

Using the correct pronoun form is seldom a problem when the sentence has just one pronoun. Problems can arise, however, when a noun and a pronoun or two pronouns are used in a compound subject or compound object. To see if you are using the correct pronoun form, read the sentence, using only one pronoun.

> **INCORRECT:** *"The Circuit" tells the story of a boy and his family. The story begins and ends as he and them pack to move yet again.*
> **CORRECT:** *"The Circuit" tells the story of a boy and his family. The story begins and ends as he and they pack to move yet again.*

Use the subject form of a pronoun when it follows a linking verb as a predicate pronoun.

You often hear the object form used in casual conversation as a predicate pronoun. ("It is him.") For this reason, the subject form may sound awkward to you, though it is preferred for more formal writing.

> **INCORRECT:** *The boy is the narrator. It is him who helps the readers feel his joy and pain.*
> **CORRECT:** *The boy is the narrator. It is he who helps the readers feel his joy and pain.*

USAGE TIP To check the form of a predicate pronoun, see if the sentence still makes sense when the subject and the predicate pronoun are reversed. *(It was he. He was it.)*

Object Pronouns Use the object form of a pronoun when it is the object of a sentence, the object of a clause, or the object of a preposition. *Me, you, him, her, it, us,* and *them* are object pronouns.

> **INCORRECT:** *We share with his family and he the frustration of not staying in one place.*
> **CORRECT:** *We share with his family and him the frustration of not staying in one place.*

Possessive Pronouns Never use an apostrophe in a possessive pronoun. *My, mine, your, yours, his, her, hers, its, our, ours, their,* and *theirs* are possessive pronouns.

Writers often confuse the possessive pronouns *its, your,* and *their* with the contractions *it's, you're,* and *they're.* Remember that the pairs are spelled differently and that they have different meanings.

> **INCORRECT:** *They're disappointment at moving again touches us. Its as if we, and not them, come home to find boxes packed. The sad circuit, or cycle, is our's.*
> **CORRECT:** *Their disappointment at moving again touches us. It's as if we, and not they, come home to find boxes packed. The sad circuit, or cycle, is ours.*

GRAMMAR PRACTICE

Write the correct pronoun form given in parentheses.

1) The life of a migrant worker would be hard for you and (I, me). **2)** (Them, They) and other workers must struggle at low-paying jobs just to survive. **3)** (They're, Their) working conditions are sometimes intolerable. **4)** Not only must workers settle for extremely low wages, but (they're, their) often unable to find any jobs for half the year. **5)** When (they, them) do, employers provide poor housing for (they, them). **6)** No sick days, holidays, or other benefits are offered to their families or (them, they). **7)** You and (I, me) might wonder why anyone would settle for such work. **8)** Many workers come from other countries, however, where (its, it's) even harder to make a living. **9)** Black and Hispanic men, women, and children make up most of the migrant work force; poor whites and (they, them) suffer equally. **10)** Some travel with (they're, their) families; others send money home.

Grammar Practice Answers

1. me
2. They
3. Their
4. they're
5. they, them
6. them,
7. I
8. it's
9. they
10. their

7.3 *Pronoun Antecedents* An antecedent is the noun or pronoun to which a personal pronoun refers. The antecedent usually precedes the pronoun.

Pronoun and Antecedent Agreement A pronoun must agree with its antecedent in

NUMBER—*singular or plural*
PERSON—*first, second, or third*
GENDER—*male or female*

Use a singular pronoun to refer to a singular antecedent; use a plural pronoun to refer to a plural antecedent.

Do not allow interrupting words to determine the number of the personal pronoun.

> **INCORRECT:** *In "In the Land of Small Dragon" it is the younger half-sister and the step-mother, not the father, who is unkind to T'âm.*
> **CORRECT:** *In "In the Land of Small Dragon" it is the younger half-sister and the step-mother, not the father, who are unkind to T'âm.*

If the antecedent is a noun that could be either male or female, use *he* or *she (him or her, his or her)* or reword the sentence to avoid the need for a singular pronoun.

> **INCORRECT:** *A reader may wonder who T'âm is. They might think she is a princess.*
> **CORRECT:** *A reader may wonder who T'âm is. He or she might think T'âm is a princess.*
> **CORRECT:** *Readers may wonder who T'âm is. They might think she is a princess.*

Be sure that the antecedent of a pronoun is clear.

In most cases, do not use a pronoun to refer to an entire idea or clause. Writing is much clearer if the exact reference is repeated.

> **UNCLEAR:** *Both this story and the Cinderella tale end happily, and it is what we hope for.*
> **CLEAR:** *Both this story and the Cinderella tale end happily, and happy endings are what we hope for.*

USAGE TIP To avoid vague pronoun references, do not use *this* or *that* alone to start a sentence. Instead, include a word that clarifies what *this* or *that* refers to—*this experience, this situation, that concept.*

Indefinite Pronouns as Antecedents When a singular indefinite pronoun is the antecedent, use *he* or *she (him or her, his or her)* or rewrite the sentence to avoid the need for a singular pronoun.

> **INCORRECT:** *Everyone at the festival rejoiced.*
> **CORRECT:** *All who were at the festival rejoiced.*

Indefinite Pronouns

Singular

another	each	everybody	neither	somebody
anybody	either	everyone	nobody	someone
anyone	one	everything	no one	something
anything			nothing	

Plural

both	few	many	several

Singular or Plural

all	any	most	none	some

GRAMMAR PRACTICE

Rewrite this paragraph to make the pronoun reference clear.

1) A tale like "In the Land of Small Dragon" is found in many countries; they remind you of Cinderella. **2)** *Mufaro's Beautiful Daughters* is one of these tales. **3)** In this book Nyasha was loved by everyone, but they usually did not like her sister. **4)** She encouraged the snake to live in her garden, where it was very comfortable. **5)** Manyara was unkind and rude, and people could not help but see it. **6)** One day a messenger arrived, and they said that the king was looking for a bride. **7)** Manyara left on her journey to the king's city before Nyasha, and she was afraid she would be late. **8)** On the way Manyara met an old woman; she reminded her to be helpful to anyone she met. **9)** Instead, she was often rude to them. **10)** Nyasha was kind and courteous, and it was rewarded in the end.

Grammar Practice Answers

1) A tale like "In the Land of Small Dragon" is found in many countries. Such tales remind me of Cinderella. **2)** *Mufaro's Beautiful Daughters* is one of these Cinderella tales. **3)** In this book Nyasha was loved by everyone, but most people did not like her sister. **4)** Nyasha encouraged the snake to live in her garden, where it was very comfortable. **5)** Manyara, the sister, was unkind and rude, and people could not help but see these qualities. **6)** One day a messenger arrived to say that the king was looking for a bride. **7)** Manyara left on her journey to the king's city before Nyasha did. Nyasha was afraid she would be late. **8)** On the way Manyara met an old woman who reminded her to be helpful to anyone she met. **9)** Instead, Manyara was often rude to strangers along her way. **10)** Nyasha was kind and courteous, and she was rewarded for it in the end.

7.4 *Pronoun Usage* The form that a pronoun takes is always determined by its function within its own clause or sentence.

Who and Whom Use *who* or *whoever* as the subject of a clause or sentence.

> **INCORRECT:** *In "The Legend of the Hummingbird," the young girl Alida falls in love with Taroo, whom is from an enemy tribe.*
> **CORRECT:** *In "The Legend of the Hummingbird," the young girl Alida falls in love with Taroo, who is from an enemy tribe.*

Use *whom* as the direct or indirect object of a verb or verbal and as the object of a preposition.

People often use *who* for *whom* when speaking informally. However, in written English the pronouns should be used correctly.

> **INCORRECT:** *First Alida meets a young boy with who she talks and picks fruit. Then she learns that his people, who Alida fears, had abandoned him on her island.*
> **CORRECT:** *First Alida meets a young boy with whom she talks and picks fruit. Then she learns that his people, whom Alida fears, had abandoned him on her island.*

WATCH OUT! Watch for prepositions and verbs that precede the word *who.*
To whom—object of a preposition.
To interview whom—object of the infinitive verb *to interview*.

In trying to determine the correct pronoun form, ignore interrupters that come between the subject and the verb.

> **INCORRECT:** *Whom do you think has the saddest fate?*
> **CORRECT:** *Who do you think has the saddest fate?*

Pronouns in Contractions Do not confuse the contractions *it's, they're, who's,* and *you're* with possessive pronouns that sound the same—*its, their, whose,* and *your.*

> **INCORRECT:** *Its sad when Alida's father arranges for her to marry someone else. Alida and Taroo both beg the god Yukiyú for help with they're tragic situation.*
> **CORRECT:** *It's sad when Alida's father arranges for her to marry someone else. Alida and Taroo both beg the god Yukiyú for help with their tragic situation.*

Pronouns with Nouns Determine the correct form of the pronoun in phrases such as *we girls* and *us boys* by dropping the noun and saying the sentence without the noun that follows the pronoun.

> **INCORRECT:** *I believe a story is best when us readers are kept in suspense.*
> **CORRECT:** *I believe a story is best when we readers are kept in suspense.*

GRAMMAR PRACTICE

Write the correct pronoun given in parentheses.

1. Many people say the hummingbird is (their, they're) favorite bird.

2. This tiny bird can beat (its, it's) wings 60 times a second.

3. People (who, whom) observe a hummingbird's wings in motion see only a blur.

4. The beating of (its, it's) wings causes a humming sound.

5. (Their, They're) tiny feet are almost useless; they must fly to travel only a few inches.

6. The hummingbird can use (its, it's) wings to move in any direction.

7. Because of (their, they're) special skeletal structure, (their, they're) able to fly backward, sideways, or even upside down.

8. (Who, Whom) could not be fascinated by this sight?

9. If (your, you're) interested in attracting hummingbirds, consider making a hummingbird feeder.

10. A hummingbird drinks nectar through (its, it's) hollow tongue.

Grammar Practice Answers

1. their
2. its
3. who
4. its
5. Their
6. its
7. their, they're
8. Who
9. you're
10. its

Grammar Handbook

8 Using Verbs Correctly

8.1 *Verb Tenses and Forms* Verb tense shows the time of an action or a condition. Writers sometimes cause confusion when they use different verb tenses in describing actions that occur at the same time.

Consistent Use of Tenses When two or more actions occur at the same time or in sequence, use the same verb tense to describe the actions.

> **INCORRECT:** *"Scout's Honor" tells about a camping group that starts in Brooklyn and went into New Jersey. The trip nearly became a disaster.*
> **CORRECT:** *"Scout's Honor" tells about a camping group that starts in Brooklyn and goes into New Jersey. The trip nearly becomes a disaster.*

A shift in tense is necessary when two events occur at different times or out of sequence. The tenses of the verbs should clearly indicate that one action precedes the other.

> **INCORRECT:** *Now that the trip is over, it seems funny. But for a while we are all miserable.*
> **CORRECT:** *Now that the trip is over, it seems funny. But for a while we were all miserable.*

Tense	Verb Form
Present	open/opens
Past	opened
Future	will/shall open
Present perfect	have/has opened
Past perfect	had opened
Future perfect	will/shall have opened

WATCH OUT! In telling a story, be careful not to shift tenses so often that the reader has difficulty keeping the sequence of events straight.

Past Tense and the Past Participle The simple past form of a verb can always stand alone. The past participle of the following irregular verbs should always be used with a helping verb.

Present Tense	Past Tense	Past Participle
be (is/are)	was/were	(have, had) been
begin	began	(have, had) begun
break	broke	(have, had) broken
bring	brought	(have, had) brought
choose	chose	(have, had) chosen
come	came	(have, had) come
do	did	(have, had) done
drink	drank	(have, had) drunk
eat	ate	(have, had) eaten
fall	fell	(have, had) fallen
freeze	froze	(have, had) frozen
give	gave	(have, had) given
go	went	(have, had) gone
lose	lost	(have, had) lost
grow	grew	(have, had) grown

> **INCORRECT:** *They have did a lot to prepare for the trip. For instance, Max have brought a compass.*
> **CORRECT:** *They had done a lot to prepare for the trip. For instance, Max had brought a compass.*

USAGE TIP Some writers use gradual shifts in verb tense (such as from the past to the past participle) to move from the past up through to the present. This can be used to show developments over a period of time as in the example above. When using this technique, be careful to use verb tenses that clearly convey your message.

GRAMMAR PRACTICE

Write the correct verb tense for each sentence.

1) In "Scout's Honor" we (seen, have seen) an attempt to build a campfire. **2)** When I camped

Grammar Practice Answers

1. have seen

with Aunt Zarefa, we (bring, brought) along dry firewood. **3)** She said the first step is to (find, found) a clear area. **4)** We (gather, gathered) fuel such as twigs and sticks. **5)** Then we (build, built) a tepee of twigs over a small pile of tinder. **6)** She asked me to (use, used) sticks to build walls around the tepee. **7)** The next task was to (place, placed) logs around the walls and lean sticks on them. **8)** After I (light, lit) a match and slipped it into the sticks, our campfire blazed. **9)** When I woke up the next day, I saw that Auntie had (use, used) water and dirt to put out the last of the fire.

8.2 *Commonly Confused Verbs* The following verb pairs are easily confused.

Let and *Leave* *Let* means "to allow or permit." *Leave* means "to depart" or "to allow something to remain where it is."

> **INCORRECT:** *"Aaron's Gift" leaves the reader imagine what to do about a wounded animal. Should you let it to die?*
> **CORRECT:** *"Aaron's Gift" lets the reader imagine what to do about a wounded animal. Should you leave it to die?*

Lie and *Lay* *Lie* means "to rest in a flat position." *Lay* means "to put or place."

> **INCORRECT:** *Almost dead, the pigeon laid down. He lied his ruffled feathers close to his body.*
> **CORRECT:** *Almost dead, the pigeon lay down. He laid his ruffled feathers close to his body.*

WATCH OUT! If you're uncertain about which verb to use, check to see whether the verb has an object. The verbs *lie, sit,* and *rise* never have objects.

Sit and *Set* *Sit* means "to be in a seated position." *Set* means "to put or place."

> **INCORRECT:** *Pidge would often set quietly and look at Aaron. Aaron was glad he'd sat out food to help the bird get well.*
> **CORRECT:** *Pidge would often sit quietly and look at Aaron. Aaron was glad he'd set out food to help the bird get well.*

Rise and *Raise* *Rise* means "to move upward." *Raise* means "to move something upward."

> **INCORRECT:** *Raising up quickly, Pidge escaped. He rose his healed wing and flapped desperately.*
> **CORRECT:** *Rising up quickly, Pidge escaped. He raised his healed wing and flapped desperately.*

Learn and *Teach* *Learn* means "to gain knowledge or skill." *Teach* means "to help someone learn."

> **INCORRECT:** *Pidge learned Aaron much about standing up for a friend.*
> **CORRECT:** *Pidge taught Aaron much about standing up for a friend.*

Here are the principal parts of these troublesome verb pairs.

Present Tense	Past Tense	Past Participle
let	let	(have, had) let
leave	left	(have, had) left
lie	lay	(have, had) lain
lay	laid	(have, had) laid
sit	sat	(have, had) sat
set	set	(have, had) set
rise	rose	(have, had) risen
raise	raised	(have, had) raised
learn	learned	(have, had) learned
teach	taught	(have, had) taught

GRAMMAR PRACTICE

Choose the correct verb from each pair of words given in parentheses.

1. Biologists have (left, let) us know that rock doves are the ancestors of pigeons like the one in "Aaron's Gift."

2. Rock doves like to (sit, set) their nests on cliff ledges, so their descendants thrive in modern cities.

3. People started (raising, rising) rock doves for food around 4500 B.C.

4. (Leave, Let) me tell you that today there are about 285 kinds of pigeons.

Grammar Practice Answers 8.1 (continued)

2. brought
3. find
4. gathered
5. built
6. use
7. place
8. lit
9. used

Grammar Practice Answers 8.2

1. let
2. set
3. raising
4. Let

5. lie
6. rise
7. laid
8. teach

9.1

1. proud
2. hardworking
3. quickly
4. stern
5. nervous
6. greatly
7. reluctantly
8. extensive

5. Pigeons are active during the day, but do they ever (lay, lie) down to sleep?

6. Some kinds of pigeons weigh as much as three pounds, so they must be strong fliers to (raise, rise) into the air.

7. When we raised pigeons, they usually (lay, laid) two eggs at a time.

8. Biologists (teach, learn) us that some pigeons use the sounds their feathers make during flight to signal each other.

❾ Using Modifiers Effectively

9.1 *Adjective or Adverb?* Use an adjective to modify a noun or a pronoun. Use an adverb to modify a verb, an adjective, or another adverb.

> **INCORRECT:** *In "Oh Broom, Get to Work," the author writes amusing about some especial boring visitors to her home.*
> **CORRECT:** *In "Oh Broom, Get to Work," the author writes amusingly about some especially boring visitors to her home.*

USAGE TIP Always determine first which word is being modified. In the preceding example, where *writes* is the word being modified, the correct choice is an adverb. A verb can only be modified by an adverb.

Use an adjective after a linking verb to describe the subject.

> **INCORRECT:** *Yo Chan and her sister felt unhappily about the many dull visitors. Only one minister seemed entertainingly.*
> **CORRECT:** *Yo Chan and her sister felt unhappy about the many dull visitors. Only one minister seemed entertaining.*

Remember that in addition to forms of the verb *be*, the following are linking verbs: *become, seem, appear, look, sound, feel, taste, grow,* and *smell.*

GRAMMAR PRACTICE

Write the correct modifier in each pair.

1) In "Oh Broom, Get to Work," Yo Chan's parents are (proud, proudly) graduates of a Christian university in Japan. **2)** Christianity was brought there by (hardworkingly, hardworking) missionaries. **3)** The religion spread (quick, quickly) throughout Japan beginning in 1549. **4)** The (stern, sternly) rulers of the nation thought that a Western religion would undermine their power. **5)** In the early 1600s the (nervously, nervous) rulers began to limit the religion. **6)** The number of people practicing Christianity dropped (great, greatly) by 1640. **7)** Missionaries were (reluctant, reluctantly) allowed back into the country in 1873. **8)** After two centuries they found some evidence of Christianity that had survived the (extensive, extensively) persecution.

9.2 *Comparisons and Negatives*

Comparative and Superlative Adjectives
Use the comparative form of an adjective when comparing two things.

Comparative adjectives are formed by adding *-er* to short adjectives *(small, smaller)* or by using the word *more* with longer adjectives *(horrible, more horrible).*

> **INCORRECT:** *"Summer of Fire" is dramaticer than many article I have read. Forest fires are one of the more scary disasters you could encounter.*
> **CORRECT:** *"Summer of Fire" is more dramatic than many articles I have read. Forest fires are one of the scarier disasters you could encounter.*

Use the superlative form when comparing three or more things.

The superlative is formed by adding *-est* to short adjectives *(tall, tallest)* or by using the word *most* with longer adjectives *(interesting, most interesting).*

> **INCORRECT:** *Which fire is threateningest? Which spreads most fast?*
> **CORRECT:** *Which fire is most threatening? Which spreads fastest?*

WATCH OUT! When using the comparative form to compare something with everything else of its kind, do not leave out the word *other*. *(Kim is shorter than any other member of her family.)*

The comparative and superlative forms of some adjectives are irregular.

Adjective	Comparative	Superlative
good	better	best
well	better	best
bad	worse	worst
ill	worse	worst
little	less or lesser	least
much	more	most
many	more	most
far	farther or further	farthest or furthest

WATCH OUT! Do not use both *-er* and *more*. Do not use both *-est* and *most*. Notice the improvement when *more* and *most* are removed from the following sentence: *The ship was more faster than the most fastest winds.*

When comparing more than two actions, use the superlative form of an adverb, which is formed by adding *-est* or by using the word *most*.

> **INCORRECT:** *Of all the park buildings, the Old Faithful Inn was considered importantest.*
> **CORRECT:** *Of all the park buildings, the Old Faithful Inn was considered most important.*

Comparative and Superlative Adverbs
When comparing two actions, use the comparative form of an adverb, which is formed by adding *-er* or the word *more*.

> **INCORRECT:** *More oftener than not, the fires spread quicklier than fire fighters could control them.*
> **CORRECT:** *More often than not, the fires spread more quickly than fire fighters could control them.*

Double Negatives To avoid double negatives, use only one negative word in a clause.

Besides *not* and *no*, the following are negative words: *never, nobody, none, no one, nothing,* and *nowhere.*

> **INCORRECT:** *No one could hardly believe the fires continued for so long. It seemed they wouldn't never stop.*
> **CORRECT:** *No one could believe the fires continued for so long. It seemed they would never stop.*

GRAMMAR PRACTICE

Rewrite the paragraph, correcting the underlined modifiers.

1) Most of the animals in Yellowstone, including the park's <u>most large</u> mammals, the bison, survived the fire. **2)** The <u>very bigger</u> bison can weigh over 1,800 pounds. **3)** They are also <u>more tall</u> than you—about six feet at the shoulder. **4)** The wild bison in the park wander <u>freer</u> than most bison on ranches. **5)** They usually seem to walk <u>slowlier</u> than other animals. **6)** However, if you get <u>too closer</u> to a bison, you might be suprised at how fast it can move. **7)** In winter, bison use their huge heads to push aside the <u>most heaviest</u> snow and find grass. **8)** They also hang around the <u>more warm</u> areas, near the geysers. **9)** Some visitors say the park bison are the <u>awesomest</u> animals they ever saw in the wild.

9.3 *Special Problems with Modifiers*
The following terms are frequently misused in spoken English, but they should be used correctly, especially in written English.

Them and *Those* *Them* is always a pronoun and never a modifier for a noun. *Those* is a pronoun when it stands alone. It is an adjective when followed by a noun.

> **INCORRECT:** *In "Flowers and Freckle Cream," Elizabeth learns that them freckles of hers aren't so bad after all.*
> **CORRECT:** *In "Flowers and Freckle Cream," Elizabeth learns that those freckles of hers aren't so bad after all.*

Grammar Practice Answers

1) Most of the animals in Yellowstone, including the park's largest mammals, the bison, survived the fire. **2)** The biggest bisons can weigh over 1,800 pounds. **3)** They are also taller than you—about six feet at the shoulder. **4)** The wild bison in the park wander more freely than most bison on ranches. **5)** They usually seem to walk more slowly than other animals. **6)** However, if you get too close to a bison, you might be surprised at how fast it can move. **7)** In winter, bison use their huge heads to push aside the heaviest snow and find grass. **8)** They also hang around the warmer areas, near the geysers. **9)** Some visitors say the park bison are the most awesome animals they ever saw in the wild.

Grammar Practice Answers

1. those
2. badly
3. Fewer
4. those
5. well
6. badly
7. that
8. those
9. little
10. well

Grammar Handbook

Bad and Badly Always use *bad* as an adjective, whether before a noun or after a linking verb. *Badly* should generally be used to modify an action verb.

> **INCORRECT:** *Grandpa saved the day when Elizabeth felt so badly. She acted bad when she refused to tell anyone what was wrong.*
> **CORRECT:** *Grandpa saved the day when Elizabeth felt so bad. She acted badly when she refused to tell anyone what was wrong.*

WATCH OUT! Avoid the use of *here* after *this* or *these*. Similarly, avoid using *there* after *that* or *those*. Notice the improvement when *here* and *there* are removed from the following sentence:

> **INCORRECT:** *I was shocked by this here story. Those there baseball managers really angered me.*

This, That, These, and Those Whether used as adjectives or pronouns, *this* and *these* refer to people and things that are nearby, and *that* and *those* refer to people and things that are farther away.

> **INCORRECT:** *All day long, Elizabeth worked outdoors in this faraway field. When she came home, she had these hateful freckles on her face.*
> **CORRECT:** *All day long, Elizabeth worked outdoors in that faraway field. When she came home, she had those hateful freckles on her face.*

Good and Well *Good* is always an adjective, never an adverb. Use *well* as either an adjective or an adverb, depending on the sentence.

When used as an adjective, *well* usually refers to a person's health. As an adverb, *well* modifies an action verb. In the expression "feeling good," *good* refers to being happy or pleased.

> **INCORRECT:** *Hoeing tobacco under the hot sun, Elizabeth did her work good. She felt well when she saw all her fine work.*
> **CORRECT:** *Hoeing tobacco under the hot sun, Elizabeth did her work well. She felt good when she saw all her fine work.*

Few and Little, Fewer and Less *Few* refers to numbers of things that can be counted; *little* refers to amounts or quantities. *Fewer* is used when comparing numbers of things; *less* is used when comparing amounts or quantities.

> **INCORRECT:** *Because she felt appreciated by Grandpa, having less freckles didn't matter. She decided that the fewer she spent on freckle cream, the better.*
> **CORRECT:** *Because she felt appreciated by Grandpa, having fewer freckles didn't matter. She decided that the less she spent on freckle cream, the better.*

GRAMMAR PRACTICE

Write the modifier from each pair in parentheses that fits the meaning of the sentence.

1. In "Flowers and Freckle Cream" Elizabeth makes one of (them, those) mail-order purchases.

2. In the 1870s big-city department stores decided that mail order was needed (bad, badly) by people on farms.

3. (Less, Fewer) rural people than today could travel to the city to shop.

4. The stores sent (these, those) customers catalogs.

5. Mail-order merchants did (good, well) by serving farm families.

6. When more people moved to the cities, mail-order business did (bad, badly).

7. Later, (this, that) kind of business was advertised in magazines.

8. Later still, (those, these) merchants began sending catalogs to city dwellers.

9. The merchants also sent catalogs to people who had (few, little) time to shop.

10. Today, the Internet works (good, well) to provide another mail-order experience.

⑩ Correcting Capitalization

10.1 *Proper Nouns and Adjectives* A common noun names a whole class of persons, places, things, or ideas. A proper noun names a particular person, place, thing, or idea. A proper adjective is an adjective formed from a proper noun. All proper nouns and proper adjectives are capitalized.

Names and Personal Titles Capitalize the name and title of a person.

Also capitalize the initials and abbreviations of titles that stand for those names. *Thomas Alva Edison, T. A. Edison, Governor James Thompson,* and *Mr. Aaron Copeland* are capitalized correctly.

> **INCORRECT:** *"President Cleveland, Where Are You?" tells about jerry's search for a trading card. Other characters include roger lussier and mr. lemire.*
> **CORRECT:** *"President Cleveland, Where Are You?" tells about Jerry's search for a trading card. Other characters include Roger Lussier and Mr. Lemire.*

Capitalize a word referring to a family relationship when it is used as someone's name *(Uncle Al)* but not when it is used to identify a person *(Jill's uncle).*

> **INCORRECT:** *Armand, Jerry's Brother, was in charge of buying their Father a gift. Last year, my Sisters and I bought a gift for aunt Marisol.*
> **CORRECT:** *Armand, Jerry's brother, was in charge of buying their father a gift. Last year, my sisters and I bought a gift for Aunt Marisol.*

WATCH OUT! Do not capitalize personal titles used as common nouns. *(We met the mayor.)*

Languages, Nationalities, Religious Terms Capitalize the names of languages and nationalities as well as religious names and terms.

Capitalize languages and nationalities, such as *French, Gaelic, Chinese,* and *Tagalog.* Capitalize religious names and terms, such as *Allah, Jehovah, the Bible,* and *the Koran*.

> **INCORRECT:** *Jerry is part of a french-american family in a small town. His family attends the local catholic church.*
> **CORRECT:** *Jerry is part of a French-American family in a small town. His family attends the local Catholic church.*

School Subjects Capitalize the name of a specific school course (Civics 101, General Science). Do not capitalize a general reference to a school subject (social studies, algebra, art).

> **INCORRECT:** *Jerry's teacher for social studies 2 was amazed at how much he knew about History.*
> **CORRECT:** *Jerry's teacher for Social Studies 2 was amazed at how much he knew about history.*

WATCH OUT! Do not capitalize minor words in a proper noun that is made up of several words (*Field Museum **of** Natural History*).

Organizations, Institutions Capitalize the important words in the official names of organizations and institutions (*Congress, Duke University*).

Do not capitalize words that refer to kinds of organizations or institutions (*college, hospital, museum*) or words that refer to specific organizations but are not their official names (*to the museum*).

> **INCORRECT:** *The smithsonian institution has old trading cards. Maybe the frenchtown historical society or another Library does too.*
> **CORRECT:** *The Smithsonian Institution has old trading cards. Maybe the Frenchtown Historical Society or another library does too.*

Geographical Names, Events, Time Periods Capitalize geographical names, as well as the names of events, historical periods and documents, holidays, and months and days, but *not* the names of seasons or directions.

Grammar Practice Answers

1. This story made me curious about President Cleveland.
2. My uncle took me to the library to find reference books, such as *The Big Book of U.S. Presidents.*
3. I learned that Cleveland was the only president to leave the White House and later return.
4. He was also the only one to get married in the White House.
5. At his marriage to Francis Folsom, thousands of citizens crowded the lawn.
6. Throughout his career, Cleveland was famous for doing what he thought right whether or not it was popular.
7. As president, like he had done as sheriff, then mayor, and then governor in New York state, he focused on reforming government.
8. Between his two terms, Cleveland worked as a lawyer in New York and spent time with his family.
9. Late one autumn night in 1891 the Clevelands welcomed their baby daughter, Ruth, the first of the couple's five children.
10. Many Americans were fascinated by the little girl, and a candy bar was named for her: "Baby Ruth."

Grammar Handbook

INCORRECT: *Stephen Grover Cleveland was born in caldwell, new jersey, on march 18, 1837.*

CORRECT: *Stephen Grover Cleveland was born in Caldwell, New Jersey, on March 18, 1837.*

Names	Examples
Continents	Africa, South America
Bodies of water	Pacific Ocean, Lake Charles, Amazon River
Political units	Maine, Japan, Brasília
Sections of a country	the South, Middle Atlantic States
Public areas	the Loop, Boston Common
Roads and structures	Park Avenue, Hoover Dam, Chrysler Building
Historical events	the War of 1812, the Emancipation Proclamation
Documents	Magna Carta, the Treaty of Paris
Periods of history	the Middle Ages, Reconstruction
Holidays	Arbor Day, New Year's Day
Months and days	May, Sunday
Seasons	summer, autumn
Directions	north, south

10.2 *Titles of Created Works* Titles need to follow certain capitalization rules.

Poems, Stories, Articles Capitalize the first word, the last word, and all other important words in the title of a poem, a story, or an article. Enclose the title in quotation marks.

INCORRECT: *Carl Sandburg's poem primer lesson talks about risks you take when you say harsh things.*

CORRECT: *Carl Sandburg's poem "Primer Lesson" talks about risks you take when you say harsh things.*

Books, Plays, Magazines, Newspapers, Films Capitalize the first word, the last word, and all other important words in the title of a book, play or musical, magazine, newspaper, or film. Underline or italicize the title to set it off.

Within a title, don't capitalize articles, conjunctions, and prepositions of fewer than five letters.

INCORRECT: Primer lesson appeared in Sandburg's book *complete poems.*

CORRECT: "Primer Lesson" appeared in Sandburg's book *Complete Poems.*

GRAMMAR PRACTICE

Correct the capitalization in the sentences below.

1. This story made me curious about president cleveland.
2. My Uncle took me to the Library to find Reference Books, such as *The Big book Of U.S. presidents.*
3. I learned that cleveland was the only president to leave the white house and later return.
4. He was also the only one to get married in the white house.
5. At his marriage to francis folsom, thousands of Citizens crowded the lawn.
6. Throughout his Career, cleveland was famous for doing what he thought Right whether or not it was popular.
7. As President, like he had done as Sheriff, then Mayor, and then Governor in new york state, he focused on reforming Government.
8. Between his two Terms, cleveland worked as a Lawyer in new york and spent time with his Family.
9. Late one Autumn night in 1891 the clevelands welcomed their baby Daughter, ruth, the first of the Couple's five Children.
10. Many americans were fascinated by the little girl, and a Candy Bar was named for her: "baby ruth."

⑪ Phrases and Clauses

11.1 Phrases
A phrase is a group of words that does not have a subject and predicate and that functions in a sentence as a single part of speech.

Prepositional Phrases When a phrase consists of a preposition, its object, and any modifiers of the object, it is called a prepositional phrase. Prepositional phrases may function as adjectives or adverbs.

> **EXAMPLE:** Adjective Phrase: *In the excerpt from* The Story of My Life, *Helen Keller tells the story of her awakening to language.*
> **EXAMPLE:** Adverb Phrase: *She had suffered in confused darkness.*

Appositive Phrases An appositive phrase identifies or provides information about a noun or pronoun.

> **EXAMPLE:** *Helen Keller, a young girl, lost her hearing and sight.*

Infinitive Phrases An infinitive phrase consists of an infinitive (*to* + a verb) along with its modifiers and objects.

> **EXAMPLE:** *For many years, Helen tried to express her thoughts and feelings.*

Participial Phrases There are two kinds of participles. The past participle is usually formed by adding *-d* or *-ed* to the present tense. Irregular verbs, however, do not follow this rule. The present participle is formed by adding *-ing* to the present tense of any verb. A participle with its objects and modifiers is called a participial phrase. Participial phrases act as adjectives.

> **EXAMPLE:** *Having read her autobiography, I can better imagine what life was like for her.*

Gerund Phrases A gerund is a verb form ending in *-ing* that functions as a noun. A gerund phrase is a group of words that includes a gerund, its modifiers, and objects.

> **EXAMPLE:** *Learning to communicate became her main goal.*

GRAMMAR PRACTICE

Identify each underlined phrase as prepositional, appositive, infinitive, participial, or gerund.

1. After reading about Helen Keller, I wanted <u>to find out more about Anne Sullivan.</u>
2. <u>Searching through the library,</u> I came across many biographies about her.
3. During her lifetime, <u>the years between 1866 and 1936,</u> she overcame her own disability and shared her strategies with others.
4. Sullivan, <u>through patience and understanding,</u> helped Helen Keller learn to use words.
5. People <u>reading of her work</u> must have wept real tears for her triumphs.
6. <u>Learning about this amazing teacher</u> was sometimes a painful experience.

11.2 Independent and Dependent (Subordinate) Clauses
A clause is a group of words that contains a subject and a verb. There are two kinds of clauses: independent clauses and dependent, or subordinate, clauses. An independent clause can stand alone as a complete sentence. A subordinate clause cannot stand alone and must be attached to an independent clause to form a complex sentence.

> **EXAMPLE:** *Independent clause: I read "Where the Girl Rescued Her Brother."*
> **EXAMPLE:** *Dependent clause: After I had finished dinner*
> **EXAMPLE:** *Complex sentence: After I had finished dinner, I read "Where the Girl Rescued Her Brother."*

Adjective and Adverb Clauses A subordinate clause may be used as an adjective. Adjective clauses are usually introduced by the relative pronouns *who, whom, whose, which,* and *that.* A subordinate clause may also be used as an adverb to modify a verb, adjective, or another adverb.

> **EXAMPLE:** *Adjective clause: Buffalo Calf Road Woman was the name of the girl who saved her brother.*
> **EXAMPLE:** *She rode into battle when she saw that her brother was surrounded.*

Grammar Practice Answers

1. infinitive
2. participial
3. appositive
4. prepositional
5. participial
6. gerund

Grammar Practice Answers

11.2

1. phrase
2. clause
3. clause
4. clause, phrase
5. clause

12.2

1. In 1925, a diphtheria epidemic broke out in Nome, Alaska. The city was not prepared.
2. More serum was needed. The town would face disaster.
3. Trains took the serum part of the way. Dog sled teams carried it on to Nome.
4. Nineteen dog sled teams worked in a relay for a week. The Nome residents cheered each team's arrival.
5. The teams working together saved the town. The people were grateful.

Noun Clauses A noun clause is a dependent (subordinate) clause used as a noun. A noun clause may be a subject, a direct object, an indirect object, a predicate noun, or the object of a preposition.

> **EXAMPLE:** *Buffalo Calf Road Woman proved that a girl can be as brave as a boy.*

GRAMMAR PRACTICE

Identify each underlined group of words as either a phrase or a clause.

1. Some Crow and Shoshone scouts tried <u>to help white soldiers defeat the Cheyenne.</u>

2. Buffalo Calf Road Woman grew worried <u>when her brother's horse was shot.</u>

3. No one imagined <u>what would happen next.</u>

4. The girl, <u>who was very brave,</u> galloped straight <u>into the fight.</u>

5. Everyone knew <u>that this was heroism.</u>

⑫ The Structure of Sentences

The structure of a sentence is determined by the number and kind of clauses it contains. Sentences are classified as simple, compound, complex, and compound-complex.

12.1 *Simple Sentences* A simple sentence is made up of one independent clause and no dependent (or subordinate) clauses.

> Jeb wrote a poem.
> INDEPENDENT CLAUSE

> Aunt Lucy is a great singer.
> INDEPENDENT CLAUSE

A simple sentence may contain a compound subject or a compound verb.

COMPOUND SUBJECT:
Jeb and Aunt Lucy are writing a song.
COMPOUND VERB:
They work and sing for hours at a time.

12.2 *Compound Sentences* A compound sentence is made up of two or more independent clauses joined together. A compound sentence does not contain any dependent clauses.

> INDEPENDENT CLAUSES

> Jeb is writing the words, and
> Aunt Lucy is writing the music.

Independent clauses can be joined with a comma and a coordinating conjunction, a semicolon, or a semicolon and a comma with a conjunctive adverb.

COMMA AND A COORDINATING CONJUNCTION:
> I have not heard the song, but I'm
> sure it will be great.

SEMICOLON:
> Aunt Lucy has great talent; she
> studied singing for many years.

SEMICOLON AND A COMMA WITH A CONJUNCTIVE ADVERB:
> Jeb has published many
> poems; however, this is his
> first attempt at song-writing.

WATCH OUT! Do not confuse a compound sentence with a simple sentence that has compound parts.

GRAMMAR PRACTICE

Rewrite each compound sentence as two simple sentences.

1) In 1925, a diphtheria epidemic broke out in Nome, Alaska, but the city was not prepared. **2)** More serum was needed, or the town would face disaster. **3)** Trains took the serum part of the way, and dog sled teams carried it on to Nome. **4)** Nineteen dog sled teams worked in a relay for a week, and the Nome residents cheered each team's arrival. **5)** The teams working together saved the town, and the people were grateful.

12.3 Complex Sentences A complex sentence is made up of one independent clause and one or more dependent clauses.

> INDEPENDENT CLAUSE
> **I would like to be an actor,** **although**
> **I've never been on stage before.**
> DEPENDENT CLAUSE

An independent clause can stand alone as a sentence. A dependent clause also has a subject and a predicate, but cannot stand alone. It is often introduced by a subordinating conjunction, such as *when, if, because,* or *until.*

GRAMMAR PRACTICE

In each of the following complex sentences, identify the independent and the dependent clauses.

1) Although beasts often appear in movies today, scary monsters are not new. **2)** As long as people have been on earth, they have told stories about strange creatures. **3)** If one looks into those old stories, one finds many different kinds of monsters. **4)** When people have been afraid of some kind of creature, it was usually a monster. **5)** Folklore usually presents monsters as horrible animals, although the creatures often have human qualities.

12.4 Compound-Complex Sentences A compound-complex sentence is made up of two or more independent clauses and one or more dependent clauses. If you start with a compound sentence, all you need to do to form a compound-complex sentence is add a dependent clause.

> COMPOUND SENTENCE:
> INDEPENDENT CLAUSES
> **The students wanted to be in the**
> **play,** but **many were too shy to audition.**

COMPOUND-COMPLEX SENTENCE:
INDEPENDENT CLAUSES
The students wanted to be in the
play, but **many were too shy to audition,**
although some finally found the
courage to do so.
DEPENDENT CLAUSE

GRAMMAR PRACTICE

In each of the following sentences, identify the independent and the dependent clauses.

1) The game started at four o'clock, and Sara was late, even though she ran all the way. **2)** When she got to the field, she was tired, and her team was impatient. **3)** Because the other team was even later, Sara was relieved, and her team forgave her. **4)** When the game began, Sara played first base, and her friend played in the outfield. **5)** Sara liked to play softball because the coach was good, and her friends played on the team.

MIXED REVIEW

Identify each sentence with **S** for simple, **CD** for compound, **CX** for complex, and **CC** for compound-complex.

1) Both children and adults like to play hangman because they can play the game together. **2)** A modern version of hangman became a popular television show. **3)** Chinese checkers is played with marbles; it is an easy game to learn. **4)** The playing board is round and has a star-like design on it. **5)** Checkers is played on a board with 64 squares. **6)** Although the game is called checkers in the United States, it is called draughts in Great Britain. **7)** Each nation has its own rules for checkers. **8)** Some people don't like to play board games; they would rather play a team sport, even though it takes more effort. **9)** Basketball is a popular sport, although soccer and softball are favorites too. **10)** Since golf is played outdoors, the weather can cause problems, and players have to stop and go inside.

Grammar Practice Answers
12.3

Independent clauses are italicized.
Dependent clauses are underlined.

1. Although beasts often appear in movies today, *scary monsters are not new.*
2. As long as people have been on earth, *they have told stories about strange creatures.*
3. If one looks into those old stories, *one finds many different kinds of monsters.*
4. When people have been afraid of some kind of creature, *it was usually a monster.*
5. *Folklore usually presents monsters as horrible animals,* although the creatures often have human qualities.

Grammar Practice Answers
12.4

Independent clauses are italicized.
Dependent clauses are underlined.

1. *The game started at four o'clock, and Sara was late,* even though she ran all the way.
2. When she got to the field, *she was tired, and her team was impatient.*
3. Because the other team was even later, *Sara was relieved, and her team forgave her.*
4. When the game began, *Sara played first base, and her friend played in the outfield.*
5. *Sara liked to play softball* because the coach was good, *and her friends played on the team.*

Mixed Review Answers

1. CX
2. S
3. CD
4. S
5. S
6. CX
7. S
8. CC
9. CX
10. CC

⑬ Punctuation

13.1 *Compound Sentences* Punctuation helps organize longer sentences that have several clauses.

Commas in Compound Sentences Use a comma before the conjunction that joins the clauses of a compound sentence.

> **INCORRECT:** *Henson reached the North Pole and he worked hard to make the most of his opportunity.*
>
> **CORRECT:** *Henson reached the North Pole, and he worked hard to make the most of his opportunity.*

Semicolons in Compound Sentences Use a semicolon between the clauses of a compound sentence when no conjunction is used. Use a semicolon before, and a comma after, a conjunctive adverb that joins the clauses of a compound sentence.

Conjunctive adverbs include *therefore, however, then, nevertheless, consequently,* and *besides.*

> **EXAMPLE:** *He made the dream of his boyhood come true; however, racism interfered with his ambition.*

USAGE TIP Even when clauses are connected by a coordinating conjunction, you should use a semicolon between them if one or both clauses contain a comma.

> **EXAMPLE:** *Matthew's father, unable to support him, sent the boy to live with an uncle; however, soon Matthew's uncle could no longer support him.*

GRAMMAR PRACTICE

Rewrite the paragraph, adding commas and semicolons where necessary.

1) "Matthew Henson at the Top of the World" describes the discovery of the North Pole but the Peary expedition wasn't the first to seek it. **2)** The earliest Arctic expedition probably took place in the late 300s B.C. a Greek explorer said he found an island six days north of Scotland. **3)** People didn't believe him they thought there was nothing but ice that far north. **4)** In the late 1500s people wanted a quick way to the Orient therefore the Englishman Martin Frobisher tried to find a northwest passage through the Arctic. **5)** In the 1770s Samuel Hearne was the first European to travel by land to the Arctic Ocean from Hudson Bay and much exploration followed his journey. **6)** In 1926 Richard Byrd and Floyd Bennett made the first flight over the North Pole the next step was to complete a submarine passage across the pole.

13.2 *Elements Set Off in a Sentence* Most elements that are not essential to a sentence are set off by commas to highlight the main idea of the sentence.

Introductory Words Use a comma to separate an introductory word or phrase from the rest of the sentence.

> **INCORRECT:** *Definitely "The First Emperor" gets me thinking about ancient China.*
>
> **CORRECT:** *Definitely, "The First Emperor" gets me thinking about ancient China.*

Use a comma to set off more than one introductory prepositional phrase, but not for a single prepositional phrase in most cases.

> **INCORRECT:** *With its images of cruel behavior this article makes me doubt that I could have survived in that world.*
>
> **CORRECT:** *With its images of cruel behavior, this article makes me doubt that I could have survived in that world.*

Interrupters Use commas to set off a word that interrupts the flow of a sentence.

> **EXAMPLE:** *What, perchance, would make a king of the weakest state want to unite all the neighboring states?*

Use commas to set off a group of words that interrupts the flow of a sentence.

> **EXAMPLE:** *The discovery of the tomb, including the soldiers guarding it, has astonished archaeologists.*

**Grammar Practice Answers
13.1**

"Matthew Henson at the Top of the World" describes the discovery of the North Pole, but the Peary expedition wasn't the first to seek it. The earliest Arctic expedition probably took place in the late 300s B.C.; a Greek explorer said he found an island six days north of Scotland. People didn't believe him; they thought there was nothing but ice that far north. In the late 1500s people wanted a quick way to the Orient; therefore the Englishman Martin Frobisher tried to find a northwest passage through the Arctic. In the 1770s Samuel Hearne was the first European to travel by land to the Arctic Ocean from Hudson Bay, and much exploration followed his journey. In 1926 Richard Byrd and Floyd Bennett made the first flight over the North Pole; the next step was to complete a submarine passage across the pole.

Nouns of Address Use commas to set off a noun in direct address at the beginning of a sentence.

> **INCORRECT:** *If I could talk with Emperor Ch'in, I'd say, "Emperor why put people in danger?"*
> **CORRECT:** *If I could talk with Emperor Ch'in, I'd say, "Emperor, why put people in danger?"*

Use commas to set off a noun in direct address in the middle of a sentence.

> **INCORRECT:** *Then I'd say, "How many people Emperor did you kill?"*
> **CORRECT:** *Then I'd say, "How many people, Emperor, did you kill?"*

Appositives Set off with commas an appositive phrase that is not necessary to the meaning of the sentence.

The following sentence could be understood without the appositive.

> **INCORRECT:** *The emperor a strong-minded person dug his own grave.*
> **CORRECT:** *The emperor, a strong-minded person, dug his own grave.*

Do not set off with commas an appositive phrase that is necessary to the meaning of the sentence.

The following sentence could not be understood without the words set off by commas:

> **INCORRECT:** *Ch'in, the warrior, seems very different from Ch'in, the worried mouse.*
> **CORRECT:** *Ch'in the warrior seems very different from Ch'in the worried mouse.*

For Clarity Use a comma to prevent misreading or misunderstanding.

> **INCORRECT:** *Excavators finally found the tomb that professors had searched for for so long.*
> **CORRECT:** *Excavators finally found the tomb that professors had searched for, for so long.*

GRAMMAR PRACTICE

Rewrite the paragraph. Add or delete commas where necessary.

1) Ch'in Shih Huang Ti "The First Emperor" sounds like a typical emperor. **2)** An emperor rules not just one but several countries by always staying alert to outside threats. **3)** Clearly his country, is the strongest one. **4)** Empires those vast political machines are formed by war. **5)** Once an empire is established however it reduces the number of wars for a while. **6)** In an empire, with strong central control everyone knows who's boss. **7)** Empires can have good effects when for example they force people to exchange languages, art, and technology. **8)** If I could, I'd say to Ch'in, "Tell me Emperor what you accomplished."

13.3 Elements in a Series Commas should be used to separate three or more items in a series and to separate adjectives preceding a noun.

Subjects, Predicates, and Other Elements
Use a comma after every item except the last in a series of three or more items.

Subjects or predicates may occur in series.

> **INCORRECT:** *In* The Story of My Life, *Helen Keller learns to fingerspell discovers that everything has a name and finds her world changed as a result.*
> **CORRECT:** *In* The Story of My Life, *Helen Keller learns to fingerspell, discovers that everything has a name, and finds her world changed as a result.*

Predicate adjectives often occur in series.

> **INCORRECT:** *As the selection begins, Helen is silent angry and careless.*
> **CORRECT:** *As the selection begins, Helen is silent, angry, and careless.*

USAGE TIP Note in the example that a comma followed by a conjunction precedes the last element in the series.

Adverbs and prepositional phrases may also occur in series.

> **INCORRECT:** *As Helen learned more words, her teacher developed new teaching plans with speed with creativity and with great success.*
> **CORRECT:** *As Helen learned more words, her teacher developed new teaching plans with speed, with creativity, and with great success.*

Grammar Practice Answers
13.2

1) Ch'in Shih Huang Ti, "The First Emperor," sounds like a typical emperor. **2)** An emperor rules not just one, but several countries by always staying alert to outside threats. **3, 4)** Clearly, his country is the strongest one. Empires, those vast political machines, are formed by war. **5)** Once an empire is established, however, it reduces the number of wars for a while. **6)** In an empire with strong central control, everyone knows who's boss. **7)** Empires can have good effects when, for example, they force people to exchange languages, art, and technology. **8)** If I could, I'd say to Ch'in, "Tell me, Emperor, what you accomplished."

Grammar Practice Answers
13.3

1. The *Story of My Life* was written by Helen Keller, writer, activist, and speaker.
2. Keller was left blind and deaf by a childhood illness, was taught to communicate by her teacher Anne Sullivan, and went on to graduate from college with honors.
3. Photographs show Helen Keller meeting with such famous persons as Mark Twain, Charlie Chaplin, and President John F. Kennedy.
4. Less well-known is Keller's love of dogs, including her shiny pug-nosed Boston terrier.

13.4

1. After reading "The Southpaw" I sent a postcard to my friend Shinobu in San Francisco, California, where I used to live.
2. Dear Shinobu,
   A girl in a story I read played baseball with a team that used to be all boys. It reminded me of you being the first girl to pitch for the Berkeley Bees!

   Yours truly,
   Elizabeth
3. Shinobu said she still remembers that day on June 14, 1966 when she first stood on the pitcher's mound.
4. I thought my uncle in Reno, Nevada might have some pictures from that day.
5. Dear Uncle Ernesto,
   Remember when you came to visit me, and we saw my friend Shinobu pitch? If you still have any of the photos you took, I'd love to see them.

   Love always,
   Elizabeth

Grammar Handbook

Two or More Adjectives In most sentences, use a comma after each adjective except the last of two or more adjectives that precede a noun.

If you can reverse the order of adjectives without changing the meaning or if you can use *and* between them, separate the two adjectives with a comma.

> INCORRECT: *Helen's eager young hands caught the flow of dark, blue water.*
> CORRECT: *Helen's eager, young hands caught the flow of dark blue water.*

GRAMMAR PRACTICE

Rewrite each sentence, inserting commas where they are needed.

1. *The Story of My Life* was written by Helen Keller, writer activist and speaker.
2. Keller was left blind and deaf by a childhood illness was taught to communicate by her teacher Anne Sullivan and went on to graduate from college with honors.
3. Photographs show Helen Keller meeting with such famous persons as Mark Twain Charlie Chaplin and President Kennedy.
4. Less well-known is Keller's love of dogs, including her shiny pug-nosed Boston terrier.

13.4 Dates, Addresses, and Letters
Punctuation in dates, addresses, and letters makes information easy to understand.

Dates Use a comma between the day of the month and the year. If the date falls in the middle of a sentence, use another comma after the year.

> INCORRECT: *I went to the game on Monday August 30 1999 a sunny day.*
> CORRECT: *I went to the game on Monday, August 30, 1999, a sunny day.*

Addresses Use a comma to separate the city and the state in an address or other location. If the city and state fall in the middle of a sentence, use a comma after the state too.

> EXAMPLE: *Janet called Richard the laughingstock of Mapesville, New Jersey.*

Parts of a Letter Use a comma after the greeting and after the closing in a letter.

> INCORRECT:
> *Dear Janet*
> *Here's the silver horseback riding trophy that you gave me.*
> *Your former friend*
> *Richard*
> CORRECT:
> *Dear Janet,*
> *Here's the silver horseback riding trophy that you gave me.*
> *Your former friend,*
> *Richard*

GRAMMAR PRACTICE

Rewrite the following sentences, correcting the comma errors.

1. After reading "The Southpaw," I sent a postcard to my friend Shinobu in San Francisco California where I used to live.
2. Dear Shinobu
   A girl in a story I read played baseball with a team that used to be all boys. It reminded me of you being the first girl to pitch for the Berkeley Bees!

   Yours truly
   Elizabeth
3. Shinobu said she still remembers that day on June 14 1996 when she first stood on the pitcher's mound.
4. I thought my uncle in Reno Nevada might have some pictures from that day.
5. Dear Uncle Ernesto
   Remember when you came to visit me and we saw my friend Shinobu pitch? If you still have any of the photos you took, I'd love to see them.

   Love always
   Elizabeth

13.5 *Quotations* Quotation marks let readers know exactly who said what. They are also used for some titles.

Quotation Marks Use quotation marks at the beginning and the end of direct quotations and to set off titles of short works.

> **INCORRECT:** *The narrator in Crow Call had never gone hunting. She said to her father, What if I don't know what to do?*
>
> **CORRECT:** *The narrator in "Crow Call" had never gone hunting. She said to her father, "What if I don't know what to do?"*

Capitalize the first word of a direct quotation, especially in a piece of dialogue.

> **INCORRECT:** *The waitress, who questioned whether they really wanted three pieces of pie, said, "you mean two?"*
>
> **CORRECT:** *The waitress, who questioned whether they really wanted three pieces of pie, said, "You mean two?"*

USAGE TIP If quoted words are from a written source and are not complete sentences, they can begin with a lowercase letter.

> **EXAMPLE:** *Mark Twain said that cauliflower was "nothing but cabbage with a college education."*

End Punctuation Place periods inside quotation marks. Place question marks and exclamation points inside quotation marks if they belong to the quotation; place them outside if they do not belong to the quotation. Place semicolons outside quotation marks.

> **INCORRECT:** *I said to my brother, "I would have been nervous too"!*
>
> *"Are you saying you're not brave"? he said.*
>
> *I responded, "Not really;" I added that I had enjoyed "Crow Call".*
>
> **CORRECT:** *I said to my brother, "I would have been nervous too!"*
>
> *"Are you saying you're not brave?" he said.*
>
> *I responded, "Not really"; I added that I had enjoyed "Crow Call."*

Use a comma to end a quotation that is a complete sentence but is followed by explanatory words.

> **EXAMPLE:** *"Have a good day," I said to the waitress as we left.*

Divided Quotations Capitalize the first word of the second part of a direct quotation if it begins a new sentence.

> **INCORRECT:** *"I know," he said. "are you scared?"*
>
> **CORRECT:** *"I know," he said. "Are you scared?"*

USAGE TIP If a capital letter would not be used, then do not use one in the divided quotation.

Do not capitalize the first word of the second part of a divided quotation if it does not begin a new sentence.

> **EXAMPLE:** *"Okay," said my father, "you can do the crow call now."*

GRAMMAR PRACTICE

Rewrite these sentences, correcting punctuation and capitalization.

1. Erik and Ron found a pamphlet called Super-Simple Cherry Pie.
2. Erik said, "to learn more, first I researched how to make a pie crust."
3. Ron noticed that "Cookbooks can be handy."
4. "The trick" Erik said "Is to avoid adding too much water to the dough."
5. Ron said, "Well maybe;" then Erik continued "You also need to flour the rolling pin."
6. "The problem is, we already ate all the cherries" muttered Ron.

13.5

1. Erik and Ron found a pamphlet called "Super-Simple Cherry Pie."
2. Erik said, "To learn more, first I researched how to make a pie crust."
3. Ron observed that cookbooks come in handy.
4. "The trick," Erik said, "is to avoid adding too much water to the dough."
5. Ron said, "Well maybe." Then Erik continued, "You also need to flour the rolling pin."
6. "The problem is we already ate all the cherries," muttered Ron.

Grammar Glossary

This glossary contains various terms you need to understand when you use the Grammar Handbook. Used as a reference source, this glossary will help you explore grammar concepts and the ways they relate to one another.

 A

Abbreviation An abbreviation is a shortened form of a word or word group; it is often made up of initials. (B.C., A.M., Maj.)

Active voice. *See* **Voice.**

Adjective An adjective modifies, or describes, a noun or pronoun. (*happy* camper, she is *small*)

A *predicate adjective* follows a linking verb and describes the subject. (The day seemed *long*.)

A *proper adjective* is formed from a proper noun. (*Jewish* temple, *Alaskan* husky)

The *comparative* form of an adjective compares two things. (*more alert, thicker*)

The *superlative* form of an adjective compares more than two things. (*most abundant, weakest*)

What Adjectives Tell	Examples
How many	*some* writers *much* joy
What kind	*grand* plans *wider* streets
Which one(s)	*these* flowers *that* star

Adjective phrase. *See* **Phrase.**

Adverb An adverb modifies a verb, an adjective, or another adverb. (Clare sang *loudly*.)

The *comparative* form of an adverb compares two actions. (*more generously, faster*)

The *superlative* form of an adverb compares more than two actions. (*most sharply, closest*)

What Adverbs Tell	Examples
How	write *carelessly* eat *quickly*
When	*Soon* I'll be home. I'll see you *later*.
Where	They traveled *far*. Put it *someplace*.

Adverb, conjunctive. *See* **Conjunctive adverb.**

Adverb phrase. *See* **Phrase.**

Agreement Sentence parts that correspond with one another are said to be in agreement.

In *pronoun-antecedent agreement*, a pronoun and the word it refers to are the same in number, gender, and person. (*Bill* mailed *his* application. The *students* ate *their* lunches.)

In *subject-verb agreement*, the subject and verb in a sentence are the same in number. (*A child cries* for help. *They cry* aloud.)

Ambiguous reference An ambiguous reference occurs when a pronoun may refer to more than one word. (Bud asked his brother if *he* had any mail.)

Antecedent An antecedent is the noun or pronoun to which a pronoun refers. (If *Adam* forgets *his* raincoat, *he* will be late for school. *She* learned *her* lesson.)

Appositive An appositive is a noun or phrase that explains one or more words in a sentence. (Cary Grant, *an Englishman*, spent most of his adult life in America.)

An *essential appositive* is needed to make the sense of a sentence complete. (A comic strip inspired the musical *Annie*.)

A *nonessential appositive* is one that adds information to a sentence but is not necessary to its sense. (O. Henry, *a short-story writer*, spent time in prison.)

Article Articles are the special adjectives *a, an,* and *the.* (*the* day, *a* fly)

A *definite article* (the word *the*) is one that refers to a particular thing. (*the* cabin)

An *indefinite article* is used with a noun that is not unique but refers to one of many of its kind. (*a* dish, *an* otter)

Auxiliary verb. *See* **Verb.**

 C

Clause A clause is a group of words that contains a verb and its subject. (*they slept*)

An *adjective clause* is a dependent (subordinate) clause that modifies a noun or pronoun. (Hugh bought the sweater *that he had admired*.)

An *adverb clause* is a dependent (subordinate) clause used to modify a verb, an adjective, or an adverb.

(Ring the bell *when it is time for class to begin.*)

A *noun clause* is a dependent (subordinate) clause that is used as a noun. (*Whatever you say* interests me.)

An *elliptical clause* is a clause from which a word or words have been omitted. (We are not as lucky as *they.*)

An *independent (main) clause* can stand by itself as a sentence. (*the flashlight flickered*)

A *dependent (subordinate) clause* does not express a complete thought and cannot stand by itself. (*while the nation watched*)

Clause	Example
Independent (main)	The hurricane struck
Dependent (subordinate)	while we were preparing to leave.

Collective noun. *See* **Noun.**

Comma splice A comma splice is an error created when two sentences are separated with a comma instead of a correct end mark. (*The band played a medley of show tunes, everyone enjoyed the show.*)

Common noun. *See* **Noun.**

Comparative. *See* **Adjective; Adverb.**

Complement A complement is a word or group of words that completes the meaning of a verb. (*The kitten finished the milk.*) *See also* **Direct object; Indirect object.**

An *objective complement* is a word or a group of words that follows a direct object and renames or describes that object. (*The parents of the rescued child declared Gus a hero.*)

A *subject complement* follows a linking verb and renames or describes the subject. (*The coach seemed anxious.*) *See also* **Noun (predicate noun); Adjective (predicate adjective).**

Complete predicate The complete predicate of a sentence consists of the main verb plus any words that modify or complete the verb's meaning. (*The student produces work of high caliber.*)

Complete subject The complete subject of a sentence consists of the simple subject plus any words that modify or describe the simple subject. (*Students of history believe that wars can be avoided.*)

Clause	Example
Complete subject	The man in the ten-gallon hat
Complete predicate	wore a pair of silver spurs.

Compound sentence part A sentence element that consists of two or more subjects, verbs, objects, or other parts is compound. (*Lou and Jay helped. Laura makes and models scarves. Jill sings opera and popular music.*)

Conjunction A conjunction is a word that links other words or groups of words.

A *coordinating conjunction* connects related words, groups of words, or sentences. (*and, but, or*)

A *correlative conjunction* is one of a pair of conjunctions that work together to connect sentence parts. (*either . . . or, neither . . . nor, not only . . . but also, whether . . . or, both . . . and*) A *subordinating conjunction* introduces a subordinate clause. (*after,*

although, as, as if, as long as, as though, because, before, if, in order that, since, so that, than, though, till, unless, until, whatever, when, where, while)

Conjunctive adverb A conjunctive adverb joins the clauses of a compound sentence. (*however, therefore, yet*)

Contraction A contraction is formed by joining two words and substituting an apostrophe for a letter or letters left out of one of the words. (*didn't, we've*)

Coordinating conjunction. *See* **Conjunction.**

Correlative conjunction. *See* **Conjunction.**

 D

Dangling modifier A dangling modifier is one that does not clearly modify any word in the sentence. (*Dashing for the train, the barriers got in the way.*)

Demonstrative pronoun. *See* **Pronoun.**

Dependent clause. *See* **Clause.**

Direct object A direct object receives the action of a verb. Direct objects follow transitive verbs. (*Jude planned the party.*)

Direct quotation. *See* **Quotation.**

Divided quotation. *See* **Quotation.**

Double negative A double negative is the incorrect use of two negative words when only one is needed. (*Nobody didn't care.*)

 E

End mark An end mark is one of several punctuation marks that can end a sentence. See the punctuation chart on page R56.

F

Fragment. *See* **Sentence fragment.**

Future tense. *See* **Verb tense.**

G

Gender The gender of a personal pronoun indicates whether the person or thing referred to is male, female, or neuter. (*My cousin plays the tuba; he often performs in school concerts.*)

Gerund A gerund is a verbal that ends in *-ing* and functions as a noun. (*Making pottery takes patience.*)

H

Helping verb. *See* **Verb (auxiliary verb).**

I

Illogical comparison An illogical comparison is a comparison that does not make sense because words are missing or illogical. (*My computer is newer than Kay.*)

Indefinite pronoun. *See* **Pronoun.**

Indefinite reference Indefinite reference occurs when a pronoun is used without a clear antecedent. (*My aunt hugged me in front of my friends, and it was embarrassing.*)

Independent clause. *See* **Clause.**

Indirect object An indirect object tells to whom or for whom (sometimes to what or for what) something is done. (*Arthur wrote Kerry a letter.*)

Indirect question An indirect question tells what someone asked without using the person's exact words. (*My friend asked me if I could go with her to the dentist.*)

Indirect quotation. *See* **Quotation.**

Infinitive An infinitive is a verbal beginning with *to* that functions as a noun, an adjective, or an adverb. (*He wanted to go to the play.*)

Intensive pronoun. *See* **Pronoun.**

Interjection An interjection is a word or phrase used to express strong feeling. (*Wow! Good grief!*)

Interrogative pronoun. *See* **Pronoun.**

Intransitive verb. *See* **Verb.**

Inverted sentence An inverted sentence is one in which the subject comes after the verb. (*How was the movie? Here come the clowns.*)

Irregular verb. *See* **Verb.**

L

Linking verb. *See* **Verb.**

M

Main clause. *See* **Clause.**

Main verb. *See* **Verb.**

Modifier A modifier makes another word more precise. Modifiers most often are adjectives or adverbs; they may also be phrases, verbals, or clauses that function as adjectives or adverbs. (*small box, smiled broadly, house by the sea, dog barking loudly*)

An *essential modifier* is one that is necessary to the meaning of a sentence. (*Everybody who has a free pass should enter now. None of the passengers got on the train.*)

A *nonessential modifier* is one that merely adds more information to a sentence that is clear without the addition. (*We will use the new dishes, which are stored in the closet.*)

N

Noun A noun names a person, a place, a thing, or an idea. (*auditor, shelf, book, goodness*)

An *abstract noun* names an idea, a quality, or a feeling. (*joy*)

A *collective noun* names a group of things. (*class, flock, group*)

A *common noun* is a general name of a person, a place, a thing, or an idea. (*valet, hill, bread, amazement*)

A *compound noun* contains two or more words. (*hometown, pay-as-you-go, screen test*)

A *noun of direct address* is the name of a person being directly spoken to. (*Lee, do you have the package? No, Suki, your letter did not arrive.*)

A *possessive noun* shows who or what owns or is associated with something. (*Lil's ring, a day's pay*)

A *predicate noun* follows a linking verb and renames the subject. (*Karen is a writer.*)

A *proper noun* names a particular person, place, or thing. (*John Smith, Ohio, Sears Tower, Congress*)

Number A word is singular in number if it refers to just one person, place, thing, idea, or action, and plural in number if it refers to more than one person, place, thing, idea, or action. (*The words he, waiter, and is are singular. The words they, waiters, and are are plural.*)

O

Object of a preposition The object of a preposition is the noun or pronoun that follows a preposition. (*The athletes cycled along the route. Jane baked a cake for her.*)

Object of a verb The object of a verb receives the action of the verb. (Sid told *stories*.)

P

Participle A participle is often used as part of a verb phrase. (had *written*) It can also be used as a verbal that functions as an adjective. (the *leaping* deer, the medicine *taken* for a fever)

The **present participle** is formed by adding *-ing* to the present form of a verb. (*Walking* rapidly, we reached the general store.)

The **past participle** of a regular verb is formed by adding *-d* or *-ed* to the present form. The past participles of irregular verbs do not follow this pattern. (*Startled*, they ran from the house. *Spun* glass is delicate. A *broken* cup lay there.)

Passive voice. *See* **Voice.**

Past tense. *See* **Verb tense.**

Perfect tenses. *See* **Verb tense.**

Person Person is a means of classifying pronouns.

A **first-person** pronoun refers to the person speaking. (*We* came.)

A **second-person** pronoun refers to the person spoken to. (*You* ask.)

A **third-person** pronoun refers to some other person(s) or thing(s) being spoken of. (*They* played.)

Personal pronoun. *See* **Pronoun.**

Phrase A phrase is a group of related words that does not contain a verb and its subject. (*noticing everything, under a chair*)

An **adjective phrase** modifies a noun or a pronoun. (The label *on the bottle* has faded.)

An **adverb phrase** modifies a verb, an adjective, or an adverb. (Come *to the fair.*)

An **appositive phrase** explains one or more words in a sentence. (Mary, *a champion gymnast,* won gold medals at the Olympics.)

A **gerund phrase** consists of a gerund and its modifiers and complements. (*Fixing the leak* will take only a few minutes.)

An **infinitive phrase** consists of an infinitive, its modifiers, and its complements. (*To prepare for a test,* study in a quiet place.)

A **participial phrase** consists of a participle and its modifiers and complements. (*Straggling to the finish line,* the last runners arrived.)

A **prepositional phrase** consists of a preposition, its object, and the object's modifiers. (The Saint Bernard does rescue work *in the Swiss Alps.*)

A **verb phrase** consists of a main verb and one or more helping verbs. (*might have ordered*)

Possessive A noun or pronoun that is possessive shows ownership or relationship. (*Dan's* story, *my* doctor)

Possessive noun. *See* **Noun.**

Possessive pronoun. *See* **Pronoun.**

Predicate The predicate of a sentence tells what the subject is or does. (The van *runs well even in winter*. The job seems *too complicated.*) *See also* **Complete predicate; Simple predicate.**

Predicate adjective. *See* **Adjective.**

Predicate nominative A predicate nominative is a noun or pronoun that follows a linking verb and renames or explains the subject. (Joan is a computer *operator*. The winner of the prize was *he*.)

Predicate pronoun. *See* **Pronoun.**

Preposition A preposition is a word that relates its object to another part of the sentence or to the sentence as a whole. (Alfredo leaped *onto* the stage.)

Prepositional phrase. *See* **Phrase.**

Present tense. *See* **Verb tense.**

Pronoun A pronoun replaces a noun or another pronoun. Some pronouns allow a writer or speaker to avoid repeating a proper noun. Other pronouns let a writer refer to an unknown or unidentified person or thing.

A **demonstrative pronoun** singles out one or more persons or things. (*This* is the letter.)

An **indefinite pronoun** refers to an unidentified person or thing. (*Everyone* stayed home. Will you hire *anybody?*)

An **intensive pronoun** emphasizes a noun or pronoun. (The teacher *himself* sold tickets.)

An **interrogative pronoun** asks a question. (*What* happened to you?)

A **personal pronoun** shows a distinction of person. (*I* came. *You* see. *He* knows.)

A **possessive pronoun** shows ownership. (*My* spaghetti is always good. Are *your* parents coming to the play?)

A **predicate pronoun** follows a linking verb and renames the subject. (The owners of the store were *they.*)

A **reflexive pronoun** reflects an action back on the subject of the sentence. (Joe helped *himself.*)

A **relative pronoun** relates a

dependent (subordinate clause) to the word it modifies. (*The draperies, which had been made by hand, were ruined in the fire.*)

Pronoun-antecedent agreement. *See* **Agreement.**

Pronoun forms

The *subject form* of a pronoun is used when the pronoun is the subject of a sentence or follows a linking verb as a predicate pronoun. (*She* fell. The star was *she.*)

The *object form* of a pronoun is used when the pronoun is the direct or indirect object of a verb or verbal or the object of a preposition. (We sent *him* the bill. We ordered food for *them.*)

Proper adjective. *See* **Adjective.**

Proper noun. *See* **Noun.**

Punctuation Punctuation clarifies the structure of sentences. See the punctuation chart below.

Quotation A quotation consists of words from another speaker or writer.

A *direct quotation* is the exact words of a speaker or writer. (Martin said, *"The homecoming game has been postponed."*)

A *divided quotation* is a quotation separated by words that identify the speaker. (*"The homecoming game,"* said Martin, *"has been postponed."*)

An *indirect quotation* reports what a person said without giving the exact words. (*Martin said that the homecoming game had been postponed.*)

Reflexive pronoun. *See* **Pronoun.**

Regular verb. *See* **Verb.**

Relative pronoun. *See* **Pronoun.**

Run-on sentence A run-on sentence consists of two or more sentences written incorrectly as one. (*The sunset was beautiful its brilliant colors lasted only a short time.*)

Sentence A sentence expresses a complete thought. The chart at the top of the next page shows the four kinds of sentences.

A *compound-complex sentence* contains one or more independent clauses and one or more dependent clauses. (*If she falls, I'll help her up, and I hope I am strong enough.*)

A *complex sentence* contains one independent (main) clause and one or more dependent (subordinate) clauses. (*Open the windows before you go to bed. If she falls, I'll help her up.*)

A *compound sentence* is made up of two or more independent clauses joined by a conjunction, a colon, or a semicolon. (*The ship finally docked, and the passengers quickly left.*)

A *simple sentence* consists of only one independent clause. (*My friend volunteers at a nursing home.*)

Punctuation	Example	
Apostrophe (')	Shows possession	Lou's garage Alva's script
	Indicates a contraction	I'll help you The baby's tired
Colon (:)	Introduces a list or quotation	three colors: red, green, and yellow
	Divides some compound sentences	This was the problem: we had to find our own way home.
Comma (,)	Separates ideas	The glass broke, and the juice spilled over.
	Separates modifiers	The lively, talented cheerleaders energized the team.
	Separates items in series	We visited London, Rome, and Paris.
Exclamation point (!)	Ends an exclamatory sentence	We had a wonderful time!
Hyphen (-)	Joins parts of some compound words	daughter-in-law, great-grandson
Period (.)	Ends a declarative sentence	Swallows return to Capistrano in spring.
	Indicates most abbreviations	min. qt. Blvd. Gen. Jan.
Question mark (?)	Ends an interrogative sentence	Where are you going?
Semicolon (;)	Divides some compound sentences	Marie is an expert dancer; she teaches a class in tap.
	Separates items in series that contain commas	Jenny visited Syracuse, New York; Athens, Georgia; and Tampa, Florida.

Sentence fragment A sentence fragment is a group of words that is only part of a sentence. (*When he arrived. Merrily yodeling.*)

Kind of Sentence	Example
Declarative (statement)	Our team won.
Exclamatory (strong feeling)	I had a great time!
Imperative (request, command)	Take the next exit.
Interrogative (question)	Who owns the car?

Simple predicate A simple predicate is the verb in the predicate. (John *collects* foreign stamps.)

Simple subject A simple subject is the key noun or pronoun in the subject. (The new *house* is empty.)

Split infinitive A split infinitive occurs when a modifier is placed between the word *to* and the verb in an infinitive. (*to quickly speak*)

Subject The subject is the part of a sentence that tells whom or what the sentence is about. (*Lou* swam.) *See also* **Complete subject; Simple subject.**

Subject-verb agreement. *See* **Agreement.**

Subordinate clause. *See* **Clause.**

Superlative. *See* **Adjective; Adverb.**

 Transitive verb. *See* **Verb.**

 Unidentified reference An unidentified reference usually occurs when the word *it, they, this, which,* or *that* is used. (In California *they* have good weather most of the time.)

V

Verb A verb expresses an action, a condition, or a state of being.

An *action verb* tells what the subject does, has done, or will do. The action may be physical or mental. (Susan *trains* guide dogs.)

An *auxiliary verb* is added to a main verb to express tense, add emphasis, or otherwise affect the meaning of the verb. Together the auxiliary and main verb make up a verb phrase. (*will* intend, *could have* gone)

A *linking verb* expresses a state of being or connects the subject with a word or words that describe the subject. (The ice *feels* cold.) Linking verbs include *appear, be (am, are, is, was, were, been, being), become, feel, grow, look, remain, seem, smell, sound,* and *taste.*

A *main verb* expresses action or state of being; it appears with one or more auxiliary verbs. (will be *staying*)

The *progressive form* of a verb shows continuing action. (She is *knitting*.)

The past tense and past participle of a *regular verb* are formed by adding -*d* or -*ed*. (*open, opened*) An *irregular verb* does not follow this pattern. (*throw, threw, thrown; shrink, shrank, shrunk*)

The action of a *transitive verb* is directed toward someone or something, called the object of a verb. (Leo *washed* the windows.) An *intransitive verb* has no object. (The leaves *scattered*.)

Verb phrase. *See* **Phrase.**

Verb tense Verb tense shows the time of an action or the time of a state of being.

The *present tense* places an action or condition in the present. (Jan *takes* piano lessons.)

The *past tense* places an action or condition in the past. (We *came* to the party.)

The *future tense* places an action or condition in the future. (You *will understand*.)

The *present perfect tense* describes an action in an indefinite past time or an action that began in the past and continues in the present. (*has called, have known*)

The *past perfect tense* describes one action that happened before another action in the past. (*had scattered, had mentioned*)

The *future perfect tense* describes an event that will be finished before another future action begins. (*will have taught, shall have appeared*)

Verbal A verbal is formed from a verb and acts as another part of speech, such as a noun, an adjective, or an adverb.

Verbal	Example
Gerund (used as a noun)	Lamont enjoys *swimming*.
Infinitive (used as an adjective, an adverb, or a noun)	Everyone wants *to help*.
Participle (used as an adjective)	The leaves *covering the drive* made it slippery.

Voice The voice of a verb depends on whether the subject performs or receives the action of the verb.

In the *active voice* the subject of the sentence performs the verb's action. (We *knew* the answer.)

In the *passive voice* the subject of the sentence receives the action of the verb. (The team *has been eliminated*.)

Speaking and Listening

Good communicators do more than just talk. They use specific techniques to present their ideas effectively, and they are attentive and critical listeners.

❶ Organization and Delivery

In school, in business, and in any community, one of the best ways to present information is to deliver it in person—speaking directly to a live audience.

Audience and Purpose

When preparing and presenting a speech, think about your purpose in speaking and your audience's level of knowledge and interest in your subject. Understanding your audience can help you tailor your speech to your audience's interests.

- **Know your audience** What kind of group are you presenting to—fellow classmates? an entire school assembly? a group of teachers? How are they different from one another? Understanding their different points of view can help you address each group in the most appropriate way.

- **Understand your purpose** Keep in mind your purpose for speaking, and select an appropriate focus and organizational structure. Are you trying to persuade the audience to do something? Are you presenting the audience with some latest research? Perhaps you simply want to entertain the audience by sharing a story or experience with them.

Writing Your Speech

If you are writing your speech beforehand, rather than working from notes or memory, use the following guidelines to help you:

- **Create a unified speech** Do this first by organizing your speech into paragraphs, each of which develops a single main idea. Then make sure that just as all the sentences in a paragraph support the main idea of the paragraph, so all the paragraphs in your speech support the main idea of the speech.

- **Use appropriate language** The subject of your speech—and the way you choose to present it—should match both your audience and the occasion. Tailor your language accordingly. For example, if you were telling a funny story to a group of friends, your speech might be informal and lighthearted. However, if you were describing your science project to a panel of judges, your speech would probably be serious, formal, and well-organized.

- **Provide evidence** Include relevant facts, statistics, and incidents; quote experts to support both your ideas and your opinions. Elaborate—or provide specific details, perhaps with visual or media displays—to clarify what you are saying.

- **Start strong, finish strong** As you begin your speech, consider using a "hook"—an interesting question or statement to capture your audience's attention. At the end, restate your main ideas simply and clearly. Perhaps conclude with a powerful example or anecdote to reinforce your message.

Prepare/Practice/Present

Confidence is the key to a successful presentation. Use these techniques to help you prepare and present your speech to your class.

Prepare

- **Review your information** Reread your written speech and review your background research—you'll feel much more confident during your speech.

- **Organize your notes** Some people prefer to include only a minimum of key points. Others prefer the entire script. Write each main point, or each paragraph, of your speech on a separate index card. Be sure to include your most important evidence and examples. It helps to number your cards.

- **Plan your visual aids** If you are planning on using visual aids, such as slides, posters, charts, graphs, video clips, overhead transparencies, or computer projections, now is the time to design them and decide how to work them into your speech.

Practice

- **Rehearse** Rehearse your speech several times, possibly in front of a practice audience. If you are using visual aids, practice handling them. Adapt your rate of speaking, pitch, and tone of voice to your audience and setting. Your style of performance should express the purpose of your speech. Use the following chart to help your style express your purpose.

TIP: It might also be helpful to time yourself during rehearsals, to ensure that your speech does not run too long.

Purpose	Pace	Pitch	Tone
to persuade	fast but clear	even	urgent
to inform	plenty of pauses	even	authoritative
to entertain	usually builds to a "punch"	varied to create characters or drama	funny or dramatic

- **Evaluate your performance** When you have finished each rehearsal, evaluate your performance. How did you do? Did you slow down for emphasis, pause to let an important point sink in, or use gestures for emphasis? Make a list of aspects of your presentation that you will try to perfect for your next rehearsal.

Present

- **Begin your speech** In order to break the tension of the opening moments, try to look relaxed and remember to smile!

- **Make eye contact** During your speech, try to make eye contact with audience members. This will not only establish the feeling of personal contact, but will help you determine if the audience understands your speech.

- **Emphasize points** To help your audience in following the main ideas and concepts of your speech, be sure to draw attention to important points. You can do this with your voice, using effective rate, volume, pitch, and tone. You can also do this with nonverbal elements, such as facial expressions, hand gestures, and props—all of which can help engage your audience's interest and hold their attention.

- **Remember to pause** A slight pause after important points will provide emphasis and give your audience time to think about what you are saying.

- **Maintain good posture** Stand up straight and avoid nervous movements that may distract the audience's attention from what you are saying.

- **Use expressive body language** A good speaker captures the attention of an audience through body language as well as through words. In front of an audience, use your entire body to help express your meaning. Lean forward when you make an important point;

move your hands and arms for emphasis. Your body language will show that you really believe in what you are saying.

② Oral Interpretation

An oral interpretation is a way to show an audience what a piece of written work means to you—whether it's yours or someone else's. The piece you interpret may be a story, poem, speech, or soliloquy. If you choose to read a scene from a play with several other speakers, your oral interpretation is called a dramatic reading.

Oral Reading
When you perform an oral reading, you use appropriate voice, facial expressions, and gestures to create a special world for your audience and bring the literature to life. There are many different types of pieces to choose from:

- **Story** This may be a brief selection from a short story or novel. You may present a monologue, a long speech offered by a single character or narrator in the piece. You may also present a dialogue, in which you take on the roles of two or more characters. Use voice and gesture to help your audience experience and understand the scene.
- **Soliloquy** This is a dramatic monologue from a story or play. It represents the unspoken thoughts of a single character, heard only by the audience and not by other characters in the scene. Use an expressive voice to help an audience understand a character's inner thoughts, emotions, and feelings.
- **Poem** Unless the poem is very long, you are likely to present the piece in its entirety (4-6 stanzas). As with a story, you may assume the voice of the poem's narrator if there is one. Recite the words

of a poem effectively, using your voice to create mood and evoke emotion from your audience.

- **Speech** Unless the speech is short, you are likely to select a brief passage from it. Choose the most powerful and dramatic part of the speech. Put yourself in the position of the speech's original orator, using voice and gesture to deliver the words passionately and persuasively.

③ Narrative Presentations

When you make a narrative presentation, you tell a story or present a subject using a story-type format. A good narrative keeps an audience both informed and entertained. It also allows you to deliver a message in a unique and creative way.

- **Establish a setting** Think about the setting of your story. Does the action take place in a home? a classroom? a neighborhood park?
- **Create a plot** What happens in your story? Is it funny? tragic? suspenseful? How do you want the events to unfold? Over what period of time?
- **Determine a point of view** Is a narrator telling the story in the third-person point of view? Who is the main character of the story? What is his or her point of view? If he or she is telling the story in the first-person point of view, make the audience believe that they are hearing the voice and opinions of a very particular person.
- **Use effective language** Include sensory details and concrete language to develop the plot and the character. Think about the adjectives you use to describe something and the verbs you use to show an action. Let your audience touch,

taste, hear, and smell what's happening in the story.

- **Employ narrative devices** Use a range of devices to keep your narrative interesting: snappy, believable dialogue; language that builds up tension in a scene because the characters seem edgy or frightened or confused; suspense to keep your audience members on the edge of their seats; sound effects and props for added realism.

- **Focus on the delivery** Once you've created your narrative, your next responsibility is to make the story come alive in presentation. Remember, it's not just what you say but how you say it. Speak clearly and confidently. Pace yourself and pause for emphasis. Vary your voice to express different emotions and moods.

GUIDELINES **HOW TO ANALYZE YOUR NARRATIVE PRESENTATION**

- Did you choose a setting that makes sense and contributes to a believable narrative?
- Does your plot help create the right mood for your audience?
- Is your character—and his or her point of view—realistic and memorable?
- Did you use strong, sensory language that allows your audience to experience the story?
- Did you use a range of narrative devices to keep your audience interested?
- Did you deliver effectively?

---

❹ Informative Presentations

When you deliver an informative presentation, you do so to explain, to teach, and perhaps to enlighten an audience with information on a particular subject.

- **Target your audience** Think about what your audience may or may not already know about the subject. Consider the best way to focus your presentation: simple and basic for beginners vs. in-depth and detailed for the more advanced.

- **Introduce the subject** Let your audience know right away what you are going to talk about. Perhaps use a "hook," something that startles or interests them, to grab their attention in the beginning.

- **Establish a framework** Pose specific, relevant questions about the subject to your audience. Use these questions as the basic structure of your speech. Keep your questions in mind as you organize your ideas and answer them completely and thoroughly.

- **Develop the topic** Use facts, details, examples, and explanations to flesh out the subject and provide the "meat" of your presentation. Be sure to use multiple authoritative sources, such as encyclopedias, newspapers, the Internet, and live experts. Having more than one knowledgeable source will make you more believable and less likely to give false information. Consider using simple but effective visual aids to illustrate your information.

- **Offer a conclusion** End your presentation with a summary of the important points raised. Consider offering your audience a last question on the subject, leaving them with something to think about when you're done.

GUIDELINES HOW TO ANALYZE YOUR INFORMATIVE PRESENTATION

- Did you take the audience's previous knowledge into consideration?
- Did you choose a specific, clearly focused topic?
- Did you present the information in a clear, organized manner?
- Did you provide evidence, examples, and supporting details, citing all sources of information?
- Did you use visual aids effectively?

❺ Oral Responses to Literature

An oral response to literature is your own personal interpretation of a piece written by someone else. It is a way to show an audience what a story means to you.

- **Select carefully** In choosing a piece for your oral response, think about the assignment, your interest, and the audience.
- **Exhibit understanding** Develop an interpretation exhibiting careful reading, understanding, and insight. Direct your reader to specific words, sentences, or paragraphs that are rich with meaning. Explore how they make you feel, what they make you think about, and why they are particularly important to the piece. Discuss the writer's techniques in developing plot, characterization, setting, or theme and how they contribute to your interpretation.
- **Organize clearly** Organize the selected interpretation around several clear ideas, premises, or images. What elements of the literature are most important? How do they relate to the piece as a whole?

What about them provides insight and meaning? Use examples and textual evidence to give weight to your interpretation.

GUIDELINES HOW TO ANALYZE YOUR ORAL RESPONSE

- Did you choose an interesting piece that you enjoy, understand, and feel strongly about?
- Did you engage in in-depth analysis and demonstrate an understanding of what the piece means to you?
- Did you direct your audience to specific parts of the piece that support your interpretation?
- Did you present your ideas in a clear, well-organized manner?
- Did your enthusiasm for the piece come through in your delivery?

❻ Persuasive Presentations

When you deliver a persuasive presentation, you clearly state your position, provide relevant evidence to support your position, and try to convince the audience to accept your position or proposal.

- **Do your research** In order to develop a clear position on a subject, you need to know enough about it to make an informed, intelligent decision. Learn about all points of view on the topic before deciding which is right for you. Consult newspapers, magazines, the Internet, and individuals with expertise on the topic to gather information.
- **State your point of view** Present your position on the subject clearly, confidently, and enthusiastically.
- **Support your position** Use strong,

supportive evidence to back up your position. Arm yourself with relevant facts, statistics, and expert quotes.

- **Provide a strong defense** Consider your audience's own biases and opinions on the subject. What kind of questions or doubts might they have? Prepare for and address them before they are raised.
- **Deliver effectively** Engage your audience. Show them that you really believe in what you are saying. Make them believe it too.

GUIDELINES | **HOW TO ANALYZE YOUR PERSUASIVE PRESENTATION**

- Did you present a clear statement or argument?
- Did you support your argument with convincing facts?
- Did you use sound logic in developing the argument?
- Did you use voice, facial expression, gestures, and posture effectively?
- Did you hold the audience's interest?

---

❼ Problems and Solutions

When delivering a presentation on problems and solutions, you need to be organized, logical, and persuasive.

- **Identify the problem** Know exactly what the problem is, and define it for your audience. Provide background information: How long has the problem existed? What are its causes? What are its effects?
- **Draw connections** Think about similar or related problems. How were they solved? How might this information help

you with your current problem? Afterward, read over your notes to help you remember what you learned.

- **Propose solutions** Offer at least two or three possible solutions. Back them up with persuasive evidence and logical analysis of how they might work.
- **Encourage discussion** Ask your audience if they have any questions or alternate suggestions. Have them discuss and evaluate what you said.

GUIDELINES | **HOW TO ANALYZE YOUR PROBLEMS/SOLUTION PRESENTATION**

- Did you provide a clear introduction to the problem?
- Did you provide sufficient background information?
- Did you explore relevant relationships?
- Did you offer several reasonable, well-supported solutions?
- Did you facilitate audience response, participation, and discussion of ideas?

---

❽ Active Listening for Information

Active listeners listen carefully and with purpose. They think about what they hear—before, during, and after any presentation—whether it's a speech, a class lecture, or even a television program.

Before Listening
- **Keep an open mind** Don't prejudge the speaker. Listen to what he or she has to say, and then evaluate it critically but fairly.
- **Prepare yourself** Review what you already know about the speaker's topic. Then think of some questions you'd like

to ask or information you'd like to learn more about.

- **Listen with purpose** Try to match how you listen with why you are listening. For example, you may listen to a joke for entertainment, while you would listen to a lesson in order to gain information. Which would you want to pay more attention to?

Listening with a Purpose		
Situation	**Reason for Listening**	**How to Listen**
Your friend tells a funny story about her pet gerbil.	For enjoyment; to provide your friend with an audience	Maintain eye contact; show you understand; react to the story.
You're listening to a talk and slide show called "Wolves of the Tundra."	For enjoyment; to learn some-thing new	Think about what you already know; listen for ideas that add to your knowledge.
Your mother explains why you can't keep an alligator as a pet.	To understand her point of view; to find opportu-nities to share your own ideas	Listen carefully; respond posi-tively to valid points; listen for opportunities to state your own reasons.
You and your friends are trying to arrange a trip to a concert.	To solve a problem	Identify goals and problems; listen closely to each other's ideas and build on them.
You are watch-ing a television program about cooking or carpentry.	To follow directions	Listen for words such as *first, second, next,* and *finally;* take notes that you can refer to later.

While Listening

- **Block out distractions** Keep your eyes on the speaker, focus your mind, and ignore outside interference.
- **Look for signals of main ideas** See the Guidelines box in the righthand column.
- **Take notes, if appropriate** Jot down phrases, main ideas, and questions that occur to you.

- **Look for relationships between ideas** Note comparisons and contrasts, causes and effects, and problems and solutions.
- **Match verbal and nonverbal communication** Pay attention to the gestures, movements, and posture of the speaker. Does he or she look confident? nervous? apologetic? Compare your impressions of the speaker's appearance with your impressions of what he or she is saying. Do the words match the physical delivery?
- **Identify tone, mood, and emotion** To aid in your comprehension, note how the speaker uses word choice and voice pitch to convey meaning. A low and deep voice might create a frightening or serious mood. A high voice could seem more comic or youthful.

TIP: If you are listening to oral instructions or directions, be sure to take notes and clarify anything that is unclear. Consider restating the information to the speaker to make sure that you understand what was said.

GUIDELINES HOW TO RECOGNIZE MAIN IDEAS

- Did you listen for ideas presented first or last?
- Did you listen for ideas repeated several times for emphasis?
- Did you note statements that begin with phrases such as "My point is . . ." or "The important thing is . . ."?
- Did you pay attention to ideas presented in a loud voice or with forceful gestures?
- In a multimedia presentation, did you note points the speaker had reproduced on a chart or on any other visual aid?

After Listening

- **Review notes taken** Make sure you understand what was said.

- **Ask questions** Clarify anything that was unclear or confusing.

- **Summarize, paraphrase, and evaluate** Restate the speaker's ideas in your own words. Clarify your reasons for agreeing or disagreeing.

GUIDELINES | **HOW TO EVALUATE WHAT YOU HEAR**

- What is the purpose of the talk and does the speaker achieve it?
- Does the information make sense? Does it contradict anything you already know?
- Are ideas presented in an interesting and logical way?
- Are points supported with facts and details?
- Do you still have any questions after hearing the talk?
- Do you agree with what the speaker said? Why or why not?

---

⑨ Critical Listening

As you listen to a speaker's ideas, you will want to analyze, evaluate, and critique those ideas. Use the following critical listening strategies as you listen to a public speaker:

- **Determine the speaker's purpose** Identify the speaker's purpose in giving the speech. Is the speaker trying to inform? to persuade? to express thoughts or feelings? to entertain?

- **Listen for the main idea** Figure out the speaker's main message before allowing yourself to be distracted by seemingly convincing facts and details of the speech.

- **Distinguish between fact and opinion** Know the difference between opinion statements such as "I think/I believe" vs. fact statements such as "Statistics show" or "It has been proven".

- **Recognize the use of rhetorical devices** Some speakers use special techniques to accomplish different purposes when they express their ideas. Noting these techniques as you listen will enable you to identify these purposes. For example, a speaker may use **repetition** of certain words or phrases, which allows him or her to emphasize ideas to draw your attention to something important. The speaker may also pose **rhetorical questions,** questions that you are not expected to respond to, to involve you in the topic. The speaker may use a third device such as an **allusion,** an indirect reference to something, for the purpose of pleasing and making a connection to a listener who recognizes the reference. Sound devices like **onomatopoeia,** where the word sounds like the thing or action it represents, can help a speaker express an idea creatively and move the audience emotionally.

---

⑩ Recognizing Persuasive Devices

An important part of critical listening is the ability to recognize persuasive devices—techniques used to persuade you to accept a particular opinion. Persuasive devices may represent faulty reasoning and provide misleading information. They are often used in advertising and in propaganda. Some persuasive devices that you should learn to recognize:

- **Inaccurate generalization** A generalization is a broad statement about a number of people or things, such as "Maps are hard to read." Although some generalizations are true, other generalizations are too broad to be true. The statement "All teenagers like junk food" is an example of an inaccurate generalization.

- **Either/Or** A writer may try to convince an audience that there are only two choices, or ways of looking at something, when in fact there may be many. The statement "If you don't join the glee club, you have no school spirit" is an example of either/or reasoning.

- **Bandwagon** A bandwagon statement appeals to people's desires to belong to a group. For example, a statement like "Everyone at your school already has this hot new watch" is an example of a bandwagon device.

- **Snob appeal** This technique appeals to people's need to feel superior to other people. A statement like "You deserve the best, so buy this jacket" relies on snob appeal.

GUIDELINES **HOW TO LISTEN CRITICALLY**

- Are you aware of the speaker's purpose in addressing you?

- Does the speaker seem confident in his or her knowledge of the subject?

- Does the speaker convince with concrete evidence rather than creative rhetoric?

- Are you able to distinguish between personal opinions and verifiable facts?

- Does the speaker use faulty or misleading persuasive devices?

- Did you clarify any information that seemed unclear or confusing?

---

11 Group Communication

Group communication can help you in school as you work on group or paired assignments; it can also help prepare you for jobs. There are many reasons to have a group discussion, from just sharing your ideas to solving problems. Participating successfully in group communication requires all of your listening, speaking, and social skills.

Assigned Roles

A group discussion stays on track and operates most effectively when each member plays a specific role. Think about what tasks need to be done, and who will do each one. Group roles often include:

- **Chairperson** Responsible for introducing the topic for discussion, explaining the agenda or goals of the meeting, participating in and keeping discussion focused, and helping resolve conflict fairly.

- **Recorder** Responsible for taking notes during discussion, participating in discussion, and organizing and copying notes to distribute to entire group later.

- **Participants** Responsible for contributing facts or ideas to discussion, responding constructively to others' ideas, reaching agreement or voting on final decision.

Guidelines for Discussion

Use these techniques to develop your group communication skills.

- **Listen attentively** Listen carefully and respectfully to each member. Pay attention to important ideas and details. Take notes about issues you want to discuss later.

- **Contribute to the discussion** Join in and share your ideas. Don't be afraid if your ideas are new or different. Share reasons for your ideas. Avoid sarcasm and contribute positive and helpful comments.
- **Compare notes** Everything we see and hear is colored by our own experiences, knowledge, and personality. Because of this, it's always a good idea to compare your perception of a spoken message with the perceptions of others

  TIP: The key to successful discussion is consideration for others. Before you speak in a group, ask yourself, "How would I feel if someone said that to me?"

GUIDELINES | **HOW TO ANALYZE GROUP DISCUSSION**

- Did you take turns speaking?
- Did you listen attentively to each speaker and take notes?
- Did you ask questions or comment on others' ideas?
- Did you speak clearly and confidently?
- Did you avoid interrupting someone who was speaking?
- Did you avoid using disrespectful language?
- Did you avoid dismissing others' ideas without evaluating them?

 Conducting Interviews

Conducting a personal interview can be an effective way to get information.

Preparing for the Interview
- Select your interviewee carefully. Think about the information you want to learn. Identify who has the kind of knowledge and experience you are looking for.
- Research any information by or about the person you will interview. The background details will help you focus and get to the point during the interview.
- Prepare a list of questions. Create open-ended questions that can't be answered simply with a "yes" or "no." Arrange your questions in order of significance, from most important to least important.

Participating in the Interview
- Consider working with a partner. You might choose one note taker and one speaker.
- Ask your questions clearly and listen carefully. Give the person you are interviewing plenty of time to answer.
- Listen interactively and flexibly. Be prepared to follow up on a response you find interesting, even if it was not on your initial list of questions.
- Avoid arguments. Be tactful and polite.
- Take notes even if you have a recording device. This will help in your write-up of the interview. Jot down main ideas or important statements that can be used as quotes.

Following up on the interview
- Summarize your notes while they are still fresh in your mind.
- Send a thank-you note to the interview subject.

  TIP: Remember that as an interviewer, your role is to listen rather than to talk about yourself. Show that you are interested in the person you are interviewing.

1 Getting Information Electronically

Electronic resources provide you with a convenient and efficient way to gather information.

1.1 Online Resources

When you use your computer to communicate with another computer or with another person using a computer, you are working "online." Online resources include commercial information services and information available on the Internet.

Commercial Information Services
You can subscribe to various services that offer information, such as the following:

- up-to-date news, weather, and sports reports

- access to encyclopedias, magazines, newspapers, dictionaries, almanacs, and databases (collections of information)

- forums, or ongoing electronic conversations among people interested in a particular topic

Internet
The Internet is a vast network of computers. News services, libraries, universities, researchers, organizations, and government agencies use the Internet to communicate and to distribute information. The Internet includes two key features:

- The **World Wide Web,** which provides information on particular subjects and links to related topics and resources

- **Electronic mail** (email), which makes possible communication among email users worldwide

What You'll Need
- To access online resources, you need a computer with a modem linked to a telephone line. Your school computer lab or resource center may be linked to the Internet or to a commercial information source.

- To use CD-ROMs, you need a computer with a CD-ROM drive.

1.2 Navigating the Web

With access to the World Wide Web, you can find virtually any piece of information once you know how to look for it. Here are some tips to get you started and keep you going.

Choose a Search Engine or a Directory
A **search engine** combs through Web sites looking for your topic. A **directory** allows you to search within a collection of sites, or databases that are grouped by subject, such as *reference, sports,* or *entertainment.*

Enter Key Words
Once you've chosen a starting point, enter the **key word** or words that describe your topic to search for your topic. By using more than one word, you will narrow your search. For example, using the key word "baseball" will find a variety of sites with information on baseball, whereas the key words "Dodgers baseball" will help you find sites with information on the specific team.

Investigate Your Options
Once you receive the results of your search, scan the site listings and their summaries to see which ones look promising. If you click on a site and it's not useful, you can always back up and try again. The sites at

the top of the list usually will be more relevant to your search than those found farther down.

Tips for Getting the Most from Your Searching

- **Note the source** Because anyone can put information on the Web, it's wise to check where the information comes from. For example, sites produced by government agencies or educational institutions tend to be more reliable than the personal Web pages of individuals.

- **Refine your search** If you're not getting the results you want, search again, using more key words or different key words.

- **Explore other avenues** One search engine may produce different results than another, and the same goes for directories.

- **Link around** Many Web sites have links to other sites with related content that you might not find searching on your own.

 CD-ROMs

A CD-ROM (compact disc–read-only memory) stores data that may include text, sound, photographs, and video.

Almost any kind of information can be found on CD-ROMs, which you can use at the library or purchase, including

- encyclopedias, almanacs, and indexes

- other reference books on a variety of subjects

- news reports from newspapers, magazines, television, or radio

- museum art collections

- back issues of magazines

- literature collections

1.4 Library Computer Services

Many libraries offer computerized catalogs and a variety of other **electronic databases.** A database is a collection of information, stored electronically and arranged for easy retrieval.

Computerized Catalogs

You may search for a book in a library by typing the title, author, subject, or key words into a computer terminal. If you enter the title of a book, the screen will display the kind of information shown below, including the book's call number and whether it is on the shelf or checked out of the library. You may also be able to search the catalogs of other libraries.

Other Electronic Resources

In addition to computerized catalogs, many libraries offer electronic versions of books, and other reference material such as **online databases** of periodical literature. They may also have a variety of indexes or other data on CD-ROM. Often these resources allow you to search for magazine or newspaper articles on any topic you choose. Ask your librarian for assistance in using these resources.

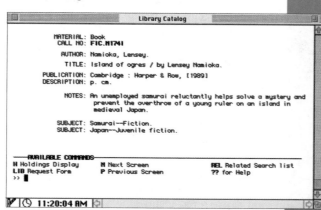

② Word Processing

Word-processing programs allow you to draft, revise, edit, format, and design your writing and to produce neat, professional-looking papers. They also allow you to share your writing with others.

②.① Revising and Editing

Improving the quality of your writing becomes easier when you use a word-processing program to revise and edit.

What You'll Need
- Computer
- Word-processing program
- Printer

Revising a Document
Most word-processing programs allow you to make the following kinds of changes:

- add or delete words
- move text from one location in your document to another
- undo a change you have made in the text
- save a document with a new name, allowing you to keep old drafts for reference
- view more than one document at a time, so you can copy text from one document and add it to another

Editing a Document
Many word-processing programs have the following features to help you catch errors and polish your writing:

- The **spell checker** automatically finds misspelled words and suggests possible corrections.
- The **grammar checker** spots possible grammatical errors and suggests ways you might correct them.

- The **thesaurus** suggests synonyms for a word you want to replace.
- The **dictionary** will give you the definitions of words so that you can be sure you have used words correctly.
- The **search and replace** feature searches your whole document and corrects every occurrence of something you want to change, such as a misspelled name.

WRITING TIP Even if you use a spell checker, you should still proofread your draft carefully to make sure you've used the right words. For example, you may have used *there* or *they're* when you meant to use *their*.

②.② Formatting Your Work

Format is the layout and appearance of your writing on the page. You may choose your formatting options before or after you write.

Formatting Type
You may want to make changes in the typeface, type size, and type style of the words in your document. For each of these, your word-processing program will most likely have several options to choose from.

These options allow you to

- **change the typeface** to create a different look for the words in your document.

Typeface
Geneva
Times
Chicago
Courier

- **change the type size** of the entire document or of just the section headings.

Size
7-point Times
10-point Times
12-point Times
14-point Times

- **change the type style** when necessary; for example, use italics or underlining for the titles of books and magazines.

Style
italic
Bold
<u>Underline</u>
SMALL CAPS

WRITING TIP Keep your format simple. Your goal is to create not only an attractive document but also one that is easy to read.

Formatting Pages

Not only can you change the way individual words look, you can also change the way they are arranged on the page. Some of the formatting decisions you make will depend on how you plan to use a printout or on the guidelines of an assignment.

- **Set the page orientation,** or select portrait (the long side runs vertically) or landscape (the long side runs horizontally).

- **Determine the number of columns.** One column is preferable for papers. Newspapers are usually two or more columns.

- **Set the line spacing,** or the amount of space you need between lines of text. Double spacing is commonly used for final drafts.

- **Set the margins,** or the amount of white space around the edges of your text. A one-inch margin on all sides is commonly used for final drafts.

- **Create a header** for the top of the page or a footer for the bottom if you want to include such information as your name, the date, or the page number on every page.

- **Determine the alignment** of your text. The screen below shows your options.

TECHNOLOGY TIP Some word-processing programs or other software packages provide preset templates, or patterns, for writing outlines, memos, letters, newsletters, or invitations. If you use one of these templates, you will not need to adjust the formatting.

2.3 Working Collaboratively

Computers allow you to share your writing electronically. Send a copy of your work via email or put it in someone's drop box if your computer is linked to other computers on a network. Then use the feedback of your peers to help you improve the quality of your writing.

Peer Editing on a Computer

The writer and the reader can both benefit from the convenience of peer editing "on screen," or at the computer.

- Be sure to save your current draft and then make a copy of it for each of your peer readers.

- You might have your peer readers enter their comments in a different typeface or type style from the one you used for your text, as shown in the example below.

- Ask each of your readers to include his or her initials in the file name.

- If your computer allows you to open more than one file at a time, open each reviewer's file and refer to the files as you revise your draft.

TECHNOLOGY TIP Some word-processing programs, such as the Writing Coach software referred to in this book, allow you to leave notes for your peer readers in the side column or in a separate text box. If you wish, leave those areas blank so that your readers can write comments or questions.

Peer Editing on a Printout

Some peer readers prefer to respond to a draft on paper rather than on the computer.

- Double-space or triple-space your document so that your peer editors can make suggestions between the lines.

- Leave extra-wide margins to give your readers room to note their reactions and questions as they read.

- Print out and photocopy your draft if you want to share it with more than one reader.

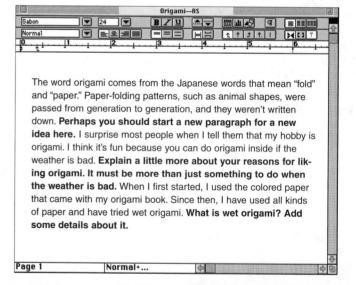

The word origami comes from the Japanese words that mean "fold" and "paper." Paper-folding patterns, such as animal shapes, were passed from generation to generation, and they weren't written down. **Perhaps you should start a new paragraph for a new idea here.** I surprise most people when I tell them that my hobby is origami. I think it's fun because you can do origami inside if the weather is bad. **Explain a little more about your reasons for liking origami. It must be more than just something to do when the weather is bad.** When I first started, I used the colored paper that came with my origami book. Since then, I have used all kinds of paper and have tried wet origami. **What is wet origami? Add some details about it.**

③ Using Visuals

Charts, graphs, diagrams, and pictures often communicate information more effectively than words alone do. Many computer programs allow you to create visuals to use with written text.

3.1 When to Use Visuals

Use visuals in your work to illustrate complex concepts and processes or to make a page look more interesting. Although you should not expect a visual to do all the work of written text, combining words and pictures or graphics can increase the understanding and enjoyment of your writing. Many computer programs allow you to create and insert graphs, tables, time lines, diagrams, and flow charts into your document. An art program allows you to create border designs for a title page or to draw an unusual character or setting for narrative or descriptive writing. You may also be able to add clip art, or pre-made pictures, to your document. Clip art can be used to illustrate an idea or concept in your writing or to enliven a page.

What You'll Need

- a graphics program to create visuals
- access to clip-art files from a CD-ROM, a computer disk, or an online service

3.2 Kinds of Visuals

The visuals you choose will depend on the type of information you want to present to your readers.

Tables

Tables allow you to arrange facts or numbers into rows and columns so that your reader can compare information more easily. In many word-processing programs, you can create a table by choosing the number of vertical columns and horizontal rows you need and then entering information in each box, as the illustration shows.

TECHNOLOGY TIP A **spreadsheet** program provides you with a preset table for your statistics and performs any necessary calculations.

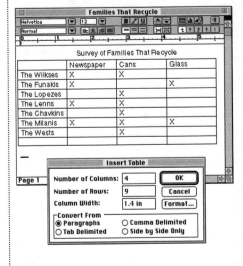

Graphs and Charts

You can sometimes use a graph or chart to help communicate complex information in a clear visual image. For example, you could use a line graph to show how a trend changes over time, a bar graph to compare statistics, or a pie chart, like the one below, to compare percentages. You might want to explore ways of displaying data in more than one visual format before deciding which will work best for you.

TECHNOLOGY TIP To help your readers easily understand the different parts of a pie chart or bar graph, use a different color or shade of gray for each section.

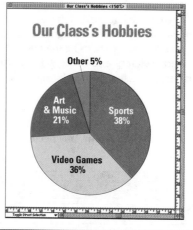

Other Visuals

Art and design programs allow you to create visuals for your writing. Many programs include the following features:

- **drawing tools** that allow you to draw, color, and shade pictures, such as the drawing below
- **clip art** that you can copy or change with drawing tools
- **page borders** that you can use to decorate title pages, invitations, or brochures
- **text options** that allow you to combine words with your illustrations
- **tools for making geometric shapes** in flow charts, time lines, and diagrams that show a process or sequence of events

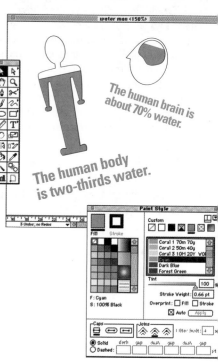

④ Creating a Multimedia Presentation

A multimedia presentation is a combination of text, sound, and visuals such as photographs, videos, and animation. Your audience reads, hears, and sees your presentation at a computer, following different "paths" you create to lead the user through the information you have gathered.

4.1 Features of Multimedia Programs

To start planning your multimedia presentation, you need to know what options are available to you. You can combine sound, photos, videos, and animation to enhance any text you write about your topic.

What You'll Need

- individual programs to create and edit the text, graphics, sound, and videos you will use
- a multimedia authoring program that allows you to combine these elements and create links between the screens

Sound

Including sound in your presentation can help your audience understand information in your written text. For example, the user may be able to listen and learn from

- the pronunciation of an unfamiliar or foreign word
- a speech
- a recorded news interview
- a musical selection
- a dramatic reading of a work of literature

Photos and Videos

Photographs and live-action videos can make your subject come alive for the user. Here are some examples:

- videotaped news coverage of a historical event
- videos of music, dance, or theater performances
- charts and diagrams
- photos of an artist's work
- photos or video of a geographical setting that is important to the written text

Research and Technology Handbook

Animation

Many graphics programs allow you to add animation, or movement, to the visuals in your presentation. Animated figures add to the user's enjoyment and understanding of what you present. You can use animation to illustrate

- what happens in a story
- the steps in a process
- changes in a chart, graph, or diagram
- how your user can explore information in your presentation

TECHNOLOGY TIP You can download photos, sound, and video from Internet sources onto your computer. This process allows you to add elements to your multimedia presentation that would usually require complex editing equipment.

(4.2) Planning Your Presentation

To create a multimedia presentation, first choose your topic and decide what you want to include. Then plan how you want your user to move through your presentation.

Imagine that you are creating a multimedia presentation about in-line skating. You know that you want to include the following items:

- photos of in-line skaters
- a text history of how in-line skating was developed
- a diagram of an in-line skate

- text on "how to skate" for beginners
- a video of a skating demonstration
- a glossary of in-line skating terms
- an audio description of safety tips

You can choose one of the following ways to organize your presentation:

- **a step-by-step method** with only one path, or order, in which the user can see and hear the information
- **a branching path** that allows users to make some choices about what they will see and hear, and in what order

A flow chart can help you figure out the path a user can take through your presentation. Each box in the flow chart below represents something about in-line skating for the user to read, see, or hear. The arrows on the flow chart show a branching path the user can follow. When boxes branch in more than one direction, it means that the user can choose which item to see or hear first.

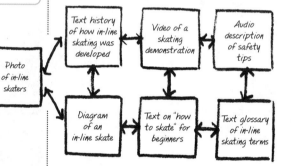

TECHNOLOGY TIP You can find CD-ROMs with videos of things like wildlife, weather, street scenes, and events, and CD-ROMs with recordings of famous speeches, musical selections, and dramatic readings.

WRITING TIP You usually need permission from the person or organization that owns the copyright on materials if you want to copy them. You do not need permission, however, if you are not making money from your presentation, if you use it only for educational purposes, and if you use only a small percentage of the original material.

4.3 Guiding Your User

Your user will need directions to follow the path you have planned for your multimedia presentation.

Most multimedia authoring programs allow you to create screens that include text or audio directions that guide the user from one part of your presentation to the next. In the example below, the user can choose between several paths, and directions on the screen explain how to make the choice.

If you need help creating your multimedia presentation, ask your school's technology adviser. You may also be able to get help from your classmates or your software manual.

The user clicks on a button to select any of these options.

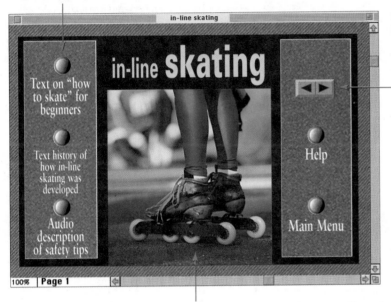

Navigational buttons take the user back and forth, one screen at a time.

This screen shows a video of a skating demonstration.

Glossary of Literary and Reading Terms

Act An act is a major unit of action in a play. *The Phantom Tollbooth,* for example, has two acts. An act may be divided into smaller sections, called scenes.

See page 319.
See also **Scene.**

Alliteration Alliteration is a repetition of consonant sounds at the beginning of words. Poets and songwriters use alliteration for emphasis or to add a musical quality. Notice the repetition of the *r* sound in the following lines:

> We rush into a rain
> That rattles double glass.
>
> —Theodore Roethke, from "Night Journey"

See page 191.

Allusion An allusion is a reference to a famous person, place, event, or work of literature. In *The Story of My Life,* Helen Keller makes an allusion to the Hebrew Bible when she says that learning about words made the world blossom for her "like Aaron's rod, with flowers."

Analogy An analogy is a point-by-point comparison between two different things in order to clarify the less familiar of the two. In "Abd al-Rahman Ibrahima," the author uses an analogy in writing about African history:

> . . . The Africans came from many countries, and from many cultures. Like the Native Americans, they established their territories based on centuries of tradition.
>
> —Walter Dean Myers, from "Abd al-Rahman Ibrahima"

Analyzing Analyzing is the process of breaking something down into its elements so that they can be examined individually. In analyzing a poem, for example, one might consider such elements as form, sound, figurative language, imagery, speaker, word choice, and theme.

Anecdote An anecdote is a short, entertaining account of a person or an event. Anecdotes are often included in larger works to amuse readers or to make a point. In "Chinatown," Laurence Yep tells an anecdote about a kickball game to illustrate his feeling of being "shunned and invisible. . . ."

See page 161.

Audience The audience of a piece of writing is the particular group of readers that the writer is addressing. A writer considers his or her audience when deciding on a subject, a purpose for writing, and the tone and style in which to write.

See page 416.

Author's perspective An author's perspective refers to an author's beliefs and attitudes. These beliefs may be influenced by such factors as the author's political views, religion, upbringing, and education. In "Bringing the Prairie Home," the author reveals her attachment to the very soil of the prairie, where she grew up.

> The Earth is like a character who has secrets; the Earth holds important clues to who we are, who we've been; who we will be.
>
> —Patricia MacLachlan, from "Bringing the Prairie Home"

See pages 363, 678.

Author's purpose An author's purpose is his or her reason for creating a particular work. The purpose may be to entertain, to inform, to express an opinion, or to persuade readers to do or believe something. An author may have more than one purpose for writing, but usually one is most important.

See pages 424, 676.

Autobiography An autobiography is the true story of a person's life, told by that person. Because autobiographies tell about real people and events, they are a form of nonfiction. Autobiographies are usually told from the first-person point of view. Helen Keller's *The Story of My Life* is an autobiography. The excerpts from *Looking Back* are considered memoir, a specific type of autobiography. A memoir relates the author's personal experiences and may be less formal in tone. Journals and diaries are other types of autobiographical writing.

See pages 97, 142, 170, 362–363, 385.

Ballad A ballad is a poem that tells a story and is meant to be sung or recited. "Barbara Frietchie" is an example of a ballad.

Biographer Anyone writing or having written a biography, or life story, of another person.

See also **Biography.**

Biography A biography is the true story of a person's life, written by another person. Because biographies tell about real people and events, they are a form of nonfiction. Biographies are usually told from the third-person point of view. "Matthew Henson at the Top of the World" is an example of biography.

See pages 97, 111, 362–363, 378.

Cast of characters In the script of a play, a cast of characters lists all the characters. It is usually found at the beginning, and the characters are usually listed in the order they appear.

See pages 319, 324.

Cause and effect Two events are related as cause and effect if one brings about—or causes—the other. The event that happens first is the cause; the one that follows from it is the effect. Writers sometimes signal cause-and-effect relationships with words and phrases such as *because, therefore, since, so that,* and *in order that.* This sentence from *Woodsong* deals with a cause and its effect: "Because we feed processed meat to the dogs, there is always the smell of meat over the kennel."

See pages 76, 446, 459, 674.

Character The people, animals, or imaginary creatures who take part in the action of a story are called characters. The most important characters are called main characters. Less important characters are called minor characters. In "The School Play," Robert is the main character, and Belinda and the others are minor characters. In good stories, characters have motivations and relationships that the reader cares about. Characters also have traits, or qualities, that help readers understand a character's personality. Examples of traits include loyalty, bravery, selfishness, and kindness.

See pages 23, 31, 45, 243–245, 319, 653.
See also **Character development.**

Character development Characters that change during a story are said to undergo character development. Main characters usually develop the most. For example, in "President Cleveland, Where Are You?" Jerry changes from acting selfishly to acting on behalf of others.

Characterization The way a writer creates and develops characters' personalities is known as characterization. A writer can develop a character in four basic ways.

1. By describing the character physically
2. By presenting the character's thoughts, speech, and actions
3. By presenting the thoughts, speech, and actions of other characters
4. By directly commenting on the character's nature

See also **Character.**

Chronological order Chronological order is the order in which events happen in time. In some stories and articles, events are related in chronological order. Other stories jump forward and backward in time.

See pages 121, 364, 378.

Cinderella tale A Cinderella tale is a version of the Cinderella story, often containing elements such as a mistreated stepchild, and a rags-to-riches plot. Cinderella tales are found in folklore all over the world. "In the Land of Small Dragon" is an example of a Cinderella tale from Vietnam.

Clarifying Clarifying is the process of stopping while reading to quickly review what has been read and to check for understanding. Clarifying helps readers keep track of events, characters, and their significance or meaning.

See pages 4, 385, 740.

Climax In a story or play, the climax, or turning point, is the point of greatest interest. At the climax, the outcome of the story becomes clear. The climax of "Tuesday of the Other June" occurs when June T. says *No* to the Other June with such strength that the astonished bully leaves her alone.

See pages 22, 319, 443, 488.
See also **Plot.**

Comedy A comedy is a dramatic work that is light and humorous. Usually it ends happily with a peaceful resolution of the main conflict. *The Phantom Tollbooth* is an example of a comedy.

See also **Drama.**

Comparison To point out what two or more things have in common is to make a comparison. Writers use comparisons to make ideas and details clearer to readers. In "Eleven," for example, the process of growing older is compared to little wooden dolls that fit together, one inside another.

See also **Metaphor; Simile.**

Conclusion Combining several pieces of information to make a guess is called drawing a conclusion. Readers draw conclusions by using information from the literature and from their own experiences.

See pages 613, 633.

Concrete poetry In a concrete poem, the arrangement of the poem's words on the page reflects the poem's subject. Note how the lines in Frank Asch's poem "Saguaro" resemble a saguaro cactus.

Conflict Conflict is a struggle between opposing forces. Almost every story is built around a central conflict faced by the main character. An external conflict is a struggle between a character and an outside force, such as society, nature, or another character. In *Woodsong,* Gary Paulsen faces an external conflict with a bear. An internal conflict is a struggle within a character's mind. It may occur when the character has to make a decision or deal with opposing feelings. Jerry's uncertainty in "President Cleveland, Where Are You?" about how to spend his money is an internal conflict.

See pages 22, 132, 319, 445.
See also **Plot.**

Connecting When readers relate the content of a literary work to what they already know or have experienced, they are connecting. Connecting helps readers identify with the experiences of the characters. For example, when they read Sandra Cisneros's story "Eleven," readers may remember times when they felt embarrassed or falsely accused.

See pages 4, 31, 281, 346.

Connotation Connotation refers to the ideas and feelings associated with a word, in contrast to the word's denotation, or dictionary definition. For example, the word *mother*, in addition to its basic meaning ("a female parent"), has a connotation of love, warmth, and security.

See page 742.

Context clues Unfamiliar words are often surrounded by words or phrases—called context—that help readers understand their meaning. A context clue may be a definition, a synonym, an example, a comparison or contrast, or any expression that enables readers to infer the word's meaning.

See page 79.

Contrast To contrast is to point out differences between things. Note how the narrator of "The All-American Slurp" contrasts Chinese and American eating habits:

> In fact we didn't use individual plates at all but picked up food from the platters in the middle of the table and brought it directly to our rice bowls.
>
> —Lensey Namioka,
> from "The All-American Slurp"

Couplet A couplet is a rhymed pair of lines in a poem. The poem "Barbara Frietchie" consists entirely of couplets.

See page 740.

Deductive reasoning In nonfiction, the structure of a text may be organized using deductive reasoning. Deductive reasoning is the process of logical reasoning from principles to specific instances; reasoning from whole to part. A text that is organized deductively begins with a generalization and advances with facts and evidence to a conclusion.

See also **Inductive reasoning.**

Denotation A word's denotation is its dictionary definition.

See page 742.
See also **Connotation.**

Description Description, also called sensory detail or imagery, is writing that helps a reader create mental pictures of scenes, events, or characters. To create descriptions, writers choose details carefully—usually details that appeal to readers' senses of sight, sound, smell, touch, and taste. Note the details in this passage from "Tuesday of the Other June" about the main character's new home:

> We went into the house, down a dim, cool hall. In our new apartment, the wooden floors clicked under our shoes, and my mother showed me everything. Her voice echoed in the empty rooms.
>
> —Norma Fox Mazer,
> from "Tuesday of the Other June"

Dialect A dialect is the particular use of language spoken in a definite place by a distinct group of people. Writers use dialect to establish setting and to develop characters.

Dialogue The words that characters speak aloud are called dialogue. Dialogue moves a plot forward and reveals the personalities of the characters. In a play, dialogue is the main way the writer tells the story. The dialogue in fiction is usually set off with quotation marks. No quotation marks are used for the dialogue in plays.

See pages 320, 337.

Diction See **Word Choice.**

Drama A drama, or play, is a form of literature meant to be performed before an audience. Dramas for stage are also called theater. In a drama, the story is presented through the dialogue and the actions of the characters. The written form of a drama is known as a script. A script usually includes dialogue, a cast of characters, and stage directions that give specific instructions about performing the play. Two important kinds of drama are comedy and tragedy. A comedy is light and humorous; a tragedy ends in disaster—most often death—for the main character and often for other important characters as well.

See pages 317–320, 321.
See also **Act; Cast of Characters; Comedy; Dialogue; Playwright; Prop; Scene; Script; Stage directions; Tragedy.**

Drawing conclusions See **Conclusion.**

Dynamic character A character in a literary work that changes significantly during the course of events is called a dynamic character.

Epic poetry An epic poem is a long narrative poem about the adventures of a hero. Epic poetry addresses universal concerns such as good and evil, life and death, and other serious subjects.

Essay An essay is a short work of nonfiction that deals with a single subject. The purpose of an essay may be to express ideas or feelings, to analyze a topic, to inform, to entertain, or to persuade. "All I Really Need to Know I Learned in Kindergarten" is an example of a personal essay, in which Robert Fulghum expresses his ideas by reflecting on incidents in his own life.

See pages 98, 473, 640.

Evaluating Evaluating is the process of judging the quality of something or someone. In evaluating a literary work, you might focus on the elements found in that type of work—for example, the plot, setting, characters, and theme of a work of fiction. You can also evaluate a work by comparing and contrasting it with similar works.

See pages 4, 216.

Exaggeration An overstating of an idea is called exaggeration. Avi uses exaggeration in "Scout's Honor" when he says a character who tripped "took off like an F-36 fighter plane."

Exposition In fiction, the plot normally begins with exposition. The exposition establishes the setting, introduces the characters, and gives the reader important background information. During this stage, the conflict may also be introduced. In "All Summer in a Day," the exposition leads up to the time when Margot tells her classmates about her memories of the sun.

See also **Plot.**

External conflict See **Conflict.**

Fable A fable is a brief story that teaches a lesson about life. In many fables, the characters are animals that act and speak like human beings. A fable often ends with a moral—a statement that summarizes its lesson. "The Wolf and the House Dog" is an example of a fable.

See also **Moral.**

Fact and opinion A fact is a statement that can be proved, such as "Mars is the fourth planet from the sun." An opinion, in contrast, is a statement that expresses a person's feelings, such as "Mars is the most beautiful planet." Opinions cannot be proved.

See pages 227, 699.

Falling action In the plot of a story, the falling action (sometimes called the resolution) occurs after the climax. During the falling action, conflicts are resolved and any loose ends are tied up. In "Ghost of the Lagoon," the falling action begins after Mako throws his spear into Tupa's side.

See pages 22, 443.
See also **Climax; Plot.**

Fantasy Literature that contains at least one fantastic or unreal element is called fantasy. The setting of a work of fantasy might be a totally imaginary world, or it might be a realistic place where very unusual or impossible things happen. *The Phantom Tollbooth* is a work of fantasy.

See pages 507–510, 552, 561.

Fiction A narrative story that uses made-up characters or events is called fiction. In some works of fiction, the entire story is made up; in others, the story is based in part on real people or events. Forms of fiction include short stories and novels. A short story can usually be read in one sitting. Novels are longer and tend to be more complicated.

See pages 21–24, 25.
See also **Character; Historical fiction; Novel; Plot; Realistic fiction; Science fiction; Setting; Short story; Theme.**

Figurative Language In figurative language, words are used to express more than their dictionary meaning. Figurative language conveys vivid images. In this passage from "The Circuit," note how the figurative language helps create a picture of working in the fields:

> The sun kept beating down. The buzzing insects, the wet sweat, and the hot dry dust made the afternoon seem to last forever. Finally the mountains around the valley reached out and swallowed the sun.
>
> —Francisco Jiménez, from "The Circuit"

See pages 192, 198.
See also **Metaphor; Personification; Simile.**

First-person point of view See *Point of View.*

Flashback A flashback is a conversation, an episode, or an event that happened before the beginning of a story. Often a flashback interrupts the chronological flow of a story to give the reader information to help in understanding a character's situation. "Crow Call" has a flashback that tells how the narrator got her shirt:

> My father had bought the shirt for me. In town to buy groceries, he had noticed my hesitating in front of Kronenberg's window. . . .
>
> —Lois Lowry, from "Crow Call"

Folklore The traditions, customs, and stories that are passed down within a culture are known as its folklore. Folklore includes various types of literature, such as legends, folk tales, myths, and fables.

See also **Fable; Folk Tale; Legend; Myth.**

Folk tale A folk tale is a simple story that has been passed down from generation to generation by word of mouth. Folk tales are usually about people, animals, or occurrences in nature and are usually set in times long past. They may include fantastical elements, like the talking animals in "Why Monkeys Live in Trees."

Foreshadowing A hint about an event that will occur later in a story is called foreshadowing. In "Lob's Girl," a stormy night foreshadows the car accident that puts Sandy in a coma.

See page 459.

Form The form of a poem is the shape the words and lines make on the page. Form is determined by the length and placement of the lines and how the lines are grouped in stanzas. "Analysis of Baseball" contains very short lines set in long stanzas. A poet may use the form of a poem to emphasize the poem's meaning. In concrete poetry, for example, the poem's shape reflects its subject.

See page 190.

Free Verse Poetry without regular patterns of rhyme or rhythm is called free verse. Free verse can sometimes sound like conversation. Note the natural flow of the following example of free verse:

> When the bird comes
> if it comes
> observe the deepest silence
> wait for the bird to enter the cage
>
> —Jacques Prévert,
> from "How to Paint the Portrait of a Bird"

See page 190.

Generalization A generalization is a statement made about a whole group. Generalizations may be untrue if they are too broad or not based on fact. For example, the statement "All Americans slurp" is a generalization that is untrue. The word *all* makes the generalization untrue.

See page 465.

Genre A type or category of literature is called a genre. There are four main literary genres: fiction, nonfiction, poetry, and drama.

Haiku Haiku is a traditional form of Japanese poetry. A haiku normally has three lines and describes a single moment, feeling, or object. In a traditional haiku, the first and third lines contain five syllables each, and the second line contains seven syllables.

See page 207.

Historical fiction Historical fiction is fiction that is set in the past. It may contain references to actual people and significant events in history. This description from the short story "The Dog of Pompeii" is true to historical fact:

> The earthquake of twelve years ago had brought down all the old structures, and since the citizens of Pompeii were ambitious to rival Naples and even Rome, they had seized the opportunity to rebuild the whole town.
>
> —Louis Untermeyer, from "The Dog of Pompeii"

See pages 697–698, 711.

Humor The quality that makes something funny is called humor. Writers create humor using exaggeration, word play, sarcasm, witty dialogue, unlikely comparisons, and other devices. In "Scout's Honor," the narrator describes the subway system map as looking "like a noodle factory hit by a bomb."

See page 424.

Idiom An idiom is an expression that has meaning different from the meaning of its individual words. For example, the idiom "in a pickle" means "having a difficult time."

Imagery Words that appeal to readers' senses are referred to as imagery. Writers usually try to describe places, characters, and events in ways that help readers imagine how they look, feel, smell, sound, and taste. In *Words on a Page*, Lenore uses imagery in the essay she reads to her class.

> And there was the beaver and the loon and the hawk circling above the treetops. And below the trout and the sturgeon slipped silently through the black water. . . . She felt the morning sun on her face and the gentle rocking of the canoe and smiled because she knew that here would always be her home.
>
> Keith Leckie, from *Words on a Page*

See pages 192, 415.

Inductive reasoning In nonfiction, the structure of a text may be organized using inductive reasoning. Inductive reasoning is the process of determining principles by logic or observation; reasoning from specific parts to whole situations. A text that is organized inductively begins with examples of specific cases. It advances by drawing logical conclusions and ends with a statement of a logical generalization.

See also **Deductive reasoning.**

Inference An inference is a logical guess based on evidence. Good readers make inferences as they read—trying to figure out more than the words say. The evidence may be facts the writer provides, or it may be experiences from a reader's own life. For example, readers of "Chinatown" can make inferences about why the narrator felt disgraceful for not excelling at sports.

See pages 198, 272, 395, 661.

Informative nonfiction Informative nonfiction is writing that provides factual information about real people, places, and events. "Summer of Fire" is an example of informative nonfiction. Newspaper and magazine articles, pamphlets, history and science textbooks, and encyclopedia articles are other examples of informative nonfiction.

See pages 99, 121, 725.

Internal conflict See **Conflict.**

Interview An interview is a meeting in which one person asks another about personal matters, professional matters, or both. Interviews may be tape-recorded, filmed, or recorded in writing. The author study for Lois Lowry includes an interview with her.

See page 99.

Irony Irony is a contrast between what is expected and what actually exists or happens. For example, readers of "The Fun They Had" may find it unexpected and ironic that the main character in the story, which is set in the year 2157, longs for the good old days when children went to school together in classrooms and passed in their homework to a teacher. The following description contains irony:

> She was thinking about the old schools they had when her grandfather's grandfather was a little boy. All the kids from the neighborhood came, laughing and shouting in the schoolyard, sitting together in the schoolroom, going home together at the end of the day. They learned the same things so they could help one another on the homework and talk about it.
>
> And the teachers were people. . . .
>
> —Isaac Asimov, from "The Fun They Had"

Legend A legend is a story that is handed down from the past and may tell about something that really happened or someone who really lived. Legends often mix fact and fiction. "The Legend of the Hummingbird" is a legend from Puerto Rico.

Limerick A limerick is a short, humorous poem usually composed of five lines. It has a rhyme scheme created by two rhyming couplets followed by a final line that rhymes with the first couplet. This rhyme scheme is known as *a-a-b-b-a*. A limerick typically has a sing-song rhythm. In some limericks, the second couplet is collapsed into one long, internally rhyming, line.

See page 566.

Literary nonfiction See **Nonfiction.**

Lyric poetry Lyric poetry is poetry that presents the thoughts and feelings of a single speaker. "I'm Nobody! Who Are You?" by Emily Dickinson is an example of lyric poetry.

Main character See **Character.**

Main idea A main idea is the most important idea that a writer wishes to express. It may be the important idea of an entire work or the important thought expressed in the topic sentence of a paragraph. A writer may need to use several paragraphs to develop a main idea. Usually, the main idea is rather general, and details give specific information that support it.

See pages 100, 111, 640.

Memoir See ***Autobiography.***

Metaphor A metaphor is a comparison of two things that have some quality in common. Unlike a simile, a metaphor does not contain a word such as *like, as, than,* or *resembles.* Instead, it states that one thing actually is something else. Lois Lowry uses a metaphor in "Crow Call" when she describes "the ribbon of road through the farm lands."

See page 192.
See also **Simile.**

Meter In poetry, a regular pattern of stressed and unstressed syllables—or a regular rhythm—is called meter. Although all poems have rhythm, not all poems have meter.

See also **Rhythm.**

Minor character See ***Character.***

Monitoring When readers pay attention to their comprehension as they are reading, they are monitoring. Monitoring, or checking comprehension, helps readers clearly understand the meaning of what they are reading.

See pages 25, 409.

Mood A mood is a feeling that a literary work conveys to readers. A mood is an emotion such as sadness, excitement, or anger. In "Ghost of the Lagoon," Armstrong Sperry creates a mood of excitement and tension as Mako prepares to meet Tupa.

See also **Tone.**

Moral A moral is a lesson taught in a literary work such as a fable. At the end of a fable, a moral is often stated directly.

Motivation A character's motivation is the reason why he or she acts, feels, or thinks in a certain way. For example, the narrator in "Scout's Honor" is motivated by a desire to prove that he is tough. A character may have a number of motivations for his or her actions. Understanding these motivations helps readers to get to know the character.

Myth A myth is a traditional story about the origins or workings of the world. Some myths explain how certain things came into being. Others explain elements of nature or social customs. The characters in myths are often superhuman beings. The events may be unlikely or realistic. Because myths have been handed down from one generation to the next for a long time, their original authors are unknown. "Arachne" is an example of a Greek myth.

See pages 768, 770.

Narrative Writing that tells a story is called a narrative. The events in a narrative may be real or imagined. Narratives that deal with real events include autobiographies and biographies. Fictional narratives include myths, short stories, and novels. A narrative may also be in the form of a poem.

Narrative poetry Narrative poetry is poetry that tells a story. Like other stories, a narrative poem contains a setting, characters, and a plot. It may also contain such elements of poetry as rhyme, rhythm, imagery, and figurative language. "The Walrus and the Carpenter" is an example of a narrative poem.

See pages 346, 740.

Narrator A narrator is the teller of a story. Sometimes a story's narrator is a character who takes part in the action; in other cases, the narrator is an outside voice. In "The Scribe," for example, the narrator is James, the main character. "The School Play," in contrast, is narrated by an outsider's voice.

See page 319.
See also **Point of view.**

Nonfiction Writing that tells about real people, places, and events is called nonfiction. There are two main types of nonfiction. Literary nonfiction is like fiction, except that the characters, setting, and plot are real rather than imaginary. Its purpose is usually to entertain or express opinions or feelings. Literary nonfiction includes autobiographies, biographies, and essays. Informative nonfiction provides factual information. Its main purpose is to inform or explain.

See pages 96–99, 100.
See also **Autobiography; Biography; Essay; Informative nonfiction.**

Novel A novel is a form of fiction that is longer and more complicated than a short story. In a novel, the setting, the plot, and the characters are developed in detail. Minor characters are developed more fully than in a short story.

See page 21.

Onomatopoeia Onomatopoeia is the use of words whose sound suggests their meaning. The words *bang* and *hiss* are examples of onomatopoeia. The onomatopoeic words in "Analysis of Baseball" include *thuds, pow,* and *thwack.*

See page 648.

Opinion See **Fact and opinion.**

Oral history An oral history is an account of an historical event as told by someone who was there at the time. Oral histories are often handed down from generation to generation by word of mouth. "Where the Girl Rescued Her Brother" is an oral history from the Cheyenne tradition.

Paraphrasing Restating an author's ideas using your own words is called paraphrasing. Paraphrasing can help you understand and remember what you read. Paraphrasing can also help you in writing research reports. By paraphrasing the information you read, you can avoid

plagiarism—the use of another's words as your own.

See page 49.

Personal essay See **Essay.**

Personification The giving of human qualities to an animal, object, or idea is known as personification. In "You Sing," trees are personified when they are said to "speak with their green tongue."

See pages 192, 346, 648.

Perspective See **Author's perspective.**

Play See **Drama.**

Playwright The author of a drama for the stage is called a playwright.

Plot The series of events in a story is called the story's plot. A plot usually centers around a central conflict—a problem faced by the main character. In a typical plot, the action that the characters take to solve the problem builds, or rises, toward a climax, an important event or decision that becomes the turning point of the story. At that point, or shortly afterward, the action falls. The problem may be solved or changed and the story ends.

See pages 22, 45, 76, 319, 443–445.

Poetic form See **Form.**

Poetry Poetry is a type of literature in which ideas, images, and feelings are expressed in few words. Most poetry is written in lines, which may be grouped in stanzas. Poets carefully select words for their sounds and meanings, combining the words in imaginative ways to present feelings, pictures, experiences, and themes vividly. In poetry, the images appeal to readers' senses, as do elements of sound, such as alliteration, rhythm, and rhyme.

See pages 189–192, 193.

Point of view The perspective from which a story is told is called the point of view. Usually, a story is told from either the first-person or the third-person point of view. In a story told from the first-person point of view, the narrator is a character in the story and uses pronouns such as *I, me,* and *we.* "Eleven" is told by the story's main character, from the first-person point of view. A story told from the third-person point of view has a narrator who is outside the story and uses pronouns such as *he, she,* and *they.* "Aaron's Gift" is told by a narrator who is not a character in the story. It is told from the third-person point of view.

See pages 281, 362.
See also **Autobiography; Biography.**

Predicting Using what you already know to make a logical guess about what might happen in the future is called predicting. Good readers gather information as they read. They combine that information with their own knowledge and experience to predict, or guess, what might happen next in the story.

See pages 4, 132, 247, 257, 337.

Primary source The information that writers of nonfiction present comes from various kinds of sources. A primary source conveys direct, firsthand knowledge. "My First Dive with the Dolphins" is a primary source because it is an account of Don C. Reed's own personal experience. Primary sources include diaries, letters, interview tapes, memoirs, journals, photographs, and other authentic artifacts.

See pages 227, 261, 363, 378.
See also **Secondary source.**

Prop The word *prop,* an abbreviation of *property,* refers to any physical object that is used in a drama or play.

Propaganda Text that uses false or misleading information to present a point of view is called propaganda. Name-calling, snob appeal, and and bandwagon appeal are three techniques of propaganda.

Prose Prose is the ordinary form of spoken and written language—that is, it is language that lacks the special features of poetry.

Purpose See *Author's purpose; Setting a purpose.*

Quest In literature, a journey or adventure that a character goes on to achieve a specific goal is called a quest. In *The Phantom Tollbooth,* Milo's adventure in the lands beyond turns into a quest when he sets out to rescue the princesses.

Questioning The process of asking questions while reading is called questioning. Good readers ask questions in an effort to understand characters and events. They then look for answers to their questions.

See pages 4, 170.

Radio play A radio play is a drama that is written specifically to be broadcast over the radio. Because the audience cannot see a radio play, sound effects are used to help listeners imagine the setting and action. The stage directions in the play's script indicate the sound effects. *Damon and Pythias* is an example of a radio play.

Realistic fiction Realistic fiction is imaginative writing set in the real, modern world. The characters act like real people who use ordinary human abilities to cope with problems and conflicts typical of modern life. "Tuesday of the Other June" is an example of realistic fiction.

See also **Fiction.**

Repetition Repetition is the use of a sound, word, or phrase more than once. Writers use repetition to bring certain ideas, sounds, or feelings to readers' attention. For example, in the poem "Chang McTang McQuarter Cat," the speaker repeats the phrase "one part" frequently as he presents the qualities of the cat.

See pages 191, 287, 395, 479.
See also **Alliteration; Rhyme.**

Resolution See *Plot; Falling action.*

Rhyme Rhyme is the repetition of similar sounds at the ends of words. In poetry, rhyme that occurs within a line is called **internal rhyme.** Rhyme that occurs at the end of lines is called **end rhyme.** Note both the internal rhymes and the end rhyme in these lines from "The Walrus and the Carpenter":

> "A pleasant <u>walk</u>, a pleasant <u>talk</u>
>   Along the briny <u>beach</u>:
> We cannot do with <u>more</u> than <u>four</u>,
>   To give a hand to <u>each</u>."
>
> —Lewis Carroll,
> from "The Walrus and the Carpenter"

See pages 191, 287, 479.

Rhyme scheme The pattern of end rhyme in a poem is called the poem's rhyme scheme. A rhyme scheme can be described by using a different letter of the alphabet to represent each rhyming sound. Note the rhyme scheme of the first four lines of "The Quarrel." This scheme is called *a-b-a-b.*

> I quarreled with my brother,   *a*
> I don't know what about,   *b*
> One thing led to another   *a*
> And somehow we fell out.   *b*
>
> —Eleanor Farjeon, from "The Quarrel"

Rhythm The rhythm of a line of poetry is the pattern of stressed and unstressed syllables in the line. A regular pattern of rhythm is called meter. Note the regular rhythm in the following lines.

> Chang McTang McQuarter Cat
> Is one part this and twenty that.
>
> —John Ciardi,
> from "Chang McTang McQuarter Cat"

See pages 191, 287, 479.
See also **Meter.**

Rising action Rising action refers to the events in a story that move the plot forward. Rising action involves conflicts and complications, and usually builds toward a climax, or turning point.

See pages 22, 443.
See also **Plot.**

Sarcasm Humor that uses words to express something opposite to their literal meaning is called sarcasm. Judith Viorst uses sarcasm in "The Southpaw." For example, when Janet writes to Richard, "Congratulations on your unbroken record," she is being sarcastic. Though Janet sounds as if she is being friendly, she is really teasing Richard, whose "unbroken record" is a series of losses.

Scanning Scanning is the process of searching through writing for a particular fact or piece of information. When readers scan, they sweep their eyes across a page looking for key words that could lead them to the information they want.

Scene In a play, a scene is a section that presents events taking place in a single setting. A new scene begins whenever the story calls for a change in time or place.

See page 319.

Scenery The painted backdrop and other structures used to create the setting for a drama are called scenery.

Science fiction Science fiction is fiction that is based on real or possible scientific developments. Although much science fiction is set in the future, the problems that the characters face may be similar to real problems that people face today. "The Fun They Had," a story about school in the 22nd century, is an example of science fiction.

See pages 216, 507–510.

Script The text of a play, motion picture, radio broadcast, or prepared speech is called a script.

Secondary source A secondary source is one that conveys indirect, secondhand knowledge. "Matthew Henson at the Top of the World" is a secondary source because the information it contains comes from Jim Haskins's reading and research. Secondary sources include most articles and reports, biographies, textbooks, and other informative nonfiction.

See pages 227, 261, 363, 378.
*See also **Primary source.***

Sensory details Words and phrases that help readers see, hear, taste, smell, and feel what a writer is describing are called sensory details, or imagery. Note the sensory details in this excerpt from "Summer of Fire":

> Boulders exploded in the heat. Sheets of flame leapt forward. Gigantic clouds of smoke ringed the horizon . . . [Snow] sifted through blackened forests and dusted herds of bison and elk.
>
> —Patricia Lauber, from "Summer of Fire"

See pages 207, 385, 648.
*See also **Description; Imagery.***

Sequence The order in which events occur or ideas are presented is called a sequence. In a narrative, events are usually presented in chronological order—the order in which they happened. A writer may use clue words and phrases—such as *then, until, after a while,* and *finally*—to help readers understand the sequence of events.

See pages 45, 444.

Setting The setting of a story, poem, or play is the time and place of the action. The time may be past, present, or future. The place may be real or imaginary. In some stories, including many fables, settings may not be clearly defined. In other stories, however, settings play an important part. For example, the desert setting of "Nadia the Willful" plays an important part in the story's action and helps to create its mood.

See pages 24, 64, 243, 246, 508, 509, 579, 585.

Setting a purpose The process of establishing specific reasons to read a work is called setting a purpose. Readers often come to a work with a purpose in mind, such as reading for entertainment, for information, or to analyze or evaluate a piece of writing. Readers can look at a work's title, headings and subheadings, and illustrations to preview the work. Previewing may also guide their purposes for reading.

See page 579.

Short story A short story is a form of fiction that can generally be read in one sitting. Like other forms of fiction, short stories contain characters, plots, settings, and themes. The plot of a short story usually involves one main conflict.

See page 21.
*See also **Fiction.***

Simile A simile is a comparison of two things that have some quality in common. A simile contains a word such as *like, as, resembles,* or *than.* Note the simile in this sentence from "The Bamboo Beads": "That night the moon was round and white as my Sunday hat."

See pages 192, 424.
See also **Metaphor.**

Skimming Skimming is the process of reading quickly to get the general idea of a work. It involves reading the title, headings, graphics, words in special print, and the first sentence of each paragraph.

Sound devices See *Alliteration; Onomatopoeia; Repetition; Rhyme; Rhythm.*

Source See *Primary source; Secondary source.*

Speaker In a poem, the speaker is the voice that talks to the reader, like the narrator in a work of fiction. The speaker is not always the poet. He or she may be a character in the poem.

See pages 192, 395.

Speech A speech is a prepared talk given in public. Lois Lowry's "Newbery Acceptance Speech" for *The Giver* is an example of a speech.

Stage A stage is the level and raised platform on which entertainers usually perform.

See page 318.

Stage directions In the script of a play, the instructions to the performers, director, and stage crew are called stage directions. They usually appear in italic type and within parentheses. Stage directions provide suggestions about such things as scenery, lighting, music, and sound effects. They may also tell performers how to move and how to speak their lines. Note the stage directions in this passage from *Damon and Pythias:*

> **Damon** *(calm and firm).* I have faith in my friend. I know he will return.
> **King** *(mocking).* We shall see!
> *(Sound: Iron door shut and locked.)*
> —Fan Kissen, from *Damon and Pythias*

See pages 318, 330.

Stanza A grouping of two or more lines within a poem is called a stanza. A stanza is similar to a paragraph in prose. "The Walrus and the Carpenter" contains 18 stanzas.

See page 190.

Static character In fiction, drama, or literary nonfiction, characters who undergo little or no change during the course of the story are referred to as static characters.

See also **Dynamic character.**

Stereotype In literature, simplistic characters defined by a single trait are called stereotypes, or clichés. Such characters do not usually demonstrate the complexities of real people. Familiar stereotypes in popular fiction include the absent-minded professor, the hard-boiled private eye, and the mustache-twirling villain. The proud, beautiful princess in fairy tales such as "King Thrushbeard" is another example:

> A king had a daughter who was unequaled for beauty, but she thought so much of herself that no suitor was good enough for her. She rejected one after another . . .
> —The Brothers Grimm, from "King Thrushbeard"

Story-mapping Creating an outline of the events that take place in a story is called story-mapping. A story map may also identify characters and setting, and the plot's conflict, resolution, and theme. Story-mapping can help you understand what you read.

See pages 330, 488.

Structure The structure of a literary work is the way in which it is organized. In poetry, structure involves the arrangement of words, lines, and stanzas. In fiction, structure involves the sequence of events in the plot. In nonfiction, the structure of a piece may be chronological or spatial order, cause and effect, or comparison and contrast. Recognizing a text's structure can help in finding the most important ideas as well as the supporting facts and details.

Style A style is a particular way of writing. It involves *how* something is said rather than *what* is said. Word choice, sentence length, tone, imagery, and use of dialogue contribute to a writer's style.

See pages 172, 426, 686.

Subject The subject of a literary work is its focus or topic. In a biography, for example, the subject is the person whose life story is being told. Subject differs from theme in that theme is a deeper meaning, usually inferred by the reader, where the subject is the main situation or set of facts described by the text.

Summarizing Summarizing is telling the main ideas of a piece of writing briefly, in one's own words. When you summarize, you condense a writer's ideas into precise statements, leaving out unimportant details. A summary may include direct quotations, important details, and statements about an underlying theme or message.

See page 341.

Surprise ending An unexpected plot twist at the end of a story is called a surprise ending. The surprise may be a sudden turn in the action, or a piece of information that gives a different perspective to the entire story. "Lob's Girl" has a surprise ending when, in the final scene, it is revealed that Lob may have been in two places at once.

Suspense Suspense is a feeling of growing tension and excitement that makes a reader curious about the outcome of a story or an event within a story. In "Ghost of the Lagoon," suspense is created as Mako sets out into Tupa's territory.

Symbol A symbol is a person, a place, or an object that stands for something other than itself. In literature, objects and images may be used to symbolize things that cannot actually be seen, such as ideas or feelings. In "Flowers and Freckle Cream," for example, the tiger lily Elizabeth receives from her grandfather may symbolize the beauty he sees in her freckled appearance.

See page 674.

Table of contents In most nonfiction books or in books arranged by chapter, or section, the book's contents are listed at the front in a table of contents. The table of contents gives the title of each section and the page number on which it starts. It can be used, like an outline, to get an overview of the material covered. It may also be used to find a specific topic covered in one section.

Tall tale A tall tale is a humorously exaggerated story about impossible events, often relating the superhuman abilities of the main character. The tales about folk heroes such as Paul Bunyan and Davy Crockett are typical tall tales.

Teleplay A play written for television is called a teleplay, or television script. In a teleplay, the stage directions usually include camera instructions. *Words on a Page* is an example of a teleplay.

Text organizers Text organizers include headings, tables of contents, and graphic elements such as charts, tables, time lines, boxes, bullets, and captions.

See page 146.

Theme A theme is the meaning or moral of a story. Writers develop themes to express their ideas about life or human nature. Sometimes themes are stated directly, but often readers must figure them out. Any lessons learned by the important characters in a story can be clues to a theme. For example, a theme of "The Scribe" might be that helping people ultimately helps you.

See pages 24, 76, 510, 611–612, 633.

Thesaurus A thesaurus is a reference tool used by writers to find the precise word to convey a certain meaning and tone. A thesaurus lists words and their synonyms, often including antonyms and other closely related words.

Third-person point of view See *Point of view.*

Title The title of a piece of writing is the name that is attached to it. A title often refers to an important aspect of the work. For example, the title of "Aaron's Gift" refers to the special importance of Aaron's effort to give a gift to his grandmother.

Tone The tone of a work shows the writer's attitude toward his or her subject. A work may have one tone throughout, such as humorous, serious, or impatient. Sometimes, however, the tone may change several times in the course of a work. For example, the tone of Don C. Reed's essay "My First Dive with the Dolphins" varies from humorous to serious.

See pages 363, 409.
See also **Mood**.

Topic sentence See *Main idea.*

Tragedy A tragedy is a dramatic work that presents the downfall of a dignified character (or characters) who is involved in historically or socially significant events. The events in a tragic plot are set in motion by a decision that is often an error in judgment. Succeeding events are linked in a cause-and-effect relationship and lead inevitably to a disastrous conclusion, usually death.

Trickster tale A folk tale that features a playful character who plays pranks on or seeks to outwit other characters is called a trickster tale. This type of tale is found in the folklore of cultures around the world. "Why Monkeys Live in Trees" is an example of a trickster tale.

Turning point See *Climax.*

Visualizing The process of forming a mental picture based on a written description is called visualizing. Readers use details of sight, sound, touch, taste, and feeling to visualize the characters, settings, and events in works of literature. Mentally picturing writers' descriptions makes reading more enjoyable and memorable.

See pages 4, 64, 511, 561

Voice A writer's unique way of writing is called voice. Voice is shaped by the choice of words, the way they are put together, and the details and thoughts the writer chooses to write about.

See page 684.

Word choice Word choice, also called diction, is the process by which writers carefully select words to give precision and impact to their writing.

See page 479.

Glossary of Words to Know

In English and Spanish

A

abundance (ə-bŭn′dəns) n. a great amount
abundancia n. gran cantidad

accumulate (ə-kyōōm′yə-lāt′) v. to gather or pile up
amontonar v. juntar o poner en montón

acknowledge (ăk-nŏl′ĭj) v. to admit or to value the existence of
reconocer v. admitir o valorar

admonishing (ăd-mŏn′ĭsh-ĭng) adj. issuing a gentle warning **admonish** v.
admonitorio(a) adj. que emite una advertencia **advertir** v.

aggression (ə-grĕsh′ən) n. threatening behavior; hostility
agresión n. conducta amenazadora; hostilidad

agitated (ăj′ĭ-tā′tĭd) adj. disturbed; upset **agitate** v.
agitado(a) adj. turbado(a); preocupado(a) **agitar** v.

allot (ə-lŏt′) v. to parcel out to; distribute to
distribuir v. repartir entre varios

ally (ă-lī′) n. a person, group, or nation that works with another to achieve shared goals
aliado n. una persona, grupo o nación que trabaja con otro para lograr metas compartidas

altitude (ăl′tĭ-tōōd′) n. an object's height above a particular level, such as ground level or sea level
altitud n. la altura de un objeto sobre un nivel particular, como el nivel del suelo o el nivel del mar

ambition (ăm-bĭsh′ən) n. a goal that is strongly desired
ambición n. una meta que se desea fuertemente

amiable (ā′mē-ə-bəl) adj. good-natured and likable
amable adj. bondadoso(a) y agradable

anguish (ăng′gwĭsh) n. severe mental pain
angustia n. dolor mental intenso

anticipate (ăn-tĭs′ə-pāt′) v. to look forward to; foresee
anticipar v. prever

anticipation (ăn-tĭs′ə-pā′shən) n. the feeling of expecting something
expectación n. espera de algo

apparatus (ăp′ə-rā′təs) n. a device or set of equipment used for a specific purpose
aparato n. una máquina o conjunto de instrumentos que se usa para un objetivo específico

apt (ăpt) adj. quick to learn or understand
apto(a) adj. hábil para aprender o comprender

ardent (är′dnt) adj. full of enthusiasm or devotion
ardiente adj. lleno(a) de entusiasmo o devoción

arrogantly (ăr′ə-gənt-lē) adv. with excessive and often undeserved pride in oneself
arrogantemente adv. con orgullo excesivo y frecuentemente inmerecido en sí mismo(a)

ascend (ə-sĕnd´) v. to move upward
subir v. mover hacia arriba

assassinate (ə-săs´ə-nāt´) v. to murder by surprise attack for political reasons
asesinar v. matar por medio de ataque por sorpresa

assure (ə-shŏŏr´) v. to promise or tell positively
asegurar v. prometer o decir positivamente

astonished (ə-stŏn´ĭsht) adj. surprised; amazed **astonish** v.
asombrado(a) adj. sorprendido(a); pasmado(a) **asombrar** v.

atone (ə-tōn´) v. to make amends
expiar v. hacer reparación

audacious (ô-dā´shəs) adj. fearlessly and recklessly daring; bold
audaz adj. intrépida y precipitadamente temerario(a); osado(a)

B

banish (băn´ĭsh) v. to send away; exile
desterrar v. echar fuera; exiliar

barren (băr´ən) adj. lacking vegetation
yermo(a) adj. sin vegetación

bazaar (bə-zär´) n. in Middle Eastern countries, an outdoor market of small shops
bazar n. en países del Oriente Medio, un mercado al aire libre de tiendas pequeñas

bear (bâr) v. to move forcefully; push
abrumar v. mover con fuerza

bellow (bĕl´ō) v. to shout in a deep voice
gritar v. levantar mucho la voz

betrayed (bĭ-trād´) adj. made a fool of; tricked **betray** v.
traicionado(a) adj. puesto(a) en ridículo; engañado(a) **traicionar** v.

bitterness (bĭt´ər-nĭs) n. a feeling of disgust or resentment
rencor n. un sentimiento de repugnancia o resentimiento

bland (blănd) adj. dull
insulso(a) adj. insípido(a)

bondage (bŏn´dĭj) n. slavery
esclavitud n. dominación

C

camouflage (kăm´ə-fläzh´) n. a disguise produced by blending in with the surroundings
camuflaje n. un disfraz que se produce entremezclándose con los alrededores

canopy (kăn´ə-pē) n. a rooflike cover; the covering formed by the branches and leaves of trees in a forest
bóveda n. una cubierta como un techo; una cubierta formada por las ramas y hojas de árboles en un bosque

chaos (kā´ŏs) n. a state of great disorder
caos n. desorden

clan (clăn) n. a family group
clan n. un grupo de familia

cleft (klĕft) adj. divided; split
partido(a) adj. dividido(a); separado(a)

coexistence (kō´ĭg-zĭs´təns) n. a state of living together in peace
coexistencia n. un estado de vivir juntos en paz

collective (kə-lĕk´tĭv) adj. done by a number of people acting as a group
colectivo(a) adj. hecho(a) por varias personas que actúan como un grupo

coma (kō´mə) n. a sleeplike state in which a person cannot sense or respond to light, sound, or touch
coma n. un estado como el sueño en que una persona no puede detectar ni responder a luz, sonido o toque

compassion (kəm-păsh′ən) *n.* sympathy for the suffering of others; pity
compasión *n.* condolencia por el sufrimiento de otros; piedad

compressed (kəm-prĕst′) *adj.* under greater than normal pressure **compress** *v.*
comprimido(a) *adj.* bajo presión mayor que la normal **comprimir** *v.*

conceal (kən-sēl′) *v.* to hide
ocultar *v.* esconder

concussion (kən-kŭsh′ən) *n.* a strong shaking
conmoción *n.* una sacudida fuerte

condescending (kŏn′dĭ-sĕn′dĭng) *adj.* displaying an attitude of patronizing superiority **condescend** *v.*
condescendiente *adj.* que muestra una actitud de superioridad **condescender** *v.*

consolidate (kən-sŏl′ĭ-dāt′) *v.* to make strong or secure
consolidar *v.* hacer fuerte o seguro(a)

contemplating (kŏn′təm-plā′tĭng) *adj.* considering carefully; pondering **contemplate** *v.*
contemplando *adj.* considerando cuidadosamente; reflexionando **contemplar** *v.*

contempt (kən-tĕmpt′) *n.* the feeling produced by something disgraceful or worthless; scorn
desprecio *n.* el sentimiento producido por algo vergonzoso o sin valor; desdén

contented (kən-tĕn′tĭd) *adj.* happy with things as they are; satisfied
contento(a) *adj.* feliz con las cosas tal como son; satisfecho(a)

cumbersome (kŭm′bər-səm) *adj.* uncomfortably heavy or bulky
abultado(a) *adj.* incómodamente pesado(a) o voluminoso(a)

curtly (kûrt′lē) *adv.* in a way that uses so few words it is either rude or almost rude
bruscamente *adv.* de manera que usa tan pocas palabras que tiende a ser descortés

cynical (sĭn′ĭkəl) *adj.* expressing scorn and mockery
cínico(a) *adj.* que expresa desdén y burla

D

decoy (dē′-koi′) *n.* an artificial bird used to attract live birds within shooting range
señuelo *n.* un ave artificial que se usa para atraer aves vivas a tiro

decree (dĭ-krē) *n.* an official order
decreto *n.* una orden oficial

dejectedly (dĭ-jĕk′tĭd-lē) *adv.* in a depressed manner
desanimadamente *adv.* de manera deprimida

deliberately (dĭ-lĭb′ər-ĭt-lē) *adv.* done in a slow, purposeful manner
deliberadamente *adv.* hecho(a) de manera lenta y resuelta

depleted (dĭ-plē′tĭd) *adj.* emptied; drained **deplete** *v.*
agotado(a) *adj.* vacío(a); reducido(a) **agotar** *v.*

deprivation (dĕp′rə-vā′shən) *n.* a lack of what is needed for survival or comfort
privación *n.* una falta de lo que se necesita para la supervivencia o el alivio

deprive (dĭ-prīv′) *v.* to take something away from
privar *v.* quitar algo de

destination (dĕs′tə-nā′shən) *n.* the place to which one intends to go
destino *n.* el lugar adonde alguien piensa ir

destitute (dĕs'tĭ-tōōt') *adj.* living in complete poverty; extremely poor
indigente *adj.* que vive en la pobreza completa; paupérrimo(a)

devise (dĭ-vīz') *v.* to form or plan in the mind; think up
idear *v.* formar o planear en la mente; inventar

disgruntled (dĭs-grŭn'tld) *adj.* not happy
descontento(a) *adj.* que no es feliz

dislodging (dĭs-lŏj'ĭng) *adj.* moving from a settled position **dislodge** *v.*
derribando *adj.* moviendo de una posición fija para que caiga **derribar** *v.*

dispense (dĭ-spĕns') *v.* to give out; distribute
dispensar *v.* repartir; distribuir

dispute (dĭ-spyōōt') *v.* to argue about; debate
disputar *v.* discutir; debatir

dissuade (dĭ-swād') *v.* to persuade someone not to do something; discourage
disuadir *v.* convencer a alguien de que no haga algo; desanimar

distorted (dĭ-stôr'tĭd) *adj.* twisted out of shape **distort** *v.*
desfigurado(a) *adj.* con la figura cambiada, usualmente de manera negativa **desfigurar** *v.*

divulge (dĭ-vŭlj') *v.* to reveal, especially something private or secret
divulgar *v.* revelar, especialmente algo privado o secreto

dominant (dŏm'ə-nənt) *adj.* having the most influence; controlling all others
dominante *adj.* que tiene la mayor influencia; que controla a todos los demás

drafting (drăf'tĭng) *n.* putting into words and writing down; composing **draft** *v.*
redactar *v.* poner por escrito; componer

dread (drĕd) *n.* deep fear; terror
pavor *n.* miedo profundo; terror

dumbfounded (dŭm'foun'dĭd) *adj.* speechless with shock; astonished **dumbfound** *v.*
pasmado(a) *adj.* sin sentido; asombrado(a) **pasmar** *v.*

dusk (dŭsk) *n.* the time of day between sunset and complete darkness
crepúsculo *n.* la hora del día entre la puesta del sol y la oscuridad completa

dwindle (dwĭn'dl) *v.* to become less and less
disminuir *v.* hacer menor

dynasty (dī'nə-stē) *n.* a series of rulers who are members of the same family
dinastía *n.* serie de soberanos pertenecientes a una familia

E

elegant (ĕl'ĭ-gənt) *adj.* beautiful in shape or style
elegante *adj.* bonito(a) en forma o estilo

embankment (ĕm-băngk'mənt) *n.* a long mound of earth or stone, sometimes built to raise a roadway or railroad above the surrounding land
terraplén *n.* un montículo largo de tierra o piedras, a veces construido para levantar una carretera o un ferrocarril encima del terreno de los alrededores

ember (ĕm'bər) *n.* a small glowing bit of burning wood
ascua *n.* un pedacito pequeño y candente de leña ardiente

emit (ĭ-mĭt') *v.* to send out; give forth, usually with force
emitir *v.* echar; expeler, usualmente con fuerza

entice (ĕn-tīs') *v.* to lure; to attract with promise of some reward
tentar *v.* atraer con la promesa de algún premio

envious (ĕn'vē-əs) *adj.* jealous
envidioso(a) *adj.* celoso(a)

erect (ĭ-rĕkt′) *adj.* firmly straight in posture; not bending or slumping
enderezarse *v.* estar parado(a)

eruption (ĭ-rŭp′shən) *n.* an outburst or throwing forth of lava, water, steam, and other materials
erupción *n.* salida explosiva de lava, agua, vapor y otros materiales

exceeding (ĭk-sē′dĭng) *n.* having more than **exceed** *v.*
exceder *v.* tener más que

except (ĭk-sĕpt′) *prep.* other than; but
excepto *prep.* menos; aparte de

expect (ĭk-spĕkt′) *v.* to look forward to something that is likely to occur
esperar *v.* anticipar algo que es probable que ocurra

expedition (ĕk′spĭ-dĭsh′ən) *n.* a journey with a goal or purpose
expedición *n.* un viaje con una meta o un propósito

expertise (ĕk′spûr-tēz′) *n.* skill or knowledge in a particular area
pericia *n.* habilidad o conocimiento en un área particular

extent (ĭk-stĕnt′) *n.* an amount or degree
punto *n.* una cantidad o un grado

extravagantly (ĭk-străv′ə-gənt-lē) *adv.* excessively; too much
extravagantemente *adv.* excesivamente; demasiado

F

faculty (făk′əl-tē) *n.* any of the powers of the mind
facultad *n.* cualquier potencia de la mente

fanfare (făn′fâr′) *n.* a loud blast of trumpets
fanfarria *n.* toque alto de trompetas

fate (fāt) *n.* a final outcome that cannot be avoided
destino *n.* hado, sino

fertile (fûr′tl) *adj.* rich in vegetation; fruitful
fértil *adj.* rico(a) en vegetación; fructífero(a)

fleeting (flē′tĭng) *adj.* passing quickly
fugaz *adj.* que pasa rápidamente

fluctuation (flŭk′chōō-ā′shən) *n.* an irregular movement or change
fluctuación *n.* un movimiento o cambio irregular

foliage (fō′lē-ĭj) *n.* plant leaves, especially tree leaves, considered as a group
follaje *n.* las hojas de plantas, especialmente las hojas de los árboles, consideradas como un grupo

forbid (fôr-bĭd′) *v.* to command someone not to do something
prohibir *v.* ordenar que alguien no haga algo

foreground (fôr′ground) *n.* the part of a scene or picture that is nearest to the viewer
primer plano *n.* la parte de una escena o un dibujo que está más cerca del espectador

forlorn (fər-lôrn′) *adj.* miserable and lonely; desolate
desolado(a) *adj.* desdichado(a) y solitario(a)

frenzied (frĕn′zēd) *adj.* wildly excited; frantic
frenético(a) *adj.* locamente excitado(a); desesperado(a)

fume (fyōōm) *v.* to burn with anger
enfurecerse *v.* arder de ira

G

gaudy (gô′dē) *adj.* bright and showy in a way that displays bad taste
llamativo(a) *adj.* vivo(a) y vistoso(a) de manera que muestra mal gusto

gesture (jĕs′chər) *v.* make a motion to express thought or emphasize words
gesticular *v.* hacer un ademán para expresar un pensamiento o enfatizar palabras

geyser (gī′zər) *n.* a natural hot spring that at times spouts water and steam into the air
géiser *n.* una fuente de agua termal natural que a veces echa agua y vapor al aire

H

harpoon (här-pōōn′) *n.* a spearlike weapon used to hunt large fish
arpón *n.* arma como una lanza para la pesca de los peces grandes

hesitantly (hĕz′ĭ-tənt-lē) *adv.* with pauses or uncertainty
en un tono indeciso *adv.* dudosamente, con vacilación

hospitality (hŏs′pĭ-tăl′ĭ-tē) *n.* a friendly and generous attitude toward guests
hospitalidad *n.* una actitud amistosa y generosa hacia los invitados

hostile (hŏs′təl) *adj.* unfavorable to health or well-being; dangerous
hostil *adj.* desfavorable a la salud o al bienestar; peligroso(a)

hover (hŭv′ər) *v.* to remain floating or suspended nearby
cernerse *v.* quedar flotando o suspendido(a) cerca

hurtle (hûr′tl) *v.* to move with great speed
abalanzarse *v.* mover con gran velocidad

hypnotic (hĭp-nŏt′ĭk) *adj.* trance-inducing
hypnotize *v.*
hipnótico(a) *adj.* que causa un trance
hipnotizar *v.*

I

idealism (ī-dē′ə-lĭz′əm) *n.* the practice of imagining that things could be absolutely perfect
idealismo *n.* la práctica de imaginar que las cosas podrían ser absolutamente perfectas

ignorance (ĭg′nər-əns) *n.* the state of being uneducated or unaware
ignorancia *n.* el estado de ser ineducado(a) o inconsciente

immense (ĭ-mĕns′) *adj.* huge; enormous
inmenso(a) *adj.* muy grande

immensely (ĭ-mĕns′lē) *adv.* to a great extent; enormously
inmensamente *adv.* en gran parte

immortal (ĭ-môr′tl) *adj.* living or lasting forever
inmortal *adj.* que vive o dura para siempre

immortality (ĭm′ôr-tăl′ĭ-tē) *n.* endless life or existence
inmortalidad *n.* vida o existencia sin fin

imp (ĭmp) *n.* a small demon
diablillo *n.* un demonio pequeño

impress (ĭm-prĕs′) *v.* to implant firmly in the mind; convey vividly
impresionar *v.* implantar firmemente en la mente; impartir vívidamente

inadvertently (ĭn′əd-vûr′tnt-lē) *adv.* by mistake or without meaning to; not deliberately
involuntariamente *adv.* por error o sin querer; no deliberadamente

incredulous (ĭn-krĕj′ə-ləs) *adj.* unbelieving
incrédulo(a) *adj.* que no cree

indicate (ĭn'dĭ-kāt') *v.* to show or express
indicar *v.* mostrar o expresar

indifferent (ĭn-dĭf'ər-ənt) *adj.* not interested; unconcerned
indiferente *adj.* no interesado(a)

indignant (ĭn-dĭg'nənt) *adj.* angry at something unjust, mean, or unworthy
indignado(a) *adj.* enojado(a)

indignantly (ĭn-dĭg'nənt-lē) *adv.* in a way that is angry, because of an insult or an attack on one's self-respect
indignadamente *adv.* de manera enojada, a causa de un insulto o un ataque

indolent (ĭn'də-lənt) *adj.* lazy
indolente *adj.* perezoso(a)

inhabitant (ĭn-hăb'ĭ-tənt) *n.* someone living in a particular place
habitante *n.* el que vive en un sitio

inquire (ĭn-kwīr') *v.* to question; ask
inquirir *v.* hacer una pregunta

insignificant (ĭn'sĭg-nĭf'ĭ-kənt) *adj.* having little or no importance
insignificante *adj.* que tiene poca importancia o sin importancia

insolent (ĭn'sə-lənt) *adj.* rude
insolente *adj.* grosero(a)

instinct (ĭn'stĭngkt') *n.* a natural or automatic way of behaving
instinto *n.* una manera de portarse natural o automática

intact (ĭn-tăkt') *adj.* whole and undamaged
intacto(a) *adj.* completo(a) y en buen estado

intricate (ĭn'-trĭ-kĭt) *adj.* full of complicated details
intrincado(a) *adj.* con detalles complicados

intrusion (ĭn-trōō'zhən) *n.* an act of coming in rudely or inappropriately
intrusión *n.* un acto de introducirse grosera o impropiamente

invisible (ĭn-vĭz'ə-bəl) *adj.* impossible to see; not visible
invisible *adj.* imposible de ver; no visible

isolated (ī'sə-lā'tĭd) *adj.* away from others; lonely **isolate** *v.*
aislado(a) *adj.* apartado(a); solitario(a) **aislar** *v.*

J

jalopy (jə-lŏp'ē) *n.* a shabby old car
carcanchita *n.* cacharro, vehículo destartalado

L

laden (lād'n) *adj.* weighed down; heavy
cargado(a) *adj.* abrumado(a); pesado(a)

lagoon (lə-gōōn') *n.* a shallow body of water separated from a sea by sandbars or coral reefs
laguna *n.* extensión de agua poco profunda separada del mar por bancos de arena o arrecifes de coral

leisurely (lē'zhər-lē) *adj.* unhurried
pausado(a) *adj.* no apurado(a)

lethargy (lĕth'ər-jē) *n.* a lack of activity; sluggishness
letargo *n.* falta de actividad; pereza

listlessly (lĭst'lĭs-lē) *adv.* without energy or interest; sluggishly
desganadamente *adv.* sin energía, interés; flojamente

loftily (lôf'tĭ-lē) *adv.* in a grand or pompous way
altaneramente *adv.* de manera elevada o presumida

luminous (lōō'mə-nəs) *adj.* full of light
luminoso(a) *adj.* lleno(a) de luz

M

magnification (măg′nə-fĭ-kā′shən) *n.* the causing of objects to appear enlarged
ampliación *n.* hacer que los objetos parezcan más grandes; aumento

maneuver (mə-nōō′vər) *n.* a movement or change in direction
maniobra *n.* un movimiento o cambio de rumbo

mannequin (măn′ĭ-kĭn) *n.* a model of the human body, used for displaying clothes
maniquí *n.* un modelo del cuerpo humano que se usa para mostrar ropa

margin (mär′jĭn) *n.* an amount or distance that allows for safety
margen *n.* una cantidad o distancia que permite más seguridad

marred (mär′d) *adj.* damaged; marked **mar** *v.*
dañado(a) *adj.* estropeado(a); con marcas que desfiguran **dañar** *v.*

marvel (mär′vəl) *v.* to feel amazement or wonder at the sight of
admirarse de *v.* sentir asombro o admiración al ver algo

mascot (măs′kŏt′) *n.* a person, an animal, or an object that is believed to bring good luck, especially one serving as the symbol of an organization (such as a sports team)
mascota *n.* una persona, animal u objeto que se cree que trae suerte, especialmente que sirve como símbolo de una organización (como un equipo de deportes)

maze (māz) *n.* a confusing network of winding paths or passageways
laberinto *n.* una red confusa de senderos o corredores

melancholy (měl′ən-kŏl′ē) *adj.* sad; gloomy
melancólico(a) *adj.* triste; lúgubre

menace (měn′ĭs) *n.* a possible danger; threat
amenaza *n.* la posibilidad de peligro

menial (mē′nē-əl) *adj.* fit for a servant
servil *adj.* apropiado(a) para un sirviente o criado

merge (mûrj) *v.* to combine or unite
unirse *v.* combinarse o fusionarse

modest (mŏd′ĭst) *adj.* not likely to call attention to oneself
discreto(a) *adj.* que no quiere llamar la atención de los demás

momentum (mō-měn′təm) *n.* the energy of an object or idea
ímpetu *n.* la energía de un objeto o idea

mope (mōp) *v.* to be gloomy or in low spirits
abatirse *v.* estar triste o sin optimismo

mortification (môr′tə-fĭ-kā′shən) *n.* a feeling of shame or humiliation
mortificación *n.* un sentimiento de vergüenza o humillación

mourn (môrn) *v.* to feel or express grief or sorrow
lamentar *v.* sentir o expresar pena o tristeza

murmur (mûr′mər) *v.* to speak so quietly that the words are difficult to make out
murmurar *v.* hablar muy bajo, de manera que no se pueda oír las palabras bien

N

naive (nä-ēv′) *adj.* as simple and believing as a young child
ingenuo(a) *adj.* sencillo(a) y creyente como un niño

nonchalantly (nŏn′shə-länt′lē) *adv.* in a casual, unconcerned way
calmadamente *adv.* de una manera despreocupada

novelty (nŏv′əl-tē) *n.* something new and unusual
novedad *n.* algo nuevo y poco usual

O

obnoxious (ŏb-nŏk′shəs) *adj.* worthy of disapproval or dislike
desagradable *adj.* que merece disgusto o desaprobación

obscure (ŏb-skyŏŏr′) *adj.* not well-known or important
recóndito(a) *adj.* desconocido(a)

obsess (əb-sĕs′) *v.* to occupy the mind of; concern excessively
obsesionar *v.* ocupar la mente excesivamente con algo

obstinacy (ŏb′stə-nə-sē) *n.* unreasonable stubbornness
obstinación *n.* terquedad, testarudez

oxygen (ŏk′sĭ-jən) *n.* one of the gases that make up air, needed for nearly all burning
oxígeno *n.* un gas que está presente en el aire, es necesario para la quema

P

palatial (pə-lā′shəl) *adj.* large and richly decorated, like a palace
palaciego(a) *adj.* grande y decorado(a) suntuosamente, como un palacio

pantomime (păn′tə-mīm′) *v.* to express oneself using only gestures and facial expressions
pantomima *n.* expresarse solamente con gestos

peal (pēl) *n.* a loud burst of noise
estruendo *n.* un ruido fuerte que ocurre de repente

peer (pîr) *v.* to look intently
escudriñar *v.* mirar intentamente

penetrate (pĕn′ĭ-trāt′) *v.* to pass through or enter into
penetrar *v.* pasar a través de o entrar en

perish (pĕr′ĭsh) *v.* to die, perhaps in an untimely or painful way
perecer *v.* morirse, quizás prematura o dolorosamente

persist (pər-sĭst′) *v.* to continue stubbornly
insistir en *v.* continuar con tenacidad

petty (pĕt′ē) *adj.* narrow-minded; shallow
mezquino(a) *adj.* de mentalidad cerrada; superficial

phosphorus (fŏs′fər-əs) *n.* a substance that glows with a yellowish or white light
fósforo *n.* una sustancia con brillo amarillento o blanco

pious (pī′əs) *adj.* showing religious feeling, especially in a way designed to draw attention
piadoso(a) *adj.* que demuestra sentimientos religiosos

poised (poĭzd) *adj.* seeming calm and well balanced **poise** *v.*
aplomado(a) *adj.* que parece tranquilo(a) y dueño de sí **tener aplomo** *v.*

pompous (pŏm′pəs) *adj.* having excessive self-esteem or showing exaggerated dignity
presuntuoso(a) *adj.* con autoestima excesiva; con una dignidad exagerada

ponder (pŏn′dər) *v.* to think about carefully
reflexionar *v.* pensar cuidadosamente en algo

practical (prăk′tĭ-kəl) *adj.* useful
práctico(a) *adj.* útil

predator (prĕd′ə-tər) *n.* an animal that hunts other animals for food
predador *n.* un animal que mata y come otros animales

premise (prĕm′ĭs) *n.* an idea that forms the basis of an argument
premisa *n.* idea que forma la base de un argumento

preservation (prĕz′ər-vā′shən) *n.* the condition of being kept perfect or unchanged
conservación *n.* la condición de mantener algo en buen estado o sin cambio

prey (prā) *v.* to have a harmful effect
explotar *v.* tener mal efecto

procedure (prə-sē′jər) *n.* a course of action
procedimiento *n.* acción de obrar

proclaim (prō-klām′) *v.* to announce officially; declare
proclamar *v.* anunciar de manera oficial; declarar

profile (prō′fīl) *n.* a side view
perfil *n.* la vista desde un lado

prop (prŏp) *n.* an object an actor uses in a play
utilería *n.* un objeto utilizado en una obra de teatro; atrezo

proposition (prŏp′ə-zish′ən) *n.* a plan offered for acceptance
propuesta *n.* un plan posible que se ofrece

prosper (prŏs′pər) *v.* to be successful; thrive
prosperar *v.* tener éxito

pummel (pŭm′əl) *v.* to beat, as with the fists
golpear *v.* dar puñetazos

Q

quest (kwĕst) *n.* a journey in search of adventure or to perform a task
búsqueda *n.* un viaje en busca de la aventura o para cumplir una tarea

quiver (kwĭv′ər) *v.* to shake with a rapid trembling movement
temblar *v.* agitarse con sacudidas rápidas y pequeñas

R

ravishing (răv′ĭ-shĭng) *adj.* unusually beautiful; delightfully pleasing
deslumbrante *adj.* muy bello(a); cautivador(a)

reef (rēf) *n.* a ridge of rocks, sand, or coral near the surface of water
arrecife *n.* una protuberancia de piedra, arena o coral cerca de la superficie del agua

regain (rē-gān′) *v.* to get back; recover
recobrar *v.* llegar al estado de antes; recuperar

reign (rān) *v.* to rule as a king or queen
reinar *v.* gobernar como un rey o una reina

relentless (rĭ-lĕnt′lĭs) *adj.* refusing to stop or give up
implacable *adj.* que se niega a parar y a dejar el intento

remotely (rĭ-mōt′lē) *adv.* to a small degree; slightly
remotamente *adv.* a un nivel bajo; un poco

repentance (rĭ-pĕn′təns) *n.* a regret for past behavior
arrepentimiento *n.* lamentar acciones en el pasado

reproduction (rē′prə-dŭk′shən) *n.* a copy; an imitation
reproducción *n.* una copia; una imitación

resentful (rĭ-zĕnt′fəl) *adj.* angry due to a feeling of being treated unfairly
resentido(a) *adj.* enojado(a) porque se siente tratado(a) injustamente

reservation (rĕz′ər-vā′shən) *n.* a doubt; an exception
reserva *n.* duda; excepción

resilient (rĭ-zĭl′yənt) *adj.* flexible and springy
elástico(a) *adj.* flexible y rebotante

restore (rĭ-stôr′) *v.* to bring back to an original condition
restaurar *v.* reconstruir una cosa para devolverla a su estado original

retort (rĭ-tôrt′) *v.* to reply, especially in a quick or unkind way
replicar *v.* responder, ser respondón

reveal (rĭ-vēl′) *v.* to bring to view; to show
revelar *v.* traer a la vista; mostrar

ricochet (rĭk′ə-shā′) *v.* to bounce off a surface
rebotar *v.* botar sobre una superficie

rival (rī′vəl) *n.* one who tries to win over another; competitor
rival *n.* el que alcanza casi el mérito de otro; competidor

rivet (rĭv′ĭt) *v.* to fasten firmly
remachar *v.* sujetar con firmeza

ruddy (rŭd′ē) *adj.* reddish; rosy
rubicundo(a) *adj.* rojizo(a); que tiene el color rojo

rummaging (rŭm′ĭ-jĭng) *adj.* searching thoroughly **rummage** *v.*
rebuscando *adj.* buscando a fondo **rebuscar** *v.*

S

sanitation (săn′ĭ-tā′shən) *n.* the creation of rules designed to protect public health
condiciones de salubridad *n.* la creación de reglas para proteger la salud del público

savor (sā′vər) *v.* to take great pleasure in
saborear *v.* apreciar con gusto

scavenging (skăv′ən-jĭng) *adj.* searching for discarded scraps **scavenge** *v.*
carroñero(a) *adj.* que hurga en los desperdicios en busca de algo **hurgar** *v.*

scornful (skôrn′fəl) *adj.* having an attitude of contempt; disdainful
desdeñoso(a) *adj.* que tiene una actitud de menosprecio

seasoned (sē′zənd) *adj.* made skillful by practice; experienced **season** *v.*
experimentado(a) *adj.* que tiene destreza como resultado de sus experiencias

sector (sĕk′tər) *n.* a part or division
sector *n.* parte o división

sentiment (sĕn′tə-mənt) *n.* emotion
sentimiento *n.* emoción

sentinel (sĕn′tə-nəl) *n.* one who keeps watch; guard
centinela *n.* alguien que monta guardia; guardia

shrine (shrīn) *n.* a place of worship
santuario *n.* templo

shunned (shŭnd) *adj.* avoided; shut out **shun** *v.*
rechazado(a) *adj.* rehuido(a); dejado(a) afuera **rechazar** *v.*

smirk (smûrk) *v.* to smile in an insulting, self-satisfied manner
sonreírse *v.* sonreír de una manera insultante, con suficiencia

smugly (smŭg′lē) *adv.* in a very self-satisfied way
presumidamente *adv.* de una manera satisfecha de sí mismo(a)

sonar (sō′när′) *n.* detection of objects by reflected sound waves
sonar *n.* la detección de objetos por medio de ondas sonoras

spectator (spĕk′tā′tər) *n.* someone who watches an event
espectador(a) *n.* alguien que mira un evento

splendor (splĕn′dər) *n.* the condition of being brilliant or magnificent
esplendor *n.* la condición de ser brillante o magnífico(a)

stalemate (stāl′māt′) *n.* a situation in which none of the people playing a game are able to win
punto muerto *n.* una situación en que ninguna de las personas que juegan puede ganar

stamina (stăm′ə-nə) *n.* the strength to withstand hardship
resistencia *n.* la fuerza necesaria para aguantar algo

status (stā′təs) *n.* one's position in society; rank
condición *n.* posición social; rango

stereotype (stĕr′ē-ə-tīp′) *n.* a fixed idea, especially about the way a group of people looks or acts
estereotipo *n.* un idea fija, especialmente sobre cómo aparece o se comporta un grupo

stoop (sto͞op) *n.* a small porch outside the main door of a building
porche *n.* un tipo de entrada a la puerta principal de un edificio con una pequeña escalinata

straddle (străd′l) *v.* to stand with a leg on either side of
sentarse *v.* estar a horcajadas

subside (səb-sīd′) *v.* to sink or settle down to a lower or normal level
disminuir *v.* bajar a un nivel más normal

succeed (sək-sēd′) *v.* to come after; follow
seguir *v.* pasar después

succulent (sŭk′yə-lənt) *adj.* tasty; delicious
suculento(a) *adj.* sabroso(a); delicioso(a)

sudden (sŭd′n) *adj.* happening without warning
repentino(a) *adj.* que ocurre sin aviso

sufficient (sə-fĭsh′ənt) *adj.* being enough; adequate
suficiente *adj.* bastante; adecuado(a)

surpass (sər-păs′) *v.* to be better or greater than
superar *v.* ser mejor o superior

surplus (sûr′pləs) *n.* extra material or supplies; leftovers
de segunda *adj.* excedente; sobrante

surveyor (sər-vā′ər) *n.* a person who determines land boundaries by measuring angles and distances
agrimensor(a) *n.* una persona que mide ángulos y distancias para determinar límites terrenales

suspicion (sə-spĭsh′ən) *n.* a feeling of doubt or mistrust
desconfianza *n.* duda o recelo

swoop (swo͞op) *v.* to move in a sudden sweep
bajar en picada *v.* descender repentinamente

systematically (sĭs′tə-măt′ĭk-lē) *adv.* in an orderly, thorough manner
sistemáticamente *adv.* de una manera ordenada y metódica

T

taboo (tə-bo͞o′) *adj.* not to be noticed or mentioned
tabú *adj.* lo que no se puede mencionar

tangible (tăn′jə-bəl) *adj.* able to be touched or grasped
tangible *adj.* que se puede tocar o agarrar

tedious (tē′dē-əs) *adj.* long, tiring, and boring
tedioso(a) *adj.* largo(a), pesado(a) y aburrido(a)

tenement (tĕn′ə-mənt) *n.* a crowded, run-down apartment building
casa de vecinos *n.* un viejo edificio de apartamentos donde la gente vive amontonada

tentative (tĕn′tə-tĭv) *adj.* uncertain; hesitant
tentativo(a) *adj.* no muy cierto(a); indeciso(a)

terrorist (tĕr′ər-ĭst) *n.* one who uses or threatens to use unlawful force
terrorista *n.* alguien que usa o amenaza usar fuerza ilegalmente

thatched (thăcht) *adj.* made of or covered with reeds or straw **thatch** *v.*
de paja *adj.* hecho(a) o cubierto(a) de paja, juncos o quincha **empajar** *v.*

thrashing (thrăsh′ĭng) *n.* moving wildly **thrash** *v.*
revolcarse *v.* moverse desordenadamente

threaten (thrĕt′n) *v.* to be a danger to
amenazar *v.* ser un peligro

tinder (tĭn′dər) *n.* a material, such as dry twigs, that is used to start a fire because it burns easily
yesca *n.* un material, como ramitas secas, que se usa para prender fuego porque se quema fácilmente

tolerate (tŏl′ə-rāt′) *v.* to put up with
tolerar *v.* aguantar, llevar con paciencia

torrent (tôr′ənt) *n.* a heavy downpour
torrente *n.* un chorro fuerte

transfusion (trăns-fyoo′zhən) *n.* an injection of blood, usually to replace a loss due to bleeding
transfusión *n.* una inyección de sangre, generalmente para reemplazar una cantidad después de sangrar

transpire (trăn-spīr′) *v.* to happen; occur
suceder *v.* pasar; ocurrir

trek (trĕk) *n.* a slow, difficult journey
recorrido *n.* viaje largo y difícil

trestle (trĕs′əl) *n.* a framework built to support a bridge
caballete *n.* armazón en el que se apoya un puente

tumult (too′mŭlt′) *n.* a noisy uproar
tumulto *n.* alboroto ruidoso

tumultuously (too-mŭl′choo-əs-lē) *adv.* in a wild and disorderly way
tumultuosamente *adv.* de manera alborotada y confundida

tyranny (tĭr′ə-nē) *n.* an extremely harsh or unjust government or authority
tiranía *n.* un gobierno o autoridad injusta o muy severa

tyrant (tī′rənt) *n.* a cruel, unjust ruler
tirano(a) *n.* un(a) gobernante cruel o injusto(a)

U

ultraviolet (ŭl′trə-vī′ə-lĭt) *adj.* consisting of invisible radiation wavelengths
ultravioleta *adj.* que consiste en ondas invisibles de radiación

unparalleled (ŭn-păr′ə-lĕld′) *adj.* having no equal; unmatched
sin paralelo *adj.* sin par; incomparable

V

vainly (vān′lē) *adv.* without success
vanamente *adv.* sin éxito

validate (văl′ĭ-dāt′) *v.* to show to be correct
validar *v.* comprobar que es correcto

vapor (vā′pər) *n.* fumes, mist, or smoke
vapor *n.* vaho, neblina o humo

vault (vôlt) *v.* to jump or to leap with the use of the hands
saltar *v.* lanzarse encima de algo, generalmente con el uso de las manos

veer (vîr) *v.* to turn aside; swerve
virar *v.* desviarse; cambiar de sentido

vent (vĕnt) *n.* an opening that allows gas, liquid, or smoke to escape
ventilación *n.* abertura para renovar el aire de un lugar

vessel (vĕs'əl) *n.* a boat or ship
navío *n.* un barco o buque

vigil (vĭj'əl) *n.* a watch kept during normal sleeping hours
vela *n.* vigilar durante las horas en que normalmente se duerme

vigorously (vĭg'ər-əs-lē) *adv.* done with force and energy
enérgicamente *adv.* con fuerza y energía

vineyard (vĭn'yərd) *n.* an area where grapevines have been planted
viña *n.* terreno plantado de vides

vinyl (vī'nəl) *n.* a tough, shiny plastic
vinilo *n.* un tipo de plástico que es fuerte y que tiene un brillo

vulgar (vŭl'gər) *adj.* crudely disrespectful and displaying bad taste
grosero(a) *adj.* con una falta de respeto y de mal gusto

W

wheeling (hwē'lĭng) *adj.* flying in curves or circles **wheel** *v.*
girante *adj.* que vuela en una curva o en círculos **girar** *v.*

whittling (hwĭt'lĭng) *adj.* carving by shaving away bits of wood with a knife **whittle** *v.*
tallando *adj.* grabando diseños en madera con un cuchillo **tallar** *v.*

withering (wĭth'ər-ĭng) *adj.* causing to dry out and shrivel up; wilting **wither** *v.*
marchitando *adj.* que seca y arruga; que se pone mustio(a) **marchitar** *v.*

Y

yearn (yûrn) *v.* to desire strongly
anhelar *v.* desear algo mucho

Pronunciation Key

Symbol	Examples	Symbol	Examples	Symbol	Examples
ă	at, gas	m	man, seem	v	van, save
ā	ape, day	n	night, mitten	w	web, twice
ä	father, barn	ng	sing, anger	y	yard, lawyer
âr	fair, dare	ŏ	odd, not	z	zoo, reason
b	bell, table	ō	open, road, grow	zh	treasure, garage
ch	chin, lunch	ô	awful, bought, horse	ə	awake, even, pencil,
d	dig, bored	oi	coin, boy		pilot, focus
ĕ	egg, ten	ŏŏ	look, full	ər	perform, letter
ē	evil, see, meal	ōō	root, glue, through		
f	fall, laugh, phrase	ou	out, cow		**Sounds in Foreign Words**
g	gold, big	p	pig, cap	KH	*German* ich, auch;
h	hit, inhale	r	rose, star		*Scottish* loch
hw	white, everywhere	s	sit, face	N	*French* entre, bon, fin
ĭ	inch, fit	sh	she, mash	œ	*French* feu, cœur;
ī	idle, my, tried	t	tap, hopped		*German* schön
îr	dear, here	th	thing, with	ü	*French* utile, rue;
j	jar, gem, badge	*th*	then, other		*German* grün
k	keep, cat, luck	ŭ	up, nut		
l	load, rattle	ûr	fur, earn, bird, worm		

Stress Marks

′ This mark indicates that the preceding syllable receives the primary stress. For example, in the word *language*, the first syllable is stressed: lăng′gwĭj.

′ This mark is used only in words in which more than one syllable is stressed. It indicates that the preceding syllable is stressed, but somewhat more weakly than the syllable receiving the primary stress. In the word *literature*, for example, the first syllable receives the primary stress, and the last syllable receives a weaker stress: lĭt′ər-ə-chŏŏr′.

Adapted from *The American Heritage Dictionary of the English Language, Third Edition;* Copyright © 1992 by Houghton Mifflin Company. Used with the permission of Houghton Mifflin Company.

Sahara Travel Display

OVERVIEW

The largest desert in the world, the Sahara is nearly the size of the United States. Although best known for its seemingly endless sand, it comprises a varied terrain that includes such features as rivers, lakes, mountains, dunes, and oases. The Sahara also supports a population of about one person per square mile, as well as many kinds of flora and fauna.

Research Questions

• What geographical features does the Sahara include?

• Who and what resides there?

• How do they survive the extreme conditions?

Investigation The class will act as a team to produce a display, suitable for travelers visiting the Sahara. The display should include information that persons planning a trip to the area would find helpful. Students will work together to make a detailed map of the desert; learn about the people of the Sahara as well as flora and fauna; research what travelers to the region should bring; and assemble the display in a useful fashion.

Wrap-up Students can act as guides or travel agents hosting visiting classes or other guests, walking them through the display and taking questions. Guides may wish to dress as characters from "Nadia the Willful" or in clothing appropriate to Sahara tourists. If possible, invite a travel agent or tour guide to speak to the class about how to design materials, and about what information is most useful to tourists.

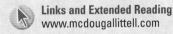
Links and Extended Reading
www.mcdougallittell.com

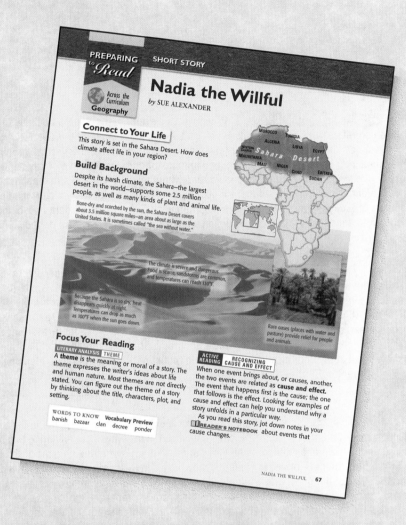

OBJECTIVES

❏ identify and represent geographical features of the Sahara

❏ research and write about the wildlife of the region

❏ describe the lives of desert nomads

❏ chart variations in climate

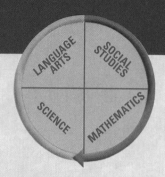

Team Teaching Assignments

CONNECT TO **LANGUAGE ARTS** Who might a traveler to the Sahara be likely to meet? Students should use reference books to learn about the lifestyle and culture of the people who make their home in this desert. Students should consider how these people adapt to the severe environment, and how it influences their housing, diet, clothing, and patterns of daily life. When did they begin to live in the desert? Working in pairs, students should read what they can find about one aspect of lifestyle or culture in this region. Next, they should make a poster about their area of research, writing paragraph-length captions for images and adding interesting quotations or fun facts. Students might include phrases in French or Arabic that a visitor to the region would find helpful. *(2–3 class periods)*

YOU WILL NEED:
- Web access (optional)
- reference books
- posterboard
- colored pens or pencils

CONNECT TO **SOCIAL STUDIES** The Sahara is a vast and surprisingly diverse landscape, covering much of the upper part of the African continent. Working in small groups, students should research land forms, geographical features, and countries and capitals located within the desert's reach. Lake Chad, the Atlas Mountains, and the Niger and Nile rivers are among the features of this extraordinary terrain. Next, students should create a large map that details these features. They may wish to first make a sketch on graph paper for greater accuracy. Students should carefully label features and make a key. Label major airports and possible routes of travel for persons planning to cross the desert. *(2–3 class periods)*

YOU WILL NEED:
- current atlas
- colored pencils or markers
- drawing paper or graph paper

CONNECT TO **SCIENCE** Various plants and animals have found a niche in the Sahara's harsh climate. Desert plants, for instance, have developed many ways of surviving in this hot, dry environment. In addition, students may be surprised to learn that the animals of the Sahara are not very different from animals in wetter climates; they have simply learned how to live in a desert environment. Gerbils, hyenas, baboons, and a variety of birds and reptiles have found a home in the Sahara. Working in two teams—for flora and for fauna—students should prepare pamphlets about the plants and animals that might be seen by visitors to the Sahara. Include sketches, descriptions, and fun facts. The pamphlets should be posted as part of the display, but photocopies should be available for visitors to take home. *(2–3 class periods)*

YOU WILL NEED:
- Web access (optional)
- reference books
- plain paper
- photocopier

CONNECT TO **MATHEMATICS** Temperatures in the Sahara can vary greatly in a single day, and rain can be so scarce as to seem nonexistent. Students should research the average daytime and nighttime temperatures per month in the Sahara, as well as the average monthly rainfall. Students can present their findings in a chart that includes bar graphs. They may wish to illustrate the charts with pictures of garments that travelers would need for day and night in that climate. Students should also find out how much water per day a traveler should expect to drink in this extreme heat, and display this amount in bottles or jars as a visual aid. *(2–3 class periods)*

YOU WILL NEED:
- reference books, especially almanacs
- graph paper or plain paper
- rulers and calculators
- bottles or jars

Polar Exploration Slide Show

OVERVIEW

The geographic North Pole lies in the Arctic Ocean at the northern end of the axis on which the earth revolves. There is no land at the North Pole, but for most of the year the ocean is frozen solid, providing a surface for travel. Across this harsh landscape, Robert E. Peary and the members of his expedition traveled by dogsled. On the last leg of the journey, Peary sent back all the members of the expedition except Matthew Henson and four Inuit.

Research Questions

• What challenges did explorers face in the early 20th century?

• Why was an expedition to the North Pole important?

• How was Peary's expedition accomplished?

Investigation Working in small groups, students will create audio-visual presentations about Henson's and Peary's 1908 expedition. They will plan a combination of text, visuals, and sounds, and present the show to classmates, families, and community members. If necessary, visuals could be displayed by using overhead transparencies as "slides".

Wrap-up When the presentations are complete, have students create a flyer or invitations specifying when and where other students, parents, and community members can view them. Distribute questionnaires to the viewers before the presentations. After the presentations, discuss the audience's answers.

 Links and Extended Reading
www.mcdougallittell.com

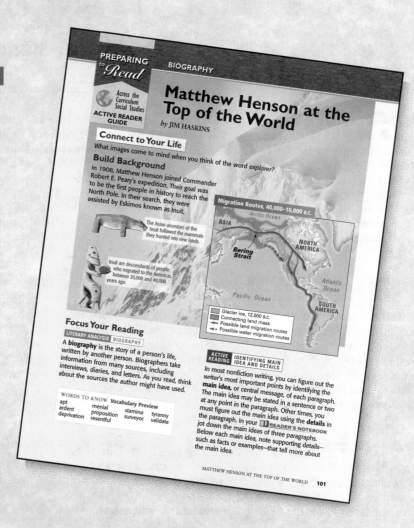

OBJECTIVES

❏ read primary and secondary source accounts and record oral readings of Peary's 1908–1909 expedition

❏ research and report on Inuit culture and the contributions of Inuits to the expedition

❏ research the ecology of the Arctic Circle and represent flora and fauna on a map

❏ present and evaluate statistics about the expedition

Team Teaching Assignments

CONNECT TO **LANGUAGE ARTS** Many explorers kept journals to record and document their accomplishments. Direct students to find and read journal entries and other primary accounts from the North Greenland expedition. Have students record readings from these primary sources. The books *Robert E. Peary and the Rush to the North Pole* by Fred L. Israel and *Dark Companion: The Story of Matthew Henson* by Bradley Robinson may be helpful resources. (Students can also use the excerpts from Henson's journal that are quoted in the selection.) The readings can play in the background while students present visuals. Students can also select appropriate music to play during parts of the presentation. You may also wish to have students complete the interdisciplinary assignments below as they create their presentations. *(3 class periods)*

YOU WILL NEED:
- Web access (optional)
- reference works on the North Greenland expedition
- audio recording equipment

CONNECT TO **SOCIAL STUDIES** Matthew Henson learned many valuable skills from the Inuit, such as how to load a sled, manage a food supply, and treat frostbite. Suggest that students devote part of their presentations to Inuits. Topics might include the following: origins of the Inuit peoples, Inuit culture then and now, and contributions of Inuit members of the North Greenland expedition. Based on their research on the expedition and on Inuit culture, students may wish to write a journal entry from the point of view of one of the Inuit members of the expedition. Caution students that, in their presentation, they must make clear to the audience that the journal entry is a work of fiction, although based on factual accounts of the expedition. Students' research could be photocopied onto an overhead transparency. *(3–4 class periods)*

YOU WILL NEED:
- Web access (optional)
- current reference books

CONNECT TO **SCIENCE** At times during the expedition, Robert Peary and his men encountered temperatures of 50 degrees below zero. Direct students to research the ecology of the Arctic circle. What plants and animals live in such an inhospitable environment? Encourage students to create a map showing the countries of the Arctic Circle and to find or create pictures of Arctic landscapes, flora, and fauna. The map could be displayed on an overhead transparency. *(3 class periods)*

YOU WILL NEED:
- Web access (optional)
- current reference books on Arctic countries
- atlas
- graphics software or art materials

CONNECT TO **MATHEMATICS** Direct students to generate statistics about the expedition. These "Fast Facts" could be displayed on an overhead transparency or incorporated into the text of the presentation. For example, Matthew Henson wrote in his journal, ". . . we couldn't carry food for more than fifty days. . . ." Help students to estimate the amount of food that the expedition needed for 50 days, and about how much the food supplies weighed. Henson wrote that during one part of the expedition, they traveled 18 to 20 hours each day. Ask students to calculate what percentage of each day the explorers traveled. The expedition set sail from New York City. Have students use an atlas and estimate how many miles the group traveled to reach the North Pole. Then tell students that the entire expedition took 275 days. Suggest that they calculate the average number of miles that the expedition covered per day. *(1–2 class periods)*

YOU WILL NEED:
- calculator
- atlas

Space Exploration Game

OVERVIEW

While humans do not have the technology that would be necessary to colonize other planets as in "All Summer in a Day," we have made tremendous advances in space exploration in the second half of the 20th century. From the launching of the first artificial satellite, *Sputnik,* in 1957 by the Soviet Union to the first-ever moon landing in 1969, made by the United States, to the first space shuttle flight in 1981, humans' ability to travel, live, and work in space is ever-increasing.

Research Questions

• What have humans accomplished in space exploration?

• What obstacles must be overcome to explore more of the universe?

Investigation Working in small groups, students will create board or computer games based on a space exploration theme. Each group will plan and execute a rules pamphlet, game board and playing pieces (or the equivalent on the computer). Games should be directed at a particular group or age level.

Wrap-up The project should culminate in a Game Day where families, other students, and community members can examine or play the games. Elimination tournament play might be arranged in which players advance as they win.

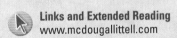

Links and Extended Reading
www.mcdougallittell.com

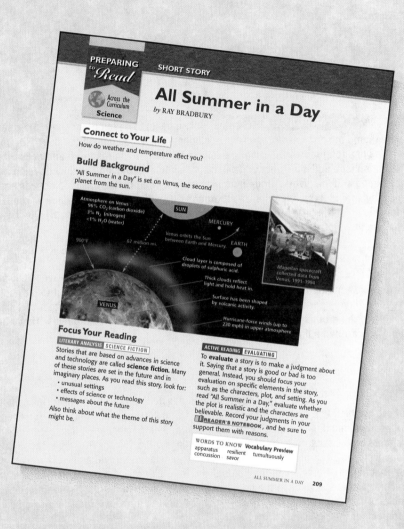

OBJECTIVES

❏ write rules for a game with a space exploration theme that fits a targeted audience

❏ research the history of space exploration and represent key events in a time line

❏ create a game board and playing pieces

❏ write and answer math problems about space travel

Team Teaching Assignments

CONNECT TO **LANGUAGE ARTS** Instruct students to develop and write the rules for a game based on the theme of space exploration. Have students examine commercial board (or computer) games and the rules of each for ideas. During brainstorming they should research and collect facts about space exploration (see activities below). They may wish to sketch ideas as they develop a game that is challenging and fun. When group members have agreed on the basic objectives and method of game play, they should write and publish a thorough guide to the rules of the game, keeping in mind the reading level of the group to which their game is targeted. You may also wish to have students complete the interdisciplinary assignments below.

YOU WILL NEED:
- board games or computer games for examination
- laser printer or art materials

CONNECT TO **SOCIAL STUDIES** The history of rocketry dates back over 1,500 years to the first use of explosives, in China. Later, the Chinese created gunpowder and used it to propel fireworks and weapons. Have students investigate the history of space travel and create a time line of key events. Encourage the groups to draw on this research as they create their games. They may wish to build their game around a time line.

YOU WILL NEED:
- Web access (optional)
- current reference materials on space exploration

CONNECT TO **SCIENCE** Probes sent to Venus have told us that the surface temperature of the planet is so high that no human could survive on its surface, even with protective equipment. After the groups have decided on the settings and goals of their games, ask them to consider what dangers explorers would face on missions to these settings. Also direct students to research the dangers of space travel in general. What challenges must people who travel and work in space overcome? (Direct students to use "Home on an Icy Planet," the Real World Link on page 588, as one resource.) Encourage students to base the conflicts that players encounter in their games on the real-life problems of space travel. Then have groups create the game boards and playing pieces (or computer graphics) for their games.

YOU WILL NEED:
- Web access (optional)
- current reference materials on space exploration
- art materials or graphics software

CONNECT TO **MATHEMATICS** Direct students to incorporate math into the scenario of their games. Tell students that the speed that a spacecraft needs to escape earth's gravity is 25,000 miles per hour (or about 7 miles per second). While in real life a spacecraft would not have a constant speed, by finding the distance from the earth to the destination and dividing by the spacecraft's average speed, students can estimate the amount of time the trip would take. Students may also wish to incorporate math problems into their games. They can write problems that players must answer correctly in order to advance in the game.

YOU WILL NEED:
- calculator

ACROSS the CURRICULUM

Oral Histories on Travel

OVERVIEW

The experience of travel has changed dramatically over the past 150 years. Innovations in production methods, such as Henry Ford's use of the assembly line in automobile factories, made cars affordable to a wider range of people starting in 1914. The invention of the jet engine in the 1930s has enabled us today to fly nonstop across the United States in just a few hours.

Research Questions

* How has travel changed over the last century?

* What transportation did Americans use in earlier times?

* What have been the most important advances in transportation technology in U.S. history so far?

Investigation Working in small groups and under supervision, students will interview some of the older members of their family, the neighborhood, or the community to gather oral histories. Students will formulate questions that will lead interview subjects to talk about their travel experiences and how they have seen transportation change over the years. These histories may be presented to the class on videotape or audiotape, in writing, or orally.

Wrap-up Schedule a day when the class's oral history presentations can be shared with families, other students, and community members. Written histories can also be displayed for a period of time on a bulletin board, and recorded histories can be made available for viewing or listening in the library.

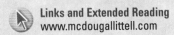
Links and Extended Reading
www.mcdougallittell.com

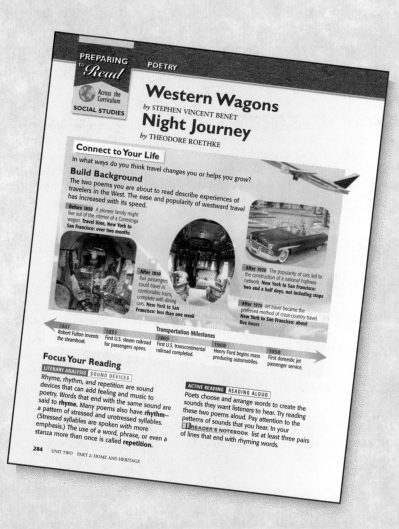

OBJECTIVES

❏ formulate interview questions and conduct oral interviews

❏ analyze interview data

❏ research the history of transportation in the United States

❏ graph the types of transportation used by interview subjects

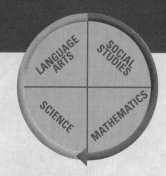

Team Teaching Assignments

CONNECT TO **LANGUAGE ARTS** Instruct each group to work together to create a list of pertinent questions to ask their interviewee. These questions should be designed to encourage the interviewee to compare travel in an earlier time to travel today, not just tell a life story. After the group has a list of questions, members can interview several subjects and decide which candidate will provide the most interesting oral history. Then the group can conduct the final interview, taping it or writing it up for presentation. You may also wish to have students complete the interdisciplinary assignments below.

YOU WILL NEED:
- audio or video recorder and tapes (optional)
- paper and pencil

CONNECT TO **SOCIAL STUDIES** American suburbs experienced rapid growth in the 1950s. One important factor contributing to the rise of the suburbs was increased car ownership, resulting from a strong economy and lower prices. Cars allowed suburbanites to live outside cities in almost rural settings, yet still have access to jobs, shopping, and entertainment in more populous areas. Ask students to consider how changes in transportation technology affect society at large and the daily lives of individuals. Direct groups to analyze the results of their interviews and write a paragraph drawing conclusions about how interview subjects' personal histories fit into the larger picture of changes in American society.

YOU WILL NEED:
- oral histories (from language arts assignment)

CONNECT TO **SCIENCE** Guide students in creating a bulletin board on important advances in transportation technology of the nineteenth and twentieth centuries. Assign each group to research a different invention, such as the steam engine, the gasoline engine, or the jet engine. Students should combine text and pictures to discuss how the type of engine was invented and how it works. Have the bulletin board on display while the groups present their oral histories.

YOU WILL NEED:
- Web access (optional)
- encyclopedias and reference books
- art materials

CONNECT TO **MATHEMATICS** Have each group poll their interviewees (or another class or other group) about all the types of transportation they have used in their lives: car, bus, subway, train, boat, bicycle, plane, etc. Then have the class create a bar graph in which one axis represents the number of people and the other represents the type of transportation used.

YOU WILL NEED:
- chart-size paper
- colored pencils
- ruler

Ancient Greece Fair

OVERVIEW

Greece has been called "the cradle of Western civilization." Foundations of Western culture such as drama, democracy, and art and architecture developed thousands of years ago in this small, mountainous area surrounded by sea. Influences from the culture of Greek antiquity are still felt today, particularly in Europe and North America. The following project could be part of a larger unit on ancient Greece.

Research Questions

- What was the culture of ancient Greece like?

- What gods and goddesses, foods, forms of entertainment, and styles of architecture were important in Greece some 2,000 years ago?

Investigation The class will work as a team to create an "ancient Greece fair" that creatively presents their research about Greek theatre, mythology, food, and architecture. Students will work together to generate posters, brochures, and other media. They will set up tables—perhaps clusters of desks—to display the materials they have created as well as books and media used in their research, with bookmarks at images that would be of particular interest to visitors. The visitors will move among the tables to explore the information. Students at each table could have a poster displaying "Ask me" questions to prompt discussion—for example: How long did plays last at ancient Greek theater festivals? Who are the most important Greek gods and goddesses? Students might also set up game or activity booths such as face-painting, posing for photos with a mythological character, an or "oracle" booth giving messages.

Wrap-up Students will invite other classes or family members to attend the ancient Greece fair, review their displays, ask questions, and take home various materials. They may wish to wear togas and sandals for the event or dress in the person of a mythological character, mortal or immortal.

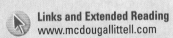 **Links and Extended Reading**
www.mcdougallittell.com

OBJECTIVES

❑ describe and define theater terms having origins in ancient Greece

❑ recognize and represent the deities and tales from Greek mythology

❑ research the foodstuffs of ancient Greece

❑ create a floor plan representing a classical Greek temple

Team Teaching Assignments

CONNECT TO **LANGUAGE ARTS** From the earliest days when *tragoidia,* or goat songs, first became part of the ancient festivals of Dionysius in Athens, performance was central to Hellenic culture. More than 2,000 years ago, Greek playwrights created the first European works of drama, some of which are still performed. Particularly well known playwrights include Aeschylus, Sophocles, Euripides, and Aristophanes. Students should research terms relevant to the drama of ancient Greece—such as, *tragedy, comedy, chorus, prologue, epilogue, proscenium, amphitheater, antagonist, protagonist,* and *mask*—and compose a glossary of terms describing their meanings and historical origins. A group of students can work to create a model or diagram of an amphitheater such as the theater at Epidaurus, and attach their definitions of theater terms to the illustration. Alternately students might be guided to perform a reading of the play in Unit Three, *Damon and Pythias.* They should prepare a program for the play which includes their glossary of theater terms. *(3–5 class periods)*

YOU WILL NEED:
- Web access (optional)
- encyclopedia
- history books
- art materials as desired

CONNECT TO **SOCIAL STUDIES** It has been said that in Western literature, only the Bible has been more influential than Greek mythology. Students should make a poster that depicts the pantheon of the thirteen primary Olympian gods and goddesses, along with their various symbols (e.g., a trident for Poseidon, an owl for Athena). Family relationships should also be noted. The poster can be displayed during the fair. In addition, students might be assigned the roles of the various Olympians, to portray during the fair. A student should dress as his or her role, carrying appropriate props and preparing a brief one-paragraph self-introduction with which to greet visitors. Next, working in pairs, students should select a favorite Greek myth, summarize it, and create a black-and-white illustration. These will be collected, photocopied, and stapled together for visitors to take home. *(4–5 class periods)*

YOU WILL NEED:
- encyclopedias
- colored pencils or markers
- posterboard
- atlas
- books of mythology
- drawing paper
- photocopier (optional)

CONNECT TO **SCIENCE** Greece is a barren and rocky country, much of it desolate and dry, with relatively little arable land. Yet the feasts of ancient Greece are legendary, and myths tell of foods coveted by gods and mortals alike. Students should use reference books to find out what the ancient Greeks ate. How did they satisfy their nutritional needs with the resources available to them? (For example, olive trees yielded oil as well as fruit; goats provided meat, milk, and cheese.) Students should make a list of these foodstuffs. Next, they should organize them in a "food pyramid" large enough so that drawings of the foods may be included. In addition, on an 8½" by 11" sheet of paper, they should make up a decorative menu for a Greek festival and photocopy it for visitors to take along. *(2–3 class periods)*

YOU WILL NEED:
- books of Greek history
- posterboard
- colored pens and pencils
- food-pyramid example
- photocopier

CONNECT TO **MATHEMATICS** The ancient Greeks applied rigorous mathematical ideals to architecture. The peripteral temple—having a colonnade on four sides—was developed in the seventh century B.C. Provide students with pictures and measurements of the most famous such temple, the Parthenon. On graph paper they should make a floor plan that represents the temple, using circles for the columns. Ask them to consider the following points: What is meant by *symmetry*? How is this temple symmetrical? Next, share with them the formula for classical proportions of column placement: x represents each of the short sides of the temple, and $2x + 1$ represents each of the long sides. How does this apply to the Parthenon? Is x an even or an odd number? What effect does this fact have on the symmetry of the temple when viewed from the front? Students should display their plans and answers to the questions, along with pictures of the temples. *(2–4 class periods)*

YOU WILL NEED:
- reference photos of the Parthenon
- graph paper
- rulers and circle templates

Book of African Empires

OVERVIEW

For more than 1,000 years—from the rise of the Ghana Empire in the fourth century until the fall of the Songhai Empire in 1591—the area surrounding the present-day African nation of Mali was dominated by powerful empires. Bordered by the continent's famous Gold Coast and comprising trade routes that reached to Europe and Asia, these empires were centers of economy, scholarship, and culture.

Research Questions

• What kingdoms and empires once dominated West Africa?

• What were their greatest natural and cultural resources?

Investigation The class will act as a team to produce a book about the empires and kingdoms of West Africa. Students will work together to generate articles, locate images, and lay out the final product. The book will include descriptions of the cultural history of the area, detailed maps, information about gold (the base of this area's historical wealth), and estimates of distances traveled by merchants and scholars. If possible, students should use a scanner and a word-processing program with a desktop publishing program. Otherwise, students may simply assemble and then photocopy the various components. The project may be bound using a three-hole punch and ribbon, or simply secured with staples.

Wrap-up Enough copies should be made so that each student may have his or her own book. In addition, students may wish to distribute books in other classrooms, and to leave copies on display in the school library. If possible, the class might visit a book bindery or printing studio, or have a professional writer visit the classroom.

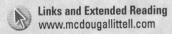

Links and Extended Reading
www.mcdougallittell.com

OBJECTIVES

❏ research and write about the empires of historical West Africa

❏ create maps that show the range of each empire

❏ describe the properties and uses of gold

❏ represent distances traveled by visitors and tradespeople

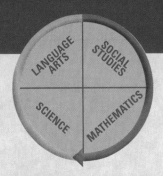

Team Teaching Assignments

CONNECT TO `LANGUAGE ARTS` Students should use reference books and the Internet to learn about the people and culture of these African empires. Students might be divided into four teams. One team will research groups key to the development of this region, such as the Arabs, the Almoravids, the Tuareg, and the Mandingos. Another will explore the importance of trade, including the extent of trade routes for salt and gold. Another will investigate the arrival of Islam and its impact on learning, art, and architecture. The fourth team will focus on the significance of Timbuktu as a center of trade and scholarship. Working in pairs, students should read what they can find about their subject. Next, they should write a feature article summarizing their findings. They might include images and intriguing facts about their area of research. *(4–5 class periods)*

YOU WILL NEED:
- Web access (optional)
- reference books
- notebook

CONNECT TO `SOCIAL STUDIES` The groups that ruled the area around present-day Mali changed over the centuries, as did their range and number. First, students should carefully draw a map of Africa, including geographical features such as lakes and rivers. They may wish to use graph paper for greater accuracy. Next, they should make one photocopy of the map for each kingdom they choose to explore. (A basic exploration might cover the empires of Ghana, Mali, and Songhai.) On each photocopy, students should label a particular kingdom and indicate its area. Approximate dates and a key would be helpful. Along with these maps, students might find it interesting to include in their book a map of Africa today. *(3–4 class periods)*

YOU WILL NEED:
- atlas
- reference books
- photocopier or scanner
- markers

CONNECT TO `SCIENCE` Gold has been a source of wealth in West Africa for centuries. Some scholars believe that gold, which has been valued since prehistoric times, was the first metal used by humans. Why have people found it so versatile? Students should do research to learn what makes this element unique. Why have people known it to be useful that gold is *chemically inactive*? What does it mean to say that gold is *ductile*? Why do the makers of jewelry and coins like the fact that gold is *malleable*? In what form is gold found? If possible, examine samples of gold wire and gold leaf, from art- or craft-supply stores. Students should compile their findings in a list of facts about gold and its properties. They may wish to accompany it with a list of uses to which gold was put in West Africa. *(1–2 class periods)*

YOU WILL NEED:
- reference books
- paper and pencils
- (optional) gold wire or gold leaf

CONNECT TO `MATHEMATICS` By the Middle Ages, the empires of this area were a center of trade across the African continent as well as into Europe, the Near East, and Asia. Today, it can take travelers a great deal of time by plane to reach Mali. However, many people visited that area centuries ago, when travel was far more difficult. Ask students to use a map and map scale to measure the distance between Timbuktu and a specific point on the African coast. Then consider: If a dromedary camel carrying a rider can travel an average of 100 miles a day, how long would it take someone to reach Timbuktu from that point? Have students calculate various round-trip distances and compile their findings in a chart called "Traveling to Timbuktu." *(1–2 class periods)*

YOU WILL NEED:
- atlas
- graph paper or plain paper
- rulers and calculators

Dolphin Field Guide

OVERVIEW

The bottlenose dolphin—the type featured in "My First Dive with the Dolphins"—inhabits temperate and tropical waters worldwide, and is not an endangered species. The bottlenose is the most abundant species of dolphin along the eastern United States from Cape Cod through the Gulf of Mexico.

Research Questions

• How do dolphins, porpoises, and whales differ?

• What are the identifying features of the bottlenose and other species of dolphins?

• How does the top swimming speed of bottlenose dolphins compare to that of other marine animals?

Investigation Working in small groups or individually, students will publish field guides to dolphins. While researching and writing their guides, students should consider, among other things, dolphin biology and habitat, how to distinguish between dolphins, porpoises, and whales, as well as how to identify the bottlenose and other species of dolphins. Each guide will be enhanced with student-selected or student-authored poetry about dolphins. Guides will also include brief articles about conservation issues.

Wrap-up When the dolphin field guides are complete, invite other students, parents, and community members to view them. Place the guides in a "lending library" in the classroom or in the school library.

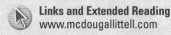

Links and Extended Reading
www.mcdougallittell.com

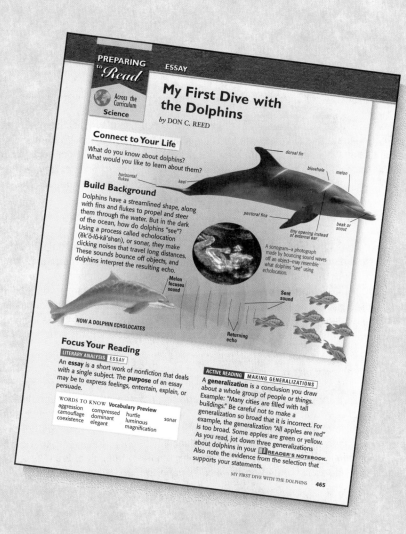

OBJECTIVES

❏ read, discuss, and write poetry about marine animals

❏ research and report on the issue of dolphin injuries from tuna fishing

❏ research and write a "field guide" to dolphins

❏ create a bar graph comparing the swimming speeds of marine animals

Team Teaching Assignments

CONNECT TO `LANGUAGE ARTS` Have students read aloud and discuss poetry about dolphins and other marine creatures such as whales, killer whales, sharks, and fish. Students may wish to include some of this poetry in their field guides, or to write their own poetry about dolphins and publish it in their guides. Two good sources for animal poetry are *The Oxford Book of Animal Poems,* edited by Michael Harrison and Christopher Stuart-Clark, and *The Beauty of the Beast: Poems from the Animal Kingdom,* edited by Jack Prelutsky. *(2 class periods)*

YOU WILL NEED:
- animal poetry anthologies

CONNECT TO `SOCIAL STUDIES` Ask students if they have noticed "dolphin-safe" labels on tuna fish cans. In the early 1990s, the American public became very concerned about the number of dolphins dying in fishing nets. The estimated number of dolphin deaths worldwide due to tuna fishing has dropped from 133,000 in 1986 to 2,000 in 1998. Direct students to research what the "dolphin-safe" label means, what fishing practices endanger dolphins, and how fishing fleets have changed their practices. Each group of students should work together to write a short report on the issue of dolphins and tuna fishing or on another current conservation issue related to dolphins for inclusion in their field guides. *(2–3 class periods)*

YOU WILL NEED:
- Web access (optional)
- current reference materials on dolphins and tuna fishing

CONNECT TO `SCIENCE` Have students form small groups and encourage them to examine sample field guides to see what type of information is included and how it is organized. Each group should create an outline of their dolphin field guide and then perform research to gather the necessary information. They will then write text and combine it with photographs and/or illustrations. Have students include any reports, fact sheets, graphs, or poetry from other team assignments and bind their field guides inside an illustrated cover. *(4 class periods)*

YOU WILL NEED:
- samples of field guides
- Web access (optional)
- reference books on dolphins
- word processor (optional)
- art materials for bookbinding

CONNECT TO `MATHEMATICS` Tell students that bottlenose dolphins can swim as fast as 20 miles per hour over short distances. Provide students with the following maximum swimming speeds of other marine animals, or have them research other animals' speeds: *gray whale: 12 mph; killer whale: 30 mph; porpoise: 24 mph; mako shark: 60 mph; sailfish: 68 mph.* Instruct each group of students to make a bar graph comparing the top speed of the bottlenose dolphin to that of other marine animals. Groups may include the bar graph in their field guide. *(1–2 class periods)*

YOU WILL NEED:
- colored pencils
- graph paper

"About Time" Bulletin Board

OVERVIEW

Time is one concept that can seem infinite. The character Milo in *The Phantom Tollbooth* feels he has too much time. He even tries "killing time." Archaeological remains tell us that in almost every ancient culture people devised ways to measure and record the passage of time.

Research Questions

• When does time seem to pass slowly and quickly for you?

• What are time zones and why do we have them?

• How did people in various cultures tell time before there were clocks?

Investigation Working in small groups, students will create a classroom bulletin board about time. The bulletin board will be made up of creative writing about time, information on time zones, descriptions of timekeeping devices through history, and calculations of the amount of time left until students' next birthdays.

Wrap-up When the bulletin board is complete, encourage students to organize a presentation on the subject for a class of younger students. They may wish to create or select a musical recording or a short picture book to use in their presentation as an attention grabber.

 Links and Extended Reading
www.mcdougallittell.com

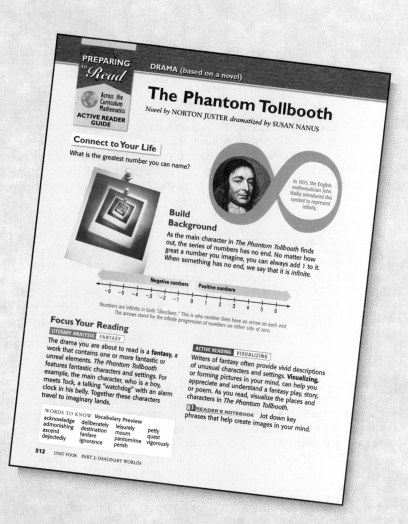

OBJECTIVES

❑ write a poem or a story about time

❑ map time zones, world cities, and their local times

❑ research and illustrate timekeeping devices through history

❑ use scientific notation to express the amount of time left until students' next birthdays

Team Teaching Assignments

CONNECT TO **LANGUAGE ARTS** Ask students if their perception of how quickly time passes is affected by what they are doing. Have them brainstorm a list of occasions when it seems that time passes slowly and those when it seems that time passes quickly. Record their responses on the board. Each student should then generate a piece of creative writing (a poem or a story) about one of the listed scenarios. Encourage students to provide vivid descriptions of what it feels like when time passes "quickly" or "slowly." *(2 class periods)*

YOU WILL NEED:
(no special materials needed)

CONNECT TO **SOCIAL STUDIES** Display a United States map with clearly marked time zones and their time differences. Quiz students about what time it is in United States time zones other than their own. Explain that there are different time zones all across the world. For example, when it is 8:00 A.M. standard time in New York City, it is 10:00 P.M. in Tokyo, Japan. Have students trace a map of the world from an atlas or an almanac. Have them label on the map the town in which their school is located. Then have them label other cities across the globe with the city's name and the local time in that city when it is 8:00 A.M. (or another time) at the students' school. *(2 class periods)*

YOU WILL NEED:
- Web access (optional)
- atlas
- chart-size paper
- colored pencils

CONNECT TO **SCIENCE** Sundials, which use the movement of the sun to indicate the time, were the first devices for telling time. The ancient Egyptians began using simple sundials as early as 3500 B.C. Sundials were followed by the development of increasingly accurate methods of telling time: water clocks, mechanical clocks, quartz clocks, and atomic clocks. Assign each group to research one of these devices and create illustrations and captions for the bulletin board explaining how it works and when and in what part(s) of the world it primarily is (or was) used. *(2–3 class periods)*

YOU WILL NEED:
- Web access (optional)
- reference books on the history of time
- art materials

CONNECT TO **MATHEMATICS** Scientific notation is a way of writing very large numbers so that they are easier to work with than when they are written out. Ask students to calculate the number of seconds until their next birthday. (Have them start by determining the number of days, and then multiplying by 86,400, the number of seconds in a day.) Then guide each student in expressing the number using scientific notation. Assign one group to create a chart titled "The Number of Seconds Until Class Members' Next Birthdays, as of [insert date and time]" for display on the bulletin board. *(2 class periods)*

YOU WILL NEED:
- calculator
- chart-size paper
- colored pencils

North America, Year 1000, Time Capsule

OVERVIEW

In *Words on a Page,* Lenore's father, Baba, fears that modern education will erase the traditions of his people. The Ojibway share with many North American first people a struggle to preserve cultures altered and diminished by European influx. In the year 1000 A.D. Europeans had not yet begun regular contact with the Americas. There were no horses on the North American continent. And none of the transplanted crops, such as apples, had arrived here. Of course, no one spoke European languages such as English and Spanish. However many of the foods we now eat, and the words that are now part of everyday English were present here. The word *moose* for example, comes from the Anishnabe word pronounced *mooz.*

Research Questions

• What was life like in the different regions of North America in 1000 A.D.?

• How do archaeologists and history keepers know about earlier time periods?

Investigation The class will act as a team to produce a time capsule that could have been created and buried in the year 1000 A.D. in one region of North America. They might choose the Northern Canadian taiga, where the Ojibway lived during that time, or they might choose a region local to their own school, and learn about a civilization or nation that lived in the area at that time. Alternatively, you might wish to have small groups research different locations and people. Each group's time capsule will include some writing—a traditional myth or legend from early history, some crafted item(s) or illustrations reflecting and crafted clothing illustrations picturing year 1000 technology.

Wrap-up Students should plan to bury the capsule with a ceremony to which other students, teachers, and members of the community are invited. If appropriate, the burial can be accompanied by traditional music and a dedication to the people it represents. The exact burial spot will also be recorded mathematically using a grid.

 Links and Extended Reading
www.mcdougallittell.com

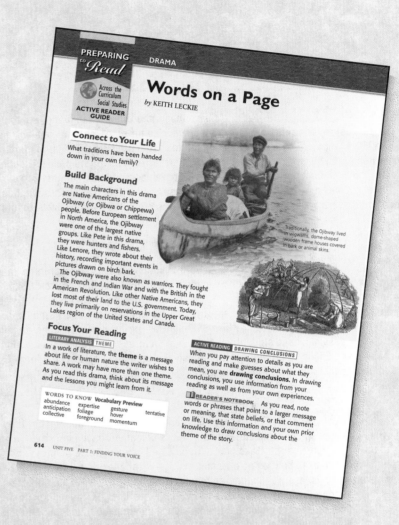

OBJECTIVES

❑ research and retell legends of ancient North America

❑ research and record Native American origins of English words, as well as the meanings of some words and phrases in Native American languages

❑ learn about and report on early clothing, crafts, and other technologies of North America

❑ create a coordinate grid that shows the exact burial spot for a time capsule

Team Teaching Assignments

CONNECT TO `LANGUAGE ARTS` Anishinabe, or the Ojibway language, is rich in oral tradition. There is a vast repertoire of Ojibway stories available for research. One small group of students should research the language. Another group should read some Ojibway stories. Students will find the Ojibway had words for many familiar phrases, for numbers, as well as for the animals around them. For the time capsule, have students create an Anishinabe/English phrase book. Another group can compile a bibliography, and short synopsis, of some Ojibwan tales or legends. If possible, pairs of students could tape record some of the stories, and place the cassette in the capsule. Note that **each** activity can be adapted to a different Native nation. *(2–3 class periods)*

YOU WILL NEED:
- Web access (optional)
- tape recorder (optional)
- books of Native American legends
- notebook

CONNECT TO `SOCIAL STUDIES` The word "Ojibway" means "puckered up" and refers to the Ojibway style of moccasin. The Ojibway made most of their clothing from buckskin. Have a small group of students research Ojibway clothing—the fabric and design. Students should create pictures of the everyday wear of the Ojibway. An alternative project would be to have a small group of students research and make an article of clothing in this style—perhaps moccasins or leggings or an example of beadwork. If possible, have students caption their pictures or crafted artifact, using both the Anishinabe and English languages. Alternatively the same activity can be adapted to a more local Native American culture. *(3–4 class periods)*

YOU WILL NEED:
- Web access (optional)
- reference books
- sewing materials (optional)

CONNECT TO `SCIENCE` The Ojibway favored woodland areas near lakes. They ate different kinds of berries and nuts as well as meat and fish. They also gathered wild rice, and celebrations of a "wild rice gathering" every year still take place. They were knowledgeable of herbs and medicinal plants. The Ojibway lived in houses built on pole frames in wigwam shape and made of birchbark and cattail mats. They were skilled fishers. Have students research the Ojibway way of life and create illustrations— preferably captioned in both Anishinabe and English—entitled "A Day in the Life of the Ojibway Year 1000" Possible topics might include; housing; plants; hunting; food; rice and berry gathering. Then have a group of students construct and decorate a "capsule" such as a large box or tube. They should place their assignments in the capsule after they have been displayed or presented in the classroom. The same activity can be adapted to a more local Native culture. *(3–4 class periods)*

YOU WILL NEED:
- Web access (optional)
- reference books
- poster paper

CONNECT TO `MATHEMATICS` Have students create a coordinate grid that shows the exact burial spot for the time capsule. First, clear a spot around the school or in another permissable location. Have pairs of students conduct a survey of the spot for burial, staking it into an archaeological grid, using popsicle sticks and twine. They should then use graph paper to create a coordinate grid with numbers running up each axis, based on the numbers of sticks along each side of the site. After a burial ceremony, students should mark their grids with an appropriate graph and label for the capsule's exact spot. An alternate activity would be to have a pair of students create a diagram with clues to the burial spot, such as: begin here; turn 90 degrees left; go one meter straight ahead, and so on. *(2–3 class periods)*

YOU WILL NEED:
- graph paper
- rulers
- popsicle sticks
- twine
- a small plot of earth to dig in

Ancient Egyptian Burial Chamber

OVERVIEW

The burial customs of ancient Egypt have long been a source of fascination. For millennia, the sandy banks of the Nile—"the long river between the deserts"—preserved these ancient wonders. Egypt's majestic pyramids, hidden tombs, mysterious mummies, and buried treasures of gilded objects both fantastic and familiar have not only tantalized the imagination but provided invaluable information about this most ancient of cultures. The following project might serve as part of a larger unit on Ancient Egypt.

Research Questions

• What can be found in the tombs of ancient Egypt?

• Who has been buried there?

• What have archaeologists and historians learned from examining the tombs?

Investigation The class will work as a team to produce a display of information about ancient Egyptian tombs. If possible, this should be housed in a sort of chamber, so that students might simulate the experience of stepping into one of the small rooms that typically housed objects in a tomb. Large appliance boxes might be used; sheets might be draped over a frame; freestanding chalkboards might be used to fence in a corner and topped with a posterboard roof. Ideally, the chamber would be dim enough so that a flashlight could be used during visits. The inside of the chamber should feature depictions and explanations of tomb objects. Also on display should be a map of pyramids and tombs along the Nile, an explanation of mummification, and a time line representing the span of kingdoms and dynasties.

Wrap-up Students will assemble the chamber and decorate it with hieroglyphics. They may wish to invite other classes to investigate the chamber. If possible, have students watch videotapes that show footage of the Nile Valley and explore its pyramids and tombs.

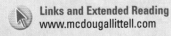

Links and Extended Reading
www.mcdougallittell.com

OBJECTIVES

❑ represent and understand the significance of tomb objects

❑ map the pyramids and tombs along the Nile

❑ explain the process of mummification

❑ create a time line that spans the dynasties of ancient Egypt

Team Teaching Assignments

CONNECT TO **LANGUAGE ARTS** Egyptian tombs were piled high with everything the deceased pharaoh and his family might need in the afterlife—furniture, dishes, headrests, jewelry, cosmetics, linens, food, games, and writing instruments—as well as statues that represented such essential figures as servants and soldiers. Of course, items specific to burial, such as sarcophagi and canopic jars, were of particular importance. Students should be given some time to browse books with pictures of these many objects. Each student should make a picture of a specific object and write a paragraph explaining its significance. If space permits, some students may wish to represent their object with sculpture rather than illustration. These representations will be displayed inside the chamber, taped or pinned to its walls or arranged on shelving. *(3–4 class periods)*

YOU WILL NEED:
- Web access (optional)
- reference books
- paper
- colored pens and pencils

CONNECT TO **SOCIAL STUDIES** Although the three pyramids of Giza, near Cairo, are by far the most recognizable of these ancient monuments, many more pyramids—as well as tombs, temples, and palaces—once dotted the banks of the Nile. Students should make a large map that represents the Nile Valley. They should accurately note the locations of the pyramid groupings of the Old Kingdom pharaohs. Next, they should note the locations of the rock tombs of the New Kingdom. They may wish to use triangles to represent pyramids and another symbol to represent tombs; these should be clearly indicated in a key. In addition, students might wish to note the locations of the Sphinx, the Colossi of Memnon, and other well-known sites and to make symbols for these on the map. The map might be hung near the chamber. *(2–4 class periods)*

YOU WILL NEED:
- atlases and encyclopedias
- colored pencils or markers
- posterboard

CONNECT TO **SCIENCE** No aspect of ancient Egypt haunts the imagination like mummies. How are the bodies preserved? What is inside of them? How much fabric was needed to wrap each one? What happened to the brain? Fortunately, scientific research can offer answers to these questions and more. Working in small groups, students should research how the ancient Egyptians embalmed and buried their dead. The class might be divided into four teams to research the following: beliefs and rituals surrounding death; preservation of the body; mummy cases; and animal mummies (millions of animals were bred for the purpose of mummification). Each group should create a poster containing important facts about its subject, as well as diagrams and illustrations. Next, each group should present the information verbally to the class, using the poster as a visual aid. Afterward, the posters might be hung on the outside of the chamber. *(3–4 class periods)*

YOU WILL NEED:
- Web access (optional)
- reference books
- posterboard
- colored pens and pencils

CONNECT TO **MATHEMATICS** For about 3,000 years, the land of Egypt was ruled by kings who, around 1400 B.C., became known as pharaohs. This span is usually divided into thirty-one dynasties. It also includes the three kingdoms of ancient Egypt: the Old Kingdom, when pyramids were first built; the Middle Kingdom, a great reunification that brought further building of pyramids; and the New Kingdom, when the empire expanded and pharaohs were interred at the Valley of the Kings. Students should create a time line that stretches from the earliest Egyptian dynasty (c. 3100 B.C.) until the land was conquered by Alexander the Great in 332 B.C. Students might label all the dynasties or simply indicate the three kingdoms as well as famous pharaohs associated with each. The time line could run along the outside of the chamber or simply hang on a bulletin board. *(3–4 class periods)*

YOU WILL NEED:
- reference books
- rulers
- pens or pencils
- paper

Index of Fine Art

Index of Skills

Literary Concepts

Act, of a play, 319, R116
Action. *See also* Conflict; Plot; Resolution.
    falling, 22, 34, 45, 443, 481, R121
    rising, 22, 34, 45, 443, 481, R127
Aesthetic language. *See* Figurative language; Sound
    devices; Word choice.
Alliteration, 191, R116. *See also* Sound devices.
Allusion, R116
Ambiguous reference, R90
Analogy, 348, 379, 675, R24
Analysis/classification, writing, R45–R46
Analyzing, R116. *See also* Analyzing *under* Reading
    and Critical Thinking Skills.
Anecdote, 154, 161, R116
Appropriate language, R96
Audience, 416, R116
Author's perspective, 161–162, 363, 684, R116
Author's purpose, 142, 409, 424, 676, R117. *See also*
    Author's purpose *under* Reading and Critical
    Thinking Skills.
Author's style. *See* Style.
Autobiography, 97, 100, 135, 142, 165, 170, 362–363,
    385, 640, R117
Ballad, R117
Bias, 363, 464, 758. *See also* Author's perspective.
Biographer, 97, 111, R117
Biography, 97, 100, 101, 111, 362–363, 378, R117
Cast of characters, 319, 324, R117
Cause and effect, 76, 154, 161, 446, 459, 674, R6, R9,
    R44–R45
Character, 23, 31, 45, 183, 243–246, 319, 343, 346,
    445, 555, 612, 633, 698, R117
    development of, R17
    main and minor, 23, 26, 31, 45, 124, 319
    and motivation, R14
    in nonfiction, 97
    real and imaginary, 698
    traits, 26, 31, 143, 161, 244, 245, 248, 257, 264,
        305, 653, 661, 735, 740, 850
Characterization, R118
Chronological order, 114, 121, 364, 378, R6, R118
Cinderella tale, R118
Clarifying, S3, 385, 740, R118
Climax, 22, 319, 443, 459, 481, 488, R118. *See also*
    Resolution; Plot.
Comedy, R118
Comparing literature, 31, 64, 76, 111, 161, 216, 227,
    287, 330, 346, 378, 409, 479, 561, 566, 572–573,
    633, 648, 684, 711, 734
Comparison, R10–R11. *See also* Metaphor; Simile.
Conclusion, 613, 633, R118. *See also* Conclusions,
    drawing, *under* Reading and Critical Thinking
    Skills.
Concrete poetry, 190, R118

Conflict, 22, 45, 124, 132, 319, 445, 459, 481, R118.
    See also Climax; Resolution; Plot.
    internal/external, 124, 132, 445, R118
Connecting, S3, 31, 281, 346, R119
Connotation, 742, R23
Context clues, 79, R20, R25
Contrast, R119
Couplet, 479, 566, 737, 740, R119
Denotation, 742, R23
Description, 264, 272, 473, R119
Details, 49, 51, 101, 111, 409, 555, 561, R6. *See also*
    Sensory details.
Dialect, R119
Dialogue, 317, 320, 333, 337, 437, R119
Diary, 97, 142
Diction, *See Word Choice.*
Drama, 317–320, 321, R120. *See also* Cast of
    characters; Dialogue; Stage directions.
Dynamic character, R120
Elaborating, 201
End rhyme. *See* Rhyme.
Entertaining, 473
Epic poetry, R120
Essay, 98, 465, 473, 640, R120
Evaluating, S3, S7, S10, S22, S24, S31, 216, R13, R14,
    R120
Evidence, R13
Exaggeration, R120
Exposition, 22, 34, 45, R120. *See also* Plot.
Expository essay, 98
External conflict. *See* Conflict.
Fable, 770, R120
Fact, 163, 164, 203, 277, 463, 699, 711, R120
Falling action. *See* Action, falling.
Fantasy, 507–510, 512, 552, 555, 561, R121
    elements of, 599
Feature story, 99
Fiction, 21–24, 25, R121. *See also* Fantasy; Historical
    fiction; Novel; Realistic fiction; Science fiction;
    Short story.
    character in, 23
    character traits and guidelines, see traits
    forms of, 21
    plot in, 22, 76, 443
    qualities of characters, see traits
    setting in, 24, 64, 76, 445, 459, 633
    theme in, 24, 76
    time in, 64
    title of, 76, 633
    types of, 21, 61
Figurative language, 192, 194, 198, 243, 648, R121
Figure of speech. *See* Idiom; Metaphor; Personification;
    Simile.
First-person point of view, 97, 112, 142, 170, 275,
    281, 362, 385
Flashback, R121

Purpose. *See* Author's purpose; Setting a purpose.

Reading and Critical Thinking Skills

Order of ideas. *See* Text structure.

Organization. *See* Text structure.

Outlining, 51, 587, 588–591, 759

Overgeneralization, 465, 473, R14

Paired activities, 45, 64, 142, 170, 198, 207, 227, 257, 287, 337, 346, 385, 395, 415, 459, 479, 561, 566, 579, 585, 661, 674, 684

Paraphrasing, 49–51, 591
    and avoiding plagiarism, 49, 758

Peer editing on a computer, R104

Peer response, using, 92, 179, 239, 301, 358, 386, 433, 693, R33

Personal response, 31, 64, 76, 89–94, 111, 132, 142, 161, 170, 198, 207, 216, 227, 257, 281, 287, 330, 337, 346, 378, 385, 395, 409, 415, 424, 459, 473, 479, 531, 552, 561, 566, 633, 640, 648, 661, 674, 684, 711, 725, 734, 740, R56–R57. *See also* Connecting.

Perspectives, different, 45, 161, 170, 216, 227, 363, 385, 424, 661, 674. *See also* Author's perspective; Point of view.

Persuading, 65, 379, 489, 662, R12–R16, R47–R48, R103–R104

Play. *See* Drama.

Plot, 22, 45, 76, 132, 319, 321, 443–445, 481, 488, 633, R126. *See also* Analyzing; Story-mapping.
    cause and effect in, 154, 161, 444, 446, 447, 459
    climax of, 22, 45, 443, 481, 488, R118
    conflict, 22, 45, 122, 132, 142, 481, 488, R118
    endings, 459
    exposition, 22, 443, R120
    falling action in, 22, 45, 443, 481, R121
    foreshadowing, 444, 447, 459, R121
    in historical fiction, 698, 711
    resolution, 22, 45, 443, 481, 488
    rising action in, 22, 45, 443, 481, 488, R127
    surprise ending, R130

Poetry, 189–192, 193, 236–241, R125
    forms, 190, 205, 207, 563, 566, R121–R122
    narrative, 343, 346, 561, 740, R124
    speaker in, 192, 391, 395, R129
    strategies for reading, 189–192, 193

Point of view, 97, 112, 170, 281, 362, 385, R126
    changing, 45, 161, 170, 216, 227, 363, 385, 424, 661, 674
    first-person, 97, 142, 170, 275, 281, 362, 385
    third-person, 281, 362, 378

Plagiarism, 49, 758

Predicting, S3, S6, S8, S26, S29, 25, 123, 132, 247, 248, 250, 255, 257, 333, 337, 455, 522, 528, 543, 549, 762, 781, R126

Prefixes. *See* Prefixes *under* Vocabulary Skills.

Previewing, 25, 100, 193

Print vs. nonprint media, 143, 217, 527, 537, 562, 634

Prior knowledge, activating, 26, 34, 45, 64, 101, 114, 124, 154, 163, 165, 194, 205, 209, 219, 248, 264, 275, 284, 322, 333, 365, 381, 391, 402, 411, 416, 418, 447, 465, 476, 481, 512, 555, 563, 574, 580, 614, 636, 643, 653, 668, 676, 678, 700, 718, 728, 737, 740

Problem solving, 340–342, 361, 386, 430–435, 653

Product label information, reading, R17

Pronunciation, key to symbols, R146

Propaganda, R13, R15

Pulled quotation, 717

Purpose. *See* Author's purpose; Setting a purpose for reading.

Questioning, S3, S6, S8, S22, S25, S31, 25, 104, 165, 170, 328, 364, 446, 450, R126

Questions
    forming and revising, 388–390
    open-ended, 735

Rate, adjusting. *See* Monitoring; Reading actively, aloud; Scanning; Skimming.

Reader's notebook, S4–S5, 26, 31, 34, 45, 52, 64, 67, 101, 111, 114, 121, 132, 135, 142, 154, 182–183, 194, 198, 205, 207, 209, 216, 219, 227, 248, 257, 264, 272, 275, 281, 284, 287, 304–305, 322, 330, 337, 343, 346, 365, 378, 381, 385, 391, 395, 402, 409, 411, 415, 418, 424, 436–437, 446, 447, 459, 465, 473, 476, 479, 481, 488, 512, 552, 555, 561, 563, 566, 574, 579, 580, 585, 598–599, 614, 633, 636, 640, 643, 648, 653, 661, 668, 674, 678, 684, 700, 711, 718, 725, 728, 734, 737, 740, 762–763, 850
    strategies for using, S4–S5, S20

Reading actively, S2–S31, 25, 26, 31, 34, 45, 52, 64, 67, 100, 101, 111, 114, 121, 132, 135, 142, 154, 193, 194, 198, 205, 207, 209, 216, 219, 227, 247, 248, 257, 264, 272, 275, 281, 284, 287, 321, 322, 330, 337, 343, 346, 365, 378, 381, 385, 391, 395, 402, 409, 411, 415, 418, 424, 446, 447, 459, 465, 473, 476, 479, 481, 488, 511, 512, 552, 555, 561, 563, 566, 574, 579, 580, 585, 613, 614, 633, 636, 640, 643, 648, 653, 661, 668, 674, 678, 684, 699, 700, 711, 718, 725, 728, 734, 737, 740
    aloud, 172, 193, 284, 287, 322, 426, 563, 566, 686
    directions, 650–652
    drama, strategies for, 317–321
    fiction, strategies for, 25
    for information, 48–51, 145–148, 201–204, 260–263, 340–342, 386, 388–390, 462–464, 588–591, 651–652, 714–717, 718, R2–R11
    model for, 4–15
    nonfiction, strategies for, 100
    poetry, strategies for, 193
    skills and strategies. *See* Active reading, strategies for.

Realistic detail, 555, 561, 698

Recalling facts, S7, 121, 725. *See also* Comprehension check; Test-taking, practice and preparation for.

Reflecting, S3, 95, 182–183, 188, 242, 304–305, 316, 361, 436–437, 442, 504, 506, 598–599, 610, 696, 762–763, 850

Rereading, 193, 207, 342, 714–717, 728

Root words. *See* Roots *under* Vocabulary Skills.

Scanning, 148, 389, R3

Sensory details, 205, 207, 281, 415, 473, 480, 643, 648, R98. *See also* Details, noting; Imagery, understanding.

Vocabulary Skills

Contrast clues, 79, R20
Definition clues, 79, R20
Denotation, 742, R23
Description clues, 79
Dictionary, using a, 149, 289, 491, 663
English/Spanish words, glossary of, R132–R146
Etymology, 386. *See also* Roots.
Example clues, 79, R20
Glossary, 51, 183, 305, 437, 599, 761, R6
 English/Spanish, R132–R146
 grammar, R90–R95
 of literary and reading terms, R116–R131
Homonyms, 289, R24, R27–R29
Homophones, 289, 553, R24
Meaning clues, 77, 79, 133, 282, 410, 491, 641, 685
Mnemonic devices, 338
Multiple meanings of words, R24
New words, learning and remembering, 386, 460, 491, 553
Personal word list, S5, 182, 304, 436, 491, 598, 762
Prefixes, 386, 397, 489, 491, R20, R27
Pronunciation, key to symbols, R146
Reference tools, 149, 289, 491, 531, 568, 663, 742, R25
Related words, 489
Restatement clues, 32, 79, 143, R20
Roots, 149, 491, 663, R21, R22
Signal words, R9
Silent letters, 338
Similar words, 491
Spanish/English words, glossary of, R132–R146
Specialized vocabulary, 568
Spelling, 32, 133, 228, 258, 338, 386, 489, 553, 685, 726, R26–R29
Standardized test practice, 46, 94, 162, 171, 181, 258, 273, 303, 308–313, 338, 410, 425, 460, 602–607, 641, 675, 735
Strategy. *See* Building vocabulary, strategies for.
Suffixes, 258, 386, 397, 491, 553, 726, R21, R27
Synonyms, 77, 112, 230, 348, 410, 712, R22
Thesaurus, using a, 531, 742
Word families, 149, 663, R22
Word list. *See* Personal word list.
Word origins, 386, 663, R22
Word parts, 32, 149, 397, R21. *See also* Prefixes; Roots; Suffixes.
Word relationships. *See also* Etymology; Related words; Word families.
 analogies and, 348, 379
Word web, 26, 391, 479

Grammar, Usage, and Mechanics

Action verb, 78, 283, R62, R95
Active voice, 123, R95
Address, commas in, R64, R88
Adjective, 332, 410, 434, 554, R78–R80, R90
 clause, R83, R90
 comparative and superlative, 380, 434, 862, R78, R90
 phrase, 425, 554, R83
 predicate, 134, R90

Adverb, 339, 410, 434, R78, R90
 clause, R83, R90
 comparative and superlative, 434, R79, R90
 phrase, 425, 554, R83
Agreement
 common problems, R70–R71
 pronoun-antecedent, R69, R74, R90
 subject-verb, 93, 162, R68–R71, R90
Ambiguous reference, R80
Antecedent-pronoun agreement, R69, R74, R90
Antonym, 230, 712, R23
Apostrophe, R65
Appositive, 490, 596, R93, R90
Article, R90
Auxiliary (helping) verb, 66, R95
Capitalization, 229, R66, R81–R82
Clause, 642, 685, R64, R83–R85, R90–R91
 adjective, R83, R90
 adverb, R83, R90–R91
 elliptical, R91
 independent and dependent, 713, 727, 736, R83–R85, R91
 noun, R76, R91
 punctuation of, 642, 685, R83, R95
 subordinate, R67, R83–R85, R91
Colon, 642, R65
Combining phrases, 475
Combining sentences, 685, 713. *See also* Conjunction.
Comma, 490, R64, R86–R89, R94
 in address, R64, R88
 in compound sentence, R64, R86
 in date, R64, R88
 in dialogue, R89
 with interrupter, R87
 with introductory phrases and clauses, R64
 with introductory words, R86–R87
 in letter, R64, R88
 with nonessential phrases and clauses, R64
 with noun of direct address, R64, R87
 with quotation marks, R89
 in series, R64, R87
 with two or more adjectives, R88
Common noun, 229
Comparative form of modifier, 359, 380, 434, R78–R79, R90. *See also* Adjective; Adverb.
Complete predicate, R63, R91
Complete subject, R63, R91
Complex sentence, 642, 685, 727, R83, R94
Compound complex sentences, 736, R85, R94
Compound predicate, 113
Compound sentence, R67, R84, R94
 punctuation of, R83
Compound subject, 113, 760, R68
Conjunction, 475, R62, R91
 coordinating, 685, R62, R67, R91
 correlative, R62, R91
 subordinating, R62, R91
Conjunctive adverb, R91
Contraction, R65, R91
Coordinating conjunction, R62, R91
Correlative conjunction, R62, R91

Dash, R65
Declarative sentence, 47
Definite article, R90
Demonstrative pronoun, R62, R83
Dependent clause, 713, 727, R93, R91
Direct object, 78, R63, R91
Direct quotation, R89, R94
Divided quotation, R89, R94
Double negative, 387, R79, R91
Ellipses, R65
End mark, R64, R91
    in quotations, R89
Essential appositive, 490, R90,
Event names, capitalizing, R66, R81–R82
Exclamation point, R64
Exclamatory sentence, 47
First word, capitalizing, R66
Fragment. *See* Sentence, fragment.
Future perfect tense, R76, R95
Future tense, R76, R95
Gender, of pronoun/antecedent, R74
Geographical names, capitalizing, R81–R82
Gerund, R92
Gerund phrase, R83, R93
Helping verb (auxiliary), 66, R95
Homonyms. *See* Homonyms *under* Vocabulary Skills.
Hyphen, R65
Imperative sentence, 47
Indefinite article, R90
Indefinite pronoun, R62, R74
Independent clause, 713, 727, R83, R91
Indirect object, R63, R92
Infinitive, R92
    phrase, R83, R93
Intensive pronoun, R62, R93
Interjection, R62, R92
Interrogative pronoun, R62, R93
Interrogative sentence, 47
Interrupters, R86
Introductory words, 675, R86
Inverted sentence, R70–R71, R92
Irregular verb, R77–R78, R95
Italics, R65
Linking verb. *See* Verb, linking.
Main clause. *See* Independent clause.
Main verb, 66, R63
Modifier, 332, 339, 380, 410, 425, 434, R38, R78–R80, R92. *See also* Adjective; Adverb.
Noun, 218, R62, R92
    abstract, R92
    clause, R83, R91
    collective, R92
    common, 229, R92
    compound, R92
    direct address, R92
    plural, R71–R72
    possessive, 302, R71–R72, R92
    predicate, 134, R92
    proper, 229, R92
    specific, R38

Noun-pronoun agreement. *See* Agreement, pronoun-antecedent.
Number, of pronoun and antecedent, R74
Object of preposition, 461, 554, R63, R92
Object of verb, 78, R63, R93. *See also* Direct object; Indirect object.
Object pronoun, 218
Organization names, capitalizing, R66, R81
Parentheses, R65
Participial phrase, R83, R93
Participle, R93, R85. *See also* Past participle; Present participle.
Parts of speech, quick reference chart, R62
Passive voice, 123, R95
Past participle, R76, R93
Past perfect tense, R76, R95
Past tense, 274, R76, R95
People's names, capitalizing, R66, R81
Period, R64
Personal pronoun, R62, R73–R75, R93
Person, of pronoun, R74, R93
Phrase, 475
    adjective, 425, 554, R83, R93
    adverb, 425, 554, R83, R93
    appositive, 490, 596, R83, R93
    gerund, R83, R93
    infinitive, R83, R93
    participial, R83, R93
    prepositional, 425, 461, 554, R63, R83, R93
    verb, 66, R83, R93
Plural nouns, R71–R72
Poetry, capitalization in, R66, R82
Possessive form, R71–R72, R93. *See also* Noun, possessive; Pronoun, possessive.
Possessive noun. *See* Noun, possessive.
Possessive pronoun. *See* Pronoun, possessive.
Precise language, 229, 332, R98
Predicate, R93
    complete, R63, R91
    compound, 113, R87
    simple, 66, R63, R95
Predicate adjective, 134, R90
Predicate noun, 134, R92, R93
Prefix. *See* Prefixes *under* Vocabulary Skills.
Preposition, 461, 554, R62, R93
Prepositional phrase, 461, 554, R63, R83, R93
Present participle, R93
Present perfect tense, R76, R95
Present tense, R76, R95
Pronoun
    demonstrative, R62, R93
    gender of, R74
    indefinite, R69, R74, R93
    intensive, R62, R93
    interrogative, R62, R93
    number of, R74
    object case of, 180, 218, R63, R73
    personal, R62, R69, R73–R75, R93
    person of, R74
    possessive, 302, R73, R93
    reflexive, R62, R93

Writing Skills, Modes, and Formats

Research and Technology

Speaking and Listening

snob appeal, R14, R104
unsupported inference, R14
Persuasive presentation, 273, 379, 562, R100–R101
Photographs in a multimedia presentation, R113
Poetry, 189–199, 198, 204, 208, 239, 240, 346
Practicing and presenting a speech, 273, R96–R101
appropriate language, R96–R98
evaluation, R97
eye contact, R97
organization, R97
pace, R97
pauses, R97
posture, R97–R98
visual aids, R97, R111–R112
Problem/solution presentation, R101
Proclamation, 77
Propaganda, R126
Public speaking, R96–R98
Questioning, R103
Radio drama, 726
Reading aloud, 77, 172, 204, 208, 227, 240, 272, 284, 287, 346, 426, 489, 563, 648, R98
Repetition, 284, 287, 740, R127
Rhetorical devices, R103
Rhyme, 284, 287, 561, 740, R127
Rhythm, 284, 287, 740
Role-playing, 32, 199, 361
Script, 347, 427, 842
Skits, performing, 46
Sound devices, 240, 284, 287, 648
Sound effects, 553
Speaking opportunities, 180, 302, 359
Speech
analyzing a, R103
audiences for, R96
drafting, R96–R97
giving, 273, 641, R96–R101
informal presentations, R99–R100
narrative presentations, R98–R99
oral interpretation, R98
oral presentation, 180
oral response to literature, R56–R57, R100
organization and delivery, R96–R98, R99
persuasive, 273, R100–R101
planning, 641, 893, R96–R97
practicing and presenting, R96–R98
preparing notes for, R97
problem and solution presentation, R101
standards for, R96–R97
writing, 77, 112, 133, 379, 562, 634, R96–R97
Staging a scene, 31, 46, 199, 427, 662, 741, 842
Storytelling, 378, 489, 842
Video technology, 143, 217, 359, 427, 504, 562, 634, R113
Visual aids, using, 641, 760, R111–R112

Viewing and Representing

Art activity, 32, 77, 122, 199, 228, 338, 379, 427, 489, 641, 649, 726
Art connection, 133, 199, 207, 489, 712, 735

Brochure, 122, 133, 342, 760
Bulletin board, 434
CD-ROM. *See* Technology.
Charting. *See also* Graphs *under* Reading and Critical Thinking Skills; Story maps; Story wheel; Venn diagrams; Word web.
cause and effect, 122, 447, 668, R44–R45
characteristics, 143, 161, 301, 850
characterization, 257, 385, 661
comparison points, 148, 217, 331, 573, 579, 586, 591
conflict and character traits, 245
connections, 26
details, 51, 52, 385, 480, 553
events, 114
fact and nonfact, 700
humor, 424
information, 143, 188
K-W-L (know, want to know, learned), 114, 700
observations, 142, 316, 649
plot, 34, 321, 322, 599
poetic form, 479
predictions, 247
problem-solution, 653
relationships, between characters, 183
sequence of events, 34, 217, 258
setting elements, 64, 76
stage directions, 330, 356
symbols, 674, 763
tone, 409
vocabulary words, 171, 273, 386
voice, 763
Collage, 610
Comparing and viewing
images, 527, 537
text, film, theatrical versions, 134, 217, 237, 527, 537, 562, 634, 635
Diagram. *See* Charting; Venn diagram; Word web.
Documentary film, 134
Drawing, 552, 741. *See also* Art activity.
Festival, storytelling, 842
Flipbook, 650–652
Formatting written work, R108–R109
Graphic organizers. *See* Charting; Graphs *under* Reading and Critical Thinking Skills; Mapmaking; Story map; Story wheel; Venn diagram; Word web.
Illustrating
biography, 380
poems, 240
scene, 474
Internet. *See* Technology.
Mapmaking, 288, 379
Map reading, 67, 101, 146–147, 165, 264, 365, 402, 447, 715, 718, 770, 788, 802, 828
Mass media
Internet, 260–263, R106–R107
magazines, 48–51, 145–148, 388–390, 462–464, 588–591
newspapers, 201–204, 340–342, 714–717
television, 304, 442, 635

Index of Titles and Authors

Page numbers that appear in italics refer to biographical information.

Acknowledgments *(continued)*

Highlights for Children: "Who's the New Kid?" by Lois Lowry, *Highlights for Children,* January 1994. Copyright © 1994 by Highlights for Children, Inc., Columbus, Ohio. Reprinted by permission.

Pantheon Books: "President Cleveland, Where Are You?," from *Eight Plus One* by Robert Cormier. Copyright © 1980 by Robert Cormier. Reprinted by permission of Pantheon Books, a division of Random House, Inc.

Jay D. Johnson: "Trading Card Talk" by Jay Johnson, *Boy's Life,* May 1994, published by the Boy Scouts of America. Reprinted by permission of Jay D. Johnson.

Brandt & Brandt Literary Agents: "Scout's Honor" by Avi. Copyright © 1996 by Avi. Originally appeared in *When I Was Your Age: Original Stories About Growing Up* (Candlewick Press, edited by Amy Ehrlich). Reprinted by permission of Brandt & Brandt Literary Agents, Inc.

Excerpt from "Scout's Honor" by Avi. Copyright © 1996 by Avi. Originally appeared in *When I Was Your Age: Original Stories About Growing Up* (Candlewick Press, edited by Amy Ehrlich). Reprinted by permission of Brandt & Brandt Literary Agents, Inc.

Curtis Brown, Ltd.: *Nadia the Willful* by Sue Alexander, first published by Alfred A. Knopf. Copyright © 1983 by Sue Alexander. Reprinted by permission of Curtis Brown, Ltd.

Excerpt from *Nadia the Willful* by Sue Alexander, first published by Alfred A. Knopf. Copyright © 1983 by Sue Alexander. Reprinted by permission of Curtis Brown, Ltd.

Random House: "Life Doesn't Frighten Me," from *And Still I Rise* by Maya Angelou. Copyright © 1978 by Maya Angelou. Reprinted by permission of Random House, Inc.

Excerpt from "Life Doesn't Frighten Me," from *And Still I Rise* by Maya Angelou. Copyright © 1978 by Maya Angelou. Reprinted by permission of Random House, Inc.

Norma Fox Mazer: "Tuesday of the Other June" by Norma Fox Mazer, from *Short Takes,* selected by Elizabeth Segel. Copyright © 1986 by Norma Fox Mazer. Reprinted by permission of Norma Fox Mazer. All rights reserved.

Harcourt Brace & Company: "Primer Lesson," from *Slabs of the Sunburnt West* by Carl Sandburg. Copyright 1922 by Harcourt Brace & Company and renewed 1950 by Carl Sandburg. Reprinted by permission of Harcourt Brace & Company.

"Older Run," from *Puppies, Dogs, and Blue Northers: Reflections on Being Raised by a Pack of Sled Dogs* by Gary Paulsen. Copyright © 1996 by Gary Paulsen. Reprinted by permission of Harcourt Brace & Company.

Walker and Company: "Matthew Henson at the Top of the World," from *Against All Opposition: Black Explorers in America* by Jim Haskins. Copyright © 1992 by Jim Haskins. Reprinted with permission from Walker and Company, 435 Hudson Street, New York, NY 10014, 1-800-289-2553. All rights reserved.

Orchard Books: Excerpt from *Summer of Fire: Yellowstone 1988* by Patricia Lauber. Text copyright © 1991 by Patricia Lauber. Published by Orchard Books, an imprint of Scholastic Inc. Reprinted by permission of Scholastic Inc.

Scott Meredith Literary Agency: "Ghost of the Lagoon" by Armstrong Sperry. Copyright © 1980 by Armstrong Sperry. Reprinted by permission of the author and the author's agents, Scott Meredith Literary Agency, L.P.

Academy Chicago Publishers: Excerpt from *The Fun of It* by Amelia Earhart. Copyright © 1932 by Amelia Earhart Putnam. Reprinted by arrangement with Academy Chicago Publishers.

Viking Penguin: "Daring to Dream," adapted excerpt from *Taking Flight: My Story* by Vicki Van Meter with Dan Gutman. Copyright © 1995 by Vicki Van Meter and Dan Gutman. Used by permission of Viking Penguin, a division of Penguin Putnam Inc.

Times Newspapers: Excerpts from "A Life in the Day of Gary Paulsen" by Caroline Scott, *The Sunday Times,* November 15, 1998. Copyright © Times Newspapers Limited, 1998. Reprinted by permission of Times Newspapers Limited.

Simon & Schuster Books for Young Readers: Excerpt from *Woodsong* by Gary Paulsen. Copyright © 1990 Gary Paulsen. Reprinted with the permission of Simon & Schuster Books for Young Readers, an imprint of Simon & Schuster Children's Publishing Division.

Unit Two

Harcourt Brace & Company: "It Seems I Test People," from *When I Dance* by James Berry. Copyright © 1988 by James Berry. Reprinted by permission of Harcourt Brace & Company.

"Saguaro," from *Cactus Poems* by Frank Asch. Copyright © 1998 by Frank Asch. Reprinted by permission of Harcourt Brace & Company.

HarperCollins Publishers and Kids Can Press: "Growing Pains," from *Hey World, Here I Am!* by Jean Little. Text copyright © 1986 by Jean Little. Used by permission of HarperCollins Publishers and Kids Can Press Ltd., Toronto.

New York Times: Excerpts from "Laureate's Mission Is to Give Voice to a Nation of Poets" by Francis X. Clines, the *New York Times,* national edition, March 17, 1998. Copyright © 1998 by The New York Times Company. Reprinted by permission.

Penguin Books: "Beautiful, seen through holes" by Issa, from *The Penguin Book of Japanese Verse,* translated by Geoffrey Bownas and Anthony Thwaite (Penguin Books, 1964). Translation copyright © Geoffrey Bownas and Anthony Thwaite, 1964. Reproduced by permission of Penguin Books Ltd.

Raymond R. Patterson: "Glory, Glory . . . ," from *26 Ways of Looking at a Black Man and Other Poems* by Raymond R. Patterson. Copyright © 1969 by Raymond R. Patterson. Reprinted by permission of the author.

Don Congdon Associates: "All Summer in a Day" by Ray Bradbury, published in *Magazine of Fantasy and Science Fiction,* March 1954. Copyright © 1954, renewed 1982 by Ray Bradbury. Reprinted by permission of Don Congdon Associates, Inc.

Excerpt from "All Summer in a Day" by Ray Bradbury, published in *Magazine of Fantasy and Science Fiction,* March 1954. Copyright © 1954, renewed 1982 by Ray Bradbury. Reprinted by permission of Don Congdon Associates, Inc.

Scott Treimel New York: "Change," from *River Winding* by Charlotte Zolotow. Copyright © 1970 by Charlotte Zolotow. Reprinted by permission of Scott Treimel New York.

Excerpt from "Change," from *River Winding* by Charlotte Zolotow. Copyright © 1970 by Charlotte Zolotow. Reprinted by permission of Scott Treimel New York.

Simon & Schuster Books for Young Readers: "Chinatown," from *The Lost Garden* by Laurence Yep. Copyright © 1991 Laurence Yep. Reprinted with the permission of Simon & Schuster Books for Young Readers, an imprint of Simon & Schuster Children's Publishing Division.

"Oh Broom, Get to Work," from *The Invisible Thread* by Yoshiko Uchida. Copyright © 1991 Yoshiko Uchida. Reprinted with the permission of Simon & Schuster Books for Young Readers, an imprint of Simon & Schuster Children's Publishing Division.

Elizabeth Ellis: "Flowers and Freckle Cream" by Elizabeth Ellis, from *Best-Loved Stories Told at the National Storytelling Festival*, edited by Jimmy Neil Smith (National Storytelling Press, 1991). Copyright © Elizabeth Ellis. Reprinted by permission of the author.

Arte Público Press: "Same Song," from *Borders* by Pat Mora (Houston: Arte Público Press—University of Houston, 1986). Copyright © 1986 by Pat Mora. Reprinted with permission from the publisher.

HarperCollins Publishers: "Aaron's Gift," from *The Witch of Fourth Street and Other Stories* by Myron Levoy. Text copyright © 1972 by Myron Levoy. Used by permission of HarperCollins Publishers.

Statue of Liberty–Ellis Island Foundation: "Your Family's History Will Come Alive," from www.ellisisland.org, Web site designed and hosted by Vanguard InterActive, Inc. Copyright © 1998 The Statue of Liberty–Ellis Island Foundation, Inc. Reprinted by permission of The Statue of Liberty–Ellis Island Foundation, Inc.

Francisco Jiménez: "The Circuit" by Francisco Jiménez, *Arizona Quarterly,* Autumn 1973. Reprinted by permission of Francisco Jiménez.

BOA Editions: "the 1st," from *Good Woman: Poems and a Memoir, 1969–1980* by Lucille Clifton. Copyright © 1987 by Lucille Clifton. Reprinted with the permission of BOA Editions, Ltd., 260 East Avenue, Rochester, NY 14604.

Brandt & Brandt Literary Agents: "Western Wagons" by Stephen Vincent Benét, from *A Book of Americans* by Rosemary and Stephen Vincent Benét, first published by Holt, Rinehart & Winston, Inc. Copyright © 1937 by Rosemary and Stephen Vincent Benét, copyright renewed © 1964 by Thomas C. Benét, Stephanie B. Mahin, and Rachel Benét Lewis. Reprinted by permission of Brandt & Brandt Literary Agents, Inc.

Doubleday: "Night Journey" by Theodore Roethke, from *The Collected Poems of Theodore Roethke.* Copyright 1940 by Theodore Roethke. Used by permission of Doubleday, a division of Random House, Inc.

Scholastic: "Ta-Na-E-Ka" by Mary Whitebird, *Scholastic Voice,* December 13, 1973. Copyright © 1973 by Scholastic Inc. Reprinted by permission.

Unit Three

Houghton Mifflin Company: *The Legend of Damon and Pythias,* from *The Bag of Fire and Other Plays* by Fan Kissen. Copyright © 1964 by Houghton Mifflin Company, renewed © 1993 by John Kissen Heaslip. Reprinted by permission of Houghton Mifflin Company. All rights reserved.

Excerpts from *The Legend of Damon and Pythias,* from *The Bag of Fire and Other Plays* by Fan Kissen. Copyright © 1964 by Houghton Mifflin Company, renewed © 1993 by John Kissen Heaslip. Reprinted by permission of Houghton Mifflin Company. All rights reserved.

Andre Deutsch Ltd.: "Cricket in the Road," from *Cricket in the Road* by Michael Anthony. Copyright © 1973 by Michael Anthony. Reprinted by permission of Andre Deutsch Ltd., London.

Marian Reiner, Literary Agent: "Mean Song," from *There Is No Rhyme for Silver* by Eve Merriam. Copyright © 1962, 1990 Eve Merriam. Used by permission of Marian Reiner, Literary Agent.

Dallas Morning News: Excerpt from "Young Peer Mediators' Effectiveness Is Hard to Dispute" by Janis Leibs Dworkis. © 1977 by Janis Leibs Dworkis. Reprinted with permission of the author.

Harold Ober Associates: "The Quarrel" by Eleanor Farjeon, from *Eleanor Farjeon's Poems for Children,* first published by Lippincott, 1951. Copyright © 1951 by Eleanor Farjeon. Reprinted by permission of Harold Ober Associates Incorporated.

Lescher & Lescher: "The Southpaw" by Judith Viorst, from *Free to Be . . . You and Me,* edited by Christopher Cerf et al. Copyright © 1974 by Judith Viorst. This usage granted by permission of Lescher & Lescher, Ltd.

Literary Estate of May Swenson: "Analysis of Baseball" by May Swenson, from *American Sports Poems* (Orchard Books, 1988). Used with permission of the Literary Estate of May Swenson.

HarperCollins Publishers: "Abd al-Rahman Ibrahima," from *Now Is Your Time!: The African-American Struggle for Freedom* by Walter Dean Myers. Copyright © 1991 by Walter Dean Myers. Used by permission of HarperCollins Publishers.

Excerpts from "Abd al-Rahman Ibrahima," from *Now Is Your Time!: The African-American Struggle for Freedom* by Walter Dean Myers. Copyright © 1991 by Walter Dean Myers. Used by permission of HarperCollins Publishers.

National Geographic Society: Excerpt from "Technology Testers" by Jane R. McGoldrick, *National Geographic World,* March 1996. Reprinted by permission of the National Geographic Society.

F. E. Albi: "Street Corner Flight" by Norma Landa Flores, from *Sighs and Songs of Aztlan,* edited by F. E. Albi and J. G. Nieto. Copyright © 1975 by F. E. Albi and J. G. Nieto. Reprinted by permission of F. E. Albi, editor.

Alfred A. Knopf: "Words Like Freedom," from *Collected Poems* by Langston Hughes. Copyright © 1994 by the Estate of Langston Hughes. Reprinted by permission of Alfred A. Knopf, Inc., a division of Random House, Inc.

Dell Publishing: "The School Play" by Gary Soto, from *Funny You Should Ask,* edited by David Gale. Copyright © 1992 by Gary Soto. Used by permission of Dell Publishing, a division of Random House, Inc.

Harcourt Brace & Company: "Ode to My Library," from *Neighborhood Odes* by Gary Soto. Copyright © 1992 by Gary Soto. Reprinted by permission of Harcourt Brace & Company.

Persea Books: Excerpts from "Who Is Your Reader?," from *The Effects of Knut Hamsun on a Fresno Boy: Recollections and Short Essays* by Gary Soto. Copyright © 1983, 1988, 2000 by Gary Soto. Reprinted by permission of Persea Books, Inc., New York.

Gary Soto and BookStop Literary Agency: "The Jacket," from *Small Faces: Stories* by Gary Soto. Text copyright © 1986 by Gary Soto. Used with permission of the author and BookStop Literary Agency. All rights reserved.

Unit Four

Random House Children's Books and Brandt & Brandt Literary Agents: "Lob's Girl," from *A Whisper in the Night* by Joan Aiken. Delacorte Press. Copyright © 1984 by Joan Aiken Enterprises. Reprinted by permission of Random House Children's Books, a division of Random House, Inc., and Brandt & Brandt Literary Agents, Inc.

National Geographic Society: Excerpts from "Animals to the Rescue" by Laura Daily, *National Geographic World,* September 1997. Reprinted by permission of the National Geographic Society.

Little, Brown and Company: "My First Dive with the Dolphins," from *The Dolphins and Me* by Don C. Reed. Text copyright © 1988 by Don C. Reed. Illustrations © 1988 by Pamela & Walter Carroll. By permission of Little, Brown and Company.

Curtis Brown, Ltd.: "A bugler named Dougal MacDougal," from *Primrose Path* by Ogden Nash. Copyright © 1935 by Ogden Nash, renewed. Reprinted by permission of Curtis Brown, Ltd.

Simon & Schuster Books for Young Readers: "Something Told the Wild Geese," from *Branches Green* by Rachel Field. Copyright 1934 Macmillan Publishing Company, copyright renewed © 1962 Arthur S. Pederson. Reprinted with the permission of Simon & Schuster Books for Young Readers, an imprint of Simon & Schuster Children's Publishing Division.

Henry Holt and Company: "Questioning Faces" by Robert Frost, from *The Poetry of Robert Frost,* edited by Edward Connery Lathem. Copyright © 1962 by Robert Frost. Copyright © 1969 by Henry Holt and Company, Inc. Reprinted by permission of Henry Holt and Company, Inc.

HarperCollins Publishers: "Zlateh the Goat," from *Zlateh the Goat and Other Stories* by Isaac Bashevis Singer. Text copyright © 1966 by Isaac Bashevis Singer. Used by permission of HarperCollins Publishers.

"Chang McTang McQuarter Cat," from *You Read to Me, I'll Read to You* by John Ciardi. Copyright © 1962 by John Ciardi. Used by permission of HarperCollins Publishers.

"Where the Sidewalk Ends," from *Where the Sidewalk Ends* by Shel Silverstein. Copyright © 1974 by Evil Eye Music, Inc. Used by permission of HarperCollins Publishers.

Samuel French, Inc.: *The Phantom Tollbooth* by Susan Nanus and Norton Juster. Copyright © 1977 by Susan Nanus and Norton Juster. Reprinted by permission of Samuel French, Inc. **Caution:** Professionals and amateurs are hereby warned that *The Phantom Tollbooth,* being fully protected under the copyright laws of the United States of America, the British Commonwealth countries, including Canada, and the other countries of the Copyright Union, is subject to a royalty. All rights, including professional, amateur, motion picture, recitation, public reading, radio, television and cable broadcasting, and the rights of translation into foreign languages, are strictly reserved. Any inquiry regarding the availability of performance rights, or the purchase of individual copies of the authorized acting edition, must be directed to Samuel French, Inc., 45 West 25th Street, New York, NY 10010, with other locations in Hollywood and Toronto, Canada.

Quotes from *The Phantom Tollbooth* by Susan Nanus and Norton Juster. Copyright © 1977 by Susan Nanus and Norton Juster. Reprinted by permission of Samuel French, Inc. **Caution:** Professionals and amateurs are hereby warned that *The Phantom Tollbooth,* being fully protected under the copyright laws of the United States of America, the British Commonwealth countries, including Canada, and the other countries of the Copyright Union, is subject to a royalty. All rights, including professional, amateur, motion picture, recitation, public reading, radio, television and cable broadcasting, and the rights of translation into foreign languages, are strictly reserved. Any inquiry regarding the availability of performance rights, or the purchase of individual copies of the authorized acting edition, must be directed to Samuel French, Inc., 45 West 25th Street, New York, NY 10010, with other locations in Hollywood and Toronto, Canada.

Houghton Mifflin Company and HarperCollins Publishers, London: "All That Is Gold," from *The Fellowship of the Ring* by J.R.R. Tolkien. Copyright © 1954, 1965 by J.R.R. Tolkien, copyright © renewed 1982 by Christopher R.

Tolkien, Michael H. R. Tolkien, John F. R. Tolkien, and Priscilla M. A. R. Tolkien. Reprinted by permission of Houghton Mifflin Company and HarperCollins Publishers, London. All rights reserved.

Jack Prelutsky: "A silly young fellow named Ben" by Jack Prelutsky. Copyright © 1989 by Jack Prelutsky. Reprinted by permission of the author.

Virginia Hamilton: "Under the Back Porch" by Virginia Hamilton. Copyright © 1992, 1999 by Virginia Hamilton Adoff. Used by permission of the author.

Ralph M. Vicinanza, Ltd.: "The Fun They Had," from *Earth Is Room Enough: Science Fiction Tales of Our Own Planet* by Isaac Asimov. Copyright © 1957 by Isaac Asimov. Published by permission of the Estate of Isaac Asimov, c/o Ralph M. Vicinanza, Ltd.

Bilingual Press: "The Sand Castle," from *Weeping Woman: La Llorona and Other Stories* by Alma Luz Villanueva. Copyright © 1994 by Alma Luz Villanueva. Reprinted by permission of Bilingual Press/Editorial Bilingüe, Arizona State University, Tempe, Arizona.

Time: Excerpt from "Home on an Icy Planet," *Time for Kids,* March 13, 1998. Copyright © 1998 Time Inc. Reprinted by permission.

Matthew Ryan Keenan: Excerpt from "Seolforis" by Matthew Ryan Keenan. Copyright © 1998 by Matthew Ryan Keenan. Reprinted by permission of the author.

Unit Five

Keith Ross Leckie: *Words on a Page* by Keith Ross Leckie. Reprinted by permission of the author.

Dutton Children's Books: "Bringing the Prairie Home" by Patricia MacLachlan, from *The Big Book for Our Planet,* edited by Ann Durell, Jean Craighead George, and Katherine Paterson. Copyright © 1993 by Dutton Children's Books. Used by permission of Dutton Children's Books, a division of Penguin Putnam Inc.

Villard Books: Excerpt from *All I Really Need to Know I Learned in Kindergarten* by Robert L. Fulghum. Copyright © 1986, 1988 by Robert L. Fulghum. Reprinted by permission of Villard Books, a division of Random House, Inc.

University of Texas Press: "Sonnet 52," from *100 Love Sonnets* by Pablo Neruda, translated by Stephen Tapscott. Copyright © Pablo Neruda 1959 and Fundación Pablo Neruda. Copyright © 1986 by the University of Texas Press. Reprinted by permission of the University of Texas Press.

Agencia Literaria Carmen Balcells: "Soneto 52," from *Cien sonetos de amor* by Pablo Neruda. Copyright © Pablo Neruda 1959 and Fundación Pablo Neruda. Reprinted by permission of Agencia Literaria Carmen Balcells, S.A.

Editions Gallimard and London Management: "How to Paint the Portrait of a Bird" by Jacques Prévert, translated by Paul Dehn. Copyright © Editions Gallimard, 1949. Reprinted by permission of Editions Gallimard and London Management, Ltd., on behalf of the estate of Paul Dehn.

Michael Manning: "Flip Out!," adapted from "Flip Books" by Michael Manning. Copyright © 1986 by Michael Manning. Reprinted by permission of the author.

Jane Dystel Literary Management: "The Scribe," from *Guests in the Promised Land* by Kristin Hunter, published by Avon Books. Copyright © 1968 by Kristin E. Lattany. Reprinted by permission of Jane Dystel Literary Management, Inc.

Harold Ober Associates: "Crow Call" by Lois Lowry, first published in *Redbook Magazine*, December 1975. Copyright © 1975 by Lois Lowry. Reprinted by permission of Harold Ober Associates Incorporated.

American Library Association: Excerpt from Newbery Award acceptance speech by Lois Lowry, June 1994. The Newbery Medal is awarded annually by the Association for Library Service to Children and is a trademark of the American Library Association. Reprinted by permission of the American Library Association.

Houghton Mifflin Company: Text excerpts from *Looking Back: A Book of Memories* by Lois Lowry. Copyright © 1998 by Lois Lowry. Reprinted by permission of Houghton Mifflin Company. All rights reserved.

Professional Publishing Services Company: "The Dog of Pompeii," from *The Donkey of God* by Louis Untermeyer. Published by arrangement with the Estate of Louis Untermeyer, Norma Anchin Untermeyer, c/o Professional Publishing Services Company. This permission is expressly granted by Laurence S. Untermeyer.

Quotes from "The Dog of Pompeii," from *The Donkey of God* by Louis Untermeyer. Published by arrangement with the Estate of Louis Untermeyer, Norma Anchin Untermeyer, c/o Professional Publishing Services Company. This permission is expressly granted by Laurence S. Untermeyer.

Los Angeles Times: Excerpt from "Remains of House in Oregon May Be Most Ancient in U.S." by Thomas H. Maugh II, *Los Angeles Times,* October 10, 1998. Copyright © 1998 Los Angeles Times Syndicate. Reprinted by permission.

Random House: Excerpt from *Lost Worlds* by Anne Terry White. Copyright © 1941 by Random House, Inc., copyright renewed 1969 by Anne Terry White. Reprinted by permission of Random House, Inc.

Dudley Randall: "Ancestors," from *After the Killing* by Dudley Randall. Copyright © 1973 by Dudley Randall. Reprinted by permission of the Estate of Dudley Randall.

Henry Morrison, Inc.: Excerpt from "The First Emperor," from *The Tomb Robbers* by Daniel Cohen. Copyright © 1980 by Daniel Cohen. Reprinted by permission of the author and his agents, Henry Morrison, Inc.

Orchard Books and Stoddart Publishing Company: *Beethoven Lives Upstairs* by Barbara Nichol, illustrated by Scott Cameron. Text copyright © 1993 by Classical Productions for Children Limited. Published by Orchard Books, an imprint of Scholastic Inc. Reprinted by permission of Scholastic Inc. and Stoddart Publishing Company Ltd.

Unit Six

Greenwillow Books: "The Boy Who Flew," from *The Robber Baby: Stories from the Greek Myths* by Anne Rockwell. Copyright © 1994 by Anne Rockwell. Reprinted by permission of Greenwillow Books, a division of William Morrow & Company, Inc.

Houghton Mifflin Company: "Arachne," from *Greek Myths* by Olivia E. Coolidge. Copyright © 1949, renewed 1977 by Olivia E. Coolidge. Reprinted by permission of Houghton Mifflin Company. All rights reserved.

Scholastic: "The Story of Ceres and Proserpina," from *Favorite Greek Myths,* retold by Mary Pope Osborne. Copyright © 1989 by Mary Pope Osborne. Reprinted by permission of Scholastic Inc.

"Why Monkeys Live in Trees," from *How Many Spots Does a Leopard Have? and Other Tales* by Julius Lester. Copyright © 1989 by Julius Lester. Reprinted by permission of Scholastic Inc.

Curbstone Press: "The Disobedient Child," from *The Bird Who Cleans the World and Other Mayan Fables* by Victor Montejo, translated by Wallace Kaufman (Curbstone Press, 1991). Copyright © 1991 by Victor Montejo. Translation copyright © 1991 by Wallace Kaufman. Reprinted with permission of Curbstone Press. Distributed by Consortium.

Clarion Books/Houghton Mifflin Company: "The Bamboo Beads," from *A Wave in Her Pocket* by Lynn Joseph. Copyright © 1991 by Lynn Joseph. Reprinted by permission of Clarion Books/Houghton Mifflin Company. All rights reserved.

Clarion Books/Houghton Mifflin Company and The Bodley Head: "The Living Kuan-yin," from *Sweet and Sour: Tales from China* by Carol Kendall and Yao-wen Li. Copyright © 1978 by Carol Kendall and Yao-wen Li. Reprinted by permission of Clarion Books/Houghton Mifflin Company and The Bodley Head, Ltd., London. All rights reserved.

Viking Penguin: *In the Land of Small Dragon* by Dang Manh Kha, as told to Ann Nolan Clark. Copyright © 1979 by Ann Nolan Clark. Used by permission of Viking Penguin, a division of Penguin Putnam Inc.

Doubleday: "King Thrushbeard," from *Grimms' Tales for Young and Old* by Jakob and Wilhelm Grimm, translated by Ralph Manheim. Copyright © 1977 by Ralph Manheim. Used by permission of Doubleday, a division of Random House, Inc.

Frederick Warne Books: "The Legend of the Hummingbird," from *Once in Puerto Rico* by Pura Belpré. Copyright © 1973 by Pura Belpré. Used by permission of Frederick Warne Books, a division of Penguin Putnam Inc.

Linda Goss: "The Frog Who Wanted to Be a Singer" by Linda Goss, from *Talk That Talk: An Anthology of African-American Storytelling*, edited by Linda Goss and Marian E. Barnes. Copyright © 1983 by Linda Goss. Reprinted by permission of the author.

BridgeWater Books: "Where the Girl Rescued Her Brother," from *The Girl Who Married the Moon*, retold by Joseph Bruchac and Gayle Ross. Text copyright © 1994 by Joseph Bruchac and Gayle Ross. Reprinted by permission of BridgeWater Books, an imprint of Troll Communications L.L.C.

Art Credits

Cover

Illustration copyright © 1999 Gary Overacre.

Front Matter

ix School Division, Houghton Mifflin Company; **x** Copyright © Reggie Holladay/SIS; **xi** Courtesy of Flannery Literary; **xii** *Spring Fair, Old Westbury Gardens*, David Peikon. Acrylic on canvas, 30" x 40". Copyright © 1998, courtesy of The Mark Humphrey Gallery, Southampton, New York; **xiv** *Pushball*, Pavel Kusnetzov. Tretiakov Gallery, Moscow, Russia/SuperStock. Copyright © Estate of Pavel Kusnetzov/Licensed by VAGA, New York; **xv** Courtesy of Gary Soto; **xvi** *Party Animals* (1995), Julia Lucich. Pastel over acrylic, 17" x 22"; **xviii** *top* Copyright © Philip & Karen Smith/Tony Stone Images; *bottom* Karen Ahola/Houghton Mifflin Company; **xx–xxi** Photos by Gordon Lewis; **S2–S7** Photos by Sharon Hoogstraten; **S8** *right* Doric pillars on Temple of Zeus Nemea, Peloponnisos, Greece. Copyright © M. Thonig/H. Armstrong Roberts; **S12** Vittoriano Rastelli/Corbis; **S13** *background* Photo by Sharon Hoogstraten; *top* Vince Streano/Corbis; *center* Corbis-Bettmann; *bottom* Farrell Grehan/Corbis; **S14** Vittoriano Rastelli/Corbis; **S16** Vince Streano/Corbis; **S18** *top* Corbis-Bettmann; *bottom* Farrell Grehan/Corbis; **S19** *left* Corbis-Bettmann; *top right* Mimmo Jodice/Corbis; *bottom right* Vanni Archive/Corbis.

Unit One

18 *background*, **20** Copyright © PhotoDisc; **21** *left* School Division, Houghton Mifflin Company; *right* From *Hatchet* by Gary Paulsen. Jacket painting by Neil Waldman. Copyright © 1987 Bradbury Press. Reprinted with the permission of Simon & Schuster Books for Young Readers, an imprint of Simon & Schuster Children's Publishing Division; **23** *left to right*, *Wee Maureen* (1926), Robert Henri. Oil on canvas, 24" x 20". Courtesy of the Pennsylvania Academy of the Fine Arts, Philadelphia. Gift of Mrs. Herbert Cameron Morris. Acc. no. 1962.17.1; *Tahitian Woman and Boy* (1889), Paul Gauguin. Oil on canvas, 37¼" x 24¼". Norton Simon Art Foundation, Pasadena, California, gift of Mr. Norton Simon, 1976; *Bobby* (ca. 1943), Jack Humphrey. Oil on masonite. Copyright © The Humphrey Estate. From the collection of John Corey; *Siri* (1970), Andrew Wyeth. Tempera on panel, 30" x 30½". Collection of the Brandywine River Museum, Chadds Ford, Pennsylvania. Copyright © 1970 Andrew Wyeth; **24** *Station Platform*, Dong Kingman. Hirshhorn Museum and Sculpture Garden, Smithsonian Institution, gift of Joseph H. Hirshhorn. Photo by John Tennant; **25** RMIP/Richard Haynes; **27** Detail of *Cake Window (Seven Cakes)* (1970–1976), Wayne Thiebaud. Copyright © Wayne Thiebaud/Licensed by VAGA, New York; **30** Courtesy of Lois Lowry; **32** Edge Productions; **33** AP/Wide World Photos; **35** Archive Photos; **36** Courtesy Smoky Mountain Knife Works; **47** Copyright © Richard Howard Photography; **49** Courtesy of Brad Kellogg; **66** Coppelia Kahn; **67** *background* Copyright © Eric A. Wessmann/Stock Boston/PNI; *inset right* Copyright © Jose Fuste Raga/The Stock Market; **68–69** *background* Copyright © Hugh Sitton/Tony Stone Images; **78** Willy Leon; **88** George Janoff; **95** *top* Copyright © PhotoDisc; *bottom* Courtesy of Flannery Literary; **96** *left* From *Summer of Fire* by Patricia

Company.

Unit Two

189 *far left* From *Poems for Youth* by Emily Dickinson. Courtesy of Little, Brown and Company; *left* From *Final Harvest* by Emily Dickinson. Courtesy of Little, Brown and Company; *center* From *Neighborhood Odes* by Gary Soto, illustrated by David Diaz. Illustrations copyright © 1992 by Harcourt, Inc. Reproduced by permission of the publisher; *right* From *Where the Sidewalk Ends* by Shel Silverstein. Copyright © 1974 Evil-Eye Music, Inc. Used by permission of HarperCollins Publishers; **190** *left* From *Nonsense Poems* by Edward Lear. Copyright © 1994 Dover Children's Thrift Classics; *center* From *Shakespeare's Sonnets*, edited by Martin Seymour-Smith. Copyright © 1963 Heinemann, London. Reprinted by permission of Heinemann Educational Publishers, a division of Reed Educational & Professional Publishing Ltd.; *right* Reprinted with permission from *Japanese Haiku*, translated by Peter Beilenson. Copyright © 1955–1956 by the Peter Pauper Press; **192** *Freedom Now,* Charles White. Collection of the California African-American Museum of Art and Culture, Los Angeles. Courtesy Heritage Gallery, Los Angeles; **193** RMIP/Richard Haynes; **194** By permission of The Houghton Library, Harvard University (MS Am 1118.3 (35). Copyright © The President and Fellows of Harvard College; **199** AP/Wide World Photos; **200** *top* Amherst College Library, Archives and Special Collections; *bottom right* Guelph (Ontario) *Daily Mercury*; **201, 202** AP/Wide World Photos; **204** Courtesy Paul M. Katz; **207** Detail of incense wrapper (Edo period, Japan; 17th–18th centuries) attributed to Ogata Korin. Wrapper mounted on hanging scroll, ink and color on gold-ground paper, 33 cm 24.1 cm. The Art Institute of Chicago, Russell Tyson Purchase Fund (1966.470). Photograph copyright © 1994 The Art Institute of Chicago. All rights reserved; **208** *top* Heibonsha Ltd., Japan; *bottom left* Lynn Saville; *bottom right* New Orleans Museum of Art: Gift of an Anonymous Donor; **209** NASA; **212, 213** *backgrounds* Copyright © 1994 Thomas Wiewandt; **213** *foreground* Detail of *Wee Maureen* (1926), Robert Henri. Oil on canvas, 24" × 20". Courtesy of the Pennsylvania Academy of the Fine Arts, Philadelphia. Gift of Mrs. Herbert Cameron Morris. Acc. no. 1962.17.1; **217** Coronet/MTI Films, St. Louis, Missouri; **218** AP/Wide World Photos; **229** Photo by K. Yep; **234–235** Copyright © 1999 Christie's Images, Ltd./PNI; **243** School Division, Houghton Mifflin Company; **244** Detail of *Wee Maureen* (1926), Robert Henri. Oil on canvas, 24" × 20". Courtesy of the Pennsylvania Academy of the Fine Arts, Philadelphia. Gift of Mrs. Herbert Cameron Morris. Acc. no. 1962.17.1; **245** *center, Bobby* (ca. 1943), Jack Humphrey. Oil on masonite. Copyright © The Humphrey Estate. From the collection of John Corey; *right* Detail of *The Case for More School Days,* C. F. Payne. First appeared in the *Atlantic Monthly*; **246** *Twilight in the Wilderness,* Frederic Edwin Church (1826–1900). Oil on canvas, 101.6 cm 162.6 cm. Copyright © 1999 The Cleveland Museum of Art, Mr. and Mrs. William H. Marlatt Fund, 1965.233; **247** RMIP/Richard Haynes; **248** Erdelyi Photo Purchased/NGS Image Collection; **250, 252, 255** Photos by Sharon Hoogstraten; **260** Copyright © Edwin Schlossberg, Inc./The Statue of Liberty–Ellis Island Foundation, Inc.; **261** The Statue of Liberty–Ellis Island Foundation, Inc.; **262** Copyright © Edwin Schlossberg, Inc./The Statue of Liberty–Ellis Island Foundation, Inc.; **274** Courtesy of the University of Santa Clara (California); **275** Courtesy of the Pacific School of Religion; **276** Photo by Sharon Hoogstraten; **283** Copyright © June Finfer/Filmedia, Ltd.; **284** *top right* Copyright © Jim Pickerell/PNI; *left, center* National Archives; *right* Woodriver Gallery/PNI; **288** *right* UPI/Corbis-Bettmann; **290** *background,* **291–296** From *Dancing Colors* by C. J. Brafford and Laine Thom. Copyright © 1992, published by Chronicle Books, San Francisco; **304** *Spring Fair, Old Westbury Gardens,*

David Peikon. Acrylic on canvas, 30" x 40". Copyright © 1998, courtesy of the Mark Humphrey Gallery, Southampton, New York; 306, 307 School Division, Houghton Mifflin Company.

Unit Three

317 *left to right* Heinemann Publishers; Copyright © Plays, Inc.; From *The Phantom Tollbooth* by Norton Juster, illustrated by Jules Feiffer. Cover illustration copyright © 1961 and renewed 1989 by Jules Feiffer. Reprinted by permission of Random House, Inc.; Movie Still Archives; *Playbill*® is a registered trademark of Playbill, Inc. All rights reserved. Used by permission; **319** *left* Detail of Chiron the centaur teaching Achilles to play the lyre (first–third century A.D.). Roman fresco from Pompeii, Museo Archeologico Nazionale, Naples, Italy. Photo copyright © Erich Lessing/Art Resource, New York; *right* Detail of statue of Diadoumenos (440 B.C.), unknown artist. Roman copy of Greek original, pentelic marble. The Metropolitan Museum of Art, Fletcher Fund, 1925 (25.78.56). Copyright © The Metropolitan Museum of Art; **320** *top left, bottom left* From *The Phantom Tollbooth* by Norton Juster, illustrated by Jules Feiffer. Illustrations copyright © 1961 and renewed 1989 by Jules Feiffer. Reprinted by permission of Random House, Inc.; *right* Copyright © 1995 Natural Photography, Ted Sacher; **321** RMIP/Richard Haynes; **322** *background* Copyright © Robert Frerck/The Stock Market; *top* Copyright © R. Sheridan/Ancient Art and Architecture Collection; *bottom* Ru Dien-Ren/Art Point Studio; **331** *top* Detail of statue of Diadoumenos (440 B.C.), unknown artist. Roman copy of Greek original, pentelic marble. The Metropolitan Museum of Art, Fletcher Fund, 1925 (25.78.56). Copyright © The Metropolitan Museum of Art; *bottom* School Division, Houghton Mifflin Company; **334** Photo by Sharon Hoogstraten; **338** Siv Brun Lie; **339** Bill Heyes; **340–341** Beatriz Terrazas/The Dallas Morning News; **347** *left* Courtesy of Henry Z. Walck, Inc.; *right* Negative no. 31415 copyright © Collection of The New-York Historical Society; **349** Copyright © Robb Helfrick/The Picture Cube/Index Stock; **351, 353** *top* Sarah Goodman; **353** *bottom* AP/Wide World Photos; **354** Sarah Goodman; **355–357** RMIP/Richard Haynes; **361** Courtesy of Gary Soto; **362** From *The Story of My Life* by Helen Keller. Copyright. Used by permission of Bantam Books, a division of Random House, Inc.; **363** *Mecklenberg County: High Cotton Mother and Child* (1978), Romare Bearden. Copyright © Romare Bearden Foundation/Licensed by VAGA, New York; **364** RMIP/Richard Haynes; **365** *top* Kneeling figure, Djenne/Dogon, Mali. Private collection/Heini Schneebeli/Bridgeman Art Library, London/New York; *center right* Chris Costello; *bottom* From *Travels and Discoveries in North and Central Africa* by Heinrich Barth. Published 1857–1858; **367, 369, 370, 372, 375** Jennifer Carney; **382** *background* Copyright © Telegraph Colour Library/FPG International; **382** *inset,* **384** Brown Brothers; **387** Courtesy of the American Foundation for the Blind, Helen Keller Archives; **388, 390** Copyright © Richard Nowitz; **392–393** Copyright © Leland Bobbe/Tony Stone Images; **396** National Portrait Gallery/Art Resources; **398** *top, center left, bottom right* Courtesy of Gary Soto; *bottom left* Corbis-Bettmann; **399** *top, bottom left* Courtesy of Gary Soto; *bottom center* Courtesy of the Jimmy Carter Library; *bottom right* Book cover from *Baseball in April and Other Stories.* Copyright © 1990 by Gary Soto. Illustration by Barry Root. Reproduced by permission of Harcourt, Inc.; **400–401** Corbis-Bettmann; **400** *top,* **401** *top* Courtesy of Gary Soto; **403** Karen Berntsen; **414** Detail of *Rainbow.* Copyright © Synthia Saint James; *bottom* A.K.G., Berlin/SuperStock; **416** *top* Detail of *Shared Hope* (1995), Paul Botello. Copyright © Social and Political Art Resource Center. Photo copyright © Robin Dunitz and James Prigoff from "Painting the Towns"; *bottom* Courtesy of Gary Soto; **417** *Shared Hope* (1995), Paul Botello. Copyright ©

Social and Political Art Resource Center. Photo copyright © Robin Dunitz and James Prigoff from "Painting the Towns"; **419–421** RMIP/Richard Haynes; **426** Courtesy of Gary Soto; **427** *top* Copyright © 1992 by Gary Soto. All rights reserved. From *The Pool Party*, provided by Gary Soto; *bottom* RMIP/Richard Haynes; **428** *top* Janjaap Dekker; *bottom left* From *Baseball in April and Other Stories.* Copyright © 1990 by Gary Soto. Illustration by Barry Root. Reproduced by permission of Harcourt, Inc. Illustration copyright © Alan Mazzetti; *bottom right* From *Taking Sides.* Copyright © 1991 by Gary Soto, reproduced by permission of Harcourt, Inc.; **429** *left to right* From *Pacific Crossing.* Copyright © 1992 by Gary Soto, reproduced by permission of Harcourt, Inc.; From *The Pool Party* by Gary Soto. Illustrations by Robert Casilla. Copyright © 1993. Used by permission of Random House Children's Books, a division of Random House, Inc.; From *Local News.* Copyright © 1998 by Gary Soto, reproduced by permission of Harcourt Inc.; From *A Fire in My Hands* by Gary Soto. Illustration by James M. Cardillo. Jacket illustration copyright © 1990 by Scholastic, Inc. Used by permission; **436** *Pushball*, Pavel Kusnetzov. Tretiakov Gallery, Moscow, Russia/SuperStock. Copyright © Estate of Pavel Kusnetzov/Licensed by VAGA, New York; **438–439** School Division, Houghton Mifflin Company.

Unit Four

444 *The Old and the New Year* (1953), Pablo Picasso. Musée d'Art et d'Histoire, St. Denis, France. Giraudon/Art Resource, New York. Copyright © 2000 Estate of Pablo Picasso/Artists Rights Society (ARS), New York; **445** Courtesy of the American Foundation for the Blind, Helen Keller Archives; **446** RMIP/Richard Haynes; **458** Detail of *Maggie* (1991), J. Rubin. Watercolor on paper; **462** Copyright © Dan Cooper/Loveland Reporter Herald; **463** Copyright © Kevin Horan/Chicago; **464** Copyright © Paula Lerner/Aurora; **465** *top* Copyright © Francois Gohier/Photo Researchers, Inc.; *center* Copyright © VCG/FPG International; **466** *background* Copyright © Leland Bobbe/Tony Stone Images; *inset* Copyright © Bill Wood/Australian Picture Library; **467, 468** Copyright © Leland Bobbe/Tony Stone Images; **469** Al Giddings Images, Inc.; **470** Copyright © Norbert Wu/Tony Stone Images; **471, 472** Copyright © Leland Bobbe/Tony Stone Images; **475** Marine World Africa USA; **476** Copyright © Jim Roetzel/Dembinsky Photo Associates; **480** *left* AP/Wide World Photos; *right* Corbis-Bettmann; **489** Detail *of I and the Village* (1911), Marc Chagall. Oil on canvas, 75⅝" x 59⅝" (192.1 cm x 151.4 cm). The Museum of Modern Art, New York. Mrs. Simon Guggenheim Fund. Photograph copyright © 2001 The Museum of Modern Art, New York; **490** Corbis/Robert Maass; **492–493, 494** Copyright © Mark Petersen/Tony Stone Images; **496** Copyright © Renee Lyon/Tony Stone Images; **497** *Rudyard Kipling*, Sir Edward Burne-Jones. National Portrait Gallery, London/SuperStock; **507** Copyright © John Lenker/Pictor; **508** Copyright © 1994 Thomas Weiwandt; **509** *left* Illustration by Peter Newell, 1902. Photo copyright © 1995 Nawrocki Stock Photo, Inc./Historical. All rights reserved; *right* From *Alice's Adventures in Wonderland* by Lewis Carroll. Illustration by Sir John Tenniel, 1865; **510** Copyright © 1995 Natural Photography, Ted Sacher; **511** RMIP/Richard Haynes; **512** *left* Copyright © Matthias Kulka/The Stock Market; *right* Library of Congress; **513** Copyright © 1995 Natural Photography, Ted Sacher; **514–516** Illustrations by Bruce Roberts; **519** From *The Phantom Tollbooth* by Norton Juster, illustrated by Jules Feiffer. Illustrations copyright © 1961 and renewed 1989 by Jules Feiffer. Reprinted by permission of Random House, Inc.; **522, 527** *bottom* Copyright © 1995 Natural Photography, Ted Sacher; **529** From *The Phantom Tollbooth* by Norton Juster, illustrated by Jules Feiffer. Illustrations copyright © 1961 and renewed 1989 by Jules Feiffer. Reprinted by permission of Random House, Inc.; **532** Illustration by Bruce Roberts; **537** *top* *left* Copyright © 1995 Natural Photography, Ted Sacher; *top right* Courtesy of Michael Domino, Basic Theatre Company; **537** *bottom right* From *The Phantom Tollbooth* by Norton Juster, illustrated by Jules Feiffer. Illustrations copyright © 1961 and renewed 1989 by Jules Feiffer. Reprinted by permission of Random House, Inc.; **541** Copyright © 1995 Natural Photography, Ted Sacher; **544, 546** From *The Phantom Tollbooth* by Norton Juster, illustrated by Jules Feiffer. Illustrations Copyright © 1961 and renewed 1989 by Jules Feiffer. Reprinted by permission of Random House, Inc.; **548** Copyright © 1995 Natural Photography, Ted Sacher; **554** Copyright © 1989 Jim Gipe; **556–560** *background* School Division, Houghton Mifflin Company; **556** Detail of illustration by Peter Newell, 1902. Photo copyright © 1995 Nawrocki Stock Photo, Inc./Historical. All rights reserved; **560** *top* Copyright © Haruki Takada/Photonica; **562** *left* Corbis-Bettmann; *right* Archive Photos/Popperfoto; **563** From *A Book of Nonsense* by Edward Lear, 1846; **564–565** Illustrations by Tim Nihoff; **567** *top* Courtesy Little Brown & Co.; *bottom right* Courtesy of Jack Prelutsky; **569** *top* From *Where the Sidewalk Ends by Shel Silverstein.* Copyright © 1974 by Evil-Eye Music, Inc. Used by permission of HarperCollins Publishers; **570** Copyright © Robert Winslow/The Viesti Collection; **571** *top* Larry Moyer; *bottom* Copyright © 1999 Courtesy of Virginia Hamilton/Photo by Ron Rovtar; **572** *left* Copyright © John Lenker/Pictor; *right* Copyright © Vera Storman/Tony Stone Images; **573** Copyright © Geoff Tompkinson/Science Photo Library/Photo Researchers, Inc.; **574–575** Copyright © John Lenker/Pictor; **575** Copyright © P. Crowther & S. Carter/Tony Stone Images; **576** *top* Copyright © Dennis Hallinan/FPG International; *bottom* Copyright © P. Crowther & S. Carter/Tony Stone Images; **577** Copyright © Jay Coneyl/Tony Stone Images; **578** *left* Copyright © P. Crowther & S. Carter/Tony Stone Images; *right* Corbis/Alex Gotfryd–Peter C. Jones; **580–581** Copyright © Vera Storman/Tony Stone Images; **582–583** Copyright © John Beatty/Tony Stone Images; **584** *top* Courtesy of Alma Luz Villanueva; *bottom* Copyright © Garry Hunter/Tony Stone Images; **586** *top right* School Division, Houghton Mifflin Company; *center left* Copyright © Mass Illusions. Photo by Will McCoy/Rainbow; *bottom right* Richard Hutchings/PhotoEdit; **588, 590–591** Courtesy of the National Engineers Week Future City Competition; **598** *Party Animals* (1995), Julia Lucich. Pastel over acrylic, 17" x 22"; **600, 601** School Division, Houghton Mifflin Company.

Unit Five

610 Karen Ahola/Houghton Mifflin Company; **611** Copyright © 1995 Natural Photography, Ted Sacher; **612** Detail of illustration copyright © Michael Paraskevas; **613** RMIP/Richard Haynes; **614** *top right* Copyright © Jim Cammack/Black Star; *center left* FPG International; *bottom* Culver Pictures; **615** Detail of poster courtesy of Christopher Pullman, WGBH; **634** From *Words on a Page,* provided by Spirit Bay Productions, Ltd. Distributed by Beacon Films; **635** Courtesy of Keith Leckie; **637** Illustrations, Students of the Harlem School of the Arts. Copyright © 1994 by Oxford University Press, Inc. From *The Sweet and Sour Animal Book* by Langston Hughes. Used by permission of Oxford University Press, Inc.; **642** Dan Lamont; **644–647** Copyright © Hideharu Naito/Photonica; **649** *left* The Granger Collection, New York; *right* Copyright © Rapho Agence Photographique/Liaison Agency; **650** RMIP/Richard Haynes; **662** John I. Lattony; **664** *top* Karen Ahola/Houghton Mifflin Company; *center left, center right* Courtesy of Lois Lowry; *bottom right* Corbis-Bettmann; **665** *top left, top right* Courtesy of Lois Lowry; *center right* From *Number the Stars* by Lois Lowry. Copyright © 1989 by Lois Lowry. Used by permission of Dell Publishing, a division of Random House, Inc.; **665** *bottom right,* **666–667** *bottom background* Corbis-Bettmann; **666** *top right,*

Myra LeBendig Foshay Learning Center, Los Angeles Unified School District

Dan Manske Elmhurst Middle School, Oakland Unified School District

Joe Olague Language Arts Department Chairperson, Alder Middle School, Fontana School District

Pat Salo Sixth-Grade Village Leader, Hidden Valley Middle School, Escondido Elementary School District

FLORIDA

Judi Briant English Department Chairperson, Armwood High School, Hillsborough County School District

Beth Johnson Polk County English Supervisor, Polk County School District

Sharon Johnston Learning Resource Specialist, Evans High School, Orange County School District

Eileen Jones English Department Chairperson, Spanish River High School, Palm Beach County School District

Jan McClure Winter Park High School, Orange County School District

Wanza Murray English Department Chairperson (retired), Vero Beach Senior High School, Indian River City School District

Shirley Nichols Language Arts Curriculum Specialist Supervisor, Marion County School District

Debbie Nostro Ocoee Middle School, Orange County School District

Barbara Quinaz Assistant Principal, Horace Mann Middle School, Dade County School District

OHIO

Joseph Bako English Department Chairperson, Carl Shuler Middle School, Cleveland City School District

Deb Delisle Language Arts Department Chairperson, Ballard Brady Middle School, Orange School District

Ellen Geisler English/Language Arts Department Chairperson, Mentor Senior High School, Mentor School District

Dr. Mary Gove English Department Chairperson, Shaw High School, East Cleveland School District

Loraine Hammack Executive Teacher of the English Department, Beachwood High School, Beachwood City School District

Sue Nelson Shaw High School, East Cleveland School District

Mary Jane Reed English Department Chairperson, Solon High School, Solon City School District

Nancy Strauch English Department Chairperson, Nordonia High School, Nordonia Hills City School District

Ruth Vukovich Hubbard High School, Hubbard Exempted Village School District

TEXAS

Gloria Anderson Language Arts Department Chairperson, Campbell Middle School, Cypress Fairbanks Independent School District

Gwen Ferguson Assistant Principal, Northwood Middle School, North Forest Independent School District

Rebecca Hadavi Parkland Middle School, Ysleta Independent School District

Patricia Jackson Pearce Middle School, Austin Independent School District

Sandy Mattox Coppell Middle School North, Coppell Independent School District

Adrienne C. Myers Foster Middle School, Longview Independent School District

Pam Potts Clute Intermediate School, Brazosport Independent School District

Frank Westermann Jackson Middle School, North East Independent School District

Bessie B. Wilson W.E. Greiner Middle School, Dallas Independent School District

Manuscript Reviewers *(continued)*

Linda C. Dahl National Mine Middle School, Ishpeming, Michigan

Mary Jo Eustis Language Arts Coordinator, Lodi Unified School District, Lodi, California

Anita Graham Muirlands Middle School, LaJolla, California

Carol Hammons English Department Chair, Washington Middle School, Salinas, California

Shirley Herzog Reading Department Coordinator, Fairfield Middle School, Fairfield, Ohio

Ellen Kamimoto Ahwahnee Middle School, Fresno, California

Maryann Lyons Literacy Specialist and Mentor Teacher, San Francisco Unified School District, San Francisco, California

Karis MacDonnell Dario Middle School, Miami, Florida

Bonnie J. Mansell Downey Adult School, Downey, California

Martha Mitchell Memorial Middle School, Orlando, Florida

Ellen Moir GATE Coordinator and teacher, Twin Peaks Middle School, Poway, California

Nancy Nachman Landmark High School, Jacksonville, Florida

Katerine L. Noether Warren E. Hyde Middle School, Cupertino, California

Gloria Perry Bancroft Middle School, Long Beach, California

Karen Williams Perry English Department Chairperson, Kennedy Junior High School, Lisle, Illinois

Julia Pferdehirt Freelance writer; former Special Education Teacher, Middleton, Wisconsin

Phyllis Stewart Rude English Department Head, Mears Junior-Senior High School, Anchorage, Alaska

Leo Schubert Bettendorf Middle School, Bettendorf, Iowa

Lynn Thomas Borel Middle School, Burlingame, California

Gertrude H. Vannoy Curriculum Liaison Specialist and Gifted and Horizon Teacher, Meany Middle School, Seattle, Washington

Richard Wagner Language Arts Curriculum Coordinator, Paradise Valley School District, Phoenix, Arizona

Stevie Wheeler Humanities Department Chair, Rincon Middle School, San Diego, California

Stephen J. Zadravec Newmarket Junior-Senior High School, Newmarket, New Hampshire